The Brief American Pageant

A History of the Republic

FOURTH EDITION

DAVID M. KENNEDY
STANFORD UNIVERSITY

THOMAS A. BAILEY

MEL PIEHL
VALPARAISO UNIVERSITY

D. C. HEATH AND COMPANY
Lexington, Massachusetts   Toronto

Cover: "Statue of Liberty 1987." Collection of Milton Bond.

Address editorial correspondence to:

D. C. Heath and Company
125 Spring Street
Lexington, MA 02173

Acquisitions Editor: James Miller
Development Editor: Lauren Johnson
Production Editor: Elizabeth Napolitano
Designer: Jan Shapiro
Photo Research: Martha Shethar, Constance S. Gardner, and Derek Wing
Cover Photo Research: Pembroke Herbert and Sandi Rygiel/Picture Research Consultants, Inc.
Production Coordinator: Charles Dutton

Published simultaneously in Canada.

Printed in the United States of America.

International Standard Book Number: 0-669-39767-9

Library of Congress Catalog Number: 94-73804

10 9 8 7 6 5 4 3 2

Preface

The American Pageant has long enjoyed a deserved reputation as one of the most accessible, popular, and effective textbooks in the field of American history. Thomas A. Bailey gave to the book a distinctive personality that mirrored his vast learning and the sparkling classroom style that he had cultivated during his nearly four decades of teaching at Stanford University. Every page of the text expresses the charm of his inventive prose, his passion for clarity, his disdain for clutter, and his mastery of the narrative form.

The Brief American Pageant, Fourth Edition, seeks to preserve the outstanding attributes of the parent text in a format suitable for one-semester courses in American history, as well as for courses that rely heavily on readings in primary sources or specialized monographs. Like the longer Tenth Edition from which it is drawn, it preserves the basic features that have made The American Pageant unique, while incorporating the rich new scholarship in social, economic, cultural, and intellectual history that has appeared in the last generation. This edition of the text continues to reflect the new historical emphasis on the experience of people—including women, the poor, blacks, Hispanics, and certain religious groups—who until recently were often neglected by historians. It is also shaped by the belief that the main drama and the urgent interest of American history reside in the public arena in which these and other groups contend and cooperate with one another. Public affairs, in short, form the spine of the text's account of American history.

That spine, however, is firmly connected to the full body of social, economic, and intellectual history that makes up the organic whole of the American past. This new edition draws out the ways in which political developments have been shaped by ideas, religious beliefs, social conditions, and economic and technological change, as well as by events in areas of the world outside the United States. It contains new or substantially revised discussions of the pre-Columbian era, Native American history, environmental history, the nature and political consequences of slavery, the role of religion in American life, urbanization and immigration in the late nineteenth century, the emergence of a consumer economy in the twentieth century, women's history, and the beginnings and the end of the Cold War. The last chapters also present substantial accounts of the major developments of the last several decades: the civil rights movement, the feminist revolution, the resurgence of immigration, the Vietnam War, Watergate, the "Reagan Revolution," the Persian Gulf War, and the election of the first "baby-boomer" president.

The "Makers of America" essays focus on the diverse ethnic and racial groups that compose our strikingly pluralistic society. They provide fascinating portraits of the lives of immigrant peoples before they arrived on American soil or, in the case of Native Americans, before contact with European and African civilizations. They also discuss the fates of those peoples over time as members of American society.

To assist students in reviewing the material, we also have maintained the chronologies that end each chapter. In addition, most of the "Varying Viewpoints" essays have been substantially revised to reflect recent scholarship and better to stimulate classroom discussion. The end-of-chapter bibliographies have been thoroughly updated; the statistical profile of the American people in the Appendix has been brought up to date; and new, improved maps and illustrations have been inserted.

A revised *Instructor's Resource Guide* is also available with this edition, featuring summaries of chapter themes; chapter outlines; suggestions and resources for lectures; and character sketches. It also includes suggestions for using the "Makers of America" and "Varying Viewpoints" features of *The Brief American Pageant,* as well as identification, multiple choice, and essay questions for the instructor's use. In addition, the student *Guidebook* assists students by focusing their attention on the central themes and major historical developments of each chapter, while presenting a variety of exercises, a glossary of key social science terms, and numerous study review questions designed to reinforce comprehension of the text.

This *Brief American Pageant,* Fourth Edition, presents the subject of American history in an engaging and lively way, without distorting the sober reality of the past. Brevity, Shakespeare noted, is the soul of wit. Though condensed, this edition seeks to preserve the bright personality that has led generations of students to discover in *The American Pageant* what Thomas A. Bailey so exuberantly taught—that the pages of history need not be dull. We hope that readers of this book will enjoy learning from it and that they will come to savor the pleasures and rewards of historical study.

D. M. K.
M. P.

Contents

Maps, Graphs, and Tables

The United States Today

⊛ Capitals of Countries

★ State Capitals

PACIFIC
OCEAN

Vancouver

Seattle
Olympia ★ Tacoma
WASHINGTON
Columbia R.
Spokane

Portland
★ Salem

OREGON

Helena ★ MONTANA
Butte
Missouri R.
Yellowstone R.

Boise ★
IDAHO

Snake R.

WYOMING

Great
Salt
Lake

Cheyenne ★

Platte R.

Reno
★ Carson City

Sacramento ★

San Francisco

NEVADA

Salt
Lake
City ★

UTAH

Denver

COLORADO

MT. WHITNEY
14,495 Ft.

CALIFORNIA

GRAND
CANYON

Hoover
Dam

Colorado R.

Los Angeles

ARIZONA

Santa Fe ★

NEW MEXICO

San Diego

Phoenix ★

Tucson

El Paso

Rio Grande

Pecos R.

HAWAII (inset)

KAUAI

NIIHAU
OAHU
Pearl Harbor ★ Honolulu
MOLOKAI
LANAI
MAUI
HAWAII
KAHOOLAWE

PACIFIC OCEAN

HAWAII

0   100   200 Miles

ALASKA (inset)

U.S.S.R.

POINT BARROW

ARCTIC OCEAN

International Dateline (U.S.S.R.)
(UNITED STATES)

ATTU

BERING SEA

Nome

ALASKA

Yukon R.
Fairbanks
MT. MCKINLEY
20,300 FT.
Anchorage

CANADA

ALEUTIAN ISLANDS

UNIMAK

KODIAK

Juneau ★

GULF OF ALASKA

0   200   400   600 Miles

MEXICO

Sail, sail thy best, ship of Democracy,
Of value is thy freight, 'tis not the Present only,
The Past is also stored in thee,
Thou holdest not the venture of thyself alone, not of
    the Western continent alone,
Earth's résumé entire floats on thy keel,
    O ship, is steadied by thy spars,
With thee Time voyages in trust,
    the antecedent nations sink or swim with thee,
With all their ancient struggles, martyrs, heroes, epics, wars,
    thou bear'st the other continents,
Theirs, theirs as much as thine, the destination-port triumphant. . . .

WALT WHITMAN
Thou Mother with Thy Equal Brood, 1872

CHAPTER 1

New World Beginnings, 33,000 B.C.–A.D. 1769

I have come to believe that this is a mighty continent which was hitherto unknown. . . .
Your Highnesses have an Other World here.

Christopher Columbus, 1498

Planetary Perspectives

About six thousand years ago—only a minute ago geologically—recorded history began among certain peoples of the ancient Middle East. Just five hundred years ago the first Europeans stumbled on the American continents. This dramatic achievement opened breathtaking new vistas and forever altered the future of both the Old World and the New.

Of the numerous new republics that eventually appeared in the Americas, the most influential has been the United States. Born a pygmy, it grew to be a giant whose liberal democratic ideals, robust economy, and achievements in science, technology, and the arts shaped lives in every corner of the planet.

The American Republic was favored by nature and history from the outset. This rare opportunity for a great social and political experiment may never come again, for few fertile and relatively uninhabited areas are left in our increasingly crowded world.

Despite its marvelous development, the United States will one day reach its peak, like Greece and Rome. Its glory eventually will fade, as did theirs. But whatever uncertainties the future may hold, the past at least is secure and richly repays examination.

The Shaping of North America

Planet earth took its present form slowly. Some 225 million years ago, a single supercontinent contained all the world's dry land. Then enormous chunks of terrain began to drift away from this colossal continent, opening the Atlantic and Indian oceans, narrowing the Pacific Ocean, and forming the great masses of Eurasia, Australia, Antarctica, and the Americas.

Continued shifting and folding of the earth's crust thrust up mountain ranges. The Appalachians were probably formed even before continental separation, perhaps 350 million years ago. The majestic

1

A Rocky Mountain Lake Near Aspen, Colorado *The geologically young Rockies form the rugged "backbone" of the North American continent.*

ranges of western North America—the Rockies, the Sierra Nevada, the Cascades, and the Coast Range—arose much more recently, geologically speaking, some 135 million to 25 million years ago.

By about 10 million years ago, nature had sculpted the basic geological shape of North America (see map following the table of contents). The continent was anchored in its northeastern corner by the massive Canadian Shield—a zone undergirded by ancient rock, probably the first part of what became the North American landmass to have emerged above sea level. A narrow eastern coastal plain, or "tidewater," region, creased by many valleys, sloped gently upward to the timeworn ridges of the Appalachians. These ancient mountains slanted away on their western side into the huge mid-continental basin that rolled downward to the Mississippi valley bottom and then rose relentlessly to the towering peaks of the Rockies. From the Rocky Mountain crest—the "roof of America"—the land fell off jaggedly into the intermountain Great Basin, bounded by the Rockies in the east and the Sierra and Cascade ranges in the west. The valleys of the

Sacramento and San Joaquin rivers and the Willamette-Puget Sound trough seamed the interiors of present-day California, Oregon, and Washington. The land at last met the foaming Pacific, where the Coast Range rose steeply from the sea.

Beginning about 2 million years ago, the Great Ice Age spread glaciers across much of northern Europe, Asia, and the Americas. In North America, thick ice sheets crept as far southward as a line stretching from Pennsylvania through the Ohio country and the Dakotas to the Pacific Northwest.

When the glaciers finally retreated, about 10,000 years ago, they left the North American landscape transformed and much as we know it today. The grinding and flushing action of the moving and melting ice pitted the rocky surface of the Canadian Shield with thousands of shallow depressions into which the melting glaciers flowed to form lakes. The same glacial action scooped out and filled the Great Lakes. When the Great Lakes eventually found an outlet to the Atlantic Ocean through the St. Lawrence River, they left the Missouri-Mississippi-Ohio river system to drain the enormous mid-continental basin between the Appalachians and the Rockies.

In the west, water from the melting glaciers filled sprawling Lake Bonneville, covering much of present-day Utah, Nevada, and Idaho. Eventually deprived of both inflow and drainage as the glaciers retreated, the giant lake became a shrinking inland sea. Bonneville grew increasingly saline and slowly evaporated, leaving an arid, mineral-rich desert, with only the Great Salt Lake as a relic of its former vastness. Today Lake Bonneville's ancient beaches are visible on mountainsides up to 1,000 feet above the dry floor of the Great Basin.

The First Discoverers of America

Besides shaping geological history, the Great Ice Age also accounted for the origins of North America's human history. Some 35,000 years ago, the congealing glaciers lowered the world's sea levels, exposing a land bridge between Eurasia and North America across the present-day Bering Strait. Across that

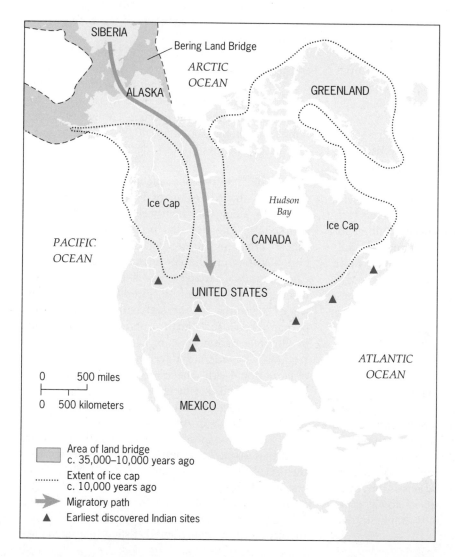

The First Discoverers of America   *For some 25,000 years, people crossed the Bering Strait land bridge from Eurasia to North America. Gradually, they dispersed southward down ice-free valleys, populating both the American continents.*

bridge ventured small bands of hunters—the first "discoverers" of America and the ancestors of the Native Americans. They continued to trek across the Eurasian isthmus for some 250 centuries, slowly peopling the American continents.

As the Ice Age ended and the glaciers melted, the sea level rose again, inundating the land bridge about 10,000 years ago. Nature thus barred the door to further immigration for many thousands of years, and this part of the human family developed its separate existence on the American continents.

Time did not stand still for these original Americans. Roaming slowly through the voiceless vastness of the awesome wilderness, they eventually reached the far tip of South America, some 15,000 miles from Siberia. By the time the Europeans arrived in 1492, perhaps 100 million persons inhabited the two American continents. Over the centuries they split into numerous tribes, with more than 2,000 separate languages and many diverse religions, cultures, and ways of life.

Incas in Peru, Mayans in Central America, and Aztecs in Mexico shaped stunningly sophisticated civilizations. Their advanced agricultural practices, based primarily on the cultivation of maize, which is Indian corn, fed large populations—perhaps as many as 25 million in Mexico alone. Though lacking such technologies as the wheel, these peoples built elaborate cities and carried on far-flung commerce. Talented mathematicians, they made strikingly accurate astronomical observations. The Aztecs also sought the favor of their gods by offering human sacrifices, sometimes cutting the hearts out of the chests of living victims.

The Earliest Americans

Agriculture accounted for the size and sophistication of the Native American civilizations in Mexico and South America. About 5000 B.C., hunter-gatherers in highland Mexico developed a wild grass into the staple of corn, which became the foundation of the large-scale, centralized Aztec and Incan nation-states. As cultivation of corn spread across the Americas from the Mexican heartland, it slowly transformed nomadic hunting bands into settled, agricultural villagers.

Corn planting reached the American Southwest by about 1200 B.C. and powerfully molded the Pueblo culture that developed there. The Pueblo peoples in the Rio Grande Valley constructed intricate irrigation systems to water their cornfields, and they built villages of terraced, multistoried buildings. Corn cultivation reached other parts of North America considerably later, and the timing of its arrival explains the relative rates of development of different Native American peoples. North and east of the Pueblos, elaborately developed "societies" in the modern sense of the word scarcely existed. The lack of dense concentrations of population or complex nation-states was among the reasons for the relative ease of the European conquest of the native North Americans.

The Mound Builders of the Ohio River Valley and the Mississippian culture of the lower Midwest did sustain some large agricultural settlements during the first millennium A.D. The Mississippian settlement at Cahokia, near present-day East St. Louis, Illinois, was home to perhaps 40,000 people in about A.D. 1100, but mysteriously declined two centuries later.

Maize cultivation reached the southeastern Atlantic seaboard region of North America about A.D. 1000, along with high-yielding strains of beans and squash. The rich diet provided by these three "sister" crops produced some of the highest population densities on the continent among the Creek, Choctaw, and Cherokee peoples. In the northeastern woodlands, the Iroquois, inspired by their legendary leader Hiawatha, in the sixteenth century created perhaps the closest North American approximation to the great nation-states of Mexico and Peru. The Iroquois Confederacy developed the political and organizational skills necessary to sustain a robust military alliance that menaced its neighbors, Native American and European alike, for well over a century (see "Makers of America," pp. 24–25).

But for the most part, native North Americans lived in scattered and impermanent settlements on the eve of the Europeans' arrival. They often encamped along rivers in the spring and then dispersed in small family bands for the winter's hunting. In more settled agricultural groups, women tended the crops while men hunted, fished, gathered fuel,

North American Indian Tribes at the Time of European Colonization   *This map illustrates the great diversity of the Indian population—and suggests the inappropriateness of identifying all the Native American peoples with the single label* Indian. *The more than 200 tribes were deeply divided by geography, language, and life-style. The heavy lines identify geographical areas that are similar in climate and terrain.*

and cleared fields for planting. This pattern of life frequently conferred substantial authority on women, and many Native Americans, including the Iroquois, developed matrilinear cultures in which power and possessions passed down the female side of the family.

Unlike the Europeans, who would soon arrive with the presumption that humans had dominion over the earth and the technologies to assert that dominion, Native Americans had neither the desire nor the means to manipulate nature aggressively. They revered the physical world and endowed nature with spiritual properties. Yet they did sometimes ignite massive forest fires, deliberately torching trees to create better hunting habitats, especially for deer. This practice accounted for the open, parklike appearance of the eastern woodlands that so amazed early European explorers.

But in a broad sense the Native Americans did not lay heavy hands on the continent because they were so few in number. In the fateful year 1492, probably no more than 10 million Native Americans padded through the whispering primeval forests and paddled across the sparkling virgin waters of North America. They were blissfully unaware that the isolation of the Americas was about to end forever, as both the land and the native peoples alike felt the full shock of the European "discovery."

Indirect Discoverers of the New World

Europeans were equally unaware of the existence of the Americas. Blond-bearded Norse seafarers from Scandinavia had visited and briefly settled in northeastern North America, probably in Newfoundland, about A.D. 1000. But no strong nation-state, yearning to expand, supported these venturesome seafarers. Their flimsy settlements consequently were soon abandoned, and their discovery was forgotten, except in Scandinavian saga and song.

For several centuries thereafter, other restless Europeans, with the growing power of ambitious

The New World as Paradise
This sixteenth-century engraving by the Flemish artist Theodore de Bry illustrates the Indian method of hunting by setting fires to drive wild game into bow range.

nation-states behind them, sought contact with a wider world, whether for conquest or trade. They thus set in motion the chain of events that led to a drive toward Asia, the exploitation of Africa, and the completely accidental discovery of the New World.

Christian crusaders of the eleventh to the fourteenth centuries rank high among America's indirect discoverers. Foiled in their military assaults on the Holy Land, they acquired a taste for the exotic delights of Asia—silk for clothing, drugs for aching flesh, perfumes for unbathed bodies, colorful draperies for gloomy castles, and sugar and spices for preserving and flavoring food. The Italian adventurer Marco Polo further whetted European appetites for Asian luxury goods when he returned from China in 1295 with news of its golden pagodas and rose-tinted pearls.

But the distance and difficulties of transportation, for which Muslim and Italian middlemen charged dearly, made European consumers and distributors eager to find a less expensive route to Asia. But their hopes for an ocean route to Asia were long frustrated. Before the mid-fifteenth century, European sailors refused to sail southward along the coast of West Africa because they could not beat their way home again against the prevailing northerly winds and south-flowing currents.

Europeans Enter Africa

About 1450, Portuguese mariners overcame these obstacles by developing the caravel, a ship that could sail against the wind, and by learning to return to Europe by way of the Azores islands, whose prevailing westward breezes carried them home.

The new world of sub-Saharan Africa, previously remote and mysterious to Europeans, now came within their questing grasp. African gold, perhaps two-thirds of Europe's supply, crossed the Sahara on camelback, and tales may have reached Europe about the flourishing West African kingdom of Mali in the Niger River Valley, with its impressive Islamic university at Timbuktu. But Europeans had no direct access to sub-Saharan Africa until the Portuguese mariners began to creep down the West African coast in the mid-fifteenth century.

The Portuguese promptly set up trading posts along the African shore for the purchase of gold—and slaves. Arab and African slave brokers had traded slaves for centuries before the Europeans arrived. They frequently charged higher prices for slaves from distant lands who could not flee to their native villages. Slave traders also deliberately separated persons from the same tribes to frustrate organized resistance.

The Portuguese adopted these long-standing slave practices in the sugar plantations that they, and later the Spanish, established on the Atlantic coastal islands of Madeira, the Canaries, São Tomé, and Principe. The Portuguese appetite for slaves was enormous, and slave trading became big business. Some 40,000 Africans were carried away to the Atlantic sugar islands in the last half of the fifteenth century. Millions more would be wrenched from their home continent after the discovery of the Americas. These fifteenth-century Portuguese adventures in Africa contained the origins of the modern plantation system, based on large-scale commercial agriculture and the wholesale exploitation of slave labor. This type of plantation economy would shape the destiny of much of the New World.

After years of cautious exploration, the Portuguese mariner Bartholomeu Días finally rounded the southernmost tip of Africa in 1498. Ten years later Vasco da Gama reached India and returned home with a small but tantalizing cargo of jewels and spices. Meanwhile, the kingdom of Spain was united as a result of the marriage of two sovereigns, Ferdinand of Aragon and Isabella of Castile. After the brutal expulsion of the Muslim Moors from Spain, the new Spanish nation was eager to outstrip its Portuguese rivals in the race for the wealth of the Indies. Because Portugal controlled the round-Africa route to India, Spain of necessity looked westward.

Columbus Comes Upon a New World

Now the stage was set for a cataclysmic shift in the course of history, not just of Europe but of all the world. Europeans clamored for more and cheaper products from the lands beyond the Mediterranean. Africa had been established as a source of cheap

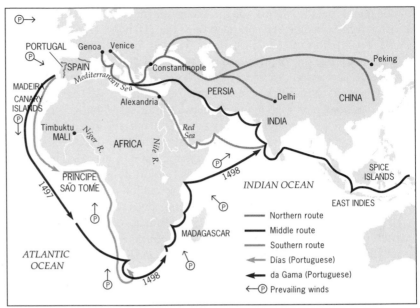

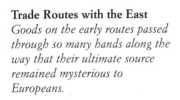

Trade Routes with the East
Goods on the early routes passed through so many hands along the way that their ultimate source remained mysterious to Europeans.

slave labor for plantation agriculture. The Portuguese had demonstrated the feasibility of long-range ocean navigation. In Spain a modern national state was taking shape, with the unity, wealth, and power to shoulder the formidable tasks of discovery, conquest, and colonization. Across the sea, vast and virginal, the New World innocently awaited its European discoverers.

The dawn of the Renaissance in the fourteenth century nurtured an ambitious spirit of optimism and adventure. Printing presses, introduced about 1450, facilitated the spread of scientific knowledge. The mariner's compass, possibly borrowed from the Arabs, eliminated some of the uncertainties of travel.

Onto this stage stepped Christopher Columbus. This skilled Italian seaman persuaded the Spanish monarchs to outfit him with three tiny but seaworthy ships. Sailing westward into the oceanic unknown, Columbus sighted land on October 12, 1492—an island in the Bahamas.

Only gradually did Europeans realize that sprawling new continents had been discovered. For decades explorers tried to get through or around the "islands" that, they assumed, blocked the ocean pathway to Asia. Columbus himself was at first so

certain that he had skirted the rim of the "Indies" that he called the native peoples Indians, a gross geographical misnomer that somehow stuck.

Columbus's discovery would eventually convulse four continents—Europe, Africa, and of course the two Americas. Thanks to his epochal voyage, an interdependent global economic system emerged on a scale undreamed of before he set sail. Its workings touched every shore washed by the Atlantic Ocean. Europe provided the markets, the capital, and the technology; Africa furnished the labor; and the New World offered its raw materials—especially its precious metals and its soil for the cultivation of sugarcane. For Europeans, as well as for Africans and Native Americans, the world after 1492 would never be the same, for better or worse.

When Worlds Collide

Two ecosystems—the fragile, naturally evolved networks of relations among organisms in a stable environment—commingled and clashed when Columbus waded ashore. The flora and fauna of the Old and New worlds had been separated for thousands of years. European explorers marveled at the strange sights that greeted them, including exotic beasts such as iguanas and "snakes with castanets" (rattlesnakes). Native New World plants such as tobacco, maize, beans, tomatoes, and especially the lowly potato eventually revolutionized the international economy and fed the rapidly growing population of the Old World. These foodstuffs were among the most important Native American gifts to the Europeans and the rest of the world. Ironically, the introduction into Africa of foods such as maize, manioc, and sweet potatoes may have fed an African population boom that numerically, though not morally, more than offset the depredations of the slave trade.

In exchange the Europeans introduced Old World crops and animals, such as cattle and horses, to the Americas. Horses reached the North American mainland through Mexico. North American tribes like the Apaches, Sioux, and Blackfoot swiftly adopted the horse, transforming their cultures into highly mobile, wide-ranging hunter societies that pursued the shaggy buffalo across the Great Plains. Columbus also brought sugarcane. Thriving in the warm Caribbean climate, it prompted a "sugar revolution" in the European diet that led to the forced migrations of millions of Africans to work the canefields and sugar mills of the New World.

Unwittingly, the Europeans also brought the germs that caused smallpox, yellow fever, and malaria—diseases that quickly devastated the Native Americans. During the Indians' millennia of separate

Seafaring Horses Come to America *The horse was first brought to the New World by the Spanish, but quickly spread across both American continents. These drawings show how horses were lowered onto Spanish ships by pulleys (right), suspended by slings to avoid falls on rough seas (upper left), and ferried ashore in smaller craft (lower left).*

existence in the Americas, most of the Old World's killer maladies had disappeared from among them. Devoid of natural resistance to Old World sicknesses, Indians died in droves. Within fifty years of the Spanish arrival, the population of the Taino natives in Hispaniola dwindled from some 5 million persons to about 200. The lethal germs spread among New World peoples with the speed and force of a hurricane, swiftly sweeping far ahead of the human invaders. Most of those afflicted never laid eyes on a European. In the century after Columbus's landfall, nearly 90 percent of Native Americans perished, a demographic catastrophe without parallel in human history. Depopulation was so severe that entire cultures and ancient ways of life were extinguished forever. Perhaps it was poetic justice that the original Americans unknowingly infected the early explorers with syphilis, injecting that lethal sexually transmitted disease for the first time into Europe.

The Spanish *Conquistadores*

Gradually, Europeans realized that the American continents held rich prizes, especially the gold and silver of the advanced civilizations in Mexico and Peru. Spain secured its title to Columbus's discoveries in the Treaty of Tordesillas (1494), dividing with Portugal the "heathen lands" of the New World.

Spain became the dominant exploring and colonizing power of the 1500s. Seeking both the glitter of gold and the glory of God, Spanish *conquistadores* ("conquerors") fanned out across the Caribbean and eventually onto the American continents (see "Makers of America: The Spanish *Conquistadores*," pp. 12–13). Some early explorers, among them Ponce de Leon, Coronado, and de Soto, ventured into territory that eventually became part of the United States. But the permanent Spanish conquests of Peru and Mexico were by far the most consequential achievements of the *conquistadores*.

In South America, the ironfisted conqueror Francisco Pizarro crushed the Incas of Peru in 1532 and added a huge horde of booty, especially silver, to Spanish coffers. This flood of precious metal touched off a price revolution in Europe in which consumer costs increased by as much as 500 percent

in the hundred years after the mid-sixteenth century. Some scholars see in this ballooning European money supply the fuel that fed the growth of the economic system known as capitalism.

The conquest of Mexico was engineered by Hernando Cortés, who set sail from Cuba in 1519 with sixteen horses and several hundred men. Approaching Mexico, he picked up a female Indian slave named Malinche, who knew both Mayan and Nahuatl, the language of the powerful Aztecs. Aided by Malinche and another interpreter, Cortés learned of the unrest within the Aztec empire and of the gold and other wealth in its capital. Tenochtitlán. "We Spanish suffer from a strange disease of the heart," Cortés allegedly told ambassadors of the Aztec ruler Montezuma, "for which the only known remedy is gold." The emissaries reported this to Montezuma, along with the astonishing fact that the newcomers rode on the backs of "deer" (horses). Believing that Cortés was the god Quetzalcoatl, whose return from the eastern sea was predicted in Aztec legends, Montezuma allowed the *conquistadores* to approach his capital unopposed.

The Spaniards were amazed by the beauty and wealth of Tenochtitlán, with its 300,000 inhabitants and marvelous temples, aqueducts, and floating gardens. Received hospitably at first, Cortés and his men were unable to contain their lust for gold. After warfare broke out on June 30, 1520, Cortés laid siege to the city. It capitulated on August 13, 1521.

The Aztec empire thus gave way to three centuries of Spanish rule. Its people suffered not only from the armed conquest but from smallpox and other epidemics that burned through the valley of Mexico. In less than a century, the native population shrank from more than 20 million to fewer than 2 million people. The temples of Tenochtitlán were destroyed to make way for the Christian cathedrals of Mexico City, built on the site of the ruined Aztec capital.

Yet the invader brought more than conquest and death. He brought his language, laws, customs, and religion, all of which proved adaptable to the people of Mexico. He intermarried with the surviving Mexicans, creating a distinctive culture of *mestizos,* people of mixed Indian and European heritage.

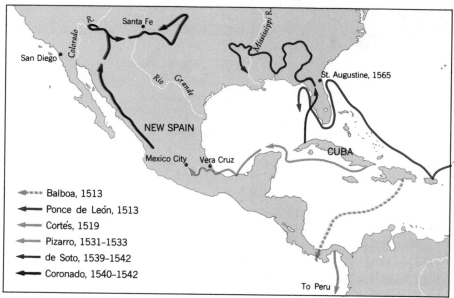

San Diego

New Spain

Mexico City   Vera Cruz

Santa Fe

Colorado R.

Rio Grande

Mississippi R.

St. Augustine, 1565

CUBA

To Peru

➤--- Balboa, 1513
➤— Ponce de León, 1513
➤— Cortés, 1519
➤— Pizarro, 1531–1533
➤— de Soto, 1539–1542
➤— Coronado, 1540–1542

Principal Early Spanish Explorations and Conquests *Note that Coronado traversed northern Texas and Oklahoma. In present-day eastern Kansas he found, instead of the great golden city he sought, a drab encampment, probably of Wichita Indians.*

To this day Mexican civilization remains a unique blend of the Old World and New, producing both ambivalence and pride among people of Mexican heritage. Cortés's translator Malinche, for example, has given her name to the Mexican language in the word *malinchista,* or "traitor." But Mexicans also celebrate Columbus Day as the *Dia de la Raza*—the birthday of a wholly new race of people.

The Spread of Spanish America

Spain's colonial empire grew swiftly and impressively. Within about half a century of Columbus's landfall, hundreds of Spanish cities and towns flourished in the Americas. Majestic cathedrals dotted the land, printing presses turned out books, and scholars studied at distinguished universities, including those at Mexico City and Lima, Peru, both founded in 1551, eighty-five years before Harvard, the first college established in the English colonies.

But how secure were these imperial possessions? Other powers were already sniffing around the edges of the Spanish domain, eager to bite off their share of the promised wealth of the new lands. The upstart English sent Giovanni Caboto (known in English as John Cabot) to explore the northeastern coast of North America in 1498. The French king dispatched Giovanni da Verrazano to probe the eastern seaboard in 1524 and Jacques Cartier to explore the St. Lawrence River in 1534. To guard sea lanes and protect their northern borderlands against such encroachments, the Spanish erected a fortress at St. Augustine, Florida, in 1565, thus founding the oldest continually inhabited European settlement in the future United States.

Farther west, the tales of Coronado's expedition of the 1540s beckoned *conquistadores* northward from Mexico into the Rio Grande and Colorado River regions. A Spanish expedition led by Don Juan de Oñate entered the Rio Grande Valley in 1598 and cruelly abused the Pueblo peoples they encountered. One of their vicious acts was to sever one foot of each survivor of the battle of Acoma in 1599. The Spaniards proclaimed the area to be the province of New Mexico in 1609 and founded its capital at Santa Fe the following year. The Spanish

The Spanish Conquistadores

In 1492, the same year that Columbus sighted America, the great Moorish city of Grenada fell after a ten-year siege. For five centuries the Christian kingdoms of Spain had tried to drive the North African Muslim Moors off the Iberian peninsula, and with the fall of Grenada they succeeded. The centuries of religious war nurtured an obsession with status and honor, bred religious zealotry and intolerance, and created a large class of men who regarded manual labor and commerce contemptuously. With the end of the "Reconquista," some of these men turned their restless gaze to Spain's New World frontier.

Between 1519 and 1540, Spanish *conquistadores* swept across the Americas in two wide arcs of con-

Indians Bearing Gifts of Gold to Balboa, by Theodore de Bry
This European painting portrays Indians happily welcoming the conquistadores *to their land; real relationships were seldom so harmonious.*

quest—one driving from Cuba through Mexico into what is now the southwestern United States, the other starting from Panama and pushing into Peru. The military conquest of this vast region was achieved by just 10,000 men, organized in a series of private expeditions. Hernando Cortés, Francisco Pizarro, and other aspiring conquerors signed contracts with the Spanish monarch, raised money from investors, and then proceeded to recruit an army. Only a minority of the *conquistadores* were nobles. About half were professional soldiers or sailors; the rest comprised peasants, artisans, and members of the middle classes. Most were in their twenties and early thirties.

Some of these motley adventurers hoped to win royal titles or favors. Others sought to ensure God's favor by spreading Christianity to the pagans. Some men aspired to escape dubious pasts, while others sought the kind of historical adventure experienced by heroes of classical antiquity. Nearly all shared a lust for gold.

But most never achieved their dreams of glory or riches. Even when an expedition captured exceptionally rich booty, the spoils were unevenly divided: men from the commander's home region often received more, and men on horseback generally got two shares to the infantryman's one. The *conquistadores* lost still more power as the crown tightened its hold on the New World, and by the 1550s the day of the *conquistadore* had ended.

Nevertheless, the *conquistadores* achieved a kind of immortality. Because of a scarcity of Spanish women in the early days of the conquest, many *conquistadores* married Indian women. Their offspring, the "new race" of *mestizos,* formed a cultural and biological bridge between Latin America's European and Indian races.

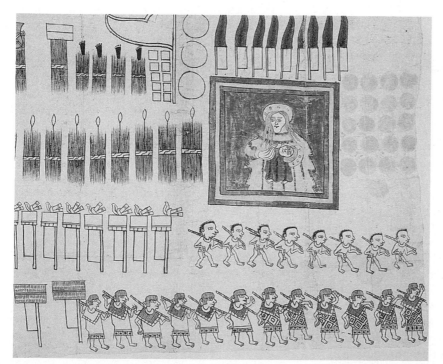

An Aztec View of the Conquest, 1531 *Produced just a dozen years after Cortés's arrival in 1519, this drawing by an Aztec artist pictures the Indians rendering tribute to their conquerors. The inclusion of the banner showing Madonna and child also illustrates that the Spanish brought their Catholic faith to the Indians as part of their conquest.*

CHRONOLOGY

c. 33,000–8000 B.C.	First humans cross over to the Americas from Asia.
c. 5000 B.C.	Corn is developed as a staple crop in highland Mexico.
c. 4000 B.C.	First civilized societies develop in the Middle East.
c. 1200 B.C.	Corn planting reaches present-day American Southwest.
c. A.D. 1000	Norse voyagers discover and briefly settle in North America.
	Corn cultivation reaches Midwest and southeastern Atlantic seaboard.
c. A.D. 1100	Mississippian settlement at Cahokia reaches its peak.
c. A.D. 1100–1300	Christian crusades arouse European interest in Asia.
1295	Marco Polo returns to Europe.
1488	Días rounds southern tip of Africa.
1492	Columbus lands in the Bahamas.
1494	Treaty of Tordesillas signed between Spain and Portugal.
1498	da Gama reaches India.
	On a mission from England Cabot explores northeastern coast of North America.
late 1400s	Spain becomes united.
1513, 1521	Ponce de Leon explores Florida.
1522	Magellan's vessel completes circumnavigation of the earth.
1532	Pizarro crushes Incas.
1539–1542	Coronado explores present-day Southwest.
1565	Spanish build fortress at St. Augustine.
late 1500s	Iroquois Confederacy founded (according to Iroquois legend).
1609	Spanish found New Mexico.
1680	Popé incites rebellion in New Mexico.
1680s	La Salle leads French expedition down Mississippi River.
1769	Serra founds first California mission at San Diego.

settlers found precious little gold, but missionaries did discover a wealth of souls to be harvested for the Christian religion. Their efforts to suppress Pueblo religious customs provoked an uprising called Popé's Rebellion in 1680. The Pueblo rebels destroyed every Catholic church in the province and killed a score of priests and hundreds of Spanish settlers. It took nearly half a century for the Spanish to reclaim New Mexico from the insurrectionary Indians.

Meanwhile, as a further hedge against the French, who had sent an expedition under Robert La Salle down the Mississippi River in the 1680s, the Spanish began around 1716 to establish a few weak settlements and missions in Texas, including the one at San Antonio later known as the Alamo. To the west, in California, no serious foreign threat loomed,

and Spain directed its attention there only belatedly. Juan Rodriguez Cabrillo had explored the California coast in 1542, but for some two centuries thereafter California slumbered undisturbed by European intruders.

Then in 1769, Spanish missionaries led by Father Junipero Serra founded at San Diego the first of a chain of twenty-one missions that wound up the coast as far as Sonoma, north of San Francisco Bay. Father Serra's brown-robed Franciscan friars toiled with zealous devotion to Christianize 300,000 native Californians and to teach them horticulture and crafts. These "mission Indians" did adopt Christianity, but they lost their native cultures and often lost their lives as well, as the white man's diseases doomed these vulnerable peoples.

The misdeeds of the Spanish in the New World obscured their substantial achievements and helped give birth to the "Black Legend." This false concept held that the conquerors merely tortured and butchered the Indians, stole their gold, infected them with smallpox, and left little but misery behind. The Spanish invaders did indeed kill, enslave, and infect countless Native Americans, but they also grafted their culture, laws, religion, and language into a vast array of native societies, laying the foundations for the proud Hispanic nations of Latin America.

Clearly the Spanish, who had more than a century's head start over the English, were genuine empire builders and cultural innovators in the New World. Compared with their Anglo-Saxon rivals, their colonial establishment was larger and richer, and endured more than a quarter of a century longer. In the last analysis, the Spanish paid the Native Americans the highest compliment of fusing with them through marriage and mixing Indian culture with their own, rather than shunning and eventually isolating the Indians, as their English adversaries would do.

Varying Viewpoints

The history of discovery and the earliest colonization raises perhaps the single most fundamental question about all American history. Should it be understood as the extension of European civilization into the New World, or as the gradual development of a uniquely "American" culture? An older school of thought tended to emphasize the Europeanization of America. Historians of that persuasion thus paid close attention to the situation in Europe, particularly in England and Spain, in the fifteenth and sixteenth centuries. They also focused on the various means by which the values and institutions of the mother continent were exported to the new lands in the western sea. Some European writers have varied this general question by asking what transforming effect the discovery of America had on Europe itself. Both of these approaches are Eurocentric.

More recently, historians have concentrated on the distinctive aspects of America, especially the interactions among the various races in the Western Hemisphere. This approach stresses the adaptations of Native American, African, and European cultures to the challenges of life in a strange new environment and emphasizes the creation of a uniquely *American* society and culture.

SELECT READINGS

Primary Source Documents

Hernando Cortés's *Letters from Mexico** have been translated into English by A. R. Pagden (1971). Bartoleme de las Casas, *Thirty Very Judicial Propositions** (1552), and Juan Gines de Sepulveda, *The Second Democrates** (1547),

reflect the Spanish *conquistadores'* efforts to understand the native peoples of the New World. See also las Casas, *The Destruction of the Indies* (1542). *The Broken Spears: The Aztec Account of the Conquest of Mexico,** edited by Miduel Leon-Portilla (1962), is an anthology of texts compiled from indigenous sources. Olaudah Equiano, *Equiano's Travels** (1789), is a fascinating account by an African in the New World in the eighteenth century.

Secondary Sources

Brian M. Fagan reviews the sketchy evidence concerning the earliest humans to arrive in the Americas in *The Great*

---

* An asterisk indicates that the document, or an excerpt from it, can be found in Thomas A. Bailey and David M. Kennedy, eds., *The American Spirit: United States History as Seen by Contemporaries, 7th ed.* (Lexington, Mass.: D.C. Heath and Company, 1991).

Journey: The Peopling of Ancient America (1987). For more on the pre-Columbian history of the Americas, see Alvin Josephy, *The Indian Heritage of America* (1968); Norman Hammond, *Ancient Maya Civilization* (1982); and Brian M. Fagan, *Kingdoms of Gold, Kingdoms of Jade: The Americas Before Columbus* (1991). Immanuel Wallerstein, *The Modern World System: Capitalist Agriculture and the Origins of the European World in the Sixteenth Century* (1974), provides a theoretical overview of the international economic background of European colonization. Early African history is sketched in J. D. Fage, *A History of West Africa* (1969).

A fascinating brief synthesis of early European contact with the Americas is J. H. Elliott, *The Old World and the New, 1492–1650* (1970). Alfred Crosby discusses *The Columbian Exchange: Biological and Cultural Consequences of 1492* (1972). A marvelously illustrated volume portraying the impact of America on the European imagination is Hugh Honour, *The New Golden Land* (1975). See also Kirkpatrick Sale, *The Conquest of Paradise: Christopher*

Columbus and the Columbian Legacy (1990), and Herman J. Viola and Carolyn Margolis, *Seeds of Change: Five Hundred Years Since Columbus* (1991). D. W. Meinig presents a geographical overview of immigration in *The Shaping of America: A Geographical Perspective on 500 Years of History. Atlantic America, 1492–1800* (1986). Various aspects of the Spanish and Portuguese conquests of America are described in James Lockhart and Stuart B. Schwartz, *Early Latin America* (1983); Charles Gibson, *Spain in America* (1966); and L. McAlister, *Spain and Portugal in the New World, 1492–1700* (1984).

Nathan Wachtel presents the Indians' view of the Spanish conquest in *The Vision of the Vanquished* (1977). The spread of Spanish America northward is traced in Philip Wayne Powell, *Soldiers, Indians and Silver: The Northward Advance of New Spain, 1550–1600* (1952), Edward H. Spicer, *Cycles of Conquest: The Impact of Spain, Mexico and the United States on the Indians of the Southwest, 1533–1960* (1962), and David J. Weber's masterful synthesis, *The Spanish Frontier in North America* (1992).

CHAPTER 2

The Planting of English America, 1500–1733

...For I shall yet live to see it [Virginia] an Inglishe nation.

Sir Walter Raleigh, 1602

England's Imperial Stirrings

As the seventeenth century dawned, scarcely a century after Columbus's landfall, the human face of much of the New World had already been profoundly transformed. Native American people had been reduced to only about 10 percent of the population of 1492, mostly by disease. Several hundred thousand African slaves toiled on Caribbean and Brazilian sugar plantations. From Florida and New Mexico southward, most of the southern lands of the New World lay firmly in the grip of imperial Spain.

But *North* America in 1600 remained largely unexplored and effectively unclaimed by Europeans. As if to herald the coming century of colonization and conflict in the northern continent, three European powers planted three primitive outposts in three distant corners of the continent within three years of one another: the Spanish at Santa Fe in 1610, the French at Quebec in 1608, and the English at Jamestown, Virginia, in 1607.

Feeble indeed were England's efforts in the 1500s to compete with the sprawling Spanish empire. As Spain's ally in the first half of the century, England took little interest in establishing its own overseas colonies. But in 1558, the Protestant Elizabeth ascended to the English throne and solidified her father King Henry VIII's break with the Catholic Church (see Ch. 3, pp. 29–30). Protestantism became dominant in England, and rivalry with Catholic Spain intensified.

An early scene of that rivalry was Ireland, where the Catholic Irish sought help from Catholic Spain to throw off the yoke of Protestant English rule. In crushing the Irish uprising with terrible ferocity, many English learned the sneering contempt for "savage" natives, an attitude they brought with them to the New World.

Encouraged by the ambitious Queen Elizabeth, hardy English buccaneers now swarmed out upon the shipping lanes to plunder Spanish treasure ships and raid Spanish settlements. The most famous of these semipiratical "sea dogs" was the courtly Francis Drake, who looted his way around the globe and returned loaded with Spanish gold in 1580.

The first English attempt at colonization, in bleak Newfoundland, collapsed when its promoter, Sir Humphrey Gilbert, lost his life at sea in 1583.

Gilbert's gallant half-brother Sir Walter Raleigh then organized a group of settlers who landed in 1585 on North Carolina's Roanoke Island. But the hapless Roanoke colony mysteriously vanished, swallowed up by the wilderness.

These pathetic English failures at colonization contrasted embarrassingly with the glories of the Spanish empire, whose profits were enriching Spain beyond its most ambitious dreams of avarice. Philip II of Spain, self-anointed foe of the Protestant Reformation, used part of his imperial gains to amass an "invincible armada" of ships for an invasion of England in 1588. But the skillful English sea dogs and a devastating storm (the "Protestant wind") scattered the crippled Spanish ships.

The defeat of the Armada marked the beginning of the end of Spanish imperial dreams, though Spain's New World empire would not fully collapse for three more centuries. England's victory also started that country well on its way to becoming master of the world oceans—a fact of enormous importance to the American people. Indeed, England now had many of the characteristics that Spain displayed on the eve of its colonizing adventure a century earlier: a strong, unified national state under a popular monarch; a measure of religious unity after a protracted struggle between Protestants and Catholics; and a vibrant sense of nationalism.

This new sense of national pride blossomed in the golden Elizabethan age of culture and politics. Shakespeare, who made occasional poetic references to England's American colonies, was only one of many contemporary patriots who expressed boundless faith in the future of the nation.

England's scepter'd isle, as Shakespeare called it, throbbed with social and economic tension as the seventeenth century opened. Its population was mushrooming, from some 3 million people in 1550 to about 4 million in 1600. In the ever-green English countryside, landlords were "enclosing" croplands

The *Mary Rose*, A Sixteenth-Century English Navy Ship *Typical of English royal navy ships of the sixteenth century was the* Mary Rose, *a 700-ton, 41-gun ship built by King Henry VIII in 1509–1510. The* Mary Rose *was sunk during a battle with a French fleet in 1545 just off the coast of Portsmouth, England, where the ship had been built. The wreck was discovered by pioneer divers in 1836, and yielded many artifacts revealing the lives and work of English sailors in the age of the Tudor monarchy. (Above left) From the painting by W. H. Bishop entitled "The Warship* Mary Rose *leaving Portsmouth Harbor—Summer 1945" showing in detail how the ship actually looked. (Above right) Personal items excavated from the* Mary Rose, *including a thimble-ring, clasp, pocket sundial, whistle, purse-hanger, comb, coins, knife-handle, seal, and rosary.*

Sir Walter Raleigh (c. 1552–1618) *Here he is shown "drinking tobacco," as smoking was first called. He is credited with introducing both tobacco and the potato into England. A dashing courtier, he launched important colonizing failures in the New World. After seducing (and marrying) one of Queen Elizabeth's maids of honor, he fell out of favor and was ultimately beheaded for treason.*

for sheep grazing, forcing many small farmers into precarious tenancy or off the land altogether. It was no accident that the woolen districts of eastern and western England—where Puritanism had taken strong root—supplied many of the earliest immigrants to America. When economic depression hit the woolen trade in the late 1500s, thousands of unemployed farmers took to the roads, often ending up as beggars and paupers in cities like Bristol and London.

At the same time, laws of primogeniture decreed that only eldest sons were eligible to inherit landed estates. Landholders' ambitious younger sons, among them Gilbert, Raleigh, and Drake, were forced to seek their fortunes elsewhere. But by the early 1600s their unsuccessful lone-wolf ventures were replaced by the joint-stock company, which enabled a considerable number of investors to pool their capital.

Peace with a chastened Spain provided the opportunity for English colonization. Population growth provided the workers. Unemployment, as well as a thirst for adventure, for markets, and for religious freedom, provided the motives. Joint-stock companies provided the financial means. The stage was now set for a historic effort to establish an English beachhead in the still uncharted North American wilderness.

England Plants the Jamestown Seedling

In 1606, two years after peace with Spain, the hand of destiny beckoned toward Virginia. A joint-stock company, known as the Virginia Company of London, received a charter from King James I of England for a settlement in the New World. The main attractions were the promise of gold and the desire to find a passage through America to the Indies. Like most joint-stock companies of the day, the Virginia Company was intended to endure for only a few years, after which its stockholders hoped to liquidate it for a profit. This arrangement put severe pressure on the luckless colonists, who were threatened with abandonment in the wilderness if they did not quickly strike it rich on the company's behalf. Few of the investors thought in terms of long-term colonization. Apparently no one even faintly suspected that the seeds of a mighty nation were being planted.

The charter of the Virginia Company is a significant document in American history. It guaranteed to the overseas settlers the same rights of Englishmen that they would have enjoyed if they had stayed at home. This precious boon was gradually extended to the other English colonies and became a foundation stone of American liberties.

Setting sail from England in late 1606, the colonists arrived in Virginia and chose a site for their settlement on the wooded but mosquito-infested banks of the James River. There, on May 24, 1607, about a hundred English settlers, all men, disembarked. They called the place Jamestown.

The early years of Jamestown proved to be a nightmare for all concerned—except the buzzards. Once ashore, the settlers died by the dozens from disease, malnutrition, and starvation. Ironically, the woods rustled with game and the rivers flopped with fish, but the greenhorn settlers, many of them self-styled "gentlemen" unaccustomed to fending for

Pocahontas (c. 1595–1617) (Detail) *Taken to England by her husband, she was received as a princess. She died when preparing to return, and her infant son ultimately reached Virginia, where hundreds of his descendants have lived, including the second Mrs. Woodrow Wilson.*

themselves, wasted valuable time grubbing for nonexistent gold when they should have been gathering provisions.

Virginia was saved from utter collapse at the start largely by the leadership and resourcefulness of an intrepid young adventurer, Captain John Smith. Taking over in 1608, he whipped the gold-hungry colonists into line with the rule "He who shall not work shall not eat." He was kidnapped in December 1607 and subjected to a mock execution by the Indian chieftain Powhatan, whose daughter Pocahontas "saved" Smith by dramatically interposing her head between his and the war clubs of his captors. Pocahontas became an intermediary between the Indians and the settlers, helping to preserve a shaky peace and provide needed food.

Still, the colonists died in droves, and survivors were driven to desperate acts. They were reduced to eating "Dogges, Catts, Ratts, and Myce" and even to digging up corpses for food. One hungry man killed, salted, and ate his wife, for which misbehavior he was executed. Of the 400 settlers who managed to make it to Virginia by 1609, only 60 survived the "starving time" winter of 1609–1610. Diseased and despairing, the colonists were ready to return to En-

gland in the spring of 1610 when a relief party suddenly arrived, headed by a new governor, Lord De La Warr.

De La Warr ordered the settlers to stay in Jamestown, imposed a harsh military regime on the colony, and soon undertook aggressive military action against the Indians. But disease continued to reap a gruesome harvest. By 1625 Virginia contained only some 1,200 hard-bitten survivors of the nearly 8,000 adventurers who had tried to start life anew in the ill-fated colony.

Cultural Clash in the Chesapeake

When the English landed in 1607, the chieftain Powhatan held loose control over a few dozen small tribes in the James River area. Powhatan at first may have considered the English potential allies in his struggle to extend his power over his Indian rivals, and he tried to be conciliatory. But relations between the Indians and the English remained tense, especially as the starving colonists took to raiding Indian food supplies.

The atmosphere grew even more strained after De La Warr arrived in 1610. He carried orders from the Virginia Company that amounted to a declaration of war against the Indians in the Jamestown region. A veteran of the vicious campaigns against the Irish, De La Warr now introduced "Irish tactics" against the Native Americans. His troops raided their villages, burned houses, confiscated provisions, and torched cornfields. A peace settlement ended this First Anglo–Powhatan War in 1614, sealed by the marriage of Pocahontas to the colonist John Rolfe—the first known interracial union in Virginia.

A fragile peace prevailed for eight years. But the Indians, pressed by the land-hungry whites and ravaged by European diseases, struck back in 1622. A series of violent attacks left 347 settlers dead, including John Rolfe. The Indians made one last effort to dislodge the Virginians in the Second Anglo–Powhatan War in 1644. They were again defeated. The peace treaty of 1646 repudiated any hope of assimilating the native peoples into Virginian society or of peacefully coexisting with them. Instead it effectively banished the Chesapeake Indians from their ancestral lands and formally separated Indian from white areas of settlement—the origins of the later reservation system. By 1669, an official census revealed that only about 2,000 Indians remained in Virginia, perhaps 10 percent of the population the original English settlers had found in 1607.

It had been the Powhatans' calamitous misfortune to fall victim to three Ds: disease, disorganization, and disposability. Like native peoples throughout the New World, they were struck down by European epidemics of smallpox and measles. They also lacked the unity to oppose the relatively well-organized and militarily disciplined whites. Finally, the Powhatans served no economic function for the Virginia colonists, having no gold, labor, or valuable commodities to offer in commerce. Indeed the Indian presence frustrated the colonists' desire for a local commodity the Europeans desperately wanted: land.

Virginia: Child of Tobacco

John Rolfe, the husband of Pocahontas, became the father of the tobacco industry and an economic savior of the Virginia colony. By 1616 he had perfected methods of raising and curing the pungent weed. A tobacco rush swept over Virginia, as crops were planted in the streets of Jamestown and even between the numerous graves. Colonists who once had hungered for food now hungered for ever more land on which to plant ever more tobacco. Relentlessly, they pressed the frontier of settlement up the river valleys to the west, further crowding the Indians.

Virginia's prosperity was built on tobacco. This "bewitching weed" played a vital role in putting the colony on firm foundations and in setting an example for other successful colonizing experiments. But tobacco—King Nicotine—was something of a tyrant. It was ruinous to the soil when greedily planted in successive years, and it also enchained the prosperity of Virginia to the fluctuating price of a single crop. Tobacco also promoted the broad-acred plantation system, and with it a brisk demand for slave labor.

In 1619, the year before the Plymouth Pilgrims landed in New England, what was described as a Dutch warship appeared off Jamestown and sold some twenty black Africans to the colonists. (The scanty record does not reveal whether they were purchased as lifelong slaves or as servants committed to limited years of servitude.) Yet blacks were too costly for most of the hard-pinched white colonists to acquire, and for decades few were brought to Virginia. In 1650 Virginia counted but 300 blacks, although by the end of the century blacks, most of them enslaved, made up approximately 14 percent of the colony's population.

Representative self-government was also born in primitive Virginia, in the same cradle with slavery and in the same year—1619. The London Company authorized the settlers to summon an assembly, known as the House of Burgesses. A momentous precedent was thus feebly established, for this assemblage was the first of many miniature parliaments to mushroom from the soil of America.

As time passed, James I grew increasingly hostile to Virginia. He detested tobacco and he distrusted the representative House of Burgesses, which he branded a "seminary of sedition." In 1624 he revoked the charter of the bankrupt Virginia Company, thus making Virginia a royal colony directly under his control.

Maryland: Catholic Haven

Maryland—the second plantation colony but the fourth English colony to be planted—was founded in 1634 by Lord Baltimore, of a prominent English Catholic family. He embarked upon the venture partly to reap financial profits and partly to create a refuge for his fellow Catholics.

Absentee proprietor Lord Baltimore hoped that the 200 settlers who founded Maryland at St. Marys on Chesapeake Bay, would be the vanguard of a vast new feudal domain. Huge estates were to be awarded to his largely Catholic relatives, and gracious manor houses, modeled on those of England's aristocracy, were intended to sprout from the fertile forests. As in Virginia, colonists proved willing to come only if offered the opportunity to acquire land of their own. Soon they were dispersed around the Chesapeake region on modest farms, and the haughty land barons, mostly Catholic, were surrounded by resentful backcountry planters, mostly

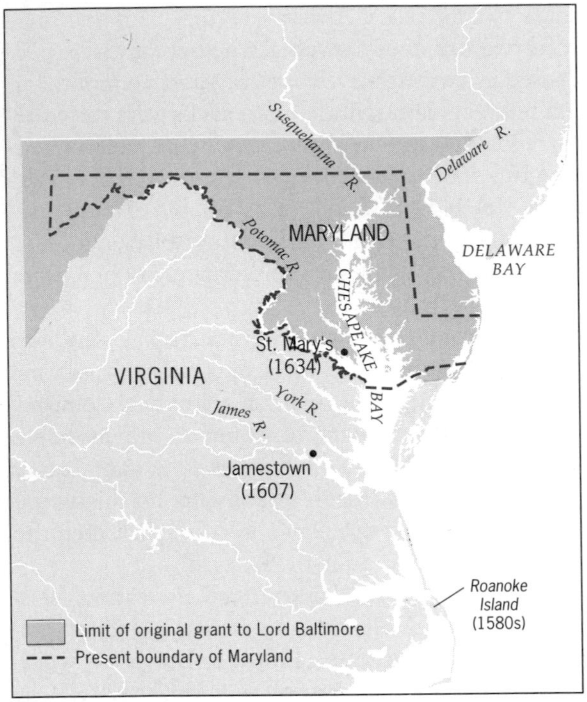
Susquehanna R.
Delaware R.
MARYLAND
Potomac R.
DELAWARE BAY
CHESAPEAKE BAY
St. Mary's (1634)
VIRGINIA
York R.
James R.
Jamestown (1607)
Roanoke Island (1580s)
Limit of original grant to Lord Baltimore
Present boundary of Maryland

Early Maryland and Virginia

Protestant. Resentment flared into open rebellion near the end of the century, and the Baltimore family for a time lost its proprietary rights.

Despite these tensions, Maryland prospered. Like Virginia, it blossomed forth in acres of tobacco. Also like Virginia, it depended for labor in its early years mainly on white indentured servants—penniless persons who bound themselves to work for a number of years to pay their passage. In both colonies it was only in the later years of the seventeenth century that black slaves began to be imported in large numbers.

Lord Baltimore permitted unusual freedom of worship both for his fellow Catholics and for Protestant settlers in Maryland. But when the heavy tide of Protestants threatened to submerge the Catholics, the Catholic settlers sought legal guarantees for their religious practice in the famed Act of Toleration, passed by the local representative assembly in 1649. This statute guaranteed toleration to all Christians, but it still decreed the death penalty for those, like Jews and atheists, who denied the divinity of Jesus. While falling far short of later standards of religious liberty, it did extend a cloak of protection to the uneasy Catholic minority.

The West Indies: Way Station to Mainland America

While the English were planting the first frail colonial shoots in the Chesapeake, they were also busily colonizing the West Indies. By the mid-seventeenth century England had secured its claim to several West Indian islands, including the large prize of Jamaica in 1655.

Sugar formed the foundation of the West Indian economy. What tobacco was to the Chesapeake, sugarcane was to the Caribbean—with one crucial difference. Tobacco was a poor man's crop that could be planted and processed easily. Sugarcane was a rich man's crop, requiring extensive planting and an elaborate refining process in a mill. Because of the need for land, and for the labor to clear it and to run the mills, sugar cultivation was a capital-intense business. Only wealthy growers with abundant capital to invest could succeed in producing the crop.

The sugar lords extended their dominion over the West Indies in the seventeenth century. To work their sprawling plantations, they imported enormous numbers of African slaves—more than a quarter of a million in the five decades after 1640. By about 1700, black slaves outnumbered white settlers in the English West Indies by nearly four to one, and the region's population has remained predominantly black ever since. West Indians thus take their place among the numerous children of the African diaspora—the vast scattering of African peoples throughout the New World in the three and half centuries following Columbus's discovery.

To control this large and potentially restive population of slaves, English authorities devised formal "codes" that defined the slaves' legal status and the masters' prerogatives. The notorious Barbados slave code of 1661 denied even the most fundamental rights to slaves and gave masters virtually complete control over their laborers.

A group of displaced English settlers from Barbados arrived in Carolina in 1670, bringing with

Early Carolina Coins   *These copper halfpennies bore the image of an elephant, an unofficial symbol of the colony, and a prayer for the Lords Proprietors.*

them a few African slaves, as well as the model of the Barbados code. In 1696, Carolina officially adopted a version of the code, which eventually inspired statutes governing slavery throughout the mainland colonies. The Caribbean islands thus served as a staging area for the slave system that would take root in British North America.

Colonizing the Carolinas

Civil wars convulsed England in the 1640s. King Charles I had dismissed Parliament in 1629, and when he recalled it in 1640, the members were mutinous. Finding their great champion in the Puritan soldier Oliver Cromwell, they ultimately beheaded Charles in 1649, and Cromwell ruled England for nearly a decade. Finally, Charles II, son of the decapitated king, was restored to the throne in 1660.

Colonization had been interrupted during this period of bloody unrest. Now, in the so-called Restoration period, empire building resumed with even greater intensity—and royal involvement. Carolina was formally created in 1670, after King Charles II granted to eight of his court favorites, the Lords Proprietors, an expanse of wilderness ribboning across the continent to the Pacific. These aristocratic founders hoped to grow foodstuffs to provision the sugar plantations in Barbados and to export non-English products like wine, silk, and olive oil.

Carolina prospered by developing close economic ties with the flourishing sugar islands of the English West Indies. Enlisting the aid of the coastal Savannah Indians, the colonists made the capture and sale of inland Indians a thriving export business. As many as 10,000 Indians were dispatched to lifelong labor in the West Indies, and others were sold to New England. The Savannahs' profitable alliance with the Carolinians finally came to an end in 1707. By 1710, after a series of bloody conflicts, the Indian tribes of coastal Carolina were all but extinct.

After much experimentation, rice emerged as the principal export crop in Carolina. Since rice was grown in Africa, the Carolinians were soon paying premium prices for West African slaves experienced in rice cultivation. The Africans' skill and their relative immunity to malaria made them ideal laborers on the hot and swampy rice plantations. By 1710 they constituted a majority of Carolinians.

Moss-festooned Charles Town—also named for King Charles II—rapidly became the busiest seaport in the South. Many high-spirited sons of English landed families, deprived of an inheritance, came to the Charleston area and gave it a rich aristocratic flavor. The village became a colorfully diverse community, to which French Protestant refugees and others were attracted by religious toleration.

Nearby, in Florida, the Catholic Spaniards bitterly resented the intrusion of these Protestant heretics. Carolina's frontier was often aflame. Armor-clad Spanish soldiers, often aided by their Indian allies, attacked English settlements during the successive Anglo-Spanish wars. But by 1700 Carolina was too strong to be wiped out.

The wild northern expanse of the huge Carolina grant bordered on Virginia. From the older colony there drifted down a ragtag group of poverty-stricken outcasts and religious dissenters, many of them expelled by the rich planters of Virginia, who belonged to the established Church of England. These small farmers, who were often "squatters" without legal right to the land, raised their tobacco and other crops on small farms with little need for slaves. Regarded as riff-raff by their snobbish neighbors, the North Carolinians earned a reputation for being irreligious and hospitable to pirates. Their location between aristocratic Virginia and aristocratic South Carolina caused the area to be dubbed "a vale of humility between two mountains of conceit." North Carolina was officially separated from South Carolina in 1712, and subsequently each segment became a royal colony.

North Carolina, unlike its sister colony, did not at first import large numbers of African slaves. But

The Iroquois

Long before the crowned heads of Europe turned their eyes and their dreams of empire toward the New World, a great military power had emerged in the Mohawk Valley of what is now New York State. The Iroquois Confederacy, dubbed by whites the League of the Iroquois, bound together five Indian nations—the Mohawks, Oneidas, Onondagas, Cayugas, and Senecas. According to Iroquois legend, it was founded in the late 1500s by two leaders, Deganawidah and Hiawatha. This proud and potent league vied with neighboring Indians for territorial supremacy and with invading Europeans for control of the fur trade, until it finally fell victim to the white man's diseases, whiskey, and muskets.

The building block of Iroquois society was the longhouse. Twenty-five feet wide and up to 200 feet long, these wooden structures sheltered from six to ten closely related nuclear families. The oldest woman in a clan was the honored matriarch, and the families' bloodlines were traced exclusively through the maternal line. Men dominated the society, but when they married they left their childhood hearth to join the longhouses of their wives.

As if sharing one great longhouse, the five nations joined in the Iroquois Confederacy but kept their own identities. Although they celebrated together and shared a common policy toward outsiders, they remained essentially independent of one another. On the eastern flank, the Mohawks, known as the Keepers of the Eastern Fire, specialized as middlemen with European traders, whereas the outlying Senecas, the Keepers of the Western Fire, became fur suppliers.

"Old Broken-Nose" *An Iroquois mask.*

Throughout the seventeenth and eighteenth centuries the Iroquois allied alternately with the British against the French and vice versa, for a time successfully working this perpetual rivalry to their advantage. But the confederacy divided during the American Revolution, with most tribes siding with the British. Their ultimate defeat left the confederacy in tatters, with most Iroquois moving to British Canada or ending up on reservations in western New York.

Reservation life was deeply demoralizing to the proud Iroquois, who sank into feuding and alcoholism. But in 1799 an Iroquois prophet named Handsome Lake arose, warning his people to mend their ways, affirm family values, and revive their old customs. Handsome Lake died in 1813, but his teachings, in the form of the Longhouse religion, survive to this day.

---

both Carolinas shared in the continuing tragedy of bloody relations between Indians and Europeans. After Tuscarora Indians fell upon the fledgling settlement of New Bern in 1711, the North Carolinians retaliated by crushing the Tuscaroras in battle and selling hundreds of them into slavery. In another ferocious encounter four years later, the South Carolinians defeated and scattered the Yamasees, thereby eliminating the last of the coastal Indian peoples in the southern colonies. In the interior Appalachian Mountains, however, the powerful Cherokees, Creeks, and Iroquois remained. (See "Makers of America: The Iroquois," pp. 24–25.) Stronger and more numerous than their coastal cousins, they managed for half a century more to contain British settlement on the coastal plain east of the mountains.

Late-Coming Georgia: The Buffer Colony

Pine-forested Georgia, with the harbor of Savannah nourishing its chief settlement, was formally founded in 1733. It proved to be the last of the thirteen colonies to be planted—126 years after Virginia and 52 years after Pennsylvania. Chronologically Georgia belongs elsewhere, but geographically it may be grouped with its southern neighbors.

Georgia was valued by the British crown chiefly as a buffer. It would serve to protect the more valuable Carolinas from inroads by vengeful Spaniards from Florida and by the hostile French from Louisiana. Georgia in truth suffered much buf-

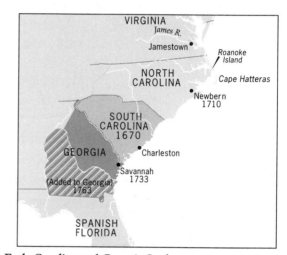

Early Carolina and Georgia Settlements

feting, especially when wars broke out between Spain and Britain in the European cockpit.

Named in honor of George II of Britain, Georgia was launched by a high-minded group of philanthropists. Aside from producing silk and wine, and strengthening the empire, they were determined to create a haven for wretched souls imprisoned for debt. The ablest of the founders was the dynamic soldier-statesman James Oglethorpe, who became keenly interested in prison reform after one of his friends died in a debtors' jail. As an able military leader, Oglethorpe repelled Spanish attacks. As an imperialist and a philanthropist, he saved "the Charity Colony" by his energetic leadership and by heavily mortgaging his own personal fortunes.

The hamlet of Savannah, like Charleston, was a melting-pot community that included German Lutherans and Scottish Highlanders, among others. All Christian worshipers except Catholics enjoyed religious toleration. Many Bible-toting missionaries arrived to work among debtors and Indians, including young John Wesley, who later returned to England and founded the Methodist Church.

Georgia grew with painful slowness and at the end of the colonial era was perhaps the least populous of the colonies. Prosperity through a large-plantation economy was thwarted by an unhealthful climate, by early restrictions on black slavery, and by demoralizing Spanish attacks.

The Plantation Colonies

Certain distinctive features were shared by all of England's southern mainland colonies: Maryland, Virginia, North Carolina, South Carolina, and Georgia. Broad-acred, these outposts of empire were all in some degree dominated by a plantation economy. Slavery was established in all the plantation colonies, though only after 1750 in reform-minded Georgia. Profitable staple crops were the rule, notably tobacco, rice, and indigo, though to a lesser extent in small-farm North Carolina. Immense acreage in the hands of a favored few fostered a strong aristocratic atmosphere, except in North Carolina and to some extent in debtor-tinged Georgia. The wide scattering of plantations and farms, often along stately rivers, made the establishment of churches and schools both difficult and expensive.

Although the tax-supported Church of England became the dominant faith, all the plantation colonies permitted some religious toleration. The plantation colonies were all in some degree expansionary. "Soul butchery" by excessive tobacco growing drove settlers westward, and the long, lazy rivers encouraged penetration of the continent—and continuing confrontation with Native Americans.

CHRONOLOGY

1585	Raleigh founds Roanoke colony.	1644	Second Anglo-Powhatan War.
1588	England defeats Spanish Armada.	1649	Act of Toleration established in Maryland.
1607	Virginia colony founded at Jamestown.	1670	Carolina colony created.
1614	First Anglo-Powhatan War ends.	1711–1713	Tuscarora War, North Carolina.
1616	Rolfe perfects cultivation of tobacco in Virginia.	1712	North Carolina officially separates from South Carolina.
1619	First black Africans arrive in Jamestown.	1715–1716	Yamasee War, South Carolina.
	Virginia House of Burgesses established.	1733	Georgia colony founded.
1634	Maryland colony founded.		
1640s	Large-scale slave-labor system established in English West Indies.		

Varying Viewpoints

Only in the last generation or so have historians begun to appreciate the *variety* of patterns of colonization in the New World. Early histories of America contrasted the alleged rapacity of the Spanish *conquistadores* with the high-minded religiosity of the Puritan settlers of New England. But recent scholarship has stressed the cultural contributions of the Spanish colonizers and their sincere, if sometimes misguided, efforts to Christianize the Native Americans.

Scholars have also shed new light on the diverse motives, methods, and consequences of the English settlements in the New World. The numbers alone tell an interesting story. Up to 1700, about 220,000 English colonists went to the Caribbean, about 120,000 to the southern mainland colonies, and only about 40,000 to the Middle Atlantic and New England colonies.

Studies such as Richard S. Dunn's *Sugar and Slaves* emphasize the importance of the Caribbean in early English colonization efforts and make clear that the desire for economic gain, more than the quest for religious freedom, fueled the migration to the islands. Similarly, works such as Edmund S. Morgan's *American Slavery, American Freedom* stress the role of economic ambition in explaining the English peopling of the Chesapeake—and the eventual importation of African slaves to that region.

Bernard Bailyn's *Voyagers to the West* demonstrates that there was scarcely a "typical" English migrant to the New World, nor a "typical" colony. English colonists migrated both singly and in families, for economic as well as religious reasons, and they established strikingly different societies in the sugar islands of the Caribbean, where they were hugely outnumbered by their black slaves; in the rice plantations of the Carolinas, where they were slightly outnumbered by African slaves; in the tobacco plantations of the Chesapeake, where slaves composed a significant but decidedly minority element in the population; and in the northern mainland colonies, where slavery was a rarity. But although they got off to a slow start, by the eighteenth century the northern mainland colonies accounted for more than half the English settlers in the New World. Explaining these surprisingly different patterns of evolution among the various English colonies is a major preoccupation of contemporary scholars.

SELECT READINGS

Primary Source Documents

Richard Hakluyt, *Divers Voyages Touching the Discovery of America and the Islands Adjacent,** edited by J. W. Jones (1850), supplied the rationale for the establishment of English colonies in North America. John Smith, "Generall Historie of Virginia," in *Travels and Works of Captain John Smith,** edited by Edward Arber (1910), is the account of the amazing, vain man who steered Jamestown through its first few years.

Secondary Sources

The immediate English background of colonization is colorfully presented in Peter Laslett, *The World We Have Lost* (1965), and in Carl Bridenbaugh, *Vexed and Troubled Englishmen, 1590–1642* (1968). A modern classic is Wallace Notestein, *The English People on the Eve of Colonization, 1603–1630* (1954). Bernard Bailyn offers a detailed statistical portrait of a single group of immigrants in *Voyagers to the West: A Passage in the Peopling of America on the Eve of the Revolution* (1986). A concise summary of his broad argument on patterns of immigration can also be found in *The Peopling of British North America: An Introduction* (1986). Karen Ordahl Kupperman, *Settling With the Indians: The Meeting of English and Indian Cultures in America, 1580–1640* (1980), and James Axtell, *The Invasion*

Within: The Conflict of Cultures in Colonial America (1985), discuss contact between Indians and Europeans. James Merrell, *The Indian's New World,* describing the wrenching experience of the Catawba Indians, is the best ethnohistorical account of a single tribe for the entire period. The Chesapeake region has received much attention, especially in Aubrey C. Land et al., *Law, Society, and Politics in Early Maryland* (1977), Thad W. Tate and David L. Ammerman, eds., *The Chesapeake in the Seventeenth Century* (1979), and Paul G. E. Clemens, *The Atlantic Economy and Colonial Maryland's Eastern Shore* (1980).

The most comprehensive account of the various colonial economies is contained in John J. McCusker and Russell R. Menard, *The Economy of British North America, 1607–1789* (1985). The role of slavery in early colonial society gets perceptive treatment in Edmund S. Morgan, *American Slavery, American Freedom* (1975). See also Winthrop Jordan's monumental *White Over Black* (1968) and Peter Wood's account of South Carolina, *Black Majority* (1974). Gary Nash analyzes relations among all three races in *Red, White, and Black: The Peoples of Early America* (1974).

CHAPTER 3

Settling the Northern Colonies, 1619–1700

God hath sifted a Nation that he might send Choice Grain into this Wilderness.

William Stoughton [of Massachusetts Bay], 1669

The Protestant Reformation Produces Puritanism

Little did the German monk Martin Luther know, when he nailed his protests against Catholic doctrines to the door of Wittenberg's castle church in 1517, that he was shaping the destiny of a yet unheralded nation. Denouncing the authority of priests and popes, Luther declared that the Bible alone was the source of God's word. He ignited a fire of religious reform (the Protestant Reformation) that licked its way across Europe for more than a century, dividing people, toppling sovereigns, and kindling the spiritual fervor of millions of men and women—some of whom helped to found America.

The reforming flame burned especially brightly in the bosom of John Calvin of Geneva. This somber and severe religious leader elaborated Luther's ideas in ways that profoundly affected the thought and character of generations of Americans yet unborn. Calvinism became the dominant theological credo not only of the New England Puritans but of other American settlers as well.

According to Calvin, God was all-powerful and all-good, while humans, because of the effects of

original sin, were weak and wicked. God was also all-knowing, and since the first moment of creation had destined some souls—the *elect*—for eternal bliss and others for eternal torment. Good works could not save those whom *predestination* had marked for the infernal fires.

But neither could the elect count on their determined salvation and lead lives of wild, immoral abandon. For one thing, no one could be certain of his or her status in the heavenly ledger. Gnawing doubts about their eternal fate caused Calvinists to seek signs of "conversion," or the receipt of God's free gift of saving grace. Those who had the intense personal experience of conversion were expected to lead "sanctified" lives, demonstrating by their holy behavior that they were among the "visible saints."

These doctrines swept into England just as King Henry VIII was breaking his ties with the Roman Catholic church in the 1530s, making himself the head of the Church of England. Henry would have been content to retain Roman rituals and creeds, but some English religious reformers sought a total purification of English Christianity. Many of these "Puritans," as it happened, came from commercially depressed woolen districts. Calvinism fed on this social unrest and provided spiritual comfort to the economically disadvantaged. Increasingly unhappy with the snaillike progress of the Protestant Reformation in England, Puritans burned with pious zeal to see the Church of England wholly de-Catholicized.

All Puritans agreed that only "visible saints" should be admitted to church membership, which meant that the "saints" had to share pews and communion rails with the damned. A tiny group of extreme Calvinists, known as Separatists, therefore vowed to break away entirely from the Church of England. King James I, who was head of both the church and the state in England, threatened to harass the more bothersome Separatists out of the land.

The Pilgrims End Their Pilgrimage at Plymouth

The most famous congregation of Separatists, fleeing royal wrath, departed for Holland in 1608. During the ensuing twelve years of toil and poverty, they were increasingly distressed by the "Dutchification" of their children. They longed to find a haven where they could live and die as Englishmen. America was the logical refuge.

A group of the Separatists in Holland, after negotiating with the Virginia Company, at length secured rights to settle under its jurisdiction. But their crowded *Mayflower*, sixty-five days at sea, missed its destination and arrived off the rocky coast of New England in 1620, with a total of 102 persons.

The Pilgrims did not make their initial landing at Plymouth Rock, as commonly supposed, but undertook a number of preliminary surveys. They finally chose for their site the shore of inhospitable Plymouth Bay. This area was outside the domain of the Virginia Company, and consequently the settlers became squatters. They were without legal right to the land, and without specific authority to establish a government.

Before disembarking, the Pilgrim Fathers drew up and signed the brief Mayflower Compact. Although setting an invaluable precedent for later written constitutions, this document was not a constitution at all. It was a simple agreement to form a crude government and to submit to the will of the majority under the regulations agreed upon. The compact was signed by forty-one adult males, eleven of them with the exalted rank of "mister," though not by the servants and two seamen. The pact was a promising step toward genuine self-government, for soon the adult male settlers were assembling to make their own laws in open-discussion town meetings—a laboratory of liberty.

The Pilgrims' first winter of 1620–1621 took a grisly toll. Only 44 out of 102 survived. Yet when the *Mayflower* sailed back to England in the spring, not a single one of the courageous band of Separatists left. As one of them wrote, "It is not with us as with other men, whom small things can discourage."

God made His children prosperous, so the Pilgrims believed. The next autumn, that of 1621, brought bountiful harvests and with them the first Thanksgiving Day in New England. In time the frail colony found sound economic legs in fur, fish, and lumber. The beaver and the Bible were the early mainstays: the one for the sustenance of the body, the other for the sustenance of the soul.

Quiet and quaint, the little colony of Plymouth was never important economically or numerically. Its population numbered only 7,000 souls by 1691, when, still charterless, it merged with its giant neighbor, the Massachusetts Bay Colony. But the tiny settlement of Pilgrims was big both morally and spiritually.

The Bay Colony Bible Commonwealth

The Separatist Pilgrims were dedicated extremists—the purest Puritans. More moderate Puritans sought to reform the Church of England from within. But their efforts faced catastrophe when Charles I dismissed Parliament in 1629 and sanctioned the anti-Puritan persecutions of the reactionary Archbishop William Laud.

In 1629, an energetic group of non-Separatist Puritans, fearing for their faith and for England's future, secured a royal charter to form the Massachusetts Bay Company. Stealing a march on both king and church, the newcomers brought their charter with them when they emigrated to the Massachusetts area. For many years they used it as a kind of constitution, out of easy reach of royal authority.

The Massachusetts Bay enterprise was singularly blessed. The well-equipped expedition of 1630, with eleven vessels carrying nearly a thousand immigrants, started the colony off on a larger scale than any of the other English settlements. Continuing turmoil in England tossed up additional enriching waves of Puritans on the shores of Massachusetts in the following decade (see "Makers of America: The English," pp. 32–33). During the "Great Migration" of the 1630s, about 75,000 refugees left England. But not all of them were Puritans, and only about 14,000 came to Massachusetts. Many were attracted to the warm and fertile West Indies, especially Barbados.

Many fairly prosperous, educated persons emigrated to the Bay Colony, including John Winthrop, a well-to-do pillar of English society. A successful attorney and manor lord in England, Winthrop eagerly accepted the offer to become governor of the Massachusetts Bay Colony, believing that he had a "calling" from God to lead the new religious experiment. He served as governor or deputy governor for nineteen years. The resources and skills of talented settlers like Winthrop helped Massachusetts prosper, and the Bay Colony rapidly shot to the fore as the biggest and the most influential of the New England outposts.

Massachusetts also benefited from a shared sense of purpose among most of the first settlers. "We shall be as a city upon a hill," a beacon to humanity, declared Governor Winthrop. The Puritan Bay colonists believed that they had a covenant with God, an agreement to build a holy society that would be a model for humankind.

Building the Bay Colony

These common convictions deeply shaped the infant colony's life. Soon after arrival the franchise was extended to all "freemen"—adult males who belonged to the Puritan congregations, which in time came to be called collectively the Congregational church. On this basis about two-fifths of adult males enjoyed the franchise in provincial affairs, a far larger proportion than in contemporary England. Town governments, which conducted much important business, were even more inclusive. There all male property holders, and in some cases other residents as well, discussed and voted on public issues.

Yet the provincial government, liberal by the standards of the time, was not a democracy. "If the people be governors," asked one Puritan clergyman, "who shall be the governed?" True, the freemen annually elected the governor and his assistants, as well as a representative assembly called the General Court. But only Puritans—the "visible saints" who were alone eligible for church membership—could be freemen. And according to the doctrine of the covenant, the whole purpose of government was to enforce God's laws—which applied to believers and nonbelievers alike. Moreover, nonbelievers as well as believers paid taxes for the government-supported church.

Religious leaders thus wielded enormous influence in the Massachusetts "Bible commonwealth." They powerfully influenced admission to church membership by conducting public interrogations of persons claiming to have experienced conversions. But the power of the preachers was not absolute. Because Puritans had suffered so much at the hands of a "political" Anglican clergy, they barred clergymen from holding formal political office. In a limited way, the Bay colonists thus endorsed the idea of the separation of church and state.

The Puritans were a worldly lot, despite—or even because of—their spiritual intensity. Like John Winthrop, they believed in the doctrine of a "calling" to do God's work on this earth. They shared in what was later called the "Protestant ethic," which involved serious commitment to work and to engagement in worldly pursuits. Legend to the contrary, they also enjoyed simple pleasures; they ate plentifully, drank heartily, sang songs occasionally, and made love monogamously.

Yet life was serious business, and hell was

The English

During the late Middle Ages, the Black Death and other epidemics that ravaged England kept the island's population in check. But by 1500, increased resistance to such diseases allowed the population to soar; and a century later, the island nation was bursting at the seams. This population explosion, combined with economic depression and religious repression, sparked the first major European migration to England's New World colonies.

Some of those who voyaged to Virginia and Maryland in the seventeenth century were independent artisans or younger members of English gentry families. But roughly three-quarters of the English migrants to the Chesapeake during this period came as servants, signed to "indentures" ranging from four to seven years. One English observer described such indentured servants as "idle, lazie, simple people," and another complained that many of those taking ship for the colonies "have been pursued by hue-and-cry for robberies, burglaries, or breaking prison."

Whereas English immigration to the Chesapeake was spread over nearly a century, most English voyagers to New England arrived within a single decade. In the twelve years between 1629 and 1642, some 14,000 Puritans swarmed to the Massachusetts Bay Colony. Fleeing a sustained economic depression and the cruel religious repression of Charles I, the Puritans came to plant a godly commonwealth in New England's rocky soil.

In contrast to the single indentured servants of the Chesapeake, the New England Puritans migrated in family groups, and in many cases whole communi-

ties were transplanted from England to America. Although they remained united by their common language and common Puritan faith, they planted a variety of English seeds in New England. The settlers of Rowley, Massachusetts, continued their Yorkshire traditions of granting families very small farming plots and maintaining vast common fields worked by and for the whole community. On the other hand, the settlers of Watertown, Massachusetts, brought with them the fervid commercial spirit of their home in East Anglia. Farmers in East Anglia, the hub of English clothmaking, engaged in a brisk land trade and tilled no common fields—practices they continued in Watertown. Political practices, too, reflected the towns' English antecedents. In Ipswich, Massachusetts, another town settled by East Anglian Puri-

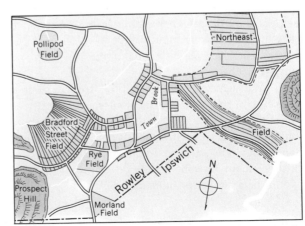

Land Use in Rowley, Massachusetts, c. 1650 *Note the small private plots and large common fields.*

tans, the ruling selectmen served long terms and ruled with an iron hand. By contrast, local politics in the town of Newbury were bitter and contentious, and officeholders were hard-pressed to win re-election; the towns' founders came from western England, a region with little tradition of local government. Although the Puritans' imperial masters eventually circumscribed the towns' precious autonomy, this diverse heritage of fiercely independent New England towns endured, reasserting itself during the American Revolution.

---

real—a hell where sinners shriveled and shrieked for divine mercy. Puritan clergyman Michael Wigglesworth's poem "Day of Doom" (1662) described the horrifying fate of the damned:

> They cry, they roar for anguish sore,
>   and gnaw their tongues for horrour,
> But get away without delay,
>   Christ pitties not your cry:
> Depart to hell, there may you yell,
>   and roar Eternally.

Trouble in the Bible Commonwealth

The Bay Colony enjoyed a high degree of social harmony, stemming from common beliefs, in its early years. But even in this tightly knit community, dissension soon appeared. Quakers, who flouted the authority of the Puritan clergy, were persecuted with fines, floggings, and banishment. In one extreme case, four Quakers were executed for their beliefs.

A sharp challenge to Puritan orthodoxy came from Anne Hutchinson. An exceptionally intelligent, strong-willed, and talkative woman, she claimed that the truly saved need not bother to obey the law of either God or man. This assertion, known as *antinomianism* (from the Greek, "against the law"), was high heresy. Brought to trial in 1638, the quick-witted Hutchinson bamboozled her clerical inquisitors for days, until she eventually stated that she had come by her beliefs through a direct revelation from God. This was even higher heresy. After the Puritan

Anne Hutchinson, Dissenter   *Mistress Hutchinson (1591–1643) held unorthodox views that challenged the authority of the clergy and the very integrity of the Puritan experiment in the Massachusetts Bay Colony.*

magistrates banished her, she traveled on foot to Rhode Island, and finally moved to New York, where she and all but one of her household were killed by Indians.

More threatening to the Puritan leaders was a personable and popular Salem minister, Roger Williams. An extreme Separatist with an unrestrained tongue, Williams demanded a clean break with the corrupt Church of England and challenged the legality of the Bay Colony's charter, which he condemned for its unfairness to the Indians. As if all this were not enough, he went on to deny the authority of civil government to regulate religious behavior—a seditious blow at the Puritan idea of government's very purpose. Their patience exhausted by 1635, the Bay Colony authorities found Williams guilty of disseminating "newe & dangerous opinions" and ordered him banished.

New England Spreads Out

Aided by friendly Indians, Roger Williams fled to the Rhode Island area in 1636, where he built a Baptist church. He established complete freedom of religion, even for Jews and Catholics, a degree of toleration far ahead of the other English settlements in the New World. He demanded no oaths regarding one's religious beliefs, no compulsory attendance at worship, and no taxes to support a state church.

Those outcasts who clustered about Roger Williams also enjoyed additional blessings. They exercised simple manhood suffrage from the start, though this boon was later modified by a property qualification. Opposed to special privilege of any kind, the malcontents and exiles who largely populated "Rogues' Island" had little in common with Roger Williams—except banishment. The Puritan clergy back in Boston sneered at Rhode Island as "that sewer" in which the "Lord's debris" had collected and rotted. Stubbornly individualistic, the squatters in "Little Rhody" finally established rights to the soil when they secured a charter from Parliament in 1644. A huge bronze statue of the "Independent Man" appropriately stands today on the dome of the state house in Providence.

The fertile valley of the Connecticut River had meanwhile attracted a sprinkling of Dutch and En-

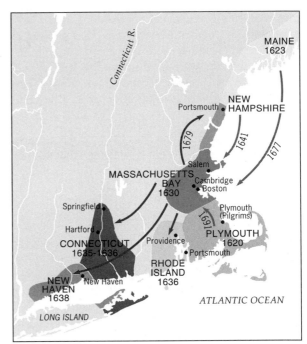

Seventeenth-Century New England Settlements *The Massachusetts Bay Colony was the hub of New England. All earlier colonies grew into it; all later colonies grew out of it.*

glish settlers. Hartford was founded in 1635, and the next year an energetic group of Boston Puritans, led by the Reverend Thomas Hooker, swarmed into the area. In 1639, the settlers of the new Connecticut River colony drafted a trailblazing document known as the Fundamental Orders, which established a regime democratically controlled by the "substantial" citizens.

Another flourishing Connecticut settlement began to spring up in New Haven in 1638. It was a prosperous community, founded by Puritans who contrived to set up an even closer church-government alliance than in Massachusetts. The colonists dreamed of making New Haven a flourishing seaport, but they fell into disfavor with Charles II because they sheltered two of the judges who had condemned his father, Charles I, to death. In 1662 the crown granted a charter that merged New Haven with the more democratic outposts in the Connecticut Valley.

Two smaller settlements grew up north of Massachusetts Bay. The fishermen and fur traders who had settled along the coast of Maine even before the founding of Plymouth were absorbed by Massachusetts Bay in 1677. The Maine territory remained part of Massachusetts for nearly a century and a half before becoming a separate state. In 1642 the Bay Colony also annexed its immediate northern neighbor, New Hampshire, under a strained interpretation of the Massachusetts charter. The king, annoyed by this display of greed, separated New Hampshire from Massachusetts in 1679 and made it a royal colony.

Puritans versus Indians

The spread of English settlements inevitably led to clashes with the Indians, who were particularly weak in New England. Shortly before the Pilgrims arrived at Plymouth in 1620, an epidemic, probably triggered by contact with English fishermen, swept through the coastal tribes and killed more than three-fourths of the native people. The deserted fields that greeted the Plymouth settlers provided grim evidence of the impact of the disease.

In no position to resist the English incursion, the local Wampanoag Indians at first befriended the settlers. Cultural accommodation was facilitated by Squanto, a Wampanoag who learned English from the ship's captain who had kidnapped him some years earlier. The Wampanoag chieftain Massasoit signed a treaty with the Plymouth Pilgrims in 1621 and helped them celebrate the first Thanksgiving after the autumn harvests that same year.

As more English settlers arrived and pushed inland into the Connecticut River Valley, confrontations between Indians and whites ruptured these peaceful relations. Hostilities exploded in 1637 between the settlers and the powerful Pequot tribe. In a brutal war the English militiamen virtually annihilated the Pequots.

During the ensuing four decades of tense peace, the Puritans made some feeble efforts to convert the remaining Indians to Christianity. But their missionary zeal never equaled that of the Spanish and French Catholics, and a mere handful of Indians were gathered into Puritan "praying towns."

The Indians' only hope for resisting English encroachment lay in intertribal unity—a pan-Indian alliance against the swiftly spreading settlements. In 1675 Massasoit's son Metacom, called "King Philip" by the English, forged such an alliance and mounted a series of coordinated assaults on English villages throughout New England. When the war ended in 1676, fifty-two Puritan towns had been attacked, and twelve destroyed entirely. Hundreds of colonists and many more Indians lay dead. Metacom was captured, drawn, and quartered. His head was carried on a pike back to Plymouth, where it was displayed for years.

King Philip's War slowed the westward march of English settlement in New England for several decades. But the war inflicted a lasting defeat on New England's Indians. Drastically reduced in numbers, disspirited, and disbanded, they never again seriously threatened the New England colonists.

Seeds of Colonial Unity and Independence

A path-breaking experiment in union was launched in 1643, when four colonies banded together to form the New England Confederation. The primary purpose of the confederation was defense against foes or potential foes, notably the Indians, the French, and the Dutch. Purely intercolonial problems, such as runaway servants and criminals who had fled from one colony to another, also came within the jurisdiction of the confederation. Each member, regardless of size, wielded two votes—an arrangement highly displeasing to the most populous colony, Massachusetts Bay.

The confederation was essentially an exclusive Puritan club. It consisted of the two Massachusetts colonies (the Bay Colony and bantam-sized Plymouth) and the two Connecticut colonies (New Haven and the scattered valley settlements). The Puritan leaders blackballed Rhode Island as well as the Maine outposts. Weak though it was, the confederation was the first notable milestone on the long and rocky road toward colonial unity.

Back in England, the king paid little attention to the American colonies during the early years of their planting. They were allowed, in effect, to become semiautonomous commonwealths. This era of benign neglect was prolonged when the crown, struggling to retain its power, became enmeshed during the 1640s in civil wars with the parliamentarians.

But when Charles II was restored to the English throne in 1660, the royalists and their Church of England allies were once more firmly in the saddle. Puritan hopes of eventually purifying the Church of England withered. Worse, Charles II was determined to take an active, aggressive hand in the management of the colonies. His plans ran headlong against the habits that decades of relative independence had bred in the colonists.

Deepening colonial defiance was nowhere more glaringly revealed than in Massachusetts. As punishment, the king gave new charters to Massachusetts' colonial rivals, Connecticut and Rhode Island. A final and crushing blow fell on the stiff-necked Bay Colony in 1684, when its precious charter was revoked by the London authorities.

Andros Promotes the First American Revolution

Massachusetts suffered further humiliation in 1686, when the Dominion of New England was created by royal authority. Unlike the homegrown New England Confederation, it was imposed from London. Embracing at first all New England, it was expanded two years later to include New York and East and West Jersey. The dominion also aimed at bolstering colonial defense in the event of war with the Indians.

More important, the Dominion of New England was designed to promote urgently needed efficiency in the administration of the English Navigation Laws. Those laws reflected the intensifying colonial rivalries of the seventeenth century. They sought to stitch England's overseas possessions more tightly to the motherland, by throttling American trade with countries not ruled by the English crown. Like colonial peoples everywhere, the Americans chafed at such confinements, and smuggling became an increasingly common and honorable occupation.

At the head of the new dominion stood autocratic Sir Edmund Andros, an able English military man, conscientious but tactless. Establishing headquarters in Puritan Boston, he generated much hostility by his open affiliation with the despised Church of England. The colonials were also outraged by his noisy and Sabbath-profaning soldiers, who were accused of teaching the people "to drink, blaspheme, curse, and damn."

Andros was prompt to use the mailed fist. He ruthlessly curbed the cherished town meetings and laid heavy restrictions on the courts, the press, and the schools. Dispensing with the popular assemblies, he taxed the people without the consent of their duly elected representatives. He also strove to enforce the unpopular Navigation Laws and suppress smuggling. Liberty-loving colonials, accustomed to unusual privileges during long decades of neglect, were goaded to the verge of revolt.

The people of old England, likewise resisting oppression, stole a march on the people of New England. In 1688–1689 they engineered the memorable Glorious (or Bloodless) Revolution. Dethroning the despotic and unpopular Catholic James II, they enthroned the Protestant rulers of the Netherlands, the Dutch king William III and his English wife, Mary, daughter of James II.

When the news of the Glorious Revolution reached America, the ramshackle Dominion of New England collapsed like a house of cards. A Boston mob, catching the fever, rose against the existing regime. Sir Edmund Andros attempted to flee in woman's clothing but was betrayed by boots protruding beneath his dress. He was then shipped off to England.

Massachusetts, though rid of the despotic Andros, did not gain as much from the upheaval as it had hoped. In 1691 it was arbitrarily made a royal colony, with a new charter and a new royal governor. The permanent loss of the ancient charter was a staggering blow to the proud Puritans, who never fully recovered. Worst of all, the privilege of voting, which had been a monopoly of church members, was now to be enjoyed by all qualified male property holders.

England's Glorious Revolution had a far-flung impact, for unrest erupted from New England to the Carolinas. The upheaval resulted in a permanent abandonment of many of the objectionable features of the Andros system, as well as a temporary breakdown of the new imperial policy of enforcing the Navigation Laws.

Yet residues remained of Charles II's effort to assert tighter administrative control over his empire. More English officials—judges, clerks, customs officials—were now staffing the courts and strolling the wharves of English America. Many were incompetent, corrupt hacks who knew little and cared less about American affairs. Appointed by influential patrons in far-off England, they blocked by their presence the rise of local leaders to positions of political power. Aggrieved Americans viewed them with mounting contempt and resentment as the eighteenth century wore on.

New Netherland Becomes New York

Late in the sixteenth century, the oppressed people of the Netherlands unfurled the standard of rebellion against Catholic Spain. After bloody and protracted fighting, they finally succeeded, with the aid of Protestant England, in winning their independence. This vigorous little lowland nation quickly emerged as a major commercial and naval power that ungratefully challenged the supremacy of its former benefactor, England.

The Dutch Republic also became a leading colonial power through the activities of the enterprising Dutch East India Company. The company's vast riches came mostly from the East Indies, where it maintained an enormous and profitable empire for three centuries. In 1609 it employed an English explorer, Henry Hudson, who ventured into Delaware Bay and New York Bay and then ascended the Hudson River, hoping that he had at last chanced upon the coveted shortcut through the continent. But, as the event proved, he merely filed a Dutch claim to the magnificently watered and wooded area.

New Netherland was permanently planted in 1623–1624 by the Dutch West India Company, the less wealthy counterpart of the East India Company. Never more than a secondary interest of the founders, the colony was exploited for its quick-profit fur trade. The company's most brilliant stroke was to buy Manhattan Island from the Indians (who did not actually "own" it) for trinkets—22,000 acres of what is now perhaps the most valuable real estate in the world for pennies per acre.

A threat to New Netherland soon came from the Swedes, who trespassed on Dutch preserves by planting the colony of New Sweden on the Delaware River in 1638. Resenting the Swedish intrusion, the Dutch dispatched a small military expedition in 1655, led by the energetic and hot-headed director-general Peter Stuyvesant, who was dubbed "Father Wooden Leg" by the Indians. The Swedish fort fell easily and the colony came to an abrupt end, leaving behind only a sprinkling of Swedish place names, log cabins (the first in America), and an admixture of Swedish blood.

Just as New Netherland absorbed New Sweden, it was soon the turn of the Dutch to be swallowed up by the English. In 1664, after Charles II had granted the area to his brother, the Duke of York, a strong English squadron appeared off the decrepit defenses of New Amsterdam. A fuming Peter Stuyvesant, short of all munitions except courage, was forced to surrender without firing a shot. New Amsterdam was thereupon renamed New York, in honor of the Duke of York. England won a splendid harbor, strategically located in the middle of the mainland colonies, and a stately Hudson River penetrating the interior. The English banner now waved triumphantly, with the removal of this foreign wedge, over a solid stretch of territory from Maine to the Carolinas.

The conquered Dutch province tenaciously retained many of the illiberal features of earlier days. An autocratic spirit survived, and the aristocratic element gained strength when certain corrupt English governors granted immense acreage to their favorites. Influential landowning families—such as the Livingstons and the De Lanceys—wielded disproportionate power in the affairs of colonial New York. These monopolistic land policies, combined with the lordly atmosphere, discouraged many European immigrants from coming. The physical growth of New York was correspondingly retarded.

Penn's Holy Experiment in Pennsylvania

A remarkable group of dissenters, commonly known as Quakers, arose in England during the mid-1600s. Their name derived from the report that they

New Amsterdam, c. 1653 *The site of latter-day New York, this colonial village was still in Dutch hands in 1653, as shown by the Dutch-style windmill.*

"quaked" when under deep religious emotion. Officially they were and still are known as the Religious Society of Friends.

Quakers were especially offensive to the authorities, both religious and civil. They refused to support the established Church of England with taxes. They built simple meetinghouses, without a paid clergy, and "spoke up" themselves in meetings when moved. Believing that they were all children in the sight of God, they kept their broad-brimmed hats on in the presence of their "betters" and addressed others with simple "thees" and "thous," rather than with conventional titles. They would take no oaths because Jesus had said, "Swear not at all." This peculiarity often embroiled them with government officials, for "test oaths" were still required to establish the fact that a person was not a Roman Catholic.

The Quakers, beyond a doubt, were a people of deep conviction. They abhorred strife and warfare and refused military service. As advocates of passive resistance, they would turn the other cheek and rebuild their meetinghouse on the site where their enemies had torn it down. Their courage and devotion to principle finally triumphed. Though at times they seemed stubborn and unreasonable, they were a simple, devoted, democratic people, contending in their own way for religious and civic freedom.

William Penn, a well-born and athletic young Englishman, was attracted to the Quaker faith in 1660, when only sixteen years old. His father, disapproving, administered a sound flogging. After various adventures in the army (the best portrait of the peaceful Quaker has him in armor), the youth firmly embraced the despised faith and suffered much persecution. The courts branded him a "saucy" and "impertinent" fellow. Several hundred of his less fortunate fellow Quakers died of cruel treatment, and thousands more were fined, flogged, or cast into "nasty stinking prisons."

Penn's thoughts naturally turned to the New World, where a sprinkling of Quakers had already fled, notably to Rhode Island, North Carolina, and New Jersey. Eager to establish an asylum for his people, he also hoped to experiment with liberal ideas in government, and at the same time make a profit. Finally, in 1681, he managed to secure from the king an immense grant of fertile land, in consideration of a monetary debt owed to his deceased father by the crown. The king called the area Pennsylvania ("Penn's Woodland") in honor of the father.

Pennsylvania was by far the best advertised of all the colonies. Its founder sent out paid agents and distributed countless pamphlets printed in English, Dutch, French, and German. Unlike the lures of many an American real estate promoter, then and later, Penn's inducements were generally truthful. He especially welcomed forward-looking spirits and substantial citizens, including industrious carpenters, masons, shoemakers, and other manual workers. His liberal land policy, which encouraged substantial holdings of land, was instrumental in attracting a heavy inflow of immigrants.

Quaker Pennsylvania and Her Neighbors

Penn formally launched his colony in 1681. His task was simplified by the presence of several thousand "squatters"—Dutch, Swedes, English, Welsh—who were already scattered along the banks of the Delaware River. Philadelphia, meaning "brotherly love" in Greek, was more carefully planned than most colonial cities and consequently enjoyed wide and attractive streets.

Penn farsightedly bought land from the Indians, including Chief Tammany, later patron saint of New York's political Tammany Hall. His treatment of the native people was so fair that the Quaker "broad brims" went among them unarmed and even employed them as baby tenders. For a brief period, Pennsylvania seemed the promised land of amicable Indian-white relations. Some southern tribes even migrated there, seeking the Quaker haven. But ironically, Quaker tolerance proved the undoing of Quaker Indian policy. As non-Quaker European immigrants flooded into the province, they undermined the Quakers' own benevolent policy toward the Indians. The feisty Scots-Irish were particularly unpersuaded by Quaker idealism. Penn's new proprietary regime was unusually liberal and included a representative assembly elected by the landowners. There was no tax-supported state church. Freedom of worship was guaranteed to all residents, although Penn, under pressure from London, was forced to deny Catholics and Jews the privilege of voting or holding office. The death penalty was imposed only for treason and murder, as compared with some 200 capital crimes in England.

William Penn Signs a Treaty with the Indians *The peace-loving Quaker founder of Pennsylvania made a serious effort to live in harmony with the Indians, but the westward thrust of white settlement eventually caused friction, as in other colonies.*

Among other noteworthy features, no provision was made by the Quakers of Pennsylvania for a military defense. No restrictions were placed on immigration, and naturalization was made easy. The humane Quakers early developed a strong dislike of black slavery, and in the genial glow of Pennsylvania some progress was made toward social reform.

With its many liberal features, Pennsylvania attracted a rich mix of ethnic groups. They included numerous religious misfits who were repelled by the harsh practices of neighboring colonies. The Quaker haven boasted a surprisingly modern atmosphere in an unmodern age, and to an unusual degree afforded economic opportunity, civil liberty, and religious freedom. Even so, there were some "blue laws" aimed at "ungodly revelers," stage plays, playing cards, dice, games, and excessive hilarity.

Under such generally happy auspices, Penn's brainchild grew lustily. The Quakers were shrewd businesspeople, and in a short time the settlers were exporting grain and other foodstuffs. Within two years Philadelphia claimed 300 houses and 2,500 people. Within nineteen years—by 1700—the colony was surpassed in population and wealth only by long-established Virginia and Massachusetts.

William Penn, who altogether spent about four years in Pennsylvania, was never fully appreciated by his colonists. His governors, some of them incompetent and tactless, quarreled bitterly with the people, who were constantly demanding greater political control. Penn himself became too friendly with James II, the deposed Catholic king. Thrice arrested for treason, thrust for a time into a debtors' prison, and racked by apoplectic seizures, he died full of sorrows. His enduring monument was not only a noble experiment in government but also a new commonwealth. Based on civil and religious liberty, and dedicated to freedom of conscience and worship, it held aloft a hopeful torch to a world of semidarkness.

Small Quaker settlements flourished next door to Pennsylvania. New Jersey was started in 1664, when two noble proprietors received the area from the Duke of York. One of the proprietors sold West New Jersey in 1674 to a group of Quakers, and East New Jersey was also acquired by Quakers a few years later. In 1702 the crown combined the two Jerseys in a royal colony.

Swedish-tinged Delaware consisted of only three counties—two at high tide, the witticism goes—and was named after Lord De La Warr, the harsh military governor who had arrived in Virginia in 1610. Harboring some Quakers, and closely associated with Penn's flourishing colony, Delaware was granted its own assembly in 1703. But until the American Revolution it remained under the governor of Pennsylvania.

The Middle Way in the Middle Colonies

The middle colonies—New York, New Jersey, Delaware, and Pennsylvania—enjoyed certain features in common.

In general, the soil was fertile and the expanse of land was broad, unlike rock-strewn New England. Pennsylvania, New York, and New Jersey came to be known as the "bread colonies" because of their heavy exports of grain.

Rivers also played a vital role. Broad, languid streams—notably the Susquehanna, the Delaware, and the Hudson—tapped the fur trade of the interior and beckoned adventuresome spirits into the backcountry. The rivers had few cascading waterfalls, unlike New England's and hence presented little inducement to manufacturing with water-wheel power.

A surprising amount of industry nonetheless flourished in the middle colonies. Virginal forests abounded for lumbering and shipbuilding. The presence of deep river estuaries and landlocked harbors stimulated both commerce and the growth of seaports, such as New York and Philadelphia. Even Albany, more than a hundred miles up the Hudson, was a port of some consequence in colonial days.

The middle colonies were in many respects midway between New England and the southern plantation group. Except in aristocratic New York, the land holdings were generally intermediate in size—smaller than in the big acreage South but larger than in small-farm New England. Local government lay somewhere between the personalized

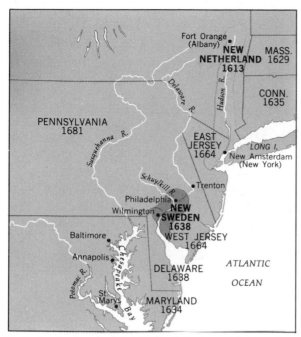

Early Settlements in the Middle Colonies, with Founding Dates

CHRONOLOGY

1517	Martin Luther begins Protestant Reformation.
1536	John Calvin of Geneva publishes *Institutes of the Christian Religion.*
1620	Pilgrims sail on the *Mayflower* to Plymouth Bay.
1624	Dutch found New Netherland.
1630	Puritans found Massachusetts Bay Colony.
1635–1636	Roger Williams, convicted of heresy, founds Rhode Island colony.
1637	Pequot War.
1638	Anne Hutchinson banished from Massachusetts colony.
1643	New England Confederation formed.
1655	New Netherland conquers New Sweden.
1664	England seizes New Netherland from Dutch.
	East and West Jersey colonies founded.
1675–1676	King Philip's War.
1681	William Penn founds Pennsylvania colony.
1686	Royal authority creates Dominion of New England.
1688–1689	Glorious Revolution overthrows Stuarts and Dominion of New England.

town meeting of New England and the diffused county government of the South. There were fewer industries in the middle colonies than in New England, but more than in the South.

Yet the middle colonies, which in some ways were the most American part of America, could claim certain distinctions in their own right. Generally speaking, the population was more ethnically mixed than that of other settlements. The people were blessed with an unusual degree of religious toleration and democratic control. Earnest and devout Quakers, in particular, made a contribution to human freedom out of all proportion to their numbers. Desirable land was more easily acquired in the middle colonies than in New England or in the tidewater South. One result was that a considerable amount of economic and social democracy prevailed, though less so in New York.

By the mid-eighteenth century, the thirteen colonies as a group revealed striking similarities, even though they had developed wide differences.

They were all basically English. They all exercised certain priceless Anglo-Saxon freedoms. They all possessed some measure of self-government, though by no means complete democracy. They all enjoyed some degree of religious toleration and educational opportunity. They all afforded unusual advantages for economic and social self-development. Finally— and perhaps most significant—they were all separated from home authority by a billowing ocean moat 3,000 miles wide.

Varying Viewpoints

For many years, historians of the first century of colonial life in English North America focused on the efforts of the colonists to stake out a social order free of the constraints of the mother country. The struggle of the Massachusetts Bay Puritans to escape the regimentation of English society and to seize the religious freedom and economic equality preferred by the American wilderness formed the centerpiece of this interpretation, which was conspicuous in the work of Perry Miller, among others. Similarly, the founding of Quaker settlements in New Jersey and Pennsylvania, and the attempt of Dutch New Yorkers to maintain their cultural heritage, revealed the discord between the colonies and the mother country.

Recent studies, including those by Gary Nash and Patricia Bonomi, have shifted the drama of early American history from the transatlantic to the domestic stage. This perspective emphasizes the contests for economic and political supremacy within the colonies, such as the efforts of the Massachusetts Bay elite to ward off the challenges of religious "heretics" and an increasingly restless lower class. Nowhere was such internal conflict so prevalent as in the ethnically diverse middle colonies, where factional conflict became the distinguishing feature of public life. Some historians even find, in the turbulent middle colonies, the seeds of the later competitive American political system.

SELECT READINGS

Primary Source Documents

John Winthrop, "A Modell of Christian Charity" (1630), in *The American Primer,* edited by Daniel Boorstin, outlines the goals of the Puritan errand into the wilderness. Winthrop's "Speech on Liberty"* (1645), in his *History of New England* (1853), established the colony's fundamental political principles. William Bradford, *Of Plymouth Plantation,** edited by Samuel E. Morison (1952), is a rich contemporary account.

Secondary Sources

New England has received more scholarly attention than any other colonial region. An incisive short account is Edmund S. Morgan's *The Puritan Dilemma: The Story of John Winthrop* (1958). A brilliant and complex intellectual history is Perry Miller's *The New England Mind* (2 vols., 1939, 1953), a work that has long been a landmark for

other scholars. Sacvan Bercovitch traces the heritage of the New England temperament in *The Puritan Origins of the American Self* (1975). Edmund S. Morgan describes the crisis that beset the original Puritans when their children displayed a lesser degree of religiosity in *Visible Saints* (1963). Economic questions receive critical attention from Bernard Bailyn in *The New England Merchants in the Seventeenth Century* (1955). Sidney Ahlstrom's *Religious History of the American People* (1972) is comprehensive. Areas outside New England are dealt with in Gary Nash, *Quakers and Politics: Pennsylvania, 1681–1726* (1971), Patricia Bonomi, *A Factious People: Politics and Society in Colonial New York* (1971), and Frederick Tolles, *Meetinghouse and Countinghouse* (1948). Timothy H. Breen, *Puritans and Adventurers* (1980), draws contrasts between Virginia and New England.

CHAPTER 4

American Life in the Seventeenth Century, 1607–1692

Being thus passed the vast ocean, and a sea of troubles before in their preparation . . . , they had now no friends to wellcome them, nor inns to entertaine or refresh their weatherbeaten bodys, no houses or much less towns to repaire too, to seeke for succore.

William Bradford, of Plymouth Plantation, 1622

The Unhealthy Chesapeake

Life in the American wilderness was nasty, brutish, and short for the earliest Chesapeake settlers. Malaria, dysentery, and typhoid took a cruel toll, cutting ten years off the life expectancy of newcomers from England. Half the people born in early Virginia and Maryland did not survive to celebrate their twentieth birthdays. Few of the remaining half lived to see their fiftieth—or even their fortieth, if they were women.

The disease-ravaged settlements of the Chesapeake grew only slowly in the seventeenth century, mostly through fresh emigration from the mother country. The great majority of immigrants were single men in their late teens and early twenties, and most perished soon after their arrival. Surviving males competed for the affections of the extremely scarce women, whom they outnumbered nearly six to one in 1650. Eligible women did not remain single for long.

Families were both few and fragile in this ferocious environment. Most men could not find mates, and most marriages were destroyed by the death of a partner within seven years. Weak family ties were reflected in the many pregnancies among unmarried young girls. In one Maryland county, more than a third of all brides were already pregnant when they spoke their marriage vows.

Yet despite these hardships, the Chesapeake colonies struggled on. The native-born adult inhabitants eventually acquired immunity to the killer diseases that had ravaged the original immigrants. The presence of more women allowed more families to form, and by the end of the seventeenth century the white population of the Chesapeake was growing on the basis of its own birthrate. As the eighteenth century opened, Virginia, with some 59,000 souls, was the most populous colony. Maryland, with about 30,000, was the third largest (after Massachusetts).

The Tobacco Economy

Though unhealthy for human life, the Chesapeake was immensely hospitable to tobacco cultivation. Profit-hungry settlers often planted tobacco before they planted corn. Seeking fresh fields, these new immigrants plunged ever farther up the river valleys. The result was continually rising tobacco production, which reached 40 million pounds a year by the end of the seventeenth century. This expansion depressed prices for the crop, but tobacco growers responded to falling prices by planting still more acres and bringing still more product to market.

More tobacco meant more labor, but where was it to come from? Families formed too slowly to provide labor by natural population increase. Indians died too quickly on contact with whites, and African slaves cost too much money. But England still had a "surplus" of displaced farmers desperate for employment. Many of them, as "indentured servants," voluntarily mortgaged the sweat of their bodies for several years to Chesapeake masters. In exchange they received transatlantic passage and eventual "freedom dues," including a few barrels of corn, a suit of clothes—and perhaps a small parcel of land.

Both Virginia and Maryland employed the "headright" system to encourage the importation of servant workers. Under its terms, the master who paid the passage of a laborer received the right to acquire fifty acres of land. Taking advantage of this system, some masters soon parlayed their investments in servants into huge fortunes in real estate. They became the great merchant-planters who came to dominate the agriculture and commerce of the southern colonies. Chesapeake planters brought some 100,000 indentured servants to the region by 1700. These "white slaves" represented more than three-quarters of all European immigrants to Virginia and Maryland in the seventeenth century.

Indentured servants led a hard but hopeful life in the early days of the Chesapeake settlements. They looked forward to becoming free and acquiring land of their own after completing their term of servitude. But as the century wore on, prime land became scarcer and the servants' lot grew harsher. Even after formal freedom was granted, penniless freed workers often had little choice but to hire themselves out for pitifully low wages to their former masters.

Frustrated Freemen and Bacon's Rebellion

An accumulating mass of footloose, impoverished freemen was drifting discontentedly about the Chesapeake region by the late seventeenth century. Mostly single young men, they were frustrated by their broken hopes of acquiring land as well as by their gnawing failure to find single women to marry.

The swelling number of these wretched bachelors rattled the established planters. Led by Governor Berkeley, the Virginia assembly in 1670 disenfranchised most of the landless knockabouts. About a thousand Virginians then broke out of control in 1676, led by a twenty-nine-year-old planter, Nathaniel Bacon. Angered by Berkeley's mild Indian policies as well as economic grievances, Bacon and his followers first attacked Indians on the frontier. They then chased Berkeley from Jamestown and put the torch to the capital. Chaos swept the raw colony, as frustrated freemen and resentful servants—described as "a rabble of the basest sort of people"—went on a rampage of plundering and pilfering.

As this civil war in Virginia ground on, Bacon suddenly died of disease. Berkeley thereupon crushed the uprising with brutal cruelty, hanging more than twenty rebels. Back in England Charles II complained, "That old fool has put to death more people in that naked country than I did here for the murder of my father."

The distant English king could scarcely imagine the depths of passion and fear that Bacon's Rebellion excited in Virginia. Bacon had ignited the smoldering unhappiness of landless former servants, and he had pitted the hardscrabble backcountry frontiersmen against the haughty gentry of the tidewater plantations. The rebellion was now suppressed, but these tensions remained. Lordly planters, surrounded by a still-seething sea of malcontents, anxiously looked about for less troublesome laborers to toil in the restless tobacco kingdom. Their eyes soon lit on Africa.

Colonial Slavery

Perhaps 10 million Africans were carried in chains to the New World in the three centuries or so following Columbus's landing. Only about 400,000 of them ended up in North America. Africans had been brought to Jamestown as early as 1619, but as late as 1670 they numbered only about 7 percent of the 50,000 people in the southern plantation colonies as a whole. For hard-pinched colonists, white servants were less costly than high-priced slaves.

Drastic change came in the 1680s. Rising prices in England shrank the pool of penniless indentured servants from England, while large planters were growing increasingly fearful of the potentially mutinous former servants in their midst. By the mid-1680s, for the first time, black slaves outnumbered white servants among the plantation colonies' new arrivals. In 1698 the Royal African Company lost its crown-granted monopoly on carrying slaves to the colonies. Enterprising Americans, especially Rhode Islanders, rushed to cash in on the lucrative slave trade, and the supply of slaves increased steeply. By 1750 blacks accounted for nearly half the population of Virginia, and in South Carolina they outnumbered whites two to one.

Most of the slaves who reached North America came from the west coast of Africa, including the area stretching from present-day Senegal to Angola. They were originally captured by African coastal tribes who traded them in crude markets to itinerant European—and American—flesh merchants. Usually branded and bound, the captives were herded aboard sweltering ships for the gruesome "middle passage," on which death rates ran as high as 20 per-

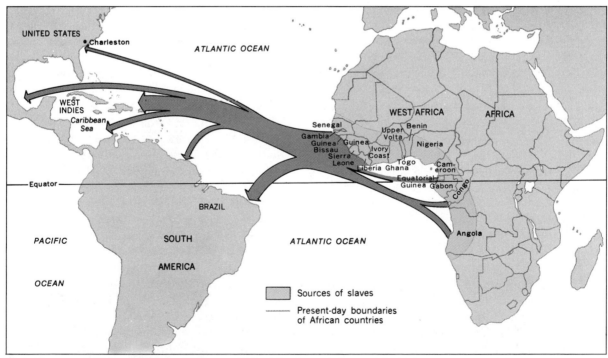

Main Sources of African Slaves, c. 1500 to c. 1800   *The three centuries of the "African Diaspora" scattered blacks all over the New World, with about 400,000 coming to North America. Boundaries shown are those of modern African states.*

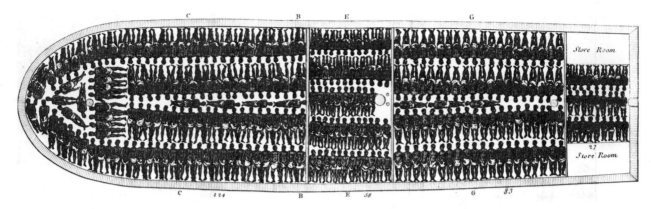

The "Middle Passage"   *Human cargo in the hold of a slave ship.*

cent. The terrified survivors were then shoved onto the auction blocks in New World ports like Newport, Rhode Island, or Charleston, South Carolina, where a giant slave market flourished for more than a century.

A few of the earliest African immigrants gained their freedom, and some even became slaveowners themselves. But as the number of Africans in their midst increased dramatically toward the end of the seventeenth century, the colonists reacted remorselessly to this supposed racial threat. The iron conditions of bondage were spelled out in slave codes that made blacks *and their children* the property (or "chattels") for life of their white masters. Not even conversion to Christianity entitled a slave to freedom. Slavery might have begun in America for economic reasons, but by the end of the seventeenth century, it was clear that racial discrimination also powerfully molded the American slave system.

Africans in America

In the deepest South, slave life was especially harsh. The climate was hostile to health, and the labor was life-draining. The widely scattered South Carolina rice and indigo plantations were lonely hells on earth where gangs of mostly male Africans toiled and perished. Only fresh imports could sustain the slave population under these cruel conditions.

Blacks in the Chesapeake region had a somewhat less cruel lot. Tobacco growing was less physically demanding, and the plantations were larger and closer to one another than rice plantations. By about 1720 the proportion of females in the Chesapeake slave population had begun to rise, making family life possible. The captive black population soon began to grow not only through new imports but also through its own fertility—making it one of the few slave societies in history to perpetuate itself by natural reproduction.

Native-born African-Americans contributed to the growth of a stable and distinctive slave culture, a mixture of African and American elements of speech, religion, and folkways (see "Makers of America: From African to African-American," pp. 48–49). On the islands off South Carolina's coast, blacks evolved a unique language, *Gullah,* that blended English with several African tongues. The ringshout, a West African religious dance performed by shuffling in a circle while answering a preacher's shouts, was brought to colonial America by slaves and eventually contributed to the development of jazz.

Slaves also helped powerfully to build the country with their labor. A few became skilled artisans—carpenters, bricklayers, and tanners. But chiefly they performed the sweaty toil of clearing swamps, grubbing out trees, and other menial tasks. Condemned to life under the lash, slaves naturally pined for freedom. Slave revolts erupted in New York City in 1712, and again in South Carolina in 1739. But in the end slaves in the South proved to be a more manageable labor force than the white indentured servants they gradually replaced. No slave rebellion in American history matched the scale of Bacon's Rebellion.

Southern Society

As slavery spread, the gaps in the South's social structure widened. The rough equality of poverty and disease of the early days was giving way to a hierarchy of wealth and status in the early eighteenth century. At the top of the social ladder perched a small but powerful covey of great planters. Owning gangs of slaves and vast domains of land, the planters ruled the region's economy and virtually monopolized political power. Yet, legend to the contrary, these seventeenth-century merchant planters were not silk-swathed cavaliers gallantly imitating the ways of English country gentlemen. For the most part they were a hardworking, businesslike lot, laboring long hours over the problems of plantation management.

Far beneath the planters in wealth, prestige, and political power were the small farmers, the largest social group. They lived a ragged, hand-to-mouth existence on their modest plots. Still lower on the social scale were landless whites, and below them indentured servants still serving out their terms. The oppressed black slaves, of course, remained enchained in society's basement.

Few cities sprouted in the colonial South, and consequently an urban professional class, including lawyers and financiers, was slow to emerge. Southern life revolved around the great plantations, distantly isolated from one another. Waterways, rather than the wretched roads, provided the principal means of transportation from one plantation to another.

The New England Family

Nature smiled more benignly on pioneer New Englanders than on their disease-plagued fellow colonists to the south. Healthier living conditions enabled settlers in seventeenth-century New England to *add* ten years to their life span by migrating from the Old World, in stark contrast to the fate of Chesapeake immigrants. The first generations of Puritan colonists enjoyed, on the average, about seventy years on this earth—not very different from the life expectancy of present-day Americans.

In further contrast with the Chesapeake colonists, New Englanders tended to migrate not as single individuals but as families, and the family remained at the center of New England life. Early marriage and fertile child-bearing enabled New England's population to grow from natural reproductive increase almost from the outset. Women typically wed by their early twenties and produced babies about every two years thereafter until menopause. A married woman could expect to experience up to ten pregnancies and rear as many as eight surviving children. A New England woman might well have dependent children living in her household from the earliest days of her marriage until the day of her death, and child raising became virtually her full-time occupation.

The longevity of the New Englanders contributed to family stability. Children received nurturing love and guidance not only from their parents but from their grandparents as well. Family stability was reflected in low premarital pregnancy rates and in the generally strong, tranquil social structure characteristic of colonial New England.

Oddly enough, the strength of New England families actually weakened the economic independence of women. In the southern colonies, men frequently died young, leaving widows with small children to support. Married women were therefore allowed to retain separate title to their property, and widows had the right to inherit their husband's estate. But in New England, Puritan lawmakers worried that women's property rights would undercut family unity. Greater longevity made widowhood less common, so women were generally denied rights of inheritance.

Life in the New England Towns

Sturdy New Englanders evolved a tightly knit society, the basis of which was small villages and farms. Puritanism especially made for unity of purpose—and for concern about the moral health of the whole community.

From African to African-American

Dragged in chains from the shores of West Africa, the first Africans in America struggled to preserve their diverse heritages from the ravages of slavery. Their sons and daughters, the first generation of American-born slaves, melded these various traditions—Guinean, Ibo, Yoruba, Angolan—into a distinctive African-American culture. Their achieve-

ment sustained them during the cruelties of enslavement and has endured to enrich American life to this day.

With the arrival of the first Africans in the seventeenth century, a cornucopia of traditions poured into the New World: handicrafts and skills in numerous trades; a plethora of languages, music, and

Gourd Fiddle; Africans Destined for Slavery *Africans taken as slaves brought the* banza, *or* banjo, *directly to the Americas. The smaller gourd fiddle is an example of a related instrument also made and played by slaves. The engraving* (right) *is an example of anti-slavery propaganda. The Africans being forced ashore by the whips of slave traders are deliberately contrasted with the national Capitol and the flag, both of which are symbols of American liberty.*

cuisines; even rice-planting techniques that conquered the inhospitable soil of South Carolina. It was North America's rice paddies, tilled by experienced West Africans, that introduced the staple into the English diet.

The first American slaves were mostly men who lived on small, isolated farms. But by the beginning of the eighteenth century, a settled slave society was emerging in the southern colonies. Laws tightened; slave traders stepped up their deliveries of human cargo; large plantations formed. Most significant, a new generation of American-born slaves joined their forebears at labor in the fields. By 1740 large groups of slaves lived together on sprawling plantations, the American-born outnumbered the African-born, and the importation of African slaves slowed.

Plantation life was a beastly cycle of endless toil for the slaves. After a day of backbreaking work, the women were expected to sit up for hours spinning, weaving, or sewing to clothe themselves and their families. Under such conditions, forging a common culture and finding a psychological weapon with which to resist their masters and preserve their dignity were daunting challenges.

Yet even with little time for society and little commonality of language and custom, a vibrant culture flowered. Women used the knitting and weaving time to discuss child-rearing and to develop close bonds. In this they carried on a West African tradition of separate female social networks. Cut off from their own religions, most slaves became Christians, but at their Sunday and nighttime prayer meetings they adapted Christianity to their own purposes, adding African-influenced music and rituals to the services. Overcoming white Protestants' prohibitions against dancing, they adopted the ringshout from their religious past. In this form of "not dancing" dancing, three or four people would stand still in a circle, clapping hands and beating time with their feet, while others circled the ring singing in unison.

Black Christianity differed from white Christianity in theology as well as fervor. Blacks rejected predestination and emphasized the lowly earthly place of Jesus and the earthly deliverance of the children of Israel, led by Moses and Joshua, from slavery in Egypt. They retained an African idea of a heaven where they would be united with their ancestors.

Thus were diverse African traditions alloyed with New World innovations, and thus was American culture endowed in its turn. Much of American music and literature, as well as religion, was born in the slave quarters, but at the bitter cost of generations of human agony.

Even territorial expansion occurred in orderly, communal fashion. New towns were legally chartered by the colonial authorities, and the distribution of land was entrusted to the steady hands of soberminded town fathers, or "proprietors." After receiving a grant of land from the colonial legislature, the proprietors usually laid out their town around a meetinghouse, which served as both the place of worship and the town hall. Also marked out was a village green, where the militia could drill. Each family received several parcels of land.

Towns of more than fifty families were required to provide elementary education, and a majority of adults knew how to read and write. As early as 1636, just six years after the colony's founding, the Massachusetts Puritans established Harvard College to train local boys for the ministry. Only in 1693, eighty-six years after the founding of Jamestown, did the Virginians establish their first college, William and Mary.

Puritans ran their own churches, and democracy in Congregational church government led logically to democracy in political government. The town meeting, in which freemen met together and each man voted, exhibited democracy in its purest form. The town meeting, observed Thomas Jefferson, was "the best school of political liberty the world ever saw."

The Changing New England Way of Life

Yet worries plagued the God-fearing pioneers of these tidy New England settlements. The pressure of a growing population was gradually dispersing the Puritans onto outlying farms, far from the control of church and neighbors. And although the core of Puritan belief still burned brightly, the passage of time was dampening the first generation's religious zeal. About the middle of the seventeenth century, alarmed preachers began scolding parishioners for their waning piety in a new form of sermon—the "jeremiad." In response to the apparent decline in conversions, troubled ministers in 1662 announced a new formula for church membership, the "Half-Way Covenant." It offered partial membership rights to persons not yet converted. This widening of church membership gradually erased the distinction between the "elect" and other members of society. In effect, strict religious purity was sacrificed somewhat to the cause of wider religious participation. Inter-

estingly, from about this time onward women made up a larger proportion of the Puritan congregations.

Women also played a prominent role in one of New England's most frightening religious episodes. A group of adolescent girls in Salem, Massachusetts, claimed to have been bewitched by certain older women. A hysterical "witch-hunt" ensued, leading to the execution in 1692 of twenty persons. Witchcraft persecutions had occurred before in Europe and America, but the reign of horror in Salem grew not only from the superstitions of the age but also from the unsettled social and religious conditions of the rapidly evolving Massachusetts village. The episode reflected the widening social stratification of New England as well as the anxieties of many religious traditionalists that the Puritan heritage was being eclipsed by Yankee commercialism. The Salem witchcraft delusion marked an all-time high in the American experience of popular passions run wild.

New England soil, like New England religion, was hard and unyielding. Scratching a living from the rock-strewn land put a premium on sharp trading and penny-pinching frugality, for which New Englanders became famous. The grudging earth also

Graveyard Art   *These New England colonists evidently died in the prime of life. Carving likenesses on grave markers was a common way of commemorating the dead.*

left the colony less ethnically mixed than its southern neighbors. European immigrants were not attracted in great numbers to a site where the soil was so stony—and the religion so sulfurous.

Yet the harsh climate and unproductive soil of New England eventually encouraged a diversified agriculture and industry. Staple products like tobacco did not flourish as they did in the South. Black slavery, although attempted, could not exist profitably on small farms. Turning away from the land, hardy men looked to the sea for a living. Hacking timber from their dense forests, they became experts in shipbuilding and commerce. They also ceaselessly exploited the self-perpetuating codfish lode off the coast of Newfoundland—the fishy "gold mines of New England." As a reminder of the importance of fishing, a handsome replica of the "sacred cod" is proudly displayed to this day in the Massachusetts State House in Boston.

And just as the land shaped New Englanders, so they shaped the land. In contrast with Native Americans, who *used* the land but recognized no right to *own* it, European settlers felt a virtual duty to "improve" the land by clearing woodlands for pasturage and tillage, building roads and fences, and laying out permanent settlements. The introduction of livestock also led colonists to clear ever more forests for pastureland, while the animals' voracious appetites and heavy hooves compacted the soil, speeding erosion and flooding.

The combination of Calvinism, soil, and climate in New England made for energy, purposefulness, sternness, stubbornness, self-reliance, and resourcefulness. Righteous men and women prided themselves on being God's chosen people. They long boasted that Boston was "the hub of the universe"—at least spiritually. A famous jingle of later days ran:

> I come from the city of Boston
> The home of the bean and the cod
> Where the Cabots speak only to Lowells
> And the Lowells speak only to God.

As flinty as their stones, as stiff as their cuffs and collars, New Englanders later cross-fertilized innumerable other communities across America with their ideals and democratic practices. The New England conscience inspired many later reformers and added something indispensable to the fiber and backbone of the American people.

The Early Settlers' Days and Ways

The cycles of the seasons and the sun set the schedules of all the earliest American colonists—men as well as women and blacks as well as whites. The overwhelming majority of colonists were farmers. They planted in the spring, tended their crops in the summer, harvested in the fall, and prepared in the winter to begin the cycle anew. They usually rose at dawn and went to bed at dusk. Chores might be performed after nightfall only if they were "worth the candle," a phrase that has persisted in American speech.

Whether slave or free, women wove, cooked, cleaned, and cared for children. Men worked the land, cut firewood, and butchered livestock as needed. Children helped with all these tasks, picking up such schooling as they could.

CHRONOLOGY	
1619	First Africans arrive in Virginia.
1636	Harvard College founded.
1662	Half-Way Covenant established to increase Congregational church membership.
1670	Virginia assembly disenfranchised landless freemen.
1676	Bacon's Rebellion, Virginia.
1680s	Mass expansion of slavery in colonies.
1689–1691	Leisler's Rebellion, New York.
1692	Salem witch trials, Massachusetts.
1693	College of William and Mary founded.
1698	Royal African Company slave trade monopoly ended.
1712	New York City slave revolt.
1739	South Carolina slave revolt.

Life was humble but comfortable by standards of the time. Compared to most seventeenth-century Europeans, Americans lived in affluent abundance. Land was relatively cheap, though somewhat less available in the planter-dominated South than elsewhere.

"Dukes don't emigrate," the saying goes, for if people enjoy wealth and security, they are not likely to risk exposing their lives in the wilderness. Similarly, the very poorest members of a society may not possess even the modest means needed to pull up stakes and seek a fresh start in life. Accordingly, most white migrants to early colonial America came neither from the aristocracy nor from the dregs of European society—with the partial exception of the impoverished indentured servants.

Seventeenth-century society in all the colonies had a certain simple sameness to it, especially in the more egalitarian New England and middle colonies. Yet many settlers, who considered themselves to be of the "better sort," tried to recreate on a modified scale the social structure they had known in the Old World. Resentment against such upper-class pretensions helped to spark outbursts such as Bacon's Rebellion in Virginia in 1676, the uprising of Maryland's Protestants toward the end of the seventeenth century, and Leisler's Rebellion in New York City from 1689 to 1691.

For their part, would-be American blue bloods resented the pretensions of the "meaner sort" and passed laws to try to keep them in their place. Massachusetts in 1651 prohibited poorer folk from "wearing gold or silver lace," and in eighteenth-century Virginia a tailor was fined and jailed for arranging to race his horse—"a sport only for gentlemen." But these efforts to reproduce the finely stratified societies of Europe proved feeble in the early American wilderness, where equality and democracy found fertile soil—at least for white people.

Varying Viewpoints

The simultaneous evolution of a rigid racial caste system and democratic political traditions in the English colonies has long perplexed students of early America. For many generations historians, most of them of Yankee stock, resolved the apparent paradox by locating the seeds of democracy in New England. The aggressive independence of the people, best expressed by the boisterous town meetings, spawned the American obsession with freedom. On the other hand, this view holds, the slave societies of the South were hierarchical, aristocratic communities under the sway of a few powerful planters.

Recent studies have questioned this interpretation. First, they point out the many undemocratic features of colonial New England. Second, they note that Washington, Jefferson, and Madison—the architects of American government and its commitment to liberty—all hailed from slaveholding Virginia. In fact, nowhere were republican principles stronger than in Virginia. This realization has sparked new speculation about the relationship between American slavery and American freedom. Some scholars, notably Edmund S. Morgan, see the willingness of wealthy planters to concede the equality and freedom of all white males as a device to ensure racial solidarity and mute class conflict. In this view, the concurrent emergence of slavery and democracy poses no paradox. Racism muffled animosity between rich and poor and fostered the devotion to equality (for whites) that became the hallmark of American democracy.

SELECT READINGS

Primary Source Documents

Adolph B. Benson, ed., *The America of 1750; Petar Kalm's Travels in North America* (1937), records the observations of a visiting Swedish naturalist with a keen eye for the behavior of human fauna. The first slave laws of Virginia are collected in Warren M. Billings, ed., *The Old Dominion in the Seventeenth Century** (1975), as are firsthand accounts of Bacon's Rebellion. See also George L. Burr, ed., *Narratives of the Witchcraft Cases, 1648–1706 (1914).**

Secondary Sources

On life and labor in the Chesapeake, consult Thad W. Tate and David L. Ammerman, eds., *The Chesapeake in the Seventeenth Century* (1979), Wesley F. Craven, *The Southern Colonies in the Seventeenth Century* (1949), and Edmund S. Morgan, *American Slavery, American Freedom* (1975), which concentrates on race and class relations. Winthrop Jordan's magnificent *White Over Black: American Attitudes Toward the Negro, 1550–1812* (1968) discusses the evolution of racial attitudes. Among the many works that scrutinize life in New England's towns and homes are Bernard Bailyn, *Education in the Forming of American Society* (1960), John Demos, *A Little Commonwealth: Family Life in Plymouth Colony* (1970), Philip Greven, *Four Generations: Population, Land, and Family in Colonial Andover, Massachusetts* (1970), Kenneth Lockridge, *New England Town: Dedham* (1970), Lyle Koehler, *A Search for Power: The "Weaker Sex" in Seventeenth-Century New England* (1980), Laurel T. Ulrich, *Good Wives: Image and Reality in the Lives of Women in Northern New England, 1650–1750* (1982), Marilynn Salmon, *Women and the Law of Property in Early America* (1986), and Philip Greven, *The Protestant Temperament* (1977), which analyzes child-rearing practices. Robert Pope examines *The Half-Way Covenant: Church Membership in Puritan New England* (1969). Witchcraft is the subject of Paul Boyer and Stephen Nissenbaum's *Salem Possessed* (1974) and John Demos's massive *Entertaining Satan* (1982). See also Carol F. Karlsen, *The Devil in the Shape of a Woman: Witchcraft in Colonial New England* (1987). A sweeping survey that emphasizes the diversity of culture already present in seventeenth-century America is E. Brooks Holifield, *Era of Persuasion: American Thought and Culture, 1521–1680* (1989). The relationship of Indians and New England whites to their environment is the subject of William Cronon's intriguing *Changes in the Land* (1983).

CHAPTER 5

Colonial Society on the Eve of Revolution, 1700–1775

Driven from every other corner of the earth, freedom of thought and the right of private judgment in matters of conscience direct their course to this happy country as their last asylum.

Samuel Adams, 1776

Conquest by the Cradle

The thirteen colonies on the North American mainland that rebelled against British rule in 1776 differed considerably in economic organization, social structure, and ways of life. Yet all of them had one outstanding feature in common: their populations were growing by leaps and bounds. In 1700 they contained fewer than 300,000 souls, about 20,000 of whom were black. By 1775, 2.5 million people inhabited the thirteen colonies, of whom about half a million were black. White immigrants made up nearly 400,000 of the increased number, and black "forced immigrants" accounted for nearly the same number of newcomers. But most of the spurt stemmed from the remarkable natural fertility of all Americans, white and black. The youthful Americans, whose average age in 1775 was about sixteen, were doubling their numbers every twenty-five years. Dr. Samuel Johnson, back in Britain, growled that the Americans were multiplying like their own rattlesnakes.

This population boom had political consequences. In 1700 there were twenty British subjects for each American colonist. By 1775 the British advantage in numbers had fallen to three to one—setting the stage for a momentous shift in the balance of power between the colonies and Britain.

The bulk of the population was cooped up east of the Alleghenies. The most populous colonies in 1775 were Virginia, Massachusetts, Pennsylvania, North Carolina, and Maryland—in that order. Only four communities could be called cities: Philadelphia, including suburbs, was first with about 34,000, with New York, Boston, and Charleston strung out behind. About 90 percent of the people lived in rural areas.

A Potpourri of Peoples

Colonial America was a melting pot, and had been from the outset. The population, although basically English in stock and language, was picturesquely mottled with numerous foreign groups.

Heavy-accented Germans constituted about 6 percent of the total population, or 150,000, by 1775.

Fleeing religious persecution, economic oppression, and the ravages of war, they had flocked to America in the early 1700s and had settled chiefly in Pennsylvania. They belonged to several different Protestant groups—primarily Lutheran—and thus further enhanced the religious diversity of the colony. Known popularly but erroneously as the Pennsylvania Dutch (a corruption of the German word *Deutsch*), they totaled about one-third of the colony's population. In Philadelphia, street signs were painted in both German and English. In the Pennsylvania backcountry, where many of them moved, German immigrants clung tenaciously to their language and customs.

The Scots-Irish (see "Makers of America: The Scots-Irish," pp. 58–59), who in 1775 numbered about 175,000, or 7 percent of the population, were an important non-English group, although they spoke English. They were not Irish at all, but turbulent Scots Lowlanders. Over many decades, they had first been transplanted to Northern Ireland, where they had not prospered. The Irish Catholics already there, hating Scottish Presbyterianism, resented the intruders and still do.

Early in the 1700s tens of thousands of embittered Scots-Irish finally abandoned Ireland and came to America, chiefly to tolerant and deep-soiled Pennsylvania. Finding the best acres already taken by Germans and Quakers, they pushed out onto the frontier. There many of them illegally but defiantly squatted on the unoccupied lands and quarreled with both Indian and white owners. It was said, somewhat unfairly, that the Scots-Irish kept the Sabbath—and all else they could lay their hands on. Pugnacious, lawless, and individualistic, they brought with them the Scottish secrets of whiskey distilling and dotted the Appalachian hills and hollows with their stills. They cherished no love for the British government that had uprooted them, and many of them—including the young Andrew Jackson—joined the embattled American Revolutionists.

Approximately 5 percent of the colonial population consisted of other European groups, including French, Welsh, Dutch, Swedes, Jews, Irish, Swiss, and Scots Highlanders. Except for the Scots Highlanders, these ethnic groups felt little loyalty to the British crown. By far the largest single non-English

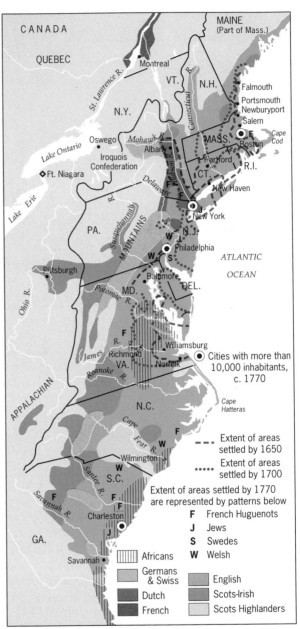

Immigrant Groups in 1775 *America was already a nation of diverse nationalities in the colonial period. This map shows the great variety of immigrant groups, especially in Pennsylvania and New York. It also illustrates the tendency of later arrivals, particularly the Scots-Irish, to push into the backcountry. The basic ethnic makeup of many of these colonial settlements persists even today, each with distinct cultural patterns and attitudes.*

group was African, accounting for nearly 20 percent of the colonial population in 1775 and heavily concentrated in the South.

The population of the thirteen colonies, though mainly Anglo-Saxon, was perhaps the most mixed to be found anywhere in the world. The South, holding about 90 percent of the slaves, already displayed its historic black-and-white racial composition. New England, mostly staked out by the original Puritan migrants, showed the least ethnic diversity. The middle colonies, especially Pennsylvania, received the bulk of later white immigrants and boasted an astonishing variety of people.

As these various immigrant groups mingled and intermarried, they laid the foundations for a new multicultural American national identity unlike anything known in Europe. White colonists were not alone in creating new societies out of diverse ethnic groups. The African slave trade long had mixed peoples from many different tribal backgrounds, giving birth to an African-American community far more variegated in its cultural origins than anything in Africa itself. Similarly, the decimation and forced migration of Indian tribes scrambled Native American peoples together in wholly new ways.

The Structure of Colonial Society

In contrast with contemporary Europe, eighteenth-century America was a shining land of equality and opportunity—with the notorious exception of slavery. No titled nobility dominated society from on high, and no pauperized underclass threatened it from below. Most white Americans, and even some free blacks, were small farmers. The cities contained a small class of skilled artisans, as well as a few shopkeepers, tradespeople, and unskilled casual laborers. The most remarkable feature of the social ladder was the rags-to-riches ease with which an ambitious colonial might rise from a lower rung to a higher one.

Yet in contrast with seventeenth-century America, colonial society on the eve of the Revolution was beginning to show signs of stratification and barriers to mobility that raised worries about the "Europeanization" of America. A new class of merchant princes in New England and the middle colonies, many of whom had made their fortunes as military suppliers in the colonial wars, roosted regally atop the social ladder. They sported imported clothing and dined at tables laid with English china and gleaming silverware. Prominent individuals

Estimated Population Elements, 1790* (based on family names)

Ethnic Groups	Number	Percentage
English and Welsh	2,605,699	66.3
Scottish (including Scots-Irish)	221,562	5.6
German	176,407	4.5
Dutch	78,959	2.0
Irish	61,534	1.6
French	17,619	0.4
All other whites	10,664	0.3
Africans	757,181	19.3
Grand total	3,929,625	100.0

* Rossiter, *A Century of Population Growth* (1909). Later estimates by Barker and Hansen (1931) are not used here because they are confused by the inclusion of Spanish and French elements *later* a part of the United States.

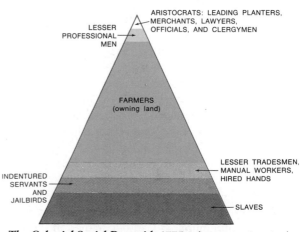

The Colonial Social Pyramid, 1775 *(an approximation)*

The Scots-Irish

As the British Empire spread its dominion across the seas in the seventeenth and eighteenth centuries, great masses of people poured into its ever-widening realms. Their migration unfolded in stages. They journeyed from farms to towns, from towns to great cities such as London and Bristol, and eventually from the seaports to Ireland, the Caribbean, and the North American colonies. Among these intrepid wanderers, few were more restless than the Scots-Irish, the settlers of the first American West. Never feeling at home in the British Empire, these perennial outsiders always headed for its most distant outposts. They migrated first from their native Scottish lowlands to Northern Ireland and then on to the New World. And even in North America, the Scots-Irish remained on the periphery, ever distancing themselves from the reach of the English crown and the Anglican church.

The Scottish migration was driven by severe poverty. Always forced to struggle with a harsh and unyielding land, poorer Scots were oppressed further in the 1600s by merciless rent increases at the hands of the landowning lairds. Adding insult to injury, the British authorities repeatedly persecuted the Presbyterian Scots, squeezing taxes from their barren purses to support the hated Anglican church.

It was not surprising, then, that some 200,000 of them immigrated to neighboring Ireland in the 1600s. So great was the exodus that Protestant Scots eventually outnumbered Catholic natives in the several northern Irish counties that compose the province of Ulster. But soon the Scots discovered that their migration had not freed them from their ancient woes. Their Irish landlords raised rents just as ferociously as their former lairds had done. Under such punishing pressures, waves of these already once-transplanted Scots, now called Scots-Irish, fled yet again, this time to America.

Most debarked in Pennsylvania, seeking the religious tolerance and abundant land of William Penn's commonwealth. But these unquiet people did not stay put for long. They fanned out from Philadelphia into the farmlands of western Pennsylvania. Blocked temporarily by the Allegheny Mountains, they then migrated south along the backbone of the Appalachian range, slowly filling the backcountry of Virginia, the Carolinas, and Georgia.

This Scottish Presbyterian church, built in 1794, still stands in Alexandria, Virginia.

Almost every Scots-Irish community, however isolated or impermanent, maintained a Presbyterian church. Religion was the bond that yoked these otherwise fiercely independent folk. In backcountry towns, churches were erected before law courts, and clerics were pounding their pulpits before civil authorities had the chance to raise their gavels. But the Scots-Irish, despite their intense faith, were no theocrats, no advocates of religious rule. Their bitter struggles with the Anglican church made them stubborn opponents of established religions in the United States, just as their seething resentment against the king of England ensured that the Scots-Irish would be well represented among the Patriots in the American Revolution.

came to be seated in churches and schools according to their social rank.

Poverty and diminished opportunity also began to appear at the bottom of society. Both Philadelphia and New York built almshouses in the 1730s to care for the destitute, although the numbers of poor people remained tiny compared with the numbers in England. In the New England countryside, the rising population meant that existing landholdings were subdivided and the average size of farms shrank drastically. Younger sons were increasingly forced to hire out as wage laborers—or eventually to seek virgin tracts of land beyond the Appalachians.

In the South the power of the great planters continued to be bolstered by their disproportionate ownership of slaves. Wealth was concentrated in the hands of the largest slaveowners, widening the gap between the prosperous gentry and the "poor whites," who were increasingly forced to become tenant farmers. In all the colonies the ranks of the lower classes were further swelled by the continuing stream of indentured servants. Far less fortunate than the voluntary indentured servants were the paupers and convicts involuntarily shipped to America. Altogether, about 50,000 "jayle birds"—including robbers, rapists, and murderers—were dumped on the colonies by the London authorities.

Least fortunate of all, of course, were the black slaves. Oppressed and degraded, the slaves were America's closest approximation to Europe's volatile lower classes, and fears of black rebellion plagued the white colonists. Some colonial legislatures, notably South Carolina's in 1760, attempted to restrict the importation of slaves, but British authorities vetoed all such efforts. Thomas Jefferson, himself a slaveholder, assailed such vetoes in an early draft of the Declaration of Independence, but his proposed clause was finally dropped, largely out of regard for southern sensibilities.

Clergy, Physicians, and Jurists

Most honored of the professions was the Christian ministry. In 1775 clergymen wielded less influence than in the early days of Massachusetts, when piety had burned more warmly. But they still occupied a position of high prestige.

Most physicians, on the other hand, were poorly trained and not highly esteemed. Not until 1765 was the first medical school established, although European centers attracted some students. Aspiring young doctors served for a while as apprentices to older practitioners and were then turned loose on their "victims." Bleeding was a favorite and often fatal remedy; when the physician was not available, a barber was often summoned.

Plagues were a constant nightmare. Especially dreaded was smallpox, which afflicted one out of five persons, including the heavily pockmarked George Washington. A crude form of inoculation was introduced in 1721, despite the objections of many physicians and some of the clergy, who opposed tampering with the will of God. Powdered dried toad was a favorite prescription for smallpox. Diphtheria was also a deadly killer, especially of young people. One epidemic in the 1730s took the lives of thousands.

At first the law profession was not favorably regarded. In this pioneering society, which required much honest manual labor, the parties to a dispute often presented their own cases in court. Lawyers were commonly regarded as noisy windbags or troublemaking rogues; an early Connecticut law classed them with drunkards and brothel keepers.

By about 1750, seaboard society had passed the pioneering stage, and trained attorneys were generally recognized as useful. Able to defend colonial rights against the crown on legal grounds, lawyers like the eloquent James Otis and the flaming Patrick Henry took the lead in the agitation that led to revolt.

Workaday America

Agriculture was the leading industry, involving about 90 percent of the people. Tobacco continued to be the staple crop in Maryland and Virginia. The fertile middle ("bread") colonies produced large quantities of grain, and by 1759 New York alone was exporting 80,000 barrels of flour a year. Seemingly the farmer had only to tickle the soil with a hoe and it would laugh with a harvest. Overall, Americans probably enjoyed an average higher standard of living than the masses of any country in history up to that time.

Fishing (including whaling), though ranking far below agriculture, was rewarding. Pursued in all the colonies, this harvesting of the sea was a major industry in New England, which exported smelly shiploads of dried cod to the Catholic countries of Europe. The fishing fleet also stimulated shipbuilding and served as a nursery for the seamen who manned the navy and merchant marine.

Yankee seamen were famous in many climes not only as skilled mariners but as tight-fisted traders. They provisioned the Caribbean sugar islands with food and forest products. They hauled Spanish and Portuguese gold, wine, and oranges to London, to be exchanged for industrial goods, which were then sold for a juicy profit in America.

Early American Doctoring, 1780   *This painting by Winthrop Chandler portrays Dr. William Glysson, a Massachusetts physician who served with the revolutionary army.*

The so-called triangular trade was infamously profitable, though small in relation to total colonial commerce. A skipper, for example, would leave a New England port with a cargo of rum and sail to the Gold Coast of Africa. Bartering the fiery liquor with African chiefs for captured African slaves, he would proceed to the West Indies with his suffocating cargo sardined below deck. There he would exchange the slaves for molasses, which he would then carry to New England, where it would be distilled into rum. He would then repeat the trip, making a handsome profit on each leg of the triangle.

Manufacturing in the colonies was of only secondary importance, although there was a surprising variety of small enterprises. Huge quantities of "kill devil" rum were distilled in Rhode Island and Massachusetts, and even some of the "elect of the Lord"

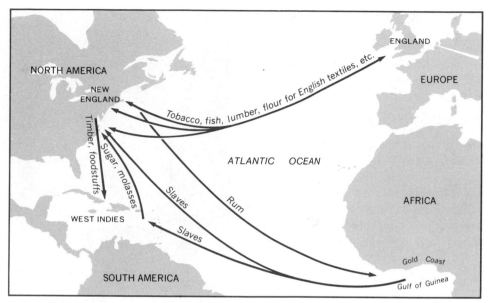

Colonial Trade Patterns, c. 1770   *Future President John Adams noted about this time that "the commerce of the West Indies is a part of the American system of commerce. They can neither do without us, nor we without them. The Creator has placed us upon the globe in such a situation that we have occasion for each other."*

developed an overfondness for it. Beaver hats, iron forges, and household goods spun and woven by women constituted other colonial manufactures. As in all colonies, strong-backed laborers and skilled crafts people were scarce and highly prized.

Lumbering was perhaps the most important single manufacturing activity. Countless cartloads of virgin timber were consumed by shipbuilders, who by 1770 were sending 400 new vessels splashing into the sea each year. Colonial naval stores—such as tar, pitch, resin, and turpentine—were highly valued. Towering trees, ideal as masts for His Majesty's Navy, were marked with the king's broad arrow for future use. The luckless colonial who was caught cutting down this reserved timber was subject to a fine.

Americans held an important flank of a thriving, many-sided Atlantic economy by the dawn of the eighteenth century. Yet strains appeared in this complex network as early as the 1730s. Fast-breeding Americans demanded more and more British products—yet the slow-growing British population early reached the saturation point for absorbing

imports from America. How, then, could the colonists sell the goods to make the money to buy what they wanted in the mother country? The answer was obvious: by seeking foreign (non-British) markets.

By the eve of the Revolution the bulk of Chesapeake tobacco was filling pipes in France and other continental countries, though it passed through the hands of British reexporters, who took a slice of the profits. More important was the trade with the West Indies, especially the French islands. West Indian purchases of North American timber and foodstuffs provided the crucial cash for the colonists to continue to make their own purchases in Britain. In 1733, bowing to pressure from influential British West Indian planters, Parliament passed the Molasses Act, aimed at squelching North American trade with the *French* West Indies. If successful, this scheme would have struck a crippling blow to American international trade and to the colonists' standard of living. American merchants responded by bribing and smuggling their way around the law.

Thus was foreshadowed the impending imperial crisis, when headstrong Americans would revolt rather than submit to the dictates of a far-off Parliament apparently bent on destroying their very livelihood.

Horsepower and Sailpower

As a sprawling and sparsely populated pioneer territory, America was cursed with oppressive problems of transportation. Not until the 1700s were there roads connecting even the major cities, and these dirt thoroughfares were treacherously poor.

Roads were often clouds of dust in summer and quagmires of mud in winter. Stagecoach travelers braved such additional dangers as tree-strewn roads, rickety bridges, carriage overturns, and runaway horses. Travel was so slow that it actually took twenty-nine days for the news of the Declaration of Independence to reach Charleston from Philadelphia.

Where man-made roads were wretched, heavy reliance was placed on God-grooved waterways. Population tended to cluster along the banks of navigable rivers. There was also much coastwise traffic, which was cheap and pleasant but slow.

Taverns sprang up along the main routes of travel as well as in the cities. Along with such attractions as bowling alleys, pool tables, and gambling equipment, taverns provided plentiful information, rumors, and gossip—frequently stimulated by alcoholic refreshment and impassioned political talk. Before a cheerful, roaring log fire all social classes would mingle, including the village loafers and drunks. Taverns were important in crystallizing public opinion, and alehouses like Boston's Green Dragon proved to be hotbeds of agitation as the revolutionary movement gathered momentum.

The Great Awakening

In all the colonial churches, religion was less fervid in the early eighteenth century than it had been a century earlier, when the colonies were first planted. The Puritan churches in particular sagged under the weight of two burdens: their elaborate theological

George Whitefield Preaching *Americans of both sexes and all races and sections were spellbound by Whitefield's emotive oratory.*

doctrines and their compromising efforts to liberalize membership requirements. Churchgoers increasingly complained about the "dead dogs" who droned out tedious sermons from the pulpit, while many ministers worried that their parishioners had gone soft and no longer embraced orthodox Calvinism. These twin trends toward clerical intellectualism and lay liberalism were sapping the spiritual vitality of many denominations.

The stage was thus set for a rousing religious revival. Known as the Great Awakening, it exploded in the 1730s and 1740s and swept through the colonies like a fire through prairie grass. The Awakening was first ignited in Northampton, Massachusetts, by a tall, delicate, and intellectual pastor, Jonathan Edwards. Perhaps the deepest theological mind ever nurtured in America, Edwards proclaimed with burning righteousness the need for complete dependence on God's grace. His preaching style was learned and closely reasoned, but his stark doctrines sparked a warmly sympathetic reaction among his parishioners in 1734.

Four years later, the itinerant English parson George Whitefield loosed a different style of evangelical preaching on America and touched off a conflagration of religious ardor that revolutionized the spiritual life of the colonies. A former alehouse attendant, Whitefield was a magnificent orator whose voice boomed sonorously over thousands of enthralled listeners in an open field. Triumphantly touring the colonies, Whitefield displayed an eloquence that reduced Jonathan Edwards to tears and even caused the skeptical and thrifty Benjamin Franklin to empty his pockets into the collection plate. During Whitefield's roaring revival meetings, countless sinners professed conversion, while hundreds of the "saved" groaned, shrieked, or rolled in the snow from religious excitation. Soon, American imitators took up Whitefield's electrifying new style of preaching and shook enormous audiences with emotional appeals.

Orthodox clergymen, known as "old lights," were deeply skeptical of the emotionalism and the theatrical antics of the revivalists. "New light" ministers, on the other hand, defended the Awakening for its role in revitalizing American religion. The Awakening left many lasting effects. Its emphasis on direct, emotive spirituality seriously undermined the older clergy, whose authority had derived from their education and erudition. The schisms the Awakening set off in many denominations increased the numbers and competitiveness of American churches. It also encouraged a fresh wave of missionary work among the Indians and black slaves. It led to the founding of "new light" centers of higher learning such as Dartmouth, Brown, Rutgers, and Princeton. Perhaps most significant, the Great Awakening was the first spontaneous mass movement of the American people. By breaking down sectional boundaries and denominational lines, it contributed to the growing sense that Americans had of themselves as a single people, united by a common history and shared experience.

Schools and Colleges

Only slowly and painfully did American colonials break away from the English idea that education was a boon reserved for the aristocratic few. In Puritan New England, education was dominated by the Congregational church, which stressed the need for Bible reading by the individual worshiper. Education, principally for boys, flourished almost from the outset in New England, which boasted an impressive number of graduates from the English universities, especially Cambridge. New Englanders, at a relatively early date, established primary and secondary schools, which varied widely in the quality of instruction and in the length of time that their doors remained open each year.

Fairly adequate primary and secondary schools were also hammering knowledge into the heads of reluctant "scholars" in the middle colonies and in the South. Some of these institutions were tax supported; others were privately operated. The South, with its white and black population diffused over wide areas, was severely handicapped in attempting to establish an effective school system. Wealthy families leaned heavily on private tutors.

The general atmosphere in the colonial schools and colleges continued grim and gloomy. The emphasis was placed on religion and on the classical languages, Latin and Greek. Independence of thinking was discouraged, and severe discipline was often administered with a switch cut from a birch tree. By 1750 there was a distinct trend toward "live" languages and other modern subjects in the colonial colleges. A significant contribution was made by Benjamin Franklin, who had a large hand in launching what became the University of Pennsylvania, the first American college free from denominational control.

Culture in the Backwoods

The dawn-to-dusk toil of pioneer life left little vitality or aptitude for artistic effort. Americans were too busy chopping down trees to sit around painting landscapes. There was no strong aesthetic tradition; many of the clergy, in fact, regarded art as an invention of the devil.

As the colonists gradually acquired some wealth and leisure time, their surplus energy went into religious and political leadership, not art. The materialistic atmosphere was not favorable to artistic endeavor. One famous painter, the noted John Trumbull of Connecticut (1756–1843), was discouraged in his youth by his father's chilling remark, "Connecticut is not Athens." Charles W. Peale (1741–1827), Benjamin West (1738–1820), and John Copley (1738–1815) all succeeded in their ambition to become famous painters, but they had to go to Britain to complete their training and find patrons for their art.

Colonial architecture, too, was largely imported from the Old World. The red-bricked Georgian style, so common in the pre-Revolutionary decades, is best exemplified by the beauty of now-restored Williamsburg, Virginia.

Colonial literature, like art, was generally undistinguished, but a few outstanding individuals produced original and enduring work. Precocious black poetess Phillis Wheatley (c. 1753–1784) was an uneducated slave girl who went to Boston and then to London. Remarkably, she overcame her handicaps and produced polished poems that reveal the influence of Alexander Pope.

Many-sided Benjamin Franklin, often called "the first civilized American," also shone as a literary light. His classic autobiography was his greatest literary achievement, but he was best known to his contemporaries for *Poor Richard's Almanack,* which he edited from 1732 to 1758. Emphasizing the homespun virtues of thrift, industry, and common sense, "Poor Richard" was most famous for his pithy sayings: "Plough deep while sluggards sleep"; "Fish and visitors stink in three days." *Poor Richard's* was well known in Europe and was more widely read in America than anything else except the Bible. As a teacher of both old and young, Franklin had an incalculable influence in shaping the American character.

Franklin's scientific efforts, including his spectacular kite-flying experiments with electricity, made him the colonies' only first-rate scientist and won him numerous honors in Europe. Among the inventions produced by his practical mind were bifocal spectacles, the Franklin stove, and the lightning rod.

Pioneer Presses

Stump-grubbing Americans were generally too poor to buy quantities of books and too busy to read them. A few fine private libraries, like that of the Byrd family in Virginia, could be found. Bustling Benjamin Franklin established in Philadelphia the first privately supported circulating library, and by 1776 there were about fifty subscription-supported public libraries.

On the eve of the Revolution there were about forty colonial newspapers, chiefly weeklies that consisted of a single large sheet folded once. The "news," especially from overseas, often lagged many weeks behind the event, and the papers devoted much column space to dull essays. Nevertheless, newspapers proved to be a powerful agency for airing colonial grievances and building up opposition to British control.

A celebrated legal case, in 1734–1735, involved John Peter Zenger, a newspaper printer. Significantly, the case arose in New York, reflecting the tumultuous give-and-take of politics in the middle colonies, where so many different ethnic groups jostled against one another. Zenger's newspaper had assailed the corrupt royal governor. Charged with seditious libel, the accused was hauled into court, where he was defended by a distinguished Philadelphia lawyer, Andrew Hamilton, then nearly eighty. Zenger argued that he had printed the truth, but the bewigged royal chief justice ruled that the mere fact of printing, irrespective of the truth, was enough to convict. Yet the jury, swayed by the eloquence of Hamilton, defied the red-robed judges and daringly returned a verdict of "not guilty." Cheers burst from the spectators.

The Zenger decision was epochal. It pointed the way to the kind of freedom of expression required by the diverse society that was colonial New York and that all America was to become. Although contrary to existing law and not accepted by other royal judges, in time it helped set a precedent against

Colonial Quilt *Crafts like quilt-making flourished in colonial America, sometimes producing beautiful folk art. This quilt depicts colonial citizens on their way to church.*

judicial tyranny in libel suits. Newspaper editors had something of a burden lifted from their backs, even though complete freedom of the press was unknown during the pre-Revolutionary era.

The Great Game of Politics

American colonials may have been backward in natural or physical science, but they were making noteworthy contributions to political science.

The thirteen colonial governments presented a varied structure. By 1775, eight of the colonies had royal governors who were appointed by the king. Three—Maryland, Pennsylvania, and Delaware—were under proprietors who themselves chose the governors. And two—Connecticut and Rhode Island—elected their own governors under self-governing charters.

Practically every colony utilized a two-house legislative body. The upper house, or council, was normally appointed by the crown in the royal colonies and by the proprietor in the proprietary colonies. It was chosen by the voters in the self-governing colonies. The lower house, the popular branch, was elected by the people—or rather by those persons who owned enough property to qualify as voters. In several of the colonies, the backcountry elements were seriously underrepresented, and they hated the ruling colonial clique perhaps more than they did kingly authority. Legislatures, in which the people enjoyed direct representation, voted such taxes as they chose for the necessary expenses of colonial government. Self-taxation through representation was a precious privilege that Americans had come to cherish above most others.

Governors appointed by the king were generally able men. But the appointees were sometimes incompetent or corrupt and included broken-down politicians badly in need of jobs. The worst of the group was impoverished Lord Cornbury, first cousin of Queen Anne, who was made governor of New York and New Jersey in 1702. He proved to be a drunkard, a spendthrift, a grafter, an embezzler, a religious bigot, and a vain fool, especially when he appeared in public dressed as a woman. Even the best appointees had trouble with the colonial legislatures, basically because the royal governor embodied a bothersome transatlantic authority some 3,000 miles away.

But the colonial assemblies were by no means defenseless. Some of them employed the trick of withholding the governor's salary unless he yielded to their wishes. Because he was normally in need of money, the power of the purse usually forced him to terms.

Administration at the local level was also varied. County government remained the rule in the plantation South; town-meeting government predominated in New England; and a modification of the two developed in the middle colonies. In the town meeting, with its open discussion and open voting, direct democracy functioned at its best. In this unrivaled cradle of self-government, Americans learned to cherish their privileges and exercise their duties as citizens of the New World commonwealths.

Yet the ballot was by no means a birthright. Religious or property qualifications for voting, with even stiffer qualifications for office holding, existed in all the colonies in 1775. The privileged upper classes, fearful of democratic excesses, were unwilling to grant the ballot to every "biped of the forest."

CHRONOLOGY

1693	College of William and Mary founded.
1721	Smallpox inoculation introduced.
1732	First edition of *Poor Richard's Almanack.*
1734	Jonathan Edwards begins Great Awakening.
1734–1735	Zenger free-press trial in New York.
1738	George Whitefield spreads Great Awakening.
1746	Princeton College founded.
1760	Britain vetoes South Carolina antislave trade measures.
1764	Paxton boys march on Philadelphia. Brown College founded.
1766	Rutgers College founded.
1768–1771	Regulator protests.
1769	Dartmouth College founded.

Perhaps half of the adult white males were thus disfranchised. But because of the ease of acquiring land and thus satisfying property requirements, the right to vote was not beyond the reach of most industrious and enterprising colonials.

By 1775 America was not yet a true democracy—socially, economically, or politically. But it was far more democratic than Britain and Europe. Colonial institutions were giving freer rein to the democratic ideals of tolerance, educational advantages, equality of economic opportunity, freedom of speech, freedom of the press, freedom of assembly, and representative government. And these democratic seeds, planted in rich soil, were to bring forth a lush harvest in later years.

Colonial Folkways

Everyday life in the colonies may now seem quaint, especially as reflected in antique shops. But judged by modern standards, it was drab and tedious. For most people, the labor was heavy and constant—from daybreak to backbreak.

Basic comforts now taken for granted were lacking. Food was plentiful, though the diet could be coarse and monotonous. Churches were unheated except for charcoal foot-warmers that the women carried. There was no running water in the houses, no plumbing, and probably not a single bathtub in all colonial America. Flickering lights were inadequate, for illumination was provided by candles and whale-oil lamps. Garbage disposal was primitive. Long-snouted hogs customarily ranged the streets to consume refuse, while buzzards, protected by law, flapped greedily over tidbits of waste.

Amusement was eagerly pursued where time and custom permitted. Militia "musters," house-raisings, quilting bees, funerals, and weddings all provided opportunities for social gatherings, which customarily involved the swilling of much strong liquor. Winter sports were common in the North, whereas the South favored hunting, horse racing, dancing, stage plays, card playing, and cock fighting.

Lotteries were universally approved, even by the clergy, and were used to raise money for churches and schools, including Harvard. Holidays were celebrated everywhere, but Christmas was frowned upon in New England as an offensive reminder of "Popery." Thanksgiving Day came to be a truly American festival, for it combined thanks to God with an opportunity for jollification, gorging, and guzzling.

The colonists in 1775 were a remarkable people: restless, energetic, ambitious, resourceful, ingenious, and independent minded. As time passed they were less willing to bow their necks to the yoke of overseas authority. With a boundless continent before them and with impressive pioneer achievements behind them, they had caught a vision of their destiny and were preparing to grasp it. Woe unto those who should try to thwart them!

Varying Viewpoints

Many historians, notably Richard Bushman, see pre-Revolutionary America as an expanding, opening society. In this view, colonial society was losing the religious discipline and social hierarchy of the founding generations, as Americans poured out onto the frontier or sailed the commercial seaways in search of fortune and adventure. These scholars portray the Great Awakening as further evidence of the erosion of social constraints. They argue that unbridled religious enthusiasm, directed by itinerant preachers, displayed the kind of questing for personal autonomy that eventually led to demands for national independence.

The opposing view, taken by Gary Nash and Kenneth Lockridge, emphasizes declining opportunities in colonial society. Pressure on land and the continued dominance of church and parental authority gave rise to a landless class, forced to till tenant plots in the countryside or find manual labor in the cities. The simmering discontent of this growing lower class, according to this interpretation, exploded first in the Great Awakening and later in the American Revolution.

SELECT READINGS

Primary Source Documents

Noting the ethnic diversity of colonial American society, Michel Guillaume Jean de Crèvecoeur's *Letters from an American Farmer* (1904)* and Benjamin Franklin's "Observations on the Increase of Mankind,"* in Jared Sparks, ed., *The Works of Benjamin Franklin* (1840), respectively celebrate and express unease at that diversity.

Franklin's entertaining *Autobiography** (1868) is an indispensable guide to the values and preoccupations of his time. It includes an account of George Whitefield's visit to Philadelphia during the Great Awakening.

Secondary Sources

Social history is painted with broad strokes in James Henretta, *The Evolution of American Society, 1700–1815* (1973), and Daniel Boorstin, *The Americans: The Colonial Experience* (1958). Richard Hofstadter takes a suggestive snapshot in *America in 1750* (1971). Immigration is discussed in Bernard Bailyn, *Voyagers to the West: A Passage in the Peopling of America on the Eve of Revolution* (1987). Black "immigrants" are studied in Philip D. Curtin, *The Atlantic Slave Trade: A Census* (1969), and indentured servants in Abbot E. Smith, *Colonists in Bondage* (1947). Jackson T. Main astutely analyzes *The Social Structure of Revolutionary America, 1763–1788* (1965). Large-scale economic patterns are traced in Edwin J. Perkins, *The Economy of Colonial America* (1980), and in Alice H. Jones, *The Wealth of a Nation to Be: The American Colonies on the Eve of the Revolution* (1980). Gary B. Nash, *The Urban Crucible: Social Change, Political Con-* *sciousness, and the Origins of the American Revolution* (1979), and Rhys Isaac, *The Transformation of Virginia, 1740–1790* (1982), both link social conflict to the Great Awakening, as does Richard L. Bushman, *From Puritan to Yankee: Character and Social Order in Connecticut, 1690–1765* (1967). Patricia Bonomi also emphasizes religious conflict as a promoter of revolutionary ideology in *Under the Cope of Heaven: Religion, Society, and Politics in Colonial America* (1986). Jon Butler challenges many standard views about the relation of religion to early American society in *Awash in a Sea of Faith* (1989). Cultural history is imaginatively presented in Howard M. Jones, *O Strange New World: American Culture in the Formative Years* (1964). Comprehensive is Henry May, *The Enlightenment in America* (1976). Colonial politics are interpreted in a most suggestive way in Bernard Bailyn, *The Origins of American Politics* (1965). More fine-grained local studies include Richard Bushman, *King and People in Provincial Massachusetts* (1985), Jackson Turner Main, *Society and Economy in Colonial Connecticut* (1985), and Daniel Blake Smith, *Inside the Great House: Planter Family Life in Eighteenth-Century Chesapeake Society* (1980).

CHAPTER 6

The Duel for North America, 1608–1763

A torch lighted in the forests of America set all Europe in conflagration.

François Voltaire, c. 1756

France Finds a Foothold in Canada

France, like England and Holland, was another late-comer in the scramble for New World real estate, and for basically the same reasons. It was convulsed during the 1500s by foreign wars and domestic strife, including the frightful clashes between Roman Catholics and Protestant Huguenots.

A new era dawned in 1598 when the Edict of Nantes, issued by the crown, granted limited toleration to French Protestants. Religious wars ceased, and in the 1600s France blossomed into the mightiest and most feared nation in Europe.

Success finally crowned the exertions of France in the New World. In 1608, the year after Jamestown was founded, the permanent beginnings of a vast empire were established at Quebec, a rocky sentinel commanding the St. Lawrence River. The leading figure was Samuel de Champlain, an intrepid soldier and explorer whose energy and leadership fairly earned him the title "Father of New France."

Champlain entered into friendly relations—a fateful friendship—with the nearby Huron Indian tribes. Yielding to their entreaties, he joined them in battle against their foes, the federated Iroquois tribes of the upper New York area. Two volleys from the "lightning sticks" of the whites routed the terrified Indians, who left behind three dead and one wounded. France, to its sorrow, thus earned the lasting enmity of the Iroquois tribes, who thereafter hampered French penetration of the Ohio Valley, ravaged French settlements, and served as allies of the British in the prolonged struggle for supremacy on the continent.

The government of New France (Canada) finally fell under the direct control of the king, after various commercial companies had faltered or failed. This royal regime was almost completely autocratic. There were no popularly elected assemblies, as in the English colonies; there was no trial by jury—merely the decision of the magistrate.

Population in Catholic New France grew with painful slowness: as late as 1750 there were only 60,000 or so whites. Landowning French peasants, unlike the dispossessed English tenant farmers who embarked for the British colonies, had little eco-

69

nomic incentive to move. Protestant Huguenots, who might have had a religious motive to migrate, were denied a refuge in this raw colony. The French government, in any case, favored its Caribbean island colonies, rich in sugar and rum, over the snow-cloaked wilderness of Canada.

New France Fans Out

New France did contain one valuable resource: the beaver. To adorn the heads of fashionable Europeans, French fur trappers ranged over the woods and waterways of North America in pursuit of beaver. These colorful *coureurs des bois* ("runners of the woods") were also runners of risks—two-fisted drinkers, free spenders, free livers and lovers. They littered the land with scores of place names, including Baton Rouge (red stick), Terre Haute (high land), Des Moines (some monks), and Grand Teton (big breast).

Singing, paddle-swinging French *voyageurs* also recruited Indians into the fur business. But the Indians were decimated by the white man's diseases and debauched by his alcohol—"firewater." Slaughtering beaver by the boatload violated many Indian religious beliefs and sadly demonstrated the shattering effect that contact with Europeans wreaked on traditional Indian ways of life.

Pursuing the sharp-toothed beaver ever deeper into the heart of the continent, French trappers and their Indian partners covered amazing distances. They trekked in a huge arc across the Great Lakes, into present-day Saskatchewan and Manitoba, along the valleys of the Platte, the Arkansas, and the Missouri rivers, west to the Rockies, and south to the border of Texas. In the process, they extinguished the beaver population in many areas, inflicting incalculable ecological damage.

French Catholic missionaries, notably the Jesuits, labored zealously to save the Indians for Christ and from the fur trappers. But though they made few permanent converts, the Jesuits played a vital role as explorers and geographers.

Other explorers sought neither souls nor fur, but empire. To check Spanish penetration into the

Life in New France, Seventeenth Century *Fur trapping and fishing were basic pursuits for both Indians and European settlers in France's American colonies.*

region of the Gulf of Mexico, ambitious Robert La Salle floated down the Mississippi in 1682 to the point where it mingles with the gulf. Three years later he tried to return to the territory he had named "Louisiana," but he failed to find the Mississippi delta. He landed instead in Spanish Texas, and in 1687 was murdered by his mutinous men.

Persistent French officials planted several fortified posts in what is now Mississippi and Louisiana, the most important of which was New Orleans (1718). Commanding the mouth of the Mississippi River, this strategic semitropical outpost tapped the fur and grain trade of the huge interior valley, especially the fertile Illinois country.

The Clash of Empires

As the seventeenth century neared its sunset, a titanic struggle was shaping up for mastery of the North American continent. It involved three nations: Britain, France, and Spain. From 1688 to 1763, four bitter wars among the great powers convulsed Europe. All four of these conflicts were world wars, in which the rival nations struggled for domination in Europe as well as the New World. The American people, whether as British subjects or as American citizens, were unable to stay out of a single one of them. Isolation from the broils of Europe was all too often a hope rather than a reality.

The first two wars, known in America as King William's War and Queen Anne's War, pitted British colonials against the French *coureurs des bois* and their Indian allies. Neither France nor England considered America worth the commitment of regular troops, so a kind of primitive guerrilla warfare prevailed. French-inspired Indians ravaged with torch and tomahawk the British colonial frontiers from New York to Massachusetts, while France's Spanish allies probed at outlying South Carolina settlements. For their part, the British colonials failed miserably in attempts to capture Quebec and Montreal but did temporarily seize the stronghold of Port Royal in Acadia.

In the Peace of Utrecht (1713), victorious Britain acquired French-populated Acadia (renamed Nova Scotia) and the wintry wastes of Newfoundland and Hudson's Bay. These immense tracts pinched the St. Lawrence settlements of France. The British also won limited trading rights in Spanish America, but these later involved much friction over smuggling. Ill feeling between Britain and Spain led to war in 1739, when the British Captain Robert Jenkins, whose ear had been sliced off by a Spanish sword, returned to London with a tale of woe on his tongue and a shriveled ear in his hand. The War of Jenkins's Ear was confined to the Caribbean and to the much-buffeted buffer colony of Georgia.

This small-scale scuffle with Spain in America soon merged with the large-scale War of Austrian Succession in Europe. Once again, France allied itself with Spain. And once again, a rustic force of New Englanders, with the help of the British fleet, captured a reputedly impregnable French fortress, Louisbourg, on Cape Breton Island, commanding the approaches to the St. Lawrence River. When the peace treaty of 1748 handed Louisbourg back to their French foe, the victorious New Englanders were outraged. The glory of their arms seemed tarnished by the wiles of Old World diplomats. Worse, Louisbourg was still a cocked pistol pointed at the heart of the American continent. France, powerful and unappeased, clung to its vast holdings in North America.

George Washington Inaugurates War with France

As the drama unfolded in the New World, the Ohio Valley became the chief bone of contention between the French and British. The Ohio country was the critical area into which the westward-pushing British would inevitably penetrate. It was the key to the continent that the French had to retain, particularly if they were going to link their Canadian holdings with those of the lower Mississippi Valley. By the mid-1700s the British colonials, painfully aware of these basic truths, were no longer so reluctant to bear the burdens of empire. Alarmed by French land-grabbing and cutthroat fur-trade competition in the Ohio Valley, they were determined to fight for their economic security and for the supremacy of their way of life in North America.

Rivalry for the lush lands of the upper Ohio Valley brought tensions to the snapping point. In 1749 a group of British colonial speculators, chiefly influential Virginians, including the Washington family, had secured rights to some 500,000 acres in this region. In the same disputed wilderness, the French were in the process of erecting a chain of forts commanding the strategic Ohio River.

In 1754 the governor of Virginia ushered George Washington, a twenty-one-year-old surveyor and fellow Virginian, onto the stage of history. Washington was sent to the Ohio country as a lieutenant colonel in command of about 150 Virginia militiamen. Encountering a small detachment of French troops in the forest about forty miles from Fort Duquesne, the Virginians fired the first shots of the globe-girdling new war. The French leader was killed, and his men retreated. An exultant Washington wrote: "I heard the bullets whistle, and believe me, there is something charming in the sound." It soon lost its charm.

The French promptly returned with reinforcements, which surrounded Washington's hastily constructed breastworks, Fort Necessity. After a ten-hour siege he was forced to surrender his entire command in July 1754—ironically the fourth of July.

With the shooting already started and in danger of spreading, the British authorities in Nova Scotia took vigorous action. Understandably fearing a stab in the back from the French Acadians, whom Britain had ruled since 1713, the British brutally uprooted some 4,000 of them in 1755. These unhappy French deportees were scattered as far south as Louisiana, where descendants of the French-speaking Acadians are now called "Cajuns" and number nearly a million.

Global War and Colonial Disunity

The first three Anglo-French colonial wars had all started in Europe, but the tables were now reversed. A fourth struggle, known as the French and Indian War, began in America. Touched off by George Washington in the wilds of the Ohio Valley in 1754, it rocked along on an undeclared basis for two years and then widened into the most far-flung conflict the world had yet seen—the Seven Years' War. It was fought not only in America but in Europe, in the West Indies, in the Philippines, in Africa, and on the ocean. The Seven Years' War was a seven-seas war.

In Europe, Britain liberally subsidized Frederick the Great of Prussia in his war against their enemy, France. The French wasted so much strength in the European bloodbath that they were unable to throw an adequate force into the New World. "America was conquered in Germany," declared British statesman William Pitt.

In previous colonial clashes, the Americans had revealed an astonishing lack of unity. Colonists who were nearest had responded much more generously with volunteers and money than those enjoying the safety of remoteness. Now, with musketballs already whining in the Ohio country, the crisis demanded concerted action.

In 1754 the British government summoned an intercolonial congress to Albany, New York, near the Iroquois country. Travel-weary delegates from only seven of the thirteen colonies showed up. The immediate purpose was to keep the Iroquois chiefs loyal to the British in the spreading war.

Famous Cartoon by Benjamin Franklin *Delaware and Georgia were omitted.*

The longer-range purpose at Albany was to bolster the common defense against France by achieving greater colonial unity. Leading this effort was wise and witty Benjamin Franklin. Before the Albany Congress had assembled, Franklin published the famous cartoon showing the separate colonies as parts of a disjointed snake, with the slogan, "Join, or die." Franklin gained the congress' approval for his well-devised scheme of colonial home rule, but it was spurned by the individual colonies and the London regime. To the colonials, it did not seem to give enough independence; to the British officials, it seemed to give too much.

Braddock's Blundering and Its Aftermath

Led by General Edward Braddock, the British stumbled badly in their opening clashes with the French and Indians. Braddock was sent to Virginia in 1755 and set out with a mixed force of 2,000 British regulars and ill-disciplined colonial militiamen to capture Fort Duquesne. Experienced in European warfare, "Bulldog" Braddock was professionally contemptuous of colonial "buckskins'" behind-the-trees method of fighting Indians.

Dragging heavy artillery through the dense forest, Braddock's expedition slowly crept to within a few miles of Fort Duquesne. There it encountered a much smaller French and Indian army. At first the enemy force was repulsed, but it quickly melted into the thickets and poured a murderous fire into the

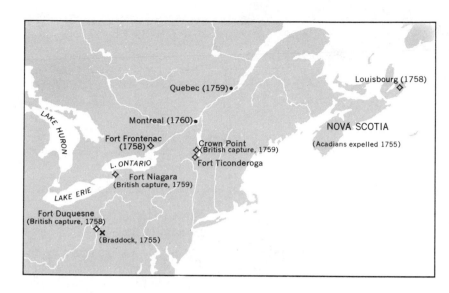

Events of 1755–1760

ranks of the redcoats. Braddock's energetic and fearless aide George Washington had two horses shot from under him and four bullet holes in his coat, and Braddock himself was mortally wounded. The entire force was routed with appalling losses.

Inflamed by this easy victory, the Indians took to a wider warpath. The whole frontier from Pennsylvania to North Carolina, left virtually naked by Braddock's bloody defeat, felt their fury. Scalping forays occurred within eighty miles of Philadelphia, and in desperation the local authorities offered bounties for Indian scalps: $50 for a woman's and $130 for a brave's.

Now that the undeclared war in America had at last merged into a world conflict, the British launched a full-scale invasion of Canada in 1756. But they unwisely tried to attack a number of exposed wilderness posts simultaneously, instead of throwing all their strength at Quebec and Montreal. Ignoring such sound strategy, defeat after defeat decimated British armies, both in America and in Europe.

Pitt's Palms of Victory

In the hour of crisis, Britain brought forth, as it repeatedly has, a superlative leader—William Pitt. A tall and imposing figure, whose flashing eyes were set in a hawklike face, Pitt was popularly known as the "Great Commoner." He drew much of his strength from the common people, who admired him so greatly that on occasion they kissed his horses.

In 1757 Pitt became a foremost leader in the London government. He wisely decided to concentrate the war effort on the vitals of Canada—the Quebec-Montreal area. Pitt first dispatched a powerful expedition in 1758 against Louisbourg. The frowning fortress, though it had been greatly strengthened, fell after a blistering siege. Wild rejoicing swept Britain, for this was the first significant British victory of the entire war.

Quebec was next on Pitt's list. For this crucial expedition he chose the thirty-two-year-old James Wolfe, who had been an officer since the age of fourteen. In a daring move, Wolfe sent a detachment up a poorly guarded part of the rocky eminence protecting Quebec. This vanguard scaled the cliff, pulling itself upward by the bushes and showing the way for the others. In the morning the two armies faced each other on the Plains of Abraham on the outskirts of Quebec, the British under Wolfe and the French under Montcalm. Both commanders fell fatally wounded, but the French were defeated and the city surrendered (see "Makers of America: The French," pp. 74–75).

The battle of Quebec ranks as one of the most significant engagements in British and American

The French

King Louis XIV's dream of a bountiful New France flickered out like a candle after the British conquered his French colonies in the eighteenth century. His former subjects in Quebec and the maritime provinces of Acadia chafed under foreign domination, and during the next two centuries many eventually found their way to the United States.

The first French to leave Canada were the Acadians, the settlers of the seaboard region that now comprises Nova Scotia, New Brunswick, Prince Edward Island, and part of Maine. In 1713 the French crown ceded this territory to the British, who demanded that the Acadians either swear allegiance to Britain or withdraw to French territory. At first doing neither, they managed to escape reprisals until *le grand derangement* ("the great displacement") in 1755, when the British expelled them at bayonet point. The Acadians fled far south to the French colony of Louisiana, where they settled among the sleepy bayous, planted sugarcane and sweet potatoes, practiced Roman Catholicism, and spoke the French dialect that came to be called Cajun (a corruption of the English word *acadian*). Their settlements were tiny and secluded, many of them accessible only by small boat.

For generations these insular people were scarcely influenced by developments outside their tight-knit communities. Not until the twentieth century did Cajun parents surrender their children to public schools and submit to a state law restricting French speech. Only in the 1930s, with a bridge-building spree engineered by Governor Huey Long, was the isolation of these bayou communities broken.

Franco-American Mill Workers in New England, c. 1910

In 1763, as the French settlers of Quebec fell under British rule, a second group began to leave Canada. By 1840 what had been an irregular southward trickle of Quebecois swelled to a steady stream of people who were driven away mostly by lean harvests.

They emigrated mostly to work in New England's lumberyards and textile mills, gradually establishing permanent settlements in the northern woods. From there they were able frequently to recross the border to visit their old homes. Like the Acadians, these later migrants stubbornly preserved their Roman Catholicism. Both groups also shared a passionate love of their French language, believing it to be the cement that bound them, their religion, and their culture together. As one French-Canadian explained: "Let us worship in peace and in our own tongue. All else may disappear but this must remain our badge."

Today, almost all Cajuns and New England French Canadians speak English. But in their ethnic communities and traditions they provide a continuing testimony to the vitality of the French influence in North American history.

* * *

history. When Montreal fell in 1760, the French flag waved in Canada for the last time. By the peace settlement at Paris (1763), French power was thrown completely off the continent of North America, leaving behind a fertile French population that is to this day a strong minority in Canada. Great Britain thus emerged as the dominant power in North America, while taking its place as the leading naval power of the world.

Restless Colonials

Britain's colonials, baptized in fire, emerged with increased confidence in their military strength. They

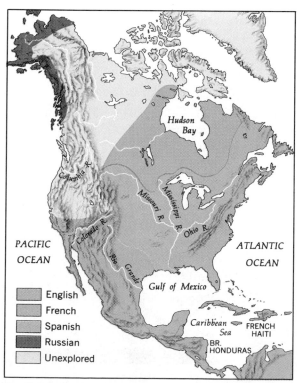

North America Before 1754

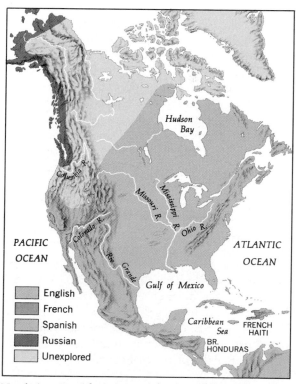

North America After 1763 *(after French losses)*

had borne the brunt of battle at first; they had fought bravely beside the crack British regulars; and they had gained valuable experience, officers and men alike. In the closing days of the conflict some 20,000 American recruits were under arms.

The French and Indian War, while bolstering colonial self-esteem, simultaneously shattered the myth of British invincibility. On Braddock's bloody field the buckskin militia had seen the demoralized regulars huddling helplessly together or fleeing their unseen enemy.

Ominously, friction had developed during the war between arrogant British officers and the raw colonial "boors." Displaying the contempt of the professional soldier for amateurs, the British refused to recognize any American militia commission above the rank of captain—a demotion humiliating to "Colonel" George Washington. They also showed the usual condescension of snobs from the civilized Old Country toward the "scum" who had confessed failure by fleeing to the "outhouses of civilization." Energetic and hard-working American settlers, on the other hand, sensed that they were the cutting edge of British civilization. They believed that they deserved credit rather than contempt for risking their lives to erect a New World empire.

British officials were further distressed by the reluctance of colonials to support the common cause wholeheartedly. American shippers developed a reasonable but lucrative trade with the Spanish and French West Indies at the very time the British navy was trying to subdue them. Other colonials, self-centered and regarding the war as remote, refused to provide men and money for the conflict until Pitt offered to reimburse the colonies for their expenditures. If the Americans had to be bribed to defend themselves against a relentless foe, would they ever unite to strike the mother country?

The curse of intercolonial disunity, present from early days, had continued throughout the recent hostilities. It had been caused mainly by enormous distances; by geographical barriers like rivers; by conflicting religions, from Catholic to Quaker; by varied national backgrounds from German to Irish; by differing types of colonial governments; by many

boundary disputes; and by the resentment that the crude backcountry settlers felt against the aristocratic bigwigs.

Yet unity received some encouragement during the French and Indian War. When soldiers and statesmen from widely separated colonies met around common campfires and council tables, they were often agreeably surprised by what they found.

CHRONOLOGY

1598	Edict of Nantes.
1608	Champlain colonizes Quebec for France.
1643	Louis XIV becomes king of France.
1682	La Salle explores Mississippi River to the Gulf of Mexico.
1689–1697	King William's War (War of the League of Augsburg).
1702–1713	Queen Anne's War (War of Spanish Succession).
1718	French found New Orleans.
1739	War of Jenkins's Ear.
1740–1748	King George's War (War of Austrian Succession).
1754	Washington battles French on frontier.
	Albany Congress.
1756–1763	French and Indian War (Seven Years' War).
1757	Pitt emerges as leader of British government.
1759	Battle of Quebec.
1763	Peace of Paris.
	Pontiac's uprising.
	Proclamation of 1763.

Despite deep-seated jealousy and suspicion, they discovered that they were all fellow Americans who generally spoke the same language and shared common ideals. Barriers of disunity began to melt, although a long and rugged road lay ahead before a nation could emerge.

Americans: A People of Destiny

The removal of the French menace in Canada profoundly affected American attitudes. While the French hawk had been hovering along the northern and western frontier, the colonial chicks had been forced to cling close to the wings of the mother hen. Now that the hawk was killed, they could range far afield with a new spirit of independence.

The French, humiliated by the British and saddened by the fate of Canada, consoled themselves with one wishful thought. Perhaps the loss of their American empire would one day result in Britain's loss of its American empire. In a sense the history of the United States began with the fall of Quebec and Montreal; the infant republic was cradled on the Plains of Abraham.

The Spanish and Indian threats were also now substantially reduced. Spain was eliminated from Florida, although entrenched in Louisiana and New Orleans. As for the Indians, the Treaty of Paris dealt a harsh blow to the Iroquois, Creeks, and other interior tribes. A violent postwar flare-up against the white men occurred in the Ohio Valley and Great Lakes region in 1763, with the Ottawa chief Pontiac as the principal leader. Catching the British napping, the Indians wiped out all but three British outposts west of the Appalachians. The whites swiftly and cruelly retaliated. One British commander ordered blankets infected with smallpox to be distributed among the Indians. Such tactics crushed the uprising and pacified the frontier.

Land-hungry American colonials were now free to burst over the dam of the Appalachian Mountains and flood out over the grassy western lands. A tiny rivulet of pioneers like Daniel Boone had already trickled into Tennessee and Kentucky; other courageous pioneers made their preparations for the long, dangerous trek over the mountains.

Then, out of a clear sky, the London government issued its Proclamation of 1763. It flatly prohibited settlement in the area beyond the Appalachians, pending further adjustments. The truth is that this hastily drawn document was not designed to oppress the colonials at all, but to work out the Indian problem fairly and prevent another bloody eruption like Pontiac's uprising.

But countless Americans, especially land speculators, were dismayed and angered. Was not the land beyond the mountains their birthright? Had they not, in addition, bought it with their blood in the recent war? In complete defiance of the proclamation, they clogged the westward trails. In 1765 an estimated 1,000 wagons rolled through the town of Salisbury, North Carolina, on their way "up west." This wholesale flouting of royal authority boded ill for the longevity of British rule in America.

The French and Indian War caused the colonials to develop a new vision of their ultimate destiny. With the path cleared for the conquest of a continent, with their birthrate high and their energy boundless, they sensed that they were a potent people on the march. And they were in no mood to be restrained.

Lordly Britons, whose suddenly swollen empire had tended to produce swollen heads, were in no mood for back talk. Puffed up over their recent victories, they were already annoyed with their unruly colonials. The atmosphere was thus conducive to a violent family quarrel.

Varying Viewpoints

The duel for North America was but one episode in the epochal story of the worldwide expansion of European commerce and culture after 1500. Dominated by the "imperial school," a group of historians who see transatlantic economic stresses as leading to revolution, scholarly inquiry has revolved around four principal questions: How did New World developments fit into the overall pattern of rivalries among the great European powers? What were the relative strengths and weaknesses of the British and French imperial systems that spelled the final triumph of the British and the defeat of the French? How well or poorly did the British Empire function? Finally, were the Americans well or badly treated in the British imperial system? In short, how economically justifiable was the eventual American Revolution?

Social historians have recently looked at the colonial rivalries in a different light. They view the social and economic dislocations wrought by war as a stimulus to class conflict and revolutionary ferment. Some scholars have also asked whether the Revolution would have occurred at all without the British victory over the French in North America. If a powerful, Catholic, hostile France had retained its foothold in Canada, the British colonials might have thought twice about challenging their mother country.

SELECT READINGS

Primary Source Documents

"The Albany Plan of the Union" was the first great statement of colonial unity; "The Proclamation of 1763" forbade settlement west of the Appalachians. Both are collected in Henry Steele Commager, *Documents of American History.*

Secondary Sources

The workings of the British mercantile system are detailed in Charles M. Andrews's vast *Colonial Period of American History* (4 vols., 1935–1938) and in Lawrence H. Gipson's still more ambitious *British Empire Before the American Revolution* (15 vols., 1936–1970). Recent efforts to analyze the colonial empire are James Henretta, *"Salutary Neglect": Colonial Administration Under the Duke of Newcastle* (1972), and Michael Kammen's especially interesting *Empire and Interest* (1970). The French colonial effort is described in George M. Wrong, *The Rise and Fall of New France* (2 vols., 1928). Calvin Martin, *Keepers of the Game* (1978), offers a provocative interpretation of the fur trade and its impact on Indian societies. The Anglo-French struggle is recounted in Howard H. Peckham, *The Colonial Wars, 1689–1762* (1964). Alan Rogers, *Empire and Liberty: American Resistance to British Authority, 1755–1763* (1974) investigates American participation in the Seven Years' War. Classic accounts are Francis Parkman's several volumes, including *Count Frontenac and New France Under Louis XIV* (1877), *Montcalm and Wolfe* (2 vols., 1884), and *A Half-Century of Conflict* (1892). Parkman's tomes are condensed in *The Battle for North America,* edited by John Tebbel (1948), and *The Parkman Reader,* edited by Samuel E. Morison (1955). An impressive biography is Douglas S. Freeman, *Young Washington* (2 vols., 1948). The youthful Washington is also treated in James T. Flexner, *George Washington: The Forge of Experience* (1965), and Bernhard Knollenberg, *George Washington: The Virginia Period* (1965).

CHAPTER 7

The Road to Revolution, 1763–1775

The Revolution was effected before the war commenced.
The Revolution was in the minds and hearts of the people.

John Adams, 1818

The Deep Roots of Revolution

In a broad sense, the American Revolution was not the same thing as the American War of Independence. The war itself lasted only eight years. But the Revolution lasted over a century and a half and began when the first permanent English settlers set foot on the new continent. Insurrection of thought usually precedes insurrection of deed. Over the years such a ferment occurred in the thinking of the colonists that the Revolution was partially completed in their minds before the musketballs began to fly. America was a revolutionary force from the day of its discovery.

Britain's colonies were settled largely by emigrants who were discontented or rebellious in spirit—by people who had failed to adjust themselves to their harsh lot in the Old World. Most of them had not been able to get along, whether socially, politically, economically, or religiously. Some of them were tired of taking off their hats and standing bareheaded in the presence of their "betters." Others wanted a larger share in government, a richer portion of this world's goods, or an opportunity to worship God in their own particular way.

The long and perilous Atlantic crossing was the first big step in the emigrants' emotional and spiritual isolation from the faraway Old World. Food shortages, epidemics, and even occasional cannibalism turned ships into "floating coffins." As a sailor's song ran:

> We ate the mice, we ate the rats,
> And through the hold we ran like cats.

Such a perilous crossing left many emotional scars. Survivors who staggered ashore on the promised land were, as a rule, spiritually isolated from the Old World. They were aware that the long arm of the London government, enfeebled by 3,000 miles of ocean, could not reach them nearly so effectively as at home. Distance weakens authority; great distance weakens authority greatly.

America's lonely wilderness likewise stimulated ideas of independence. Back in Britain some villagers had lived near graveyards that contained the bones of their ancestors of a thousand years past. Born into such conservative surroundings, the poor peasants did not question the social rut in which they found themselves. But in the New World they were not held down by the scowl of their overlords.

Rugged pioneering conditions changed patterns of living and consequently habits of thought. Before long, Americans were eating Indian corn, wearing Indian moccasins and buckskin, and, in extreme instances on the frontier, uttering the war whoop as they scalped their fallen Indian foe. Hacking a home out of the wildwood with an ax developed self-confidence, individualism, and a spirit of independence.

As the Americans matured, they acquired privileges of self-government enjoyed by no other colonial peoples. They set up thirteen parliaments of their own and emulated the parliamentary methods of Britain. Ultimately they came to regard their own legislative bodies as more or less on a footing with the great Parliament in London.

The Mercantile Theory

Britain's empire was acquired in a "fit of absent-mindedness," as the old saying goes, and there is much truth in it. Not one of the original thirteen colonies, except Georgia, was formally planted by the British government. The others were haphazardly founded by trading companies, religious groups, land speculators, and others.

Britain controlled the colonies through simple machinery. The principal imperial agency, the Board of Trade, made recommendations that were often enacted into law by Parliament or adopted by the Privy Council (the king's advisers).

The theory that shaped and justified British exploitation of the American colonies was called mercantilism. According to mercantile doctrine, colonies existed only to benefit the mother country. They should help the imperial power to achieve economic (and military) self-sufficiency by exporting more than they imported. Colonists were regarded more or less as tenants. They were expected to produce tobacco and other products needed in Britain and not to bother their heads with dangerous dreams of economic independence or self-government.

Specifically, how were the American colonies to benefit Britain? First, they were to ensure Britain's naval supremacy by furnishing ships, ships' stores, sailors, and trade. In addition, they were to provide a profitable consumer's market for British manufacturers' goods. Finally, they were to keep gold and silver money within the empire by growing products, such as sugar, that otherwise would have to be bought from foreigners. The idea of "buy British" would thus be promoted in a manner that foreshadowed later protective tariffs.

Mercantilist Trammels on Trade

Parliament passed numerous measures to enforce the mercantile system. The first of these, the Navigation Law of 1651, was aimed at rival Dutch shippers. This measure, and subsequent Navigation Laws, restricted commerce to and from the colonies to British vessels. Such regulation kept money within the empire and bolstered the British—and colonial—merchant marine.

An alert Parliament from time to time enacted additional laws favorable to Britain. European goods consigned to America had to be landed first in Britain, where customs duties could be collected and where the British middleman would get his cut of the profit. Still other curbs required certain "enumerated" products, notably tobacco, to be shipped to Britain and not to foreign markets, even though prices in Europe might be higher. Settlers were also forbidden to manufacture for export such products as woolen cloth and beaver hats, because the colonies were supposed to complement and not compete with British industry.

Americans also felt the pinch in the area of currency. No banks existed in the colonies, and the money problem on the eve of the Revolution was acute. Industrious colonials were now busily buying more goods from Britain than they were selling there, so the difference had to be made up in hard cash. Every year gold and silver money, much of it in Spanish coins from the West Indies, was drained out of the colonies. The colonials simply did not have enough left for the convenience of everyday purchases. Barter became necessary, and even butter, nails, pitch, and feathers were used for purposes of exchange.

The Female Combatants *Britain is symbolized as a lady of fashion, and her rebellious daughter as an Indian princess.*

The Merits of Mercantilism

Americans have long regarded the British mercantile system as thoroughly selfish and deliberately oppressive. The truth is that until 1763 the Navigation Laws imposed no intolerable burden, partly because they were laxly enforced. Ingenious colonial merchants early learned to disregard or evade restrictions they found vexatious. Some of the early American fortunes, like that of John Hancock, were amassed by wholesale smuggling.

Americans also reaped direct benefits from the mercantile system. London paid liberal bounties to colonials who produced ships' parts and ships' stores, even though British competitors complained heatedly. Virginia tobacco planters were guaranteed a monopoly in the British market for their pungent yellow leaf, and tobacco growing was outlawed in Britain and Ireland.

American colonials enjoyed the undiluted rights of Englishmen and the protection of the British government at little cost. A strong army of British redcoats and the mightiest navy in the world sheltered them against the French, Dutch, Spanish, Indians, and pirates—without a penny of tax.

"Prosperity trickles down" is a common saying; and it is true that the Americans enjoyed a generous share of Britain's profits under the time-honored mercantile system. The average American was probably better off economically than the average British person at home. If the colonies existed for the benefit of Britain, it was hardly less true that Britain existed for the benefit of the colonies. The well-meaning officials in London were working for the welfare of the empire as a whole, and they gave overall unity to its policies. A wise person does not disembowel or starve the goose that lays the golden eggs. Mistakes were made by the British authorities, but they were not, until revolt had erupted, the mistakes of malice.

The Menace of Mercantilism

But when painted in its rosiest colors, the mercantile system burdened the colonials with annoying liabilities. Economic initiative was stifled because Americans were not at complete liberty to buy, sell, ship, or manufacture under conditions that they found most

Currency problems came to a boil when dire need finally forced many of the colonies to issue paper money, which unfortunately depreciated. British merchants and creditors, understandably worried, squawked so loudly that Parliament was compelled to act. It restrained the colonial legislatures from printing paper currency and from passing lax bankruptcy laws—practices that might result in defrauding British merchants. The Americans, who felt that their welfare was again being sacrificed, reacted angrily. Another burning grievance was thus heaped upon the pile of combustibles already smoldering.

London officialdom kept a watchful eye on legislation passed by the colonial assemblies, and the Privy Council vetoed any laws that conflicted with British regulations or policy. This "royal veto" was used sparingly—only 469 times in connection with 8,563 laws. But the colonists nevertheless felt aggrieved when they were forbidden to make reforms they deemed desirable, such as curbing the degrading trade in African slaves.

profitable. The southern colonies, as "pets," were generally favored over the northern ones, chiefly because they grew non-British products like tobacco, sugar, and rice. Revolution was one seed that sprouted vigorously from the stony soil of New England, for the proud descendants of the Puritans resented being treated like unwanted relatives.

One-crop Virginians also nursed rankling grievances. Forced to sell their tobacco in Britain, they were at the mercy of British merchants, who often gouged them. Many of the fashionable Virginia planters were plunged into debt by the falling price of tobacco and were forced to buy their necessities in Britain by mortgaging future crops. Countless Virginians welcomed the opportunity to end their economic bondage to the mother country.

Finally—and of supreme importance—mercantilism was debasing to the Americans. They were to be kept in a state of perpetual economic adolescence and never allowed to come of age. As Benjamin Franklin wrote in 1775:

> We have an old mother that peevish is grown;
> She snubs us like children that scarce walk
>   alone;
> She forgets we're grown up and have sense of
>   our own.

Revolution broke out, as Theodore Roosevelt later remarked, because Britain failed to recognize an emerging nation when it saw one.

The Stamp Tax Uproar

The costly Seven Years' War, which ended in 1763, marked a new relationship between Britain and its transatlantic colonies. A revolution in British colonial policy precipitated the American Revolution.

Victory-flushed Britain emerged from the conflict possessing one of the biggest empires in the world—and also, less happily, the biggest debt. It amounted to £140 million, about half of which had been incurred in defending the American colonies. British officials wisely had no intention of asking the colonials to help pay off this crushing burden. But London felt that the Americans should be asked to defray one-third the cost of maintaining a garrison of

some 10,000 redcoats, presumably for the colonies' own protection.

Prime Minister George Grenville aroused the resentment of the colonials in 1763 by ordering the British navy to enforce the Navigation Laws. He also secured from Parliament the so-called Sugar Act of 1764, the first law ever passed by that body for raising revenue in the colonies for the crown. Among various provisions, it increased the duty on foreign sugar imported from the West Indies. After bitter protests from the colonials, the duties were lowered substantially, and the agitation died down. But resentment was kept burning by the Quartering Act of 1765. It required certain colonies to provide food and quarters for British troops.

Then in the same year, 1765, Grenville proposed the most odious measure of all: a stamp tax, to raise revenues to support the new military force. The Stamp Act required the use of stamped paper or the affixing of stamps, certifying payment of tax. Involved were about fifty trade items and certain types of commercial and legal documents, including playing cards, pamphlets, newspapers, diplomas, bills of lading, and marriage licenses.

Grenville regarded all these measures as reasonable and just. He was simply asking the Americans to pay their fair share for colonial defense, through taxes that were already familiar in Britain. In fact, Englishmen for two generations had endured a stamp tax far heavier than that passed for the colonies.

Yet the Americans were angrily aroused at what they regarded as Grenville's fiscal aggression. The new laws pinched their pocketbooks and, even more ominously, menaced the local liberties they had come to assume as a matter of right. Thus, some colonial assemblies defiantly refused to comply with the Quartering Act or voted for only a fraction of the supplies that it called for.

Worse still, Grenville's noxious legislation seemed to jeopardize the basic rights of the colonists as Britons. Both the Sugar Act and the Stamp Act provided for trying offenders in the hated admiralty courts, where juries were not allowed. The burden of proof was on the defendants, who were assumed to be guilty unless they could prove themselves innocent. Trial by jury and the doctrine of "innocent until proved guilty" were ancient privileges that British people everywhere, including the American colonials, held most dear. And why was a British army needed at all in the colonies, now that the French were expelled from the continent and Pontiac's warriors crushed? Could its real purpose be to whip rebellious colonials themselves into line? Many Americans began to sniff the strong scent of a conspiracy to strip them of their historic liberties. They lashed back violently, and the Stamp Act became the target that drew their most ferocious fire.

Angry throats raised the cry, "No taxation without representation." Taking the high ground of principle, the agitated colonials vividly recollected the theories of popular government developed during England's own Puritan revolution a century earlier. American firebrands hurled these doctrines back at their British masters, who were stunned at the keenness of the colonials' historical memory.

The Americans made a distinction between "legislation" and "taxation." They conceded the right of Parliament to legislate about matters that affected the entire empire, including the regulation of trade. But they steadfastly denied the right of Parliament, in which no Americans were seated, to impose taxes on Americans. Only their own elected colonial legislatures, the Americans insisted, could legally tax them.

Grenville dismissed these American protests as hairsplitting absurdities. The power of Parliament was supreme and undivided, he asserted, and in any case the Americans *were* represented in Parliament. Elaborating the theory of "virtual representation," Grenville claimed that every member of Parliament represented all British subjects, even those Americans in Boston or Charleston who had never voted for a member of the London Parliament. The Americans scoffed at the notion of virtual representation.

Thus the principle of no taxation without representation was supremely important, and the colonials clung to it with tenacious consistency. When the British replied that the soverign power of government could not be divided between "legislative" authority in London and "taxing" authority in the colonies, they forced the Americans to deny the authority of Parliament altogether and to begin to consider their own political independence. This chain of logic eventually led to revolutionary consequences.

Parliament Forced to Repeal the Stamp Act

Among colonial outcries against the hated stamp tax, the most conspicuous was the Stamp Act Congress, held in New York City in 1765. Twenty-seven distinguished delegates from nine colonies petitioned the king and Parliament to repeal the repugnant legislation. The Stamp Act Congress made little splash in America at the time, but it was one more significant step toward intercolonial unity.

More effective than the congress was the widespread adoption of nonimportation agreements against British goods. Homespun woolen garments became fashionable, and the eating of lamb chops was discouraged so that the wool-bearing sheep would be allowed to mature. Nonimportation agreements were in fact a promising stride toward union; they spontaneously united the American people for the first time in common action.

Violence also attended colonial protests. Crying, "Liberty, property, and no stamps," ardent sons and daughters of liberty enforced the nonimportation agreements against violators, often with a generous coat of tar and feathers. They ransacked the houses of unpopular officials and hanged stamp agents on liberty poles, albeit in effigy.

Shaken by violence, the machinery for collecting the tax broke down. On that dismal day in 1765 when the new act was to go into effect, the stamp agents had all been forced to resign, and there was no one to sell the stamps. While flags flapped at half-mast, the law was openly and flagrantly defied—or rather, nullified.

Britain was hard hit. Merchants, manufacturers, and shippers suffered from the colonial nonimportation agreements, and hundreds of laborers were thrown out of work. Loud demands converged on Parliament for repeal of the Stamp Act. But many of the members could not understand why 7.5 million Britons had to pay heavy taxes to protect the colonies, whereas some 2 million colonials refused to pay for only one-third of the cost of their own defense.

After a stormy debate, and as a matter of expedience and not of right, Parliament in 1766 reluctantly repealed the Stamp Act. At the same time, and by an overwhelming vote, it saved face by passing the Declaratory Act. This futile measure proclaimed that Parliament had the right "to bind" the colonies "in all cases whatsoever." A bare assertion of this right was but a feeble victory for British authority, for the unruly colonials had proved that the London government could be forced to yield to boycotts and mob action.

The Townshend Tea Tax and the Boston "Massacre"

Control of the British ministry was now seized by the gifted but erratic "Champagne Charley" Townshend, a man who could deliver brilliant speeches in Parliament even while drunk. Rashly promising to pluck feathers from the colonial goose with a minimum of squawking, he persuaded Parliament in 1767 to pass the Townshend Acts. The most important of these new regulations was a light import duty on glass, white lead, paper, and tea. Townshend made this tax, unlike the Stamp Act, an indirect customs duty payable at American ports.

Flushed with their recent victory over the stamp tax, the colonists were in a rebellious mood. The impost on tea was especially irksome, for an estimated 1 million people drank the refreshing brew twice a day.

The new Townshend revenues, worse yet, would be used to pay the salaries of the royal governors and judges in America. The ultrasuspicious Americans, who had beaten the royal governors into line by controlling the purse, regarded Townshend's tax as another attempt to enchain them. Their worst fears took on a greater reality when the London government, after passing the Townshend taxes, suspended the New York legislature for failure to comply with the Quartering Act.

Nonimportation agreements, previously potent, were quickly revived against the Townshend Acts. But they proved less effective than those devised against the Stamp Act. The colonials, again enjoying prosperity, took the new tax less seriously than might have been expected, largely because it was light and indirect. They found, moreover, that they could secure smuggled tea at a cheap price, and consequently smugglers increased their activities, especially in Massachusetts.

British officials, faced with a breakdown of law and order, landed two regiments of troops in Boston in 1768. A clash between citizens and soldiers was inevitable. On the evening of March 5, 1770, a crowd of some sixty townspeople set upon a squad of about ten "bloody backs," one of whom was hit by a club and another of whom was knocked down. Acting apparently without orders but under extreme provocation, the troops opened fire and killed or wounded eleven "innocent" citizens. One of the first to die was Crispus Attucks, described by contemporaries as a "mulatto" and as a leader of the mob. Both sides were in some degree to blame, and in the subsequent trial only two of the soldiers were found guilty of manslaughter.

The so-called Boston Massacre further inflamed the colonials against the British. Massacre Day was observed in Boston as a patriotic holiday until 1776, when the more glorious Fourth of July eclipsed it.

The Seditious Committees of Correspondence

By 1770 King George III was strenuously attempting to restore the declining power of the British monarchy. Earnest, industrious, stubborn, and lustful for power, he surrounded himself with cooperative "yes men," notably his corpulent prime minister, Lord North.

The ill-timed Townshend Acts had failed to produce revenue, though producing near-rebellion. Net proceeds from the tax in one year were £295, and during that time the annual military costs to Britain in the colonies had mounted to £170,000. Nonimportation agreements, though feebly enforced, were pinching British manufacturers. The government of Lord North, bowing to various pressures, finally persuaded Parliament to repeal the Townshend revenue duties. But the threepence tax on tea was retained to keep alive the principle of parliamentary taxation.

The BLOODY MASSACRE perpetuated in King—Street B... ... on ... ... by a party of the 29th R...

BUTCHER'S HALL

Engrav'd Printed & Sold by Paul Revere Boston

The Boston Massacre, 1770 *This widely reprinted engraving by Paul Revere was both art and propaganda.*

Flames of discontent, stirred by periodic incidents involving British officials, were continually fanned by a master propagandist and engineer of rebellion, Samuel Adams, a cousin of John Adams. Unimpressive in appearance, his friends had to buy him a presentable suit of clothes when he left Massachusetts on intercolonial business. Zealous, tenacious, and courageous, he cherished a deep faith in the common people. Skillful also as a pamphleteer, he became known as the "Penman of the Revolution."

Samuel Adams's signal contribution was to organize in Massachusetts the local committees of correspondence. After he had formed the first one in Boston during 1772, some eighty towns in the colony speedily set up similar organizations. Their chief function was to spread propaganda and information by exchanging letters and thus keep alive opposition to British policy.

Intercolonial committees of correspondence were the next logical step. Virginia led the way in 1773 by creating such a body as a standing committee of the House of Burgesses. Within a short time every colony had established a central committee through which it could exchange ideas and information with other colonies. These intercolonial groups, which were supremely significant in stimulating and disseminating sentiment in favor of united action, evolved directly into the first American congresses.

Tea Parties at Boston and Elsewhere

Thus far—that is, by 1773—nothing had happened to make rebellion inevitable. Nonimportation was weakening. Increasing numbers of colonials were reluctantly paying the tea tax, because the legal tea was now cheaper than the smuggled tea and cheaper than tea in England.

A new ogre entered the picture in 1773. The powerful British East India Company, overburdened with 17 million pounds of unsold tea, was facing bankruptcy. If it collapsed, the London government would lose heavily in tax revenue. The ministry therefore decided to assist the company by awarding it a complete monopoly of the American tea business. The terms thus granted would enable the giant corporation to sell the coveted leaves more cheaply than ever before, even with the threepence tax added. But to many American consumers, principle was more important than price.

The new tea monopoly seemed to the Americans like a shabby attempt to trick them into acceptance of the detested tax with the bait of cheaper tea. Once more the colonials rose in wrath. Not a single one of the several thousand chests of tea shipped by the company reached the consignees. At Annapolis, Maryland, protesters burned both the cargo and the vessel.

Boston was host to the most famous tea party of all. A band of white townfolk, disguised as Indians, boarded the three tea ships on December 16, 1773. They smashed open 342 chests and dumped the "cursed weed" into Boston harbor, while a silent crowd watched approvingly from the wharves as salty tea was brewed for the fish.

Parliament Passes the "Intolerable Acts"

An outraged Parliament responded speedily to the Boston Tea Party with measures that brewed a revolution. By huge majorities in 1774 it passed a series of "Repressive Acts," which were designed to chastise Boston in particular, Massachusetts in general.

Most drastic of all was the Boston Port Act. It closed the tea-stained harbor until damages were paid and order could be ensured. By other "Intolerable Acts"—as they were called in America—many of the chartered rights of colonial Massachusetts were swept away. Restrictions were likewise placed on the precious town meetings. Contrary to previous practice, enforcing officials who killed colonials in line of duty could now be sent to England for trial. There, suspicious Americans assumed, they would be likely to get off scot-free.

By a fateful coincidence, the Intolerable Acts were accompanied in 1774 by the Quebec Act. Passed at the same time, it was erroneously regarded in English-speaking America as one of the "repressive" measures. Actually, the Quebec Act was a good law in bad company. For many years, the British government had debated how it should administer the 60,000 or so conquered French subjects in Canada, and it had finally framed this farsighted and statesmanlike measure. The French Canadians were guaranteed their Catholic religion. They were also permitted to retain many of their old customs and institutions, which did not include a representative assembly or trial by jury in civil cases. In addition, the old boundaries of the Province of Quebec were now extended southward all the way to the Ohio River.

The Quebec Act, from the viewpoint of the French Canadians, was a shrewd and conciliatory measure. If Britain had only shown as much foresight in dealing with its English-speaking colonies, it might not have lost them.

But from the viewpoint of the American colonials as a whole, the Quebec Act was especially noxious. All the other "repressive" laws slapped directly at Massachusetts, but this one had a much wider range. It seemed to set a dangerous precedent in America against jury trials and popular assemblies. It alarmed land speculators, who were distressed to see the huge trans-Allegheny area snatched from their grasp. It aroused anti-Catholics, who were shocked by the extension of Roman Catholic jurisdiction southward into a huge region that had once been earmarked for Protestantism—a region about as large as the thirteen original colonies.

The Continental Congress and Bloodshed

American dissenters, outraged by the Quebec Act and the other Intolerable Acts, responded sympathetically to the plight of Massachusetts. Their most significant action was the summoning of a Continental Congress, which met in Philadelphia from September 5 to October 26, 1774. John Adams played a stellar role at the First Continental Congress. Eloquently swaying his colleagues to a revolutionary

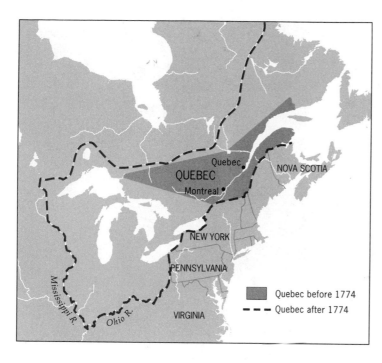

Quebec Before and After 1774 *Young Alexander Hamilton voiced the fears of many colonists when he warned that the Quebec Act of 1774 would introduce "priestly tyranny" into Canada, making that country another Spain or Portugal. "Does not your blood run cold," he asked, "to think that an English Parliament should pass an act for the establishment of arbitrary power and Popery in such a country?"*

course, he helped defeat by the narrowest of margins a proposal by moderates for a species of American home rule under British direction.

The most significant action of the Congress was the creation of The Association. Unlike previous nonimportation agreements, this one called for a *complete* boycott of British goods. But still there was no genuine drive toward independence—merely an effort to bring about a repeal of the offensive legislation and a return to the happy days before parliamentary taxation.

But the deadly drift toward war continued. The petitions of the Continental Congress were rejected, after considerable debate, by strong majorities in Parliament. In America, chickens squawked and tar kettles bubbled as violators of The Association were tarred and feathered. Muskets were being collected, men were openly drilling, and a clash seemed imminent.

In April 1775, the British commander in Boston sent a detachment of troops to nearby Lexington and Concord. They were to seize stores of colonial gunpowder and also to bag the "rebel" ringleaders, Samuel Adams and John Hancock. At Lexington the colonial Minute Men refused to disperse rapidly enough, and shots were fired that killed eight Americans and wounded several more. The redcoats pushed on to Concord, whence they were forced to retreat by the homespun Americans, whom Emerson immortalized:

> By the rude bridge that arched the flood,
> Their flag to April's breeze unfurled,
> Here once the embattled farmers stood,
> And fired the shot heard round the world.*

The bewildered British, fighting off murderous fire from militiamen crouched behind thick stone walls, finally regained the sanctuary of Boston. Licking their wounds, they could count about 300 casualties, including some 70 killed. Britain now had a war on its hands.

---

* Ralph Waldo Emerson, *Concord Hymn.*

Imperial and Colonial Pluses and Minuses

Aroused Americans had brashly rebelled against a mighty empire. The population odds were about three to one against the rebels—some 7.5 million Britons to 2.5 million colonials. The odds in monetary wealth and naval power were overwhelmingly in favor of Britain.

Black people were only a partial asset to the American cause, for they could hardly be expected to fight for a society that had enslaved them. Still, about 5,000 saw military service, whether as freedmen or as slaves promised freedom, and in a number of engagements they fought bravely. Even larger numbers, often guaranteed freedom with no strings attached, fled to enemy lines and left the country when the British departed.

Britain then boasted a professional army of some 50,000 men, as compared with the numerous but wretchedly trained American militia. George III, in addition, hired some 30,000 German soldiers—so-called Hessians. The British also enlisted the services of about 50,000 American Loyalists and many Indians, who inflamed long stretches of the frontier.

Yet Britain was weaker than it seemed at first glance. British troops had to be detached to watch the latent volcano of oppressed Ireland. Recently defeated France was bitterly awaiting an opportunity to stab Britain in the back. The London government, under the stubborn George III and his pliant minister Lord North, was confused and inept.

Many earnest and God-fearing Britons had no desire to kill their American cousins. Many British Whigs believed that the battle for their own liberties was being fought in America. If George III triumphed, his rule at home might become more tyrannical. This outspoken sympathy in Britain, though plainly that of a minority, encouraged the Americans. If they continued their resistance long enough, the Whigs might come to power and deal generously with them.

Britain's army in America had to operate under endless difficulties. The generals were second-rate; the soldiers, though on the whole capable, were brutally treated. Provisions were often scarce, rancid, and wormy.

Other handicaps loomed. The redcoats had to conquer the Americans; a draw would be a victory

Abigail Adams *The wife of revolutionary leader and future president John Adams, she was a prominent patriot in her own right. She was also among the first Americans to see, however faintly, the implications of revolutionary ideas for changing the status of women.*

for the colonials. Britain was operating some 3,000 miles from its home base, and distance added greatly to the delays and uncertainties arising from storms and other mishaps.

America's geographical expanse was enormous: roughly 1,000 by 600 miles. The united colonies had no urban nerve center like France's Paris. British armies captured every city of any size, yet like a boxer punching a feather pillow, they made little more than a dent in the entire country. The Americans wisely traded space for time.

The revolutionists were also blessed with outstanding leadership. George Washington was a giant among men. Master diplomat Benjamin Franklin eventually secured open foreign aid from France. In a class by himself was Marquis de Lafayette, a young French noble who loved glory and liberty. Lafayette became a major general in the colonial army at age nineteen, and the services of the teenage "French gamecock" secured further aid from France.

Other conditions aided the Americans. They were fighting defensively on their own terrain. In agriculture, the colonies were mainly self-sustaining. Colonial "buckskins" were a tough, self-reliant people. Their marksmen, far superior to the British, could hit a man's head at 200 yards. In addition, the Americans enjoyed the moral advantage that came from belief in a just cause.

Yet the American rebels were badly organized for war. Almost fatally lacking in unity, the new nation lurched forward uncertainly like an uncoordinated centipede. Even the Continental Congress, which directed the conflict, was hardly more than a debating society, and it grew feebler as the struggle dragged on. Disorganized colonials fought almost the entire war before adopting a written constitution—the Articles of Confederation—in 1781.

Economic difficulties were almost insuperable. With metallic money drained away and taxation an explosive issue, a cautious Continental Congress was forced to finance the war with "Continental" paper money. As this currency poured from the presses, it depreciated until the expression "not worth a Continental" became current. Inflation of the currency skyrocketed prices, hitting especially hard the families of soldiers at the front. Debtors easily acquired handfuls of the semiworthless money and gleefully paid their debts "without mercy."

A Thin Line of Heroes

Basic military supplies in the colonies were dangerously scanty, especially firearms and powder. Benjamin Franklin seriously proposed going back to the bow and arrow. Even where food was accumulated, wagons were often not available to haul it. At Valley Forge, in the winter of 1777–1778, the shivering American soldiers were without bread for three successive days.

Manufactured goods were generally in short supply in agricultural America, and clothing and shoes were appallingly scarce. The path of the patriot fighting men was often marked by bloody snow. At frigid Valley Forge, during one anxious period, 2,800 men were barefooted or nearly naked.

American militiamen were numerous but also highly unreliable. Able-bodied American males—perhaps several hundred thousand of them—had

CHRONOLOGY	
1651	First Navigation Law to control colonial commerce.
1696	Board of Trade assumes governance of colonies.
1763	French and Indian War (Seven Years' War) ends.
1764	Sugar Act.
1765	Quartering Act.
	Stamp Act.
	Stamp Act Congress.
1766	Declaratory Act.
1767	Townshend Acts passed.
	New York legislature suspended by Parliament.
1768	British troops occupy Boston.
1770	Boston Massacre.
	All Townshend Acts except tea tax repealed.
1772	Committees of correspondence formed.
1773	British East India Company granted tea monopoly.
	Boston Tea Party.
1774	Intolerable Acts.
	Quebec Act.
	First Continental Congress.
	The Association boycotts British goods.
1775	Battle of Lexington and Concord.

received rudimentary training, and many of these recruits served for short terms in the rebel armies. But poorly trained plowboys, though better shots, could not stand up in the open field against professional British troops advancing with bare bayonets. Many of these undisciplined warriors would, in the words of Washington, "fly from their own shadows."

A few thousand regulars—perhaps 7,000 or 8,000 at war's end—were finally whipped into shape by stern drillmasters. Notable among them was an organizational genius, the salty German Baron von Steuben. He spoke no English when he reached America, but he soon taught his men that bayonets were not for broiling beefsteaks over open fires. As they gained experience, these soldiers of the Continental line could hold their own in open battle against crack British troops.

Morale in the revolutionary army was badly undermined by American profiteers. These grasping gentry, putting profits before patriotism, sold to the British because the invader could pay in gold. Speculators forced prices sky-high; and some Bostonians made profits of 50 percent to 200 percent on army clothing while the American army was freezing at Valley Forge. Washington never had as many as 20,000 effective troops in one place at one time, despite bounties of land and other inducements. Yet if the rebels had thrown themselves into the struggle with revolutionary zeal, they could easily have raised many times that number.

The harsh truth is that only a select minority of colonials attached themselves to the cause of independence with a spirit of selfless devotion. These were the dedicated souls who bore the burden of battle and the risks of defeat; these were the freedom-loving patriots who deserved the gratitude and esteem of generations yet unborn.

Varying Viewpoints

Historians once assumed that the Revolution was just another chapter in the unfolding story of human liberty—a kind of divinely ordained progress toward perfection in human affairs. This approach is often called the Whig view of history.

At the beginning of this century, the concept was sharply challenged by so-called progressive historians, who argued that not God but a sharp struggle among different social groups brought about change. For example, Carl Becker saw the Revolution as stemming from class conflict and ending in a truly transformed social order. As one of them put it, the Revolution was not only about home rule but about "who should rule at home."

Since World War II two broad interpretations of the Revolution have contended with each other. One view, advanced by such scholars as Gary Nash and Edward Countryman, builds on Becker's work and emphasizes class conflict. Attacks on political elites and resentment toward wealth are taken as evidence that American society was breeding revolutionary change from within, apart from British provocations.

A generally more influential view was most prominently developed by Bernard Bailyn. Arguing that colonial society was *already* fairly democratic before 1776 (at least for white men), Bailyn asks why a revolution occurred at all, and what it consisted of. His answer emphasizes neither British economic affronts nor domestic political friction, but deep-seated ideological and even psychological factors. Inspired by their reading of mainly seventeenth-century English political theorists, the hypersensitive colonists regarded British moves in the 1760s as part of a government conspiracy to deprive them of both their livelihoods and their liberty. Opposition to this "ministerial plot" drove the Americans to armed insurrection and further inspired them to define the essence of the Revolution in terms of an ideology of liberty that has colored American thought and political action ever since.

SELECT READINGS

Primary Source Documents

Adam Smith's *An Inquiry into the Nature and Causes of the Wealth of Nations** (1776) is a penetrating analysis of British mercantilism. Patrick Henry's "Speech before the Virginia House of Burgesses against the Stamp Act"* (1765) was an influential statement of colonial opposition to British policy, as was John Dickinson's response to the Townshend Acts, *Letters from a Farmer in Pennsylvania* (1768). For contemporary accounts of the beginning of hostilities, see Peter Force, ed, *American Archives,* Fourth Series, Vol. 2 (1839).*

Secondary Sources

Edmund S. Morgan, *The Birth of the Republic, 1763–1789* (1959), is among the best brief accounts of the revolutionary era. It stresses the happy coincidence of the revolutionaries' principles and their interests. Lawrence Gipson, *The Coming of the Revolution, 1763–1775* (1954), summarizes his 15-volume masterwork (cited in Chapter 6). Merrill Jensen, *The Founding of a Nation* (1968), is a more recent attempt at synthesis, as is Robert Middlekauff's *The Glorious Cause: The American Revolution, 1763–1789*

(1982). Bernhard Knollenberg examines the effects of the British tightening of the imperial system in the 1760s in *Origin of the American Revolution, 1759–1766* (1960), as does Michael Kammen in *Empire and Interest* (1970). John Shy imaginatively explores an important aspect of the imperial system's effect on America in *Toward Lexington: The Role of the British Army in the Coming of the American Revolution* (1965). Clinton Rossiter, *Seedtime of the Republic* (1953), stresses the importance of ideas in pushing the Revolution forward, as does Bernard Bailyn's seminal *Ideological Origins of the American Revolution* (1967), which also emphasizes the colonists' fears of a conspiracy against their liberties. Edward A. Countryman emphasizes class conflict in *The American Revolution* (1987). Two books take a psychological approach to the problem of the revolutionary generation's assault on established authority: Kenneth S. Lynn, *A Divided People* (1977), and Jay Fliegelman, *Prodigals and Pilgrims: The American Revolution Against Patriarchal Authority, 1750–1800* (1982).

CHAPTER 8

America Secedes from the Empire, 1775–1783

These are the times that try men's souls. The summer soldier and the sunshine patriot will, in this crisis, shrink from the service of their country; but he that stands it now, deserves the love and thanks of man and woman.

Thomas Paine, December 1776

Congress Drafts George Washington

Bloodshed at Lexington and Concord, in April 1775, was a clarion call to arms. About 20,000 musket-bearing Minute Men swarmed around Boston, there to coop up the outnumbered British.

The Second Continental Congress met in Philadelphia the next month, on May 10, 1775; and this time the full slate of thirteen colonies was represented. The conservative element in the congress was still strong, despite the shooting in Massachusetts. There was no real sentiment for independence—merely a desire to continue fighting in the hope that king and Parliament would consent to a redress of grievances. The congress hopefully drafted new appeals to the British people and king—appeals that were spurned. Anticipating a possible rebuff, the delegates also adopted measures to raise money and to create an army and a navy.

Perhaps the most important single action of the congress was to select George Washington, one of its members already in officer's uniform, to head the hastily improvised army besieging Boston. This choice was made with considerable misgivings. The tall, powerfully built, dignified, blue-eyed Virginia planter, then forty-three, had never risen above the rank of a colonel in the militia. His largest command had numbered only 1,200 men, and that had been some twenty years earlier. Falling short of true military genius, Washington would actually lose more pitched battles than he won.

But the distinguished Virginian was gifted with outstanding powers of leadership and immense strength of character. He radiated patience, courage, self-discipline, and a sense of justice. He was a great moral force rather than a great military mind—a symbol and a rallying point. People instinctively trusted him. As a man of wealth, by inheritance and by marriage, Washington could not be accused of being a fortune seeker. He insisted on serving without pay, though he kept a careful expense account amounting to more than $100,000.

The Continental Congress initially selected Washington more for political reasons than for his leadership qualities. Americans from other sections distrusted the large New England army gathering around Boston, and prudence suggested a commander from Virginia.

Washington at Verplanck's Point, New York, 1782, Reviewing the French Troops After the Victory at York-town, by John Trumbull, 1790   *This noted American artist accentuated Washington's already imposing height (6 feet, 2 inches) by showing him towering over his horse. Washington so appreciated this portrait of himself that he hung it in his dining room at his home at Mount Vernon, Virginia.*

Bunker Hill and Hessian Hirelings

The clash of arms continued on a strangely contradictory basis. On the one hand, the Americans were emphatically affirming their loyalty to the king and earnestly voicing their desire to patch up existing difficulties. On the other hand, they were raising armies and shooting down His Majesty's soldiers. This curious war of inconsistency was fought for fourteen long months—from April 1775 to July 1776—before the fateful plunge into independence was taken.

Gradually the tempo of warfare increased. In May 1775 a tiny American force, under Ethan Allen and Benedict Arnold, surprised and captured the British garrisons at Ticonderoga and Crown Point, on the scenic lakes of upstate New York. A priceless store of powder and artillery for the siege of Boston was thus secured.

In June 1775, the colonials seized a hill, now known as Bunker Hill (actually Breed's Hill), from which they menaced the enemy in Boston. The British blundered bloodily when they launched a frontal attack with 3,000 men. Sharpshooting Americans, numbering 1,500 and strongly entrenched, mowed down the advancing foe with frightful slaughter. But their scanty store of powder finally gave out, and they were forced to abandon the hill in disorder. With two more such victories, remarked the French foreign minister, the British would have no army left in America.

Following Bunker Hill, the king slammed the door on all hope of reconciliation. In August 1775 he formally proclaimed the colonies in rebellion. The next month he widened the chasm by hiring thousands of German troops, shocking colonials who feared the so-called Hessians' exaggerated reputation for butchery and bestiality. Actually, the Hessian hirelings turned out to be more interested in booty than in duty. Hundreds of them deserted and remained in America as respected citizens.

The Abortive Conquest of Canada

The unsheathed sword continued to take its toll. In October 1775, on the eve of a cruel winter, the British burned Falmouth (Portland), Maine. In that same autumn the rebels daringly undertook a two-pronged invasion of Canada. American leaders believed, erroneously, that the conquered French were explosively restive under the British yoke. A successful assault on Canada would add a fourteenth colony, while depriving Britain of a valuable base for striking at the colonies in revolt. But this large-scale attack, involving some 2,000 American troops, contradicted the claim of the colonials that they were merely fighting defensively for a redress of grievances. Invasion northward was undisguised offensive warfare.

The bold stroke for Canada narrowly missed success. One invading column under the Irish-born General Richard Montgomery, formerly of the British army, pushed up the Lake Champlain route and captured Montreal. He was joined at Quebec by the bedraggled army of General Benedict Arnold, whose men had been reduced to eating dogs and shoe leather during their grueling march through the Maine woods. An assault on Quebec, launched on the last day of 1775, was beaten off. The able Montgomery was killed; the dashing Arnold was wounded in one leg. Scattered remnants under his command retreated up the St. Lawrence River, reversing Montgomery's route. French-Canadian leaders, who had been generously treated by the British in the Quebec Act of 1774, showed no real desire to welcome the plundering anti-Catholic invaders.

Bitter fighting continued in the colonies, though the Americans still disclaimed all desire for independence. In January 1776 the British set fire to the Virginia town of Norfolk. In March they were finally forced to evacuate Boston, taking with them the leading friends of the king. (Evacuation Day is still celebrated annually in Boston.) In the South the rebellious colonials won two victories in 1776: one in February against some 1,500 Loyalists at Moore's Creek Bridge, in North Carolina, and the other in June against an invading British fleet at Charleston harbor.

Thomas Paine Preaches Common Sense

Why did Americans continue to deny any intention of independence? Loyalty to the empire was deeply ingrained; colonial unity was poor; and open rebellion was dangerous, especially against a formidable Britain. Irish rebels of that day were customarily hanged, drawn, and quartered. American rebels might have fared no better. As late as January 1776—five months before independence was declared—the king's health was being toasted by the officers of Washington's mess near Boston. "God save the king" had not yet been replaced by "God save the Congress."

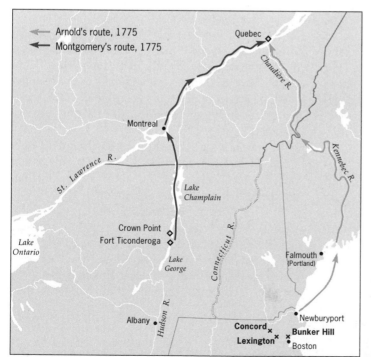

Revolution in the North, 1775–1776
Benedict Arnold's troops were described as "pretty young men" when they sailed from Massachusetts. They were considerably less pretty on their arrival in Quebec, after eight weeks of struggling through wet and frigid forests, often without food. "No one can imagine," one of them wrote, "the sweetness of a roasted shotpouch (ammunition bag) to the famished appetite."

Gradually the Americans were shocked into an awareness of their inconsistency. Their eyes were opened by harsh British acts such as the burning of Falmouth and Norfolk, and especially by the hiring of the Hessians. Early in 1776 came the publication of *Common Sense,* one of the most influential pamphlets ever written. Its author was the radical Thomas Paine, once an impoverished corset-maker's apprentice, who had come over from Britain a year earlier. His tract became a whirlwind best seller, and within a few months reached the astonishing total of 120,000 copies in circulation.

Paine flatly branded the shilly-shallying of the colonials as contrary to "common sense." Why not throw off the cloak of inconsistency? Nowhere in the physical universe did the smaller heavenly body control the larger one. Then why should the tiny island of Britain control the vast continent of America? As for the king, whom the Americans professed to revere, he was nothing but "the Royal Brute of Great Britain." America had a sacred mission—a moral obligation to the world—to set itself up as an independent, democratic republic, untainted by association with corrupt and monarchical Britain.

Paine's passionate protest was eloquent and radical. He helped thousands of American waverers, hesitant to break with Britain, to see that their cause embraced *both* self-determination and democracy. He also forcefully reminded them that they could not hope for open aid from France as long as they swore allegiance to the British king. The French crown was interested in destroying the British Empire, not in helping to reconstruct it under a plan of reconciliation.

Jefferson's "Explanation" of Independence

Members of the Philadelphia Congress, instructed by their respective colonies, gradually edged toward a clean break. On June 7, 1776, fiery Richard Henry Lee of Virginia moved that "These United Colonies are, and of right ought to be, free and independent states. . . ." After considerable debate, the motion was adopted nearly a month later, on July 2, 1776.

The passing of Lee's resolution was the formal "declaration" of independence by the American colonies, and technically this was all that was needed to cut the British tie. John Adams wrote confidently that ever thereafter July 2 would be celebrated annually with fireworks. But something more was required. An epochal rupture of this kind called for some formal explanation to "a candid world." An inspirational appeal was also needed to enlist other British colonies in the Americas, to invite assistance from foreign nations, and to rally resistance to the crown at home.

Shortly after Lee made his memorable motion on June 7, Congress appointed a committee to prepare an appropriate statement. The task of drafting it fell to Thomas Jefferson, a tall, freckled, sandy-haired Virginia lawyer of thirty-three. Despite his youth, he was already recognized as a brilliant writer, and he measured up splendidly to his opportunity. After some debate and amendment, the Declaration of Independence was formally approved by the Congress on July 4, 1776.

Jefferson's pronouncement, couched in a lofty style, was magnificent. He gave his appeal universality by invoking the "natural rights" of mankind—not just British rights. He argued persuasively that because the king had flouted these rights, the colonials were justified in cutting their connection. He then set forth a long list of the presumably tyrannous misdeeds of George III. The overdrawn bill of indictment included imposing taxes without consent, dispensing with trial by jury, abolishing valued laws, establishing a military dictatorship, maintaining standing armies in peacetime, cutting off trade, burning towns, hiring mercenaries, and inciting hostility among the Indians.*

Jefferson's withering blast was admittedly one-sided. He owned many slaves, and his affirmation that "all men are created equal" was to haunt him and his fellow citizens for generations.

The formal declaration of independence cleared the air as a thundershower does on a muggy day. Foreign aid could be solicited with greater hope of success. Those patriots who defied the king were now rebels, not loving subjects shooting their way into reconciliation. They must all hang together,

---

* For an annotated text of the Declaration of Independence, see the Appendix.

Franklin is said to have grimly remarked, or they would all hang separately. Or, in the eloquent language of the great declaration, "We mutually pledge to each other our lives, our fortunes and our sacred honor."

Patriots and Loyalists

The War of Independence was a civil war between two factions of Americans as well as a war between Americans and the British. Besides battling the British redcoats, the American rebels, called Patriots or Whigs, fought Americans loyal to the king, called Loyalists or Tories.

Like many revolutions, the American Revolution was a minority movement. Many colonists were apathetic or neutral, including the Byrds of Virginia, who sat on the fence. The opposing forces contended not only against each other but also for the allegiance and support of the civilian population. In this struggle for the hearts and minds of the people, the Patriot militia proved to be far more successful than the inept British. The British military proved able to control only those areas where it could maintain a massive military presence. Elsewhere, as soon as the redcoats had marched on, the rebel militiamen appeared and took up the task of "political education"—sometimes by coercive means. Often lacking

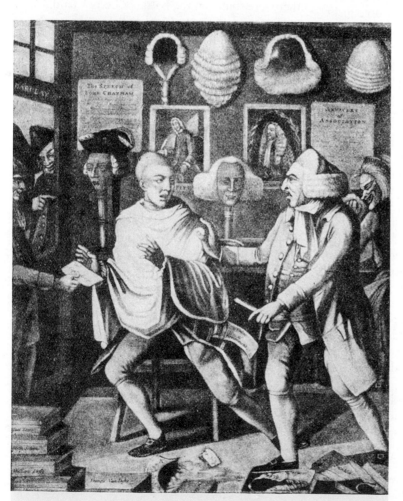

THE PATRIOTIC BARBER OF NEW-YORK

Revolutionary Shaving   *This Tory cartoon ridicules the Patriots for carrying their cause even into the barber's chair. The patriotic barber has threatened to half-shave a Tory captain.*

bayonets but always loaded with political zeal, the ragtag militia units convinced many colonists, even those indifferent to independence, that the British army was an unreliable friend and that they had better throw in their lot with the Patriot cause.

Loyalists, numbering perhaps 20 percent of the American people, remained true to their king. Some 50,000 Loyalist volunteers at one time or another bore arms for the British. They also helped the king's cause by serving as spies, by inciting the Indians, and by keeping Patriot soldiers at home to protect their families.

Conservative Americans—the people of education and wealth, of culture and caution—generally remained loyal. They were also more numerous among the older generation, for young people make revolutions. Loyalists also included the king's officers and other beneficiaries of the crown—people who knew which side their daily bread came from. Loyalists were most numerous where the Anglican church was strongest, except in Virginia, where debt-burdened Anglican aristocrats flocked into the rebel camp. The king's followers were well entrenched in aristocratic New York City and Charleston, and also in Quaker Pennsylvania and New Jersey, where General Washington felt that he was fighting in "the enemy's country." Loyalists were least numerous in New England, where Presbyterianism and Congregationalism flourished, producing strong support for rebellion.

Before independence was declared in 1776, persecution of the Loyalists was relatively mild. But after the Declaration of Independence, Loyalists were more roughly handled. A Patriot definition of a Tory betrayed the bitterness many felt: "A Tory is a thing whose head is in England, and its body in America, and its neck ought to be stretched." A few noncombatant Loyalists were hanged, and other were imprisoned. About 80,000 loyal supporters of George III were driven out or fled, and their estates were confiscated to finance the war. But no reign of terror comparable to that of the later French and Russian revolutions occurred. Some 50,000 Loyalist volunteers at one time or another bore arms for the British. Ardent Loyalists had their hearts in their cause; it was a major blunder of the haughty British not to make full use of them in the fighting.

General Washington at Bay

With Boston evacuated in March 1776, the British concentrated on New York as a base of operations. Here was a splendid seaport, centrally located, where the king could count on cooperation from the numerous Loyalists. An awe-inspiring British fleet appeared off New York in July 1776. It consisted of some 500 ships and 35,000 men—the largest armed force to be seen in America until the Civil War. General Washington, dangerously outnumbered, could muster only 18,000 ill-trained troops with which to meet the crack army of the invader.

Disaster befell the Americans in the summer and fall of 1776. Out-generaled and outmaneuvered, they were routed at the Battle of Long Island, where panic seized the raw recruits. By the narrowest of margins, and thanks to a favoring wind and fog, Washington escaped to Manhattan Island. Retreating northward, he crossed the Hudson River to New Jersey and finally reached the Delaware River with the British close at his heels. Tauntingly, enemy buglers sounded the fox-hunting call, so familiar to Virginians of Washington's day. The Patriot cause was at low ebb when the rebel remnants fled across the river, after collecting all available boats to forestall pursuit.

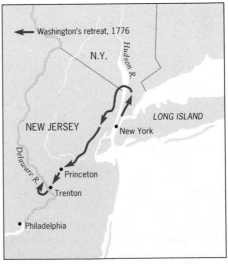

New York and New Jersey, 1776–1777

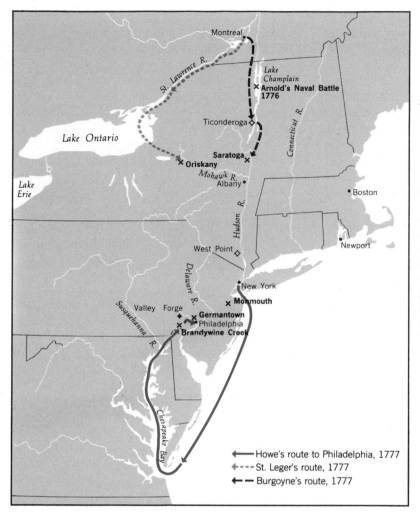

New York-Pennsylvania Theater, 1777–1778 *Distinguished members of the Continental Congress fled from Philadelphia in near panic as the British army approached. Thomas Paine reported that at three o'clock in the morning the streets were "as full of Men, Women, and Children as on a Market Day." John Adams had anticipated that "I shall run away, I suppose, with the rest," since "we are too brittle ware, you know, to stand the dashing of balls and bombs." Adams got his chance to decamp with the others into the interior of Pennsylvania and tried to put the best face on things. "This tour," he commented, "has given me an opportunity of seeing many parts of this country which I never saw before."*

The wonder is that Washington's adversary, General William Howe, did not speedily crush the demoralized American forces. But he was no military genius, and he well remembered the horrible slaughter at Bunker Hill, where he had commanded. The country was rough, supplies were slow in coming, and as a professional soldier Howe did not relish the rigors of winter campaigning.

Washington, who was now almost counted out, stealthily recrossed the ice-clogged Delaware River. At Trenton, on December 26, 1776, he surprised and captured a thousand Hessians who were sleeping off the effects of their Christmas celebration. A week later, leaving his campfires burning as a ruse, he

slipped away and inflicted a sharp defeat on a smaller British detachment at Princeton.

Burgoyne's Blundering Invasion

London officials adopted an intricate scheme for capturing the vital Hudson River valley in 1777. If successful, the British would sever New England from the rest of the states and paralyze the American cause. The main invading force, under an actor-playwright-soldier, General ("Gentleman Johnny") Burgoyne, would push down the Lake Champlain route from Canada. General Howe's troops in New York, if needed, could advance up the Hudson River to meet Burgoyne near Albany. A third and much smaller British force, commanded by Colonel St. Leger, would come in from the west by way of Lake Ontario and the Mohawk Valley.

British planners did not reckon with General Benedict Arnold. Retreating slowly from Quebec, Arnold had heroically kept his army in the field and assembled a small fleet on Lake Champlain. The British finally constructed a fleet that defeated Arnold's tiny flotilla. But winter was descending and the British were forced to retire to Canada.

Starting over in the spring of 1777, General Burgoyne began his fateful invasion with 7,000 regular troops, a heavy baggage train, and many officers' wives. Progress was painfully slow, for sweaty axmen had to chop a path through the forest, while American militiamen began to gather like hornets on Burgoyne's flanks.

Meanwhile, astonished eyebrows rose as General Howe took the main British army toward Philadelphia at a time when it seemed obvious he should be starting up the Hudson River from New York to join Burgoyne. Scholars now know that Howe wanted to engage and destroy Washington's army, apparently assuming he had ample time to assist Burgoyne directly should he be needed.

General Washington, keeping a wary eye on the British in New York, hastily transferred his army to the vicinity of Philadelphia. There, late in 1777, he was defeated in two pitched battles, at Brandywine Creek and Germantown. Pleasure-loving General Howe then settled down comfortably in the lively capital, leaving Burgoyne to flounder through the wilds of upstate New York. Benjamin Franklin, recently sent to Paris as an envoy, truthfully jested that Howe had not captured Philadelphia but that Philadelphia had captured Howe. Washington finally retired to winter quarters at Valley Forge, a strong hilly position some twenty miles northwest of Philadelphia, and there his frostbitten and hungry men were short of about everything except misery. This rabble was nevertheless whipped into a professional army by the recently arrived Prussian drill-master, the profane but patient Baron von Steuben.

Burgoyne meanwhile had begun to bog down north of Albany, while a host of American militiamen, scenting the kill, swarmed about him. In a series of sharp engagements, in which General Arnold was again shot in the leg previously wounded at Quebec, the British army was trapped. Meanwhile the Americans had driven back St. Leger's force at Oriskany. Unable to advance or retreat, Burgoyne was forced to surrender his entire command at Saratoga, on October 17, 1777, to the American General Horatio Gates.

Saratoga ranks high among the decisive battles of both American and world history. The victory immensely revived the faltering colonial cause. Even more important, it made possible the urgently needed foreign aid from France, which in turn helped ensure American independence.

The Colonial War Becomes a World War

France, thirsting for revenge against the British, was eager to inflame the quarrel that had broken out in America. After the shooting at Lexington in April 1775, French agents undertook to blow on the embers. They secretly provided the Americans with life-saving amounts of powder and other munitions. About 90 percent of all the gunpowder used by the Americans during the first two and a half years of the war came from French arsenals.

Secrecy enshrouded all these French schemes. Open aid to the American rebels might provoke Britain into a declaration of war; and France, still weakened by its recent defeat, was not ready to fight. It feared that the American rebellion might fade out, for the colonies were proclaiming their desire to patch up differences. But the Declaration of Independence in 1776 showed that the Americans really meant business; and the smashing victory at Saratoga seemed to indicate that they had an excellent chance of winning their freedom.

After the humiliation at Saratoga in 1777, the British Parliament belatedly passed a measure that in effect offered the Americans home rule within the empire. This was essentially all that the colonials had ever asked for—except independence. If the French were going to break up the British Empire, they would have to bestir themselves. Wily and bespectacled old Benjamin Franklin, whose simple fur cap and witty sayings had captivated the French public, played skillfully on France's fears of reconciliation.

Seeing an opportunity to undo the victor's peace of 1763, and fearing a reconciliation between Britain and her colonies, France offered the Americans a treaty of alliance in 1778. This was the first entangling military alliance in the experience of the republic, and one that later caused prolonged trouble.

Britain and France thus came to blows in 1778, and the shot fired at Lexington rapidly widened into a global conflagration. Spain entered the fray against Britain in 1779, as did Holland. Catherine the Great of Russia lined up the remaining European neutrals into the "Armed Neutrality," which maintained an attitude of passive hostility toward Britain.

To the British, the struggle in the New World seemed secondary. The Americans deserve credit for having kept the war going, with secret French aid, until 1778. But they did not achieve their independence until the conflict erupted into a multipower world war that was too big for Britain to handle. From 1778 to 1783, France provided the rebels with large sums of money, immense amounts of equipment, about one-half of America's regular armed forces, and practically all of the new nation's naval strength.

France's entrance into the conflict forced the British to change their basic strategy in America. With powerful French fleets in American waters, Britain could no longer blockade the colonial coast and command the seas. To shorten their lines of supply, the British evacuated Philadelphia in 1778 and regrouped in New York City. Henceforth, except for the Yorktown interlude in 1781, Washington remained in the New York area, hemming in the British.

Blow and Counterblow

In the summer of 1780 a powerful French army of 6,000 regular troops, commanded by the Comte de Rochambeau, arrived in Newport, Rhode Island. Preparations were then made for a Franco-American attack on New York.

Improving American morale was staggered later in 1780, when General Benedict Arnold turned traitor. A leader of undoubted dash and brilliance, he was ambitious, greedy, unscrupulous, and suffering from a well-grounded but petulant feeling that his valuable services were not fully appreciated. He plotted with the British to sell out the key stronghold of West Point, which commanded the Hudson River, for £6,300 and an officer's commission. By the sheerest accident the plot was detected in the nick of time, and Arnold fled to the British. "Whom can we trust now?" cried General Washington in anguish.

The British meanwhile had devised a plan to roll up the colonies, beginning with the South, where the Loyalists were numerous. Georgia was ruthlessly overrun in 1778–1779. Charleston, South Carolina, fell in 1780. The surrender of the city to the British involved the capture of 5,000 men and 400 cannon and was a heavier loss to the Americans, in relation to existing strength, than Burgoyne was to the British.

Warfare now intensified in the Carolinas, where Patriots bitterly fought their Loyalist neighbors. It was not uncommon for prisoners on both sides to be butchered in cold blood after they had thrown down their arms. The tide turned late in 1780 and early in 1781, when American riflemen wiped out a British detachment at King's Mountain and then defeated a smaller force at Cowpens. In the Carolina campaign of 1781, General Nathanael Greene,

War in the South, 1780–1781

a Quaker-reared tactician, distinguished himself by his strategy of delay. Standing and then retreating, he exhausted his foe, General Cornwallis, in vain pursuit. By losing battles but winning campaigns, the "Fighting Quaker" finally succeeded in clearing most of Georgia and South Carolina of British troops.

The Land Frontier and the Sea Frontier

The West was ablaze during much of the war. Indian allies of George III, hoping to protect their land, were busy attacking and burning frontier settlements; they were egged on by British agents branded as "hair buyers" because they allegedly paid bounties for American scalps. The anti-American Iroquois were led by Mohawk chief Joseph Brant, a convert to Anglicanism who believed that a victorious Britain would restrain American expansion into the West. Brant and the British ravaged large areas of backcountry Pennsylvania and New York until defeated by an American force in 1779.

Yet the tide of westward-moving pioneers did not halt its flow. Eloquent testimony is provided by place names in Kentucky, such as Lexington (named after the battle) and Louisville (named after America's new ally, Louis XVI).

In the wild Illinois country the British were vulnerable to attack, for they held scattered posts that they had captured from the French. An audacious frontiersman, George Rogers Clark, conceived the idea of seizing these forts by surprise. With the blessing of Virginia and £1,200 in depreciated currency, he floated down the Ohio River in 1778–1779 with about 175 men and captured in quick succession Kaskaskia, Cahokia, and Vincennes.

America's infant navy, commanded by daring officers such as hard-fighting Scotsman John Paul Jones, was more successful in destroying British merchant shipping than in engaging Britain's powerful fleets. More numerous and damaging than ships of the regular American navy were swift privateers—privately owned and armed ships authorized by Congress to prey on enemy shipping. Over 1,000 of these legalized pirates captured some 600 British prizes. Although they diverted manpower from the main war effort and involved Americans in speculation and graft, privateers brought in urgently needed gold, harassed the enemy, and raised American morale. Merchant ships were compelled to sail in convoy, and British shippers and manufacturers brought increasing pressure on Parliament to end the war on honorable terms.

Yorktown and the Final Curtain

One of the darkest periods of the war was 1780–1781, before the last decisive victory. Inflation of the currency was continuing at full gallop, and the government was virtually bankrupt. Despair was prevalent; disunion was increasing among the states; and mutiny over back pay was spreading in the army.

Meanwhile, British General Cornwallis was blundering into a trap. After futile operations in Virginia, he had fallen back to Chesapeake Bay at Yorktown to await seaborne supplies and reinforcements. He assumed Britain would continue to control the sea. But these few fateful weeks just happened to be one of the brief periods during the war when British naval superiority slipped away.

The French were now prepared to cooperate energetically in a brilliant stroke. Admiral de Grasse, operating with a powerful fleet in the West Indies, advised the Americans that he was free to join with them in an assault on Cornwallis at Yorktown. Quick to seize this opportunity, General Washington made a swift march of more than 300 miles to the Chesapeake from the New York area. Accompanied by Rochambeau's French army, he beset the British by land, while de Grasse blockaded them by sea after beating off the British fleet. Completely cornered, Cornwallis surrendered his entire force of 7,000 men, on October 19, 1781, as his band appropriately played "The World Turn'd Upside Down." The triumph was no less French than American: the French provided essentially all the seapower and about half of the regular troops in the besieging army of some 16,000 men.

Stunned by news of the disaster, Prime Minister Lord North cried, "Oh God! It's all over! It's all over!" But it was not. George III stubbornly planned to continue the struggle, for Britain was far from being crushed. It still had 54,000 troops in North America, including 32,000 in the United States.

Washington returned with his army to New York, there to continue keeping a vigilant eye on the British force of 10,000 men.

Fighting actually continued for more than a year after Yorktown, with Patriot-Loyalist warfare in the South especially savage. "No quarter for Tories" was the common battle cry. One of Washington's most valuable contributions was to keep the languishing cause alive, the army in the field, and the states together during these critical months. Otherwise, a satisfactory peace treaty might never have been signed.

Peace at Paris

After Yorktown, the war-weary British were increasingly ready to come to terms. In addition to their losses in America, they had suffered heavy reverses in India and in the West Indies. Lord North's ministry collasped in March 1782, temporarily ending the personal rule of George III. A Whig ministry, rather favorable to the Americans, replaced the Tory regime of Lord North.

Three American peace negotiators had meanwhile gathered at Paris: the aging but astute Benjamin Franklin; the flinty John Adams, vigilant for New England interests; and the impulsive John Jay of New York, deeply suspicious of Old World intrigue. The three envoys had explicit instructions from Congress to make no separate peace, and to consult with their French allies at all stages of the negotiations. But the American representatives chafed under this directive. They well knew that it had been written by a subservient Congress, with the French Foreign Office indirectly guiding the pen.

France was in a painful position. It had induced Spain to enter the war on its side, and the Spanish also coveted the immense trans-Allegheny area. Wanting an America that would be independent but feeble, the French joined the scheme to keep the new republic cooped up east of the Allegheny Mountains.

But John Jay was unwilling to play France's game. Suspiciously alert, he perceived that the French could not satisfy the conflicting ambitions of both Americans and Spaniards. He saw signs—or thought he did—indicating that the Paris Foreign

The Reconciliation Between Britannia and Her Daughter America   *America (represented by an Indian) is invited to buss (kiss) her mother.*

Office was about to betray America's trans-Allegheny interests to satisfy those of Spain. He therefore secretly made separate overtures to London, contrary to his instructions from Congress. The hard-pressed British, eager to entice one of their enemies from the alliance, speedily came to terms with the Americans. A preliminary treaty of peace was signed in 1782, the final peace the next year.

By the Treaty of Paris of 1783, the British formally recognized the independence of the United States. In addition, they granted generous boundaries, stretching majestically to the Mississippi on the west, to the Great Lakes on the north, and to Spanish Florida on the south. (Spain had recently captured Florida from Britain.) The Yankees, though now divorced from the empire, were to retain a share in the priceless fisheries of Newfoundland. The Canadians, of course, were profoundly displeased.

The Americans, for their part, had to yield important concessions. Loyalists were not to be further persecuted, and Congress was to *recommend* to the state legislatures that confiscated Loyalist property be restored. As for the debts long owed to British creditors, the states were bound to put no lawful obstacles in the way of their collection. Unhappily for future harmony, the assurances regarding both debts and Loyalists were not carried out in the manner hoped for by London.

A New Nation Legitimized

Britain's terms were liberal almost beyond belief. The enormous trans-Allegheny area was thrown in as a virtual gift, for George Rogers Clark had captured only a small segment of it. Why the generosity? Had the United States beaten Britain to its knees?

The key to the riddle may be found in the Old World. At the time the peace terms were drafted, Britain was trying to seduce America from her French alliance, so it made the terms as alluring as possible. The shaky Whig ministry, hanging on by its fingernails for only a few months, was more friendly to the Americans than were the Tories. It was determined, by a policy of liberality, to salve recent wounds, reopen old trade channels, and prevent future wars over the coveted trans-Allegheny region. This far-visioned policy was regrettably not followed by the successors of the Whigs.

In spirit, the Americans made a separate peace—contrary to the French alliance. In fact, they did not. The Paris Foreign Office formally approved the terms of peace, though disturbed by the lone-wolf course of its American ally. France was immensely relieved by the prospect of bringing the costly conflict to an end, and of freeing itself from its embarrassing promises to the Spanish crown.

America alone gained from the world-girdling war. The British, though soon to stage a comeback, were battered and beaten. The French gained sweet revenge but plunged headlong down the slippery slope to bankruptcy and revolution. In truth, fortune smiled benignly on the Americans. Snatching their independence from the furnace of world conflict, they began their national career with a splendid territorial birthright and a priceless heritage of freedom. Seldom, if ever, has any people been so favored.

CHRONOLOGY

1775	Battle of Lexington and Concord.		1778	Formation of French-American alliance.
	Second Continental Congress.		1778–1779	Clark's victories in the West.
	Battle of Bunker Hill.		1781	Battle of King's Mountain.
	Failed invasion of Canada.			Battle of Cowpens.
1776	Paine's *Common Sense.*			Greene leads Carolina campaign.
	Declaration of Independence.			Battle of Yorktown.
	Battle of Trenton.		1782	North's ministry collapses in Britain.
1777	Battle of Brandywine.		1783	Treaty of Paris.
	Battle of Germantown.			
	Battle of Saratoga.			

Varying Viewpoints

As the first colonial struggle for "national liberation," the Revolutionary War has long captured the attention of military historians. Early accounts concentrated on the engagements between British regulars and the Continental Army, and the war's place in the context of European rivalries. The French alliance, the dramatic battles at Saratoga and Yorktown, and the terrible winter at Valley Forge receive the greatest emphasis in most of these studies.

During the period of the Cold War, the proliferation of guerrilla conflicts in the developing nations prompted scholars to emphasize another distinctive feature of the war for American independence—the "triangularity" of the revolutionary struggle. Focusing on the efforts of the Patriot militia to disrupt British supply lines and win the loyalty of the general public, recent accounts, most notably those of John Shy and Charles Royster, portray the conflict less as a battle between two armies than as a contest between the British and the militia for control of the civilian population. By forcing the apathetic majority to associate actively with the Patriot cause, the militia won this war for the hearts and minds of the people and made it unlikely that the British could have recovered the loyalty of the colonists, even had they achieved a military victory.

SELECT READINGS

Primary Source Documents

Thomas Paine's fiery *Common Sense** (1776) is the manifesto of the Revolution. "The Declaration of Independence"* (1887) is one of the foundations of American political theory. See also the "Treaty of Peace with Great Britain" (1783), in Henry Steele Commager, *Documents of American History*.

Secondary Sources

The war is sketched in John R. Alden, *A History of the American Revolution* (1969), and in Don Higgenbotham's excellent military history, *The War of American Independence: Military Attitudes, Policies, and Practice, 1763–1789* (1971). On the implications of the revolutionary conflict, see John Shy, *A People Numerous and Armed: Reflections on the Military Struggle for American Independence* (1976), and Charles Royster, *A Revolutionary People at War: The Continental Army and the American Character* (1980). Carl Becker's classic *The Declaration of Independence* (1922) is masterful; on the same subject see also Garry Wills, *Inventing America: Jefferson's Declaration of Independence* (1980). The role of the Loyalists is treated in William H. Nelson, *The American Tory* (1961), Robert M. Calhoun, *The Loyalists in Revolutionary America* (1973), Mary Beth Norton, *The British-Americans: The Loyalist Exiles in England* (1972), Sheila L. Skemp, *William Franklin: A Man in the Middle* (1990), and Bernard Bailyn's unusually sensitive biography of the governor of colonial Massachusetts, *The Ordeal of Thomas Hutchinson* (1974). Attention to the social history of the Revolution has been largely inspired by John E. Jameson's seminal *The American Revolution Considered as a Social Movement* (1926). Jackson T. Main, *The Social Structure of Revolutionary America* (1969), takes the exploration further along the same lines, with conclusions somewhat at variance with Jameson's. Women in the revolutionary era are the subject of Linda K. Kerber, *Women of the Republic: Intellect and Ideology in Revolutionary America* (1980), and Mary Beth Norton, *Liberty's Daughters: The Revolutionary Experience of American Women* (1980). Michael Kammen brilliantly evokes the ways that the Revolution has been enshrined in the national memory in *A Season of Youth: The American Revolution and the Historical Imagination* (1978).

CHAPTER 9

The Confederation and the Constitution, 1776–1790

This example of changing the constitution by assembling the wise men of the state, instead of assembling armies, will be worth as much to the world as the former examples we have given it.

Thomas Jefferson

A Revolution of Sentiments

The American Revolution was not a revolution in the sense of a radical or total change. It did not suddenly and violently overturn the entire political and social framework, as later occurred in the French and Russian revolutions. What happened was accelerated evolution rather than outright revolution.

Yet some striking changes were ushered in, affecting social customs, political institutions, ideas about society and government and even gender roles. The exodus of some 80,000 substantial Loyalists paved the way for new Patriot elites to emerge. It also cleared the field for the "leveling" ideas of unbridled democracy to sweep across the land.

Equality was everywhere the watchword. When a group of Continental Army officers in 1783 formed an exclusive military order, the Society of the Cincinnati, they were roundly denounced for their aristocratic pretensions. Most states reduced (but usually did not eliminate altogether) property-holding requirements for voting. Social democracy was further stimulated by the growth of trade organizations for artisans and laborers.

A protracted fight for separation of church and state resulted in notable gains. The well-entrenched Congregational church continued to be legally established in some New England states, but the Anglican church, tainted by association with the British crown, was humbled. De-Anglicized, it re-formed as the Protestant Episcopal church and was everywhere disestablished. The bitter struggle for divorce between religion and government in Virginia was prolonged to 1786, when free-thinking Thomas Jefferson and his co-reformers, including the Baptists, won a complete victory with the passage of the Virginia Statute for Religious Freedom.

The egalitarian sentiments unleashed by the war likewise challenged the institution of slavery. Philadelphia Quakers in 1775 founded the world's first antislavery society. The Continental Congress in 1774 called for the complete abolition of the slave trade, a summons to which most of the states responded positively. Several northern states went further and either abolished slavery outright or provided for the gradual emancipation of blacks. Even

Charleston Slave Advertisement

in slave-burdened Virginia, a few idealistic masters freed their human chattels. In this still sadly incomplete revolution of sentiments, symbolized and inspired by the Declaration of Independence, were to be found the first frail sprouts of the later abolitionist movement.

Likewise incomplete was the extension of the doctrine of equality to women. Some women did serve (disguised as men) in the military, and New Jersey's new constitution in 1776 even temporarily enabled women to vote. But though Abigail Adams teased her husband John in 1776 that "the ladies" were determined "to foment a rebellion" of their own if they were not given political rights, most of the women in the revolutionary era were still doing traditional women's work.

Yet women did not go untouched by revolutionary ideals. Republican ideology advanced the concept of "civic virtue"—the idea that democracy depended on the unselfish commitment of each citizen to the public good. Mothers, whom society

trusted with education of the young, were often cited as the very models of proper republican behavior. The idea of "republican motherhood" thus took root, elevating women to a newly prestigious role as special keepers of the nation's conscience.

Constitution Making in the States

The Continental Congress in 1776 called upon the colonies to draft new constitutions. In effect, Congress was asking the colonies to summon themselves into being as new states, whose sovereignty, according to the theory of republicanism, would rest on the authority of the people. In most of the states, constitution writers worked tirelessly to capture the democratic spirit of the age on black-inked parchment.

Massachusetts contributed one especially noteworthy innovation when it called a special convention to draft its constitution and then submitted the final draft directly to the people for ratification. This procedure was later imitated in the drafting and ratification of the federal Constitution.

The newly penned state constitutions enjoyed many features in common. As *written* documents, they were intended to represent a *fundamental* law, superior to the transient whims of ordinary legislation. Most of these documents included bills of rights, specifically guaranteeing long-prized liberties against later legislative encroachment. All of them deliberately created weak executive and judicial branches. A generation of quarreling with His Majesty's officials had implanted a deep distrust of despotic governors and arbitrary judges. But the legislatures, presumably the most democratic branch of government, were given sweeping powers.

The democratic character of the new state legislatures was vividly reflected by the presence of many members from the recently enfranchised poorer western districts. Their influence was powerfully felt in their several successful movements to relocate state capitals from the haughty eastern seaports into the less pretentious interior. These geographical shifts portended political shifts with which many of the more conservative Americans grew increasingly uncomfortable.

Economic Crosscurrents

Economic changes begotten by the war were likewise noteworthy, but not overwhelming. States seized control of former crown lands, and although rich speculators had their day, many of the large Loyalist holdings were confiscated and eventually cut up into small farms. Roger Morris's huge estate in New York, for example, was sliced into 250 parcels—thus accelerating the spread of economic democracy. The frightful excesses of the French Revolution were avoided, partly because cheap land was easily available. People do not chop off heads so readily when they can chop down trees. It is significant that in the United States economic democracy, broadly speaking, preceded political democracy.

A sharp stimulus was given to manufacturing by the prewar nonimportation agreements and later by the war itself. Goods that had formerly been imported from Britain were mostly cut off, and the ingenious Yankees were forced to make their own. Ten years after the Revolution the busy Brandywine Creek, south of Philadelphia, was turning the waterwheels of numerous mills along an eight-mile stretch. Yet America remained overwhelmingly a nation of soil-tillers.

Economically speaking, independence had drawbacks. Much of the coveted commerce of Britain was still reserved for the loyal parts of the empire; and now that the Americans were aliens, they were forced to find new customers. Fisheries were disrupted, and bounties for ships' stores had abruptly ended. In some respects, the hated British Navigation Laws were more disagreeable after independence than before.

New commercial outlets fortunately compensated partially for the loss of old ones. Americans could now trade freely with foreign nations, subject to local restrictions—a boon they had not enjoyed in the old days of mercantilism. Enterprising Yankee shippers ventured boldly—and profitably—into the Baltic and China seas.

Yet the general economic picture was far from being rosy. War had spawned demoralizing extravagance, speculation, and profiteering, with profits for some as indecently high as 300 percent. Runaway inflation had been ruinous to many citizens, and Congress had failed in its feeble attempts to curb economic laws by fixing prices. The average citizen was probably worse off financially at the end of the shooting than before.

A Shaky Start Toward Union

What would the Americans do with the independence they had so dearly won? Prospects for erecting a lasting regime were far from bright. It is always difficult to set up a new government, but it is doubly difficult to set up a new type of government. The picture was further confused in America by leaders preaching "natural rights" and looking suspiciously at all persons clothed with authority. America was more a name than a nation, and unity ran little deeper than the color on the map.

Disruptive forces stalked the land. The departure of the conservative Tories left the political system inclined toward experiment and innovation. Patriots had fought the war with a high degree of disunity, but they had at least enjoyed the unifying cement of a common cause. Now even that was gone. It would have been almost a miracle if any government fashioned in all this confusion had long endured.

Hard times, the bane of all regimes, set in shortly after the war and hit bottom in 1786. As if other troubles were not enough, British manufacturers, with dammed-up surpluses, began flooding the American market with cut-rate goods. War-baby American industries, in particular, suffered industrial colic from such ruthless competition.

Yet hopeful signs could be discerned. The thirteen sovereign states were basically alike in governmental structure and functioned under similar constitutions. Americans enjoyed a rich political inheritance, derived partly from Britain and partly from their own homegrown devices for self-government. Finally, they were blessed with political leaders of a high order in men such as George Washington, James Madison, John Adams, Thomas Jefferson, and Alexander Hamilton.

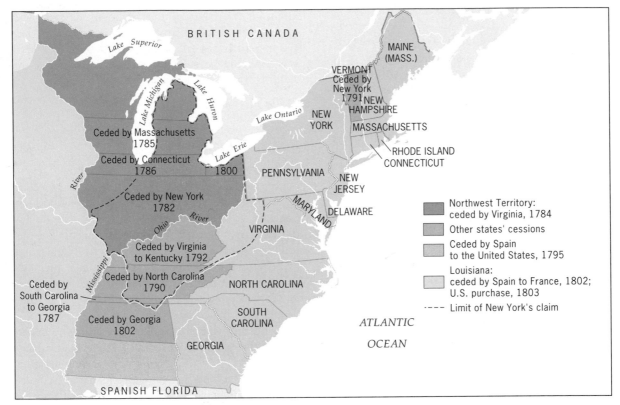

Western Land Cessions to the United States, 1782–1802

Creating a Confederation

The Second Continental Congress of revolutionary days was little more than a conference of ambassadors from the thirteen states. In nearly all respects the states were sovereign, for they coined money, raised armies and navies, and erected tariff barriers.

Shortly before declaring independence in 1776, Congress appointed a committee to draft a written constitution for the new nation. The finished product was the Articles of Confederation. Adopted by Congress in 1777, it was translated into French after the battle of Saratoga so as to convince France that America had a genuine government in the making. In due course this new constitution was sent out to the states for their approval. But final action was delayed for four years, until 1781, less than eight months before the victory at Yorktown.

The chief apple of discord was western lands. Six of the jealous states, including Pennsylvania and

Maryland, had no holdings beyond the Appalachian Mountains. Seven, notably New York and Virginia, were favored with enormous acreage, on the basis of earlier sea-to-sea charter grants. The six land-hungry states argued that the more fortunate states would not have retained possession of this splendid prize if all the other states had not fought for it also. A major complaint was that the land-blessed states could sell their trans-Appalachian tracts and thus pay off pensions and other debts incurred in the common cause. States without such holdings would have to tax themselves heavily to defray these obligations. Why not turn the whole western area over to the central government?

Unanimous approval of the Articles of Confederation by the thirteen states was required, and land-hungry Maryland stubbornly held out until March 1, 1781. It at length gave in when New York surrendered her western claims and Virginia seemed about to do so. To sweeten the pill, Congress pledged itself to dispose of these vast areas for the "common benefit." It further agreed to carve from the new public domain not colonies but a number of "republican" states, which in time would be admitted to the union on terms of complete equality with all the others. This extraordinary commitment faithfully reflected the anticolonial spirit of the Revolution, and the pledge was later fully redeemed in the famed Northwest Ordinance of 1787.

Fertile public lands thus transferred to the central government proved to be an invaluable bond of union. The states that had thrown their heritage into the common pot had to remain in the Union if they were to reap their share of the advantages from the land sales. An army of westward-moving pioneers purchased their farms from the federal government, directly or indirectly, and they learned to look to the national capital, rather than to the state capitals—with a consequent weakening of local influence. Finally, a uniform national land policy was made possible.

The Articles of Confederation: America's First Constitution

The Articles of Confederation provided for a loose confederation or "firm league of friendship." Thirteen independent states were thus linked together for joint action in dealing with common problems, such as foreign affairs. A clumsy Congress was to be the chief agency of government. There was no executive branch—George III had left a bad taste—and the vital judicial arm was left almost exclusively to the states, which remained sovereign.

Congress, though dominant, was closely hobbled by the suspicious states. All bills dealing with specified subjects of importance required at least a two-thirds vote; any amendment of the Articles themselves required an almost-impossible unanimous vote. Purposely designed to be weak, Congress was crippled by its lack of power to regulate commerce, which left the states free to establish conflictingly different laws regarding tariffs and navigation. With no power to enforce its tax-collection program,

Congress could only set a tax quota for the individual states and ask them please to contribute their shares voluntarily.

Despite their defects, the Articles of Confederation were a significant steppingstone toward the present Constitution. They clearly outlined the general powers that were to be exercised by the central government, such as making treaties and establishing a postal service. As the first written constitution of the republic, the Articles kept alive the flickering ideal of union and held the states together—until such time as they were ripe for the establishment of a strong constitution by peaceful, evolutionary methods. The anemic Articles represented what the states regarded as an alarming surrender of their power. Without this intermediary jump, they probably would never have consented to the breathtaking leap from the old boycott Association of 1774 to the Constitution of the United States.

Landmarks in Land Laws

Handcuffed though the Congress of the Confederation was, it succeeded in passing supremely farsighted pieces of legislation. These related to an immense part of the public domain recently acquired from the states, commonly known as the Old Northwest. This area of land lay northwest of the Ohio River, east of the Mississippi River, and south of the Great Lakes.

The first of these red-letter laws was the Land Ordinance of 1785. It provided that the acreage of the Old Northwest should be sold and that the proceeds should be used to help pay off the national debt. The vast area was to be surveyed before sale and settlement, thus forestalling endless confusion and lawsuits. It was to be divided into townships six miles square, each of which in turn was to be split into thirty-six sections of one square mile each. The sixteenth section of each township was set aside to be sold for the benefit of the public schools—a priceless gift to education in the Northwest.

Even more noteworthy was the Northwest Ordinance of 1787, which established governments for the Old Northwest. This law came to grips with the problem of how a nation should deal with its colonial peoples—the same problem that had bedev-

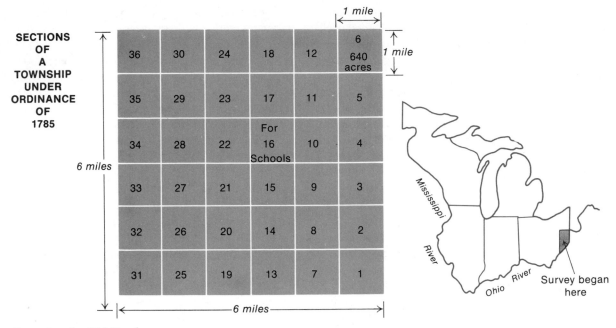

Surveying the Old Northwest

iled the king and Parliament in London. The solution provided by the Northwest Ordinance was a judicious compromise: temporary tutelage, then permanent equality. First, there would be two evolutionary territorial stages, during which the area would be subordinate to the federal government. Then, when a territory could boast 60,000 inhabitants, it might be admitted by Congress as a state, with all the privileges of the thirteen charter members. (This is precisely what the Continental Congress had promised the states when they surrendered their lands in 1781.) The ordinance also forbade slavery in the Old Northwest—a pathbreaking gain for freedom.

The wisdom of Congress in handling this explosive problem deserves warm praise. If it had attempted to chain the new territories in permanent subordination, a second American Revolution almost certainly would have erupted in later years, fought this time by the West against the East. Congress thus neatly solved the seemingly insoluble problem of empire. The scheme worked so well that its basic principles were ultimately carried over from the Old Northwest to other frontier areas.

The World's Ugly Duckling

Foreign relations, especially with London, continued troubled during these anxious years of confederation. Britain flatly declined to send a minister to America, to make a commercial treaty, or to repeal its ancient Navigation Laws. Lord Sheffield argued that Britain would win back America's trade anyhow, as commerce would naturally return to old channels. The British also shut off their profitable West Indian trade from the United States.

Along the northern border British agents intrigued with the disgruntled Allen brothers to annex Vermont to Canada. Redcoats continued to hold a chain of trading posts on American soil, maintaining a profitable fur trade and keeping the Indians lined up on the side of the king as a barrier against future American attacks on Canada.

Maddened by these grievances, some patriotic Americans demanded that the United States force the British into line by imposing restrictions on their imports to America. But Congress could not control commerce, and the states refused to adopt a uniform tariff policy.

Spain, though recently an enemy of Britain, was openly unfriendly to the new republic. It controlled the mouth of the all-important Mississippi, down which the pioneers of Tennessee and Kentucky were forced to float their produce. In 1784 Spain closed the river to American commerce, threatening the West with strangulation. Spain likewise claimed a large area north of the Gulf of Mexico, including Florida, granted to the United States by the British in 1783. At Natchez, on disputed soil, Britain held an important fort. It also schemed with the neighboring Indians to hem in the Americans east of the Appalachians. Spain and Britain together, radiating their influence out among resentful Indian peoples, prevented America from exercising effective control over about half of its total territory.

Even America's wartime ally France demanded the repayment of money loaned during the war, and restricted trade with its bustling West Indies ports. North African pirates, including the arrogant Dey of Algiers, ravaged America's Mediterranean commerce and enslaved Yankee sailors. The British purchased protection for their subjects, but as an independent nation the United States was too weak to fight and too poor to bribe.

John Jay, secretary for foreign affairs, hoped that these insults would at least humiliate the American people into framing a new government at home that would be strong enough to command respect abroad.

The Horrid Specter of Anarchy

Economic storm clouds continued to hang low in the mid-1780s. An alarming uprising, known as Shays's Rebellion, flared up in western Massachusetts in 1786 and set off widespread fear of further insurrection. Impoverished backcountry farmers, many of them Revolutionary War veterans, were losing their farms through mortgage foreclosures and tax delinquencies. Led by Captain Daniel Shays, a veteran of the Revolution, these desperate debtors demanded cheap paper money, lighter taxes, and a suspension of mortgage foreclosures. Hundreds of angry agitators, again seizing their muskets, attempted to enforce their demands.

Massachusetts authorities responded with drastic action. Supported partly by contributions from wealthy citizens, they raised a small army under General Benjamin Lincoln. Several skirmishes occurred—at Springfield three Shaysites were killed, and one was wounded—and the movement collapsed. Daniel Shays, who believed that he was fighting anew against tyranny, was condemned to death but later pardoned.

Shays's followers were crushed—but the nightmarish memory lingered on. The outbursts of these and other distressed debtors struck fear in the hearts of the propertied class, who began to suspect that the Revolution had raised up a Frankenstein's monster of "mobocracy."

How critical were conditions under the confederation? Conservatives, anxious to safeguard their wealth and position, naturally exaggerated the seriousness of the nation's plight. They were eager to persuade their fellow citizens to scrap the Articles of Confederation, under which the states were sovereign, in favor of a muscular central government, in which the federal authority would be sovereign. But the poorer states'-rights people, who favored at most a simple amending of the Articles, pooh-poohed the talk of anarchy. Many of them were debtors who feared that a powerful federal government would force them to pay their creditors.

Yet friends and critics of the confederation agreed that it needed strengthening. Popular toasts were "cement to the union" and "a hoop to the barrel." The chief differences arose over how this goal should be attained and how a maximum amount of states' rights could be reconciled with a strong central government.

A Convention of "Demi-Gods"

Control of commerce touched off the chain reaction that led to a constitutional convention. Interstate squabbling over this issue had become so alarming by 1786 that Virginia issued a call for a convention at Annapolis. When delegates from only five states showed up, nothing could be done about the ticklish commerce question. A thirty-one-year-old New Yorker, Alexander Hamilton, brilliantly saved the convention from failure by engineering a call for another convention to meet the next year in Philadelphia to bolster the entire fabric of the Articles of Confederation.

Congress was reluctant to take a step that might be the signing of its own death warrant. But after six states appointed delegates anyhow, Congress belatedly issued the call for a convention *"for the sole and express purpose of revising"* the Articles of Confederation.

Every state chose representatives, except independent-minded Rhode Island, a stronghold of paper-moneyites. These leaders were all appointed by the state legislatures, whose members had been elected by voters who could qualify as property holders. This double distillation inevitably brought together a select group of propertied men.

A quorum of the fifty-five emissaries from twelve states finally convened at Philadelphia on May 25, 1787, in the imposing red-brick statehouse. The smallness of the assemblage facilitated intimate acquaintance and hence compromise. Sessions were held in complete secrecy, with armed sentinels posted at the doors. Delegates knew that they would generate heated differences, and they did not want to advertise their own dissensions or put crippling arguments into the mouths of the opposition.

The caliber of the participants was extraordinarily high—"demi-gods," Jefferson called them. The crisis was such as to induce the ablest men to drop their personal pursuits and come to the aid of their country. Most of the members were lawyers, and most of them fortunately were old hands at constitution making in their own states.

George Washington, towering austere and aloof among the "demi-gods" was unanimously elected chairman. His enormous prestige as "the Sword of the Revolution" served to quiet overheated tempers. Benjamin Franklin, then eighty-one, added the urbanity of an elder statesman, although he was inclined to be indiscreetly talkative in his declining years. James Madison, then thirty-six and a profound student of government, made contributions so notable that he has been dubbed "the Father of the Constitution." Alexander Hamilton, then only thirty-two, was present as an advocate of a super-

powerful central government. His five-hour speech in behalf of his plan, though the most eloquent of the convention, left only one delegate convinced—himself.

Most of the flaming revolutionary leaders of 1776 were absent. Thomas Jefferson, John Adams, and Thomas Paine were in Europe; Samuel Adams and John Hancock were not elected by Massachusetts. Patrick Henry, ardent champion of states' rights, was chosen as a delegate from Virginia but declined to serve, declaring that he "smelled a rat." It was perhaps well that these architects of revolution were absent. The time had come to yield the stage to leaders interested in fashioning solid political systems.

Patriots in Philadelphia

The fifty-five delegates were a conservative, well-to-do body: lawyers, merchants, shippers, land speculators, and moneylenders. Not a single spokesperson was present from the poorer debtor groups. They were young (the average age was about forty-two) but experienced statesmen. Above all, they were nationalists, more interested in preserving and strengthening the young Republic than in further stirring the roiling cauldron of popular democracy.

The delegates hoped to crystallize the evaporating pools of revolutionary idealism into a stable political structure that would endure. They strongly desired a firm, dignified, and respected government. They believed in republicanism but sought to protect the American democratic experiment from its weaknesses abroad and excesses at home. They aimed to clothe the central authority with genuine power, especially in controlling tariffs, so that the United States could wrest satisfactory commercial treaties from foreign nations.

Other motives were present in the stately Philadelphia hall. Delegates were determined to preserve the union, forestall anarchy, and ensure security of life and property against dangerous uprisings by the "mobocracy." Above all, they sought to curb the unrestrained democracy rampant in the various states. The specter of the recent outburst in Massachusetts was especially alarming, and in this sense,

Daniel Shays was a founding father. Grinding necessity extorted the Constitution from a reluctant nation. There were fifty-five delegates; fear occupied the fifty-sixth chair.

Hammering Out a Bundle of Compromises

Some of the travel-stained delegates, when they first reached Philadelphia, decided upon a daring step. They would completely *scrap* the old Articles of Confederation, despite explicit instructions from Congress to *revise*. Technically, these bolder spirits were determined to overthrow the existing government of the United States by peaceful means. The sovereign states were in danger of losing their sovereignty.

A scheme proposed by populous Virginia, and known as "the large-state plan," was first pushed forward as the framework of the Constitution. Its essence was that representation in both houses of a bicameral Congress should be based on population—an arrangement that would naturally give the larger states an advantage. Tiny New Jersey, suspicious of Virginia, countered with "the small-state plan." This provided for equal representation in a unicameral Congress by states, regardless of size and population.

After bitter and prolonged debate, the "Great Compromise" of the convention was hammered out and agreed upon. The larger states were conceded representation by population in the House of Representatives (Art. I, Sec. II, para. 3; see Appendix at end of this book), and the smaller states were appeased by equal representation in the Senate (see Art. I, Sec. III, para. 1). Each state, no matter how poor or small, would have two senators. The big states, which would have to bear the major burden of taxation, obviously yielded more. As a sop to them, the delegates agreed that every tax bill or revenue measure must originate in the House, where population counted more heavily (see Art. 1, Sec. VII, para. 1). This critical compromise broke the logjam, and from then on success seemed within reach.

The Constitution as drafted was a bundle of compromises; they stand out in every section. A vital compromise was the method of electing the president indirectly by the Electoral College, rather than by direct means (see Art. II, Sec. I, para. 2).

Gouverneur Morris (1752–1816), by James Sharples, 1810 *A delegate from Pennsylvania to the Constitutional Convention of 1787, he spoke more frequently than any other member and served as principal draftsman of that superbly written document. A wealthy and rock-ribbed conservative, he had joined the revolutionary movement with reluctance and to the end feared the "riotous mob."*

Sectional jealousy also intruded. Should the voteless slave of the southern states count as a person in apportioning direct taxes and also representation in the House of Representatives? The South, not wishing to be deprived of influence, answered "yes." The North replied "no," arguing that counting slaves for purposes of representation was unfair. As a compromise between total representation and none at all, it was decided that a slave might count as three-fifths of a person. Hence the memorable, if illogical, "three-fifths compromise" (see Art. I, Sec. II, para. 3).

Most of the states wanted to shut off the African slave trade. But slaveholding South Carolina and Georgia raised vehement protests. In another compromise the convention stipulated that the slave trade might continue until the end of 1807, at which time Congress could end the importation of slaves

Strengthening the Central Government

Under Articles of Confederation	Under Federal Constitution
A loose confederation of states	A firm union of people
1 vote in Congress for each state	2 votes in Senate for each state; representation by population in House (see Art. I, Secs. II, III)
⅔ vote (9 states) in Congress for all important measures	Simple majority vote in Congress, subject to presidential veto (see Art. I, Sec. VII, para. 2)
Laws executed by committees of Congress	Laws executed by powerful president (see Art. II, Secs. II, III)
No congressional power over commerce	Congress to regulate both foreign and interstate commerce (see Art. I, Sec. VIII, para. 3)
No congressional power to levy taxes	Extensive power in Congress to levy taxes (see Art. I, Sec. VIII, para. 1)
No federal courts	Federal courts, capped by Supreme Court (see Art. III)
Unanimity of states for amendment	Amendment less difficult (see Art. V)
No authority to act directly upon individuals and no power to coerce states	Ample power to enforce laws by coercion of individuals and to some extent of states

(see Art. I, Sec. IX, para. 1). It did so as soon as the prescribed interval had elapsed. Meanwhile all the new state constitutions except Georgia's forbade overseas slave trade.

Safeguards for Conservatism

Heated clashes among the delegates have been overplayed. The area of agreement was actually large; otherwise the convention would have speedily disbanded. Economically, the members of the Constitutional Convention generally saw eye to eye; they demanded sound money and the protection of private property. Politically, they were in basic agreement; they favored a stronger government, with three branches and with checks and balances among them—what critics called a "triple-headed monster." Finally, the convention was virtually unanimous in believing that manhood-suffrage democracy—government by "democratick babblers"—was something to be feared and fought.

Daniel Shays, the prime bogeyman, still frightened the conservative-minded delegates. They deliberately erected safeguards against the excesses of the "mob," and they made these barriers as strong as they dared. The awesome federal judges were to be appointed for life. The powerful president was to be elected *indirectly* by the Electoral College; the lordly senators were to be chosen *indirectly* by state legislatures (see Art. I, Sec. III, para. 1). Only in the case of one-half of one of the three great branches—the House of Representatives—were qualified (propertied) citizens permitted to choose their officials by *direct* vote (see Art. I, Sec. II, para. 1).

Yet the new charter also contained democratic elements. Above all, it stood foursquare on the two great principles of republicanism: that the only legitimate government was one based on the consent of the governed, and that the powers of the government should be limited. "We the people," the Preamble began, in a ringing affirmation of these republican doctrines.

At the end of seventeen muggy weeks—May 25 to September 17, 1787—only forty-two of the original fifty-five members remained to sign the Constitution. Three of the forty-two, refusing to do so, returned to their states to resist ratification. The remainder, adjourning to the City Tavern, appropriately celebrated the occasion.

The Clash of Federalists and Antifederalists

The founding fathers early foresaw that nationwide acceptance of the Constitution would not be easy to obtain. A formidable barrier was unanimous ratifica-

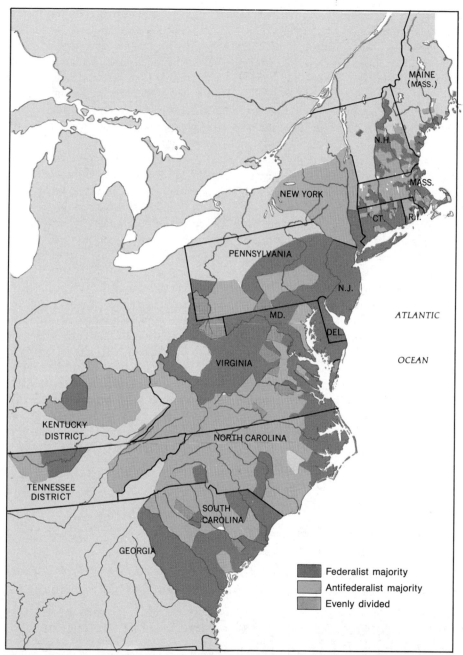

MAINE
(MASS.)

N.H.

MASS.

NEW YORK

CT.   R.I.

PENNSYLVANIA

N.J.

MD.

DEL.

ATLANTIC

OCEAN

VIRGINIA

KENTUCKY
DISTRICT

NORTH CAROLINA

TENNESSEE
DISTRICT

SOUTH
CAROLINA

GEORGIA

Federalist majority

Antifederalist majority

Evenly divided

The Struggle over Ratification   *This mottled map shows that federalist support tended to cluster around the coastal areas, which had enjoyed profitable commerce with the outside world, including the export of grain and tobacco. Impoverished frontiersmen, suspicious of a powerful new central government under the Constitution, were generally antifederalists.*

tion by all thirteen states, as required for amendment by the still-existent Articles of Confederation. But since absent Rhode Island was certain to veto the Constitution, the delegates boldly adopted a different scheme. They stipulated that when nine states had registered their approval through specially elected conventions, the Constitution would become the supreme law of the land in those states ratifying (see Art. VII).

This was extraordinary, even revolutionary. It was in effect an appeal over the heads of Congress that had called the convention, and over the heads of the legislatures that had chosen its members, to the people—or those of the people who could vote. In this way the framers could claim greater popular sanction for their handiwork. Congress reluctantly submitted the document to the states on this basis, without recommendation of any kind.

The American people were somewhat shocked, so well had the secrets of the convention been kept. The public had expected the old Articles of Confederation to be patched up; now it was handed a frightening document in which, many thought, the precious jewel of state sovereignty was swallowed up. One of the hottest debates of American history forthwith erupted. The antifederalists, who opposed the stronger federal government, were arrayed against the federalists, who naturally favored it.

A motley crowd gathered in the antifederalist camp. It consisted primarily, though not exclusively, of the states'-rights devotees, the backcountry pioneers, the one-horse farmers, the work-soiled artisans, the ill-educated and illiterate—in general, the poorer classes. They were joined by paper-moneyites and debtors, many of whom feared that a potent central government would force them to pay off their debts—and at full value.

Silver-buckled federalists were more respectable; they generally embraced the cultured and propertied groups. Most of them lived in the settled areas along the seaboard, not in the raw backcountry. They were in outlook rather closely akin to the conservative Loyalists of revolutionary days. In fact, many of the remaining former Loyalists vigorously supported the Constitution; without them it might have failed to be ratified.

Antifederalists, their worst fears aroused, voiced vehement objections to the "gilded trap" known as the Constitution. They cried with much truth that it had been drawn up by the aristocratic elements and hence was antidemocratic. They likewise charged that the sovereignty of the states was being submerged, and that the freedoms of the individual were jeopardized by the absence of a bill of rights. They decried the dropping of annual elections for congressional representatives; the setting up of a

REDEUNT SATURNIA REGNA.

On the erection of the Eleventh PILLAR of the great National DOME, we beg leave most sincerely to felicitate " OUR DEAR COUNTRY."

Rise it will.

The foundation good—it may yet be SAVED.

A Triumphant Cartoon   *It appeared in the* Massachusetts Centinel *on August 2, 1788. Note the two laggards, especially the sorry condition of Rhode Island.*

federal stronghold ten miles square (later the District of Columbia); the creation of a standing army; the omission of any reference to God; and the highly questionable procedure of ratifying with only two-thirds of the states.

The Great Debate in the States

Special elections, some apathetic but others hotly contested, were held in the various states for members of the ratifying conventions. The candidates—federalist or antifederalist—were elected on the basis of pledges for or against the Constitution.

The newly forged document was quickly accepted by four small states, for they had come off much better than they expected. Pennsylvania, number two on the list of ratifiers, was the first large state to act, but not until high-handed irregularities had been employed by the federalist legislature in calling a convention. These included the forcible seating of two antifederalist members, their clothes torn and their faces red with rage, in order to complete a quorum.

Massachusetts, the second most populous state, provided an acid test. If the Constitution had failed there, the entire movement might easily have bogged down. The Boston ratifying convention at first contained an antifederalist majority, including weatherbeaten Shaysites and the suspicious Samuel Adams, who now distrusted change. The absence of a bill of rights especially alarmed the antifederalists, but the federalists gave solemn assurances that the first Congress would add such a safeguard by amendment. Massachusetts then ratified by the narrow margin of 187 to 168.

Three more states fell into line. Nine states—all but Virginia, New York, North Carolina, and Rhode Island—had now taken shelter under the "new federal roof," and the document was officially adopted on June 21, 1788. But such rejoicing was premature so long as the four dissenters, conspicuously New York and Virginia, remained outside the fold.

The Four Laggard States

Proud Virginia, the biggest and most populous state, provided fierce antifederalist opposition. There the college-bred federalist orators, for once, encountered worthy antagonists, including the fiery Patrick Henry. He professed to see in the fearsome parchment the death warrant of liberty. George Washington, James Madison, and John Marshall, on the federalist side, lent influential support. The new Union was going to be formed anyhow, and Virginia could not very well continue comfortably as an independent state. After a close and exciting debate in the state convention, ratification carried, 89 to 79.

New York, which also experienced an uphill struggle, was the only state that permitted a manhood-suffrage vote for the members of the ratifying convention. The result was a heavy antifederalist majority. Alexander Hamilton at heart favored a much stronger central government than that under debate, but he contributed his sparkling personality and persuasive eloquence to whipping up support. He also joined John Jay and James Madison in penning a masterly series of articles for the New York newspapers. Though designed as propaganda, these essays remain the most penetrating commentary ever written on the Constitution and are still widely sold in book form as *The Federalist*.

New York finally yielded. Realizing that the state could not prosper apart from the Union, the convention ratified the document by the close count of 30 to 27.

Last-ditch dissent developed in only two states. A hostile convention met in North Carolina, then adjourned without taking a vote. Rhode Island did not even summon a ratifying convention. The two most ruggedly individualist centers of the colonial era—homes of the "otherwise minded"—thus ran true to form. They were to change their course, albeit unwillingly, only after the new government had been in operation for some months.

The battle for ratification, despite much apathy, was close and extremely bitter in some localities. No lives were lost, but riotous disturbances broke out in New York and Pennsylvania, involving bruises and bloodshed. There was much behind-the-scenes pressure on delegates who had promised their constituents to vote against the Constitution. The last four states ratified, not because they wanted to but because they had to. They could not safely exist apart from the Union.

Hamiltonian Frigate *A victory parade in New York City honoring Hamilton and the ratification of the Constitution. At the key New York ratifying convention at Poughkeepsie, Hamilton, by sheer eloquence and cogent argument, turned a two-thirds majority against the Constitution into a majority of three in favor of it.*

A Conservative Triumph

The minority had triumphed—doubly. A militant minority of American radicals had engineered the military revolution that cast off the unwritten British constitution. A militant minority of conservatives—now embracing many of the earlier radicals—had engineered the peaceful revolution that overthrew the inadequate constitution known as the Articles of Confederation. Eleven states, in effect, had seceded from the confederation, leaving two out in the cold.

A majority had not spoken. Only about one-fourth of the adult white males in the country, chiefly the propertied people, had voted for delegates to the ratifying conventions. Careful estimates indicate that if the new Constitution had been submitted to a manhood-suffrage vote, as in New York, it would have encountered much more opposition, probably defeat.

Conservatism was victorious. Safeguards had been erected against mob-rule excesses, and the democratic gains of the Revolution were conserved in the face of possible anarchy. Radicals like Patrick Henry, who had overthrown British rule, had in turn been overthrown by American conservatives. The result was a kind of peaceful counterrevolution. It restored the economic and political stability of colonial years and set the drifting ship of state on a more promising course.

Yet if the architects of the Constitution were conservative, it is worth emphasizing that what they conserved was the principle of popular, democratic government, made forever sacred in the fires of the Revolution. By ingeniously embedding the doctrine of self-rule in a self-limiting system of checks and balances, the Constitution reconciled the potentially conflicting principles of liberty and order. It preserved the ideals of the Revolution even while setting boundaries to them. One of the distinctive—and enduring—paradoxes of American history was thus revealed: conservatives and radicals alike have championed the heritage of democratic revolutionism.

CHRONOLOGY

1774	Continental Congress calls for abolition of slave trade.
1775	Philadelphia Quakers found world's first antislavery society.
1776	New Jersey constitution temporarily gives women the vote.
1777	Articles of Confederation adopted by Congress.
1780	Massachusetts adopts first constitution drafted in convention and ratified by popular vote.
1781	Articles of Confederation put into effect.
1783	Military officers form Society of the Cincinnati.
1785	Land Ordinance of 1785.
1786	Virginia Statute for Religious Freedom.
	Shays's Rebellion.
	Meeting of five states to discuss revision of the Articles of Confederation.
1787	Northwest Ordinance.
	Constitutional Convention in Philadelphia.
1788	Ratification by nine states guarantees a new government under the Constitution.

Varying Viewpoints

Charles Beard's book, *An Economic Interpretation of the Constitution of the United States* (1913), has long defined the area around which debate on the constitutional period has revolved. Beard described the Constitution as the "reactionary" phase of the revolutionary era—a shrewd maneuver by conservative property owners to curtail the democratic excesses let loose in 1776.

Most modern scholars, if they accept Beard's argument at all, accept it only with severe qualifications. The most recent discussions of the Constitution have been cast in terms of reflections on the ancient riddle of republicanism: does republican self-government rest on the virtue of the people or on the formal political institutions that control human behavior? Writing about the "ideological origins" of the Revolution, Bernard Bailyn saw disputes over the principles of republicanism—not economic and social conflict—as the force driving the evolution of American institutions. Building on Bailyn's interpretation, scholars such as Gordon Wood have concluded that the Constitution was actually a bold experiment in channeling selfish human instincts toward the common good. By constructing a strong, balanced national government to rule an "extensive republic," the founding fathers challenged the conventional wisdom that a republic could survive only if extended over a small area with a homogeneous population. Therefore it was the federalists, rather than their fearful antifederalist opponents, who fulfilled the Revolution and carried out its most advanced ideas.

SELECT READINGS

Primary Source Documents

A comparison of the text of the Articles of Confederation (1781), in Henry Steele Commager, *Documents of American History,* with the Constitution* makes an intriguing study. See also Madison, Hamilton, and Jay's explanations of the Constitution in *The Federalist Papers,* especially "Federalist No. 10."*

Secondary Sources

John Fiske, in *The Critical Period of American History* (1888), portrayed America under the Articles of Confederation as a crisis-ridden country. His view has been sharply qualified by Merrill Jensen in *The New Nation* (1950). Jack N. Rakove's *The Beginning of National Politics* (1979) offers a history of the Continental Congress that substantially revises Jensen's work. Especially learned is Gordon S. Wood's massive and brilliant study of the entire period, *The Creation of the American Republic, 1776–1787* (1969). Edmund S. Morgan also looks at both England and America in *Inventing the People: The Rise of Popular Sovereignty in England and America* (1988). An influential transatlantic perspective on the roots of American republicanism is J. G. A. Pocock, *The Machiavellian Moment: Florentine Political Thought and the Atlantic Republican Tradition* (1975). On the Constitutional Convention, see Richard Bernstein's superb synthesis of current scholarship, *Are We to Be a Nation? The Making of the Constitution* (1987). Among fine studies inspired by the bicentennial of the Constitution are John P. Reid, *Constitutional History of the American Revolution: The Authority of Rights* (1986), Ruth Bloch, *Visionary Republic: Millennial Themes in American Thought, 1756–1800* (1986), and Leonard Levy, *Original Intent and the Framers' Constitution* (1988). Robert A. Rutland's *The Ordeal of the Constitution* (1966) describes the ratification struggle. Charles A. Beard shocked conservatives with *An Economic Interpretation of the Constitution of the United States* (1913). It has been seriously weakened by two blistering attacks: Robert E. Brown, *Charles Beard and the Constitution* (1956), and Forrest McDonald, *We the People: The Economic Origins of the Constitution* (1958). Michael A. Kammen, *A Machine That Would Go of Itself* (1987), examines the changing attitudes toward the Constitution throughout American history.

CHAPTER 10

Launching the New Ship of State, 1789–1800

I shall only say that I hold with Montesquieu, that a government must be fitted to a nation, as much as a coat to the individual; and, consequently, that what may be good at Philadelphia may be bad at Paris, and ridiculous at Petersburg [Russia].

Alexander Hamilton, 1799

A New Ship on an Uncertain Sea

When the Constitution was launched in 1789, the republic was continuing to grow at an amazing rate. Population was still doubling about every twenty-three years, and the first official census of 1790 recorded almost 4 million souls. Cities had blossomed proportionately: Philadelphia numbered 42,000; New York, 33,000; Boston, 18,000; Charleston, 16,000; and Baltimore, 13,000.

America's population was still about 90 percent rural, despite the flourishing cities; all but 5 percent lived east of the Appalachian Mountains. The trans-Appalachian overflow was concentrated chiefly in Kentucky, Tennessee, and Ohio, all of which were welcomed as states within fourteen years. Foreign travelers everywhere looked down their noses at the roughness and crudity resulting from ax-and-rifle pioneering life. Yet, critical though they might be, they were impressed by evidences of energy, self-confidence, and material well-being.

The new ship of state, despite these promising signs of fair weather, did not spread its sails to the most favorable breezes. Within twelve troubled years the American people had risen up and thrown overboard their first two constitutions: the British constitution and the Articles of Confederation. A decade of constitution smashing and law breaking was not the best training for government making. Americans had come to regard a central authority, replacing that of George III, as a necessary evil—something to be distrusted, watched, and curbed.

People of the western waters, in the stump-studded clearings of Kentucky, Tennessee, and Ohio, were restive and dubiously loyal. The mouth of the Mississippi, their life-giving outlet, lay in the hands of unfriendly Spaniards. Smooth-tongued Spanish and British agents, jingling gold, moved freely among the settlers and held out seductive promises of independence.

Finances of the infant government were likewise precarious. The revenue had declined to a trickle, while the public debt, with interest heavily in arrears, was mountainous. Worthless paper money, both state and national, was as plentiful as metallic money was scarce. The Americans, moreover, were brashly attempting to erect a republic on an immense scale, something that no other people had attempted

Evolution of the Cabinet

Original Members	Added, 1798–1913	Added, 1947–1989
Secy. of state, 1789	Secy. of navy, 1798 (lost cabinet status, 1947)	Secy. of defense, 1947 (subordinate members, without cabinet rank, are secys. of army, navy, and air force)
Secy. of treasury, 1789		
Secy. of war, 1789 (lost cabinet status, 1947)	Postmaster general, 1829 (lost cabinet status, 1970)	Secy. of health, education, and welfare, 1953 (divided, 1979)
Attorney general, 1789 (not head of Justice Dept. until 1870)	Secy. of interior, 1849	Secy. of housing and urban development, 1965
	Secy. of agriculture, 1889	Secy. of transportation, 1966
	Secy. of commerce and labor, 1903 (office divided, 1913)	Secy. of energy, 1977
	Secy. of commerce, 1913	Secy. of health and human services, 1979
	Secy. of labor, 1913	Secy. of education, 1979
		Secy. of veterans' affairs, 1989

and that traditional political theory held to be impossible. The eyes of a skeptical world were on the upstart United States, and the bejeweled monarchs of Europe in particular feared that the new republic would provide a dangerous example for their long-oppressed subjects.

Washington's Profederalist Regime

General Washington, the esteemed war hero, was unanimously drafted as president by the Electoral College in 1789—the only presidential nominee ever to be honored by unanimity.

His presence was imposing: 6 feet 2 inches, 175 pounds, broad and sloping shoulders, strongly pointed chin, and pockmarks (from smallpox) on nose and cheeks. Much preferring the quiet of Mount Vernon to the turmoil of politics, he was perhaps the only president who did not in some way angle for this exalted office. Balanced rather than brilliant, he commanded his followers by strength of character rather than by the arts of the politician.

Washington's long journey from Mount Vernon to New York City, the temporary capital, was a triumphal procession. He was greeted by roaring cannon, pealing bells, flower-carpeted roads, and singing and shouting citizens. With appropriate ceremony, he solemnly and somewhat nervously took the oath of office on April 30, 1789, on a crowded balcony overlooking Wall Street.

The Constitution does not mention a cabinet; it merely provides that the president "may require" written opinions of the heads of the executive branch departments (see Art. II, Sec. II, para. 1). But this system proved so cumbersome, and involved so much homework, that cabinet meetings gradually evolved during the Washington administration. At first there were only three department heads: Secretary of State Thomas Jefferson, Secretary of the Treasury Alexander Hamilton, and Secretary of War Henry Knox.

The Bill of Rights

Drawing up a bill of rights headed the list of tasks facing the new government. Many antifederalists had sharply criticized the Constitution drafted at Philadelphia for its failure to provide guarantees of individual rights such as freedom of religion and trial by jury. Many states had ratified the federal Constitution with the understanding that it would soon be amended to include such guarantees.

The proposed amendments were drafted and submitted to Congress by James Madison, whose scholarly and political skills had made him the leading figure in the new body. Adopted by the necessary number of states in 1791, the first ten amendments to the Constitution, popularly known as the Bill of Rights, safeguard some of the most precious American principles. Among these are protections for free-

Confidence in the Constitution *This late-eighteenth-century printer's cut caught the spirit of optimism and hope that prevailed in the infant republic.*

dom of religion, speech, and the press; the right to bear arms and to be tried by a jury; and the right to assemble and petition the government for redress of grievances. The Bill of Rights also prohibits cruel and unusual punishments and arbitrary government seizure of private property.

To guard against the danger that enumerating such rights might lead to the conclusion that they were the only ones protected, Madison inserted the crucial Ninth Amendment. It declares that specifying certain rights "shall not be construed to deny or disparage others retained by the people." To reassure states'-righters, he included the equally significant Tenth Amendment, which reserves all rights not explicitly delegated or prohibited by the federal Constitution "to the States respectively, or to the people." By preserving a strong central government while specifying certain protections for minority and individual liberties, Madison's amendments partially swung the federalist pendulum back in an antifederalist direction. (See Amendments I–X, in the Appendix.)

The first Congress also nailed other newly sawed governmental planks into place. It created effective federal courts under the Judiciary Act of 1789. The act organized the Supreme Court, with a chief justice and five associates, as well as federal district and circuit courts, and established the office of attorney general. New Yorker John Jay, Madison's collaborator on *The Federalist Papers,* became the first chief justice of the United States.

Hamilton Revives the Corpse of Public Credit

The key figure in the new government was smooth-faced Treasury Secretary Alexander Hamilton, a thirty-four-year-old native of the British West Indies. Hamilton's genius was unquestioned, but critics claimed he loved his adopted country more than his countrymen. Doubt about his character and his loyalty to the republican experiment always swirled about his head. Hamilton regarded himself as a kind of prime minister in Washington's cabinet and on occasion thrust his hands into the affairs of other departments, including that of his arch-rival, Thomas Jefferson.

A financial wizard, Hamilton set out immediately to correct the economic vexations that had crippled the Articles of Confederation. His plan was to shape the fiscal policies of the administration in such a way as to favor the wealthier groups. They, in turn, would gratefully lend the government monetary and moral support. The new federal regime would flourish, the propertied classes would grow fat, and prosperity would trickle down to the masses.

The youthful financier's first objective was to bolster the national credit. Without public confidence in the government, Hamilton could not secure the funds with which to float his risky schemes. He therefore boldly urged Congress to "fund" the entire national debt at par and to assume completely the debts incurred by the states during the recent war.

"Funding at par" meant that the federal government would pay off its debts at face value, plus accumulated interest—a then-enormous total of more than $54 million. So many people believed the infant Treasury incapable of meeting those obligations that government bonds had depreciated to ten to fifteen cents on the dollar. Yet speculators held fistfuls of them, and when Congress passed Hamilton's measure in 1790, they grabbed for some more. Some of them galloped into rural areas ahead of the news, buying for a song the depreciated paper holdings of farmers, war veterans, and widows. Hamilton was willing, even eager, to have the new government shoulder additional obligations. While pushing the funding scheme, he urged Congress to assume the debts of the states, totaling some $21.5 million.

The secretary made a convincing case for "assumption." The state debts could be regarded as a proper national obligation, for they had been incurred in the war for independence. But foremost in Hamilton's thinking was the belief that assumption would chain the states more tightly to the "federal chariot." Thus, the secretary's maneuver would shift the attachment of wealthy creditors from the states to the federal government. The support of the rich for the national administration was a crucial link in Hamilton's political strategy of strengthening the central government.

States burdened with heavy debts, such as Massachusetts, were delighted by Hamilton's proposal. States with small debts, such as Virginia, were less happy. The stage was set for some old-fashioned horse trading. Virginia did not want the state debts assumed, but it did want the forthcoming federal district*—now the District of Columbia—to be located on the Potomac River. Hamilton persuaded a reluctant Jefferson to line up enough votes in Congress for assumption. In return, Virginia would have the federal district on the Potomac. The bargain was carried through in 1790.

Customs Duties and Excise Taxes

The new ship of state thus set sail dangerously overloaded. The national debt had swelled to $75 million owing to Hamilton's insistence on honoring the outstanding federal and state obligations alike. But Hamilton, "Father of the National Debt," was not greatly worried. His objectives were as much politi-

Alexander Hamilton, Secretary of the Treasury *Everyone recognized Hamilton's talents and leadership, but many feared his fierce ambition and disdain for popular government.*

cal as economic. He believed that, within limits, a national debt was a "national blessing"—a kind of cement of union. The more creditors to whom the government owed money, the more people there would be with a personal stake in the success of his ambitious enterprise.

Where was the money to come from to pay interest on this huge debt and to run the government? Hamilton's first answer was customs duties, derived from a tariff. Tariff revenues, in turn, depended on a vigorous foreign trade, another crucial link in Hamilton's overall economic strategy for the new republic.

The first tariff law, which imposed a low tariff of about 8 percent on dutiable imports, was speedily passed by the First Congress in 1789, even before Hamilton was sworn in. Revenue was by far the main goal, but the measure was also designed to erect a low protective wall around infant industries, which

---

* Authorized by the Constitution, Art. I, Sec. VIII, para. 17.

bawled noisily for more shelter than they received. Hamilton had the vision to see that the Industrial Revolution would soon reach America, and he argued strongly in favor of more protection for the well-to-do manufacturing groups—another vital element in his economic program. But Congress was still dominated by agricultural and commercial interests, and it voted only two slight increases in the tariff during Washington's presidency.

Hamilton, with characteristic vigor, sought additional internal revenue and in 1791 secured from Congress an excise tax on a few domestic items, notably whiskey. The new levy of seven cents a gallon was borne chiefly by the distillers who lived in the mountains and the western backcountry. Whiskey flowed so freely on the frontier that it was used for money.

Hamilton Battles Jefferson for a Bank

As the capstone for his financial system, Hamilton proposed a powerful Bank of the United States. With the Bank of England as his model, Hamilton wanted the bank to be a private institution with the government as its major stockholder. The federal Treasury would deposit its surplus monies there. The bank would provide a convenient strong-box for federal funds, stimulate business by keeping money in circulation, and print a badly needed sound paper currency.

Jefferson, whose written opinion Washington requested, argued vigorously against the bank. There was, he insisted, no specific authorization in the Constitution for such a financial octopus. He was convinced that all powers not specifically granted to the central government were reserved to the states, as provided in the about-to-be-ratified Bill of Rights (see Art. X). He therefore concluded that the states, not Congress, had the power to charter banks. Believing that the Constitution should be interpreted "literally" or "strictly," Jefferson and his states'-rights disciples zealously embraced the theory of "strict construction."

Hamilton, also at Washington's request, prepared a brilliantly reasoned reply to Jefferson's arguments. He boldly invoked that clause of the Constitution that stipulates that Congress may pass any laws "necessary and proper" to carry out the powers vested in the various governmental agencies (see Art. I, Sec. VIII, para. 18). The government was explicitly empowered to collect taxes and regulate trade. In carrying out these basic functions, Hamilton argued, a national bank would be not only "proper" but "necessary." By inference or by implication—that is, by virtue of some "implied powers"—Congress would be fully justified in establishing the Bank of the United States. In short, Hamilton contended for a "loose" or "broad" interpretation of the Constitution. He and his federalist followers thus evolved the theory of "loose construction" by invoking the "elastic clause" of the Constitution—a precedent for enormous federal powers.

Hamilton's financial views prevailed. His eloquent and realistic arguments were accepted by Washington, who reluctantly signed the bank measure into law. This explosive issue had been debated with much heat in Congress, where the old North-South cleavage again appeared ominously. The most enthusiastic support for the bank naturally came from the commercial and financial centers of the North, whereas the strongest opposition arose from the agricultural South.

The Bank of the United States, as created by Congress in 1791, was chartered for twenty years. Located in Philadelphia, it was to have a capital of $10 million, one-fifth of it owned by the federal government.

Mutinous Moonshiners in Pennsylvania

The Whiskey Rebellion, which flared up in southwestern Pennsylvania in 1794, sharply challenged the new national government. Hamilton's excise bore harshly on these homespun pioneer folk. They regarded it not as a tax on a luxury but as a burden on an economic necessity and a medium of exchange. Even preachers of the gospel were paid in "Old Monongahela rye." Defiant distillers finally erected whiskey poles, similar to the liberty poles of antistamp tax days in 1765, and raised the cry "liberty and no excise." Boldly tarring and feathering revenue officers, they brought collections to a halt.

President Washington, once a revolutionist, was alarmed by what he called these "self-created societies." With the warm encouragement of Hamilton, he summoned the militia of several states. Anxious moments followed the call, for there was much doubt as to whether men in other states would muster to crush a rebellion in a sister state. Despite some opposition, an army of about 13,000 rallied to the colors, and two widely separated columns marched briskly forth in a gorgeous, leaf-tinted Indian summer. When the troops reached the hills of western Pennsylvania, they found no insurrection. The "Whiskey Boys" were overawed, dispersed, or captured.

The Whiskey Rebellion was small—some three rebels were killed—but its consequences were large. George Washington's government, now substantially strengthened, commanded a new respect. Yet the numerous foes of the federalists condemned the administration for its brutal display of force—for having used a sledge hammer to crush a gnat.

The Emergence of Political Parties

Almost overnight Hamilton's fiscal feats had established the government's sound credit rating. The Treasury could now borrow needed funds in the Netherlands on favorable terms. But Hamilton's financial successes—funding, assumption, the excise, the bank, suppression of the Whiskey Rebellion—created some political liabilities. All these schemes encroached sharply upon states' rights. Many Americans, dubious about the Constitution in the first place, might never have approved it if they had foreseen how the states were going to be overshadowed by the federal colossus. Now, out of resentment against Hamilton's revenue-raising and centralizing policies, an organized opposition began to build. What once was a personal feud between Hamilton and Jefferson developed into a full-blown and often bitter political rivalry.

National political parties, in the modern sense, were unknown to America when George Washington took the inaugural oath. There had been Whigs and Tories, federalists and antifederalists, but these groups were factions rather than parties. They had sprung into existence over hotly contested special issues; they had faded away when their cause had triumphed or had become hopelessly lost.

The founders at Philadelphia had not envisioned the existence of permanent political parties. Organized opposition to the government seemed tainted with disloyalty, an affront to the spirit of national unity that the glorious cause of the Revolution had inspired.

The notion of a formal party apparatus was thus a novelty in the 1790s, and when Jefferson and Madison first organized their opposition to the Hamiltonian program, they did not anticipate creating a long-lived popular party. But as their antagonism toward Hamilton endured, and as the boisterous newspapers spread both their political message and Hamilton's, primitive semblances of political parties emerged. The two-party system has existed in the United States since that time. Their competition for power has actually proved to be among the indispensable ingredients of a sound democracy.

The Impact of the French Revolution

When Washington's first administration ended, early in 1793, domestic controversies had already formed two political camps—Hamiltonian Federalists and Jeffersonian Democratic-Republicans. As his second term began, foreign policy issues brought the differences between them to a fever pitch.

Only a few weeks after Washington's inauguration in 1789, the curtain had risen on the first act of the French Revolution. Twenty-six years were to pass before the seething continent of Europe settled back into a peace of exhaustion. Few non-American events have left a deeper scar on American political and social life.

Most Americans, except a few ultraconservative Federalists, applauded the early, peaceful stages of the French Revolution, which involved a successful attempt to impose constitutional shackles on King Louis XVI. The Revolution entered upon a more ominous phase in 1792, when France declared war on hostile Austria. Late in that year the electrifying news reached America that French citizen armies had hurled back the invading foreigners, and that France had proclaimed itself a republic. Americans enthusiastically sang "The Marseillaise" and other rousing French revolutionary songs, and they renamed thoroughfares to honor revolutionary principles.

But centuries of pent-up poison could not be purged without baleful results. The guillotine was set up and the king beheaded in 1793. Christianity was abolished, and the head-rolling Reign of Terror was begun. Back in America, God-fearing Federalist aristocrats nervously fingered their tender white necks and eyed the Jeffersonian masses apprehensively. Lukewarm Federalist approval of the early Revolution turned, almost overnight, to heated opposition to "blood-drinking cannibals."

Sober-minded Jeffersonians regretted the bloodshed. But they felt, with Jefferson, that one could not expect to be carried from "despotism to liberty in a feather bed," and that a few thousand aristocratic heads were a cheap price to pay for human freedom.

Such gloating was shortsighted, for peril loomed ahead. The earlier battles of the French Revolution had not hurt America directly, but now Britain was sucked into the titanic conflict. The conflagration speedily spread to the New World, where it vitally affected the expanding young American republic.

Washington's Neutrality Proclamation

Ominously, the Franco-American alliance of 1778 was still on the books, and many Jeffersonian Democratic-Republicans favored honoring it. Aflame with the liberal ideals of the French Revolution, Jeffersonians were eager to enter the conflict against Britain, the recent foe, at the side of France, the recent friend.

But level-headed President Washington was not swayed by the clamor of the crowd. Backed by Hamilton, he perceived that war had to be avoided at all costs. Accordingly, Washington boldly issued his Neutrality Proclamation in 1793, shortly after the outbreak of war between Britain and France. This epochal document not only proclaimed the government's official neutrality in the widening conflict but sternly warned American citizens to be impartial toward both armed camps. It was America's first formal declaration of aloofness from Old World quarrels and as such proved to be a major prop of the spreading isolationist tradition.

The pro-French Jeffersonians were enraged by the Neutrality Proclamation; the pro-British Federalists were heartened. A few days earlier an impetuous, thirty-year-old representative of the French republic, Citizen Edmond Genêt, had landed at Charleston, South Carolina. With unrestrained zeal, he undertook to outfit privateers and otherwise take advantage of the existing Franco-American alliance. The giddy-headed envoy was soon swept away by his enthusiastic reception by the Jeffersonian Democratic-Republicans. He foolishly came to believe that the Neutrality Proclamation did not reflect the true wishes of the American people, and he consequently embarked upon unneutral activity not authorized by

The Contrast *Adaptation of a British cartoon. C. C. Coffin,* Building a Nation, *1882.*

the French alliance. After he had threatened to appeal over the head of "Old Washington" to the sovereign voters, the president demanded Genêt's withdrawal and the Frenchman was replaced by a less impulsive emissary.

Jay's Treaty Ends Embroilments with Britain

President Washington's far-visioned policy of neutrality was sorely tried by the British. For ten years they had been retaining the chain of northern frontier posts on United States soil, all in defiance of the peace treaty of 1783. British agents openly sold firearms and firewater to the Indians, who continued to attack pioneers invading their lands. When General "Mad Anthony" Wayne crushed the Northwest Indians at the Battle of Fallen Timbers on August 20, 1794, the fleeing foe left British arms and a few of their Canadian allies dead on the battlefield. In the Treaty of Greenville in 1795, the Indians, finally abandoned by their red-coated friends, ceded their claims to a vast virgin tract in the Ohio country.

On the sea frontier, the British were eager to starve out the French West Indies and naturally expected the United States to defend them under the Franco-American alliance. Hard-boiled commanders of the Royal Navy, acting under instructions from London in 1793, struck savagely. They seized about 300 American merchant ships in the West Indies, impressed scores of seamen into service on British

vessels, and threw hundreds of others into foul dungeons. A mighty outcry arose, chiefly from outraged Jeffersonians, that America should once again fight George III in defense of its liberties.

President Washington, in a last desperate gamble to avert war, sent John Jay to London in 1794. The Jeffersonians were acutely unhappy over the choice, partly because they feared that so notorious a Federalist and Britain-lover would sell out his country. Arriving in London, Jay gave the Jeffersonians further cause for alarm when, at the presentation ceremony, he routinely kissed the queen's hand.

Unhappily, Jay entered the negotiations with weak cards, which were further weakened by Hamilton. The latter, fearful of war with Britain, secretly supplied the British with the details of America's bargaining strategy. Not surprisingly, Jay won few concessions. The British did promise to evacuate the chain of posts on U.S. soil—a pledge that inspired little confidence, since it had been made before in Paris (to the same John Jay!) in 1783. In addition, Britain consented to pay damages for the recent seizures of American ships. But the British stopped short of pledging anything about *future* maritime seizures and impressments, or about supplying arms to Indians. And they forced Jay to give ground by binding the young nation to pay the debts still owed to British merchants on pre-Revolutionary accounts.

When the Jeffersonians learned of Jay's concessions, their rage was fearful to behold. The treaty seemed like an abject surrender to Britain, as well as a betrayal of the Jeffersonian South. Southern planters would have to pay the major share of the pre-Revolutionary debts, while rich Federalist shippers were collecting damages for recent British seizures. Jeffersonian mobs hanged, burned, and guillotined in effigy that "damn'd archtraitor, Sir John Jay." His unpopular pact, more than any other issue, vitalized the newborn Democratic-Republican party of Thomas Jefferson.

Jay's treaty had other unforeseen consequences. Fearing that the treaty foreshadowed an Anglo-American alliance, Spain moved hastily to strike a deal with the United States. Pinckney's treaty of 1795 granted the Americans virtually everything they demanded, including free navigation of the Mis-

American Posts Held by the British After 1783

sissippi and the large disputed territory north of Florida.

Exhausted after the diplomatic and partisan battles of his second term, President Washington decided to retire. His choice contributed powerfully to establishing a two-term tradition for American presidents.* In his farewell address to the nation in 1796, Washington strongly advised the avoidance of "permanent alliances" like the still-vexatious French Treaty of 1778. Contrary to general misunderstanding, Washington did not oppose all alliances, but favored only "temporary alliances" for "extraordinary emergencies."

Washington's contributions as president were enormous, even though the sparkling Hamilton at times seemed to outshine him. The central government, its fiscal feet now under it, was solidly established. The West was expanding. The merchant marine was plowing the seas. Above all, Washington had kept the nation out of both overseas entanglements and foreign wars. The experimental stage had passed and the presidential chair could now be turned over to a less impressive figure. But republics are notoriously ungrateful. When Washington left office in 1797, he was showered with the brickbats of partisan abuse, quite in contrast with the bouquets that had greeted his coming.

"Bonny Johnny" Adams Becomes President

Who should succeed the exalted "Father of His Country"? Alexander Hamilton was the best-known Federalist now that Washington had bowed out. But his financial policies, some of which had fattened the speculators, had made him so unpopular that he could not hope to be elected president. The Federalists were forced to turn to the experienced but ungracious vice president John Adams, a rugged chip off old Plymouth Rock. The Democratic-

Republicans rallied behind their master organizer and leader, Thomas Jefferson.

Political passions ran feverishly high in the presidential campaign of 1796. The presence of Washington had hitherto imposed some restraints on partisan attacks; now the lid was off. Cultured Federalists referred to the Jeffersonians as "fire-eating salamanders, poison-sucking toads." Federalists and Democratic-Republicans even drank their liquor in separate taverns. The Jeffersonians again assailed the too-forceful crushing of the Whiskey Rebellion and, above all, the negotiation of Jay's hated treaty.

John Adams, with most of his support in New England, squeezed through by the narrow margin of 71 votes to 68 in the Electoral College. Jefferson, as runner-up, became vice president.*

One of the ablest statesmen of his day, Adams at sixty-two was sharp-featured, bald, short (5 feet 7 inches), and thickset ("His Rotundity"). He impressed observers as a man of stern principles who did his duty with stubborn devotion. Although learned and upright, he was a tactless and prickly intellectual aristocrat, with no appeal to the masses and no desire to cultivate any. Many citizens regarded him with "respectful irritation."

The crusty New Englander suffered from other handicaps. He had stepped into Washington's shoes, which no successor could hope to fill. In addition, Adams was hated by Hamilton, who had resigned from the Treasury in 1795 and now headed the war faction of the Federalist party. The famed financier even secretly plotted with certain members of the cabinet against the president, who had a conspiracy rather than a cabinet on his hands. Most ominous of all, Adams inherited a violent quarrel with France— a quarrel that foreshadowed blazing gunpowder.

Unofficial Fighting with France

The French were infuriated by Jay's treaty. They condemned it as the initial step toward an American

---

* Not broken until 1940 by Franklin D. Roosevelt, and made a part of the Constitution in 1951 by the Twenty-second Amendment. (See the text of the Constitution in Appendix.)

* The possibility of such an inharmonious two-party combination in the future was removed by the Twelfth Amendment to the Constitution in 1804. (See text in Appendix.)

Preparation for War to Defend Commerce   *The building of the frigate* Philadelphia. *In 1803 this frigate ran onto the rocks near Tripoli harbor, and about 300 officers and men were imprisoned by the Tripolitans. The ship was refloated for service against the Americans, but Stephen Decatur led a party of men that set it afire.*

alliance with Britain, their relentless foe. French warships, in retaliation, began to seize defenseless American merchant vessels, altogether about 300 by mid-1797.

President Adams kept his head, temporarily, even though the nation was mightily aroused. Trying to reach an agreement with the French, he appointed a diplomatic commission of three men, including John Marshall, the future chief justice. When they reached Paris in 1797, Adams's envoys were secretly approached by three French go-betweens, later referred to as X, Y, and Z in the published dispatches. The French spokesmen demanded an unneutral loan of 32 million florins, plus what amounted to a bribe of $250,000 for the privilege of merely talking with Talleyrand, the French foreign minister.

These terms were intolerable. The American trio knew that bribes were standard diplomatic devices in Europe, but they gagged at paying a quarter of a million dollars for mere talk, without any assurances of a settlement. Negotiations quickly broke down.

War hysteria swept through the United States, catching up President Adams. The slogan of the hour became "Millions for defense, but not one cent for tribute." Despite considerable Jeffersonian opposition in Congress, war preparations were pushed along at a feverish pace. The Navy Department was created; the three-ship navy was expanded; the United States Marine Corps was established.

Bloodshed was confined to the sea, and principally to the West Indies. In two and one-half years of undeclared hostilities (1798–1800), American privateers and men-of-war of the new navy captured over eighty armed vessels flying the French colors, though several hundred Yankee merchantmen were lost to the enemy. Evidently only a slight push would plunge both nations into a full-dress war.

Adams Puts Patriotism Above Party

Embattled France, her hands full in Europe, wanted no war. An outwitted Talleyrand realized that to fight the United States would add one more foe to his enemies. The British, who were lending the Americans cannon and other war supplies, were actually driven closer to their wayward cousins than they were to be again for many years. Talleyrand therefore let it be known, through roundabout channels, that if the Americans would send a new minister, he would be received with proper respect.

Adams unexpectedly exploded a bombshell when, early in 1799, he submitted to the Senate the name of a new minister to France. Hamilton and his war-hawk faction were enraged. But public opinion—Jeffersonian and reasonable Federalist alike—was favorable to one last try for peace.

America's envoys (now three) found the political skies brightening when they reached Paris early in 1800. The ambitious "Little Corporal," the Corsican Napoleon Bonaparte, had recently seized dictatorial power. He was eager to free his hands of the American squabble so that he might continue to redraw the map of Europe, and perhaps create a New World empire in Louisiana. The distresses and ambitions of the Old World were again working to America's advantage.

After much haggling, a memorable treaty known as the Convention of 1800 was signed in Paris. France agreed to grant a divorce from the twenty-two-year-old marriage of (in)convenience, but as a kind of alimony the United States agreed to pay the damage claims of American shippers. So ended the nation's only peacetime military alliance for a century and a half. Its troubled history does much to explain the traditional antipathy of the American people to foreign entanglements.

Adams, flinty to the end, deserves immense credit for his belated push for peace, even though

moved in part by jealousy of Hamilton. He not only avoided the hazards of war but unwittingly smoothed the path for the peaceful purchase of Louisiana three years later. If America had drifted into a full-blown war with France in 1800, Napoleon would not have been willing to sell Louisiana on any terms in 1803.

President Adams, the bubble of his popularity pricked by peace, was aware of his signal contribution to the nation. He later suggested as the epitaph for his tombstone (not used): "Here lies John Adams, who took upon himself the responsibility of peace with France in the year 1800."

The Federalist Witch Hunt

Exulting Federalists had meanwhile capitalized on the anti-French frenzy to drive through Congress in 1798 a sheaf of laws designed to reduce or gag their Jeffersonian foes.

The first of these oppressive laws was aimed at supposedly pro-Jeffersonian "aliens." The Federalist Congress, hoping to discourage the "dregs" of Europe, erected a disheartening barrier. They raised the residence requirements for aliens who desired to become citizens from a tolerable five years to a severely restrictive fourteen. This drastic new law violated the traditional American policy of open-door hospitality and speedy assimilation.

Two additional Alien Laws struck heavily at undesirable immigrants. The president was empowered to deport dangerous foreigners in time of peace, and to deport or imprison them in time of hostilities. This was an arbitrary grant of power contrary to American tradition and to the spirit of the Constitution, even though the stringent Alien Laws were never enforced.

The "lockjaw" Sedition Act, the last of the harsh Federalist measures, was a direct slap at two priceless freedoms guaranteed in the Constitution by the Bill of Rights—freedom of speech and freedom of the press (First Amendment). This law provided that anyone who impeded the policies of the government or falsely defamed its officials, including the president, would be liable to a heavy fine and imprisonment. Severe though the measure was, the Federalists believed that it was justified. The verbal violence of the day was unrestrained, and foul-penned editors, some of them exiled aliens, assailed Adams's anti-French policy in vicious terms.

Many outspoken Jeffersonian editors were indicted under the Sedition Act, and ten were brought to full trial. All of them were convicted, often by packed juries swayed by prejudiced Federalist judges.

The Sedition Act, at least in spirit, was in direct conflict with the Constitution. But the Supreme Court, dominated by Federalists, was of no mind to declare this Federalist law unconstitutional. (The law expired, in March 1801, to much rejoicing from Jeffersonians.) This high-handed attempt by the Federalists to crush free speech and silence the opposition party undoubtedly made many converts for the Jeffersonian cause.

Yet the Alien and Sedition Acts, despite pained outcries from the Jeffersonians, commanded widespread popular support. Anti-French hysteria played directly into the hands of witch-hunting conservatives. In the congressional elections of 1798–1799, the Federalists, riding a wave of popularity, scored the most sweeping victory of their entire history.

The Virginia (Madison) and Kentucky (Jefferson) Resolutions

Resentful Jeffersonians naturally refused to take the Alien and Sedition Acts lying down. Jefferson himself feared that if the Federalists managed to choke free speech and free press, they would then wipe out other precious constitutional guarantees. His own fledgling political party might even be stamped out of existence.

Fearing prosecution for sedition, Jefferson secretly wrote a series of resolutions, which the Kentucky legislature approved in 1798 and 1799. His friend and fellow Virginian James Madison drafted a similar but less extreme statement, which was adopted by the Virginia legislature in 1798.

Both Jefferson and Madison stressed the compact theory—a theory popular among English political philosophers in the seventeenth and eighteenth centuries. As applied to America by the Jeffersonians, this concept meant that the thirteen sovereign states, in creating the federal government, had entered into a "compact," or contract, regarding its jurisdiction. The national government was consequently the agent or creation of the states. Because water can rise no higher than its source, the individual states were the final judges of whether their agent had broken the "compact" by overstepping the authority originally granted. Invoking this logic, Jefferson's Kentucky resolutions concluded that the federal regime had exceeded its constitutional powers, and that with regard to the Alien and Sedition Acts "nullification" was the "rightful remedy."

No other state legislatures, despite Jefferson's hopes, fell into line. Some of them flatly refused to endorse the Virginia and Kentucky resolutions. Others, chiefly in Federalist states, added ringing condemnations. Many Federalists argued that the people, not the states, had made the original compact, and that it was up to the Supreme Court—not the states—to nullify unconstitutional legislation passed by Congress. This practice, though not specifically authorized by the Constitution, was finally adopted by the Supreme Court in 1803.

The Virginia and Kentucky resolutions were a brilliant formulation of the extreme states'-rights view regarding the Union. They were later used by southerners to support nullification—and ultimately secession. Yet neither Jefferson nor Madison, as founding fathers of the Union, had any intention of breaking it up: they were groping for ways to preserve it. Their resolutions were basically campaign documents designed to crystallize opposition to the Federalist party and to unseat it in the upcoming presidential election of 1800. The only real nullification that Jefferson had in view was the nullification of Federalist abuses.

Federalists versus Democratic-Republicans

As the presidential contest of 1800 approached, the differences between Federalists and Democratic-Republicans were sharply etched. As might be expected, federalists of the pre-Constitutional period (1787–1789) became Federalists in the 1790s. Largely welded by Hamilton into an effective group by 1793, they openly advocated rule by the "best people." "Those who own the country," remarked

John Jay, "ought to govern it." With their intellectual arrogance and Tory tastes, Hamiltonians distrusted full-blown democracy as the fountain of all mischiefs and feared the "swayability" of the untutored common folk.

Federalists also advocated a strong central government with the power to crush democratic excesses like Shays's Rebellion, protect the lives and estates of the wealthy, and subordinate the sovereignty-loving states. They believed the national government should support private enterprise, not interfere with it. This attitude came naturally to the seaboard merchants, manufacturers, and shippers who made up the majority of Federalist support. If a gunner had fired cannonballs 50 miles inland, he would have hit few Hamiltonians.

Federalists were also pro-British in foreign affairs. Many of them still harbored mildly Loyalist sentiments from revolutionary days and saw foreign trade with Britain as a key to the success of Hamilton's financial policies.

Leading the anti-Federalists, who eventually came to be known as Democratic-Republicans or sometimes simply Republicans, was Thomas Jefferson. Lanky and relaxed in appearance, lacking personal aggressiveness, weak-voiced and unable to deliver a rabble-rousing speech, he became a master political organizer through his ability to lead men rather than drive them. His strongest appeal was to the middle class and to the underprivileged—the "dirt" farmers, the laborers, the artisans, and the small shopkeepers.

Liberal-thinking Jefferson, with his aristocratic head set on a farmer's frame, was a bundle of inconsistencies. By one set of tests he should have been a Federalist, for he was a Virginia aristocrat and slave-owner who lived in an imposing hilltop mansion at Monticello. A so-called traitor to his upper class, Jefferson cherished uncommon sympathy for the common people, especially the down-trodden, the oppressed, and the persecuted. As he wrote in 1800, "I have sworn upon the altar of God eternal hostility against every form of tyranny over the mind of man."

Jeffersonian Democratic-Republicans demanded a weak central regime. They believed that the best government was one that governed least, and that the bulk of power should be retained by the

Monticello, Jefferson's Self-Designed Architectural Marvel

states. There the people could keep a more vigilant eye on their public servants. The national debt should be paid off, and government should provide no special privileges for special classes, especially manufacturers. Agriculture, to Jefferson, was the favored branch of the economy. He regarded farming as essentially ennobling; it kept people away from wicked cities and close to the sod. Most of his followers naturally came from the agricultural South and Southwest.

Above all, Jefferson advocated the rule of the people. But he did not propose thrusting the ballot into the hands of *every* adult white male. He favored government *for* the people, but not by *all* the people. Since the ignorant were incapable of self-government, only those literate enough to inform themselves about citizenship should have the ballot. Universal education would have to precede universal suffrage. Jefferson had a profound faith in the reasonableness and teachableness of the masses and in their collective wisdom once taught. His enduring appeal was to America's better self.

The open-minded Jefferson championed free speech, because without free speech the misdeeds of tyranny could not be exposed. Although he suffered foul abuse from the Federalist press, he said that he would choose "newspapers without a government" rather than "a government without newspapers."

Jeffersonian Democratic-Republicans, unlike the Federalist "British boot lickers," were basically pro-French. They believed that it was to America's advantage to support the liberal ideals of the French Revolution, rather than applaud the reaction of the British Tories.

So as the young republic's first full decade of nationhood came to a close, the founders' hopes seemed already imperiled. Conflicts over domestic politics and foreign policy undermined the unity of the revolutionary era and called into question the very survivability of the American democracy. As the presidential election of 1800 approached, the danger loomed that the fragile and battered American ship of state would founder on the rocks of controversy. The shores of history are littered with the wreckage of nascent nations torn asunder before they could grow to stable maturity. Why should the United States expect to enjoy a happier fate?

CHRONOLOGY

1798	Constitution formally put into effect.
	Judiciary Act of 1789.
	Washington elected president.
	French Revolution begins.
1790	First official census.
1791	Bill of Rights adopted.
	Vermont becomes fourteenth state.
	Bank of the United States created.
	Excise tax passed.
1792–1793	Federalist and Democratic-Republican parties formed.
1793	Louis XVI beheaded; radical phase of French Revolution.
	Washington's Neutrality Proclamation.
1794	Whiskey Rebellion.
	Battle of Fallen Timbers.
	Jay's treaty with Britain.
1795	Treaty of Greenville: Indians cede Ohio.
	Pinckney's treaty with Spain.
1796	Washington's farewell address.
1797	Adams becomes president.
	XYZ Affair.
1798	Alien and Sedition Acts.
1798–1799	Kentucky and Virginia resolutions.
1798–1800	Undeclared war with France.
1800	Convention of 1800: peace with France.

Varying Viewpoints

Underlying all debates about the so-called federalist era of the 1790s is one fundamental question: what allowed the United States, barely a nation in anything more than name at the conclusion of the Revolutionary War, to survive the explosive conflicts of its first decade and emerge as a coherent, viable polity? The earliest students of the period emphasized the philosophical differences between Hamiltonians and Jeffersonians and simply presumed that democratic (that is, Jeffersonian) ideas were destined to predominate.

This high-minded approach was challenged in

the early years of the twentieth century by historians who stressed the economic rivalries at the root of federalist-age political debates. They saw the Hamiltonian-Jeffersonian dispute over political principles as a smokescreen for battles between creditors and debtors, commercial interests and agrarian interests, and northern merchants and southern planters. In this view, it was not so much democracy, but capitalism, that inevitably triumphed.

More recent students have swung the pendulum back toward ideological factors. Scholars such as Drew McCoy and Lance Banning see the turmoil as a continuation of the debate over the meaning of republicanism that gave rise to the Revolution and the Constitution. But later scholarship emphasizes that virtually all participants in that debate believed in some version of republican values. Thus, in this view, the new nation survived the *apparent* divisiveness of the 1790s because *all* parties were, at bottom, republicans. Following this line of argument leads to a deeper question: what factors in the earlier revolutionary era, or even before, had so "republicanized" American thinking?

SELECT READINGS

Primary Source Documents

"The Report on Manufactures" (in Daniel Boorstin, ed., *American Primer*), the last of Alexander Hamilton's messages to Congress, presented the case for the development of American industry. Thomas Jefferson expounded his views in *Notes on the State of Virginia* (1784). For further study of the Hamiltonian-Jeffersonian debate, see Henry Cabot Lodge, ed., *The Works of Alexander Hamilton** (1904), and Paul L. Ford, ed., *The Writings of Thomas Jefferson** (1985). Important salvos in the battle between national power and state sovereignty, and between Federalists and Jeffersonians, were the Virginia and Kentucky resolutions* (1798) and the reply of Rhode Island* (1799). Washington's farewell address* (1796) established the foundation for American attitudes about party politics and foreign policy. See also Benjamin Franklin Bache's stinging editorial on Washington's retirement, Philadelphia *Aurora** (1797).

Secondary Sources

Perceptive introductions are provided by Marcus Cunliffe's succinct *The Nation Takes Shape, 1789–1837* (1959) and John C. Miller's more detailed *The Federalist Era, 1789–1801* (1960). For the origins of party politics, see William N. Chambers, *Political Parties in the New Nation* (1963), and Richard Hofstadter's thoughtful *The Idea of a Party System* (1969). Among the new interpretations of that subject, stressing the ideology of republicanism, are Drew McCoy, *The Elusive Republic: Political Economy in Jeffersonian America* (1980), and Lance Banning, *The Jeffersonian Persuasion* (1978). For a trenchant analysis of Jeffersonianism, see Joyce Appleby, *Capitalism and a New Social Order: The Republican Vision* (1984). Also illuminating is Gerald Stourzh, *Alexander Hamilton and the Idea of Republican Government* (1970). Thomas P. Slaughter focuses on *The Whiskey Rebellion: Frontier Epilogue to the American Revolution* (1986). A comprehensive biography is James T. Flexner, *George Washington and the New Nation, 1783–1793* (1969). Consult also Forrest McDonald, *The Presidency of George Washington* (1974), and Garry Wills, *Cincinnatus: George Washington and the Enlightenment* (1984). Of special interest is Richard H. Kohn, *Eagle and Sword: The Federalists and the Creation of the Military Establishment in America, 1783–1802* (1975). On Adams, consult Page Smith, *John Adams* (2 vols.) (1962), and Stephen G. Kurtz, *The Presidency of John Adams* (1957). John C. Miller, *Crisis in Freedom* (1951), and James M. Smith, *Freedom's Fetters* (1956), treat the Alien and Sedition Acts, as does Leonard Levy, *Legacy of Suppression* (1960).

CHAPTER 11

The Triumph of Jeffersonian Democracy, 1800–1809

Timid men . . . prefer the calm of despotism to the boisterous sea of liberty.

Thomas Jefferson, 1796

Federalist and Democratic-Republican Mudslingers

In the critical presidential contest of 1800, Adams and Jefferson were again the standard bearers of their respective parties. The Federalists labored under heavy handicaps. Their Alien and Sedition Acts had aroused a host of enemies, although most of them were dyed-in-the-wool Jeffersonians.

The most damaging blow to the Federalists, however, was the refusal of Adams to give them a rousing fight with France. Their feverish war preparations had swelled the public debt and required disagreeable new taxes, including a stamp tax. After all these unpopular measures, the war scare had petered out, and the country was left with an all-dressed-up-but-no-place-to-go feeling.

Thrown on the defensive, the Federalists concentrated their fire on Jefferson himself, who became the victim of one of America's earliest "whispering campaigns." He was accused of having robbed a widow and her children of a trust fund and of having fathered numerous mulatto children by his own slave women. As a liberal in religion, Jefferson had earlier incurred the wrath of the orthodox clergy, largely through his successful struggle to separate church and state in Virginia. From the New England stronghold of Federalism and Congregationalism, the preachers thundered against his "atheism," although he believed in God. Old ladies of Federalist families, fearing Jefferson's election, even buried their Bibles or hung them in wells.

The Jeffersonian "Revolution of 1800"

Jefferson won by a majority of seventy-three electoral votes to sixty-five. But the austere and presumably unpopular Adams polled more electoral strength than he had gained four years earlier—except for New York. The Empire State fell into the Jeffersonian basket, and with it the election, largely because Aaron Burr, a master wire puller, turned New York to Jefferson by the narrowest of margins. The Vir-

The Providential Detection (Federalist Propaganda) *The American eagle snatches the Constitution from Jefferson, who is about to burn it (together with the works of Voltaire, Paine, and others) on the altar to French Revolutionary despotism.*

ginian polled the bulk of his strength in the South and West, particularly in states where manhood suffrage had been adopted.

Jeffersonians rejoiced wildly over the end of the "Federalist Reign of Terror." Some of them, with alcoholic enthusiasm, bawled the song "Jefferson and Liberty":

> Lord! how the Federalists will stare
> At Jefferson, in Adams's chair!

But Jeffersonian joy was dampened by an unexpected deadlock. Through a technicality Jefferson, the presidential candidate, and Burr, his vice-presidential running mate, received the same number of electoral votes for the presidency. Under the Constitution the tie could be broken only by the House of Representatives (see Art. II, Sec. I, para. 2).

This body was controlled for several more months by the lame duck Federalists, who had been swept into office during the French war scare and who were eager to elect Burr.*

Voting in the House moved slowly to a climax. As ballots were taken in wearisome succession, representatives snored in their seats. The deadlock was broken when a few Federalists, despairing of electing Burr and hoping for moderation from Jefferson,

---

* A "lame duck" has been humorously defined as a politician whose political goose has been cooked at the recent elections. The possibility of another such tie was removed by the Twelfth Amendment in 1804 (for text, see Appendix). Before then, each elector had two votes, with the second-place finisher becoming vice president.

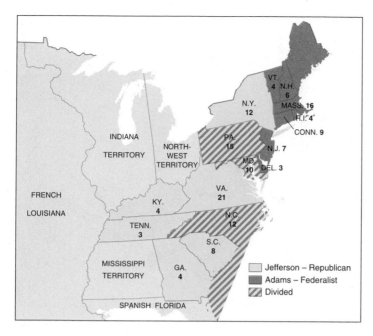

Presidential Election of 1800 (with electoral vote by state) *New York was the key state in this election, and Aaron Burr helped to swing it away from the Federalists with tactics that anticipated the political machines of a later day. Federalists complained that Burr "travels every night from one meeting of Republicans to another, haranguing . . . them to the most zealous exertions. [He] can stoop so low as to visit every low tavern that may happen to be crowded with his dear fellow citizens." But Burr proved that the price was worth it. "We have beat you," Burr told kid-gloved Federalists after the election, "by superior Management."*

refrained from voting. The election then went to the rightful candidate.

Jefferson later claimed that the election of 1800 was a "revolution" comparable to that of 1776. But it was no revolution in the sense of a massive popular upheaval or an upending of the political system. What *was* revolutionary was the peaceful and orderly transfer of power on the basis of an election whose results all parties accepted. This was a remarkable achievement for a raw young nation, especially after all the partisan bitterness that had agitated the country during Adams's presidency. Americans could take justifiable pride in the vigor of their experiment in democracy.

The Federalist Finale

John Adams proved to be the last Federalist president. His party sank slowly into the mire of political oblivion and ultimately disappeared completely in the days of Andrew Jackson.

Whatever their shortcomings, the Federalists were a party of the elite. They boasted a high concentration of brains, talent, and ability. Their political and financial leaders had built enduring foundations for the new government. Their diplomats, with

a strong helping hand from Europe's distresses, had signed advantageous treaties with Britain, Spain, and France. Their leaders had kept the peace during a crucial period when peace had to be kept.

After all the turmoil of the American Revolution, a conservative party served a valuable function in preserving democratic gains and fending off anarchy. The Federalists provided a welcome breathing spell, a chance for the nation to get its bearings. They served, in the words of historian Henry Adams, great-grandson of John Adams, as the "half-way house between the European past and the American future."

But by 1800 the Federalists, blessed with more talent than wisdom, were out of place. The bustling new republic knew instinctively where it was going. It was eager to take the high road over the mountains that would one day lead to the fulfillment of its democratic experiment. The Federalists lost out because they were content to mark time and failed to get in step with the westward march of progress. They were unable or unwilling to unbend and appeal to the common people. They could not adapt—so they died, like the dinosaur. Distinguished though their past service had been, it was no substitute for a capacity to grapple democratically with future problems. The victorious Jeffersonians were prepared to keep the Federalist edifice while ousting the Federalist architects.

Responsibility Breeds Moderation

"Long Tom" Jefferson was inaugurated president on March 4, 1801, in the swampy village of Washington, the crude new national capital. Tall (6 feet 2 inches), with large hands and feet, reddish hair ("the Red Fox"), and prominent cheekbones and chin, he was an arresting figure. Believing that the customary pomp did not befit his democratic ideals, he spurned a horse-drawn coach and simply walked over to the Capitol from his boarding house.

The inaugural address, beautifully phrased, was a classic statement of democratic principles. Seeking to allay Federalist fears of a bull-in-the-china-closet overturn, Jefferson calmly stated, "We are all Republicans, we are all Federalists." As for foreign affairs, he pledged "honest friendship with all nations, entangling alliances with none."

With its rustic setting, Washington lent itself admirably to the simplicity and frugality of the Jeffersonian Democratic-Republicans. In this respect, it contrasted sharply with the elegant atmosphere of Federalist Philadelphia, the former, temporary capital.

As a widower, Jefferson was shockingly unconventional. He would receive callers in sloppy attire—once in a dressing gown and slippers. He also began the tradition, unbroken for 112 years, of sending messages to Congress to be read by a clerk. Personal appearances, in the Federalist manner, suggested too strongly a monarchical speech from the throne.

As if plagued by an evil spirit, Jefferson was forced to reverse many of the political principles he had so vigorously championed. There were in fact two Thomas Jeffersons. One was the private citizen and philosopher who developed brilliant ideas in his study. The other was the public official, who made the disturbing discovery that bookish theories worked out differently in the noisy arena of practical politics. The open-minded Virginian was therefore consistently inconsistent; it is easy to quote one Jefferson to refute the other.

Mad Tom in a Rage *A Federalist cartoon shows Jefferson, assisted by brandy and the devil, trying to pull down the federal edifice erected by Washington and Adams. Jefferson says that the federal government is stronger than he thought, while the devil assures his "son" that he will help.*

As a practical politician, Jefferson proved able and successful. He was especially effective in the informal atmosphere of a dinner party, where he wooed congressional representatives while personally pouring imported wines and serving French food.

In part, Jefferson had to rely on his charm because his party was so weak-jointed. Denied the power to dispense patronage, the disappointed Democratic-Republicans could not build a political following. Opposition to the Federalists was the chief glue holding them together, and as the Federalists faded, so did Democratic-Republican unity. The era of well-developed, well-disciplined political parties still lay in the future.

At the outset, Jefferson was determined to undo the Federalist abuses begotten by the anti-French hysteria. The hated Alien and Sedition Acts had already expired. The incoming president speedily pardoned the "martyrs" serving sentences under the Sedition Act, and the government returned many fines. Shortly after Congress met, the Jeffersonians enacted the new naturalization law of 1802, which reduced the unreasonable requirement of fourteen years of residence to five years.

Jefferson actually kicked away only one substantial prop of the Hamiltonian system. He hated the excise tax, which bred bureaucrats and bore heavily on his farmer following, and he early persuaded Congress to repeal it.

Except for excising the excise tax, the Jeffersonians left the Hamiltonian framework essentially intact. They launched no attack on the Bank of the United States, and they did not repeal the mildly protective Federalist tariff.

Paradoxically, Jefferson's moderation thus further cemented the gains of the "Revolution of 1800." That revolution had consisted above all in the peaceful replacement of one governing party by another. By shrewdly absorbing many major Federalist programs, Jefferson showed that a change of regime need not be disastrous for the defeated group. His restraint pointed the way toward the two-party system that was later to become a characteristic feature of American politics.

The "Dead Clutch" of the Judiciary

The "deathbed" Judiciary Act of 1801 was one of the last important laws passed by the expiring Federalist Congress. It created sixteen new federal judgeships and other judicial offices. President Adams remained at his desk until nine o'clock in the evening of his last day in office, allegedly signing the commissions of the Federalist "midnight judges." (Actually only three commissions were signed on his last day.)

This Federalist-sponsored Judiciary Act, though a long-overdue reform, aroused bitter resentment. "Packing" of these lifetime posts with anti-Jeffersonian partisans was, in Democratic-Republican eyes, a brazen attempt by the defeated party to entrench itself in one of the three powerful branches of government. Jeffersonians condemned the midnight judges in violent language.

The newly elected Democratic-Republican Congress bestirred itself to repeal the Judiciary Act of 1801 in the year after its passage. Jeffersonians thus swept sixteen benches from under the recently appointed midnight judges.

Jeffersonians likewise had their knives sharpened for the scalp of Chief Justice John Marshall, whom Adams had appointed to the Supreme Court in the dying days of his term. The lanky Marshall, with his rasping voice and steel trap mind, was a cousin of Thomas Jefferson. As a Virginia Federalist, he was cordially disliked by the states'-rights Jeffersonians. He served for about thirty days under a Federalist administration, and thirty-four years under the administrations of the Jeffersonian Democratic-Republicans and their successors. The Federalist party died out, but Marshall went on handing down Federalist decisions serenely for many more years. He probably did more than Hamilton to engraft the Hamiltonian concept of a powerful central government upon the American political and economic system.

One of the midnight judges of 1801 presented John Marshall with a historic opportunity. When obscure William Marbury, whom President Adams had named a justice of the peace for the District of Columbia, learned that his commission was being held up by Secretary of State James Madison, he sued for its delivery. Chief Justice John Marshall knew that his Jeffersonian rivals, entrenched in the executive branch, would hardly spring forward to enforce a writ to deliver the commission to his fellow Federalist Marbury. He therefore dismissed Marbury's suit, avoiding a direct showdown. But the wily Marshall snatched a victory from the jaws of this judicial defeat. In explaining his ruling, Marshall said that the part of the Judiciary Act of 1789 on which Marbury tried to base his appeal was unconstitutional. The act had attempted to assign to the Supreme Court powers that the Constitution had not foreseen.

In this self-denying opinion, Marshall greatly magnified the authority of the Court—and slapped at the Jeffersonians. Until the case of *Marbury* v. *Madison* (1803), controversy had clouded the question of who had the final authority to determine the meaning of the Constitution. Jefferson in the Kentucky resolutions (1798) had tried to assign that right to the individual states. But now his cousin on the Court had cleverly promoted the contrary principle of "judicial review"—that the black-robed tribunal of the Supreme Court alone had the last word on the question of constitutionality. In this epochal case, Marshall inserted the keystone into the arch that supports the tremendous power of the Supreme Court in American life.*

The Pacifist Jefferson Turns Warrior

As a passionate champion of freedom, Jefferson distrusted large standing armies as an invitation to dictatorship. Trusting the ill-trained militia, Jefferson reduced the military establishment to a mere police force of 2,500 officers and men. The navy was also reduced to a peacetime footing.

But harsh realities forced a penny-pinching Jefferson to change his tune on navies and war. Pirates of the North African states had long made a national industry of blackmailing and plundering merchant ships that ventured into the Mediterranean. Preceding Federalist administrations had been forced to buy protection. At the time of the French crisis of 1798, when Americans were shouting, "Millions for defense, but not one cent for tribute," twenty-six barrels of blackmail dollars were being shipped to Algiers.

The showdown came in 1801. The Pasha of Tripoli, dissatisfied with his share of protection money, informally declared war on the United States by cutting down the flagstaff of the American consulate. A challenge was thus thrown squarely into the face of Jefferson—the noninterventionist, the pacifist, the critic of a big-ship navy, and the political foe of Federalist shippers. He reluctantly rose to the

occasion by dispatching the infant navy to "the shores of Tripoli," as related in the song of the U.S. Marine Corps. After four years of intermittent fighting, marked by hair-raising exploits, Jefferson succeeded in extorting a treaty of peace from Tripoli in 1805. It was secured at the bargain price of only $60,000—a sum representing ransom payments for captured Americans.

The Louisiana Godsend

A secret pact, fraught with peril for America, was signed in 1800. Napoleon Bonaparte induced the king of Spain to cede to France, for attractive considerations, the immense trans-Mississippi region of Louisiana, which included the New Orleans area.

Rumors of the transfer were partially confirmed in 1802, when the Spaniards at New Orleans withdrew the right of deposit guaranteed America by the treaty of 1795. Deposit privileges were vital to frontier farmers who floated their produce down the Mississippi to its mouth, there to await oceangoing vessels. A roar of anger rolled up the mighty river and into its tributary valleys. American pioneers talked wildly of descending upon New Orleans, rifles in hand.

Thomas Jefferson, both pacifist and anti-entanglement, was again on the griddle. Louisiana in the grip of Spain posed no real threat; America could seize the territory when the time was ripe. But Louisiana in the iron fist of Napoleon, the preeminent military genius of his age, foreshadowed a dark and blood-drenched future.

Hoping to quiet the clamor of the West, Jefferson moved decisively. Early in 1803 he sent James Monroe to Paris to join forces with the regular minister there, Robert R. Livingston. The two envoys were instructed to buy New Orleans and as much land to the east as they could get for a maximum of $10 million.

At this critical juncture, Napoleon suddenly decided to sell all Louisiana and abandon his dream of a New World empire. Two developments prompted his change of mind. First, he had failed to reconquer the sugar-rich island of Santo Domingo, for which Louisiana was to serve as a granary. Infuriated ex-slaves, ably led by a gifted black revolution-

---

* The next invalidation of a federal law by the Supreme Court came fifty-four years later with the explosive Dred Scott decision (see pp. 286–287).

ary, Toussaint L'Ouverture, had put up a stubborn resistance. Santo Domingo could not be reconquered, except perhaps at a staggering cost. Second, Bonaparte was about to end the twenty-month lull in his deadly conflict with Britain. Because the British controlled the seas, he feared that he might be forced to make them a gift of Louisiana. Rather than drive America into the arms of Britain by attempting to hold the area, he decided to sell the huge wilderness to the Americans and pocket the money for his schemes nearer home. Napoleon hoped that the United States, strengthened by Louisiana, would one day grow up to be a military and naval power that would thwart the ambitions of the lordly British in the New World. The distresses of France in Europe were again paving the way for America's diplomatic successes.

Events now moved dizzily. Suddenly, out of a clear sky, the French foreign minister asked the American minister Livingston how much he would give for all Louisiana. Scarcely able to believe his ears (he was partially deaf anyhow), Livingston nervously entered upon the negotiations. After about a week of haggling, the treaties were signed on April 30, 1803, ceding Louisiana to the United States for about $15 million.

Out-Federalizing the Federalists in Louisiana

When the news of the bargain reached America, Jefferson was startled. He had authorized his envoys to offer not more than $10 million for New Orleans, and as much to the *east* in the Floridas as they could get. Instead, they had signed three treaties that pledged $15 million for New Orleans and a vast wilderness entirely to the *west*—an area that would more than double the United States. They had bought a wilderness to get a city.

Once again the two Jeffersons wrestled with each other: the theorist and the former strict constructionist versus the realist and public official. Where in his beloved Constitution was the president authorized to negotiate treaties incorporating a huge new expanse into the Union—an expanse containing some 50,000 red, white, and black inhabitants?

There was no such clause. So Jefferson shamefacedly submitted the treaties to the Senate, while privately admitting that the purchase was unconstitutional.

The senators were less finicky than Jefferson. Reflecting enthusiastic public support, they registered their prompt approval of the transaction. Land-hungry Americans were not disposed to split constitutional hairs when confronted with perhaps the most magnificent real estate bargain in history—828,000 square miles at about three cents an acre.

What really worried the Federalists was that the signing of the Louisiana treaties was the signing of their own political death warrant. New states would be carved from the immense area—states that would out-vote the thirteen charter members, including Federalist New England. The Jeffersonian agrarians would then become unassailable. At Williams College in Massachusetts, a debating group voted fifteen to one that the purchase of Louisiana was undesirable. A few Federalist extremists even threatened to secede from the Union.

The purchase of Louisiana—the most glorious achievement of Jefferson as president—was a triumph for which neither he nor anyone else could claim much direct credit. Napoleon, for reasons purely selfish, dumped this rich prize into the laps of Livingston, Monroe, and Jefferson. Louisiana was so desirable that Jefferson found it less embarrassing to reverse himself on strict construction than to lose the magnificent windfall.

Louisiana in the Long View

Jefferson's bargain with France was epochal. By scooping up Louisiana, America secured at one bloodless stroke the western half of the richest river valley in the world, and further laid the foundations of a future major power. The ideal of a great agrarian democracy, as envisioned by Jefferson, would have elbowroom in the vast "Valley of Democracy." At the same time, the transfer established a precedent that was to be followed repeatedly: the acquisition of foreign territory and peoples by purchase.

The extent of the huge new area was more fully unveiled by a series of explorations under the direction of Jefferson. He was keenly interested in the unexplored natural treasures of his purchase. In the

Exploring the Louisiana Purchase and the West *Seeking to avert friction with France by purchasing all of Louisiana, Jefferson bought trouble because of the vagueness of the boundaries. The disputants included Spain in the Floridas, Spain and Mexico in the Southwest, and Great Britain in Canada.*

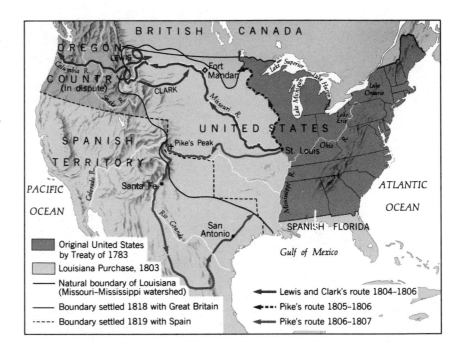

spring of 1804, Jefferson sent Meriwether Lewis and William Clark up the "Great Muddy" Missouri River through the Rockies to the mouth of the Columbia River. This hazardous venture into the uncharted western wilderness bolstered America's claim to Oregon, while further opening the West to trade and exploration. Zebulon M. Pike, in 1805–1806, explored the headwaters of the Mississippi River, and in 1807 ventured into the southern portion of the Louisiana territory.

Jefferson's reluctant purchase of Louisiana proved to be a landmark in American foreign policy. Overnight he avoided a possible rupture with France, and the consequent entangling alliance with Britain. The nation was thus able to continue the noninterventionist policies of the founding fathers, though it later quarreled with Spain and Britain over the vague boundaries of Louisiana, north, south, and west.

The Louisiana godsend likewise boosted national unity. Once-proud Federalists, now mere sectionalists, sank ever lower in public esteem as they were reduced to whining impotence. A few of their more extreme members attempted to plot with scheming Aaron Burr for the secession of New En-

gland and New York. But the intrigue failed, largely owing to the vigilance of Alexander Hamilton, who subsequently provoked Burr to a duel. The pistol with which Burr killed Hamilton in 1804 blew the brightest brain out of the Federalist party—and destroyed its one remaining hope of effective leadership.

A once restive West, which now toasted the "immortal Jefferson," was more securely riveted to the Union by the purchase. People of the western waters were grateful to the federal government for having safeguarded their interests, particularly in securing the mouth of the Mississippi. A new spirit of nationalism surged through the West.

Aaron Burr, turning his disunionist plottings to the trans-Mississippi West, was arrested in 1806 for treason. Tried the next year at Richmond, Virginia, he was freed after the presiding judge, Chief Justice Marshall, had infuriated the Jeffersonians by what seemed to be bias in favor of the accused. The government's case collapsed when two witnesses to the same overt act of treason could not be found, as required by the Constitution (see Art. III, Sec. III). Burr's schemes are still somewhat shrouded in mystery, but he apparently planned to separate the west-

Intercourse or Impartial Dealings *A cartoon by "Peter Pencil" (1809) shows Jefferson being victimized by both Britain (left) and France (right).*

ern part of the United States from the eastern and unite it with to-be-conquered Spanish territory west of the Louisiana Purchase. The very fact that so dashing a figure as Burr could muster only three-score followers was significant. It indicated, among other things, that the West was developing a deeper sense of loyalty to the Washington government.

America: A Nutcrackered Neutral

Jefferson was triumphantly reelected in 1804, with 162 electoral votes to only 14 for his Federalist opponent. His success was not so much due to republicanizing the Federalists, as he fondly supposed, as to federalizing the Democratic-Republicans. The iron hand of reality gradually forced him, quite unintentionally, to kill off the opposition party by stealing many of its principles and embracing them as his own. As was said, he caught the Federalists bathing and made off with their clothes.

But the laurels of Jefferson's first administration soon withered under the blasts of the new storm that broke in Europe. After unloading Louisiana in 1803, Napoleon deliberately provoked a renewal of his war with Britain—a conflict that crashed to an awesome close eleven years later.

For two years a maritime United States—the number one neutral carrier since 1793—enjoyed juicy commercial pickings. But a setback came in 1805. At the Battle of Trafalgar, Britain's Admiral Nelson achieved immortality by smashing the combined French and Spanish fleets off the coast of Spain, thereby ensuring Britain's supremacy on the seas. At the Battle of Austerlitz in Austria, Napoleon crushed the combined Austrian and Russian armies, thereby ensuring his mastery of the land. Like the tiger and the shark, France and Britain were supreme in their chosen elements.

Unable to hurt each other directly, the two antagonists were forced to strike indirect blows. Britain ruled the waves and waived the rules. The London government, beginning in 1806, issued a series of Orders in Council. These edicts closed the ports under French continental control to foreign shipping, including American, unless the vessels first stopped at a British port. There they would pay the necessary fees and, if acceptable, secure clearance papers. Napoleon struck back in a series of decrees.

In effect, they ordered the seizure of all merchant ships, including American, that entered British ports.

British Man Stealing

Even more galling to American pride than the seizure of wooden ships was the seizure of flesh-and-blood American seamen. Impressment—the forcible enlistment of sailors—was a crude form of conscription that the British, among others, had employed for over four centuries. Clubs and stretchers (for men knocked unconscious) were standard equipment of press-gangs from His Majesty's man-hungry ships.

The London authorities themselves set limits to this ugly practice. They claimed the right to impress only British subjects on their own soil, in their own harbors, or on merchant ships on the high seas. But many Americans looked like Britons, and the benefit of the doubt was seldom given to an experienced seaman in those short-handed days. The result was that some 6,000 bona fide U.S. citizens, according to the best estimates, were impressed by the "piratical man stealers" of Britain from 1808 to 1811 alone.

Britain had its back to the wall, and its desperate plight colored its views. The British feared that they would lose the war with Napoleon if they gave up the hoary method of conscription—and they would fight before they did. Their determination was highlighted in 1807 when a British warship, seeking deserters, fired on a U.S. frigate, the *Chesapeake,* killing three Americans and wounding eighteen. Infuriated Federalists and Democratic-Republicans alike now joined in an outburst of national wrath. Jefferson could easily have led a united nation into war, but he chose instead to use the *Chesapeake* outrage diplomatically to force the British to renounce impressment altogether, which they refused to do.

Jefferson's Backfiring Embargo

National honor would not permit a slavish submission to British and French mistreatment. Yet a large-scale foreign war was contrary to the settled policy of the new republic—and in addition it would be futile. The navy was weak, thanks largely to Jefferson's anti-

navalism; and the army was even weaker. A disastrous defeat would not improve America's plight.

The warring nations in Europe depended heavily upon the United States for raw materials and foodstuffs. In his eager search for an alternative to war, Jefferson seized upon this essential fact. He reasoned that if America voluntarily cut off its exports, the offending powers would be forced to come, hat in hand, and agree to respect U.S. rights.

Responding to the presidential lash, Congress hastily passed the Embargo Act late in 1807. This rigorous law forbade the export of all goods from the United States, whether in American or in foreign ships. It was a compromise between submission and shooting.

Jefferson, the onetime strict constructionist, had once more flip-flopped into the camp of the loose constructionists. In the interests of the Federalist shippers, whom he disliked, he was rereading the Constitution with strange bifocals. To him, it now meant that Congress, under its authority to "regulate" commerce, could go so far as to stop foreign trade altogether. Regulation thus became strangulation.

Federalist New England could well have prayed for relief from its newly found Virginia friend, "Mad Tom" Jefferson. Forests of dead masts gradually filled once-flourishing harbors; docks that had once rumbled were deserted (except for illegal trade); and soup kitchens cared for some of the hungry unemployed. Jeffersonian Democratic-Republicans probably hurt the commerce of New England, which they avowedly were trying to protect, far more than Britain and France together were doing.

Farmers of the South and West, the strongholds of Jefferson, suffered no less disastrously than New England. They were alarmed by the mounting piles of exportable cotton, grain, and tobacco. Tart-tongued John Randolph of Virginia remarked that enacting the embargo was like cutting off one's toes to cure one's corns. Jefferson in truth seemed to be waging war on his fellow citizens rather than on the offending belligerents.

The American people, from the days of the colonial Navigation Acts, have never submitted meekly to unpopular legislation. Though basically

The Ograbme (Embargo) *As a snapping turtle, it halts overseas shipments.*

law abiding, they habitually flout laws that are opposed by large numbers of the population. An enormous illicit trade mushroomed in 1808, especially along the Canadian border, where bands of armed Americans on loaded rafts overawed or overpowered federal agents. Irate citizens cynically transposed the letters of "embargo" to read "o grab me," "go bar 'em," and "mobrage," while they heartily denounced the "dambargo."

Jefferson nonetheless induced Congress to pass iron-toothed enforcing legislation. It was so inquisitorial and tyrannical as to cause some Americans to think more kindly of George III, whom Jefferson had berated in the Declaration of Independence. One indignant New Hampshire poet burst out in song:

> Our ships all in motion,
> Once whiten'd the ocean;
>   They sail'd and return'd with a cargo;
> Now doom'd to decay
>   They are fallen a prey,
> To Jefferson, worms, and EMBARGO.

New England seethed with talk of secession; and Jefferson later admitted that he felt the foundations of government tremble under his feet.

An alarmed Congress, bowing to the storm of public anger, finally repealed the embargo on March 1, 1809, three days before Jefferson's retirement. A half-loaf substitute was provided by the Non-Intercourse Act. This measure formally reopened trade with all the nations of the world, except the two most important, Britain and France. Though thus watered down, economic coercion continued to be the policy of the Jeffersonians from 1809 to 1812, when the nation finally plunged into war.

The Wooden Gun Embargo: A Successful Failure

Why did the embargo, Jefferson's most daring act of statesmanship, collapse after fifteen dismal months? First of all, the president underestimated the bulldog determination of the British, as others have, and overestimated their dependence on America's trade. Bumper grain crops blessed the British Isles during these years, and the revolutionary Latin American republics unexpectedly threw open their ports for compensating commerce.

The hated embargo was not continued long enough or tightly enough to achieve the desired results. But leaders must know the temper of their people, and Jefferson should have foreseen that such a self-crucifying weapon could not possibly command public support. The Americans, notoriously people of action, did not take kindly to the passive type of heroism. They much preferred commercial activity, with all its risks, to enforced inactivity, with no chance of profit.

A crestfallen Jefferson himself admitted that the embargo was three times more costly than war. The irony is that with only a fraction of its cost to the country, he could have built a fairly strong navy. Such a fighting force would have won more respect for American rights on the high seas, and might well have prevented the War of 1812.

The embargo further embroiled relations with both Britain and France. It embittered the British, partly because it hit them more forcibly than it did Napoleon. The French despot naturally applauded the embargo, for it was an indirect American blockade of his foe.

A stoppage of exports hurt Federalist shipping but temporarily revived the Federalist party. Gaining new converts, its leaders hurled their nullification of the embargo into the teeth of the "Virginia lordlings" in Washington. In 1804, the discredited Federalists had polled only 14 electoral votes out of 176; in 1808, the embargo year, the figure rose to 47 out of 175.

Curiously enough, New England plucked a new prosperity from the ugly jaws of the embargo. With shipping tied up and imported goods scarce, the resourceful Yankees reopened old factories and erected new ones. The real foundations of modern America's industrial might were laid behind the protective wall of the embargo, followed by nonintercourse and the War of 1812. Jefferson, the avowed critic of factories, may have unwittingly done more for American manufacturing than Alexander Hamilton, the outspoken friend of factories.

Jefferson's embargo, followed in modified form by nonintercourse, undeniably pinched Britain. Many British importers and manufacturers suffered severe losses, especially those dependent on American cotton. As thousands of factory workers were thrown out of jobs, agitation mounted for a repeal of the restrictions that had brought on the embargo. A

CHRONOLOGY	
1800	Jefferson defeats Adams for presidency.
1801	Jefferson inaugurated president.
	Judiciary Act of 1801.
1801–1805	Naval war with Tripoli.
1802	Revised naturalization law.
	Judiciary Act of 1801 repealed.
1803	*Marbury* v. *Madison.*
	Louisiana Purchase.
1804	Jefferson reelected.
1804–1806	Lewis and Clark expedition.
1805	Peace treaty with Tripoli.
1805–1806	Pike's explorations.
1806	Burr treason trial.
1807	*Chesapeake* affair.
	Embargo Act.
1809	Non-Intercourse Act replaces Embargo Act.

petition to Parliament in 1812, from the city of Birmingham alone, bore 20,000 names on a sheet of parchment 150 feet long. So strong was public pressure that two days before Congress declared war in June 1812 the British foreign secretary announced that the offensive Orders in Council would be immediately suspended. The supreme irony is that Jefferson's policy of economic coercion did win in the end, but America was not patient enough to wait for it to work and thus reap the reward of her sacrifices.

The Living Jefferson

Thomas Jefferson retained much of his popularity, even though it was severely tarnished by the embargo. One public toast ran: "May he receive from his fellow citizens the reward of his merit, a halter [hangman's noose]." But his grip on his party was such that he could easily have won a third nomination and election. The international crisis was still acute; and although Jefferson was sixty-five years old, he was mentally alert and physically vigorous. He lived eighteen more years, relieved to have escaped what he called the "splendid misery" of the presidential penitentiary.

Jefferson, rather than Washington, was the real father of the two-term tradition. Unlike the first president, who had no serious constitutional qualms, he feared that more than two terms might open the door to dictatorship. Yet Jefferson strongly favored the nomination and election of a kindred spirit, his friend and fellow Virginian, the quiet, intellectual, and unassuming James Madison.

Although bitterly assailed, Jefferson left office with the consolation that he had remained true to the guiding star of the other founding fathers. He had kept the country out of a serious foreign war. Despite numerous reversals of policy under the whiplash of practicality, he never lost his faith in democracy and in the common people. He brought a renovation rather than a revolution; the real revolution that did occur was in his own thinking. If the Federalists were the stepping-stone between monarchical Europe and republican America, then the Jeffersonians were the stepping-stone between aristocratic federalism and democratic Jacksonianism.

Thomas Jefferson and John Adams died on the same day—appropriately the Fourth of July 1826. The last words of Adams, then ninety-one, were: "Thomas Jefferson still survives." He was wrong, for three hours earlier Jefferson had breathed his last breath. But Thomas Jefferson still survives in the democratic ideals and liberal principles of the great nation that he risked his all to found and that he served so long and faithfully.

Varying Viewpoints

The Jeffersonian era has long presented observers with a series of paradoxes, none greater than the question of how the man who proclaimed, "We are all Republicans, we are all Federalists," came to preside over one of the most bitterly partisan periods in American history.

Some scholars play down the importance of party conflict in this era. Stressing the early parties' lack of concern for organizing the electorate, these accounts note that the Jeffersonians and the Federalists distrusted parties; saw them only as temporary, necessary evils; and looked forward to their elimination. Thus, historians such as James S. Young argue that the Jeffersonian era possessed no true party system.

Others, among them Noble E. Cunningham, see the organizations of the early national period as the prototypes of the modern American party system. Conceding that the Federalists and Jeffersonians never became mass-based organizations like the later Jacksonian parties, this interpretation emphasizes the innovations of the period. The Jeffersonians created a partisan press, maintained control of Congress by dominating committee chairmanships, and pioneered campaign tactics like stump speaking and door-to-door canvassing.

Most important, their experiences in the two decades after the ratification of the Constitution led both groups to accept, grudgingly, the idea that party competition was inevitable and potentially beneficial in a republican society. This realization paved the way for the evolution of a full-blown two-party system in the 1830s.

SELECT READINGS

Primary Source Documents

Jefferson's "First Inaugural Address" (1801), in Henry Steele Commager, *Documents of American History,* echoed the themes of Washington's farewell and set the tone for his presidency. Reuben G. Thwaites, ed., *Original Journals of the Lewis and Clark Expedition** (1904), chronicles the explorers' adventures. For the political flavor of the age, see the debate over the Embargo Act* (1807). For constitutional history, read the decision of John Marshall in *Marbury* v. *Madison** (1803).

Secondary Sources

A monument of American historical writing is Henry Adams, *History of the United States During the Administrations of Jefferson and Madison* (9 vols., 1889–1891), available in a one-volume abridgement edited by Ernest Samuels. Especially fascinating are Adams's epilogue and prologue on the United States in 1800 and 1817. A brief introduction is given in Marshall Smelser, *The Democratic Republic, 1801–1815* (1968). Problems with the judiciary can be traced in Albert J. Beveridge's still-respected *Life of John Marshall* (4 vols., 1919). A more recent and succinct analysis is Richard E. Ellis, *The Jeffersonian Crisis: Courts and Politics in the New Republic* (1971). Politics are treated in a broad, imaginative context in James S. Young, *The Washington Community, 1800–1829* (1966), and more traditionally in Noble E. Cunningham's rebuttal, *The Process of Government Under Jefferson* (1979). Daniel Boorstin vividly evokes the intellectual climate of the age in *The Lost World of Thomas Jefferson* (1948). On Jefferson himself, see Dumas Malone's monumental study, *Jefferson and His Times* (5 vols., 1948–1981). A briefer standard biography is Merrill D. Peterson, *Thomas Jefferson and the New Nation* (1970). Peterson has also scrutinized *The Jefferson Image in the American Mind* (1960). John C. Miller, *The Wolf by the Ears: Thomas Jefferson and Slavery* (1977), probes the third president's attitudes on an important question.

CHAPTER 12

James Madison and the Second War for Independence, 1809–1815

The existing war—the child of prostitution. May no American acknowledge it legitimate.

A Federalist toast during the War of 1812

Madison: Dupe of Napoleon

Scholarly James Madison took the presidential oath on March 4, 1809, as the awesome conflict in Europe was roaring to its climax. Madison was small of stature (5 feet 4 inches), light of weight (about 100 pounds), bald of head, and weak of voice. Despite a distinguished career as a legislator, as president he fell tragically short of providing vigorous executive leadership. Crippled also by factions within his cabinet, he was unable to dominate his party, as Jefferson had once done.

The Non-Intercourse Act of 1809—the limited substitute for the embargo aimed solely at Britain and France—would expire in about a year. Congress, desperately attempting to uphold American rights, adopted in 1810 a bargaining measure known as Macon's Bill No. 2. While permitting American trade with all the world, it dangled an attractive lure. If either Britain or France repealed its commercial restrictions, America would restore nonimportation against the nonrepealing nation. In short, the United States would bribe the belligerents into respecting its rights.

This opportunity was made to order for Napoleon, a past master of deceit. He was eager to

have nonimportation clamped down once more on the British, because it would serve as a partial blockade, which he would not have to raise a finger to enforce. He was hopeful that such a boycott would embroil the Americans in war with Britain, for then they would be serving as his indirect allies to weaken his archenemy. Accordingly, he blandly announced, in August 1810, that his objectionable decrees had been repealed.

Responsible Americans, rising above self-delusion, should have examined the hollow-sounding French announcement with extreme caution. Napoleon, prince of liars, had no intention whatever of repealing his damaging decrees. But Madison, frantically seeking to wrest recognition of American rights from Britain, accepted French bad faith as good faith. He formally announced in November 1810 that France had complied with the terms of Macon's Bill No. 2 and that nonimportation would consequently be reestablished against Britain.

Madison's decision was fateful. Britons were angered by America's apparent willingness to be the dupe and partner of Napoleon. Once Madison had aligned his nation against Britain commercially, he

153

found himself gravitating toward France politically—and edging toward the whirlpool of war.

War Whoops Arouse the War Hawks

The complexion of the Twelfth Congress, which met late in 1811, differed markedly from that of its predecessor. Recent elections had swept away many of the older "submission men" and replaced them with young hotheads, chiefly from the South and West. The youthful newcomers—"the boys," John Randolph called them—were on fire for a new war with the old enemy. Not having had a conflict in their own generation, these war hawks were weary of hearing how their fathers had "whipped" the British singlehandedly. They won control of the House of Representatives and elevated to the speakership the tall (6 feet 2 inches), eloquent, and magnetic Henry Clay of Kentucky, the gallant "Harry of the West," then only thirty-four years old.

Western war hawks were especially eager to wipe out a dangerously renewed Indian threat to the pioneer settlers who were streaming steadily into the western wilderness. As this white flood washed through the green forests, more and more Indians were pushed farther and farther toward the setting sun. Two remarkable Shawnee brothers, Tecumseh and the Prophet, concluded that if this onrushing tide were ever to be stopped, that time had come. They began to weld together a far-flung confederacy of all the tribes east of the Mississippi. Their warriors foreswore liquor in order to be fit for the last-ditch battle with the intruders.

White frontierspeople and their war-hawk representatives in Congress were convinced that British "scalp buyers" were nourishing the Indians' growing strength. Seizing the initiative, General William Henry Harrison advanced upon Tecumseh's headquarters at Tippecanoe in present-day Indiana on November 7, 1811. He forced the Indians from the village and burned it to the ground. Fighting alongside the British, Tecumseh was killed at the Battle of the Thames in 1813. With him perished the dream of an Indian confederacy.

In the South, meanwhile, Andrew Jackson inflicted a similar, crushing defeat on the Creek Indians at the Battle of Horseshoe Bend on March 27,

Henry Clay (1777–1852), daguerreotype by Mathew Brady, 1849 *A glamorous, eloquent, and ambitious member of the House and Senate for many years, Clay was thrice an unsuccessful candidate for the highest office in the land. "Sir," he declared in the Senate in 1850, "I would rather be right than be President." But it was his inability to straddle the growing conflict over slavery, rather than his conscience, that kept him from attaining the highest office.*

1814. These victories effectively quashed Indian resistance to white expansion east of the Mississippi. The way now lay open for a surge of settlement into the Ohio country and the southwestern frontier.

Besides defeating Tecumseh's rebellion, Harrison's victory at Tippecanoe made the blood course faster in the veins of the impetuous war hawks. People like Representative Felix Grundy of Tennessee, three of whose brothers had been killed, cried that there was only one way permanently to defeat the Indians: wipe out their Canadian base. Canada was a lush prize—so near, so desirable, and apparently so defenseless. "On to Canada, on to Canada" was the war hawks' ominous chant. Less vocal southern expansionists also cast a coveted eye on Florida, then weakly held by Britain's ally Spain.

The war hawks wanted "free trade and sailors' rights" as well as free land. It may seem strange that settlers beyond the mountains, many of whom had never seen a body of salt water larger than a salt lick, should want to fight for maritime rights. But the proud, nationalistic westerners were outraged by the manhandling of American sailors and by the British Orders in Council that dammed up their agricultural products from shipment to Europe. Westerners also joined many of their fellow citizens in believing that only a vigorous assertion of American rights could demonstrate the viability of American nationhood—and of democracy as a form of government. If America could not fight to protect itself, its experiment in republicanism would be discredited in the eyes of a scoffing world.

Militant war hawks, with scattered but essential support from other sections, finally engineered a declaration of war in June 1812. The vote in the House was 79 to 49, in the Senate 19 to 13. The close tally revealed a dangerous degree of national disunity. Representatives from the pro-British maritime and commercial centers, as well as from the middle Atlantic states, almost solidly opposed hostilities. Thus the West and Southwest, mostly landlocked, presented the sea-fronting East with a war for a free sea that the East vehemently resented.

Mr. Madison's War

But why fight Britain rather than France, which had committed nearly as many maritime offenses? The traditional Republican attachment to France partly explains the choice of foe, as does the visibility of British impressments and the British arming of the Indians, who were smashing into pioneer cabins on the frontier.

The choice prize of Canada also beckoned from the north. Americans fondly (but wrongly) believed that taking Canada would be absurdly simple, a "frontiersman's frolic." If this northern mirage had not been so inviting, the administration would have waited a few more months and thereby learned of London's intention to repeal the Orders in Council. In fact, the announcement of the intention to repeal was made two days *before* Congress voted for war. Had there been an Atlantic cable, the war hawks probably could not have forced a declaration of hostilities through the Senate.

Seafaring New England damned the war for a free sea. The news of the declaration of war was greeted with muffled bells, flags at half-mast, and public fasting.

Why the opposition? To New Englanders, impressment was an old and exaggerated wrong. New England shippers and manufacturers were still raking in money, and profits dull patriotism. Pro-British New England Federalists also sympathized with Britain and resented the Virginia dynasty's sympathy with Napoleon, whom they regarded as the "Corsican butcher" and "the anti-Christ of the age."

Federalists also condemned the War of 1812 because they opposed the acquisition of Canada, which would merely add more agrarian states from the wild Northwest. This, in turn, would increase the voting strength of the Jeffersonian Democratic-Republicans. New England Federalists were determined, wrote one versifier:

> To rule the nation if they could,
> But see it damned if others should.

The bitterness of New Englanders against "Mr. Madison's War" led them to treason or near-treason. In a sense America fought two enemies simultaneously: old England and New England. New England gold holders probably lent more dollars to the British than to the Federal treasury. New England farmers sent huge quantities of supplies and foodstuffs to Canada, enabling British armies to invade New York. New England governors stubbornly refused to permit their militias to serve outside their own states.

Fight over Canada on Land and Lakes

The War of 1812, largely because of widespread disunity, ranks as one of America's worst-fought wars. There was no burning national anger, as there had been in 1807, following the *Chesapeake* outrage. War hawks in Congress were no more than a zealous minority. President Madison, although supporting their aims, knew that there was serious disunity. The supreme lesson of this conflict was the folly of leading a divided and apathetic people into war.

The republic was dangerously unprepared, despite warnings going back nineteen years to the outbreak of the European war in 1793. The nation was still suffering from its own embargo and nonintercourse, which it had partially enforced for the better part of four years. Congress had shortsightedly permitted the Bank of the United States to expire in 1811, at a time when a powerful financial institution was needed.

The regular army was scandalously inadequate, for it was ill-trained, ill-disciplined, and widely scattered. It had to be supplemented by the even more poorly trained militia, who were sometimes distinguished by speed of foot in leaving the battlefield. Some of the ranking generals were semisenile heirlooms from the Revolutionary War, rusting on their laurels and lacking in vigor and vision.

The offensive strategy in Canada was poorly conceived. Had the Americans captured Montreal, the center of population and transportation, everything to the west would have died, just as the leaves of a tree wither when the trunk is girdled. But instead of laying ax to the trunk, the Americans frittered away their strength in the three-pronged invasion of 1812. The trio of invading forces that set out from Detroit, Niagara, and Lake Champlain were all beaten back shortly after they had crossed the Canadian border.

By contrast, the British and Canadians displayed energy from the outset. Early in the war they captured the American fort of Mackinac, which commanded the upper Great Lakes and the Indian-inhabited area to the south and west. Their brilliant defensive operations were led by the inspired British general Isaac Brock, and assisted (in the American camp) by "General Mud" and "General Confusion."

When several American land invasions of Canada were again hurled back in 1813, Americans looked for success on water. Control of the Great Lakes was vital, and an energetic American naval officer, Oliver Hazard Perry, managed to build a fleet of green-timbered ships on the shores of Lake Erie, manned by even greener seamen. When he captured a British fleet in a furious engagement on Lake Erie, he reported to his superior, "We have met the enemy and they are ours." Perry's victory and his slogan infused new life into the drooping American cause. Forced to withdraw from Detroit and Fort Malden, the retreating redcoats were overtaken by General Harrison's army and beaten at the Battle of the Thames in October 1813.

Despite these successes, the Americans by late 1814, far from invading Canada, were grimly defending their own soil against the invading British. In Europe, the diversionary power of Napoleon was destroyed in mid-1814, and the dangerous despot was marooned on the Mediterranean isle of Elba. The United States, which had so brashly provoked

The Three U.S. Thrusts of 1812 *The thin red line delineates the Canadian boundary.*

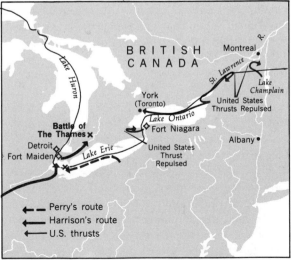

Campaigns of 1813 *The thin red line denotes the Canadian boundary.*

war behind the protective skirts of Napoleon, was now left to face the music alone. As thousands of redcoated veterans began to pour into Canada, Europe's distresses, for once, failed the Americans.

Assembling some 10,000 crack troops, the British prepared in 1814 for a crushing blow into New York, along the familiar lake-river route. In the absence of roads, the invader was forced to bring supplies over the Lake Champlain waterway. A weaker American fleet, commanded by the thirty-year-old Thomas Macdonough, challenged the British. The ensuing battle was desperately fought near Plattsburgh, on September 11, 1814, on floating slaughterhouses. The American flagship at one point was in grave trouble. But Macdonough, unexpectedly turning his ship about with cables, confronted the enemy with a fresh broadside and came away the victor.

The results of this heroic naval battle were momentous. The invading British army was forced to retreat. Macdonough thus saved at least upstate New York from conquest, New England from further disaffection, and the Union from possible dissolution. He also profoundly affected the concurrent negotiations of the Anglo-American peace treaty in Europe.

Washington Burned and New Orleans Defended

A second formidable British force, numbering about 4,000, landed in the Chesapeake Bay area in August 1814. Advancing rapidly on Washington, it easily dispersed some 6,000 panicky militia at Bladensburg ("the Bladensburg races"). The invaders then entered the capital and set fire to most of the public buildings, including the Capitol and the White House ("the Yankee Palace"). President Madison and his aides, chased into the surrounding hills like frightened rabbits, witnessed from afar the billowing smoke. The British fleet next appeared off Baltimore, a nest for privateers, but was beaten off by the doughty defenders at Fort McHenry, despite "bombs bursting in air." At the same time, the American land defenders, though driven back at first, caused the attacking army to withdraw. The memory of the Chesapeake campaign was further kept alive when Francis Scott Key, a detained American anxiously watching the bombardment at Baltimore from a British ship, was inspired to write the words of "The Star-Spangled Banner."

A third British blow of 1814, aimed at New Orleans, menaced the entire Mississippi Valley. Gaunt and hawk-faced Andrew Jackson, fresh from crushing the southwest Indians at the Battle of Horseshoe Bend in what is now Alabama, was placed in command. His hodgepodge force consisted of 7,000 sailors, regulars, pirates, and Frenchmen, as well as militiamen from Louisiana, Kentucky, and Tennessee. Among the defenders were two Louisiana regiments of free black volunteers, numbering about 400 men. The Americans threw up their entrenchment, and in the words of a popular song:

> Behind it stood our little force—
> None wished it to be greater;
> For ev'ry man was half a horse,
> And half an alligator.

The overconfident British, numbering some 8,000 battle-seasoned veterans, blundered badly. They made the mistake of launching a frontal assault, on January 8, 1815, on the entrenched American riflemen and cannoneers. The attackers suffered the most devastating defeat of the entire war, losing over 2,000 killed and wounded in half an hour, compared with some 70 for the Americans. This slaughter was as useless as it was horrible, for the treaty of peace had been signed at Ghent, in Europe, two weeks earlier. But Jackson became more than ever the hero of the West.

The "glorious news" from New Orleans reached Washington early in February 1815, and about two weeks later came the tidings of the treaty of peace. Naive citizens promptly concluded that the British, beaten to their knees by Jackson, had hastened to make terms.

Ship Duels and Privateer Prizes

Man for man and ship for ship the American navy did much better than the army. But the results of its heroism have been exaggerated.

Britain's navy in 1812 boasted more than 800 men-of-war. Of these oaken craft, 219 were ships-of-the-line of the 74-gun class, and 296 were frigates of roughly the 44-gun class. America, by contrast, had only sixteen ships in its entire navy, the largest of which were a few 44-gun frigates, unable to stand up to British ships-of-the-line. There could obviously be no saltwater fleet engagements in the slam-bang Trafalgar tradition; the only fleet battles were fought on the interior lakes.

American frigates and smaller sloops did clash with the enemy in a series of spectacular duels. In the frigate class, the Americans won four out of five of the single-ship contests, and in the sloop class, eight out of nine. American craft on the whole were more skillfully handled, had better gunners, and were manned by non-press-gang crews who were burning to avenge numerous indignities. The American frigates were specially designed superfrigates, notably the *Constitution* ("Old Ironsides"). They had thicker sides, heavier firepower, and larger crews, of which one sailor in six was a free black.

Commemorative Buckler   *The buckler on the sword from the* U.S.S. Constitution *commemorates the ship's famous battle with the* Guerrière *in 1812.*

The British were deeply humiliated by their naval defeats, all the more so because they had sneered at America's "few fir-built frigates, manned by a handful of bastards and outlaws." In a few months they lost more warships to the Yankees than the French and Spanish together had captured in years of fighting.

Swift and annoying American privateers—the "militia of the sea"—numbered about 500. They were in fact much more damaging than the regular navy and had an important bearing on the coming of peace. Built to fly from stronger ships rather than fight them, these speedy craft captured or destroyed some 1,350 British merchantmen, even pursuing them into the English Channel and the Irish Sea. Assisted by fast-sailing sloops of the navy, Yankee privateers were so destructive that Lloyd's of London refused to insure unconvoyed British merchantmen crossing the Irish Sea.

Yet the American privateers were a mixed blessing. They lost scores of their own craft and diverted valuable manpower from the navy and army. But they brought urgently needed wealth into the country, boosted sagging morale, and slowed British operations in Canada and elsewhere by capturing arms and supplies. Moreover, the privateers brought the war home to British manufacturers, merchants, and shippers, who in turn exerted strong pressure on Parliament to end this costly conflict.

Its wrath aroused, the Royal Navy finally retaliated by throwing a ruinous naval blockade along America's coast, and by landing raiding parties almost at will. American economic life, including fishing, was crippled. Customs revenues were choked off, and near the end of the war the bankrupt Treasury was unable to meet its maturing obligations.

The Treaty of Ghent

Tsar Alexander I of Russia, hard-pressed by Napoleon's army and not wanting his British ally to fritter away its strength in America, proposed mediation between the clashing Anglo-Saxon cousins in 1812. The tsar's feeler eventually set in motion the machinery that brought five American peacemakers to the quaint Belgian city of Ghent in 1814. The bickering group was headed by early-rising, puritanical John Quincy Adams, son of John Adams, who deplored the late-hour card playing of his high-living colleague Henry Clay.

Confident after their military successes, Britain's envoys made sweeping demands for a neutralized Indian buffer state in the Great Lakes region, control of the Great Lakes, and a substantial part of conquered Maine. The Americans flatly rejected these terms, and the talks appeared stalemated. But news of British reverses in upstate New York and at Baltimore, and increasing war-weariness in Britain, made London more willing to compromise. Preoccupied with the Congress of Vienna and still-dangerous France, the British lion resigned itself to licking its wounds. Revenge against its upstart American offspring would be sweet—but expensive. Once again European distress brought American diplomatic success, for the War of 1812 was "won" by the United States, so far as it was won at all, in Europe.

The Treaty of Ghent, signed on Christmas Eve in 1814, was essentially an armistice. Both sides simply agreed to stop fighting and to restore conquered territory. No mention was made of those grievances for which America had ostensibly fought: Indian relations, search and seizure, Orders in Council, impressment, and confiscations. These maritime omissions have often been cited as further evidence of the insincerity of the war hawks. Rather, they are proof that the Americans did not defeat the British decisively. With neither side able to impose its will, the treaty negotiations—like the war itself—ended as a virtual draw.

The news from Ghent triggered an outburst of rejoicing in the United States. Many Americans had rather expected to lose some territory, so dark was the military outlook early in 1815. But when the treaty arrived, the public mood rocketed from gloom to glory. The popularity of the pact was so overwhelming that it was unanimously approved by the Senate. A slogan of the hour became "Not one inch of territory ceded or lost"—a watchword that contrasted strangely with "On to Canada" at the outset of the war.

"I've often heard of your Wasps and Hornets but little thought such diminutive insects could give me such a Sting!!!"

A Wasp on a Frolic   *U.S. sloops-of-war* Wasp *and* Hornet *sting John Bull's pride. The* Wasp *captured the* Frolic.

Federalist Grievances and the Hartford Convention

Defiant New England remained a problem. It was by far the most prosperous section during the conflict, owing largely to illicit trade with the enemy in Canada and to the absence of a British blockade until 1814. But the embittered opposition of the Federalists to the war continued unabated. Late in 1812, when the first wartime presidential election was held, unhappy Federalists combined with disaffected Democratic-Republicans and almost unseated President Madison. If the state of Pennsylvania alone had been transferred to their electoral column, they would have won.

As the war dragged on, New England extremists became more vocal. A small minority of them proposed secession from the Union, or at least a separate peace with Britain. Ugly rumors were afloat about "Blue Light" Federalists—treacherous New Englanders who supposedly flashed lanterns on the shore so that blockading British cruisers would be alerted to the attempted escape of American ships.

The most spectacular manifestation of Federalist discontent was the ill-omened Hartford Convention. Late in 1814, when the capture of New Orleans seemed imminent, Massachusetts issued a call for a convention at Hartford, Connecticut. The states of Massachusetts, Connecticut, and Rhode Island dispatched full delegations, and New Hampshire and Vermont sent partial representation. This group of prominent men, twenty-six in all, met in complete secrecy for about three weeks—December 15, 1814, to January 5, 1815—to discuss their grievances and to seek redress for their wrongs.

In truth, the Hartford Convention was less radical than the alarmists supposed. Its immediate goal was to secure financial assistance from Washington, because the shores of New England were then being menaced by blockading British squadrons. A minority of the delegates gave vent to much wild talk of secession, but they were outvoted by the moderate Federalists.

Three special envoys from Massachusetts, bearing demands of the Hartford Convention for financial support to promote defense, and proposed constitutional amendments aimed at hobbling Congress, journeyed to the burned-out capital of Washington. The trio arrived just in time to be overwhelmed by the glorious news from New Orleans, followed by that from Ghent. Pursued by the sneers and jeers of the press, they slunk away into obscurity and disgrace.

The Hartford resolutions, as it turned out, were the death song of the Federalist party. In 1816, the next year, the Federalists nominated their last presidential candidate. He was lopsidedly defeated by James Monroe, yet another Virginian.

Unhappily, the stench of treason has clung to the Hartford Convention. The taint was not justified by its formal resolutions. Yet if the War of 1812 had not ended when it did, the convention might well have paved the way for treasonable courses.

Federalist doctrines of disunity, which long survived the party, blazed a fateful trail. Until 1815, there was far more talk of nullification and secession in New England than in any other section, including the South. The outright flouting of the Jeffersonian embargo and the later crippling of the war effort were the two most damaging acts of nullification in America prior to the events leading to the Civil War.

The Second War for American Independence

The War of 1812 was a small war, in which about 6,000 Americans were killed or wounded. It was but a footnote to the mighty European conflagration. In 1812, when Napoleon invaded Russia with about 500,000 men, Madison tried to invade Canada with about 5,000 men. But if the American conflict was globally unimportant, its results were highly important to the United States.

Americans wrested no formal recognition of their rights on the high seas, but informally they did. No longer did British aristocrats jeer at the "striped bunting" over "American cockboats." The republic had shown that it would resent, sword in hand, what it regarded as grievous wrongs. Other nations developed a new respect for American fighting men. Naval officers such as Perry and Macdonough were the most effective type of negotiators; the hot breath of their broadsides spoke the most eloquent diplomatic language. America's diplomats abroad were henceforth treated with less scorn. In a diplomatic sense, if not in a military sense, the conflict could be called the Second War for American Independence.

A new nation, moreover, was welded in the fiery furnace of armed conflict. Sectionalism, now identified with discredited New England Federalists, was given a black eye. The painful events of the war glaringly revealed, as perhaps nothing else could have done, the folly of sectional disunity. In a sense, the most conspicuous casualty of the war was the Federalist party.

The nation thrilled to the victories of its warriors. A brilliant naval tradition, already well launched, was strengthened by the exploits of the gallant seamen. The ineptitude of insubordinate or fleeing militia was forgotten. The battle-singed regular army, which in the closing months of the war had fought bravely and well, had won its spurs. New war heroes emerged, such as Andrew Jackson and William Henry Harrison, both of whom were to become president.

The Indians in the South had been crushed by Jackson at Horseshoe Bend (1814), and those in the North by Harrison at the Battle of the Thames (1813). Left in the lurch by their British friends at Ghent, the Indians were forced to make such terms as they could. They reluctantly consented, in a series of treaties, to relinquish vast areas of forested land north of the Ohio River.

Manufacturing increased behind the fiery wooden wall of the British blockade. In an economic sense, as well as in a diplomatic sense, the War of 1812 may be regarded as the Second War for American Independence. The industries that were thus stimulated by the fighting rendered America less dependent on Europe's workshops.

International Legacies

Regrettably, the war revived and intensified bitterness toward Britain. The uglier incidents of the conflict, notably the burning of Washington, added fuel to a century of Britain hating and Britain baiting. Mutual suspicion and hate were perhaps the most enduring heritages of this frustrating little war. Few Americans could have guessed in 1815 that it was to be the nation's last armed conflict with Britain.

Canadian patriotism and nationalism, no less than American patriotism and nationalism, received a powerful stimulus from the clash. The outnumbered Canadians, fighting bravely in defense of their homeland against the Yankee invader, won their full share of the laurels. Their stirring song, "The Maple Leaf," ringingly recalls these battles, including Chippewa and Lundy's Lane, which Americans regard as their victories.

Many Canadians felt betrayed by the Treaty of Ghent. They were especially aggrieved by the failure to secure an Indian buffer state, or even mastery of the Great Lakes. Canadians fully expected the frustrated Yankees to return, and for a time the Americans and British engaged in a naval armaments race on the Great Lakes. But in 1817 the Rush-Bagot

CHRONOLOGY	
1810	Macon's Bill No. 2.
	Napoleon supposedly repeals blockade decrees.
	Madison declares boycott of British goods.
1811	Battle of Tippecanoe.
1812	United States declares war on Britain.
	Madison reelected president.
1812–1813	American invasions of Canada fail.
1813	Battle of the Thames.
	Battle of Lake Erie.
1814	Battle of Plattsburgh.
	British burn Washington.
	Battle of Horseshoe Bend.
	Treaty of Ghent signed.
1814–1815	Hartford Convention.
1815	Battle of New Orleans.
1817	Rush-Bagot agreement.

agreement between Britain and the United States severely limited naval armament on the lakes. Better relations brought the last border fortifications down in the 1870s, with the happy result that the United States and Canada now share the world's longest unfortified boundary—5,527 miles long.

After Napoleon's final defeat at Waterloo in 1815, Europe slumped into a peace of exhaustion. Deposed monarchs returned to battered thrones, as the Old World took the rutted road back to conservatism, illiberalism, and reaction.

But the American people were largely unaffected by these European developments. Freed from the humiliating side blows of the belligerents, they no longer had to scan the Atlantic horizon for approaching sails—sails that might bring news of impending calamities. Americans thrilled to a new sense of nationality. They were like subject peoples attaining their majority, and for the first time shaking off the shackles of colonialism. Turning their backs on the Old World, they faced resolutely toward the untamed West. Unlike monarchy-cursed Europe, they were ready to take the high road toward democracy, liberalism, and freedom. The steady tramp, tramp of the westward-moving pioneers came to be the giant drumbeat of a new destiny.

Varying Viewpoints

The causes and consequences of the War of 1812 have long sparked spirited debate. Was war the result of western war-hawk expansionism or of British provocations on the high seas? Most recent historians emphasize the naval issue. The young nation's pride and independence, they argue, could not tolerate John Bull's repeated affronts. The Jeffersonian Democratic-Republicans accepted the need for war because they believed that the future of their party, and indeed of the entire American experiment in republican government, rested on the infant nation's ability to prove that it could meet external challenges.

Perhaps of more interest, scholars also see the first vague outlines of an American identity emerging from the smoke of the War of 1812. Henry Adams's magisterial *History* made this theme a central motif; Adams found evidence of a distinctive American character even in the tactics and techniques of Yankee seamen. The war does appear to have dissolved many localisms and to have begun the forging of a genuine national consciousness—thus paving the way for an upsurge of expansionism and nationalism in the so-called Era of Good Feelings.

SELECT READINGS

Primary Source Documents

See James Madison's "War Message"* (1812), in James D. Richardson, ed., *Messages and Papers of the Presidents* (1896), Vol. I, pp. 500–504; and the protest of thirty-four Federalist representatives, *Annals of Congress** 12 Cong., I sess., II cols. 2219–2221 (1812). Timothy Dwight offers a participant's view of the opposition to the war in *The History of the Hartford Convention** (1833).

Secondary Sources

An important recent work that sets the War of 1812 in a broad context of early American history is J. C. A. Stagg, *Mr. Madison's War: Politics, Diplomacy and Warfare in the Early American Republic* (1983). Also see Steven Watts, *The Republic Reborn: War and the Making of Liberal America, 1790–1820* (1987). On the causes of the war, Julius W.

Pratt, *Expansionists of 1812* (1925), stresses western pressures; Bradford Perkins, *Prologue to War: England and the United States, 1805–1812* (1961), and Reginald Horsman, *The Causes of the War of 1812* (1962), discuss free seas; and Roger H. Brown, *The Republic in Peril: 1812* (1964), emphasizes the need for saving the republican form of government. The relevant volumes of Henry Adams's nine-volume *History of the United States* (1889–1891) still contain magnificent reading, both on the war and on the peace. Federalist reaction to Democratic-Republican foreign policy is vividly etched in David H. Fischer, *The Revolution of American Conservatism* (1965), and James M. Banner, *To the Hartford Convention: The Federalists and the Origins of Party Politics in Massachusetts* (1970).

CHAPTER 13

The Postwar Upsurge of Nationalism, 1815–1824

The American continents . . . are henceforth not to be considered as subjects for future colonization by any European powers.

James Monroe, December 2, 1823

Nascent Nationalism

The most impressive by-product of the War of 1812 was a heightened nationalism—the spirit of nation-consciousness or national oneness. America may not have fought the war as one nation, but it emerged one nation.

A weak nationalism had existed since revolutionary days, but the vibrant new nationalism of the postwar era was composed of many additional ingredients. It sprang partly from pride in recent victories, partly from the setback suffered by Federalist sectionalism and states'-rightism, partly from a lessening of economic and political dependence on Europe, and partly from an exulting confidence in the future. Swelling numbers of citizens—although probably not yet a majority—were coming to regard themselves as first of all Americans and secondarily as citizens of their respective states.

The changed mood even manifested itself in the birth of a distinctively national literature. Washington Irving and James Fenimore Cooper attained international recognition in the 1820s, significantly as the nation's first writers of importance to use American scenes and themes. School textbooks, often British in an earlier era, were now being written by Americans for Americans. In the world of magazines, the highly intellectual *North American Review* began publication in 1815—the year of the triumph at New Orleans. Even American painters increasingly celebrated the glories of native landscapes on their canvases.

A fresh nationalistic spirit could be recognized in many other areas as well. A more handsome capital began to rise from the ashes of Washington. The army was expanded to 10,000 men. The navy covered itself with glory in 1815 when the naval heroes of the late war administered a thorough beating to the piratical plunderers of North Africa. These gratifying victories, inspired by the spirit of nationalism, further inflamed nationalism.

The rising tide of nation-consciousness also touched finance. The War of 1812 demonstrated the folly of permitting the Bank of the United States to expire in 1811, as weak state banks flooded the country with depreciated bank notes. Borrowing

Washington D.C., 1824   *This view of the Capitol building, much smaller than it is today, reveals the rustic conditions of the early days in the nation's capital.*

Hamiltonian arguments, Republicans in Congress revived the institution in 1816, while the dying Federalist minority denounced it as unconstitutional. The Second Bank of the United States—the "moneyed monster," to its enemies—further broadened nationalism as it thrust its numerous branches out across state boundaries.

The American System

Nationalism likewise manifested itself in manufacturing. Patriotic Americans took pride in the factories that had recently mushroomed, largely as a result of the self-imposed embargoes and the war.

When hostilities ended in 1815, British competitors began to dump the contents of their bulging warehouses on the United States, often cutting their prices below cost in an effort to strangle the American war-baby factories in the cradle. The infant industries bawled lustily for protection.

A nationalist Congress, out-federalizing the old Federalists, responded by passing the pathbreaking Tariff of 1816. The legislators were impressed with the desirability of saving the new industries for the national defense, while at the same time promoting the general welfare. The Tariff of 1816, significantly, was the first in American history with aims that were primarily protective. Its rates—roughly 20 to 25 percent on the value of dutiable imports—were not high enough to provide completely adequate safeguards, but the law was a bold beginning. A strongly protective trend was started that stimulated the appetites of the protected for more protection.

The battle in Congress over the Tariff of 1816 reflected North-South sectional crosscurrents. Thirty-four-year-old Representative John C. Calhoun of South Carolina—slender, handsome, black-haired, intense, and intellectual—played a stellar role in the debates. A recent war hawk and an ardent nationalist, he supported the tariff bill with all his eloquence and vigor. In 1816 there was some likelihood that the future of his native South lay in manufacturing, as well as in the intensive cultivation of cotton. But within a few years Calhoun became a relentless foe of a highly protective tariff. He sadly concluded that it was being used to enrich a few Yan-

Daguerreotype of Daniel Webster (1782–1852), by South-worth and Hawes *Premier orator and statesman, he served many years in both houses of Congress and also as secretary of state. Often regarded as presidential timber, he was somewhat handicapped by an overfondness for good food and drink and was frequently in financial difficulties. His devotion to the Union was inflexible. "One country, one constitution, and one destiny," he declaimed in 1837.*

kee manufacturers, rather than to build up the economic self-sufficiency and well-being of the entire nation.

Calhoun encountered a worthy adversary in Daniel Webster of New Hampshire, also thirty-four. Stocky, bushy-browed, and dark-haired, "Black Dan" Webster eloquently opposed the highly protective duties of the Tariff of 1816. He took this stand even though he was later to be a zealous nationalist and an ardent champion of high protection. The explanation is simple. Manufacturing in New England had not yet pushed shipping into a back seat, and the shippers of Webster's New Hampshire district feared that a tariff would interfere with their carrying trade. New England, though favoring some protection, was not yet completely willing to exchange the mainsail for the loom—but that day was slowly dawning.

Nationalism was further highlighted by Henry Clay's grandiose plan for developing a profitable home market. Still radiating the nationalism of war-hawk days, Clay threw himself behind an elaborate scheme known by 1824 as the American System. This system began with the protective tariff, behind which eastern manufacturing would flourish. Revenues gushing from the tariff would provide funds for roads and canals, especially in the fast-developing Ohio Valley. Through these new arteries of transportation would flow foodstuffs and raw materials from the South and West to the North and East. In exchange, a stream of manufactured goods would flow in the return direction.

Persistent and eloquent demands by Henry Clay and others for internal improvements struck a responsive chord with the public, especially in the road-poor West. The recent attempts to invade Canada had all failed partly because of oath-provoking roads—or no roads at all.

But attempts to secure federal funding for roads and canals stumbled on Republican constitutional scruples. Congress passed Calhoun's Bonus Bill in 1817, which would have parceled out $1.5 million to the states for internal improvements. But President Madison sternly vetoed the measure as unconstitutional, forcing the individual states to undertake building programs on their own. Madison's successor, James Monroe, generally followed the same line of negative reasoning. Jeffersonian Republicans, who had gulped down Hamiltonian loose construction on other important problems, choked on the idea of direct federal support for intrastate internal improvements. They were supported by the turncoat New England Federalists, now strict constructionists, who also opposed federal roads and canals because they would further drain away population and create competing states beyond the mountains.

The So-Called Era of Good Feelings

James Monroe—6 feet tall, somewhat stooped, courtly, and mild mannered—was nominated for the presidency in 1816 by the Republicans. They thus undertook to continue the so-called Virginia dynasty of Washington, Jefferson, and Madison. The fading

Federalists ran a candidate for the last time in their checkered history, and he was crushed by 183 electoral votes to 34.

The death of the once-proud Federalist party was due to various shortcomings and misfortunes. A list would include its disgraceful war record, its inability to choke down the new nationalistic program, and the theft of its tenets by the Jeffersonians. Many Federalists followed their stolen principles into the opposition camp; others gradually crawled away to the political graveyard.

In James Monroe, the man and the times auspiciously met. As the last president to wear an old-style cocked hat, he straddled two generations: the bygone age of the founding fathers and the emergent age of nationalism. Never brilliant, and perhaps not great, the serene Virginian with gray-blue eyes was in intellect and personal force among the least distinguished of the first eight presidents. But the times called for sober administration, not heroics. And Monroe was an experienced, level-headed executive, with an ear-to-the-ground talent for interpreting popular rumblings.

President Monroe further cemented emerging nationalism with a goodwill tour in 1817 that took him to New England. The heartwarming welcome he received even in "the enemy's country" ushered in the "Era of Good Feelings," as the Monroe administrations commonly have been called.

The Era of Good Feelings, unfortunately, was something of a misnomer. Considerable tranquility and prosperity did in fact smile upon the early years of Monroe, but the period was a troubled one. The acute issues of the tariff, the bank, internal improvements, and the sale of public lands were being hotly contested. Sectionalism was crystallizing, and the conflict over slavery was beginning to raise its hideous head.

A vanquished Federalist party was gasping its dying breaths, leaving the field to the triumphant Republicans and one-party rule. But where there is only one party, or where one of the parties enjoys a lopsided majority, the tendency is for factions to develop and fight among themselves. By the early 1820s an "Era of Inflamed Feelings" was dawning. Political giants—men like Clay, Calhoun, Jackson, and John Quincy Adams—were elbowing for power and championing the clashing economic interests of their respective sections.

The Panic of 1819 and the Curse of Hard Times

Much of the goodness went out of the good feelings in 1819, when a paralyzing economic panic descended. It brought deflation, depression, bankruptcies, bank failures, unemployment, soup kitchens, and over-crowded pesthouses known as debtors' prisons.

This was the first national financial panic since President Washington took office. It was to be followed by a succession of others every twenty or so years, in what seemed an inevitable cycle. Many factors contributed to the catastrophe of 1819, but looming large was overspeculation in frontier lands. The Bank of the United States, through its western branches, had become deeply involved in this popular type of outdoor gambling.

Financial paralysis from the panic, which lasted in some degree for several years, gave a rude setback to the nationalistic ardor. Various parts of the country tended to drift back toward the old sectionalism as they concentrated on bailing themselves out. The West was especially hard hit. When the pinch came, the Bank of the United States forced the speculative ("wildcat") western banks to the wall and foreclosed mortgages on countless farms.

A more welcome child of the panic was fresh legislation to govern the sale of public lands. The plight of the western farmer, combined with the evils of land speculation, laid bare the defects of the Land Act of 1800, as amended in 1804. By its terms, the pioneer could buy a minimum of 160 acres at $2 an acre over a period of four years, with a down payment of $80. When hard times came, entire communities would default on their installments. An improved Land Act of 1820 lightened the burden somewhat. It permitted the buyer to secure 80 virgin acres at a minimum of $1.25 an acre in cash—for a total cost of $100. There was less acreage but less outlay.

The Panic of 1819 also created backwashes in the political and social world. It hit especially hard at the poorer classes—the one-suspender men and their families—and hence helped cultivate the seedbed of Jacksonian democracy. It also directed attention to the inhumanity of imprisoning debtors. In extreme cases, often overplayed, mothers were torn from their infants for owing a few dollars. Mounting agitation against imprisonment for debt bore fruit in remedial legislation in an increasing number of states.

Growing Pains of the West

Beyond a doubt the West, out of which had swooped the war hawks of 1812, was by far the most nationalistic of the sections. Being new, it had no long-established states'-rights tradition. Moreover, it had early learned to lean on the national government, from which it had secured most of its land, directly or indirectly. It was a mixing bowl within the huge American melting pot, for people from all the sections rubbed elbows on the frontier.

Marvelous indeed had been the onward march of the West; nine frontier states had joined the original thirteen between 1791 and 1819. With an eye to preserving the North-South sectional balance, most

of these commonwealths had been admitted alternately, free or slave. (See Admission of States, in Appendix.)

Why this explosive expansion? In part, it was simply a continuation of the generations-old westward movement, which had been going on since early colonial days. In addition, the siren call of cheap lands—"the Ohio fever"—had a special appeal to European immigrants. Newcomers from abroad were beginning to shuffle down the gangplanks in impressive numbers, especially after the war of embargoes and bullets ended. Land exhaustion in the older tobacco states, where the soil was "mined" rather than cultivated, likewise drove people westward. Glib-tongued speculators, accepting small down payments, make it easier to buy new holdings.

The western boom was stimulated by additional developments. Acute distress during the embargo years turned many saddened faces toward the setting sun. The crushing of the Indians in the Northwest and South, by Generals Harrison and Jackson, pacified the frontier and opened up vast virgin tracts of land. The building of highways improved the land routes to the Ohio Valley. Note-

Wagons West *This busy scene on the Frederick Road, leading westward from Baltimore, was typical as pioneers flooded into the newly secured West in the early 1800s.*

worthy was the Cumberland Road, begun in 1811, which ran ultimately from western Maryland to Illinois. The use of the first steamboat on western waters, also in 1811, heralded a new era of upstream navigation. But the West, despite the inflow of settlers, was still weak in population and influence. To make its voice heard, it was forced to ally itself with other sections.

Slavery and Sectional Balance

Sectional tensions were nakedly revealed in 1819, when the territory of Missouri knocked on the doors of Congress for admission as a slave state. This fertile and well-watered area contained sufficient population to warrant statehood. But the House of Representatives stymied the plans of the Missourians by passing the incendiary Tallmadge amendment. It stipulated that no more slaves should be brought into Missouri and also provided for the gradual emancipation of children born to slave parents already there. A mounting roar of anger burst from slaveholding southerners.

Southerners saw in the Tallmadge amendment, which was defeated in the Senate, an ominous threat to the sectional balance. When the Constitution was adopted in 1788, the North and South were running neck and neck in wealth and population. But with every passing decade, the North was becoming wealthier and more thickly settled—an advantage reflected in an increasing northern majority in the House of Representatives. Yet in the Senate, with eleven states free and eleven slave, the southerners had maintained equality. They were therefore in a good position to thwart any northern effort to interfere with the expansion of slavery, and they did not want to lose this veto.

The future of the slave system caused southerners profound concern. Missouri was the first state entirely west of the Mississippi River to be carved out of the Louisiana Purchase, and the Missouri emancipation amendment might set a damaging precedent for all the rest of the area. Even more disquieting was another possibility. If Congress could abolish the "peculiar institution" in Missouri, might it not attempt to do likewise in the older states of the South? The wounds of the Constitutional Convention of 1787 were once more ripped open.

Burning moral questions also protruded, even though the main issue was political and economic balance. A small but growing group of antislavery agitators in the North seized the occasion to raise an

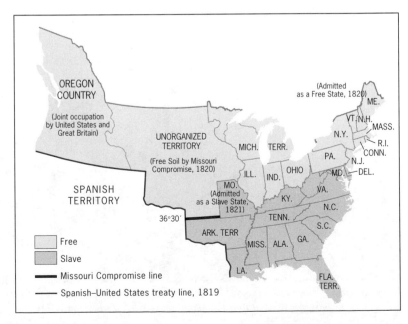

The Missouri Compromise and Slavery, 1820–1821   *In the 1780s Thomas Jefferson had written of slavery in America: "Indeed I tremble for my country when I reflect that God is just; that his justice cannot sleep forever; that . . . the Almighty has no attribute which can take side with us in such a contest." Now, at the time of the Missouri Compromise, Jefferson feared that his worst forebodings were coming to pass. "I considered it at once," he said of the Missouri question, "as the knell of the Union."*

outcry against the evils of slavery. They were determined that the plague of human bondage should not spread further into the virgin territories.

The Uneasy Missouri Compromise

Deadlock in Washington was at length broken in 1820 by the time-honored American solution of compromise—actually a bundle of three compromises. Congress, despite abolitionist pleas, agreed to admit Missouri as a slave state. But at the same time, free-soil Maine, which until then had been a part of Massachusetts, was admitted as a separate state. The balance between North and South was thus kept at twelve states each and remained there for fifteen years. Although Missouri was permitted to retain slaves, all future bondage was prohibited in the remainder of the Louisiana Purchase north of the line of 36° 30′—the southern boundary of Missouri.

Neither North nor South was acutely displeased, although neither was completely happy. Fortunately, the Missouri Compromise lasted thirty-four years—a vital formative period in the life of the young republic—and during that time it preserved the shaky compact of the states. Yet the embittered dispute over slavery heralded the future breakup of the Union. Ever after, the morality of the South's peculiar institution was an issue that could not be swept under the rug. The Missouri Compromise only ducked the question—it did not resolve it. Sooner or later, Thomas Jefferson predicted, it will "burst on us as a tornado."

The Missouri dispute proved to be another serious setback to nationalism and a tremendous stimulus to sectionalism—in the North, South, and West. From this time forward, the embattled South began to develop a nationalism of its own. Needing sectional reinforcements, it cast flirtatious eyes upon the adolescent West, which in turn was seeking allies. Meanwhile, with every passing decade, the North was becoming stronger in population, wealth, industry, and transportation—all of which added up to military strength.

Subsequent generations have tended to sneer at the architects of the Missouri solution as weak "appeasers." Yet compromise and statesmanship are often Siamese twins. Compromise made the Union in 1789; compromise saved the Union until 1860. When compromise broke down, the Union broke up.

The Missouri Compromise and the concurrent Panic of 1819 should have dimmed the political star of President Monroe. Certainly both unhappy events had a dampening effect on the Era of Good Feelings. But smooth-spoken James Monroe was so popular, and the Federalist opposition so weak, that he received every electoral vote except one in the election of 1820. Unanimity remained an honor reserved for George Washington.

John Marshall and Judicial Nationalism

Upsurging nationalism of the post-Ghent years, despite setbacks, was further reflected and strengthened by the Supreme Court.

The august tribunal was dominated by the tall, thin, and aggressive Chief Justice John Marshall, a "deathbed" Federalist appointee of John Adams's expiring administration. He had served at Valley Forge during the Revolution, and while suffering from cold and hunger, had been painfully impressed with the drawbacks of feeble central authority. Before Marshall mounted the Supreme Court bench in 1801, the judiciary had been the weakest and most timid of the three arms of the federal government. But he boldly asserted the doctrine of judicial review of congressional legislation in the case of *Marbury* v. *Madison* (1803).* And long before the end of his thirty-four years of service, he had made the judiciary, in some respects, the strongest branch of the national government.

Marshall, whose formal legal schooling had lasted only six weeks, was a judicial statesman rather than a strictly impartial judge. He examined a case through the colored lenses of his Federalist philosophy, and undertook to find legal precedents to support his Hamiltonian preconceptions. Sure of his ground, he wrote some of his most important decisions even before the lawyers had concluded their arguments.

---

* See pp. 143–144.

For over three decades, the ghost of Alexander Hamilton spoke through the lanky, black-robed justice. As a shaper of the Constitution in the direction of a more potent central government, Marshall ranks as the foremost of the molding fathers. As a wealthy businessman and land speculator, he instinctively shared Hamilton's preference for the propertied class. As a Virginia aristocrat, he deplored democratic excesses and opposed universal manhood suffrage and the rule of the "unwashed masses."

The Supreme Court Curbs States' Rights

One group of Marshall's decisions—perhaps the most famous—bolstered the power of the federal government at the expense of the states. A notable case in this category was *McCulloch* v. *Maryland* (1819). The suit involved an attempt by the state of Maryland to destroy a branch of the Bank of the United States by imposing a tax on its notes. John Marshall, speaking for the Court, declared the bank constitutional by invoking the Hamiltonian doctrine of implied powers (see p. 127). At the same time, he strengthened federal authority and slapped at state infringements when he denied the rights of Maryland to tax the bank. With ringing emphasis, he affirmed "that the power to tax involves the power to destroy" and "that a power to create implies a power to preserve."

Marshall's ruling on this case gave the doctrine of loose construction its most famous formulation. The Constitution, he said, derived from the consent of the people and thus permitted the government to act for their benefit. He further argued that the Constitution was "intended to endure for ages to come and, consequently, to be adapted to the various crises of human affairs." Finally, he declared: "Let the end be legitimate, let it be within the scope of the Constitution, and all means which are appropriate, which are plainly adapted to that end, which are not prohibited, but consist with the letter and spirit of the Constitution, are constitutional."

Two years later (1821) the case of *Cohens* v. *Virginia* gave Marshall one of his greatest opportunities. The Cohens, found guilty by Virginia courts of illegally selling lottery tickets, appealed to the highest tribunal. Virginia won, in that the conviction of the Cohens was upheld. But it lost, in that Marshall resoundingly asserted the right of the Supreme Court to review the decisions of the state supreme courts in all questions involving powers of the federal government. The states' rights people were aghast.

Hardly less significant in Marshall's career was the celebrated "steamboat case," *Gibbons* v. *Ogden* (1824). The suit grew out of an attempt by the state of New York to grant to a private concern a monopoly of waterborne commerce between New York and New Jersey. Marshall sternly reminded the upstart state that the Constitution conferred on Congress alone the control of interstate commerce (see Art. I, Sec. VIII, para. 3). He thus struck another blow at states' rights, while upholding the sovereign powers of the federal government. Interstate streams were thus cleared of this judicial snag, while the departed spirit of Hamilton may have applauded.

Judicial Dikes Against Democratic Excesses

Another sheaf of Marshall's decisions bolstered judicial barriers against democratic or demagogic attacks on property rights.

The notorious case of *Fletcher* v. *Peck* (1810) arose when a Georgia legislature, swayed by bribery, granted 35 million acres in the Yazoo River country (present-day Mississippi) to private speculators. The next legislature, yielding to an angry public outcry, canceled the crooked transaction. But the Supreme Court, with Marshall presiding, decreed that the legislative grant was a contract (even though fraudulently secured), and that the Constitution forbids state laws "impairing" contracts (see Art. I, Sec. X, para. 1). The decision is perhaps most noteworthy as further protecting property rights against popular pressures. It is also one of the earliest clear assertions of the right of the Court to invalidate state laws conflicting with the federal Constitution.

A similar principle was upheld in the case of *Dartmouth College* v. *Woodward* (1819), perhaps the best-remembered of Marshall's decisions. The college had been granted a charter by King George III in 1769, but the democratic New Hampshire state legislature had seen fit to change it. Marshall put the states firmly in their place when he ruled that the original charter must stand. It was a contract, and the Constitution protected contracts against state encroachments. The *Dartmouth* decision had the fortunate effect of safeguarding business enterprise from domination by the states. But it had the unfortunate effect of creating a precedent that enabled chartered corporations, in later years, to escape the handcuffs of needed public control.

Marshall's decisions are felt even today. In this sense his nationalism was the most tenaciously enduring of the era. He buttressed the federal Union and helped to create a stable, nationally uniform environment for business. In an age when white manhood suffrage was flowering and America was veering toward popular control, Marshall almost single-handedly shaped the Constitution along conservative, centralizing lines that ran somewhat counter to the dominant spirit of the new country. Through him the conservative Hamiltonians triumphed from the tomb.

Sharing Oregon and Acquiring Florida

The yeasty nationalism of the years after the War of 1812 was likewise reflected in foreign policy. To this end, the nationalistic President Monroe teamed with his nationalistic secretary of state, John Quincy Adams, the cold and scholarly son of the frosty and bookish ex-president. The younger Adams, a statesman of the first rank, happily rose above the ingrown Federalist sectionalism of his native New England and proved to be one of the great secretaries of state.

To its credit, the Monroe administration negotiated the much-underrated Treaty of 1818 with Britain. This multisided agreement permitted Americans to share the coveted Newfoundland fisheries with their Canadian cousins. It also fixed the vague northern limits of Louisiana along the forty-ninth parallel from the Lake of the Woods to the Rocky Mountains. The treaty further provided for a ten-year joint occupation of the untamed Oregon country, without a surrender of the rights or claims of either America or Britain.

To the south lay semitropical Spanish Florida, which many Americans believed geography and providence had destined to become part of the United States. Americans already claimed west

Florida, where uninvited American settlers had torn down the hated Spanish flag in 1810. Congress ratified this grab in 1812, and during the War of 1812, a small American army seized the Mobile region. But the bulk of Florida remained, tauntingly, under Spanish rule.

When an epidemic of revolutions broke out in South America, Spain was forced to denude Florida of troops to fight the rebels. With Spanish authority weakened, bands of Indians, runaway slaves, and white outcasts raided across the border into American territory and then fled to safety behind the surveyor's line.

General Andrew Jackson, idol of the West and scourge of the Indians, reappeared in 1817. The Monroe administration formally commissioned Jackson to punish the Florida outlaws and, if necessary, to pursue them into Spanish territory. But he was to respect all posts under the Spanish flag.

Early in 1818 Jackson swept across the Florida border with all the fury of an avenging angel. He hanged two Indian chiefs without ceremony and, after hasty military trials, executed two British subjects for assisting the Indians. He also seized the two most important Spanish posts in the area, St. Marks and Pensacola, where he deposed the Spanish governor.

Jackson had clearly exceeded his instructions from Washington. Alarmed, President Monroe consulted his cabinet. Its members were for disavowing or disciplining the overzealous Jackson—all except the lone wolf John Quincy Adams, who refused to howl with the pack. An ardent patriot and nationalist, the flinty New Englander finally won the others over to his point of view. He emphatically told the Spanish that their alternatives were to control the area or cede it to the United States.

Distressed in Latin America and at home, and believing that they were going to lose Spanish Florida in any case, the Spanish decided to dispose of the alligator-infested area while they could still get something for it. In the mislabeled Florida Purchase Treaty of 1819, Spain ceded Florida as well as shadowy Spanish claims to Oregon, in exchange for America's abandonment of equally shadowy claims to Texas, soon to become part of independent Mexico. The hitherto vague western boundary of

Louisiana was made to run zigzag along the Rockies to the forty-second parallel and then to turn due west to the Pacific, dividing Oregon from Spanish holdings.

The Menace of Monarchy in America

After the Napoleonic nightmare, the rethroned autocrats of Europe banded together in a kind of monarchical protective association. Determined to restore the good old days, they undertook to stamp out the democratic tendencies that had sprouted from soil they considered richly manured by the ideals of the French Revolution. The world must be made safe *from* democracy.

The crowned despots acted promptly. With complete ruthlessness, they smothered the embers of rebellion in Italy (1821) and in Spain (1823). According to the European rumor factory, they were also gazing across the Atlantic. Russia, Austria, Prussia, and France, acting in partnership, would presumably send powerful fleets and armies to the revolted colonies of Spanish America, and there restore the autocratic Spanish king to his ancestral domains.

Many Americans were alarmed. Sympathetic to democratic revolutions everywhere, they had cheered when the Latin American republics rose from the ruins of monarchy. Americans feared that if the European powers intervened in the New World, the cause of republicanism would suffer irreparable harm. The physical security of the United States— the mother lode of democracy—would be endangered by the proximity of powerful and unfriendly forces.

The southward push of the Russian bear, from the chill region now known as Alaska, had already publicized the menace of monarchy to North America. In 1821 the tsar of Russia issued a decree extending Russian jurisdiction over 100 miles of the open sea down to the line of 51°, an area that embraced most of the coast of present-day British Columbia. The energetic Russians had already established trad-

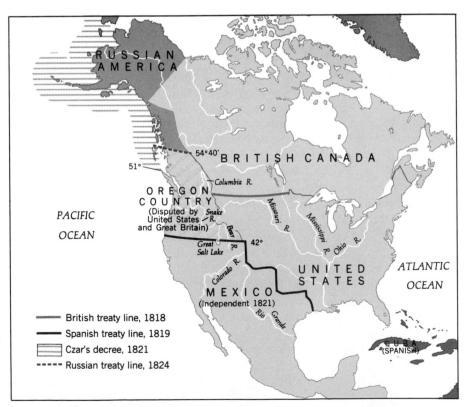

The West and Northwest, 1819–1824 *The British Hudson's Bay Company moved to secure its claim to the Oregon country in 1824, when it sent a heavily armed expedition led by Peter Skene Ogden into the Snake River country. In May 1825 Ogden's party descended the Bear River "and found it discharged into a large Lake of 100 miles in length"—one of the first documented sightings by white explorers of Great Salt Lake. (The mountain man Jim Bridger is usually credited with being the first white man to see the lake.)*

ing posts almost as far south as the entrance to San Francisco Bay, and the fear prevailed in the United States that they were planning to cut the republic off from California, its prospective window on the Pacific.

Great Britain, still mistress of the seas, was now beginning to play a lone-hand role on the complicated international stage. In particular, it recoiled from joining hands with the continental European powers in crushing the newly won liberties of the Spanish-Americans. These revolutionists had thrown open their monopoly-bound ports to outside trade, and British shippers, as well as Americans, had found the profits sweet.

Accordingly, in August 1823, George Canning, the haughty British foreign secretary, approached the American minister in London with a startling proposition. Would not the United States join with Britain in a joint declaration and specifically warn the European despots to keep their harsh hands off the Latin American republics? The American minister, lacking instructions, referred this fateful scheme to his superiors in Washington.

Mr. Monroe and His Doctrine

Reactions in America to the Canning proposal varied. The intimate advisers of President Monroe, including the aged Jefferson and Madison, recommended that the republic lock arms with hitherto distrusted Britain. The one notable exception was again the lone-wolf nationalist, Secretary Adams, who was hardheaded enough to beware of Britons bearing gifts. Why should the lordly British, with the mightiest navy afloat, need America as an ally—an America that had neither naval nor military strength? Such a union, argued Adams, was undignified—like a tiny American "cockboat" sailing "in the wake of the British man-of-war."

Adams, ever alert, thought that he detected a joker in the Canning proposal. If Canning could seduce the United States into supporting existing territorial arrangements in the New World, America's hands would be morally tied against expansion into Cuba or Britain's Caribbean possessions. He suspected—correctly—that European powers had no definite plans for invading the Americas. Know-

ing that the British navy would not permit hostile fleets to interfere with South American markets, Adams decided it was safe for Uncle Sam to blow a defiant nationalistic blast at all Europe.

The Monroe Doctrine was born late in 1823, when the nationalistic Adams won the nationalistic Monroe over to his way of thinking. The president, in his regular annual message to Congress on December 2, 1823, incorporated a stern warning to the European powers. Its two basic features were (1) noncolonization and (2) nonintervention.

Monroe first directed his verbal blast primarily at Russia in the Northwest. He proclaimed, in effect, that the era of colonization in the Americas had ended and that henceforth there would be a permanently closed season. What the great powers had they might keep, but neither they nor any other Old World powers could seize or otherwise acquire more.

At the same time Monroe sounded a trumpet blast against foreign intervention. He was clearly concerned with regions to the south, where fears were felt for the fledgling Latin American republics. Monroe bluntly warned the crowned heads of Europe to keep their hated monarchical systems out of this hemisphere. For its part, the United States would not intervene in the war that the Greeks were then fighting against the Turks for their independence.

Monroe's Doctrine Appraised

Monroe's ringing declaration quickened the patriotic pulse of nationalistic America. The American people were thrilled, even though they had no effective army or navy, to shake their collective fists at all the European despots and loudly warn them to stay away. While gratifying national pride and striking a blow for democratic rule, Monroe was also striking a blow for the "almighty dollar," as represented by the freshly opened Latin American markets.

Reactions in Britain were mixed. The British press, likewise savoring the juicy Latin American markets, was generally favorable to Monroe's forceful warning. But Canning was irked, for he perceived that the Monroe Doctrine was aimed at possible land grabbing by Britain, as well as by Europe. "Hands off" applied to all outside powers, including proud Britain.

The ermined monarchs of Europe were angered. Having resented the incendiary American experiment from the beginning, they were now deeply offended by Monroe's high-flown pronouncement—all the more so because of the gulf between America's loud pretensions and her weak military strength. But though offended by the upstart Yankees, the European powers found their hands tied, and their frustration increased their annoyance. Even if they had worked out plans for invading the Americas, they would have been helpless before the booming broadsides of the British navy.

Monroe's solemn warning, when issued, made little splash in the newly hatched republics to the south. Anyone could see that Uncle Sam was only secondarily concerned about his neighbors, because he was primarily concerned about defending himself against future invasion. Only a relatively few educated Latin Americans knew of the message, and they generally recognized that the British navy—not the paper pronouncement of James Monroe—stood between them and a hostile Europe.

In truth, Monroe's message actually did not have very much contemporary significance. Americans applauded it, and then forgot it as they turned back to such activities as felling trees and fighting Indians. Not until 1845 did President Polk revive it, and not until midcentury did it become an important national dogma.

The Monroe Doctrine might more accurately have been called the Self-Defense Doctrine. President Monroe was concerned basically with the security of his own country—not Latin America. The United States has never willingly permitted a powerful foreign nation to secure a foothold near its strategic Caribbean vitals. Yet in the absence of the British navy or other allies, the strength of the Monroe Doctrine has never been greater than America's power to eject the trespasser. But attaching Monroe's name to the Self-Defense Doctrine has given it the prestige that comes from a distinguished personage.

The Monroe Doctrine has had a long career of ups and downs. It was never law—domestic or inter-

CHRONOLOGY	
1810	*Fletcher* v. *Peck* case.
1815	*North American Review* founded.
	Battle of New Orleans.
1816	Second Bank of the United States founded.
	Protectionist Tariff of 1816.
	Monroe elected president.
1817	Madison vetoes Calhoun's Bonus Bill.
1818	Treaty of 1818 with Britain.
	Jackson invades Florida.
1819	Panic of 1819.
	Spain cedes Florida to United States.
	McCulloch v. *Maryland* case.
	Dartmouth College v. *Woodward* case.
1820	Missouri Compromise.
	Land Act of 1820.
	Monroe reelected.
1821	*Cohens* v. *Virginia* case.
1823	Secretary Adams proposes Monroe Doctrine.
1824	Russo-American Treaty of 1824.
	Gibbons v. *Ogden* case.
1825	Erie Canal completed.

national. It was not, technically speaking, a pledge or an agreement. It was merely a simple, personalized statement of the policy of President Monroe. And Monroe's presidential successors have ignored, revived, distorted, or expanded the original version.

But the Monroe Doctrine in 1823 was largely an expression of the post-1812 nationalism energizing the United States. Although directed at a specific menace in 1823, and hence a kind of period piece, the doctrine proved to be the most famous of all the long-lived offspring of that nationalism. While giving vent to a spirit of patriotism, it simultaneously deepened the illusion of isolationism. Many Americans falsely concluded, then and later, that the republic was in fact isolated from European dangers simply because it wanted to be, and because, in a nationalistic outburst, Monroe had publicly warned the Old World powers to stay away.

Varying Viewpoints

The Era of Good Feelings at first generated little ill feelings among historians, who generally agreed in seeing the period in terms not of conflict but of consolidation. There were then few irreconcilable controversies, but rather a remarkable consensus on laying the new nation's institutional base. In effect, the era set up a political program for the future, defined the power of the Supreme Court and its relation to the other branches of government, stabilized national boundaries, and established basic elements of foreign policy in the Monroe Doctrine.

More recently, historians have uncovered the tensions seething under the calm surface of the period. One-party rule masked deep divisions over economic and sectional issues that would soon erupt into bitter struggles over the tariff, expansion, and, especially, slavery. The tenuous Missouri Compromise revealed the fragility of the era's buoyant nationalism.

SELECT READINGS

Primary Source Documents

See James Madison's "War Message"* (1812), in James D. Richardson, ed., *Messages and Papers of the Presidents* (1896), Vol. I, pp. 500–504, and the protest of thirty-four Federalist representatives, *Annals of Congress** 12 Cong., I sess., II cols. 2219–2221 (1812). Timothy Dwight offers a participant's view of the opposition to the war in *The History of the Hartford Convention** (1833).

Secondary Sources

An excellent introduction is George Dangerfield, *The Awakening of American Nationalism, 1815–1828* (1965), which supplements his *Era of Good Feelings* (1952). Perry Miller, *The Life of the Mind in America* (1965), contains suggestive insights on legal thought and the role of the legal profession in the Marshall era. This and other topics are astutely placed in context by Lawrence Friedman in *A History of American Law* (1973). George R. Taylor's classic *Transportation Revolution* (1955) remains a valuable source on that subject. Glover Moore, *The Missouri Controversy, 1819–1821* (1953), and Charles S. Sydnor, *The Development of Southern Sectionalism, 1819–1848* (1948), place the Missouri Compromise in a broader context. On the Monroe Doctrine, the best single volume is Dexter Perkins, *A History of the Monroe Doctrine* (1955). On Calhoun, consult Richard N. Current, *John C. Calhoun* (1963), and John Niven, *John C. Calhoun and the Price of Union* (1988).

CHAPTER 14

The Rise of Jacksonian Democracy, 1824–1830

In the full enjoyment of the gifts of Heaven and the fruits of superior industry, economy, and virtue, every man is equally entitled to protection by law; but when the laws undertake to add to those natural and just advantages artificial distinctions . . . and exclusive privileges . . . the humble members of society — the farmers, mechanics, and laborers . . . have a right to complain of the injustice of their government.

Andrew Jackson, 1832

Politics for the People

Democracy was something of a taint in the days of the lordly Federalists. But by the 1820s, if not before, aristocracy was becoming the object of public scorn, and democracy was becoming respectable. Politicians were now forced to unbend and curry favor with the voting masses. Lucky indeed was the aspiring office seeker who could boast of birth in a log cabin. The semiliterate frontiersman Davy Crockett of Tennessee was elected to Congress mainly on the basis of his bear-hunting prowess. Even the wealthy and prominent citizens who continued to fill most high offices had to forsake all social pretensions and cultivate the common touch if they hoped to win elections.

Jeffersonian democracy had proclaimed that the people should be governed as little as possible; Jacksonian democracy now added that whatever governing was to be done should be done directly by the people. The common man was at last moving to the center of the national political stage. Instead of

the old divine right of kings, America was now witnessing the divine right of the people.

The New Democracy, so called, was based on universal white manhood suffrage rather than the old property qualifications. The frontier state of Vermont, admitted to the Union in 1791, was the first to place the ballot in the hands of all adult white males. This trend continued, notably in the West, where land was so easily obtained as to render almost meaningless the old property qualifications. Property tests for office holding were also widely abolished, and even judges were now being popularly elected. The South trailed other regions in giving up property requirements, but it, too, eventually extended suffrage and the right to hold office to all white men.

Nourishing the New Democracy

What caused this lush flowering of political democracy? In part it was simply the logical outgrowth of

177

Canvassing For a Vote   *Politicians in the Jacksonian era had to take their message to the common man, as shown in this painting by George Caleb Bingham.*

the egalitarian ideas that had taken root in colonial days and been lavishly fertilized during the revolutionary era. More immediately, the Panic of 1819 and the Missouri Compromise of 1820 rank high on the list of the New Democracy's nutrients.

The economic downturn was blamed by many workers and farmers on banking irregularities and speculation. In particular, the panic nurtured burning resentment at the government-granted privileges of the banks. Farmers unable to pay their debts often lost their farms; overextended bankers protected their property by simply suspending payment on their bank notes, which left their customers holding worthless paper. These types of practices reeked of favoritism and seemed to mock the democratic principles of equality and fair play. The desire to purge the land of this kind of corruption and restore the republican ideals of Jefferson's day invigorated the interest of many Americans in politics—especially the followers of Andrew Jackson. They sought control of government in order to tear the banks from its

protective embrace, to substitute hard money for bank notes, and even to abolish the banks altogether. Opposed to the Jacksonians were those persons who favored the current banking system and, more generally, who believed that the federal government had a legitimate role to play in promoting economic growth.

The Missouri Compromise likewise awakened many Americans, especially white southerners, to the importance of politics. The spectacle of organized northern resistance to admission of Missouri as a slave state aroused fears in the white South about further federal aggressions against states' rights— especially the right to perpetuate slavery. Many white southerners became involved in politics in order to prevent that result.

Economic distress and the slavery issue together raised the political stakes in the 1820s, ushering in a whole new chapter in the history of American politics. The deference, apathy, and virtually nonexistent party organizations of the Era of Good

Feelings gave way to the boisterous democracy, frenzied vitality, and strong political parties of the Jacksonian era. Voter turnout rose dramatically, from about 25 percent of eligible voters in the presidential election of 1824 to 78 percent in the election of 1840. A new style of politicking emerged, as candidates made increasing use of banners, badges, parades, barbecues, free drinks, and baby kissing in an effort to "get out the vote." The old suspicion of political parties as illegitimate disrupters of society's natural harmony was replaced by an acceptance of the sometimes wild contentiousness of political life. Vigorous political conflict even came to be celebrated as necessary for the health of democracy.

Everywhere the people flexed their political muscles. To an increasing degree, members of the Electoral College were being chosen directly by the people, rather than by state legislatures. Presidential nominations by a congressional caucus, meeting secretly, were now condemned as furtive, elitist, and subversive of democracy. Crying "Down with King Caucus," the voters in 1824 turned against the candidate (Crawford) who had been selected by the congressional clique. For a brief period, nominations were made by some of the state legislatures. But these did not seem democratic either, and in 1831 the first of the circuslike national nominating conventions was held (by the short-lived but significant Anti-Masonic party). Here the people appeared to exercise greater control, though their will was often thwarted by paunchy bosses in smoke-filled rooms.

The Adams-Clay "Corrupt" Bargaining

The woods were full of presidential timber in 1824. Four candidates towered above the others: Andrew Jackson of Tennessee, the tall, silver-maned, and hollow-cheeked "Old Hero" of New Orleans; Henry Clay of Kentucky, the gamy and gallant "Harry of the West"; William H. Crawford of Georgia, a giant of a man, able but ailing; and John Quincy Adams of Massachusetts, highly intelligent, experienced, and aloof.

All four rivals professed to be Republicans. Well-organized parties had not yet emerged, as illustrated by the fact that John C. Calhoun appeared as the vice-presidential candidate on both the Adams and the Jackson tickets.

The results of the noisy campaign were interesting but confusing. Jackson, the war hero, clearly had the strongest personal appeal, especially in the West. Foreshadowing the themes that would later shape his presidency, his campaign appealed for the salvation of republicanism from the forces of corruption and privilege in government. He polled almost as many popular votes as his next two rivals combined, but he failed to win a majority of the electoral vote. In such a deadlock the House of Representatives, as directed by the Twelfth Amendment (see Appendix), must choose among the top three candidates. Clay was thus eliminated, yet as the popular Speaker of the House, he was in a position to throw the election to the candidate of his choice.

Clay reached his fateful decision by a process of elimination. Crawford, recently felled by a paralytic stroke, was out of the picture. Clay hated the "military chieftain" Jackson, who in turn bitterly resented Clay's public denunciation of his Florida foray in 1818. The only candidate left was the puritanical Adams, with whom Clay—a free-living gambler and duelist—had never established cordial personal relations. But the two men had much in common politically: both were fervid nationalists and advocates of the American System. Shortly before the final ballot in the House, Clay met privately with Adams and assured him of his support.

Decision day came early in 1825. The House of Representatives met amid tense excitement, with sick members being carried in on stretchers. On the first ballot, thanks largely to Clay's behind-the-scenes influence, Adams was elected president. A few days later, the victor announced that Henry Clay would be the new secretary of state.

Masses of angered Jacksonians, most of them common folk, roared in protest against the "corrupt bargain." Jackson condemned Clay as the "Judas of the West," and John Randolph of Virginia said that Clay "shines and stinks like . . . a rotten mackerel by moonlight." No positive evidence has yet been unearthed to prove that Adams and Clay entered into a formal bargain, corrupt or otherwise. But appearances were so damning as to render denials

Presidential Election of 1824

Candidates	Electoral Vote	Popular Vote	Popular Percentage
Jackson	99	153,544	42.16
Adams	84	108,740	31.89
Crawford	41	46,618	12.95
Clay	37	47,136	12.99

unconvincing. Both men erred, the one by offering the post in circumstances sure to arouse suspicion, and the other by accepting it.

A Yankee Misfit in the White House

John Quincy Adams was a chip off the old family glacier. Short (5 feet 7 inches), thickset, and billiard-bald, he was even more frigidly austere than his president-father, John Adams. Shunning people, he often went for early morning swims, sometimes stark naked, in the then-pure Potomac River. Essentially a closeted thinker rather than a politician, he was irritable, sarcastic, and tactless. Yet few individuals have ever come to the presidency with a more brilliant record in statecraft, especially in foreign affairs. He ranks as one of the most successful secretaries of state, yet one of the least successful presidents.

A man of puritanical honor, Adams entered upon his four-year "sentence" in the White House smarting under charges of "bargain," "corruption," and "usurpation." Less than one-third of the voters had voted for Adams. As the first "minority president," he would have found it difficult to win popular support even under the most favorable conditions. Possessing almost none of the arts of the politician, he had achieved high office by commanding respect rather than by courting popularity. In an earlier era, an aloof John Adams could win the votes of propertied men by sheer ability. But with the raw New Democracy in the driver's seat, his cold-fish son could hardly hope for success at the polls.

Adams's nationalistic views contributed to his woes in the White House. The old Jeffersonian Democratic-Republican party was breaking into fragments, most of which tended to coalesce around a common hatred of the Adams-Clay partnership. The flinty president refused to recognize that the popular tide was turning away from the post-Ghent nationalism toward states' rights and sectionalism. Confirmed nationalist that he was, Adams urged upon Congress in his first annual message the construction of roads and canals. He renewed George Washington's proposal for a national university and went so far as to advocate federal support for an astronomical observatory.

The public reaction to these proposals was prompt and unfavorable. To many workaday Americans grubbing out stumps, astronomical observatories seemed like a scandalous waste of public funds. The South in particular bristled. If the federal government could meddle in local concerns like education and roads, it might even try to lay its hand on the "peculiar institution" of black slavery.

The Tricky "Tariff of Abominations"

The touchy tariff issue became one of Adams's biggest headaches. Congress had increased the general tariff in 1824 from about 23 percent on dutiable goods to about 37 percent. But wool manufacturers, dissatisfied with their share of protection, held out for still-higher barriers.

Ardent Jacksonites, seeking to unhorse Adams, proposed a politically designed bill that would push duties as high as 45 percent on manufactured items and impose a heavy duty on certain raw materials, notably wool. They thought that New Englanders, who needed these materials, would vote against the entire measure, thus giving Adams a political black eye and boosting Jackson. But the New Englanders spoiled this clever little game. They were so anxious to preserve the principle of protection that they choked down the dishonest Tariff of 1828. Daniel Webster, who had earlier fought the mild Tariff of 1816, and John C. Calhoun, who had sponsored it, had by this time completely reversed their positions. They and others now clearly saw that the future of New England lay in the factory, rather than on the waves, while the destiny of the South lay in the cotton fields.

Tariff Inequalities, North and South, 1832 *The protective tariff under which the North grows fat and prosperous brings economic hardship to the South.*

Southerners, as heavy consumers of manufactured goods, were shocked by what they regarded as the outrageous rates of the Tariff of 1828. Hotheads promptly branded it the "Tariff of Abominations," and several southern states adopted formal protests.

Why did the South, especially South Carolina, react so angrily against the tariff? Underlying the outcry were growing anxieties about possible federal interference with the institution of slavery. The congressional debate on the Missouri Compromise had kindled these anxieties, and they were further fed by an ominous slave rebellion in Charleston in 1822, led by a free black, Denmark Vesey. The South Carolinians, still closely tied to the British West Indies, also knew full well how their slaveowning West Indian cousins were feeling the mounting pressure of British abolitionism on the London government. Abolitionism in America might similarly use the power of the government in Washington to suppress slavery in the South. If so, now was the time, and the tariff was the issue, for taking a strong stand on principle against all federal encroachments on states' rights.

Nearer the surface was the real economic distress of the old South—the seaboard area first set-

tled. It was now the least flourishing of all the sections. Its overcropped acres were petering out, and the price of cotton was falling sharply. Southerners were seeking a scapegoat for their economic distress, but there was also a sound basis for their belief that the "Yankee tariff" discriminated against them. They sold their cotton and other farm produce in a world market completely unprotected by tariffs and were forced to buy their manufactured goods in an American market heavily protected by tariffs.

The plight of the South may be illustrated by a hypothetical case. Suppose that in 1828 an English manufacturer sold shoes in South Carolina at $1.25 a pair, whereas a Massachusetts shoemaker, paying higher wages, would have to charge $1.50 for a pair of equal quality. South Carolinians would naturally buy the British footwear. But if a tariff of $0.50 a pair were levied on foreign shoes at the Charleston customshouse, the British shoes would cost $1.75 a pair. The Massachusetts shoemaker could safely raise the price to anything less than $1.75—say, $1.74—and still undercut the British competitor by selling the cheapest shoes in South Carolina. South Carolinians would thus be forced to pay higher prices, while the profits of the Yankee manufacturer were commensurately fattened.

The South also objected to other consequences of towering tariffs. If higher prices led Americans to buy fewer British textiles, the British would in turn buy less southern cotton with which to make the textiles. Southerners thus would suffer both as consumers and producers, as importers and exporters.

South Carolinians took the lead in protesting against the Tariff of Abominations. Their legislature went so far as to publish in 1828, though without formal endorsement, a pamphlet known as "The South Carolina Exposition." It had been secretly written by John C. Calhoun, one of the few topflight political theorists ever produced by America. (As vice-president, he was forced to conceal his authorship.) "The Exposition" boldly denounced the recent tariff as unjust and unconstitutional. Going a stride beyond the Kentucky and Virginia resolutions of 1798, it bluntly proposed that the states should nullify the tariff—that is, they should declare it null and void within their borders.

Calhoun found himself caught in an awkward straddle. Still a Unionist and a nationalist, he was also a southern sectionalist. He therefore desperately sought a formula that would protect the minority in the South from the "tyranny of the majority" in the North and West. Seizing upon nullification, he undertook by this explosive device to preserve the Union and prevent secession. Calhoun's aim was to salvage the Union by quieting the fears of those forces that might one day destroy it.

Calhoun's "Exposition," at least immediately, was a false alarm. No other state joined South Carolina in its heated antitariff protest. But the disruptive theory of nullification was further publicized, and the even more dangerous doctrine of secession was foreshadowed. South Carolina was not then prepared to force the controversy to a showdown. The election of Carolina-born Andrew Jackson to the presidency had occurred two weeks earlier, and the Old Hero—a fellow cotton planter and slaveowner—was expected to sympathize with the plight of the South.

The Jacksonian "Revolution of 1828"

The presidential campaign for Andrew Jackson had started early. It began on February 9, 1825, the day of John Quincy Adams's controversial election by the House, and continued noisily for nearly four years.

Even before the election of 1828, the temporarily united Republicans of the Era of Good Feelings had split into two camps. One was the National

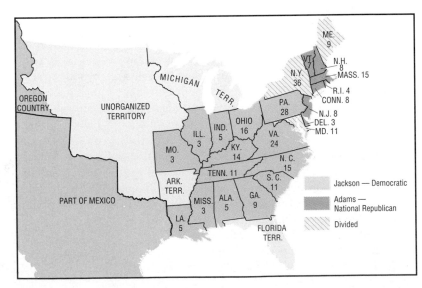

Presidential Election of 1828 (with electoral vote by state) *Jackson swept the South and West, while Adams retained the old Federalist stronghold of the Northeast. Yet Jackson's inroads in the Northeast were decisive. He won twenty of New York's electoral votes and all twenty-eight of Pennsylvania's. If those votes had gone the other way, Adams would have been victorious—by a margin of one vote.*

Republicans, with the ultranationalistic Adams as their standard bearer. The other was the Democratic-Republicans, with the fiery Jackson heading their ticket.

"Shall the people rule?" was the chief issue of 1828, at least to Jacksonians. They argued that the will of the voters had been thwarted in 1825 by the backstairs "bargain" of Adams and Clay. The only way to right the wrong was to seat Jackson, who would then bring about "reform" by sweeping out the "dishonest" Adams gang.

Mudslinging reached a disgraceful level, partly as a result of the taste of the new mass electorate for bare-knuckle politics. Adams would not stoop to gutter tactics, but many of his backers were less squeamish. They described Jackson's mother as a prostitute, recounted "Old Hickory's" numerous duels and his hanging of six militiamen, and branded him an adulterer for marrying his wife, Rachel, before her divorce was officially granted.

Jackson men also hit below the belt. A billiard table that President Adams had purchased with his own money became, in the mouths of rabid Jacksonites, "gambling furniture" in the "presidential palace." Jackson campaigners mocked Adams's long service on the federal payroll, and even accused him of serving as a pimp for a Russian nobleman while minister to Russia.

When the nasty campaign was over, General Jackson was as victorious at the ballot box as he had been on the battlefield. The popular tally was 647,286 votes for him to 508,064 for Adams, with an electoral count of 178 to 83. Support for Jackson came mainly from the West and South, and to a considerable extent from the sweat-stained laborers of the eastern seaboard. Generally speaking, the common people—though by no means all of them—voted for the Hero of New Orleans. Adams won the backing of his own New England and the propertied "better elements" of the Northeast.

The election of 1828 has often been called the "Revolution of 1828." Actually, as in 1800, no upheaval or landslide swept out the incumbent. But the concept of a *political* revolution in 1828 is not completely farfetched. It was a peaceful revolution, achieved by ballots instead of bullets, by counting heads instead of crushing them. In the struggle between the poorer masses and the entrenched classes, the homespun folk scored a resounding triumph. America hitherto had been ruled by an elite of brains and wealth, whether aristocratic Federalist shippers or aristocratic Jeffersonian planters. Jackson's victory accelerated the transfer of national power from the countinghouse to the farmhouse, from the East to the West, and from the snobs to the mobs. The plowholders were now ready to take over the government—their government.

The Advent of Old Hickory Jackson

Andrew Jackson cut a striking figure—tall (6 feet 1 inch), gaunt, and with bushy iron-gray hair brushed high above a prominent forehead, craggy eyebrows, and blue eyes. His irritability and emaciated condition (140 pounds) probably had resulted in part from long-term bouts with dysentery, malaria, tuberculosis, and lead poisoning from two bullets that he carried in his body from near-fatal duels. His autobiography was largely written in his lined face.

To a considerable degree, Jackson personified the new West. He reflected its individualism, its jack-of-all-trades versatility, its opportunism, its energy, its directness, and its prejudices. He was a genuine folk hero—an uncommon common man. Born in the Carolinas and early orphaned, "Mischievous Andy" grew up without parental restraints. As a youth, he displayed much more interest in brawling and cockfighting than in his scanty opportunities for reading and spelling. Although he ultimately learned to express himself in writing with vigor and clarity, his grammar was always rough-hewn and his spelling was often original.

The youthful Carolinian had the foresight to emigrate "up West" to Tennessee, where a fighting man was more highly regarded than a writing man. There—through native intelligence, force of personality, and powers of leadership—he became a judge and a member of Congress. His passions were so terrible that on occasion he would choke into silence when he tried to speak. He won his greatest fame as a commander of militia troops, who dubbed him Old Hickory in honor of his toughness. Afflicted with a

"BORN TO COMMAND."

OF VETO MEMORY.

HAD I BEEN CONSULTED.

KING ANDREW THE FIRST.

"King Andrew the First" *Jackson is here assailed as a tyrant who tramples underfoot the Constitution, the courts, and domestic welfare.*

violent temper, he early became involved in numerous duels, stabbings, and other bloody frays. But, rough and forthright as democracy itself, he made things happen.

The first president from the West, and the first without a college education, except Washington, Jackson was unique. His university was adversity. He had risen from the masses, but he was not one of them, except insofar as he shared many of their prejudices. Essentially a frontier aristocrat, he owned many slaves, cultivated broad acres, and lived in one of the finest mansions in America—the Hermitage, near Nashville, Tennessee.

As befitted an authentic man of the people and hero of the one-suspender man, Jackson's political

ideas had a stark simplicity. He was suspicious of the federal government as a bastion of privilege, an institution dangerously removed from popular scrutiny. He was therefore determined to reduce it "to that simple machine which the Constitution created," which meant, among other things, hostility to the active federal economic role envisioned by Henry Clay's American System. Conversely, he and especially his followers were generally friendly toward the frothy democracy bubbling up in the states and looked with some favor on economic activism on the part of state governments.

While president, Jackson proved to be a storm center. As a former military man, he demanded prompt and loyal support from his subordinates. Cherishing strong ideas as to his constitutional prerogatives, he ignored the Supreme Court on several conspicuous occasions. He likewise defied or dominated Congress as few presidents have done. Jackson's six predecessors combined had wielded the veto ten times; during his two terms he employed it twelve times, sometimes on grounds of personal distaste rather than constitutional principle. Jackson's modest use of the veto ax was perfectly legitimate, but his numerous enemies condemned him as "King Andrew the First."

Jackson's inauguration symbolized the newly won ascendancy of the masses. "Hickoryites" poured into Washington from far places, sleeping on hotel floors and in hallways. They were curious to see their hero take office, and perhaps to pick up a well-paying office for themselves. Nobodies mingled with notables as the White House, for the first time, was thrown open to the multitude. A milling crowd of clerks, shopkeepers, hobnailed artisans, and grimy laborers surged in, wrecking the china and furniture, and threatening the "people's champion" with cracked ribs. Jackson was hastily spirited through a side door, and the White House miraculously emptied itself when the word was passed that huge bowls of well-spiked punch had been placed on the lawns. Such was the "inaugural brawl."

To conservatives, this orgy seemed like the end of the world. "King Mob" reigned triumphant as Jacksonian vulgarity replaced Jeffersonian simplicity. Faint-hearted traditionalists shuddered, drew their blinds, and recalled the opening scenes of the French Revolution.

Jackson Nationalizes the Spoils System

Under Jackson the spoils system—that is, rewarding political supporters with appointment to public office—was introduced into the federal government on a large scale. Its name came from Senator William Marcy's remark in 1832, "To the victors belong the spoils of the enemy." The system had already secured a firm hold in New York and Pennsylvania, where well-greased political machines were run by professional politicians who made a full-time occupation out of politics by ladling out the "gravy" of office.

A housecleaning of some kind in Washington was clearly needed. No party overturn had occurred since the defeat of the Federalists in 1800. A few office holders, their commissions signed by President Washington, were lingering on into their eighties, drawing breath and salary but doing little else. Elected as a reformer, Jackson believed that the swiftest road to reform was to sweep out the Adams-Clay gang and bring in his own trusted henchmen. Furiously aroused against his foes, he agreed that the old Adams "barnacles" must "be scraped clean from the Ship of State."

Jackson fully shared the view of the New Democracy that "every man is as good as his neighbor"—perhaps "equally better." Because this was believed to be so, and the routine of office was thought to be simple enough for any upstanding American to learn quickly, why encourage the development of an aristocratic, bureaucratic, officeholding class? The New Democracy also trumpeted the ideal of "rotation in office," which was designed to let as many citizens as possible share in the experience of government. This was a polite way of saying "throw the rascals out and put our rascals in."

The spoilsmen now had their inning. Office seekers hounded Jackson at every turn and even invaded his privacy; for every appointee there were seemingly ten disappointees. In view of such pressures, one may marvel that he removed so few incumbents rather than so many. During his eight years, only about one-fifth of the old civil servants were dismissed, leaving more than 9,000 out of the original 11,000. The "clean sweeps" were to come in later administrations.

Even so, a demoralizing practice was begun on a national scale. Fitness, merit, and the ideal of public service were subordinated, while offices were prostituted to political ends. The questions were not "What can he do for the country?" but "What has he done for the party?" and "Is he loyal to Jackson?"

Scandal inevitably accompanied the new system. Men who had openly bought their posts by campaign contributions were appointed to high office. Illiterates, incompetents, and plain crooks were given positions of public trust; they lusted for the spoils of office rather than the toils of office. Samuel Swartwout, despite ample warnings of his untrustworthiness, was awarded the high-salaried post of collector of the customs of the port of New York. Nearly nine years later he "Swartwouted out" for Britain, leaving his accounts more than a million dollars short—the first person to steal a million from the federal government.

Finally, the spoils system built up a potent, personalized political machine. Its delicate gears were lubricated by gifts from expectant party members and by percentage levies on the salaries of office holders—a kind of political job insurance. The system at length secured such a tenacious hold that more than half a century passed before its grip could be partially loosened.

Cabinet Crises and Nationalistic Setbacks

Jackson's cabinet was mediocre; its members were used primarily as executive clerks. The only person of conspicuous ability was the smooth-tongued and keen-witted secretary of state, Dutch-descended Martin Van Buren of New York, who shone as a gifted conciliator and wire puller. A balding, sharp-featured man, he was affectionately addressed by Jackson as "Matty." But he was known to his enemies as the "Little Magician."

The official cabinet of six was privately supplemented by an extra-official cabinet of about thirteen ever-shifting members. It grew out of Jackson's informal meetings with his advisers, some of whom were newspaperpeople who kept him in touch with the fickle public opinion. The enemies of the president branded these shirt-sleeved cronies "the Kitchen Cabinet."

The regular cabinet was wrecked in 1831, as a result of the "Eaton malaria." Secretary of War Eaton had married the daughter of a Washington boardinghouse keeper, pretty Peggy O'Neale, whom the tongue of scandal had perhaps unfairly linked with the male boarders. She was consequently snubbed by the ladies of Jackson's official family, conspicuously by the blue-blooded wife of Vice President Calhoun. The president, whose own spouse had been victimized by scandalmongers, was chivalrously aroused in behalf of Peggy Eaton's chastity. With a zeal worthy of a better cause, he tried to force the social acceptance of the black-haired beauty. But the all-conquering general finally had to acknowledge defeat in the "Petticoat War" at the hands of the female phalanx.

The Eaton scandal played directly into the hands of Secretary Van Buren. As a fancy-free widower, he further curried favor with Jackson by paying marked attention to Peggy Eaton. Jackson turned increasingly against Calhoun, and finally broke with him completely. Followers of the South Carolinian were purged from the cabinet in 1831. Calhoun himself, resigning the vice presidency the next year, entered the Senate as a champion of South Carolina.

It would be absurd to say that Peggy Eaton caused the Civil War. But up to this time Calhoun had publicly been a strong nationalist, despite his secret espousal of nullification in "The South Carolina Exposition" of 1828. As vice president, he thought himself in line for the presidency after Jackson had served one term. The open break with the incumbent, though foreshadowed earlier, blighted his hopes. He gradually abandoned his weakening nationalism and became an inflexible defender of southern sectionalism. Seeking extreme medicines for protecting the states and preserving the Union, the "Great Nullifier" contributed to the almost fatal illness of the Union.

Jackson himself dealt nationalism a body blow by his hostility to localized roads and canals. True, he signed a number of measures that appropriated federal funds for ambitious internal improvements. But his states' rights principles rebelled against spending money from the pinched Washington Treasury for roads built entirely within individual states and unrelated to an interstate network. He headlined his antagonism in 1830, when he vigorously vetoed a bill for improving the Maysville Road, which lay completely within Henry Clay's Kentucky. This setback slapped at the internal improvements aspect of the American System, so ardently championed by Clay, the "corrupt bargainer" whom Jackson never forgave. Old Hickory's veto was also a signal victory for eastern and southern states'-rightism in its struggle with Jackson's own West.

The Webster-Hayne Forensic Duel

Sectional jealousies found a spectacular outlet in the Senate during 1829–1830. Hidebound New England, resenting the marvelous expansion of the West, was determined to call a halt. The lavish distribution of western acreage was draining off eastern population, while further upsetting the political balance. Late in 1829, therefore, a New England senator introduced a resolution designed to curb the sale of public lands.

Sectional passions flared angrily in the Senate, as the western senators sprang furiously to the defense of their interests. The South, seeking allies in its controversies with the Northeast, promptly sided with the West. Its most persuasive spokesman was Robert Y. Hayne, of South Carolina, one of the silver-tongued orators of his generation.

Hayne's oratorical effort in the Senate was impressive. He roundly condemned the obvious disloyalty of New England during the War of 1812, as well as its selfish inconsistency on the protective tariff. Airing in detail the grievances of the South, he reserved his heavy fire for the Tariff of Abominations (1828). He then acclaimed Calhoun's dangerous doctrine of nullification as the only means of safeguarding the minority interests of his section.

The "Godlike Daniel" Webster, spokesman for New England, now took the floor and began a nine-day running debate with Hayne in January 1830. Matchless orator and leader of the American bar,

"The man who has filled the measure of his Country's Glory."
JEFFERSON.

Jackson,

DEMOCRACY,

And our Country.

"The Union must be Preserved."

A Jackson Campaign Poster, 1832 *Note the emphasis on democracy and union.*

Webster awed audiences with his majestic presence. He had craglike brows, flashing eyes, a sonorous voice, a noble head, and a deep-chested frame.

After defending New England with vigor, if not complete candor, Webster, the ex-Federalist, passed on to the larger issue of the Union. Insisting that the *people* and not the *states* had framed the Constitution (here he was on shaky historical ground*), he decried the insidious doctrine of nullification. Either the Supreme Court would judge the constitutionality of laws, or the republic would be

---

* The original preamble of the Constitution of 1787 had read: "We the people of the states of"—and then they were listed by name. But when it was objected that all the states might not ratify, the formula "We the people of the United States" was adopted. (For the text of the Preamble, see Appendix.)

torn by revolution. If each of the twenty-four states was free to go its separate way in obeying or rejecting federal statutes, there would be no union but only a "rope of sand." Webster's concluding outburst, which brought tears to his listeners' eyes, was a magnificent tribute to the Union, ending with those imperishable words: "Liberty and Union, now and forever, one and inseparable."

Websterian Cement for the Union

Webster did not overpower Hayne with his thunderous oratory; Hayne did not defeat Webster with his seductive eloquence. There were no official judges. The polished southerner was sounder on historical and economic grounds; the impassioned New Englander was sounder on constitutional practicalities and common sense—on things as they were rather than as they had been. Each section was satisfied with its champion.

The impact of Webster's reply was spectacular. About 40,000 copies were printed in three months, and arguments for the Union were seared into the minds of countless northerners. Among them was young Abraham Lincoln, just turning twenty-one and moving from Indiana to the Illinois frontier. Webster's inspirational peroration was printed in the school readers and was memorized by tens of thousands of impressionable lads—the Boys in Blue who in 1861–1865 were willing to lay down their lives for the Union.

Webster, beyond a doubt, had a large hand in winning the Civil War. He probably did more than any other person to arouse the oncoming generation of northerners to fight for the ideal of Union. His admirers have claimed that the nation was saved hardly less by the thunder of Webster's replies to Hayne than by the thunder of General Grant's replies to the cannonading of General Lee.

Hot-tempered Old Hickory had meanwhile been keeping strangely silent on southern grievances. States'-rights leaders, at a Jefferson Day banquet in 1830, schemed to smoke him out. Their strategy was to devise a series of toasts in honor of Jefferson, one-time foe of centralization, that would lean toward states' rights and nullification. The plotters assumed that the Old Hero—a fellow southerner—would be swept along by the tenor of the toasts and speak up in favor of states' rights.

Jackson, forewarned and inwardly fuming, had carefully prepared his response. At the proper moment he rose to his full height, fixed his eyes on Calhoun, and with dramatic intensity proclaimed:

> "Our Union: It must be preserved!"

The southerners were dumbfounded, and Calhoun haltingly replied, in part:

> "The union, next to our liberty, most dear!"

Some seventy other anticlimactic toasts followed, but in effect the party was over.

Jackson's military ire was aroused. As commander-in-chief, he would stand for no back talk from the states or particularly from the hated Calhoun. But, as fate decreed, the showdown with defiant South Carolina was postponed for over two years.

CHRONOLOGY

1822	Vesey slave rebellion, South Carolina.
1824	Lack of electoral majority for presidency throws election into the House of Representatives.
1825	House elects John Quincy Adams president.
1828	Tariff of 1828 (Tariff of Abominations).
	Jackson elected president.
1830	Maysville Road veto.
	Webster-Hayne debate.
1831	Anti-Masonic party holds first national convention.
	Eaton affair.
1832	Calhoun resigns as vice president.

Varying Viewpoints

Aristocratic nineteenth-century historians damned Andrew Jackson as a backwoods barbarian. They criticized Jacksonianism as democracy run riot—an irresponsible, backcountry outburst that overturned the electoral system and raised hob with the national financial structure. Early twentieth-century progressive historians followed the lead of Frederick Jackson Turner in his famous 1893 essay "The Significance of the Frontier in American History." They saw the frontier as the fount of democratic virtue, and they hailed Jackson as a popular hero sprung from the forests of the West. But with the publication of Arthur M. Schlesinger, Jr.'s *The Age of Jackson* in 1945, the focus of the debate on Jacksonianism shifted. Contending that the urban working people of the Northeast formed the backbone of Jackson's support, Schlesinger argued that its identification with a social class, rather than a geographical section, was the most important characteristic of Jacksonianism.

Soon after Schlesinger's book appeared, the discussion again shifted ground. The ethnocultural school, led by Lee Benson, argued that social class was less important than ethnic and religious conflict in shaping political life, especially at the local level. In the 1980s, however, Sean Wilentz and other scholars began to reclaim some of Schlesinger's interpretation. Wilentz argues that artisans and other small producers were threatened by big, impersonal institutions and large-scale employers that began to drive them out of business. Thus Jackson's attack on the Bank of the United States symbolized the antagonism these individuals felt toward the emergent corporate economy and determined their strong allegiance to Jackson.

This interpretation is conspicuous in Charles Sellers's *The Market Revolution: Jacksonian America, 1815–1846* (1992), which raises a fascinating question: What was the relationship between American democracy and free-market capitalism? They are often assumed to be twins, born from the common parentage of freedom and opportunity, reared in the wide-open young republic, and mutually supporting one another ever since. But perhaps, Sellers suggests, they were actually adversaries, with Jacksonians inventing mass democracy in order to hold capitalist expansion in check. Yet if this interpretation is correct, how can one explain the phenomenal growth of the capitalist economy in the years immediately following the triumphs of Jacksonianism?

SELECT READINGS

Primary Source Documents

Davy Crockett's *Exploits and Adventures in Texas** (1836) is a lively description of the democratic political order of Jacksonian America. C. W. Janson, *The Stranger in America, 1793–1806** (1807), exposes the seamier aspects of American egalitarianism. On the Tariff of Abominations and its implications, see the "Webster-Hayne Debate"* (1830). Webster's reply to Hayne is one of the greatest specimens of American political oratory.

Secondary Sources

A still-living classic treatise on the Jacksonian period is Alexis de Tocqueville, *Democracy in America* (1835, 1840). General introductions are Glyndon G. Van Deusen, *The Jacksonian Era* (1959), and Edward Pessen, *Jacksonian America: Society, Personality, and Politics* (rev. ed., 1978). The latter volume sharply disputes Tocqueville's findings. Marvin Meyers, *The Jacksonian Persuasion* (1957), and John William Ward, *Andrew Jackson: Symbol for an Age* (1955), examine the broader cultural significance of Old Hickory and his supporters. Arthur M. Schlesinger, Jr., in his seminal *The Age of Jackson* (1945), stresses the support of eastern labor for Jackson, a view that has come under attack in Lee Benson, *The Concept of Jacksonian Democracy: New York as a Test Case* (1961). On the evolution of mass-based political parties, see Richard P. McCormick, *The Second American Party System* (1966), and two books by Ronald P. Formisano, *The Birth of Mass Political Parties: Michigan, 1827–1861* (1971) and *The Transformation of Political Culture: Massachusetts Parties, 1790s–1840s* (1983). Samuel Flagg Bemis, *John Quincy Adams and the Union* (1956), is the second volume of a distinguished biography, as is Robert V. Remini, *Andrew Jackson and the Course of American Freedom, 1822–1832* (1981). A masterful analysis of the period's most celebrated statesmen is Merrill D. Peterson, *The Great Triumvirate: Webster, Clay, and Calhoun.* The standard work on tariffs is Frank W. Taussig, *The Tariff History of the United States* (1931).

CHAPTER 15

Jacksonian Democracy at Flood Tide, 1830–1840

The vain threats of resistance by those who [in South Carolina] have raised the standard of rebellion shew their madness and folly. . . . In forty days, I can have within the limits of So. Carolina fifty thousand men. . . . The Union will be preserved.

Andrew Jackson, 1832

"Nullies" in South Carolina

The abominable Tariff of 1828 continued to rankle with hot-blooded South Carolinians. They persisted in seeing it not only as economically punitive in the short run but as a possible entering wedge for later federal interference with slavery in the southern states. The nullifiers—"nullies," they were called—tried strenuously to muster the necessary two-thirds vote for nullification in the South Carolina legislature. But they were blocked by a determined minority of Unionists, scorned as "submission men."

Back in Washington, Congress touched off the fuse by passing the new Tariff of 1832, which fell far short of meeting all southern demands. The measure did pare away the worst of the "abominations" of 1828, and it did lower the imposts to about the level of the moderate Tariff of 1824—roughly 35 percent, or a reduction of 10 percent. Yet the new law was frankly protective and to many southerners it had a disquieting air of permanence.

South Carolina was now nerved for drastic action. Nullifiers and Unionists clashed head-on in the state election of 1832. Nullies, defiantly wearing the state symbol of palmetto ribbons on their hats,

emerged with more than a two-thirds majority. The state legislature then called for a special convention. Several weeks later the delegates, meeting in Columbia, solemnly declared the existing federal tariff to be null and void within South Carolina. The hotheaded assemblage also called upon the state legislature to undertake any necessary military preparations. Finally, the convention defiantly threatened to take South Carolina out of the Union if the Washington regime attempted to collect the customs duties by force.

President-General Jackson, his military instincts rasped, reacted violently. Hating Calhoun and pledged to uphold the Union, he privately threatened to hang the nullifiers. But fortunately for compromise, he was much less pugnacious in public.

Conciliatory Henry Clay of Kentucky had no desire to see his old enemy Jackson win new laurels by crushing the Carolinians and returning with Calhoun's scalp dangling from his belt. Clay therefore threw his small influence behind a compromise bill that would gradually reduce the Tariff of 1832 by about 10 percent.

The compromise Tariff of 1833 finally squeezed through Congress. But at the same time, and partly as a face-saving device, Congress passed the Force Bill, known among Carolinians as the "Bloody Bill." It authorized the president to use the army and navy, if necessary, to collect federal tariff duties.

Militant South Carolinians welcomed this opportunity to extricate themselves without loss of face from a dangerously tight corner. To the consternation of the Calhounites, no other southern states had sprung to their support. Moreover, an appreciable Unionist minority within South Carolina was gathering guns, organizing militia, and nailing the Stars and Stripes to flagpoles. Faced with civil war within and invasion from without, the Columbia convention met again and repealed the ordinance of nullification. As a final but futile gesture of fist shaking, it nullified the unnecessary Force Act and adjourned.

A Victory for Both Union and Nullification

Although neither Jackson nor the Nullies won a clear-cut victory, South Carolina actually emerged with colors flying. Confronted with overwhelming odds, it had forced a reduction of the tariff to as reasonable a level as it could have expected. It had not only saved face but surrendered no principle. Unrepentant and defiant, it felt that it had won; and the people of Charleston—the "Cradle of Secession"—gave a gala "victory ball" for the volunteer troops. But ominously the South Carolinians gradually abandoned nullification in favor of the more extreme remedy of secession.

Later generations, gazing back through the smoke of the Civil War, have condemned the "appeasement" of South Carolina in 1833 as sheer folly. Unbloody and unbowed, it could have been voted the state most likely to secede. (In 1860 it was the first to go.) If Jackson had only strangled the serpent of secession in the nest, so the argument runs, there might have been no costly Civil War.

Yet force was the risky solution. The flare-up in South Carolina was no mere Whiskey Rebellion, and the nation was not yet ready to drink the cup of blood. Violence tends to beget violence. Armed invasion might have aroused other southern states and touched off a civil war, at a time when the Unionists were even worse prepared for fighting than in 1861. Force is a confession that statesmanship has failed. Reasonable compromise was in the American tradition, and in 1833 any other course seemed unwise.

The Bank as a Political Football

A man of violent dislikes, President Jackson came to share the prejudices of his own West against the "moneyed monster," the Bank of the United States (BUS). Hated Henry Clay especially aroused Jackson's ire by supporting a premature move in the Senate to recharter the Bank in 1832—four years early.

Clay's scheme was to ram a recharter bill through Congress and then send it on to the White House. If Jackson signed it, he would alienate his worshipful western followers. If he vetoed it, as seemed certain, he would presumably lose the presidency in the forthcoming election by alienating the wealthy and influential groups in the East. President Jackson growled privately, "The Bank . . . is trying to kill me, but I will kill it."

The recharter bill slid through Congress on greased skids, as planned, but was killed by a scorching veto from Jackson. The Old Hero assailed the plutocratic and monopolistic bank as unconstitutional. Of course, the Supreme Court had earlier declared it constitutional in the case of *McCulloch* v. *Maryland* (1819), but Jackson acted as though he regarded the executive branch as superior to the judicial branch. He had sworn to uphold the Constitution as he understood it, not as his foe John Marshall understood it.

Jackson's veto message went on to condemn the bank as not only antiwestern but anti-American. A substantial minority of its stockholders were foreigners, chiefly Britons, for whom Americans still harbored a war-born hate. Thus, at one bold stroke, Jackson succeeded in mobilizing the prejudices of the West against the East. He was setting the log cabin against the business office, the apprehensive debtor against the steely-eyed creditor. More than that, he was arousing the "native" American against the foreigner, the states'-righter against the centralizer.

The gods continued to misguide Henry Clay. Delighted with the financial fallacies of Jackson's message, but blind to its political appeal, he arranged to have thousands of copies printed as a campaign document. The president's sweeping accusations may indeed have seemed demagogic to the moneyed men of the country, but they made good sense to the common men. The bank issue was now thrown into the noisy arena of the Clay-Jackson presidential canvass of 1832.

Brickbats and Bouquets for the Bank

What of Jackson's vigorous charges? The bank was undeniably antiwestern in its strong hostility to the wobbly "wildcat banks" that provided financial fuel—often volatile paper—for western expansion. It had foreclosed on many western farms and had thus drained "tribute" into eastern coffers. For that era it was a mammoth superbank—a "monster monopoly"—and hence out of touch with the sweaty New Democracy. It was undeniably plutocratic, run by an elite moneyed aristocracy, headed by the able but high-handed Nicholas Biddle (dubbed "Czar Nicholas I"). The bank was also in some degree autocratic and tyrannical, especially when it turned the screws on the weak "rag money" banks.

The charge that the bank was a "hydra of corruption" contained much truth. Biddle cleverly lent funds where they would make influential friends. In 1831 alone, a total of fifty-nine members of Congress borrowed sums from "Biddle's bank" totaling about a third of a million dollars. Even a dog does not ordinarily bite the hand that feeds it. During one period Daniel Webster was a director of the bank, its chief paid counsel, its debtor in the sum of thousands of dollars, and a member of the Senate, where he eloquently battled for his employer's interests. Judicious loans by Biddle to newspaper editors likewise ensured a "good press" and led to the sneer "Emperor Nick of the Bribery Bank." Whomever he could not corrupt, it was believed, he crushed.

Yet the bank had much to commend it. A financially sound organization, it imposed some restraint on fly-by-night western banks—banks that often consisted of little more than a few chairs and a suitcase full of printed notes. It reduced bank fail-

ures and, at a time when the country was flooded with depreciated paper money, issued sound bank notes ("old Nick's money"). It promoted economic expansion by making credit and sound currency reasonably abundant. It was a safe depository for the funds of the Washington government, which it also served by transferring and disbursing money. But paradoxically, the bank's enormous economic power made it politically vulnerable.

The bank, in short, was a highly important and useful institution, but one whose very existence seemed to sin against the egalitarian credo of American democracy. Its officers were not only arrogant but also neglectful of their responsibilities to society in the management of a public trust.

Old Hickory Crushes Clay in 1832

Clay, as a National Republican, and Jackson, as a Democrat, were the chief gladiators in the presidential contest of 1832. The gaunt old general, who had earlier favored one term for a president and rotation in office, was easily persuaded by his cronies not to rotate himself out of office.

Novel features made the campaign of 1832 especially memorable. For the first time, a third party entered the field—the newborn Anti-Masonic party, which opposed the fearsome secrecy of the Masonic order. The Anti-Masonic party quickly became a potent political force in New York and spread its influence throughout the middle Atlantic and New England states. The Anti-Masons appealed to long-standing American suspicions of secret societies, which they condemned as citadels of privilege and monopoly—a note that harmonized with the democratic chorus of the Jacksonians. But since Jackson himself was a Mason, and publicly gloried in his membership, the Anti-Masonic party was also an anti-Jackson party. Moreover, the Anti-Masons attracted support from many evangelical Protestant groups seeking to use political power to effect moral and religious reforms, such as prohibiting mail deliveries on Sundays, and otherwise keeping the Sabbath holy. This moral busybodiness was anathema to the Jacksonians, who were generally opposed to all government meddling in social and economic life.

"Race Over Uncle Sam's Course" *Clay, with his American System, is supposed to gain the White House as Jackson, with his veto club and Van Buren as running mate, falls on the bank issue in 1832. A falsely optimistic Whig cartoon.*

A further novelty of the presidential contest in 1832 was the calling of national nominating conventions (three of them) to name candidates. The Anti-Masons and a group of National Republicans added still another innovation when they adopted formal platforms, publicizing their positions on the issues.

Henry Clay and his overconfident National Republicans enjoyed impressive advantages. Ample funds flowed into their campaign chest, including $50,000 in "life insurance" from the BUS. Most of the newspaper editors, some of them "bought" with Biddle's bank loans, dipped their pens in acid when they wrote of Jackson.

Yet Jackson won easily over the sparkling Kentuckian. The popular count stood at 687,502 to 530,189, the electoral count at 219 to 49. A Jacksonian wave swept over the West and South, washed into Pennsylvania and New York, and even broke into rock-ribbed New England.

Badgering Biddle's Bank

A vindictive Jackson was not one to let the financial octopus die in peace. He was convinced that he now had a "mandate" from the voters, and he had good reason to fear that the slippery Biddle might try to manipulate the bank (as he did) so as to force its recharter. Jackson therefore decided to weaken the bank by "removing" federal deposits from its vaults. By slowly siphoning off the government's funds, he would bleed the bank dry and ensure its demise when its charter expired in four years.

"Removing" the deposits involved nasty complications. Jackson, his dander up, was forced to reshuffle his cabinet before he could find a secretary of the treasury who would bend to his iron will. Surplus federal funds henceforth were placed in several dozen state institutions—the so-called pet banks or Jackson's pets.

Compelled to retrench after losing federal deposits, Biddle called in loans with unnecessary severity. A number of wobblier banks were driven to the wall by "Biddle's Panic." The teetering financial structure received an additional shock in 1836 when Jackson issued a "Specie Circular" requiring all public lands to be purchased with "hard" metallic money. This drastic step was long overdue, but coming at that time it gave the speculative bubble another sharp prick. Hard money brought hard feelings and hard times for the West.

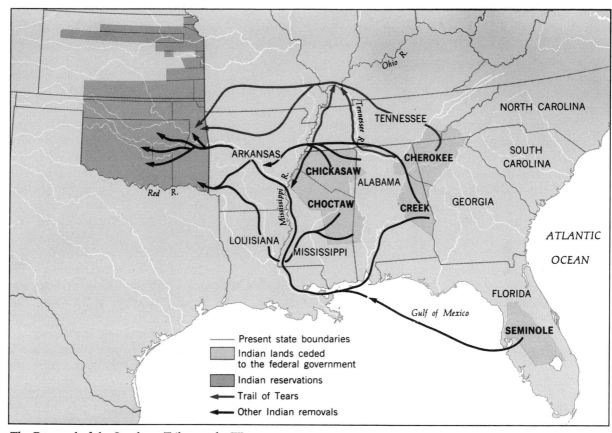

The Removal of the Southern Tribes to the West

Transplanting the Tribes

Wondrous indeed was the continued expansion of the American population. The unflagging fertility of the people, reinforced by immigration, brought the total figure to nearly 13 million by 1830—or more than three times that of 1790.* Most of the states east of the Mississippi had been admitted, leaving "island" Indian populations surrounded by white neighbors who coveted their land.

More than 125,000 Native Americans dwelled in the forests and prairies east of the Mississippi in the 1820s. Federal policy toward them varied. Beginning in the 1790s, the Washington government

ostensibly recognized the tribes as separate nations and agreed to acquire land from them through formal treaties. In practice, however, the Indians were repeatedly coerced or tricked into ceding huge tracts of territory to whites.

Yet many white Americans also felt respect and admiration for the Indians and believed they could be assimilated into white society. Much energy was therefore devoted to "civilizing" and Christianizing the Indians, and many denominations sent missionaries into Indian villages.

Although many tribes violently resisted white encroachment, others followed the path of accommodation. The Cherokees of Georgia made especially remarkable efforts. They adopted a system of

---

* For population figures since 1790, see Appendix.

settled agriculture, missionaries opened schools on their lands, and the Indian Sequoyah devised a Cherokee alphabet. Some Cherokees became prosperous cotton planters and even turned to slaveholding. Nearly 1,300 blacks toiled for their Native American masters in the Cherokee nation in the 1820s.

The Cherokees' attempts at assimilation apparently did not reduce the whites' hostility. In 1828 the Georgia legislature declared the Cherokee tribal council illegal and asserted its own jurisdiction over Indian affairs and Indian lands. The Cherokees appealed this move to the Supreme Court, which thrice upheld the rights of the Indians. But President Jackson, who clearly wanted to open Indian lands to white settlement, refused to recognize the Court's decisions. In a callous sneer at the Indians' defender, Jackson reportedly snapped, "John Marshall has made his decision; now let him enforce it."

Professing concern for the Indians' welfare, Jackson proposed a bodily removal of the remaining eastern tribes—chiefly Cherokee, Creek, Choctaw, Chickasaw, and Seminole—beyond the Mississippi.

Emigration was supposed to be voluntary because it would be "cruel and unjust to compel the aborigines to abandon the graves of their fathers," Jackson declared.

Jackson's policy sounded noble, but it led to the forced uprooting of more that 100,000 Indians. After Congress passed the Indian Removal Act in 1830, countless Indians died on the "Trail of Tears" to the newly established Indian Territory (present-day Oklahoma). The Bureau of Indian Affairs was established in 1836 to administer relations with America's original inhabitants, but as land-hungry whites pushed rapidly westward, the government's guarantees of a "permanent" Indian settlement went up in smoke.

Suspicious of white intentions from the start, Black Hawk led Indian resistance to removal in Illinois and Wisconsin, until his braves were forcibly crushed by regular army and militia troops in 1832. In Florida, the Seminoles, under the leadership of Osceola, retreated into the swampy Everglades, and for seven years (1835–1842) waged a bitter guerrilla war that took the lives of 1,500 soldiers and proved

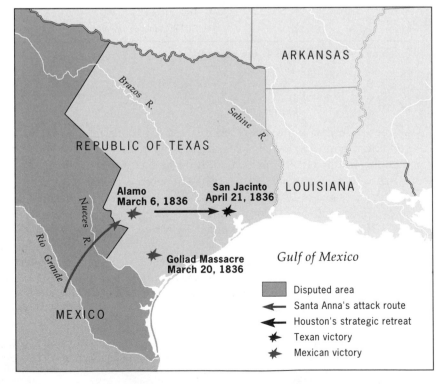

The Texas Revolution, 1835–1836 *General Houston's strategy was to retreat and use defense in depth. His line of supply from the United States was shortened as Santa Anna's lengthened. The Mexicans were forced to bring up supplies by land because the Texas navy controlled the sea. This force consisted of only four small ships, but it was big enough to do the job.*

to be the costliest Indian conflict in the American experience. After their defeat, some Seminoles fled deeper into the Everglades, where their descendants now live, while the majority were moved to Oklahoma.

The Lone Star of Texas Flickers

Americans, greedy for land, continued to covet the vast expanse of Texas, which the United States had abandoned to Spain when acquiring Florida in 1819. The Spanish authorities were desirous of populating this virtually unpeopled area, but before they could carry through their contemplated plans, the Mexicans won their independence. A new regime in Mexico City thereupon concluded arrangements in 1823 for granting a huge tract of land to Stephen Austin, with the understanding that he would bring in 300 American families. Immigrants were to be of the established Roman Catholic faith and were to become properly Mexicanized.

These two restrictions were largely ignored. Hardy Texan pioneers remained Americans at heart, resenting the trammels imposed by a "foreign" government. They were especially annoyed by the presence of Mexican soldiers, many of whom were ragged ex-convicts.

Energetic and prolific, Texas-Americans numbered about 30,000 by 1835 (see "Makers of America: Mexican or Texican?" pp. 198–199). Among the adventurers who had migrated to Texas were Davy Crockett, the fabulous rifleman, and James Bowie, the presumed inventor of the murderous knife that bears his name. A distinguished latecomer and leader was an ex-governor of Tennessee, Sam Houston. His life had been temporarily shattered in 1829 when his bride of a few weeks left him and he took up transient residence with the Arkansas Indians, who dubbed him "Big Drink."

The pioneer individualists who came to Texas were not easy to push around. Friction rapidly increased between Mexicans and Texans over such issues as slavery, immigration, and local rights. Slavery was a particularly touchy issue. Mexico emancipated its slaves in 1830 and prohibited their further importation into Texas, as well as further settlement by troublesome Americans. The Texans refused to

Samuel ("Sam") Houston (1793–1863)   *After a promising career in Tennessee as a soldier, lawyer, congressman, and governor, Houston became the chief leader and hero of Texas rebels. Elected to the Senate and the governorship of Texas, he was forced into retirement when his love for the Union caused him to spurn the Confederacy in the Civil War.*

honor this decree. They kept their slaves in bondage, and new American settlers kept bringing more slaves into Texas. The explosion finally came in 1835, when Mexican dictator Santa Anna wiped out all local rights and started to raise an army to suppress the upstart Texans.

Early in 1836 the Texans declared their independence and unfurled their Lone Star flag—with Sam Houston as commander-in-chief. Santa Anna, at the head of about 6,000 men, swept ferociously into Texas. Trapping a band of nearly 200 pugnacious Texans at the Alamo in San Antonio, he wiped them out to a man after a thirteen-day siege. A short time later a band of about 400 surrounded and defeated American volunteers, having thrown down their arms at Goliad, were butchered as "pirates."

Mexican or Texican?

Moses Austin, born a Connecticut Yankee in 1761, was determined to be Spanish—if that was what it took to acquire cheap land and freedom from pesky laws. In 1798 he tramped into untracked Missouri, still part of Spanish Louisiana, and pledged his allegiance to the king of Spain. He was not pleased when the Louisiana Purchase of 1803 restored him to American citizenship. In 1820, his old Spanish passport in his saddlebag, he rode into Spanish Texas and asked for permission to establish a colony of 300 families.

The Spanish authorities had previously banned American settlement in Texas. But they somewhat reluctantly allowed these "right sorts" to enter the

Mexican Forces Assault the Alamo
The defenders fought bravely but were overwhelmed by Santa Anna's army. Among those who died defending the historic mission were Colonel William Travis, Captain James Bowie, and former Congressman David Crockett.

territory, hoping that they might help "civilize" the land and wrest it from the Indians.

Upon Moses Austin's death in 1821, the task of realizing his dream fell to his twenty-seven-year-old son, Stephen. "I bid an everlasting farewell to my native country," Stephen Austin said, and he crossed into Texas on July 15, 1821, "determined to fulfill rigidly all the duties and obligations of a Mexican citizen." Soon he learned fluent Spanish and was signing his name as "Don Estévan F. Austin."

Austin fell just three families short of recruiting the 300 that his father had contracted to bring to Texas. The original settlers were nevertheless dubbed "the Old Three Hundred," the Texas equivalent of New England's *Mayflower* Pilgrims or the "first families of Virginia." Mostly Scots-Irish southerners from the trans-Appalachian frontier, the Old Three Hundred were cultured folk by frontier standards; all but four of them were literate. Other settlers followed, from Europe as well as America. Within ten years the "Anglos" (many of them French and German) outnumbered the Mexican residents, or *tejanos,* ten to one. They soon evolved a distinctive Texan culture, which included the mounted Texas Rangers, and cattle ranchers who ran huge operations on the limitless prairies.

The original Anglo-Texans brought with them the old Scots-Irish frontiersman's hostility to officialdom and authority. When the Mexican government tried to impose its will on the Anglo-Texans in the 1830s, they protested. Like the American revolutionaries of the 1770s, who at first demanded only the rights of Englishmen, the Texans began by asking simply for Mexican recognition of their rights as guaranteed by the Mexican constitution of 1824. But bloodshed at the Alamo in 1836, like that at Lexington in 1775, transformed protest into rebellion.

Texas lay—and still lies—along the frontier where Hispanic and Anglo-American cultures met, mingled, and clashed. In part, the Texas revolution was a contest between those two cultures. But it was also a contest about philosophies of government, pitting liberal frontier ideals of freedom against the conservative concept of centralized control. Stephen Austin sincerely tried to "Mexicanize" himself and his followers—until the Mexican government grew too arbitrary and authoritarian. Some of those who adhered to this philosophy were not "Anglos" but *tejanos.* Seven *tejanos* died at the Alamo, and several others signed the Texas declaration of independence.

Lorenzo de Zavala, an ardent Mexican liberal who had long resisted the centralizing tendencies of Mexico's dominant political party, was designated vice president of the Texas republic's interim government in 1836. Like the Austins, these *tejanos* and Mexicans had sought in Texas an escape from overbearing governmental authority. Their role in the revolution underscores the fact that the uprising was a struggle between defenders of local rights and agents of central authority as much as it was a fight between Anglo and Mexican cultures.

Texan war cries—"remember the Alamo!" "remember Goliad!" and "death to Santa Anna!"—swept up into the United States. Scores of vengeful Americans seized their rifles and rushed to the aid of relatives, friends, and compatriots. But despite their efforts, the Lone Star was in grave danger of being dimmed forever as General Sam Houston's small army continued its thirty-seven-day eastward retreat.

But Houston proved equal to the occasion. A commanding figure of a man and a natural leader of the Texans, he lured the pursuers onward to San Jacinto, near the site of the city that now bears his name. The invaders numbered about 1,300 men, the Texans about 900. Suddenly, on April 21, 1836, Houston turned, wiping out the invading force. The captured Santa Anna was forced to sign two treaties.

By their terms he agreed to withdraw Mexican troops and to recognize the Rio Grande as the extreme southwestern boundary of Texas. When released, he repudiated the whole agreement as illegal and as extorted under duress.

Texas: An International Derelict

Mexico no doubt had a genuine grievance against the United States. The Texans, though courageous, could hardly have won their independence without unneutral help of men and supplies from their American cousins. The Washington government, as the Mexicans bitterly complained, had a solemn obligation under international law to enforce its leaky neutrality statutes. But American public opinion, overwhelmingly favorable to the Texans, openly nullified the existing legislation. The federal authorities were powerless to act.

Jackson's heart was torn by the Texas issue. He disliked the Mexican overlords and admired the heroism of Sam Houston, his old comrade-in-arms against the Indians. But he was in no haste to recognize Texas formally as an independent republic. To do so would touch off the whole explosive issue of slavery, at a time when he was trying to engineer the election of his handpicked successor, Martin Van Buren. But after Van Buren had come safely under the wire, Jackson extended the right hand of recognition on the day before he left office in 1837.

Texas had every reason to expect a union with the United States, for what nation in its right mind would refuse so princely a dowry? The radiant Texan bride, officially petitioning for annexation in 1837, presented herself for marriage. But the expectant groom, Uncle Sam, was jerked back by the black hand of the slavery issue. Antislavery crusaders in the North were opposing annexation with increasing vehemence; they contended that the whole scheme was merely a conspiracy cooked up by the southern "slavocracy" to bring new slave pens into the Union.

Texas was left in a dangerous predicament. Fearing the return of the "villain," Santa Anna, it understandably went so far as to send feelers out to Britain and France for support. An ugly situation, involving balance-of-power politics, began to develop below the underbelly of the United States.

The Birth of the Whigs and the Election of 1836

New political parties were gelling as the 1830s lengthened. As early as 1828, the Democratic-Republicans of Jackson had unashamedly adopted the once-tainted name of "Democrats." Jackson's opponents condemned him as "King Andrew the First" and began to coalesce as Whigs—a name deliberately chosen to recollect eighteenth-century British and revolutionary American opposition to the monarchy.

The Whig party contained so many diverse elements that it was mocked at first as "an organized incompatibility." Hatred of Jackson and his "executive usurpation" was its only apparent cement in its formative days. The Whigs first emerged as an identifiable group in the Senate in opposition to Jackson's bank policies. Thereafter, the Whigs rapidly evolved into a potent national political force by attracting other groups alienated by Jackson: supporters of Clay's American System; southern states'-righters offended by Jackson's stand on nullification; the larger northern industrialists and merchants; and eventually many of the evangelical Protestants associated with the Anti-Masonic party.

As the presidential election of 1836 neared, the still-ramshackle organization of the Whigs showed in their inability to nominate a single presidential candidate. Their long-shot strategy was instead to run several prominent "favorite sons" who would so scatter the vote that no candidate would win a majority.

Martin Van Buren of New York, a smooth-as-silk politician, was Jackson's choice for "appointment" as his successor. Leaving nothing to chance, Jackson carefully rigged the nominating convention and rammed his favorite down the throats of the delegates. Van Buren was supported by the Jacksonites without wild enthusiasm, even though he had promised "to tread generally" in the military-booted footsteps of his predecessor.

Van Buren, the dapper "Little Van," squirmed into office by the close popular vote of 765,483 to 735,795. The Electoral College margin was more comfortable, 170 votes to 124.

In retrospect, the Jackson years were yeasty ones. The rough-hewn general—through forthrightness, energy, and strength of character—left a lasting imprint on the presidency. He demonstrated anew the value of strong executive leadership; he led the common people into national politics; he united them into the powerful and long-lived Democratic party; and he proved that they could be trusted with the vote. Reasserting the power of the presidency, he amazed weak-kneed politicians by showing that the courageous course often wins the most votes.

The other side of the ledger is less satisfying. Jackson cannot escape blame for his encouragement of the spoils system and especially for the damage he inflicted on the nation's financial system. It is true that the BUS was a powerful and ultimately corrupting monopoly that needed to have its wings clipped. But chopping off its head instead of clipping its wings deprived the nation of a sound central bank just as it was entering an era of rapid industrialization.

Big Woes for the "Little Magician"

Martin Van Buren, the eighth president, was the first to be born under the American flag. Bland of face, bald of head, slender of figure, the adroit little New Yorker has been described as "a first-class second-rate man." An accomplished wire puller and spoilsman—"the wizard of Albany"—he was also a statesman of wide experience in both legislative and administrative life. In intelligence, education, and training, he was above the average of the presidents since Jackson. The myth of his complete mediocrity sprouted from a series of misfortunes over which he had no control.

From the outset, the new politician-president labored under severe handicaps. As a machine-made candidate, he incurred the resentment of many Democrats. Jackson, the master showman, had been the dynamic type of executive whose administration had resounded with furious quarrels and cracked heads. Easygoing Martin Van Buren seemed to rattle about in the military boots of his testy predecessor. The people felt let down. Inheriting Jackson's mantle without his popularity, the polished New Yorker also inherited the ex-president's numerous and vengeful enemies.

Worst of all, Van Buren inherited the makings of a searing depression from Jackson. Much of his energy had to be devoted to the purely negative task of battling the panic, and there were not enough rabbits in the "Little Magician's" tall silk hat. Hard times ordinarily blight the reputation of a president—and Van Buren was no exception.

Depression Doldrums and the Independent Treasury

The panic of 1837 was a symptom of the financial sickness of the times. Its basic cause was rampant speculation prompted by a mania of get-rich-quick-ism. Gamblers in western lands were doing a "land-office business" on borrowed capital, much of it in the shaky currency of wildcat banks. The speculative craze spread to canals, roads, railroads, and slaves.

But speculation alone did not cause the crash. Jacksonian finance, including the Bank War and the Specie Circular, gave an additional jolt to an already teetering structure. Failures of wheat crops, ravaged by the Hessian fly, deepened the distress. Grain prices were forced so high that mobs in New York City, three weeks before Van Buren took the oath, stormed warehouses and broke open flour barrels.

Financial stringency abroad likewise left its imprint on America. Late in 1836, while Jackson was still president, the failure of two prominent British banks created tremors, and these in turn caused British investors to call in foreign loans. The resulting pinch in the United States, combined with other setbacks, heralded the beginning of the panic.

Hardship was acute and widespread. American banks collapsed by the hundreds, including some "pet banks," which carried down with them several millions in government funds. Commodity prices drooped, sales of public lands fell off, and customs revenues dried to a rivulet. Factories closed their doors; unemployed workers milled in the streets.

The Whigs came forward with proposals for active government remedies for the economy's ills. They called for the expansion of bank credit, higher tariffs, and subsidies for internal improvements. But Van Buren, shackled by the Jacksonian philosophy of keeping the government's paws off the economy, scorned all such ideas.

The beleaguered Van Buren tried to apply vintage Jacksonian medicine to the ailing economy through his controversial "Divorce Bill." Convinced that some of the financial fever was fed by the injection of federal funds into private banks, he championed the principle of "divorcing" the government from banking altogether. By establishing a so-called independent treasury, the government could lock its surplus money in vaults. Government funds would thus be safe, but they would also be denied to the banking system as reserves, thereby shriveling available credit resources. Van Buren's desire for political purity triumphed over enlightened economics.

Van Buren's "divorce" scheme was never highly popular. It was supported only lukewarmly by his fellow Democrats, many of whom longed for the risky but lush days of the "pet banks." The new policy was condemned by the Whigs, primarily because it would dampen their hopes for a revived Bank of the United States. After a prolonged struggle, the Independent Treasury Bill passed Congress in 1840. Repealed the next year by the victorious Whigs, the scheme was reenacted by the triumphant Democrats in 1846 and then continued until merged with the Federal Reserve System in the next century.

"Tippecanoe" versus "Little Van"

Martin Van Buren, though panic tainted, was renominated by the Democrats in 1840, albeit without terrific enthusiasm. They had no acceptable alternative to what the Whigs called "Martin Van Ruin."

The Whigs, hungering for the spoils of office, scented victory in the breeze. Pangs of the panic were still being felt; and voters blindly blamed their woes on the party in power. The Whigs turned again not to their ablest statesman—Clay or Webster—but to their presumably ablest vote getter: General William Henry Harrison, a coarse-featured military chieftain, with a long, thin face and medium build (5 feet 8 inches).

The aging hero, nearly sixty-eight when the campaign ended, was a small-bore candidate. Despite an inflated reputation, he had been only moderately successful in civilian and military life, notably at the battles of Tippecanoe (1811) and the Thames (1813). "Old Tippecanoe" was then living quietly in a sixteen-room mansion, located on a 3,000-acre farm near North Bend, Ohio. His views on current issues were only vaguely known. He was nominated primarily because he was issueless and

enemyless—and a most unfortunate precedent was thus set. John Tyler of Virginia, an afterthought, was selected as his vice presidential running mate.

The Whigs played the political game in the 1840 campaign with the cards close to their vests. They published no platform, because they feared making bothersome commitments and were unwilling to reveal the deep divisions within their own patchwork party. They hoped to sweep their hero in by a frothy huzza-for-Harrison campaign.

A dull-witted Democratic editor played directly into Whig hands. Stupidly insulting the West, he sneered at Harrison as an impoverished old farmer who would be content with a pension, a log cabin, and a barrel of hard cider—the poor westerner's champagne. Whigs gleefully took up the challenge and, stressing the hard cider and log cabin theme, turned the campaign into a huge political revival meeting.

A nonexistent candidate rapidly began to take shape in the hands of Whig mythmakers. The real Harrison was not low born, but from one of the FFVs (first families of Virginia). He was not poverty stricken; he did not live in a one-room log cabin; he did not swill down gallons of hard cider (he evidently preferred whiskey); and he did not plow his fields with his own "huge paws."

Whig propagandists made merry with little "Matty" Van Buren, the "Flying Dutchman." Although reared in poverty, he was denounced as a supercilious aristocrat who wore corsets and ate French food with golden teaspoons from golden plates. Jackson's rough-timbered Democratic party, deeply rooted in the West, was thus saddled with a simpering dandy from the aristocratic East. As a jeering Whig campaign song proclaimed:

> Old Tip, he wears a homespun shirt,
> He has no ruffled shirt, wirt, wirt.
> But Matt, he has the golden plate,
> And he's a little squirt, wirt, wirt.

The Log Cabins and Hard Cider of 1840

Eager Democrats, who had hurrahed Jackson into the White House, now discovered to their chagrin that this was a game two could play. Acres of Whig audiences and miles of Whig marchers shouted such slogans as "Harrison, two dollars a day and roast beef" and "With Tip and Tyler we'll bust Van's biler [boiler]." Log cabins were dished up in every conceivable form. Bawling Whigs, stimulated by fortified cider, rolled huge inflated balls from village to village and state to state—balls that represented the snowballing majority for "Tip and Ty." As they pushed, they sang:

> Tippecanoe, and Tyler too.
> And with them we'll beat little Van, Van, Van,
> Oh! Van is a used-up man.

Claptrap was king, as the electoral debauch reached an all-time intellectual low. There was little sober discussion of the issues. Democrats inquired earnestly about the bank, internal improvements, and the tariff. The replies were "log cabin," "hard cider," and "Harrison is a poor man." Van Burenites,

protesting futilely, drowned in a wave of apple juice as America experienced its first mass-turnout election.

Harrison won by the surprisingly close margin of 1,275,016 popular votes to 1,129,102, but by the overwhelming electoral count of 234 to 60. The hard-ciderites had seemingly received a mandate to go to Washington, tear down the White House, and erect a log cabin.

Basically, the vote was a protest against hard times—a thunderous shout of "Out with the old and in with the new." But the blatant bunkum and silly slogans set an unfortunate example for future campaigns. Democracy calls for hard thinking, not hard cider; for dignity, not delirium. Yet a well-organized and well-entrenched political party was hooted out of office not because of its policies or principles but by an inane hoopla campaign.

Politics for the Common Man   *Artist George Caleb Bingham here gently satirizes the drinking and wheeler-dealing that sometimes marred the electoral process in the boisterous age of Jacksonian politics.*

The Democrats were baffled. They complained with much bitterness and no little truth that they had been shouted down, sung down, lied down, and drunk down. Yet, though outsloganed, they had kept their ranks intact. Even in defeat they were a stronger party than the Whigs. Though temporarily overdosed with hard cider, they would be heard from again.

The Two-Party System Emerges

The Jeffersonians of an earlier day had been so successful in absorbing the programs of their Federalist opponents that a full-blown two-party system had never truly emerged in the subsequent Era of Good Feelings. The idea had prevailed that parties of any kind smacked of conspiracy and "faction" and were injurious to the health of the body politic in a virtuous republic.

But the American political world changed dramatically in the era of the New Democracy. One of Andrew Jackson's most lasting legacies was the impetus he gave to the formation of a vigorous and durable two-party system, which had fully come of age by 1840.

Both parties, the Democrats as well as the Whigs, grew out of the rich soil of Jeffersonian republicanism, and each laid claim to different aspects of the republican inheritance. Jacksonians glorified the liberty of the individual and were fiercely on guard against the inroads of "privilege" into government. Whigs trumpeted the natural harmony of society and the value of community over individualism and self-interest, and were willing to use government to realize their objectives.

Democrats clung to states' rights and federal restraint in social and economic affairs as their basic doctrines. Whigs tended to favor a renewed national bank, protective tariffs, internal improvements, public schools, and, increasingly, moral reforms, such as the prohibition of liquor and eventually the abolition of slavery.

The two parties were thus separated by real differences of philosophy and policy. But they also had much in common. Both were mass-based "catchall" parties that tried deliberately to mobilize as many voters as possible for their cause. Although

CHRONOLOGY	
1823	Mexico opens Texas to American settlers.
1830	Indian Removal Act.
	Jackson vetoes bill to improve Maysville Road.
1832	Jackson defeats Clay for presidency.
	Bank War: Jackson vetoes bill rechartering Bank of the United States.
	Tariff of 1832.
	Black Hawk War.
1833	South Carolina nullification crisis.
	Compromise Tariff of 1833.
	Jackson removes federal deposits from Bank of the United States.
1835–1839	Southeastern Indians removed on "Trail of Tears."
1836	Bank of the United States expires.
	Specie Circular issued.
	Bureau of Indian Affairs established.
	Texas wins independence from Mexico.
	Van Buren elected president.
1837	Seminole Indians defeated and removed from Florida.
	United States recognizes Texas but refuses annexation.
	Panic of 1837.
1840	Independent treasury established.
	Harrison defeats Van Buren for presidency.

it is true that Democrats tended to be more humble folk and Whigs more prosperous, both parties nevertheless commanded the loyalties of all kinds of Americans, from all social classes and in all sections. The social diversity of the two parties fostered horse-trading compromises *within* each party that prevented either from assuming extreme or radical positions. By the same token, the geographical diversity of the two parties retarded the emergence of purely sectional political parties—temporarily suppressing,

through compromise, the ultimately uncompromisable issue of slavery. When the two-party system began to creak in the 1850s, the Union was mortally imperiled.

Varying Viewpoints

As the debate over Jacksonianism shifted from a concern with geography to a consideration of social class, and later to an analysis of religion and ethnicity, historical evaluations of the rival parties also changed. Patrician historians of the nineteenth century made the Whigs the champions of enlightened civilization against the excesses of the Jacksonian rabble. The progressive historians of the early years of this century reversed those assessments. They praised the Jacksonians as the representatives of freedom and equality, and

damned the Whigs as self-serving, aristocratic snobs. That view held sway until recent times, when historians began exploring the operation of the party system on a local level and the variations in party positions from state to state. Studies such as those by Ronald Formisano and Michael Holt stress the two parties' connections with various religious and immigrant groups, and have encouraged a more balanced assessment of the merits of both parties.

SELECT READINGS

Primary Source Documents

An incisive commentary on Jacksonian politics is novelist James Fenimore Cooper's *The American Democrat** (1838). On the Bank War, see Andrew Jackson's "Veto Message" (July 10, 1832), in James D. Richardson, ed., *Messages and Papers of the Presidents* (1896), vol. II, pp. 576 ff,* and Daniel Webster's "Speech on Jackson's Veto of the U.S. Bank Bill" (1832), in Richard Hofstadter, ed., *Great Issues in American History.*

Secondary Sources

A thorough introduction to the Jacksonian era is the concluding volume of Robert V. Remini's biography, *Andrew Jackson and the Course of American Democracy, 1833–1845* (1984). Incisive analysis can be found in Richard Hofstadter's essay on Jackson in *The American Political Tradition* (1948). A superior monograph is William W. Freehling, *Prelude to Civil War: The Nullification Controversy in South Carolina* (1966). Jacksonian banking policy

is broadly treated in John McFaul, *The Politics of Jacksonian Finance* (1972). Robert V. Remini focuses on the political conflict over economic issues in *Andrew Jackson and the Bank War* (1967). Jackson's Indian policies are scrutinized in Ronald N. Satz, *American Indian Policy in the Jacksonian Ear* (1975), and Michael P. Rogin's heavily psychoanalytic *Fathers and Children: Andrew Jackson and the Subjugation of the American Indians* (1975). Important political transformations are handled in the Ronald P. Formisano and Richard P. McCormick volumes cited in Chapter 14. See also the opening chapters of Michael F. Holt's *The Political Crisis of the 1850s* (1978). Daniel W. Lowe provides a stimulating analysis of Jackson's opponents in *The Political Culture of the American Whigs* (1980). The color of the frothy presidential campaign of 1840 comes through in Robert G. Gunderson, *The Log-Cabin Campaign* (1957).

CHAPTER 16

Forging the National Economy, 1790–1860

The progress of invention is really a threat [to monarchy]. Whenever I see a railroad I look for a republic.

Ralph Waldo Emerson, 1866

The Westward Movement

The rise of Andrew Jackson, the first president from beyond the Appalachian Mountains, exemplified the inexorable westward march of the American people. The West, with its raw frontier, was the most typically American part of the nation. As Ralph Waldo Emerson wrote in 1844, "Europe stretches to the Alleghenies; America lies beyond."

The republic was young, and so were the people. As late as 1850, half of Americans were under the age of thirty. They were also restless and energetic, seemingly always on the move, and always westward. By 1840 the demographic center had crossed the Alleghenies. On the eve of the Civil War, it had marched beyond the Ohio River.

Legend portrays an army of muscular axmen triumphantly carving civilization out of the western woods. But in reality life was downright grim for most pioneer families. Poorly fed, ill clad, housed in hastily erected shanties, they were perpetual victims of disease, depression, and premature death. Above all, unbearable loneliness haunted them, especially the women. These women settlers were often cut off

from human contact, even their neighbors, for whole days or even weeks, while confined to the cramped orbit of a dark cabin erected in a secluded clearing. Breakdowns and even madness were all too frequently the "opportunities" that the frontier offered to pioneer women.

Frontier life could be tough and crude for men as well. No-holds-barred wrestling, which permitted such niceties as the biting off of noses and the gouging out of eyes, was a popular entertainment. Pioneering Americans, marooned by geography, were often ill informed, superstitious, provincial, and fiercely individualistic. Emerson's popular lecture-essay "Self-Reliance" struck a deeply responsive chord. The literature of the period abounded with portraits of heroically unique, isolated figures such as James Fenimore Cooper's Natty Bumppo and Herman Melville's Captain Ahab—just as Jacksonian politics aimed to emancipate the lone-wolf, enterprising businessperson. Yet even in this heyday of rugged individualism, there were important exceptions. Pioneers, in tasks clearly beyond their own

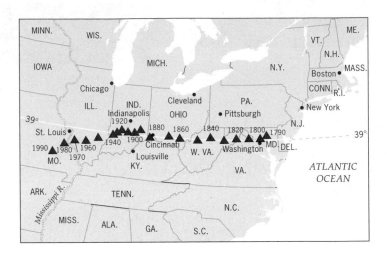

Westward Movement of the Center of Population, 1790–1990 *Note the remarkable equilibrium of the north-south pull from 1790 onward, and the strong spurt west and south after 1940. The 1980 census revealed that the nation's center of population had at last moved west of the Mississippi River.*

individual resources, would call on neighbors for log rolling and barn raising and ask their governments for help in building internal improvements.

Shaping the Western Landscape

The westward movement also molded the physical environment. Pioneers in a hurry often exhausted the land and then pushed on leaving behind barren and rain-gutted fields. In the Kentucky bottomlands, settlers discovered that they could burn off the native cane and plant "Kentucky bluegrass," which made ideal pasture for livestock.

Pioneers altered the environment of the American West in additional ways. By the 1820s American fur-trappers were setting their traplines all over the vast Rocky Mountain region. Each summer, trappers would come down from the mountains and swap their beaver pelts for manufactured goods from the East. Trade in buffalo robes also flourished until the massive bison herds were virtually annihilated. On the California coast, other traders pursued sea-otter pelts until the once-bountiful otters were near extinction. Some historians have called this aggressive and often heedless exploitation of the West's natural bounty "ecological imperialism."

Yet Americans in this period also reverenced nature and admired its beauty. Indeed the spirit of nationalism fed the growing appreciation of the uniqueness of the American wilderness. Searching for distinctive American characteristics in this nation-conscious age, many observers found the wild, western land to be among the young nation's defining attributes. Devotion to the pristine, natural beauty of the American wilderness became in time a national mystique, animating literature and painting, and eventually kindling a conservation movement.

George Catlin, a painter and student of Native American life, was among the first Americans to advocate the preservation of nature as a deliberate national policy. Appalled at the reckless slaughter of the buffalo, Catlin proposed the creation of a national park to preserve nature and wildlife—a goal that bore fruit with the establishment of Yellowstone National Park in 1872.

The March of the Millions

As the American people moved West, they also multiplied at an amazing rate. By midcentury the population was still doubling approximately every twenty-five years, as in colonial days.

By 1860 the original thirteen states had more than doubled in number: thirty-three stars graced the American flag. The United States was the fourth most populous nation in the Western world, exceeded only by three European countries—Russia, France, and Austria.

Urban growth continued explosively. In 1790 only two American cities could boast 20,000 or more souls: Philadelphia and New York. By 1860 there were 43; and about 300 other places claimed over 5,000 inhabitants apiece. New York was the metropolis; New Orleans, the "Queen of the South"; and Chicago, the swaggering lord of the Midwest, destined to be "hog butcher for the world."

Such overrapid urbanization unfortunately brought undesirable by-products. It intensified the problems of smelly slums, feeble street lighting, inadequate policing, impure water, foul sewage, ravenous rats, and improper garbage disposal. Hogs poked their scavenging snouts about many city streets as late as the 1840s. Boston in 1823 pioneered with a sewage system; and New York in 1842 abandoned wells for a piped-in water supply. The city thus unknowingly eliminated the breeding places of many disease-carrying mosquitoes.

A continuing high birthrate accounted for most of the increase in population, but by the 1840s the tides of immigration were adding hundreds of thousands more. Before this decade, immigrants had been flowing in at the rate of about 60,000 a year, but suddenly the influx was tripled in the 1840s, and then quadrupled in the 1850s. During these two feverish decades, over a million and a half Irish, and nearly as many Germans, swarmed down the gangplanks. Why did they come?

The immigrants came partly because Europe seemed to be running out of room. The population of the Old World more than doubled in the nineteenth century, and Europe began to generate a great seething pool of apparently "surplus" people. They were displaced and footloose in their homelands before they felt the tug of the American magnet. Indeed, at least as many people moved about *within* Europe as crossed the Atlantic.

Although many of these people went elsewhere, it was America that beckoned most strongly to the struggling masses of Europe. About 35 million of the nearly 60 million who abandoned Europe in the century after 1840 headed for "the land of freedom and opportunity," where no aristocratic caste or state church suppressed the individual. Much-read letters sent home by immigrants—"America letters"—described in glowing terms the richer life: low taxes, no compulsory military service, and "three meat meals a day." The introduction of transoceanic steamships also meant that the immigrants could come speedily, in a matter of ten or twelve days instead of ten or twelve weeks. They were still jammed into unsanitary quarters, thus suffering an

appalling death rate, but the nightmare was more endurable because it was shorter.

The Emerald Isle Moves West

Ireland, already groaning under the heavy hand of British overlords, was prostrated in the mid-1840s. A terrible rot attacked the potato crop, on which the people had become dangerously dependent, and about one-fourth of them were swept away by disease and hunger. Starved bodies were found dead by the roadsides with grass in their mouths. All told, about 2 million perished.

Tens of thousands of destitute souls, fleeing the Land of Famine for the Land of Plenty, flocked to America in the "Black Forties." Ireland's great export has been population; and the Irish take their place beside the Africans and the Jews as a dispersed people (see "Makers of America: The Irish," pp. 210–211).

These uprooted newcomers swarmed into the larger seaboard cities, such as Boston and New York, which rapidly became the largest Irish city in the world.

The luckless Irish received no red-carpet treatment. They were scorned by the older American stock, especially "proper" Protestant Bostonians, who regarded the scruffy Catholic newcomers as a social menace. Barely literate "Biddies" (Bridgets) took jobs as kitchen maids. Broad-shouldered "Paddies" (Patricks) were pushed into pick-and-shovel drudgery on canals and railroads, where thousands left their bones as victims of disease and accidental explosions. It was said that an Irishman lay buried under every railroad tie. As wage-depressing competitors for jobs, the Irish were hated by native workers. "No Irish Need Apply" was a sign commonly posted at factory gates, and was often abbreviated to NINA. The Irish, in turn, fiercely resented the blacks, with whom they shared society's basement. Race riots between black and Irish dockworkers flared up in several port cities, and the Irish were generally cool to the abolitionist cause.

The friendless "famine Irish" were forced to fend for themselves. The Ancient Order of Hibernians, a semisecret society founded in Ireland to fight rapacious landlords, served as a benevolent society

The Irish

During the wars that ravaged Europe from 1793 to 1815, Irish tenant farmers had prospered—but only temporarily. When peace came, wheat prices plummeted and hard-pressed landlords, aided by British police, forced their tenants off the land. Many displaced Irish farmers sought work in England; a few went to America. Then in 1845, a blight that ravaged the potato crop sounded the final knell for the Irish peasantry. The resultant famine spread desolation throughout the island. In five years, about 2 million people died. Another million sailed for America.

Of the emigrants, most were young and literate in English. Families typically pooled money to send strong young sons to the New World, where they would earn wages to pay the fares for those who remained behind. These "famine Irish" mostly remained in the port cities of the Northeast, abandoning the farmer's life for the squalor and congestion of the urban metropolis.

The Irish newcomers were poorly prepared for urban life. They found progress up the economic ladder painfully slow. Their work as domestic servants or construction laborers was dull and arduous, and mortality rates were astoundingly high. Escape from the potato famine hardly guaranteed a long life to an Irish-American; a gray-bearded Irishman was a rare sight in nineteenth-century America.

But it was their Roman Catholicism, even more than their penury and their perceived fondness for alcohol, that earned the Irish the distrust and resentment of their native-born, Protestant American neighbors. The cornerstone of social and religious life for Irish immigrants was the parish. Worries about safeguarding their children's faith inspired the construction of parish schools, financed by the parents' hard-earned pennies.

Just Off the Boat *Most poverty-stricken Irish peasants arrived in America with no more than the few goods they could carry on their back. Yet within a few generations Irish-Americans came to play a prominent role in America's cities, politics, and Catholic church life.*

If Ireland's green fields scarcely equipped its sons and daughters for the scrap and scramble of economic life in America's cities, life in the old country had instilled in them an aptitude for politics. Irish-Catholic resistance against centuries of British Anglican domination had instructed many Irish in the ways of mass politics. That political experience readied them for the boss system of political "machines" in America's northeastern cities. Irish voters soon became a bulwark of the Democratic party, reliably supporting the party of Jefferson and Jackson in cities such as New York and Boston. As Irish-Americans like New York's "Honest John" Kelly themselves became bosses, white-collar jobs in government service opened up to the Irish. They became building inspectors, aldermen, and even policemen—an astonishing irony for a people driven from their homeland by the nightsticks and bayonets of the British police.

in America, aiding the downtrodden. It also helped to spawn the "Molly Maguires," a shadowy Irish miners' union that rocked the Pennsylvania coal districts in the 1860s and 1870s.

The Irish tended to remain in low-skill occupations but gradually improved their lot, usually by acquiring modest amounts of property. The education of children was cut short as families struggled to save money to purchase a home. But for humble Irish peasants, cruelly cast out of their homeland, owning property was a grand "success."

Politics quickly attracted these gregarious Gaelic newcomers. They soon began to gain control of powerful city machines, notably New York's Tammany Hall, and reaped the patronage rewards. Before long, beguilingly brogued Irishmen dominated police departments in many big cities, where they now drove the "Paddy wagons" that had once carted their brawling forebears to jail.

The German Forty-Eighters

The influx of refugees from Germany between 1830 and 1860 was hardly less spectacular than that from Ireland. During these troubled years, over a million and a half thrifty Germans stepped onto American soil (see "Makers of America: The Germans," pp. 212–213). The bulk of them were uprooted farmers, displaced by crop failures and by other hardships. But a strong sprinkling were liberal political refugees. Saddened by the collapse of the democratic revolutions of 1848, they had decided to leave the autocratic fatherland and flee to America—the brightest hope of democracy.

Germany's loss was America's gain. Zealous liberals like the lanky and public-spirited Carl Schurz, a relentless foe of slavery and public corruption, contributed richly to the elevation of American political life.

Irish and German Immigration by Decade

Years	Irish	German	All Others	Totals
1820–1830	Unknown	Unknown	Unknown	151,824
1831–1840	207,381	152,454	239,290	599,125
1841–1850	780,719	434,626	497,906	1,713,251
1851–1860	914,119	951,667	732,428	2,598,214
1861–1870	435,778	787,468	1,091,578	2,314,824
1871–1880	436,871	718,182	1,657,138	2,812,191
1881–1890	655,482	1,452,970	3,138,161	5,246,613
1891–1900	388,416	505,152	2,793,996	3,687,564

The Germans

Between 1820 and 1920, a sea of Germans lapped at America's shores and seeped into its very heartland. Their numbers surpassed those of any other immigrant group, even the prolific and often detested Irish. Yet this Germanic flood, unlike its Gaelic equivalent, stirred little panic in the hearts of native-born Americans, because the Germans largely stayed to themselves, far from the crowded northeastern cities.

These "Germans" actually hailed from many different Old World lands, because there was no unified nation until 1871, when the ruthless and crafty Prussian Otto von Bismarck assembled the German state out of a mosaic of independent principalities, kingdoms, and duchies. Until that time, "Germans" came to America as Prussians, Bavarians, Hessians, Rhinelanders, Pomeranians, and Westphalians. They arrived at different times and for many different reasons. Some, particularly the so-called Forty-Eighters—the refugees from the failed democratic revolution of 1848—hungered for the democracy they had failed to win in Germany. Others, particularly Jews, Pietists, and Anabaptist groups like the Amish and the Mennonites, coveted religious freedom.

Typical German immigrants arrived with fatter purses than their Irish counterparts. Small land-owners or independent artisans in their native countries,

"Little Germany" *Cincinnati's "Over-the-Rhine" district, 1887.*

they did not have to settle for bottom-rung industrial employment in the grimy factories of the Northeast and instead could afford to push on to the open spaces of the West.

In Wisconsin these immigrants found a home away from home, a place with a climate, soil, and geography much like those of central Europe. Milwaukee, a crude frontier town before their arrival, became the "German Athens." It boasted a German theater, German beer gardens, a German volunteer fire company, and a German-English academy. In distant Texas, German settlements such as New Braunfels and Friedrichsburg flourished. When the famous landscape architect and writer Frederick Law Olmsted stumbled upon these prairie outposts of Teutonic culture in 1857, he was shocked to be "welcomed by a figure in a blue flannel shirt and pendant beard, quoting Tacitus."

These German colonizers of America's heartland also formed religious communities, none more distinctive or durable than the Amish settlements of Pennsylvania, Indiana, and Ohio. The Amish took their name from their founder and leader, the Swiss Anabaptist Jacob Ammann. Like other Anabaptist groups, they shunned extravagance and reserved baptism for adults, repudiating the tradition of infant baptism practiced by most Europeans. For this they were persecuted, even imprisoned, in Europe. Seeking escape from their oppression, some 500 Amish ventured to Pennsylvania in the 1700s, followed by 3,000 in the years from 1815 to 1865.

In America they formed enduring religious communities—isolated enclaves where they could shield themselves from the corruption and the conveniences of the modern world. To this day the German-speaking Amish travel in horse-drawn carriages and farm without heavy machinery. The Amish remain a stalwart, traditional community in a rootless, turbulent society, a living testament to the religious ferment and social experiments of the antebellum era.

Many of these Germanic newcomers, unlike the Irish, possessed a modest amount of material goods. Most of them pushed out to the lush lands of the Midwest, notably Wisconsin, where they settled and established model farms.

The hand of Germans in shaping American life was widely felt in still other ways. They had fled from the militarism and wars of Europe and consequently came to be a bulwark of isolationist sentiment in the upper Mississippi Valley. Better educated on the whole than the stump-grubbing Americans, they strongly supported public schools, including their *Kindergarten* (children's garden). They likewise did much to stimulate art and music. As outspoken champions of freedom, they became relentless enemies of slavery during the fevered years before the Civil War.

Yet the Germans—often dubbed "damned Dutchmen"—were occasionally regarded with suspicion by their old-stock American neighbors. Seeking to preserve their language and culture, they sometimes settled in compact colonies and kept aloof from the surrounding community. Accustomed to the "Continental Sunday" and uncurbed by Puritan tradition, they made merry on the Sabbath and drank huge quantities of an amber beverage called *bier* (beer), which dates its real popularity in America to their coming. Their Old World drinking habits, like those of the Irish newcomers, spurred advocates of temperance in the use of alcohol to redouble their reform efforts.

Flare-ups of Antiforeignism

The invasion by this so-called immigrant rabble in the 1840s and 1850s inflamed the hates of American "nativists." Not only did the newcomers take jobs from "native" Americans, but the bulk of displaced Irishmen were Roman Catholics, as were a substantial minority of the Germans. The Church of Rome was still widely regarded by many old-line Americans as a foreign church.

Roman Catholics were now on the move. Seeking to protect their children from Protestant indoctrination in the public schools, they began in the 1840s to construct an entirely separate Catholic school system—an enormously expensive undertaking for a poor immigrant community, but one that revealed the strength of its religious commitment. A negligible minority during colonial days, Catholics became a powerful religious group with the enormous influx of the Irish and Germans in the 1840s and 1850s. In 1840 they ranked fifth, behind the Baptists, Methodists, Presbyterians, and Congregationalists. By 1850, with some 1.8 million communicants, they had bounded into first place—a position they have never lost.

"Native" Americans were alarmed by these mounting figures. They professed to believe that in due time the "alien riffraff" would "establish" the Catholic church at the expense of Protestantism and would introduce "popish idols." The noisier American nativists rallied for political action. In 1849 they

formed the Order of the Star-Spangled Banner, which soon developed into the formidable Know-Nothing party—a name derived from its secretiveness. Nativists agitated for rigid restrictions on immigration and naturalization and for laws authorizing the deportation of alien paupers. They also promoted a lurid anti-Catholic literature, most of it pure fiction. The authors, sometimes posing as "escaped nuns," described sin as they imagined it behind convent walls. One of these books—Maria Monk's *Awful Disclosures* (1836)—sold over 300,000 copies.

Even uglier was occasional mass violence. As early as 1834 a Catholic convent near Boston was burned by a howling mob, and in ensuing years there were a few scattered attacks on Catholic schools and churches. The most frightful flare-up occurred during 1844 in Philadelphia, where the Irish Catholics fought back against the threats of the nativists. The City of Brotherly Love did not quiet down until two Catholic churches had been burned and some thirteen citizens had been killed and fifty wounded in several days of fighting. These outbursts of intolerance, though infrequent and generally localized in the larger cities, remain an unfortunate blot on the record of America's treatment of minority groups.

Crooked Voting   *A bitter nativist cartoon charging Irish and German immigrants with "stealing" elections.*

Immigrants were undeniably making America a more pluralistic society—one of the most ethnically and racially varied in the history of the world. Why, in fact, were cultural clashes not more frequent and more violent? Part of the answer lies in the robust American economy. Its vigorous growth in these years ensured that immigrants could claim their share of wealth without decreasing the wealth of others. Their hands and brains, in fact, helped fuel economic expansion. Immigrants and the American economy, in short, needed one another. Without the newcomers, a preponderantly agricultural United States might well have been condemned to watch in envy as the Industrial Revolution swept through nineteenth-century Europe.

The March of Mechanization

A gifted group of British inventors, beginning about 1750, perfected a series of machines for the mass production of textiles. This enslavement of steam multiplied the power of human muscles some ten thousandfold, and ushered in the modern factory system—and with it the so-called Industrial Revolution.

The factory system gradually spread from Britain—"the world's workshop"—to other lands. It took a generation or so to reach western Europe, and then the United States. Why was the youthful American republic, destined to be an industrial giant, so slow to embrace the machine?

For one thing, virgin soil in America was cheap. Land-starved descendants of land-starved peasants were not going to coop themselves up in smelly factories when they might till their own acres in God's fresh air and sunlight. Labor was therefore generally scarce, and enough nimble hands to operate the machines were hard to find. Money for capital investment, moreover, was not plentiful in pioneering America. Raw materials lay undeveloped, undiscovered, or unsuspected.

Just as labor was scarce, so were consumers. The young country at first lacked a domestic market large enough to make factory-scale manufacturing profitable.

Long-established British factories, which provided cutthroat competition, posed another problem. Their superiority was attested by the fact that a few unscrupulous Yankee manufacturers, out to make a dishonest dollar, stamped their own products with faked English trademarks.

The British also enjoyed a monopoly of the textile machinery, whose secrets they were anxious to hide from foreign competitors. Parliament enacted laws, in harmony with the mercantilistic system, forbidding the export of the machines or the emigration of mechanics able to reproduce them.

Although a number of small manufacturing enterprises existed in the early republic, the future industrial colossus was still snoring. Not until well past the middle of the nineteenth century did the value of the output of the factories exceed that of the farms.

Whitney Ends the Fiber Famine

Samuel Slater has been acclaimed the "Father of the Factory System" in America, and seldom can the paternity of a movement more properly be ascribed

Eli Whitney (1765–1825) *Few men have been so pivotal in American history. Whitney's cotton gin revolutionized southern agriculture, ushering in the cotton-and-slave kingdom of the early nineteenth century. His system of interchangeable parts revolutionized northern industry, giving the North economic and technological superiority in the Civil War, which ultimately extinguished slavery.*

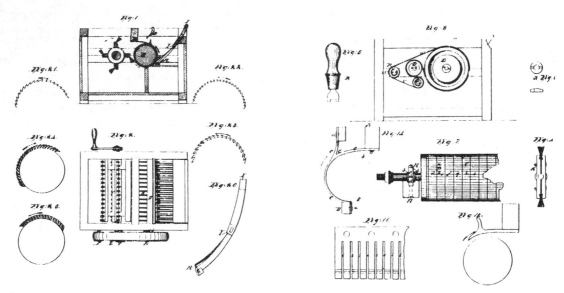

Whitney's Cotton Gin *Shown here as it was pictured in Whitney's application for a U.S. patent, the gin was artfully simple. Wire brushes on a rotating wheel pulled the cotton fibers through slots too narrow to allow seeds to pass. A second set of brushes removed the fibers. Whitney's gin made possible the mass cultivation of upland or short-staple cotton, which was unprofitable to raise when its seeds had to be laboriously removed by hand. Before Whitney's invention, cotton growing had been largely confined to long-staple or Sea Island cotton, which could grow in hot, humid coastal areas; now short-staple cotton cultivation spread across the southern interior, and so did slavery.*

to one person. A skilled British mechanic of twenty-one, he was attracted by bounties being offered by his country to workers familiar with the textile machines. After memorizing the plans for the machinery, he escaped in disguise to America, where he won the backing of Moses Brown, a Quaker capitalist in Rhode Island. Laboriously reconstructing the essential apparatus with the aid of a blacksmith and a carpenter, he put into operation in 1791 the first efficient American machinery for the spinning of cotton thread.

The ravenous mechanism was now ready, but where was the cotton fiber? Handpicking one pound of lint from three pounds of seed was a full day's work for one slave, and this process was so expensive that cotton cloth was relatively rare.

Another mechanical genius, Massachusetts-born Eli Whitney, now made his mark. After graduating from Yale, he journeyed to Georgia to serve as a private tutor while preparing for the law. There he

was told that the poverty of the South would be relieved if someone could only invent a workable device for separating the seed from the short-staple cotton fiber. Within ten days in 1793, he constructed a crude machine called the cotton gin (short for en*gin*e), which was fifty times more efficient than the handpicking process.

Few machines have ever wrought so wondrous a change. The gin affected not only the history of America but that of the world. Almost overnight the raising of cotton became highly profitable, and the South was tied hand and foot to the throne of king cotton. Human bondage had been dying out, but the insatiable demand for cotton reriveted the chains on the limbs of the downtrodden southern blacks.

Both South and North prospered. Slave-driving planters cleared more acres for cotton, pushing the cotton kingdom westward off the depleted tidewater plains, over the Piedmont, and onto the black loam bottomlands of Alabama and Mississippi.

Humming gins poured out avalanches of snowy fiber for the spindles of the Yankee machines. The American phase of the Industrial Revolution, which first blossomed in cotton textiles, was well on its way.

Factories at first flourished most actively in New England, though branching out into the more populous areas of New York, New Jersey, and Pennsylvania. The South, increasingly wedded to the production of cotton, could boast of comparatively little manufacturing. Its capital was bound up in slaves; its local consumers for the most part were desperately poor.

New England was singularly favored as an industrial center for several reasons. Her narrow belt of stony soil discouraged farming and hence made manufacturing more attractive than elsewhere. A relatively dense population provided labor and accessible markets; shipping brought in capital; and snug seaports made easy the import of raw materials and the export of the finished products. Finally, the rapid rivers—most notably the Merrimack in Massachusetts—provided abundant water power to turn the cogs of the machines. By 1860 more than 400 million pounds of southern cotton were pouring annually into the gaping maws of over 1,000 mills, mostly in New England.

Marvels in Manufacturing

America's factories spread slowly until about 1807, when there began the fateful sequence of the embargo, nonintercourse, and the War of 1812. The stoppage of European commerce drove both capital and labor from the waves onto the factory floor. Generous bounties were offered by local authorities for homegrown goods. "Buy American" and "wear American" became popular slogans, and patriotism prompted the wearing of baggy homespun garments. President Madison donned some at his inauguration, where he was said to have been a walking argument for the better processing of native wool.

But the manufacturing boomlet broke abruptly with the peace of Ghent in 1815, as British competitors unloaded their dammed-up surpluses at ruinously low prices. Responding to pained outcries, Congress provided some relief when it passed the mildly protective Tariff of 1816—among the earliest

political contests to control the shape of the economy.

As the factory system flourished, it embraced numerous other industries in addition to textiles. Prominent among them was the manufacturing of firearms, and here the wizardly Eli Whitney again appeared with an epochal contribution. Frustrated in his earlier efforts to monopolize the cotton gin, he turned to the mass production of muskets for the U.S. Army. Up to this time each part of a firearm had been hand-tooled, and if the trigger of one broke, the trigger of another might or might not fit. About 1798 Whitney seized upon the idea of having machines make each part, so that all the triggers, for example, would be as much alike as the successive imprints of a copperplate engraving. Journeying to Washington, he reportedly dismantled ten of his new muskets in the presence of skeptical officials, scrambled the parts together, and then quickly reassembled ten different muskets.

The principle of interchangeable parts was widely adopted by 1850, and it ultimately became the basis of modern mass-production, assembly-line methods. It gave to the North the vast industrial plant that ensured its eventual military preponderance over the South. The Yankee Eli Whitney, by perfecting the cotton gin, gave slavery a renewed lease on life, and perhaps made inevitable the Civil War. The same Whitney, by popularizing the principle of interchangeable parts, caused factories to flourish in the North and contributed heavily to the winning of that war by the Union.

The sewing machine, invented by Elias Howe in 1846 and perfected by Isaac Singer, gave another strong boost to northern industrialization. The sewing machine became the foundation of the ready-made clothing industry, which took root about the time of the Civil War. It drove many a seamstress from the shelter of the private home to the factory where, like a human robot, she tended the clattering mechanism.

Each momentous new invention seemed to stimulate still more imaginative inventions. For the decade ending in 1800 only 306 patents were registered in Washington, but the decade ending in 1860 saw the amazing total of 28,000. Yet in 1838 the clerk of the Patent Office had resigned in despair, complaining that all worthwhile inventions had been discovered.

Technical advances spurred equally important changes in the form and legal status of business organizations. The principle of limited liability aided the concentration of capital by permitting the individual investor, in cases of legal claims or bankruptcy, to risk no more than his or her own share of the corporation's stock. Laws of "free incorporation," first passed in New York in 1848, meant that business-people could create corporations without applying for individual charters from the legislature.

Samuel F. B. Morse's telegraph was among the inventions that tightened the sinews of an increasingly complex business world. A distinguished but poverty-stricken portrait painter, Morse finally secured from Congress, to the accompaniment of the usual jeers, an appropriation of $30,000 to support his experiment with "talking wires." In 1844 Morse strung a wire forty miles from Washington to Baltimore and tapped out the historic message, "What hath God wrought?" The invention brought fame and fortune to Morse, as he put distantly separated people in almost instant communication with one another.

Workers and "Wage Slaves"

One ugly offspring of the factory system was an increasingly acute labor problem. Hitherto manufacturing had been done in the home, or in the small shop, where the master craftsman and his apprentice, rubbing elbows at the same bench, could maintain an intimate and friendly relationship. The Industrial Revolution submerged this personal association in the impersonal ownership of stuffy factories in "spindle cities." Around these, like tumors, the slumlike hovels of the "wage slaves" tended to cluster.

Clearly the early factory system did not shower its benefits evenly on all. While many owners waxed fat, workingpeople often wasted away at their workbenches. Hours were long, wages were low, and meals were skimpy and hastily gulped. Workers were forced to toil in unsanitary buildings that were poorly ventilated, lighted, and heated. They were forbidden by law to form labor unions to raise wages, for such cooperative activity was regarded as a crim-

inal conspiracy. Not surprisingly, only twenty-four recorded strikes occurred before 1835.

Especially vulnerable to exploitation were child workers. In 1820, half the nation's industrial toilers were children under ten years of age. Victims of factory labor, many children were mentally blighted, emotionally starved, physically stunted, and even brutally whipped in special "whipping rooms." In Samuel Slater's mill of 1791, the first machine tenders were seven boys and two girls, all under twelve years of age.

By contrast, the lot of most adult wage workers improved markedly in the 1820s and 1830s. In the full flush of Jacksonian democracy, many of the states granted the laboring man the vote. Brandishing the ballot, workers pushed for such goals as the ten-hour day, better wages and working conditions, public education, and an end to the inhumane practice of imprisonment for debt.

Employers, abhorring the rise of the rabble in politics, fought the ten-hour day to the last ditch. But labor registered a red-letter gain in 1840 when President Van Buren established the ten-hour day for federal employees on public works. In ensuing years a number of states gradually fell into line by reducing the hours for workingpeople.

Day laborers at last learned that their strongest weapon was to lay down their tools, even at the risk of prosecution under the law. Dozens of strikes erupted in the 1830s and 1840s, most of them for higher wages, some for the ten-hour day. The workers lost more strikes than they won, for the employer could resort to such tactics as importing strikebreakers—often derisively called "scabs" or "rats," and often fresh off the boat from the Old World. Labor long raised its voice against the unrestricted inpouring of wage-depressing and union-busting immigrant workers.

Labor's early and painful efforts at organization had netted some 300,000 trade unionists by 1830. But such encouraging gains were dashed on the rock of hard times following the severe depression of 1837. A hope-giving legal victory came in 1842 when the Massachusetts Supreme Court ruled in the case of *Commonwealth* v. *Hunt* that labor unions were not illegal conspiracies, provided that their methods were "honorable and peaceful." This enlightened decision did not legalize the strike overnight throughout the country, but it was a significant signpost of the times. Trade unions still had nearly a century to go before they could meet management on relatively even terms.

Women and the Economy

Women also were sucked into the clanging mechanism of factory production. They typically toiled six days a week, earning a pittance for dreary stints of twelve or thirteen hours—"from dark to dark." The Boston Associates' textile mills at Lowell, Massachusetts, employed New England farm girls, carefully supervised on and off the job by watchful matrons. Escorted regularly to church from their company boardinghouses, forbidden to form unions, they were as disciplined and docile a labor force as any employer could wish.

But factory jobs of any kind were still unusual for women. Opportunities for women to be economically self-supporting were scarce and consisted mainly of nursing, domestic service, and especially teaching. The dedicated Catharine Beecher, daughter of a famous preacher and sister of Harriet Beecher Stowe, tirelessly urged women to enter the teaching profession. She eventually succeeded beyond her dreams, as men left teaching for other lines of work and schoolteaching became a thoroughly "feminized" occupation.

In 1850, about 10 percent of white women were working for pay outside their own homes. Estimates are that about 20 percent of all women had been employed at some time prior to marriage. The vast majority of working women were single. Upon marriage, they left their paying jobs and took up their new work (without wages) as wives and mothers. In the home they were enshrined in a "cult of domesticity," a widespread cultural creed that glorified the traditional functions of the homemaker. From their pedestal, married women commanded immense moral power, and they increasingly made decisions that altered the character of the family itself.

Women's changing roles and the spreading Industrial Revolution brought some important changes in the life of the nineteenth-century home— the traditional "women's sphere." Love, not parental arrangement, more and more frequently determined the choice of a spouse—yet parents often retained the power of veto. Families thus became more closely knit and affectionate, providing the emotional refuge that made the threatening impersonality of big-city industrialism tolerable to many people.

Most striking, families grew smaller. The average household had nearly six members at the end of the eighteenth century but fewer than five members a century later. The fertility rate, or number of births to women age 14 to 45, dropped sharply among white women in the years after the Revolution and, in the course of the nineteenth century as a whole, fell by half. Birth control was still a taboo topic for polite conversation, and contraceptive technology was primitive, but clearly some form of family limitation was being practiced quietly and effectively in countless families, rural and urban alike. Women undoubtedly played a large part—perhaps the leading part— in decisions to have fewer children. This newly assertive role for women has been called "domestic feminism," because it signified the growing power and independence of women, even while they remained trapped in the cult of domesticity.

Smaller families, in turn, meant child-centered families, since where children are fewer, parents can lavish more care on them individually. European visitors to the United States in the nineteenth century often complained about the unruly behavior of American "brats." But though American parents may have increasingly spared the rod, they did not spoil their children. What Europeans saw as permissiveness was in reality the consequence of an emerging new idea of child-rearing, in which the child's will was not to be simply broken, but shaped. In the little republic of the family, as in the republic at large, good citizens were raised not to be meekly obedient to authority, but to be independent individuals who could make their own decisions on the basis of internalized moral standards. Thus, the outlines of the "modern" family were clear by midcentury: it was small, affectionate, and child centered, and provided a special arena for the talents of women. Feminists of a later day might decry the stifling atmosphere of the Victorian home, but to many women of the time it seemed a big step upward from the conditions of

Textile Workers of Lawrence (Massachusetts)   *Engraving by painter Winslow Homer. Born in Boston in 1836, Homer first became famous as a magazine illustrator. His drawings of battlefield scenes for* Harper's Weekly *during the Civil War made the conflict come to life for thousands of home-bound readers. He abandoned illustration in 1876 and gained even greater renown as a painter in oils and watercolors, especially with his depictions of marine scenes and life among blacks.*

grinding toil—often alongside men in the fields—in which their mothers had lived.

Western Farmers Reap a Revolution in the Fields

As smoke-belching factories altered the eastern skyline, flourishing farms were changing the face of the West. The trans-Appalachian region—especially the Ohio-Indiana-Illinois tier—was fast becoming the nation's breadbasket. Before long, it would become a granary to the world.

Pioneer farmers first hacked a clearing out of the forest and then planted their painfully furrowed fields to corn. The yellow grain was amazingly versatile. It could be fed to hogs ("corn on the hoof") or distilled into liquor ("corn in the bottle"). Both these

products could be transported more easily than the bulky grain itself, and they became the early western farmer's staple market items. So many hogs were butchered, traded, or shipped at Cincinnati that the city was known as the "Porkopolis" of the West.

Most western produce was at first floated down the Ohio-Mississippi river system to feed the booming cotton kingdom. Spurred on by the easy availability of the seemingly boundless acres, these soil tillers continuously sought ways to bring more and more acres into cultivation. Frustrated by thickly matted soil that snagged and snapped fragile wooden plows, farmers rejoiced in 1837 when John Deere finally produced a sharp steel plow light enough to be pulled by horses, rather than oxen.

In the 1830s Virginia-born Cyrus McCormick contributed the most wondrous contraption of all: a mechanical mower-reaper. The clattering cogs of McCormick's horse-drawn machine were to the western farmers what the cotton gin was to the southern planters. Seated on his red-chariot reaper, a single husbandman could do the work of five men with sickles and scythes.

No other American invention cut so wide a swath. It made ambitious capitalists out of humble plowmen, who now scrambled for more acres on which to plant more fields of billowing wheat. Large-scale ("extensive"), specialized, cash-crop agriculture came to dominate the West. With it followed mounting indebtedness, as farmers bought more land and more machinery to work it. Soon hustling farmer-businesspeople were annually harvesting a larger crop than the South could devour. They began to dream of markets elsewhere—in the mushrooming factory towns of the East, or across the faraway Atlantic. But they were still largely landlocked. Commerce moved north and south on the river systems. Before it could begin to move east-west in bulk, a transportation revolution would have to occur.

Highways and Steamboats

In 1789, when the Constitution was launched, primitive methods of travel were still in use. Waterborne commerce, whether along the coast or on the rivers, was slow, uncertain, and often dangerous. Stagecoaches and wagons lurched over bone-shaking roads. Passengers would be routed out to lay nearby fence rails across muddy stretches, and occasionally horses would drown in muddy pits while wagons sank slowly out of sight.

Cheap and efficient carriers were imperative if raw materials were to be transported to the factories, and if the finished product was to be delivered to the consumer.

A promising change came in the 1790s, when a private company completed the Lancaster turnpike, a broad, hard-surfaced highway that thrust sixty-two miles westward from Philadelphia to Lancaster, Pennsylvania. The highly successful Lancaster Pike returned dividends as high as 15 percent annually to its stockholders, attracted a rich trade to Philadelphia, stimulated the westward migration of the can-

vas-covered Conestoga wagons, and touched off a turnpike-building boom that lasted about twenty years.

Western road-building, always expensive, encountered opposition from states'-righters who opposed federal aid to local projects. Eastern states also protested against being bled of their populations. Westerners scored a notable triumph in 1811 when the federal government began to construct the elongated National Road, or Cumberland Road. When finally completed in 1852, after interruptions caused by the War of 1812 and states'-rights shackles on internal improvements, the highway stretched 591 miles from Cumberland, Maryland, to Vandalia, Ilinois.

The steamboat craze, which overlapped the turnpike-building era, was touched off by an ambitious painter-engineer named Robert Fulton. In 1807 Fulton installed a powerful steam engine in a vessel that posterity came to know as the *Clermont,* which was also dubbed "Fulton's Folly" by a dubious public. Belching sparks from its single smokestack, the quaint little ship steadily churned up the Hudson River from New York City to Albany, making the 150-mile trip in thirty-two hours.

The success of the steamboat was sensational. People could now in large degree defy wind, wave, tide, and downstream current. Within a few years Fulton had changed all of America's navigable streams into two-way arteries, thereby doubling their carrying capacity. Hitherto, keelboats had been pushed up the Mississippi, with quivering poles and raucous profanity, at less than one mile an hour—a process that was prohibitively expensive. Now the steamboats could churn rapidly against the current, ultimately attaining speeds in excess of ten miles an hour. The mighty Mississippi had finally met its master.

By 1820 there were some sixty steamboats on the Mississippi and its tributaries; by 1860 about 1,000 of them were luxurious river palaces. Chugging steamboats played a vital role in the opening of the West and South, both of which were richly endowed with navigable rivers. Like bunches of grapes on a vine, population clustered along the banks of the broad-flowing streams. Cotton growers and other farmers made haste to take up the now-profitable virgin soil. Not only could they float their produce out to market but, hardly less important, they could ship in, at low cost, their shoes, hardware, and other manufactured necessities.

Canals and Iron Horses

A canal-cutting craze paralleled the boom in turnpikes and steamboats. Led by dynamic Governor DeWitt Clinton, New York State started the trend when it dug the Erie Canal linking the Hudson River to the Great Lakes.

Begun in 1817, the canal eventually ribboned 363 miles. On its completion in 1825, a garland-bedecked canal boat glided from Buffalo, on Lake Erie, to the Hudson River and on to New York harbor. There, with colorful ceremony, Governor Clinton emptied a cask of water from the lake to symbolize "the marriage of the waters."

The water from Clinton's cask baptized an Empire State. Mule-drawn passengers and bulky freight could now be handled with cheapness and dispatch at the dizzy speed of five miles an hour. The cost of shipping a ton of grain from Buffalo to New York City fell from $100 to $5, and the time of transit from about twenty days to six.

Ever-widening economic ripples followed the completion of the Erie Canal. The value of land along the route skyrocketed, and new cities—such as Rochester and Syracuse—blossomed. Industry in the state boomed. The new profitableness of farming in the old Northwest—notably in Ohio, Michigan, Indiana, and Illinois—attracted thousands of European immigrants to the unaxed and untaxed lands now available. Flotillas of steamships soon plied the Great Lakes, connecting with waiting canal barges at Buffalo. Interior waterside villages such as Cleveland, Detroit, and Chicago exploded into mighty cities.

Other profound economic and political changes followed the canal's completion. The price of potatoes in New York City was cut in half, and many dispirited New England farmers, no longer able to face this ruinous competition, abandoned their rocky holdings and went elsewhere. Some became mill hands, thus speeding the industrialization of America. Others, finding it easy to go west over the Erie Canal, took up new farmlands south of the Great Lakes, where they were joined by thousands of New Yorkers and other northerners. Still others shifted to fruit, vegetable, and dairy farming. The transformations in the Northeast showed how long-established local market structures could be swamped by the emerging behemoth of a continental economy.

The most significant contribution to the development of such an economy proved to be the railroad. It was fast, reliable, cheaper than canals to construct, and not frozen over in winter. Able to go almost anywhere, even through the Appalachian barrier, it defied terrain and weather. The first railroad appeared in the United States in 1828. By 1860, only thirty-two years later, the United States boasted 30,000 miles of railroad track, three-fourths of it in the rapidly industrializing North.

At first the railroad faced strong opposition from vested interests, especially canal backers. Anxious to protect its investment in the Erie Canal, the New York legislature in 1833 prohibited the railroads from carrying freight—at least temporarily. Early railroads were also considered a dangerous public menace, for flying sparks could set fire to haystacks and houses, and appalling railway accidents could turn the wooden "miniature hells" into flaming funeral pyres for their riders.

Railroad pioneers had to overcome other obstacles as well. Arrivals and departures were conjectural, and numerous differences in gauge (the distance between the rails) meant frequent changes of trains for passengers. In 1840 there were seven transfers between Philadelphia and Charleston. But gauges gradually became standardized, safety devices were adopted, and the Pullman "sleeping palace" was introduced in 1859. America at long last was being bound together with ribs of iron, later to be made of steel.

The Transport Web Binds the Union

More than anything else, the desire of the East to tap the West stimulated the "transportation revolution." Until about 1830, the produce of the western region drained southward to the cotton belt or to the

The Stourbridge Lion   *On August 8, 1829, at Honesdale, Pennsylvania, this smoke-belching beast made the first successful trip in America by a steam locomotive.*

heaped-up wharves of New Orleans. The steamboat vastly aided the reverse flow of finished goods up the watery western arteries and helped bind West and South together. But the truly revolutionary changes in commerce and communication came in the three decades before the Civil War, as canals and railroad tracks radiated out from the East, across the Appalachians, and into the blossoming heartland. The ditchdiggers and tie layers were attempting nothing less than a conquest of nature itself. They would offset the "natural" flow of trade on the interior rivers by laying down an impressive grid of "internal improvements."

The builders succeeded beyond their wildest dreams. The Mississippi was increasingly robbed of its traffic, as goods moved eastward on chugging trains, puffing lake boats, and mule-tugged canal

barges. Governor Clinton had in effect picked up the mighty Father of Waters and flung it over the Appalachians, forcing it to empty into the sea at New York City. By the 1840s Buffalo was handling more western produce than New Orleans. Between 1836 and 1860, grain shipments through Buffalo increased a staggering sixtyfold. New York City became the seaboard queen of the nation, a gigantic port through which a vast hinterland poured its wealth and to which it daily paid economic tribute.

By the eve of the Civil War, a truly continental economy had emerged. The principle of division of labor, which spelled productivity and profits in the factory, applied on a national scale as well. Each region now specialized in a particular type of economic activity. The South raised cotton for export to New England and old England; the West grew grain

Railroads in Operation in 1850

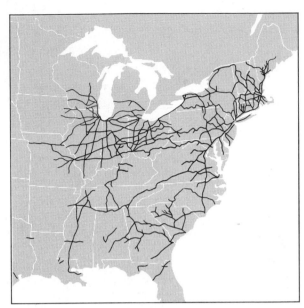

Railroads in Operation in 1860

and livestock to feed factory workers in the East and Europe; the East made machines and textiles for the South and West.

The economic pattern thus woven had fateful political and military implications. Many southerners regarded the Mississippi as a silver chain that naturally linked together the upper valley states and the cotton kingdom. They were convinced, as secession approached, that some or all of these states would have to secede with them or be strangled. But they overlooked the man-made links that now bound the upper Mississippi Valley to the East in intimate commercial union. Southern rebels would have to fight not only northern armies but the tight bonds of an interdependent continental economy. Economically, the two northerly sections were Siamese twins.

The emergence of a specialized, continental-scale economy also had far-reaching social effects. As more and more Americans—mill hands as well as farmers, women as well as men—linked their economic fate to the burgeoning market economy, the self-sufficient households of colonial days were transformed. Most families had once raised all their own food, spun their own wool, and bartered with

their neighbors for the few necessities they could not make themselves. In growing numbers, they now scattered to work for wages in the mills, or they planted just a few crops for sale at market and used the money to buy goods made by strangers in far-off factories. As store-bought fabrics, candles, and soap replaced homemade products, a quiet revolution occurred in the household division of labor and status. Traditional women's work was rendered superfluous and devalued. The home itself, once a center of economic production in which all family members cooperated, grew into a place of refuge from the world of work, a refuge that became increasingly the special and separate sphere of women.

Wealth and Poverty

Revolutionary advances in manufacturing and transportation brought increased prosperity to all Americans, but they also widened the gulf between the rich and the poor. Millionaires had been rare in the early days of the republic, but by the eve of the Civil War several specimens of colossal financial success were strutting across the national stage. Spectacular was the case of fur trader and real-estate speculator John Jacob Astor, who left an estate of $30 million on his death in 1848.

Cities bred the greatest extremes of economic inequality. Unskilled workers, then as always, fared worst. Many of them came to make up a floating mass of "drifters," buffeted from town to town by the shifting prospects for menial jobs. These wandering workers accounted, at various times, for up to half the population of the brawling industrial centers. Although their numbers were large, they left little behind them but the homely fruits of their transient labor. Largely unstoried and unsung, they are among the forgotten men and women of American history.

Many myths about "social mobility" grew up over the buried memories of these luckless day laborers. Mobility did exist in industrializing America—but not in the proportions that legend often portrays. Rags-to-riches success stories were relatively few.

Yet America, with its dynamic society and its wide open spaces, undoubtedly provided more "opportunity" than did the contemporary countries of the Old World—which is why millions of immigrants packed their bags and headed for New World shores. Moreover, a rising tide lifts all boats, and the improvement in overall standards of living was real. Wages for unskilled workers in labor-hungry America rose about 1 percent a year from 1820 to 1860. This general prosperity helped to defuse the potential class conflict that otherwise might have exploded—and that did explode in many European countries.

Cables, Clippers, and Pony Riders

A new pattern of American foreign trade also emerged in the antebellum years, though businesses concentrated on developing the wondrously rewarding domestic market. (Foreign commerce seldom added up to more than 7 percent of the national product.) Abroad as at home, cotton was king and regularly accounted for more than half the value of all American exports. After the repeal of the British exclusionary Corn Laws in 1846, the wheat gathered by McCormick's reapers began to play an increasingly important role in trade with Britain. Americans generally exported agricultural products and imported manufactured goods—and they generally imported more than they exported.

A crucial step came in 1858 when Cyrus Field, called "the greatest wire puller in history," stretched a telegraph cable under the deep North Atlantic waters from Newfoundland to Ireland. Although this initial cable went dead after three weeks of public rejoicing, a heavier cable laid in 1866 permanently provided transatlantic intercommunication.

The United States merchant marine encountered rough sailing during much of the early nineteenth century. American vessels had been repeatedly laid up by the embargo, the War of 1812, and the panics of 1819 and 1837. American naval designers made few contributions to maritime progress. A pioneer American steamer, the *Savannah,* had crept across the Atlantic in 1819, but it used sail most of the time and was pursued for a day by a British captain who thought it afire.

In the 1840s and 1850s, a golden age dawned for American shipping. Yankee naval yards, notably Donald McKay's at Boston, began to send down the ways sleek new crafts called clipper ships. Long, narrow, and majestic, they glided across the sea under towering masts and clouds of canvas. In a fair breeze they could outrun any steamer.

The stately clippers sacrificed cargo space for speed, and their captains made killings by hauling high-value cargoes in record times. They wrested much of the tea-carrying trade between East Asia and Britain from their slower-moving British competitors, and they sped thousands of impatient adventurers to the gold fields of California and Australia.

But the hour of glory for the clipper was relatively brief. On the eve of the Civil War the British had clearly won the world race for maritime ascendancy with their iron tramp steamers ("tea-kettles"). Though slower and less romantic than the clipper, these vessels were steadier, roomier, more reliable, and hence more profitable.

No story of rapid American communication would be complete without including the far West. By 1858 horse-drawn overland stages, immortalized in Mark Twain's *Roughing It,* were a familiar sight. Their dusty tracks stretched from the bank of the muddy Missouri River clear to California.

Even more dramatic was the Pony Express, established in 1860 to carry mail speedily the 2,000 lonely miles from St. Joseph, Missouri, to Sacra-mento, California. Daring, lightweight riders, leaping onto wiry ponies saddled at stations approximately ten miles apart, could make the trip in an amazing ten days. These unarmed horsemen galloped on, summer or winter, day or night, through dust or snow, past Indians and bandits. The speeding postmen missed only one trip, though the whole enterprise lost money heavily and folded after only eighteen legend-leaving months.

Just as the clippers had succumbed to steam, so were the express riders unhorsed by Morse's clacking keys, which began tapping messages to California in 1861. The swift ships and the fleet ponies ushered out a dying technology of wind and muscle. In the future, machines would be in the saddle.

Varying Viewpoints

Economic history was once simply a tale of industrious inventors and inventive industrialists. But economics has become a sophisticated science, and so has the story of the material past. Historians now seek to know just why economic growth occurred. Many scholars emphasize the plentiful resources of the United States. These resources, especially abundant land, limited the industrial labor supply, thus driving up wages and inducing manufacturers to adopt labor-saving machinery. Thus the natural plenty of the continent set off a chain reaction that unleashed explosive economic growth.

Other historians stress the contribution of human resources to America's economic progress. They focus on the large population of natives and immigrants to till the soil and fill the factories, the exploitation of slaves, legal and political innovations such as the tariff and the general incorporation laws, and the technical genius of the American people.

Historians are also increasingly interested in the question, which people benefited most from economic growth? This is known as the "welfare" question, as distinct from the fact of growth alone. Recently, labor historians, such as Sean Wilentz, have described the emergence of an increasingly self-conscious working class in antebellum America. These studies reveal the efforts of urban workers to protect themselves from the dislocations of industrialization and to secure a fair share of the benefits of economic development.

SELECT READINGS

Primary Source Documents

Seth Luther, *An Address to the Working-Men of New-England** (1833), is the eloquent appeal of an uneducated working-class labor reformer. On the transportation revolution, see John H. B. Latrobe's *Western Waters** (1871) and Mark Twain's classic *Life on the Mississippi* (1883). Lemuel Shaw's decision of 1842 in *Commonwealth v. Hunt*, 4 Metc. III (in Henry Steele Commager, *Documents of American History*) is regarded as the "Magna Carta of American labor organization."

Secondary Sources

Solid introductions are George R. Taylor, *The Transportation Revolution, 1815–1860* (1951), Clarence H. Danhoff, *Change in Agriculture: The Northern United States, 1820–1870* (1969), and Douglas C. North, *Economic Growth in the United States, 1790–1860* (1961). The events of the period are placed in a larger context of economic history in Stuart Bruchey, *The Roots of American Economic Growth, 1607–1861* (1965), and Albert W. Niemi, *U.S. Economic History: A Survey of the Major Issues* (1975). The laboring classes are chronicled in Joseph Rayback, *History of American Labor* (1966). Consult also Herbert Gutman's path-breaking *Work, Culture, and Society in Industrializing America* (1976) and Sean Wilentz's insightful *Chants Democratic: New York City and the Rise of the American Working Class, 1788–1850* (1984). The experiences of women workers are the focus of Thomas Dublin, *Women at Work: The Transformation of Work and Community in Lowell, Massachusetts, 1826–1860* (1979), and Christine Stansell, *City of Women: Sex and Class in New York, 1789–1860* (1986). On the introduction of technology, see the provocative anthology edited by S. B. Saul, *Technological Change: The U.S. and Britain in the Nineteenth Century* (1970). Ideological aspects of this process are described in John F. Kassen, *Civilizing the Machine: Technology and Republican Values in America, 1776–1900* (1976). On railroads, consult Robert Fogel, *Railroads and American Economic Growth* (1964), which presents the startling thesis that the iron horse in fact did little to promote growth. For a different view, see Albert Fishlow, *American Railroads and the Transformation of the Ante-Bellum Economy* (1965).

CHAPTER 17

The Ferment of Reform and Culture, 1790–1860

We [Americans] will walk on our own feet; we will work with our own hands; we will speak our own minds.

Ralph Waldo Emerson, "The American Scholar," 1837

Reviving Religion

Church attendance was still a regular ritual for about three-fourths of the 23 million Americans in 1850. Alexis de Tocqueville declared that there was "no country in the world where the Christian religion retains a greater influence over the souls of men than in America." Yet the old Calvinist rigor had long been seeping out of the nation's churches.

The rationalist ideas of the French Revolutionary era had done much to soften the older orthodoxy. Many of the founding fathers, including Paine, Jefferson, and Franklin, embraced the liberal doctrines of Deism, which relied on reason rather than revelation, on science rather than the Bible. Deists rejected the concept of original sin and denied Christ's divinity, but believed in a Supreme Being who had endowed human beings with a capacity for moral behavior.

Deism helped to inspire an important spin-off from Puritanism—the Unitarian faith, which began to gather momentum in New England at the end of the eighteenth century. Unitarians held that God existed in only *one* person (hence *uni*tarian) and not in the orthodox Trinity. Denying the divinity of Jesus, Unitarians stressed the essential goodness of human nature, the possibility of salvation through good works, and God as a loving Father rather than a stern Creator. Embraced by many leading thinkers (including Ralph Waldo Emerson), the Unitarian movement appealed mostly to intellectuals whose rationalism and optimism contrasted sharply with the Calvinist doctrines of predestination and human depravity.

A boiling reaction against the growing liberalism in religion set in about 1800. A fresh wave of roaring revivals, beginning on the southern frontier but soon rolling even into the cities of the Northeast, sent the Second Great Awakening surging across the land. The Second Awakening was one of the most momentous episodes in the history of American religion, a tidal wave of spiritual fervor that left in its wake countless converted souls, shattered and reorganized churches, and numerous new sects. The Second Great Awakening was spread to the masses on the frontier by huge "camp meetings" where as many

229

A Camp Meeting at Sing Sing, New York *Note the preacher with uplifted hands under the canopy at the left. A British visitor wrote in 1839 of a revival meeting: "In front of the pulpit there was a space railed off and strewn with straw, which I was told was the anxious seat, and on which sat those who were touched by their consciences."*

as 25,000 people would gather for an encampment of several days. In the East, many converts were moved to engage in missionary work among the Indians, in Hawaii, and in Asia. Everywhere the Second Awakening encouraged an effervescent evangelicalism that bubbled up into innumerable areas of American life—including prison reform, the temperance cause, the women's movement, and the crusade to abolish slavery.

Methodists and Baptists reaped the biggest harvest of souls from the fields fertilized by revivalism. Both sects stressed personal conversion (contrary to predestination), relatively democratic control of church affairs, and rousing emotionalism. As a frontier jingle ran:

> The devil hates the Methodist
> Because they sing and shout the best.

Many prominent evangelists spread the spirit of revival across the American continent. Powerful Peter Cartwright (1785–1872), one of the Methodist "circuit riders" or traveling frontier preachers, ranged for a half-century from Tennessee to Illinois, calling upon sinners to repent. This ill-educated but sinewy servant of the Lord not only lashed the devil with his bellowing voice but with his fists knocked out rowdies who tried to break up his meetings. Bell-voiced Charles Grandison Finney, the greatest of the revival preachers, abandoned his career as a lawyer to become an evangelist after a deeply moving conversion experience as a young man. Finney held huge crowds spellbound with the power of his oratory. He led massive revivals in Rochester and New York City in 1830 and 1831. Holding out the promise of a perfect Christian kingdom on earth, Finney denounced both alcohol and slavery. He eventually served as president of Oberlin College in Ohio, which he helped to make a hotbed of revivalist activity and abolitionism.

Denominational Diversity

Revivals also furthered the fragmentation of religious faiths. Western New York, where many descendants of New England Puritans had settled, was so blistered by sermonizers preaching "hell-fire and damnation" that it came to be known as the "Burned-Over District." Millerites, or Adventists, mustered several hundred thousand adherents from the superheated soil of the Burned-Over District in the 1840s. The failed doomsday prophecy of their eloquent leader, William Miller, dampened but did not destroy the movement.

Like the First Great Awakening, the Second Great Awakening tended to widen the lines between classes and regions. The more prosperous and conservative denominations in the East were little touched by revivalism; Episcopalians, Presbyterians, Congregationalists, and Unitarians continued to rise mostly from the wealthier, better-educated levels of society. Methodists, Baptists, and the members of the other new denominations spawned by the swelling evangelistic fervor tended to come from less prosperous, less "learned" communities in the rural South and West.

Religious diversity further reflected social cleavages when the churches faced up to the slavery issue. By 1844–1845 both the southern Baptists and the southern Methodists had split with their northern brethren over human bondage. In 1857 the Presbyterians, North and South, parted company. The secession of the southern churches foreshadowed the secession of the southern states. First the churches split, then the political parties split, and then the Union split.

A Desert Zion in Utah

The smoldering spiritual embers of the Burned-Over District kindled one especially ardent flame in 1830. In that year Joseph Smith—a tall, powerfully built visionary—reported that he had received some golden plates from an angel. When deciphered, they constituted the Book of Mormon, and the Church of Jesus Christ of Latter-Day Saints (Mormons) was launched. It was a native product, a new religion destined to spread its influence worldwide.

After establishing a religious oligarchy, Smith ran into serious opposition from his non-Mormon neighbors, first in Ohio and then in Missouri and Illinois. His cooperative sect rasped rank-and-file Americans, who were individualistic and dedicated to free enterprise. The Mormons aroused further antagonism by voting as a unit and by openly but understandably drilling their militia for defensive purposes. Accusations of polygamy likewise arose and increased in intensity, for Joseph Smith was reputed to have several wives.

Continuing hostility finally drove the Mormons to desperate measures. In 1844 Joseph Smith and his brother were murdered and mangled by a mob in Carthage, Illinois, and the movement seemed near collapse. But the falling torch was seized by a remarkable Mormon Moses named Brigham Young, an aggressive leader, eloquent preacher, and gifted administrator. Determined to escape further persecution, Young in 1846–1847 led his oppressed and despoiled Latter-Day Saints over vast rolling plains to Utah as they sang "Come, Come, Ye Saints."

Overcoming pioneer hardships, the Mormons soon made the desert bloom like a new Eden by means of ingenious and cooperative methods of irrigation. The crops of 1848, threatened by hordes of crickets, were saved when flocks of gulls appeared, as if by a miracle, to gulp down the invaders. (A monument to the sea gulls stands in Salt Lake City today.)

Semiarid Utah grew remarkably. By the end of 1848 some 5,000 settlers had arrived, and other large bands were to follow them. Many dedicated Mormons in the 1850s actually made the 1,300-mile trek across the plains pulling two-wheeled carts.

Under the rigidly disciplined management of Brigham Young, the community became a prosperous frontier theocracy and a cooperative commonwealth. Young married as many as twenty-seven women—some of them wives in name only—and begot fifty-six children.

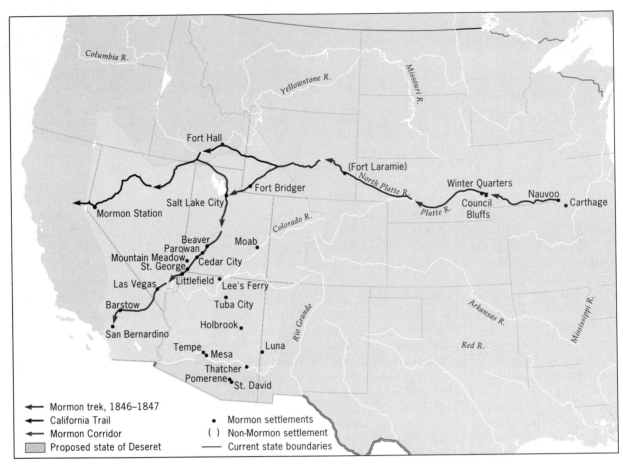

The Mormon World *After Joseph Smith's murder in 1844, the Mormons abandoned their thriving settlement at Nauvoo, Illinois (which had about 20,000 inhabitants in 1845), and set out for the valley of the Great Salt Lake, then still part of Mexico. When the Treaty of Guadalupe Hidalgo in 1848 brought the vast Utah Territory into the United States, the Mormons rapidly expanded their desert colony, which they called Deseret, especially along the "Mormon Corridor" that stretched from Salt Lake to southern California.*

A crisis developed when the Washington government was unable to control the hierarchy of Brigham Young, who had been made territorial governor in 1850. A federal army marched in 1857 against the Mormons, who harassed its lines of supply and rallied to die in their last dusty ditch. Fortunately, the quarrel was finally adjusted without serious bloodshed. The Mormons later ran afoul of the antipolygamy laws passed by Congress in 1862 and 1882, and their marital customs delayed statehood for Utah until 1896.

Free Schools for a Free People

Tax-supported primary schools were scarce in the early years of the republic. They had the odor of pauperism about them, since they existed chiefly to educate the children of the poor—the so-called ragged

School Days *School teaching in the early nineteenth century was a poorly paid occupation that was often pursued by single men who were not very well-educated themselves. This drawing depicts John Pounds (1766–1839), who taught school "while also earning an honest substance by mending shoes."*

schools. Advocates of "free" public education met stiff opposition.

Well-to-do, conservative Americans gradually saw the light. If they did not pay to educate "other folkses brats," the brats might grow up into a dangerous, ignorant rabble—armed with the vote. Taxation for education was an insurance premium that the wealthy paid for stability and democracy.

Tax-supported public education, though lagging in the slavery-cursed South, triumphed between 1825 and 1850. Grimy-handed laborers wielded increased influence and demanded instruction for their children. Most important was the gaining of manhood suffrage for whites in Jackson's day. A free vote cried aloud for free education. A civilized nation that was both ignorant and free, declared Thomas Jefferson, "never was and never will be."

The famed little red schoolhouse—with one room, one stove, one teacher, and often eight grades—became the shrine of American democracy. Regrettably, it was an imperfect shrine. Early free schools stayed open only a few months of the year. Schoolmasters, most of them men in this era, were too often ill trained, ill tempered, and ill paid. These knights of the blackboard often "boarded around" in the community, and some knew scarcely more than their older pupils. They usually taught only the "three Rs—readin', 'ritin', and 'rithmetic."

Reform was urgently needed. Into the breach stepped Horace Mann (1796–1859), a brilliant and idealistic graduate of Brown University. As secretary of the Massachusetts Board of Education, he campaigned effectively for more and better schoolhouses, longer school terms, higher pay for teachers, and an expanded curriculum. His influence radiated out to other states, and impressive improvements were chalked up. Yet education remained an expensive luxury for many communities. As late as 1860 the nation counted only a few hundred public secondary schools—and nearly a million white adult illiterates. Black slaves in the South were legally forbidden to receive instruction in reading or writing, and even free blacks, in the North as well as the South, were usually excluded from the schools.

Educational advances were aided by improved textbooks, notably those of Noah Webster (1758–1843), a Yale-educated Connecticut Yankee who was known as the "Schoolmaster of the Republic." He devoted twenty years to his famous dictionary, published in 1828, which helped to standardize the American language.

Equally influential was Ohioan William H. McGuffey (1800–1873), a teacher-preacher of rare power. His grade-school readers, first published in the 1830s, sold 122 million copies in the following decades. *McGuffey's Readers* hammered home lasting lessons in morality, patriotism, and idealism.

Higher Goals for Higher Learning

Higher education was likewise stirring. The religious zeal of the Second Great Awakening led to the planting of many small, denominational, liberal arts colleges, chiefly in the South and West.

The first state-supported universities sprang up in the South, beginning with North Carolina in 1795. Federal land grants nourished the growth of state institutions of higher learning. Conspicuous among the early group was the University of Virginia, founded in 1819 by Thomas Jefferson, who also designed its beautiful architecture.

Women's higher education was frowned upon in the early decades of the nineteenth century. A woman's place was in the home, and training in needlecraft seemed more important than training in algebra. In an era when the clinging-vine bride was the ideal, coeducation was regarded as frivolous. Prejudices also prevailed that too much learning injured the feminine brain, undermined health, and rendered a young lady unfit for marriage. The teachers of Susan B. Anthony, the future feminist, refused to instruct her in long division.

Women's schools at the secondary level began to attain some respectability in the 1820s, thanks in part to the dedicated work of Emma Willard (1787–1870). In 1821 she established the Troy (New York) Female Seminary. Oberlin College in Ohio shocked traditionalists in 1837 when it opened its doors to women as well as men. (Oberlin had already created shock waves by admitting black students.) In the same year, Mary Lyon established an outstanding women's school, Mount Holyoke Seminary (later College), in South Hadley, Massachusetts.

Traveling lecturers helped to carry learning to the masses through the lyceum lecture associations, which numbered about 3,000 by 1835. The lyceums provided platforms for speakers on science, literature, and moral philosophy. Talented talkers such as Emerson journeyed thousands of miles on the lyceum circuits, casting their pearls of civilization before appreciative audiences.

Magazines flourished in the pre–Civil War years, but most of them withered after a short life. The *North American Review,* founded in 1815, was the long-lived leader of the intellectuals. *Godey's Lady's Book,* founded in 1830, survived until 1898 and attained the enormous circulation (for those days) of 150,000. It was devoured devotedly by millions of women.

An Age of Reform

As the republic grew, reform campaigns of all types flourished in sometimes bewildering abundance. There was not a "reading man" who was without some scheme for a new utopia in his "waistcoat pocket," claimed Ralph Waldo Emerson. Reformers promoted rights for women as well as miracle medicines, communal living, polygamy, celibacy, rule by prophets, and guidance by spirits. Societies were formed against alcohol, tobacco, and the transit of mail on Sunday. Eventually overshadowing all other reforms was the crusade against slavery.

Some reformers were simply cranks, but most were intelligent, inspired idealists, usually touched by the fire of evangelical religion then licking through the pews and pulpits of American churches. The optimistic promises of the Second Great Awakening inspired countless souls to do battle against earthly evils. These modern idealists dreamed anew the old Puritan vision of a perfected society: free from cruelty, war, intoxicating drink, discrimination, and—ultimately—slavery. Women were particularly prominent in these reform crusades, especially in their own struggle for suffrage. For many middle-class women, the campaigns provided an excellent opportunity to escape the confines of home and enter the arena of public affairs.

In part, the practical, activist Christianity of these reformers resulted from their desire to reaffirm traditional values as they plunged ever further into a world disrupted and transformed by the turbulent forces of a market economy. Often blissfully unaware that they were witnessing the dawn of the industrial era, they either ignored the problems of factory workers or blamed them on bad habits. Reformers sometimes applied conventional virtue to refurbishing an older order—while events hurtled them headlong into the new.

Imprisonment for debt continued to be a nightmare. As late as 1830 hundreds of penniless persons were languishing in filthy holes, sometimes for owing less than one dollar. The poorer working classes were especially hard hit by this merciless practice. But as the embattled laborer won the ballot and asserted himself, state legislatures gradually abolished the debtors' prison.

Criminal codes in the states were likewise being softened. The number of capital offenses was being reduced, and brutal punishments, such as whipping and branding, were being slowly eliminated. A refreshing idea was taking hold that prisons should reform as well as punish—hence "reformatories," "houses of correction," and "penitentiaries" (for penance).

Sufferers from so-called insanity were still being treated with incredible cruelty. The mentally deranged were considered willfully perverse and depraved, and often treated like beasts in jails or poorhouses. A quiet New England teacher-author, Dorothea Dix (1802–1887) spent eight years observing these conditions at first hand, and then presented her damning reports to the Massachusetts legislature in 1843. Her description of cells so foul that visitors were driven back by the stench turned legislative stomachs and hearts. Her persistent prodding

resulted in improved conditions and in a gain for the concept that the demented were not willfully perverse but mentally ill.

Agitation for peace also gained some momentum in the pre–Civil War years. In 1828 the American Peace Society was formed, with a ringing declaration of war on war. The American peace crusade, linked with the European crusade, was making promising progress by midcentury, when it was set back by the bloodshed of the Crimean War in Europe and the Civil War in America.

Demon Rum: The "Old Deluder"

The ever-present drink problem also attracted dedicated reformers. Weddings all too often became disgraceful brawls, and occasionally a drunken mourner would fall into the open grave at a funeral. Widespread heavy drinking caused labor inefficiency and increased the danger of accidents on the job. Drunkenness also fouled the sanctity of the family, threatening the spiritual welfare and physical safety of women and children.

After earlier and feebler efforts, the American Temperance Society was formed at Boston in 1826. Within a few years about a thousand local groups sprang into existence. They implored drinkers to sign the temperance pledge and organized children's clubs, known as the "Cold Water Army." Temperance crusaders also made effective use of pictures, pamphlets, and lurid lecturers, some of whom were reformed drunkards.

The most popular anti-alcohol tract of the era was T. S. Arthur's melodramatic novel, *Ten Nights in a Barroom and What I Saw There* (1854). It described in shocking detail how a once-happy village was ruined by Sam Slade's tavern. The book was second only to Stowe's *Uncle Tom's Cabin* as a best seller in the 1850s, and it enjoyed a highly successful run on the stage.

Early foes of demon drink adopted two major lines of attack. One was to stiffen the individual's will to resist the wiles of the little brown jug. The moderate reformers thus stressed temperance rather than "teetotalism," or the total elimination of intoxicants. But less patient zealots gradually came to believe that temptation should be removed by legislation. Prominent among this group was Neal S. Dow of Maine, a blue-nosed reformer who, as a mayor of Portland and an employer of labor, had often witnessed the debauching effect of alcohol.

Dow—the "Father of Prohibition"—sponsored the so-called Maine Law of 1851. This drastic new statute, hailed as "the law of Heaven Americanized," prohibited the manufacture and sale of intoxicating liquor. Other states in the North followed Maine's example, and by 1857 about a dozen had passed various prohibitory laws.

By the eve of the Civil War the prohibitionists had registered inspiring gains, despite hostility in many localities. There was much less drinking among women than earlier in the century and probably much less per capita consumption of hard liquor.

Women in Revolt

When the nineteenth century opened, it was still a man's world, in both America and Europe. A wife was supposed to immerse herself in her home and subordinate herself to her husband. Like black slaves, she could not vote; like black slaves, she could be legally beaten by her overlord "with a reasonable instrument." When she married, she could not retain title to her property; it passed to her husband. Although faring better than European women, women in America were still the "submerged sex" in the early part of the century.

But as the decades unfolded, women increasingly emerged to breathe the air of freedom and self-determination. In contrast to colonial times, many women avoided marriage altogether. Indeed, about 10 percent of adult women were unmarried at the time of the Civil War.

Gender differences were strongly emphasized, largely because the burgeoning market economy was increasingly separating women and men into sharply distinct economic roles. Women were thought to be physically and emotionally weak, but also artistic and refined. Endowed with finely tuned moral sensibilities, they were the keepers of society's conscience, with special responsibility for the young. Men were considered strong but crude, always in danger of slipping into some savage or beastly way of life if not guided by the gentle hands of their loving ladies.

But if sex roles were sharply separated, men and women could still be regarded as equals. As a sign of the prestigious position of American women, tourist Alexis de Tocqueville noted that in his native France rape was punished only slightly, whereas in America it was one of the few crimes punishable by death.

The home was woman's special sphere. But some women increasingly felt that the glorified sanctuary was in fact a gilded cage. They yearned to tear down the bars that separated the private world of women from the public world of men.

Clamorous female reformers began to gather strength as the century neared its halfway point. Most were broad-gauge crusaders; while demanding rights for women, they joined in the general reform movement of the age, fighting for temperance and the abolition of slavery. Like men, they had been touched by the evangelical spirit that offered the alluring promise of earthly reward for human

Stellar Suffragists *Elizabeth Cady Stanton* (left) *and Susan B. Anthony* (right) *were two of the most persistent battlers for women's rights.*

endeavor. Neither foul eggs nor foul words, when hurled by disapproving men, could halt women heartened by these doctrines.

The woman's rights movement was mothered by some arresting characters. Prominent among them was Lucretia Mott, a sprightly Quaker whose ire had been aroused when she and her fellow female delegates to the London antislavery convention of 1840 were not recognized. Elizabeth Cady Stanton, a mother of seven who had insisted on leaving the word *obey* out of her marriage ceremony, shocked fellow feminists by going so far as to advocate suffrage for women. Quaker-reared Susan B. Anthony, a militant lecturer for women's rights, fearlessly exposed herself to rotten garbage and vulgar epithets. She became such a conspicuous advocate of female rights that progressive women everywhere were called "Suzy Bs."

Other feminists challenged the man's world. Dr. Elizabeth Blackwell, a pioneer in a previously forbidden profession for women, was the first female graduate of a medical college. Precocious Margaret Fuller edited a transcendentalist journal, *The Dial,* and took part in the struggle to bring unity and republican government to Italy. The talented Grimké sisters, Sarah and Angelina, championed antislavery. Lucy Stone retained her maiden name after marriage—hence the latter-day "Lucy Stoners," who follow her example. Amelia Bloomer revolted against the current "street-sweeping" female attire by donning a short skirt with Turkish trousers—"bloomers," they were called—amid much bawdy ridicule about "bloomerism" and "loose habits." A jeering male rhyme of the times jabbed:

> Gibbey, gibbey gab
> The women had a confab
> And demanded the rights
> To wear the tights
> Gibbey, gibbey gab.

Fighting feminists met at Seneca Falls, New York, in a memorable Woman's Rights Convention (1848). The defiant Mrs. Stanton read a "Declaration of Sentiments," which in the spirit of the Declaration of Independence declared that "all men *and women* are created equal." One resolution formally demanded the ballot for females. Amid scorn and denunciation from press and pulpit, the Seneca Falls meeting launched the modern women's rights movement.

The crusade for women's rights was eclipsed by that against slavery in the decade before the Civil War. Any white male over twenty-one could vote; women could not. Yet women were being gradually admitted to colleges, and some states, beginning with Mississippi in 1839, were even permitting wives to own property after marriage.

Wilderness Utopias

Bolstered by the spirit of the age, various reformers, ranging from the high-minded to the "lunatic fringe," set up more than forty communities of a cooperative, communistic, or "communitarian" nature. Seeking human betterment, a wealthy and idealistic Scottish textile manufacturer, Robert Owen, founded in 1825 a communal society of about a thousand people at New Harmony, Indiana. Little harmony prevailed in the colony, which, in addition to hard-working visionaries, attracted a sprinkling of radicals, lazy theorists, and outright scoundrels. The enterprise sank in a morass of contradiction and confusion.

Brook Farm in Massachusetts, comprising 200 acres of grudging soil, was started in 1841 with the brotherly and sisterly cooperation of about twenty intellectuals. They prospered reasonably well until 1846, when they lost by fire a large new communal building shortly before its completion. The whole experiment in "plain living and high thinking" then collapsed in debt. The Brook Farm experiment inspired Nathaniel Hawthorne's classic novel *The Blithedale Romance* (1852), whose main character was modeled on Margaret Fuller.

A more radical experiment was the Oneida Colony, founded in New York in 1848. It practiced free love ("complex marriage"), birth control, and the eugenic selection of parents to produce superior offspring. The leader finally fled to Canada to escape persecution for adultery. This curious enterprise flourished for more than thirty years, largely because its artisans made superior steel traps and Oneida

Community (silver) plate. In 1879–1880 the group embraced monogamy and abandoned communism.

Among the longest-lived communitarian sects were the Shakers. Led by Mother Ann Lee, they began in the 1770s to set up a score or so of religious communities. They attained a membership of about 6,000 in 1840, but since their customs opposed both marriage and sexual relations, they were virtually extinct by 1940.

Artistic Endeavors and Achievements

Architecturally, America contributed little of note in the first half of the century. The rustic republic, still under pressure to erect shelters in haste, was continuing to imitate European models. Public buildings and other important structures followed Greek and Roman styles, which seemed curiously out of place in a wilderness setting. A remarkable Greek revival came between 1820 and 1850. About midcentury, strong interest developed in a revival of Gothic forms, with their emphasis on pointed arches and large windows.

Talented Thomas Jefferson, architect of revolution, was probably the ablest American architect of his generation. He brought a classical design to his Virginia hilltop home, Monticello—perhaps the most stately mansion in the nation. The quadrangle of the University of Virginia at Charlottesville, another of Jefferson's creations, remains one of the finest examples of classical architecture in America.

Painting, like the theater, suffered from the Puritan prejudice that art was a sinful waste of time—and often obscene. When Edward Everett, the eminent Boston scholar and orator, placed a statue of Apollo in his home, he had its naked limbs draped.

Competent painters nevertheless emerged. Gilbert Stuart (1775–1828) wielded his brush in Britain, in competition with the best artists. He produced several portraits of Washington, all of them somewhat idealized and dehumanized. Charles Willson Peale (1741–1827) painted some sixty portraits of Washington, who patiently sat for about fourteen of them. John Trumbull (1756–1843), who had fought in the Revolutionary War, recaptured its scenes and spirit on scores of striking canvases.

During the nationalistic upsurge after the War of 1812, American painters turned increasingly from human subjects to romantic mirrorings of local landscapes. The Hudson River School excelled in this type of art. At the same time, portrait painters gradually encountered some unwelcome competition from the invention of a crude photograph known as the daguerreotype, perfected about 1839 by a Frenchman, Louis Daguerre.

The Blossoming of a National Literature

"Who reads an American book?" sneered a British critic in 1820. The painful truth was that the nation's rough-hewn, pioneering civilization gave little encouragement to imaginative literature. America produced political essays, sermons, and autobiographies, but imported or plagiarized much of its reading matter from England.

A genuinely American literature received a strong boost from the wave of nationalism that followed the Revolutionary War and especially the War of 1812. By 1820 the older seaboard areas were sufficiently removed from tree chopping so that literature could be supported as a profession. The Knickerbocker Group in New York blazed brilliantly across the literary heavens, enabling America for the first time to boast of a literature to match its magnificent landscapes.

Washington Irving (1783–1859), born in New York City, was the first American to win international recognition as a literary figure. Steeped in the traditions of New Netherland, he published in 1809 his *Knickerbocker's History of New York,* with its amusing caricatures of the Dutch. When the family business failed, Irving was forced to turn to the goose-feather pen. In 1819–1820 he published *The Sketch Book,* which brought him immediate fame at home and abroad. Combining a pleasing style with delicate charm and quiet humor, he used English as well as American themes, and included such immortal Dutch-American tales as "Rip Van Winkle" and "The Legend of Sleepy Hollow." Europe was amazed to find at last an American with a feather in his hand, not in his hair.

The novelist James Fenimore Cooper (1789–1851) gained world fame and made New

World themes internationally respectable. He first achieved fame in 1821 with his novel *The Spy*—an absorbing tale of the American Revolution. His fame rests most enduringly on the *Leatherstocking Tales.* A deadeye rifleman named Natty Bumppo, one of nature's noblemen, meets with Indians in stirring adventures like *The Last of the Mohicans.* Some Europeans who read Cooper's novels came to think of all American people as born with tomahawk in hand. Cooper was exploring the viability of America's republican experiment by contrasting the values of "natural men" from the wilderness with the artificiality of modern civilization.

A third member of the Knickerbocker Group in New York was the belated Puritan William Cullen Bryant (1794–1878), transplanted from Massachusetts. At age sixteen he wrote the meditative and melancholy "Thanatopsis" (published in 1817), which was one of the first high-quality poems produced in the United States. Critics could hardly believe that it had been written on "this side of the water."

Trumpeters of Transcendentalism

A golden age in American literature dawned in the second quarter of the nineteenth century, when an amazing outburst shook New England. One of the mainsprings of this literary flowering was transcendentalism, especially around Boston, which preened itself as "the Athens of America."

The transcendentalist movement of the 1830s resulted in part from a liberalizing of the strait-jacket Puritan theology. It also owed much to foreign influences, including the German romantic philosophers and the religions of Asia. The transcendentalists rejected the prevailing theory, derived from John Locke, that all knowledge comes to the mind through the senses. Truth, rather, "transcends" the senses: it cannot be found by observation alone. Every person possesses an inner light that can illuminate the highest truth and put him or her in direct touch with God, or the "Oversoul."

These mystical doctrines of transcendentalism defied precise definition, but they underlay concrete beliefs. Foremost was a stiff-backed individualism in matters religious as well as social. Closely associated was a commitment to self-reliance, self-culture, and self-discipline. These traits naturally bred hostility to authority and to formal institutions of any kind, as well as to all conventional wisdom. Finally came exaltation of the dignity of the individual, whether black or white—the mainspring of a whole array of humanitarian reforms.

Best known of the transcendentalists was Boston-born Ralph Waldo Emerson (1803–1882). Tall, slender, and intensely blue-eyed, he mirrored serenity in his noble features. Trained as a Unitarian minister, he early forsook his pulpit and ultimately reached a wider audience by pen and platform. He was a never-failing favorite as a lyceum lecturer, and for twenty years took a western tour every winter. Perhaps his most thrilling public effort was a Phi Beta Kappa address, "The American Scholar," delivered at Harvard College in 1837. This brilliant appeal was an intellectual Declaration of Independence, for it urged American writers to throw off European traditions and delve into the riches of their own backyards.

Hailed as both a poet and a philosopher, Emerson was not of the highest rank as either. He was more influential as a practical philosopher, and through his fresh and vibrant essays enriched thousands of humdrum lives. Catching the individualistic mood of the republic, he stressed self-reliance, self-improvement, optimism, and freedom. The secret of Emerson's popularity lay largely in the fact that his ideals reflected those of an expanding America. By the 1850s he was an outspoken critic of slavery, and he ardently supported the Union cause in the Civil War.

Henry David Thoreau (1817–1862) was Emerson's close associate—a poet, a mystic, a transcendentalist, and a nonconformist. Condemning a government that supported slavery, he refused to pay his Massachusetts poll tax, and was jailed for a night.* A gifted prose writer, he is well known for *Walden: Or Life in the Woods* (1854). The book is a record of Thoreau's two years of simple existence in a hut that he built on the edge of Walden Pond, near Concord,

---

* The story (probably apocryphal) is that Emerson visited Thoreau at the jail and asked, "Why are you here?" The reply came, "Why are you not here?"

Massachusetts. A stiff-necked individualist, he believed that he should reduce his bodily wants so as to gain time for a pursuit of truth through study and meditation. Thoreau's *Walden* and his essay "On the Duty of Civil Disobedience" exercised a strong influence in furthering idealistic thought, both in America and abroad. His writings later encouraged Mohandas Gandhi to resist British rule in India and, still later, inspired the development of American civil rights leader Martin Luther King, Jr.'s thinking about nonviolence.

Bold, brassy, and swaggering was the open-collared figure of Brooklyn's Walt Whitman (1819–1892). In his famous collection of poems, *Leaves of Grass* (1855), he gave free rein to his gushing genius with what he called a "barbaric yawp." Highly romantic, emotional, and unconventional, he dispensed with titles, stanzas, rhymes, and at times even regular meter. He handled sex with shocking frankness, and his book was banned in Boston.

Whitman's *Leaves of Grass* was at first a financial failure. The only three enthusiastic reviews that it received were written by the author himself—anonymously. But in time the once-withered *Leaves of Grass,* revived and honored, won for Whitman an enormous following in both America and Europe.

Leaves of Grass gained for Whitman the informal title "Poet Laureate of Democracy." Singing with transcendental abandon of his love for the masses, he caught the exuberant enthusiasm of an expanding America that had turned its back on the Old World:

> All the Past we leave behind;
> We debouch upon a newer, mightier world, varied
>   world;
> Fresh and strong the world we seize—world of
>   labor and the march—
> Pioneers! O Pioneers!

Here at last was the native art for which critics had been crying.

Glowing Literary Lights

Certain other literary giants were not actively associated with the transcendentalist movement, though not completely immune to its influences. Professor

Henry Wadsworth Longfellow (1807–1882), a man who for many years taught modern languages at Harvard College, was one of the most popular poets ever produced in America. His wide knowledge of European literature supplied him with many themes, but some of his most admired poems—"Evangeline," "Hiawatha," and "The Courtship of Miles Standish"—were based on American traditions. Immensely popular in Europe, Longfellow was the only American ever to be honored with a bust in the Poets' Corner of Westminster Abbey.

A fighting Quaker, John Greenleaf Whittier (1807–1892), was the uncrowned poet laureate of the antislavery crusade. His poems cried aloud against inhumanity, injustice, and intolerance, against

> The outworn rite, the old abuse,
> The pious fraud transparent grown.

Undeterred by insults and the stonings of mobs, Whittier helped arouse a calloused America on the slavery issue. A great conscience rather than a great poet or intellect, Whittier was preeminently the poet of human freedom.

Many-sided Professor James Russell Lowell (1819–1891), who succeeded Professor Longfellow at Harvard, is remembered as a political satirist in his *Biglow Papers,* especially those of 1846 dealing with the Mexican War. Written partly as poetry in the Yankee dialect, the *Papers* condemned in blistering terms the alleged slavery-expansion designs of the Polk administration.

The scholarly Dr. Oliver Wendell Holmes (1809–1894), who taught anatomy with a sparkle at Harvard Medical School, was a prominent poet, essayist, novelist, lecturer, and wit. A nonconformist and a fascinating conversationalist, he shone among a group of literary lights who regarded Boston as "the hub of the universe." His poem "The Last Leaf," in honor of the last "white Indian" of the Boston Tea Party, came to apply to himself. Dying at the age of eighty-five, he was the "last leaf" among his distinguished contemporaries.*

---

* Oliver Wendell Holmes had a son of the same name who became a distinguished justice of the Supreme Court (1902–1932) and who lived to be ninety-four, less two days.

The most noteworthy literary figure produced by the South before the Civil War, unless Edgar Allan Poe is regarded as a southerner, was novelist William Gilmore Simms (1806–1870). Eighty-two books flowed from his ever-moist pen, winning for him the title "the Cooper of the South." His themes dealt with the southern frontier in colonial days and with the South during the Revolutionary War.

Literary Individualists and Dissenters

Not all writers in these years believed so keenly in human goodness and social progress. Edgar Allan Poe (1809–1849), who spent much of his youth in Virginia, was an eccentric genius. Orphaned at an early age, cursed with ill health, and married to a child-wife of thirteen who fell fatally ill of tuberculosis, he suffered hunger, cold, poverty, and debt. Failing at suicide, he took refuge in the bottle and dissipated his talent early. Poe was a gifted lyric poet, as "The Raven" attests. A master stylist, he also excelled in the short story, especially of the horror genre, in which he shared his fantastic nightmares with fascinated readers. If he did not invent the modern detective novel, he at least set new high standards in tales like "The Gold Bug."

Poe was fascinated by the ghostly and ghastly, as in "The Fall of the House of Usher" and other stories. He reflected a morbid sensibility distinctly at odds with the usually optimistic tone of American culture. Partly for this reason, Poe has perhaps been even more prized by Europeans than by his own countrymen. His brilliant career was cut short when he was found drunk in a Baltimore gutter and shortly thereafter died.

Two other writers reflected the continuing Calvinist obsession with original sin and with the never-ending struggle between good and evil. In somber Salem, Massachusetts, Nathaniel Hawthorne grew up in an atmosphere heavy with the memories of his Puritan forebears and the tragedy of his father's premature death on an ocean voyage. His masterpiece was *The Scarlet Letter* (1850), which described the Puritan practice of forcing an adultress to wear a scarlet *A* on her clothing. The tragic tale chronicles the psychological effects of sin on the guilty heroine and her secret lover (the father of her baby), a minister of the gospel in Puritan Boston. In *The Marble Faun* (1860), Hawthorne dealt with a group of young American artists who witness a mysterious murder in Rome. The book explores the concepts of the omnipresence of evil and the dead hand of the past weighing upon the present.

Herman Melville (1819–1891), an orphaned and ill-educated New Yorker, went to sea as a youth and served eighteen adventuresome months on a whaler. "A whale ship was my Yale College and my Harvard," he wrote. Jumping ship in the South Seas, he lived among cannibals, from whom he providentially escaped uneaten. His masterpiece, *Moby Dick* (1851), is a complex allegory of good and evil, told in terms of the conflict between a whaling captain,

Herman Melville *After experiencing early success as a writer of South Seas adventure novels, Melville lost popularity after the publication of* Moby Dick *and spent the last third of his life in poverty and despair. Only in the twentieth century was he recognized as one of America's greatest novelists.*

CHRONOLOGY

1770s	First Shaker communities formed.
1794	Thomas Paine publishes *The Age of Reason.*
1795	University of North Carolina founded.
1800	Second Great Awakening begins.
1819	Jefferson founds University of Virginia.
1821	Cooper publishes *The Spy,* his first successful novel.
	Emma Willard establishes Troy (New York) Female Seminary.
1825	New Harmony commune established.
1826	American Temperance Society founded.
1828	American Peace Society founded.
	Noah Webster publishes dictionary.
1830	Joseph Smith founds Mormon church.
	Godey's Lady's Book first published.
1830–1831	Finney conducts revivals in eastern cities.

1835	Lyceum movement flourishes.
1837	Emerson delivers "The American Scholar" address.
	Mary Lyon establishes Mount Holyoke Seminary.
	Oberlin College admits female students.
1841	Brook Farm commune established.
1843	Dorothea Dix petitions Massachusetts legislature on behalf of the insane.
1846–1847	Mormon migration to Utah.
1848	Seneca Falls Woman's Rights Convention held.
	Oneida commune established.
1850	Hawthorne publishes *The Scarlet Letter.*
1851	Melville publishes *Moby Dick.*
	Maine passes first law prohibiting liquor.
1855	Whitman publishes *Leaves of Grass.*

Ahab, and a giant white whale, Moby Dick. Captain Ahab, who lost a leg to the marine monster, swore revenge. His pursuit finally ends when Moby Dick rams and sinks Ahab's ship, leaving only one survivor. The whale's exact identity and Ahab's motives remain obscure. In the end the sea, like the terrifyingly impersonal and unknowable universe of Melville's imagination, simply rolls on.

Moby Dick was widely ignored at the time of its publication; people were accustomed to more straightforward and upbeat prose. A disheartened Melville continued to write unprofitably for some years, part of the time eking out a living as a customs inspector, and then died in relative obscurity and poverty. Ironically, his brooding masterpiece about the mysterious white whale had to wait until the more jaded twentieth century for readers and for proper recognition.

Portrayers of the Past

A distinguished group of American historians was emerging at the same time that other writers were winning distinction. Energetic George Bancroft (1800–1891), who as secretary of the navy helped found the Naval Academy at Annapolis in 1845, has deservedly received the title "Father of American History." He published a spirited, superpatriotic history of the United States to 1789 in six (originally ten) volumes (1834–1876), a work that grew out of his vast researches in dusty archives in Europe and America.

Two other historians are read with greater pleasure and profit today. William H. Prescott (1796–1859) published classic accounts of the conquest of Mexico (1843) and Peru (1847). Francis Parkman (1823–1893) penned a brilliant series of volumes, beginning in 1851. In epic style he chronicled the struggle between France and Britain in colonial times for the mastery of North America.

Early American historians of prominence were almost without exception New Englanders, largely because the Boston area provided well-stocked libraries and a stimulating literary tradition. These writers numbered abolitionists among their relatives and friends, and hence were disposed to view unsympathetically the slave-cursed South. The writing of American history for generations to come was to suffer from an antisouthern bias perpetuated by this early "made in New England" interpretation.

Varying Viewpoints

Early chronicles of the antebellum period universally lauded the era's reformers, portraying them as idealistic crusaders intent on improving American society. After World War II, however, some historians began to detect selfish and even conservative motives underlying the apparent benevolence of the reformers. This view described the advocates of reform as anxious upper-class men and women threatened by the ferment of life in America. The pursuit of reforms like prohibition, asylums, and mandatory education represented a means of asserting "social control." In this vein, David H. Donald identified one reform movement as "the anguished protest of an aggrieved class against a world they never made."

The wave of reform activity in the 1960s prompted a reevaluation of the reputations of the antebellum reformers. These more recent interpretations find much to admire in the authentic religious commitments of the reformers and especially in the participation of women, who sought various social improvements as an extension of their function as protectors of the home and family.

The role of women has been particularly scrutinized in recent years, as scholars animated by the modern feminist movement seek to reconstruct the feminine past. Here the work of Nancy Cott has been especially influential, with its stress on women's efforts to create and nurture networks of strong, affective human associations that would sustain communitarian values.

SELECTED READINGS

Primary Source Documents

Alexis de Tocqueville's *Democracy in America* (1835, 1840) has stood for a century and a half as the classic analysis of the American character. Joseph Smith, *The Pearl of Great Price** (1829), contains an account of the Mormon leader's religious visions, which capture the religious restiveness of the age. William H. McGuffey, *Fifth Eclectic Reader** (1879), was the most popular school text of the age. On the women's movement, see the "Seneca Falls Manifesto"* (1848), which laid the foundations of the feminist movement. Catharine Beecher and Harriet Beecher Stowe, *The American Woman's Home** (1869), discusses the role of women. Stowe's classic novel, *Uncle Tom's Cabin* (1852), offers an emotional appeal against slavery and a fascinating portrait of slavery, religion, and family life in antebellum America.

Secondary Sources

A magisterial synthesis is Daniel Boorstin, *The Americans: The National Experience* (1965). Satisfying detail is found in two Russell B. Nye books: *The Cultural Life of the New Nation, 1776–1830* (1960), and *Society and Culture in America, 1830–1860* (1974). Alexis de Tocqueville's classic account of life in the republic is brilliantly analyzed by

James R. Schlieffer in *The Making of Tocqueville's "Democracy in America"* (1980). Sydney E. Ahlstrom, *Religious History of the American People* (1972), is sweeping. On revivalism, see Paul Johnson, *A Shopkeeper's Millennium: Society and Revivals in Rochester, New York, 1815–1837* (1978), and Michael Barkun's *Crucible of the Millennium: The Burned-Over District of New York in the 1840s* (1986). Richard L. Bushman describes the origins of Mormonism in *Joseph Smith and the Beginnings of Mormonism* (1984), and Leonard J. Arrington analyzes the most celebrated Mormon leader in *Brigham Young: American Moses* (1984). On reformers, see Ronald Walters, *American Reformers, 1815–1860* (1978).

Women's history for this period has blossomed in a number of studies, including Ellen Carol DuBois, *Feminism and Suffrage* (1978), Barbara J. Berg, *The Remembered Gate: Origins of American Feminism—The Woman and the City, 1800–1860* (1977), Ruth Bordin, *Women and Temperance* (1981), Estelle B. Freedman, *Their Sisters' Keepers: Women's Prison Refirm in America, 1830–1930* (1981), and emphasizing intellectual and literary history, Ann Douglas, *The Feminization of American Culture* (1977). Family history is covered in Steven Mintz and Susan Kellogg, *Domestic Revolutions: A Social History of American Family Life* (1988), Joseph F. Kett, *Rites of Passage: Adolescence in America* (1976), Lewis Perry, *Childhood, Marriage, and Reform: Henry Clarke Wright, 1797–1870* (1980), Carl N. Degler, *At Odds: Women and the Family in America from the Revolution to the Present* (1980), and Mary P. Ryan, *Cradle of the Middle Class: The Family in Oneida County, New York* (1981).

CHAPTER 18

The South and the Slavery Controversy,
1793–1860

If you put a chain around the neck of a slave, the other end fastens itself around your own.

Ralph Waldo Emerson, 1841

"Cotton Is King!"

When George Washington first took the presidential oath, the economic wheels of the South were creaking badly. The region was burdened with depressed prices, unmarketable products, overcropped lands, and the dead weight of an unprofitable slave system. Some southern statesmen, including Thomas Jefferson, were talking openly of freeing their slaves, and confidently predicting that slavery would gradually die of economic anemia.

But the introduction of Whitney's cotton gin in 1793 changed the scene. The newly popularized short-staple cotton, which brought a premium price, gradually became the dominant southern crop, eclipsing tobacco, rice, and sugar. Slavery was reinvigorated, the slave was chained to the gin, and the planter was chained to the slave.

As time passed, the cotton kingdom developed into a huge agricultural factory, pouring out avalanches of the fluffy fiber. Quick profits drew planters to the virgin bottomlands of the gulf states. As long as the soil was still vigorous, the yield was bountiful and the rewards were high. Caught up in an economic spiral, the planters bought more slaves and land to grow more cotton, so as to buy still more slaves and land.

Northern shippers reaped a large part of the profits from the cotton trade. They would load bulging bales of cotton at southern ports, transport them to Britain, sell them for pounds sterling, and buy needed manufactured goods for sale in the United States. To a large degree the prosperity of both North and South rested on the bent backs of southern slaves.

Cotton accounted for half the value of all American exports after 1840. It even held foreign nations in partial bondage. Britain's most important single manufacture in the 1850s was cotton cloth, from which about one-fifth of its population, directly or indirectly, drew its livelihood. About 75 percent of this precious supply of fiber came from the white-carpeted acres of the South.

Southern leaders were fully aware that Britain was tied to them by cotton threads, and this dependence gave them a heady sense of power. In their eyes "cotton was king," the gin was his throne, and the black slaves were his henchmen. If war should ever break out between North and South, northern warships would presumably cut off the outflow of cotton. Fiber-famished British factories would then close their gates, starving mobs would force the London government to break the blockade, and the South would triumph. Cotton was a powerful monarch indeed.

Slaves of the Slave System

Before the Civil War the South was in some respects not so much a democracy as an oligarchy—or a government by the few, in this case heavily influenced by a planter aristocracy. In 1850 only 1,733 families owned more than 100 slaves each, and this select group provided the cream of the political and social leadership of the section and nation. Here was the mint-julep South of the tall-columned and white-painted plantation mansion—the "big house," where dwelt the "cottonocracy."

The planter aristocrats, with their blooded horses and Chippendale chairs, enjoyed a lion's share of southern wealth. They could educate their children in the finest schools, often in the North or abroad. Their money provided the leisure for study, reflection, and statecraft, as was notably true of men like John C. Calhoun (a Yale graduate) and Jefferson Davis (a West Point graduate).

The plantation system also shaped the lives of southern women. The mistress of a great plantation commanded a sizable household of mostly female slaves, passing out daily orders to cooks, maids, seamstresses, laundresses, and personal servants. Some mistresses showed tender regard for their bondswomen, while others treated their slaves atrociously. But virtually no slaveholding women believed in abolition, and relatively few protested when the husbands and children of their slaves were sold.

Despite the occasional benevolent relations between owners and slaves, the moonlight-and-magnolia tradition concealed much that was worrisome, distasteful, and sordid. Plantation agriculture was wasteful, largely because king cotton and his money-hungry subjects despoiled the good earth. Quick profits led to excessive cultivation or "land butchery," which in turn caused a heavy leakage of population to the West and Northwest.

The economic structure of the South became increasingly monopolistic. As the land wore thin, many small farmers sold their holdings to more prosperous neighbors. The big got bigger and the small

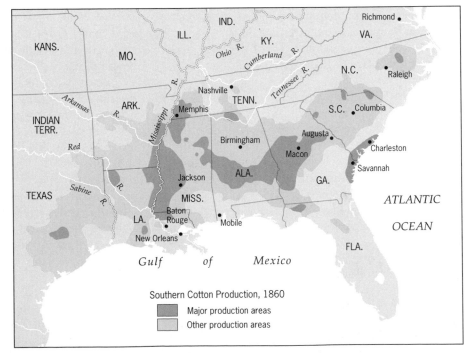

Southern Cotton Production, 1860

Major production areas

Other production areas

smaller. When the Civil War finally erupted, a large number of southern farms had passed from the hands of the families that had originally cleared them.

Another cancer in the bosom of the South was the financial instability of the plantation system. The temptation to overspeculate in land and slaves caused many planters, including Andrew Jackson in his later years, to plunge in beyond their depth. The slaves represented a heavy investment of capital, perhaps $1,200 each in the case of "prime field hands"; and they might deliberately injure themselves or run away.

Dominance by king cotton likewise led to a dangerous dependence on a one-crop economy, whose price level was at the mercy of world conditions. The whole system discouraged a healthy diversification of agriculture and inhibited the development of manufacturing.

Southern planters resented watching the North grow fat at their expense. They were pained by the heavy outward flow of commissions and interest to northern middlemen, bankers, agents, and shippers. True souls of the South, especially by the 1850s, deplored the fact that when born they were wrapped in Yankee-made swaddling clothes, and that they spent the rest of their lives in servitude to Yankee manufacturing. When they died, they were laid in coffins made with Yankee nails, and were buried in graves dug with Yankee shovels. The South furnished only the corpse and the hole in the ground.

The cotton kingdom also repelled large-scale European immigration, which added so richly to the manpower and wealth of the North. In 1860 only 4.4 percent of the southern population was foreign born, as compared with 18.7 percent for the North.

The White Majority

Only a handful of southern whites lived in Greek-pillared mansions. Below those 1,733 families in 1850 who owned 100 or more slaves were the less wealthy slaveowners. They totaled in 1850 some 345,000 families, representing about 1,725,000 white persons. Over two-thirds of these families—255,268 in all—owned fewer than ten slaves each. All told, only about one-fourth of white southerners owned slaves or belonged to a slaveowning family.

The smaller slaveowners did not own a majority of the slaves, but they made up a majority of masters. With the striking exception that their households contained a slave or two, or perhaps an entire slave family, the style of their life resembled that of small farmers in the North more than it did that of the southern planter aristocracy. They lived in modest farmhouses and sweated beside their slaves in the cotton fields, laboring nearly as hard as those they held in bondage.

Beneath the slaveowners was the great body of whites who owned no slaves at all. By 1860 their numbers had swelled to 6,120,825—three-quarters of the southern white population. Shouldered off the richest bottomlands by the mighty planters, they scratched a simple living from the thinner soils of the backcountry and the mountain valleys. These red-necked farmers participated in the market economy

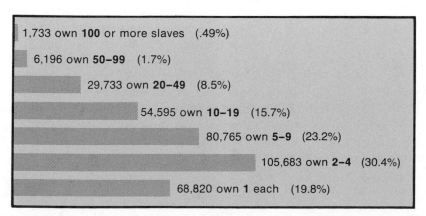

1,733 own **100** or more slaves (.49%)

6,196 own **50–99** (1.7%)

29,733 own **20–49** (8.5%)

54,595 own **10–19** (15.7%)

80,765 own **5–9** (23.2%)

105,683 own **2–4** (30.4%)

68,820 own **1** each (19.8%)

Slaveowning Families, 1850
Ralph Waldo Emerson, a New Englander, declared in 1856: "I do not see how a barbarous community and a civilized community can constitute a state. I think we must get rid of slavery or we must get rid of freedom."

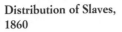

Distribution of Slaves,
1860

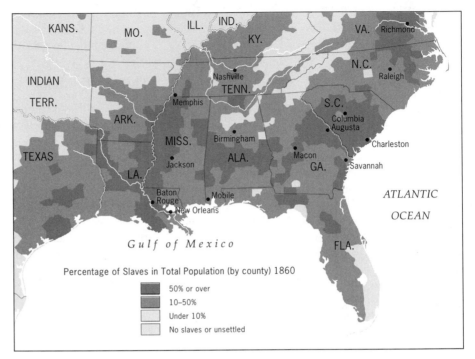

scarcely at all. As subsistence farmers, they raised corn and hogs, not cotton, and often lived isolated lives, punctuated by local socializing and the fervent experience of religious revival meetings. Some of the least prosperous nonslaveholding whites were scorned even by slaves as "poor white trash," "hill-billies," or "crackers."

All these whites without slaves had no direct stake in the preservation of slavery, yet they were among the stoutest defenders of the system. Why? The answer is not far to seek.

The carrot on the stick ever dangling before their eyes was the hope of buying a slave or two and of parlaying their holdings into riches—all in accord with the American dream of upward social mobility. They also took fierce pride in their presumed racial superiority, which would be watered down if the slaves were freed. Many of the poorer whites were hardly better off economically than the slaves, but even the most wretched could take perverse comfort

from the knowledge that they out-ranked someone in status: the still more wretched African-American slave. Thus did the logic of economics join with the illogic of racism in buttressing the slave system.

In a special category among white southerners were the mountain whites, more or less marooned in the valleys of the Appalachian range that stretched from western Virginia to northern Georgia and Alabama. As independent small farmers, hundreds of miles distant from the heart of the cotton kingdom and rarely if ever in sight of a slave, these mountain people had little in common with the whites of the flatlands. Many of them, including future President Andrew Johnson of Tennessee, hated both the haughty planters and their gangs of blacks. When the Civil War came, the tough-fibered mountain men constituted a vitally important peninsula of Unionism jutting down into the secessionist southern sea. They ultimately played a significant role in crippling the Confederacy.

Slave Nurse and Young White Master *Southern whites would not allow slaves to own property or exercise civil rights, but, paradoxically, they often entrusted them with the raising of their own precious children. Many a slave "mammy" served as a surrogate mother for the offspring of the planter class.*

Free Blacks: Slaves Without Masters

Precarious in the extreme was the standing of the South's free blacks, who numbered about 250,000 by 1860. In the upper South, the free black population traced its origins to a wavelet of emancipation inspired by the idealism of revolutionary days. In the deeper South, many free blacks were mulattoes, usually the emancipated children of a white planter and his black mistress. Throughout the South were some free blacks who had purchased their freedom with earnings from labor after hours.

These free blacks in the South were a kind of "third race." These people were prohibited from certain occupations, and always vulnerable to being hijacked back into slavery by unscrupulous slave traders. As free men and women, they were walking examples of what might be achieved by emancipation, and hence were resented and detested by defenders of the slave system.

Free blacks were also unpopular in the North, where about another 250,000 of them lived. Several states forbade their entrance, most denied them the right to vote, and some barred them from public schools. Much of the agitation in the North against the spread of slavery into the new territories in the 1840s and 1850s grew out of race prejudice, not humanitarianism.

Antiblack feeling was in fact frequently stronger in the North than in the South. It was sometimes observed that white southerners, who were often suckled and reared by black nurses, liked black people as individuals but despised the race. The white northerner, on the other hand, often professed to like the race but disliked individual blacks.

Plantation Slavery

In society's basement in the South of 1860 were nearly 4 million black human chattels. Their numbers had quadrupled since the dawn of the century, as the booming cotton economy created a seemingly unquenchable demand for slave labor. Despite the ending of the legal slave trade by Congress in 1808, the price of "black ivory" was so high that thousands of slaves were smuggled illegally into the South. Yet the huge bulk of the increase came not from imports but instead from natural reproduction—a fact that distinguished slavery in America from other New World societies and implied much about the tenor of the regime and the conditions of family life under slavery.

Above all, the planters regarded the slaves as investments, into which they had sunk nearly $2 billion by 1860. Slaves were the primary form of wealth in the South, and as such they were cared for as any asset is cared for by a prudent capitalist. Masters sometimes hired cheap Irish wage laborers to perform dangerous work rather than risk the life of a valuable slave, worth $1,800 by 1860 (a price that had quintupled since 1800).

Slavery was profitable for the great planters, though it hobbled the economic development of the region as a whole. The profits from the cotton boom sucked ever more slaves from the upper to the lower South. Thousands of blacks from the exhausted plantations of the Old South, especially Virginia, were "sold down the river" to the cotton frontier of the lower Mississippi Valley. By 1860 the Deep South states of South Carolina, Florida, Mississippi, Alabama, and Louisiana each had a majority or near-majority of blacks, and accounted for about half of all slaves in the South.

The open "breeding" of slaves was not encouraged. However, white masters, all too frequently, would force their attention on female slaves, fathering a sizable mulatto population, most of which remained enchained, thus increasing the slave population.

Slave auctions were brutal sights. The open selling of human flesh under the hammer was among the most revolting aspects of slavery. On the auction block, families were separated with distressing frequency, usually for economic reasons such as bankruptcy or the division of "property" among heirs. The sundering of families in this fashion was perhaps slavery's greatest psychological horror. Abolitionists decried the practice, and Harriet Beecher Stowe seized on the emotional power of this theme by putting it at the heart of the plot of *Uncle Tom's Cabin*.

Life Under the Lash

White southerners often romanticized about the happy life of their singing, dancing, banjo-strumming, joyful "darkies." But how did the slaves actually live? There is no simple answer to this question. Conditions varied greatly from region to region, from large plantation to small farm, and from master to master. Everywhere, of course, slavery meant hard work, ignorance, and oppression. The slaves—both men and women—usually toiled from dawn to dusk in the fields, under the watchful eyes and ready whip-hand of a white overseer or black "driver." They had no civil or political rights, and even minimal protection from murder or unusually cruel punishment was difficult to enforce, since slaves were forbidden to testify in court.

Floggings were common, for the whip was the substitute for the wage-incentive system and the most visible symbol of the planter's mastery. Strong-willed slaves were sometimes sent to "breakers," whose technique consisted mostly in lavish laying on of the lash. As an abolitionist song of the 1850s lamented:

> To-night the bond man, Lord
> Is bleeding in his chains;
> And loud the falling lash is heard
> On Carolina's plains!

But savage beatings made sullen laborers, and lash marks hurt resale values. There are, to be sure, sadistic monsters in any population, and the planter class contained its share. But for financial as well as humane reasons, the typical planter did not customarily brutalize or beat to death a valuable slave. For better or worse, slaves were generally treated like the expensive "property" their owners considered them to be.

By 1860 most slaves were concentrated in the "black belt" of the Deep South that stretched from South Carolina and Georgia into the new southwest states of Alabama, Mississippi, and Louisiana. A majority of blacks lived on larger plantations that harbored communities of twenty or more slaves. In some counties of the Deep South, especially along the lower Mississippi River, blacks accounted for more than 75 percent of the population. There the family life of slaves tended to be relatively stable, and a distinctive African-American culture developed. Forced separation of spouses, parents, and children was evidently more common on smaller plantations and in the upper South. Slave marriage vows sometimes proclaimed, "Until death or *distance* do you part."

With impressive resilience, blacks managed to sustain family life in slavery, and most slaves were

The Cruelty of Slavery (left) *Held captive in a net, a slave sits on the Congo shore, waiting to be sold and shipped.* (above) *The device was riveted around a slave's neck. Its attached bells, like a cowbell, made it impossible for the wearer to hide from his or her owner.*

raised in stable two-parent households. Continuity of family identity across generations was evidenced in the widespread practice of naming children for grandparents or adopting the surname not of a current master, but of a forebear's master. African-Americans also displayed their African cultural roots when they avoided marriage between first cousins, a practice the ingrown planter aristocracy allowed.

African roots were also visible in the slaves' religious practices. Though heavily Christianized by itinerant evangelists of the Second Great Awakening, blacks in slavery molded their own distinctive religious forms from a mixture of Christian and African elements. They emphasized those aspects of the Christian heritage that seemed most pertinent to their own situation—especially the captivity of the Israelites in Egypt. One of the most haunting spirituals implored:

> Tell old Pharaoh
> "Let my people go."

And another lamented:

> Nobody knows de trouble I've had
> Nobody knows but Jesus

African practices also persisted in the "responsorial" style of preaching, in which the congregation frequently punctuates the minister's remarks with assents and *amens*—an adaptation of the give-and-take between caller and dancers in the African ring-shout dance.

The Burdens of Bondage

Slavery was intolerably degrading to the victims, who were deprived of the dignity and sense of responsibility that come from independence and the right to make choices. Slaves were denied an education, because reading brought ideas, and ideas brought discontent. Many states passed laws forbidding their instruction, and perhaps nine-tenths of adult slaves at the beginning of the Civil War were illiterate. For all slaves—indeed for virtually all blacks, slave or free—the American dream of bettering one's lot through study and hard work was a cruel and empty mockery.

Not surprisingly, victims of the "peculiar institution" devised countless ways to throw sand in its gears. They often slowed the pace of their labor to the barest minimum that would spare them the lash, thus fostering the myth of black "laziness" in the minds of whites. They filched food from the "big house" and pilfered other goods that had been produced by their labor. They sometimes sabotaged expensive equipment and occasionally even put poison in their master's food.

The slaves also universally pined for freedom. Many took to their heels as runaways, frequently in search of a separated family member. Others rebelled, though never successfully. In 1800 an armed insurrection led by a slave named Gabriel in Richmond, Virginia, was foiled by informers, and in 1822 Denmark Vesey, a free black, organized another ill-fated rebellion in Charleston. In both cases the rebels were betrayed by informers and hanged. In 1831 Nat Turner, a visionary black preacher, led an uprising that slaughtered about sixty Virginians, mostly women and children. Reprisals were swift and bloody.

The dark taint of slavery also left its mark on the whites. It fostered the brutality of the whip, the bloodhound, and the branding iron. White southerners increasingly lived in a state of imagined siege, surrounded by potentially rebellious blacks inflamed by abolitionist propaganda from the North. Their fears bolstered an intoxicating theory of biological racial superiority and turned the South into a reactionary backwater in an era of progress. The defenders of slavery were forced to degrade themselves, along with their victims. As Booker T. Washington, a distinguished black leader and ex-slave, later observed, whites could not hold blacks in a ditch without getting down there with them.

Early Abolitionism

The inhumanity of the "peculiar institution" gradually caused antislavery societies to sprout forth. Abolitionist sentiment first stirred at the time of the Rev-

olution, especially among leading Quakers. Because of the widespread loathing of blacks, some of the earliest abolitionist efforts focused on transporting blacks back to Africa. The American Colonization Society was founded for this purpose in 1817, and in 1822 the Republic of Liberia was established for former slaves on the West African coast.

In the 1830s the abolitionist movement took on new energy and momentum, mounting to the proportions of a crusade. American abolitionists took heart in 1833 when their British counterparts unchained the slaves in the West Indies. Most important, the religious spirit of the Second Great Awakening now inflamed the hearts of many abolitionists against the sin of slavery.

Prominent among them was lanky, tousle-haired Theodore Dwight Weld, who had been evangelized by Charles Grandison Finney in the 1820s. In 1832 Weld enrolled at Lane Theological Seminary in Cincinnati, which was presided over by the formidable Lyman Beecher, father of novelist Harriet Beecher Stowe, feminist Catharine Beecher, and preacher-abolitionist Henry Ward Beecher. Expelled along with several other students in 1834 for organizing an eighteen-day debate on slavery, Weld and his fellow "Lane Rebels"—full of the energy and idealism of youth—fanned out across the Old Northwest preaching the antislavery gospel. Weld also assembled a potent propaganda tract, *American Slavery as It Is* (1839), which greatly influenced Harriet Beecher Stowe's *Uncle Tom's Cabin.*

Radical Abolitionism

On New Year's Day 1831 a shattering abolitionist blast came from the bugle of William Lloyd Garrison, a mild-looking reformer of twenty-six. A spiritual child of the Second Great Awakening, Garrison published in Boston the first issue of his militantly antislavery newspaper the *Liberator.* With this mighty paper broadside, Garrison triggered a thirty-year war of words and in a sense fired one of the opening guns of the Civil War.

Stern and uncompromising, Garrison proclaimed in strident tones that under no circumstances would he tolerate the poisonous weed of slavery:

Frederick Douglass *The former Maryland slave became the most prominent African-American leader of the nineteenth century. His autobiography,* A Narrative of the Life of Frederick Douglass, *is considered a literary classic.*

> I will be as harsh as truth and as uncompromising as justice. . . . I am in earnest—I will not equivocate—I will not excuse—I will not retreat a single inch—and I WILL BE HEARD!

Other dedicated abolitionists rallied to Garrison's standard, and in 1833 they founded the American Anti-Slavery Society. Prominent among them was eloquent Wendell Phillips, a Boston patrician known as "abolition's golden trumpet."

Black abolitionists distinguished themselves as living monuments to the cause of African-American freedom. Their ranks included the incendiary David Walker, who advocated violent revolt against white supremacy. Also noteworthy were Sojourner Truth, a freed black woman who fought tirelessly for black emancipation and women's rights, and Martin Delany, one of the few black leaders who advocated black recolonization in Africa.

The greatest of the black abolitionists was Frederick Douglass. Escaping from bondage in 1838 at the age of twenty-one, Douglass was "discovered" by the abolitionists three years later when he gave a stunning impromptu speech at an antislavery meeting in Massachusetts. Thereafter he lectured widely for the cause, despite frequent beatings and threats against his life. In 1845 he published his classic autobiography, *Narrative of the Life of Frederick Douglass.*

Douglass was as flexibly practical as Garrison was stubbornly principled. Garrison often appeared to be more interested in his own righteousness than in the substance of the slavery evil itself, and repeatedly demanded that the "virtuous" North secede from the "wicked" South. Renouncing politics, on the Fourth of July 1854, he publicly burned a copy of the Constitution as "a covenant with death and an agreement with hell." Douglass, on the other hand, along with other abolitionists, increasingly looked to politics to end the blight of slavery. These political abolitionists backed the Liberty party in 1840, the Free Soil party in 1848, and eventually the Republican party in the 1850s. In the end, most abolitionists, including even the pacifistic Garrison himself, followed out the logic of their beliefs and supported a frightfully costly fratricidal war as the price of emancipation.

High-minded and courageous, the abolitionists were men and women of goodwill and various colors who faced the cruel choice that people in many ages have had thrust upon them: when is evil so enormous that it must be denounced, even at the risk of precipitating bloodshed and butchery?

The South Lashes Back

Antislavery sentiment was not unknown in the South, but after about 1830 the voice of white southern abolitionism was silenced. Nat Turner's rebellion sent a wave of hysteria sweeping over the white cotton fields, and planters in increasing numbers slept with pistols by their pillows.

The nullification crisis in 1832 further implanted haunting fears in white southern minds, conjuring up nightmares of black incendiaries and abolitionist devils. Jailings, whippings, and lynchings now greeted rational efforts to discuss the slavery problem in the South.

Proslavery whites responded by launching a massive defense of slavery as a positive good. In doing so they forgot their own section's previous doubts about the morality of the "peculiar institution." Slavery, they claimed, was supported by the authority of the Bible and the wisdom of Aristotle. It was good for the Africans, who were lifted from the "barbarism of the jungle" and clothed with the blessings of Christian civilization.

Slavemasters did indeed encourage religion in the slave quarters, emphasizing those teachings that encouraged obedience. White apologists also pointed out that master-slave relationships really resembled those of a family. On many plantations, especially those in the Old South of Virginia and Maryland, this argument had a certain plausibility.

Southern whites were quick to contrast the "happy" lot of their "servants" with that of the overworked northern wage slaves, including sweated women and stunted children. The blacks mostly toiled in the fresh air and sunlight, not in dark and stuffy factories. They did not have to worry about slack times or unemployment, as did the "hired hands" of the North. Provided with a jail-like form of Social Security, they were cared for in sickness and old age, unlike the northern workers, who were set adrift when they had outlived their usefulness.

These curious proslavery arguments only widened the chasm between a backward-looking South and a forward-looking North—and indeed much of the rest of the Western world. The southerners reacted to the pressure of their own fears and the merciless nagging of the northern abolitionists. Increasingly the white South turned in upon itself and grew hotly intolerant of any embarrassing questions about the status of slavery.

Regrettably, also, the controversy over free people endangered free speech in the entire country.

CHRONOLOGY

1793	Whitney's cotton gin transforms southern economy.
1800	Gabriel slave rebellion in Virginia.
1808	Congress outlaws slave trade.
1817	American Colonization Society formed.
1822	Republic of Liberia established in Africa.
	Vesey slave rebellion in Charleston.
1829	Walker publishes *Appeal to the Colored Citizens of the World.*
1831	Garrison begins publishing the *Liberator.*
	Nat Turner slave rebellion in Virginia.
1831–1832	Virginia legislature debates slavery and emancipation.
1833	British abolish slavery in the West Indies.
	American Anti-Slavery Society founded.
1834	Abolitionist students expelled from Lane Theological Seminary.
1835	U.S. Post Office orders destruction of abolitionist mail.
	Broadcloth Mob attacks Garrison.
1836	House of Representatives passes gag resolution.
1837	Mob kills abolitionist Lovejoy in Alton, Illinois.
1839	Weld publishes *American Slavery as It Is.*
1840	Liberty party organized.
1845	Douglass publishes *Narrative of the Life of Frederick Douglass*
1848	Free Soil party organized.

Piles of petitions poured in upon Congress from the antislavery reformers; and in 1836 sensitive southerners drove through the House the so-called gag resolution. It required all such antislavery appeals to be tabled without debate.

Southern whites likewise resented the flooding of their mails with incendiary abolitionist literature. In 1835 a mob in Charleston, South Carolina, looted the local post office and burned a pile of abolitionist propaganda. Capitulating to southern pressures, the Washington government in 1835 ordered southern postmasters to destroy abolitionist material and called on southern state officials to arrest federal postmasters who did not comply. Such was "freedom of the press" as guaranteed by the Constitution.

The Abolitionist Impact in the North

Abolitionists—especially the extreme Garrisonians—were for a long time unpopular in many parts of the North. Northerners had been brought up to revere the Constitution and to regard the clauses on slavery as a lasting bargain. The ideal of Union, hammered home by the thundering eloquence of Daniel Webster and others, had taken deep root; and Garrison's wild talk of secession grated harshly on northern ears.

The North also had a heavy economic stake in Dixie. By the late 1850s the southern planters owed northern bankers and other creditors about $300 million, and much of this immense sum would be lost—as, in fact, it later was—should the Union dissolve. New England textile mills were fed with cotton raised by the slaves, and a disrupted labor system might cut off this vital supply and bring unemployment. The Union during these critical years was partly bound together with cotton threads, tied by lords of the loom in collaboration with the so-called lords of the lash. It was not surprising that strong hostility developed in the North against the boat-rocking tactics of the radical antislaveryites.

Repeated tongue lashings by the extreme abolitionists provoked many mob outbursts in the North, some led by respectable gentlemen. A gang of young toughs broke into Lewis Tappan's New York house in 1834 and demolished its interior while a crowd in the street cheered. In 1835 Garrison, with a rope tied around him, was dragged through the streets of Boston by the so-called Broadcloth Mob but escaped almost miraculously. Reverend Elijah P. Lovejoy, of Alton, Illinois, not content to assail slavery, impugned the chastity of Catholic women. His printing press was destroyed four times, and in 1837 he was killed by a mob, thus becoming "the martyr abolitionist." So unpopular were the antislavery zealots that ambitious politicians, like Lincoln, usually avoided the taint of Garrisonian abolition like the plague.

Yet by the 1850s the abolitionist outcry had made a deep dent in the northern mind. Many citizens had come to see the South as the land of the unfree and the home of a hateful institution. Few northerners were prepared to abolish slavery outright, but a growing number, including Abraham Lincoln, opposed extending it to the territories in the West. People of this stamp, commonly called "free-soilers," swelled their ranks as the Civil War approached.

Varying Viewpoints

Ulrich Bonnell Phillips made three key arguments in his landmark study *American Negro Slavery* (1918). He claimed that slavery was an unprofitable and dying economic institution; that slavery was a benign institution run by kindly, paternalistic masters; and that blacks were passive by nature and did not abhor their enslavement. Scholars no longer accept Phillips's views of slavery's unprofitability or black racial inferiority, but they still debate the nature of the master-slave relationship and its effect on the slave personality.

Beginning in the late 1950s, historians such as Stanley Elkins emphasized the harshness of the slave system, which they even compared to the Nazi concentration camps, and its "infantilizing" effect on the slaves' personalities. Recently, scholars such as Eugene Genovese have criticized these views. Without diminishing the deprivations and pains of slavery, these students of the "peculiar institution" concede that slavery embraced a strange form of paternalism, a system that reflected not the benevolence of southern slaveholders but their need to protect and coax work out of their often recalcitrant "investments."

Other historians agree with Elkins that slavery was a brutal institution, but differ with his portrait of the slaves as passive victims. Kenneth Stampp stressed the frequency and variety of violent and peaceful slave resistance. Scholars such as Herbert Gutman and Lawrence Levine emphasize the tenacity with which slaves maintained their own culture, despite the hardships of bondage. Pointing to the slaves' capacity for active initiative, they see the "Sambo" stereotype as an act, an image that the slaves cleverly employed in order to confound their masters without incurring punishment.

The reputation of the abolitionists, both moderate and extreme, has greatly improved, reflecting the changed atmosphere generated by the civil rights struggles of the 1960s and 1970s. Once vilified as irresponsible provokers of a needless war, they are now commonly hailed as champions of human rights.

SELECT READINGS

Primary Source Documents

Two influential abolitionist documents are Theodore Dwight Weld, *American Slavery As It Is** (1839), and the inaugural editorial of William Lloyd Garrison's *Liberator** (1831). Roy P. Basler, ed., *The Collected Works of Abraham Lincoln* (1933), contains the Great Emancipator's assessment of abolitionism in 1854. For southern perspectives, see James Henry Hammond's famous "Cotton Is King" speech, *Congressional Globe,* 36 Cong., 1 sess., p. 961 (March 3, 1858).*

Secondary Sources

A good introduction to southern history is Clement Eaton, *A History of the Old South: The Emergence of a Reluctant Nation* (1975). Wilbur J. Cash, *The Mind of the South* (1941), is an engagingly written classic. Always incisive is C. Vann Woodward, *The Burden of Southern History* (1960) and *American Counterpoint* (1971). The literature on slavery and African-Americans is enormous; the best place to start is John Hope Franklin, *From Slavery to Freedom* (5th ed., 1980), and consult also Nathan Irving Huggins's sometimes lyrical *Black Odyssey* (1977). The modern debate on slavery began with Ulrich B. Phillips's classic *American Negro Slavery* (1918); a darker view of the same subject is found in Kenneth M. Stampp, *The Peculiar Institution* (1956). Consult also Stanley Elkins's stimulating essay, *Slavery* (2d ed., 1968), which has interesting obser-

vations on the abolitionists. A major study of the slaves and their relations to their masters is Eugene Genovese, *Roll, Jordan, Roll* (1974). Carl N. Degler compares slavery and race relations in Brazil and the United States in *Neither Black Nor White* (1971). Vincent Harding, *There Is a River: The Black Struggle for Freedom in America* (1981), discusses slave resistance and revolt. Two studies compare the development of race relations in South Africa and the United States: George M. Frederickson, *White Supremacy: A Comparative Study in American and South African History* (1981), and John Cell, *The Highest Stage of White Supremacy: The Origins of Segregation in South Africa and the American South* (1981). See also Sterling Stuckey, *Slave Culture: Nationalist Theory and the Foundations of Black America* (1987). David B. Davis provides indispensable background to the history of abolitionism in *The Problem of Slavery in Western Culture* (1966) and *The Problem of Slavery in the Age of Revolution* (1975). The best brief history of the abolitionists is James B. Stewart, *Holy Warriors* (1976). Aileen Kraditor is favorably disposed toward Garrison in *Means and Ends in American Abolitionism: Garrison and His Critics* (1977). White attitudes toward race and slavery can be studied in Winthrop Jordan's masterful *White Over Black* (1968) and George Frederickson's insightful *The Black Image in the White Mind* (1971). The most prominent black abolitionist is portrayed in Waldo E. Martin, Jr., *The Mind of Frederick Douglass* (1984), and William S. McFeely, *Frederick Douglass* (1990).

CHAPTER 19

Manifest Destiny and Its Legacy, 1841–1848

Our manifest destiny [is] to overspread the continent allotted by Providence for the free development of our yearly multiplying millions.

John L. O'Sullivan, 1845*

The Accession of "Tyler Too"

A horde of hard-ciderites descended upon Washington in 1841, clamoring for the spoils of office. The real leaders of the Whig party regarded President William Henry Harrison, "Old Tippecanoe," as little more than an impressive figurehead. Daniel Webster, as secretary of state, and Henry Clay, the uncrowned king of the Whigs and their ablest spokesman in the Senate, would grasp the helm.

Unluckily for Clay and Webster, their schemes soon hit a fatal snag. Before the new term had fairly started, Harrison came down with pneumonia and died after only four weeks in the White House—the shortest administration by far in American history.

The "Tyler too" part of the Whig ticket, hitherto only a rhyme, now claimed the spotlight. Six feet tall, slender, blue-eyed, and fair-haired, with classical features and a high forehead, Tyler was a Virginia gentleman of the old school—gracious and kindly, yet stubbornly attached to principle. He had earlier

resigned from the United States Senate, quite unnecessarily, rather than accept distasteful instructions from the Virginia legislature. Still a lone wolf, he had forsaken the Jacksonian Democratic fold for that of the Whigs, largely because he could not stomach the dictatorial tactics of Jackson.

Tyler's enemies accused him of being a Democrat in Whig clothing, but this charge was only partially true. The Whig party, like the Democratic party, was something of a catchall, and the accidental president belonged to the minority wing, which embraced a number of Jeffersonian states'-righters. Tyler had in fact been put on the ticket partly to attract the vote of this influential group.

It was true, however, that on virtually every major issue the obstinate Virginian was at odds with the majority of his Whig party, which was probank, pro–protective tariff, and pro–internal improvements. "Tyler too" rhymed with "Tippecanoe," but there the harmony ended. As events turned out, President Harrison, the Whig, served for only four weeks, while Tyler, the ex-Democrat who was still largely a Democrat at heart, served for 204 weeks.

---

* Earliest known use of the term *Manifest Destiny,* sometimes called "manifest desire."

John Tyler: A President Without a Party

After their hard-won, hard-cider victory, the Whigs brought their not-so-secret platform out of Clay's waistcoat pocket. To the surprise of no one, it outlined a strongly nationalistic program.

Financial reform came first. The Whig Congress hastened to pass a law ending the independent treasury system, and President Tyler, disarmingly agreeable, signed it. Clay next drove through Congress a bill for a Fiscal Bank, which would establish a new Bank of the United States.

Tyler's hostility to a centralized bank was notorious, and Clay—the "Great Compromiser"—would have done well to conciliate him. But the Kentuckian, robbed repeatedly of the presidency by lesser men, was in an imperious mood and riding for a fall. When the bank bill reached the presidential desk, Tyler flatly vetoed it on both practical and constitutional grounds. A drunken mob gathered late at night near the White House and shouted insultingly, "Huzza for Clay!" "A bank! A bank!" "Down with the veto!"

Whig extremists, boiling with indignation, condemned Tyler as "His Accidency" and as "Executive Ass." To the delight of Democrats, the stiff-necked Virginian was formally expelled from his party by a caucus of Whig congressmen, and a serious attempt to impeach him was made in the House of Representatives. His entire cabinet resigned in a body, except Secretary of State Webster, who was in the midst of delicate negotiations with Britain.

The proposed Whig tariff also felt the prick of the president's well-inked pen. Tyler vetoed a tariff bill that included a scheme for distributing revenues from sale of public land to the states. But he reluctantly signed the revised Clayite Tariff of 1842, pushing rates back down to the moderately protective level of 1832, about 32 percent.

Manipulating the Maine Maps

Hatred of Britain during the nineteenth century came to a head periodically and had to be lanced by treaty settlement or by war. The sore had festered ominously in the late 1830s, especially because of private American involvement in an unsuccessful Canadian rebellion in 1837. When an American steamer, the *Caroline,* attempted to deliver supplies to Canadian insurgents, British troops sank the ship in the Niagara River, killing one American.

Then, Anglo-American controversy exploded in the early 1840s over the disputed Maine boundary. The St. Lawrence River is icebound several months of the year, as the British, remembering the War of 1812, well knew. They were determined, as a defensive precaution against the Yankees, to build a road westward from the seaport of Halifax to Quebec. But the proposed route ran through disputed territory—claimed also by Maine under the misleading peace treaty of 1783. Tough-knuckled lumberjacks from both Maine and Canada entered the disputed no-man's-land of the tall-timbered Aroostook River Valley. Ugly fights flared up and both sides summoned the local militia. The small-scale lumberjack clash, dubbed the "Aroostook War," threatened to widen into a full-dress shooting war.

As the crisis deepened in 1842, the London Foreign Office took an unusual step. It sent to Washington a nonprofessional diplomat, the conciliatory financier Lord Ashburton, who had married a wealthy American woman. He speedily established cordial relations with Secretary Webster, who had recently been lionized during a visit to England.

The two statesmen, their nerves eventually frayed by protracted negotiations in the heat of a Washington summer, finally agreed to compromise on the Maine boundary. On the basis of a rough, split-the-difference arrangement, the Americans were to retain some 7,000 square miles of the 12,000 square miles of wilderness in dispute. The British got less land, but won the desired Halifax-Quebec route.

An overlooked bonus was won in the same treaty when the British, in adjusting the boundary to the west, surrendered 6,500 square miles. The area was later found to contain the priceless Mesabi iron range of Minnesota.

The Lone Star of Texas Shines Alone

During the uncertain eight years since 1836, Texas had led a precarious existence. Mexico, refusing to recognize its independence, regarded the Lone Star republic as a province in revolt, to be reconquered in

A Texas Party, Early Nineteenth Century   *Texas was a meeting ground of Hispanic and Anglo-American cultures, creating a unique way of life that has been called "Texican."*

the future. Mexican officials loudly threatened war if the American eagle should gather the fledgling republic under its protective wings.

The Texans were forced to maintain a costly military establishment. Vastly outnumbered by their Mexican foes, the Texans could not tell when Mexico would strike again. Mexico actually did make two half-hearted raids, which, though ineffectual, foreshadowed more fearsome efforts. Confronted with such perils, Texas was driven to open negotiations with Britain and France, in the hope of securing the defensive shield of a protectorate. In 1839 and 1840, the Texans concluded treaties with France, the Dutch Republic, and Belgium.

Britain was intensely interested in an independent Texas. Such a republic would check the southward surge of the American colossus, whose bulging biceps posed a constant threat to nearby British possessions in the New World.

British abolitionists were also busily intriguing for a foothold in Texas. If successful in freeing the few blacks there, they presumably would inflame the nearby slaves of the South. In addition, British merchants regarded Texas as a potentially important free-trade area—an offset to the tariff-walled United States. British manufacturers likewise perceived that those vast Texan plains constituted one of the great cotton-producing areas of the future. An independent Texas would relieve British looms of their fatal dependence on American fiber—a supply that might be cut off in time of crisis by embargo or war.

The Delayed Texas Nuptials

Partly because of the fears aroused by British schemers, Texas became a leading issue in the presidential campaign of 1844. The proexpansion Democrats under James K. Polk finally triumphed over the Whigs under Henry Clay, the hardy perennial candidate. Lame-duck President Tyler thereupon interpreted the narrow Democratic victory, with dubious accuracy, as a "mandate" to acquire Texas.

Eager to marry his troubled administration to this splendid and promising prize, Tyler deserves much of the credit for shepherding Texas into the fold. Many "conscience Whigs" feared that Texas in the Union would be red meat to nourish the lusty "slave power." Tyler despaired of securing the needed two-thirds vote for a treaty in the Senate, and he therefore arranged for annexation by a joint resolution. This solution required only a simple majority in both houses of Congress. After a spirited debate, the resolution passed early in 1845, and Texas was formally invited to become the twenty-eighth star on the American flag.

Mexico angrily charged that the Americans had despoiled it of Texas. This was to some extent true in 1836, but hardly true in 1845, for the area was no longer Mexico's to be despoiled of. As the years stretched out, realistic observers could see that the Mexicans would not be able to reconquer their lost province. Yet Mexico left the Texans dangling by denying their right to dispose of themselves as they chose.

By 1845 the Lone Star republic had become a danger spot, inviting foreign intrigue that menaced the American people. The republic's continued existence as an independent nation threatened to involve the United States in a series of ruinous wars, both in America and in Europe.

What other power would have spurned the imperial domain of Texas? The bride was so near, so rich, so fair, so willing. Whatever the peculiar circumstances of the Texas revolution, the United States can hardly be accused of unseemly haste in achieving annexation. Nine long years were surely a decent wait between the beginning of the courtship and the nuptials.

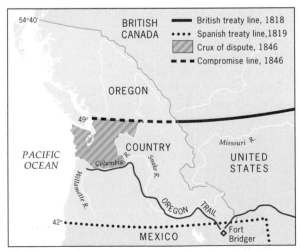

The Oregon Controversy

Oregon Fever Populates Oregon

The so-called Oregon Country was an enormous wilderness. It sprawled magnificently west of the Rockies to the Pacific Ocean, and north of California to the line of 54° 40'—the present southern tip of the Alaska panhandle. All or substantial parts of this immense area were claimed at one time or another by four nations: Spain, Russia, Britain, and the United States.

Two claimants dropped out of the scramble. Spain, though the first to raise its banner in Oregon, bartered away its claims to the United States in the so-called Florida Treaty of 1819. Russia retreated to the line of 54° 40' by the treaties of 1824 and 1825 with America and Britain. These two remaining rivals now had the field to themselves.

British claims to Oregon were strong—at least to that portion north of the Columbia River. They were based squarely on prior discovery and exploration, on treaty rights, and on actual occupation. The most important colonizing agency was the far-flung Hudson's Bay Company, which was trading profitably with the Indians of the Pacific Northwest for their furs.

Americans, for their part, could also point pridefully to exploration and occupation. Captain Robert Gray in 1792 had stumbled upon the majestic Columbia River, which he named after his ship; and the famed Lewis and Clark expedition of 1804–1806 had ranged overland through the Oregon Country to the Pacific. This shaky American toehold was ultimately strengthened by the presence of missionaries and other settlers, a sprinkling of whom reached the grassy Willamette River Valley, south of the Columbia, in the 1830s. These men and women of God were instrumental in saving the soil of Oregon for the United States. They stimulated interest in a faraway domain that countless Americans had earlier assumed would not be settled for centuries.

Scattered American and British pioneers in Oregon continued to live peacefully side by side. At the time of negotiating the Treaty of 1818, the United States had sought to divide the vast domain by the forty-ninth parallel. But the British, who regarded the Columbia River as the St. Lawrence of the West, were unwilling to yield this vital artery. A scheme for peaceful "joint occupation" was thereupon adopted, pending a future settlement.

The handful of Americans in the Willamette Valley was suddenly multiplied in the early 1840s, when "Oregon fever" seized hundreds of restless pioneers. In increasing numbers their creaking covered wagons jolted over the 2,000-mile Oregon Trail as the human rivulet widened into a stream. By 1846 about 5,000 Americans had settled south of the Columbia River.

The British, in the face of this rising torrent of humanity, could muster only 700 or so subjects north of the Columbia. Losing out lopsidedly in the population race, they were beginning to see the wisdom of arriving at a peaceful settlement before being engulfed by their neighbors.

A curious fact is that only a relatively small segment of the Oregon Country was in actual controversy by 1845. The area in dispute consisted of the rough triangle between the Columbia River on the south and the forty-ninth parallel on the north (most of the present state of Washington). Britain had repeatedly offered the line of the Columbia; America had repeatedly offered the forty-ninth parallel. The whole fateful issue was now tossed into the presidential election of 1844, where it was largely overshadowed by the question of annexing Texas.

A Mandate (?) for Manifest Destiny

The two major parties nominated their presidential standard bearers in May 1844. Ambitious but often-frustrated Henry Clay, easily the most popular man in the country, was enthusiastically chosen by the Whigs at Baltimore. The Democrats, meeting later in the same city, nominated James K. Polk of Tennessee, America's first "dark horse" or "surprise" presidential candidate. Speaker of the House of Representatives for four years and governor of Tennessee for two terms, Polk was a determined, industrious, ruthless, and intelligent public servant. Whigs attempted to jeer him into oblivion with the taunt, "Who is James K. Polk?" They soon found out.

The campaign of 1844 was in part an expression of the mighty emotional upsurge known as Man-

ifest Destiny. Countless citizens in the 1840s and 1850s, feeling a sense of mission, believed that Almighty God had "manifestly" destined the American people for a hemispheric career. They would irresistibly spread their uplifting and ennobling democratic institutions over at least the entire continent, and possibly over South America as well. Land greed and ideals—"empire" and "liberty"—were thus conveniently conjoined.

Expansionist Democrats were strongly swayed by the intoxicating spell of Manifest Destiny. They came out flat-footedly in their platform for the "reannexation of Texas"* and the "reoccupation of Oregon," all the way to 54° 40'. The Whigs countered with such slogans as "Hooray for Clay" and "Polk, Slavery, and Texas, or Clay, Union, and Liberty."

On the crucial issue of Texas, the acrobatic Clay tried to ride two horses at once. The "Great Compromiser" compromised away the presidency when he stated that he favored annexing slaveholding Texas (an appeal to the South) but that he also favored postponement (an appeal to the North). By straddling the issue this way, Clay alienated ardent antislaveryites.

In the stretch drive, "Dark Horse" Polk nipped Henry Clay at the wire, 170 to 105 votes in the Electoral College and 1,338,464 to 1,300,097 in the popular column. Clay would have won if he had not lost New York by a scant 5,000 votes. There the tiny antislavery Liberty party absorbed nearly 16,000 votes, many of which would otherwise have gone to the unlucky Kentuckian. Ironically, the anti-Texas Liberty party, by helping to elect the pro-Texas Polk, hastened the annexation of Texas. The victorious Democrats proclaimed that they had received a mandate from the voters to take Texas, and three days before leaving office President Tyler signed the joint resolution of annexation.

---

* The United States had given up its claims to Texas in the so-called Florida Purchase Treaty with Spain in 1819 (see p. 171). The slogan "Fifty-four forty or fight" was evidently not coined until two years later, in 1846.

Polk the Purposeful

"Young Hickory" Polk, unlike "Old Hickory" Jackson, was not an impressive figure. Of middle height (5 feet 8 inches), lean, white-haired (worn long), gray-eyed, and stern-faced, he took life seriously and drove himself mercilessly into a premature grave. His burdens were increased by an unwillingness to delegate authority. Methodical and hard working but not brilliant, he was shrewd, narrow-minded, conscientious, and persistent. "What he went for he fetched," wrote a contemporary. Purposeful in the highest degree, he developed a positive four-point program, and with remarkable success achieved it completely in less than four years.

Polk's first goal was to lower the tariff. Robert Walker, his secretary of the treasury, lobbied through Congress a tariff-for-revenue bill that lowered the average rates of the Tariff of 1842 from about 32 percent to 25 percent. The Walker Tariff of 1846 proved to be an excellent revenue producer.

A second objective of Polk's was the restoration of the independent treasury, which was unceremoniously dropped by the Whigs in 1841. Probank Whigs in Congress raised a storm of opposition, but victory at last rewarded the president's efforts in 1846. The third and fourth points on Polk's "must list" were the acquisition of California and the settlement of the Oregon dispute.

"Reoccupation" of the "whole" of Oregon had been promised northern Democrats in the campaign of 1844. But southern Democrats, once they had annexed Texas, rapidly cooled off. Polk, himself a southerner, had no intention of insisting on the 54° 40′ pledge of his own platform. But feeling bound by the offers of his predecessors, he again proposed the compromise line of 49°.

Fortunately for peace, British antiexpansionists ("Little Englanders") were now persuaded that the Columbia River after all was not the St. Lawrence of the West. Early in 1846 the British came around and themselves proposed the line of 49°. The senators speedily accepted the offer and approved the subsequent treaty, despite a few diehard shouts of "Fifty-four forty forever!"

Satisfaction with the Oregon settlement among Americans was not unanimous. The northwestern states, hotbeds of Manifest Destiny and "fifty-four

President Polk's Flimsy House of Cards *He appears to be hatching troublesome eggs relating to vexatious issues.*

fortyism," joined the antislavery forces in condemning what they regarded as a base betrayal by the South. Why *all* of Texas and not *all* of Oregon? Because, sneered the expansionist Senator Thomas Hart Benton of Missouri, "Great Britain is powerful and Mexico is weak."

So Polk, despite all the campaign bluster, got neither "fifty-four forty" nor a fight. But he did get something that in the long run was better: a reasonable compromise without shedding a drop of blood.

Misunderstandings with Mexico

Faraway California was another worry of Polk's. He and other disciples of Manifest Destiny had long coveted its verdant valleys, and especially the spacious bay of San Francisco. This splendid harbor was widely regarded as America's future gateway to the Pacific Ocean.

The population of California in 1845 was curiously mixed. It consisted of some 7,000 sun-blessed Spanish-Mexicans, plus more than ten times as many dispirited Indians. There were fewer than 1,000 foreigners, mostly Americans, some of whom had "left their consciences" behind them as they rounded Cape Horn. Given time, these transplanted Yankees might yet bring California into the Union by "playing the Texas game."

Polk was eager to buy California from Mexico. But relations with Mexico City were dangerously embittered, partly over unpaid damage claims by U.S. citizens but mostly over Texas. After threatening war if the United States should acquire the Lone Star republic, the Mexican government had completely broken diplomatic relations following annexation.

Deadlock with Mexico over Texas was further tightened by a question of boundaries. During the long era of Spanish-Mexican occupation, the southwestern boundary of Texas had been the Nueces River. But the expansive Texans, on rather farfetched grounds, were claiming the more southerly Rio Grande instead. Polk, for his part, felt a strong obligation to defend Texas in its claim, once it was annexed.

The Mexicans were far less concerned about this boundary quibble than the United States. In their eyes all of Texas was still theirs, although temporarily in revolt, and a dispute over the two rivers seemed pointless. Yet Polk was careful to keep American troops out of virtually all of the explosive no-man's-land between the Nueces and the Rio Grande, as long as there was any real prospect of peaceful adjustment.

The golden prize of California continued to cause Polk much anxiety. Disquieting rumors (now known to have been ill-founded) were circulating that Britain was about to buy or seize California—a grab that Americans could not tolerate under the Monroe Doctrine. In a last desperate throw of the dice, Polk dispatched John Slidell to Mexico City as minister late in 1845. The new envoy, among other alternatives, was instructed to offer a maximum of $25 million for California and territory to the east.

But the proud Mexicans would not even permit Slidell to present his "insulting" proposition.

American Blood on American (?) Soil

A frustrated Polk was now prepared to force a showdown. On January 13, 1846, he ordered 4,000 men, under General Zachary Taylor, to march from the Nueces River to the Rio Grande, provocatively near Mexican forces. Polk's presidential diary reveals that he expected at any moment to hear of a clash. When none occurred after an anxious wait, he informed his cabinet on May 9, 1846, that he proposed to ask Congress to declare war on the basis of (1) unpaid claims and (2) Slidell's rejection. These, at best, were rather flimsy pretexts. Two cabinet members spoke up and said that they would feel better satisfied if Mexican troops should fire first.

That very evening, news of bloodshed arrived. On April 25, 1846, Mexican troops had crossed the Rio Grande and attacked General Taylor's command, with a loss of sixteen Americans killed or wounded.

Polk, further aroused, sent a vigorous war message to Congress. He declared that despite "all our efforts" to avoid a clash, hostilities had been forced upon the country by the shedding of "American blood on the American soil." A patriotic Congress overwhelmingly voted for war, and enthusiastic volunteers cried, "Ho for the Halls of the Montezumas!" and "Mexico or Death!" Inflamed by the war fever, even antislavery Whig centers joined with the rest of the nation, though they later condemned "Jimmy Polk's war." As James Russell Lowell of Massachusetts lamented,

> Massachusetts, God forgive her,
> She's akneelin' with the rest.

In his message to Congress Polk was making history—not writing it. If he had been a historian, he would have explained that American blood had been shed on soil that the Mexicans had good reason to regard as their own. A gangling, rough-featured Whig congressman from Illinois, one Abraham Lincoln, introduced certain resolutions that requested information as to the precise spot on American soil where American blood had been shed. He pushed his "spot" resolutions with such persistence that he

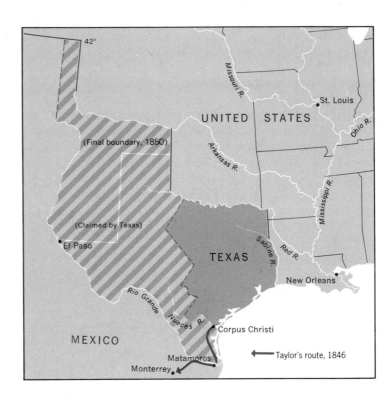

Texas, 1845–1846 *Texas President Mirabeau Buonaparte Lamar, flushed with imperial dreams, tried to secure the Texas claim to the large striped area on this map by leading a military expedition in 1841 against the Mexicans at Santa Fe. But the weak and outgunned "army" of the Lone Star republic, made up mostly of American drifters and adventurers, was speedily smashed. The Texans drew in their horns thereafter, and with renewed vigor sought annexation to the United States, rather than further expansion to the west of their precariously independent nation.*

came to be known as the "spotty Lincoln" who could die of "spotted fever."

Did Polk provoke war? California was an imperative point in his program, and Mexico would not sell it at any price. The only way to get it was to use force or wait for an internal American revolt. But in 1846, patience had ceased to be a virtue as far as Polk was concerned. Bent on grasping California by fair means or foul, he pushed the quarrel to a bloody showdown.

Both sides, in fact, were spoiling for a fight. Hotheaded Americans, especially southwestern expansionists, were eager to teach the Mexicans a lesson. The Mexicans, in turn, were burning to humiliate the "Bullies of the North." Possessing a considerable standing army, heavily overstaffed with generals, they boasted of invading the United States, freeing the black slaves, and lassoing whole regiments of Americans. They were hoping that the quarrel with Britain over Oregon would blossom into a full-dress war, as it came near doing, and further pin down the hated *yanquis*. A conquest of Mexico's vast and arid expanses seemed fantastic, espe-

cially in view of the bungling American invasion of Canada in 1812.

The Mastering of Mexico

Polk wanted California—not war. But when war came he hoped to fight it on a limited scale and then pull out when he had won the prize. The dethroned Mexican dictator Santa Anna, then exiled with his teenage bride in Cuba, let it be known that if the American blockading squadron would permit him to slip into Mexico, he would sell out his country. Polk agreed to this discreditable intrigue. But the double-crossing Santa Anna, once he returned to Mexico, proceeded to rally his countrymen to a desperate defense of their soil.

American operations in the Southwest and in California were completely successful. In 1846 General Stephen W. Kearny led a detachment of 1,700 troops over the famous Santa Fe Trail from Fort Leavenworth to Santa Fe. This sunbaked outpost, with its drowsy plazas, was easily captured. But before Kearny could reach California, the fertile

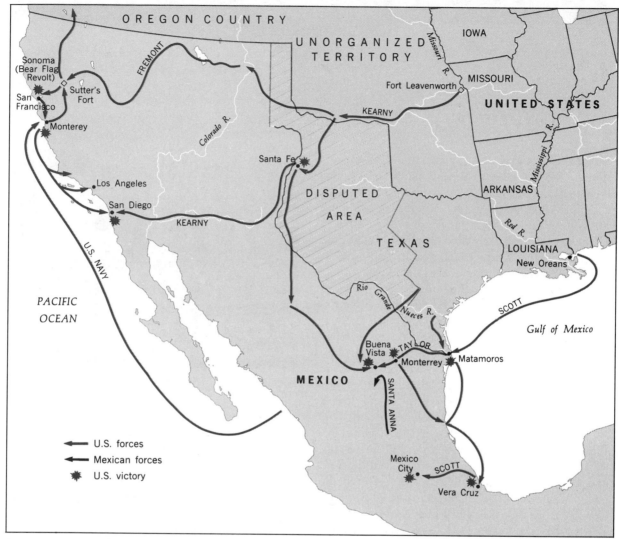

Major Campaigns of the Mexican War

province was won. When war broke out, Captain John C. Frémont, the dashing explorer, just "happened" to be there with several dozen well-armed men. In helping to overthrow Mexican rule in 1846, he collaborated with American naval officers and with the local Americans, who had hoisted the banner of the short-lived California Bear Flag Republic.

General Zachary Taylor meanwhile had been spearheading the main thrust. Known as "Old Rough and Ready" because of his iron constitution

and incredibly unsoldierly appearance—he sometimes wore a Mexican straw hat—he fought his way across the Rio Grande into Mexico. After several gratifying victories, he reached Buena Vista. There, on February 22–23, 1847, his weakened force of 5,000 men was attacked by some 20,000 march-weary troops under Santa Anna. The Mexicans were finally repulsed with extreme difficulty, and overnight Zachary Taylor became the "Hero of Buena Vista."

The Californios

When the United States acquired the Mexican Cession in 1848, it took in a vast land that stretched from the deserts of the Southwest to the fruited valleys and port cities of California. There dwelled some 13,000 Californios—descendants of the Spanish and Mexican conquerors who had once ruled California.

The Spanish had first arrived in California in 1769, extending their New World empire and outracing Russian traders to bountiful San Francisco Bay. Father Junipero Serra, an enterprising Franciscan friar, soon established twenty-one missions along the coast. Indians in the iron grip of the missions were encouraged to adopt Christianity and often forced to toil endlessly as farmers and herders, in the process suffering disease and degradation. These maltreated mission Indians occupied the lowest rungs on the ladder of Spanish colonial society.

On the loftiest rungs perched the Californios. Pioneers from the Mexican heartland of New Spain, they had trailed Serra to California, claiming land and civil offices in their new home. Yet even the proud Californios had deferred to the all-powerful Franciscan missionaries until Mexico threw off the Spanish colonial yoke in 1826, and began a process of transferring power from the missions to secular (that is, governmental) authorities.

This "secularization" program attacked and eroded the immense power of the Franciscans, who had self-confidently commanded their rich fiefdoms and resisted even minor efforts to reform their harsh treatment of the Indians. But during the 1830s nearly all of their lands and assets were confiscated by the Californios, who established vast *ranchos* that they ruled until the Mexican War.

The Californios' glory faded in the wake of the

Indians Dancing at the Mission in San Jose, 1806

American victory. Overwhelmed by the inrush of Anglo golddiggers after the discovery at Sutter's Mill in 1848, the Californios saw their recently acquired lands and political power slip through their fingers. When the Civil War broke out in 1861, so harshly did the word *yankee* ring in their ears that many Californios supported the South.

By 1870 the Californios' brief ascendancy had utterly vanished—a short and sad tale of riches to rags in the face of the Anglo onslaught. Half a century later, beginning in 1910, hundreds of thousands of young Mexicans would swarm into California and the Southwest. They would enter a region liberally endowed with Spanish architecture and artifacts, bearing the names of Spanish missions and Californios' *ranchos*. But they would find it a land dominated by Anglos, a place far different from that which their California ancestors had settled so hopefully in earlier days.

Sound American strategy now called for a crushing blow at the enemy's vitals—Mexico City. General Taylor, though a good leader of modest-sized forces, could not win decisively in the semi-deserts of northern Mexico. The command of the main expedition, which pushed inland from the coastal city of Vera Cruz early in 1847, was entrusted to General Winfield Scott. A handsome giant of a man, Scott had emerged as a hero from the War of 1812 and had later earned the nickname of "Old Fuss and Feathers" because of his resplendent uniforms and strict discipline. Scott succeeded in battling his way up to Mexico City by September 1847 in one of the most brilliant campaigns in American military annals. He proved to be the most distinguished general produced by his country between 1783 and 1861.

Fighting Mexico for Peace

Polk was anxious to end the shooting as soon as he could secure his territorial goals. Accordingly, he sent along with Scott's invading army the chief clerk of the State Department, Nicholas P. Trist. Grasping a fleeting opportunity to negotiate, Trist signed the Treaty of Guadalupe Hidalgo on February 2, 1848, and forwarded it to Washington.

The terms of the treaty were breathtaking. They confirmed the American title to Texas and yielded the enormous area stretching westward to Oregon and the ocean and embracing coveted California. This total expanse, including Texas, was about one-half of Mexico. The United States agreed to pay $15 million for the land and to assume the claims of its citizens against Mexico in the amount of $3,250,000 (see "Makers of America: The Californios," p. 266).

Polk submitted the treaty to the Senate. Speed was imperative. The antislavery Whigs in Congress —dubbed "Mexican Whigs" or "Conscience Whigs"—were condemning this "damnable war" with increasing heat. Having secured control of the House in 1847, they were even threatening to vote down supplies for the armies in the field. If they had done so, Scott probably would have been forced to retreat, and the fruits of victory might have been tossed away.

Another peril impended. A swelling group of expansionists, intoxicated by Manifest Destiny, was clamoring for all of Mexico. If America had seized it, the nation would have been saddled with an expensive and vexatious problem. Farseeing southerners like Calhoun, alarmed by the mounting anger of antislavery agitators, realized that the South would do well not to be too greedy. The treaty was finally approved by the Senate, 38 to 14. Oddly enough, it was condemned both by opponents who wanted all of Mexico and by opponents who wanted none of it.

Profit and Loss in Mexico

As wars go, the Mexican War was a small one. It cost some 13,000 American lives, most of them taken by disease. But the fruits of the fighting were enormous.

America's total expanse, already vast, was increased by about one-third (counting Texas)—an addition even greater than that of the Louisiana Purchase. A sharp stimulus was given to the spirit of Manifest Destiny for, as the proverb has it, the appetite comes with eating.

As fate ordained, the Mexican War was the blood-spattered schoolroom of the Civil War. The campaigns provided priceless field experience for most of the officers destined to become leading generals in the forthcoming conflict, including Captain Robert E. Lee and Lieutenant Ulysses S. Grant. The Military Academy at West Point, founded in 1802, fully justified its existence through the well-trained officers. Useful also was the navy, which did valuable work in throwing a crippling blockade around Mexican ports. The Marine Corps, in existence since 1798, won new laurels, and to this day sings, in its stirring hymn, about the halls of Montezuma.

The army waged war without defeat and without a major blunder, despite formidable obstacles and a half-dozen or so achingly long marches. Chagrined British critics, as well as other foreign skeptics, reluctantly revised upward their estimate of Yankee military prowess. Opposing armies, moreover, emerged with increased respect for each other. The Mexicans, though poorly led, fought heroically. At Chapultepec, near Mexico City, the teenage lads of the military academy there (*los niños*) perished to a boy.

A Cartoon from *Yankee Doodle*, 1847 *This satiric drawing was symbolic of the "lick all creation" spirit of the times.*

PLUCKED:

OR.

THE MEXICAN EAGLE BEFORE THE WAR!   THE MEXICAN EAGLE AFTER THE WAR!

Long-memoried Mexicans have never forgotten that their northern enemy tore away about half of their country. The argument that they were lucky not to lose all of it, and that they had been paid something for their land, did not lessen their bitterness. The war also marked an ugly turning point in the relations between the United States and Latin America as a whole. Hitherto, Uncle Sam had been regarded with some complacency, even friendliness. Henceforth, he was increasingly feared as the "Colossus of the North." Suspicious neighbors to the south condemned him as a greedy and untrustworthy bully, who might next despoil them of their soil.

Most ominous of all, the war rearoused the snarling dog of the slavery issue, and the beast did not stop yelping until drowned in the blood of the

CHRONOLOGY

1841	Harrison dies after four weeks in office.
	Tyler assumes presidency.
1842	Aroostook War over Maine boundary.
	Webster-Ashburton treaty.
1844	Polk defeats Clay in "Manifest Destiny" election.
1845	United States annexes Texas.
1846	United States settles Oregon dispute with Britain.

1846	United States and Mexico clash over Texas boundary.
	Kearny takes Santa Fe.
	Frémont conquers California.
	Wilmot Proviso passes House of Representatives.
1846–1848	Mexican War.
1847	Battle of Buena Vista.
	Scott takes Mexico City.
1848	Treaty of Guadalupe Hidalgo.

Civil War. Abolitionists assailed the Mexican conflict as one provoked by the southern "slavocracy" for its own evil purposes.

Quarreling over slavery extension also erupted on the floors of Congress. In 1846, shortly after the shooting started, Polk requested an appropriation of $2 million with which to buy a peace. Representative David Wilmot of Pennsylvania, fearful of the southern "slavocracy," introduced a fateful amendment. It stipulated that slavery should never exist in any of the territory wrested from Mexico.

The disruptive Wilmot amendment twice passed the House, but not the Senate. Southern members, unwilling to be robbed of prospective slave states, fought the restriction tooth and nail. Antislavery forces, in Congress and out, battled no less bitterly for the exclusion of slaves. The Wilmot Proviso soon came to symbolize the burning issue in the territories.

In a broad sense, the opening shots of the Mexican War were the opening shots of the Civil War. President Polk left the nation the splendid physical heritage of California and the Southwest, but also the ugly moral heritage of an embittered slavery dispute. Mexicans could later take some satisfaction in knowing that the territory wrenched from them had proved to be a frightful apple of discord that could well be called Santa Anna's revenge.

Varying Viewpoints

Historians have long probed for the real meaning behind the pulse-stirring phrase *Manifest Destiny.* Some have emphasized the idealistic impulses behind continental expansion. Others have stressed the supposed "superiority" of Anglo-Saxon culture over Native American and Spanish civilizations. Still other writers have seen American expansion as simply another chapter in the familiar story of territorial conquest. In recent years, many historians, no doubt influenced by the general reappraisal of America's relations with the rest of the world, have stressed the "imperialistic" forces behind America's territorial growth. These writers identify economic considerations—the quest for markets, the desire for cheap land, the demands for the expansion of slavery—as the motivations for conquest. Scholars have also begun to show more interest in, and sympathy for, the people displaced or absorbed in America's sweep to the western sea. They condemn the racial doctrines that had for several generations been used to justify expansionism.

SELECTED READINGS

Primary Source Documents

The colorful reminiscences of the pioneers are collected in Dale Morgan, ed., *Overland in 1846: Diaries and Letters of the California-Oregon Trail** (1963). For women's perspectives see Sandra Myres, *Ho for California! Women's Overland Diaries from the Huntington Library* (1980). The outbreak and conduct of the Mexican War come alive in the fascinating *Diary of James K. Polk,* edited by Milo Milton Quaife (1910).

Secondary Sources

A brief introduction is Ray A. Billington, *The Far Western Frontier, 1830–1860* (1956); more comprehensive is his *Westward Expansion* (rev. ed., 1974). Still useful is Albert K. Weinberg, *Manifest Destiny* (1935), though it should be supplemented by Frederick Merk, *Manifest Destiny and Mission in American History* (1963). For the Pacific region, see Francis Parkman's classic *The California and Oregon Trail* (1849), and Norman A. Graebner's general account, *Empire on the Pacific* (1955). On the conflict with Mexico, see K. Jack Bauer, *The Mexican-American War, 1846–1848* (1974). The other side's perspective is given in Gene M. Brack, *Mexico Views Manifest Destiny, 1821–1846* (1976). John H. Schroeder analyzes an important aspect of the conflict in *Mr. Polk's War: American Opposition and Dissent, 1846–1848* (1973). Paul H. Bergeron scrutinizes

Polk's administration in *The Presidency of James K. Polk* (1987). David M. Pletcher gives an overall view in *The Diplomacy of the Annexation of Texas, Oregon, and the Mexican War* (1973). Robert W. Johannsen uses the war to investigate American culture in *To the Halls of the Montezumas: The Mexican War in the American Imagination* (1985). Unusually colorful social history of the westward movement is provided in John Mack Faragher, *Women and Men on the Overland Trail* (1979), and John D. Unruh, Jr., *The Plains Across: The Overland Emigrants and the Trans-Mississippi West, 1840–1860* (1979). Julie Roy Jeffrey focuses on *Frontier Women* (1979). William R. Brock summarizes the politics of the 1840s in *Parties and Political Conscience: American Dilemmas, 1840–1850* (1979).

CHAPTER 20

Renewing the Sectional Struggle, 1848–1854

Secession! Peaceable secession! Sir, your eyes and mine are never destined to see that miracle.

Daniel Webster, 1850

The Popular Sovereignty Panacea

The year 1848, highlighted by a rash of revolutions in Europe, was filled with unrest in America. The Treaty of Guadalupe Hidalgo had officially ended the war with Mexico, but it had initiated a new and perilous round of political warfare in the United States. The vanquished Mexicans had been forced to relinquish an enormous tract of real estate from Texas to California. The acquisition of this huge domain raised anew the burning issue of extending slavery into the territories. Northern antislaveryites had rallied behind the Wilmot Proviso, which flatly prohibited slavery in any territory acquired in the Mexican War. Southern senators had blocked the passage of the proviso, but the issue would not die. Ominously, debate over slavery in the area of the Mexican Cession threatened to disrupt the ranks of both Whigs and Democrats and split national politics along North-South sectional lines.

Each of the two great political parties was a vital bond of national unity, for each enjoyed powerful support in both North and South. If they should be replaced by two purely sectional groupings, the Union would be in peril. To politicians, the wisest strategy seemed to be to sit on the lid of the slavery issue and ignore the boiling beneath. Even so, the cover bobbed up and down in response to the agitation of zealous northern abolitionists and hotheaded southern "fire-eaters."

President Polk, broken in health, had pledged himself to a single term. The Democratic National Convention in Baltimore turned to aging General Lewis Cass, an experienced but pompous senator whose enemies dubbed him "General Gass." The Democratic platform was silent on the burning issue of slavery in the territories. But Cass himself was a well-known advocate of "popular sovereignty," the doctrine that the people of a territory, under the principles of the Constitution, should themselves determine the status of slavery.

Popular sovereignty had a persuasive appeal. The public liked it because it accorded with the democratic tradition of self-determination. Politicians liked it because it seemed a comfortable compromise between a ban on slavery in the territories and southern demands that Congress protect slavery in the territories. Popular sovereignty tossed the slavery problem into the laps of the people in the various territories. Advocates of the doctrine thus hoped to dissolve the most stubborn national issue of the day into a series of local issues. Yet popular sovereignty had one fatal defect: it might serve to spread the blight of slavery.

Meeting in Philadelphia, the Whigs turned away from controversial Henry Clay and nominated Zachary Taylor, the "Hero of Buena Vista," who had never held civil office or even voted for president. As usual, the Whigs pussyfooted in their platform. Eager to win at any cost, they dodged all troublesome issues and merely extolled the homespun virtues of their candidate. Taylor had not committed himself on the issue of slavery extension, but as a wealthy Louisiana sugar planter he owned scores of slaves.

Aroused by the conspiracy of silence in the Democratic and Whig platforms, ardent antislavery men organized the Free Soil party. It stood foursquare for the Wilmot Proviso and against slavery in the territories. The new party nominated ex-President Van Buren and adopted the slogan, "Free soil, free speech, free labor, and free men."

With the slavery issue officially shoved under the rug by the two major parties, politicians on both sides were happy to focus on personalities. The amateurish Taylor had to be carefully watched, lest his indiscreet pen puncture his puffed-up military reputation. Taylor won with 1,360,967 popular and 163 electoral votes compared with Cass's 1,222,342 popular and 127 electoral votes. Free-soiler Van Buren polled 291,263 votes and won no states, but apparently diverted enough Democratic strength from Cass in the crucial state of New York to throw the election to Taylor.

Sectional Balance and the Underground Railroad

The South of 1850 was relatively well off. It had seated in the White House the war hero Zachary Taylor, a Virginia-born, slaveowning planter from Louisiana. It had a majority in the cabinet and on the supreme bench. If outnumbered in the House, the South had equality in the Senate, where it could hope to exercise a veto voice. Its cotton fields were expanding, and the price of the snowy fiber was profitably high. Few sane people, North or South,

believed that slavery was seriously threatened where it already existed below the Mason-Dixon line. The fifteen slave states could easily veto any proposed constitutional amendment.

Yet the South was deeply worried, as it had been for several decades, by the ever-tipping political balance. There were then fifteen slave states and fifteen free states. The admission of California, now knocking at the door after the gold rush of 1848–1849, would destroy the delicate equilibrium in the Senate, perhaps forever. The fate of California might well establish a precedent for the rest of the Mexican Cession territory.

Texas nursed an additional grievance of its own. It claimed a huge area east of the Rio Grande and north to the forty-second parallel, part of present New Mexico. The federal government was proposing to detach this prize, while hot-blooded Texans were threatening to descend upon Santa Fe and seize what they regarded as rightfully theirs. The explosive quarrel foreshadowed shooting.

Many southerners were also angered by the nagging agitation in the North for the abolition of slavery in the District of Columbia. They looked with alarm on the prospect of a ten-mile-square oasis of free soil, thrust between slaveholding Maryland and slaveholding Virginia.

Even more disagreeable to the South was the loss of runaway slaves, many of whom were assisted north by the Underground Railroad. It consisted of an informal chain of "stations" (antislavery homes), through which scores of "passengers" (runaway slaves) were spirited by "conductors" (usually white and black abolitionists) from the slave states to the free-soil sanctuary of Canada.

The most amazing of these "conductors" was a runaway slave from Maryland, fearless Harriet Tubman. During nineteen forays into the South, she rescued more than 300 slaves, including her aged parents, and deservedly earned the title "Moses." Lively imaginations later exaggerated the role of the Underground Railroad, but its existence is a fact.

By 1850 southerners were demanding a new and more stringent fugitive-slave law. The old one, passed by Congress in 1793, had proved inadequate to cope with runaways, especially since unfriendly state authorities failed to cooperate.

Resurrection of Henry Box Brown *Brown, a slave, was shipped to Philadelphia abolitionists from Virginia in a box.*

Estimates indicate that the South in 1850 was losing perhaps 1,000 runaways a year, out of its total of some 4 million slaves. In fact, more blacks probably gained their freedom by self-purchase or voluntary emancipation than by escaping. But the moral judgment implied by the Underground Railroad infuriated slaveowners, and they demanded federal redress.

Twilight of the Senatorial Giants

Southern fears were such that Congress was confronted with catastrophe in 1850. Free-soil California was banging on the door for admission, and fire-eaters in the South were voicing ominous threats of secession. The crisis brought into the congressional forum the most distinguished assemblage of statesmen since the Constitutional Convention of 1787—the Old Guard of the dying generation and the young gladiators of the new. That "immortal trio"—Clay, Calhoun, and Webster—appeared together for the last time.

Henry Clay, now seventy-three years of age, played a crucial role by proposing a series of compromises. Ably seconded by Senator Stephen A. Douglas of Illinois, the "Little Giant," Clay urged that both the North and the South make concessions.

Senator John C. Calhoun, then sixty-eight and dying of tuberculosis, championed the South in his last formal speech. Too weak to deliver it himself, he sat bundled up in the Senate chamber, his eyes glowing within a stern face, while a younger colleague read his fateful words. Rejecting Clay's proposed concessions, Calhoun's passionate plea was to leave slavery alone, return runaway slaves, give the South its rights as a minority, and restore the political balance. Calhoun died in 1850, before the debate was over, uttering the sad words, "The South! The South! God knows what will become of her."

Daniel Webster, now sixty-eight years old and ailing, next took the Senate spotlight to uphold Clay's compromise measures in his last great speech. Webster urged all reasonable concessions to the South, including a new fugitive-slave law. Because climate would prevent the spread of cotton production to the Mexican Cession territory, Webster argued, it was unnecessary to legislate on slavery there.* The old orator's eloquent plea visibly strengthened Union sentiment, and especially pleased northern banking and commercial centers,

---

* Webster was wrong here; within 100 years California had become one of the great cotton-producing states of the Union.

Compromise of 1850

Concessions to the North	Concessions to the South
California admitted as a free state	The remainder of the Mexican Cession area to be formed into the territories of New Mexico and Utah, without restriction on slavery, hence open to popular sovereignty
Territory disputed by Texas and New Mexico to be surrendered to New Mexico	Texas to receive $10 million from the federal government as compensation
Abolition of the slave trade (but not slavery) in the District of Columbia	A more stringent Fugitive Slave Law, going beyond that of 1793

which stood to lose millions of dollars by secession. But the abolitionists, who had mistakenly regarded Webster as one of them, upbraided him as a traitor.

The stormy congressional debate of 1850 was not finished, for the Young Guard from the North were yet to have their say. Led by wiry Senator William Seward of New York, this new generation of antislavery politicians seemed more interested in purifying the Union than in patching and preserving

A Seward Caricature   *He later became Lincoln's foremost rival for the presidency, and still later his secretary of state.*

it. Seward flatly opposed further concessions to the South, appealing to a moral "higher law" than the Constitution to exclude slavery from the territories.

As the great debate in Congress ran its heated course, deadlock seemed certain. In response to the threats of Texas to seize Santa Fe, blunt old President Taylor seemed ready to lead an army into Texas and hang all the "damned traitors." If the troops had marched, the South probably would have seceded, and the Civil War might have erupted in 1850.

Breaking the Congressional Logjam

At the height of the controversy in 1850, President Taylor unknowingly made compromise possible by dying suddenly. The colorless vice president, Millard Fillmore, took the reins. As presiding officer of the Senate, he had been impressed with the arguments for conciliation, and he gladly signed the series of compromise measures that passed Congress after seven long months of stormy debate.

The struggle to get these measures accepted by the country was hardly less heated than in Congress. In the northern states, "Union savers" like senators Clay, Webster, and Douglas orated on behalf of the compromise. The ailing Clay himself delivered more than seventy speeches. Their cause was aided by a growing feeling of goodwill and by an upsurge of prosperity.

But southern fire-eaters were still violently opposed to concessions. In mid-1850 an assemblage of southern extremists met in Nashville, Tennessee,

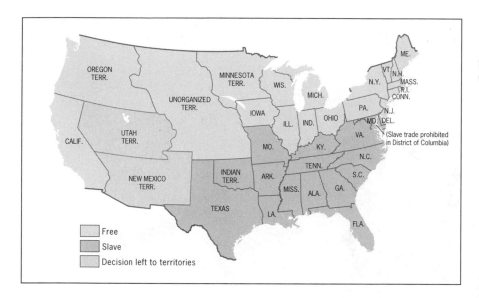

Slavery After the Compromise of 1850

to condemn the compromise. But the convention proved to be a dud, and southern opinion reluctantly accepted the verdict of compromise.

Like the calm after a storm, a second Era of Good Feelings dawned. Both North and South were determined that the compromises should finally bury the explosive issue of slavery. But this placid period of reason proved all too brief.

Balancing the Compromise Scales

Who got the better deal in the Compromise of 1850? The answer is clearly the North. California, as a free state, tipped the Senate balance permanently against the South. The territories of New Mexico and Utah were open to slavery on the basis of popular sovereignty. But the iron law of nature—the "highest law" of all—had loaded the dice in favor of free soil. The southerners urgently needed more slave territory to restore the "sacred balance." If they could not carve new states out of the recent conquests from Mexico, where else could they get them? In the Caribbean, was one answer.

Even the apparent gains of the South rang hollow. Disgruntled Texas was to be paid $10 million toward discharging its indebtedness, but in the long run this was a modest sum. The immense area in dispute had been torn from the side of slaveholding Texas, and was almost certain to be free. The South had halted the drive toward abolition in the District of Columbia, at least temporarily, by permitting the outlawing of the slave *trade* in the federal district. But even this move was an entering wedge toward complete emancipation in the nation's capital.

Most alarming of all, the drastic new Fugitive Slave Law of 1850—"the Bloodhound Bill"—stirred up a storm of opposition in the North. The fleeing slaves could not testify in their own behalf, and they were denied a jury trial. These harsh practices threatened to create dangerous precedents for white Americans. The federal commissioner who handled the case would receive $5 if the runaway were freed and $10 if not—an arrangement that strongly resembled a bribe. Freedom-loving northerners who aided the slave to escape were liable to heavy fines and jail sentences. They might even be ordered to join the slave catchers, and this possibility rubbed salt into old sores.

So savage was this "man-stealing law" that it touched off an explosive chain reaction in the North. Many shocked moderates, hitherto passive, were driven into the swelling ranks of the abolitionists.

The Underground Railroad stepped up its timetable, and infuriated northern mobs rescued slaves from their pursuers. Massachusetts, in a move toward nullification suggestive of South Carolina in

A Ride for Liberty *This famous painting by New England artist Eastman Johnson brilliantly evokes the anxiety of fleeing slaves.*

1832, made it a penal offense for any state official to enforce the new federal statute. Other states passed "personal liberty laws," which denied local jails to federal officials and otherwise hampered enforcement. The abolitionists rent the heavens with their protests against the man-stealing statute. A meeting presided over by William Lloyd Garrison in 1851 declared, "We execrate it, we spit upon it, we trample it under our feet."

Beyond question, the Fugitive Slave Law was an appalling blunder on the part of the South. No single irritant of the 1850s was more persistently galling to both sides, and none did more to awaken in the North a spirit of antagonism against the South. The southerners in turn were embittered because the northerners would not in good faith execute the law—the one real and immediate southern "gain"

from the Great Compromise. Slave catchers, with some success, redoubled their efforts.

Should the shooting showdown have come in 1850? From the standpoint of the secessionists, yes; from the standpoint of the Unionists, no. Time was fighting for the North. With every passing decade this huge section was forging further ahead in population and wealth—in crops, factories, foundries, ships, and railroads.

Delay also added immensely to the moral strength of the North—to its will to fight for the Union. In 1850 thousands of northern moderates were unwilling to pin the South to the rest of the nation with bayonets. But the inflammatory events of the 1850s did much to bolster the Yankee will to resist secession, whatever the cost. This one feverish decade gave the North time to accumulate the physical and moral strength that provided the margin of victory. Thus the Compromise of 1850, from one point of view, won the Civil War for the Union.

Defeat and Doom for the Whigs

Meeting in Baltimore, the Democratic convention in 1852 chose as its nominee an obscure New Hampshire lawyer-politician, Franklin Pierce, the second "dark horse" candidate in American history. Weak and indecisive, Pierce was called the "fainting general" by his opponents because he had fallen off a horse during the Mexican War. Chosen because he was acceptable to the slavery wing of the Democratic party, Pierce came out for the finality of the Compromise of 1850, Fugitive Slave Law and all.

The Whigs, also convening in Baltimore, foolishly bypassed figures associated with the Compromise of 1850, such as President Fillmore and Senator Webster. Having won in the past only with military heroes, they turned to another, "Old Fuss and Feathers," General Winfield Scott. The huge and haughty Scott's personality repelled the masses, and Democrats cried exultantly, "We Polked 'em in '44; we'll Pierce 'em in '52."

Luckily for the Democrats, the Whig party was hopelessly split. Antislavery Whigs swallowed Scott but deplored his platform, which endorsed the hated Fugitive Slave Law. Southern Whigs, who doubted Scott's loyalty to the Compromise of 1850 and especially to the Fugitive Slave Law, accepted the platform but spat on the candidate. Stabbed in the back by his fellow Whigs in the South, Scott received 1,385,453 popular votes, but only 42 electoral votes. The pliant Pierce won in a landslide, with 1,601,117 popular votes and 254 electoral votes.

The election of 1852 was fraught with frightening significance, though it may have seemed tame at the time. It marked the effective end of the disorganized Whig party and, within a few years, its complete death. The Whigs were governed at times by the crassest opportunism, and they won only two presidential elections (1840, 1848) in their colorful career, both with war heroes. They finally choked to death trying to gag down the Fugitive Slave Law. But their great contribution—and a noteworthy one indeed—was to help implant and uphold the ideal of Union through leaders like Clay and Webster. Both of these statesmen, by unhappy coincidence, died during the 1852 campaign. But the good that they had done lived after them and contributed powerfully to the eventual preservation of a united United States.

The Expansionist Legacy of the Mexican War

At the outset the Pierce administration displayed vigor in pursuing expansion. The new president's cabinet contained aggressive southerners, including Secretary of War Jefferson Davis, future president of the Confederacy. The people of Dixie were determined to acquire more slave territory, and the compliant Pierce was their willing tool.

The intoxicating victories of the Mexican War stimulated the lust for new slave territory among "slavocrats." Many Americans were also looking for potential canal routes across Central America in Nicaragua and Panama, and favored expansion into the islands flanking them, notably Spain's Cuba.

Southerners took a special interest in Nicaragua. A brazen American adventurer, William Walker, tried repeatedly to grab control of this Central American country in the 1850s. Backed by an armed force largely recruited in the South, he installed himself as president in July 1856 and promptly legalized slavery. One southern newspaper proclaimed to the planter aristocracy that Walker—the "gray-eyed man of destiny"—"now offers Nicaragua to you and your slaves." But a coalition of Central American nations formed an alliance to overthrow him. President Pierce withdrew diplomatic recognition, and the gray-eyed man's destiny was to crumple before a Honduran firing squad in 1860.

Nicaragua was also of vital concern to Britain. Fearing that the grasping Yankees would monopolize trade there, the British seized a solid foothold at Greytown, the eastern end of the proposed Nicaraguan canal route, and an ugly armed clash threatened. But the crisis was surmounted in 1850 by the Clayton-Bulwer Treaty, which stipulated that neither America nor Britain would secure exclusive control over any future isthmian waterway.

America had become a Pacific power with the acquisition of California and Oregon. American shippers already traded with China, and they urged Washington to push for commercial intercourse with Japan, which had been closed to the European world for over 200 years.

The Washington government responded in 1853 by dispatching to Japan a fleet of awesome, smoke-belching warships commanded by Commodore Matthew C. Perry. By a judicious display of force and tact, Perry persuaded the Japanese in 1854 to sign a memorable treaty that proved to be the beginning of an epochal relationship.

Sugar-rich Cuba, lying off the nation's southern doorstep, was the prime objective of Manifest Destiny in the 1850s. Supporting a large population of enslaved blacks, it was coveted by the South as the most desirable slave territory available. Carved into several states, it would once more restore the political balance in the Senate.

Cuba was a kind of heirloom—the most important remnant of Spain's mighty empire. Polk, the expansionist, had offered the Spanish $100 million for Cuba, but they had replied that they would see it sunk into the ocean before they would sell it to the Americans at any price. With purchase out of the question, seizure was apparently the only way to pluck the ripening fruit.

Private adventurers from the South now undertook to shake the tree of Manifest Destiny. During 1850–1851, two "filibustering" expeditions, each numbering several hundred armed men, descended upon Cuba. These feeble efforts were repelled, and fifty of the invaders were summarily shot or strangled.

When Spanish officials in Cuba seized an American steamer in 1854, southern-dominated President Pierce decided to provoke a war with Spain and seize Cuba. An incredible cloak-and-dagger episode followed. The secretary of state instructed the American ministers to Spain, Britain, and France to meet in Ostend, Belgium, and draw up a top-secret plan to acquire Cuba. Their document, known as the Ostend Manifesto, urged that the United States should offer $120 million for Cuba; if Spain refused to sell, the United States would "be justified in wresting" the island from the Spanish.

When the secret Ostend Manifesto leaked out, northern free-soilers rose in an outburst of wrath against the "manifesto of brigands." The red-faced Pierce administration was forced to drop its brazen schemes for Cuba. The shackled black hands of Harriet Beecher Stowe's Uncle Tom, who had already roused the North, held the South back from Cuba.

Pacific Railroad Promoters and the Gadsden Purchase

Acute transportation problems were another legacy of the Mexican War. The newly acquired prizes of California and Oregon might just as well have been islands some 8,000 miles west of the nation's capital. The sea routes to and from the isthmus of Panama, to say nothing of those around South America, were too long. Covered-wagon travel past bleaching animal bones was possible but slow and dangerous. A popular song recalled:

> They swam the wide rivers and crossed the tall peaks,
> And camped on the prairie for weeks upon weeks.
> Starvation and cholera and hard work and slaughter,
> They reached California spite of hell and high water.

Feasible land transportation was imperative—or the newly won possessions on the Pacific Coast might break away. Camels were even proposed as the answer, but a transcontinental railroad was clearly the only real solution to the problem. The South, losing the economic race with the North, was eager to extend a railroad through the adjacent southwestern territory all the way to California. The best route across the Southwest ran slightly south of the Mexican border. Secretary of War Jefferson Davis had South Carolina railroad man James Gadsden appointed minister to Mexico. He negotiated a treaty in 1853, which ceded to the United States the Gadsden Purchase area for $10 million. The transaction aroused northern criticism, but the Senate approved the pact.

Southerners now argued that because their proposed line ran through the organized New Mex-

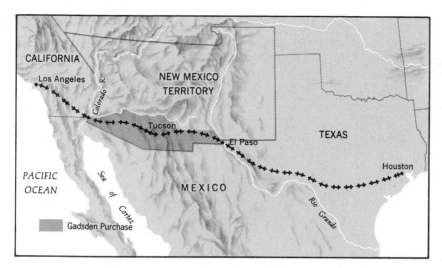

Gadsden Purchase, 1853
Future Southern Pacific Railroad (completed in 1882) is shown.

ico territory, the southern route should be built first. Northern railroad boosters quickly replied that if organized territory was the test, then Nebraska should be organized. But the southerners in Congress greeted all schemes for organizing the Nebraska territory with apathy or hostility. Why should the South help create new free-soil states, and thus cut its own throat by facilitating a northern railroad?

Douglas's Kansas-Nebraska Scheme

At this point in 1854, Senator Stephen A. Douglas of Illinois delivered a counterstroke to offset the Gadsden thrust for southern expansion westward. A squat, bull-necked, and heavy-chested figure, the "Little Giant" radiated the energy and breezy optimism of the self-made man. An ardent booster for the West, he longed to break the North-South deadlock over westward expansion and stretch a line of settlements across the continent. He had also invested heavily in Chicago real estate and railway stock and was eager to have the Windy City become the eastern terminus of the proposed Pacific railroad. He would thus endear himself to Illinois voters, benefit his section, and enrich his own purse.

A veritable "steam engine in breeches," Douglas threw himself behind a legislative scheme that would enlist the support of a reluctant South. The proposed Territory of Nebraska would be carved into two territories, Kansas and Nebraska. Their status regarding slavery would be settled by popular sovereignty—a democratic concept to which Douglas and his western constituents were deeply attached. Kansas, which lay due west of slaveholding Missouri, would presumably choose to become a slave state. But Nebraska, lying west of free-soil Iowa, would presumably become a free state.

Douglas's Kansas-Nebraska scheme ran headlong into a formidable political obstacle. The Missouri Compromise of 1820 had forbidden slavery in the proposed Nebraska Territory, which lay north of the sacred 36° 30′ line. The only way to open the region to popular sovereignty was to repeal the ancient compact outright. This bold step Douglas was prepared to take, even at the risk of shattering the uneasy truce patched up by the Compromise of 1850.

Many southerners, who had not conceived of Kansas as slave soil, rose to the bait. Here was a chance to gain one more slave state. The pliable President Pierce, under the thumb of southern advisers, threw his full weight behind the Kansas-Nebraska Bill.

But the Missouri Compromise, now thirty-four years old, could not be brushed aside lightly. Whatever Congress passes it can repeal, but by this time the North had come to regard the sectional pact as almost as sacred as the Constitution itself. Free-soil members of Congress struck back furiously. They met their match in the violently gesticulating Douglas, who was the ablest rough-and-tumble debater of his generation. Employing twisted logic and oratorical fireworks, he rammed the bill through Congress, with strong support from many southerners. So heated were political passions that bloodshed was barely averted. Some members carried a concealed revolver or a bowie knife—or both.

Douglas's motives in prodding anew the snarling dog of slavery have long puzzled historians. His personal interests have already been mentioned. In addition, his foes accused him of angling for the presidency in 1856. Yet his admirers have argued in his defense that if he had not championed the ill-omened bill, someone else would have.

The truth seems to be that Douglas acted somewhat impulsively and recklessly. His heart did not bleed over the issue of slavery, and he declared repeatedly that he did not care whether it was voted up or down in the territories. What he failed to perceive was that hundreds of thousands of his fellow citizens in the North *did* feel deeply on this moral issue. They regarded the repeal of the Missouri Compromise as an intolerable breach of faith, and they would henceforth resist to the last trench all future southern demands for slave territory.

Genuine leaders, like skillful chess players, must foresee the possible effects of their moves. Douglas predicted a "hell of a storm," but he grossly underestimated its proportions. His critics in the North, branding him a "Judas" and a "traitor," greeted his name with frenzied boos, hisses, and "three groans for Doug." But he still enjoyed a high degree of popularity among his following in the Democratic party, especially in Illinois, a stronghold of popular sovereignty.

Douglas Hatches a Slavery Problem *Note the already hatched Missouri Compromise, Squatter Sovereignty, and filibustering (in Cuba), and the about-to-hatch Free Kansas and Dred Scott decision. So bitter was the outcry against Douglas at the time of the Kansas-Nebraska controversy that he claimed with exaggeration that he could have traveled from Boston to Chicago at night by the light from his burning effigies.*

CHRONOLOGY

1848	Treaty of Guadalupe Hidalgo ends U.S.-Mexican War.
	Taylor defeats Cass and Van Buren for presidency.
1849	California gold rush.
1850	Compromise of 1850.
	Clayton-Bulwer Treaty with Britain.
	Fillmore assumes presidency after Taylor's death.
1852	Pierce defeats Scott for presidency.
1853	Gadsden Purchase from Mexico.
1854	Commodore Perry opens Japan.
	Ostend Manifesto proposes seizure of Cuba.
	Kansas-Nebraska Act.
	Republican party organized.
1856	William Walker becomes president of Nicaragua and legalizes slavery.

Congress Legislates a Civil War

The Kansas-Nebraska Act—a curtain raiser to a terrible drama—was one of the most momentous measures ever to pass Congress. By one way of reckoning, it led directly down the slippery slope to civil war.

Antislavery northerners were angered by what they condemned as an act of bad faith by the "Nebrascals" and their "Nebrascality." All future compromise with the South would be immeasurably more difficult, and without compromise there was bound to be conflict.

Henceforth the Fugitive Slave Law of 1850, previously enforced in the North only halfheartedly, was a dead letter. The Kansas-Nebraska Act wrecked two compromises: that of 1820, which it repealed specifically, and that of 1850, which northern opinion repealed indirectly. Emerson wrote, "The Fugitive [Slave] Law did much to unglue the eyes of men, and now the Nebraska Bill leaves us staring."

Northern abolitionists and southern fire-eaters alike were stirred to new outbursts. The growing legion of antislaveryites gained numerous recruits, who resented the grasping move by the "slavocracy" for Kansas. The southerners, in turn, became inflamed when the free-soilers attempted to control Kansas, contrary to the presumed "deal."

The proud Democrats—a party now over half a century old—were shattered by the Kansas-Nebraska Act. They did elect a president in 1856, but he was the last one they were to boost into the White House for twenty-eight long years.

Undoubtedly the most durable offspring of the Kansas-Nebraska blunder was the new Republican party. It sprang up spontaneously in the Midwest, notably in Wisconsin and Michigan, as a mighty moral protest against the gains of slavery. Gathering together dissatisfied elements, it soon included disgruntled Whigs (among them Abraham Lincoln), Democrats, Free-Soilers, Know-Nothings, and other foes of the Kansas-Nebraska Act. The hodgepodge party spread eastward with the rapidity of a prairie fire and with the zeal of a religious crusade. Unheard of and unheralded at the beginning of 1854, it elected a Republican speaker of the House of Representatives within two years. Never really a third-party movement, it erupted with such force as to become almost overnight the second major political party—and a purely sectional one.

At long last the dreaded sectional rift had appeared. The new Republican party would not be allowed south of the Mason-Dixon line. Countless southerners subscribed wholeheartedly to the sentiment that it was "a nigger-stealing, stinking, putrid, abolition party." The Union was in dire peril.

Varying Viewpoints

Historical analysts of the 1850s have long been preoccupied with the mounting controversy over slavery. Why, they have asked, did the long-simmering issue finally boil to a head in the decade of the 1850s, eventually exploding in the brutal Civil War of 1861–1865? Many scholars, most notably David M. Potter, have argued that the irreconcilable differences between free and slave societies—moral, political, economic, and social—increasingly eroded the ties between the sections and inexorably set the United States on the road to civil war. In this process no event was more

important than the breakdown of the Jacksonian party system.

Historians of the ethnocultural school, especially Michael Holt, have challenged this traditional view. In their view, it was a temporary *consensus* between the two parties on almost all *other* national issues that shoved slavery to the fore, encouraging the emergence of Republicans in the North and secessionists in the South. In the absence of regular, national two-party conflict over economic issues, purely regional parties (like the Republicans) identified their opponents not simply as competitors for power but as threats to their way of life, even to the life of the republic itself. This approach thus suggests an answer to the question of why the Civil War came when it

did: sectional strife had existed at least since the Missouri Compromise, but, paradoxically, it was only with the collapse of traditional partisan conflict in the 1850s that it led to war.

SELECT READINGS

Primary Source Documents

The *Congressional Globe* for 1850 contains the dramatic orations of a dying generation of American statesmen on the Compromise of 1850. See the speeches by Webster,* Calhoun,* and Clay (in Richard Hofstadter, ed., *Great Issues in American History*). The debate on the Kansas-Nebraska Bill can be found in the 1854 volume of the same source, which includes addresses by Stephen A. Douglas* and his Republican opponent, Salmon P. Chase.*

Secondary Sources

The best account of the events of the 1850s is David M. Potter's masterful *The Impending Crisis, 1848–1861* (1976). A concise summary of the events leading to the war is also available in the opening chapters of James M. McPherson, *Battle Cry of Freedom: The Civil War Era* (1988). Comprehensive treatments may be found in James G. Randall and David Donald, *The Civil War and Recon-*

struction (rev. ed., 1969), and William Freehling, *Road to Disunion: Secessionists at Bay, 1776–1854* (1990). David Potter offers illuminating insights in *The South and the Sectional Conflict* (1968). The standard work is Holman Hamilton, *Prologue to Conflict: The Crisis and Compromise of 1850* (1964). The emergence of the Republican party can be studied in Eric Foner's brilliant discussion of ideology, *Free Soil, Free Labor, Free Men* (1970), William Gienapp, *The Origins of the Republican Party, 1852–1856* (1987), and Michael Holt's perceptive *Forging a Majority: The Formation of the Republican Party in Pittsburgh* (1969). Foner's ideas can be pursued further in his *Politics and Ideology in the Age of Civil War* (1980), while Holt has developed his views in *The Political Crisis of the 1850s* (1978), an unusually provocative book. Richard H. Sewell, *Ballots for Freedom: Antislavery Politics in the United States, 1837–1860* (1976), is a standard work.

CHAPTER 21

Drifting Toward Disunion, 1854–1861

A house divided against itself cannot stand.
I believe this government cannot endure permanently half slave and half free.

Abraham Lincoln, 1858

Stowe and Helper: Literary Incendiaries

Sectional tensions were further strained in 1852, and later, by an inky phenomenon. Harriet Beecher Stowe, a wisp of a woman and the mother of a half-dozen children, published her heartrending novel *Uncle Tom's Cabin.* Dismayed by the passage of the Fugitive Slave Law, she was determined to awaken the North to the wickedness of slavery by laying bare its terrible inhumanity, especially the cruel splitting of families. Her book was distinguished by powerful imagery and touching pathos. "God wrote it," she explained in later years—a reminder that the sources of her antislavery sentiments lay in the religious crusades of the Second Great Awakening.

The success of the novel at home and abroad was sensational. Several hundred thousand copies were published in the first year, and the totals soon ran into the millions as the tale was translated into more than a score of languages. It was also put on the stage in "Tom shows" for lengthy runs. No other novel in American history—perhaps in all of history—can be compared with it as a political force. To millions of people it made slavery appear almost as evil as it really was.

When Mrs. Stowe was introduced to President Lincoln in 1862, he reportedly remarked, "So you're the little woman who wrote the book that made this great war." The truth is that *Uncle Tom's Cabin* helped start the Civil War—and win it.

Uncle Tom, endearing and enduring, left a profound impression on the North. Thousands of readers swore that henceforth they would have nothing to do with the enforcement of the Fugitive Slave Law. The tale was devoured by millions of impressionable youths in the 1850s—the later Boys in Blue who volunteered to fight the Civil War through to its grim finale. The memory of a beaten and dying Uncle Tom helped sustain their determination to wipe out the plague of slavery.

Another trouble-brewing book appeared in 1857, five years after the debut of Uncle Tom. Entitled *The Impending Crisis of the South,* it was written by Hinton R. Helper, a nonaristocratic white from North Carolina. Hating both slavery and blacks, he attempted to prove by an array of statistics that indirectly the nonslaveholding whites were the ones who suffered most from the millstone of slavery. Helper's

Cover of Children's Edition of *Uncle Tom's Cabin,* **1853**
Harriet Beecher Stowe's antislavery novel was the all-time best seller in nineteenth-century America, and the stage version became equally popular.

book, with its "dirty allusions," was banned in the South, where book-burning parties were held. But in the North thousands of copies, many in condensed form, were distributed as campaign literature by the Republicans.

The North-South Contest for Kansas

The rolling plains of Kansas had meanwhile been providing a horrible example of the workings of popular sovereignty. Newcomers who ventured into Kansas were a motley lot. Most of the northerners were just ordinary westward-moving pioneers. But a small part of the inflow was financed by groups of northern abolitionists or free-soilers, especially the New England Emigrant Aid Company, which sent about 2,000 persons to the troubled area to forestall the South—and also to make a profit. Shouting "Ho

for Kansas," many of them carried the deadly new breech-loading Sharps rifles, nicknamed "Beecher's Bibles" after the prominent clergyman who had helped raise money for their purchase. Many of the Kansas-bound pioneers sang Whittier's marching song (1854):

> We cross the prairie as of old
>   The pilgrims crossed the sea,
> To make the West, as they the East,
>   The homestead of the free!

Southern spokesmen, now more than ordinarily touchy, raised furious cries of betrayal. They had supported the Kansas-Nebraska scheme of Douglas with the informal understanding that Kansas would become slave and Nebraska free. The northern "Nebrascals" were now apparently out to "abolition-ize" *both* Kansas and Nebraska.

Quick to respond in kind, a few southern hot-heads attempted to "assist" small groups of well-armed slaveowners in moving to Kansas. But despite such efforts slavery never really came to Kansas. The census of 1860 found only 2 slaves among 107,000 souls in the territory, and only 15 in Nebraska. There was much force in the charge that the whole quarrel revolved around "an imaginary Negro in an impossible place."

Crisis conditions in Kansas rapidly worsened. When the day came in 1855 to elect members of the first territorial legislature, proslavery "border ruffi-ans" poured in from Missouri to vote early and often. The slavery supporters triumphed and then set up their own puppet government at Shawnee Mission. The free-soilers, unable to stomach this fraudulent conspiracy, established an extralegal regime of their own in Topeka. Confused Kansans thus had their choice between two governments—one based on fraud, the other on illegality. Tension mounted in 1856 when a gang of proslavery raiders shot up and burned a part of the free-soil town of Lawrence. This outrage was but the prelude to a bloodier tragedy.

Kansas in Convulsion

The fanatical figure of John Brown now stalked upon the Kansas battlefield. Spare, gray-bearded, iron-willed, and narrowly ignorant, he was dedicated to the abolitionist cause. The power of his glittering gray eyes was such, so he claimed, that his stare could force a dog or cat to slink out of a room. Brooding over the recent attack on Lawrence, "Old Brown" of Osawatomie led a band of his followers to Pottawatomie Creek, in May 1856. There they literally hacked to pieces five surprised men, allegedly proslaveryites. This fiendish butchery brought vicious retaliation from proslavery forces. Civil war in Kansas thus flared forth in 1856, and continued intermittently until it merged with the large-scale Civil War of 1861–1865.

The proslavery forces intensified the conflict in 1857 when they attempted to bring Kansas into the Union under a tricky document known as the Lecompton Constitution. Although the majority of Kansans were free-soilers, the vote on the proposed constitution was arranged so that it was impossible to prohibit all black bondage and still obtain statehood. With infuriated free-soilers boycotting the election, the slaveryites approved the constitution with slavery late in 1857.

The new president, James Buchanan, just as much under southern influence as Pierce, threw the weight of his administration behind the notorious Lecompton Constitution. But Senator Douglas, who had championed true popular sovereignty, would have none of this semipopular fraudulency. Deliberately tossing away his strong support in the South for the presidency, Douglas fought courageously for a fair popular vote on the *entire* Lecompton Constitution. The free-soil voters thereupon snowed it under at the polls, ending Kansas's hopes for statehood until 1861.

President Buchanan, by antagonizing the numerous Douglas Democrats in the North, hopelessly divided the once-powerful Democratic party. Until then, it had been the only remaining *national* party, for the Whigs were dead and the Republicans were sectional. With the disruption of the Democrats came the snapping of one of the last important strands in the rope that was barely binding the Union together.

"Bully" Brooks and His Bludgeon

"Bleeding Kansas" also splattered blood on the floor of the United States Senate. Tall and imposing Senator Charles Sumner of Massachusetts delivered a blistering speech in 1856 entitled, "The Crime Against Kansas," in which he condemned proslavery men as "hirelings picked from the drunken spew and vomit of an uneasy civilization." The speech also insulted white-haired Senator Butler of South Carolina.

Butler's hot-tempered nephew, South Carolina Congressman Preston Brooks, took vengeance into

SOUTHERN CHIVALRY — ARGUMENT versus CLUB'S.

Sumner Beaten by Brooks *Note that the cartoonist has two of the senators smiling or laughing and one of them preventing interference with his cane. Note also that Sumner is defending himself with a quill pen while Brooks is wielding a club.*

his own hands. On May 22, 1856, he approached Sumner, then sitting at his Senate desk, and pounded the orator with a heavy cane until it broke. The victim fell bleeding and unconscious to the floor, suffering serious injuries to his head and nervous system.

Bleeding Sumner thus joined Bleeding Kansas as a political issue. South Carolina triumphantly reelected Brooks, and Massachusetts did the same for Sumner, even though the battered abolitionist was unable to take his seat. Sumner's abusive speech sold by the thousands in the North, while southern admirers deluged Brooks with canes to replace the one he had broken.

The Sumner-Brooks clash and the ensuing reactions revealed how dangerously inflamed passions were becoming, North and South. It was ominous that the cultured Sumner should have used the language of a barroom bully and that the gentlemanly Brooks should have employed the tactics and tools of a thug. Emotion was displacing thought. The blows rained on Sumner's head were, broadly speaking, among the first blows of the Civil War.

"Old Buck" versus "The Pathfinder"

With bullets whining in Kansas, Democrats met in Cincinnati to nominate the presidential standard bearer of 1856. Both weak-kneed President Pierce and dynamic Senator Douglas were too blackened by the Kansas-Nebraska Act to win the election, so the party turned to a well-to-do Pennsylvania lawyer, James Buchanan, who had fortunately been abroad as minister to London during the recent Kansas-Nebraska uproar. Although his "Kansasless" neutrality made him acceptable to the party, "Old Buck" was mediocre, irresolute, and confused—a pygmy in a time that called for giants.

The fast-growing Republican party, meeting in Philadelphia, passed over "Higher Law" Seward, their most conspicious leader, and chose a dashing but erratic explorer-soldier-surveyor, John C. Frémont. Republicans hoped that the "Pathfinder of the West," who was also untarred with the Kansas brush, would blaze them a path to the White House. Vigorously condemning the extension of slavery into the territories, Republicans sang:

> Arise, arise ye brave!
> And let our war-cry be
> Free speech, free press, free soil, free men,
> Fré-mont and victory!

A bland Buchanan, although polling less than a majority of the popular vote, won handily. His tally in the Electoral College was 174 to 114 for Frémont, with third-party candidate Millard Fillmore garnering 8. The popular vote was 1,832,955 for Buchanan to 1,339,932 for Frémont, with 871,731 for Fillmore.

Democrats had lifted the hapless "Old Buck" into office, but it was the infant Republicans who could rightfully claim a "victorious defeat" in 1856. The new party had made an astonishing showing against the well-oiled Democratic machine. Whittier pointedly asked:

> Then sound again the bugles,
> Call the muster-roll anew;
> If months have well-nigh won the field,
> What may not four years do?

The question cast a long shadow forward, as politicians, North and South, peered anxiously toward 1860.

The Dred Scott Bombshell

The Dred Scott decision, handed down by the Supreme Court on March 6, 1857, abruptly ended the two-day presidential honeymoon of the unlucky bachelor, James Buchanan. Basically, the case was simple. Dred Scott, a black slave, had lived with his master for five years in Illinois and Wisconsin Territory. Backed by interested abolitionists, he sued for freedom on the basis of his long residence on free soil.

The Supreme Court proceeded to turn a simple legal case into a complex political issue. It ruled, not surprisingly, that Dred Scott was a black slave and not a citizen, and hence could not sue in federal courts.* The tribunal could then have thrown out the

---

* This part of the ruling, denying blacks their citizenship, seriously menaced the precarious position of the South's quarter-million free blacks.

case on these technical grounds alone. But a majority decided to go further, under the leadership of emaciated Chief Justice Taney from the slave state of Maryland.

Taney's thunderclap rocked the free-soilers back on their heels. A majority of the Court decreed that because a slave was private property, he or she could be taken into *any* territory and legally held there in slavery. The reasoning was that the Fifth Amendment clearly forbade Congress to deprive people of their property without due process of law. The Court, to be consistent, went further. The Missouri Compromise, banning slavery north of 36° 30′, had been repealed three years earlier by the Kansas-Nebraska Act. But its spirit was still venerated in the North. Now the Court had ruled that the Compromise of 1820 had been unconstitutional all along: Congress had no power to ban slavery from the territories, regardless of even what the territorial legislatures might want.

Southerners were delighted with this unexpected victory. Champions of popular sovereignty, including Senator Douglas and most northern Democrats, were aghast. Another lethal wedge was thus driven between the northern and southern wings of the once-united Democratic party.

Foes of slavery extension, especially the Republicans, were infuriated by the Dred Scott setback. Because a majority of the court were southerners, Republicans considered the opinion purely political, and declared it no more binding than the views of a "southern debating society." Southerners, in turn, wondered how long they could remain joined to a section that refused to honor the Supreme Court, to say nothing of the constitutional compact that had established it.

The Financial Crash of 1857

Bitterness caused by the Dred Scott decision was deepened by hard times, which dampened a period of feverish prosperity. Late in 1857, a financial panic burst about Buchanan's harassed head. The storm was not so bad economically as the panic of 1837, but psychologically it was probably the worst of the nineteenth century.

The North, including the grain growers, was hardest hit. The South, enjoying favorable cotton prices abroad, rode out the storm with flying colors. Panic conditions seemed further proof that cotton *was* king, and that its economic kingdom was stronger than that of the North. This fatal delusion helped drive the overconfident southerners closer to a shooting showdown.

Financial distress in the North, especially in agriculture, gave new vigor to the demand for free farms of 160 acres from the public domain. Eastern industrialists, worried about losing their labor force, together with southern slaveholders, fearful of filling the territories with free-soilers, had long blocked the scheme. In 1860 Congress finally passed a homestead act that made public lands available at the nominal sum of twenty-five cents an acre. But it was stabbed to death by the veto pen of Buchanan, near whose elbows sat southern sympathizers.

The panic of 1857 also created a clamor for higher tariff rates. The Tariff of 1857 had lowered duties to about 20 percent, but hardly were the revised rates on the books when the financial distress descended like a black pall. Northern manufacturers blamed their misfortunes on the low tariff and appealed for relief. Thus the panic gave the Republicans two surefire issues for 1860: protection for the unprotected and farms for the farmless.

An Illinois Rail Splitter Emerges

The Illinois senatorial election of 1858 now claimed the national spotlight. Senator Douglas's term was about to expire, and the Republicans decided to run against him a rustic Springfield lawyer, one Abraham Lincoln. The Republican candidate—6 feet 4 inches in height and 180 pounds in weight—presented an awkward but arresting figure. His legs, arms, and neck were grotesquely long; his head was crowned by coarse, black, and unruly hair; and his face was sad, sunken, and weather beaten.

Lincoln was no silver-spoon child of the elite. Born in 1809 in a Kentucky log cabin to impoverished parents, he attended a frontier school for not more than a year; being an avid reader, he was mainly self-educated. All his life he said "git," "thar," and "heered." Although narrow-chested and somewhat stoop-shouldered, he shone in his frontier community as a wrestler and weight lifter, and spent some time, among other pioneering pursuits, as a splitter of logs for fence rails. A superb teller of earthy and amusing stories, he would also periodically plunge into protracted periods of melancholy.

Lincoln's private and professional life was not especially noteworthy. He married "above himself" socially, into the influential Todd family of Kentucky; and the temperamental outbursts of his highstrung wife, known by her enemies as the "she wolf," helped to school him in patience and forbearance. After reading a little law, he gradually emerged as one of the dozen or so better-known trial lawyers in Illinois, although still accustomed to carrying important papers in his stovepipe hat. He was widely referred to as "Honest Abe," partly because he would refuse cases that he could not conscientiously defend.

The rise of Lincoln as a political figure was less than rocketlike. After making his mark in the Illinois legislature as a Whig politician of the logrolling variety, he served one undistinguished term in Congress, 1847–1849. Until 1854, when he was forty-five years of age, he had done nothing to establish a claim to statesmanship. But the passage of the Kansas-Nebraska Act in that year lighted within him unexpected fires. After mounting the Republican bandwagon, he emerged as one of the foremost politicians and orators of the Northwest. At the Philadelphia convention of 1856, where Frémont was nominated, Lincoln actually received 110 votes for the vice-presidential nomination.

The Great Debate: Lincoln versus Douglas

Lincoln, as Republican nominee for the Senate seat, boldly challenged Douglas to a series of joint debates. This was a rash act, because the stumpy senator was probably the nation's most devastating debater. Douglas promptly accepted Lincoln's chal-

Lincoln and Douglas Debate, 1858   *Thousands of people attended each of the seven Lincoln-Douglas debates. Douglas is shown here sitting to Lincoln's right in the debate at Charleston, Illinois, in September. On one occasion, Lincoln quipped that Douglas's logic would prove that a horse chestnut was a chestnut horse.*

lenge, and seven meetings were arranged from August to October 1858.

The most famous debate came at Freeport, Illinois, where Lincoln neatly impaled his opponent on the horns of a dilemma. Suppose, he queried, the people of a territory should vote slavery down? The Supreme Court in the Dred Scott decision had decreed that they could not. Who would prevail, the Court or the people?

Douglas replied that no matter how the Supreme Court ruled, slavery would stay down if the people voted it down. Laws to protect slavery would have to be passed by the territorial legislatures. These would not be forthcoming in the absence of popular approval, and black bondage would soon disappear. Douglas, in truth, had American history on his side. Where public opinion does not support the federal government, as in the case of Jefferson's embargo, the law is almost impossible to enforce.

The upshot was that Douglas defeated Lincoln for the Senate seat. The "Little Giant's" loyalty to popular sovereignty, which still had a powerful appeal in Illinois, probably was decisive. But in winning Illinois, Douglas further split his splintering Democratic party. After his opposition to the Lecompton Constitution for Kansas, and his further defiance of the Supreme Court at Freeport, southern Democrats were determined to break up the party (and the Union) rather than accept him. For his part, Lincoln had lost the election but shambled into the national spotlight in company with the most prominent northern politicians. The Lincoln-Douglas debate platform thus proved to be one of the preliminary battlefields of the Civil War.

John Brown: Murderer or Martyr?

The gaunt, grim figure of John Brown of Kansas notoriety now appeared again in a more terrible way. His crackbrained scheme was to invade the South secretly with a handful of followers, call upon the slaves to rise, furnish them with arms, and establish a kind of black free state as a sanctuary. Brown secured several thousand dollars for firearms from northern abolitionists, and finally arrived in hilly western Virginia with some twenty men. He seized the federal arsenal at scenic Harpers Ferry in October 1859,

incidentally killing seven innocent people, including a free black, and injuring ten or so more. But the slaves failed to rise, and the wounded Brown and the remnants of his tiny band were quickly captured. "Old Brown" was convicted of murder and treason, after a hasty but legal trial.

But Brown—"God's angry man"—was given every opportunity to pose and to enjoy martyrdom. Though probably of unsound mind, he was clever enough to see that he was worth much more to the abolitionist cause dangling from a rope than in any other way. So the hangman's trap was sprung, and Brown plunged not into oblivion but into world fame. A memorable marching song of the impending Civil War ran:

> John Brown's body lies a-mould'ring in
>   the grave,
> His soul is marching on.

The effects of Harpers Ferry were calamitous. In the eyes of the South, already embittered, "Osawatomie Brown" was a wholesale murderer and an apostle of treason. Many southerners asked how they could possibly remain in the Union while a "murderous gang of abolitionists" were financing armed bands to "Brown" them. Moderate northerners, including Republican leaders, openly deplored this mad exploit. But the South naturally concluded that the violent abolitionist view was shared by the entire North, dominated by "Brown-loving" Republicans.

Abolitionists and other ardent free-soilers were infuriated by Brown's execution. On the day of his death, free-soilers in the North tolled bells, fired guns, half-masted flags, and held mass meetings. Some spoke of "Saint John" Brown, and Ralph Waldo Emerson compared the new martyr-hero with Jesus. The gallows became a cross. E. C. Steman wrote,

> And Old Brown,
> Osawatomie Brown,
> May trouble you more than ever
> When you've nailed his coffin down!

The ghost of the martyred Brown would not be laid to rest.

Democrats Divide and Republicans Rally

Beyond question the presidential election of 1860 was the most fateful in American history. Deeply divided, the Democrats met in Charleston. Northern Democrats looked to Douglas as their leader, but southern fire-eaters regarded him as a traitor. Cotton-state delegates walked out of the convention after a bitter platform fight. The southerners' departure from the Democratic convention was the first tragic act of secession. It became habit forming.

The Democrats tried again in Baltimore. With northern Douglas Democrats firmly in the saddle, the cotton-state delegates again took a walk, and the rest of the convention enthusiastically nominated their hero. Angered southern Democrats promptly organized a rival convention in Baltimore and selected as their nominee the stern-jawed vice president, John C. Breckinridge, from the border state of Kentucky. Their platform favored the extension of slavery into the territories and the annexation of slave-populated Cuba.

A middle-of-the-road group, fearing for the Union, hastily organized the Constitutional Union party. It consisted mainly of old Whigs and Know-Nothings. This "gathering of graybeards" met in Baltimore and nominated John Bell of Tennessee for the presidency on a platform of "the Union, the Constitution, and the enforcement of the law."

With their opponents split hopelessly into three factions, elated Republicans scented victory in the breeze. The best-known of the contenders at their convention in Chicago was William H. Seward. But Seward's radical utterances, including his "irrepressible conflict" speech at Rochester in 1858, fatally marred his prospects. Lincoln, the favorite son of Illinois, was a stronger candidate because he had fewer enemies than Seward. Overtaking Seward on the third ballot, he was nominated amid scenes of wild excitement.

The Republican platform appealed to almost every important nonsouthern group. To the free-soilers, it promised the nonextension of slavery; to the northern manufacturers, a protective tariff; to the immigrants, no abridgment of rights; and to westerners and farmers, internal improvements at federal expense.

Southern secessionists promptly served notice that the election of the "baboon" Lincoln would split the Union. Although Lincoln was in fact no abolitionist, he campaigned quietly and issued no new statements in response to these threats. The most active opposition to southern extremism came from "little Doug" Douglas, who waged a vigorous speaking campaign, even in the South, and threatened to put the hemp with his own hands around the neck of the first secessionist.

The returns, breathlessly awaited, proclaimed a sweeping victory for Lincoln (see map, p. 291).

The Electoral Upheaval of 1860

Awkward "Abe" Lincoln had run a curious race. To a greater degree than any other president (except John Quincy Adams), he was a minority president. Sixty percent of the voters preferred some other candidate. He was also a sectional president, for in ten southern states, where he was not allowed on the ballot, he polled no popular votes. The election of 1860 was virtually two elections: one in the North, the other in the South. South Carolinians rejoiced over Lincoln's victory; they now had their excuse to secede. In winning the North the "rail splitter" had split off the South.

Douglas, though scraping together only 12 electoral votes, made an impressive showing. He drew important strength from all sections, and ranked a fairly close second in the popular-vote column. In fact, the Douglas Democrats and the Breckinridge Democrats together amassed 366,484 more popular votes than Lincoln. But Lincoln's electoral vote victory did not occur because his opponents were divided. Even if all the Democrats and Constitutional Unionists had united behind Douglas, Lincoln would have carried the populous northern states, and therefore would have won 169 to 134 instead of 180 to 123.

Significantly, the verdict at the ballot box did not indicate a strong sentiment for secession. Breckinridge, while favoring the extension of slavery, was

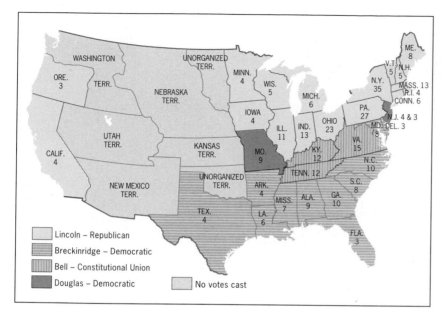

Presidential Election of 1860 (with electoral vote by state)
A surprising fact is that Lincoln, often rated among the greatest presidents, ranks near the bottom in percentage of popular votes. In all the eleven states that seceded, he received only a scattering of one state's votes— about 1.5 percent in Virginia.

no disunionist. He polled fewer votes in the slave states than Douglas and Bell combined. Although southern hotheads saw Lincoln's victory as the end of slavery, more rational southerners could see that their section still controlled the Supreme Court, both houses of Congress, and sufficient states to block any attempt to end slavery by constitutional amendment.

The Secessionist Exodus

But a tragic chain reaction of secession now began to explode. South Carolina had threatened to go out if the "Illinois baboon" were elected, and in December 1860 a special convention called by the legislature carried out the threat by voting unanimously to secede. During the next six weeks, six other states of the lower South followed South Carolina over the precipice.

With the eyes of destiny upon them, the seven seceders, formally meeting in Montgomery, Alabama, in February 1861, created a government known as the Confederate States of America. As their president they chose Jefferson Davis, a dignified and austere former secretary of war and U.S. senator from Mississippi.

As the Union disintegrated, the crisis was deepened by the lame duck interlude.* Although elected president in November 1860, Lincoln could not take office until four months later, March 4, 1861. As a private citizen, Lincoln watched seven states pull out of the Union during this period of protracted uncertainty.

Meanwhile, aging President Buchanan chose to wring his hands rather than secessionist necks. Even though he has been blamed for his inaction, there were good reasons for not resorting immediately to force. The tiny standing army of 15,000 men was widely scattered, fighting Indians in the West.

---

* The lame duck period was shortened to ten weeks in 1933 by the Twentieth Amendment (see Appendix).

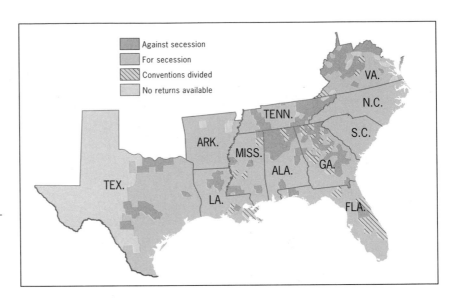

Southern Opposition to Secession, 1860–1861 (showing vote by county)
This county vote shows the opposition of the antiplanter, antislavery mountain whites in the Appalachian region. There was also considerable resistance to secession in Texas, where Governor Sam Houston, who led the Unionists, was deposed by secessionist hotheads.

Public opinion in the North, at that time, was far from willing to unsheathe the sword. Fighting would merely shatter all prospects of adjustment, and until the guns began to boom there was still a flickering hope of reconciliation rather than a contested divorce. The weakness lay not so much in Buchanan as in the Constitution and in the Union itself. Ironically, Lincoln as president essentially continued Buchanan's wait-and-see policy.

The Collapse of Compromise

Impending bloodshed spurred final, frantic attempts at compromise, most notably by Senator James Henry Crittenden of Kentucky. Crittenden proposed several constitutional amendments designed to appease the South. Slavery in the territories was to be prohibited north of 36° 30', but south of that line it was to be given federal protection in all territories existing or "hereafter to be acquired" (such as Cuba). Future states, north or south of 36° 30', could come into the Union with or without slavery, as they should choose. In short, the slavery supporters were to be guaranteed full rights in the southern territories, as long as they were territories, regardless

of the wishes of the majority under popular sovereignty. Federal protection in a territory south of 36° 30' might conceivably, though improbably, turn the entire area permanently to slavery.

Lincoln flatly rejected the Crittenden scheme, which offered some slight prospect of success, and all hope of compromise fled. For this refusal he must bear a heavy responsibility. Yet he had been elected on a platform that opposed the extension of slavery, and he felt that as a matter of principle he could not afford to yield, even though gains for slavery in the territories might be only temporary. Larger gains might come later in Cuba and Latin America. Crittenden's proposal, said Lincoln, "would amount to a perpetual covenant of war against every people, tribe, and state owning a foot of land between here and Tierra del Fuego."

As for the supposedly spineless "Old Fogy" Buchanan, how could he have prevented the Civil War by starting a civil war? No one has yet come up with a satisfactory answer. If he had used force on South Carolina in December 1860, the fighting almost certainly would have erupted three months sooner than it did, and under less favorable circumstances for the Union. The North would have appeared as the heavy-handed aggressor. And the crucial Border States, so vital to the Union, might have been driven into the arms of their "wayward sisters."

Farewell to Union

Secessionists who parted company with their sister states left for a number of avowed reasons, mostly relating in some way to slavery. They were alarmed by the inexorable tipping of the political balance against them—"the despotic majority of numbers." The "crime" of the North, observed James Russell Lowell, was the census returns. Southerners were also dismayed by the triumph of the new sectional Republican party, which seemed to threaten their rights as a slaveholding minority. They were weary of free-soil criticism, abolitionist nagging, and northern interference, ranging from the Underground Railroad to John Brown's raid. "All we ask is to be let alone," declared President Jefferson Davis in an early message to his congress.

Many southerners supported secession because they felt sure that their departure would be unopposed, despite "Yankee yawp" to the contrary. They were confident that the clodhopping and cod-fishing Yankee would not or could not fight. They believed that northern manufacturers and bankers, so heavily dependent on southern cotton and markets, would not dare to cut their own economic throats with their own swords. But should war come, the immense debt owed to northern creditors by the South—happy thought—could be promptly repudiated, as it later was.

Southern leaders regarded secession as a golden opportunity to cast aside their generations of "vassalage" to the North. An independent Dixie could develop its own banking and shipping, trade directly with Europe, and forever rid itself of the threat of high tariffs. For decades these issues had pitted the manufacturing North against the agrarian South.

The principles of self-determination—of the Declaration of Independence—seemed to many southerners to apply perfectly to them. Few, if any, of the seceders felt that they were doing anything wrong or immoral. The thirteen original states had

CHRONOLOGY

1852	Harriet Beecher Stowe publishes *Uncle Tom's Cabin.*
1854	Kansas-Nebraska Act.
1856	Buchanan defeats Frémont and Fillmore for presidency.
	Sumner beaten by Brooks in Senate chamber.
	Brown's Pottawatomie Creek massacre.
1856–1860	Civil war in "Bleeding Kansas."
1857	Dred Scott decision.
	Lecompton Constitution rejected.
	Panic of 1857.
	Hinton R. Helper publishes *The Impending Crisis of the South.*
1858	Lincoln-Douglas debates.
1859	Brown raids Harpers Ferry.
1860	Lincoln wins four-way race for presidency.
	South Carolina secedes from the Union.
	Crittenden Compromise fails.
1861	Seven seceding states form the Confederate States of America.

voluntarily entered the Union and now seven—ultimately eleven—southern states were voluntarily withdrawing from it.

Historical parallels ran even deeper. In 1776, thirteen American colonies, led by the rebel George Washington, had seceded from the British Empire by throwing off the yoke of King George III. In 1860–1861, eleven American states, led by the rebel Jefferson Davis, were seceding from the Union by throwing off the yoke of "King" Abraham Lincoln. With that burden gone, the South was confident that it could work out its own peculiar destiny more quietly, happily, and prosperously.

Varying Viewpoints

Few issues have generated as much heat among American historians as the causes of the war for southern independence. The very names chosen to describe the conflict—notably "Civil War" and "War Between the States"—reveal much about various authors' points of view. Opinions have naturally differed according to section, but in general the appraisals of the war have gone through four phases.

The so-called nationalist school in the late nineteenth century found slavery and Union to be the fundamental causes of the bloodletting, and approved the war because it ended slavery and preserved the Union. In the early twentieth century, some writers, notably Charles Beard, argued that the war was not about slavery per se, but about the basic economic conflict between an industrial North and an agricultural South.

After the disappointing results of World War I, some historians argued that the Civil War itself had been a great mistake, traceable not to any fundamentally "irreconcilable conflict," whether racial or economic, but to the breakdown of political institutions and the ineptitude of a blundering generation of leaders. But since World War II, a "neonationalist" view has generally prevailed. It pictures the Civil War as an all but inevitable clash between two cultures and two sets of social values, ending in victory for the forces of virtue and progress.

SELECT READINGS

Primary Source Documents

Harriet Beecher Stowe's *Uncle Tom's Cabin* (1852) and Hinton R. Helper's *The Impending Crisis of the South** (1852) are vivid and important. The Lincoln-Douglas debates* (1858) frame the issues of the 1850s and remain classics of American oratory.

Secondary Sources

For comprehensive treatment of events leading up to the Civil War, refer to Chapter 20 for the titles by David M. Potter, James M. McPherson, James G. Randall, David Donald, Kenneth M. Stampp, and Roy F. Nichols. Richly detailed is Allan Nevins, *The Emergence of Lincoln* (2 vols., 1950). Lincoln's rise is developed in Don E. Fehrenbacher,

Prelude to Greatness (1962). On the Lincoln-Douglas debates see Harry V. Jaffa, *Crisis of the House Divided* (1959). Don E. Fehrenbacher brilliantly and thoroughly dissects *The Dred Scott Case* (1978). The final moments before the fighting began are scrutinized in David M. Potter, *Lincoln and His Party in the Secession Crisis* (1942), and Kenneth M. Stampp, *And the War Came* (1950). Stephen B. Oates paints a vivid portrait of John Brown in *To Purge This Land with Blood* (1970). Thomas J. Pressley reviews the copious literature about the war in *Americans Interpret Their Civil War* (1954). George Forgie offers a psychoanalytic explanation of the coming of the war in *Patricide in the House Divided: A Psychological Interpretation of Lincoln and His Age* (1979).

CHAPTER 22

Girding for War: The North and the South, 1861–1865

I consider the central idea pervading this struggle is the necessity that is upon us, of proving that popular government is not an absurdity. We must settle this question now, whether in a free government the minority have the right to break up the government whenever they choose. If we fail it will go far to prove the incapability of the people to govern themselves.

Abraham Lincoln, May 7, 1861

President of the Disunited States of America

Abraham Lincoln solemnly took the oath of office on March 4, 1861, after having slipped into Washington at night, partially disguised to thwart assassins. He thus became president, not of the United States of America, but of the disunited states of America. Seven had departed; eight more were teetering on the edge. The girders of the unfinished Capitol dome loomed nakedly in the background, as if to symbolize the imperfect state of the Union.

Lincoln's inaugural address was firm yet conciliatory; there would be no conflict unless the South provoked it. Secession, the president declared, was wholly impracticable, because, "Physically speaking, we cannot separate."

Here Lincoln put his finger on a profound geographical truth. The North and South were bound inseparably together. If they had been divided by the Pyrenees Mountains or the Danube River, a sectional separation would have been more feasible. But both the Appalachian Mountains and the mighty Mississippi River ran the wrong way.

Uncontested secession would only create new controversies. What share of the national debt should the South be forced to take with it? What portion of the jointly held federal territories, if any, should the Confederate states be allotted—areas so largely purchased with southern blood? How would the fugitive-slave issue be dealt with? The Underground Railroad would certainly redouble its activity, and it would have to transport its passengers only across the Ohio River, not all the way to Canada. Was it conceivable that all such problems could have been solved without ugly armed clashes?

A united United States had hitherto been the top-dog republic in the Western Hemisphere. If this powerful democracy should break into two hostile nations, the European powers would be delighted. They could gleefully transplant to America their hoary concept of the balance of power. Playing the no less hoary game of divide and conquer, they could incite one snarling fragment of the disunited states against the other. The colonies of the European powers in the New World, notably those of Britain, would thus be made safer against the rapacious Yankees. And European imperialists, with no unified republic to stand across their path, could the more easily defy the Monroe Doctrine and seize territory in the Americas.

South Carolina Assails Fort Sumter

The issue of the divided Union came to a head over the matter of federal forts in the South. As the seceding states left, they had seized the United States arsenals, mints, and other public property within their borders. When Lincoln took office, only two significant forts in the South still flew the Stars and Stripes. The more important of the pair was square-walled Fort Sumter, in Charleston Harbor, with fewer than 100 men.

Ominously the choices presented to Lincoln by Fort Sumter were all bad. This stronghold had provisions that would last only a few weeks—until the middle of April 1861. If no supplies were forthcoming, its commander would have to surrender without firing a shot. Lincoln, quite understandably, did not feel that such a weak-kneed course squared with his obligation to protect federal property. But if he sent

reinforcements, the South Carolinians would undoubtedly fight back; they could not tolerate a federal fort blocking the mouth of their most important Atlantic seaport.

After agonizing indecision, Lincoln adopted a middle-of-the-road solution. He notified the South Carolinians that an expedition would be sent to *provision* the garrison, though not to *reinforce* it. But to southern eyes "provision" spelled "reinforcement."

A Union naval force next started on its way to Fort Sumter—a move that the South regarded as an act of aggression. On April 12, 1861, the cannon of the Carolinians opened fire on the fort, while crowds in Charleston applauded and waved handkerchiefs. After a thirty-four-hour bombardment, which took no lives, the dazed garrison surrendered.

The firing on the fort electrified the North, which at once responded with cries of "Remember Fort Sumter" and "Save the Union." Hitherto countless northerners had been saying that if the southern states wanted to go, they should not be pinned to the rest of the nation with bayonets. "Wayward sisters, depart in peace" was a common sentiment.

But the assault on Fort Sumter provoked the North to a fighting pitch: the fort was lost, but the Union was saved. Lincoln had contrived to win a

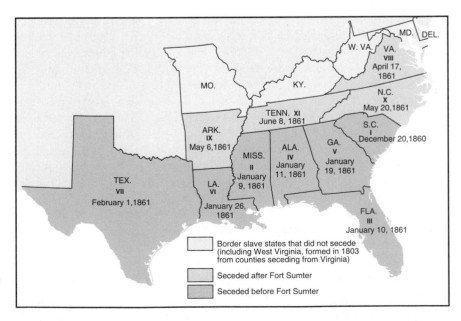

Seceding States (with dates and order of secession)
Note the long period of time between the secession of South Carolina, the first state to go, and that of Tennessee, the last state to leave the Union. These six months were a time of terrible trial for moderate southerners. When a Georgia statesman pleaded for restraint and negotiations with Washington, he was rebuffed with the cry: "Throw the bloody spear into this den of incendiaries!"

great strategic victory. Southerners had wantonly fired upon the glorious Stars and Stripes, and honor demanded an armed response. Lincoln promptly (April 15) issued a call to the states for 75,000 militiamen; and volunteers sprang to the colors in such enthusiastic numbers that many were turned away—a mistake not often repeated. On April 19 and 27 the president proclaimed a leaky blockade of southern seaports.

The call for troops, in turn, aroused the South much as the attack on Fort Sumter had aroused the North. Lincoln was now waging war—from the southern view an aggressive war—on the Confederacy. Virginia, Arkansas,and Tennessee, all of which had earlier voted down secession, reluctantly joined their embattled sister states, as did North Carolina. Thus the seven became eleven as the "submissionists" and "Union shriekers" were overcome. Richmond, Virginia, replaced Montgomery, Alabama, as the Confederate capital.

The Crucial Border States

The only slave states left were the crucial Border States. This group consisted of Missouri, Kentucky, Maryland, Delaware, and later West Virginia—the "mountain white" area that somewhat illegally tore itself from the side of Virginia in mid-1861. If the North had fired the first shot, some or all of these doubtful states probably would have seceded, and the South might well have succeeded. The Border group actually boasted a white population more than half that of the entire Confederacy. Lincoln reportedly said that he hoped to have God on his side, but he *had* to have Kentucky.

In dealing with the Border States, the president used methods of dubious legality. In Maryland he declared martial law where needed and sent in troops, because this state threatened to cut off Washington from the North. He also deployed Union soldiers in western Virginia and notably in Missouri, where they fought beside Unionists in a local civil war within the larger Civil War.

Any official statement of the North's war aims was profoundly influenced by the teetering Border States. At the very outset Lincoln was obliged to declare publicly that he was not fighting to free the blacks. An antislavery declaration would no doubt have driven the Border States into the welcoming arms of the South. Lincoln insisted repeatedly—even though weakening his moral cause—that his primary purpose was to preserve the Union at all costs. Thus the war began not as one between slave soil and free soil, but one for the Union—with slaveholders on both sides and many proslavery sympathizers in the North.

Slavery also colored the character of the war in the West. In the Indian Territory (present-day Oklahoma), most of the Five Civilized Tribes—the Cherokees, Creeks, Choctaws, Chickasaws, and Seminoles—sided with the Confederacy. Some of these Indians, notably the Cherokees, owned slaves and thus felt themselves to be making common cause with the slaveowning South. These Native Americans sent delegates to the Confederate Congress and supplied troops to the Confederate army. Most of the Plains Indians, however, sided with the Union.

Unhappily, the conflict between "Billy Yank" and "Johnny Reb" was a brothers' war. There were many northern volunteers from the southern states, and many southern volunteers from the northern states. The "mountain whites" of the South sent north some 50,000 men, and the loyal slave states contributed some 300,000 soldiers to the Union. In many a family of the Border States, one brother rode north to fight with the Blue, another south to fight with the Gray. Senator Crittenden of Kentucky, who wrote the abortive Crittenden Compromise, had two sons: one became a general in the Union army, the other a general in the Confederate army.

The Balance of Forces

When war broke out, the South seemed to have great advantages. The Confederacy could fight defensively behind interior lines. The North had to invade the vast territory of the Confederacy, conquer it, and drag it bodily back into the Union. In fact, the South did not have to win the war in order to win its independence. If it merely fought the invaders to a draw and thereby discouraged them, Confederate independence would be won. Fighting on their own soil for self-determination and preservation of their way of life, southerners at first enjoyed an advantage in morale as well.

Militarily, the South had the most talented officers right from the beginning of the war. Most conspicuous among a dozen or so first-rate commanders was gray-haired General Robert E. Lee, whose knightly bearing and sense of honor embodied the southern ideal. President Lincoln had unofficially offered him the command of the northern armies, but when Virginia seceded Lee felt honor-bound to go with his native state. Lee's chief lieutenant for much of the war was black-bearded Thomas J. ("Stonewall") Jackson, a gifted tactical theorist whose use of "foot cavalry" made him a master of speed and deception.

Besides their brilliant leaders, ordinary southerners were also bred to fight. Accustomed to managing horses and bearing arms from boyhood, they made excellent cavalrymen and foot soldiers. Their high-pitched rebel yell ("yeeeahhh") was designed to strike terror into the hearts of fuzz-chinned Yankee recruits.

As one immense farm, the South seemed to be handicapped by the scarcity of its factories. Yet by seizing federal weapons, running Union blockades, and developing their own ironworks, southerners managed to obtain sufficient weaponry. "Yankee ingenuity" was not confined to Yankees.

Nevertheless, as the war dragged on, grave shortages of shoes, uniforms, and blankets did appear in the South. Even with immense stores of food on southern farms, civilians and soldiers often went hungry because of supply problems. "Forward, men! They have cheese in their haversacks," cried one southern officer as he attacked the Yankees. Much of the hunger was caused by a breakdown of the South's rickety transportation system, especially where the railroad tracks were cut or destroyed by the Yankee invaders.

The economy was the greatest southern weakness; it was the North's greatest strength. The North was not only a huge farm but a sprawling factory as well. Yankees boasted about three-fourths of the nation's wealth, including three-fourths of the 30,000 miles of railroads.

The North also controlled the sea. With its vastly superior navy, it established a blockade that choked off southern supplies and eventually shattered southern morale. Its sea power also enabled the North to exchange huge quantities of grain for munitions and supplies from Europe, thus adding the factories of Europe to its own.

The Union also enjoyed a much larger reserve of manpower. The loyal states had a population of some 22 million; the seceding states had 9 million people, including about 3.5 million slaves. Adding to the North's population strength was the large immigrant population from Europe, which continued to pour into the area even during the war. Over 800,000 newcomers arrived between 1861 and 1865, most of them British, Irish, and German. Large numbers of them were induced to enlist in the Union armies. Altogether about one-fifth of the Union forces were foreign born, and in some units military commands were given in four different languages.

Whether immigrant or native, ordinary northern boys were much less prepared than their southern counterparts for military life. Yet the northern "clodhoppers" and "shopkeepers" eventually adjusted themselves to soldiering and became known for their discipline and determination.

The North was much less fortunate in its higher commanders. It was forced to use a costly trial-and-error method to sort out effective leaders from the many incompetent political officers, until it finally uncovered a general, Ulysses Simpson Grant, who would crunch his way to victory.

In the long run, as the northern strengths were brought to bear, they outweighed those of the South. But when the war began, the chances for southern independence were unusually favorable—certainly better than the prospects for success of the thirteen colonies in 1776. The turn of a few events could easily have produced a different outcome.

The might-have-beens are fascinating. *If* the Border States had seceded, *if* the uncertain states of the upper Mississippi Valley had turned against the Union, *if* a wave of northern defeatism had demanded an armistice, and *if* Britain and/or France had broken the blockade, the South probably would have won. All of these possibilities almost became

Recruiting Immigrants for the Union Army   *This poster in several languages appeals to immigrants to enlist. Immigrant resources provided the Union with both industrial and military muscle.*

realities, but none of them actually occurred. Successful revolutions, including the American Revolution of 1776, have generally succeeded because of foreign intervention. The South counted on it, did not get it, and lost.

Dethroning King Cotton

Of all the Confederacy's potential assets, none counted more heavily than the prospect of foreign intervention on behalf of the South. Europe's ruling classes, which had long abhorred the incendiary example of American democracy, were openly sympathetic to the semifeudal, aristocratic South.

In contrast, the masses of working people in Britain, and to some extent in France, were pulling and praying for the North. Many of them had read *Uncle Tom's Cabin,* and they sensed that the war—though at the outset officially fought only over the question of union—might extinguish slavery if the North emerged victorious. The hostility of British common folk to any official intervention had a sobering effect on the British government. Yet the fact remained that British textile mills depended on the American South for 75 percent of their cotton supplies. Humanitarian sympathies aside, southerners counted on hard economic need to bring Britain to their aid. Why did king cotton fail them?

It failed in part because the South had been so lavishly productive in the immediate prewar years of 1857–1860. Enormous exports of cotton in those years had piled up surpluses in British warehouses. When the shooting started in 1861, British manufacturers had on hand a heavy oversupply of fiber. The real pinch did not come until about a year and a half later, when thousands of hungry operatives were thrown out of work. But by this time Lincoln had announced his slave-emancipation policy, and the "wage slaves" of Britain would not demand a war for the slaveowners of the South.

The direst effects of the "cotton famine" in Britain were relieved in several ways. Hunger among unemployed workers was partially eased when certain kindhearted Americans sent over several cargoes of foodstuffs. As Union armies penetrated the South, they captured or bought considerable supplies of cotton and shipped them to Britain; and the Confederates also ran a limited quantity through the blockade. In addition, the cotton growers of Egypt and India, responding to high prices, increased their output. Finally, booming war industries in Britain, which supplied both North and South, relieved unemployment.

The North's king wheat and king corn proved to be more potent potentates than king cotton. Blessed with ideal weather and the efficient harvesting of McCormick's mechanical reaper, the North produced bountiful crops during the war years. The grain was purchased by Britain, which suffered a series of bad harvests at the same time. The British became so dependent on the northern granary that they were unwilling to cut off this precious supply by breaking the blockade.

The Decisiveness of Diplomacy

America's diplomatic front has seldom been so critical as during the Civil War. The South never wholly abandoned its dream of foreign intervention, and Europe's rulers schemed to take advantage of America's distress.

The first major crisis with Britain came over the *Trent* affair, late in 1861. A Union warship cruising on the high seas north of Cuba stopped a British mail steamer, the *Trent,* and forcibly removed two Confederate diplomats who were on their way to Europe.

Britons were outraged: upstart Yankees could not do this kind of thing to the mistress of the seas. War preparations buzzed, as redcoated troops embarked for Canada with bands blaring, "I Wish I Was in Dixie." The London Foreign Office prepared an ultimatum demanding surrender of the prisoners and an apology. But luckily, slow communications gave passions on both sides a chance to cool. Lincoln came to see the *Trent* prisoners as "white elephants," and reluctantly released them.

Another major crisis in Anglo-American relations arose over the unneutral building in Britain of Confederate commerce raiders, notably the *Alabama.* These vessels were not warships within the meaning of loopholed British law, because they left their shipyards unarmed and picked up their guns elsewhere. The *Alabama* escaped in 1862 to the Portuguese Azores, and there took on weapons and a crew from two British ships that followed it.

The *Alabama* lighted the skies from Europe to East Asia with the burning hulks of Yankee merchantmen. All told, this "British pirate" captured over sixty vessels. Competing British shippers were delighted, while an angered North had to divert naval strength from its blockade for wild goose chases. The barnacled *Alabama* finally accepted a challenge from a stronger Union cruiser off the coast of France in 1864, and was quickly destroyed.

The Sinking of the *Alabama*, 1864   *The French impressionist painter Édouard Manet witnessed the fight between a Union battleship and the famous Confederate raider. He painted this version of the sinking after the event.*

The *Alabama* was beneath the waves, but the issue of British-built Confederate raiders stayed afloat. Under prodding by the American minister Charles Francis Adams, the British gradually perceived that allowing such ships to be built was a dangerous precedent that might be used against them. In 1863 London openly violated its own leaky laws and seized another raider being built for the South. But despite greater official efforts by Britain to remain truly neutral, Confederate commerce-destroyers, chiefly British-built, captured more than 250 Yankee ships, severely crippling the American merchant marine. Angered Americans talked openly of securing revenge by seizing Canada when the war was over.

Foreign Flare-ups

A final Anglo-American crisis was touched off in 1863 by the Laird rams—two Confederate warships being constructed in Great Britain. Designed to destroy the wooden ships of the Union navy with their iron rams and large-caliber guns, they were far more dangerous than the swift and lightly armed *Alabama*. If delivered to the South, they probably would have sunk the blockading squadrons and then brought northern cities under their fire. In angry retaliation, the North doubtless would have invaded Canada, and a full-dress war with Britain would have erupted. But Minister Adams took a hard line, warning that "this is war" if the rams were released. At the last minute the London government relented, and bought the two ships for the Royal Navy. Everyone seemed satisfied—except the disappointed Confederates. Britain also eventually repented its sorry role in the *Alabama* business. It agreed in 1871 to submit the *Alabama* dispute to arbitration, and in 1872 paid American claimants $15.5 million for damages caused by wartime commerce raiders.

Emperor Napoleon III of France, taking advantage of America's preoccupation with its own internal problems, dispatched a French army to occupy Mexico City in 1863. The following year he installed on the ruins of the crushed republic his puppet, Austrian Archduke Maximilian, as emperor of Mexico. Both sending the army and enthroning Maximilian were done in flagrant violation of the Monroe Doctrine. Napoleon was gambling that the Union would collapse and thus America would be too weak to enforce its "hands-off" policy in the Western Hemisphere.

The North, as long as it was convulsed by war, pursued a walk-on-eggs policy toward France. But when the shooting stopped in 1865, Secretary of State William Seward, speaking with the authority of nearly a million bayonets, prepared to march south. Napoleon realized that his costly gamble was doomed. He reluctantly took "French leave" of his ill-starred puppet in 1867, and Maximilian soon crumpled ingloriously before a Mexican firing squad.

President Davis versus President Lincoln

The Confederate government, like king cotton, betrayed fatal weaknesses. Its constitution, borrowing liberally from that of the Union, had one deadly defect. Created by secession, it could not logically deny future secession to its states. Jefferson Davis, while making his bow to states' rights, had in view a well-knit central government. But determined states'-rights supporters fought him bitterly to the end. The Richmond regime even encountered difficulty in persuading certain state troops to serve outside their own borders.

Sharp-featured President Davis—tense, humorless, legalistic, and stubborn—was repeatedly in hot water. Although an eloquent orator and an able administrator, he at no time enjoyed real personal popularity and was often at loggerheads with his congress. At times there was serious talk of impeaching him. Unlike Lincoln, Davis was somewhat imperious and inclined to defy rather than lead public opinion. Suffering acutely from neuralgia and other nervous disorders (including a tic), he overworked himself with the details of both civil government and military operations. No one could doubt his courage, sincerity, integrity, and devotion to the South, but the task proved beyond his powers.

Lincoln also had his troubles, but on the whole they were less prostrating. The North enjoyed the prestige of a long-established government, financially stable and fully recognized both at home and abroad. Lincoln, the inexperienced prairie politician, proved superior to the more experienced but less flexible Davis. Able to relax with droll stories at critical times, "Old Abe" grew as the war dragged on. Tactful, quiet, patient, yet firm, he developed a genius for interpreting and leading a fickle public opinion. Holding aloft the banner of Union with inspiring utterances, he revealed charitableness toward the South and forbearance toward backbiting colleagues. "Did [Secretary] Stanton say I was a damned fool?" he reportedly replied to a talebearer. "Then I dare say I must be one, for Stanton is generally right and he always says what he means."

Limitations on Wartime Liberties

When inaugurated, Lincoln laid his hand on the Bible and swore a solemn oath to uphold the Constitution. Then, driven by sheer necessity, he proceeded to tear a few holes in that hallowed document. He sagely concluded that if he did not do so, and patch the parchment later, there might not be a Constitution of a *united* United States to mend. The rail splitter was no hairsplitter.

Congress was not in session when war erupted, so Lincoln gathered the reins into his own hands. Brushing aside legal objections, he boldly proclaimed a blockade. (His action was later upheld by the Supreme Court.) He arbitrarily increased the size of the federal army—something that only Congress can do under the Constitution (see Art. I, Sec. VIII, para. 12). (Congress later approved.) He suspended the privilege of the writ of habeas corpus, so that anti-Unionists might be summarily arrested.

Lincoln's regime was also guilty of many other high-handed acts. For example, it arranged for "supervised" voting in the Border States. There the intimidated citizen, holding a colored ballot indicating his party preference, had to march between two lines of armed troops. The federal officials also ordered the suspension of certain newspapers and the arrest of their editors on grounds of obstructing the war.

Jefferson Davis was less able than Lincoln to exercise arbitrary power, mainly because of confirmed states'-righters who revealed an intense spirit of localism. To the very end of the conflict the owners of horse-drawn vans in Petersburg, Virginia, prevented the joining of the incoming and outgoing tracks of a militarily vital railroad. The South seemed willing to lose the war before it would surrender local rights—and it did.

Volunteers and Draftees: North and South

Ravenous, the gods of war demanded men—lots of men. Northern armies were at first manned solely by volunteers, with each state assigned a quota based on population. But in 1863, after volunteering had slackened off, Congress passed a federal conscription law for the first time on a nationwide scale in the United States. The provisions were grossly unfair to the poor. Rich boys, including young John D. Rockefeller, could hire substitutes to go in their places, or purchase exemption outright by paying $300.

The draft was especially damned in the Democratic strongholds of the North, notably in New York City. A frightful riot broke out in 1863, touched off largely by underprivileged and anti-black Irish-Americans who shouted. "Down with Lincoln!" and "Down with the draft!" For several days the city was at the mercy of a burning, drunken, pillaging mob, and scores of lives were lost, the victims including many lynched blacks. Elsewhere in the North, conscription met with resentment and an occasional minor riot.

Yet over 90 percent of the Union troops were volunteers, since social and patriotic pressures to enlist were strong. As able-bodied men became scarcer, generous bounties for enlistment were offered by federal, state, and local authorities.

With money flowing so freely, an unsavory crew of "bounty brokers" and "substitute brokers" sprang up at home and abroad. They combed the poorhouses of the British Isles and western Europe;

President Davis, the Acrobat, on Rope of Cotton *The "Confederacy" is a fuse bomb; the flag reads, "Let Us Alone," a Davis theme. The cotton rope is unraveling.*

The New York Draft Riot, 1863 *Irish workers resented competition for jobs by "nagurs." The free blacks in turn called the Irish "white niggers."*

and many an Irishman or German was befuddled with whiskey and induced to enlist. A number of the slippery "bounty boys" deserted, volunteered elsewhere, and netted another handsome haul. The rolls of the Union army recorded about 200,000 deserters of all classes, and the Confederate authorities were plagued with a problem of similar dimensions.

Like the North, the South relied mainly on volunteers. But since the Confederacy was much less populous, it scraped the bottom of its manpower barrel much more quickly. The Richmond regime, robbing both "cradle and grave" (ages seventeen to fifty), was forced to resort to conscription as early as April 1862, nearly a year earlier than the Union.

Confederate draft regulations also worked serious injustices. As in the North, a rich man could hire a substitute or purchase exemption. Slaveowners or overseers with twenty slaves might also claim exemption. These special privileges, later modified, made for bad feelings among the less prosperous, many of whom complained that this was "a rich man's war and a poor man's fight."

No large-scale draft riots broke out in the South, as in New York City. But the Confederate conscription agents often found it prudent to avoid those areas inhabited by sharp-shooting mountain whites, who were branded "Tories," "traitors," and "Yankee lovers."

The Dollar Goes to War

Blessed with a lion's share of the wealth, the North rode through the financial breakers much more smoothly than the South. Excise taxes on tobacco and alcohol were substantially increased by Congress. An income tax was levied for the first time in the nation's experience.

Customs receipts likewise proved to be important revenue raisers. Early in 1861, after enough antiprotection southern members had seceded, Congress passed the Morrill Tariff Act. It increased the existing duties some 5 to 10 percent, but these modest rates were soon pushed sharply upward by the necessities of war. The increases were designed partly to raise additional revenue and partly to provide more protection for the prosperous manufacturers who were being plucked by the new internal taxes. A protective tariff thus became identified with the Republican party, as American industrialists, mostly Republicans, waxed fat on these welcome benefits.

The Washington Treasury also issued green-backed paper money, totaling nearly $450 million at face value. This printing-press currency was inadequately supported by gold, and hence its value was determined by the nation's credit. Greenbacks thus fluctuated with the fortunes of Union arms, and at one low point were worth only thirty-nine cents on the gold dollar.

Yet borrowing far outstripped both greenbacks and taxes as a money raiser. The Federal Treasury netted $2,621,916,786 through the sale of bonds, which bore interest and were payable at a later date.

A financial landmark of the war was the National Banking System, authorized by Congress in 1863. Launched partly as a stimulant to the sale of government bonds, it was also designed to establish a standard bank-note currency. (The country was then flooded with depreciated "rag money" issued by unreliable bankers.) Banks that joined the National Banking System could buy government bonds and issue sound paper money backed by them. The war-born National Banking System thus turned out to be the first significant step taken toward a unified banking network since 1836, when the "monster" Bank of the United States was killed by Andrew Jackson. Spawned by the war, this new system continued to function for fifty years.

An impoverished South was beset by different financial problems. Customs duties were choked off as the coils of the Union blockade tightened. Large issues of Confederate bonds were sold at home and abroad, amounting to nearly $400 million. The Richmond regime also increased taxes sharply and imposed a 10 percent levy on farm produce. But in general, the states'-rights southerners were vigorously opposed to heavy direct taxation by the central authority: only about 1 percent of the total income was raised this way.

As revenue began to dry up, the Confederate government was forced to print blue-backed paper money with complete abandon. "Runaway inflation" occurred as southern presses continued to grind out the poorly backed treasury notes, totaling in all more than $1 billion. One breakfast for three in Richmond in 1864 cost $141. The Confederate paper dollar finally sank to the point where it was worth only 1.6 cents when Lee surrendered. Overall, the war inflicted a 9,000 percent inflation rate on the Confederacy, contrasted with 80 percent for the Union.

"Shoddy" Millionaires in the North

Wartime prosperity in the North was nothing short of miraculous. New factories, sheltered by the friendly umbrella of the new protective tariffs, mushroomed forth. Soaring prices, resulting from inflation, unfortunately pinched the day laborer and the white-collar worker to some extent. But the manufacturers and businesspeople raked in "the fortunes of war." The Civil War spawned a millionaire class for the first time in American history.

Yankee "sharpness" appeared at its worst. Dishonest agents, putting profits above patriotism, palmed off aged and blind horses on government purchasers. Unscrupulous northern manufacturers supplied shoes with cardboard soles, and fast-disintegrating uniforms of reprocessed or "shoddy" wool, rather than virgin wool. Hence the reproachful term "shoddy millionaires."

Newly invented laborsaving machinery enabled the North to expand economically, even though the cream of its manpower was being drained off to the fighting front. The sewing machine wrought wonders in fabricating uniforms and military footwear. Clattering mechanical reapers, which numbered about 250,000 by 1865, proved hardly less potent than thundering guns. They not only released tens of thousands of farm boys for the army but fed them while there.

Other industries were humming. The discovery of petroleum gushers in 1859 had led to a rush of "Fifty-Niners" to Pennsylvania. The result was the birth of a new industry, with its "petroleum plutocracy" and "coal oil Johnnies." Pioneers continued to push westward during the war, altogether an estimated 300,000 people. Major magnets were free gold nuggets and free lands under the Homestead Act of 1862. Strong propellants were the federal draft agents. The only major northern industry to suffer was the ocean-carrying trade, which fell prey to the *Alabama* and other raiders.

The war also opened new opportunities for women. The booming military demand for shoes and clothing, combined with the availability of new technology such as the sewing machine, and the unavailability of male workers who had gone to war drew numerous women into industrial employment. Female workers increased their proportion of the manufacturing labor force from one-fourth to one-third during the conflict.

Other women went to the fighting front—or close behind it. America's first female physician, Dr. Elizabeth Blackwell, helped to organize the United States Sanitary Commission to provide medical supplies and assistance to the armies in the field. Here many women acquired the organizational skills and the self-confidence that would propel the women's movement forward after the war. Still others, such as the heroically energetic Clara Barton, helped to transform nursing from a lowly service into a respected profession, and in the process opened up another major category of employment for women in the postwar era.

A Crushed Cotton Kingdom

Dismally different was the plight of the South, which fought to exhaustion. The suffocation caused by the blockade, together with the destruction by invaders, took a terrible toll. Possessing 30 percent of the national wealth in 1860, the South claimed only 12 percent in 1870. Transportation collapsed. The South was even driven to the economic cannibalism of pulling up rails from the less-used lines to repair the main ones. Window weights were melted down into bullets; gourds replaced dishes; pins became so scarce that they were loaned with reluctance.

To the brutal end, the South revealed remarkable resourcefulness and spirit. Women buoyed up their menfolk, many of whom had seen enough of war at first hand to be heartily sick of it. A proposal was made by a number of women that they cut off their long hair and sell it abroad. But the project was not adopted, partly because of the blockade. The self-sacrificing women took pride in denying themselves the silks and satins of their northern sisters.

At war's end, the northern captains of industry had conquered the southern lords of the manor. A crippled South left the capitalistic North free to work its own way, with high tariffs and other benefits. The industrial giants of the North, ushering in the full-fledged Industrial Revolution, were destined for increased dominance over American economic and political life. Hitherto the agrarian "slavocracy" of the South, by using sectional alliances, had partially checked the rising plutocracy of the North. Now cotton capitalism had lost out to industrial capitalism. The South of 1865 was to be rich in little but amputees, war heroes, ruins, and memories.

CHRONOLOGY

1861	Confederate governments formed.		Homestead Act.
	Lincoln takes office.	1862–1864	*Alabama* raids northern shipping.
	Fort Sumter fired upon	1863	Union enacts conscription.
	Four Upper South states secede.		New York City draft riot.
	Morrill Tariff Act passed.		National Banking System established.
	Trent affair.	1863–1864	Napoleon III installs Archduke Maximilian as emperor of Mexico.
	Lincoln suspends writ of habeas corpus.	1864	*Alabama* sunk by Union warship.
1862	Confederacy enacts conscription.		

Varying Viewpoints

When the Civil War ended, slavery was officially defunct, secession was a dead issue, and industrial growth was surging forward. Charles Beard later hailed the war as the "Second American Revolution" because it had transformed the legal and institutional structure of government and placed the levers of power firmly in the hands of a new business class.

But did the bloody conflict neatly bisect the nation's history? In recent years many scholars have questioned the concept that the war constituted a dramatic turning point. Slavery may have disappeared formally, but blacks remained a scandalously subordinated social group. Regional differences persisted, as they do even to the present day. Thomas Cochran even argued that the Civil War may have *retarded* overall industrialization. As for the rising commercial class of the postwar Gilded Age, many historians now point to its antecedents in both the Whig and Jacksonian movements. History, it seems, is a mighty stream that in time partially submerges even momentous events such as the Civil War beneath the surface of its relentless flow.

SELECT READINGS

Primary Source Documents

The Constitution of the Confederacy* (1861) makes an interesting contrast to the United States Constitution. Two diaries that describe life behind the Confederate lines are those of John B. Jones, published as Earl S. Miers, ed., *A Rebel War Clerk's Diary** (1958), and Paul B. Barringer, *The Natural Bent** (1949). Lincoln's Gettysburg Address (1863) (in Henry Steele Commager, *Documents of American History*) poetically proclaims the president's highest war aims, as does his Second Inaugural Address (1865), in Roy P. Basler, ed., *The Collected Works of Abraham Lincoln* (1953), Vol. VIII, pp. 332–333.

Secondary Sources

The best one-volume biography is Stephen B. Oates, *With Malice Toward None: The Life of Abraham Lincoln* (1977). An excellent collection is Don E. Fehrenbacher, *Lincoln in Text and Context: Collected Essays* (1987). See also Garry Wills, *Lincoln at Gettysburg: The Words That Remade America* (1992). Home-front politics are treated in James A. Rawley, *The Politics of Union* (1974), and Joel Silbey, *A Respectable Minority: The Democratic Party in the Civil War Era* (1977). See also Jean H. Baker, *Affairs of Party: The Political Culture of the Northern Democrats in the Mid-Nineteenth Century* (1983). Lincoln's problems are analyzed in LaWanda Cox, *Lincoln and Black Freedom* (1981). Eugene C. Murdoch analyzes the military draft in the North in *One Million Men* (1971). Iver Bernstein treats *The New York City Draft Riots* (1990). Gerald F. Linderman examines the motivations of soldiers in *Embattled Courage: The Experience of Combat in the Civil War* (1987). Mary E. Massey presents the interesting story of women in the Civil War in *Bonnet Brigades* (1966); that topic also figures in Anne Firor Scott's *The Southern Lady* (1970). On the Confederacy, see Charles P. Roland, *The Confederacy* (1960), and Emory M. Thomas, *The Confederate Nation, 1861–1865* (1979). Economic matters are handled in Ralph L. Andreano, ed., *The Economic Impact of the American Civil War* (1962), and David T. Gilchrist and W. David Lewis, eds., *Economic Change in the Civil War* (1965). The war's literary legacy is keenly analyzed in Edmund Wilson's classic *Patriotic Gore* (1962) and Daniel Aaron's *The Unwritten War: American Writers and the Civil War* (1973). For a fascinating discussion of northern intellectuals and the conflict, consult George M. Frederickson, *The Inner Civil War* (1965).

CHAPTER 23

The Furnace of Civil War, 1861–1865

My paramount object in this struggle is to save the Union, and is not either to save or to destroy slavery.

Abraham Lincoln, 1862

Bull Run Ends the "Ninety-Day War"

When President Lincoln, on April 15, 1861, issued his call to the states for 75,000 militiamen, he envisioned them serving for only ninety days. He reaffirmed that he had "no purpose, directly or indirectly, to interfere with slavery in the States where it exists." He hoped, with a swift flourish of federal force, to show the folly of secession and rapidly return the rebellious states to the Union. Northern newspapers, also eager for a quick resolution of the crisis, raised the cry "On to Richmond!"

In this expectant atmosphere, a Union army of some 30,000 men drilled near Washington in the summer of 1861. It was ill prepared for battle, but the press and the public clamored for action. Lincoln eventually concluded that an attack on a smaller Confederate force at Bull Run (Manassas Junction), some thirty miles southwest of Washington, might be worth a try. If successful, it would demonstrate the superiority of Union arms. It might even lead to the capture of the Confederate capital at Richmond, 100 miles to the south. If Richmond fell, secession would be thoroughly discredited and the Union could be restored without damage to the economic and social system of the South.

Raw Yankee recruits marched or straggled out of Washington toward Bull Run on July 21, 1861, as if they were headed for a sporting event. Congressmen and spectators trailed along with their lunch baskets to witness the fun. At first the battle went well for the Yankees. But "Stonewall" Jackson's gray-clad warriors stood like a stone wall (here he won his nickname), and Confederate reinforcements arrived unexpectedly. Panic seized the green Union troops, many of whom fled in shameful confusion. The Confederates, themselves too exhausted or disorganized to pursue, feasted on captured lunches.

The "military picnic" at Bull Run, though not decisive militarily, had significant psychological and political consequences. Victory was worse than defeat for the South because it inflated an already dangerous overconfidence. Many southern soldiers promptly deserted, feeling that the war would be over shortly. Southern enlistments fell off sharply, and preparations for a protracted conflict slackened. Defeat was better than victory for the Union, because it dispelled all illusions of a one-punch war and caused the northerners to buckle down to the staggering task at hand. It also set the stage for a war that would be waged not merely for the cause of Union but also, eventually, for the abolitionist ideal of emancipation.

"Tardy George" McClellan and the Peninsula Campaign

Northern hopes brightened later in 1861, when General George B. McClellan was given command of the Army of the Potomac, as the major Union force near Washington was now called. Red-haired and red-mustached, strong and stocky, McClellan was a brilliant, thirty-four-year-old West Pointer.

Cocky George McClellan embodied a curious mixture of virtues and defects. He was a superb organizer and drillmaster, and he injected splendid morale into the Army of the Potomac. Hating to sacrifice his troops, he was idolized by his men, who affectionately called him "Little Mac." But he was a perfectionist who seems not to have realized that an army is never ready to the last button, and that wars cannot be won without running some risks. He consistently but erroneously believed that the enemy outnumbered him, partly because his intelligence

reports from the head of Pinkerton's Detective Agency were unreliable. He was overcautious—Lincoln once accused him of having "the slows"—and he addressed the president in an arrogant tone that a less forgiving person than Lincoln would never have tolerated. Privately the general referred to his chief as a "baboon." After threatening to "borrow" the army if it was not going to be used, Lincoln finally issued firm orders to move.

A reluctant McClellan at last decided upon a waterborne approach to Richmond. Choosing the route up the narrow peninsula formed by the James and York rivers, he warily advanced toward the Confederate capital in the spring of 1862 with about 100,000 men. After taking a month to capture historic Yorktown, which bristled with imitation wooden cannons, he finally came within sight of the spires of Richmond. Then General Robert E. Lee launched a devastating counterattack—the Seven Days' Battles—June 26–July 2, 1862. The Confederates slowly drove McClellan back to the sea. The Union forces abandoned the Peninsula Campaign as a costly failure, and Lincoln temporarily abandoned McClellan as commander of the Army of the

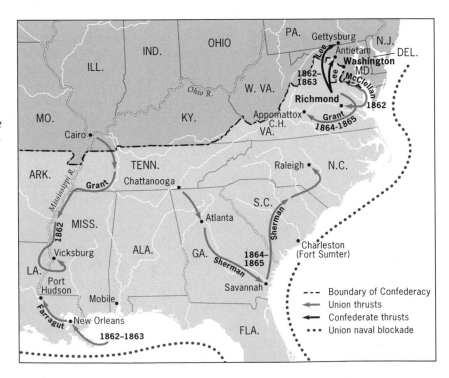

Main Thrusts, 1861–1865
Northern strategists at first believed that the rebellion could be snuffed out quickly by a swift, crushing blow. But the stiffness of southern resistance to the Union's early probes revealed that the conflict would be a war of attrition, long and bloody.

Potomac—though Lee's army had suffered some 20,000 casualties to McClellan's 10,000.

Lee had achieved a brilliant, if bloody, triumph. Yet the ironies of his accomplishment are striking. If McClellan had succeeded in taking Richmond and ending the war in mid-1862, the Union would probably have been restored with minimal disruption of slavery, which would have survived at least for a time. By his successful defense of Richmond and defeat of McClellan, Lee had in effect ensured that the war would endure until slavery was uprooted and the old South thoroughly destroyed. Lincoln himself now declared that the rebels "cannot experiment for ten years trying to destroy the government and if they fail still come back into the Union unhurt." He began to draft an emancipation proclamation.

Union strategy now turned toward total war. As finally developed, the northern military plan had six components: first, slowly suffocate the South by blockading its coasts; second, liberate the slaves and hence undermine the very economic foundations of the old South; third, cut the Confederacy in half by seizing control of the Mississippi River backbone; fourth, chop it to pieces by sending troops through Georgia and the Carolinas; fifth, decapitate it by capturing its capital at Richmond; and sixth (this was Ulysses Grant's idea, especially), try everywhere to engage the enemy's main strength and grind it into submission.

The War at Sea

The blockade started leakily; it was not clamped down all at once but extended by degrees. Blockading was simplified by concentrating on the principal ports and inlets. Only at such places were dock facilities available for loading bulky bales of cotton. The blockade was also strengthened when Britain recognized it as binding and warned its shippers that they ignored it at their peril.

Blockade running soon became riskily profitable, as the growing scarcity of southern goods drove prices skyward. The most successful runners were swift, gray-painted steamers, scores of which were specially built in Scotland. A leading rendezvous was the West Indies port of Nassau, in the British Bahamas, where at one time thirty-five of the speedy ships were counted. But the lush days of blockade running finally passed as Union squadrons gradually pinched off the leading southern ports, from New Orleans to Charleston.

The most alarming Confederate threat to the blockade came in 1862. Resourceful southerners raised and reconditioned a former wooden United States warship, the *Merrimack,* and plated its sides with old iron railroad rails. Renamed the *Virginia,* this clumsy but powerful monster easily destroyed two wooden ships of the Union navy in the Virginia waters of Chesapeake Bay; it also threatened the entire Yankee blockading fleet. (Actually the homemade ironclad was not a seaworthy craft.)

A tiny Union ironclad, the *Monitor,* built in about 100 days, arrived on the scene in the nick of time. For four hours, on March 9, 1862, the little "Yankee cheesebox on a raft" fought the wheezy *Merrimack* to a standstill. Britain and France had already built several powerful ironclads, but the first battle test of these new craft heralded the doom of wooden warships. A few months after the historic battle, the Confederates destroyed the *Merrimack* to keep it from the grasp of advancing Union troops.

The Pivotal Point: Antietam

Robert E. Lee, having broken the back of McClellan's assault on Richmond, next moved northward. Emboldened by a victory at the Second Battle of Bull Run (August 29–30, 1862), Lee daringly thrust into Maryland. He hoped to strike a blow that would not only encourage foreign intervention but also seduce the still wavering Border State and its sisters from the Union. The Confederate troops sang lustily:

> Thou wilt not cower in the dust,
>   Maryland! my Maryland!
> Thy gleaming sword shall never rust,
>   Maryland! my Maryland!

But the Marylanders did not respond to the siren song. The presence among the invaders of so many blanketless, hatless, and shoeless soldiers dampened the state's ardor for the Confederate cause.

Events finally converged toward a critical battle at Antietam Creek, Maryland. Lincoln, responding to popular pressures, hastily restored "Little Mac" to active command of the main northern army. His soldiers tossed their caps skyward and hugged his horse as they hailed his return. McClellan succeeded in halting Lee at Antietam on September 17, 1862, in one of the bloodiest and most bitter days of the war. Antietam was more or less a draw militarily. But Lee, finding his thrust parried, retired across the Potomac.

The landmark Battle of Antietam was one of the most decisive engagements of world history— probably the most decisive of the Civil War. Jefferson Davis was perhaps never again so near victory as on that fateful summer day. The British and French governments were on the verge of diplomatic mediation, a species of interference sure to be angrily resented in the North. But both Paris and London cooled off when the Union displayed unexpected power at Antietam, and their chill deepened with the passing months.

Bloody Antietam was also the long-awaited "victory" that Lincoln needed for launching his Emancipation Proclamation. The abolitionists had long been clamoring for action. By midsummer of 1862, with the Border States safely in the fold, Lincoln was ready to move. But he believed that to issue such an edict on the heels of a series of military disasters would be folly.

The halting of Lee's offensive was just enough of a victory to justify Lincoln's issuing, on September 23, 1862, the preliminary Emancipation Proclamation. This hope-giving document announced that on January 1, 1863, the president would issue a final proclamation. On the scheduled date he fully redeemed his promise, and the Civil War became more of a moral crusade. It also became more of what Lincoln called a "remorseless revolutionary struggle." After January 1, 1863, he said, "The character of the war will be changed. It will be one of subjugation. . . . The [old] South is to be destroyed and replaced by new propositions and ideas."

A Proclamation Without Emancipation

Lincoln's Emancipation Proclamation of 1863 declared "forever free" the slaves in those Confederate states still in rebellion. The blacks in the loyal Border States were not affected, nor were those in specific

Confederate Corpses at Antietam   *Unknown to Lee, who had dangerously divided his army, McClellan had somehow obtained a copy of the Confederate battle plan. The Union forces thus had a great tactical advantage, and the result was appalling slaughter. The twelve-hour fight at Antietam Creek ranks as the bloodiest day of the war, with more than 10,000 Confederate casualties and even more on the Union side. "At last the sun went down and the battle ended," one historian wrote, "smoke heavy in the air, the twilight quivering with the anguished cries of thousands of wounded men."*

conquered areas in the South—all told, about 800,000. The tone of the document was dull and legalistic: there was no clarion call for a holy war to achieve freedom. Lincoln in fact is on record, as late as February 1865, as favoring cash compensation to the owners of all slaves.

The presidential pen did not formally strike the shackles from a single slave. Where Lincoln could presumably free the slaves—that is, in the loyal Border States—he refused to do so, lest he spur disunion. Where he could not—that is, in the Confederate states—he tried to. In short, where he *could* he would not, and where he *would* he could not. Thus the Emancipation Proclamation was stronger on proclamation than emancipation.

Yet much unofficial do-it-yourself liberation did take place. Thousands of jubilant slaves, learning of the proclamation, flocked to the invading Union armies, stripping already run-down plantations of their work force. But many fugitives would have come anyhow, as they had from the war's outset. Actually, Lincoln did not go so far as legislation already passed by Congress for freeing enemy-owned slaves. His immediate goal was not so much to liberate the slaves as to strengthen the moral cause of the Union at home and abroad. This he succeeded in doing. At the same time Lincoln's proclamation clearly foreshadowed the ultimate doom of slavery. This was legally achieved by action of the individual states and by their ratification of the Thirteenth Amendment in 1865, eight months after the Civil War had ended. (For text, see Appendix.)

Public reactions to the long-awaited proclamation of 1863 were varied. "God bless Abraham Lincoln," exulted the antislavery editor Horace Greeley in his New York *Tribune*. But many ardent abolitionists complained that Lincoln had not gone far enough. On the other hand, formidable numbers of northerners, especially in the Old Northwest and the Border States, felt that he had gone too far. A Democratic rhymester sneered:

> Honest old Abe, when
>   the war first began,
> Denied abolition was
>   part of his plan;
> Honest old Abe has since
>   made a decree,

> The war must go on
>   till the slaves are all free.
> As both can't be honest,
>   will someone tell how,
> If honest Abe then,
>   is he honest Abe now?

Opposition mounted in the North against supporting an "abolition war." Many Boys in Blue, especially from the Border States, had volunteered to fight for the Union, not against slavery. Desertions increased sharply. The crucial congressional elections in the autumn of 1862 went heavily against the administration, particularly in New York, Pennsylvania, and Ohio. Democrats even carried Lincoln's Illinois, although they failed to secure control of Congress.

The Emancipation Proclamation caused an outcry to rise from the South that "Lincoln the fiend" was trying to stir up the "hellish passions" of a slave insurrection. Aristocrats of Europe, noting that the proclamation applied only to rebel slaveholders, were inclined to sympathize with southern protests. But the Old World working classes, especially in Britain, reacted otherwise. They sensed that the proclamation spelled the ultimate doom of slavery, and many laborers were more determined than ever to oppose intervention. Gradually the diplomatic position of the Union improved.

The North now had much the stronger moral cause. In addition to preserving the Union, it had committed itself to freeing the slaves. The moral position of the South was correspondingly weakened.

Blacks Battle Bondage

As Lincoln moved to emancipate the slaves, he also took steps to enlist blacks in the armed forces. Although some African-Americans had served in the Revolution and the War of 1812, the regular army contained no blacks at the war's outset, and the War Department refused to accept those free northern blacks who tried to volunteer. (The Union navy, however, enrolled many blacks, mainly as cooks, stewards, and firemen.)

But as manpower ran low and emancipation was proclaimed, black enlistees were accepted, sometimes over ferocious protests from northern as well as southern whites. By war's end some 180,000 blacks served in the Union armies, most of them from the slave states, but many from the free-soil North. They accounted for about 10 percent of the total enlistments in the Union forces, on land and sea, and included two Massachusetts regiments raised largely through the efforts of the ex-slave Frederick Douglass.

Black fighting men unquestionably had their hearts in the war against slavery that the Civil War had become after Lincoln proclaimed emancipation. Participating in about 500 engagements, they received twenty-two Congressional Medals of Honor —the highest military award. Their casualties were extremely heavy; more than 38,000 died, whether from battle, sickness, or reprisals from vengeful masters. Many were put to death as slaves in revolt, as not until 1864 did the South recognize them as prisoners of war. In one notorious case, several black soldiers were massacred after they had formally surrendered at Fort Pillow, Tennessee. Thereafter vengeful black units cried "Remember Fort Pillow" as they swung into battle, and vowed to take no prisoners.

For reasons of pride, prejudice, and principle, the Confederacy could not bring itself to enlist slaves until a month before the war ended, and then it was too late. Meanwhile tens of thousands were impressed into labor battalions, the building of fortifications, the supplying of armies, and other war-connected activities. Slaves moreover were "the stomach of the Confederacy," for they kept the farms going while the white men fought.

Through the "grapevine," the blacks learned of Lincoln's Emancipation Proclamation. Yet the bulk of them, whether because of fear, loyalty, lack of leadership, or strict policing, never rose in revolt. But tens of thousands did rebel "with their feet," when they abandoned their plantations upon the approach or arrival of Union armies, with or without emancipation proclamations. About 25,000 joined Sherman's march through Georgia in 1864, and their presence in such numbers created problems of supply and discipline.

Lee's Last Lunge at Gettysburg

After Antietam, Lincoln replaced McClellan as commander of the Army of the Potomac with General A. E. Burnside, whose ornate side-whiskers came to be known as "burnsides" or "sideburns." Protesting his unfitness for this responsibility, Burnside proved it when he launched a rash frontal attack on Lee's

Black Union Soldiers   *These former slaves, recruited into the Union army in Tennessee, helped to man an artillery battery during the battle of Nashville.*

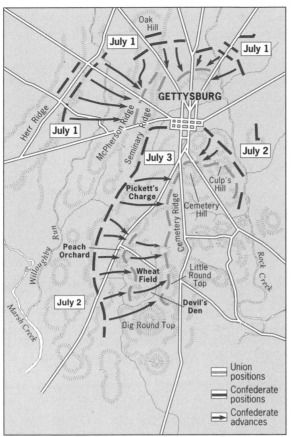

The Battle of Gettysburg, 1863 *With the failure of Pickett's charge, the fate of the Confederacy was sealed—though the Civil War dragged on for almost two more bloody years.*

strong position at Fredericksburg, Virginia, on December 13, 1862. A chicken could not have lived in the line of fire, remarked one Confederate officer. More than 10,000 northern soldiers were killed or wounded in "Burnside's Slaughter Pen."

A new slaughter pen was prepared when General Burnside yielded his command to "Fighting Joe" Hooker, an aggressive officer but a headstrong subordinate. At Chancellorsville, Virginia, May 2–4, 1863, Lee daringly divided his numerically inferior force and sent Stonewall Jackson to attack the Union flank. The strategy worked. Hooker, temporarily dazed by a near hit from a cannon ball, was badly beaten but not crushed. This victory was probably Lee's most brilliant, but it was dearly bought. Jack-

son was mistakenly shot by his own men in the gathering dusk and died a few days later. "I have lost my right arm," lamented Lee. Southern folklore relates how Jackson outflanked the angels while getting into Heaven.

Lee now prepared to follow up his brilliant victory by invading the North again, this time through Pennsylvania. A decisive blow would add strength to the noisy peace movement in the North and would also encourage foreign intervention—still a southern hope. Quite by accident, the northern army, now under General George G. Meade, took its stand on the rolling hills near quiet little Gettysburg, Pennsylvania. There his 92,000 men in blue locked horns in furious combat with Lee's 76,000 gray-clad warriors. The battle seesawed across the green slopes for three agonizing days, July 1–3, 1863, and the outcome was in doubt until the very end. The failure of General George Pickett's magnificent but futile charge finally broke the back of the Confederate attack—and the Confederate cause.

Pickett's charge has been called the "high tide of the Confederacy." It defined both the northernmost point reached by any significant southern force and the last real chance for the Confederacy to win the war. After Gettysburg, Lincoln spurned southern efforts to reach a negotiated peace settlement between the parties. From now on the southern cause was doomed. Yet the men of Dixie fought on for nearly two years longer, through sweat, blood, and weariness of spirit.

Later in that dreary autumn of 1863, with the graves still fresh, Lincoln journeyed to Gettysburg to dedicate the cemetery. He read a two-minute address, following a two-hour speech by the orator of the day. Lincoln's noble remarks were branded by the London *Times* as "ludicrous" and by Democratic editors as "dishwatery" and "silly." The address attracted relatively little attention at the time, but the president was speaking for the ages.

The War in the West

Events in the western theater of the war at last provided Lincoln with an able general who did not have to be shelved after every reverse. Ulysses S. Grant had been a mediocre student at West Point, although he did do well in mathematics and horsemanship. After fighting creditably in the Mexican War, he was stationed at isolated frontier posts, where boredom and loneliness drove him to drink. Resigning from the army to avoid a court martial for drunkenness, he failed at various business ventures, and when war came, he was working in his father's leather store in Illinois for $50 a month.

Grant did not cut much of a figure. Shy and silent, he was short, stooped, awkward, stubble-bearded, and sloppy in dress. He managed with some difficulty to secure a colonelcy in the volunteers. From then on his military experience—com-

bined with his boldness, resourcefulness, and doggedness—catapulted him on a meteoric rise.

Grant's first signal success came in the northern Tennessee theater. After heavy fighting, he captured Fort Henry and Fort Donelson on the Tennessee and Cumberland rivers in February 1862. When the Confederate commander at Fort Donelson asked for terms, Grant bluntly demanded "an unconditional and immediate surrender."

Grant's triumph in Tennessee was crucial. It not only riveted Kentucky more securely to the Union but also opened the gateway to the strategically important region of Tennessee, as well as to

General Ulysses S. Grant and General Robert E. Lee *Trained at West Point, Grant (left) proved to be a better general than a president. Oddly, he hated the sight of blood and recoiled from rare beef. Lee (right), a gentlemanly general in an ungentlemanly business, remarked when the Union troops were bloodily repulsed at Fredericksburg, "It is well that war is so terrible, or we should get too fond of it."*

Georgia and the heart of Dixie. Grant next attempted to exploit his victory by capturing the junction of the main Confederate north-south and east-west railroads in the Mississippi Valley at Corinth, Mississippi. But a Confederate force foiled his plans in a gory battle at Shiloh, just over the Tennessee border from Corinth, on April 6–7, 1862.

Lincoln resisted all demands for the removal of "Unconditional Surrender" Grant, saying, "I can't spare this man; he fights." When talebearers later told Lincoln that Grant drank too much, the president allegedly replied, "Find me the brand, and I'll send a barrel to each of my other generals."

Other Union thrusts were in the making. In the spring of 1862 a flotilla commanded by David G. Farragut joined with a northern army to strike the South a staggering blow by seizing New Orleans. With Union gunboats both ascending and descending the Mississippi, the eastern part of the Confederacy was left with a precarious back door. Through this narrowing entrance, between Vicksburg and Port Hudson, flowed herds of vitally needed cattle and quantities of other provisions from Louisiana

and Texas. The fortress of Vicksburg, located on a hairpin turn of the Mississippi, was the South's sentinel protecting the lifeline to the western sources of supply.

General Grant was now given command of the Union forces attacking Vicksburg, and in the teeth of grave difficulties displayed rare skill and daring. This was his best-fought campaign of the war. Vicksburg at length surrendered, on July 4, 1863, with the garrison reduced to eating mules and rats. Five days later came the fall of Port Hudson, the last southern bastion on the Mississippi. The spinal cord of the Confederacy was now severed and, in Lincoln's poetic phrase, the Father of Waters at last flowed "unvexed to the sea."

The Union victory at Vicksburg (July 4, 1863) came the day after the Confederate defeat at Gettysburg. The political significance of these back-to-back military successes was epochal. Reopening the Mississippi helped to quell strong peace agitation in the areas of southern Ohio, Indiana, and Illinois in the Ohio River Valley. Confederate control of the Mississippi had cut off that region's usual trade routes down the Ohio-Mississippi river system to New Orleans, thus adding economic pain to that border section's already shaky support for the abolition war. The twin victories also conclusively tipped the diplomatic scales in favor of the North, as Britain stopped delivery of the Laird rams to the Confederates and as France killed a deal for the sale of six naval vessels to the Richmond government. By the end of 1863 all confederate hopes for foreign help were irretrievably lost.

Sherman Scorches Georgia

General Grant, the victor of Vicksburg, was now transferred to the east Tennessee theater. There, in November 1863, he won a series of desperate engagements in the vicinity of Chattanooga, including Missionary Ridge and Lookout Mountain ("the Battle Above the Clouds"). Chattanooga was captured, the state was cleared of Confederates, and the way was thus opened for an invasion of Georgia. Grant was rewarded by being made general-in-chief.

Georgia's conquest was entrusted to General William Tecumseh Sherman. Red-haired and red-

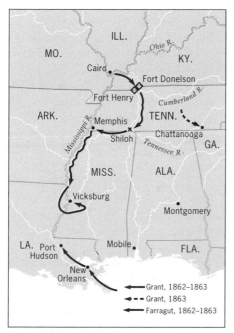

The Mississippi River and Tennessee, 1862–1863

bearded, grim-faced and ruthless, he captured and burned Atlanta in September 1864. He then daringly left his supply base, lived off the country for some 250 miles, and emerged at Savannah on the sea.

Sherman's hated "Blue Bellies," 60,000 strong, cut a sixty-mile swath of destruction through Georgia. They burned buildings, leaving only the blackened chimneys ("Sherman's Sentinels"). They tore up railroad rails, heated them red-hot, and twisted them into "iron doughnuts" and "Sherman's hairpins." They bayoneted family portraits and ran off with valuable "souvenirs." "War . . . is all hell," admitted Sherman later, and he proved it by his efforts to "make Georgia howl." His major purpose was twofold: to destroy supplies destined for the Confederate army, and to weaken the morale of the men at the front by waging war on their homes.

Sherman was a pioneer practitioner of total war. His success in "Shermanizing" the South was attested by increasing numbers of Confederate desertions. Although effective, his methods were unquestionably brutal. At times the discipline of his army broke down, as roving soldiers ("Sherman's bummers") engaged in an orgy of pillaging. "Sherman the Brute" was universally damned in the South.

Sherman's March, 1864–1865

After seizing Savannah as a Christmas present for Lincoln, Sherman's army veered north into South Carolina, where the destruction was even more vicious. Many Union soldiers believed that this state, the "hell-hole of secession," had wantonly provoked the war. The capital city, Columbia, burst into flames, in all probability the handiwork of the Yankee invader. Crunching northward, Sherman's conquering army had rolled deep into North Carolina by the time the war ended.

The Politics of War

Presidential elections come by the calendar, not by the crisis. The election of 1864 fell most inopportunely in the midst of war.

Political infighting in the North added greatly to Lincoln's cup of woe. Factions within his own party, distrusting his ability or doubting his commitment to abolition, sought to tie his hands or even remove him from office. Conspicuous among these critics was a group led by his overambitious secretary of the treasury, Salmon Chase. Especially burdensome to Lincoln was the creation of the Congressional Committee on the Conduct of the War, formed in late 1861. It was dominated by "radical" Republicans who resented the expansion of presidential power in wartime and who pressed Lincoln zealously on emancipation.

Most dangerous of all to the Union cause were the northern Democrats. Deprived of the talent that had departed with the southern wing of the party, those Democrats remaining in the North were left with the taint of association with the seceders. Tragedy befell the Democrats—and the Union— when their gifted leader, Stephen A. Douglas, died of typhoid fever seven weeks after the war began. Unshakably devoted to the Union, he probably could have kept much of his following on the path of loyalty.

Lacking a leader, the Democrats divided. A large group of "War Democrats" patriotically supported the Lincoln administration, but tens of thousands of "Peace Democrats" did not. At the extreme were the so-called Copperheads, named for the poisonous snake that strikes without a rattle. Copperheads openly obstructed the war through attacks against the draft, against Lincoln, and especially, after 1863, against emancipation. They denounced the president as the "Illinois Ape" and condemned the "Nigger War."

Notorious among the Copperheads was sometime congressman from Ohio Clement L. Vallandigham. This tempestuous character possessed brilliant oratorical gifts and unusual talents for stirring up trouble. A southern partisan, he publicly demanded an end to the "wicked and cruel" war, and was convicted and sentenced to prison by a military tribunal for treasonable utterances. Lincoln decided that if Vallandigham liked the Confederates so much, he ought to be banished to their lines. This was done. But Vallandigham was not so easily silenced. Working his way to Canada, he ran for the governorship of Ohio on foreign soil, and polled a substantial but insufficient vote.

The Election of 1864

As the election of 1864 approached, Lincoln's precarious authority depended on his retaining Republican support while spiking the threat from the Peace Democrats and the Copperheads.

Facing defeat, the Republican party executed a clever maneuver. Joining with the War Democrats, it proclaimed itself to be the Union party. Thus the Republican party passed temporarily out of existence.

Lincoln's renomination at first encountered surprisingly strong opposition. Hostile factions whipped up considerable agitation to shelve him in favor of Secretary of the Treasury Chase. Lincoln was accused of lacking force, of being overready to compromise, of not having won the war, and of having shocked many sensitive souls by his ill-timed and earthy jokes. ("Prince of Jesters," one journal called him.) But the "ditch Lincoln" move collapsed, and he was nominated by the Union party without serious dissent.

Lincoln's running mate was ex-tailor Andrew Johnson, a loyal War Democrat from Tennessee who had been a small slaveowner when the conflict began. He was placed on the Union party ticket to "sew up" the election by attracting War Democrats and voters in the Border States and not with proper regard for the possibility that Lincoln might die in office.

Embattled Democrats—regulars and Copper-

The Copperhead Party *The cartoon shows the party in favor of a vigorous prosecution of peace.*

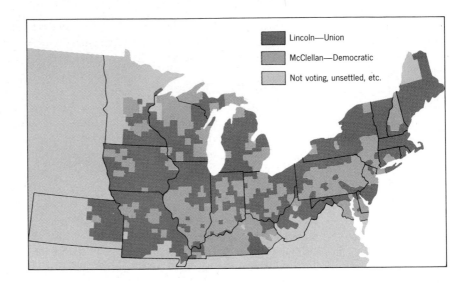

Presidential Election of 1864 (showing popular vote by county) *Lincoln also carried California, Oregon, and Nevada, but there was a considerable McClellan vote in each.*

Lincoln—Union
McClellan—Democratic
Not voting, unsettled, etc.

heads—nominated the deposed and overcautious war hero, General McClellan. The Copperheads managed to force into the Democratic platform a plank denouncing the prosecution of the war as a failure. But McClellan, who could not otherwise have faced his old comrades-in-arms, repudiated this defeatist declaration.

The campaign was noisy and heated. Lincoln's reelection was at first gravely in doubt. The war was going badly, and Lincoln himself gave way to despondency, fearing that his defeat was imminent. But the atmosphere of gloom was changed electrically, as balloting day neared, by a succession of northern victories. Admiral Farragut captured Mobile, Alabama, after defiantly shouting the now famous, "Damn the torpedoes! Go ahead." General Sherman seized Atlanta. General ("Little Phil") Sheridan laid waste the verdant Shenandoah Valley of Virginia so thoroughly that, in his words, "A crow could not fly over it without carrying his rations with him."

The president pulled through, but nothing more than necessary was left to chance. At election time many northern soldiers were furloughed home to support Lincoln. Other soldiers were permitted to cast their ballots at the front.

Lincoln, bolstered by the so-called bayonet vote, vanquished General McClellan by 212 electoral

votes to 21, with the loss of only Kentucky, Delaware, and New Jersey. But "Little Mac" ran a much closer race than the electoral count indicates. He netted a surprising 45 percent of the popular vote, 1,803,787 to Lincoln's 2,206,938, piling up much support in the southerner-infiltrated states of the Old Northwest, in New York, and also in his native state of Pennsylvania (see map above).

One of the most crushing defeats suffered by the South was the defeat of the northern Democrats in 1864. The removal of Lincoln was the last ghost of a hope for a Confederate victory, and the southern soldiers would wishfully shout, "Hurrah for McClellan!" When Lincoln triumphed, desertions from the sinking southern ship increased sharply.

Grant Outlasts Lee

Grant was now brought in from the West over Meade, who was blamed for failing to pursue the defeated but always dangerous Lee. Lincoln needed a general who, employing the superior resources of the North, would have the intestinal stamina to drive straight ahead, regardless of casualties. A soldier of bulldog tenacity, Grant was the man for this meat-grinder type of warfare. His overall basic strategy was to assail the enemy's armies simultaneously, so that they could not assist one another and hence could be destroyed piecemeal. His personal motto was "When in doubt, fight." Lincoln urged him "to chew and choke, as much as possible."

A grimly determined Grant, with more than 100,000 men, struck for Richmond. He engaged Lee in a series of furious battles in the wilderness of Virginia, during May and June 1864, notably in the leaden hurricane of the "Bloody Angle" and "Hell's Half Acre." In this Wilderness Campaign Grant suffered about 50,000 casualties, or nearly as many men as Lee had at the start. But Lee lost about as heavily in proportion.

In a ghastly gamble, on June 3, 1864, Grant ordered a frontal assault on the impregnable position of Cold Harbor. The Union soldiers advanced to almost certain death with papers pinned on their backs bearing their names and addresses. In a few minutes, about 7,000 men were killed or wounded.

Public opinion in the North was appalled by this "blood and guts" type of fighting. Critics cried that "Grant the Butcher" had gone insane. But his basic strategy of hammering ahead seemed brutally necessary; he could trade two men for one and still beat the enemy to its knees. "I propose to fight it out on this line," he wrote, "if it takes all summer." It

did—and it also took all autumn, all winter, and a part of the spring.

Early in 1865 the Confederates, tasting the bitter dregs of defeat, tried desperately to negotiate for peace between the "two countries." But Lincoln could accept nothing short of Union, and the southerners could accept nothing short of independence. So the war had to grind on—amid smoke and agony—to its terrible climax.

The end came with dramatic suddenness. Rapidly advancing northern troops captured Richmond and cornered Lee at Appomattox Court House in Virginia in April 1865. Grant—stubble-bearded and informally dressed—met with Lee on Palm Sunday and granted generous terms of surrender. Among other concessions, the hungry Confederates were allowed to keep their own horses to use for spring plowing.

Tattered southern veterans—"Lee's Ragamuffins"—wept as they took leave of their beloved commander. The elated Union soldiers cheered, but they were silenced by Grant's stern admonition, "The war is over; the rebels are our countrymen again."

Lincoln himself traveled to conquered Rich-

The Assassination of Abraham Lincoln at Ford's Theater, 1865 *John Wilkes Booth* (left) *shot Lincoln* (top center) *from behind, then leaped to the stage and escaped. Many heard him shout,* "Sic Semper Tyrannus!" *("Thus Ever to Tyrants!"), the state motto of Virginia.*

mond and sat in Jefferson Davis's evacuated office just forty hours after the Confederate president had left it. As he walked the blasted streets of the city, crowds of freed slaves gathered to see and touch "Father Abraham." One black man fell to his knees before the Emancipator, who said to him, "Don't kneel to me. This is not right. You must kneel to God only, and thank Him for the liberty you will enjoy hereafter." Sadly, as many freed slaves would discover, the hereafter of their full liberty was a long time coming.

The Martyrdom of Lincoln

On the night of April 14, 1865 (Good Friday), only five days after Lee's surrender, Ford's Theater in Washington witnessed its most sensational drama. A half-crazed, fanatically prosouthern actor, John Wilkes Booth, slipped behind Lincoln as he sat in his box and shot him in the head. After lying unconscious all night, the Great Emancipator died the following morning.

Lincoln expired in the arms of victory at the very pinnacle of his fame. From the standpoint of his reputation, his death could not have been better timed if he had hired the assassin. A large number of his countrymen had not suspected his greatness, and many others had even doubted his ability. But his dramatic death helped to erase the memory of his shortcomings and caused his nobler qualities to stand out in clearer relief.

The full impact of Lincoln's death was not at once apparent to the South. Hundreds of bedraggled ex-Confederate soldiers cheered, as did some southern civilians and northern Copperheads, when they learned of the assassination. But as time wore on, increasing numbers of southerners perceived that Lincoln's death was a calamity for them. Belatedly they recognized that his kindliness and moderation would have been the most effective shields between them and vindictive treatment by the victors. The assassination unfortunately embittered the North, partly because of the fantastic rumor that Jefferson Davis had plotted it.

A few historians have argued that if the rail splitter had lived he would have suffered Andrew Johnson's fate of being impeached by the embittered members of his own party who demanded harsh treatment of the South. Lincoln no doubt would have clashed with Congress; in fact, he had already found himself in some hot water. But the surefooted and experienced Lincoln could hardly have blundered into the same quicksands that engulfed Johnson. Lincoln was a victorious president; and there is no arguing with victory. Enjoying battle-tested powers of leadership, he possessed in full measure tact, sweet reasonableness, and an uncommon amount of common sense. Andrew Johnson, hot-tempered and impetuous, lacked all of these priceless qualities.

Ford's Theater, with its tragic murder of Lincoln, set the stage for the terrible ordeal of Reconstruction.

The Aftermath of the Nightmare

The Civil War took a grisly toll in gore, about as much as all of America's subsequent wars combined. Over 600,000 men died in action or of disease, and in all, over 1 million were killed or seriously wounded. To its lasting hurt, the nation lost the cream of its young manhood and potential leadership.

Direct monetary costs of the conflict totaled about $15 billion. But this colossal figure does not include continuing expenses, such as pensions and interest on the national debt. The intangible costs—dislocations, disunities, wasted energies, lowered ethics, blasted lives, bitter memories, and burning hates—cannot be calculated.

The greatest constitutional decision of the century, in a sense, was written in blood and handed down at Appomattox Court House, near which Lee surrendered. The extreme states'-righters were crushed. The national government, tested in the fiery furnace of war, emerged unbroken. Nullification and secession, those twin nightmares of previous decades, were laid to rest.

Beyond doubt the Civil War—the nightmare of the republic—was the supreme test of American democracy. It finally answered the question, in the words of Lincoln at Gettysburg, whether a nation dedicated to such principles "can long endure." The preservation of democratic ideals, though not an officially announced war aim, was subconsciously one of the major objectives of the North.

Victory for the Union also provided inspiration to the champions of democracy and liberalism the world over. The great English Reform Bill of 1867, under which Britain became a true political democracy, was passed two years after the Civil War ended. American democracy had proved itself, and its success was an additional argument used by the disfranchised British masses in securing similar blessings for themselves.

The "lost cause" of the South was lost, but few Americans today would argue that the end result was not for the best. The shameful cancer of slavery was sliced away by the sword, and African-Americans were at last in a position to claim their rights to life, liberty, and the pursuit of happiness. The nation was again united politically, though for many generations it remained divided spiritually by the passions of the war. Grave dangers were averted by a Union victory, including the indefinite prolongation of the "peculiar institution," the unleashing of the slave power on weak Caribbean neighbors, and the transformation of the area from Panama to Hudson's Bay into an armed camp, with several heavily armed and hostile states constantly snarling and sniping at one another. America still had a long way to go to make the promises of freedom a reality for all its citizens, black and white. But emancipation laid the necessary groundwork, and a united and democratic United States was free to fulfill its destiny as the dominant republic of the hemisphere—and eventually of the world.

Varying Viewpoints

Why did the North win the Civil War? The usual answer is that superior industry and transportation tipped the scales in the Union's favor. This line of reasoning leads to the conclusion that this was the first "modern" war, in which victory turned at least as much on home-front economic mobilization as on battlefield prowess.

Another approach focuses on military strategy. Historians of this persuasion argue that Union successes in the western theater more than compensated for the early debacles in Virginia. Victories in the West allowed the emergence of tacticians such as Grant and Sherman, who were better equipped to wage a modern total war than the valiant but old-fashioned Confederate generals.

A third answer emphasizes political leadership. In this view, the Lincoln administration was able through political skill to maintain control at home and prevent unfavorable foreign intervention in the conflict. The government of Jefferson Davis had no such domestic or diplomatic success. One historian even suggested that if the North and South had traded presidents, the Confederacy would have won its independence. Even today, heated debate continues over the relative importance of battlefront and behind-the-lines factors in accounting for the North's crushing victory.

SELECT READINGS

Primary Source Documents

Abraham Lincoln's reply in 1862 to Horace Greeley's "Prayer of Twenty Millions"* (*Collected Works of Abraham Lincoln,* edited by Roy P. Basler, 1953) is an early statement of the president's war aims. See also, in the same collection, the Emancipation Proclamation (1863). Reminiscences of the military struggle include Eliza Andrews, *The War-Time Journal of a Georgia Girl** (1908) and *Memoirs of General William T. Sherman** (1887), and C. Vann Woodward, ed., *Mary Chestnut's Civil War* (rev. ed., 1981). See also Stephen Crane's classic war novel *The Red Badge of Courage* (1895).

Secondary Sources

The most compelling single-volume account of the war is James M. McPherson, *Battle Cry of Freedom: The Civil War Era* (1988). An able survey is James G. Randall and David Donald, *The Civil War and Reconstruction* (rev. ed., 1969). Greater detail appears in James G. Randall, *Lincoln the President* (4 vols., 1945–1955). Other capable one-volume studies include Peter J. Parish, *The American Civil War* (1975), and James M. McPherson, *Ordeal by Fire: The*

Civil War and Reconstruction (1982). See also the multivolume study by Shelby Foote, *The Civil War* (3 vols., 1958–1974), and Allan Nevin's monumental *Ordeal of the Union* (8 vols., 1947–1971). Bruce Catton has a series of a dozen or so books on aspects of the Civil War, all readable and knowledgeable, including *A Stillness at Appomattox* (1953) and *This Hallowed Ground* (1956). Russell T. Weigley, *The American Way of War* (1973), puts military history in the broader context. Herman Hattaway and Archer Jones discuss *How the North Won* (1983). An intriguing analysis of Confederate strategy is Grady McWhiney and Perry D. Jamison, *Attack and Die* (1982). Bell I. Wiley's descriptions of common soldiers, *The Life of Johnny Reb* (1943) and *The Life of Billy Yank* (1952), are classics. See also Benjamin Quarles, *The Negro in the Civil War* (1953), and James M. McPherson's collection of documents, *The Negro's Civil War* (1965). On the abolitionists' role in securing emancipation, see James M. McPherson, *The Struggle for Equality* (1964). The two leading Civil War generals are masterfully treated in Douglas S. Freeman, *R. E. Lee* (4 vols., 1934–1935), and William S. McFeely, *Grant* (1981).

CHAPTER 24

The Ordeal of Reconstruction, 1865–1877

With malice toward none, with charity for all, with firmness in the right as God gives us to see the right, let us strive on to finish the work we are in, to bind up the nation's wounds, to care for him who shall have borne the battle and for his widow and orphan, to do all which may achieve and cherish a just and lasting peace among ourselves and with all nations.

Abraham Lincoln, Second Inaugural Address, March 4, 1865

The Problems of Peace

The battle was done, the buglers silent. Bone-weary and bloodied, the American people, North and South, now faced the staggering challenges of peace. Four questions loomed large. How would the South, physically devastated by war and socially revolutionized by emancipation, be rebuilt? How would the liberated blacks fare as free men and women? How would the southern states be reintegrated into the Union? And who would direct the process of Reconstruction—the southern states themselves, the president, or Congress?

Other questions clamored for answers. What should be done with the captured Confederate ringleaders? During the war a popular northern song had been "Hang Jeff Davis to a Sour Apple Tree," and some northerners did think Davis and others should be tried for treason. But no trials were ever held. Davis served only two years in prison, and President Johnson pardoned all "rebel" leaders as a Christmas present in 1868. Congress removed their civil disabilities thirty years later.

Dismal indeed was the picture presented by the war-wracked South when the rattle of musketry faded. Not only had an age perished, but a civilization had collapsed, in both its economic and its social structure. The moonlight-and-magnolia Old South, largely imaginary in any case, had forever gone with the wind.

Handsome cities of yesteryear, like Charleston and Richmond, were gutted. An Atlantan returned to his once-fair hometown and remarked, "Hell has laid her egg, and right here it hatched."

Economic life had creaked to a halt. Banks and business houses had locked their doors, ruined by runaway inflation. Factories were smokeless, silent, dismantled. The transportation system had broken down completely. Efforts to untwist the rails corkscrewed by Sherman's soldiers proved bumpily unsatisfactory.

Agriculture—the economic lifeblood of the South—was almost hopelessly crippled. Once-white cotton fields now yielded a lush harvest of nothing

Ruins of Richmond, April 1865 *The devastation of Richmond and other southern cities has been compared with the bomb-destroyed cities of Europe during World War II.*

but green weeds. The slave-labor system had collapsed, seed was scarce, and livestock had been driven off by plundering Yankees. Pathetic instances were reported of men hitching themselves to plows, while women and children gripped the handles.

The princely planter aristocrats were humbled by the war—at least temporarily. Reduced to proud poverty, they faced charred and gutted mansions, lost investments, and almost worthless land. Their investment of more than $2 billion in slaves, their primary form of wealth, had evaporated with emancipation.

Beaten but unbent, many high-spirited white southerners remained dangerously defiant. They cursed the "damnyankees" and spoke of "your government" in Washington instead of "our government." Conscious of no crime, these former Confederates continued to believe that their view of secession was correct and that the "lost cause" was still a just war. One popular anti-Union song ran:

I'm glad I fought agin her, I only wish we'd won,
And I ain't axed any pardon for anything I've done.

Such attitudes boded ill for the prospects of painlessly binding up the republic's wounds.

Unfettered Freedmen

Confusion abounded in the still-smoldering South about the precise meaning of "freedom" for blacks. Emancipation took effect haltingly and unevenly in different parts of the conquered Confederacy, and in some regions planters stubbornly protested that slavery was legal until state legislatures or the Supreme Court might act. For many slaves, the shackles of bondage were not struck off in a single mighty blow; long-suffering blacks often had to struggle out of their chains link by link.

The variety of responses to emancipation, by whites as well as blacks, illustrated the sometimes startling complexity of the master-slave relationship. Unbending loyalty to "ole Massa" prompted many slaves to help their owners resist the liberating Union armies. Blacks blocked the door of the "big house" with their bodies, or stashed the plantation silverware under mattresses in their own humble huts, where it would be safe from the plundering "bluebellies." On other plantations, pent-up bitterness burst violently forth on the day of liberation. A group of Virginia slaves laid twenty lashes on the back of their former master—a painful dose of his own favorite medicine. Newly emancipated slaves sometimes eagerly accepted the invitation of Union troops to join in the pillaging of their master's possessions. One freedman said that he felt that he was entitled to steal a chicken or two, since the whites had robbed him of his labor and his children.

Emancipation followed by reenslavement, or worse, was the bewildering lot of many blacks, as Union armies marched in and out of various locali-ties. A North Carolina slave estimated that he had celebrated emancipation about twelve times. As blacks in one Texas county flocked to the free soil of the liberated county next door, their owners bush-whacked them with rifle fire as they swam for free-dom across the river that marked the county line. The next day, trees along the riverbank were bent with swinging corpses—a grisly warning to others dreaming of liberty.

Prodded by the bayonets of Yankee armies of

NOON AT THE PRIMARY SCHOOL FOR FREEDMEN, VICKSBURG, MISSISSIPPI.—[SEE PAGE 326.]

Primary School for Freedmen in Vicksburg, Mississippi, 1866 Top: *Outdoor recess at school.* Bottom: *Teaching the pupils; note the wide range of ages.*

326 Chapter 24 ★ The Ordeal of Reconstruction, 1865–1877

occupation, all masters were eventually forced to recognize their slaves' permanent freedom. The once-commanding planter would assemble his former human chattels in front of the porch of the "big house" and announce their liberty. This "Day of Jubilo" was the occasion of wild rejoicing. Tens of thousands of blacks naturally took to the roads. They sought long-separated loved ones, as formalizing a "slave marriage" was the first goal of many newly free men and women. Others traveled in search of economic opportunity in the towns or in the still-wild West. Many moved simply to test their new freedom.

Desperately trying to bootstrap themselves up from slavery, blacks assembled in "Conventions of Freedmen" to fight to make their freedom a reality. Led by ministers of God and freeborn blacks from the North, these conventions expressed surprisingly moderate views. But moderation could not guarantee a warm reception by embittered white southerners. The freed blacks would need all the friends—and the power—they could find in Washington.

The Freedmen's Bureau

Abolitionists had long preached that slavery was a degrading institution. Now the emancipators had to face the brutal truth that the former slaves were in many ways indeed degraded. The freedmen were overwhelmingly unskilled, unlettered, without property or money, and with scant knowledge of how to survive as free people. To cope with this problem throughout the conquered South, Congress created the Freedmen's Bureau in 1865.

On paper at least, the bureau was intended to be a kind of primitive welfare agency. It was to provide food, clothing, and education both to freedmen and to white refugees. It was also authorized to distribute up to forty acres of abandoned or confiscated land to black settlers. The bureau achieved its greatest successes in education. It taught an estimated 200,000 blacks how to read. Many former slaves had a passion for learning, partly because they wanted to close the gap between themselves and the whites and partly because they longed to read the Word of God.

But in other areas the bureau's accomplishments were meager—or even mischievous. It distrib-

uted virtually no land. Its local administrators often collaborated with planters in expelling blacks from towns and cajoling them into signing labor contracts to work for their former masters. Yet the white South resented the bureau as a meddlesome federal interloper that threatened to upset white racial dominance. President Andrew Johnson, who shared the white-supremacist views of most white southerners, repeatedly tried to kill it, and it expired in 1872.

Johnson: The Tailor President

Few presidents have ever been faced with a more perplexing sea of troubles than that confronting Andrew Johnson. What manner of man was this medium-built, dark-eyed, black-haired Tennessean, now chief executive by virtue of the bullet that killed Lincoln?

No citizen, not even Lincoln, has ever reached the White House from humbler beginnings. Born to impoverished parents in North Carolina and early orphaned, Johnson never attended school but was apprenticed to a tailor at age ten. Ambitious to get ahead, he taught himself to read, and later his wife taught him to write and do simple arithmetic. Like many a self-made man, he was inclined to overpraise his maker.

Johnson early became active in politics in Tennessee, where he had moved when seventeen years old. He shone as an impassioned champion of the poor whites against the planter aristocrats and excelled as a two-fisted stump speaker before angry and heckling crowds. Elected to Congress, he refused to secede with his own state, and was then appointed war governor after Tennessee was partially "redeemed" by Union armies.

Political exigency next thrust Johnson into the vice presidency. Lincoln's Union party in 1864 needed to attract support from the War Democrats and other prosouthern elements, and Johnson, a Democrat, seemed to be the ideal man.

"Old Andy" Johnson was no doubt a man of parts—unpolished parts. He was intelligent, able, forceful, and steadfastly devoted to duty and the Constitution. Yet the man who had raised himself from the tailor's bench to the president's chair was a misfit. A southerner who did not understand the

Johnson as a Parrot *He was constantly invoking the Constitution.*

North, a Tennessean who had earned the distrust of the South, a Democrat who had never been accepted by the Republicans, a president who had never been elected to the office, he was not at home in a Republican White House. Hotheaded, contentious, and stubborn, he was the wrong man in the wrong place at the wrong time. A Reconstruction policy devised by the angels might well have failed in his tactless hands.

Presidential Reconstruction

Even before the shooting war had ended, the political war over Reconstruction had begun. Abraham Lincoln believed that the southern states had never legally withdrawn from the Union. Their formal restoration to the Union would therefore be relatively simple. Accordingly, Lincoln in 1863 proclaimed his "10 percent" Reconstruction plan. It decreed that a state could be reintegrated into the Union when 10 percent of its voters in the presidential election of 1860 had taken an oath of allegiance to the United States and pledged to abide by emancipation. The next step would be formal erection of

a state government. Lincoln would then recognize the purified regime.

Lincoln's proclamation provoked a sharp reaction in Congress, where Republicans feared the restoration of the planter aristocracy to power and the possible reenslavement of the blacks. Republicans therefore rammed through Congress in 1864 the Wade-Davis Bill, which required that 50 percent of a state's voters take an oath of allegiance and demanded stronger safeguards for emancipation than Lincoln's as the price of readmission. Republicans were outraged when Lincoln pocket-vetoed this bill by refusing to sign it after Congress had adjourned.

The controversy surrounding the Wade-Davis Bill had revealed deep differences between the president and Congress. Unlike Lincoln, many in Congress insisted that the seceders had indeed left the Union—had "committed suicide" as republican states—and had therefore forfeited all their rights. They could be readmitted only as "conquered provinces" on such conditions as Congress should decree.

The episode further revealed differences among two emerging Republican factions, moderates and radicals. The majority moderate group tended to agree with Lincoln that the seceded states should be restored to the Union as simply and swiftly as reasonable—though on Congress's terms, not the president's. The minority radical group believed that before the South could be restored its social structure should be uprooted, the haughty planters punished, and the helpless blacks protected by federal power.

Some radicals hoped that spiteful Andy Johnson, who shared their hatred for the planter aristocracy, would also share their desire to reconstruct the South with a rod of iron. But Johnson soon disillusioned them. He quickly recognized several of Lincoln's 10 percent governments, and on May 29, 1865, he issued his own Reconstruction proclamation. It disfranchised certain leading Confederates, though they might petition him for personal pardons, and called for special state conventions, which were required to repeal secession, repudiate all Confederate debts, and ratify the slave-freeing Thirteenth Amendment.

Johnson, savoring his dominance over the high-toned aristocrats who now begged his favor, granted pardons in abundance. Bolstered by the political resurrection of the planter elite, the recently rebellious states moved rapidly in the second half of 1865 to organize governments. But as the pattern of the new governments became clear, Republicans of all stripes grew furious.

The Baleful Black Codes

Among the first acts of the new southern regimes sanctioned by Johnson was the passage of the iron-toothed Black Codes. These laws were designed to regulate the affairs of the emancipated blacks, much as the slave statutes had done in pre–Civil War days. The Black Codes aimed, first of all, to ensure a stable labor supply. Severe penalties were therefore imposed on blacks who "jumped" their labor contracts, which usually committed them to work for the same employer for one year, and generally at pittance wages.

The codes also sought to restore as nearly as possible the preemancipation system of race relations. Freedom was legally recognized, as were some other privileges, such as the right to marry. But all the codes forbade blacks to serve on juries or vote, and some even barred them from renting or leasing land.

These oppressive laws mocked the ideal of freedom, so recently purchased by buckets of blood. The Black Codes imposed terrible burdens on the blacks, struggling against ignorance and poverty to make their way as free persons. Thousands of impoverished former slaves slipped into virtual peonage as sharecropper farmers, as did many landless whites.

The Black Codes made an ugly impression in the North. If the former slaves were being reenslaved, people asked one another, had not the Boys in Blue spilled their blood in vain? Had the North really won the war?

Congressional Reconstruction

These questions grew more insistent when the congressional delegations from the newly reconstituted southern states presented themselves in the Capitol in December 1865. To the shock and disgust of the Republicans, many former Confederate leaders were on hand to claim their seats.

The appearance of these ex-rebels was a natural but costly blunder. Voters of the South, seeking able representatives, had turned instinctively to their experienced statesmen. But most of the southern leaders were tainted by active association with the "lost cause." Among them were four former Confederate generals, five colonels, and various members of the Richmond cabinet and Congress. Worst of all, there was the shrimpy but brainy Alexander Stephens, ex–vice president of the Confederacy, still under indictment for treason.

The presence of these "whitewashed rebels" infuriated the Republicans in Congress. The war had been fought to restore the Union, but not on these kinds of terms. Many Republicans balked at giving up the political advantage they had enjoyed while the South had been "out" from 1861 to 1865. On the first day of the congressional session, December 4, 1865, they banged shut the door in the face of the newly elected southern delegations.

Looking to the future, the Republicans were

Principal Reconstruction Proposals and Plans

Year(s)	Proposal or Plan
1864–1865	Lincoln's 10 percent proposal
1865–1866	Johnson's version of Lincoln's proposal
1866–1867	Congressional plan: 10 percent plan with Fourteenth Amendment
1867–1877	Congressional plan of military Reconstruction: Fourteenth Amendment plus black suffrage, later established nationwide by Fifteenth Amendment

alarmed to realize that a restored South would be stronger than ever in national politics. Before the war a black slave had counted as three-fifths of a person in apportioning congressional representation, but now, owing to full counting of free blacks, the eleven rebel states were entitled to twelve more votes in Congress, and twelve more presidential electoral votes, than they had previously enjoyed. Again, angry voices in the North raised the cry: "Who won the war?"

Republicans had good reason to fear that ultimately they might be elbowed aside. Southerners might join hands with Democrats in the North and win control of Congress or maybe even the White House. If this happened, they could perpetuate the Black Codes, perhaps even formally reenslave the blacks. They could dismantle the economic program of the Republican party, and possibly even repudiate the national debt. President Johnson thus deeply provoked the congressional Republicans when he announced on December 6, 1865, that the recently rebellious states had satisfied his conditions and that in his view the Union was now restored.

Johnson Clashes with Congress

A clash between president and Congress was now inevitable. It exploded into the open in February 1866, when the president vetoed a bill (later repassed) extending the life of the controversial Freedmen's Bureau.

Aroused, the Republicans swiftly struck back. In March 1866 they passed the Civil Rights Bill, which conferred on the blacks the privileges of American citizenship and struck at the Black Codes. President Johnson resolutely vetoed this forward-looking measure, but in April congressmen steam-rollered it over his veto—something they repeatedly did henceforth. The hapless president, dubbed "Sir Veto" and "Andy Veto," had his presidential wings clipped short, as Congress assumed the dominant role in running the government.

The Republicans now undertook to rivet the principles of the Civil Rights Bill into the Constitution as the Fourteenth Amendment. The proposed amendment, as approved by Congress and sent to the states in June 1866, was sweeping. It (1) con-ferred civil rights, including citizenship but excluding the franchise, on the freedmen; (2) reduced proportionately the representation of a state in Congress and in the Electoral College if it denied the blacks the ballot; (3) disqualified from federal and state office former Confederates who as federal office-holders had once sworn to "support the Constitution of the United States"; and (4) guaranteed the federal debt, while repudiating all Confederate debts. (See text of Fourteenth Amendment in Appendix.)

The radical faction was disappointed that the Fourteenth Amendment did not grant the right to vote, but all Republicans agreed that no state should be welcomed back into the Union fold without first ratifying the Fourteenth Amendment. Yet President Johnson advised the southern states to reject it, and

An Inflexible President *This Republican cartoon shows Johnson knocking blacks out of the Freedmen's Bureau by his veto.*

all of the "sinful eleven," except Tennessee, defiantly spurned the amendment.

Swinging 'Round the Circle with Johnson

As 1866 lengthened, the battle grew between Congress and the president. Now the issue was whether Reconstruction was to be carried on with or without the drastic Fourteenth Amendment. The Republicans demanded nothing less.

The crucial congressional elections of 1866—more crucial than some presidential elections—were fast approaching. President Johnson was naturally eager to escape from the clutch of Congress by securing a majority favorable to his soft-on-the-South policy. Invited to dedicate a Chicago monument to Stephen A. Douglas, he undertook to speak at various cities en route in support of his views.

Johnson's famous "swing around the circle," beginning in the late summer of 1866, was a serio-comedy of errors. The president delivered a series of "give 'em hell" speeches, in which he accused the radicals in Congress of having planned large-scale antiblack riots and murder in the South. As he spoke, hecklers hurled insults at him. Reverting to his stump-speaking days in Tennessee, he shouted back angry retorts, amid cries of "You be damned" and "Don't get mad, Andy." The dignity of his high office sank to a new low.

As a vote getter, Johnson was highly successful—for the opposition. His inept speechmaking heightened the cry "Stand by Congress" against the "Tailor of the Potomac." When the ballots were counted, the Republicans had rolled up more than a two-thirds majority in both houses of Congress.

Republican Reconstruction

The Republicans now had a veto-proof Congress and virtually unlimited control of Reconstruction policy. But moderates and radicals still disagreed over the best course to pursue in the South.

The radicals in the Senate were led by courtly and principled Charles Sumner, and in the House by crusty and vindictive Thaddeus Stevens, both devoted not only to black freedom but to racial equality. Still opposed to rapid restoration of the southern states, the radicals wanted to keep them out as long as possible, and to apply federal power to bring about a drastic social and economic transformation in the South.

Moderate Republicans, more attuned to time-honored Republican principles of states' rights and self-government, preferred policies that restrained the states from abridging citizens' rights, rather than policies that directly involved the federal government in individual lives. The actual policies adopted by Congress showed the influence of both these schools of thought, though the moderates, as the majority faction, had the upper hand. And one thing both groups had come to agree on by 1867 was the necessity to enfranchise black voters, even if it took federal troops to do it.

Against a backdrop of vicious and bloody race riots that had erupted in several southern cities, Congress passed the Military Reconstruction Act of March 2, 1867. This drastic legislation divided the South into five military districts, each commanded by a Union general and policed by blue-clad soldiers, about 20,000 all told.

Congress additionally laid down stringent requirements for the readmission of the seceded states. The wayward states were required to ratify the Fourteenth Amendment, giving the former slaves their rights as citizens, and to guarantee in their state constitutions full suffrage for their former adult male slaves. Yet the act, reflecting moderate sentiment, stopped short of giving the freedmen land or education at federal expense. The overriding purpose of the moderates was to create an electorate in southern states that would vote those states back into the Union on acceptable terms and thus free the federal government from direct responsibility for the protection of black rights. As later events would demonstrate, this approach proved woefully inadequate to the cause of justice for the blacks.

The radical Republicans, still worried that unrepentent states, once readmitted, would amend their constitutions to withdraw the ballot from the blacks, sought the ironclad safeguard of black suffrage in the federal Constitution. This goal was finally achieved by the Fifteenth Amendment, passed by Congress in 1869 and ratified by the required number of states in 1870. (For text, see Appendix.)

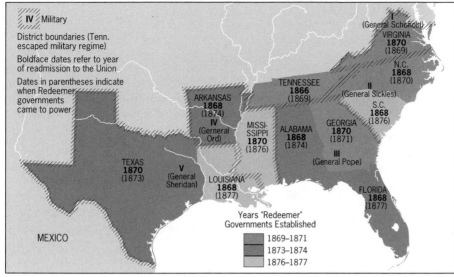

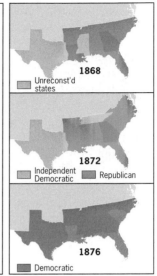

Military Reconstruction, 1867 (five districts and commanding generals)   *For many white southerners, military Reconstruction amounted to turning the knife in the wound of defeat. An often-repeated story of later years had a southerner remark, "I was sixteen years old before I discovered that* damnyankee *was two words."*

Presidential Electoral Vote by Party

Military Reconstruction of the South not only usurped certain functions of the president as commander-in-chief but set up a martial regime of dubious legality. The Supreme Court had already ruled, in the case *Ex parte Milligan* (1866), that military tribunals could not try civilians, even during wartime, in areas where the civil courts were open. Peacetime military rule seemed starkly contrary to the spirit of the Constitution, but for the time being the Supreme Court avoided giving offense to the Republican Congress.

Prodded into line by federal bayonets, the southern states got on with the task of constitution making. By 1870 all of them had reorganized their governments and had been accorded full rights. The hated "bluebellies" were withdrawn from police work only when the new regimes—usually called "radical" regimes—appeared to be firmly entrenched. Finally, in 1877, the last federal muskets were removed from state politics, and the "solid" Democratic South congealed.

The passage of the three Reconstruction Amendments—the Thirteenth, Fourteenth, and Fifteenth—delighted former abolitionists but deeply disappointed advocates of women's rights. Women had played a prominent part in the prewar abolitionist movement, and in the eyes of many women the struggle for black freedom and the crusade for women's rights were one and the same. Now, feminist leaders reeled with shock when the Fourteenth Amendment, which defined equal national citizenship, for the first time inserted the word *male* into the Constitution. When the Fifteenth Amendment proposed to prohibit denial of the vote on the basis of "race, color, or previous condition of servitude," women's rights leaders Susan B. Anthony and Elizabeth Cady Stanton wanted the word *sex* added to the list. They lost this battle, too. Fifty years would pass before the Constitution granted women the right to vote.

The Realities of Radical Reconstruction in the South

The blacks now had freedom, of a sort. By 1867 Republican hesitation over black voting had given way to a hard determination to enfranchise the former slaves wholesale and immediately, while thousands of white southerners were being denied the right to vote. By glaring contrast most of the northern states, before ratification of the Fifteenth Amendment in 1870, withheld the ballot from their tiny black minorities. White southerners naturally concluded that the Republicans were hypocritical in insisting that blacks in the South be allowed to vote.

How well did the radical regimes rule? Black voters made up a majority of the electorate in five states, but only in South Carolina did blacks predominate in the lower house of the legislature. Many of the newly elected black legislators were literate and able; more than a few came from the ranks of the prewar free blacks who had acquired considerable education. More than a dozen black congressmen and two black United States senators, Hiram Revels and Blanche K. Bruce, both of Mississippi, did creditable work in the national capital.

Yet in many southern capitals, former slaves held offices, to the bitter resentment of their one-time masters. Some untutored blacks fell under the control of white "scalawags" (southerners who collaborated in creating the new regimes) and "carpetbaggers" (northerners who had come south at war's end to seek their fortune).

In many radical regimes, graft did indeed run rampant. This was especially true in South Carolina and Louisiana, where conscienceless promoters and other pocket-padders used politically inexperienced blacks as cat's-paws. The worst "black-and-white" legislatures purchased, as "legislative supplies," such "stationery" as hams, perfumes, suspenders, bonnets, corsets, champagne, and a coffin. Yet this kind of corruption was no more outrageous than the scams and felonies being perpetrated in the North at the same time, especially in Boss Tweed's New York.

The radical legislatures also passed much desirable legislation. For the first time in southern history, steps were taken toward establishing adequate public schools. Tax systems were streamlined; public works were launched; and property rights were guaranteed to women. Many of these reforms were so welcome that they were retained by the all-white "redeemer" governments that later returned to power.

The Ku Klux Klan

Deeply embittered, some southern whites resorted to savage measures against "radical rule." Many whites resented the success and ability of black legislators as much as they resented alleged corruption. A number of secret organizations mushroomed forth, the most notorious of which was the "Invisible Empire of the South," or Ku Klux Klan, founded in Tennessee in 1866. Besheeted night riders, their horses' hoofs muffled, would approach the cabin of an "upstart" black and hammer on the door. In ghoulish tones one thirsty horseman would demand a bucket of water. Then, under pretense of drinking, he would pour the whole bucket into a rubber attachment concealed beneath his mask and gown, smack his lips, and declare that this was the first water he had

Persons in United States Lynched [by race], 1882–1970*

Year	Whites	Blacks	Totals
1882	64	49	113
1885	110	74	184
1890	11	85	96
1895	66	113	179
1900	9	106	115
1905	5	57	62
1910	9	67	76
1915	13	56	69
1920	8	53	61
1925	0	17	17
1930	1	20	21
1935	2	18	20
1940	1	4	5
1945	0	1	1
1950	1	1	2
1965	0	0	0

* There were no lynchings in 1965–1970. In every year from 1882 (when records were first kept) to 1964, the number of lynchings corresponded roughly to the figures here given. The worst year was 1892, when 161 blacks and 69 whites were lynched (total 230); the next worst was 1884, when 160 whites and 51 blacks were lynched (total 211).

tasted since he was killed at the Battle of Shiloh. If fright did not produce the desired effect of intimidating black voters, force was employed.

Such tomfoolery and terror proved partially effective. Many ex-bondsmen and white carpetbaggers, quick to take a hint, shunned the polls. Those stubborn souls who persisted in their "upstart" ways were flogged, mutilated, or even murdered.

Congress, outraged by this night-riding lawlessness, passed the harsh Force Acts of 1870 and 1871. Federal troops were able to stamp out much of the "lash law," but by this time the Invisible Empire had already done its work of intimidation.

Attempts to empower the blacks politically failed miserably. The white South, for many decades, openly flouted the Fourteenth and Fifteenth Amendments. Wholesale disfranchisement of the blacks, starting conspicuously about 1890, was achieved by intimidation, fraud, and trickery. Among various underhanded schemes were the literacy tests, unfairly administered by whites to the advantage of illiterate whites. In the eyes of white southerners, the goal of white supremacy fully justified dishonorable devices.

Johnson Walks the Impeachment Plank

Radicals meanwhile had been sharpening their hatchets for President Johnson. Not content with curbing his authority, they decided to remove him altogether by constitutional processes.*

As an initial step, Congress in 1867 passed the Tenure of Office Act—as usual over Johnson's veto. Contrary to precedent, the new law required the president to secure the consent of the Senate before he could remove his appointees, once they had been approved by that body. One purpose was to freeze into the cabinet the secretary of war, Edwin M. Stanton, a holdover from the Lincoln administration. Although outwardly loyal to Johnson, he was secretly serving as a spy and informer for the radicals.

Another purpose was to goad Johnson into breaking the law, and thus establish grounds for his impeachment. An aroused Johnson, eager to get a test case before the Supreme Court, abruptly dismissed the two-faced Stanton early in 1868.

A radical-influenced House of Representatives struck back swiftly. By a count of 126 to 47, it voted to impeach Andrew Johnson for "high crimes and misdemeanors," as called for by the Constitution. Most of the specific accusations grew out of the president's so-called violation of the ("unconstitutional") Tenure of Office Act. Two additional articles related to Johnson's verbal assaults on the Congress, involving "disgrace, ridicule, hatred, contempt, and reproach."

A Not Guilty Verdict for Johnson

With evident zeal, the radical-led Senate now sat as a court to try Johnson on the dubious impeachment charges. The House conducted the prosecution. The trial aroused intense public interest and, with 1,000 tickets printed, proved to be the biggest show of 1868. Johnson kept his dignity and sobriety and maintained a discreet silence. His battery of attorneys was extremely able, whereas the House prosecutors, including oily-tongued Benjamin F. Butler and embittered Thaddeus Stevens, bungled their case.

On May 16, 1868, the day for the first voting in the Senate, the tension was electric, and heavy breathing could be heard in the galleries. By a margin of only one vote, the radicals failed to muster the two-thirds majority for Johnson's removal.

The radicals were infuriated. "The country is going to the Devil!" cried the crippled Stevens as he was carried from the hall. But the nation, though violently aroused, accepted the verdict with a good temper that did credit to its political maturity. In a less stable republic, an armed uprising might have erupted against the president.

The nation thus narrowly avoided a bad precedent that would have gravely weakened one of the three branches of the federal government. Johnson was clearly guilty of bad speeches, bad judgment, and bad temper, but not of high crimes and misde-

---

* For impeachment, see Art. I, Sec. II, para. 5; Art. I, Sec. II, paras. 6, 7; Art. II, Sec. IV, in Appendix.

meanors. From the standpoint of the radicals, his greatest crime had been to stand inflexibly in their path.

The Purchase of Alaska

Johnson's administration, though largely reduced to a figurehead, achieved its most enduring success in the field of foreign relations.

The Russians by 1867 were in a mood to sell the vast and chilly expanse now known as Alaska. The region had been ruthlessly "furred out" and was a growing economic liability. The Russians were therefore eager to unload their "frozen asset" on the Americans, primarily because they wanted to strengthen further the republic as a barrier against their ancient enemy, Britain.

In 1867 Secretary of State Seward, an ardent expansionist, signed a treaty with Russia that transferred Alaska to the United States for the bargain price of $7.2 million. But Seward's enthusiasm for these frigid lands was not shared by his ignorant or uninformed countrymen, who jeered at "Seward's Folly," "Seward's Icebox," "Frigidia," and "Walrussia." The American people, still preoccupied with Reconstruction and other internal vexations, were economy minded and antiexpansionist.

Then why did Congress and the American public sanction the purchase? For one thing Russia, alone among the powers, had been conspicuously friendly to the North during the recent Civil War. Americans did not feel that they could offend their great and good friend, the tsar, by hurling his walrus-covered icebergs back into his face. Besides, the territory was rumored to be teeming with furs, fish, and gold, and it might yet "pan out" profitably—as it later did, with natural resources, including oil and gas.

The Heritage of Reconstruction

Many white southerners regarded Reconstruction as a more grievous wound than the war itself. It left an angry scar that would take generations to heal. They resented the upending of their social and racial system, the humiliation of being ruled by blacks, and

the insult of federal intervention in their local affairs. Yet given the explosiveness of the issues that had caused the war, and the bitterness of the fighting, the wonder is that Reconstruction was not far harsher than it was. Northern policy makers groped for the right policies, influenced as much by southern responses to defeat and emancipation as by any specific plans of their own.

CHRONOLOGY

1863	Lincoln announces 10 percent Reconstruction plan.
1864	Lincoln vetoes Wade-Davis Bill.
1865	Johnson proclaims presidential Reconstruction.
	Congress refuses to seat southern congressmen.
	Freedmen's Bureau established.
	Southern states pass Black Codes.
1866	Congress passes Civil Rights Bill over Johnson's veto.
	Congress passes Fourteenth Amendment.
	Johnson-backed candidates lose congressional election.
	Ex parte Milligan case.
	Ku Klux Klan founded.
1867	Military Reconstruction Act.
	Tenure of Office Act.
	United States purchases Alaska from Russia.
1868	Johnson impeached and acquitted.
	Johnson pardons Confederate leaders.
1870	Fifteenth Amendment ratified.
1870–1871	Force Acts.
1872	Freedmen's Bureau ended.
1877	Military Reconstruction ends.

The Republicans acted from a mixture of idealism and political expediency. They wanted both to protect the freed slaves and to promote the fortunes of the Republican party. In the end their efforts backfired badly. Republican Reconstruction conferred only fleeting benefits on the blacks, envenomed the whites, and virtually extinguished the Republican party in the South for nearly 100 years.

In the light of hindsight, the Republican Reconstruction program seems too narrowly conceived. Moderate Republicans in particular never appreciated the efforts necessary to make the freed slaves completely independent citizens, or the lengths to which southern whites would go to preserve their system of racial dominance. Had Thaddeus Stevens's radical program of drastic economic reforms and heftier protection of political rights been enacted, things might well have been different. But ingrained American resistance to tampering with property rights and violating the principle of local self-government, combined with spreading indifference in the North to the plight of the blacks, formed too formidable an obstacle.

Varying Viewpoints

Few topics have triggered as much intellectual warfare as the "dark and bloody ground" of Reconstruction. The period provoked questions—sectional, racial, and constitutional—about which people felt deeply and remain deeply divided even today. Scholarly argument goes back to the early years of the twentieth century, when historian William A. Dunning and his students wrote about Reconstruction as a kind of national disgrace, foisted upon a prostrate South by vindictive, self-seeking radical Republican politicians.

A second cycle of scholarship in the 1920s was impelled by widespread suspicion that the Civil War itself had been a tragic and unnecessary blunder. Scholars such as Howard Beale questioned the motives of northern politicians. The radical Republicans' false concern for the slaves, Beale and others believed, masked their real desire to exploit southern labor and ensure a Republican political presence in the defeated South.

After World War II, Kenneth Stampp, among others, turned this view on its head. Influenced by the modern civil rights movement, he argued that Reconstruction had been a noble attempt to extend American principles of equity and justice. By the early 1970s the view that the radical Republicans and carpetbaggers were heroes had become orthodoxy, and it generally holds sway today. Yet some scholars, such as Michael Benedict and Leon Litwack, disillusioned with the inability to achieve full racial justice in the 1960s, began once more to scrutinize the motives of northern politicians immediately after the Civil War and to claim that Reconstruction had never been very radical.

More recently, Eric Foner has powerfully reasserted the argument that Reconstruction was a truly radical and praiseworthy attempt to establish an interracial democracy. Drawing on the work of black scholar W. E. B. Du Bois, Foner compared American Reconstruction to South Africa, the Caribbean, and other areas once marked by slavery. Even if Reconstruction did not achieve full equality, Foner has contended, it did allow blacks to form political organizations and churches, to vote, and to establish some measure of economic independence. Many of the benefits were taken away during the Gilded Age, but the constitutional principles and organizations developed during Reconstruction provided the foundation for the modern civil rights movement, which some have called the Second Reconstruction.

SELECT READINGS

Primary Source Documents

Booker T. Washington's classic autobiography *Up from Slavery** (1901) records one freedman's experiences. Contemporary comments on the process of Reconstruction include the laments of editor Edwin L. Godkin, *The Nation* (December 7, 1871, p. 364),* and Frederick Douglass, *Life and Times of Frederick Douglass** (1882), as well as the debates in the *Congressional Globe* (1867–1868)* between radicals like Thaddeus Stevens and moderates like Lyman Trumbull.

Secondary Sources

Eric Foner, *Reconstruction: America's Unfinished Revolution, 1863–1877* (1988), is a superb synthesis of current scholarship. Overall accounts may be found in James G. Randall and David Donald, *The Civil War and Reconstruction* (rev. ed., 1969), and James McPherson, *Ordeal by Fire: The Civil War and Reconstruction* (1981), perhaps the best brief introduction. Lincoln's early efforts at Reconstruction are handled in Peyton McCrary, *Abraham Lincoln and Reconstruction* (1978). Following up the story of national politics is Eric L. McKitrick, *Andrew Johnson and Reconstruction: Principle and Prejudice, 1865–1866* (1963). Sympathetic to the radical Republicans are James M. McPherson, *The Struggle for Equality* (1964), and Hans L. Trefousse, *The Radical Republicans* (1969). See also David

Montgomery, *Beyond Equality: Labor and the Radical Republicans, 1862–1872* (1967). Conditions in the South are analyzed in W. E. B. Du Bois's controversial classic *Black Reconstruction* (1935) and in Leon F. Litwack's brilliantly evocative *Been in the Storm So Long* (1979), a revealing study of the initial responses, by both blacks and whites, to emancipation. Race relations are the subject of Joel Williamson, *The Crucible of Race* (1984). Consult also Thomas Holt, *Black over White: Negro Political Leadership in South Carolina During Reconstruction* (1977). C. Vann Woodward's *The Strange Career of Jim Crow* (rev. ed., 1974) is a classic study of the origins of segregation. His views drew criticism in Harold O. Rabinowitz, *Race Relations in the Urban South, 1865–1890* (1977). Richard N. Current rehabilitates the maligned carpetbaggers in *Those Terrible Carpetbaggers* (1988). Fresh scholarship is presented in Kenneth M. Stampp and Leon Litwack, eds., *Reconstruction: An Anthology of Revisionist Writings* (1969). Eric Foner looks at emancipation in comparative perspective in *Nothing But Freedom* (1983). A comprehensive study of the climax of this troubled period is William Gillette, *Retreat from Reconstruction, 1869–1879* (1979). Also see Michael Perman, *The Road to Redemption: Southern Politics, 1869–1879* (1984).

CHAPTER 25

Politics in the Gilded Age, 1869–1896

Grant . . . had no right to exist. He should have been extinct for ages. . . . That, two thousand years after Alexander the Great and Julius Caesar, a man like Grant should be called—and should actually and truly be—the highest product of the most advanced evolution, made evolution ludicrous. . . . The progress of evolution, from President Washington to President Grant, was alone evidence enough to upset Darwin. . . . Grant . . . should have lived in a cave and worn skins.

Henry Adams, *The Education of Henry Adams,* 1907

The "Bloody Shirt" Elects Grant

Disillusionment ran deep among idealistic Americans in the era after the Civil War. They had spilled their blood for Union, emancipation, and Abraham Lincoln, who had promised "a new birth of freedom." Instead, they got a bitter dose of corruption, petty politics, and Ulysses S. Grant, a great soldier but an inept politician.

Wrangling between Congress and Andrew Johnson had soured the people on professional politicians, and the notion still prevailed that a good general was bound to make a good president. Stubbly bearded General Grant, with his slightly stooped body measuring a shade over 5 feet 8 inches, was by far the most popular northern hero to emerge from the war. Unfortunately, this hard-riding soldier was a greenhorn in the political arena. He had almost no political experience, and his one presidential vote had been cast for the Democratic ticket in 1856.

The Republicans, now freed from the Union party coalition of war days, enthusiastically nomi-

nated Grant for the presidency in 1868. The party's platform sounded a clarion call for continued Reconstruction of the South under the glinting steel of federal bayonets.

Expectant Democrats, meeting in their own nominating convention, denounced military Reconstruction but could agree on little else. Wealthy eastern delegates demanded that federal war bonds be redeemed in gold, while the poorer midwesterners backed the "Ohio Idea" calling for redemption in greenbacks. Agrarian Democrats thus hoped to make loans less costly by keeping more money in circulation.

Midwestern delegates got the progreenback platform but not the candidate. The nominee, former New York governor Horatio Seymour, sank the Democrats' scant hopes for success by repudiating the Ohio Idea plank. Republicans whipped up enthusiasm for Grant by energetically "waving the bloody shirt"—that is, reviving gory memories of the

337

Civil War—which became for the first time a prominent feature of a presidential campaign. "Vote as you shot" was a powerful Republican slogan aimed at Union army veterans.

Grant won, with 214 electoral votes to 80 for Seymour. But despite his great popularity, the former general scored a majority of only 300,000 in the popular vote (3,013,421 to 2,706,829). Most white voters apparently supported Seymour, and the ballots of three still-unreconstructed southern states (Mississippi, Texas, and Virginia) were not counted. An estimated 500,000 former slaves gave Grant his margin of victory. To remain in power, the Republican party had to continue to control the South—and to keep the ballot in the hands of the grateful freedmen. Republicans could not take future victories "for Granted."

The Era of Good Stealings

The population of the republic continued to vault upward by vigorous leaps, despite the awful bloodletting of the Civil War. Census takers reported over 39 million people in 1870, a gain of 26.6 percent over the previous decade, as the immigrant tide surged again. The United States was now the third-largest nation of the Western world, ranking behind Russia and France.

But the moral stature of the republic fell regrettably short of its physical stature. The war and its aftermath bred waste, extravagance, speculation, and graft. The whole atmosphere was fetid. The Man in the Moon, it was said, had to hold his nose when passing over America. Railroad promoters sometimes left gullible bond buyers with only "two streaks of rust and a right of way." Unscrupulous stock-market manipulators were a cinder in the public eye. Too many judges and legislators put their power up for hire. Cynics defined an honest politician as one who, when bought, would stay bought.

Notorious in the financial world were two millionaires, "Jubilee Jim" Fisk and Jay Gould. This crafty pair concocted a plot in 1869 to corner the gold market. Their slippery game would work only if the federal Treasury refrained from selling gold. The conspirators worked on President Grant directly,

Boss Tweed Manipulates Ballots *Another Nast cartoon had Tweed ask, "As long as I count the votes, what are you going to do about it?"*

and also through his brother-in-law, who received $25,000 for his complicity. On "Black Friday" (September 24, 1869), Fisk and Gould madly bid the price of gold skyward, while scores of honest businesspeople were driven against a wall. The bubble finally broke when the Treasury, contrary to Grant's supposed assurances, was compelled to release gold. A congressional probe concluded that Grant had done nothing crooked, though he had acted stupidly and indiscreetly.

The infamous Tweed Ring in New York City vividly displayed the ethics (or lack of ethics) typical of the age. Burly "Boss" Tweed—240 pounds of rascality—employed bribery, graft, and fraudulent elections to milk the metropolis of as much as $200 million.

Tweed's luck finally ran out. The *New York Times* secured damning evidence in 1871 and courageously published it, though offered $5 million not to do so. Gifted cartoonist Thomas Nast pilloried Tweed mercilessly, after spurning a heavy bribe to desist. A New York attorney, Samuel J. Tilden, headed the prosecution and gained fame that later paved the path to his presidential nomination. Unbailed and unwept, Tweed died behind bars.

A Carnival of Corruption

More serious than Boss Tweed's sticky fingers was the corrupt atmosphere in the federal government. President Grant's cabinet was a nest of grafters and incompetents, and favor seekers even haunted the White House, plying Grant himself with cigars, wine, and horses.

The easy-going Grant was first tarred by the Crédit Mobilier scandal. Union Pacific Railway insiders had formed the Crédit Mobilier construction company and then cleverly hired themselves at inflated prices to build rail lines, thereby earning dividends of 348 percent in one year. Fearing that Congress might blow the whistle, the company furtively distributed shares of its valuable stock to key congressmen. A newspaper exposé and congressional investigation of the scandal in 1872 led to the censure of two congressmen and the revelation that the vice president of the United States had accepted Crédit Mobilier stock and dividends.

The breath of scandal in Washington also reeked of alcohol. A sprawling Whiskey Ring robbed the Treasury of millions in excise tax revenues, and when President Grant's private secretary turned up among the culprits, the president volunteered a written statement to the jury that helped the thief escape. Further rottenness in the Grant administration turned up in 1876, when Secretary of War Belknap resigned after impeachment by the House for pocketing bribes from Indian suppliers. Grant, ever loyal to his crooked cronies, accepted Belknap's resignation "with great regret."

The Liberal Republican Revolt of 1872

By 1872 a powerful wave of disgust with Grantism was beginning to build up throughout the nation, even before some of the worst scandals had been exposed. Reform-minded citizens banded together in the Liberal Republican party. Voicing the slogan "Turn the rascals out," they urged purification of the Grant administration and an end to military Reconstruction.

The Liberal Republicans muffed their chance when their Cincinnati nominating convention astounded the country by nominating the brilliant but erratic Horace Greeley for the presidency. Although Greeley was a fearless editor of the *New York Tribune,* he was dogmatic, emotional, petulant, and notoriously unsound in his political judgments.

More astonishing still was the action of the office-hungry Democrats, who endorsed Greeley's candidacy. In swallowing Greeley the Democrats ate crow in large gulps, for the eccentric editor had long blasted them as traitors, slave whippers, saloon keepers, horse thieves, and idiots. Yet Greeley pleased the Democrats, North and South, when he pleaded for a clasping of hands across "the bloody chasm." The Republicans dutifully renominated Grant, and the voters were thus presented with a choice between two candidates who had made their careers in fields other than politics and who were both eminently unqualified, by temperament and lifelong training, for high political office. In the mud-spattered campaign, Greeley was denounced as an atheist, a free-lover, and a vegetarian, while Democrats derided Grant as a drunken swindler. But the regular Republicans, chanting "Grant us another term," pulled the president through. The count in the electoral column was 286 to 66, in the popular column 3,596,745 to 2,843,446.

Liberal Republican agitation frightened the regular Republicans into cleaning their own house before they were thrown out of it. The Republican Congress in 1872 passed a general amnesty act, removing political disabilities from all but some 500 former Confederate leaders. Congress also moved to reduce high Civil War tariffs and to fumigate the Grant administration with mild civil service reform. Like many American third parties, the Liberal Republicans left some enduring footprints, even in defeat.

Depression and Demands for Inflation

The evil repute of the scandal-scarred Grant years was worsened by the paralyzing panic that broke in 1873. Bursting with startling rapidity, the crash was one of those periodic plummets that roller-coastered the economy in this age of unbridled capitalist expansion. Boom times became gloom times as more than 15,000 businesses went bankrupt; and in New York City an army of unemployed riotously battled the police.

Hard times were especially distressing to debtors, who began to clamor for inflationary policies. Proponents of inflation breathed new life into the issue of greenbacks. During the war $450 million of the folding money had been issued, but it had depreciated under a cloud of popular mistrust and dubious legality.* By 1868 the Treasury had already withdrawn $100 million of the "battle-born currency" from circulation, and "hard money" people everywhere looked forward to its complete disappearance. But now afflicted agrarian and debtor groups—"cheap money" supporters—clamored for a reissuance of the greenbacks. They reasoned that

more money meant cheaper money and, hence, rising prices and easier-to-pay debts. Creditors, of course, reasoning from the same premises, advocated precisely the opposite policy.

The hard money advocates carried the day in 1874 when they persuaded the confused Grant to veto a bill to print more paper money. They scored another victory in the Resumption Act of 1875, which pledged the government to the further withdrawal of greenbacks from circulation, and to the redemption of all paper currency in gold at face value, beginning in 1879.

Down but not out, debtors now looked for relief to another precious metal, silver. The "sacred white metal," they claimed, had received a raw deal. In the early 1870s, the Treasury stubbornly and unrealistically maintained that an ounce of silver was worth only 1/16 as much as an ounce of gold, though open-market prices for silver were higher. Silver miners thus stopped offering their shiny product for sale to the federal mints. With no silver flowing into the federal coffers, Congress formally dropped the coinage of silver dollars in 1873. Fate then played a sly joke when new silver discoveries later in the 1870s shot production up and forced silver prices down. Westerners from silver-mining states joined with debtors in assailing the "Crime of '73," demanding a return to the "Dollar of our daddies." This demand, like the demand for more greenbacks, was essentially a call for inflation.

Republicans resisted this call and counted on Grant to hold the line against it. The Treasury began to accumulate gold stocks against the appointed day for resumption of metallic-money payments. Coupled with the reduction of greenbacks, this policy was called "contraction." It had a noticeable deflationary effect—the amount of money per capita in circulation actually *decreased* between 1870 and 1880, from $19.42 to $19.37. Contraction probably worsened the impact of the depression. But the new policy did restore the government's credit rating, and it brought the embattled greenbacks up to their full face value. When Redemption Day came in 1879, few greenback holders bothered to exchange the lighter and more convenient bills for gold.

The fate of silver disappointed the friends of easy money. "Soft money" advocates demanded the

---

* The Supreme Court in 1870 declared the Civil War Legal Tender Act unconstitutional. With the concurrence of the Senate, Grant thereupon added to the bench two justices who could be counted on to help reverse that decision, which happened in 1871. This is how the Court grew to its current size of nine justices.

unlimited coinage of all silver mined at the old value-ratio of 16 to 1. "Sound money" champions scornfully rejected the coinage of any silver at all. A compromise was struck with the Bland-Allison Act of 1878, which instructed the Treasury to buy and coin between $2 and $4 million worth of silver bullion each month. But the government dampened the hopes of inflationists when it stuck to a policy of buying only the legal minimum.

Republican hard money policy had a political backlash. It helped elect a Democratic House of Representatives in 1874, and in 1878 it spawned a Greenback Labor Party that polled over a million votes and elected fourteen members of Congress.

Pallid Politics in the Gilded Age

The political see-saw was delicately balanced throughout most of the Gilded Age (a sarcastic name given to the post–Civil War era by Mark Twain in 1873). Even a slight nudge could tip the teeter-totter to the advantage of the opposition party. Every presidential election was a squeaker, and the majority party in the House of Representatives switched six times in the eleven sessions between 1869 and 1891. Wobbling in such shaky equilibrium, politicians tiptoed timidly, producing a political record that was often trivial and petty.

Few significant economic issues separated the major parties. Democrats and Republicans saw very nearly eye-to-eye on major questions such as the tariff, currency, and civil-service reform. Yet despite their rough agreement on these national matters, the two parties were ferociously competitive with each other. They were tightly and efficiently organized, and they commanded fierce loyalty from their partisans. Voter turnouts reached heights of nearly 80 percent in the three decades after the Civil War, a figure unmatched before or since. On election day, droves of the party faithful tramped behind marching bands to the polling places, and "ticket splitting," or failing to vote the straight party line, was as rare as a silver dollar.

How can this apparent paradox of political consensus and partisan fervor be explained? The answer lies in the sharp ethnic and cultural differences in the membership of the two parties—in distinctions of style and tone, and especially of religious sentiment. Republican voters tended to adhere to those creeds that traced their lineage to Puritanism. They stressed strict codes of personal morality and believed that government should play a role in regulating both the economic and the moral affairs of the community as a whole. Democrats, among whom immigrant Lutherans and Roman Catholics figured heavily, were likely to adhere to faiths that took a less stern view of human weakness. Their religions professed toleration of differences in an imperfect world, and they spurned government efforts to impose a single moral standard on the entire society. These differences in temperament and religious values often produced raucous political contests at the local level, where issues such as prohibition and education loomed large.

Democrats had a solid electoral base in the South and in the northern industrial cities, which were packed with immigrants and controlled by well-oiled political machines. Republicans could usually count on winning the Midwest and the rural and small-town Northeast. Grateful freedmen in the South contributed significant numbers of votes to the Republicans. Another important bloc of Republican ballots came from the members of the Grand Army of the Republic (GAR)—a politically potent fraternal organization of several hundred thousand Union veterans of the Civil War. The lifeblood of both parties was patronage—disbursing jobs by the bucketful in return for votes, kickbacks, and party service.

Boisterous infighting beset the Republican party in the 1870s and 1880s. A "Stalwart" faction, led by handsome and imperious Senator Roscoe ("Lord Roscoe") Conkling of New York, unblushingly embraced the time-honored system of swapping civil service jobs for votes. Opposed to the Conklingites were the so-called Half-Breeds, who flirted coyly with civil service reform, but whose real quarrel with the Stalwarts was over who should grasp the ladle that dished out the spoils. The champion of the Half-Breeds was James G. Blaine, a radiantly personable congressman from Maine with a fine physical presence, a thrilling speaking voice, and an elastic conscience. A perennial contender for the presidency, Blaine was inclined to demagoguery in his pursuit of the office. But despite all the color of their personalities, Conkling and Blaine succeeded only in stalemating each other and deadlocking their party.

The Hayes-Tilden Standoff, 1876

Hangers-on around Grant, like fleas urging their ailing dog to live, begged the "Old Man" to try for a third term in 1876. The general, blind to his own ineptitudes, showed a disquieting willingness. But the House, by a lopsided bipartisan vote of 233 to 18, spiked the third-term boom. It passed a resolution that sternly reminded the country—and Grant—of the antidictator implications of the two-term tradition.

With Grant out of the running, and with the Conklingites and Blaineites checkmating each other, the Republicans turned to a compromise candidate, Rutherford B. Hayes, who was obscure enough to be dubbed "the Great Unknown." His foremost qualification was the fact that he hailed from the electorally doubtful but potent state of Ohio, where he had served three terms as governor. So crucial were the "swing" votes of Ohio in the cliff-hanging presidential contests of the day that the state produced more

than its share of presidential candidates. A political saying of the 1870s went:

> Some are born great,
> Some achieve greatness
> And some are born in Ohio.

Pitted against the humdrum Hayes was the Democratic nominee Samuel J. Tilden, who had risen to fame as the man who bagged Boss Tweed in New York. Campaigning against Republican scandal and for sweeping civil service reform, Tilden racked up 184 electoral votes of the needed 185, with 20 votes in four states doubtful because of irregular returns. Surely Tilden could pick up at least one of these, especially in view of the fact that he had polled 247,448 more popular votes than Hayes, 4,284,020 to 4,036,572.

Both parties scurried to send "visiting statesmen" to the contested southern states of Louisiana, South Carolina, and Florida. All three disputed states submitted two sets of returns, one Democratic and one Republican. As the weeks drifted by, the paralysis tightened. Here were the makings of an epochal constitutional crisis. The Constitution merely specifies that the electoral returns from the states shall be sent to Congress, and in the presence

Hayes-Tilden Disputed Election of 1876 (with electoral vote by state) *Nineteen of the twenty disputed votes composed the total electoral count of Louisiana, South Carolina, and Florida. The twentieth was one of Oregon's three votes, cast by an elector who turned out to be ineligible because he was a federal officeholder (a postmaster), contrary to the Constitution (see Art. II, Sec. I, para. 2).*

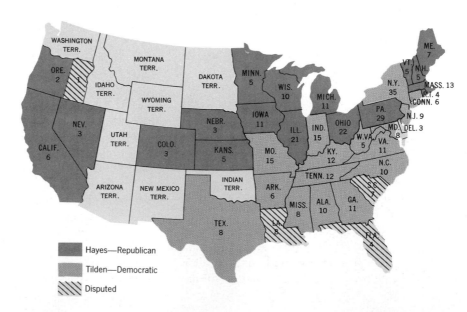

Hayes—Republican
Tilden—Democratic
Disputed

of the House and Senate they shall be *opened* by the president of the Senate (see the Twelfth Amendment). But who should *count* them? On this point the Constitution was silent. If counted by the president of the Senate (a Republican), Republican returns would be selected. If counted by the Speaker of the House (a Democrat), the Democratic returns would be chosen.

The Compromise of 1877 and the End of Reconstruction

Clash or compromise was the stark choice. The danger loomed that there would be no president on Inauguration Day, March 4, 1877. "Tilden or Blood!" cried Democratic hotheads, and some of their "Minute Men" began to drill with arms. But behind the scenes frantically laboring statesmen gradually hammered out an agreement in the Henry Clay tradition—the Compromise of 1877.

The election deadlock itself was to be broken by the Electoral Count Act, which passed Congress early in 1877. It set up an electoral commission consisting of fifteen men selected from the Senate, the House, and the Supreme Court.

In February 1877, about a month before inauguration day, the Senate and House met together in an electric atmosphere to settle the dispute. The roll of the states was tolled off alphabetically. When Florida was reached—the first of the three southern states with two sets of returns—the disputed documents were referred to the electoral commission, which sat in a nearby chamber. After prolonged discussion the members agreed, by the partisan vote of eight Republicans to seven Democrats, to accept the Republican returns. Outraged Democrats in Congress, smelling defeat, undertook to launch a filibuster "until hell froze over."

Renewed deadlock was avoided by the rest of the complex Compromise of 1877, already partially concluded behind closed doors. The Democrats reluctantly agreed that Hays might take office in return for his withdrawing intimidating federal troops from the two states in which they remained, Louisiana and South Carolina. Among various concessions, the Republicans assured the Democrats a place at the presidential patronage trough and support for a bill subsidizing the Texas and Pacific Rail-road's construction of a southern transcontinental line. Not all of these promises were kept in later years, including the Texas and Pacific subsidy. But the deal held together long enough to break the dangerous electoral standoff.

The compromise bought peace at a price. Violence was averted by sacrificing the black freedmen in the South. With the Hayes-Tilden deal, the Republican party quietly abandoned its commitment to black equality. That commitment had been weakening, in any case. The Civil Rights Act of 1875 was in a sense the last feeble gasp of the congressional radical Republicans. The act supposedly guaranteed equal accommodations in public places and prohibited racial discrimination in jury selection, but the law was born toothless and stayed that way for nearly a century. The Supreme Court pronounced much of the act unconstitutional in the *Civil Rights Cases* (1883), declaring that the Fourteenth Amendment prohibited only *government* violations of civil rights, not the denial of civil rights by *individuals.*

Hayes clinched the bargain by withdrawing the last federal troops that were propping up carpetbag governments, and the bayonet-backed Republican regimes collapsed as the blue-clad soldiers departed.

The Democratic South speedily solidified and swiftly suppressed the now friendless blacks. For generations to come, southern blacks were condemned to eke out a threadbare living under conditions scarcely better than slavery. They were segregated in woefully inferior schools, denied the ballot by fraud and intimidation, and legally separated from whites in virtually all public facilities, including railroad cars and even restrooms.

The Supreme Court validated the South's strictly segregationist social order in the case of *Plessy v. Ferguson* (1896). It ruled that "separate but equal" facilities were constitutional under the "equal protection" clause of the Fourteenth Amendment. But in reality the quality of African-American life was grotesquely unequal to that of whites. It would take a second Reconstruction, nearly a century later, to redress the racist imbalance of southern society.

Labor Troubles and Chinese Immigration

Rutherford ("Rutherfraud") B. Hayes's title to the presidency was clouded by the dubious election deal

The Chinese

In the late nineteenth century the burgeoning industries and booming frontier towns of the United States' Pacific Coast hungered for laborers. In faraway Asia the Chinese answered the call. Contributing their muscle to the building of the West, they dug in the gold mines and helped to lay the transcontinental railroads that stitched together the American nation.

The first wave of Chinese came in response to the discovery of gold in California in 1848. The fortune-hungry immigrants who sailed into San Francisco named the city the "golden mountain."

The California boom coincided with the culmination of years of tumult and suffering in China. As the once great Chinese empire disintegrated, European imperial powers forced their way into the unstable country. Faced with economic hardship and political turmoil, more than 2 million Chinese left their homeland between 1840 and 1900 for destinations as diverse as Southeast Asia, Peru, Hawaii, and Cuba, with more than 300,000 entering the United States. Although their number included a few merchants and artisans, most were unskilled country folk.

The Chinese America of the late-nineteenth-century West was overwhelmingly a bachelor society. Women of good repute rarely made the passage. Of the very few Chinese women who did venture to California at this time, most became prostitutes.

Although a stream of workers returned to China, many Chinese stayed. "Chinatowns" sprang

Central Pacific Railroad Workers in the 1860s

up wherever economic opportunities presented themselves. Chinese in these settlements spoke their own language, enjoyed the fellowship of their own compatriots, and sought safety from prejudice and violence. Many immigrant clubs and associations were American adaptations of the Chinese tradition of loyalty to clan. The poorest and most alienated individuals also established *tongs*—literally, "meeting halls"—secret societies that acquired a sinister reputation among non-Chinese.

After 1882 the Chinese Exclusion Act barred nearly all Chinese from the United States for six decades. Many of the bachelors died or returned home. Slowly, however, those men and the few women who remained raised families and reared a new generation of Chinese-Americans. Like their immigrant parents, this second generation suffered from discrimination. They had to eke out a living in jobs despised by Caucasian laborers or take daunting risks in small entrepreneurial ventures. Yet many hard-working Chinese did manage to open their own restaurants, laundries, and other small businesses. These enterprises formed a solid economic foundation for their small community and remain a source of livelihood for many Chinese-Americans even today.

that brought him to office. His term was also marred by turbulent labor disturbances that rumbled throughout the country. The explosive atmosphere was largely a by-product of the long years of depression and deflation following the panic of 1873. Mass disorders convulsed a number of major eastern cities in 1877. The paralyzing railroad strikes of that year, which verged on civil war in places like Baltimore and Pittsburgh, forced Hayes to call out federal troops. Order was restored only after scores of rioters had been killed or injured.

Economic unrest swept to California and included hard-working Chinese laborers among its victims. (see "Makers of America: The Chinese," pp. 344–345). By 1880 the Golden State counted 75,000 of these Asian newcomers, about 9 percent of its entire population. Mostly poor, uneducated males from southern China, they had originally come to America to dig in the gold fields and to sledge-hammer the tracks of the transcontinental railroads across the West. Perhaps half of those who arrived before the 1880s eventually returned home, but those who remained in America faced extraordinary hardships. They worked at the most menial jobs, often as cooks, laundrymen, or domestic servants. Without women or families, they lived lonely lives, bereft of the children who in other communities eased their parents' assimilation into the United States through their exposure to the English language and American customs in school.

In San Francisco, Irish-born demagogue Denis Kearney incited his followers, many of them recently arrived European immigrants, to violent abuse of the hapless Chinese. Taking to the streets, gangs of Kearneyites terrorized the Asians by shear-ing off precious pigtails. Some victims were murdered outright.

Congress finally responded to all this uproar in 1879, when it passed a bill severely restricting the influx of Chinese immigrants. But Hayes, ever the man of honor, vetoed this discriminatory measure on the grounds that it violated the existing treaty with China. Angry Californians burned the president in effigy. Once the scrupulous Hayes was out of the way, in 1882, Congress slammed the door on Chinese laborers with the enactment of the Chinese Exclusion Act, and the door stayed closed until 1943.

Hayes accomplished little that was lasting—except writing "finished" to Reconstruction. His legislative record was negligible, and his political record was a disaster. As the presidential campaign of 1880 approached, Hayes was a man without a party. Denounced as "Granny" Hayes and a "Goody Two-Shoes" reformer, he was openly repudiated by the old-line politicians.

The Garfield Interlude

Deadlocked for thirty-five ballots by the usual Stalwart–Half-Breed standoff, Republicans finally broke the impasse when they nominated for the presidency in 1880 a dark horse candidate, James A. Garfield of Ohio. Born in a log cabin in the electorally powerful state of Ohio, "Boatman Jim" had struggled up from poverty by driving mules along the towpaths of the Ohio canal. Delegates appeased spoilsmen by nominating for the vice-presidency a notorious Stalwart, Senator Conkling's henchman Chester A. Arthur of New York. The platform declared emphatically for the protective tariff and somewhat feebly for reform of the civil service.

Wrathful Democrats, still seething over having been robbed of the presidency in 1876, nominated another former Civil War general, Winfield S. Hancock. Both Hancock and Garfield shunned real controversy like leprosy during the campaign. Turning their backs on deepening economic and social injustices, Republicans strove desperately to wring another presidency from the bloody shirt by verbally refighting the Civil War. Energetic Democrats, equally oblivious to deepening economic and social injustices, harped on Garfield's alleged receipt of stock dividends in the Crédit Mobilier scandal.

Garfield, "the Canal Boy," barely scraped across the electoral reefs. He polled only 39,213 more votes than Hancock—4,453,295 to 4,414,082 —but his margin in the electoral column was a comfortable 214 to 155. The new president was an able and generous man, and a devoted son who turned and kissed his mother after taking the inaugural oath. But Garfield was soon besieged by patronage-hungry Republicans and by political conflict between his new secretary of state, James G. Blaine, and Blaine's Stalwart nemesis, Senator Roscoe Conkling.

Then, as the political battle was raging, tragedy struck. A disappointed and mentally deranged office-seeker, Charles J. Guiteau, shot President Garfield in the back in a Washington railroad station. The victim lingered in agony for eleven weeks and died on September 19, 1881. Guiteau, when seized, reportedly cried, "I am a Stalwart. Arthur is now President of the United States."

Garfield's death accomplished what he would have been unlikely to achieve in life: it shocked politicians and the public into reforming the spoils system. It was shameful but true that only Garfield's unwitting martyrdom forced correction of the system's most flagrant abuses.

Chester Arthur Takes Command

Garfield's death was rendered all the more shocking by the low repute of his successor. Chester Arthur had no apparent qualifications for the presidency. He was a wealthy, handsome widower who enjoyed a richly stocked wine cellar and a wardrobe that included eighty pairs of trousers, and his previous political experience consisted almost entirely of service as a spoilsman in Conkling's sprawling New York political machine.

But observers at first underestimated Arthur. The responsibilities of the highest office in the land lifted "Prince" Arthur to new, unexpected heights. He prosecuted with vigor certain post office frauds and gave his former Conklingite cronies a frosty reception when they came seeking favors.

Disgust with the circumstances of Garfield's murder churned the public's clamor for civil service reform into an irresistible wave. The Republican party itself began to reveal a previously undetected enthusiasm for reform. Republicans lost control of the House in the midterm elections of 1882, and they rightly feared further political hemorrhaging if they failed to find a cure for the ravages that the spoils system was inflicting on the body politic.

The Pendleton Act of 1883—the so-called Magna Carta of civil service reform—was the medicine finally applied to the long-suffering organs of the federal government. It prohibited, at least on paper, financial assessments on job holders, including lowly scrubwomen. It established a merit system of making appointments to office on the basis of aptitude rather than "pull." It set up a Civil Service Commission charged with administering open competitive examinations to applicants for posts in the classified service. Offices not "classified" by the president remained the fought-over footballs of politics.

Ironically, the success of the new antispoils law depended largely on the cooperation of a seasoned former spoilsman, President Arthur. Fortunately, he cooperated with vigor. By 1884 he had classified nearly 14,000 federal offices, or about 10 percent of the total. A century later, about 90 percent of the federal offices were classified.

Civil service reform was a necessary idea whose time had come. Yet like many well-intentioned reforms, it bred unintended problems of its own. The law skimmed off much of the cream of federal patronage and put it safely beyond the reach of grasping politicians. They were now forced to look elsewhere for money, "the mother's milk of politics."

Increasingly, they turned to the bulging coffers of the big corporations. A new breed of boss emerged—less skilled at mobilizing small armies of immigrants and other voters on election day, but more adept at milking dollars from manufacturers and lobbyists. The Pendleton Act partially divorced politics from patronage, but it helped drive politicians into "marriages of convenience" with big-business leaders.

President Arthur's surprising display of integrity unfortunately offended too many powerful Republicans. His ungrateful party turned him out to pasture, and in 1886 he died of a cerebral hemorrhage.

The Blaine-Cleveland Mudslingers of 1884

James G. Blaine's persistence in pursuit of the presidential nomination finally paid off in 1884. The dashing down-easter, blessed with almost every political asset except a reputation for honesty, was clearly the choice of the Republican convention in Chicago. But many reform-minded Republicans gagged on Blaine's candidacy.

Blaine's enemies publicized the fishy-smelling "Mulligan letters," written by Blaine to a Boston businessman and linking the powerful politician to a corrupt deal involving federal favors to a southern railroad. At least one of the damning documents ended with the furtive warning "Burn this letter." Some reformers, unable to swallow Blaine, bolted to the Democrats. They were sneeringly dubbed *Mugwumps,* a word of Indian derivation apparently meaning "holier than thou."

Victory-starved Democrats turned enthusiastically to a noted reformer, Grover Cleveland. A burly bachelor with a soup-strainer mustache and a taste for chewing tobacco, Cleveland was a solid but not brilliant lawyer of forty-seven. He had rocketed from the Buffalo mayor's office to the governorship of New York and the presidential nomination in three short years. He enjoyed a well-deserved reputation for probity in office.

Unfortunately, Cleveland's admirers soon got something of a shock. Resolute Republicans, digging for dirt in the past of bachelor Cleveland, unearthed the report that he had been involved in an amorous affair with a Buffalo widow, to whom an illegitimate

son, now eight years old, had been born. Democratic elders, who had launched the campaign on a high ethical plane, were demoralized. They hurried to Cleveland and urged him to lie like a gentleman, but their ruggedly honest candidate insisted, "Tell the truth."

The campaign of 1884 sank to perhaps the lowest level in American experience, as the two parties grunted and shoved for the hog trough of office. Few fundamental differences separated them. Even the bloody shirt had faded to a pale pink.* Personalities, not principles, claimed the headlines. Enormous crowds of Democrats surged through city streets, chanting—to the rhythm of left, left, left, right, left—"Burn, burn, burn this letter!" Republicans taunted in return, "Ma, ma, where's my pa?" Defiant Democrats shouted back, "Gone to the White House, ha, ha, ha!"

The contest hinged on the state of New York, where Blaine blundered badly in the closing days of the campaign. A witless Republican clergyman damned the Democrats as the party of "rum, Romanism, and rebellion"—insulting at one stroke the national origin, faith, and patriotism of New York's numerous Irish-Americans. Blaine was present but lacked the presence of mind to repudiate the statement immediately. The pungent phrase, shortened to "RRR," stung and stuck. Blaine's silence seemed to give consent, and the wavering Irishmen who deserted his camp helped to account for Cleveland's paper-thin plurality of about 1,000 votes in New York State.

Cleveland swept the solid South and squeaked into office with 219 to 182 electoral votes and 4,879,507 to 4,850,293 popular votes.

"Old Grover" Takes Over

Bull-necked Cleveland in 1885 was the first Democrat to take the oath of presidential office since Buchanan, twenty-eight years earlier. Huge question

---

* Neither Blaine nor Cleveland had served in the Civil War. Cleveland had hired a substitute to go in his stead while he supported his widowed mother and two sisters. Blaine was the only candidate nominated by the Republicans from Grant through McKinley (1868–1900) who had not been a Civil War officer.

"I Want My Pa!" *Malicious anti-Cleveland cartoon.*

carpings of Democratic bosses and fired almost two-thirds of the 120,000 federal employees, including 40,000 incumbent (Republican) postmasters.

Military pensions gave Cleveland painful political headaches. The Union had tried to treat its veterans generously, but by the 1880s the pension legislation contained gaping loopholes and was aggressively abused. With its ready access to Treasury dollars, and strong backing from the politically powerful GAR, the pension system attracted grafters and fraudulent claimants as honey attracts flies. Hundreds of dubious private pension bills were regularly logrolled through Congress and sent to the White House. The conscientious Cleveland carefully read and weighed each bill on its merits, vetoed several hundred of them, and then laboriously penned individual veto messages for Congress. He courageously risked the retribution of the GAR in 1887 when he vetoed a bill adding several hundred thousand new pensioners to the rolls.

marks hung over his portly frame (5 feet 11 inches, 250 pounds). Could the "party of disunion" be trusted to govern the Union? Would desperate Democrats, ravenously hungry after twenty-four years of exile, trample the frail sprouts of civil service reform in a stampede to the patronage trough? Could Cleveland restore a measure of respect and power to the maligned and enfeebled presidency?

Cleveland was not a suave or skillful political leader. A staunch apostle of the hands-off creed of *laissez-faire,* the new president summed up his political philosophy in 1887 when he vetoed a bill to provide seeds for drought-ravaged Texas farmers. "Though the people support the government," he declared, "the government should not support the people." As tactless as a mirror and as direct as a bulldozer, Cleveland was outspoken, unbending, and profanely hot tempered.

At the outset Cleveland narrowed the North-South chasm by naming to the cabinet two former Confederates. As for the civil service, Cleveland was whipsawed between the demands of the Democratic faithful for jobs and the demands of the Mugwumps, who had helped elect him, for reform. Believing in the merit system, Cleveland at first favored the cause of the reformers; but he eventually caved in to the

Cleveland Battles for a Lower Tariff

During the Civil War, tariff schedules had been jacked up to new high levels, and by 1881 the Treasury was running an annual surplus amounting to an embarrassing $145 million. Most of the government's income, in those preincome tax days, came from the tariff.

Congress could reduce the vexatious surplus in two ways. One was to squander it on pensions and "pork-barrel" bills, and thus curry favor with veterans and other self-seeking groups. The other was to lower the tariff—something the big industrialists vehemently opposed. As Grover Cleveland studied the subject, he was much impressed by the arguments for downward revision of the tariff schedules. After much hesitation Cleveland saw his duty and overdid it.

Rejecting the advice of Democratic politicians, the president decided to prod the hornet's nest of the tariff issue. With his characteristic bluntness, Cleveland tossed his appeal for lower tariffs like a bombshell into the lap of Congress in late 1887. The annual message of the president had always been devoted to a review of the year's events, but Cleveland aimed his fire solely at the tariff.

The response was electric. Cleveland succeeded admirably in smoking the issue out into the open. Democrats were deeply depressed at the obstinacy of their chief. Republicans rejoiced at his apparent recklessness. The old warrior Blaine gloated, "There's one more president for us in [tariff] protection." For the first time in years, a real issue divided the two parties and would dominate the upcoming presidential election of 1888.

Harrison Ousts Cleveland in 1888

Dismayed Democrats, seeing no alternative, somewhat dejectedly nominated Cleveland in their St. Louis convention. Eager Republicans turned to Benjamin Harrison of Indiana, whose grandfather was former president William Henry ("Tippecanoe") Harrison.

The campaign proceeded on a fairly high level, despite some feeble flapping of the bloody shirt and some further probing of Cleveland's private life. The tariff was the prime issue. The two parties flooded the country with some 10 million pamphlets on the subject.

The British Lion's tail came in for some energetic twisting, especially when a California man claiming English birth wrote to the British minister in Washington, Sir Lionel Sackville-West, for advice on how to vote. The foolish diplomat replied, in effect, that a vote for Cleveland, with his low-tariff policies, was a vote for Britain, the champion of free trade. Republicans jubilantly trumpeted the indiscreet letter and made it a front-page sensation. The crucial Irish vote in New York, normally Democratic, began to slip away.

In an impressive demonstration of the post–Pendleton Act alliance of politics and big business, Republicans raised a war chest of some $3 million—the heftiest yet—largely by "frying the fat" out of nervous industrialists. The money was widely used to line up corrupt "voting cattle" known as "repeaters" and "floaters." In Indiana, always a crucial swing state, votes were shamelessly purchased for as much as $20 each.

On election day, Harrison nosed out Cleveland, 233 to 168 electoral votes. A change of about 7,000 ballots in New York would have reversed the outcome. Cleveland actually polled more popular votes, 5,537,857 to 5,447,129. Such are the curiosities of the Electoral College.

Republicans Return Under Harrison

The incoming president, stocky, heavily bearded Benjamin Harrison, was an honest and earnest party man, but he was also personally brusque and abrupt. He could charm a crowd of 10,000 with his oratory, but "the White House Ice Chest" would chill them individually with a clammy handshake.

After their four-year fast, Republicans licked their lips hungrily for the bounty of federal office. For the second time, the headstrong and ambitious "Plumed Knight," James G. Blaine, received the secretaryship of state as a consolation prize for failing to attain the presidency. The new president also named to the Civil Service Commission a bespectacled and violently energetic New Yorker, Theodore Roosevelt, as a reward for the eager-beaver politician's oratory in the campaign.

Republicans in the House of Representatives were eager to get on with squandering the surplus dollars produced by the high tariffs. But they had only three votes more than the necessary quorum of 163 members, and the Democrats were preparing to continue their obstructive practices of refusing to answer roll calls, demanding roll calls to determine the presence of a quorum, and making numerous delaying motions.

Into this explosive cockpit stepped the new Republican Speaker of the House, Thomas B. Reed of Maine. A hulking figure who towered 6 feet 3 inches, he had already made his mark as a masterful debater. Cool and collected, he spoke with a harsh nasal drawl and wielded a verbal harpoon of sarcasm. One congressman who had declaimed that he would "rather be right than president," like Henry Clay, was silenced by Reed's rasping sneer that he would "never be either." Opponents cringed at "the crack of his quip."

Believing that the majority should legislate and not be crippled by a filibustering minority, Reed single-handedly changed the House rules early in 1890. He ignored Democratic speakers who demanded quorum counts, and counted as present Democrats who had not answered the roll call. With "Czar" Reed and his iron gavel firmly in charge, the Fifty-first, or "Billion-Dollar," Congress—the first in history to appropriate that sum—gave birth to a bumper crop of expensive legislative babies.

Political Gravy for All

President Harrison, himself a Civil War general, was disposed to deal generously with his old comrades-in-arms. He appointed as commissioner of pensions a Civil War amputee who promised to drive a six-mule team through the Treasury surplus. He cut a wide swath, and a Treasury surplus has never been a problem since his day.

The Billion-Dollar Congress cooperated by opening wide the federal purse in the Pension Act of 1890. It showered pensions on Union Civil War veterans, raising the number of pensioners from 676,000 in 1891 to 970,000 in 1895, and the cost from $81 million to $135 million in 1893. This policy of liberality toward old soldiers helped Republican politicians by solving the Treasury surplus problem and thus justifying the continuing high tariff. The handouts also secured the votes of the aging veterans of the GAR for the GOP (Grand Old Party).

"Czar" Reed's imperious gavel drove additional bills through Congress. The pioneering Sherman Anti-Trust Act of 1890, though a feeble bludgeon, helped to quiet the mounting uproar against bloated corporations.

The Sherman Silver Purchase Act of 1890 arose from the acute unhappiness of western miners over the limited silver-purchase program under the Bland-Allison Law of 1878. Debt-burdened farmers were also clamoring for the unlimited coinage of silver in order to inflate the currency, thus making for higher prices and easier debt payments. The "gold bug" East looked with conservative horror on any such tampering with the money supply but hungered for the profits that might be reaped from a boost in the tariff schedules. In a huge logrolling operation, eastern protectionists agreed to support a silver bill in exchange for western backing for a higher protectionist tariff. The Sherman Silver Purchase Act provided for the Treasury to buy 4.5 million ounces

of silver monthly with notes redeemable in either silver or gold.

High-tariff Republicans reaped their political reward with the McKinley Tariff Bill of 1890, which boosted rates to their highest peacetime level yet—an average of 48.4 percent on dutiable goods. Sponsored in the House by William McKinley of Ohio, the "high priest of high protection," the bill also gave a bounty of two cents a pound to American sugar producers and raised tariffs on agricultural products—a hollow gesture to farmers because foreign growers could never compete with soil-rich Americans.

With some eastern manufacturers raising prices even before the law went into effect, the sweeping McKinley Act brought new woes to the farmer. Mounting discontent against "Bill" McKinley and his McKinley Bill caused voters to rise in wrath, especially in the midwestern farm belt. The congressional landslide of 1890 reduced the Republican membership of the House from 166 to a scant 88 members, as compared with 235 Democrats. Ominously for conservatives, the new Congress also included nine members of the Farmers' Alliance, the militant organization of southern and western farmers.

Unhorsing President Harrison in 1892

Discontent over Republican high-tariff policies gave the Democrats high hopes as the presidential election of 1892 approached. Their man of destiny was portly but energetic former President Grover Cleveland. He had built up a profitable law practice in New York City and, after hobnobbing with his wealthy clientele, had become increasingly conservative. Yet such was his reputation that he was nominated at Chicago on the first ballot.

Gathering in Minneapolis, the Republicans renominated cold-fish President Harrison, even though he was cordially disliked by party bosses. Their platform championed the protective tariff.

The campaign of 1892 also featured the new People's Party (Populists), which represented frustrated farmers in the West and South. Meeting in Omaha, the Populists adopted a platform that denounced the "prolific womb of governmental injustice." It demanded free and unlimited coinage of silver at the ratio of 16 to 1, a graduated income tax, and government ownership of the telephone and telegraph, as well as the railroads. As their presidential candidate the Populists nominated the well-respected Civil War veteran, General James B. Weaver.

An epidemic of nationwide strikes in the summer of 1892 raised the prospect that the Populists could bring aggrieved workers together with indebted farmers in a revolutionary joint assault on the capitalist order. At Andrew Carnegie's Homestead steel plant near Pittsburgh, company officials called in 300 armed Pinkerton detectives in July to crush a strike by steelworkers angry over pay cuts. Defiant strikers, armed with rifles and dynamite, forced their assailants to surrender after a vicious battle in which ten people were killed and some sixty wounded. Troops were eventually summoned, and both the strike and the union were broken. But this unsavory episode—lead instead of bread—doubtless cost the Republicans thousands of votes.

With this unexpected boost from the Pinkerton Agency, Cleveland thus unhorsed Harrison. "Old Grover" polled a total of 277 electoral votes to his opponent's 145, and 5,556,918 popular votes to 5,176,108. Cleveland, like Andrew Jackson, received a popular plurality three times, though he took office only twice.

The Populists made a remarkable showing in the 1892 presidential election. Singing "Good-by, Party Bosses," they rolled up 1,029,846 popular votes and 22 electoral votes for General Weaver. They thus became one of the few third parties in U.S. history to break into the electoral column. But they fell far short of an electoral majority. Industrial laborers, especially in the urban East, did not rally to the Populist banner in appreciable numbers. Populist electoral votes came from six midwestern and western states, four of which (Kansas, Colorado, Idaho, and Nevada) fell completely into the Populist basket.

Grover, Grim Times, and Gold

Grover Cleveland took office once again in 1893, the only president ever reelected after defeat. He was the same old bull-necked and bull-headed Cleveland, with a little more weight, polish, conservatism, and self-assertiveness.

But if it was the same old Grover, it was not the same old country. Hardly had Cleveland seated himself in the presidential chair when the devastating Panic of 1893 burst about his burly frame. Lasting for about four years, it was in some respects the worst depression of the nineteenth century. Contributing causes were no doubt the splurge of overspeculation, labor disorders, and the current agricultural depression. Free-silver agitation had also damaged American credit abroad, and the usual pinch on American finances had come when European banking houses began to call in loans from the United States.

Distress was acute and widespread. About 8,000 American business houses collapsed in six months, and dozens of railroad lines went into the hands of receivers. Business executives "died like flies under the strain," wrote Henry Adams. Soup kitchens were set up for the unemployed, while gangs of hoboes wandered aimlessly about the country. Local charities did their feeble best, but the federal government, bound by the let-nature-take-its-course philosophy of the times, saw no legitimate way to relieve the suffering masses.

Cleveland, who had earlier been bothered by a surplus, now faced a growing deficit. Owners of the paper currency issued under the Sherman Silver Purchase Act were presenting the notes for gold, and by law the notes had to be reissued. New holders would then repeat the process, thus draining away gold in an "endless chain" operation.

Alarmingly, the gold reserve in the Treasury dropped below $100 million, which was popularly regarded as the safe minimum for supporting about $350 million in outstanding paper money. Cleveland saw no alternative but to halt the bleeding away of gold by engineering a repeal of the Sherman Silver Purchase Act of 1890. For this purpose he summoned Congress into an extra session in the summer of 1893.

In Congress debate over the repeal of the silver act was heated. An eloquent young congressman from Nebraska, the thirty-three-year-old William Jennings Bryan, held the galleries spellbound for three hours as he championed the cause of free silver.

Presidential Election of 1892 (showing vote by county)
Note the concentration of Populist strength in the semiarid farming regions of the western half of the country. People living in territories (unsettled areas—see key) could not vote.

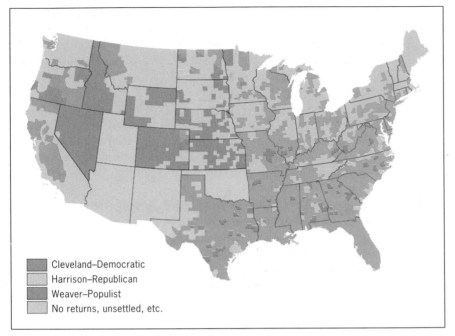

Cleveland–Democratic
Harrison–Republican
Weaver–Populist
No returns, unsettled, etc.

The friends of silver announced that "hell would freeze over" before Congress passed the repeal measure. But an angered Cleveland used his office-giving power to break the filibuster in the Senate. He thus alienated the Democratic silverites and disrupted his party at the very outset of his administration.

Furthermore, the repeal of the Sherman Silver Purchase Act failed to stop the hemorrhaging of gold from the Treasury. The gold reserve sank to a dismaying $41 million in February 1894. The United States was now in grave danger of going off the gold standard—a move that would render the nation's currency volatile and unreliable as a measure of value and that could mortally cripple America's international trade. Two Treasury bond issues totaling over $100 million were floated in 1894, but the gold drain continued relentlessly.

Early in 1895 Cleveland turned in desperation to J. P. Morgan, "the banker's banker," and a Wall Street syndicate. After tense negotiations at the White House, the bankers agreed to lend the government $65 million in gold. They were obviously in business for profit, so they charged a commission amounting to about $7 million. But they did make a

significant concession when they agreed to obtain one-half of the gold abroad and take the necessary steps to dam it up in the leaky Treasury. The loan, at least temporarily, helped restore confidence in the nation's finances.

But the bond deal stirred up a storm. The Wall Street ogre, especially in the eyes of the silverites and other debtors, symbolized all that was wicked and grasping. Cleveland's secretive dealings with mighty "Jupiter" Morgan were savagely condemned as a "sellout" of the national government. But Cleveland was certain that he had done no wrong. Sarcastically denying that he was "Morgan's errand boy," he asserted: "Without shame and without repentance I confess my share of the guilt."

Cleveland suffered further embarrassment with the passage of the Wilson-Gorman Tariff in 1894. The Democrats had pledged to lower tariffs, but by the time the measure got through Congress, it had been so loaded with special-interest protection that it lowered rates only slightly below those of the McKinley Tariff. An outraged Cleveland grudgingly let the bill, which also contained a 2 percent tax on incomes over $4,000, become law without his signa-

CHRONOLOGY

1868	Grant defeats Seymour for presidency.	1881	Garfield assassinated; Arthur assumes presidency.
1869	Fisk and Gould corner the gold market.	1882	Chinese Exclusion Act.
1871	Tweed scandal in New York.	1883	Pendleton Act sets up Civil Service Commission.
1872	Crédit Mobilier scandal.	1884	Cleveland defeats Blaine for presidency.
	Liberal Republicans break with Grant.	1888	Harrison defeats Cleveland for presidency.
	Grant defeats Greeley for presidency.	1890	Billion Dollar Congress.
1873	Panic of 1873.		Sherman Silver Purchase Act of 1890.
1875	Whiskey Ring scandal.		McKinley Tariff Bill.
	Civil Rights Act of 1875.	1892	Cleveland defeats Harrison and Weaver for presidency.
	Resumption Act passed.	1893	Depression of 1893 begins.
1876	Hayes-Tilden election standoff and crisis.	1894	Wilson-Gorman Tariff.
1877	Compromise of 1877; Reconstruction ends.	1895	Morgan loans $65 million in gold to federal government.
	Railroad strikes paralyze nation.		Supreme Court declares income tax unconstitutional.
1880	Garfield defeats Hancock for presidency.		

ture. When the income tax provision was struck down by a five-to-four Supreme Court decision in 1895,* the Populists and other impoverished groups found further proof that the courts were only the tools of the plutocrats.

Democratic political fortunes naturally suffered. The tariff dynamite that had blasted the Republicans out of the House in 1890 now dislodged the Democrats, with a strong helping hand from the depression. Revitalized Republicans, singing "The

Soup House" and "Times Are Mighty Hard," won the congressional elections of 1894 in a landslide and now had 244 votes to 105 for the Democrats. Republicans looked forward to the 1896 presidential elections with glee.

Despite his gruff integrity and occasional courage, Grover Cleveland failed utterly to cope with the serious economic crisis that hit the nation in 1893. He was tied down in office by the same threads that held all the presidents of the day to Lilliputian levels. Grant, Hayes, Garfield, Arthur, and Harrison are often referred to as the "forgettable presidents." Bewhiskered and bland in person, they left mostly blanks—or blots—on the nation's political record. In this dull galaxy even such a dim light as Cleveland shone like a bright star. What little political vitality

---

* It violated the "direct tax" clause. See Art. I, Sec. IX, para. 4, Appendix. The Sixteenth Amendment to the Constitution, adopted in 1913, permitted an income tax.

existed was to be found in local settings, or in Congress, which overshadowed the White House during most of the Gilded Age.

As the nineteenth century drew to a close, observers were asking, "Why are the 'best men' not in politics?" One answer was that they had been lured away from public life by the lusty attractions of the booming industrial economy. Talented men

ached for profits, not the presidency; they dreamed of controlling corporations, not Congress. What the nation lost in political leadership, it gained in an astounding surge of economic growth. Although still in many ways a political dwarf, the United States was about to stand up before the world as an industrial colossus.

Varying Viewpoints

Historians have long been harsh in their appraisal of the Gilded Age political system. Taking their cue from contemporary satirical commentaries such as Henry Adams's *Democracy* and Mark Twain and Charles Dudley Warner's *The Gilded Age,* they have condemned the politicians of the era as petty, corrupt, and self-serving. Such a view is conspicuous in Charles and Mary Beard's *The Rise of American Civilization* (4 vols., 1927–1942), perhaps the most influential American history text ever written. It is equally evident in Vernon Louis Parrington's classic literary history *Main Currents in American Thought* (3 vols., 1927–1930), where the entire era is contemptuously dismissed as the time of "the Great Barbecue." As leaders of the so-called progressive school of historical writing, the Beards and Parrington were fiercely antibusiness and warmly prolabor, profarmer, and proreform.

Yet the generation of political leaders from Grant to Cleveland did succeed in largely healing the terrible wounds of the Civil War and presided over an unprecedented burst of economic expan-

sion. These were no small achievements, even if they were purchased at the high price of the abandonment of the ex-slaves and the exploitation of industrial workers. Moreover, the late nineteenth century witnessed an unparalleled degree of mass political participation, as "army-style" parties mobilized millions of citizens to take part in the electoral process. Ethnocultural historians such as Richard Jensen and Paul Kleppner have explained the high level of political participation by citing the cultural values aroused by local issues like prohibition and education. Yet they have not fully explained the relation between the passions supposedly stirred by these "cultural" questions and the persistence of the major parties in focusing on bread-and-butter economic issues at the national level. The shadow of progressive historiography still lies long across the American historical imagination, preventing a sympathetic, comprehensive appraisal of the genuine accomplishments of the Gilded Age political system, in both the local and the national arenas.

SELECT READINGS

Primary Source Documents

Henry Adams penned some perceptive and sour observations on the era in his autobiographical *Education of Henry Adams* (1907) and in his novel *Democracy* (1880). See also the classic satire by Mark Twain and Charles Dudley Warner, *The Gilded Age* (1873).

Secondary Sources

The scandal-rocked Grant era is treated with brevity in James G. Randall and David Donald, *The Civil War and Reconstruction* (rev. ed., 1969), and at greater length in William Gillette, *Retreat from Reconstruction* (1979), and James M. McPherson, *Ordeal by Fire* (1981). Southern politics is detailed in J. Morgan Kousser, *The Shaping of Southern Politics* (1974), whereas William Gillette, *The Right to Vote* (1965), discusses the North. On the party systems, see Paul Kleppner, *The Third Electoral System, 1835–1892* (1979), Morton Keller, *Affairs of State: Public Life in Nineteenth-Century America* (1977), and Richard Jensen, *The Winning of the Mid-West* (1971). Money questions are treated in Irwin Unger, *The Greenback Era* (1964), Walter

T. K. Nugent, *Money and American Society, 1865–1880* (1968), and Allen Weinstein's account of the "Crime of '73," *Prelude to Populism* (1970). C. Vann Woodward sharply analyzes the Compromise of 1877 in *Reunion and Reaction* (rev. ed., 1956). California receives special attention in Alexander Saxton, *The Indispensable Enemy: Labor and the Anti-Chinese Movement in California* (1975).

CHAPTER 26

Industry Comes of Age, 1865–1900

The railroads are not run for the benefit of the dear public. That cry is all nonsense.
They are built for men who invest their money and expect to get a fair percentage on the same.

William H. Vanderbilt, 1882

The Iron Colt Becomes an Iron Horse

The feverish years after the Civil War witnessed an unparalleled outburst of railroad construction. When Lincoln was shot in 1865, there were only 35,000 miles of steam railways in the United States, mostly east of the Mississippi. By 1900 the figure had spurted up to 192,556 miles, or more than that for all Europe combined.

Transcontinental railroad building was so costly and risky as to require governmental subsidies. Congress began to advance liberal money loans to two favored cross-continent companies in 1862 and added enormous donations of acreage paralleling the tracks. Granting land was a cheap way to subsidize a much-desired transportation system, because it avoided new taxes for direct cash grants. All told, Washington rewarded the railroads with 155,504,994 acres, and the western states contributed 49 million more—a total area larger than Texas.

Deadlock in the 1850s over the location of the proposed transcontinental railroad was broken when the South seceded, leaving the field to the North. In 1862, the year after the guns first spoke at Fort Sumter, Congress made provision for starting the long-awaited line. One weighty argument for action was the urgency of bolstering the Union, already disrupted, by binding the Pacific Coast more securely to the rest of the republic.

The Union Pacific Railroad—note the word *Union*—was thus commissioned by Congress to thrust westward from Omaha, Nebraska. The laying of rails began in earnest after the Civil War ended in 1865; and with juicy loans and land grants available, the "groundhog" promoters made all possible haste.

Sweaty construction gangs, containing many Irish "Paddies" (Patricks), worked at a frantic pace. On one record-breaking day, a sledge-and-shovel army of some 5,000 men laid ten miles of track. A favorite song was:

> Then drill, my Paddies, drill;
> Drill, my heroes, drill;
> Drill all day,
> No sugar in your tay,
> Workin' on the U.P. Railway.

***Snow Sheds on the Central Pacific Railroad in the Sierra Nevada Mountains,* by
Joseph H. Becker, c. 1869**   *This painting suggests the obstacles of climate and terrain
that confronted the builders of the Central Pacific Railroad in California's Sierra Nevada
mountains.*

When hostile Indians attacked, the laborers
would drop their picks and seize their rifles. Relaxation and conviviality were provided by the tented
towns, known as "hells on wheels," which sprang up
at rail's end, sometimes numbering as many as 10,000
men and a sprinkling of painted prostitutes. The fabulous profits of the huge enterprise were reaped by
the insiders of the Crédit Mobilier construction company. They slyly pocketed $73 million for some $50
million worth of construction while bribing congressmen to look the other way.

Rail laying at the California end was undertaken by the Central Pacific Railroad. This line
pushed boldly eastward from boomtown Sacra-
mento, over and through the towering, snow-clogged
Sierra Nevada. Four farseeing men—the so-called
Big Four—were the chief financial backers of the
enterprise. The quartet included the heavyset, enter-

prising ex-governor Leland Stanford of California,
who had useful political connections, and the burly,
energetic Collis P. Huntington, an adept lobbyist.

The Central Pacific, which was granted the
same princely subsidies as the Union Pacific, had the
same incentive to haste. Some 10,000 pig-tailed Chinese laborers sweated from dawn to dusk under their
basket hats. Hundreds lost their lives in premature
explosions and other mishaps. The rocky Sierra
Nevada presented a formidable barrier; and the
nerves of the Big Four were strained when their
workers could chip only a few inches a day through
rocky tunnels, while the Union Pacific was sledge-
hammering westward across the plains.

A "wedding of the rails" was finally consum-
mated near Ogden, Utah, in 1869, as two locomotives gently kissed cowcatchers. The colorful ceremony included the breaking of champagne bottles

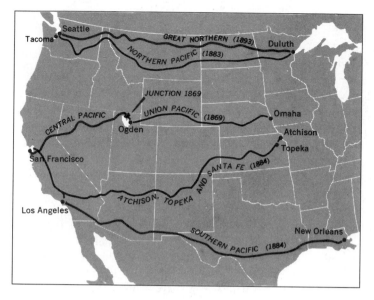

Early Pacific Railway Lines (with completion dates)   *The Great Northern line claimed several distinctions: it was the last-built of the major transcontinental roads, the only one constructed without lavish federal subsidies, and the most northerly. Its larger-than-life promoter, James J. Hill, once declared: "You can't interest me in any proposition in any place where it doesn't snow. . . . No man on whom the snow does not fall ever amounts to a tinker's dam."*

and the driving of a last ceremonial (golden) spike, with ex-governor Stanford clumsily wielding a silver sledgehammer.* In all, the Union Pacific built 1,086 miles, and the Central Pacific 689 miles.

Completion of the transcontinental line welded the West Coast more firmly to the Union and facilitated a flourishing trade with Asia. It penetrated the arid barrier of the deserts, paving the way for the phenomenal growth of the Great West. Americans compared this great achievement with the Declaration of Independence and the emancipation of the slaves; jubilant Philadelphians again rang the cracked bell of Independence Hall.

Binding the Country with Railroad Ties

With the westward trail now blazed, four other transcontinental lines were completed before the century's end. None of them secured monetary loans from the federal government, as did the Union Pacific and the Central Pacific. But all of them except the Great Northern received generous grants of land.

The Northern Pacific Railroad, stretching from

Lake Superior to Puget Sound, reached its terminus in 1883. Two other lines ran parallel to some extent in New Mexico, Arizona, and California. One—the Atchison, Topeka, and Santa Fe—which stretched through the southwestern deserts to California, was completed in 1884. The other, the Southern Pacific, ribboned from New Orleans to San Francisco and was consolidated in the same year. The South had finally won its direct route to the West Coast.

The last of the five nineteenth-century transcontinental railroads, the Great Northern, ran from Duluth to Seattle. Its creator was James J. Hill, a far-visioned Canadian-American who perceived that the prosperity of his railroad depended on the prosperity of the area that it served. Hill's sound organization enabled his railroad to ride through later financial storms with flying colors.

Hill's sense of responsibility and public duty made him an exception in the romantic but often sordid railroad business. Pioneer builders were often guilty of gross over-optimism, laying down rails that went "from nowhere to nothing" in order to get the lavish federal land bounties. When prosperity failed to smile, they went into bankruptcy, carrying down with them the savings of trusting investors. Many of the large railroads of the post–Civil War decades passed through seemingly endless bankruptcies, mergers, or reorganizations.

---

* The spike was promptly removed and is now exhibited at the Stanford University Museum.

Railroad Consolidation and Mechanization

The success of the western lines was facilitated by welding together and expanding the older eastern networks, notably the New York Central. The genius in this enterprise was "Commodore" Cornelius Vanderbilt, who daringly turned from steamboating to a new career in railroading in his late sixties. Though ill-educated, ungrammatical, coarse, and ruthless, he was clear-visioned. Offering superior service at lower rates, he amassed a fortune of $100 million, of which he contributed $1 million to the founding of Vanderbilt University in Tennessee.

Two significant new improvements proved a boon to the railroads. One was the steel rail, which Vanderbilt helped popularize when he replaced the old iron tracks of the New York Central with the tougher metal. Steel was safer and more economical because it could bear a heavier load. A standard gauge of track width likewise came into wide use during the postwar years, thus eliminating the expense and inconvenience of numerous changes from one line to another.

Other refinements played a vital role in railroading. The Westinghouse air brake, generally adopted in the 1870s, was a marvelous contribution to efficiency and safety. The Pullman Palace Cars, advertised as "gorgeous traveling hotels," were introduced on a considerable scale in the 1860s.

Revolution by Railways

The metallic fingers of the railroads intimately touched countless phases of American life. For the first time, a sprawling nation became united in a physical sense, bound with ribs of iron and steel. By stitching North America together from sea to sea, the transcontinental lines created an enormous market for American raw materials and manufactured goods—a huge empire of commerce that beckoned to foreign and domestic investors alike.

More than any other single factor, the railroad network spurred the amazing industrialization of the post–Civil War years. The puffing locomotives opened up fresh markets for manufactured goods and sped raw materials to the factory. The forging of the rails themselves provided the largest single backlog for the adolescent steel industry.

The screeching iron horse likewise stimulated mining and agriculture, especially in the West. It took farmers out to their land, carried the fruits of their toil to market, and brought them their manufactured necessities. Clusters of farm settlements

William Vanderbilt, Robber Baron *This caricature from a contemporary newspaper cover takes aim at railroad magnate Vanderbilt's infamous comment, "The public be damned!"*

paralleled the railroads, just as earlier they had followed the rivers.

Railways were a boon for cities and played a leading role in the great cityward movement of the last decades of the century. The iron monsters could carry food to enormous concentrations of people and at the same time ensure them a livelihood by providing both raw materials and markets.

Railroad companies also stimulated the mighty stream of immigration. Seeking settlers to whom their land grants might be sold at a profit, they advertised seductively in Europe and sometimes offered free transportation to prospective buyers.

The land also felt the impact of the railroad—especially the broad, ecologically fragile midsection of the continent. Settlers following the railroads plowed up the tallgrass prairies of Iowa, Illinois, Kansas, and Nebraska and planted well-drained, rectangular cornfields. On the shortgrass prairies of the high plains in the Dakotas and Montana, range-fed cattle rapidly displaced the buffalo, which were hunted to near-extinction. The white pine forests of Michigan, Wisconsin, and Minnesota disappeared into lumber that was sped by rail to prairie farmers who used it to build houses and fences.

Time itself was bent to the railroads' needs. Until the 1880s every town in the United States had its own "local" time, dictated by the sun's position. When it was noon in Chicago, it was 11:50 A.M. in St. Louis and 12:18 P.M. in Detroit. For railroad operators worried about keeping schedules and avoiding wrecks, this patchwork of local times was a nightmare. Thus on November 18, 1883, the major rail lines decreed that the continent would henceforth be divided into four "time zones." Most communities quickly adopted railroad "standard" time.

Finally, the railroad, more than any other single factor, was the maker of millionaires. A raw new aristocracy, consisting of "lords of the rail," replaced the old southern "lords of the lash." The rail lines became the playthings of Wall Street; and colossal wealth was amassed by stock speculators and railroad wreckers like "Jubilee Jim" Fisk.

Wrongdoing in Railroading

Corruption lurks nearby when fabulous fortunes can be amassed overnight. The fleecings administered by the railroad construction companies, such as the Crédit Mobilier, were but the first of the bunco games that the railroad promoters learned to play. Methods soon became more refined, as fast-fingered financiers executed multimillion-dollar maneuvers beneath the noses of a bedazzled public. Jay Gould was the most adept of these ringmasters of rapacity. For nearly thirty years he boomed and busted the stocks of the Erie, the Kansas Pacific, the Union Pacific, and the Texas and Pacific in an incredible circus of speculative skullduggery.

One of the favorite devices of the moguls of manipulation was "stock watering." The term originally referred to the practice of making cattle thirsty by feeding them salt, and then having them bloat themselves with water before they were weighed in for sale. Using a variation of this technique, railroad stock promoters grossly inflated their claims about a given line's assets and profitability and sold stocks and bonds far in excess of the railroad's actual value. "Promoters' profits" were often the tail that wagged the iron horse itself. Railroad managers were forced to charge extortionate rates and wage ruthless competitive battles in order to pay off the exaggerated financial obligations with which they were saddled.

The public interest was frequently trampled underfoot as the railroad titans waged their brutal wars. Crusty old Cornelius Vanderbilt, when told that the law stood in his way, reportedly exclaimed: "Law! What do I care about the law? Hain't I got the power?" His son, William H. Vanderbilt, when asked in 1883 about the discontinuance of a fast mail train, reportedly snorted, "The public be damned!"

While abusing the public, the railroaders blandly bought and sold people in public life. They bribed judges and legislatures, elected their own agents to high office, and showered free passes on journalists and politicians.

Railroad kings were, for a time, virtual industrial monarchs. As manipulators of a huge natural monopoly, they exercised more direct control over the lives of more people than did the president of the United States—and their terms were not limited to four years. They increasingly shunned the crude bloodletting of cutthroat competition and began to cooperate with one another to rule the railroad dominion. Sorely pressed to show at least some returns on their bloated investments, they entered into defensive alliances to protect precious profits.

The earliest form of combination was the "pool"—an agreement to divide the business in a given area and share the profits. Other rail barons granted secret rebates or kickbacks to powerful shippers in return for steady and assured traffic. Often they slashed their rates on competing lines, but they more than made up the difference on noncompeting ones, where they might actually charge more for a short haul than for a long one.

Government Bridles the Iron Horse

It was neither healthy nor politically acceptable that so many people should be at the mercy of so few. Impoverished farmers, especially in the Midwest, began to wonder if the nation had not escaped from the slavery power only to fall into the hands of the money power, as represented by the railroad plutocracy.

But the American people, though quick to respond to political injustice, were slow to combat economic injustice. Dedicated to free enterprise and the principle that competition is the soul of trade, they remembered that Jefferson's ideals were hostile to governmental interference with business. Above all, there shimmered the "American dream": the hope that in a catch-as-catch-can economic system, anyone might become a millionaire.

The depression of the 1870s finally goaded the embattled farmers into protesting against being "railroaded" into bankruptcy. Under pressure from organized agrarian groups like the Grange (Patrons of Husbandry), many midwestern legislatures tried to regulate the railroad monopoly.

The scattered state efforts screeched to a halt in 1886. The Supreme Court, in the famed *Wabash* case, decreed that individual states had no power to regulate interstate commerce. If the mechanical monster were to be corralled, the federal government would have to do the job.

Congress ignored President Cleveland's grumbling indifference and passed the epochal Interstate Commerce Act in 1887. It prohibited rebates and pools and required the railroads to publish their rates openly. It also forbade unfair discrimination

against shippers and outlawed charging more for a short haul than a long one over the same line. Most important, it set up the Interstate Commerce Commission (ICC) to enforce and administer the new legislation.

Despite acclaim, the Interstate Commerce Act emphatically did not represent a popular victory over corporate wealth. One of the leading corporation lawyers of the day, Richard Olney, shrewdly noted that the new commission "can be made of great use to the railroads. It satisfies the popular clamor for a government supervision of railroads, at the same time that such supervision is almost entirely nominal. . . . The part of wisdom is not to destroy the Commission, but to utilize it."

What the new legislation did do was provide an orderly forum where competing business interests could resolve their conflicts in peaceable ways. The country could now avoid ruinous rate wars among the railroads, and outraged, "confiscatory" attacks on the lines by pitchfork-prodded state legislatures. This was a modest accomplishment but by no means an unimportant one. The Interstate Commerce Act tended to stabilize, not revolutionize, the existing business system.

Yet the act still ranks as a red-letter law. It was the first large-scale attempt by Washington to regulate business in the interest of society at large. It foreshadowed the doom of freewheeling, buccaneering business practices and served full notice that there was a public interest in private enterprise that the government was bound to protect.

Miracles of Mechanization

Postwar industrial expansion, partly a result of the railroad network, rapidly began to assume gigantic proportions. When Lincoln was elected in 1860, the republic ranked only fourth among the manufacturing nations of the world. By 1894 it had bounded into first place. Why the sudden upsurge?

Liquid capital, previously scarce, was now becoming abundant. The word *millionaire* had not been coined until the 1840s, and in 1861 only a handful of men were in this class. But the Civil War, partly through profiteering, created immense fortunes; and these accumulations could now be combined with the customary borrowings from foreign capitalists.

The amazing natural resources of the nation were now about to be fully exploited, including coal, oil, and iron. Unskilled labor, both homegrown and imported, was now cheap and plentiful. Steel, the keystone industry, came to be based largely on the sweat of low-priced immigrant labor, working in two twelve-hour shifts, seven days a week.

American ingenuity at the same time played a vital role in the second American Industrial Revolution. American inventiveness flowered luxuriantly in the postwar years: between 1860 and 1890 some 440,000 patents were issued. Business operations were facilitated by the cash register, the stock ticker, and the typewriter ("literary piano"), which attracted women to industry. Urbanization was speeded by the refrigerator car, the electric dynamo, and the electric railway that displaced animal-drawn cars.

The ingenious telephone was introduced in 1876 by Alexander Graham Bell, a teacher of the deaf who said that if he could make the mute talk, he could make iron speak. His invention had a great social impact on the nation, especially as many women were beckoned from the home to become the "number please" operators in the gigantic communications network.

The most versatile inventor of all was Thomas A. Edison, who ran a veritable invention factory in New Jersey. He is perhaps best known for his perfection in 1879 of the electric light, which he unveiled after trying some 6,000 filaments. He invented, perfected, or did useful exploratory work on the phonograph, the mimeograph, the dictaphone, and the moving picture. "Genius," he said, "is one percent inspiration and ninety-nine percent perspiration."

The Trust Titan Emerges

Despite pious protests to the contrary, competition was the bugbear of most business leaders of the day. Tycoons such as Andrew Carnegie, the steel king, John D. Rockefeller, the oil baron, and J. Pierpont Morgan, the bankers' banker, exercised their genius in devising ways to circumvent competition. Carnegie developed "vertical integration" of produc-

tion by directly controlling every phase of his steelmaking operation. His miners scratched the ore from the earth in Minnesota's Mesabi range; Carnegie ships floated it across the Great Lakes; Carnegie railroads delivered it to the blast furnaces at Pittsburgh. When the molten metal finally poured from the glowing crucibles into the waiting ingot molds, no other hands but those in Carnegie's employ had touched the product.

Rockefeller pursued the less justifiable technique of "horizontal integration," which simply meant consolidating with competitors to monopolize a given market. He perfected a device for controlling bothersome rivals—the "trust." Stockholders in various smaller oil companies assigned their stock to the board of directors of Rockefeller's Standard Oil Company. It then consolidated and concerted the operations of the previously competing enterprises. "Let us prey" was said to be Rockefeller's unwritten motto. Ruthlessly wielding vast power, Standard Oil soon cornered virtually the entire world petroleum market. Weaker competitors, left out of the trust agreement, were forced to the wall. Rockefeller's stunning success inspired many imitators, and the word *trust* came to be generally used to describe any large-scale business combination.

The imperial Morgan devised still other schemes for eliminating "wasteful" competition. The depression of the 1890s drove into his welcoming arms many bleeding businesspeople, wounded by cutthroat competition. His prescribed remedy was to consolidate rival enterprises and to ensure future harmony by placing officers of his own banking syndicate on their various boards of directors. These came to be known as "interlocking directorates."

The Supremacy of Steel

"Steel is king!" might well have been the exultant war cry of the new industrialized generation. The mighty metal ultimately held together the new civilization, from skyscrapers to coal scuttles, while providing it with food, shelter, and transportation. Steel making, notably rails for railroads, typified the dominance of heavy industry, which concentrated on making capital goods, as distinct from the production of consumer goods such as clothes and shoes.

Now taken for granted, steel was a scarce commodity in the wood-and-brick America of Abraham Lincoln. Yet within an amazing twenty years the United States had outdistanced all foreign competitors and was pouring out more than one-third of the world's supply of steel.

What wrought the transformation? Chiefly the invention in the 1850s of a method of making cheap steel—the Bessemer process. It was named after a derided British inventor, although an American had stumbled on it a few years earlier. William Kelly, a Kentucky manufacturer of iron kettles, discovered that cold air blown on red-hot iron caused the metal to become white-hot by igniting the carbon and thus eliminating impurities.

Kingpin among steelmasters was Andrew Carnegie, an undersized, charming Scotsman. As a tow-headed lad, he was brought to America by his impoverished parents in 1848 and got a job as a bobbin boy at $1.20 a week. Mounting the ladder of success so fast that he was said to have scorched the rungs, he forged ahead by working hard, doing the extra chore, cheerfully assuming responsibility, and smoothly cultivating influential people.

After accumulating some capital, Carnegie entered the steel business in the Pittsburgh area. By 1900 he was producing one-fourth of the nation's Bessemer steel, and his partners were dividing the profits of $40 million a year, with the "Napoleon of the smokestacks" himself receiving a cool $25 million. These were the preincome tax days, when millionaires were really rich and profits represented take-home pay.

Into the picture now stepped the financial giant of the age, J. Pierpont Morgan. "Jupiter" Morgan had made a legendary reputation for himself and his Wall Street banking house by financing the reorganization of railroads, insurance companies, and banks. An impressive figure of a man, with massive shoulders, shaggy brows, piercing eyes, and a bulbous, acne-cursed red nose, he had established an enviable reputation for integrity. He did not believe that "money power" was dangerous, except when in dangerous hands—and he did not regard his hands as dangerous.

The force of circumstances brought Morgan and Carnegie into collision. By 1900 the canny little Scotsman, weary of turning steel into gold, was eager to sell his holdings. Morgan had meanwhile plunged heavily into the manufacture of steel pipe tubing. Carnegie, cleverly threatening to invade the same business, was ready to ruin his rival if he did not receive his price. The steelmaster's agents haggled with the imperious Morgan for eight agonizing hours, and the financier finally agreed to buy out Carnegie for over $400 million. Fearing that he would die "disgraced" with so much wealth, Carnegie dedicated the remaining years of his life to giving it away for public libraries, pensions for professors, and other such philanthropic purposes—in all disposing of about $350 million.

Morgan moved rapidly to expand his new industrial empire. He took the Carnegie holdings, added others, "watered" the stock liberally, and in 1901 launched the enlarged United States Steel Corporation. Capitalized at $1.4 billion, it thus became America's first billion-dollar corporation—a larger sum than the total estimated wealth of the nation in 1800. The Industrial Revolution, with its hot Bessemer breath, had come into its own.

Rockefeller Grows an American Beauty Rose

Another new industry was born almost overnight when in 1859 the first oil well—"Drake's Folly" in Pennsylvania—poured out its liquid "black gold." Kerosene, derived from petroleum, was the first major product of the infant oil industry. Replacing whale oil as the fuel for America's lamps, kerosene became the country's fourth most valuable export by the 1870s.

But what technology gives, technology takes away. By 1885, Thomas Edison's new electric light bulbs had rendered kerosene largely obsolete. Oil might thus have remained a modest, even a shrinking industry but for yet another turn of the technological tide—the invention of the automobile. By 1900 the gasoline-burning internal combustion engine had clearly bested its rivals, steam and electricity, and the oil business got a new, long-lasting, and hugely profitable lease on life.

John D. Rockefeller—lanky, shrewd, ambitious, abstemious (he neither drank, smoked, nor swore)—came to dominate the oil industry. Born to a family of precarious income, he became a successful businessman at age nineteen. One upward stride led to another, and in 1870 he organized the Standard Oil Company of Ohio, nucleus of the great trust formed in 1882. Locating his refineries in Cleveland, he sought to squeeze out middlemen and competitors.

Pious and parsimonious, Rockefeller flourished in an era of completely free enterprise. Operating "just to the windward of the law," he pursued a policy of rule or ruin. By 1877 Rockefeller controlled 95 percent of America's oil refineries.

Rockefeller—"Reckafellow," as Carnegie once called him—showed little mercy. A kind of primitive savagery prevailed in the jungle world of big business, where only the fittest survived. Or so Rockefeller believed. His son later explained that the giant American Beauty rose could be produced "only by sacrificing the early buds that grew up around it." His father pinched off the small buds with complete ruthlessness. Employing spies and extorting secret rebates from the railroads, he even forced the lines to pay him rebates on the freight bills of his competitors!

Rockefeller thought he was simply obeying a law of nature. "The time was ripe" for aggressive consolidation, he later reflected. "It had to come, though all we saw at the moment was the need to save ourselves from wasteful conditions. . . . The day of combination is here to stay. Individualism has gone, never to return."

On the other side of the ledger, Rockefeller's oil monopoly did turn out a superior product at a relatively cheap price. It achieved important economies, both at home and abroad, by its large-scale methods of production and distribution. This, in truth, was the tale of the other trusts as well. The efficient use of expensive machinery called for bigness, and consolidation proved more profitable than ruinous price wars.

Other trusts blossomed along with the American Beauty of oil. These included the sugar trust, the tobacco trust, the leather trust, and the harvester trust, which amalgamated some 200 competitors. The meat industry arose on the backs of bawling western herds, and meat kings like Gustavus F. Swift

and Philip Armour took their place among the new royalty. Wealth was coming to dominate the commonwealth.

These untrustworthy trusts, and the "pirates" who captained them, were disturbingly new. They eclipsed an older American aristocracy of modestly successful merchants and professionals. An arrogant class of "new rich" was now elbowing aside the patrician families in the mad scramble for power and prestige. Not surprisingly, the ranks of the antitrust crusaders were frequently spearheaded by the "best men"—genteel old-family do-gooders who were not radicals but conservative defenders of their own vanishing influence.

The Gospel of Wealth

Monarchs of yore invoked the divine right of kings, and America's industrial plutocrats took a somewhat similar stance. Some candidly credited heavenly help, and the body of ideas with which they justified their social position came to be known as the "Gospel of Wealth." "Godliness is in league with riches," preached the Episcopal bishop of Massachusetts, and hardfisted John D. Rockefeller piously acknowledged that "the good Lord gave me my money." But most defenders of this wide-open capitalism relied more heavily on the survival-of-the-fittest theories of Charles Darwin. "The millionaires are a product of natural selection," concluded Yale Professor William Graham Sumner. "They get high wages and live in luxury, but the bargain is a good one for society." Despite plutocracy and deepening class divisions, the captains of industry provided material progress.

Self-justification by the wealthy inevitably involved contempt for the poor. Many of the rich, especially the newly rich, had pulled themselves up by their own bootstraps; hence they concluded that those who stayed poor must be lazy and lacking in enterprise. The Reverend Russell Conwell of Philadelphia became rich by delivering his lecture "Acres of Diamonds" thousands of times. In it he said, "There is not a poor person in the United States who was not made poor by his own shortcomings." Such attitudes were a formidable roadblock to social reform.

Washington as Seen by the Trusts   *"What a funny little government," John D. Rocke-feller observes in this satirical cartoon. His own wealth and power are presumed to dwarf the resources of the federal government.*

Plutocracy, like the earlier slavocracy, took its stand firmly on the Constitution. The clause that gave Congress sole jurisdiction over interstate commerce was a godsend to the monopolists; their high-priced lawyers used it time and again to thwart controls by the state legislatures. Giant trusts likewise sought refuge behind the Fourteenth Amendment, which had been originally designed to protect the rights of ex-slaves as persons. The courts ingeniously interpreted a corporation to be a legal "person" and decreed that, as such, it could not be deprived of its property by a state without "due process law" (see Art. XIV, para. 1).

Great industrialists likewise sought to incorporate in "easy states," like New Jersey, where the restrictions on big business were mild or nonexistent. For example, the Southern Pacific Railroad, with much of its trackage in California, was incorporated in Kentucky.

Government Tackles the Trust Evil

At long last the masses of the people began to mobilize against monopoly. They first tried to control the trusts through state legislation, as they had earlier attempted to curb the railroads. Failing here, as before, they were forced to appeal to Congress. After prolonged pulling and hauling, the Sherman Anti-Trust Act of 1890 was finally signed into law.

The Sherman Act flatly forbade combinations in restraint of trade, without any distinction between "good" trusts and "bad" trusts. Bigness, not badness, was the sin. The law proved ineffective, largely because it had only baby teeth or no teeth at all, and because it contained legal loopholes through which clever corporation lawyers could wriggle. But it was unexpectedly effective in one respect. Contrary to its original intent, it was used to curb labor unions or labor combinations that were deemed to be restraining trade.

Early prosecutions of the trusts by the Justice Department under the Sherman Act of 1890, as it turned out, were neither vigorous nor successful. Not until 1914 were the paper jaws of the Sherman Act fitted with reasonably sharp teeth. Until then, there was some question as to whether the government would control the trusts or the trusts the government.

But the iron grip of monopolistic corporations was being threatened. A revolutionary new principle had been written into the law books by the Sherman Anti-Trust Act of 1890, as well as by the Interstate Commerce Act of 1887. Private greed must henceforth be subordinated to public need.

The South in the Age of Industry

The industrial tidal wave that washed over the North after the Civil War caused only feeble ripples in the backwater of the South. The plantation system had degenerated into a pattern of absentee land ownership. White and black sharecroppers now tilled the soil for a share of the crop, or they became tenants, in bondage to landlords who controlled needed credit and supplies.

Southern agriculture received a welcome boost in the 1880s, when machine-made cigarettes replaced the roll-your-own variety and tobacco consumption shot up. James Buchanan Duke took full advantage of the new technology to mass-produce the dainty "coffin nails." In 1890, in what was becoming a familiar pattern, he absorbed his main competitors into the American Tobacco Company. The cigarette czar later showed such generosity to Trinity College, near his birthplace in Durham, North Carolina, that the trustees gratefully changed its name to Duke University.

Industrialists tried to coax the agricultural South out of the fields and into the factories, but with only modest success. The region remained overwhelmingly rural. Prominent among the boosters of a "new South" was silver-tongued Henry W. Grady, editor of the Atlanta *Constitution.* He tirelessly exhorted the ex-Confederates to become "Georgia Yankees" and outplay the North at the commercial and industrial game.

Yet formidable obstacles lay in the path of southern industrialization. One was the paper barrier of regional rate-setting systems imposed by the northern-dominated railroad interests. Railroads gave preferential rates to manufactured goods moving southward from the North, but in the opposite direction they discriminated in favor of southern raw materials. The net effect was to keep the South in a kind of "third world" servitude to the Northeast—as a supplier of raw materials to the manufacturing metropolis, unable to develop a substantial industrial base of its own.

A bitter example of this economic discrimination against the South was the "Pittsburgh plus" pricing system in the steel industry. Rich deposits of coal and iron ore near Birmingham, Alabama, worked by low-wage southern labor, should have given steel manufacturers there a competitive edge, especially in southern markets. But the steel lords of Pittsburgh brought pressure to bear on the compliant railroads. As a result, Birmingham steel, no matter where it was delivered, was charged a fictional fee, as if it had been shipped from Pittsburgh. This stunting of the South's natural economic advantages throttled the growth of the Birmingham steel industry.

In manufacturing cotton textiles the South fared considerably better. Southerners had long resented shipping their fiber to New England, and now their cry was, "Bring the mills to the cotton." Beginning about 1880, northern capital began to erect cotton mills in the South, largely in response to tax benefits and the prospect of cheap and nonunionized labor.

The textile mills proved a mixed blessing to the economically blighted South. Cheap labor was the South's major attraction for potential investors, and keeping labor cheap became almost a religion among southern industrialists. Mills took root in the chronically depressed piedmont region, where poor "hillbillies"—all of them white, for blacks were excluded from employment in the mills—worked from dawn to dusk amid the whirring spindles. Paid at half the rate of their northern counterparts, they were often habitually in debt to the company store.

The Impact of the New Industrial Revolution on America

Economic miracles wrought during the decades after the Civil War enormously increased the wealth of the republic. The standard of living rose sharply, and well-fed American workers enjoyed more physical comforts than their co-workers in any other powerful nation. Urban centers mushroomed as the insatiable factories demanded more American labor, and as immigrants swarmed like honeybees to the

The Poles

As the United States industrialized in the half-century following the Civil War, its smoke-belching factories beckoned across the Atlantic for badly needed labor. Few groups answered the call in greater numbers than the Poles. Between 1870 and the start of World War I, some 2 million Polish-speaking peasants boarded steamships for America.

Earlier Polish immigrants, who came in very small numbers, included prominent officers in the American Revolutionary army. But the Polish peasants who poured into the United States in the late nineteenth century came primarily to stave off starvation and to earn money to buy land. Known in their homeland as *za chlebem* ("for-bread") emigrants, they belonged to the mass of central and eastern European peasants who had been forced off their farms by growing competition from the large-scale, mechanized agriculture of western Europe and the United States. An exceptionally high birthrate among the Catholic Poles compounded this economic pressure, creating an army of land-poor and landless peasants who left their homes seasonally or permanently in search of work.

Poland had been carved up by the great European powers in the late eighteenth century. Poles fleeing Prussian rule arrived first in America, having been driven out of their homeland in part by the anti-Catholic policies that the German imperial government pursued in the 1870s. Fleeing religious persecution as well as economic turmoil, many of these early immigrants arrived in the United States intending to stay. Most of those who came later from Austrian and Russian Poland simply hoped to earn enough money to return home and to buy land.

The first wave of Polish immigrants had established a thriving network of self-help and fraternal

Polish Coal Miners, c. 1905 *It was common practice in American mines to segregate mining crews by ethnicity and race.*

associations, organized around Polish Catholic parishes. Often Polish-American entrepreneurs helped their European compatriots to make travel arrangements or to find jobs in the United States. One of the most successful of these, the energetic Chicago grocer Anton Schermann, is credited with "bringing over" 100,000 Poles and helping to earn the Windy

City the nickname the American Warsaw.

Most of the Poles arriving in the United States in the late nineteenth century headed for booming industrial cities such as Buffalo, Pittsburgh, Detroit, Milwaukee, and Chicago. In 1907, four-fifths of the men toiled as unskilled laborers in coal mines, meat-packing factories, textile and steel mills, oil refineries, and garment-making shops. Although married women usually stayed home, children and single girls often joined their fathers and brothers on the job.

Most Polish immigrants ultimately decided to remain in the United States and gradually assimilated to American life. Relatively few Poles returned to the independent Poland that emerged after World War I. That nation's absorption into the Communist bloc after World War II led most Polish Americans to cling still more tightly to their American identity. Rather than returning to the Old World, they pushed for landmarks like Chicago's Pulaski Highway to memorialize their culture in the New World.

---

new jobs (see "Makers of America: The Poles," pp. 368–369).

Early Jeffersonian ideals were withering before the smudgy blasts from the smokestacks. As agriculture declined in relation to manufacturing, America could no longer aspire to be a nation of small free-hold farms. Jefferson's concepts of free enterprise, neither helped nor hindered by Washington, were being thrown out the factory window.

Older ways of life also wilted in the heat of the factory furnaces. The very concept of time was revolutionized. Rural American migrants and peasant European immigrants, used to living by the languid clock of nature, now had to regiment their lives by the factory whistle. The seemingly arbitrary discipline of industrial labor did not come easily and sometimes was forcibly taught by corporate managers.

Probably no single group was more profoundly affected by the new industrial age than women. Sucked into industry by recent inventions, chiefly the typewriter and the telephone switchboard, millions of stenographers and "hello girls" achieved a new economic independence. Careers for women also meant delayed marriages and smaller families.

The clattering machine age likewise accentuated class division. "Industrial buccaneers" flaunted bloated fortunes, and their rags-to-riches spouses displayed glittering diamonds. Such extravagances evoked bitter criticism. Some of it was envious but

much of it rose from the small and increasingly vocal group of Socialists and other radicals, many of whom were recent European immigrants. The existence of an oligarchy of money was amply demonstrated by the fact that by 1900 about one-tenth of the people owned and controlled nine-tenths of the nation's wealth.

Finally, strong pressures for foreign trade developed as the tireless machine threatened to flood the domestic market. American products radiated out all over the world—notably the five-gallon kerosene can of the Standard Oil Company. The flag follows trade, and empire tends to follow the flag—a harsh lesson that America was soon to learn.

In Unions There Is Strength

Sweat of the laborer lubricated the vast new industrial machine. Yet wageworkers did not share proportionately with their employers the benefits of the age of big business.

The worker, suggestive of the Roman galley slave, was becoming a lever puller in a giant mechanism. Individual originality and creativity were being stifled, and less value than ever before was being placed on manual skills. Before the Civil War the worker might have toiled in a small plant, whose owner hailed the employee in the morning by first name and inquired after the family's health. But now the factory hand was employed by a corporation—

Striking Streetcar Workers, 1895   *The depression of 1893–1897 brought a rash of labor unrest across the U.S. These Brooklyn streetcar workers struck to protest wage reductions and layoffs by their company.*

depersonalized, bodiless, soulless, and often conscienceless. The vast new railroad network could shuttle unemployed workers, including blacks and immigrants, into areas where wages were high, and thus beat standards down. Inpouring Europeans further worsened conditions. During the 1880s and 1890s and later, the labor market had to absorb several hundred thousand unskilled workers a year.

Individual workers were powerless to battle singlehandedly against giant industry. The corporation could dispense with the individual worker much more easily than the worker could dispense with the corporation. Employers could pool vast wealth through thousands of stockholders, import strikebreakers ("scabs"), and employ thugs to beat up labor organizers. In 1886 Jay Gould reputedly boasted, "I can hire one-half of the working class to kill the other half."

Corporations had still other weapons in their arsenals. They could call upon the conservative federal courts to issue injunctions against strikers, and then request state or federal authorities to send in troops if defiance continued. Employers could lock the doors of their plants (a process called the "lockout") and starve rebellious workers into submission. They could compel them to sign "ironclad oaths" or "yellow dog contracts"—agreements not to join a labor union—as a condition of employment. They could put the names of labor agitators on a "black list" and circulate it among fellow employers. A corporation might even own the "company town" or "company store," which often sank workers into perpetual debt—a status that strongly resembled serfdom.

The public, annoyed by recurrent strikes, grew deaf to the outcry of the worker. Carnegie and Rockefeller had battled their way to the top, and the view was common that the laborer could do likewise. Somehow the strike seemed like a foreign importation—socialistic and hence unpatriotic. Big business might combine into trusts to raise prices, but the worker must not combine into unions to raise wages.

Labor Limps Along

Labor unions, which had been few and disorganized in 1861, were given a strong boost by the Civil War. By 1872 there were several hundred thousand organized workers and thirty-two national unions, including such craftsmen as bricklayers, typesetters, and shoemakers.

The National Labor Union, organized in 1866, represented a giant bootstride by the workers. It lasted six years and attracted the impressive total of some 600,000 members, including the skilled, unskilled, and farmers. Its keynote was social reform, although it agitated for such specific goals as the eight-hour day and the arbitration of industrial disputes. It finally succeeded in winning an eight-hour day for government workers, but the devastating depression of the 1870s dealt it a knockout blow. Wage reductions in 1877 touched off a series of strikes on the railroads that were so violent as to verge on civil war.

A new organization—the Knights of Labor—seized the torch dropped by the defunct National Labor Union. Officially known as the Noble and Holy Order of the Knights of Labor, it began inauspiciously in 1869 as a secret society, with a private ritual, passwords, and a grip.

The Knights of Labor, like the National Labor Union, sought to include all workers in "one big union." Their slogan was: "An injury to one is the concern of all." A welcome mat was rolled out for the skilled and unskilled, for men and women, for whites and underprivileged blacks, some 90,000 of whom joined. The Knights excluded only liquor dealers, professional gamblers, lawyers, bankers, and stockbrokers.

Setting up broad goals, the embattled Knights campaigned for economic and social reform, including producers' cooperatives and codes for safety and health. The ordinary workday was then ten hours or more, and the Knights waged a determined campaign for the eight-hour stint.

Under the eloquent but often erratic leadership of Terence V. Powderly, an Irish-American of nimble wit and fluent tongue, the Knights won a number of strikes for the eight-hour day. When the Knights staged a successful strike against Jay Gould's Wabash Railroad in 1885, membership mushroomed to about three-quarters of a million workers.

Unhorsing the Knights of Labor

Despite their outward success, the Knights were riding for a fall. They became involved in a number of May Day strikes in 1886, about half of which failed. A focal point was Chicago, which contained about 80,000 Knights. The city was also honeycombed with a few hundred anarchists, many of them foreign-born, who were advocating a violent overthrow of the American government.

Tensions rapidly built up to the bloody Haymarket Square episode. Labor disorders had broken out, and on May 4, 1886, the Chicago police advanced on a meeting called to protest alleged brutalities by the authorities. Suddenly a dynamite bomb was thrown that killed or injured several dozen persons, including police.

Hysteria swept the Windy City. Eight anarchists were rounded up, although nobody proved that they had anything to do directly with the bomb. But the judge and jury held that since they had preached incendiary doctrines, they could be charged with conspiracy. Five were sentenced to death, one of whom committed suicide, and the other three were given stiff prison terms. They were eventually pardoned in 1892 by Illinois Governor John P. Altgeld, a German-born Democrat of strong liberal tendencies.

The Haymarket Square bomb helped blow the props from under the Knights of Labor. They were associated in the public mind, though mistakenly, with the anarchists. The eight-hour movement suffered correspondingly, and subsequent strikes by the Knights met with scant success. By the 1890s the Knights had melted away to 100,000 members, and these gradually fused with other protest groups of that decade.

The A.F. of L. to the Fore

The elitist American Federation of Labor, born in 1886, was largely the brainchild of squat, square-jawed Samuel Gompers. This colorful Jewish cigar maker, born in a London tenement and removed from school at age ten, was brought to America when thirteen. Taking his turn at reading informative literature to his fellow cigar makers in New York, he was pressed into overtime service because of his strong voice. Rising spectacularly in the labor ranks, he was elected president of the American Federation of Labor every year except one from 1886 to 1924.

Gompers adopted a down-to-earth approach, soft-pedaling attempts to engineer sweeping social reform. A bitter foe of socialism, he kept the federation squarely on the cautious path of conservatism.

He had no quarrel with capitalism as such, but he wanted labor to win its fair share. All he wanted, he said simply, was "more." His objectives were better wages and hours, as well as other improved conditions for the worker.

The A.F. of L. thus established itself on solid but narrow foundations. Although attempting to speak for all workers, it fell far short of being representative of them. Composed of skilled craftsmen, like the carpenters and bricklayers, it was willing to let unskilled laborers, including women and especially blacks, shift for themselves. The A.F. of L. weathered the Panic of 1893 reasonably well, and by 1900 it could boast a membership of 500,000.

Labor disorders continued throughout the years from 1881 to 1900, during which there was an alarming total of over 23,000 strikes. These disturbances involved 6,610,000 workers, with a total loss to both employers and employees of $450 million. The strikers lost about half their strikes and won or compromised the remainder. Perhaps the gravest weakness of organized labor was that it still embraced only a small minority of all working people—about 3 percent in 1900.

But attitudes toward labor had begun to change perceptibly by 1900. The public was beginning to concede the right of workers to organize, to bargain collectively, and to strike. As a sign of the times, Labor Day was made a legal holiday by act of Congress in 1894. A few enlightened industrialists had come to perceive the wisdom of avoiding costly economic warfare by bargaining with the unions and signing agreements. But the vast majority of employ-

CHRONOLOGY

1862	Congress authorizes a transcontinental railroad.
1866	National Labor Union organized.
1869	Transcontinental railroad joined at Ogden, Utah.
	Knights of Labor organized.
1870	Standard Oil Company organized.
1876	Bell invents the telephone.
1879	Edison invents the electric light.
1886	Haymarket Square bombing.
	Wabash case.
	American Federation of Labor formed.
1887	Interstate Commerce Act.
1890	Sherman Anti-Trust Act.
1901	United States Steel Corporation formed.

ers continued to fight organized labor, which achieved its grudging gains only after recurrent strikes and frequent reverses. Several trouble-fraught decades were to pass before labor was to gain a position of relative equality with capital. If the age of big business had dawned, the age of big labor was still some distance over the horizon.

Varying Viewpoints

The capitalists who forged an industrial America in the late nineteenth century were once called "captains of industry"—a respectful title that bespoke the awe due their wondrous material accomplishments. But these economic innovators have never been universally admired. During the Great Depression of the 1930s, when the entire industrial order they had created seemed to have collapsed utterly, it was fashionable to speak of them as "robber barons"—a term implying scorn for their high-handed methods. This sneer often issued from the lips and pens of left-wing critics like Matthew Josephson, who sympathized with the working classes that were allegedly brutalized by the factory system.

Criticism has also come from writers nostalgic

for a preindustrial past. These critics see in industrialization a stripping away of the traditions, values, and pride of native farmers and immigrant craftspeople. Conceding that economic development elevated the standard of living for working Americans, this interpretation contends that the Industrial Revolution diminished their "quality of life." Accordingly, historians such as Herbert Gutman and David Montgomery portray labor's struggle for control of the workplace as the central drama of industrial expansion.

Nevertheless, even these historians concede that class-based protest has never been as powerful a force in America as in certain European countries. In the 1960s, historians led by Stephan Thernstrom began to test the long-standing belief that greater social mobility had dampened class tensions in the United States. Looking at such factors as occupation, wealth, and geographic mobility, they concluded that, although relatively few Americans had leaped from rags to riches, large

numbers had experienced small improvements in their economic and social status. These studies also found that race and ethnicity often affected one's chance for success.

In recent years such studies have been criticized by certain historians, among them James Henretta, who pointed out the difficulties involved in defining social status. They observed that lower wages did not necessarily equal lower social status, and some ethnic groups, such as the Italians and Irish, may have put greater emphasis on acquiring land or small businesses rather than on professional education. Meanwhile, leftist historians such as Michael Katz argued that the degree of social mobility in the United States has been overrated. They maintained that the fundamental inequality of an industrial capitalistic class system, in which a working class sells its labor and a business class controls resources, persisted even in America's seemingly fluid society.

SELECT READINGS

Primary Source Documents

Andrew Carnegie's "Wealth,"* *North American Review* (June 1889), gives the philosophy of the Gilded Age's greatest entrepreneur. Henry Grady's Boston speech (1889), in Joel C. Harris, *Life of Henry W. Grady* (1890), dramatizes the plight of the South. Samuel Gompers penned his "Letter on Labor in Industrial Society," an open letter to Judge Peter Grossup, in 1894 (in Richard Hofstadter, *Great Issues in American History*). William Dean Howells's novel *The Rise of Silas Lapham* (1885) treats the moral impact of the new business culture on one New England businessman and his family.

Secondary Sources

A useful survey is Nell Painter, *Standing at Armageddon* (1987). See also Samuel P. Hays, *The Response to Industrialism, 1885–1914* (1957). Stuart Bruchey puts the period in context in *The Growth of the Modern Economy* (1975). Business is the subject of Alfred D. Chandler, Jr., *The Visible Hand: The Managerial Revolution in American Business* (1978), and Saul Engelbourg, *Power and Morality:*

American Business Ethics, 1840–1914 (1980). The thought and attitudes characteristic of the new industrial age are examined by Richard Hofstadter, *Social Darwinism in American Thought* (rev. ed., 1955), and Daniel T. Rodger, *The Work Ethic in Industrial America, 1850–1920* (1978). C. Vann Woodward has provided a masterful analysis of *Origins of the New South, 1877–1913* (1951). For labor, see Gerald Grob, *Workers and Utopia* (1961), David Montgomery's innovative *Workers' Control in America: Studies in the History of Work, Technology, and Labor Struggles* (1979), and Herbert Gutman's stimulating *Work, Culture, and Society in Industrializing America* (1976) and *Power and Culture: Essays on the American Working Class* (1987). On female workers, see David Katzman, *Seven Days a Week: Women and Domestic Service in Industrializing America* (1978), and Alice Kessler-Harris, *Out to Work: A History of Wage-Earning Women in the United States* (1982). For a discussion of labor and race, see Gerald David Jaynes, *Branches Without Roots: Genesis of the Black Working Class in the American South, 1862–1882* (1986).

CHAPTER 27

America Moves to the City, 1865–1900

What shall we do with our great cities? What will our great cities do with us . . . ? [T]he question . . . does not concern the city alone. The whole country is affected . . . by the condition of its great cities.

Lyman Abbot, 1891

The Urban Frontier

Born in the country, America moved to the city in the decades following the Civil War. By the year 1900 the United States' upsurging population nearly doubled from its level of some 40 million people enumerated in the census of 1870. Yet in the very same period the population of American cities *tripled.* By the end of the nineteenth century, four of ten Americans were city dwellers.

This cityward drift affected not only the United States but most of the Western world. European peasants, pushed off the land in part by competition from cheap American foodstuffs, were pulled into cities—in both Europe and America—by the new lure of industrial jobs. A revolution in agriculture thus fed the industrial and urban revolutions.

The growth of American metropolises was spectacular. In 1860 no city in the United States could boast a million inhabitants; by 1890 New York, Chicago, and Philadelphia had spurted past the million mark. By 1900 New York, with some 3.5 million people, was the second largest city in the world, outranked only by London.

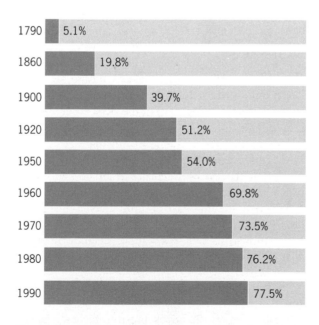

1790	5.1%
1860	19.8%
1900	39.7%
1920	51.2%
1950	54.0%
1960	69.8%
1970	73.5%
1980	76.2%
1990	77.5%

The Shift to the City *Percentage of total population living in cities of twenty-five hundred or more. Note the slowing of the cityward trend in the 1970s.*

New York's Mulberry Street, 1904 *Outside the teeming tenement buildings, crowded city streets became places of work, play, and rough-and-tumble Americanization for many of the nation's recent immigrants.*

Cities grew both up and out. The cloud-brushing skyscraper allowed more people and workplaces to be packed onto a parcel of land. Appearing first as a ten-story building in Chicago in 1885, the skyscraper was made usable by the perfecting of the electric elevator. An opinionated Chicago architect, Louis Sullivan (1856–1924), contributed formidably to the further development of the skyscraper with his famous principle that "form follows function."

Cities also spread out, turning many Americans into commuters who were carted daily by mass-transit electric trolleys between urban job and suburban home. The compact and communal "walking city" gave way to the immense and impersonal megalopolis, carved into distinctly different districts for business, industry, and residential neighborhoods—which in turn were segregated by race, ethnicity, and social class.

Rural America could not compete with the siren song of the city. Industrial jobs, above all, drew country folks off the farms and into factory centers. But the urban lifestyle also held powerful attractions.

The predawn milking of cows had little appeal when compared with the late-night glitter of city lights. Electricity, indoor plumbing, and telephones all made life in the big city more alluring. Engineering marvels like the skyscraper and New York's awesome Brooklyn Bridge, a harplike suspension span dedicated in 1883, further added to the seductive glamour of the gleaming cities.

Cavernous department stores such as Macy's in New York and Marshall Field's in Chicago attracted urban shoppers and heralded the dawning era of consumerism. They also accentuated widening class divisions. When Carrie Meeker, novelist Theodore Dreiser's fictional heroine in *Sister Carrie* (1900), escapes from rural boredom to Chicago, the city's dazzling department stores awaken her to a richer, more elegant way of life.

The move to the city also introduced new American lifestyles. Household products sold in bulk at the local store, without wrapping, gave way to city goods that came in throwaway bottles, boxes, bags, and cans. Apartment houses had no adjoining barnyards where residents might toss garbage to the hogs. Waste disposal, in short, was an issue new to the age of urban consumerism.

The jagged skyline of America's perpendicular civilization could not fully conceal the canker sores of feverish growth. Criminals flourished like lice in the teeming asphalt jungles. Impure water, uncollected garbage, unwashed bodies, and droppings from draft animals enveloped many cities in a satanic stench.

The cities were monuments of contradiction. They represented "humanity compressed," remarked one observer, "the best and the worst combined, in a strangely composite community." They harbored merchant princes and miserable paupers, stately banks and sooty factories, green-grassed suburbs and stinking tenements. The glaring contrasts that assaulted the eye in New York reminded one visitor of "a lady in ball costume, with diamonds in her ears, and her toes out at the boots."

Worst of all were the human pigsties known as slums. They seemed to grow ever more crowded, more filthy, and more rat-infested, especially after the perfection in 1879 of the "dumbbell" tenement. So named because of the outline of its floor plan, the dumbbell was usually seven or eight stories high, with shallow, sunless, and ill-smelling air shafts providing minimal ventilation. Several families were sardined onto each floor of the barrackslike structures, and they shared a malodorous toilet in the hall. Small wonder that slum dwellers strove mightily to escape their wretched surroundings—as many of them did. The slums remained foul places, inhabited by successive waves of newcomers, but to a remarkable degree hardworking people moved up and out of them. The most successful families left the inner city altogether and headed for the semirural suburbs. These leafy "bedroom communities" eventually ringed the brick-and-concrete cities with a greenbelt of affluence.

The New Immigration

The powerful pull of the American urban magnet was felt even in faraway Europe. A brightly colored stream of immigrants continued to pour in from the old "mother continent." In each of the three decades from the 1850s through the 1870s, more than 2 million migrants had stepped onto America's shores. By the 1880s the stream had swelled to a rushing torrent, as more than 5 million cascaded into the country.

Until the 1880s, most immigrants had come from the British Isles and western Europe, chiefly Germany and Scandinavia. They were usually Protestant, except for the Catholic Irish and many Catholic Germans, and boasted a comparatively high rate of literacy. They fit relatively easily into American society.

But in the 1880s the character of the immigrant stream changed drastically. The so-called New Immigrants—Italians, Croats, Slovaks, Greeks, Poles—came from southern and eastern Europe. Many of them worshiped in Roman Catholic or Eastern Orthodox churches or in Jewish synagogues. Heavily illiterate and impoverished, they hived together in the "Little Italys" and "Little Polands" of the jam-packed cities. The New Immigrants totaled only 19 percent of newcomers in the 1880s, but by the first decade of the next century they constituted an astonishing 66 percent of the total inflow.

Why were these bright-shawled and quaint-jacketed strangers hammering on the gates? In part, they left their old countries because Europe seemed to have no room for them. Rapid population growth, American food imports, and European industrialization shook the peasantry loose from its ancient habitats and customary occupations, creating a vast, footloose army of the unemployed. Europeans by the millions drained out of the countryside and into European cities. Most stayed there, but some kept moving and left Europe altogether. About 60 million Europeans abandoned the old continent in the nineteenth and early twentieth centuries. More than half of them moved to the United States. But that striking fact should not obscure the important truth that masses of people were already in motion in Europe before they felt the tug of the American magnet. Immigration to America was, in many ways, a by-product of the urbanization of Europe.

"America fever" proved highly contagious in Europe. The United States was often painted as a

The Italians

Who were the New Immigrants? Who were these southern and eastern European birds of passage that flocked to the United States between 1880 and 1920? Prominent and typical among them were Italians, some 4 million of whom sailed to the United States during the four decades of the New Immigration.

They came from the southern provinces of their native land, the heel and toe of the Italian boot. These areas had lagged behind the prosperous, industrial northern region. Unification had raised hopes of progress in the downtrodden south, but progress came slowly.

Southern peasants tilled their fields without fertilizer or machinery, using hand plows and rickety hoes that had been passed down for generations. From such disappointed and demeaned conditions, southern Italians set out for the New World. Almost all of them were young men who intended to spend only a few months in America, stuff their pockets with dollars, and return home. Almost half of Italian immigrants did indeed repatriate—as did comparable numbers of the other New Immigrants, with the conspicuous exception of the Jews, who had fled their native lands to escape religious persecution.

Almost all Italian immigrants sailed through New York harbor, sighting the Statue of Liberty as they debarked from crowded ships. Many soon moved on to other large cities, but so many remained that, in the early years of the twentieth century, more Italians resided in New York than in Florence, Venice, and Genoa combined. Although they huddled in the cities, these immigrants did not, however, abandon their rural upbringings entirely. Much to their neighbors' consternation, they often kept chickens in vacant lots and raised vegetables in small

Italian Immigrant Woman and Children Doing Piecework at Home in New York, c. 1910

garden plots nestled between decaying tenement houses.

Those who bade a permanent farewell to Italy clustered in tightly knit communities that boasted opera clubs, Italian-language newspapers, and courts for playing bocci—a version of lawn bowling imported from the Old Country. Pizza emerged from the hot wood-burning ovens of these Little Italys, its aroma and flavor wafting its way into the hearts and stomachs of all Americans.

Italians typically earned their daily bread as industrial laborers—most famously as longshoremen and construction workers. They owed their prominence in the building trades to the "padrone system." The *padrone,* or labor boss, met immigrants upon arrival and secured jobs for them in New York, Chicago, or wherever there was an immediate demand for industrial labor.

Lacking education, the Italians, as a group, remained in blue-collar jobs longer than some of their fellow New Immigrants. Many of them, valuing vocation over schooling, sent their children off to work as early in their young lives as possible. Before

World War I, fewer than 1 percent of Italian children were enrolled in high school. Over the next fifty years, Italian-Americans and their offspring gradually prospered, moving out of the cities into the more affluent suburbs. Many served heroically in World War II and availed themselves of the GI Bill to finance the college education and professional training that their immigrant forebears had lacked.

---

land of fabulous opportunity in the "America letters" of friends and relatives already transplanted.

The land of the free was also blessed with freedom from military conscription and religious persecution. Beginning in the 1880s, savage treatment of minorities in Europe, especially Russian Jews, drove tens of thousands of battered refugees to American shores. Virtually unique among the New Immigrants, Jews often had experience with city life in Europe, and many of them brought their urban skills of tailoring and shopkeeping to American cities, especially New York.

The New Immigrants struggled heroically to preserve their traditional cultures. Catholics expanded their parochial school system, and Jews established Hebrew schools. Foreign-language newspapers, parishes, theaters, restaurants, and social clubs all attested to the desire to keep old ways alive. Yet time took its toll on these efforts to conserve the customs of the Old World in the New. The children of the immigrants grew up speaking fluent English, sometimes mocking the broken grammar of their parents. They often rejected the Old Country manners of their mothers and fathers in their desire to plunge headlong into the mainstream of American life.

Reactions to the New Immigration

America's government system, nurtured in wide-open spaces, was ill suited to the cement forests of the great cities. Beyond minimal checking to weed

out criminals and the insane, the federal government did virtually nothing to ease the assimilation of immigrants into American society. State governments, usually dominated by rural representatives, did even less. City governments, overwhelmed by the sheer scale of rampant urban growth, proved woefully inadequate to the task. By default, the business of ministering to the immigrants' needs fell to the unofficial "governments" of the urban political machines, led by "bosses" such as New York's notorious Boss Tweed.

Taking care of the immigrants was big business, indeed. Trading jobs and services for votes, a powerful boss might claim the loyalty of thousands of followers. In return for their support at the polls, the boss provided employment on the city's payroll, found housing for new arrivals, tided over the needy with gifts of food and clothing, patched up minor scrapes with the law, and helped get schools, parks, and hospitals built in immigrant neighborhoods. Reformers gagged at this cynical exploitation of the immigrant vote, but the political boss provided valuable assistance that was forthcoming from no other source.

The nation's social conscience gradually awakened to the plight of the cities and their immigrant masses. Prominent in this awakening were Protestant clergymen such as Walter Rauschenbusch of New York City and Washington Gladden of Columbus, Ohio, who sought to apply the lessons of Christianity to the slums and factories. Preaching the "social gospel," they both insisted that the churches tackle the burning social issues of the day.

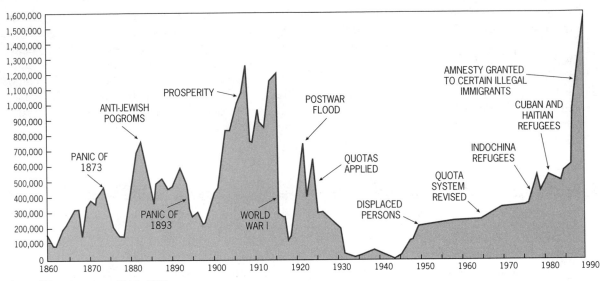

Annual Immigration, 1860–1990

One middle-class woman who was deeply dedicated to uplifting the urban masses was Jane Addams (1860–1935). Born into a prosperous Illinois family, Addams was one of the first generation of college-educated women, and sought proper outlets for her large talents. Inspired by a visit to England, in 1889 she established Hull House in Chicago as the most prominent American settlement house. Located in a poor immigrant neighborhood of Greeks, Italians, Russians, and Germans, Hull House offered instruction in English, counseling to help newcomers cope with American big-city life, child-care services for working mothers, and cultural activities of all kinds for neighborhood residents.

Soft-spoken but tenacious, Jane Addams became a kind of urban American saint in the eyes of many admirers. She was a broad-gauge reformer who courageously condemned war as well as poverty, and she eventually won the Nobel Peace Prize in 1931.

Following Jane Addams's lead, women founded settlement houses in other cities as well—notably Lillian Wald's Henry Street Settlement in New York, which opened its doors in 1893. The settlement houses became centers of women's activism and social reform on behalf of women, children, blacks, and consumers. The women of Hull House, for example, successfully lobbied in 1893 for an Illinois antisweatshop law that protected women workers and prohibited child labor. They were led by Florence Kelley, a guerrilla warrior in the urban jungle who battled for decades on behalf of the underprivileged at both the Hull House and Henry Street settlements.

The pioneering work of Addams, Wald, and Kelley vividly demonstrated that the city was the frontier of opportunity for women, just as the wilderness had been the frontier of opportunity for men. The urban frontier opened boundless new possibilities for women—as social workers and secretaries, store clerks and seamstresses, telephone operators and bookkeepers. More than a million women joined the workforce in the single decade of the 1890s. As America moved to the city, women moved nearer to economic independence.

Narrowing the Welcome Mat

Antiforeignism, or "nativism," earlier touched off by the Irish and German arrivals in the 1840s and 1850s, bared its ugly face in the 1880s with fresh ferocity. The New Immigrants had come for much the same reasons as the Old—to escape the poverty

Jane Addams (1860–1935) *Besides founding the Hull House settlement, Jane Addams helped develop the modern profession of social work and became a strong advocate for international peace during and after World War I.*

and squalor of Europe and to seek new opportunities in America. But "nativists" viewed the eastern and southern Europeans as culturally and religiously exotic hordes and often gave them a rude reception. The newest newcomers aroused widespread alarm. Their high birthrate, common among people with a low standard of living and sufficient youth and vigor to pull up stakes, raised worries that the original Anglo-Saxon stock would soon be outbred and outvoted. Still more horrifying was the prospect that it would be "mongrelized" by a mixture of "inferior" southern European blood and that the fairer Anglo-Saxon types would disappear. One New England writer cried out in anguish:

> O Liberty, white Goddess! is it well
> To leave the gates unguarded?

"Native" Americans voiced additional fears. They blamed the immigrants for the degradation of urban government. Trade unionists assailed the alien arrivals for their willingness to work for "starvation" wages that seemed to them like princely sums, and for importing in their intellectual baggage such dangerous doctrines as socialism, communism, and anarchism. Many business leaders, who had welcomed the flood of cheap manual labor, began to fear that they had embraced a Frankenstein's monster.

Antiforeign organizations, reminiscent of the "Know-Nothings" of antebellum days, were now revived in a different guise. Notorious among them was the American Protective Association (APA), which was created in 1887 and soon claimed a million members. In seeking its nativist goals, the APA urged voting against Roman Catholic candidates for office and sponsored the publication of lustful fantasies about runaway nuns.

Organized labor was quick to throw its growing weight behind the move to choke off the rising tide of foreigners. Frequently used as strikebreakers, the wage-depressing immigrants were hard to unionize because of the language barrier. Labor leaders argued, not illogically, that if American industry was entitled to protection from foreign goods, the American worker was entitled to protection from foreign laborers.

Congress finally nailed up partial bars against the inpouring immigrants. The first restrictive law, in 1882, banged the gate in the faces of paupers, criminals, and convicts, all of whom had to be returned at the expense of the greedy or careless shipper. Congress further responded to pained outcries from organized labor when in 1885 it prohibited the importation of workers under contract—usually for substandard wages.

In later years other federal laws lengthened the list of undesirables to include the insane, polygamists, prostitutes, alcoholics, anarchists, and persons carrying contagious diseases. A proposed literacy test, long a favorite of nativists because it favored the Old Immigrants over the New, met vigorous opposition. It was not enacted until 1917, after three presidents had vetoed it on the grounds that literacy was more a measure of opportunity than of intelligence.

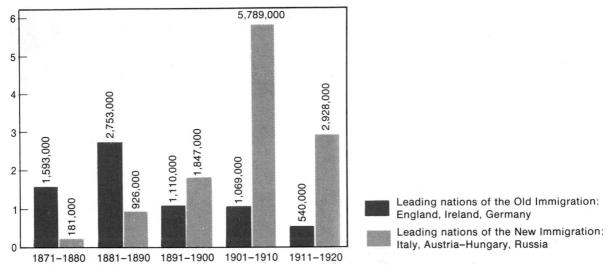

Old and New Immigration (by decade) *In the 1970s, the sources of immigration to the United States shifted yet again. The largest number of immigrants came from Latin America (especially Mexico), the next largest from Asia. The old "mother continent" of Europe accounted for only 10 percent of the immigrants to America in the 1980s.*

The year 1882, in addition to the first federal restrictions on immigration, brought forth a law to bar completely one ethnic group—the Chinese (see pp. 344–345). Hitherto America had gathered to her ample breast the oppressed and underprivileged of all races and creeds. Hereafter the gates would be padlocked against defective undesirables—plus the Chinese.

Four years later, in 1886, the Statue of Liberty arose in New York harbor, a gift from the people of France. On its base were inscribed the words of Emma Lazarus:

> Give me your tired, your poor
> Your huddled masses yearning to breathe
>   free,
> The wretched refuse of your teeming shore.

To many nativists, those noble words described only too accurately the "scum" washed up by the New Immigrant tides. Yet the uprooted immigrants, unlike "natives" lucky enough to have had parents who caught an earlier ship, became American citizens the hard way. They stepped off the boat, many of them full-grown and well muscled, ready to put their shoulders to the nation's industrial wheels. The republic owes much to these latercomers—for their brawn, their brains, their courage, and the yeasty diversity they brought to American society.

Churches Confront the Urban Challenge

The swelling size and changing character of the urban population posed sharp challenges to American churches, which, like other national institutions, had grown up in the country. Protestant churches, in particular, suffered heavily from the shift to the city, where many of their traditional doctrines and pastoral approaches seemed irrelevant.

As they lost their bearings in the new urban world, some churches were tending to become merely sacred diversions or amusements. Reflecting the wealth of their prosperous parishioners, many of the old-line churches were distressingly slow to raise their voices against social and economic vices. John D. Rockefeller was a pillar of the Baptist church; J. Pierpont Morgan, of the Episcopal church. Cynics remarked that the Episcopal church had become "the Republican party at prayer." The mounting emphasis was on materialism; too many devotees worshiped at the altar of avarice. Money was the accepted measure of achievement, and the new gospel of wealth proclaimed that God caused the righteous to prosper.

Into this spreading moral vacuum stepped a new generation of urban revivalists. Most conspicuous was a former Chicago shoe salesman, Dwight Lyman Moody. Proclaiming a gospel of kindness and forgiveness, Moody was a modern urban circuit rider who took his message to countless American cities in the 1870s and 1880s. Clad in a dark business suit, the bearded and rotund Moody held huge audiences spellbound. He contributed powerfully to adapting the old-time religion to the realities of city life. The Moody Bible Institute, founded in Chicago in 1889, carried on his work after his death in 1899.

Simultaneously, the Roman Catholic and Jewish faiths were gaining enormous strength from the New Immigration. By 1900 the Roman Catholics had increased their lead as the largest single denomination, numbering nearly 9 million communicants. Roman Catholics and Jewish groups kept the common touch better than many of the leading Protestant churches. Cardinal James Gibbons (1834–1921) of Baltimore, an urban Catholic leader devoted to American unity, was immensely popular with Roman Catholics and Protestants alike. Acquainted with every president from Johnson to Harding, he employed his liberal sympathies to assist the American labor movement.

By 1890 the variety-loving American could choose from 150 religious denominations, two of them newcomers. One was the band-playing Salvation Army, whose soldiers without swords invaded America from England in 1879 and established a beachhead on the street corners. Appealing frankly to the down-and-outers, the so-called Starvation Army did much practical good, especially with free soup.

The other important new faith was the Church of Christ, Scientist (Christian Science), founded by Mary Baker Eddy in 1879, after she had suffered much ill health. Preaching that the true practice of Christianity heals sickness, she set forth her views in a book entitled *Science and Health with Key to the Scriptures* (1875), which sold an amazing 400,000 copies before her death in 1910. Appealing especially to America's hurried, nerve-wracked urban residents, Christian Science became an influential church that embraced several hundred thousand worshipers.

Although a few new churches managed to grow, traditional religion received serious blows from modern books on comparative religion and historical criticism of the Bible. Most unsettling of all was *On the Origin of Species* (1859), in which the English naturalist Charles Darwin set forth the sensational theory that humans had slowly evolved from lower forms of life. Evolution cast serious doubt on a literal interpretation of the Bible, which relates how God created the heavens and the earth in six days.

Darwinism eventually created rifts in the churches and colleges of the post–Civil War era. Conservative believers, or Fundamentalists, stood firmly on the Scripture as the inspired and infallible Word of God, whereas "Modernists" valued the Bible's ethical teachings but refused to accept it as either history or science. Modernist clergymen were removed from their pulpits; teachers of biology who embraced evolution were dismissed from their chairs. As time wore on, an increasing number of liberal thinkers were able to reconcile Darwinism with Christianity by regarding evolution as a newer and grander revelation of the ways of the Almighty. But Darwinism undoubtedly did much to loosen religious moorings and promote unbelief.

The Lust for Learning

Public education continued its upward climb. The ideal of tax-supported elementary schools was still gathering strength. Beginning about 1870, more and more states were making at least a grade-school education compulsory, and this gain, incidentally, helped check the frightening abuses of child labor.

Spectacular indeed was the spread of the high schools, especially by the 1880s and 1890s. By 1900 there were some 6,000 tax-supported high schools. In addition, the taxpayers of the states were providing free textbooks in increasing numbers during the last two decades of the century.

Other trends were noteworthy. Teacher training schools, then called "normal schools," experienced a striking expansion after the Civil War. Kindergartens, earlier borrowed from Germany, also began to gain strong support. The New Immigration in the 1880s and 1890s brought vast new strength to the Catholic parochial schools, which were fast becoming a major pillar of the nation's educational structure.

Public schools, though showering benefits on children, excluded millions of adults. This deficiency was partially remedied by the Chautauqua movement, launched in 1874 on the shores of Lake Chautauqua in New York. The organizers achieved gratifying success through nationwide public lectures, often held in tents and featuring such well-known speakers as Mark Twain. In addition, there were extensive Chautauqua courses of home study, for which 100,000 persons enrolled in 1892 alone.

Crowded cities, despite their cancers, generally provided better educational facilities than the old one-room, one-teacher red schoolhouse. The success of the public schools is confirmed by the falling of the illiteracy rate from 20 percent in 1870 to 10.7 percent in 1900. Americans were developing a profound faith in formal education, often misplaced, as the sovereign remedy for their ills.

Booker T. Washington and Education for Black People

War-torn and impoverished, the South lagged far behind other regions in public education, and African-Americans suffered most severely. A staggering 44 percent of nonwhites were illiterate in 1900. Some help came from northern philanthropists, but the foremost champion of black education was an ex-slave, Booker T. Washington, who had slept under a board sidewalk to save pennies for his schooling. Called in 1881 to head the black normal and industrial school at Tuskegee, Alabama, he began with forty students in a tumbledown shanty. Undaunted by adversity, he taught his people useful trades so that they could gain self-respect and economic opportunity. But he stopped short of advocating social equality with whites.

A stellar member of the Tuskegee faculty, beginning in 1896, was slave-born George Washington Carver, who as an infant in Missouri was kidnapped and ransomed for a horse worth $300. He became an internationally famous agricultural chemist who helped the economy of the South by discovering hundreds of new uses for the lowly peanut (shampoo, axle grease), sweet potato (vinegar), and soybean (paints).

Other African-American leaders, notably Dr. W. E. B. Du Bois, assailed Booker T. Washington as an "Uncle Tom," who was condemning their race to manual labor and perpetual inferiority. Born in Massachusetts, Du Bois was a mixture of African, French, Dutch, and Indian blood ("Thank God, no Anglo-Saxon," he would add). After a determined struggle, he earned a Ph.D. at Harvard, the first of his race to achieve this goal. He demanded full equality for blacks, social as well as economic, and helped to found the National Association for the Advancement of Colored People (NAACP) in 1910. Rejecting Washington's gradualism and separatism, he demanded that the "talented tenth" of the black community be given full and immediate access to the mainstream of American life. An exceptionally skilled historian, sociologist, and poet, he died as a self-exile in Africa in 1963, at the age of ninety-five.

The Hallowed Halls of Ivy

Colleges and universities also shot up like lusty young saplings in the decades after the Civil War. The educational battle for women, only partially won before the war, now turned into a rout of masculine diehards. Women's colleges, such as Vassar, were gaining ground; and universities open to both genders were blossoming forth, notably in the Midwest. By 1900 every fourth college graduate was a woman.

The almost phenomenal growth of higher education owed much to the Morrill Act of 1862. This enlightened law, passed after the South had seceded, provided a generous grant of the public lands to the states for support of education. "Land-grant colleges," most of which became state universities, in turn bound themselves to provide certain services, such as military training. The Hatch Act of 1887, supplementing the Morrill Act, provided federal funds for the establishment of agricultural experiment stations in connection with the land-grant colleges.

Private philanthropy richly supplemented federal grants to higher education. Many of the new industrial millionaires, developing tender social consciences, donated immense fortunes to educational enterprises. In the twenty years from 1878 to 1898 these money barons gave away about $150 million. Noteworthy among the new private universities of high quality to open their doors were Cornell (1865) and Leland Stanford Junior (1891), the latter founded in memory of the deceased fifteen-year-old only child of a builder of the Central Pacific Railroad. The University of Chicago, opened in 1892, speedily forged into a front-rank position, owing largely to the lubricant of Rockefeller's oil millions.

Towering among the new professionalized institutions of higher education was the Johns Hopkins University, opened in 1876, which developed the nation's first high-grade graduate school. Several generations of American scholars, repelled by snobbish English cousins and attracted by painstaking Continental methods, had attended German universities. Now reputable scholars no longer had to go abroad for a gilt-edged graduate degree; Dr. Woodrow Wilson, among others, received his Ph.D. from Johns Hopkins.

The old cut-and-dried classical curriculum in the colleges was on the way out, as the new industrialization brought insistent demands for "practical" courses and specialized training in the sciences. The elective system, which permitted students to choose more courses in cafeteria fashion, was gaining popularity. It received a powerful boost in the 1870s, when Dr. Charles W. Eliot, a vigorous young chemist, became president of Harvard College and embarked upon a lengthy career of educational statesmanship.

Winds of "dangerous doctrines" threatened to shipwreck freedom of teaching in the colleges. Disagreeable incidents involved the dismissal of professors who taught evolution or expressed hostility to high tariffs. For many years, some of the big business alumni of Yale vainly sought the bald scalp of the low-tariff economist and sociologist William Graham Sumner.

Medical schools and medical science after the Civil War were prospering. Despite the enormous sale of patent medicines and Indian remedies— "good for man or beast"—the new scientific gains were reflected in improved public health. Revolutionary discoveries abroad, such as those of the French scientist Louis Pasteur and the English physician Joseph Lister, left their imprint on America. As a result of new health-promoting precautions, including campaigns against public spitting, life expectancy at birth was measurably increased.

One of America's most brilliant intellectuals, the slight and sickly William James (1842–1910), served for thirty-five years on the Harvard faculty. Through his numerous writings he made a deep mark on many fields. His *Principles of Psychology* (1890) helped to establish the modern discipline of psychology. In *The Will to Believe* (1897) and *The Varieties of Religious Experience* (1902), he explored the philosophy and psychology of religion. In his most famous work, *Pragmatism* (1907), he colorfully described America's greatest contribution to the history of philosophy. The concept of pragmatism held that truth was to be tested, above all, by the practical consequences of an idea, by action rather than theories. This kind of reasoning aptly expressed the philosophical temperament of a nation of doers.

The Appeal of the Press

Well-stocked public libraries—the poor people's university—were making encouraging progress, especially in Boston and New York. The magnificent Library of Congress building, which opened its doors in 1897, provided thirteen acres of floor space in the largest and costliest edifice of its kind in the world. A new era was inaugurated by the generous gifts of Andrew Carnegie. This open-handed Scotsman, book-starved in his youth, contributed $60 million for the construction of public libraries all over the country. By 1900 there were about 9,000 free circulating libraries in America, each with at least 300 books.

Roaring newspaper presses, spurred by the

invention of the linotype in 1885, more than kept pace with the demands of a word-hungry public. But the heavy investment in machinery and plant was accompanied by a growing fear of offending advertisers and subscribers. Bare-knuckle editorials were, to an increasing degree, being supplanted by feature articles and noncontroversial syndicated material. The day of slashing journalistic giants like Horace Greeley was passing.

Sensationalism, at the same time, was beginning to debase the public taste. The semiliterate immigrants, combined with strap-hanging urban commuters, created a profitable market for news that was simply and punchily written. Sex, scandal, and other human-interest stories burst into the headlines, as a vulgarization of the press accompanied the growth of circulation. Critics complained in vain of "presstitutes."

Two new journalistic tycoons emerged. Joseph Pulitzer, Hungarian-born and near-blind, was a leader in the techniques of sensationalism in St. Louis and especially with the New York *World*. His use of the colored comic supplements, featuring the "Yellow Kid," gave the name of *yellow journalism* to his lurid sheets. A close and ruthless competitor was youthful William Randolph Hearst, who had been expelled from Harvard College for a crude prank. Able to draw on his California father's mining millions, he built up a powerful chain of newspapers, beginning with the San Francisco *Examiner* in 1887.

Unfortunately, the influence of Pulitzer and Hearst was not altogether wholesome. Although both championed many worthy causes, both prostituted the press in their struggle for increased circulation; both "stooped, snooped, and scooped to conquer."

Apostles of Reform

Magazines partly satisfied the public appetite for good reading, notably old standbys like *Harper's,* the *Atlantic Monthly,* and *Scribner's Monthly.* Possibly the most influential journal was the liberal and highly intellectual *Nation,* which was read largely by professors, preachers, and publicists as "the weekly Day of Judgment." Launched in 1865 by the Irish-born Edwin L. Godkin, a merciless critic, it crusaded militantly for civil service reform, honesty in government, and a moderate tariff.

Another journalist-author, Henry George, was an original thinker who left an enduring mark. Poor in formal schooling, he was rich in idealism and in the milk of human kindness. After seeing poverty at its worst in India, and land grabbing at its greediest in California, he took pen in hand. His classic treatise, *Progress and Poverty* (1879), undertook to solve "the great enigma of our times"—"the association of progress with poverty." According to George, property owners unjustifiably profited from the pressure of growing population on a fixed supply of land. A single 100 percent tax on those profits would eliminate unfair inequalities and stimulate economic growth.

George soon became a most controversial figure. His book broke into the best-seller lists and ultimately sold some 3 million copies, to the horror of the propertied classes. George also lectured widely in America, where he influenced thinking about the maldistribution of wealth, and in Britain, where he left an indelible mark on Fabian socialism.

Edward Bellamy, a quiet Massachusetts Yankee, was another journalist-reformer of remarkable power. In 1888 he published a socialistic novel, *Looking Backward,* in which the hero, falling into a hypnotic sleep, awakens in the year 2000. He "looks backward" and finds that the social and economic injustices of 1887 have melted away under an idyllic government, which has nationalized big business to serve the public interest. To a nation already alarmed by the trust evil, the book had a magnetic appeal and sold over a million copies. Scores of Bellamy Clubs sprang up to discuss this mild utopian socialism, and they heavily influenced American reform movements near the end of the century.

Postwar Writing

As literacy increased, so did book reading. Post–Civil War Americans devoured millions of "dime novels," usually depicting the wilds of the West. Paint-bedaubed Indians and quick-triggered gunmen such as "Deadwood Dick" shot off vast quantities of gunpowder, and virtue invariably triumphed. These lurid "paperbacks" were frowned upon by

Emily Dickinson (1830–1886) *A great American poet, she never married but pursued intense intellectual relationships with several men, including the abolitionist Thomas Wentworth Higginson.*

An even more popular writer was Horatio ("Holy Horatio") Alger, a Puritan-reared New Englander, who in 1866 forsook the pulpit for the pen. He wrote more than a hundred volumes of juvenile fiction that sold over 100 million copies. His stock formula was that virtue, honesty, and industry are rewarded by success, wealth, and honor—a kind of survival of the purest, especially nonsmokers, nondrinkers, nonswearers, and nonliars. Although Alger's own bachelor life was criticized, he implanted morality and the conviction that there is always room at the top (especially if one is lucky enough to save the life of the boss's daughter and marry her).

In poetry Walt Whitman was one of the few luminaries of yesteryear who remained active. Although shattered in health by service as a Civil War nurse, he brought out successive—and purified—revisions of his hardy perennial, *Leaves of Grass*. The assassination of Lincoln inspired him to write two of the most moving poems in American literature, "O Captain! My Captain!" and "When Lilacs Last in the Dooryard Bloom'd."

The curious figure of Emily Dickinson, one of America's most gifted lyric poets, did not emerge until 1886, when she died and her poems were discovered. A Massachusetts recluse, she wrote over a thousand short lyrics on odd scraps of paper. Only two were published during her lifetime, and those without her consent. As she wrote:

> How dreary to be somebody!
> How public, like a frog
> To tell your name the livelong day
> To an admiring bog!

Literary Landmarks

In novel writing, the romantic sentimentality of a youthful era was giving way to a rugged realism that reflected more faithfully the materialism of an industrial society. American authors now turned increasingly to the course human comedy and tragedy of the world around them to find their subjects.

The daring feminist author Kate Chopin (1851–1904) wrote candidly about adultery, suicide, and women's ambitions in *The Awakening* (1899).

parents, but goggle-eyed youths read them in haylofts or in schools behind the broad covers of geography books. The king of dime novelists was Harlan F. Halsey, who made a fortune by dashing off about 650 novels, often one in a day.

General Lewis Wallace—lawyer, soldier, and author—was a colorful figure. Having fought with distinction in the Civil War, he sought to combat the prevailing wave of Darwinian skepticism with his novel *Ben Hur: A Tale of the Christ* (1880). A phenomenal success, the book sold an estimated 2 million copies in many languages, including Arabic and Chinese, and later appeared on stage and screen. It was the *Uncle Tom's Cabin* of the anti-Darwinists, who found in it support for the Holy Scriptures.

Largely ignored in her own day, Chopin was rediscovered by later readers who found in her work the feminist yearnings that stirred beneath the surface of "respectability" in the Gilded Age.

Mustachioed Mark Twain (1835–1910) had leapt to fame with *The Celebrated Jumping Frog of Calaveras County* (1867) and *The Innocents Abroad* (1869). He teamed up with Charles Dudley Warner in 1873 to write *The Gilded Age.* An acerbic satire on post–Civil War politicians and speculators, the book gave a name to an era. With his scanty formal schooling in frontier Missouri, Twain typified a new breed of American authors in revolt against the elegant refinements of the old New England school of writing. Christened Samuel Langhorne Clemens, he had served for a time as a Mississippi river boat pilot and later took his pen name, Mark Twain, from the boatman's cry that meant two fathoms. After a brief stint in the armed forces, Twain journeyed to California, a trip he described, with a mixture of truth and tall tales, in *Roughing It* (1872).

Many other books flowed from Twain's busy pen. His *The Adventures of Tom Sawyer* (1876) and *The Adventures of Huckleberry Finn* (1884) rank among American masterpieces. His later years were soured by bankruptcy growing out of unwise investments, and he was forced to take to the lecture platform and amuse what he called "the damned human race." Twain made his most enduring contribution in recapturing frontier realism and humor in the authentic American dialect.

Another author who wrote out of the West and achieved at least temporary fame and fortune was Bret Harte (1836–1902). A foppishly dressed New Yorker, Harte struck it rich in California with gold-rush stories, especially "The Luck of Roaring Camp" and "The Outcasts of Poker Flat." Catapulted suddenly into notoriety by those stories, he never again matched their excellence or their popularity. He lived out his final years in London as little more than a hack writer.

William Dean Howells (1837–1920), a printer's son from Ohio, could boast of little schoolhouse education, but his busy pen carried him high into the literary circles of the East. In 1871 he became the editor of the prestigious Boston-based *Atlantic Monthly* and was subsequently presented with honorary degrees from six universities, including Oxford. He wrote about ordinary people and about contemporary and sometimes controversial social themes. *A Modern Instance* (1882) deals with the once-taboo subject of divorce; *The Rise of Silas Lapham* (1885) describes the trials of a newly rich paint manufacturer caught up in the caste system of Brahmin Boston. *A Hazard of New Fortunes* (1890) portrays the reformers, strikers, and Socialists in Gilded-Age New York.

Stephen Crane (1871–1900), the fourteenth son of a Methodist minister, also wrote about the seamy underside of life in urban, industrial America. His *Maggie: A Girl of the Streets* (1893), a brutal tale about a poor prostitute driven to suicide, was too grim to find a publisher. Crane had to have it printed privately. He rose quickly to prominence with *The Red Badge of Courage* (1895), the stirring story of a bloodied young Civil War recruit under fire. Crane himself had never seen a battle and wrote entirely from the printed Civil War records. He died of tuberculosis in 1900, when only twenty-nine.

Henry James (1843–1916), brother of Harvard philosopher William James, was a New Yorker who turned from law to literature. Taking as his dominant theme the confrontation of innocent Americans with subtle Europeans, James penned a remarkable number of brilliant novels, including *Daisy Miller* (1879), *The Portrait of a Lady* (1881), and *The Wings of the Dove* (1902). In *The Bostonians* (1886) he wrote one of the first novels about the rising feminist movement. James frequently made women his central characters, exploring their inner reactions to complex situations with a deftness that marked him as a master of "psychological realism." Long a resident of England, he became a British subject shortly before his death.

Candid portrayals of contemporary life and social problems were the literary order of the day by the turn of the century. Jack London (1876–1916), famous as a nature writer of such books as *The Call of the Wild* (1903), turned to depicting a possible fascistic revolution in *The Iron Heel* (1907). Frank Norris (1870–1902), like London a Californian, wrote *The Octopus* (1901), an earthy saga of the stranglehold of the railroad and corrupt politicians on California wheat ranchers.

Conspicuous among the new "social novelists" rising in the literary firmament was Theodore Dreiser (1871–1945), a homely, gangling writer from Indiana. He burst upon the literary scene in 1900 with *Sister Carrie,* a graphically realistic narrative of a poor working girl in Chicago and New York. She becomes one man's mistress, then elopes with another, and finally strikes out on her own to make a career on the stage. The fictional Carrie's disregard for prevailing moral standards so offended Dreiser's publisher that the book was soon withdrawn from circulation.

The New Morality

Victoria Woodhull, who was real flesh and blood, also shook the pillars of conventional morality when she publicly proclaimed her belief in free love in 1871. Woodhull was a beautiful and eloquent divorcée, sometime stockbroker, and tireless feminist propagandist. Together with her sister Tennessee Claflin she published a far-out weekly periodical, *Woodhull and Claflin's Weekly.* The sisters again shocked "respectable" society in 1872 when their journal struck a blow for the new morality by charging that Henry Ward Beecher, the most famous preacher of his day, had for years been carrying on an adulterous affair.

Pure-minded Americans sternly resisted these affronts to their moral principles. Their foremost champion was a portly crusader, Anthony Comstock, who made lifelong war on the "immoral." Armed after 1873 with a federal statute—the notorious Comstock Law—this self-appointed defender of sexual purity boasted that he had confiscated no fewer than 202,679 "obscene pictures and photos"; 4,185 "boxes of pills, powders, etc., used by abortionists"; and 26 "obscene pictures, framed on walls of saloons."

The antics of Woodhull and Claflin and Anthony Comstock exposed to daylight the battle going on in late-nineteenth-century America over sexual attitudes and the place of women. Switchboards and typewriters in the booming cities became increasingly the tools of women's liberation. Economic freedom encouraged sexual freedom, and the "new morality" began to be reflected in soaring divorce rates, the spreading practice of birth control, and increasingly frank discussion of sexual topics. By 1913, said one popular magazine, the chimes had struck "sex o'clock in America."

Families and Women in the City

The new urban environment was hard on families. Paradoxically, the crowded cities were emotionally isolating places. Urban families had to go it alone, separated from clan, kin, and village. Many families cracked under the strain of providing the virtually exclusive arena for intimate companionship. The late nineteenth-century urban era launched the "divorce revolution" that transformed the United States' social landscape in the twentieth century.

Urban life also dictated changes in work habits and even family size. Not only fathers but mothers and even children as young as ten years old often worked, and usually in widely scattered locations. In the city more children meant more mouths to feed, more crowding in sardine-tin tenements, and more human baggage to carry in the uphill struggle for social mobility. Not surprisingly, birthrates were still dropping and family size continued to shrink as the nineteenth century lengthened. Marriages were being delayed, and more couples learned the techniques of birth control.

Women were growing more independent in the urban environment, and in 1898 they heard the voice of a major feminist prophet, Charlotte Perkins Gilman. In that year the freethinking and original-minded Gilman published *Women and Economics.* In this classic of feminist literature, Gilman called on women to abandon their dependent status and contribute to the larger life of the community through productive involvement in the economy. Rejecting all claims that biology gave women a fundamentally different character from men, she argued that "our highly specialized motherhood is not so advantageous as believed." She advocated centralized nurseries and cooperative kitchens to facilitate women's participation in the workforce—anticipating by more than half a century the day-care centers and convenience-food services of a later day.

Fiery feminists also continued to insist on the ballot. They had been demanding the vote since before the Civil War, but many high-minded female reformers had temporarily shelved the cause of women to battle for the rights of blacks. In 1890 militant suffragists formed the National American Women's Suffrage Association. Its founders included aging pioneers like Elizabeth Cady Stanton, who had helped organize the first women's rights convention in 1848, and her long-time comrade Susan B. Anthony, the radical Quaker who had courted jail by trying to cast a ballot in the 1872 presidential election.

By 1900 a new generation of women had taken command of the suffrage battle. Their most effective leader was Carrie Chapman Catt, a pragmatic and businesslike reformer of relentless dedication. Significantly, under Catt the suffragists deemphasized the argument that women deserved the vote, as a matter of right, because they were in all respects the equals of men. Instead, Catt stressed the desirability of giving women the vote if they were to continue to discharge their traditional duties as homemakers and mothers in the increasingly public world of the city.

By thus linking the ballot to a traditional definition of women's role, suffragists registered encouraging gains as the new century opened, despite continuing showers of rotten eggs and the jeers of male critics. Women were increasingly permitted to vote in local elections, particularly on issues related to the schools. Wyoming Territory—later called "the Equality State"—granted the first unrestricted suffrage to women in 1869. This important breach in the dike once made, many states followed Wyoming's example. Paralleling these triumphs, most of the states by 1890 had passed laws to permit wives to own or control their property after marriage.

Prohibition of Alcohol and Social Progress

Alarming gains by Demon Rum spurred the temperance reformers to redoubled zeal. Especially obnoxious to them was the shutter-doored corner saloon, appropriately called "the poor man's club." It helped keep both him and his family poor. Liquor consumption had increased during the nerve-wracking days of the Civil War; and immigrant groups, accustomed to alcohol in the Old Country, were hostile to restraints.

The National Prohibition party, organized in 1869, polled a sprinkling of votes in some of the ensuing presidential elections. Militant ladies entered the alcoholic arena, notably when the Woman's Christian Temperance Union (WCTU) was organized in 1874. The white ribbon was its symbol of purity; the saintly Frances E. Willard—also a champion of planned parenthood—was its leading spirit. Less saintly was a muscular and mentally deranged "Kansas Cyclone," Carrie A. Nation, whose first husband had died of alcoholism. With her hatchet she boldly smashed saloon bottles and bars, and her "hatchetations" brought considerable disrepute to the prohibition movement by the violence of her one-woman crusade.

But rum was now on the run. The potent Anti-Saloon League was formed in 1893, with its members singing "The Lips That Touch Liquor Must Never Touch Mine." The great triumph—but only a temporary one—came in 1919, when the national prohibition amendment (Eighteenth) was attached to the Constitution.

Banners of other social crusaders were aloft. The American Society for the Prevention of Cruelty to Animals was created in 1866, after its founder had witnessed brutality to horses in Russia. The American Red Cross was launched in 1881, with the dynamic Clara Barton, an "angel" of Civil War battlefields, as a leading spirit.

Artistic Triumphs

America still lacked artists to match its magnificent mountains. Artistic activity had been rare in the rustic years of the republic, largely because of an absence of leisure and wealth. The nation now had both, but the results were unspectacular. Perhaps the roar of industrial civilization repelled the delicate muses.

Yet several portrait painters of distinction emerged, notably James Whistler (1834–1903). He did much of his work in Britain, including the celebrated portrait of his mother. Another gifted portrait painter, likewise self-exiled in Britain, was John Singer Sargent (1856–1925).

Other brush wielders, no less talented, brightened the artistic horizon. Self-taught George Inness

(1825–1894) became America's leading landscape artist. Thomas Eakins (1844–1916) attained a high degree of realism in his painting. Winslow Homer (1836–1910) was perhaps the greatest painter of the group. Earthily American and largely resistant to foreign influences, he revealed rugged realism and boldness of conception. His canvases of the sea and of fisherfolk were masterly, and probably no American artist has excelled him in portraying the awesome power of the ocean. Perhaps the most gifted sculptor yet produced by America was Augustus Saint-Gaudens (1848–1907). Born in Ireland of an Irish mother and a French father, he became an adopted American. Among his most moving works is the Robert Gould Shaw memorial in Boston, which depicts the young white officer leading his black troops into battle in the Civil War.

Music, too, was gaining popularity. America of the 1880s and 1890s was assembling high-quality symphony orchestras, notably in Boston and Chicago. The famed Metropolitan Opera House of New York was erected in 1883. In its fabled "Diamond Horseshoe" the newly rich would flaunt their jewels, gowns, and furs. A marvelous discovery was the reproduction of music by mechanical means. The phonograph, though a squeakily imperfect instrument when invented by the deaf Edison, had by 1900 reached over 150,000 homes.

In addition to skyscraper-builder Louis Sullivan, the most famous American architect of the age was Henry H. Richardson, a Bostonian who spread his immense influence throughout the eastern half of the United States. He popularized a distinctive ornamental style that came to be known as "Richardsonian." His masterpiece and most famous work was the Marshall Field Building (1885) in Chicago.

A revival of classical architectural forms—and a setback for realism—came with the great Columbian Exposition in Chicago in 1893. This so-called dream of loveliness, which was visited by 27 million people, did much to raise American artistic standards and promote city planning.

The Business of Amusement

Fun and frolic were not neglected by the workaday American. The legitimate stage still flourished, as appreciative audiences responded to the lure of the footlights. Vaudeville, with its coarse jokes and graceful acrobats, continued to be immensely popular during the 1880s and 1890s.

The circus—high-tented and multiringed—finally emerged full-blown. Phineas T. Barnum, the master showman who had early discovered that "the public likes to be humbugged," joined hands with James A. Bailey in 1881 to stage the "Greatest Show on Earth."

Colorful "Wild West" shows, first performed in 1883, were even more distinctively American. Headed by the knightly, goateed, and free-drinking William F. ("Buffalo Bill") Cody, the troupe included war-whooping Indians, live buffalo, and deadeye sharpshooters. Among them was the girlish Annie Oakley. Rifle in hand, at thirty paces she could perforate a tossed-up card half a dozen times before it fluttered to the ground. (Hence the term "Annie Oakley" for a punched ticket, later for a free pass.)

Baseball, already widely played before the Civil War, was clearly emerging as the national pastime, if not a national mania. A league of professional players was formed in the 1870s, and in 1888 an all-star baseball team toured the world, using the pyramids as a backstop while in Egypt. The trend toward spectator sports was well exemplified by football, a rugged game that used the dangerous flying wedge formation. The Yale-Princeton game of 1893 drew 50,000 cheering spectators, while foreigners jeered that the nation was getting "sports on the brain."

Even pugilism, with its long background of bare-knuckle brutality, gained a new and gloved respectability in 1892. Agile "Gentleman Jim" Corbett, a scientific boxer, wrested the world championship from the aging and alcoholic John L. Sullivan, the fabulous "Boston Strong Boy."

Two crazes swept the country in the closing decades of the century. Croquet became enormously popular, though condemned by moralists of the "naughty nineties" because it exposed feminine ankles and promoted flirtation. The low-framed "safety" bicycle came to replace the high-seated model. By 1893 a million bicycles were in use.

Basketball was invented in 1891 by James Naismith, a YMCA instructor in Springfield, Massachusetts. Designed as an active indoor sport that could be played during the winter months, it spread rapidly and enjoyed enormous popularity in the next century.

The land of the skyscraper was plainly becoming more standardized, owing largely to the new industrialization. To an increasing degree, Americans were falling into the ways of lockstep living—playing, reading, thinking, and talking alike. They were eating the same canned food and wearing the same ready-made clothes. But what they had lost in variety, they had gained in efficiency. They were still inseparably wedded to the ideal of unlimited human progress, and they still glimpsed, with invincible optimism, the unexplored vistas that stretched into the future.

CHRONOLOGY

1869	Wyoming Territory grants women the right to vote.
1871	*Woodhull and Claflin's Weekly* published.
1873	Comstock Law passed.
1874	Woman's Christian Temperance Union (WCTU) organized.
	Chautauqua movement takes shape.
1876	Johns Hopkins University graduate school established.
1879	Henry George publishes *Progress and Poverty.*
	Dumbbell tenement introduced.
	Mary Baker Eddy establishes Christian Science.
	Salvation Army begins work in America.
1881	Booker T. Washington becomes head of Tuskegee Institute.
	American Red Cross founded.
1882	First immigration-restriction laws passed.
1883	Brooklyn Bridge completed.
1884	Mark Twain publishes *The Adventures of Huckleberry Finn.*
1885	Louis Sullivan builds the first skyscraper in Chicago.
	Linotype invented.
1886	Statue of Liberty erected in New York harbor.
1887	American Protective Association (APA) formed.
1888	Edward Bellamy publishes *Looking Backward.*
1889	Jane Addams founds Hull House in Chicago.
	Moody Bible Institute established in Chicago.
1890	National American Women's Suffrage Association formed.
1893	Lillian Wald opens Henry Street Settlement in New York.
	Anti-Saloon League formed.
1897	Library of Congress opens.
1898	Charlotte Perkins Gilman publishes *Women and Economics.*
1900	Theodore Dreiser publishes *Sister Carrie.*
1910	National Association for the Advancement of Colored People (NAACP) founded.

Varying Viewpoints

The late nineteenth century witnessed great ferment in American society as patterns of living that had endured for generations began to break down. For people who flooded into cities, the security and cohesion of their small-town experience gave way to the uncertainty and impersonality of urban existence. Influxes of immigrants from southern and eastern Europe brought to America new customs and religions—Catholic, Orthodox, and Jewish. An active feminist movement challenged women's traditional roles. Darwin's theories seemed to undermine religious belief. In a world of endless upheaval, many Americans groped for stability and reassurance.

Some became reformers. They joined social crusades and meliorist movements such as the Anti-Saloon League and the Woman's Christian Temperance Union (WCTU). Churches sent missionaries, often women, into tenements, slums, and Indian reservations.

Other Americans placed more faith in science and technical expertise than in moral uplift. Doctors, teachers, social workers, and others formed professional societies and applied their innovative scientific methods to curing social ills. Even high culture was affected, as artists, musicians, and literary critics tried to shape the public's tastes.

Historians have interpreted these varied responses to the emergence of an urban society in different lights. Through much of our present century, most scholars stressed the disinterested humanitarianism, the idealism, and the religious benevolence of the reformers, and the virtues of scientific progress. But in the 1960s historians such as Paul Boyer, Michael Katz, and David Rothman began to argue that charitable organizations, the prohibition campaigns, and such new institutions as asylums and orphanages aimed to control the lower social orders as much as help them. In the same vein, some women's historians have portrayed professionalism less as a device to rationalize highly skilled occupations and more as a move to shore up the male status of doctors and others.

In recent years, this historical appraisal itself has been criticized. Certain women's historians, among them Estelle Freedman, argued that at least some social welfare movements—for example, settlement houses and the campaign for separate prisons for women—resulted from the genuine desire of middle-class women to help their less fortunate sisters.

SELECT READINGS

Primary Source Documents

Jacob Riis, *How the Other Half Lives** (1890), is a vivid account of life in America's slums. In *A Hazard of New Fortunes* (1890), William Dean Howells penned one of the first "urban novels" in American literature. Frances Willard's *Glimpses of Fifty Years** (1880) is the memoir of a leading prohibitionist. Victoria Woodhull, *The Scarecrows of Sexual Slavery** (1874), provocatively illustrates some changing ideas about women's role. Henry James's novel *The Bostonians* (1886) vividly portrays feminists and suffragists.

Secondary Sources

The Rise of the City, 1878–1898 (1933) is a classic study by Arthur M. Schlesinger. More recent are Gunther Barth, *City People: The Rise of Modern City Culture in Nineteenth-Century America* (1980), Blake McKelvey, *The*

Urbanization of America, 1860–1915 (1963), Howard Chudacoff, *The Evolution of American Urban Society* (1975), and Sam Bass Warner, *The Urban Wilderness* (1972). See also Kenneth T. Jackson, *Crabgrass Frontier: The Suburbanization of America* (1985), and Eric H. Monkkonen, *America Becomes Urban: The Development of Cities and Towns, 1780–1980* (1988). Maldwyn Jones, *American Immigration* (1960), is a well-written introduction, as is Thomas J. Archdeacon, *Becoming American* (1983). Oscar Handlin, *The Uprooted* (1951), is an imaginative account of the immigrant experience. John Higham examines the nativist reaction in *Strangers in the Land* (1955). Black thought for this period is illuminated by three studies: August Meier, *Negro Thought in America, 1880–1915* (1963), Louis R. Harlan, *Booker T. Washington: The Making of a Black Leader, 1865–1901* (1972), and Elliott M. Rudwick, *W. E. B. Du Bois: A Study in Minority Group Leadership* (1960). On women and the family, consult Carl Degler, *At Odds: Women and the Family from the Revolution to the Present* (1980), Steven Mintz, *A Prison of Expectations: The Family in Victorian Culture* (1983), Aileen Kraditor, *Ideas of the Woman Suffrage Movement* (1965), Eleanor Flexner, *Century of Struggle* (1959), and Rosalind Rosenberg, *Beyond Separate Spheres* (1982). James Turner probes one aspect of the conflict between science and religion in *Without God; Without Creed: The Origins of Unbelief in America* (1985). Two fascinating studies document the rise of a "new" middle-class mentality: Burton J. Bledstein, *The Culture of Professionalism* (1976), and Thomas Haskell, *The Emergence of Professional Social Science* (1977). See also Alexandra Oelson and John Voss, eds., *The Organization of Knowledge in Modern America, 1860–1920* (1979).

CHAPTER 28

The Great West and the Agricultural Revolt, 1865–1900

Up to our own day American history has been in a large degree the history of the colonization of the Great West. The existence of an area of free land, its continuous recession, and the advance of American settlement westward, explain American development.

Frederick Jackson Turner, 1893

The Indian Barrier to the West

When the Civil War crashed to a close, the frontier line was still wavering westward. A long fringe of settlement, bulging outward here and there, ran roughly north through central Texas and onward to the Canadian border. Between this jagged line and the settled areas on the Pacific slope, there were virtually no white people. The only notable exceptions were the islands of Mormons in Utah, some trading posts and gold camps, and several scattered Spanish-Mexican settlements in the Southwest.

Sprawling in expanse, the Great West was a rough square that measured about 1,000 miles on each side. Embracing mountains, plateaus, deserts, and plains, it was the habitat of the Indian, the buffalo, the wild horse, the prairie dog, and the coyote. Thirty-five years later—that is, by 1900—the entire domain had been carved into states and the three territories of Arizona, New Mexico, and the "Indian Territory," or Oklahoma. Pioneers flung themselves greedily on this enormous prize, as if to ravish it.

Native Americans, to their misfortune, stood in the path of the white settlers. Diverse tribes of buffalo-hunting Indians roamed the spacious western plains in 1860. In three centuries the Spanish-introduced horse had transformed the culture of the Plains Indians, causing the tribes to become more nomadic and more warlike. The Plains Indians had become skilled riders and fighters.

When white soldiers and settlers had edged onto the plains in the two or three decades before the Civil War, they triggered an environmental cycle that set the Indian tribes against one another and ultimately undermined the foundations of Native American culture. By hunting and by grazing their own livestock on the prairie grasses, whites steadily shrank the Great Plains bison population. As the mammoth buffalo herds dwindled, competition and warfare among Indian peoples intensified. Pushed off their own traditional lands, the Sioux expanded at the expense of other Plains peoples like the Crows, Kiowas, and Pawnees.

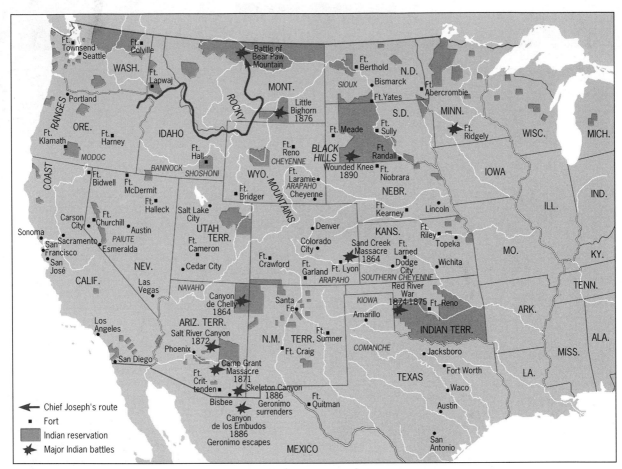

Indian Wars, 1860–1890 *Surrendering in 1877, Chief Joseph of the Nez Percés declared: "Our chiefs are killed. . . . The old men are all dead. . . . The little children are freezing to death. . . . I want to have time to look for my children. . . . Hear me, my chiefs. My heart is sick and sad. From where the sun now stands I will fight no more forever."*

The federal government tried to sign treaties with the "chiefs" of various tribes, but the white treaty makers misunderstood both Indian government and Indian society. Living in scattered bands, Native Americans recognized no authority outside their immediate family, or perhaps a village elder, and resisted white attempts to confine them to a defined territory. When the federal government in the 1860s tried to herd the Plains Indians onto the "Great Sioux Reservation" in the Dakotas and the Indian Territory of Oklahoma, the stage was set for the final drama of Indian-white conflict in North America.

From 1868 to about 1890, almost incessant warfare between Indians and whites raged in the various parts of the West. The fighting was fierce and harrowing, especially the winter campaigning in sub-zero weather. Regular army troops, mostly Civil War veterans led by generals such as Sherman, Sheridan, and Custer, met formidable adversaries in the well-armed Plains Indians, who rode swift ponies and enjoyed baffling mobility. The army's ranks included four crack black units—about one-fifth of all soldiers assigned to the frontier during these years.

The Indian wars in the West were often brutal affairs. Aggressive whites sometimes shot peaceful

Geronimo (c. 1829–1909) *He was the most famous Apache leader.*

The spectacular Great Sioux War of the 1870s began when Colonel George Armstrong Custer led a "scientific" expedition into the Black Hills of South Dakota (part of the Sioux reservation) and announced that he had discovered gold. Hordes of greedy gold seekers rushed to the Dakota Territory. The aggrieved Sioux took to the warpath, led by the influential and wily Sitting Bull.

Colonel Custer's Seventh Cavalry set out to suppress the Indians and force them onto the reservation. Attacking what turned out to be a superior force of some 2,500 well-armed warriors led by Crazy Horse near the Little Big Horn River in present-day Montana, the "White Chief with Yellow Hair" and his 264 officers and men were completely wiped out in 1876 when two supporting columns failed to come to their rescue. White military reinforcements later arrived, and the Indians who defeated Custer were relentlessly crushed in a series of battles across the northern plains.

The Nez Percé Indians of Idaho were likewise goaded into warfare in 1877, when gold-crazed white miners trespassed upon their beaver streams. Chief Joseph, a noble and unusually humane leader, finally surrendered after a tortuous, 1,700-mile three-month trek across the Continental Divide toward Canada, where he hoped to join forces with Sitting Bull. Betrayed into believing they would be returned to their ancestral lands in Idaho, the Nez Percé instead were sent to a dusty reservation in Kansas, where 40 percent of them perished from disease.

Fierce Apache tribes of Arizona and New Mexico were the most difficult to subdue. Led by Geronimo, whose eyes blazed hatred of the whites, they were pursued into Mexico by federal troops using the sun-flashing heliograph, a communication device, which impressed the Indians as "big medicine." Scattered remnants of the warriors were finally persuaded to surrender after the Apache women had been exiled to Florida. The Apaches ultimately became successful ranchers and farmers in Oklahoma.

This relentless fire-and-sword policy of the whites at last shattered the spirit of the Indians. The vanquished Native Americans were finally ghettoized in reservations, there to eke out an existence as wards of the government.

Indians on sight. At Sand Creek, Colorado, in 1864, Colonel J. M. Chivington's militia massacred in cold blood some 400 Indians who apparently thought they had been promised immunity. Indian women were shot praying for mercy, children had their brains dashed out, and braves were tortured, scalped, and mutilated.

Cruelty begot cruelty. In 1866 a Sioux war party ambushed Captain William Fetterman's command of eighty-one soldiers and civilians in Wyoming's Big Horn Mountains, killing every man and mutilating the corpses. As a result, the federal government temporarily abandoned its attempt to construct the Bozeman Trail through Montana, and the cycle of ferocious warfare intensified.

The Plains Indians

The last of the native peoples of North America to bow before the military might of the whites, the Indians of the northern Great Plains long defended their lands and their ways of life against the American cavalry. After the end of the Indian wars, toward the close of the nineteenth century, the Plains tribes struggled on, jealously guarding their communities against white encroachment.

Before Europeans first appeared in North America in the sixteenth century, the vast plain from northern Texas to Saskatchewan was home to some thirty different tribes. There was no typical Plains Indian; each tribe spoke a distinct language, practiced its own religion, and formed its own government.

Indians had first trod the arid plains to pursue sprawling herds of antelope, elk, and buffalo, but they were not exclusively hunters. The women were expert farmers, coaxing lush gardens of pumpkins, squash, corn, and beans from the dry but fertile soil. Still, the shaggy pelt and heavy flesh of the buffalo constituted the staff of life on the plains. Hunted by men, the great bison were butchered by women, who made use of every part of the beast.

The nomadic Plains Indians had roamed the countryside in small bands for many centuries, gathering together in the summer for religious ceremonies, socializing, and communal buffalo hunts. Then in the sixteenth century, the mounted Spanish *conquistadores* ventured into the New World, and their steeds quickly spread over the plains. The horse

Arapaho Chief Hail Wearing Ghost Dance Shirt, c. 1890
The Ghost Dance cult originated among the Paiute Indians in the 1870s and spread swiftly throughout the western tribes. It held out the promise of a revival of traditional Indian culture and revenge on the invading whites, but it was ruthlessly suppressed by the U.S. authorities. Ghost dance shirts like this one were thought to be impermeable to bullets.

revolutionized Indian societies, turning the Plains tribes into efficient hunting machines that promised to banish hunger from the prairies.

The European invasion put an end to the short-lived era of prosperity provided by the horse. After many battles the Plains Indians found themselves crammed together on tiny reservations, clinging with tired but determined fingers to their traditions. Although much of Plains Indian culture persists to this day, the Indians' free-ranging way of life has passed into memory. As Black Elk, an Ogalala Sioux, put it, "Once we were happy in our own country and we were seldom hungry, for then the two-leggeds and the four-leggeds lived together like relatives, and there was plenty for them and for us. But then the Wasichus [white people] came, and they made little islands for us . . . and always these islands are becoming smaller, for around them surges the gnawing flood of Wasichus."

The defeat of the Indians was engineered by a number of factors. Of cardinal importance was the railroad, which shot an iron arrow through the heart of the West. The Indians were also ravaged by the white people's diseases and liquor, to which they showed little resistance. Finally, the virtual extermination of the buffalo resulted in the near-extermination of the Plains Indians.

Bellowing Herds of Bison

Tens of millions of buffalo blackened the western prairies when the white Americans first arrived. These shaggy, lumbering animals were the staff of life for the Native Americans (see "Makers of America: The Plains Indians," pp. 398–399). Their flesh provided food; their dried dung provided fuel ("buffalo chips"); their hides provided clothing, lariats, bowstrings, and harnesses.

When the Civil War closed, there were still some 15 million of these meaty beasts grazing on the western plains. In 1868 a Kansas Pacific locomotive had to wait eight hours for a herd to amble across the tracks. William "Buffalo Bill" Cody killed over 4,000 animals in eighteen months while employed by the Kansas Pacific.

With the building of the railroad, the massacre of the herds began in deadly earnest. The creatures were slain for their hides, for a few choice cuts of meat, or simply for amusement. "Sportsmen" on lurching railroad trains would lean out the windows and blaze away at the brutes to satisfy their lust for slaughter or excitement.

With such wholesale butchery, fewer than 1,000 buffalo were left by 1885, and the species was barely saved from extinction. The whole story is a shocking example of the greed and waste that accompanied the conquest of a continent.

The End of the Trail

By the 1880s the national conscience began to stir uneasily over the plight of the Indians. Helen Hunt Jackson, a Massachusetts writer of children's literature, pricked the moral sense of Americans in 1881 when she published *A Century of Dishonor.* The book chronicled the sorry record of governmental ruthlessness and chicanery in dealing with the Indians. Her later novel *Ramona* (1884), a story of injustice to the California Indians, sold some 600,000 copies and further inspired sympathy for the Indians.

Debate see-sawed. Humanitarians wanted to treat the Indians kindly and persuade them thereby to "walk the white man's road." Yet hard-liners insisted on the current policy of forced containment and brutal punishment. Neither side showed much respect for traditional Native American culture. Christian reformers, who often administered educational facilities on the reservations, sometimes withheld precious food to force the Indians to give up their tribal religion and assimilate to white society. In 1884 these zealous white souls joined with military men in successfully persuading the federal government to outlaw the sacred Sun Dance. When the "Ghost Dance" cult later spread to the Dakota Sioux, the army bloodily stamped it out in 1890 at the so-called Battle of Wounded Knee. In the fighting thus provoked, an estimated 200 Indian men, women, and children were killed, as well as 29 invading soldiers.

The misbegotten offspring of the movement to reform Indian policy was the Dawes Severalty Act of 1887. Reflecting the forced-civilization views of the reformers, the act dissolved many tribes as legal entities, wiped out tribal ownership of land, and set up individual Indian family heads with 160 free acres. If the Indians behaved themselves like "good white settlers," they would get full title to their holdings, as well as citizenship, in twenty-five years. The probationary period was later extended, but full citizenship was granted to all Indians in 1924.

The federal efforts at forced assimilation included boarding schools for Indian children, beginning in 1879 with the Carlisle Indian School in Pennsylvania. "Kill the Indian and save the man" was the motto for these schools, where Native American children, separated from their tribe, were taught English and inculcated with white values and customs.

The Dawes Act struck directly at the organization of the tribe and tried to make rugged individualists out of the Indians. Whatever its good intentions, this legislation did much to accelerate the already advanced decay of traditional Indian culture. The Dawes Act remained the cornerstone of the government's official Indian policy until 1934, when the Indian Reorganization Act ("the Indian New Deal")

reversed the individualistic approach and belatedly tried to restore the tribal basis of Indian life.

Under these new federal policies, defective though they were, the Indian population started to mount slowly. The total number had been reduced by 1887 to about 243,000—the result of bullets, bottles, and bacteria—but the census of 1990 counted some 1.5 million Native Americans, urban and rural.

Mining: From Dishpan to Ore-Breaker

The conquest of the Indians and the coming of the railroad were life-giving boons to the mining frontier. The golden gravel of California continued to yield "pay dirt," and in 1858 an electrifying discovery convulsed Colorado. Avid "Fifty-Niners" or "Pike's Peakers" rushed west to rip at the ramparts of the Rockies. Many miners failed, and returned "busted" and weary to the East. But others stayed on in Colorado to strip silver or discover nonmetallic wealth in the form of golden grain.

Fifty-Niners also poured feverishly into Nevada in 1859, after the fabulous Comstock lode had been uncovered. A fantastic amount of gold and silver, worth more than $340 million, was mined by the "Kings of the Comstock" from 1860 to 1890. The scantily populated state of Nevada, "child of the Comstock lode," was prematurely railroaded into the Union in 1864, partly to provide three electoral votes for President Lincoln.

Smaller "lucky strikes" drew frantic gold and silver seekers into Montana, Idaho, and other western states. Boomtowns, known as "Helldorados," sprouted from the desert sands like magic. Every third cabin was a saloon, where sweat-stained miners drank adulterated liquor ("rotgut") in the company of accommodating women. Lynch law and hempen vigilante justice, as in early California, preserved a crude semblance of order. And when the "diggings" petered out, the gold seekers decamped, leaving picturesque "ghost towns," such as Virginia City, Nevada, silhouetted in the desert. Begun with a boom, these towns ended with a whimper.

Once the loose surface gold was gobbled up, ore-breaking machinery was imported to smash the gold-bearing quartz. This operation was so expensive that it could ordinarily be undertaken only by corporations pooling the wealth of stockholders. Gradually the age of big business came to the mining industry. Dusty, bewhiskered miners, dishpans in hand, were replaced by the impersonal corporations, with their costly machinery and trained engineers.

Yet the mining frontier had played a vital role in subduing the continent. Magnetlike, it attracted population and wealth, while advertising the wonders of the Wild West. The amassing of precious metals helped finance the Civil War, facilitated the building of railroads, and enabled the Treasury to resume specie payments in 1879. The miners also injected the silver issue into American politics. "Silver senators," representing the thinly peopled "acreage states" of the West, used their disproportionate influence to promote the interests of the silver miners. Finally, the mining frontier added to American folklore and literature, as the writings of Bret Harte and Mark Twain so colorfully attest.

Beef Bonanzas and the Long Drive

When the Civil War ended, the grassy plains of Texas supported several million tough, long-horned cattle. These scrawny beasts were killed primarily for their hides. There was no way of getting their meat profitably to market.

The problem of marketing was neatly solved when the transcontinental railroads thrust their iron fingers into the West. Cattle could now be shipped bodily to the stockyards and, under "beef barons" such as the Swifts and Armours, the highly industrialized meat-packing business sprang into existence as a main pillar of the economy. Drawing upon the gigantic stockyards at Kansas City and Chicago, the packers could ship their fresh products to the East Coast in the newly perfected refrigerator cars.

A spectacular feeder of the new slaughterhouses was the "long drive." Texas cowboys—black, white, and Mexican—drove herds, numbering from 1,000 to 10,000 head, slowly over the unfenced and unpeopled plains until they reached a railroad terminal. The bawling beasts grazed en route on the free government grass. Favorite terminal points were fly-specked "cow towns" like Dodge City and Abilene (Kansas), Ogallala (Nebraska), and Cheyenne (Wyoming). From 1866 to 1888, bellowing herds totaling over 4 million steers were driven northward from the beef bowl of Texas.

What the Lord giveth, the Lord also taketh away. The railroad made the long drive; and the railroad unmade the long drive, primarily because the locomotives ran both ways. The same rails that bore the cattle from the open range to the kitchen range brought out the homesteader and the sheepherder. Both of these intruders, amid flying bullets, built barbed-wire fences that were too numerous to be cut down by the cowboys. Furthermore, the terrible winter of 1886–1887, with blinding blizzards reaching 68° below zero, left thousands of dazed cattle starving and freezing. Overexpansion and overgrazing likewise took their toll, as the cowboys slowly gave way to plowboys.

The only escape for the stockman was to make cattle raising a big business and avoid the perils of overproduction. Breeders learned to fence their ranches, lay in winter feed, import blooded bulls, and produce fewer and meatier animals. They also learned to organize. The Wyoming Stock-Growers' Association, especially in the 1880s, virtually controlled the territory and its legislature.

This was the heyday of the cowboy. The equipment of the lone cowhand—from "shooting irons" and ten-gallon hat to chaps and high-heeled boots—served a useful, not an ornamental, function. A "genuwine" gun-toting cowpuncher, riding where men were men and smelled like horses, could justifiably boast of his toughness.

These bowlegged Knights of the Saddle, with colorful trappings and cattle-lulling songs, became an authentic part of American folklore. Many of them, perhaps 5,000, were blacks, who especially enjoyed the new-found freedom of the open range.

The Farmer's Frontier

The miners and cattlemen created the romantic legend of the West, but it was the sober sodbuster who wrote the final chapter of frontier history. A new day dawned for western farmers with the Homestead Act of 1862. The law provided that a settler could acquire as much as 160 acres of land (a quarter section) by living on it for five years, improving it, and paying a nominal fee averaging about $30.

The Homestead Act marked a drastic departure from previous policy. Before the act, public land had been sold primarily for revenue; now it was to be given away to encourage a rapid filling of empty spaces and to provide a stimulus to the family farm—"the backbone of democracy." During the forty years after its passage, about half a million families took advantage of the Homestead Act to carve out new homes in the vast open stretches. Yet five times that many families *purchased* their land from the railroads, land companies, or the states.

The Homestead Act often turned out to be a cruel hoax. The standard 160 acres, quite adequate in the well-watered Mississippi basin, frequently proved quite inadequate on the rain-scarce Great Plains. Thousands of homesteaders, perhaps two out of three, were forced to give up the one-sided struggle against drought.

Naked fraud was spawned by the Homestead Act and similar laws. Perhaps ten times more of the public domain wound up in the clutches of land-grabbing promoters than in the hands of bona fide farmers. Unscrupulous corporations would use "dummy" homesteaders—often immigrants bribed with cash or beer—to grab the best properties, containing timber, minerals, and oil. Settlers would later swear that they had "improved" the property by erecting a "twelve-by-fourteen" dwelling, which turned out to measure twelve by fourteen *inches.*

The railways also played a major role in developing the agricultural West, largely through the profitable marketing of crops. Some railroad companies induced Americans and European immigrants to buy the cheap lands earlier granted by the government. The Northern Pacific Railroad at one time had nearly 1,000 paid agents in Europe distributing leaflets in various languages.

Agriculture expanded once the myth of the great American desert was shattered. Pioneer explorers had assumed that the soil must be barren, simply because it was not heavily watered and did not support immense forests. But once the prairie sod was broken with heavy iron plows pulled by four yokes of oxen, the earth proved astonishingly fruitful.

Lured by higher wheat prices resulting from crop failures elsewhere in the world, settlers in the 1870s rashly pushed still farther west, onto the poor, marginal lands beyond the one-hundredth meridian. Geologist John Wesley Powell, explorer of Arizona's Grand Canyon, warned in 1874 that land westward of the one-hundredth meridian was too arid for farming without massive irrigation projects.

Ignoring Powell's advice, farmers heedlessly chewed up the crusty earth in western Kansas, eastern Colorado, and Montana. They quickly went broke as a six-year drought in the 1880s further desiccated the already dusty region. In the wake of the drought, some pioneers tried the dry farming technique of frequent shallow cultivation. This practice pulverized the surface soil and contributed to the "Dust Bowl" several decades later (see p. 517).

Other adaptations to the western environment were more successful. Tough strains of wheat, resistant to cold and drought, were imported from Russia and blossomed into billowing yellow carpets. Barbed wire, perfected by Joseph F. Glidden in 1874, solved the problem of how to build fences on the treeless prairies. Eventually, federally financed irrigation projects on a colossal scale caused the great American desert to bloom. In the long run, hydraulic engineers had more to do with shaping the modern West than all the trappers, miners, cavalrymen, and cowboys there ever were.

The Great West experienced a fantastic growth of population from the 1870s to the 1890s. A parade of new western states proudly joined their eastern sisters. Boomtown Colorado, offspring of the Pikes Peak gold rush, was greeted in 1876 as "the Centennial State." In 1889–1890 a Republican Congress, eagerly seeking more Republican electoral and congressional votes, admitted in a wholesale lot six new states: North Dakota, South Dakota, Montana, Washington, Idaho, and Wyoming. The Mormon Church formally banned polygamy in 1890, but not until 1896 was Utah deemed worthy of admission. Only Oklahoma, New Mexico, and Arizona remained to be formed into states from contiguous territory on the mainland of North America.

In a last gaudy fling, the federal government made available to settlers vast stretches of fertile plains formerly occupied by the Indians in the district of Oklahoma ("the beautiful land"). Scores of overeager and well-armed "sooners," illegally jumping the gun, had entered Oklahoma Territory. They had to be evicted repeatedly by federal troops, who on occasion would shoot the intruders' horses. On April 22, 1889, all was in readiness for the legal opening, and some 50,000 "boomers" were poised expectantly on the boundary line. At high noon the bugle shrilled, and a horde of "Eighty-Niners" poured in on lathered horses or careening vehicles. That night a lonely spot on the prairie had mushroomed into the tented city of Guthrie, with over 10,000 souls. By the end of the year Oklahoma boasted 60,000 inhabitants, and Congress made it a territory. In 1907 it became "the Sooner State."

The Folding Frontier

In 1890—a watershed date—the superintendent of the census announced that for the first time in America's experience a frontier line was no longer discernible. All the unsettled areas had been invaded by isolated bodies of settlement. As the nineteenth century neared its sunset, the westward-tramping American people were disturbed to find that their fabled free land was going or had gone. The secretary of war had prophesied in 1827 that 500 years would be needed to fill the West; but when the nation learned that its land was not inexhaustible, the seeds were planted in the public mind for the belated conservation movement that blossomed in later decades.

The frontier was more than a place: it was also a state of mind and a symbol of opportunity. Its passing ended a romantic phase of the nation's internal development and created new economic and psychological problems. Traditionally footloose, Americans were notorious for their mobility. The nation's farmers, unlike the peasants of Europe, have seldom remained rooted to their soil. The land, sold for a profit as settlement closed in, was often the settler's most profitable crop.

Much has been said about the frontier as a "safety valve." The theory is that when hard times came, the unemployed who cluttered the city pavements merely moved west, took up farming, and prospered. In truth, relatively few city dwellers, at least in the populous eastern centers, migrated to the frontier during depressions. Most of them did not know how to farm; few of them could raise enough money to transport themselves west and then pay for livestock and expensive machinery.

But the safety valve theory does have some validity. Free acreage did lure to the West a host of immigrants who otherwise might have remained in the eastern cities to clog the markets. And the very *possibility* of westward migration may have induced urban employers to maintain wage rates high enough to discourage workers from leaving.

The westward movement did not end in the 1890s; yet by then it was no longer a movement to the farming, ranching, or mining frontiers. The historic cityward movement began well before 1890 and continued through the twentieth century, in the West as elsewhere. The ironic fact is that though the wilderness frontier may not have provided much of a safety valve for cooped-up urbanites, the city served as a major safety valve for failed farmers and busted miners.

United States history cannot be properly understood unless it is viewed in light of the westward-moving experience. As Frederick Jackson Turner wrote, "American history has been in a large degree the history of the colonization of the Great West." The story of settling and taming the trans-Mississippi West in the late nineteenth century was but the last chapter in the colonizing of various American "wests" since Columbus.

And yet the trans-Mississippi West formed a distinct chapter in that saga and retains its uniqueness even today. There the Native American peoples made their last struggle against colonization, and there most Native Americans live today. There "Anglo" culture collided most directly with Hispanic culture, and the Southwest remains the most Hispanicized region in America. There America faced Asia across the Pacific, and there most Asian-Americans dwell today. There the scale and severity of the environment posed their largest challenges to human ambitions, and there the environment continues to mold social and political life, as well as the American imagination, as in no other part of the nation.

The westward-moving pioneers and the country they confronted have assumed mythic proportions in the American mind. For better or worse, those pioneers planted the seeds of civilization in the immense western wilderness. The life we live, they dreamed of; the life they lived, we can only dream.

The Farm Becomes a Factory

After the Civil War, if not earlier, the immense grain-producing areas of the Mississippi Valley found themselves in the throes of an agricultural revolution. Prices were so favorable that the farmers were concentrating on a single money-crop, such as wheat or corn. They could use their profits to buy their foodstuffs at the country store, instead of raising them themselves. They could secure their manufactured goods in town or by mail order, perhaps from the Chicago firm of Aaron Montgomery Ward, established in 1872, with its first catalog a single sheet.

Large-scale farmers were now both specialists and businesspeople. As cogs in the vast industrial machine, they were intimately tied in with banking, railroading, and manufacturing. They had to buy expensive machinery to plant and to harvest their crops. A powerful steam engine could drag behind it simultaneously the plow, seeder, and harrow. The speed of harvesting wheat was immensely increased in the 1870s by the twine binder and then in the 1880s by the combine—the combined reaper-thresher, which was drawn by twenty to forty horses and which both reaped and bagged the grain.

This amazing mechanization of agriculture in the postwar years was almost as striking as the mechanization of industry. As modernization drove many marginal farmers off the land, those who remained achieved miracles of production, making America the world's breadbasket and butcher shop. The farm was attaining the status of a factory—an outdoor grain factory. Bonanza wheat farms of the Minnesota–North Dakota area, for example, were enor-

Wheat Harvesters, 1890   *Harvest time required long hours of labor by all members of a farm family and their hired hands. Here, a mother and daughter have come out from the farmhouse kitchen to join the field workers in posing for a photographer.*

mous. By 1890 there were at least a half-dozen of them larger than 15,000 acres, with communication by telephone from one part to another. These bonanza farms foreshadowed the gigantic agribusinesses of the next century.

Agriculture was a big business from the outset in California's phenomenally productive (and phenomenally irrigated) Central Valley. California farms, carved out of giant Spanish-Mexican land grants and the railroads' huge holdings, were from the outset more than three times larger than the national average. With the advent of the railroad refrigerator car in the 1880s, California fruits and vegetable crops, raised on sprawling tracts by ill-paid Mexican and Chinese farmhands, sold at a handsome profit in the rich urban markets of the East.

Deflation Dooms the Debtor

Once the farmers became chained to a one-crop economy—wheat or corn—they were in the same leaky boat as southern cotton growers. They were no longer the masters of their own destinies. American grain growers found themselves engaged in a fiercely competitive business because the price of their product was determined in a world market by the world output. If the wheat fields of Argentina, Russia, and other foreign countries smiled, the price of the farmers' grain would fall and American sodbusters would face ruin, as they did in the 1880s and 1890s.

Low prices and a deflated currency were the chief worries of the frustrated farmers—north, south, and west. If a family had borrowed $1,000 in 1855, when wheat was worth about a dollar a bushel, they expected to pay back the equivalent of 1,000 bushels, plus interest, when the mortgage fell due. But if they let their debt run to 1890, when wheat had fallen to about fifty cents a bushel, they would have to pay back the price of 2,000 bushels for the $1,000 they had borrowed, plus interest. This unexpected burden struck them as unjust, though their steely-eyed creditors often branded the complaining farmers as slippery and dishonest rascals.

The deflationary pinch on the debtor flowed partly from the static money supply. There were simply not enough dollars to go around, and as a result,

prices were forced down. In 1870 the currency in circulation for each person was $19.42; in 1890 it was only $22.67. Yet during these twenty years, business and industrial activity, increasing manyfold, had intensified the scramble for available currency.

The forgotten farmers were caught on a treadmill. Despite unremitting toil, they operated year after year at a loss and lived off their fat as best they could. In a vicious circle, their farm machinery increased their output of grain, lowered the price, and drove them even deeper into debt. Mortgages engulfed homesteads at an alarming rate; by 1890 Nebraska alone reported more than 100,000 farms blanketed with mortgages. The repeated crash of the sheriff-auctioneer's hammer kept announcing to the world that another sturdy American husbandman had become landless in a landed nation.

Ruinous rates of interest, running from 8 to 40 percent, were charged on mortgages, largely by agents of eastern loan companies. The windburned sons and daughters of the sod, who felt that they deserved praise for developing the country, cried out in despair against the loan sharks and the Wall Street octopus.

Farm tenancy rather than farm ownership was spreading like stinkweed. The trend was especially marked in the sharecropping South. By 1880 one-fourth of all American farms were operated by tenants. The United States was ready to feed the world, but under the new industrial feudalism the farmers were sinking into a status suggesting Old World serfdom.

Unhappy Farmers

Even Mother Nature ceased smiling, as her powerful forces conspired against agriculture. Mile-wide clouds of grasshoppers, leaving "nothing but the mortgage," periodically ravaged prairie farms. The terrible cotton-boll weevil was also wreaking havoc by the early 1890s.

The good earth was going sour. Floods added to the waste of erosion, which had already washed the topsoil off millions of once-lush southern acres. A long succession of droughts seared the trans-Mississippi West, beginning in the summer of 1887. Whole towns were abandoned. "Going home to the wife's folks" and "in God we trusted, in Kansas we busted" were typical laments of many impoverished farmers, as they fled their weather-beaten shacks and sun-baked sod houses.

To add to their miseries, the soil tillers were gouged by their governments—local, state, and national. Their land was overassessed and they paid painful local taxes, while wealthy easterners concealed their stocks and bonds in safe-deposit boxes. Protective tariffs of these years, while pouring profits into the pockets of the manufacturer, imposed heavy burdens on agriculture, especially in the South. Cotton producers or grain growers had to sell their low-priced, unprotected product in a fiercely competitive world market, while buying high-priced, manufactured goods in a protected home market.

The farmers were also "farmed" by the corporations, processors, and railroads. Trusts raised prices on farmers' supplies to extortionate levels, while storage rates for their grain at warehouses and elevators were pushed up by the operators. The railroad octopus often pushed freight rates so high that the farmers sometimes lost less if they burned their corn for fuel than if they shipped it.

Farmers still made up nearly one-half the population in 1890, but they were hopelessly disorganized. The manufacturers and the railroad barons knew how to combine to promote their interests, and so, increasingly, did industrial workers. But the farmers were by nature independent and individualistic—dead set against consolidation or regimentation. They never did organize successfully to restrict production until forced to by the federal government nearly half a century later, in Franklin Roosevelt's New Deal days. Meanwhile, they were slowly being goaded into a large-scale political uprising.

The Farmers Take Their Stand

Agrarian unrest had flared forth earlier, in the Greenback movement shortly after the Civil War. Prices sagged in 1868, and a host of farmers unsuccessfully sought relief from low prices and high indebtedness by demanding an inflation of the currency with paper money.

The National Grange of the Patrons of Husbandry—better known as the Grange—was orga-

nized in 1867. Its leading spirit was Oliver H. Kelley, a shrewd and energetic Minnesota farmer then working as a clerk in Washington. A primary objective at first was to stimulate the minds of the farm folk by social, educational, and fraternal activities. The Grangers gradually raised their goals from self-improvement to improvement of the farmers' collective plight. In a determined effort to escape the clutches of the trusts, they established cooperatives for both consumers and producers.

Embattled Grangers also went into politics, enjoying their most gratifying success in the grain-growing regions of the upper Mississippi Valley, chiefly in Illinois, Wisconsin, Iowa, and Minnesota. There, through state legislation, they strove to regulate railway rates and the storage fees charged by railroads and by the operators of warehouses and grain elevators. Many of the state courts, notably in Illinois, were disposed to recognize the principle of public control of private business for the general welfare. A number of the so-called Granger Laws, however, were badly drawn, and they were bitterly fought through the high courts by the well-paid lawyers of the "interests." Following judicial reverses, most severely at the hands of the Supreme Court in the famous *Wabash* decision of 1886 (see p. 362), the Grangers' influence faded.

Farmers' grievances likewise found a vent in the Greenback Labor party, which combined the inflationary appeal of the earlier Greenbackers with a program for improving the lot of labor. In 1878, the high-water mark of the movement, the Greenback-Laborites polled over a million votes and elected fourteen members of Congress. In the presidential election of 1880 the Greenbackers ran General James B. Weaver, an old Granger who spoke to perhaps a half-million citizens in 100 or so speeches but polled only 3 percent of the popular vote.

The Passionate Populist Crusade

A striking manifestation of rural discontent, cresting in the late 1880s, came through the Farmers' Alliances, north and south, white and black. Like the Grangers, these groups sponsored picnics and other social gatherings; they bestirred themselves in politics; they organized cooperatives of various kinds;

The Grange Awakening the Sleepers
The farmer tries to arouse the apathetic public to the dangers of the onrushing railroad monopoly.

and they sought to break the strangling grip of the railroads and manufacturers. By about 1890 the members of the Farmers' Alliances probably numbered about 1 million hard-bitten souls.

A new grouping—the People's party—began to emerge spectacularly in the early 1890s. Better known as the Populists, these zealous folk attracted countless recruits from the Farmers' Alliances. The higher the foreclosure rate on mortgages, the deeper the anger of the farmers. Numerous fiery prophets sprang forward to lead the Populists. Among these assorted characters loomed an eloquent red-haired "spellbinder," Ignatius Donnelly of Minnesota, who was three times elected to Congress.

The queen of the "calamity howlers" was undeniably Mary Elizabeth ("Mary Yellin'") Lease, a tall, athletically built woman who was called "the Kansas Pythoness." In 1890 she made an estimated

160 speeches denouncing Wall Street, and reportedly cried that Kansans should raise "less corn and more hell." The big-city New York *Evening Post* snarled, "We don't want any more states until we can civilize Kansas." To many easterners, complaint, not corn, was the westerners' chief crop.

Yet the Populists, despite their peculiarities, were not to be laughed aside. In deadly earnest, they were leading an impassioned crusade to relieve the misfortunes of the farmer. Smiles faded from Republican and Democratic faces alike as countless thousands of Populists sang, "Good-bye, My Party, Good-bye."

Populists made their dramatic entry into politics in the campaign of 1892. Their scorching platform, adopted by a wildly enthusiastic convention in Omaha, worried conservatives. It called for the unlimited coinage of silver, a graduated income tax, and government ownership of the telephone, telegraph, and railroads.

In 1892 Populists chose the eloquent old Greenbacker, General James B. Weaver, as their presidential candidate. Campaigning vigorously, Weaver remarkably garnered over a million votes and 22 electoral votes. The new party's strength came primarily from six states in the Midwest and West. Although they attempted to reach a national audience concerned about the trusts, the Populists proved unable to reach beyond their rural and regional base.

The South, although a hotbed of agrarian agitation, proved especially unwilling to throw in its lot with a new party. Race was the reason. More than a million southern black farmers were organized in the Colored Farmers' National Alliance. They shared a host of grievances with poor white farmers, and for a time the common economic goals of black and white farmers promised to overcome their racial differences. Precisely that prospect alarmed the conservative white "Bourbon" elite in the South, which played cynically upon historic racial antagonisms for its own political advantage.

Southern blacks were heavy losers. The Populist-inspired reminder of potential black political strength led to the near-total extinction of what little African-American suffrage remained in the South. Literacy tests and poll taxes were used to deny blacks the ballot. The notorious "grandfather clause" exempted from those requirements anyone whose forebear had voted in 1860—when, of course, black slaves had not voted at all. More than half a century would pass before southern blacks could again vote in considerable numbers. Accompanying the disfranchisement were more severe Jim Crow laws, designed to enforce racial segregation in public places, including hotels and restaurants, and backed up by atrocious lynchings and other forms of intimidation. Such were the bitterly ironic fruits of the Populist crusade in the South.

Coxey's Army and the Pullman Strike

The Panic of 1893 and the long, severe depression that followed strengthened the arguments of Populists and other reformers that farmers and laborers were being ground under by an oppressive economic and political system. Ragged armies of the unemployed, victims of the depression, began staging demonstrations to protest their grievances.

The most famous of these marches was that of "General" Jacob S. Coxey, a wealthy Ohio quarry owner, who started for Washington in 1894 with a small "army" of his followers, alarming eastern conservatives. His platform included a demand that the government relieve unemployment by an inflationary public works program, supported by some $500 million in legal tender notes, to be issued by the Treasury. Coxey himself rode in a carriage with his wife and infant son, appropriately named Legal Tender Coxey, while his "army" tramped along behind, singing:

> We're coming, Grover Cleveland,
>   500,000 strong,
> We're marching on to Washington
>   to right the nation's wrong.

The "Commonweal Army" of Coxeyites finally straggled into the nation's capital. But the "invasion" took on the aspects of a comic opera when "General" Coxey and his "lieutenants" were arrested for walking on the grass.

The depression also intensified labor protests, sometimes leading to violent flare-ups. Most frightening was the crippling Pullman strike of 1894 in Chicago. Eugene V. Debs, an impetuous but personally lovable labor leader, had helped organize the American Railway Union of about 150,000 members. The Pullman Palace Car Company, which maintained a model town near Chicago for its employees, was hit hard by the depression and cut wages about one-third. But it did not reduce rent for the company houses. The workers finally struck—in some places overturning Pullman cars—and paralyzed railway traffic from Chicago to the Pacific Coast.

The conflict in Chicago was serious but not completely out of hand. At least this was the judgment of Governor Altgeld of Illinois, a friend of the downtrodden who had pardoned the Haymarket Square anarchists the year before (see p. 371). But Attorney General Olney, an archconservative and an ex-railroad attorney, urged the dispatch of federal troops on the legal grounds that the strikers were interfering with the transit of the United States mail. Cleveland supported Olney, declaring, "If it takes the entire army and navy to deliver a postal card in Chicago, that card will be delivered."

To the delight of conservatives, the Pullman strike was crushed by bayonet-supported intervention from Washington. Debs and his leading associates, who had defied a federal court injunction to cease striking, were sentenced to six months' imprisonment for contempt of court. Ironically, the lean labor agitator spent much of his enforced leisure reading radical literature, and he emerged from prison to become the leader of the Socialist movement in America.

Embittered cries of "government by injunction" now burst from organized labor. This was the first time that such a legal weapon had been used conspicuously by Washington to break a strike, and it was all the more distasteful because defiant laborites who were held in contempt could be imprisoned without jury trial. Signs multiplied that employers were striving to smash labor unions by court action. Nonlabor elements of the country, including the Populists and other debtors, were likewise incensed. They saw in the brutal Pullman episode further proof of an unholy alliance between big business and the courts.

Golden McKinley and Silver Bryan

The long-standing grievances of the farmers and laborers, aggravated by the immediate sufferings of depression, gave ominous significance to the election of 1896. Discontented debtors and unemployed workers looked for political salvation, while defenders of the status quo feared upheaval.

The leading candidate for the Republican presidential nomination was former Congressman McKinley of Ohio, sponsor of the ill-starred tariff bill of 1890 (see p. 350). He had established a creditable Civil War record, having risen to the rank of major; he hailed from the electorally potent state of Ohio; and he could point to long years of honorable service in Congress, where he had made a great many friends by his kindly and conciliatory manner.

As a presidential candidate, McKinley was the creation of a fellow Ohioan, Marcus Alonzo Hanna.

Mark Hanna had made his fortune in the iron business, and he now coveted the role of president maker. Hanna, as a wholehearted Hamiltonian, believed that a prime function of government was to aid business. As a conservative in business, he was a confirmed "standpatter," content not to rock the boat. He believed that in some measure prosperity "trickled down" to the laborer, whose dinner pail was full when business flourished. Critics assailed this idea as equivalent to feeding the horses in order to feed the sparrows.

A hardfisted Hanna, although something of a novice in politics, organized his preconvention campaign for McKinley with consummate skill and with a liberal outpouring of his own money. The convention steamroller, well lubricated with Hanna's dollars, nominated McKinley on the first ballot at St. Louis in June 1896. The Republican platform declared for the gold standard, even though McKinley's voting record in Congress had been embarrassingly friendly to silver.

Dissension riddled the Democratic camp. Cleveland no longer led his party; dubbed "the Stuffed Prophet," he was undeniably the most unpopular man in the country. Labor-debtor groups remembered too vividly the silver-purchase repeal, the Pullman strike, and the backstairs Morgan bond deal. Ultraconservative in finance, Cleveland was now more a Republican than a Democrat on the silver issue.

Rudderless, the Democratic convention met in Chicago in July 1896, with the silverites in command. Shouting insults at the absent Cleveland, they refused to endorse their own administration. They had the enthusiasm and the numbers; all they lacked was a leader.

A new Moses suddenly appeared in the person of William Jennings Bryan of Nebraska. Then only thirty-six years of age and known as "the Boy Orator of the Platte," * he stepped confidently onto the platform before 15,000 people. His masterful presence was set off by handsome features, a smooth-shaven jaw, and raven-black hair. He radiated honesty, sin-

---

* One contemporary sneered that Bryan, like the Platte River, was "six inches deep and six miles wide at the mouth."

"The Sacrilegious Candidate" *A hostile cartoonist makes sport of Bryan's notorious Cross of Gold speech in 1896.*

cerity, and energy. He had a good mind but not a brilliant one; he was less a student of books than of human nature; and he possessed broad human sympathies. His was a great heart rather than a great head, a great voice rather than a great brain.

In Chicago the setting was made to order for a magnificent oratorical effort. A hush fell over the convention as Bryan stood before it. With an organ-like voice that rolled into the outer corners of the huge hall, he delivered a fervent plea for silver. Rising to supreme heights of eloquence, he thundered, "We will answer their demands for a gold standard by saying to them: 'You shall not press down upon the brow of labor this crown of thorns, you shall not crucify mankind upon a cross of gold.'"

The Cross of Gold speech was a sensation. Swept off its feet in a tumultuous scene, the Democratic convention nominated Bryan the next day on the fifth ballot. The platform declared for the unlimited coinage of silver at the ratio of 16 ounces of silver to 1 of gold, though the market ratio was about

William Jennings Bryan, 1896 *The premier orator of his day, this spellbinding speaker was the presidential candidate of both the Democratic and Populist parties in 1896.*

32 to 1. This meant that the silver in a dollar would be worth about fifty cents.

Democratic "gold bugs," unable to swallow Bryan, bolted their party over the silver issue. Conservative Senator Hill of New York, when asked if he was a Democrat still, reportedly replied, "Yes, I am a Democrat still—*very* still." The Democratic minority, including Cleveland, charged that the Populist-silverites had stolen both the name and the clothes of their party. They nominated a lost-cause ticket of their own, and many of them, including Cleveland, hoped for a McKinley victory.

Populists were left out in the cold, for the Democratic majority had appropriated their main plank—"16 to 1," that "heaven-born ratio." The bulk of the confused "Popocrats," rather than submit to a hard-money McKinley victory, endorsed Bryan in their convention. Singing "The Jolly Silver Dollar of the Dads," they became in effect the "Demo-Pop" party. But many of the original Populists refused to support Bryan and went down with their colors nailed to the mast.

Class Conflict: Plowholders versus Bondholders

Mark Hanna smugly assumed that he could make the tariff the focus of the campaign. But Bryan, a dynamo of energy, forced the free trade issue into a back seat when he took to the stump in behalf of free silver. Sweeping through twenty-seven states and traveling 18,000 miles, he made between 500 and 600 speeches—36 in one day—and even invaded the East, "the enemy's country." Vachel Lindsay caught the spirit of his oratorical orgy:

> Prairie avenger, mountain lion,
> Bryan, Bryan, Bryan, Bryan,
> Gigantic troubadour, speaking like a siege gun,
> Smashing Plymouth rock with his boulders
>   from the West.*

---

* Reprinted with permission of Macmillan Publishing Company, Inc., from *Collected Poems*, by Vachel Lindsay. Copyright 1920 by Macmillan Publishing Company, Inc., renewed 1948 by Elizabeth C. Lindsay.

Bryan created panic among eastern conservatives with his threat of converting their holdings overnight into fifty-cent dollars. "In God we trust, with Bryan we bust," the Republicans sneered. Widespread fear of Bryan and the "silver lunacy" enabled "Dollar Mark" Hanna, now chairman of the Republican National Committee, to shine as a money raiser. He "shook down" the trusts and plutocrats, and piled up an enormous "slush fund" for a "campaign of education"—or of propaganda, depending on one's point of view. The Republicans amassed the most formidable political campaign chest thus far in American history. At all levels—national, state, and local—it amounted to about $16 million, as contrasted with about $1 million for the poorer Democrats (roughly "16 to 1"). With some justification, the Bryanites accused Hanna of buying the election and of floating McKinley into the White House on a tidal wave of greenbacks. The Republicans definitely had the edge in money and mud.

Bryan's cyclonic campaign, launched with irresistible enthusiasm, began to lose steam as the weeks passed. Fear was probably the strongest ally of Hanna, the worst enemy of Bryan, who allegedly had "silver on the brain." Some Republican businesspeople threatened layoffs or wage reductions if Bryan triumphed. Such were some of the "dirty tricks" of the "Stop Bryan, Save America" crusade.

Hanna's campaign methods paid off, for on election day McKinley triumphed decisively. The vote was 271 to 176 in the Electoral College, and 7,102,246 to 6,492,559 in the popular column. Responding to fear, hope, and excitement, an unprecedented outpouring of voters flocked to the polls. McKinley ran strongly in the populous East, where he carried every county of New England, and in the upper Mississippi Valley. Bryan's states, concentrated in the debt-burdened South and the trans-Mississippi West, involved more acreage than McKinley's but less population.

The free-silver election of 1896 was probably the most significant since Lincoln's victories in 1860 and 1864. Despite Bryan's strength in the South and West, the results vividly demonstrated his lack of appeal to the unmortgaged farmer and especially the eastern urban laborer. Many wage earners in the East voted for their jobs and full dinner pails, threatened

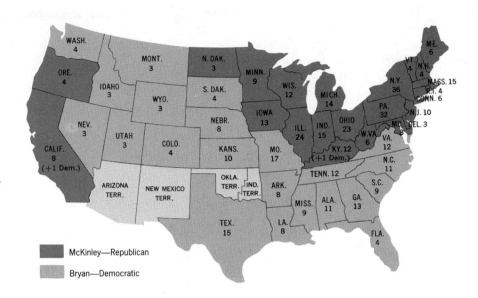

Presidential Election of 1896 (with electoral vote by state)   *This election tolled the death knell of the Gilded Age political system, with its razor-close elections, strong party loyalties, and high voter turnouts. For years after 1896, Republicans predominated and citizens showed declining interest in either joining parties or voting.*

■ McKinley—Republican

■ Bryan—Democratic

as they were by free silver, free trade, and fireless factories. Living precariously on a fixed wage, the factory workers had no reason to favor inflation, which was the heart of the Bryanites' program.

The Bryan-McKinley battle heralded the advent of a new era in American politics. The outcome was a resounding victory for big business, the big cities, middle-class values, and financial conservatism. Bryan's defeat marked the last serious effort to win the White House with mostly agrarian votes. The future of presidential politics lay not on the farms, with their dwindling population, but in the mushrooming cities.

The smashing Republican victory of 1896 also heralded a Republican grip on the White House for sixteen consecutive years—indeed, for all but eight of the next thirty-six years. McKinley's election thus imparted a new character to the American political system. The long period of Republican political dominance that it ushered in was accompanied by diminishing voter participation in elections, a weakening of party organizations, and the fading away of issues such as the money question and civil service reform, which came to be replaced by concern for industrial regulation and the welfare of labor. Schol-

ars have dubbed this new political era the period of the "fourth party system."*

Republican Standpattism Enthroned

An eminently "safe" McKinley took the inaugural oath in 1897. Though a man of considerable ability, he was an ear-to-the-ground politician who seldom got far out of line with majority opinion. His cautious, conservative nature caused him to shy away from the flaming banner of reform. Business was

---

* The first party system, marked by doubts about the very legitimacy of parties, embraced the Federalist-Republican clashes of the 1790s and early 1800s. The second party system took shape with the emergence of mass-based politics in the Jacksonian era, pitting Democrats against Whigs. The third party system was characterized by the precarious equilibrium between Republicans and Democrats, as well as the high electoral participation, that lasted from the end of the Civil War to McKinley's election. The fourth party system is described above. The fifth party system emerged in Franklin Roosevelt's New Deal, which initiated a long period of Democratic ascendancy. Each of these systems, except the fifth, has lasted about forty years. Debate continues as to whether the nation has now entered or is about to enter the era of the sixth party system.

CHRONOLOGY

1858	Pike's Peak gold rush.
1859	Nevada Comstock lode discovered.
1862	Homestead Act.
1864	Sand Creek massacre.
	Nevada admitted to the Union.
1867	National Grange organized.
1876	Battle of Little Big Horn.
	Colorado admitted to the Union.
1877	Nez Percé Indian war.
1881	Helen Hunt Jackson publishes *A Century of Dishonor.*
1884	Federal government outlaws Indian Sun Dance.
1885–1890	Farmers' Alliances formed.
1887	Dawes Severalty Act.
1889	Oklahoma opened to settlement.
1889–1890	North Dakota, South Dakota, Montana, Washington, Idaho, and Wyoming admitted to the Union.
1890	Census Bureau declares frontier line ended.
	Emergence of People's party (Populists).
	Battle of Wounded Knee.
1893	Frederick Jackson Turner publishes "The Significance of the Frontier in American History."
1894	Coxey's "Commonweal Army" marches on Washington.
	Pullman strike.
1896	McKinley defeats Bryan for presidency.
	Utah admitted to the Union.
1897	Dingley Tariff Act.
1900	Gold Standard Act.
1907	Oklahoma admitted to the Union.
1924	Indians granted U.S. citizenship.
1934	Indian Reorganization Act.

given a free rein, and the trusts, which had trusted him in 1896, were allowed to develop more mighty muscles without serious restraints.

As soon as McKinley took office, the tariff issue, which had played second fiddle to silver in the "Battle of '96," quickly forced itself to the fore. In due course the Dingley Tariff Bill was jammed through the House in 1897. The proposed new rates were high, but not enough to satisfy the paunchy lobbyists, who once again descended upon the Senate. Over 850 amendments were tacked onto the overburdened bill. The resulting piece of patchwork finally established the average rates at 46.5 percent, substantially higher than the Democratic Wilson-Gorman Act of 1894 and in some categories even higher than the McKinley Act of 1890. (See the chart in Appendix.)

With the return of prosperity under McKinley in 1897, the money issue that had dominated politics and economics since the Civil War gradually faded. The Gold Standard Act of 1900, passed over last-ditch silverite opposition, provided that paper currency was to be freely redeemed in gold. Electrifying discoveries of new gold deposits in Canada (Klondike), Alaska, South Africa, and Australia, along with new gold-extracting processes, created a moderate inflation and finally took care of the currency needs of an explosively expanding nation.

In retrospect, a controlled expansion of American currency in the 1880s and 1890s was clearly desirable. Agrarian debtors had a good cause: relief from social and economic hardship through an inflation of the dollar supply. But the free-silver fixation not only discredited the case for needed currency expansion but seriously set back the movement for agrarian reform. The tide of "silver heresy" rapidly receded, and the "Popocratic" fish were left gasping high and dry on a golden-sanded beach.

Varying Viewpoints

For more than half a century, the Turner thesis dominated historical writing about the American West. In his famous essay of 1893, "The Significance of the Frontier in American History," historian Frederick Jackson Turner argued that the frontier experience molded both region and nation. Not only the West, Turner suggested, but the national character itself had been uniquely shaped by the westward movement. The pioneers had brought the raw West into the embrace of civilization. And on the ever-moving frontier, *Europeans* had been transformed into tough, inventive, and self-reliant *Americans* in the struggle to overcome the hazards of the wilderness, including distance, deserts, and Indians.

Turner's essay implied that the West, once having been ushered into the temple of civilization, would lose its distinctive regional identity with the closing of the frontier. His thesis also posed a provocative question: what forces might forge a distinctively American national character now that the testing ground of the frontier had been plowed and tamed?

In recent years several so-called New Western historians have sharply challenged Turner's suggestion that the West lost its regional distinctiveness after 1890, when the superintendent of the census declared the frontier line no longer recognizable. Scholars such as Patricia Nelson Limerick, Donald Worster, and Richard White insist that the twentieth-century West is a unique part of the national mosaic, a region whose history, culture, and identity remain every bit as distinct as those of New England or the Old South. But whereas Turner saw the frontier as the principal shaper of the region's character, the New Western historians emphasize ethnic and racial confrontation, topography, climate, and the roles of government and big business as the factors that have made the modern West.

These historians thus reject Turner's emphasis on the triumphal "civilizing" of a "wild" West by Europeans, who were reshaped on the frontier into ruggedly individualistic Americans. As the New Western scholars see it, European settlers did not tame the West but rather conquered it by suppressing the Native American and Hispanic peoples who had preceded them into the region. But those conquests were not complete, so the argument goes, and the West thus remains, uniquely among American regions, an unsettled arena of commingling and competition among those groups.

As for the West's role in creating a *national* identity, Turner's hypothesis is surely among the most important and stimulating ever proposed about the formative influences on U.S. society. But as the frontier era recedes ever further into the past, scholars are less persuaded that the Turner thesis adequately explains the national character. Americans are still conspicuously different from Europeans and other peoples, even though Turner's frontier disappeared more than a century ago.

SELECT READINGS

Primary Source Documents

Black Elk Speaks, edited by John G. Neihardt (1932), is an eloquent Indian statement about the Sioux experience. Theodore Roosevelt, *Hunting Trips of a Ranchman** (1885), offers the future president's views on the Indian question. Mary Lease's famous call to arms is recorded in William E. Connelley, ed., *History of Kansas, State and People** (1928).

Secondary Sources

Vivacious chapters appear in Ray A. Billington, *Westward Expansion* (rev. ed., 1974). Walter Prescott Webb, *The Great Plains* (1931), is a classic. Robert V. Hine, *The American West* (2d ed., 1984), is a useful survey. Patricia Nelson Limerick traces regional themes across time in *Legacy of Conquest: The Unbroken Past of the American West* (1987). Richard White's fresh account, *"It's Your Misfortune and None of My Own": A New History of the American West* (1991), emphasizes the role of the federal government, corporations, and the market economy in the region's development and pays special attention to the twentieth century, as does Donald Worster, *Rivers of Empire: Water, Aridity, and the Growth of the American West* (1986). Native Americans are discussed in Robert Utley, *The Indian Frontier of the American West, 1846–1890* (1984), and in Dee Brown's *Bury My Heart at Wounded Knee: An Indian History of the American West* (1970). Consult also Francis P. Prucha, *The Great Father: The United States Government and the American Indians* (1984); Frederick E. Hoxie, *A Final Promise: The Campaign to Assimilate the Indians* (1984); Thomas Berger's novel *Little Big Man* (1964); and Albert Hurtado, *Indian Survival on the California Frontier* (1988). The military history of the "Indian Wars" is covered in S. L. A. Marshall, *Crimsoned Prairie* (1972). Two intriguing studies of cross-cultural perception are Robert F. Berkhofer, Jr., *The White Man's Indian* (1978), and Richard Drinnon, *Facing West: The Metaphysics of Indian Hating and Empire Building* (1980). William Cronon explores the relationship between Chicago and the development of the "Great West" in *Nature's Metropolis* (1991). A powerful work on the farmers' protest is Lawrence Goodwyn, *Democratic Promise* (1976), abridged as *The Populist Moment* (1978). See also John D. Hicks's classic *The Populist Revolt* (1931); Walter T. K. Nugent, *The Tolerant Populists* (1963); Steven Hahn, *The Roots of Southern Populism* (1983); and Bruce Palmer, *"Man over Money": The Southern Populist Critique of American Capitalism* (1980). Kevin Starr probes the cultural history of California in both *Americans and the California Dream, 1850–1915* (1973) and *Inventing the Dream: California Through the Progressive Era* (1985). Henry Nash Smith, *Virgin Land: The American West as Symbol and Myth* (1950), is a landmark study of particular interest to students of literature. Charles Hoffman examines *The Depression of the Nineties* (1970). The election of 1896 is analyzed in Robert F. Durden, *The Climax of Populism: The Election of 1896* (1965), and Stanley L. Jones, *The Presidential Election of 1896* (1964). Also informative are Paul W. Glad, *McKinley, Bryan, and the People* (1964), and H. Wayne Morgan, *William McKinley and His America* (1963).

CHAPTER 29

The Path of Empire, 1890–1909

We assert that no nation can long endure half republic and half empire, and we warn the American people that imperialism abroad will lead quickly and inevitably to despotism at home.

Democratic National Platform, 1900

Imperialist Stirrings

From the end of the Civil War to the 1880s, the indifference of most Americans to the outside world was almost unbelievable. But then in the sunset decades of the nineteenth century, a momentous shift occurred in U.S. foreign policy. The new diplomacy mirrored the far-reaching changes that were reshaping industry, agriculture, and the social structure.

The republic was becoming increasingly outward looking as exports of both manufactured goods and agricultural products shot up. Many Americans believed the United States had to expand or explode. Their country was bursting with a new sense of power generated by the booming increase in population, wealth, and industrial production—and it was trembling from the hammer blows of labor violence and agrarian unrest. Overseas markets might provide a safety valve to relieve such pressures.

Other forces also stimulated overseas expansion. The lurid "yellow press" of Joseph Pulitzer and William Randolph Hearst whetted the popular taste for excitement abroad. Missionaries, inspired by

books like the Reverend Josiah Strong's *Our Country: Its Possible Future and Its Present Crisis,* looked overseas for new vineyards to till. Strong trumpeted the superiority of Anglo-Saxon civilization and summoned Americans to spread their religion and their civilization to "backward" peoples. At the same time, aggressive Americans like Theodore Roosevelt and Congressman Henry Cabot Lodge were interpreting Darwinism to mean that the earth belonged to the strong and fit—that is, to Uncle Sam. This view was strengthened as such latecomers to the colonial scramble as Japan, Germany, and Russia scooped up leavings from the banquet table of earlier diners. If America was to survive in the competition of modern nation-states, perhaps it, too, would have to become an imperial power.

The development of a new steel navy also focused attention overseas. Captain Alfred Thayer Mahan's book of 1890, *The Influence of Sea Power upon History, 1660–1783,* argued that control of the sea was the key to world dominance. Mahan helped to stimulate the naval race among the great powers that gained momentum around the turn of the century. Red-blooded Americans joined in the demands for a mightier navy and for an American-built isthmian canal between the Atlantic and the Pacific.

America's new international interest manifested itself in a number of diplomatic crises or near-wars in the late 1880s and early 1890s. The American and German navies nearly came to blows in 1889 over the faraway Samoan Islands in the South Pacific. The lynching of eleven Italians in New Orleans in 1891 brought America and Italy to the brink of war, until the United States agreed to pay compensation. In the ugliest affair, American demands on Chile after the deaths of two American sailors in the port of Valparaiso in 1892 made hostilities between the two countries seem inevitable. The threat of attack by Chile's modern navy spread alarm on the Pacific Coast, until American power finally forced the Chileans to pay an indemnity. A simmering argument between the United States and Canada over seal hunting near the Pribilof Islands off the coast of Alaska was resolved by arbitration in 1893. The willingness of Americans to risk war over such distant and minor disputes demonstrated the aggressive new national mood.

This new American belligerence combined with old-time anti-British feeling to create a serious crisis between the United States and Britain in 1895–1896. The jungle boundary between British Guiana and Venezuela had long been in dispute, but the discovery of gold in the area brought the conflict to a head. President Cleveland and his pugnacious secretary of state, Richard Olney, stepped into the affair with a smashing note to Britain that invoked the Monroe Doctrine. "Today the United States is practically sovereign on this continent," it declared. "Its infinite resources combined with its isolated position render it master of the situation. . . ."

British officials, unimpressed, shrugged off Olney's blast as just another twist of the Lion's tail and took four months to respond that the affair was none of America's business. President Cleveland—"mad clear through," as he put it—sent a bristling special message to Congress that called for a U.S. commission to determine where the line ought to go. Then, he implied, if the British would not accept the

rightful boundary, the United States would fight for it. The entire country, irrespective of political party, was swept off its feet in an outburst of hysteria.

Fortunately, sober second thoughts prevailed on both sides of the Atlantic. Shifts in the European balance of power had left Britain in a state of insecure isolation, and an American war would be a disaster. London backed off and consented to arbitrate the Venezuelan dispute. With their eyes wide open to the European peril, the chastened British inaugurated an era of "patting the Eagle's head," which replaced a century or so of America's "twisting the Lion's tail." Sometimes called the Great Rapprochement—or reconciliation—between the United States and Britain, the new Anglo-American cordiality became a cornerstone of both nations' foreign policies as the twentieth century opened.

Spurning the Hawaiian Pear

Enchanted Hawaii had early attracted the attention of Americans. In the morning years of the nineteenth century, the breeze-brushed islands were a way station and provisioning point for Yankee shippers, sailors, and whalers. In 1820 came the first New England missionaries, who preached the twin blessing of Protestant Christianity and protective calico. Americans gradually came to regard the Hawaiian Islands as a virtual extension of their own coastline. The State Department, beginning in the 1840s, sternly warned other powers to keep their hands off the islands. America's grip was further tightened in 1887 by a treaty with the native government guaranteeing priceless naval-base rights at spacious Pearl Harbor.

But trouble, both economic and political, was brewing in the languid insular paradise. Sugar cultivation went sour in 1890 when the McKinley Tariff erected barriers against the Hawaiian product. White planters, mostly Americans, were further alarmed by the increasingly autocratic tendencies of Queen Liliuokalani, who insisted that native Hawaiians should control Hawaii. Desperate whites, though only a tiny minority, organized a successful revolt early in 1893. It was openly assisted by American troops, who landed under the unauthorized orders of the expansionist American minister in

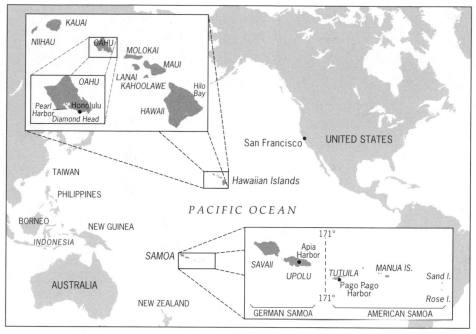

The Pacific *The enlargements show the Hawaiian Islands and the Samoas, both areas of American imperialistic activity in the late nineteenth century.*

Honolulu. "The Hawaiian pear is now fully ripe," he wrote exultantly to his superiors in Washington, "and this is the golden hour for the United States to pluck it."

A treaty of annexation was rushed to Washington, but before it could be railroaded through the Senate, Republican President Harrison's term expired and Democratic President Cleveland came in. Suspecting that his powerful nation had gravely wronged the deposed Queen Liliuokalani, "Old Grover" abruptly withdrew the treaty. When the subsequent probe revealed the damning fact that a majority of the Hawaiian natives did not favor annexation at all, the sugar-coated move for annexation had to be abandoned for five more years. The Hawaiian pear continued to ripen until 1898.

War with Spain over Cuba

Cuba's masses, frightfully misgoverned, again rose against their Spanish oppressors in 1895. The roots of their revolt were partly economic. Sugar production—the backbone of the island's prosperity—was crippled when the American tariff of 1894 restored high duties on the toothsome product.

Driven to desperation, the insurgents adopted a scorched-earth policy, torching cane fields and sugar mills and even dynamiting passenger trains. American sympathies went out to the Cuban underdogs. Aside from pure sentiment, the United States had an investment stake of about $50 million in Cuba and an annual trade stake of about $100 million.

Fuel was added to the Cuban conflagration in 1896 with the coming of the Spanish General ("Butcher") Weyler. He undertook to crush the rebellion by herding many civilians into barbed-wire reconcentration camps, where they could not give assistance to the armed *insurrectos*. Lacking proper sanitation, these enclosures turned into deadly pestholes, where the victims died like dogs.

The atrocities in Cuba were made to order for the sensational new yellow journalism. William R. Hearst and Joseph Pulitzer, then engaged in a titanic

The Explosion of the *Maine*, February 15, 1898 *Encouraged and amplified by the "yellow press," the outcry over the tragedy of the* Maine *helped to drive the country into an impulsive war against Spain.*

duel for circulation, attempted to outdo each other with screeching headlines and hair-raising "scoops." Lesser competitors zestfully followed suit.

Where atrocity stories did not exist, they were invented. Hearst sent the gifted artist Frederic Remington to Cuba to draw sketches, and when the latter reported that conditions were not bad enough to warrant hostilities, Hearst is alleged to have replied, "You furnish the pictures and I'll furnish the war." Among other outrages, Remington depicted Spanish customs officials brutally disrobing and searching an American woman. Most readers of Hearst's *Journal,* their indignation soaring, had no way of knowing that such tasks were performed by female attendants.

Early in 1898 Washington sent the battleship *Maine* to Cuba, ostensibly for a "friendly visit" but actually to protect and evacuate Americans if a dan-

gerous flare-up should again occur. Tragedy struck on February 15, 1898, when the *Maine* mysteriously blew up in Havana harbor, with a loss of 260 officers and men.

Two investigations of the iron coffin were undertaken, one by U.S. naval officers, and the other by Spanish officials. The Spanish commission stated that the explosion had been internal and presumably accidental; the American commission reported that the blast had been caused by a submarine mine. Not until 1976 did Admiral Hyman G. Rickover, under U.S. Navy auspices, present overwhelming evidence that the initial explosion had resulted from spontaneous combustion in one of the coal bunkers adjacent to a powder magazine. Ironically, this is essentially what the Spanish commission had concluded in 1898.

But Americans in 1898, now war-mad, blindly accepted the unlikely explanation of Spanish government treachery. The battle cry of the hour became:

Remember the *Maine!*
To hell with Spain!

Nothing would do but to hurl the "dirty" Spanish flag from the hemisphere.

The national war fever burned higher, even though American diplomats had already gained Madrid's agreement to Washington's two basic demands: a revocation of reconcentration and an armistice with the Cuban rebels. The cautious McKinley did not want hostilities. Neither did Mark Hanna and Wall Street, for war might unsettle business. As "Wobbly Willy" McKinley hesitated, the jingoistic yellow press and the frenzied public denounced him. Fight-hungry Theodore Roosevelt snarled that the "white-livered" occupant of the White House did not have "the backbone of a chocolate eclair."

The president, recognizing the inevitable, finally yielded and gave the people what they wanted. McKinley also perceived that the Democrats would make political capital out of his resistance to war, and it seemed to him better to break up the remnants of Spain's empire than to break up the Grand Old Party. On April 11, 1898, McKinley sent his war message to Congress, urging armed intervention to free the oppressed Cubans. The legislators responded uproariously with what was essentially a declaration of war. In a burst of self-righteousness, they likewise adopted the hand-tying Teller Amendment. This proviso proclaimed to the world that when America had overthrown Spanish misrule, she would give the Cubans their freedom—a declaration that caused imperialistic Europeans to smile skeptically.

Dewey's May Day Victory at Manila

The American people plunged into the war light-heartedly, like schoolchildren off to a picnic. Bands blared incessantly "There'll Be a Hot Time in the Old Town Tonight" and "Hail, Hail, the Gang's All Here," thus leading foreigners to believe that those were the national anthems.

But such jubilation seemed premature to European observers. Except for ally-seeking Britain, the Old World powers generally favored Spain in the war, and they looked with skepticism on America's underprepared army and relatively small navy. But the new American steel navy, now fifteen years old and ranking fifth among the fleets of the world, was in much better trim than Spain's navy. Although formidable on paper, it was in wretched condition.

The war got off to a splendid start for American forces. On February 25, 1898, Assistant Secretary of the Navy Theodore Roosevelt had cabled Commodore George Dewey, commanding the American Asian squadron at Hong Kong, to descend upon Spain's Philippines in the event of war. Dewey carried out his orders magnificently on May 1, 1898. Sailing boldly with his six warships at night into the fortified harbor of Manila, he trained his guns the next morning on the ten-ship Spanish fleet, one of whose craft was only a moored hulk without functioning engines. The entire collection of antiquated and overmatched vessels was quickly destroyed, with a loss of nearly 400 Spaniards killed and wounded, and without the loss of a single life in Dewey's fleet.

George Dewey, quiet and taciturn, became a national hero overnight. An amateur poet blossomed forth with:

Oh, dewy was the morning
Upon the first of May,
And Dewey was the Admiral
Down in Manila Bay,
And dewy were the Spaniards' eyes,
Them orbs of black and blue;
And dew we feel discouraged?
I dew not think we dew!

Yet Dewey was in a perilous position. He had destroyed the enemy fleet, but he could not storm the forts of Manila with his sailors. His nerves frayed, he was forced to wait in the steaming-hot bay while reinforcements were slowly assembled in America. The appearance of German warships in Manila harbor added to the tension.

Long-awaited American troops, finally arriving in force, captured Manila on August 13, 1898. They collaborated with the Filipino insurgents, commanded by their well-educated, part-Chinese leader,

Emilio Aguinaldo. Dewey, to his later regret, had brought this shrewd and magnetic revolutionist from exile in Asia, so that he might weaken Spanish resistance.

These thrilling events in the Philippines had meanwhile focused attention on Hawaii. An impression spread that America needed the archipelago as a coaling and provisioning way station, in order to send supplies and reinforcements to Dewey. A joint resolution of annexation was rushed through Congress and approved by McKinley on July 7, 1898.

The Confused Invasion of Cuba

Shortly after the outbreak of war, the Spanish government ordered a fleet of warships to Cuba. Panic seized the eastern seaboard of the United States. American vacationers abandoned their seaside cottages while nervous investors moved their securities to inland depositories. But the Spanish commander, Admiral Cervera, knew that his wretchedly prepared ships were courting suicide. He finally found refuge in Santiago harbor, where he was blockaded by the much more powerful American fleet.

Sound strategy seemed to dictate that an American army be sent in from the rear to drive out Cervera. Command of the invading force was entrusted to the grossly overweight General William R. Shafter, a leader so blubbery and gout-stricken that he had to be carried about on a door.

The "Rough Riders," a part of the invading army, now charged onto the stage of history. This colorful regiment of volunteers, short on discipline but long on dash, consisted largely of western cowboys and other hardy characters, with a sprinkling of former polo players and ex-convicts. Commanded by Colonel Leonard Wood, the group was organized principally by the glory-hungry Roosevelt, who had resigned from the Navy Department to serve as a lieutenant colonel.

About the middle of June a bewildered American army of 17,000 men finally embarked at Tampa, Florida, amid scenes of indescribable confusion. Shafter's landing near Santiago, Cuba, was made without serious opposition. Brisk fighting broke out on July 1 at El Caney and San Juan Hill, up which

Colonel Roosevelt and his Rough Riders charged, with strong support from two crack black regiments. They suffered heavy casualties, but the colorful colonel, having the time of his life, shot a Spaniard with his revolver, and rejoiced to see his victim double up like a jackrabbit. He later wrote a book on his exploits, which, humorist Finley Peter Dunne's fictional "Mr. Dooley" remarked, ought to have been entitled *Alone in Cubia* [*sic*].

The success of the American army spelled doom for the Spanish fleet. After a running chase, on July 3, the foul-bottomed Spanish fleet was entirely destroyed, as the wooden decks caught fire and the blazing infernos were beached. About 500 Spaniards were killed, as compared with 1 American. "Don't cheer, men," admonished Captain Philip of the *Texas,* "the poor devils are dying." Shortly thereafter Santiago surrendered.

Hasty preparations were now made for a descent upon Puerto Rico before the war should end. The American army there met little resistance. By this time Spain had satisfied its honor, and on August 12, 1898, it signed an armistice.

If the Spaniards had held out a few months longer in Cuba, the American army might have melted away. The inroads of malaria, typhoid, dysentery, and yellow fever became so severe that hundreds were incapacitated—"an army of convalescents." Others suffered from eating the spoiled canned meat known as "embalmed beef."

One of the war's worst scandals was the high death rate from sickness, especially typhoid fever. This disease was rampant in the unsanitary training camps located in the United States. All told, nearly 400 men lost their lives to bullets, over 5,000 to bacteria and other causes.

America's Course (Curse?) of Empire

Late in 1898 the Spanish and American peace negotiators met in Paris. War-wracked Cuba, as expected, was freed from her Spanish overlords. The Americans had little difficulty in securing the remote Pacific island of Guam, which they had captured early in the conflict. They also picked up Puerto Rico, the last crumb of Spain's once-magnificent

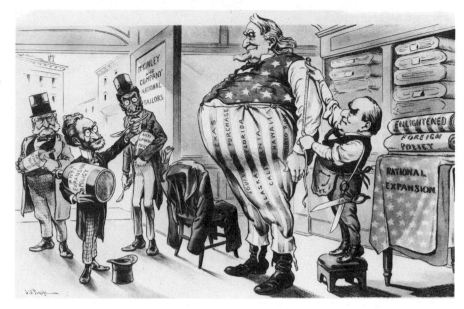

Imperial Uncle Sam
Tailored by William McKinley, an overstuffed Uncle Sam dismisses the anti-imperial protests of reformers Carl Schurz and Oswald Ottendorfer, as well as New York World *publisher Joseph Pulitzer.*

American empire. It was to prove a difficult morsel for Uncle Sam to digest (see "Makers of America: The Puerto Ricans," pp. 424–425).

Knottiest of all was the problem of the Philippines, a veritable apple of discord. These lush islands not only embraced an area larger than the British Isles but contained a completely alien population of some 7 million souls. McKinley was confronted with a devil's dilemma. He did not feel that America could honorably give the islands back to Spanish misrule, especially after it had fought a war to free Cuba. And America would be turning its back upon its responsibilities, he believed, if it simply pulled up anchor and sailed away.

Other alternatives open to McKinley were trouble-fraught. The ill-prepared native Filipinos, if left to govern themselves, might fall into anarchy. One of the major powers might then try to seize them, possibly aggressive Germany, and the result might be a world war into which the United States would be sucked. Seemingly the least of the evils consistent with national honor and safety was to acquire all the Philippines, and then perhaps give "the little brown brothers" their freedom later.

President McKinley, ever sensitive to public opinion, kept a carefully attuned ear to the ground. The rumble that he heard seemed to call for the entire group of islands. Zealous Protestant missionaries were eager for new converts from Spanish Catholicism.* Wall Street had generally opposed the war; but awakened by the booming of Dewey's guns, it was clamoring for profits in the Philippines.

A tormented McKinley, so he was later reported as saying, finally went down on his knees seeking divine guidance. An inner voice seemed to tell him to take all the Philippines and Christianize and civilize them. Accordingly, he decided for outright annexation of the islands. The deed was accomplished by negotiators in Paris after the Americans agreed to pay Spain $20 million, because Manila had been captured a day *after* the armistice was signed and the islands could not properly be listed among the spoils of war.

The signing of the pact of Paris—a trouble-fraught document—touched off one of the most impassioned debates of American history. Except for glacial Alaska, coral-reefed Hawaii, and a handful of Pacific atolls, the republic had hitherto acquired only contiguous territory on the continent. All previous acquisitions had been thinly peopled and capable of

---

* The Philippines were substantially Christianized by Catholics before the founding of Jamestown in 1607.

The Puerto Ricans

At dawn on July 26, 1898, the U.S. warship *Gloucester* steamed into Puerto Rico's Guánica harbor, fired at the Spanish blockhouse, and landed some 3,300 troops. Within days, the Americans had taken possession of the militarily strategic Caribbean island 1,000 miles southeast of Florida. In so doing they set in motion changes on the island that ultimately brought a new wave of immigrants to U.S. shores.

Puerto Rico had been a Spanish possession since Christopher Columbus claimed it for Castile in 1493. The Spaniards enslaved many of the island's 40,000 Taino Indians and set them to work on farms and in mines. Many Tainos died of exhaustion and disease, and in 1511 the Indians rebelled. The Spaniards crushed the uprising, killed thousands of Indians, and began importing African slaves—thus establishing the basis for Puerto Rico's multiracial society.

The first Puerto Rican immigrants to the United States arrived as political exiles in the nineteenth century. From their haven in America, they agitated for the island's independence from Spain. In 1897 Spain finally granted the island local autonomy; ironically, however, the Spanish-American War the following year placed it in American hands. Puerto Rican political emigrés in the United States returned home, but they were soon replaced by poor islanders looking for work.

When Congress granted Puerto Ricans U.S. citizenship in 1917, thereby eliminating immigration hurdles, many islanders hurried north to find jobs. Over the ensuing decades, Puerto Ricans went to work in Arizona cotton fields, New Jersey soup factories, and Utah mines. The majority, however, clustered in New York City and found work in the city's

The First Puerto Ricans *The Spanish* conquistadores *treated the native Taino Indian peoples in Puerto Rico with extreme cruelty, and the Indians were virtually extinct by the mid-1500s.*

cigar factories, shipyards, and garment industry. Migration slowed somewhat after the 1920s as the Great Depression shrank the job market on the mainland and as World War II made travel hazardous.

When World War II ended in 1945, the sudden advent of cheap air travel sparked an immigration explosion. As late as the 1930s, the tab for a boat trip to the mainland exceeded the average Puerto Rican's yearly earnings. But with an airplane surplus after World War II, the six-hour flight from Puerto Rico to New York cost under $50. The Puerto Rican population on the mainland quadrupled between 1940 and 1950 and tripled again by 1960. In 1970, 1.5 million Puerto Ricans lived in the United States, one-third of the island's total population.

U.S. citizenship and affordable air travel made it easy for Puerto Ricans to return home. Thus to a far greater degree than most immigrant groups, Puerto Ricans kept one foot in the United States and the other on their native island. By some estimates, 2 million people a year journeyed to and from the island during the postwar period. Puerto Rico's gubernatorial candidates sometimes campaigned in New York for the thousands of voters who were expected to return to the island in time for the election.

Puerto Ricans have fared better economically in the United States than on the island, where, in 1970, 60 percent of all inhabitants lived below the poverty line. In recent years Puerto Ricans have attained more schooling, and many have attended college. Invigorated by the civil rights movement of the 1960s, Puerto Ricans also have become more politically active, electing growing numbers of congressmen and state and city officials.

---

ultimate statehood. But in the Philippines the nation had on its hands a distant tropical area, thickly populated by Asians of a different race, tongue, and government institutions.

An Anti-Imperialist League sprang into being to fight the McKinley administration's expansionist moves. The organization counted among its members some of the most prominent people in America, including the presidents of Stanford and Harvard Universities, the philosopher William James, and the novelist Mark Twain. The anti-imperialist blanket even stretched over such strange bedfellows as labor leader Samuel Gompers and steel titan Andrew Carnegie. "Goddamn the United States for its vile conduct in the Philippine Isles!" burst out the usually mild-mannered Professor James. The Harvard philosopher could not believe that the United States could "puke up its ancient soul in five minutes without a wink of squeamishness."

Anti-imperialists had still other arrows in their quiver. The Filipinos panted for freedom; and to annex them would violate the "consent of the governed" philosophy of the Declaration of Independence. Finally, annexation would propel the United States into the political and military cauldron of East Asia.

Yet the expansionists or imperialists could sing a seductive song. They appealed to patriotism and played up possible trade profits. Manila, in fact, might become another Hong Kong. Rudyard Kipling, the British poet laureate of imperialism, urged America down the slippery path:

> Take up the White Man's burden—
> Ye dare not stoop to less—
> Nor call too loud on Freedom
> To cloak your weariness.

In short, the wealthy Americans must help to uplift (and exploit) the underprivileged, underfed, and underclad of the world.

In the Senate the Spanish treaty ran into such heated opposition that it seemed doomed to defeat.

But it received last-minute support from a surprising source—William Jennings Bryan. Bryan argued that the war would not officially end until America ratified the pact, and the sooner it accepted the document, the sooner it could give the islands their independence. Bryan's foes assumed that he was attempting to fasten the stigma of imperialism on the Republicans and then sweep into the presidency in 1900 on the flaming banner of anti-imperialism.

After Bryan used his personal influence with certain Democratic senators, the treaty was approved on February 6, 1899, with only one vote to spare. But the responsibility, as Bryan had foreseen, rested primarily on the Republicans.

Perplexities in Puerto Rico and Cuba

Puerto Rico was a poverty-stricken island, the fertility of whose 1 million inhabitants, including many blacks, outran that of their soil. By the Foraker Act of 1900, Congress accorded the Puerto Ricans a limited degree of popular government, and in 1917 granted them U.S. citizenship. Although the American regime worked wonders in education, sanitation, good roads, and other physical improvements, many of the inhabitants continued to clamor for independence. Many ultimately moved to New York City, where they added to the complexity of the melting pot.

A thorny legal problem was posed by the question: did the Constitution follow the flag? Did American laws, including tariff laws, apply with full force to the newly acquired possessions, chiefly the Philippines and Puerto Rico? Beginning in 1901 with the Insular Cases, a badly divided Supreme Court decreed, in effect, that the flag outran the Constitution, and that the outdistanced document did not extend with full force to the new windfalls.

Cuba, scorched and chaotic, presented another headache. An American military government, set up under the administrative genius of General Leonard Wood of Rough Rider fame, wrought miracles in government, finance, education, agriculture, and public health. Under his leadership a frontal attack was launched on yellow fever. Spectacular experiments were performed by Dr. Walter Reed and others upon American soldiers, who volunteered as human guinea pigs; and the stegomyia mosquito was proved to be the lethal carrier.

The United States, honoring its self-denying Teller Amendment of 1898, withdrew from Cuba in 1902. Old World imperialists could scarcely believe their eyes. But the federal government could not turn this rich and strategic island completely loose on the international sea; a grasping power like Germany might secure dangerous lodgment near America's soft underbelly. The Cubans were therefore forced to write into their own Constitution of 1901 the so-called Platt Amendment.

The hated restriction severely hobbled the Cubans. They bound themselves not to impair their independence by treaty or by contracting a debt beyond their resources. They further agreed that the United States might intervene with troops to restore order and to provide mutual protection. Finally, the Cuban government promised to sell or lease needed coaling or naval stations, ultimately two and then only one (Guantánamo), to its powerful "benefactor." The United States is still there on about 28,000 acres under an agreement that can be revoked only by the consent of both parties.

New Horizons in Two Hemispheres

In essence the Spanish-American War was a kind of gigantic coming-out party. Dewey's thundering guns advertised the fact that the nation had already become a world power.

The war itself was short (113 days), spectacular, low in casualties, and successful—despite the bungling. American prestige rose sharply, and European powers grudgingly accorded the republic more respect.

An exhilarating new spirit thrilled America. National pride was touched and cockiness was increased by what John Hay called a "splendid little war."* America did not start the war with imperialistic motives, but after falling through the cellar door of imperialism in a drunken fit of idealism, it wound up with imperialistic and colonial fruits in its grasp.

---

* Anti-imperialist William James called it "our squalid war with Spain."

By taking on the Philippine Islands, the United States became a full-fledged East Asian power. Hereafter these distant islands were to be a "heel of Achilles"—a kind of indefensible hostage given to Japan, as events proved in 1941. With singular short-sightedness, the Americans assumed dangerous commitments that they were later unwilling to defend by proper naval and military outlays.

But the lessons of unpreparedness were not altogether lost. Captain Mahan's big-navyism seemed vindicated, and popular support grew for more and better battleships. A master organizer, Elihu Root, took over the reins of the War Department. He established a general staff and founded the War College in Washington.

One of the happiest results of the conflict was the further closing of the "bloody chasm" between North and South. Thousands of patriotic southerners had flocked to the Stars and Stripes, and the gray-bearded General Joseph ("Fighting Joe") Wheeler—a Confederate cavalry hero—was given a command in Cuba. He allegedly cried, in the heat of battle, "To hell with the Yankees! Dammit, I mean the Spaniards."

"Little Brown Brothers" in the Philippines

Unhappily, the liberty-loving Filipinos were tragically deceived. They had assumed that they, like the Cubans, would be granted their freedom after the war. Bitterness toward the American troops erupted into open insurrection on February 4, 1899, under Emilio Aguinaldo.

The war with the Filipinos, unlike the "splendid" little set-to with Spain, was sordid and prolonged. It involved more savage fighting, more soldiers killed, and far more scandal. Anti-imperialists redoubled their protests. In their view the United States, having plunged into war with Spain to free Cuba, was now fighting 10,000 miles away to rivet shackles on a people who asked for nothing but liberty—in the American tradition.

As the ill-equipped Filipino armies were defeated, they melted into the jungle to wage a vicious guerrilla warfare. Many of the outgunned Filipinos used barbarous methods, and inevitably the infuriated American troops responded in kind.

Atrocity tales shocked and rocked the United States, for such methods did not reflect America's better self. Uncle Sam's soldiers were goaded to such extremes as the painful "water cure"—that is, forcing water down the victim's throat until he yielded information or died. Reconcentration camps were established that strongly suggested those of "Butcher" Weyler in Cuba. America, having begun the Spanish war with noble ideals, thus had now dirtied its hands. One New York newspaper published a reply to Rudyard Kipling's famous poem:

> We've taken up the white man's burden
>   Of ebony and brown;
> Now will you kindly tell us, Rudyard,
>   How we may put it down?

The backbone of the Filipino insurrection was finally broken in 1901, when Aguinaldo was captured. But sporadic fighting dragged on for many dreary months.

McKinley's "benevolent assimilation" of the Philippines proceeded with painful slowness. Millions of American dollars were poured into the islands to improve roads, sanitation, and public health. Important economic ties, including trade in sugar, developed between the two peoples. American teachers—"pioneers of the blackboard"—set up an unusually good school system and helped make English a second language. But all this vast expenditure, which profited America little, was ill received. The Filipinos, who hated compulsory civilization, preferred less sanitation and more liberty. Like caged hawks, they beat against their gilded bars until they finally got their freedom, on the Fourth of July, 1946.

Hinging the Open Door in China

Exciting events had meanwhile been brewing in China. Following its defeat by Japan in 1894–1895, the imperialistic European powers, notably Russia and Germany, moved in. Like vultures descending upon a wounded whale, they began to tear away valuable leaseholds and economic spheres of influence from the Manchu government.

A growing group of Americans viewed the vivisection of China with alarm. Churches were worried about their missionary vineyards; manufacturers and exporters feared that Chinese markets would be monopolized by Europeans. An alarmed American public, prodded by the press and by certain free-trade Britons, demanded that Washington do something. Secretary of State John Hay finally decided upon a dramatic move.

In the summer of 1899, Hay dispatched to all the great powers a communication soon known as the Open Door note. He urged them to announce that in their leaseholds or spheres of interest they would respect certain Chinese rights and the ideal of fair competition. Hay's proposal caused much squirming in the leading world capitals, but all the great powers eventually accepted, though subject to the condition that the others acquiesce unconditionally.

Open door or not, patriotic Chinese did not care to be used as a doormat by the Europeans. In 1900 a superpatriotic group known as the "Boxers" broke loose with the cry, "Kill foreign devils." Over 200 missionaries and other ill-fated whites were murdered, and a number of foreign diplomats were besieged in the capital, Beijing (Peking).

A multinational rescue force of some 18,000 soldiers, including about 2,500 Americans, arrived in the nick of time. Such participation in a joint military operation, especially in Asia, was plainly contrary to the nation's time-honored principles of nonentanglement and noninvolvement.

The victorious allied invaders acted angrily and vindictively. They assessed prostrate China an excessive indemnity of $333 million, of which America's share was to be $24.5 million. When Washington discovered that this sum was much more than enough to pay damages and expenses, it remitted about $18 million. The Beijing government, appreciating this gesture of goodwill, set aside the money to educate a selected group of Chinese students in the United States. These bright young people later played a significant role in the westernization of Asia.

Secretary Hay now let fly another paper broadside in 1900, announcing that henceforth the Open Door would embrace the territorial integrity of China. Defenseless China was spared partition during these troubled years. But its salvation was proba-

bly due not to Hay's fine phrases but to the strength of the competing powers.

Imperialism or Bryanism in 1900?

President McKinley's renomination by the Republicans in 1900 was a foregone conclusion. He had piloted the country through a victorious war; he had acquired rich, though burdensome, real estate; he had established the gold standard; and he had brought the promised prosperity of the full dinner pail.

An irresistible vice-presidential boom had developed for "Teddy" Roosevelt (TR), the cowboy-hero of San Juan Hill. Capitalizing on his war-born popularity, he had been elected governor of New York, where the local political bosses had found him headstrong and difficult to manage. They therefore devised a scheme to kick the colorful colonel upstairs into the vice-presidency.

This plot to railroad Roosevelt worked beautifully. Gesticulating wildly, he attended the nominating convention, where his western-style cowboy hat made him stand out like a white crow. To the accompaniment of cries of "we want Teddy," he received a unanimous vote, except for his own. A frantic Hanna reportedly moaned that there would be only one heartbeat between that wild-eyed "madman"—"that damned cowboy"—and the presidency of the United States.

William Jennings Bryan was the odds-on choice of the Democrats, meeting at Kansas City. The Democratic platform proclaimed, as did Bryan, that the "paramount" issue was Republican overseas imperialism.

McKinley, the soul of dignity, sat safely on his front porch, as before. Bryan, also as before, took to the stump in a cyclonic campaign, assailing both imperialism and Republican-fostered trusts. Lincoln, he charged, had abolished slavery for 3.5 million Africans; McKinley had reestablished it for 7 million Filipinos.

Republicans responded by charging that "Bryanism," not imperialism, was the paramount issue. By this accusation they meant that Bryan would rock the boat of prosperity once he got into office with his free-silver lunacy and other dangerous ideas. The voters were much less concerned about imperialism than about "four years more of the full dinner pail."

McKinley triumphed by a much wider margin than in 1896; 7,218,491 to 6,356,734 popular votes and 292 to 155 electoral votes. Victory for the Republicans was not a mandate for or against imperialism. If there was any mandate at all it was for the two Ps: prosperity and protection.

TR: Brandisher of the Big Stick

Kindly William McKinley had scarcely served another six months when, in September 1901, he was murdered by a deranged anarchist. Roosevelt became president at age forty-two, the youngest thus far in American history.

What manner of man was Theodore Roosevelt, the red-blooded blueblood? Born into a wealthy and distinguished New York family, he had fiercely built up his spindly, asthmatic body by a stern and self-imposed routine of exercise. Graduating from Harvard with Phi Beta Kappa honors, he published at the age of twenty-four the first of some thirty volumes of muscular prose. Then came busy years, which involved duties as a ranch owner and bespectacled cowboy ("Four-Eyes") in the Dakotas, followed by various political posts. When fully developed, he was a barrel-chested 5 feet 10 inches, with prominent teeth, squinty eyes, droopy mustache, and piercing voice.

The Rough Rider's high-voltage energy was electrifying. Believing that it was better to wear out than to rust out, he would shake the hands of some 6,000 persons at one stretch or ride horseback many miles in a day as an example for portly cavalry officers. Incurably boyish and bellicose, Roosevelt never ceased to preach the virile virtues and to denounce civilized softness, with its pacifists and other "flubdubs" and "mollycoddles." An ardent champion of military and naval preparedness, he adopted as his pet proverb, "Speak softly and carry a big stick, [and] you will go far."

Wherever Roosevelt went, there was a great stir. At a wedding he eclipsed the bride; at a funeral, the corpse. Shockingly unconventional, he loved to break hoary precedents—the hoarier the better. He loved people and mingled with those of all ranks from Catholic cardinals to professional prize fighters, one of whom blinded a Rooseveltian eye in a White House bout.

An outspoken moralizer and reformer, Roosevelt preached righteousness from the White House pulpit. Yet he was an opportunist who would compromise rather than butt his head against a stone wall. He was, in reality, much less radical than his blustery actions would indicate. A middle-of-the-roader, he stood just a little left of center and bared his mulelike molars at liberals and reactionaries alike.

Roosevelt rapidly developed into a master politician with an idolatrous personal following. A magnificent showman, he was always front-page copy; and his cowboyism, his bear shooting, his outsize teeth, and his pince-nez glasses were ever the delight of cartoonists.

Above all, Roosevelt was a direct-actionist. He believed that the president should lead. He had no real respect for the delicate checks and balances among the three branches of government. The president, he felt, may take any action in the general interest that is not specifically forbidden by the laws of the Constitution.

Building the Panama Canal

Foreign affairs absorbed much of Roosevelt's bullish energy. Having traveled extensively in Europe, he enjoyed a far more intimate knowledge of the outside world than most of his predecessors.

The Spanish-American War had emphasized the need of constructing the long-talked-about canal across the Central American isthmus. An isthmian canal would plainly augment the strength of the navy by increasing its mobility. Such a waterway would also make easier the defense of such recent acquisitions as Puerto Rico, Hawaii, and the Philippines, while facilitating the operations of the American merchant marine.

Initial obstacles in the path of the canal builders were legal rather than geographical. By the terms of the ancient Clayton-Bulwer Treaty, con-

Big Stick in the Caribbean *In 1901 Roosevelt declared: "If a man continually blusters . . . a big stick will not save him from trouble; and neither will speaking softly avail, if back of the softness there does not lie strength, power. . . . If the boaster is not prepared to back up his words his position becomes absolutely contemptible."*

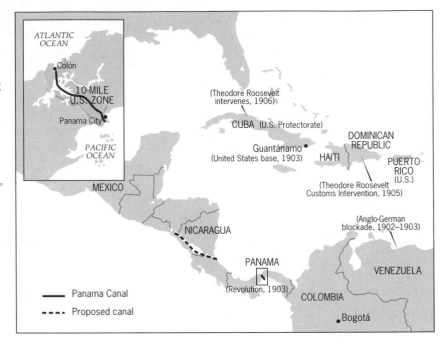

cluded with Britain in 1850, the United States could not secure exclusive control over such a route. But by 1901 America's British cousins were willing to yield ground. Confronted with an unfriendly Europe and bogged down in the South African Boer War, they conceded the Hay-Pauncefote Treaty in 1901. It not only gave the United States a free hand to build the canal but conceded the right to fortify it as well.

Legal barriers now removed, the next question was: where should the canal be dug? Many American experts favored the Nicaraguan route, but agents of an old French canal company were eager to salvage something from their costly failure at S-shaped Panama. Represented by a young, energetic, and unscrupulous engineer, Philippe Bunau-Varilla, the New Panama Canal Company suddenly dropped the price of its holdings from $109 million to the fire sale price of $40 million.

After much debate, Congress in June 1902 finally decided on the Panama route. The scene now shifted to Colombia, of which Panama was an unwilling part. A treaty highly favorable to the United States was negotiated with the agent of the Bogotá government, but it was unanimously rejected by the Colombian senate, which wanted more money for the valuable isthmian strip. Impatient Panamanians, who had rebelled numerous times, were ripe for another revolt. They had counted on a wave of prosperity to follow construction of the canal, and they feared that the United States would now turn to the Nicaraguan route. Scheming Bunau-Varilla was no less disturbed by the prospect of losing the company's $40 million. Working hand in glove with the Panama revolutionists, he helped incite a rebellion on November 3, 1903. Colombian troops were gathered to crush the uprising, but U.S. naval forces would not let them cross the isthmus.

Roosevelt moved rapidly to make steamy Panama a virtual outpost of the United States. Three days after the uprising he hastily extended the right hand of recognition. Fifteen days later, Bunau-Varilla, who was now the Panamanian minister despite his French citizenship, signed the Hay–Bunau-Varilla treaty in Washington. The price of the canal strip was left the same, but the zone was widened from six to ten miles. The French company gladly pocketed its $40 million from the U.S. Treasury.

Theodore Roosevelt and His Big Stick in the Caribbean, 1904 *Roosevelt's policies seemed to be turning the Caribbean into a Yankee pond.*

Critics charged that Roosevelt's "cowboy diplomacy" represented thinly disguised imperialism. European imperialists, who were old hands at this kind of thing, could now raise their eyebrows sneeringly at America's superior moral pretension. But Roosevelt heatedly defended himself against charges of evildoing. He claimed that he had received a "mandate from civilization" to start the canal, and that Colombia had wronged the United States by not permitting itself to be thus benefited.

Active work was begun on "making the dirt fly" in 1902, but grave difficulties were encountered, ranging from labor troubles to landslides. The organization was finally perfected under an energetic but autocratic West Point engineer, Colonel George Washington Goethals. At the outset, sanitation proved to be more important than excavation. Colonel William C. Gorgas, the quiet and determined exterminator of yellow fever in Havana, ulti-mately made the Canal Zone "as safe as a health resort."

Americans finally succeeded where Frenchmen had failed. In 1914 the colossal canal project was completed at an initial cost of about $400 million.

TR's Perversion of Monroe's Doctrine

Latin American debt defaults created the conditions for further Rooseveltian involvement in affairs south of the border. Nations such as Venezuela and the Dominican Republic were chronically in arrears in their payments to European creditors, particularly Britain and Germany. Roosevelt feared that if the Germans or others got their foot in the door as bill collectors, they might remain in Latin America. He therefore devised a devious policy of "preventive intervention," better known as the Roosevelt corol-lary of the Monroe Doctrine. He declared that in the event of future financial malfeasance by the Latin American nations, the United States itself would intervene, take over the customshouses, pay off the debts, and keep the troublesome powers on the other side of the Atlantic. In short, no outsiders could push the Latin nations around except Uncle Sam, Policeman of the Caribbean.

This new brandishing of the Big Stick in the Caribbean became effective in 1905. It was formalized two years later by a treaty with the Dominican Republic giving the United States supervisory powers over Dominican tariff collections.

Roosevelt's rewriting of Monroe's doctrine did more than any other single step to promote the "Bad Neighbor" policy begun in these years. As time wore on, the new corollary was used to justify wholesale interventions and repeated landings of the marines, all of which helped turn the Caribbean into a "Yankee pond." To Latin Americans it seemed as though the Monroe Doctrine, far from providing a shield, was a cloak behind which the United States sought to strangle them.

Roosevelt on the World Stage

Booted and spurred, Roosevelt charged into international affairs far beyond Latin America. The outbreak of war between Russia and Japan gave him a chance to perform as a global statesman. The Russian Bear, having lumbered across Asia, was seeking to bathe its frostbitten paws in the ice-free ports of China's Manchuria, particularly Port Arthur. In Japanese eyes, Manchuria and Korea in tsarist hands were pistols pointed at Japan's strategic heart. With the Russians threatening a permanent occupation of Manchuria, the Japanese suddenly began war in 1904 by a devastating surprise attack on the Russian fleet at Port Arthur. They proceeded to administer a humiliating series of beatings to the inept Russians. But as the war dragged on, Japan began to run short of men and yen—a weakness it did not want to betray to the enemy. Tokyo officials therefore approached Roosevelt in the deepest secrecy and asked him to help sponsor peace negotiations.

Roosevelt agreed and shepherded the delegates of the two sides together at Portsmouth, New Hampshire, in 1905. The Japanese presented stern de-

mands for a huge indemnity and the entire strategic island of Sakhalin, while the Russians stubbornly refused to concede the depth of their defeat. Blustering at both sides behind the scenes, Roosevelt forced through an accord in which the Japanese received no indemnity and only the southern half of Sakhalin.

For achieving this agreement, as well as for helping arrange an international conference at Algeciras, Spain, in 1906 to mediate North African disputes, Roosevelt received the Nobel Peace Prize in 1906. But the price of TR's diplomatic glory was high for U.S. foreign relations. Two historic friendships withered on the windswept plains of Manchuria. America's relations with Russia, once friendly, soured as the Russians implausibly accused Roosevelt of robbing them of military victory. Japan, once America's protégé, felt robbed of its indemnity. Both newly powerful, Japan and America now became rivals in Asia, as fear and jealously between them grew.

Japanese Laborers in California

The population of America's Pacific Coast was directly affected by the Russo-Japanese War. A new restlessness swept over the rice paddies of Japan, largely as a result of the dislocation and tax burdens caused by the recent conflict. Numerous Japanese laborers, with their wives and children, began to pour into the spacious valleys of California. By 1906 approximately 70,000 Japanese dwelt along the Pacific Coast. Nervous Californians, confronted by another "yellow peril," were fearful of being drowned in an Asian sea.

A showdown on the Japanese influx came in 1906. Following the frightful earthquake and fire of that year in San Francisco, the local school authorities, pressed for space, decreed that Japanese children should attend a special school.

Instantly, the Japanese school incident brewed an international crisis. The people of Japan, highly sensitive on questions of race, regarded this discrimination as an insult to them and their beloved children. On both sides of the Pacific, irresponsible war talk sizzled in the yellow press—the real yellow peril. Roosevelt, who as a Rough Rider had relished shooting, was less happy over the prospect that California might stir up a war that all the other states would have to fight. He therefore invited the entire San Francisco Board of Education to come to the White House.

TR finally broke the deadlock, but not until he had brandished his big stick and bared his teeth. The Californians were induced to repeal the offensive school order and to accept what came to be known as "the Gentlemen's Agreement." This secret understanding was worked out, during 1907–1908, by an exchange of diplomatic notes between Washington and Tokyo. The Japanese, for their part, agreed to

---

CHRONOLOGY

1820	New England missionaries arrive in Hawaii.
1889	Samoa crisis with Germany.
	Pan-American Conference.
1890	Mahan publishes *The Influence of Sea Power upon History.*
1891	New Orleans crisis with Italy.
1892	Valparaiso crisis with Chile.
1893	White planter revolt in Hawaii.
	Cleveland refuses Hawaii annexation.
1895	Cubans revolt against Spain.
1895–1896	Venezuelan boundary crisis with Britain.
1898	*Maine* explosion in Havana harbor.
	Spanish-American War.
	Teller Amendment.
	Dewey's victory at Manila Bay.
	Hawaii annexed.
1899	Senate ratifies treaty acquiring the Philippines.
	Aguinaldo launches rebellion against United States.
	First American Open Door note.
1900	Boxer Rebellion and U.S. expedition to China.
	Second Open Door note.
	Hawaii receives territorial status.
	McKinley defeats Bryan for presidency.

1901	McKinley assassinated; Roosevelt assumes presidency.
	Filipino rebellion defeated.
	Hay-Pauncefote Treaty.
	Supreme Court Insular Cases.
	Platt Amendment.
1902	Colombian senate rejects canal treaty.
	U.S. troops leave Cuba.
1903	Panamanian revolution against Colombia.
	Hay–Bunau-Varilla treaty.
1904	Roosevelt declares his corollary to the Monroe Doctrine.
1904–1914	Construction of the Panama Canal.
1905	Roosevelt mediates Russo-Japanese peace treaty.
	United States takes over Dominican Republic customs.
1906	Japanese education crisis in San Francisco.
	Roosevelt arranges Algeciras conference.
1906–1909	U.S. marines occupy Cuba.
1907	Great White Fleet.
1907–1908	"Gentlemen's Agreement" with Japan.
1908	Root-Takahira agreement.
1917	Puerto Ricans granted U.S. citizenship.

stop the flow of laborers to the American mainland by withholding passports. Caucasian Californians, their fears allayed, henceforth slept easier.

Roosevelt worried that his intercession between California and Japan might be interpreted in Tokyo as prompted by fear of the Japanese. Accordingly, he hit upon a dramatic scheme to impress the Japanese with the heft of his big stick. He daringly decided to send the entire battleship fleet on a highly visible voyage around the globe.

Late in 1907 sixteen smoke-belching battleships started from Virginia waters. Their commander pointedly declared that he was ready for "a feast, a frolic, or a fight." The Great White Fleet—to the accompaniment of cannonading champagne corks—received tumultuous welcomes in Latin America, Hawaii, New Zealand, and Australia.

As events turned out, an overwhelming reception in Japan was the high point of the trip. Tens of thousands of kimonoed schoolchildren had been trained to wave tiny American flags and sing "The Star-Spangled Banner"—reportedly in English. In the happy diplomatic atmosphere created by the visit of the fleet, the Root-Takahira agreement of 1908 was reached with Japan. The United States and Japan solemnly pledged themselves to respect each other's territorial possessions in the Pacific and to uphold the Open Door in China. The once fight-thirsty Roosevelt, who thus went out of his way to avoid a fight with Japan, regarded the battleship cruise as his most important contribution to peace.

Varying Viewpoints

Disagreement marks historical appraisals of America's emergence as a great power at the turn of the twentieth century. Many writers believe that the United States did not enter the great power game as just another player, but rather introduced a distinctive new style of diplomatic play and perhaps even a new set of rules. But judgments differ about these alleged innovations. An older school of thought stresses the idealism that America brought to the world arena, and regards the territorial imperialism of the 1890s as some kind of aberration. More recently, "New Left" revisionists such as William Appleman Williams and Walter LaFeber have argued that territorial imperialism was really only a small part of the larger pattern of America's overseas expansionism. America's special contribution to international life, they charge, was the self-serving notion of "informal empire" typified by a worldwide Open Door doctrine. This strategy shunned formal territorial possession and instead sought to dominate foreign raw materials, markets, and investments.

Historians disagree further about the motivating impulses of American diplomacy. The revisionists have stressed economic factors, arguing that the United States sought foreign markets to solve the problems of domestic overproduction and recurring business depressions. They thus try to link the two most striking developments of the age: the amazing industrialization of America and the republic's emergence as a great world power. Such a revisionist interpretation has been sharply challenged by scholars who argue that foreign policy is much too complex to be explained by economic factors alone.

SELECT READINGS

Primary Source Documents

Examples of yellow journalism include Joseph Pulitzer's New York *World* and William R. Hearst's New York *Journal.* Particularly interesting is the editorial in the *World* of February 13, 1897,* and the article by Charles Duval in the *Journal* of October 10, 1897.* McKinley's War Message,* in James D. Richardson, ed., *Messages and Papers of the Presidents* (1899), vol. X, pp. 139ff., outlines the American rationale for intervention. The anti-imperialist answer can be found in Charles E. Norton's article in *Public Opinion,* June 23, 1898, pp. 775–776.* For the intrigue surrounding the independence of Panama and the building of the canal, see *Foreign Relations of the United States** (1903) and Theodore Roosevelt to Albert Shaw, October 10, 1903,* in *The Letters of Theodore Roosevelt,* edited by Elting E. Morison (1951), vol. 3, p. 628.

Secondary Sources

Main outlines are sketched in Foster Rhea Dulles, *America's Rise to World Power, 1898–1954* (1955), and in Thomas G. Paterson, *American Foreign Policy: A Brief History* (3d ed., 1988). Two general (and quite contrasting) interpretations of modern American foreign policy are George F. Kennan, *American Diplomacy* (1951), and William Appleman Williams, *The Tragedy of American Diplomacy* (1959). Consult also Williams's *The Roots of the Modern American Empire* (1961), Ernest R. May, *Imperial Democracy* (1961), and Walter LeFeber, *The New Empire* (1963). On the Spanish-American War itself, see Frank Freidel, *The Splendid Little War* (1958), and David F. Trask, *The War With Spain in 1898* (1981). David F. Healey examines *The United States in Cuba, 1898–1902* (1963), and Leon Wolff paints a grim picture of American involvement in the Philippines in *Little Brown Brother* (1961). For more on the Philippine imbroglio, see Stuart C. Miller,

"Benevolent Assimilation": The American Conquest of the Philippines, 1899–1903 (1982), and Stanley Karnow, *In Our Image: America's Empire in the Philippines* (1989). For the Open Door, consult A. Whitney Griswold, *The Far Eastern Policy of the United States* (1938), and Marilyn B. Young, *The Rhetoric of Empire: America's China Policy, 1895–1901* (1968). On relations with Japan, see Charles E. Neu, *An Uncertain Friendship: Theodore Roosevelt and Japan, 1906–1909* (1967) and *The Troubled Encounter: The United States and Japan* (1975). Also valuable are two books by Akira Iriye, *Across the Pacific* (1967) and *Pacific Estrangement: Japanese and American Expansion, 1897–1911* (1972). James Reed discusses *The Missionary Mind and American East Asian Policy, 1911–1915* (1983). Also see William R. Hutchinson, *Errand to the World: American Protestant Thought and Foreign Missions* (1987). On the treatment of the Japanese in the United States, see Ronald Takaki, *Strangers from a Different Shore* (1989). The canal issue is analyzed in David McCullough, *The Path between the Seas* (1977); Walter LeFeber, *The Panama Canal* (1978); and Richard H. Collin, *Theodore Roosevelt's Caribbean: The Panama Canal, the Monroe Doctrine, and the Latin American Context* (1990). For Roosevelt himself, see Howard K. Beale, *Theodore Roosevelt and the Rise of America to World Power* (1956), John M. Blum, *The Republican Roosevelt* (new ed., 1977), and G. Wallace Chessman, *Theodore Roosevelt and the Politics of Power* (1969). Especially good on the youthful TR are Edmund Morris, *The Rise of Theodore Roosevelt* (1979), and David McCullough, *Mornings on Horseback* (1981).

CHAPTER 30

Progressivism and the Republican Roosevelt, 1901–1912

When I say I believe in a square deal I do not mean . . . to give every man the best hand. If the cards do not come to any man, or if they do come, and he has not got the power to play them, that is his affair. All I mean is that there shall be no crookedness in the dealing.

Theodore Roosevelt, 1905

Progressive Roots

Nearly 76 million Americans greeted the new century in 1900. Of them, almost one in seven was foreign born. In the fourteen years of peace that remained before the Great War of 1914 engulfed the globe, 13 million more migrants would carry their bundles down the gangplanks to the land of promise.

Hardly had the twentieth century dawned on the ethnically and racially mixed American people than they were convulsed by a reform movement, the like of which the nation had not seen since the 1840s. The new crusaders, who called themselves "progressives," waged war on many evils, notably monopoly, corruption, inefficiency, and social injustice. The progressive army was large, multicolored, and widely deployed, but the real heart of the movement, explained one progressive reformer, was to "use the government as an agency of human welfare."

The ground swell of the new reformist wave went far back—to the Greenback Labor party of the 1870s and the Populists of the 1890s, to the mounting unrest throughout the land as grasping industrialists concentrated more and more power in fewer

and fewer hands. An outworn philosophy of hands-off individualism seemed increasingly out of place in the modern machine age. Progressive theorists were insisting that society could no longer afford the luxury of a limitless "let-alone" policy (laissez-faire). The people, through government, must substitute mastery for drift.

Well before 1900, perceptive politicians and writers had begun to pinpoint targets for the progressive attack. Bryan, Altgeld, and the Populists loudly branded the "bloated trusts" with the stigma of corruption and wrongdoing. In 1894 Henry Demarest Lloyd charged headlong into the Standard Oil Company with his book entitled *Wealth Against Commonwealth*. Eccentric Thorstein Veblen assailed the new rich with his prickly pen in *The Theory of the Leisure Class* (1899), a savage attack on "predatory wealth" and "conspicuous consumption."

Other pen-wielding knights likewise entered the fray. The keen-eyed and keen-nosed Danish immigrant Jacob A. Riis, a reporter for the *New York Sun,* shocked middle-class Americans in 1890 with

Child Workers *Two young girls tend a thread-winding machine. The boy is already a veteran coal miner.*

How the Other Half Lives. His account was a damning indictment of the dirt, disease, vice, and misery of those rat-gnawed human rookeries known as the New York slums. Novelist Theodore Dreiser used his blunt prose to batter promoters and profiteers in *The Financier* (1912) and *The Titan* (1914).

Socialists, now swelling in numbers, must take high rank among the caustic critics of existing injustices. Many of them were European immigrants, and they received much of their inspiration from abroad, where countries such as Germany were launching daring experiments in state socialism.

High-minded messengers of the social gospel also contributed mightily to the upsurging wave of reform, as did the ever-growing women's movement. Feminists in multiplying numbers added social justice to suffrage on their list of needed reforms. With urban pioneers such as Jane Addams blazing the way, women entered the fight to clean up corrupt city governments, to protect women on the clanging factory floor, to keep children out of the smudgy mills and sooty mines, and to ensure that only safe food

products found their way to the family table. Much of progressivism reflected the new public concerns of women, born of their changing role in the still-stretching cities.

Raking Muck with the Muckrakers

Beginning about 1902 the exposing of evil became a flourishing industry among American publishers. A group of aggressive ten- and fifteen-cent popular magazines surged to the front, notably *McClure's, Cosmopolitan, Collier's,* and *Everybody's.* Waging fierce circulation wars, they dug deep for the dirt that the public loved to hate. Enterprising editors financed extensive research and encouraged pugnacious writing by their bright young reporters, whom President Roosevelt branded as "muckrakers" in 1906.

In 1902 a brilliant New York reporter, Lincoln Steffens, launched a series of articles in *McClure's* entitled "The Shame of the Cities." He fearlessly unmasked the corrupt alliance between big business and municipal government. Steffens was followed in the same magazine by Ida M. Tarbell, who published a devastating but factual exposé of the Standard Oil Company.

Muckrakers fearlessly assailed the malpractices of life insurance companies and tariff lobbies. They roasted the beef trust, the "money trust," the railroad barons, and the corrupt amassing of American fortunes. David G. Phillips shocked an already startled nation by his series in *Cosmopolitan* entitled "The Treason of the Senate" (1906). He boldly charged that seventy-five of the ninety senators did not represent the people at all but the railroads and trusts.

Some of the most effective fire of the muckrakers was directed at social evils. The ugly list included the immoral "white slave" traffic in women, the rickety slums, and the appalling number of industrial accidents. The sorry subjugation of America's 9 million blacks was spotlighted in Ray Stannard Baker's *Following the Color Line* (1908). The abuses of child labor were brought luridly to light by John Spargo's *The Bitter Cry of the Children* (1906).

Vendors of potent patent medicines (often heavily spiked with alcohol) likewise came in for bitter criticism. These conscienceless vultures, who sold incredible quantities of adulterated or habit-forming drugs, were exposed by muckraking attacks in *Collier's,* reinforced by the research of Dr. Harvey W. Wiley, chief chemist of the Department of Agriculture.

Full of sound and fury, the muckrakers signified much about the nature of the progressive reform movement. They were long on lamentation and short on sweeping remedies. To right social wrongs they counted on publicity and an aroused public conscience, not drastic political change. They sought not to overthrow capitalism but to cleanse it. The cure for the ills of American democracy, they earnestly believed, was more democracy.

Political Progressivism

Progressive reformers were mainly middle-class men and women who felt themselves squeezed from above and below. They sensed pressure from the new giant corporations, the restless immigrant hordes, and the aggressive labor unions. The progressives simultaneously sought two goals: to use state power to curb the trusts, and to stem the Socialist threat by generally improving the common person's conditions of life and labor. Progressives emerged in both major parties, in all regions, and at all levels of government. The truth is that progressivism was less a minority movement and more a majority mood.

One of the first objectives of progressives was to regain the power that had slipped from the hands of the people into those of the "interests." These ardent reformers pushed for direct primary elections so as to undercut power-hungry party bosses. They favored the "initiative" so that voters could directly propose legislation themselves, thus bypassing the boss-bought state legislatures. Progressives also agitated for the referendum. This device would place laws on the ballot for final approval by the people, especially laws that had been railroaded through a compliant legislature by free-spending agents of big business. The recall would enable the voters to remove faithless elected officials, particularly those who had been bribed by bosses or lobbyists. The secret Australian ballot was likewise being introduced more widely in the states to counteract boss rule.

Direct election of U.S. senators became a favorite goal of progressives, especially after muckrakers had exposed the scandalous tie-in between greedy corporations and Congress. Direct election was finally achieved by the Seventeenth Amendment to the Constitution, approved in 1913 (see Appendix). But the expected improvement of the Senate "millionaire's club" was slow in coming.

Woman suffrage, the goal of feminists for many decades, likewise received powerful new support from the progressives early in the 1900s. The political reformers believed that women's votes would elevate the political tone; foes of the saloon felt that they could count on the support of enfranchised females. Many of the states, especially the more liberal ones in the West, gradually extended the vote to women. But by 1910 nationwide female suffrage was still a decade away.

Progressivism in the Cities and States

Progressives scored some of their most impressive gains in the cities. Frustrated by the inefficiency and

Suffragists Put the Pressure on Washington *Success finally crowned their effort with the ratification of the Nineteenth Amendment in 1920.*

corruption of machine-oiled city government, many localities followed the pioneering example of Galveston, Texas. In 1901 it had appointed expert-staffed commissions to manage urban affairs. Other communities adopted the city manager system, also designed to take politics out of municipal administration. Some of these "reforms" obviously valued efficiency more highly than democracy, as control of civic affairs was further removed from the people's hands.

Urban reformers likewise attacked "slumlords," juvenile delinquency, and wide-open prostitution (vice-at-a-price), which flourished in red-light districts unchallenged by bribed police. Public-spirited city dwellers also moved to halt the corrupt sale of franchises for streetcars and other public utilities.

Progressivism naturally bubbled up to the state level, notably in Wisconsin, which became a yeasty laboratory of reform. Pompadoured Robert M. ("Fighting Bob") La Follette was an undersized but over-engined crusader who emerged as the most militant of the progressive Republican leaders. Elected

governor in 1901 after a desperate fight with the railroad and timber interests, he perfected a scheme for regulating public utilities while laboring in close association with experts on the faculty of the University of Wisconsin at Madison.

Other states marched steadily toward the progressive camp as they undertook to regulate railroads and trusts, chiefly through public utilities commissions. Oregon was not far behind Wisconsin, and California made giant bootstrides under the stocky Hiram W. Johnson. Elected Republican governor in 1910, this dynamic prosecutor of grafters helped break the dominant grip of the Southern Pacific Railroad on California politics and then, like La Follette, set up a political machine of his own.

In these and other states, fired-up progressives tackled head-on a whole array of social problems. One of the most remarkable features of this era was the energy and confidence with which reformers did battle with a host of evils. They finally secured the enactment of safety and sanitation codes for industry and closed certain harmful trades to juveniles. Progressives further protected the toiler with workmen's compensation laws protecting injured laborers and laws setting maximum hours and minimum wages.

Steaming and unsanitary sweatshops were a public scandal in many cities. The issue was thrust into the public eye in 1911, when a fire at the Triangle Shirtwaist Company in New York City incinerated 146 women workers, mostly girls. Lashed by the public outcry, the legislature of New York and later other legislatures passed laws regulating the hours and conditions of toil in such firetraps. In the landmark case of *Muller* v. *Oregon* (1908), crusading attorney Louis D. Brandeis persuaded the Supreme Court to accept the constitutionality of laws protecting women workers, because of "women's peculiar structures." Although that reasoning seemed sexist by later standards, progressives at the time hailed Brandeis's achievement as a triumph.

But crusaders for these humane measures did not always have smooth sailing. One dismaying setback came in 1905, when the Supreme Court in *Lochner* v. *New York* invalidated a New York law establishing a ten-hour day for bakers. Yet the reformist progressive wave finally washed up into the judiciary, and in 1917 the Court upheld a ten-hour law for factory workers. Gradually, the concept of the employer's responsibility to society was replacing the old dog-eat-dog philosophy of unregulated free enterprise.

Corner saloons, with their shutter doors, naturally attracted the ire and fire of progressives. By 1900 cities such as New York and San Francisco had one saloon for about every 200 people. Antiliquor campaigners received powerful support from several militant organizations, notably the Woman's Christian Temperance Union (WCTU). Pious Frances E. Willard, one of its founders, would fall on her knees in prayer on saloon floors. She found a vigorous ally in the Anti-Saloon League, which was aggressive, well organized, and well financed.

Caught up in the crusade, some states and numerous counties passed "dry" laws that controlled, restricted, or abolished alcohol. The big cities were generally "wet," for they had a large immigrant vote accustomed to the free flow of wine and beer in the Old Country. When World War I erupted in 1914, nearly one-half of the population lived in "dry" territory. Demon Rum was groggy and

was to be floored—temporarily—by the Eighteenth Amendment in 1919.

TR's Square Deal for Labor

Theodore Roosevelt, though something of an imperialistic busybody abroad, was touched by the progressive wave at home. Like other reformers, he feared that the "public interest" was being submerged in the drifting seas of indifference. Everybody's interest was nobody's interest. Roosevelt decided to make it his. His sportsman's instincts spurred him into demanding a "square deal" for capital, labor, and the public at large. Broadly speaking, his program embraced three Cs: control of the corporations, consumer protection, and conservation of natural resources.

The square deal for labor received its acid test in 1902, when a crippling strike broke out in the anthracite coal mines of Pennsylvania. Some 140,000 besooted workers, many of them illiterate immigrants, had long been frightfully exploited and accident plagued. They demanded, among other improvements, a 20 percent increase in pay and a reduction in the working day from ten to nine hours.

Unsympathetic mine owners, confident that a chilled public would react against the miners, refused to arbitrate or even negotiate. One of their spokesmen, the multimillionaire George F. Baer, wrote that workers would be cared for "not by the labor agitators, but by the Christian men to whom God in his infinite wisdom has given the control of the property interests of this country." Closed minds meant closed coal mines.

As coal supplies dwindled, factories and schools were forced to shut down, and even hospitals felt the icy grip of winter. Desperately seeking a solution, Roosevelt threatened to seize the mines and operate them with federal troops. Faced with this first-time ever threat to use federal bayonets against capital, rather than labor, the owners grudgingly consented to arbitration. A compromise decision ultimately gave the miners a 10 percent pay boost and a working day of nine hours. But their union was not officially recognized as a bargaining agent.

Keenly aware of the mounting antagonisms between capital and labor, Roosevelt urged Congress to create a new Department of Commerce and

Labor. This goal was achieved in 1903. (Ten years later the agency was split into two.) An important arm of the newly born Department of Commerce and Labor was the Bureau of Corporations, which was authorized to probe businesses engaged in interstate commerce. The bureau was highly useful in helping to break the stranglehold of monopoly and in clearing the road for the era of "trustbusting."

TR Corrals the Corporations

The sprawling railroad octopus sorely needed restraint. The Interstate Commerce Commission, created in 1887 as a feeble sop to the public, had proved woefully inadequate. Railroad barons could simply appeal the commission's decisions on rates to the federal courts—a process that might take ten years.

Spurred by the former-cowboy president, Congress passed effective railroad legislation, beginning with the Elkins Act of 1903. This curb was aimed primarily at the rebate evil. Heavy fines could now be imposed both on the railroads that gave rebates and on the shippers that accepted them.

Still more effective was the Hepburn Act of 1906. Free passes, with their hint of bribery, were severely restricted. The once-infantile Interstate Commerce Commission was expanded, and its reach was extended to include express companies, sleeping-car companies, and pipelines. For the first time, the commission was given real molars when it was authorized, on complaint of shippers, to nullify existing rates and stipulate maximum rates.

Roosevelt, as a trustbuster, first burst into the headlines in 1902 with an attack on the Northern Securities Company, a railroad holding company organized by financial titan J. P. Morgan and empire builder James J. Hill. These moguls of money sought to achieve a virtual monopoly of the railroads in the Northwest. Roosevelt was therefore challenging the most regal potentates of the industrial aristocracy.

The railway promoters appealed to the Supreme Court, which in 1904 upheld Roosevelt's antitrust suit and ordered the Northern Securities Company to be dissolved. The *Northern Securities* decision jolted Wall Street and angered big business but greatly enhanced Roosevelt's reputation as a trust-smasher. Roosevelt's big stick crashed down on other giant monopolies, as he initiated over forty legal proceedings against the beef, sugar, fertilizer, harvester, and other monopolies.

Much mythology, however, has inflated Roosevelt's reputation as a trustbuster. The Rough Rider understood the political popularity of monopoly smashing, but he did not consider it sound economic policy. Combination and integration, he felt, were the hallmarks of the age, and to try to stem the tide of economic progress by political means he considered the rankest folly. Bigness was not necessarily badness; so why punish success? Roosevelt's real purpose in assaulting the Goliaths of industry was symbolic: to prove conclusively that the government, not private business, ruled the country. He believed in regulating, not fragmenting, the big business combines. The threat of dissolution, he felt, might make the sultans of the smokestacks more amenable to federal regulation—as it did.

In truth, Roosevelt never swung his trust-crushing stick with maximum force. His successor, William Howard Taft, actually "busted" more trusts than TR did. In one celebrated instance in 1907, Roosevelt even gave his personal blessing to J. P. Morgan's plan to have U.S. Steel absorb the Tennessee Coal and Iron Company, without fear of antitrust reprisals. When Taft then launched a suit against U.S. Steel in 1911, the political reaction from TR was explosive.

Caring for the Consumer

Roosevelt backed a noteworthy measure in 1906 that benefited both corporations and consumers. Big meat packers were being shut out of certain European markets because some American meat—from the small packinghouses, claimed the giants—had been found to be tainted. Foreign governments were even threatening to ban all American meat imports by throwing out the good beef with the bad botulism.

At the same time, American consumers hungered for safer canned products. Their appetite for reform was whetted by Upton Sinclair's sensational novel *The Jungle,* published in 1906. Sinclair intended his revolting tract to focus attention on the plight of the workers in the big canning factories, but instead he appalled the public with his description of disgustingly unsanitary food products. (As he put it, he aimed for the nation's heart, but hit its stomach.) The book described in nauseating detail the filth, disease, and putrefaction in Chicago's damp, ill-ventilated slaughterhouses. A cynical jingle of the time ran:

> Mary had a little lamb,
> And when she saw it sicken,
> She shipped it off to Packingtown,
> And now it's labeled chicken.

Backed by a nauseated public, Roosevelt induced Congress to pass the Meat Inspection Act of 1906. It decreed that the preparation of meat shipped over state lines would be subject to federal inspection from corral to can. Although the largest packers resisted certain features of the act, they grudgingly accepted it as an opportunity to drive their smaller, fly-by-night competitors out of business. At the same time, they could receive the government's seal of approval on their exports. As a companion to the Meat Inspection Act, the Pure Food and Drug Act of 1906 was designed to prevent the adulteration and mislabeling of foods and pharmaceuticals.

Earth Control

Wasteful Americans, assuming that their natural resources were inexhaustible, had looted and polluted their incomparable domain with unparalleled speed and greed. Westerners were especially eager to accelerate the destructive process, for they panted to build up the country, and the environmental consequences be hanged. But even before the end of the nineteenth century, far-visioned leaders saw that such a squandering of the nation's birthright would have to be halted or America would sink from resource richness to despoiled squalor.

A first feeble step toward conservation was the Desert Land Act of 1877, under which the federal government sold arid soil cheaply on condition that the purchaser irrigate the thirsty soil in three years. More successful was the Forest Reserve Act of 1891, authorizing the president to set aside public forest land as national forests and other reserves. Under this statute some 46 million acres of magnificent trees were rescued from the lumberman's saw in the 1890s and preserved for posterity.

A new day in the history of conservation dawned with the advent of Roosevelt. Huntsman, naturalist, rancher, lover of the great out-of-doors, he was appalled by the pillaging of natural resources. Other dedicated conservationists, notably Gifford Pinchot, head of the federal Division of Forestry, had broken important ground before him. But Roosevelt seized the banner of leadership and charged into the fray with all the weight of his prestige, his energy, his firsthand knowledge, and his invective.

The thirst of the desert still unslaked, Congress responded to the whip of the Rough Rider by passing the landmark Newlands Act of 1902. Washington was authorized to collect money from the sale of public lands in the sun-baked western states and then use these funds for the development of irrigation projects. Settlers repaid the cost of reclamation from their now-productive soil, and the money was put into a fund to finance more such enterprises.

Roosevelt pined to preserve the nation's shrinking forests. By 1900 only about a quarter of the once-vast virgin timberlands remained standing. Lumbermen had already logged off most of the virgin timber from Maine to Michigan, and the sharp thud of their axes was beginning to split the silence in the great fir forests of the Pacific slope. Roosevelt proceeded to set aside in federal reserves some 125 millions acres, or almost three times the acreage thus saved from the saw by his three predecessors. He similarly earmarked millions of acres of coal deposits, as well as water resources useful for irrigation and power.

Conservation, including reclamation, may have been Roosevelt's most enduring tangible achievement. The superactive president took conservation out of the conversation stage, threw the force of his colorful personality behind it, dramatized it, and aroused public opinion to a constructive crusade. He was buoyed in this effort by an upwelling national mood of concern about the disappearance of the frontier. City dwellers, worried that too much civilization might not be good for the soul, snapped up Jack London's *Call of the Wild* (1903) and other books about nature. Groups like the outdoor-oriented Boy Scouts of America and the Sierra Club, founded in 1892, reflected the growing national interest in America's natural heritage.

Conservationist forces were not all of one mind. The building of a dam in the Hetch Hetchy Valley in Yosemite National Park in 1913 laid bare a deep division that persists to this day. To the preservationists of the Sierra Club, including famed naturalist John Muir, Hetch Hetchy was a "temple" of nature that should be held inviolable by the civilizing hand of humanity. But other conservationists, like President Roosevelt and his chief forester, Gifford Pinchot, believed that "wilderness was waste" and wanted to *use* nature intelligently. They sought to combine recreation, sustained-yield logging, watershed protection, and summer stock grazing on the same expanse of federal land.

Rational use of resources meant large-scale and long-term planning as well as efficient administrative techniques. Roosevelt's conservation policies, like many of his business policies, meant working hand in glove with the biggest resource users. The one-man-and-a-mule logger and the one-man-and-a-dog sheepherder were inevitably shouldered aside by the combined strength of big business and big government.

The "Roosevelt Panic" of 1907

Roosevelt was handily elected president in his own right in 1904 and entered his new term buoyed up by his enormous personal popularity. Yet the conservative Republican bosses grew increasingly restive as Roosevelt in his second term called ever more loudly for regulating the corporations, taxing incomes, and protecting workers. Roosevelt, meanwhile, had partly defanged himself after his election in 1904 by announcing that under no circumstances would he be a candidate for a third term.

Roosevelt suffered a sharp setback in 1907, when a short but punishing panic descended on Wall Street. The financial flurry featured frightened "runs" on banks, suicides, and criminal indictments against speculators.

The financial world hastened to blame Roosevelt for the storm. It cried that this "quack" had

unsettled industry with his boat-rocking tactics, and branded the current distress the "Roosevelt panic." The hot-tempered president angrily lashed back at his critics when he accused "certain malefactors of great wealth" of having deliberately engineered the monetary crisis to force the government to relax its assaults on trusts.

Fortunately, the panic of 1907 paved the way for long-overdue fiscal reforms. Precipitating a currency shortage, the flurry laid bare the need for a more elastic medium of exchange. Congress in 1908 responded by passing the Aldrich-Vreeland Act, which authorized national banks to issue emergency currency backed by various kinds of collateral. The path was thus smoothed for the epochal Federal Reserve Act of 1913 (see p. 455).

The Rough Rider Thunders Out

Still warmly popular in 1908, Roosevelt could easily have won a second presidential nomination and almost certainly the election. But he felt bound by his impulsive postelection promise after his victory in 1904.

The departing president thus naturally sought a successor who would carry out "my policies." The man of his choice was amiable, ample-girthed, and huge-framed William Howard Taft, secretary of war and a mild progressive. As an heir apparent, he had often been called upon in Roosevelt's absence to "sit on the lid"—all 350 pounds of him. At the Republican convention of 1908 in Chicago, Roosevelt used his control of the party machinery—the "steamroller"—to push through Taft's nomination on the first ballot. Three weeks later, in mile-high Denver, in the heart of silver country, the Democrats nominated twice-beaten William Jennings Bryan.

The dull campaign of 1908 featured both the rotund Taft and the now-balding "Boy Orator" trying to claim the progressive Roosevelt mantle. The solid Judge Taft read cut-and-dried speeches while Bryan griped that Roosevelt had stolen his policies from the Bryanite camp. The prosperous voters chose stability with Roosevelt-endorsed Taft, who polled 321 electoral votes to 162 for Bryan. The victor's popular count was 7,675,320 to 6,412,294. The election's only surprise came from the Socialists, who

Baby, Kiss Papa Good-by   *Roosevelt leaves his baby, "My Policies," in the hands of his chosen successor, William Howard Taft. Friction between Taft and Roosevelt would soon erupt, however, prompting Roosevelt to return to politics and challenge Taft for the presidency.*

amassed 420,793 votes for Eugene V. Debs, the hero of the Pullman strike of 1894.

Roosevelt, ever in the limelight, left soon after the election for a lion hunt in Africa. His numerous enemies clinked glasses while toasting "Health to the lions," and a few irreverently prayed that some lion would "do its duty." But TR survived, still bursting with energy at the age of fifty-one in 1909.

Roosevelt was branded by his adversaries as a wild-eyed radical, but his reputation as an eater of errant industrialists now seems inflated. He fought many a sham battle, and the number of laws that he inspired was certainly not in proportion to the amount of noise he emitted. He was often under attack from the reigning business lords, but the more enlightened of them knew that they had a friend in the White House. Roosevelt should be remembered first and foremost as the cowboy who started to tame the bucking bronco of adolescent capitalism, thus ensuring it a long adult life.

TR's enthusiasm and perpetual youthfulness, like an overgrown Boy Scout's, appealed to the young of all ages. "You must always remember," a British diplomat cautioned his colleagues, "that the president is about six." He served as a political lightning rod to protect capitalists against popular indignation—and against socialism, which Roosevelt regarded as "ominous." He strenuously sought the middle road between unbridled individualism and paternalistic collectivism. His conservation crusade, which tried to mediate between the romantic wilderness-preservationists and the rapacious resource-predators, was probably his most typical and his most lasting achievement.

Several other contributions of Roosevelt lasted beyond his presidency. First, he greatly enlarged the power and prestige of the presidential office—and masterfully developed the technique of using the big stick of publicity as a political bludgeon. Second, he helped to shape the progressive movement and beyond it the liberal reform campaigns later in the century. His square deal, in a sense, was the grandfather of the New Deal later launched by his fifth cousin, Franklin D. Roosevelt. Finally, to a greater degree than any of his predecessors, TR opened the eyes of Americans to the fact that they shared the world with other nations. As a great power they had fallen heir to great responsibilities—and had been seized by ambitions—from which there was no escaping.

Taft: A Round Peg in a Square Hole

William Howard Taft, with his ruddy complexion and upturned mustache, at first inspired widespread confidence. "Everybody loves a fat man," the saying goes, and the jovial Taft, with "mirthquakes" of laughter bubbling up from his abundant abdomen, was personally popular. He had graduated second in his class at Yale and had established an admirable reputation as a lawyer and judge, though widely regarded as hostile to labor unions. He had been a trusted administrator under Roosevelt—in the

Philippines, at home, and in Cuba, where he had served capably as a troubleshooter.

But "good old Will" suffered from lethal political handicaps. Roosevelt had led the conflicting elements of the Republican party by the sheer force of his personality. Taft, in contrast, had none of the arts of a dashing political leader, and none of Roosevelt's zest for the fray. Recoiling from the clamor of controversy, he generally adopted an attitude of passivity toward Congress. He was a poor judge of public opinion, and his candor made him a chronic victim of "foot-in-mouth" disease.

"Peaceful Bill" was no doubt a mild progressive, but at heart he was more wedded to the status quo than to change. Significantly, his cabinet did not contain a single representative of the party's "insurgent" wing, which was on fire for reform of current abuses, especially the tariff.

The Dollar Goes Abroad as a Diplomat

The brand of "dollar diplomacy" was stamped, somewhat unfairly, on the foreign affairs of the Taft administration. This concept had two sides: (1) using foreign policy to protect Wall Street dollars invested abroad, and (2) using Wall Street dollars to uphold foreign policy. The first aspect was grossly overplayed by Taft's critics; the second aspect was widely misunderstood.

Though ordinarily lethargic, Taft bestirred himself to use the lever of American investments to boost American diplomacy. Washington warmly encouraged Wall Street bankers to pump their surplus dollars into foreign areas of strategic concern to the United States, especially in East Asia and in the regions critical to the security of the Panama Canal. New York bankers would thus strengthen American defenses and foreign policies, while bringing further prosperity to their homeland—and to themselves. The almighty dollar thus supplanted the big stick.

China's Manchuria was the object of Taft's most spectacular effort to inject the reluctant dollar into the East Asian theater. Newly ambitious Japan and imperialistic Russia, recent foes, controlled the railroads of this strategic province. President Taft saw in the Manchurian railway monopoly a possible strangulation of Chinese economic interests, and a consequent slamming of the Open Door in the faces of U.S. merchants. In 1909 Secretary of State Knox blunderingly proposed that a group of American and foreign bankers buy the Manchurian railroads, and then turn them over to China under a self-liquidating arrangement. Both Japan and Russia, unwilling to be jockeyed out of their dominant position, bluntly rejected Knox's overtures. Taft was showered with ridicule.

Another dangerous new trouble spot was the revolution-riddled Caribbean—now virtually a Yankee lake. Hoping to head off trouble, Washington urged Wall Street bankers to pump dollars into the financial vacuums in Honduras and Haiti to keep out foreign funds.

But dollar diplomacy did not bring an end to armed Caribbean intervention. Sporadic disorders in palm-fronded Cuba, Honduras, and the Dominican Republic brought American forces to these countries to restore order. A revolutionary upheaval in Nicaragua, perilously close to the nearly completed canal, resulted in the landing of 2,500 marines in 1912.

Taft the Trustbuster

Taft managed to gain some fame as a smasher of monopoly. The ironic truth is that the colorless Taft brought ninety suits against the trusts during his four years in office, compared with some forty-four for Roosevelt in seven and a half years.

By fateful happenstance the most sensational judicial actions during the Taft regime came in 1911. In that year the Supreme Court ordered dissolution of the mighty Standard Oil Company, which was judged to be a combination in restraint of trade in violation of the Sherman Anti-Trust Act of 1890. At the same time the Court handed down its famous "rule of reason." This doctrine held that only those combinations that "unreasonably" restrained trade were illegal. This fine-point proviso ripped a huge hole in the government's antitrust net.

Even more explosively, in 1911 Taft decided to press an antitrust suit against the U.S. Steel Corporation. This initiative infuriated Roosevelt, who had personally been involved in one of the mergers that prompted the suit. Once Roosevelt's protégé, President Taft was increasingly taking on the role of his antagonist. The stage was being set for a bruising confrontation.

Taft Splits the Republican Party

Lowering the barriers of the high protective tariff—the "mother of trusts"—was high on the agenda of the progressive members of the Republican party, and they at first thought they had a friend and ally in Taft. Meeting in special session in March 1909, the House passed a moderately reductive bill, but senatorial reactionaries, led by Senator Nelson Aldrich of Rhode Island, tacked on hundreds of upward tariff revisions. Only such items as hides, sea moss, and canary-bird seed were left on the duty-free list.

After much handwringing, Taft signed the Payne-Aldrich Bill, thus betraying his campaign promises and outraging the progressive wing of his party, heavily drawn from the Midwest. Taft rubbed salt in the wound by proclaiming it "the best bill that the Republican party ever passed."

Taft revealed a further knack for shooting himself in the foot in his handling of conservation. The portly president was a dedicated conservationist, and his contributions actually equaled or surpassed those of Roosevelt. He set up the Bureau of Mines to control mineral resources, rescued millions of acres of western coal lands from exploitation, and protected water-power sites from private development.

But those praiseworthy accomplishments were largely erased in the public mind by the noisy Ballinger-Pinchot quarrel that erupted in 1910. When Secretary of the Interior Ballinger opened public lands in Wyoming, Montana, and Alaska to corporate development, he was sharply criticized by Gifford Pinchot, chief of the Agriculture Department's Division of Forestry and a stalwart Rooseveltian. When Taft dismissed Pinchot on the narrow grounds of insubordination, a storm of protest arose from conservationists and from Roosevelt's friends, who were legion. The whole unsavory episode further widened the growing rift between the president and the former president, one-time bosom friends.

The reformist wing of the Republican party was now up in arms, while Taft was being pushed increasingly into the embrace of the standpat Old Guard. By the spring of 1910, the Grand Old Party was split wide open, owing largely to the clumsiness of Taft. A suspicious Roosevelt returned triumphantly to New York in June 1910 and shortly thereafter stirred up a tempest. In a flaming speech at Osawatamie, Kansas, he proclaimed a doctrine—popularly known as the "New Nationalism"—that urged the national government to increase its power to remedy economic and social abuses.

Weakened by these internal divisions, the Republicans lost badly in the congressional elections of 1910. The Democrats emerged from their landslide victory with 228 seats to only 161 for the once-dominant Republicans. In a further symptom of the reforming temper of the times, a Socialist representative, Austrian-born Victor L. Berger, was elected from Milwaukee.* The Republicans, by virtue of holdovers, retained the Senate, 51 to 41, but the insurgents in their midst were numerous enough to make that hold precarious.

The Taft-Roosevelt Rupture

The insurgent uprising in Republican ranks had meanwhile been blossoming into a full-fledged revolt. Early in 1911 the National Progressive Republican League was formed, with the fiery, white-maned Senator La Follette of Wisconsin its leading candidate for the Republican presidential nomination. The assumption was that Roosevelt would not permit himself to be "drafted."

But the restless Rough Rider began to change his views about third terms as he saw Taft, hand in glove with the hated Old Guard, discard "my policies." In February 1912 Roosevelt formally wrote to seven state governors that he was willing to accept the Republican nomination. His reasoning was that the third-term tradition applied to three *consecutive elective* terms. Exuberantly he cried, "My hat is in the ring!" and "The fight is on and I am stripped to the buff!"

Roosevelt forthwith seized the Progressive banner, while La Follette, who had served as a convenient pathbreaker, was protestingly elbowed aside.

* He was eventually denied his seat in 1919, during a wave of anti-Red hysteria.

Roosevelt the Take-Back Giver

Girded for battle, the Rough Rider clattered into the presidential primaries then being held in many states. He shouted through half-clenched teeth that the president had fallen under the thumb of the reactionary bosses, and that although Taft "means well, he means well feebly." The once-genial Taft, now in a fighting mood, branded the Roosevelt supporters "emotionalists and neurotics."

A Taft-Roosevelt explosion was near in June 1912, when the Republican convention met in Chicago. The Rooseveltites, who were about 100 delegates short of winning the nomination, challenged the right of some 250 Taft delegates to be seated. Most of these contests were arbitrarily settled in favor of Taft, whose supporters held the throttle of the convention steamroller. The Roosevelt adherents, crying "fraud" and "naked theft," in the end refused to vote, and Taft triumphed.

Roosevelt, the good sportsman, proved to be a poor loser. Having tasted for once the bitter cup of defeat, he was now on fire to lead a third-party crusade.

CHRONOLOGY

1901	Commission system established in Galveston, Texas.
	Progressive Robert La Follette elected governor of Wisconsin.
1902	Lincoln Steffens and Ida Tarbell publish muckraking exposés.
	Anthracite coal strike.
	Newlands Act.
1903	Department of Commerce and Labor established.
	Elkins Act.
1904	*Northern Securities* case.
	Roosevelt defeats Parker for presidency.
1905	*Lochner* v. *New York.*
1906	Hepburn Act.

1906	Upton Sinclair publishes *The Jungle.*
	Meat Inspection Act.
	Pure Food and Drug Act.
1907	"Roosevelt panic."
1908	*Muller* v. *Oregon.*
	Taft defeats Bryan for presidency.
1909	Payne-Aldrich Tariff.
1910	Ballinger-Pinchot affair.
1911	Triangle Shirtwaist Company fire.
	Standard Oil antitrust case.
	U.S. Steel Corporation antitrust suit.
1912	Taft wins Republican nomination over Roosevelt.
1913	Seventeenth Amendment passed (direct election of U.S. senators).

Varying Viewpoints

Debate about progressivism has revolved around a question that is simple to ask but devilishly difficult to answer: who were the progressives? It was once taken for granted that progressive reformers were simply the heirs of the Jeffersonian-Jacksonian-Populist reform tradition, oppressed and downtrodden common people who finally erupted in wrath and demanded their due. In his influential *Age of Reform,* Richard Hofstadter debunked that view. Progressive leaders, he argued, were middle-class people motivated more by psychological "status anxiety" than by the real problems of industrialization.

By contrast, New Left writers, notably Gabriel Kolko, argue that progressivism was dominated by older business elites who successfully perverted "reform" to their own conservative ends. Still other scholars, such as Samuel P. Hays and Robert Wiebe, suggest that the progressives were members of a newly emergent social class possessed of the new techniques of scientific expertise and organizational knowhow. In this view, the movement was not characterized by conflict at all, but was simply an effort to rationalize and modernize many social institutions ("reform without a fight"). Yet the argument that progressives paved the way to a scientific, bureaucratic future is severely qualified by Otis Graham's study showing that less than half the surviving progressives approved the later reforms of the New Deal. Where did the progressives—and progressivism—go?

SELECT READINGS

Primary Source Documents

Lincoln Steffens's *The Shame of the Cities** (1904) is an exemplary muckraking document, as is Upton Sinclair's notorious novel *The Jungle* (1906). For a less-than-gracious assessment of the muckrakers, see Theodore Roosevelt, "The Man with the Muckrake," *Putnam's Monthly and The Critic,* vol. I (October 1906), pp. 42–43.* A revealing account of municipal politics is George Washington Plunkitt's *Plunkitt of Tammany Hall** (1905). See also the decision of the Supreme Court on state bakery regulations in *Lochner* v. *New York,* 198 U.S. 45 (1905). Oliver Wendell Holmes, Jr.'s thundering dissent in the *Lochner* case is reprinted in Richard Hofstadter, *Great Issues in American History.*

Secondary Sources

A brief introduction is John W. Chambers, *The Tyranny of Change: America in the Progressive Era, 1900–1917* (1980). Perceptive interpretations are Samuel P. Hays, *The Response to Industrialism, 1885–1914* (1957), Robert H. Wiebe, *The Search for Order* (1967), Richard Hofstadter, *The Age of Reform* (1955), and David B. Danbom, *The World of Hope* (1987). Especially provocative are James Weinstein, *The Corporate Ideal in the Liberal State* (1968), and Gabriel Kolko, *The Triumph of Conservatism* (1963). Consult also Alfred D. Chandler, Jr., *The Visible Hand* (1977), and Morton Keller, *Regulating a New Economy: Public Policy and Economic Change in America, 1900–1933* (1990).

The progressive concern with poverty is analyzed in Roy Lubove, *The Progressives and the Slums* (1962), Allen F. Davis, *Spearheads for Reform: The Social Settlements and the Progressive Movement, 1890–1914* (1967), and James Patterson, *America's Struggle Against Poverty, 1900–1980* (1981). See also Mina Carson, *Settlement Folk: Social Thought and the American Settlement Movement, 1885–1930* (1990). On education, see David B. Tyack, *The One Best System: A History of American Urban Education* (1974), and Lynn Gordon, *Gender and Higher Education in the Progressive Era* (1990). On religion consult Martin E. Marty, *Modern American Religion: The Irony of It All, 1893–1919* (1986); T. J. Jackson Lears takes a different perspective in *No Place of Grace: Antimodernism and the*

Transformation of American Culture (1981). Municipal reform is the subject of Marin J. Schiesl, *The Politics of Efficiency* (1977), and two useful anthologies, Bruce Stave, ed., *Urban Bosses, Machines, and Progressive Reformers* (1972), and Blaine A. Brownell and Warren E. Stickle, eds., *Bosses and Reformers* (1973). On conservation, see Samuel P. Hays, *Conservation and the Gospel of Efficiency* (1959). Socialism is discussed in Nick Salvatore, *Eugene V. Debs: Citizen and Socialist* (1982), and Mari Jo Buhle, *Women and American Socialism, 1897–1920* (1981). Another perspective on women in the period is given in Rosalind Rosenberg, *Beyond Separate Spheres* (1982). The Taft era is summarized in Paolo Coletta, *The Presidency of William Howard Taft* (1973). Otis Graham traces the progressive legacy in *Encore for Reform: The Old Progressives and the New Deal* (1967).

CHAPTER 31

Wilsonian Progressivism at Home and Abroad, 1912–1916

This is not a day of triumph; it is a day of dedication. Here muster not the forces of party, but the forces of humanity. . . . I summon all honest men, all patriotic, all forward-looking men, to my side. God helping me, I will not fail them, if they will but counsel and sustain me!

Thomas Woodrow Wilson, Inaugural Address, 1913

The Emergence of Dr. Thomas Woodrow Wilson

Office-hungry Democrats—the "outs" since 1897—were jubilant over the disruptive Republican brawl at Chicago. If they could come up with an outstanding reformist leader, they had an excellent chance to win the White House. Such a leader appeared in Dr. Woodrow Wilson, once a mild conservative but now a militant progressive. Beginning professional life as a brilliant academic lecturer on government, he had risen in 1902 to the presidency of Princeton University, where he had achieved some sweeping educational reforms.

Wilson entered politics in 1910 when New Jersey bosses, needing a respectable "front" candidate for the governorship, offered him the nomination. They expected to lead the academic novice by the nose, but to their surprise, Wilson waged a passionate reform campaign in which he assailed the "predatory" trusts and promised to return government to the people. Riding the crest of the progressive wave, the "schoolmaster in politics" was swept into office.

Once in the governor's chair, Wilson drove through the legislature a sheaf of forward-looking measures that made reactionary New Jersey one of the more liberal states. Filled with righteous indignation, Wilson revealed irresistible reforming zeal, burning eloquence, superb powers of leadership, and a refreshing habit of appealing over the heads of the scheming bosses to the sovereign people. Now a figure of national eminence, Wilson was being widely mentioned for the presidency.

When the Democrats met at Baltimore in 1912, Wilson was nominated on the forty-sixth ballot, aided by William Jennings Bryan's switch to his side. The Democrats gave Wilson a strong reform platform to run on, including calls for antitrust legislation, monetary changes, and tariff reductions.

The "Bull Moose" Campaign of 1912

Surging events had meanwhile been thrusting Roosevelt to the fore as a candidate for the presidency on a third-party Progressive ticket. The fighting ex-cow-

GOP Divided by Bull Moose Equals Democratic Victory

boy, angered by his recent rebuff, was eager to lead the charge. A pro-Roosevelt Progressive convention, with about 2,000 delegates from forty states, assembled in Chicago during August 1912. Dramatically symbolizing the rising political status of women, as well as Progressive support for the cause of social justice, settlement-house pioneer Jane Addams placed Roosevelt's name in nomination for the presidency.

Fired-up Progressives entered the campaign with righteousness and enthusiasm. Roosevelt boasted that he felt "as strong as a bull moose," and hence the bull moose took its place with the jackass and the elephant in the American political zoo.

Roosevelt and Taft were bound to slit each other's political throats; by dividing the Republican vote they virtually guaranteed a Democratic victory. The two antagonists tore into each other as only former friends can. "Death alone can take me out now," cried the once-jovial Taft, as he branded Roosevelt a "dangerous egotist" and a "demagogue." Roosevelt, fighting mad, assailed Taft as a "fathead" with the brain of a "guinea pig."

Beyond the clashing personalities, the overshadowing question of the 1912 campaign was which of two varieties of progressivism would prevail—Roosevelt's New Nationalism or Wilson's New Freedom. Both men favored a more active government role in economic and social affairs, but they disagreed sharply over specific strategies. Roosevelt preached the theories spun out by the progressive thinker Herbert Croly in his book, *The Promise of American Life* (1910). Both Croly and TR favored

continued consolidation of trusts and labor unions, paralleled by the growth of powerful regulatory agencies in Washington. Roosevelt and his "bull moosers" also campaigned for woman suffrage and a broad program of social welfare, including minimum-wage laws and social insurance. Clearly the bull moose Progressives looked forward to the kind of activist welfare state that Franklin Roosevelt's New Deal would one day make a reality.

Wilson's New Freedom, by contrast, favored small enterprise, entrepreneurship, and the free functioning of unregulated and unmonopolized markets. The Democrats shunned social welfare proposals and pinned their economic faith on competition—on the "man on the make," as Wilson put it. The keynote of Wilson's campaign was not regulation but fragmentation of the big industrial combines, chiefly by means of vigorous enforcement of the antitrust laws. The election of 1912 thus offered the voters a choice not merely of policies but of political and economic philosophies—a rarity in U.S. history.

The heat of the campaign cooled a bit when, in Milwaukee, Roosevelt was shot in the chest by a fanatic. The Rough Rider suspended active campaigning for more than two weeks after delivering, with bull moose gameness and a bloody shirt, his scheduled speech.

Woodrow Wilson: A Minority President

Former professor Wilson won handily, with 435 electoral votes and 6,296,547 popular votes, The third-party candidate, Roosevelt, finished second, with 88 electoral votes and 4,118,571 popular votes. Taft won only 8 paltry electoral votes and 3,486,720 popular votes.

The election figures are fascinating. Wilson, with only 41 percent of the popular vote, was clearly a minority president, though his party won a majority in Congress. His popular total was actually smaller than Bryan had amassed in any of his three defeats, despite the increase in population. Taft and Roosevelt together polled over one and a quarter million more votes than the Democrats. Progressivism rather than Wilson was the runaway winner. Although the Democratic total obviously included many conservatives in the solid South, still the combined progressive vote for Wilson and Roosevelt exceeded the tally of the more conservative Taft. To the progressive totals must be added some support for the Socialist candidate, hardy Eugene V. Debs, who rolled up 900,672 votes, or more than twice as many as he had netted four years earlier. Starry-eyed Socialists dreamed of being in the White House within eight years.

Roosevelt's lone-wolf course was tragic both for himself and for his former Republican associates. The Progressive party, which was primarily a one-man show, had no future because it had elected few candidates to state and local offices. Without patronage plums to hand out to the faithful workers, death by slow starvation was inevitable. Yet the Progressives made a tremendous showing for a hastily organized third party and helped spur the enactment of many of their pet reforms by the Wilsonian Democrats.

As for the Republicans, they were thrust into unaccustomed minority status in Congress for the next six years and were frozen out of the White House for eight years. Taft himself had a fruitful old age. He taught law for eight pleasant years at Yale University and in 1921 became chief justice of the Supreme Court—a job for which he was far more happily suited than the presidency.

Wilson: The Idealist in Politics

(Thomas) Woodrow Wilson, the second Democratic president since 1861, looked like the ascetic intellectual he was, with his clean-cut features, pinched-on eyeglasses, and trim figure (5 feet 11 inches and 179 pounds). Born in Virginia shortly before the Civil War, and reared in Georgia and the Carolinas, the professor-politician was the first man from one of the seceded southern states to reach the White House since Zachary Taylor, sixty-four years earlier.

The impact of Dixieland on young "Tommy" Wilson was profound. He sympathized with the Confederacy's gallant attempt to win its independence, a sentiment that partly inspired his ideal of self-determination for minority peoples in other countries. Steeped in the traditions of Jeffersonian democracy, he shared Jefferson's faith in the masses—if they were properly informed.

Son of a Presbyterian minister, Wilson was reared in an atmosphere of fervent piety. He later used the presidential pulpit to preach his inspirational political sermons. A moving orator, Wilson could rise on the wings of spiritual power to soaring eloquence. Skillfully using a persuasive voice, he

The Presidential Vote, 1912

Candidate	Party	Electoral Vote	Popular Vote	Approximate Percentage
Woodrow Wilson	Democratic	435	6,296,547	41
Theodore Roosevelt	Progressive	88	4,118,571	27
William H. Taft	Republican	8	3,486,720	23
Eugene V. Debs	Socialist	—	900,672	6
E. W. Chafin	Prohibition	—	206,275	1
A. E. Reimer	Socialist-Labor	—	28,750	0.2

relied not on arm waving but on sincerity and moral appeal. As a lifelong student of finely chiseled words, he turned out to be a "phraseocrat" who coined many noble epigrams. Someone has remarked that he was born halfway between the Bible and the dictionary, and never got away from either.

A profound student of government, Wilson believed that the chief executive should play a dynamic role. He was convinced that Congress could not function properly unless the president, like a kind of prime minister, got out in front and provided leadership. He enjoyed dramatic success, as both governor and president, in appealing over the heads of legislators to the sovereign people.

Splendid though Wilson's intellectual equipment was, he suffered from serious defects of personality. Though jovial and witty in private, he could be cold and standoffish in public. Incapable of unbending and acting the showman, like "Teddy" Roosevelt, he lacked the common touch. He loved humanity in the mass rather than the individual in person. His academic background caused him to feel most at home with scholars, although he had to work with politicians. An austere and somewhat arrogant intellectual, he looked down his nose through pince-nez glasses upon lesser minds, including journalists. He was especially intolerant of stupid senators, whose "bungalow" minds made him "sick."

Wilson's burning idealism—especially his desire to reform ever-present wickedness—drove him forward faster than lesser spirits were willing to go. His sense of moral righteousness was such that he often found compromise difficult: black was black, wrong was wrong, and one should never compromise with wrong. Wilson's Scottish Presbyterian ancestors had passed on to him an inflexible stubbornness. When convinced that he was right, he would break before he would bend, unlike Theodore Roosevelt.

Wilson Attacks the "Triple Wall of Privilege"

Few presidents have arrived at the White House with a clearer program than Wilson's or one destined to be so completely achieved. The new president called for an all-out assault on what he called the "triple wall of privilege": the tariff, the banks, and the trusts.

Wilson tackled the tariff first. In a precedent-shattering move, the president appeared in person before a joint session of Congress in 1913 and presented his appeal with stunning eloquence and effectiveness. Moved by Wilson's aggressive leadership, the House swiftly passed the Underwood Tariff Bill, which provided for a substantial reduction of rates. It was also a landmark in tax legislation. Under authority granted by the recently ratified Sixteenth Amendment, Congress enacted a graduated income tax, beginning with a modest levy on incomes over $3,000 (then considerably higher than the average family's income). By 1917 revenue from the income tax shot ahead of receipts from the tariff. This gap has since been vastly widened.

A second bastion of the triple wall of privilege was the antiquated and inadequate banking and currency system, long since outgrown by the republic's lusty economic expansion. The most serious shortcoming of the country's financial structure, as exposed by the panic of 1907, was the inelasticity of the currency. Banking reserves were heavily concentrated in New York and a handful of other large cities and could not be mobilized in times of financial stress into areas that were badly pinched.

In 1911 a special commission headed by moss-back Republican Senator Aldrich recommended a gigantic bank with numerous branches—in effect, a third Bank of the United States. Democratic banking reformers preferred the findings of a House committee chaired by Congressman Arsene Pujo, which traced the tentacles of the "money monster" into the hidden vaults of American banking and business. President Wilson's confidant, progressive-minded Massachusetts attorney Louis D. Brandeis, further fanned the flames of reform with his incendiary though scholarly book *Other People's Money and How the Bankers Use It* (1914).

In June 1913, in a second dramatic personal appearance before Congress, the president ringingly endorsed sweeping Democratic reform proposals for a decentralized bank in government hands, as opposed to Republican demands for a huge private bank. Again appealing to the sovereign people, Wilson scored another triumph. In 1913 he signed the epochal Federal Reserve Act, the most important piece of economic legislation between the Civil War and the New Deal.

The new Federal Reserve Board, appointed by the president, oversaw a nationwide system of twelve regional reserve districts, each with its own central bank. Though these regional banks were actually bankers' banks, owned by member financial institutions, the final authority of the Federal Reserve Board guaranteed a substantial measure of public control. The board was also empowered to issue paper money—Federal Reserve notes—backed by commercial paper, such as the promissory notes of businesspeople. Thus, the amount of money in circulation could be swiftly increased as needed for the legitimate requirements of business.

The Federal Reserve Act was a red-letter achievement. It carried the nation with flying banners through the financial crises of the World War of 1914–1918. Without it, the republic's progress toward the modern economic age would have been seriously retarded.

Without pausing for breath, Wilson pushed toward the last remaining rampart in the triple wall of privilege—the trusts. A third personal appearance before Congress in 1914 led to the Federal Trade Commission Act of 1914. The new law empowered a presidentially appointed commission to turn a searchlight on industries engaged in interstate commerce, such as the meat packers. The commissioners were expected to crush monopoly in the cradle by rooting out unfair trade practices, including unlawful competition, false advertising, mislabeling, adulteration, and bribery.

The knot of monopoly was further cut by the Clayton Anti-Trust Act of 1914. It lengthened the shopworn Sherman Act's list of business practices that were deemed objectionable, including price discrimination and interlocking directorates (whereby the same individuals served as directors of supposedly competing firms).

The Clayton Act also conferred long-overdue benefits on labor. The law sought to exempt labor and agricultural organizations from antitrust prosecutions under the Sherman Act, while explicitly

legalizing strikes and peaceful picketing. Union leader Samuel Gompers hailed the act as the Magna Carta of labor because it legally lifted human labor out of the category of "a commodity or article of commerce." But the rejoicing was premature, as conservative judges in later years continued to clip the wings of the union movement.

Wilsonian Progressivism at High Tide

Energetically scaling the triple wall of privilege, Woodrow Wilson had treated the nation to a dazzling demonstration of vigorous presidential leadership. He proved nearly irresistible in his first eighteen months in office. For once, a political creed was matched by deed, as the progressive reformers racked up victory after victory.

Standing at the peak of his powers at the head of the progressive forces, Wilson pressed ahead with further reforms. The Federal Farm Loan Act of 1916 made credit available to farmers at low rates of interest—as long demanded by the Populists. The Warehouse Act of 1916 authorized loans on the security of staple crops—another Populist idea. Other laws benefited rural America by providing for highway construction and the establishment of agricultural extension work in the state colleges.

Sweaty laborers also made gains as the progressive wave foamed forward. Sailors, treated brutally from cat-o'-nine-tails days onward, were given relief by the La Follette Seaman's Act of 1915. It required decent treatment and a living wage on American merchant ships.

Wilson further helped the workers with the Workingmen's Compensation Act of 1916, granting assistance to federal civil service employees during periods of disability. In the same year the president approved an act restricting child labor on products flowing into interstate commerce, though the standpat Supreme Court soon invalidated the law. The Adamson Act of 1916 aided railroad workers by establishing an eight-hour day for all employees on trains in interstate commerce, with extra pay for overtime.

Wilson earned the enmity of businesspeople and bigots but endeared himself to progressives when in 1916 he nominated for the Supreme Court the prominent reformer Louis D. Brandeis—the first Jew to be called to the high bench. Yet even Wilson's progressivism had its limits, and it clearly stopped short of better treatment for blacks. The southern-bred Wilson actually presided over accelerated segregation in the federal bureaucracy. When a delegation of black leaders personally protested to him, the schoolmasterish president virtually froze them out of his office.

Despite these limitations, Wilson knew that to be reelected in 1916, he needed to identify himself clearly as the candidate of progressivism. Wilson's election in 1912 had been something of a fluke, owing largely to the Taft-Roosevelt split in the Republican ranks. To remain in the White House, the president would have to woo the bull moose voters into the Democratic fold.

New Directions in Foreign Policy

In one important area, Wilson chose not to answer the trumpet call of the bull moosers. In contrast to Roosevelt and even Taft, Wilson recoiled from an aggressive foreign policy. Hating imperialism, he was repelled by TR's big stickism. Suspicious of Wall Street, he detested the so-called dollar diplomacy of Taft.

In office only a week, Wilson declared war on dollar diplomacy. He proclaimed that the government would no longer offer special support to American investors in Latin America and China. Shivering from this Wilsonian bucket of cold water, American bankers pulled out of the Taft-engineered six-nation loan to China the next day. Wilson's anti-imperialism also produced the Jones Act of 1916, which granted territorial status and promised eventual independence for the Philippines.

Wilson also partially defused a menacing crisis with Japan in 1913. The California legislature, still seeking to rid the Golden State of Japanese settlers, prohibited them from owning land. Tokyo, understandably irritated, lodged vigorous protests. Wilson dispatched Secretary of State William Jennings Bryan to plead with the California legislature to soften its stand, and tensions eased somewhat.

Events in the Caribbean soon forced Wilson to eat some of his anti-imperialist words. In response to disorders in Haiti in 1914–1915, the president reluctantly dispatched marines to protect American lives and property. In 1916 he stole a page from Roosevelt's corollary to the Monroe Doctrine and concluded a treaty with Haiti that provided U.S. supervision of Haiti's finances and police. In the same year, Wilson sent the leathernecked marines to the riot-rocked Dominican Republic, and that debt-cursed land came under the shadow of the American eagle's wings. In 1917 Wilson purchased from Denmark the Virgin Islands in the West Indies. Increasingly the Caribbean Sea, with its vital approaches to the now-completed Panama Canal, was taking on the earmarks of a Yankee preserve.

Moralistic Diplomacy in Mexico

Rifle bullets whining across the southern border served as a constant reminder that all was not quiet in Mexico. For decades Mexico had been sorely exploited by foreign investors in oil, railroads, and mines. By 1913 American capitalists had sunk about a billion dollars into the underdeveloped but richly endowed country.

But if Mexico was rich, the Mexicans were poor. Fed up with their miserable lot, they at last revolted. Their revolution took an ugly turn in 1913, when a conscienceless clique murdered the popular new revolutionary president and installed General Victoriano Huerta, a full-blooded Indian, in the president's chair. All this chaos accelerated a massive migration of Mexicans to the United States. More than a million Spanish-speaking newcomers tramped across the southern border in the first three decades of the twentieth century. Settling mostly in Texas, New Mexico, Arizona, and California, they helped to create a unique borderland culture that blended Mexican and American folkways.

The revolutionary bloodshed also menaced American lives and property in Mexico. Cries for intervention burst from the lips of American jingoes such as publisher William Randolph Hearst, owner of a Mexican ranch larger than Rhode Island.

Wilson stood firm against demands for inter-

The United States in the Caribbean *This map explains why many Latin Americans accused the United States of turning the Caribbean Sea into a Yankee lake. It also suggests that Uncle Sam was much less "isolationist" in his own backyard than he was in faraway Europe or Asia.*

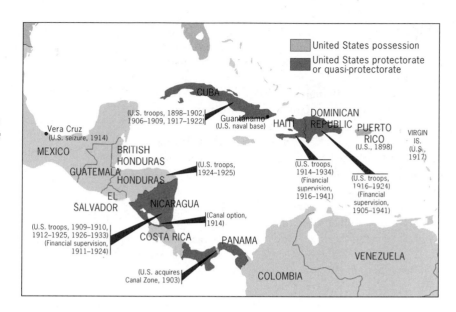

vention, but he also refused to recognize the murderous government of "that brute" Huerta. "I am going to teach the South American republics to elect good men," the former professor declared. He put his munitions where his mouth was in 1914, when he allowed American arms to flow to Huerta's principal rivals, white-bearded Venustiano Carranza and swarthy Francisco ("Pancho") Villa.

The Mexican volcano erupted at the Atlantic seaport of Tampico in April 1914, when a small party of American sailors was arrested. The Mexicans promptly released the captives and apologized, but they refused the hotheaded American admiral's demand for a salute of twenty-one guns. Wilson then ordered the navy to seize the Mexican port of Vera Cruz. Huerta as well as Carranza hotly condemned this high-handed Yankee intervention.

Just as a full-dress shooting conflict seemed inevitable, Wilson was rescued by an offer of mediation from the ABC powers—Argentina, Brazil, and Chile. Huerta collapsed in July 1914 under pressure from within and without. He was succeeded by his arch-rival, Carranza, still fiercely resentful of Wilson's military meddling. The whole sorry episode did not augur well for the future of United States–Mexican relations.

Pancho Villa, a bloodthirsty combination of bandit and Robin Hood, had meanwhile emerged as the chief rival of President Carranza, whom Wilson reluctantly supported. Villa displayed his hatred of the gringos in early 1916, when his followers killed eighteen U.S. citizens in Mexico, and later killed seventeen more during a raid across the border into Columbus, New Mexico.

General John J. ("Black Jack")* Pershing, a ramrod-erect veteran of the Cuban and Philippine campaigns, was ordered to break up the bandit band. His hastily organized force of several thousand horse-borne troops penetrated deep into rugged Mexico with surprising speed. They clashed with Carranza's forces and mauled the Villistas but missed capturing Villa himself. As the threat of war with Germany loomed larger, the invading army was withdrawn in January 1917.

A Precarious Neutrality

Europe's powder magazine, long smoldering, blew up in the summer of 1914, when the flaming pistol of

---

* So called from his earlier service as an officer with the crack black Tenth Cavalry.

a Serb patriot killed the heir to the throne of Austria-Hungary. An outraged Viennese government, backed by Germany, forthwith presented a stern ultimatum to Serbia.

An explosive chain reaction followed. Russian mobilization in support of Serbia threatened Germany in the east, even as the tsar's ally, France, confronted Germany in the west. In alarm, the Germans struck suddenly at France through unoffending Belgium. Great Britain in turn was sucked into the conflagration on the side of France.

Almost overnight most of Europe was locked in a fight to the death. On one side were arrayed the Central Powers: Germany and Austria-Hungary, and later Turkey and Bulgaria. On the other side were the Allies, principally France, Britain, and Russia, and later Japan and Italy. Americans thanked God for the ocean moats and self-righteously congratulated themselves on having had ancestors wise enough to have abandoned the hell pits of Europe. Americans felt strong, snug, smug, and secure—but not for long.

Peace-loving President Wilson sorrowfully issued the routine neutrality proclamation and called on Americans to be neutral in thought as well as deed. But such scrupulous evenhandedness proved difficult.

Both sides wooed the United States, the great neutral in the West. The British enjoyed the boon of close cultural, linguistic, and economic ties with America and had the added advantage of controlling most of the transatlantic cables. Their censors sheared away war stories harmful to the Allies and drenched the United States with tales of German bestiality.

Some German-American immigrants expressed noisy sympathy for the fatherland, but most Americans were anti-German from the outset. With his villainous upturned mustache, Kaiser Wilhelm II seemed the embodiment of arrogant autocracy, an impression strengthened by Germany's ruthless strike at neutral Belgium. Inept German plans for industrial sabotage in the United States further inflamed opinion against the kaiser and Germany. Yet the great majority of Americans earnestly hoped to stay out of the horrible war.

America Earns Blood Money

When Europe burst into flames in 1914, the United States was bogged down in a worrisome business recession. But as fate would have it, British and French war orders soon pulled American industry out of the morass of hard times and onto a peak of war-born prosperity. Part of this boom was financed by American bankers, notably the Wall Street firm of J. P. Morgan and Company, which eventually advanced to the Allies the enormous sum of $2.3 billion during the period of American neutrality. The Central Powers protested bitterly against the immense trade between America and the Allies, but this traffic did not in fact violate the international neutrality laws. Germany was technically free to trade with the United States, but the tight British naval blockade prevented it from doing so.

Hard-pressed Germany did not tamely consent to being starved out. In retaliation for the British blockade, in February 1915 Berlin announced a submarine war area around the British isles. The subma-

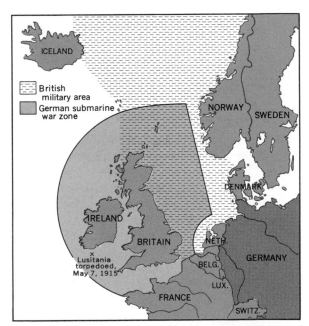

British Military Area (declared November 3, 1914), and German Submarine War Zone (declared February 4, 1915)

rine was a weapon so new that existing international law could not be made to fit it. The old rule that a warship must stop and board a merchantman could hardly apply to submarines, which could easily be rammed or sunk if they surfaced.

The cigar-shaped marauders posed a dire threat to the United States—so long as Wilson insisted on maintaining America's neutral rights. Berlin officials declared that they would try not to sink *neutral* shipping, but they warned that mistakes would probably occur. Wilson now determined on a policy of calculated risk. He would continue to claim profitable neutral trading rights, while hoping that no high-seas incident would force his hand to grasp the sword of war. He emphatically warned Germany that it would be held to "strict accountability" for any attacks on American vessels or citizens.

The German submarines meanwhile began their deadly work. In the first months of 1915, they sank about ninety ships in the war zone. Then the submarine issue became acute when the British passenger liner *Lusitania* was torpedoed and sank off the coast of Ireland on May 7, 1915, with the loss of 1,198 lives, including 128 Americans.

The *Lusitania* was carrying 4,200 cases of small-arms ammunition, a fact the Germans used to justify the sinking. But Americans were swept by a wave of shock and anger at this act of "mass murder" and "piracy." The eastern United States, closer to the war, seethed with talk of fighting, but the rest of the country showed a strong distaste for hostilities. The peace-loving Wilson had no stomach for leading a disunited nation into war, and instead relied on a series of increasingly strong notes to bring the German warlords sharply to book. "There is such a thing," he said, "as a man being too proud to fight."

Yet Wilson, sticking to his verbal guns, made some diplomatic progress. After another British liner, the *Arabic,* was sunk in August 1915, with the loss of two American lives, Berlin reluctantly agreed not to sink unarmed and unresisting passenger ships *without warning.*

This pledge appeared to be violated in March 1916, when the Germans torpedoed a French passenger steamer, the *Sussex.* The infuriated Wilson informed the Germans that unless they renounced the inhuman practice of sinking merchant ships without warning he would break diplomatic relations—an almost certain prelude to war.

Germany reluctantly knuckled under to President Wilson's *Sussex* ultimatum, agreeing not to sink passenger ships and merchant vessels without giving warning. But the Germans attached a long string to their *Sussex* pledge: the United States would have to persuade the Allies to modify what Berlin regarded as their illegal blockade. This, obviously, was something that Washington could not do. Wilson promptly accepted the German pledge, without accepting the "string." He thus won a temporary but precarious diplomatic victory—precarious because Germany could pull the string whenever it chose, and the president might suddenly find himself hauled over the cliff of war.

Wilson Wins Reelection in 1916

Against this ominous backdrop, the presidential campaign of 1916 gathered speed. Both the bull moose Progressives and the Republicans met in Chicago. The Progressives uproariously renominated Theodore Roosevelt, but the Rough Rider, who loathed Wilson and all his works, had no stomach for splitting the Republicans again and ensuring the reelection of his hated rival. In refusing to run, he sounded the death knell of the Progressive party.

Roosevelt's Republican admirers also clamored for "Teddy," but the Old Guard detested the renegade who had ruptured the party in 1912. Instead, they drafted Supreme Court Justice Charles Evans Hughes, a cold intellectual who had achieved a solid record when he was governor of New York. The Republican platform condemned the Democratic tariff, assaults on the trusts, and Wilson's wishy-washiness in dealing with both Mexico and Germany.

The richly bewhiskered Hughes ("an animated feather duster") left the judicial bench for the campaign stump, where he was not at home. In anti-German areas of the country he assailed Wilson for not standing up to the kaiser, whereas in isolationist areas he took a softer line. This fence-straddling operation led to the jeer, "Charles Evasive Hughes."

AMERICA FIRST

Wilson, That's All !

HENRY HEININGER CO. PUB. N. Y.

Wilson Campaign Poster, 1916   *This poster presents Wilson's campaign theme of patriotism.*

Hughes was further plagued by Roosevelt, who was delivering a series of skin-'em-alive speeches against "that damned Presbyterian hypocrite Wilson." Frothing for war, TR privately sneered at Hughes as a "whiskered Wilson"; the only difference between the two, he said, was "a shave."

Wilson, nominated by acclamation at the Democratic convention in St. Louis, ignored Hughes on the theory that one should not try to murder a man who is committing suicide. His campaign was built on the slogan, "He kept us out of war."

Democratic orators warned that by electing Hughes the nation would be electing a fight—with a certain frustrated Rough Rider leading the charge. A Democratic advertisement appealing to American workers read:

You are Working;
  —Not Fighting!
Alive and Happy;
  —Not Cannon Fodder!
Wilson and Peace with Honor?
  or
Hughes with Roosevelt and War?

On election day, Hughes swept the East and looked like a surefire winner. Wilson went to bed that night prepared to accept defeat, while New York newspapers displayed huge portraits of "The President-Elect—Charles Evans Hughes."

But the rest of the country turned the tide. Midwesterners and westerners, attracted by Wilson's progressive reforms and antiwar policies, flocked to the polls for the president. The final result, in doubt for several days, hinged on California, which Wilson carried by some 3,800 votes out of about a million cast.

Wilson barely squeaked through, with a final vote of 277 to 254 in the Electoral College and 9,127,695 to 8,533,507 in the popular column. The prolabor Wilson had received strong support from the working class and from ex–bull moosers, whom Republicans failed to lure back into their camp. Wilson had not specifically promised to keep the country out of war, but probably enough voters relied on such implicit assurances to ensure his victory. Their hopeful expectations were soon rudely shattered.

Varying Viewpoints

Wilson's achievement in realizing his New Freedom reforms in 1913 and 1914 undeniably constitutes one of the most noteworthy examples of presidential leadership. Yet the precise character of Wilson's accomplishment remains something of a puzzle. Some historians conclude that Wilson, having beaten Roosevelt in the election, proceeded to implement Roosevelt's program. These scholars point especially to the New Nationalist flavor of the Federal Reserve Act and the Federal Trade Commission. Other analysts claim that the Clayton Anti-Trust Act was faithful in following Wilson's campaign pledges and reflected his "real" political beliefs. Still other critics, noting especially Wilson's appointment of businesspeople to the new governmental bodies, charge that the rhetoric of progressive reform was simply a cloak for the consolidation of conservative rule. This dispute again illustrates the difficulty of defining *progressive*.

No issue, however, reveals the ambiguity of that term as well as the debate over the nation's entry into World War I. Was Wilson's conduct of foreign policy consistent with the principles of his New Freedom? Was United States intervention in the brutal European war a repudiation of the progressive program or the logical culmination of it? These questions continue to spark controversy today.

SELECT READINGS

Primary Source Documents

Theodore Roosevelt's "Acceptance Speech"* at the Progressive convention of 1912, and Woodrow Wilson's collection of campaign speeches, *The New Freedom** (1913), give the substance and flavor of the critical 1912 campaign. Louis D. Brandeis, *Other People's Money and How the Bankers Use It** (1914), expresses the philosophy of a key

Wilson adviser. On the *Lusitania* incident, see *Foreign Relations of the United States,* 1915, Supplement, pp. 394–395, 420.*

Secondary Sources

See the titles by John W. Chambers, Samuel P. Hays, Richard Hofstadter, and Robert Wiebe cited in Chapter 30. John M. Cooper, Jr.'s *The Warrior and the Priest* (1983) deftly contrasts Wilson and Theodore Roosevelt. Biographies of Wilson include August Heckscher's voluminous *Woodrow Wilson: A Biography* (1991), Arthur Link's five-volume *Wilson* (1947–1965), and John M. Blum's *Woodrow Wilson and the Politics of Morality* (1956). Particularly interesting is Alexander and Juliette George's psychological study, *Woodrow Wilson and Colonel House* (1956).

The road to World War I finds comprehensive treatment in Ernest May, *The World War and American Isolation, 1914–1917* (1959), and Daniel M. Smith, *The Great Departure: The United States and World War I, 1914–1920* (1965). Special studies of value include Thomas A. Bailey and Paul B. Ryan, *The Lusitania Disaster* (1975), and Burton I. Kaufman, *Efficiency and Expansion* (1974). Social and intellectual currents are described in Henry F. May, *The End of American Innocence: A Study of the First Years of Our Own Time, 1912–1917* (1959). Michael C. Adams, *The Great Adventure: Male Desire and the Coming of World War I* (1990), is a provocative work that tries to link Victorian gender ideology to the martial enthusiasm of the early twentieth century.

CHAPTER 32

The War to End War, 1917–1918

The world must be made safe for democracy. Its peace must be planted upon the tested foundations of political liberty. We have no selfish ends to serve. We desire no conquest, no dominion. We seek no indemnities for ourselves, no material compensation for the sacrifices we shall freely make.

Woodrow Wilson, war message, April 2, 1917

War by Act of Germany

Destiny dealt cruelly with Woodrow Wilson. The lover of peace, as fate would have it, was forced to lead a hesitant and peace-loving nation into war. As the last days of 1916 slipped through the hourglass, the president made one final futile attempt to mediate between the embattled belligerents. On January 22, 1917, he delivered one of his most moving addresses, realistically declaring that only a negotiated "peace without victory" would prove durable.

Germany's warlords responded with a blow of the mailed fist. On January 31, 1917, they announced to an astonished world that they intended to wage *unlimited* submarine warfare, sinking *all* ships, including America's, in the war zone.

The Germans thus jerked viciously on the string they had attached to their *Sussex* pledge in 1916. Wilson, his bluff now called, broke diplomatic relations but refused to move toward war unless the Germans undertook "overt" acts against American lives and property. To defend American interests short of war, the president asked Congress for authority to arm American merchant ships. When a

band of midwestern senators launched a filibuster to block the measure, Wilson denounced them as a "little group of willful men" who were rendering a great nation "helpless and contemptible." But their obstructionism was a powerful reminder of the continuing strength of American isolationism.

Meanwhile, the sensational Zimmerman note was intercepted and published on March 1, 1917, infuriating Americans, especially westerners. German foreign secretary Zimmerman had secretly proposed a German-Mexican alliance, tempting anti-Yankee Mexico with thoughts of recovering Texas, New Mexico, and Arizona.

On the heels of this provocation came the long-dreaded "overt" acts in the Atlantic, where German U-boats sank four unarmed American merchant vessels in the first two weeks of March. As one Philadelphia newspaper observed, the "difference between war and what we have now is that now we aren't fighting back." Simultaneously came the rousing news that a revolution in Russia had toppled the cruel regime of the tsars. America could now fight foursquare for democracy on the side of the Allies, without the black sheep of Russian despotism in the Allied fold.

Subdued and solemn, Wilson at last stood before a hushed joint session of Congress on the evening of April 2, 1917, and asked for a declaration of war. He had lost his gamble that America could pursue the profits of neutral trade without being sucked into the ghastly maelstrom. A myth developed in later years that America was dragged unwittingly into war by munitions makers and Wall Street bankers, desperate to protect their profits and loans. Yet the weapons merchants and financiers were already thriving, unhampered by wartime government restrictions and heavy taxation. Their slogan might well have been "Neutrality forever." The simple truth is that British harassment of American commerce had been galling but endurable; Germany had resorted to the mass killing of civilians. The difference was like that between a gang of thieves and a gang of murderers. President Wilson had drawn a clear, if risky, line against the depredations of the submarine. The German high command, in a last desperate throw of the dice, chose to cross it. In a figurative sense, America's war declaration of April 6, 1917, bore the unambiguous trademark "Made in Germany."

Wilsonian Idealism Enthroned

"It is a fearful thing to lead this great peaceful people into war," Wilson said in his war message. It was fearful indeed, not least of all because of the formidable challenge it posed to Wilson's leadership skills. Ironically, it fell to the scholarly Wilson, deeply respectful of American traditions, to shatter one of the most sacred of those traditions by entangling America in a distant European war.

How could the president arouse his fellow citizens to shoulder this unprecedented burden? No fewer than six senators and fifty representatives (including the first congresswoman, Jeannette Rankin of Montana) had voted against the war resolution. Wilson could whip up no enthusiasm, especially in the landlocked Midwest, by fighting to make the world safe from the submarine. The president would have to proclaim more glorified aims.

Wilson's burning idealism led him instinctively to an inspired decision. Radiating the spiritual fervor of his Presbyterian ancestors, he declared the twin goals of "a war to end war" and a crusade "to make the world safe for democracy." Flourishing the sword of righteousness, Wilson virtually hypnotized the nation with his lofty ideals. He contrasted the selfish war aims of the other belligerents, Allied and enemy alike, with America's shining altruism. America, he preached, did not fight for the sake of riches or territorial conquest. The republic sought only to shape an international order in which democracy could flourish without fear of power-crazed autocrats and militarists.

In Wilsonian idealism, the personality of the president and the necessities of history were perfectly matched. The high-minded Wilson genuinely believed in the principles he so eloquently intoned. And probably no other appeal could have successfully converted the American people from their historic hostility to involvement in European squabbles. Americans, it seemed, could be either isolationists or crusaders, but nothing in between.

Wilson's appeal worked—perhaps too well. Holding aloft the torch of idealism, the president fired up the public mind to a fever pitch. "Force, force to the utmost, force without stint or limit," he cried, while the country responded less elegantly with, "Hang the Kaiser!" Lost on the gale was Wilson's earlier plea for "peace without victory."

Fourteen Potent Wilsonian Points

Wilson quickly came to be recognized as the moral leader of the Allied cause. He scaled a summit of inspiring oratory on January 8, 1918, when he delivered his famed Fourteen Points Address to an enthusiastic Congress. Though one of his primary purposes was to keep reeling Russia in the war, Wilson's eloquence inspired all the drooping Allies to make mightier efforts and demoralized the enemy governments by holding out alluring promises to their dissatisfied minorities.

The first five of the Fourteen Points were broad in scope: (1) A proposal to abolish secret treaties pleased liberals of all countries. (2) Freedom of the seas appealed to the Germans, as well as to

Americans who distrusted British sea power. (3) A removal of economic barriers among nations was comforting to Germany, which feared postwar vengeance. (4) Reduction of armament burdens was gratifying to taxpayers everywhere. (5) An adjustment of colonial claims in the interests of both native peoples and the colonizers was reassuring to the anti-imperialists.

Other points among the fourteen proved to be no less seductive. They held out the promise of independence ("self-determination") to oppressed minority groups, such as the Poles, millions of whom lay under the heel of Germany and Austria-Hungary. The capstone point, number fourteen, foreshadowed the League of Nations—an international organization that Wilson hoped would provide a system of collective security. Wilson earnestly prayed that this new scheme would effectively guarantee the political independence and territorial integrity of all countries, whether large or small.

Yet Wilson's appealing points, though raising hopes the world over, were not everywhere applauded. Certain leaders of the Allied nations, with an eye to territorial booty, were less than enthusiastic. Hard-nosed Republicans at home grumbled, and some of them openly sneered at the "fourteen commandments" of "God Almighty Wilson."

Creel Manipulates Minds

Mobilizing the mind for war, both in America and abroad, was an urgent task facing the Washington authorities. For this purpose, the Committee on Public Information was created. It was headed by a youngish journalist, George Creel, who, though outspoken and tactless, was gifted with zeal and imagination. His job was to sell America on the war, and sell the world on Wilsonian war aims.

The Creel organization, employing 150,000 workers at home and overseas, proved that words were indeed weapons. It sent out an army of 75,000 "four-minute men"—often longer-winded than that—who delivered countless speeches containing much "patriotic pep."

Creel's propaganda took varied forms. Posters were splashed on billboards in the "battle of the fences," as artists "rallied to the colors." Millions of

Anti-German Propaganda   *The government relied extensively on emotional appeals and hate propaganda to rally support for the war, which most Americans regarded as a distant "European" affair.*

leaflets and pamphlets, which contained the most pungent Wilsonisms, were showered like confetti upon the world. Propaganda booklets with red-white-and-blue covers were printed by the millions.

Hang-the-kaiser movies, carrying such titles as *The Kaiser, the Beast of Berlin* and *To Hell with the Kaiser,* revealed the "Hun" in his bloodiest colors. Arm-waving conductors by the thousands led huge audiences in songs that poured scorn on the enemy and glorified the "boys" in uniform.

Creel typified American war mobilization, which relied more on aroused passion and voluntary compliance than on formal laws. But he rather oversold the ideals of Wilson, and led the world to expect too much. When the president proved to be a mortal and not a god, the resulting disillusionment at home and abroad was disastrous.

Enforcing Loyalty and Stifling Dissent

German-Americans numbered over 8 million, counting those with at least one parent foreign born, out of a total population of 100 million. On the whole they proved to be gratifyingly loyal to the United States. Yet rumormongers were quick to spread tales of spying and sabotage: even trifling epidemics of diarrhea were blamed on German agents. A few German-Americans were tarred, feathered, and beaten; in one extreme case a German Socialist in Illinois was lynched by a drunken mob.

As emotion mounted, hate hysteria swept the nation against Germans and things Germanic. Orchestras found it unsafe to present German-composed music, such as that of Wagner or Beethoven. The teaching of the German language was short-sightedly discontinued in many high schools and colleges. Sauerkraut became "liberty cabbage" and hamburger became "liberty steak."

Both the Espionage Act of 1917 and the Sedition Act of 1918 reflected current fears about Germans and antiwar Americans. Especially visible among the 1,900 prosecutions undertaken under these laws were antiwar Socialists and members of the radical union Industrial Workers of the World. Kingpin Socialist Eugene V. Debs was convicted under the Espionage Act in 1918 and sentenced to ten years in the federal penitentiary. IWW leader William D. ("Big Bill") Haywood and ninety-nine associates were similarly convicted. There was also mild press censorship, and some magazines such as the *Masses* were denied mailing privileges.

These prosecutions form an ugly chapter in the history of American civil liberty. With the dawn of peace, presidential pardons were rather freely granted, like that given to Eugene Debs by President Harding in 1921. Yet a few victims lingered behind bars into the 1930s.

The Nation's Factories Go to War

Victory was no foregone conclusion, especially since the republic, despite ample warning, was caught flat-footedly unready for its leap into global war. The pacifistic Wilson had only belatedly backed some mild preparedness measures beginning in 1915, including a shipbuilding program and a modest beefing up of the army to about 100,000 regulars. It would take a herculean effort to mobilize America's daunting but disorganized resources and throw them into the field quickly enough to bolster the Allied war effort.

Towering obstacles confronted economic mobilizers. Sheer ignorance was among the biggest roadblocks. No one knew precisely how much steel or explosive powder the country was capable of producing. Old ideas also proved to be liabilities, as traditional fears of big government hamstrung efforts to orchestrate the economy from Washington.

Late in the war, and after some bruising political battles, Wilson succeeded in imposing some order on this economic confusion. In March 1918 he appointed lone-eagle stock speculator Bernard Baruch to head the War Industries Board. But the War Industries Board never had more than feeble formal powers. Even in a globe-girdling crisis, the American preference for laissez-faire and for a weak central government proved amazingly strong.

Perspiring workers were urged to put forth their best efforts, spurred by the slogan "Labor will win the war." Women were encouraged to enter industry and also agriculture, where they were called "farmerettes." Women's war work at last prompted the president to endorse woman suffrage as "a vitally necessary war measure." Nearly a century of struggle was crowned with success when women received the right to vote with the passage of the Nineteenth Amendment in 1920. (For text, see Appendix.) Tens of thousands of southern blacks were drawn to the North by the magnet of war industries—the small-scale beginnings of a migration of immense sociological significance.

Samuel Gompers and his powerful American Federation of Labor gave loyal support to the war effort. Yet labor harbored grievances, as high inflation kept pace with wartime wage increases. Some 6,000 strikes occurred during the war. More than a thousand cases were brought before the National War Labor Board, which served as the supreme court for labor disputes.

Women Ordnance Plant Workers with Pneumatic Hammers, 1918 *A minority of women had long been in the workforce, but World War I drew more of them into heavy industrial labor.*

Some of the most crippling labor sabotage was engineered by the left-wing IWW members, or "Wobblies." As transient laborers in such industries as fruit and lumber, the Wobblies were the victims of some of the worst working conditions in the country. When they protested, many of the Wobblies were arrested, beaten up, or run out of town.

Forging a War Economy

Mobilization relied more on the heated emotions of patriotism than on the cool majesty of the laws. The largely voluntary and somewhat haphazard character of economic war organization testified eloquently to ocean-insulated America's safe distance from the fighting—as well as to the still modest scale of government power in the Progressive-Era republic.

As the larder of democracy, America had to feed itself and its allies. By a happy inspiration, the man chosen to head the Food Administration was the Quaker humanitarian Herbert C. Hoover, already a hero for his successful charitable drive to feed the starving people of war-wracked Belgium.

In common with other American war administrators, Hoover preferred to rely on voluntary compliance rather than on formal edicts. Instead of rationing food supplies, he waged a whirlwind propaganda campaign through posters, billboards, newspapers, pulpits, and movies. To save food for export, Hoover proclaimed wheatless Wednesdays and meatless Tuesdays—all on a voluntary basis. Even children, when eating apples, were urged to be "patriotic to the core."

Food surpluses were also piled up through the use of backyard "victory gardens," and by restricting the use of foodstuffs for manufacturing alcoholic beverages. The wartime drive against German-descended brewers aided in the passage of the Eighteenth Amendment in 1919, which prohibited all alcoholic drinks—temporarily.

Thanks to the superheated patriotic wartime spirit, Hoover's voluntary approach worked, as farm production increased by one-fourth, and food exports to the Allies tripled in volume. Hoover's methods were widely imitated in other war agencies. The Fuel Administration exhorted Americans to save fuel with "heatless Mondays" and "gasless Sundays." The Treasury Department sponsored huge parades and invoked slogans such as "Halt the Hun" to promote four great Liberty Loan drives, followed by a Victory Loan campaign in 1919. Together, these efforts netted the then-fantastic sum of about $21 billion, or two-thirds of the current cost of the war to the United States. The remainder was raised by increased taxes, which, unlike the loan subscriptions, were obligatory.

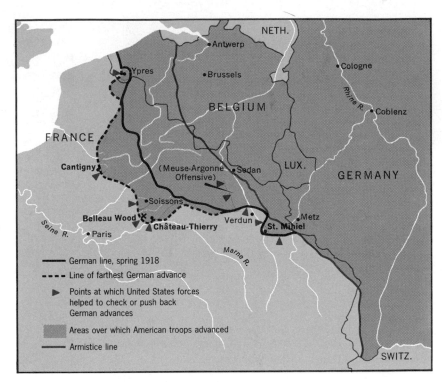

Major U.S. Operations in France, 1918 *One doughboy recorded in his diary his baptism of fire at St. Mihiel: "Hiked through dark woods. No lights allowed, guided by holding on the pack of the man ahead. Stumbled through underbrush for about half mile into an open field where we waited in soaking rain until about 10:00 P.M. We then started on our hike to the St. Mihiel front, arriving on the crest of a hill at 1:00 A.M. I saw a sight which I shall never forget. It was the zero hour and in one instant the entire front as far as the eye could reach in either direction was a sheet of flame, while the heavy artillery made the earth quake."*

Despite the Wilson administration's preference for voluntary means of mobilizing the economy, the government on occasion reluctantly exercised its sovereign formal power, notably when it took over the nation's railroads following indescribable traffic snarls in late 1917. Washington also launched a gigantic shipbuilding program, but it was largely too late to make a substantial contribution.

Making Plowboys into Doughboys

Most citizens, at the outset, did not dream of sending a mighty force to France. They expected that America would use its navy to uphold freedom of the seas, ship war materials to the Allies, and supply them with loans. But in April and May of 1917, the European associates confessed that they were scraping the bottom not only of their money chests, but, more ominously, of their manpower barrels. A huge American army would have to be raised, trained, and transported, or the whole western front would collapse.

Conscription was the only answer to the need for raising an immense army with all possible speed. Wilson disliked a draft, but he eventually accepted and eloquently supported conscription as a disagreeable and temporary necessity. After six weeks of criticism and doomsaying, Congress grudgingly consented and passed conscription.

The draft act required the registration of all males between the ages of eighteen and forty-five. The draft machinery, on the whole, worked effectively. No "draft dodger" could purchase his exemption or hire a substitute, as during the Civil War, though there were many exemptions for men in key industries such as shipbuilding.

Within a few frantic months the army was increased from about 200,000 men to over 4 million. For the first time women were admitted to the armed forces: some 11,000 to the navy and 269 to the marine corps.

Recruits were supposed to receive six months of training in America and two more months overseas. But so great was the urgency that many dough-

Over There   *American troops ("doughboys") man a machine gun in a bomb-blasted forest.*

boys were swept swiftly into battle scarcely knowing how to handle a rifle, much less a bayonet.

America Helps Hammer the Hun

Russia's collapse underscored the need for haste. As the communistic Bolsheviks removed their beaten country from the war, Germany moved its forces to the front in France.

Berlin's calculations as to American tardiness were surprisingly accurate. No significantly effective American fighting force reached France until about a year after Congress declared war. The Germans hoped to deliver the knockout blow to the Allies before American reinforcements could arrive.

Despite shipping shortages that plagued the Allies, France gradually began to bustle with American doughboys. The first trainees to reach the front were used as replacements in the Allied armies. The newcomers soon made friends with the French girls—or tried to—and one of the most sung-about

women in history was the fabled "Mademoiselle from Armentieres." Doughboys made up hundreds of stanzas; one of the printable ones was:

> She was true to me, she was true to you,
> She was true to the whole damned army, too.

The dreaded German drive on the western front exploded in the spring of 1918. Spearheaded by about half a million troops, the enemy rolled forward with terrifying momentum. So dire was the peril that Allies for the first time united under a supreme commander, the quiet French Marshal Ferdinand Foch.

At last the ill-trained "Yanks" were coming—and not a moment too soon. Late in May 1918, the forward-rolling Germans, smashing to within forty miles of Paris, threatened to knock out France. Newly arrived American troops, numbering fewer than 30,000, were thrown into the breach at Château-Thierry, right in the teeth of the German advance. This was a historic moment—the first significant engagement of American troops in a European war. With their arrival, it was clear that a new American giant had arisen in the West to replace the dying Russian titan in the East.

American weight in the scales was now being felt. By July 1918 the awesome German drive had spent its force, and keyed-up American boys participated in a Foch counteroffensive in the Second Battle of the Marne. This engagement marked the beginning of a German withdrawal that was never effectively reversed. In September 1918 nine American divisions (about 243,000 men) joined four French divisions to push the Germans from the St. Mihiel salient, a German dagger in France's flank.

The Americans, dissatisfied with merely bolstering the British and French, finally acquired their own army under General John J. Pershing, and their own sector of the front stretching from the Swiss border to meet the French lines. As part of the last mighty Allied assault, involving several million men, Pershing's army undertook the Meuse-Argonne offensive, from September 26 to November 11, 1918. This battle, the most titanic thus far in American history, lasted forty-seven days and engaged 1.2 million American troops. With especially heavy fighting in the rugged Argonne Forest, the killed and wounded mounted to 120,000, or 10 percent of the Americans involved.

Victory was in sight—and fortunately so. The slowly advancing American armies in France were eating up their supplies so rapidly that they were in grave danger of running short. But the battered Germans were reeling under the sledgehammer blows of the Allies and suffering from critical food shortages caused by the British blockade. Propaganda leaflets, containing seductive Wilsonian promises, were raining upon their crumbling lines from balloons, shells, and rockets.

Berlin was now ready to hoist the white flag. Seeking a peace based on the Fourteen Points, the Germans turned to the presumably softhearted Wilson in October 1918. In stern responses the president made it clear that the kaiser must be thrown overboard before an armistice could be negotiated. The war-weary Germans then forced the disgraced kaiser to flee to Holland.

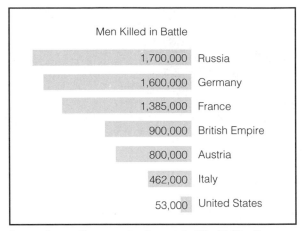

Men Killed in Battle

1,700,000	Russia
1,600,000	Germany
1,385,000	France
900,000	British Empire
800,000	Austria
462,000	Italy
53,000	United States

Approximate Comparative Losses in World War I

The exhausted Germans laid down their arms at eleven o'clock on the eleventh day of the eleventh month of 1918, and an eerie, numbing silence fell over the western front. War-taut America burst into a delirium of around-the-clock rejoicing, as streets were jammed with laughing, whooping, milling, dancing masses. The war to end wars had ended.

The United States' main contribution to the ultimate victory had been foodstuffs, munitions, credits, oil, and manpower—but not battlefield victories. The "Yanks" fought only two major battles, at St. Mihiel and the Meuse-Argonne. It was the *prospect* of endless U.S. troop reserves, rather than America's actual military performance, that eventually demoralized the battered Germans.

Ironically enough, General Pershing in some ways depended more on the Allies than they depended on him. Most of the U.S. Army's supplies and weapons were purchased from the British and French. The United States was no arsenal of democracy in this war; that role awaited it in the next global conflict, two decades later.

Wilson Steps Down from Olympus

Woodrow Wilson had helped to win the war. What role would he now play in shaping the peace? Expectations ran extravagantly high. As the fighting in Europe crashed to a close, the American president

Wilson in Dover, England, 1919   *Hailed by many Europeans in early 1919 as the savior of the Western world, Wilson was a fallen idol only a few months later, when his own countrymen repudiated the peace treaty he had helped to craft.*

towered at the peak of his popularity and power. No other man had ever occupied so dizzy a pinnacle as moral leader of the world. Wilson also had behind him the prestige of victory and the economic resources of the mightiest nation on earth. But at this fateful moment, his sureness of touch deserted him, and he began to make a series of tragic fumbles.

Under the slogan "Politics is adjourned," partisan political strife had been kept below the surface during the war crisis. Hoping to strengthen his hand at the Paris peace table, Wilson broke the truce by personally appealing for a Democratic victory in the congressional elections of November 1918. But the maneuver backfired when voters instead returned a narrow Republican majority to Congress. Having staked his personal prestige on the outcome, Wilson went to Paris as a diminished leader. Unlike all the parliamentary statesmen at the table, he did not command a legislative majority at home.

Wilson's decision to go in person to Paris to help make the peace infuriated Republicans, who saw it as flamboyant grandstanding. He further ruffled Republican feathers when he neglected to include a single Republican senator in his official peace delegation. The logical choice was the new chairman of the Senate Committee on Foreign Relations, slender and aristocratically bewhiskered Henry Cabot Lodge of Massachusetts, a Harvard Ph.D. But including Lodge would have been problematic for the president. The senator's mind, quipped one critic, was like the soil of his native New England: "naturally barren but highly cultivated." Wilson loathed him, and the feeling was warmly reciprocated. An accomplished author, Lodge had been known as "the scholar in politics" until Wilson came on the scene. The two men were at daggers drawn, personally and politically.

Hammering Out the Treaty

Woodrow Wilson, the great prophet arisen in the West, received tumultuous welcomes from the masses of France, England, and Italy late in 1918 and early in 1919. But the realistic statesmen of Italy and France were determined that Wilsonian idealism should not upset their finespun imperialistic plans.

Almost from the outset, the Paris Conference of great and small nations fell into the hands of an inner clique, known as the Big Four. Wilson, representing the richest and freshest great power, more or less occupied the driver's seat. He was joined by Vittorio Orlando of Italy, David Lloyd George of Britain, and cynical, hard-bitten Georges Clemenceau, the seventy-eight-year-old "organizer of victory" known as "the Tiger of France."

Speed was urgent when the conference opened on January 18, 1919. Europe seemed to be slipping into anarchy; the red tide of communism was licking westward from Bolshevist Russia.

Wilson's ultimate goal was a world parliament to be known as the League of Nations, but he first bent his energies to preventing any cynical parceling out of the former colonies and protectorates of the vanquished powers. He forced through a compromise between naked imperialism and Wilsonian idealism, in which the victors received conquered territory only as trustees of the League of Nations. But in practice this half-loaf compromise was little more than the old prewar colonialism, thinly disguised.

Wilson envisioned the League of Nations as containing an assembly with seats for all nations and a council to be controlled by the great powers. He gained a signal victory over the skeptical Old World diplomats in February 1919, when they agreed to make the League Covenant, Wilson's brainchild, an integral part of the final peace treaty.

On a quick trip to America, Wilson discovered that certain Republican senators, led by Senator Lodge, were sharpening their knives. To them the League was either a useless "sewing circle" or an overpotent "super-state." They were joined by a dozen or so isolationists, led by Senators William Borah of Idaho and Hiram Johnson of California, who were known as "irreconcilables" or "the battalion of death."

Thirty-nine Republican senators or senators-elect—enough to defeat the treaty—proclaimed that the Senate would not approve the League of Nations in its existing imperfect form. These difficulties delighted Wilson's Allied adversaries in Paris. They were now in a stronger bargaining position, because Wilson would have to beg them for changes in the covenant that would safeguard the Monroe Doctrine and other American interests dear to the senators.

As soon as Wilson was back in Paris, hard-headed Premier Clemenceau pressed French demands for the German-inhabited Rhineland and the Saar valley, a rich coal area. Faced with fierce Wilsonian opposition to this violation of self-determination, France settled for a compromise whereby the Saar basin would remain under the League of Nations for fifteen years and then a popular vote would determine its fate.* In exchange for dropping its demands for the Rhineland, France got a security treaty in which both Britain and America pledged to come to its aid in the event of another German invasion. The French later felt betrayed when the pact was quickly pigeonholed by the U.S. Senate, which shied away from all entangling alliances.

Wilson's next battle was with Italy over Fiume, a valuable seaport inhabited by both Italians and Yugoslavs. When Italy demanded Fiume, Wilson insisted that the seaport go to Yugoslavia and appealed over the heads of Italy's leaders to the country's masses. The maneuver fell flat. The Italian delegates went home in a huff, and the Italian masses turned savagely against Wilson.

Another crucial struggle was with Japan over China's Shantung peninsula and the German islands in the Pacific, which the Japanese had seized during the war. Japan was conceded the strategic Pacific islands under a League of Nations mandate,† but Wilson fiercely opposed Japanese control of Shantung as a violation of self-determination for its 30 million Chinese residents. But when the Japanese threatened to walk out, Wilson reluctantly accepted a compromise whereby Japan kept Germany's economic holdings in Shantung and pledged to return the peninsula to China at a later date. The Chinese were outraged by this imperialistic solution, while Clemenceau jeered that Wilson "talked like Jesus Christ and acted like Lloyd George."

---

* The Saar population voted overwhelmingly to rejoin Germany in 1935.

† In due time the Japanese illegally fortified these islands—the Marshalls, Marianas, and Carolines—and used them as bases against the United States in World War II.

The Peace Treaty that Bred a New War

A completed Treaty of Versailles, after more weeks of wrangling, was handed to the Germans in June 1919—almost literally on the point of a bayonet. Loud and bitter cries of betrayal burst from their throats—charges that Adolf Hitler would soon reiterate during his meteoric rise to power.

Wilson, of course, was guilty of no conscious betrayal. But he had been forced to compromise away some of his less cherished Fourteen Points in order to salvage the more precious League of Nations. He was much more like the mother who had to throw her sickly younger children to the pursuing wolves in order to save her sturdy firstborn child.

Greeted a few months earlier with frenzied acclaim in Europe, Wilson was now a fallen idol, condemned alike by disillusioned liberals and frustrated imperialists. He was keenly aware of some of the injustices that had been forced into the treaty. But he was hoping that a potent League of Nations, led by America, would iron out the inequities.

Yet the richly condemned treaty had much to commend it. Not least among its merits was its liberation of millions of minority peoples, such as the Poles, from the yoke of an alien dynasty. Wilson's critics to the contrary, the settlement was almost certainly a fairer one because he had gone to Paris.

Wilson's Battle for the League

At home in America, the Treaty of Versailles and the League of Nations were showered with brickbats from all sides. Superpatriots, with their strong isolationist convictions, raised a furious outcry against entanglement in a newfangled "League of Notions." Rabid Hun-haters, regarding the pact as not harsh enough, voiced their discontent. Professional liberals, like the editors of the *Nation,* thought it too harsh—and a gross betrayal to boot. German-Americans, Italian-Americans, Irish-Americans, and other "hyphenated Americans" were aroused because the peace settlement was not sufficiently favorable to their native lands.

Despite mounting discontent, a strong majority of the people still seemed favorable to the treaty, with the "Wilson League" firmly riveted in Part I of the pact. At this time—early July 1919—Senator Lodge had no real hope of defeating the Treaty of Versailles. His strategy was merely to amend it in such a way as to "Americanize," "Republicanize," or "senatorialize" it.

Lodge effectively used delay to confuse and divide public opinion. He read the entire 264-page treaty aloud in the Senate Foreign Relations Committee and held protracted hearings in which people of various nationalities aired their grievances.

With the treaty bogged down in the Senate, Wilson decided to appeal directly to the people with a spectacular speechmaking tour in September 1919. Physicians and friends warned the increasingly frail president against making the strenuous trip, but he declared that he was willing to die, like the doughboys he had sent into battle, for the sake of the new world order.

The presidential tour got off to a rather lame start in the Midwest, where German-American influence was strong and hostile "irreconcilable" senators Borah and Johnson dogged Wilson's trail. But the Rocky Mountain region and the Pacific Coast, areas that had elected Wilson in 1916, welcomed him with heartwarming outbursts. The high point—and the breaking point—of the return trip was at Pueblo, Colorado, September 25, 1919. Wilson, with tears coursing down his cheeks, pleaded for the League of Nations as the only real hope of preventing future wars. That night he collapsed from physical and nervous exhaustion.

Wilson was whisked back in the "funeral train" to Washington where several days later a stroke paralyzed one side of his body. During the next few weeks he lay in a darkened room in the White House, as much a victim of the war as the unknown soldier buried at Arlington. For seven and a half months he did not meet his cabinet.

Defeat Through Deadlock

Senator Lodge, coldly calculating, was now at the helm. After failing to amend the treaty outright, he came up with fourteen formal reservations to protect American sovereignty and guard Congress's war-declaring power against the League. Wilson, hating

Lodge, saw red at the mere suggestion of the *Lodge* reservations, which he insisted "emasculated" the entire pact.

Although too feeble to lead, Wilson was still strong enough to obstruct Lodge's proposal. When the day finally came for voting in the Senate, he sent word to all true Democrats to vote *against* the treaty with the odious Lodge reservations attached. Loyal Democrats in the Senate, on November 19, 1919, blindly did Wilson's bidding. Combining with the irreconcilables, mostly Republicans, they rejected the treaty with the Lodge reservations appended, 55 to 39.

In the face of strong public indignation at this outcome, the Senate was forced to vote a second time in March 1920. There was only one possible path to success. Unless the Senate approved the pact with the Lodge reservations, the entire document would be rejected. But the sickly Wilson signed the treaty's death warrant by again sending word to all loyal Democrats to vote down the treaty with the obnoxious Lodge reservations. On a fateful March 19, 1920, the treaty netted a simple majority but failed to get the necessary two-thirds majority by a count of 49 yeas to 35 nays.

Who defeated the treaty? The Lodge-Wilson personal feud, traditionalism, isolationism, disillusionment, and partisanship all contributed to the confused picture. But Wilson himself must bear a substantial share of the responsibility. He asked for all or nothing—and got nothing.

The "Solemn Referendum" of 1920

Wilson's own pet solution for the deadlock was to settle the treaty issue by appealing to the people for a "solemn referendum" in the presidential election of 1920. This was sheer folly, for a true mandate on the League in the noisy arena of politics was clearly an impossibility.

Gathering in Chicago, jubilant Republicans devised a masterfully ambiguous platform that could appeal to both pro-League and anti-League sentiment in the party. As the leading presidential contestants killed one another off, a group of Senate bosses, meeting rather casually in the historic "smoke-filled" Room 404 of the Hotel Blackstone, informally decided on affable, malleable Senator Warren G. Harding of Ohio. To run with the "folksy," back-slapping former newspaper editor, the party nominated frugal, grim-faced Governor Calvin ("Silent Cal") Coolidge of Massachusetts.

Meeting in San Francisco, Democrats nominated earnest Governor James M. Cox of Ohio, who strongly supported the League. His running mate was assistant navy secretary Franklin D. Roosevelt, a young, handsome, vibrant New Yorker.

Democratic attempts to make the campaign a referendum on the League were thwarted by Senator Harding, who issued muddled and contradictory statements on the issue from his front porch. Both pro-League and anti-League Republicans claimed that Harding's election would advance their cause, while the candidate suggested that if elected he would work for a vague Association of Nations—*a* league but not *the* League.

With newly enfranchised women swelling the vote totals, Harding was swept into power with a prodigious plurality of over 7 million votes—16,143,407 to 9,130,328 for Cox. The electoral count was 404 to 127. Eugene V. Debs, federal prisoner number 9653 at the Atlanta Penitentiary, rolled up the largest vote ever for the left-wing Socialist party—919,799.

Public desire for a change found vent in a resounding repudiation of "high and mighty" Wilsonism. People were tired of professional highbrowism, star-reaching idealism, bothersome do-goodism, moral overstrain, and constant self-sacrifice. Eager to lapse back into "normalcy," they were willing to accept a second-rate president—and they got a third-rate one.

Although the election could not be considered a true referendum, Republican isolationists successfully turned Harding's victory into a death sentence for the League. Politicians increasingly shunned the League as they would a leper. When the legendary Wilson died in 1924, admirers knelt in the snow outside his Washington home. His "great vision" of a league for peace had died long before.

The Betrayal of Great Expectations

America's spurning of the League was tragically shortsighted. The republic had helped to win a costly war, but it blindly kicked the fruits of victory under the table. Whether a strong international organization would have averted World War II in 1939 will always be a matter of dispute. But there can be no doubt that the orphaned League of Nations was undercut at the start by the refusal of the mightiest power on the globe to join it. The Allies themselves were largely to blame for the new world conflagration that flared up in 1939, but they found a convenient justification for their own shortcomings by pointing an accusing finger at Uncle Sam.

The ultimate collapse of the Treaty of Versailles must be laid, at least in some degree, at America's doorstep. This complicated pact, tied in with the four other peace treaties through the League Covenant, was a top-heavy structure designed to rest on a four-legged table. The fourth leg, the United States, was never put into place. This rickety structure teetered for over a decade and then crashed in ruins—a debacle that played into the hands of German demagogue Adolf Hitler.

No less ominous events were set in motion when the Senate spurned the Security Treaty with France. The French, fearing that a new generation of Germans would follow in their fathers' goose steps, undertook to build up a powerful military force. Predictably resenting the presence of strong French armies, Germany began to rearm illegally. The seething cauldron of uncertainty and suspicion brewed an intoxicant that helped inflame the fanatical following of dictator Hitler.

The United States, as the tragic sequel proved, hurt its own cause when it buried its head in the sands. Granted that the conduct of its Allies had been disillusioning, it had its own ends to serve by carrying through the Wilsonian program. It would have been well advised if it had forthrightly assumed its war-born responsibilities and had resolutely played the role of global leader into which it had been thrust by the iron hand of destiny. In the interests of its own security, if for no other reason, the United States should have used its enormous strength to shape world-shaking events. Instead, it permitted itself to drift along aimlessly and dangerously toward the abyss of a second and even more bloody international disaster.

CHRONOLOGY

1915	Council of National Defense established.
1917	Germany resumes unrestricted submarine warfare.
	Zimmerman note.
	United States enters World War I.
	Espionage Act of 1917.
1918	Wilson proposes the Fourteen Points.
	Sedition Act of 1918.
	Battle of Château-Thierry.
	Second Battle of the Marne.

	Meuse-Argonne offensive.
	Armistice ends World War I.
1919	Paris Peace Conference and Treaty of Versailles.
	Wilson's pro-League tour and collapse.
	Eighteenth Amendment (prohibition of alcohol) passed.
1920	Final Senate defeat of Versailles Treaty.
	Harding defeats Cox for presidency.
	Nineteenth Amendment (woman suffrage) passed.

Varying Viewpoints

Was Woodrow Wilson a starry-eyed idealist or a hard-nosed realist? For three-quarters of a century, this question has hung over discussions of the president's wartime diplomacy and peacemaking, especially his proposal for a League of Nations. Wilson's detractors charge that the American leader naively tried to impose his own high-minded legal and moral concepts on international affairs, which often do not operate according to the rules of law and morality. Some New Left writers have claimed that Wilson's diplomacy revealed an objectionable purpose of another kind: a thrust to open the world to American economic penetration.

Wilson's defenders usually emphasize that his lofty principles were tempered by pragmatism. They stress the give-and-take character of some of his proposals, such as the mandates for former colonial territories. Apologists also point out that the League did embody the modern, and presumably "realistic," concept of "collective security." Recently, writers such as Arno Mayer and N. Gordon Levin, Jr., have attempted to rehabilitate Wilson. They credit him with an immensely sophisticated grasp of the way certain ideals—such as free trade, reduced armaments, and political stability—would benefit both the world and the profit margins of American businesspeople. To them Woodrow Wilson now appears to be a farseeing visionary who perceived the compatibility of his high principles with America's own material interests.

SELECT READINGS

Primary Source Documents

John J. Pershing, *My Experiences in the World War** (1931), recounts American fighting tactics. Wilson's "Fourteen Points Address" to Congress on January 8, 1918* *(Congressional Record,* 65 Cong., 2 sess., p. 691), defined the nation's war aims. The dealings at the Versailles Conference are described in the words of Wilson's personal adviser, *The Intimate Papers of Colonel House** (1928). William E. Borah, *"Speech on the League of Nations"* (1919), in Richard Hofstadter, *Great Issues in American History,* reveals the isolationist position. Ernest Hemingway's *A Farewell to Arms* (1929) is an outstanding war novel.

Secondary Sources

The home front is emphasized in David M. Kennedy, *Over Here: The First World War and American Society* (1980). Economic mobilization is covered in Robert Cuff, *The War Industries Board* (1973), Daniel R. Beaver, *Newton D. Baker and the American War Effort* (1966), and Charles Gilbert, *American Financing of World War I* (1970). The abuse of civil liberties is soberly analyzed in Harry N. Scheiber, *The Wilson Administration and Civil Liberties, 1917–1921* (1960), and Paul L. Murphy, *World War I and the Origin of Civil Liberties in the United States* (1979). Military matters are handled in Edward M. Coffman, *The War to End All Wars: The American Military Experience in World War I* (1968), and Arthur E. Barbeau and Florette Henri, *Unknown Soldiers: Black American Troops in World War One* (1974). The war experiences of women are captured in Maurine W. Greenwald, *Women, War, and Work* (1980). Works of cultural history include Stanley Cooperman, *World War I and the American Novel* (1966), Stuart Rochester, *American Liberal Disillusionment in the Wake of World War I* (1977), and Paul Fussell, *The Great War and Modern Memory* (1975). On the peace, see Arthur S. Link, *Woodrow Wilson: Revolution, War, and Peace* (1979), and two studies by Thomas A. Bailey, *Woodrow Wilson and the Lost Peace* (1944) and *Woodrow Wilson and the Great Betrayal* (1945). Consult also N. Gordon Levin, Jr., *Woodrow Wilson and World Politics* (1968), and Arno J. Mayer, *Politics and Diplomacy of Peacemaking* (1967). The end of this troubled period is sketched in Burl Noggle, *Into the Twenties: The U.S. From the Armistice to Normalcy* (1974).

CHAPTER 33

American Life in the "Roaring Twenties," 1919–1929

America's present need is not heroics but healing; not nostrums but normalcy; not revolution but restoration; . . . not surgery but serenity.

Warren G. Harding, 1920

Insulating America from the Radical Virus

Bloodied by the war and disillusioned by the peace, Americans turned inward in the 1920s. Shunning diplomatic commitments to foreign countries, they also denounced "radical" foreign ideas, condemned "un-American" lifestyles, and clanged shut the immigration gates against foreign peoples. They partly sealed off the domestic economy from the rest of the world and plunged headlong into a dizzying decade of homegrown prosperity.

Hysterical fears of red Russia continued to color American thinking for several years after the Bolshevik revolution of 1917, which spawned a tiny Communist party in America. Tensions were heightened by an epidemic of strikes that convulsed the republic at war's end, many of them the result of high prices and frustrated union-organizing drives. Upstanding Americans jumped to the conclusion that labor troubles were fomented by bomb-and-whisker Bolsheviks. A general strike in Seattle in 1919, though modest in its demands and orderly in its methods, prompted a call from the mayor for federal troops to head off "the anarchy of Russia."

The big "red scare" of 1919–1920 resulted in a nationwide crusade against left-wingers whose Americanism was suspect. Attorney General A. Mitchell Palmer, who perhaps "saw red" too easily, earned the title of the "Fighting Quaker" by his excess zeal in rounding up suspects. When a bomb shattered both Palmer's nerves and his Washington home in June 1919, the "Fighting Quaker" was dubbed the "Quaking Fighter." Late in December 1919, a shipload of 249 alleged alien radicals was deported on the *Buford* ("Soviet Ark") to the "workers' paradise" of Russia. A still unexplained bomb blast in Wall Street in September of 1920 killed thirty-eight people and wounded several hundred others.

Various states joined the pack in the outcry against radicals. In 1919–1920 a number of legislatures passed criminal syndicalism laws. These antired statutes, some of which were born of the war, made unlawful the mere *advocacy* of violence to secure social change. Critics protested that mere words were not criminal deeds, that there was a great gulf between throwing fits and throwing bombs, and that "free screech" was for the nasty as well as the nice. Violence was done to traditional American concepts of free speech as IWWs and other radicals were vigorously prosecuted. The hysteria went so far that in 1920 five members of the New York legislature, all lawfully elected, were denied their seats simply because they were Socialists.

The red scare was a godsend to conservative businesspeople, who used it to break the backs of the fledgling unions. Labor's call for the "closed," or all-union, shop was denounced as "Sovietism in disguise." Employers, in turn, hailed their own anti-union campaign for the "open" shop as "the American plan."

Antiredism and antiforeignism were reflected in a notorious case regarded by liberals as a "judicial lynching." Nicola Sacco, a shoe-factory worker, and Bartolomeo Vanzetti, a fish peddler, were convicted in 1921 of the murder of a Massachusetts paymaster and his guard. The jury and judge were probably prejudiced in some degree against the defendants because they were Italians, atheists, anarchists, and draft dodgers.

Liberals and radicals the world over rallied to the defense of the two aliens doomed to die. The case dragged on for six years until 1927, when the condemned men were electrocuted. Communists and other radicals were thus presented with two martyrs in the "class struggle," while many American liberals hung their heads.

Hooded Hoodlums of the KKK

A new Ku Klux Klan, spawned by the postwar reaction, mushroomed fearsomely in the early 1920s. Despite the familiar sheets and hoods, it more closely resembled the antiforeign "nativist" movements of the 1850s than the antiblack night riders of the 1860s. It was antiforeign, anti-Catholic, antiblack, anti-Jewish, antipacifist, anticommunist, anti-internationalist, antievolutionist, antibootlegger, antigambling, antiadultery, and anti–birth control. It was also pro–Anglo-Saxon, pro-"native" American, and pro-Protestant. In short, the besheeted Klan betokened

KKK Parade of 40,000 Men in Washington, 1925

an extremist, ultraconservative uprising against many of the forces of diversity and modernity that were transforming American culture.

As reconstituted, the Klan spread with astonishing rapidity, especially in the Midwest and the "Bible Belt" South. At its peak in the mid-1920s, it enrolled about 5 million dues-paying members and wielded potent political influence. The Klan's most impressive displays were "konclaves" and huge flag-waving parades. The chief warning was the burning of the fiery cross. The principal weapon was the lash, supplemented by tar and feathers.

This reign of hooded horror, so repulsive to the best American ideals, collapsed rather suddenly in the late 1920s. Decent people at last recoiled from the orgy of ribboned flesh and terrorism, and scandalous embezzling by Klan officials resulted in a congressional investigation. The bubble was punctured when the movement was exposed, not as a crusade, but as a vicious racket based on a $10 initiation fee. At bottom, the KKK was an alarming manifestation of the intolerance and prejudice so common in the

	Immigrants from N. and W. Europe	Immigrants from other countries, principally S. and E. Europe
Average annual inflow, 1907–1914	176,983	685,531
Quotas under Act of 1921	198,082	158,367
Quotas under Act of 1924	140,999	21,847
Quotas under National-Origins Provision of 1929	132,323	20,251
Quotas under McCarran-Walter Act of 1952	125,165	29,492

Annual Immigration and Quota Laws

anxiety-plagued minds of the 1920s. America needed no such cowardly apostles, whose white sheets concealed dark purposes.

Stemming the Foreign Flood

Isolationist America of the 1920s, ingrown and provincial, had little use for the immigrants who began to flood into the country again as peace settled soothingly on the war-torn world. Some 800,000 stepped ashore in 1920–1921, about two-thirds of them from southern and eastern Europe. The "one hundred-percent Americans," gagging at the sight of this resumed "new immigration," once again cried that the famed poem at the base of the Statue of Liberty was all too literally true: They claimed that a sickly Europe was indeed vomiting on America "the wretched refuse of its teeming shore."

Congress temporarily plugged the breach with the Emergency Quota Act of 1921. Newcomers from Europe were restricted in any given year to a definite quota, which was set at 3 percent of the persons of their nationality who had been living in the United States in 1910. This national-origins system was relatively favorable to the immigrants from southern and eastern Europe, for by 1910 immense numbers of them had already arrived.

This stopgap legislation of 1921 was replaced, after additional reflection, by the Immigration Act of 1924. Quotas for foreigners were cut from 3 percent to 2 percent. The national-origins base was shifted from the census of 1910 to that of 1890, when comparatively few southern Europeans had arrived.* The purpose was clearly to freeze America's existing ethnic composition, which was largely northern European. A flagrantly discriminatory section of the Immigration Act of 1924 slammed the door absolutely against Japanese immigrants. Exempt from the quota system were Canadians and Latin Americans.

The quota system effected an epochal departure in American policy. Immigration henceforth died down to a comparative trickle. Quotas thus caused America to sacrifice something of its tradition of freedom and opportunity, as well as much of its color and variety.

The Immigration Act of 1924 marked the end of an era—a period of virtually unrestricted immi-

---

* Five years later the Immigration Act of 1929, using 1920 as the quota base, virtually cut immigration in half by limiting the total to 152,574 a year. In 1965 Congress abolished the national-origins quota system.

gration that in the previous century had brought some 35 million newcomers to the United States, mostly from Europe. The immigrant tide was now cut off; but by the 1920s it left on American shores a patchwork of ethnic communities separated from the larger society and each other by language, religion, and customs. Many Italians, Jews, Poles, and others lived in isolated enclaves with their own houses of worship, newspapers, and theaters. Efforts to organize labor unions repeatedly foundered on the rocks of ethnic rivalries—often played upon by cynical employers. Ethnic variety thus undermined class and political solidarity in America.

The Prohibition Experiment

One of the last peculiar spasms of the progressive reform movement was prohibition, loudly supported by crusading churches and by women. The arid new order was authorized in 1919 by the Eighteenth Amendment (for text, see Appendix), as implemented by the Volstead Act passed by Congress later that year. Together these laws made the world "safe for hypocrisy."

The legal abolition of alcohol was fairly popular in the Midwest, and especially so in the South. Southern whites were eager to keep stimulants out of the hands of blacks, lest they burst out of "their place." But despite the overwhelming ratification of the "dry" amendment, strong opposition persisted in the larger eastern cities. Concentrated colonies of "wet" foreign-born peoples hated to abandon their Old World drinking habits. Yet most Americans assumed that prohibition had come to stay. Everywhere there were last wild flings, as the nation prepared for a permanent "alcoholiday."

But prohibitionists were naive in the extreme. They overlooked the tenacious American tradition of strong drink and of weak control by the central government, especially over private lives. They forgot that the federal authorities had never satisfactorily enforced a law where the majority of the people—or a strong minority—were hostile to it. Lawmakers could not legislate away a thirst.

Prohibition simply did not prohibit. The old-time "men only" corner saloons were replaced by thousands of "speakeasies," each with its tiny grilled

window through which the thirsty spoke softly before the barred door was opened. Hard liquor, especially the cocktail, was drunk in staggering volume by both sexes. Largely because of the difficulties of transporting and concealing bottles, beverages of high alcoholic content were popular. Foreign rumrunners, often from the West Indies, had their inning, and countless cases of liquor leaked down from Canada.

"Home brew" and "bathtub gin" became popular, as law-evading adults engaged in "alky cooking" with toy stills. The worst of the homemade "rotgut" produced blindness, even death.

Yet the "noble experiment" was not entirely a failure. Bank savings increased, and absenteeism in industry decreased, presumably because of the newly sober ways of formerly soused bar-flies. On the whole, probably less liquor was consumed than in the days before prohibition, though strong drink continued to be available. As the legendary tippler remarked, prohibition was "a darn sight better than no liquor at all."

The Golden Age of Gangsterism

Prohibition spawned shocking crimes. The lush profits of illegal alcohol led to bribery of the police, many of whom were induced to see and smell no evil. Violent gang wars broke out in the big cities between rivals seeking to corner the rich market in booze. Rival triggermen used their sawed-off shotguns and chattering "typewriters" (machine guns) to "erase" bootlegging competitors who were trying to "muscle in" on their "racket." In the gang wars of the 1920s in Chicago, about 500 low characters were murdered.

Chicago was by far the most spectacular example of lawlessness. In 1925 "Scarface" Al Capone, a grasping and murderous booze distributor, began six years of gang warfare that netted him millions of blood-spattered dollars. He zoomed through the streets in an armor-plated, bulletproof car.

Gangsters rapidly moved into other profitable and illicit activities: prostitution, gambling, and narcotics. Racketeers even invaded the ranks of local labor unions as organizers and promoters. Organized crime had come to be one of the nation's most gigantic businesses. By 1930 the annual "take" of the underworld was estimated to be from $12 billion to $18 billion—several times the income of the federal government.

Criminal callousness sank to new depths in 1932 with the kidnapping for ransom, and eventual murder, of the infant son of aviator hero Charles A. Lindbergh. The entire nation was inexpressibly shocked and saddened, prompting Congress to pass the so-called Lindbergh Law, making interstate abduction in certain circumstances a death penalty offense.

Monkey Business in Tennessee

Education in the 1920s continued to make giant bootstrides. More and more states were requiring young people to remain in school until age sixteen or eighteen, or until graduation from high school. The proportion of seventeen-year-olds who finished high school almost doubled in the 1920s, to more than one in four.

The most revolutionary contribution to educational theory during these yeasty years was made by mild-mannered Professor John Dewey, who served on the faculty of Columbia University from 1904 to 1930. By common consent one of America's few front-rank philosophers, he set forth the principles of "learning by doing" that formed the foundation of so-called progressive education with its greater "permissiveness." He believed that the workbench was as essential as the blackboard, and that "education for life" should be a primary goal of the teacher.

Science also scored wondrous advances in these years. A massive public health program, launched by the Rockefeller Foundation in the South in 1909, had virtually wiped out the ancient affliction of hookworm by the 1920s. Better nutrition and health care helped to increase the life expectancy of a newborn infant from fifty years in 1901 to fifty-nine years in 1929.

Yet both science and progressive education in the 1920s were subjected to unfriendly fire from Fundamentalists. These old-time religionists charged that the teaching of Darwinian evolution was destroying faith in God and the Bible, while contributing to the moral breakdown of youth in the

The Fundamentalist Outcry *Radicalism and science are both condemned.*

Jazz Age. Numerous attempts were made to secure laws prohibiting the teaching of evolution, "the bestial hypothesis," in the public schools, and three southern states adopted such measures. The trio included Tennessee, in the heart of the so-called Bible Belt South, where evangelical religion was especially robust.

The stage was set for the memorable "Monkey Trial" at the hamlet of Dayton, in eastern Tennessee, in 1925. A likable high school biology teacher, John T. Scopes, was indicted for teaching evolution. Batteries of newspaper reporters armed with notebooks and cameras, descended upon the quiet town to witness the spectacle. Scopes was defended by nationally known attorneys, and William Jennings Bryan, an ardent Presbyterian Fundamentalist, joined the prosecution. Taking the stand as an expert on the Bible, Bryan was made to appear foolish by the famed criminal lawyer, Clarence Darrow. Five days after the trial was over, Bryan died of a stroke, no doubt brought on by the heat and strain.

This historic clash between theology and biology proved inconclusive. Scopes, the forgotten man of the drama, was found guilty and fined $100. But the supreme court of Tennessee, while upholding the law, set aside the fine on a technicality.* The Fundamentalists at best won only a hollow victory, for the absurdities of the trial cast ridicule on their cause. Yet even though increasing numbers of Christians were coming to reconcile the revelations of religion with the findings of modern science, Fundamentalism, with its emphasis on literal reading of the Bible, remained a vibrant force in American spiritual life. It was especially strong in the Baptist church and in the rapidly growing Churches of Christ, organized in 1906.

The Mass-Consumption Economy

Prosperity—real, sustained, and widely shared—put much of the "roar" into the twenties. The economy kicked off its war harness in 1919, faltered a few steps in the recession of 1920–1921, and then sprinted forward for nearly seven years. Both the recent war and Treasury Secretary Andrew Mellon's tax policies favored the rapid expansion of capital investment. Ingenious machines, powered by relatively cheap energy from newly tapped oil fields, dramatically increased the productivity of the laborer. Assembly-line production reached such perfection in Henry Ford's famed Rouge River plant near Detroit that a finished automobile emerged every ten seconds.

Great new industries suddenly sprouted forth. Supplying electrical power for the humming new machines became a giant business in the 1920s. Above all the automobile, once the horseless chariot of the rich, now became the carriage of the common citizen. By 1930 Americans owned almost 30 million cars.

The nation's deepening "love affair" with the automobile headlined a momentous shift in the character of the economy. American manufacturers seemed to have mastered the problems of production; their worries now focused on consumption. Could they find the mass markets for the goods they had contrived to spew forth in such profusion?

Responding to this need, a new arm of American commerce came into being: advertising. By persuasion and ploy, allure and sexual suggestion, advertisers sought to make Americans chronically discontented with their paltry possessions and want more, more, more.

In this commercialized atmosphere, even sports were becoming a big business. Ballyhooed by the "image makers," home-run heroes like George H. ("Babe") Ruth were far better known than most statesmen. In 1921 a Jersey City crowd paid more than a million dollars to watch heavyweight champion Jack Dempsey knock out challenger George Carpentier—the first in a series of million-dollar "gates" in the golden 1920s.

Buying on credit was another innovative feature of the postwar economy. "Possess today and pay tomorrow" was the message directed at buyers. Once-frugal descendants of Puritans went ever deeper into debt to own all kinds of newfangled marvels—refrigerators, vacuum cleaners, and especially cars and radios—now. Prosperity thus accumulated an overhanging cloud of debt, and the economy became increasingly vulnerable to disruptions of the credit structure.

Putting America on Rubber Tires

A new industrial revolution slipped into high gear in America in the 1920s. Thrusting out steel tentacles, it changed the daily life of the people in unprecedented ways. Machinery was the new messiah—and the automobile was its principal prophet.

Of all the inventions of the era, the automobile cut the deepest mark. It heralded an amazing new industrial system, based on assembly-line methods and mass-production techniques.

Americans adapted rather than invented the gasoline engine; Europeans can claim the original honor. By the 1890s a few daring American inventors and promoters, including Henry Ford and Ransom E. Olds (Oldsmobile), were developing the infant automotive industry. By 1910 there were sixty-nine companies with a total annual production of 181,000 units. Soon an enormous industry sprang into being, as Detroit became the motorcar capital of America.

---

* The Tennessee law was not formally repealed until 1967.

Best known of the new crop of industrial wizards was Henry Ford, who more than any other individual, put America on rubber tires. His high and hideous Model T ("Tin Lizzie") was cheap, rugged, and reasonably reliable, though rough and clattering. The parts of Ford's "flivver" were highly standardized, but the behavior of this "rattling good car" was so individualized that it became the butt of numberless jokes.

Lean and silent Henry Ford, who was said to have wheels in his head, erected an immense personal empire on the cornerstone of his mechanical genius. Ill educated, this multimillionaire mechanic was socially and culturally narrow; "history is bunk," he once testified. But he devoted himself with one-track devotion to he gospel of standardization. After two early failures, he grasped and applied fully the techniques of assembly-line production— "Fordism." He is supposed to have remarked that the purchaser could have his automobile in any color —just as long as it was black. So economical were his methods that in the mid-1920s he was selling the Ford roadster for $260—well within the purse of a thrifty worker.

The flood of Fords was phenomenal. In 1914 the "Automobile Wizard" turned out his five hundred thousandth Model T. By 1930 his total had riscn to 20 million. By 1929, when the great bull market collapsed, 26 million motor vehicles were registered in the United States. This figure, averaging 1 for every 4.9 Americans, represented far more automobiles than existed in all the rest of the world.

The Advent of the Gasoline Age

The impact of the self-propelled carriage on various aspects of American life was tremendous. A gigantic new industry emerged, dependent on steel, but displacing steel from its kingpin role. Employing directly or indirectly about 6 million people by 1930, it was a major prop of the nation's prosperity. Thousands of new jobs, moreover, were created by supporting industries. The lengthening list would include rubber, glass, and fabrics, to say nothing of thousands of service stations and garages. America's standard of living, responding to this infectious prosperity, rose to an enviable level.

New industries boomed lustily; older ones grew sickly. The petroleum business experienced an explosive development. Hundreds of oil derricks shot up in California, Texas, and Oklahoma, as these states expanded wondrously and the wilderness frontier became an industrial frontier. The once-feared railroad octopus, on the other hand, was hard hit by the competition of passenger cars, buses, and trucks. An age-old story was repeated: one industry's gains were another industry's pains.

Other effects were widely felt. Speedy marketing of perishable foodstuffs, such as fresh fruits, was accelerated. Countless new roads ribboned out to meet the demand of the American motorist for smoother and faster highways, often paid for by taxes on gasoline. The era of mud ended as the nation made haste to construct the finest network of hard-surfaced roadways in the world. Lured by new seductiveness in advertising and encouraged by the perfecting of installment-plan buying, countless Americans with shallow purses acquired the habit of riding as they paid.

Zooming motorcars were agents of social change. At first a luxury, they rapidly became a necessity. Essentially devices for needed transportation, they soon developed into a badge of freedom and equality—a necessary prop for self-respect. Women were further freed from their dependence on men. Isolation among the sections was broken down, and the less attractive states lost population at an alarming rate. Buses made possible the consolidation of schools and to some extent of churches. The sprawling suburbs spread out still farther from the urban core, as America became a nation of commuters.

Virtuous home life partially broke down as joy-riders of all ages forsook the ancestral hearth for the wide-open spaces. The morals of flaming youth sagged correspondingly—at least in the judgment of their elders.

Yet no sane American would plead for a return of the old horse and buggy, complete with fly-breeding manure. The automobile contributed notably to improved air and environmental quality, despite its later notoriety as a polluter. Life might be cut short on the highways, and smog might poison the air, but the automobile brought more convenience, pleasure, and excitement into people's lives than almost any other single invention.

Humans Develop Wings

Gasoline engines also provided the power that enabled humans to fulfill their age-old dream of sprouting wings. After near-successful experiments by others with heavier-than-air craft, the Wright brothers, Orville and Wilbur, performed "the miracle at Kitty Hawk," North Carolina. On a historic day—December 17, 1903—Orville Wright took aloft a feebly engined plane that stayed airborne for twelve seconds and 120 feet. Thus the air age was launched by two obscure bicycle repairmen.

As aviation gradually got off the ground, the world slowly shrank. The public was made increasingly air-minded by unsung heroes—often martyrs—who appeared as stunt fliers at fairs and other public gatherings. Airplanes—"flying coffins"—were used with marked success for various purposes during the Great War of 1914–1918. Shortly thereafter private companies began to operate passenger lines with airmail contracts, which were in effect a subsidy from Washington. The first transcontinental airmail route was established from New York to San Francisco in 1920.

In 1927 modest and skillful Charles A. Lindbergh, the so-called Flyin' Fool, electrified the world by making the first solo west-to-east conquest of the Atlantic. Seeking a prize of $25,000, the lanky stunt flier courageously piloted his single-engined plane, the *Spirit of St. Louis,* from New York to Paris in a grueling thirty-three hours and thirty-nine minutes.

Lindbergh's exploit swept Americans off their feet. Fed up with the cynicism and debunking of the Jazz Age, they found in this wholesome and handsome youth a genuine hero. "Lucky Lindy" received an uproarious welcome in the "hero canyon" of lower Broadway, as 1,800 tons of ticker tape and other improvised confetti showered upon him. Lindbergh's achievement—it was more than a stunt—did much to dramatize and popularize flying, while giving a strong boost to the infant aviation industry.

The impact of the airplane was tremendous. It provided the soaring American spirit with yet another dimension and increased the tempo of an already breathless civilization. The floundering railroad received another sharp setback through the loss of passengers and mail. A lethal new weapon was given to the gods of war with the coming of city-busting aerial bombs. The Atlantic Ocean was shriveling to about the size of the Aegean Sea in the days of Socrates, while isolation behind ocean moats was becoming a bygone dream.

The Radio Revolution

The speed of the airplane was far eclipsed by the speed of radio waves. Guglielmo Marconi, an Italian, invented wireless telegraphy in the 1890s, and his brainchild was used for long-range communication during World War I.

Next came the voice-carrying radio, a triumph of many minds. A red-letter day was posted in November 1920, when the Pittsburgh station KDKA broadcast the news of the Harding landslide. In harmony with American free enterprise, radio programs were generally sustained by bothersome commercials, as contrasted with the drabber government-owned systems of Europe.

Like other marvels, the radio not only created a new industry but added richness to the fabric of American life. More joy was given to leisure hours, and many children who had been lured from the fireside by the automobile were brought back by the radio. The nation was better knit together. Various sections heard Americans with standardized accents, and countless millions "tuned in" on perennial comedy favorites like "Amos 'n' Andy." Advertising was further perfected as an art.

Educationally and culturally, radio made a significant contribution. Politicians had to adjust their speaking technique to the new medium, and millions rather than thousands of voters heard their pleas. A host of listeners became ringside participants in world-shaking events. Finally, the music of famous artists and symphony orchestras was beamed into countless homes.

Hollywood's Filmland Fantasies

The flickering movie was the fruit of numerous geniuses, including Thomas A. Edison. As early as

The Guardian of Morality
Women's new one-piece bathing suits were a sensation in the 1920s. Here a check is carefully made to ensure that not too much leg is showing.

the 1890s, this novel contraption, though still in crude form, had attained some popularity in the naughty peep-show penny arcades. The real birth of the movie came in 1903, when the first story sequence reached the screen. This breathless melodrama—*The Great Train Robbery*—was featured in the five-cent theaters, popularly called "nickelodeons." Spectacular among the first full-length classics was D. W. Griffith's *The Birth of a Nation* (1915), which glorified the Ku Klux Klan of Reconstruction days and defamed blacks.

A fascinating industry was thus launched. Hollywood, California, quickly became the movie capital of the world, for it enjoyed a maximum of sunshine and other advantages. The motion picture really arrived during the World War of 1914–1918, when it was used as an engine of anti-German propaganda.

A new era began in 1927 with the success of the first "talkie"—*The Jazz Singer,* starring the white performer Al Jolson in blackface. The age of the "silents" was ushered out as theaters everywhere were wired for sound. About the same time, reasonably satisfactory color films were produced.

Movies eclipsed all other new forms of amusement in the phenomenal growth of their popularity.

Movie stars commanded much larger salaries than the president of the United States, in some cases as much as $100,000 for a single picture.

Critics bemoaned the vulgarization of popular taste wrought by the technologies of radio and movies, but the effects of the new mass media were not all negative. Much of the rich diversity of immigrant cultures was lost, as children, especially, forsook Grandma's storytelling for the downtown movie theater or popular radio shows like "Amos 'n' Andy." The standardization of tastes and language hastened entry into the American mainstream—and set the stage for the emergence of a working-class political coalition that, for a time, would overcome the divisive ethnic differences of the past.

The Dynamic Decade

Far-reaching changes in lifestyles and values paralleled the dramatic upsurge of the economy. The census of 1920 revealed that for the first time most Americans no longer lived in the countryside but in urban areas. Women continued to find new opportunities for employment in the cities, though they tended to cluster in a few low-paying jobs (such as retail clerking and office typing) that quickly became classified as "women's work." An organized birth control movement, led by fiery feminist Margaret Sanger, openly championed the use of contraceptives. A National Women's Party began in 1923 to campaign for an Equal Rights Amendment to the Constitution. To some defenders of traditional ways, it seemed that the world had suddenly gone mad.

Even before the war, one observer thought the chimes had "struck sex o'clock in America," and the 1920s witnessed what many old-timers thought was a veritable erotic eruption. Advertisers exploited sexual allure to sell everything from soap to car tires. Once-modest maidens now proclaimed their new freedom as "flappers" in bobbed tresses and dresses. Young women appeared with hemlines elevated, stockings rolled, breasts taped flat, cheeks rouged, and lips a "crimson gash" that held a dangling cigarette. Thus did the flapper symbolize a yearned-for and devil-may-care independence (some said wild abandon) in American women. Still more adventuresome females shocked their elders when they sported the new one-piece bathing suits.

Justification for this new sexual frankness could be found in the recently translated writings of Dr. Sigmund Freud. This Viennese physician appeared to argue that sexual repression was responsible for a variety of nervous and emotional ills. Thus not pleasure alone, but health, demanded sexual gratification and liberation.

Many taboos flew out the window as sex-conscious Americans let themselves go. As unknowing Freudians, teenagers pioneered the sexual frontiers. Glued together in syncopated embrace, they danced to jazz music squeaking from phonographs. In an earlier day a kiss had been the equivalent of a proposal of marriage. But in the new era exploratory young folk sat in darkened movie houses or took to the highways and byways in automobiles—branded "houses of prostitution on wheels" by straitlaced elders. There the youthful "neckers" and "petters" poached upon the forbidden territory of each other's bodies.

If the flapper was the goddess of the "era of wonderful nonsense," jazz was its sacred music. With its virtuoso wanderings and tricky syncopation, jazz moved up from New Orleans along with migrating

blacks during World War I. Tunes such as W. C. Handy's "St. Louis Blues" became instant classics, as the wailing saxophone became the trumpet of the new era. Blacks such as Handy, "Jelly Roll" Morton, and Joseph ("Joe") King Oliver gave birth to jazz, but the entertainment industry soon spawned all-white bands—notably Paul Whiteman's. Caucasian impresarios cornered the profits, though not the creative soul, of America's most native music.

A new racial pride also blossomed in the northern black communities that grew so rapidly during and after the war. Harlem in New York City, counting some 100,000 African-American residents in the 1920s, was one of the largest black communities in the world. Harlem sustained a vibrant, creative culture that nourished poets like Langston Hughes, whose first volume of verse, *Weary Blues,* appeared in 1926. Harlem in the 1920s also spawned at least one messianic leader, Marcus Garvey. A colorful West Indian, Garvey founded the United Negro Improvement Association (UNIA) to promote the resettlement of American blacks in Africa. His Black Star Steamship Company, intended to transport his numerous followers to the new African Eden, went bankrupt in 1923, and Garvey was eventually convicted of fraud and imprisoned. But his vigor and visibility did much to cultivate feelings of self-confidence and self-reliance among blacks, and his example proved important to the later founding of the Nation of Islam (Black Muslim) movement.

Literary Liberation

In literature, also, an older era seemed to have ground to a halt with the recent war. By the dawn of the 1920s most of the custodians of an aging genteel culture had died—Henry James in 1916, Henry Adams in 1918, and William Dean Howells (the "dean of American literature") in 1920. A few novelists who had been popular in the previous decades continued to thrive, notably the well-to-do, cosmopolitan New Yorker Edith Wharton and the Virginia-born Willa Cather, esteemed for her stark but sympathetic portrayals of pioneering on the prairies.

But in the decade after the war, a new generation of writers burst upon the scene. Many of them hailed from ethnic and regional backgrounds different from that of the Protestant New Englanders who traditionally had dominated American cultural life. The newcomers exhibited the energy of youth, the ambition of excluded outsiders, and, in many cases, the smoldering resentment of ideals betrayed. They bestowed on American literature a new vitality, imaginativeness, and artistic quality.

A patron saint of many young authors was H. L. Mencken, the "Bad Boy of Baltimore," who admired their critical attitude toward American society. In the pages of his green-covered monthly *American Mercury,* Mencken assailed marriage, patriotism, democracy, prohibition, Rotarians, and the middle-class American "booboisie." The South he contemptuously dismissed as "the Sahara of the Bozart" (a bastardization of *beaux arts,* French for the "fine arts"), and he scathingly attacked do-gooders as "Puritans." Puritanism, he jibed, was "the haunting fear that someone, somewhere, might be happy."

The war had jolted many young writers out of their complacency about traditional values and literary standards. With their pens they probed for new codes of morals and understanding, as well as fresh forms of expression. F. Scott Fitzgerald, a handsome Minnesota-born Princetonian then only twenty-four years old, became an overnight celebrity when he published *This Side of Paradise* in 1920. The book became a kind of Bible for the young. It was eagerly devoured by aspiring flappers and their ardent wooers, many of whom affected an air of bewildered abandon toward life. Catching the spirit of the hour (often about 4 A.M.), Fitzgerald found "All gods dead, all wars fought, all faiths in man shaken." He followed this melancholy success with *The Great Gatsby* (1925), a brilliant evocation of the glamour and cruelty of an achievement-oriented society. Theodore Dreiser's masterpiece of 1925 explored much the same theme: *An American Tragedy* dealt with the murder of a pregnant working girl by her socially ambitious young lover.

Ernest Hemingway, who had seen action on the Italian front in 1917, was among the writers most affected by the war. He responded to pernicious propaganda and the overblown appeal of patriotism by devising his own lean, word-sparing style. Hemingway spoke with a voice that was to have many imitators but no real equals. In *The Sun Also Rises* (1926)

F. Scott Fitzgerald and His Wife, Zelda   *They are shown here in the happy, early days of their stormy marriage.*

he told of disillusioned, spiritually numb American expatriates in Europe. In *A Farewell to Arms* (1929) he crafted one of the finest novels in any language about the war experience. A troubled soul, he finally blew out his brains with a shotgun blast in 1961.

Other writers turned to a critical probing of American small-town life. Sherwood Anderson dissected various fictional personalities in *Winesburg, Ohio* (1919), finding them all in some way warped by their cramped psychological surroundings. But the chief chronicler of midwestern life was spindly, red-haired, heavy-drinking Sinclair Lewis, a hot-headed journalistic product of Sauk Centre, Minnesota. A master of satire, he sprang into prominence in 1920 with *Main Street,* the story of one woman's unsuccessful war against provincialism. In *Babbitt* (1922) he affectionately pilloried George F. Babbitt, a prosperous, vulgar, middle-class real estate broker who slavishly conformed to the respectable materialism of his group. The word *Babbittry* was quickly coined to describe his all-too-familiar lifestyle.

William Faulkner, a dark-eyed, pensive Mississippian, penned a bitter war novel, *Soldier's Pay,* in 1926. He then turned his attention to a fictional chronicle of an imaginary, history-rich Deep South county. In powerful books like *The Sound and the Fury* (1929) and *As I Lay Dying* (1930), Faulkner peeled back layers of time and consciousness from the constricted souls of his tormented southern characters.

Nowhere was innovation in the 1920s more obvious than in poetry. Ezra Pound, a brilliantly erratic Idahoan who deserted America for Europe, rejected what he called "an old bitch civilization, gone in the teeth," and proclaimed his doctrine: "make it new." Pound strongly influenced Missouri-born and Harvard-educated T. S. Eliot, who took up residence in England. In "The Waste Land" (1922) Eliot produced one of the most impenetrable but influential poems of the century. Robert Frost, a San Francisco-born poet, wrote hauntingly about his adopted New England.

On the stage, Eugene O'Neill, a New York dramatist and Princeton dropout of globe-trotting background, laid bare Freudian notions of sex in plays like *Strange Interlude* (1928). A prodigious playwright, he wrote more than a dozen productions in the 1920s, and won the Nobel Prize in 1936.

O'Neill arose from New York's Greenwich Village, which before and after the war was a seething cauldron of writers, painters, musicians, actors, and other would-be artists. After the war, a black cultural renaissance also took root uptown in Harlem, led by such gifted writers as Claude McKay and Langston Hughes, and jazzmen like Louis Armstrong. They proudly exulted in their black culture. Although many whites frequented the black jazz joints, black writers were yet to win a wide audience among white readers.

Architecture also married itself to the new materialism and functionalism. Long-range city planning was being intelligently projected, and architects such as Frank Lloyd Wright were advancing the theory that buildings should grow from their sites and not slavishly imitate Greek and Roman importations.

The Machine Age outdid itself in New York City in 1931 when it thrust upward the cloud-brushing Empire State Building, 102 stories high.

Wall Street's Big Bull Market

The boom of the golden twenties showered genuine benefits on Americans, and their incomes and living standards assuredly rose, but there always seemed to be something fantastic about it all. People sang, somewhat incredulously:

> My sister she works in the laundry,
>   My father sells bootlegger gin,
> My mother she takes in the washing,
>   My God! how the money rolls in!

Signals abounded that the economic joy ride might end in a crash; even in the best years of the 1920s several hundred banks failed annually. This something-for-nothing craze was well illustrated by real estate speculation, especially the fantastic Florida boom that culminated in 1925. Numerous underwater lots were sold to eager purchasers for preposterous sums. The whole wildcat scheme collapsed when the peninsula was devastated by a hurricane.

The stock exchange provided even greater sensations. Speculation ran wild, and an orgy of boom-or-bust trading pushed the bull market up to dizzy peaks, as Wall Street gamblers gored one another and fleeced greedy lambs. The stock market became a veritable gambling den.

As the 1920s lurched forward, everybody seemed to be buying stocks "on margin"—that is, with a small down payment. Barbers, stenographers, and elevator boys cashed in on "hot tips" picked up while on duty. One valet was reported to have parleyed his wages into a quarter of a million dollars. "The cash register crashed the social register" as rags-to-riches Americans eagerly worshiped at the altar of the ticker-tape machine. So powerful was the intoxicant of quick profits that few heeded the voices raised in certain quarters to warn that this kind of tinsel prosperity could not last forever.

Little was done by Washington to curb money-mad speculators. In the wartime days of Wilson, the national debt had rocketed from the 1914 figure of

$1,188,235,400 to the 1921 peak of $23,976,250,608. Conservative principles of money management pointed to a diversion of surplus funds to reduce this financial burden.

The burdensome taxes inherited from the war were especially distasteful to Secretary of the Treasury Mellon, as well as to his fellow millionaires. Their theory was that such high levies forced the rich to invest in tax-exempt securities rather than in factories that provided prosperous payrolls. The Mellonites also argued, with considerable persuasiveness, that high taxes not only discouraged business but also brought a smaller net return to the Treasury than moderate taxes.

Seeking to succor the "poor" rich people, Mellon helped engineer a series of tax reductions from 1921 to 1926. Congress followed his lead by repealing the excess-profits tax, abolishing the gift tax, and reducing excise taxes, the surtax, the income tax, and estate taxes. In 1921 a wealthy American with an income of $1 million had paid $663,000 in income taxes; in 1926 the same person paid about $200,000. Mellon's spare-the-rich policies thus shifted much of the tax burden from the wealthy to middle-income groups.

Mellon, lionized by conservatives as the "greatest secretary of the treasury since Hamilton," remains a controversial figure. True, he reduced the national debt by $10 billion—from about $26 billion to $16 billion. But foes of the emaciated multimillionaire charged that he should have bitten a larger chunk out of the debt, especially while the country was pulsating with prosperity. He was also accused of indirectly encouraging the bull market. If he had absorbed more of the national income in taxes, there would have been less money left for frenzied speculation. His refusal to do so typified the single-mindedly probusiness regime that dominated the political scene throughout the postwar decade.

CHRONOLOGY

1903	Wright brothers fly the first airplane.
	First story-sequence motion picture.
1919	Eighteenth Amendment (prohibition) ratified.
	Seattle general strike.
	Anderson publishes *Winesburg, Ohio*.
1919–1920	Red scare.
1920	Radio broadcasting begins.
	Fitzgerald publishes *This Side of Paradise*.
	Lewis publishes *Main Street*.
1921	Sacco-Vanzetti trial.
	Emergency Quota Act of 1921.
	Bureau of the Budget created.
1922	Lewis publishes *Babbitt*.
	Eliot publishes "The Waste Land."

1923	Equal Rights Amendment (ERA) proposed.
1924	Immigration Act of 1924.
1925	Scopes trial.
	Florida real estate boom.
	Fitzgerald publishes *The Great Gatsby*.
	Dreiser publishes *An American Tragedy*.
1926	Hemingway publishes *The Sun Also Rises*.
1927	Lindbergh flies the Atlantic solo.
	First talking motion pictures.
	Sacco and Vanzetti executed.
1929	Faulkner publishes *The Sound and the Fury*.
	Hemingway publishes *A Farewell to Arms*.

Varying Viewpoints

Many historians have depicted the 1920s as a great watershed in the history of American culture, seeing it as the "first decade of modern America." Frederick Lewis Allen's immensely popular book *Only Yesterday* (1931) probably did more than any other single work to project the image of the 1920s as a decade that witnessed what Allen called a "revolution in manners and morals." The census finding in 1920 that a majority of Americans now lived in urban areas, the seeming defeat of religious Fundamentalism at the Scopes trial, the emergence of the flapper, and the shift from a capital-goods to a consumer-goods economic base are often cited as evidence of this social transformation. The advertising executive at the wheel of a Ford seemed to have replaced the farmer behind a plow as the typical American.

But the modern, transformative character of the 1920s has perhaps been exaggerated. The

Great Depression amply demonstrated that familiar problems of the business cycle remained. Mounting evidence points to the persistence of ethnic identities and immigrant and minority cultural traits. Changes in sexual behavior and the roles of women had roots deep in the industrializing, urbanizing era of the nineteenth century. Folklore to the contrary, prohibition *did* diminish the consumption of alcohol by Americans. The political strength of the "Moral Majority" and other Fundamentalist and evangelical groups in the 1980s and 1990s demonstrate the continued vitality of "old-time religion." And rural culture, manifested in widespread suspicion of cities and the popularity of country and western music, still lives. In retrospect, the changes of the 1920s look less like a revolutionary break and more like just another evolutionary chapter in the long process of modernization.

SELECT READINGS

Primary Source Documents

For the fallout from the Red scare, see Walter Lippman's eloquent plea for the lives of the Italian-American radicals Sacco and Vanzetti in the New York *World** (August 19, 1927). The life of automaker and business magnate Henry Ford is told in his *My Life and Work** (1922). For caustic fictional versions of those conditions, see Sinclair Lewis's novels, *Main Street* (1920), *Babbitt* (1922), and *Arrowsmith* (1925).

Secondary Sources

The best introduction to the 1920s is William Leuchtenburg, *The Perils of Prosperity, 1914–1932* (1958). Frederick Lewis Allen, *Only Yesterday* (1931), is an evocative recollection of the texture of life in the decade. Equally informative are Robert S. Lynd and Helen M. Lynd's classic sociological studies, *Middletown* (1929) and *Middletown in Transition* (1937). Robert K. Murray, *Red Scare* (1955), is authoritative. Immigration restriction is dealt with in John

Higham, *Strangers in the Land* (1955). The standard work on the revived Klan is David M. Chalmers, *Hooded Americanism* (rev. ed., 1981). The changing experiences of women are discussed in Winnifred Wandersee, *Women's Work and Family Values, 1920–1940* (1981); Lois Scharf and Joan M. Jensen, eds., *Decades of Discontent: The Women's Movement, 1920–1940* (1983); Nancy F. Cott, *The Grounding of Modern Feminism* (1987); and Phyllis Palmer, *Domesticity and Dirt: Housewives and Domestic Servants in the United States, 1920–1945* (1990). Fundamentalism is treated in George M. Marsden, *Fundamentalism and American Culture: The Rise of Twentieth-Century Evangelicalism, 1870–1925* (1980), and in Lawrence W. Levine's sensitive study of William Jennings Bryan, *Defender of the Faith* (1965). On the economy, see George H. Soule, *Prosperity Decade* (1947), and Daniel Nelson, *Frederick Winslow Taylor and the Rise of Scientific Management* (1980). Changing sexual attitudes are analyzed in

David M. Kennedy, *Birth Control in America: The Career of Margaret Sanger* (1970), and Linda Gordon, *Woman's Body, Woman's Right: A Social History of Birth Control in America* (1976). Gilbert Osofsky describes the background of the "Harlem renaissance" in *Harlem: The Making of a Ghetto, 1890–1930* (1966). Three stimulating literary histories are Frederick J. Hoffman, *The Twenties: American Writing in the Postwar Decade* (1955), Alfred Kazin, *On Native Grounds* (1942), and Daniel J. Singal, *The War Within: From Victorian to Modernist Thought in the South, 1919–1945* (1982). David M. Kennedy, *Over Here: The First World War and American Society* (1980), pays special attention to the literature that emerged from the war experience.

CHAPTER 34

The Politics of Boom and Bust, 1920–1932

We in America today are nearer to the final triumph over poverty than ever before in the history of any land. We have not yet reached the goal—but . . . we shall soon, with the help of God, be in sight of the day when poverty will be banished from this nation.

Herbert Hoover, 1928

The Republican "Old Guard" Returns

Handsome President Harding—with erect figure (6 feet), broad shoulders, high forehead, bushy eyebrows, and graying hair—was one of the best-liked men of his generation. An easygoing, warm-handed first-namer, he exuded graciousness and love of people. Yet the amiable, smiling exterior concealed a weak, flabby interior.

Harding, like Grant, was unable to detect moral halitosis in his evil associates, and he was soon surrounded by his poker-playing, shirt-sleeved cronies of the "Ohio gang." He hated to hurt people's feelings, especially those of his friends, by saying "no"; and designing political leeches capitalized on this weakness. He "was not a bad man," said one Washington observer. "He was just a slob."

Well-intentioned but weak-willed, Harding was a perfect "front" for enterprising industrialists. A McKinley-style old order settled heavily back into place at war's end, crushing the reform seedlings that had sprouted in the Progressive Era. This new Old Guard hoped to improve on the old business doctrine of laissez-faire. Their plea was not simply for

government to keep hands off business but for government to help guide business along the path to profits. They subtly and effectively achieved their ends by putting the courts and the administrative bureaus into the safekeeping of fellow standpatters.

The Supreme Court was a striking example of this trend. Harding lived less than three years as president, but he appointed four of the nine justices. In the first years of the 1920s, the Supreme Court axed progressive legislation. It killed a federal child labor law, stripped away many of labor's hard-won gains, and rigidly restricted governmental intervention in the economy. In the landmark case of *Adkins* v. *Children's Hospital* (1923), the Court reversed its own reasoning in *Muller* v. *Oregon* (see p. 441), and invalidated a minimum wage law for women. Its strained ruling was that because females now had the vote (Nineteenth Amendment), they could no longer be protected by special legislation. The contradictory premises of the *Muller* and *Adkins* cases framed a debate over gender differences that would continue for the rest of the century: were women sufficiently different from men that they merited special legal and social treatment, or were they effectively equal in the eyes of the law and therefore undeserving of special protection and preferences?

Corporations, under Harding, could once more relax and expand. Antitrust laws were often ignored, circumvented, or feebly upheld by friendly prosecutors in the attorney general's office. The Interstate Commerce Commission, to single out one agency, came to be dominated by members who were sympathetic to the managers of the railroads.

Big industrialists, striving to lessen competition, now had a free hand to set up trade associations. Cement manufacturers, for example, would use these agencies to agree upon standardization of product, publicity campaigns, and a united front in dealing with the railroads and labor. Although many of these associations ran counter to the spirit of existing antitrust legislation, their formation was encouraged by Secretary of Commerce Herbert Hoover. His sense of engineering efficiency was shocked by the waste resulting from cutthroat competition.

The Aftermath of War

Wartime government controls on the economy were swiftly dismantled. The War Industries Board disappeared with almost indecent haste. With its passing, progressive hopes for more government regulation of big business evaporated.

Washington likewise returned the railroads to private management in 1920. The Esch-Cummins Transportation Act of 1920 encouraged private consolidation of the railroads and obligated the federal Interstate Commerce Commission to guarantee their profitability. The new philosophy was not to save the country from the railroads, as in the days of the Populists, but to save the railroads for the country.

The federal government also tried to pull up anchor and get out of the shipping business. The Merchant Marine Act of 1920 authorized the Shipping Board, which controlled about 1,500 vessels, to dispose of much of the hastily built wartime fleet at bargain basement prices.

Labor, suddenly deprived of its wartime crutch of friendly government support, limped along badly in the postwar decade. A bloody strike in the steel

Race Riot, Chicago, 1919 *The policeman apparently arrived too late to spare this victim from being pelted by stones from an angry mob.*

industry was ruthlessly broken in 1919, partly by exploiting ethnic and racial divisions among the steelworkers, and partly by branding the strikers as dangerous "Reds." The Railway Labor Board, a successor body to the wartime labor boards, ordered a wage cut of 12 percent in 1922, provoking a two-month strike. It ended when Attorney General Harry Daugherty, who fully shared Harding's big-business bias, clamped on the strikers one of the most sweeping injunctions in American history. Unions wilted in this hostile political environment, and membership dropped by nearly 30 percent between 1920 and 1930.

Vicious race riots also rocked the republic in the years following the Great War. The prospect of fat pay envelopes in smoking war plants had sucked thousands of blacks out of the South into such northern industrial cities as New York and Chicago. The war thus kicked off a historic exodus that redistributed America's black population, with lasting social and political effects. But in the immediate postwar period, blacks were brutally taught that the North was not a promised land. A racial reign of terror descended on Chicago in the summer of 1919, leaving twenty-three blacks and fifteen whites dead. Clashes also inflamed Knoxville, Omaha, Washington, and other cities.

Needy veterans were among the few nonbusiness groups to reap lasting gains from the war. In 1921 Congress created the Veterans' Bureau to operate hospitals and provide vocational rehabilitation for the disabled. The American Legion, founded in Paris in 1919 by Colonel Theodore Roosevelt, Jr., became known for its militant conservatism and aggressive lobbying for veterans' benefits. It pressed fervently for "adjusted compensation" to make up for the wages veterans had "lost" while in uniform. Harding vetoed one such bill in 1922, but in 1924 Congress passed the Adjusted Compensation Act over President Calvin Coolidge's veto. It gave every former soldier a paid-up insurance policy due in twenty years—adding about $3.5 billion to the total cost of the war.

Isolationism and the Washington Conference

Isolation was enthroned in Washington during the Harding administration. With the Senate "irreconcilables" holding a hatchet over its head, the U.S. government continued to regard the League of Nations as a thing unclean.

But disarmament was one international issue on which Harding set isolationism aside and seized the initiative. He was prodded by businesspeople unwilling to dig deeper into their pockets for money to finance the ambitious naval building program started during the war. A deadly contest was shaping up with Britain and Japan, which watched with alarm as the oceans filled with American vessels. Britain still commanded the world's largest navy, but the clatter of American riveters proclaimed that the United States would soon overtake it. Tensions ran especially high in East Asia, where the Japanese were growing increasingly restive. Anxieties were further heightened by a long-standing Anglo-Japanese alliance (signed in 1902), which apparently obligated

the British to join with Japan in the event of war between Japan and the United States.

Public agitation in America, fed by these worries, brought about the headline-making Washington Disarmament Conference in 1921–1922. The double agenda included naval disarmament and the situation in East Asia.

At the outset, Secretary of State Charles Evans Hughes submitted a comprehensive plan for declaring a ten-year "holiday" on construction of battleships, and even for scrapping some of the huge dreadnoughts already built or being built. He proposed that the scaled-down navies of America and Britain should enjoy parity in battleships and aircraft carriers, with Japan on the small end of a 5-5-3 ratio.

Complex bargaining followed in the wake of Hughes's proposals. The Five-Power Naval Treaty of 1922 embodied Hughes's ideas on ship ratios, but only after face-saving compensation was offered to the Japanese. Both the British and the Americans conceded that they would refrain from fortifying their East Asian possessions, including the Philippines. The Japanese were not subjected to such restraints in their possessions. In addition, a four-power treaty replaced the Anglo-Japanese alliance. The new pact bound Britain, Japan, France, and the United States to preserve the status quo in the Pacific—another concession to the Japanese. Finally, the Washington Conference gave chaotic China— "the sick man of East Asia"—a shot in the arm with the Nine-Power Treaty of 1922, whose signatories agreed to nail wide open the Open Door in China.

The Hardingites boasted of this globe-shaking achievement in disarmament, but their satisfaction was somewhat illusory. No restrictions had been placed on small warships, and the other powers churned ahead with the construction of cruisers, destroyers, and submarines, while penny-pinching Uncle Sam lagged dangerously behind. Ominously, the American people seemed content to rely for their security on words and wishful thinking rather than weapons and hardheaded realism.

A similar sentimentalism welled up later in the decade, when Americans clamored for the "outlawry of war," on the theory that if nations would only pledge to forswear war, swords could be beaten into plowshares. The Kellogg-Briand Pact, declaring war illegal, was signed by Coolidge's secretary of state and the French foreign minister in 1928 and was ultimately ratified by sixty-two nations. It was delusory in the extreme. Lacking both muscles and teeth, it was a diplomatic derelict, and virtually useless in a showdown. Yet it accurately—and dangerously—reflected the American mind in the 1920s, which was all too ready to be lulled into a false sense of security. This mood took even deeper hold in the ostrichlike neutralism of the 1930s.

Hiking the Tariff Higher

A comparable lack of realism afflicted foreign economic policy in the 1920s. Businessmen, shortsightedly obsessed with the dazzling prospects in the prosperous home market, sought to keep that market to themselves by flinging up high, virtually unclimbable, tariff walls around the United States. With glib lobbyists in full attendance, Congress passed the Fordney-McCumber Tariff Law of 1922, which boosted schedules from the average of 27 percent under Wilson's Underwood Tariff of 1913 to an average of 38.5 percent.

The high-tariff course thus charted by the Republican regimes set off an ominous chain reaction. European producers felt the squeeze, for the American tariff walls prolonged the postwar chaos. An impoverished Europe needed to sell its manufactured goods to the United States, particularly if it hoped to achieve economic recovery and to pay its huge war debt to Washington. America needed to give foreign nations a chance to make a profit from it so that they could buy its manufactured articles and repay debts. International trade, Americans were slow to learn, is a two-way street. In general, they could not sell to others in quantity unless they bought from them in quantity—or lent them more U.S. dollars.

Erecting tariff walls was a game that two could play. The American example spurred European nations, throughout the feverish 1920s, to pile up higher barriers themselves. The whole vicious circle further deepened the international economic distress, providing one more rung on the ladder by which Adolf Hitler scrambled to power.

The Stench of Scandal

The loose morality and get-rich-quickism of the Harding era manifested themselves spectacularly in a series of scandals.

Early in 1923 the head of the Veterans' Bureau, Colonel Charles R. Forbes, was caught with his hand in the till and resigned. An appointee of the gullible Harding, he and his accomplices looted the government to the tune of about $200 million, chiefly in connection with the building of veterans' hospitals. He was sentenced to two years in a federal penitentiary.

Most shocking of all was the Teapot Dome scandal, an affair that involved priceless naval oil reserves at Teapot Dome (Wyoming) and Elk Hills (California). In 1921 the slippery secretary of the interior, Albert B. Fall, induced his careless colleague, Secretary of the Navy Denby, to transfer these valuable properties to the Interior Department. Harding indiscreetly signed the secret order. Fall then quietly leased the lands to oilmen Harry F. Sinclair and Edward L. Doheny, but not until he had received a bribe ("loan") of $100,000 from Doheny and about three times that amount in all from Sinclair.

Teapot Dome, no tempest in a teapot, finally came to a whistling boil. Details of the crooked transaction leaked out in March 1923. Fall, Sinclair, and Doheny were indicted in 1924. Fall was found guilty of taking a bribe and sentenced to one year in jail. The two bribe givers were acquitted, though Sinclair served time in jail for "shadowing" jurors and for refusing to testify before a Senate committee.

Other scandals erupted. Persistent reports about the underhanded doings of Attorney General Daugherty brought a Senate investigation in 1924 of the illegal sale of pardons and liquor permits. Forced to resign, the accused official was tried in 1927 but was released after a jury twice failed to agree on a verdict. During the trial, Daugherty hid behind the trousers of the now-dead Harding by implying that persistent probing might uncover crookedness in the White House.

Harding was mercifully spared the full revelation of these iniquities. Just as the scandals were

The Cash Register Chorus *Business croons its appreciation of "Coolidge prosperity."*

breaking, he died in San Francisco on August 2, 1923, of pneumonia and thrombosis.

The brutal fact is that Harding simply was not a strong enough man for the presidency—as he himself privately admitted. Such was his weakness that he tolerated people and conditions that subjected the republic to its worst disgrace since the days of President Grant.

Calvin Coolidge: A Yankee in the White House

News of Harding's death was sped to Vice President Coolidge, then visiting at his father's New England farmhouse. By the light of two kerosene lamps the elder Coolidge, a justice of the peace, used the old family bible to administer the presidential oath to his son.

This homespun setting was symbolic of Coolidge. Quite unlike Harding, the stern-faced Vermonter, with his thin nose and tightly set lips, embodied the New England virtues of honesty, morality, industry, and frugality. His dour, serious visage prompted the acerbic observation that he had been "weaned on a pickle."

Coolidge seemed to be a crystallization of the commonplace. A painfully shy individual of average height (5 feet 10 inches), he was blessed with only mediocre powers of leadership. He would occasionally flash a dry wit in private; but his speeches, delivered in a nasal New England twang, were invariably boring. A staunch apostle of the status quo, he became the "high priest of the great god Business." He believed that "the man who builds a factory builds a temple" and that "the man who works there worships there." Coolidge "luck" held during his five and a half prosperity-blessed years.

Ever a profile in caution, Coolidge slowly gave the Harding regime a badly needed moral fumigation. Teapot Dome had scalded the Republican party badly, but so transparently honest was the vinegary Vermonter that the scandalous oil did not rub off on him.

Frustrated Farmers

Sun-bronzed farmers were squarely in a boom-or-bust cycle in the postwar decade. While the fighting had raged, they had raked in money, hand over gnarled fist; but peace ended high farm prices.

Machines also threatened to plow the farmer under an avalanche of his own overabundant crops. The gasoline-engine tractor was working a revolution on American farms. This steel mule was to cultivation and sowing what the McCormick reaper was to harvesting. Blue-denimed farmers could sit on their chugging mechanical chariots and harrow many acres in a single day. They could grow bigger crops on larger areas, using fewer horses and hired hands. The wartime boom had encouraged them to bring vast new tracts under cultivation, especially in the "wheat belt" of the upper Midwest. But such improved efficiency and expanded agricultural acreage helped to pile up more price-dampening surpluses. A withering depression swept through agricultural districts in the 1920s, when one farm in four was sold for debt or taxes.

Schemes abounded for bringing relief to the hard-pressed farmers. A bipartisan "farm bloc" from

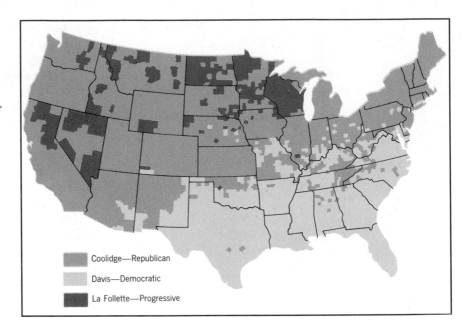

Presidential Election of 1924 (showing popular vote by county) *Note the concentration of La Follette's votes in the old Populist strongholds of the Midwest and the mountain states. His ticket did especially well in the grain-growing districts battered by the postwar slump in agricultural prices.*

Coolidge—Republican
Davis—Democratic
La Follette—Progressive

the agricultural states sprouted up in Congress in 1921 and succeeded in driving through some helpful laws. Noteworthy was the Capper-Volstead Act, which exempted farmers' marketing cooperatives from antitrust prosecution. The farm bloc's favorite proposal was the McNary-Haugen Bill, pushed energetically from 1924 to 1928. It sought to keep agricultural prices high by authorizing the government to buy up surpluses and sell them abroad. Government losses were to be made up by a special tax on the farmers. Congress twice passed the bill, but frugal Coolidge twice vetoed it. Farm prices stayed down, and the farmers' political temperatures stayed high, reaching fever pitch in the election of 1924.

A Three-Way Race for the White House in 1924

Self-satisfied Republicans, chanting "Keep cool and keep Coolidge," nominated "Silent Cal" for the presidency at their convention in Cleveland in the simmering summer of 1924. Squabbling Democrats had more difficulty choosing a candidate when they met in New York's sweltering Madison Square Garden. Reflecting many of the cultural tensions of the decade, the party was hopelessly split between

"wets" and "drys," urbanites and farmers, Fundamentalists and Modernists, northern liberals and southern standpatters, immigrants and old-stock Americans.

Deadlocked for an unprecedented 102 ballots, the convention at last turned wearily, sweatily, and unenthusiastically to John W. Davis. A wealthy corporation lawyer connected with the Wall Street banking house of J. P. Morgan and Company, the polished nominee was no less conservative than cautious Calvin Coolidge.

The field was now wide open for a liberal candidate. The white-pompadoured Senator Robert ("Fighting Bob") La Follette of Wisconsin sprang forward to lead a new Progressive grouping. He gained the endorsement of the American Federation of Labor and enjoyed the support of the Socialist party, but his major constituency was made up of the price-pinched farmers. La Follette's new Progressive party, only a shadow of the robust progressive coalition of prewar days, called for government ownership of railroads and relief for farmers, lashed out at monopoly and antilabor injunctions, and urged a constitutional amendment to limit the Supreme Court's power to invalidate laws passed by Congress.

La Follette turned in a respectable showing, polling nearly 5 million votes. But "Cautious Cal" and the oil-bespattered Republicans slipped easily back into office, overwhelming Davis, 15,718,211 votes to 8,385,283. The electoral count stood at 382 for Coolidge, 136 for Davis, and 13 for La Follette, all from his home state of Wisconsin.

Foreign Policy Flounderings

Isolation continued to reign in the Coolidge era. Despite presidential proddings, the Senate proved unwilling to allow America to adhere to the World Court—the judicial arm of the still-suspect League of Nations. Coolidge only half-heartedly—and unsuccessfully—pursued further naval disarmament after the loudly trumpeted agreements worked out at the Washington Conference in 1922.

A glaring exception to the United States' inward-looking indifference to the outside world in the 1920s was the armed interventionism in the Caribbean and Central America. American troops were withdrawn (after an eight-year stay) from the Dominican Republic in 1924, but they remained in Haiti from 1914 to 1934. President Coolidge in 1925 briefly removed American bayonets from troubled Nicaragua, where they had glinted intermittently since 1909, but in 1926 he sent them back, 5,000 strong, and they stayed until 1933. American oil companies clamored for a military expedition to Mexico in 1926 when the Mexican government began to assert its sovereignty over oil resources. Coolidge kept cool and defused the Mexican crisis with some skillful diplomatic negotiating. But his mailed-fist tactics elsewhere bred sore resentments south of the Rio Grande, where critics loudly assailed "*yanqui* imperialism."

Overshadowing all other foreign policy problems in the 1920s was the knotty issue of international debts, a complicated tangle of private loans, Allied war debts, and German reparations. The key knot in the debt tangle was the $10 billion that the U.S. Treasury had loaned to the Allies during and immediately after the war. Uncle Sam held their IOUs—and he wanted to be paid. The Allies, in turn, protested that they had held up a wall of flesh and bone against the common foe until America the Unready had entered the fray. America, they argued, should write off its loans as war costs, just as the Allies had been tragically forced to write off the lives of millions of young men. And the final straw, protested the Europeans, was that America's postwar tariff walls made it almost impossible for them to sell the goods to earn the dollars to pay their debts.

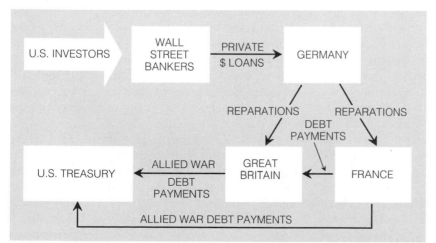

Aspects of the Financial Merry-Go-Round, 1921–1933 *Great Britain, with a debt of over $4 billion to the U.S. Treasury, had a huge stake in proposals for inter-Allied debt cancellation, but France's stake was even larger. Less prosperous than Britain in the 1920s, and more battered by the war, which had been fought on its soil, France owned nearly $3.5 billion to the United States, and additional billions to Britain.*

Unraveling the Debt Knot

America's tightfisted insistence on getting its money back helped to harden the hearts of the Allies against conquered Germany. The French and the British demanded that the Germans make enormous reparations payments, totaling some $32 billion, as compensation for war-inflicted damages. The Allies hoped to settle their debts to America with the money received from Germany. The French, seeking to extort lagging reparations payments, sent troops into Germany's industrialized Ruhr valley in 1923. Berlin responded by permitting its currency to inflate astronomically. At one point in October 1923, a loaf of bread cost 480 million marks, or about $120 million in preinflation money. German society teetered on the brink of mad anarchy, and the whole international house of financial cards threatened to flutter down in colossal chaos.

Sensible statesmen now urged that war debts and reparations alike be drastically scaled down or even canceled outright. But to Americans such proposals smacked of "welshing" on a debt. Scrooge-like, Calvin Coolidge turned aside suggestions of debt cancellation with a typically terse question: "They hired the money, didn't they?" The Washington administration proved especially unrealistic in its dogged insistence that there was no connection whatever between debts and reparations.

Reality finally was partly recognized in the Dawes Plan of 1924. Negotiated largely by Charles Dawes, about to be Coolidge's running mate, it rescheduled German reparations payments and opened the way for further American private loans to Germany. The whole financial cycle now became still more complicated as U.S. bankers loaned money to Germany, Germany paid reparations to France and Britain, and the former Allies paid war debts to the United States. Clearly the source of this monetary merry-go-round was the flowing well of American credit. When that well dried up after the great crash in 1929, the tangled jungle of international finance quickly turned into a desert.

The United States never did get its money, but it harvested a bumper crop of ill will. Throughout Europe Uncle Sam was caricatured as Uncle Shylock, greedily whetting his knife for the last pound of Allied flesh. The bad taste left in American mouths by the whole sorry episode contributed powerfully to the storm-cellar neutrality legislation passed by Congress in the 1930s.

The Triumph of Herbert Hoover, 1928

Poker-faced Calvin Coolidge, the tight-lipped "Sphinx of the Potomac," apparently bowed himself out of the 1928 presidential race when he tersely announced, "I do not choose to run." His logical successor was super-Secretary (of Commerce) Herbert Hoover. He was nominated on a platform that clucked contentedly over both prosperity and prohibition.

Still-squabbling Democrats nominated Alfred E. Smith, the wisecracking, glad-handing governor of New York. "Al (cohol)" Smith was soaking wet on prohibition, abrasively urban, and Roman Catholic in an overwhelmingly Protestant—and unfortunately prejudiced—land. Many dry, rural, and Fundamentalist Democrats gagged on his candidacy, and they saddled Smith with a dry running mate and a dry platform.

Radio figured prominently in this campaign for the first time, and it helped Hoover more than Smith. The New Yorker had more personal sparkle, but he could not project it through the radio. Iowa-born Hoover, with his double-breasted dignity, came out of the microphone better than he went in.

Chubby-faced, ruddy-complexioned Herbert Hoover, with his painfully high starched collar, was a living example of the American success story, and an intriguing mixture of two centuries. As a poor orphan boy who had worked his way through Stanford University, he had absorbed the nineteenth-century copybook maxims of industry, thrift, and self-reliance. As a fabulously successful mining engineer and businessman, he had honed to a high degree the efficiency doctrines of the Progressive Era.

A small-town boy from Iowa and Oregon, he had traveled and worked overseas extensively. His experiences abroad had further strengthened his faith in American individualism, free enterprise, and small government.

As befitted America's newly mechanized civilization, Hoover was the ideal businessperson's candidate. A self-made millionaire, he recoiled from anything suggesting socialism, paternalism, or "planned economy." Yet as secretary of commerce, he had exhibited some progressive instincts. He endorsed labor unions and supported federal regulation of the new radio industry. He even flirted for a time with the idea of government-owned radio, similar to the British Broadcasting Corporation (BBC).

Despite the best efforts of Hoover and Smith, below-the-belt tactics were employed by their lower-level campaigners. Religious bigotry raised its hideous head over Smith's Catholicism. A whispering campaign claimed that "A vote for Al Smith is a vote for the Pope" and that the White House, under Smith, would become a branch of the Vatican.

Hoover triumphed in a landslide. He bagged 21,391,993 popular votes to 15,016,169 for his embittered opponent, while rolling up an electoral count of 444 to 87. A huge Republican majority was returned to the House of Representatives. Tens of thousands of dry southern Democrats—"Hoovercrats"—rebelled against Al Smith. Hoover swept all the border states and carried five states of the former Confederacy.

President Hoover's First Moves

Prosperity in the late 1920s smiled broadly as the Hoover years began. Soaring stocks on the bull market continued to defy the laws of financial gravity. But two immense groups of citizens were not getting their share of the riches flowing from the national cornucopia: the unorganized wage earners and especially the disorganized farmers.

Hoover's administration, in line with its philosophy of promoting self-help, responded to the outcry of the farmers with the Agricultural Marketing Act. Passed by Congress in June 1929, it was designed to help the farmers help themselves, largely through producers' cooperatives. It set up a Federal Farm Board, with a revolving fund of half a billion dollars at its disposal. Money was lent generously to farm organizations seeking to buy, sell, and store agricultural surpluses.

Herbert Hoover Campaigning in Tennessee, 1928 *A gifted administrator and public policy analyst, Hoover was stiff and uncomfortable on the campaign trail. His lack of political skills hurt him badly when the Great Depression began in 1929.*

In 1930 the Farm Board itself created both the Grain Stabilization Corporation and the Cotton Stabilization Corporation. The prime goal was to bolster sagging prices by buying up surpluses. But the two agencies were soon suffocated by an avalanche of farm produce, as wheat dropped to fifty-seven cents a bushel and cotton to five cents a pound.

Farmers had meanwhile clutched at the tariff as a possible straw to keep their heads above the water of financial ruin. But the Hawley-Smoot Tariff of 1930, which started out as a modest measure to assist farmers, acquired more than a thousand amendments and turned into the highest protective tariff in the nation's peacetime history. The average duty was raised from 38.5 percent to nearly 60 percent. To angered foreigners, the Hawley-Smoot Tariff seemed a declaration of economic warfare. It widened the yawning trade gaps and plunged both America and other nations deeper into the terrible depression that had already begun. It forced the United States further into the bog of economic isolationism, which played directly into the demagogic hands of Adolf Hitler.

The Great Crash Ends the Golden Twenties

When Herbert Hoover confidently took the presidential oath on March 4, 1929, America's productive colossus—stimulated by the automobile, radio, movie, and other new industries—was roaring along at a dizzy speed that suggested a permanent plateau of prosperity. Prices on the stock exchange continued to spiral upward and create a fool's paradise of paper profits. A few prophets of disaster raised warning voices, but they were drowned out by the mad chatter of the ticker-tape machine.

A catastrophic crash came on "Black Tuesday," October 29, 1929, when 16,410,030 shares of stock were sold in a save-who-may scramble. Wall Street became a wailing wall as gloom and doom replaced boom. Losses, even in blue-chip securities, were fantastic. By the end of 1929—two months after the initial crash—stockholders had lost $40 billion in paper values, or more than the total cost of World War I to the United States.

The stock market collapse heralded a business depression, at home and abroad, that was the most prolonged and withering in American or world experience. No other industrialized nation suffered so severe a setback. By the end of 1930, more than 4 million workers in the United States were jobless; two years later the figure had about tripled. Hungry and despairing workers pounded pavements in search of nonexistent jobs ("We're firing, not hiring"). When employees were not discharged, wages and salaries were often slashed.

The misery and gloom were incalculable, as forests of dead factory chimneys stood starkly against

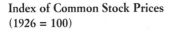
Index of Common Stock Prices
(1926 = 100)

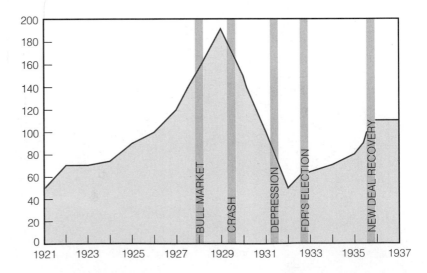

the sky. Over 5,000 banks collapsed in the first three years of the depression, carrying down with them the life savings of tens of thousands of widows and retired citizens. Countless thousands of honest, hard-working people lost their homes and farms to the forecloser's hammer. Bread lines formed, soup kitchens dispensed food, and apple sellers stood shivering on street corners trying to peddle their wares for five cents. Families felt the stress, as jobless fathers nursed their guilt and shame at not being able to provide for their households. Breadless breadwinners often blamed themselves for their plight, despite abundant evidence that the economic system, not individual initiative, had broken down. Mothers meanwhile nursed fewer babies, as hard times reached even into the nation's bedrooms, precipitating a decade-long dearth of births. As cash registers gathered cobwebs, the song "My God, How the Money Rolls In" gave way to "Brother, Can You Spare a Dime?"

Hooked on the Horn of Plenty

What caused the Great Depression? One basic explanation was overproduction by both farm and factory. Ironically, the depression of the 1930s, was one of abundance, not want. It was the "great glut" or the "plague of plenty."

The nation's ability to produce goods had clearly outrun its capacity to consume or pay for them. Too much money was going into the hands of a few wealthy people, who in turn invested it in factories and other agencies of production. Not enough was going into salaries and wages, where revitalizing purchasing power could be more quickly felt.

This already bleak picture was further darkened by economic anemia abroad. Britain and the Continent had never fully recovered from the upheaval of World War I. A drying up of international trade, moreover, had been hastened by the shortsighted Hawley-Smoot Tariff of 1930.

By 1930 the depression had become a national calamity. Through no fault of their own, a host of industrious citizens had lost everything. The blighting effect of all this dazed despair on the spirit was incalculable and long lasting. Hitherto the people had grappled with storms, trees, stones, and other physical obstacles. But the depression was a baffling wraith they could not grasp. Panhandlers begged for food or "charity soup." In extreme cases "ragged individualists" slept under "Hoover blankets" (old newspapers), fought over the contents of garbage cans, or cooked their findings in old oil drums in tin-and-paper shantytowns cynically named "Hoovervilles." The very foundations of America's social structure trembled.

Rugged Times for Rugged Individualists

Hoover's exalted reputation as a wonder worker and efficiency engineer crashed about as dismally as the stock market. The perplexed president was impaled on the horns of a cruel dilemma. As a deservedly famed humanitarian, he was profoundly distressed by the widespread misery about him. Yet as a "rugged individualist," deeply rooted in an earlier era of free enterprise, he shrank from the heresy of government handouts. Convinced that industry, thrift, and self-reliance were the virtues that had made America great, he feared that a government doling out doles would weaken, or perhaps destroy, the national fiber.

The president at last worked out a compromise between the old hands-off philosophy and the "soul-destroying" direct dole then being used in Britain. He would assist the hard-pressed railroads, banks, and rural credit corporations, in the hope that if financial health were restored at the top of the economic pyramid, unemployment would be relieved at the bottom on a trickle-down basis.

Early in 1932 Congress, responding to Hoover's belated appeal, established the Reconstruction Finance Corporation (RFC). With an initial working capital of half a billion dollars, this agency became a government lending bank. It was designed to provide indirect relief by assisting insurance companies, banks, agricultural organizations, railroads, and even hard-pressed state and local governments. But to preserve individualism and character, there would be no loans to individuals from this "billion-dollar soup kitchen."

"Pump-priming" loans by the RFC were no doubt of widespread benefit, though the organization was established many months too late for maxi-

Home Relief Station, **by Louis Ribak** *Destitute and despairing, millions of hard-working Americans like these had to endure the degradation and humiliation of going on relief as the pall of depression descended over the land.*

mum usefulness. Projects that it supported were largely self-liquidating, and the government as a banker actually profited to the tune of many millions of dollars. Giant corporations so obviously benefited from this assistance that the RFC was dubbed—rather unfairly—"the millionaires' dole."

Hoover's administration also provided some indirect benefits for labor. After stormy debate, Congress passed the Norris–La Guardia Anti-Injunction Act in 1932, and Hoover signed it. The measure outlawed "yellow dog" (antiunion) contracts and forbade the federal courts to issue injunctions to restrain strikes, boycotts, and peaceful picketing.

The truth is that Herbert Hoover, despite criticism of his "heartlessness," did inaugurate a significant new policy. In previous panics the masses had been forced to "sweat it out." Slow though Hoover was to abandon this nineteenth-century bias, by the end of his term he had traveled a long way toward government assistance for needy citizens—a road that Franklin Roosevelt was to take all the way.

Routing the Bonus Army in Washington

Many veterans of World War I were numbered among the hard-hit victims of the depression. They began to clamor for the premature payment of the deferred "adjusted compensation" (see p. 495) voted by Congress in 1924 and payable in 1945.

Thousands of impoverished veterans, both of war and of unemployment, prepared to move on Washington, there to demand of Congress the immediate payment of their *entire* bonus. The "Bonus Expeditionary Force" (BEF), which mustered about 20,000 souls, converged on the capital in the summer of 1932. These supplicants promptly set up unsanitary public camps on vacant lots—a gigantic Hooverville.

Following riots that cost two lives, Hoover ordered the army to evacuate the unwanted guests. The eviction was carried out by General Douglas MacArthur with bayonets and tear gas, and with far more severity than Hoover had planned. A few of the former soldiers were injured as the torch was put to their pathetic shanties in the inglorious "Battle of Anacostia Flats." An eleven-month-old "bonus baby" allegedly died from exposure to tear gas.

This brutal episode brought down additional condemnation on the once-popular Hoover, who by now was the most loudly booed man in the country. The Democrats, not content with his vulnerable record, employed professional "smear" artists to drive him from office. The existing panic was unfairly branded "the Hoover depression." In truth, Hoover had been oversold as a superman—and the public grumbled when his magician's wand failed to produce rabbits. The time was ripening for the Democratic party—and Franklin D. Roosevelt—to cash in on Hoover's calamities.

Japanese Aggressors and Latin American Good Neighbors

The Great Depression, which brewed enough distress at home, added immensely to difficulties abroad. Rampaging Japan stole the East Asian spotlight. In September 1931, the Japanese imperialists, noting that the Western world was badly mired down in depression, lunged into Manchuria. Alleging provocation, they rapidly overran the coveted Chinese province and proceeded to bolt shut the Open Door in the conquered area.

Peaceful peoples were stunned by this act of naked aggression. Numerous indignant Americans, though by no means a majority, urged strong measures, ranging from boycotts to blockades. Possibly a tight blockade by the League of Nations, backed by the United States, would have brought Japan sharply to book. But the League was handicapped in taking two-fisted action by the nonmembership of the United States. Washington flatly rebuffed initial attempts in 1931 to secure American cooperation in applying economic pressures.

Hoover and Secretary of State Henry L. Stimson decided in the end to fire only paper bullets at the Japanese aggressors. The so-called Stimson doctrine, proclaimed in 1932, declared that the United States would not recognize any territorial acquisitions achieved by force. Righteous indignation—or a preach-and-run policy—would substitute for vigor-

ous initiatives. But there was no real sentiment for stronger measures among a depression-ridden people who remained strongly isolationist during the 1930s.

Hoover's arrival at the White House brought a more hopeful turn to relations with America's southern neighbors. The new president was deeply interested in the lands below the Rio Grande; shortly after his election he had undertaken a goodwill tour of Latin America—on a U.S. battleship.

Hoover strove to abandon the interventionist twist given to the Monroe Doctrine by Theodore Roosevelt. In 1932 he negotiated a new treaty with Haiti that provided for the complete withdrawal of American bayonets by 1934. Further pleasing omens came early in 1933, when the last marine leathernecks sailed away from Nicaragua after an almost continuous stay of some twenty years.

Herbert Hoover, the engineer in politics, thus engineered the foundations of the "Good Neighbor" policy. Upon them rose an imposing edifice in the days of his successor, Franklin Roosevelt.

Varying Viewpoints

Many American historians have been "liberals," and this political preference has strongly colored writing about the 1920s. The three Republican presidents of the decade are therefore often seen as a mere reactionary interlude in the forward march of liberal reform that is supposedly the main theme of American society in the present century. Such an interpretation is conspicuous in John D. Hick's *Republican Ascendancy.*

Yet later historians raised many questions about this judgment. As scholars increasingly distinguished progressivism from the New Deal, they naturally asked what, if anything, the 1920s "interrupted." And when "New Left" critics in the 1960s pooh-poohed the reform character of progressivism and of the New Deal itself, they implicitly suggested that the 1920s carried forward the essentially *conservative* course of modern American history.

Herbert Hoover's changing historical reputation illustrates these trends. Long criticized as a doctrinaire, *laissez-faire* conservative, Hoover was partly rehabilitated in the 1970s when skepticism about big, activist government spread in the wake of Vietnam and the Watergate scandal. Hoover's historical standing will probably continue to serve as a kind of barometer of attitudes toward government. And debate continues as to whether the 1920s represented a conservative triumph, a conservative debacle, or simply another episode, however dramatic, in the ongoing saga of a highly individualistic, business-oriented capitalist society.

SELECT READINGS

Primary Source Documents

Herbert Hoover, *American Individualism* (1922), contains the philosophy of the man and his times. See also Hoover's "Rugged Individualism" speech (1928), in Richard Hofstadter, *Great Issues in American History.* As the Great Depression descended, Hoover fought to maintain his principles in a noteworthy speech at New York's Madison Square Garden (*New York Times,* November 1, 1932).* On foreign affairs, see "The Stimson Doctrine" (1931), in Henry Steele Commager, ed., *Documents of American History.*

Secondary Sources

A lively introduction to the postwar decade is Burl Noggle, *Into the Twenties: The United States from Armistice to Normalcy* (1974). On Harding see Robert K. Murray's balanced *The Harding Era* (1969). David M. Kennedy, *Over Here: The First World War and American Society* (1980), discusses postwar race relations and demobilization, as well as the international economic aftermath of the war, a subject treated at greater length in Joan Hoff Wilson, *American Business and Foreign Policy, 1920–1933* (1971). The complicated international financial tangle of the 1920s is deftly discussed in Herbert Feis, *The Diplomacy of the Dollar* (1950), and in the early chapters of Charles Kindleberger, *The World in Depression* (1973). The best brief biography of Hoover is Joan Hoff Wilson, *Herbert Hoover: Forgotten Progressive* (1975). Brilliantly unsympathetic toward Hoover is Arthur M. Schlesinger, Jr., *The Crisis of the Old Order, 1919–1933* (1957). More favorable is David Burner, *Herbert Hoover: A Public Life* (1979). On the depression itself, consult John K. Galbraith's breezy *The Great Crash, 1929* (1955), Peter Temin's trenchant *Did Monetary Factors Cause the Great Depression?* (1976), Robert McElvaine's *The Great Depression* (1984), and Lester V. Chandler's comprehensive *America's Greatest Depression* (1970).

CHAPTER 35

The Great Depression and the New Deal, 1933–1938

The country needs and . . . demands bold, persistent experimentation. It is common sense to take a method and try it. If it fails, admit it frankly and try another. But above all, try something.

Franklin D. Roosevelt, campaign speech, 1932

FDR: A Politician in a Wheelchair

Voters were in an ugly mood as the presidential campaign of 1932 neared. Countless factory chimneys remained ominously cold, while more than 11 million unemployed workers and their families sank ever deeper into the pit of poverty.

Herbert Hoover, sick at heart, was renominated by the Republican convention in Chicago without great enthusiasm. The rising star in the Democratic firmament was Governor Franklin Delano Roosevelt of New York, a fifth cousin of Theodore Roosevelt. Like the Rough Rider, he had been born to a wealthy New York family, had graduated from Harvard, had been elected as a kid-gloved politician to the New York legislature, had served as governor of the Empire State, had been nominated for the vice-presidency (though not elected), and had served capably as assistant secretary of the navy.

Infantile paralysis, while putting steel braces on Franklin Roosevelt's legs, put additional steel into his soul. Until 1921, when the dread disease struck, young Roosevelt—tall (6 feet 2 inches), athletic, classic-featured, and as handsome as a Greek god—impressed observers as charming and witty yet at times a superficial and arrogant "lightweight." But suffering humbled him; courageously fighting his way back from complete helplessness to a hobbling mobility, he schooled himself in patience, tolerance, compassion, and strength of will. He once remarked that after trying for two years to wiggle one big toe, all else seemed easy.

Another of Roosevelt's great personal and political assets was his wife, Eleanor. The niece of Theodore Roosevelt, she was Franklin Roosevelt's distant cousin as well as his spouse. Tall, ungainly, and toothy, she overcame the misery of an unhappy childhood and emerged as a champion of the dispossessed—and ultimately as the "conscience of the New Deal." She was to become the most active First Lady in history. Through her lobbying of her husband, her speeches, and her syndicated newspaper column, she powerfully influenced the policies of the national government. Always, she battled for the impoverished and the oppressed. At one meeting in Birmingham, Alabama, she confounded local

Eleanor Roosevelt *She was America's most active First Lady and commanded enormous popularity and influence during the Roosevelt presidency. Here she emerges, miner's cap in hand, from an Ohio coal mine.*

authorities and flouted the segregation statutes by deliberately straddling the aisle separating the black and white seating sections. Sadly, her personal relationship with her husband was often rocky due to his occasional infidelity. Condemned by conservatives and loved by liberals, she was one of the most controversial—and consequential—public figures of the twentieth century.

Roosevelt's political appeal was amazing. His commanding presence and his golden speaking voice, despite a sophisticated accent, combined to make him the premier American orator of his generation. He could turn on charm in private conversations as one would turn on a faucet. As a popular

depression governor of New York, he had sponsored heavy state spending to relieve human suffering. Though favoring frugality, he believed that money, rather than humanity, was expendable. He revealed a deep concern for the plight of the "forgotten man"— a phrase he used in a 1932 speech—although he was assailed by the rich as a "traitor to his class."

Exuberant Democrats met in Chicago in June 1932 and speedily nominated Roosevelt, who flew daringly through stormy weather to Chicago to accept the nomination in person. He electrified the delegates and the public with these words: "I pledge you, I pledge myself to a new deal for the American people."

Roosevelt Routs Hoover in 1932

In the campaign that followed, Roosevelt consistently preached a New Deal for the forgotten man, but he was annoyingly vague and somewhat contradictory. Many of his speeches were ghost-written by the "Brains Trust" (popularly the "Brain Trust"), a small group of reform-minded intellectuals. They were predominantly youngish college professors, who, as a kind of kitchen cabinet, later authored much of the New Deal legislation. Roosevelt rashly promised a balanced budget and berated heavy Hooverian deficits. All this was to make ironic reading in later months.

Hoover had been swept into office on the rising tide of prosperity; he was swept out by the receding tide of depression. The flood of votes totaled 22,809,638 for Roosevelt and 15,758,901 for Hoover; the electoral count stood at 472 to 59. Hoover won only six rock-ribbed Republican states.

One striking feature of the election was a heavy shift of blacks from the Republican party of Lincoln to the Roosevelt camp. Beginning with the election of 1932, they became, notably in the great urban centers of the North, a vital element in the Democratic party.

Defeated and repudiated, the grim-faced Hoover remained president during four long months, until March 4, 1933. But he was helpless to embark upon any long-term policies without Roo-

Roosevelt Speaks on Radio, 1932 *FDR's smooth, confident radio voice made him seem like an intimate friend to millions of distressed Americans during the Great Depression, especially when he delivered his "fireside chats."*

sevelt's cooperation. In two meetings with Roosevelt on the war-debt issue, Hoover tried to bind his successor to an anti-inflationary policy that would have made impossible many of the later New Deal experiments. But Roosevelt refused to assume responsibility without authority, and airily remarked to the press, "It's not my baby."

With Washington deadlocked, the vast and vaunted American economic machine clanked to a virtual halt. One worker in four tramped the streets, feet weary and hands idle. Banks were locking their doors all over the nation, as people nervously stuffed paper money under their mattresses. Hooverites, then and later, accused Roosevelt of deliberately permitting the depression to worsen, so that he could emerge the more spectacularly as a savior.

FDR and the Three Rs: Relief, Recovery, and Reform

Great crises often call forth gifted leaders; and the hand of destiny tapped Roosevelt on the shoulder. On a dreary inauguration day, March 4, 1933, his vibrant voice provided the American people with inspirational new hope. He denounced the "money changers" who had brought on the calamity, and declared that the government must wage war on the Great Depression as it would wage war on an armed foe. His clarion note was: "Let me assert my firm belief that the only thing we have to fear is fear itself."

Roosevelt moved decisively. Now that he had full responsibility, he boldly declared a nationwide banking holiday, March 6–10, as a prelude to opening the banks on a sounder basis. He then summoned the overwhelmingly Democratic Congress into special session to cope with the national emergency. For the so-called Hundred Days (March 9–June 16, 1933), members hastily ground out an unprecedented basketful of remedies.

Roosevelt's New Deal program was sparked by three Rs—relief, recovery, and reform. Short-range goals were relief and immediate recovery, especially in the first two years. Long-range goals were permanent recovery and reform of current abuses, particularly those that had produced the boom-and-bust catastrophe. The three-R objectives often overlapped and got in one another's way. But in all this haste and topsy-turviness, the gigantic New Deal program lurched forward.

Firmly ensconced in the driver's seat, President Roosevelt cracked the whip. A green Congress so fully shared the panicky feeling of the country that it was ready to rubber-stamp bills drafted by White House advisers. More than that, Congress gave the president extraordinary blank-check powers: some laws expressly delegated legislative authority to the chief executive.

Roosevelt was delighted to accept executive leadership. He was inclined to do things by intuition—off the cuff. He was like the quarterback, as he put it, whose next play depends on the success of the previous play. So desperate was the mood of the action-starved public that *any* movement, even in the wrong direction, seemed better than no movement at all.

The frantic Hundred Days Congress passed many essentials of the New Deal's three Rs, though

Principal New Deal Acts During Hundred Days Congress, 1933
(Items in parentheses indicate secondary purposes.)

Recovery	*Relief*	*Reform*
FDR closes banks, March 6, 1933		
Emergency Banking Relief Act, March 9, 1933		
(Beer Act)	(Beer Act)	Beer and Wine Revenue Act, March 22, 1933
(CCC)	Unemployment Relief Act, March 13, 1993, creates Civilian Conservation Corps (CCC)	
FDR orders gold surrender, April 5, 1933		
FDR abandons gold standard, April 19, 1933		
(FERA)	Federal Emergency Relief Act, May 12, 1933, creates Federal Emergency Relief Administration (FERA)	
(AAA)	Agricultural Adjustment Act (AAA), May 12, 1933	
(TVA)	(TVA)	Tennessee Valley Authority Act (TVA), May 18, 1933
		Federal Securities Act, May 27, 1933
Gold-payment clause repealed, June 5, 1933		
(HOLC)	Home Owners' Refinancing Act, June 13, 1933, creates Home Owners' Loan Corporation (HOLC)	
National Industrial Recovery Act, June 16, 1933, creates National Recovery Administration (NRA), Public Works Administration (PWA)	(NRA; PWA)	(NRA)
(Glass-Steagall Act)	(Glass-Steagall Act)	Glass-Steagall Banking Reform Act, June 16, 1933, creates Federal Deposit Insurance Corporation

For later New Deal measures, see p. 520.

important long-range measures were added in later sessions. These reforms owed much to the legacy of the pre–World War I progressive movement. Many of them were long overdue, side-tracked by World War I and the Old Guard reaction of the 1920s. The New Dealers, sooner or later, embraced such progressive ideas as unemployment insurance, old-age insurance, minimum-wage regulations, conservation and development of natural resources, and restrictions on child labor. Many of these forward-looking measures had been adopted a generation or so earlier by the more advanced countries of western Europe.

In the area of social welfare, the United States, in the eyes of many Europeans, remained a backward nation.

Roosevelt Tackles Money and Banking

Banking chaos cried aloud for immediate action. Congress pulled itself together, and in an incredible eight hours had the Emergency Banking Relief Act of 1933 ready for Roosevelt's busy pen. The new law clothed the president with power to regulate banking transactions and foreign exchange and to reopen solvent banks.

Roosevelt, the master showman, next turned to the radio to deliver the first of his thirty famous "fireside chats." As some 35 million people hung on his soothing words, he gave assurances that it was now safer to keep money in a reopened bank than "under the mattress." Confidence returned with a gush, as banks unlocked their doors.

The Hundred Days Congress also buttressed public reliance on the banking system by enacting the memorable Glass-Steagall Banking Reform Act. This measure provided for the Federal Deposit Insurance Corporation, which insured individual deposits up to $5,000 (later raised).

Roosevelt moved swiftly elsewhere on the financial front, seeking to protect the melting gold reserve and to prevent panicky hoarding. He ordered all private holdings of gold to be surrendered to the Treasury in exchange for paper currency and then took the nation off the gold standard.

The goal of Roosevelt's "managed currency" was inflation, which he believed would relieve debtors' burdens and stimulate new production. Roosevelt's principal instrument for achieving inflation was gold buying. He instructed the Treasury Department to purchase gold, ratcheting the dollar price of gold up from $21 an ounce in 1933 to $35 an ounce in 1934, a price that held for nearly four decades. This policy did increase the dollars in circulation, as holders of gold cashed it in at the newly elevated prices, although "sound money" critics assailed the "baloney dollar." The gold-buying scheme came to an end in February 1934, when FDR returned the nation to a limited gold standard for the purposes of international trade only. Thereafter

(until 1971—see p. 619), the United States pledged itself to pay foreign bills, if requested, in gold at the rate of one ounce of gold for every $35 due. But domestic circulation of gold continued to be prohibited, and gold coins became collectors' items.

Creating Jobs for the Jobless

Overwhelming unemployment clamored for prompt remedial action. One of four workers was jobless when FDR took his inaugural oath—the highest level of unemployment in the nation's history. Roosevelt had no hesitancy about using federal money to assist the unemployed, and at the same time to prime the pump of industrial recovery. (A farmer has to pour a little water into a dry pump to start the flow.)

The Hundred Days Congress responded to Roosevelt's spurs when it created the Civilian Conservation Corps (CCC). This agency provided employment in fresh-air government camps for about 3 million uniformed young men. Their work included reforestation, fire fighting, flood control, and swamp drainage. The recruits were required to help their parents by sending home most of their pay. Both human resources and natural resources were thus conserved, though there were minor complaints of "militarizing" the nation's youth.

The first major effort of the new Congress to grapple with the millions of adult unemployed was the Federal Emergency Relief Act. Its chief aim was immediate relief rather than long-range recovery. The resulting Federal Emergency Relief Administration (FERA) was handed over to zealous Harry L. Hopkins, a pauper-thin, shabbily dressed, chain-smoking New York social worker who had earlier won Roosevelt's friendship and who became one of his most influential advisers. Hopkins's agency finally granted about $3 billion to the states for direct dole payments or preferably for wages on work projects.

Immediate relief was also given to two large and hard-pressed special groups by the Hundred Days Congress. One section of the Agricultural Adjustment Act (AAA) made available many millions of dollars to help farmers meet their mortgages. Another law created the Home Owners' Loan Corporation (HOLC). Designed to refinance mortgages on nonfarm homes, it ultimately assisted about a million badly pinched households, while simultaneously bailing out mortgage-holding banks.

Harassed by the continuing plague of unemployment, FDR himself established the Civil Works Administration (CWA) under Hopkins's direction late in 1933. Designed to provide temporary jobs during the cruel winter emergency, it employed tens of thousands of jobless people in leaf raking and other make-work tasks. The CWA served a useful purpose, although it was heavily criticized as "boondoggling."

Direct relief from Washington to needy families helped pull the nation through the ghastly winter of 1933–1934. But the disheartening persistence of unemployment and suffering demonstrated that emergency relief measures must be not only continued but supplemented. One danger signal was the appearance of various demagogues, notably a magnetic "microphone messiah," Father Coughlin, a Catholic priest in Michigan who began broadcasting in 1930 with the slogan of "Social Justice." His anti–New Deal harangues to some 40 million radio fans finally became so anti-Semitic, fascistic, and demagogic that he was silenced in 1942 by his superiors.

Also notorious among the new brood of agitators were those who capitalized on popular discontent to make pie-in-the-sky promises. Most conspicuous of these individuals was Senator Huey P. ("Kingfish") Long of Louisiana, who used his rabble-rousing talents to publicize his "Share our wealth" program, which promised to make "every man a king." Every family was to receive $5,000, supposedly at the expense of the prosperous. Fear of Long's becoming a fascist dictator ended when he was shot by an assassin in the Louisiana state capitol in 1935.

Another Pied Piper was gaunt Dr. Francis E. Townsend of California, a retired physician whose savings had recently been wiped out. He attracted the pathetic support of perhaps 5 million "senior citizens" with his fantastic plan. Each person sixty years of age or over was to receive $200 a month, provided that the money was spent within the month. One estimate had the scheme costing one-half of the national income.

Partly to quiet the ground swell of unrest produced by such crackbrained proposals, Congress authorized the Works Progress Administration (WPA) in 1935. The objective was employment on useful projects. Launched under the supervision of the ailing but energetic Hopkins, this remarkable agency ultimately spent about $11 billion on thousands of public buildings, bridges, and hard-surfaced roads. It controlled crickets in Wyoming and built a monkey pen in Oklahoma City. Critics sneered that WPA meant "We Provide Alms," but the fact is that over a period of eight years nearly 9 million persons were given jobs, not handouts.

Agencies of the WPA also found part-time occupations for needy high school and college students and for such unemployed white-collar workers as actors, musicians, and writers. John Steinbeck, future Nobel Prize novelist, counted dogs in his California county. Cynical taxpayers condemned lessons in tap dancing, as well as the painting of scenes on post office walls. But much precious talent was nourished, self-respect was preserved, and more than a million pieces of art were created, many of them publicly displayed.

A Helping Hand for Industry and Labor

A daring attempt to stimulate a nationwide comeback was initiated when the Hundred Days Congress authorized the National Recovery Administration (NRA). This ingenious scheme was by far the most complex and far-reaching effort by the New Dealers to combine immediate relief with long-range recovery and reform. Triple-barreled, it was designed to assist industry, labor, and the unemployed.

Individual industries—over 200 in all—were to work out codes of "fair competition," under which hours of labor would be reduced so that employment could be spread over more people. A ceiling was placed on the maximum hours of labor; a floor was placed under wages to establish minimum levels.

Labor, under the NRA, was granted additional benefits. Workers were formally guaranteed the right to organize and bargain collectively through representatives *of their own choosing*—not through handpicked agents of the company's choosing. The hated "yellow dog," or antiunion, contract was expressly forbidden, and certain safeguarding restrictions were placed on the use of child labor.

Industrial recovery through the NRA fair competition codes would be painful at best, for these called for self-denial by both management and labor. Patriotism was aroused by mass meetings and huge parades, which included 200,000 marchers on New York City's Fifth Avenue. A handsome blue eagle was designed as the symbol of the NRA, and merchants subscribing to a code displayed it in their windows with the slogan "We do our part." A newly formed professional football team was christened the Philadelphia Eagles. Such was the enthusiasm for the NRA that for a brief period there was a marked upswing of business activity, although Roosevelt had warned, "We cannot ballyhoo our way to prosperity."

But the high-flying blue eagle gradually fluttered to earth. Too much self-sacrifice was expected of labor, industry, and the public for such a scheme to work. Critics began to brand the NRA "Nuts Running America," symbolized by what Henry Ford called "that damn Roosevelt buzzard."

Complete collapse was imminent when, in 1935, the Supreme Court shot down the dying eagle in the famed *Schechter* "sick chicken" decision. The learned justices unanimously held the Congress could not "delegate legislative powers" to the executive. They further declared that congressional control of interstate commerce could not properly apply to a local fowl business, like that of the Schechter brothers in Brooklyn and New York. Roosevelt was incensed by this "horse and buggy" interpretation of the Constitution, but actually the Court helped him out of a bad jam.

The same act of Congress that hatched the blue-eagled NRA also authorized the Public Works Administration (PWA), likewise intended both for industrial recovery and for unemployment relief. The agency was headed by acid-tongued Secretary of the Interior Harold L. Ickes, a former bull mooser. Long-range recovery was the primary purpose of the new agency, and in time over $4 billion was spent on some 34,000 projects, which included public buildings, highways, and parkways. One spectacular achievement was the Grand Coulee Dam on the Columbia River—the largest structure erected by humans since the Great Wall of China.

Under Roosevelt the outlawed liquor industry returned to life. The Hundred Days Congress legalized and taxed "light" wine and beer (3.2% alcohol), providing new employment and federal revenue. Prohibition was officially repealed by the Twenty-first Amendment late in 1933 (see Appendix)—and the saloon returned.

Paying Farmers Not to Farm

Ever since the war-boom days of 1918, farmers had suffered from low prices and overproduction, especially in grain. During the depression conditions became desperate as countless mortgages were foreclosed, as corn was burned for fuel, and as embattled farmers tried to prevent shipment of crops to glutted markets. In Iowa several counties were placed under martial law.

A radical new approach to farm recovery was embraced when the Hundred Days Congress established the Agricultural Adjustment Administration (AAA). Through "artificial scarcity" this agency was to establish "parity prices" for basic commodities. "Parity" was the price set for a product that gave it the same real value, in purchasing power, that it had enjoyed during the period from 1909 to 1914. The AAA would eliminate price-depressing surpluses by paying growers to reduce their crop acreage. The millions of dollars needed for these payments were to be raised by taxing processors of farm products, such as flour millers, who in turn would shift the burden to consumers.

Unhappily, the AAA got off to a wobbly start. It was begun after much of the cotton crop for 1933 had been planted, and balky mules, trained otherwise, were forced to plow under countless young plants. Several million squealing pigs were purchased and slaughtered. Much of their meat was distributed to persons on relief, but some of it was used for fertilizer. This "sinful" destruction of food, at a time

The Dust Bowl Migrants

Black dust rolled across the southern Great Plains in the 1930s, darkening the skies above a landscape already desolated by the Great Depression. Its soil depleted by erosion, exhausted by overintensive farming, and parched by drought, the prairie of Oklahoma, Arkansas, northern Texas, and western Missouri became a dust bowl. The thirsty land offered up neither crops nor livelihood to the sturdy people whose forebears had staked out homesteads there. The desiccated earth exhaled only black dust and a dry wind that blew hundreds of thousands of people—the so-called Okies and Arkies—out of the Dust Bowl forever.

They headed mainly for California, piling aboard buses, hopping freight trains, or buying space in westbound cars. Most journeyed in their own autos, cramming their meager possessions into old jalopies and sputtering down the highway. But unlike the aimless, isolated Joad family of John Steinbeck's classic novel *The Grapes of Wrath,* most Dust Bowl migrants knew where they were headed. Although many had lost everything in the depression, they had relatives or friends who had migrated to California before the crash and had sent back word about its abundant promise.

But when Okies arrived in California, they often were greeted with billboards proclaiming "NO JOBS in California . . . If YOU are looking for work—KEEP OUT." Still, they refused to believe that the depression could sully the Golden State's bright promise. Some went to cities, but many of them favored the

An Okie Family Hits the Road in the 1930s

San Joaquin Valley, the southern part of central California's agricultural kingdom. The migrants chose it for its familiarity. The valley shared much in common with the southern plains—aridity, cotton growing, newfound deposits of oil, and abundant land.

During the 1930s the San Joaquin Valley also proved all too familiar in its poverty. Food, shelter, and clothing were scarce; the winter months, without work and without heat, proved nearly unendurable for the migrants. John Steinbeck, writing in a San Francisco newspaper, exposed the tribulations of the Dust Bowl refugees: "First the gasoline gives out. And without gasoline a man cannot go to a job even if he could get one. Then the food goes. And then in the rains, with insufficient food, the children develop colds. . . ."

Eventually, the Farm Security Administration—a New Deal agency—set up camps to house the Okies. A fortunate few purchased land and erected makeshift homes, creating tiny "Okievilles" or "Little Oklahomas." Most Okies eventually escaped seasonal farm labor, securing regular jobs in defense industries. But the "Okievilles" remained to form the bedrock of a still-thriving subculture in California—one that brought the Dust Bowl's country and western music, pecan pie, and evangelical religion to the Far West.

---

when thousands of citizens were hungry, increased condemnation of the American economic system by many left-leaning critics. The much-criticized AAA was itself plowed under in 1936 by the Supreme Court, which declared its regulatory taxation provisions unconstitutional.

The New Deal recovered from this blow by passing the Soil Conservation and Domestic Allotment Act (1936), which paid subsidies to farmers if they planted soil-conserving crops such as soybeans or let land lie fallow. The Second Agricultural Adjustment Act (1938) linked parity payments to acreage restrictions on commodities such as cotton and wheat. Other provisions of the new AAA were designed to give farmers not only a fairer price but a more substantial share of the national income. Both goals were partially achieved.

Dust Bowls and Black Blizzards

Mother Nature meanwhile had been providing some unplanned scarcity. Late in 1933 a prolonged drought struck the states of the trans-Mississippi Great Plains. Rainless weeks were followed by furious, whining winds, while the sun was darkened by millions of tons of powdery topsoil torn from homesteads in Missouri, Texas, Kansas, Arkansas, and Oklahoma—an area soon dubbed the Dust Bowl. Despondent citizens sat on front porches with pro-

tective masks on their faces, watching the farms swirl by. Some of the dust darkened faraway Boston.

Burned and blown out of the Dust Bowl, tens of thousands of refugees fled their ruined acres (see "Makers of America: The Dust Bowl Migrants," pp. 516–517). In five years about 350,000 Oklahomans

Dust Bowl Refugees *Family of "Okies" in California.*

and Arkansans—"Okies" and "Arkies"—trekked to southern California in "junkyards on wheels." The dismal story of these human tumbleweeds was realistically portrayed in John Steinbeck's best-selling novel *The Grapes of Wrath* (1939), which proved to be the *Uncle Tom's Cabin* of the Dust Bowl.

Zealous New Dealers, sympathetic toward these desperate soil tillers, made various efforts to relieve their burdens. The Frazier-Lemke Farm Bankruptcy Act, passed in 1934, made possible a suspension of mortgage foreclosures for five years. It was voided the next year by the Supreme Court, but a revised version was upheld. In 1935 the president set up the Resettlement Administration to help farmers move to better land. And more than 200 million young trees were successfully planted on the bare prairies as windbreaks by the young men of the CCC.

Native Americans also felt the far-reaching hand of New Deal reform. Commissioner of Indian Affairs John Collier ardently sought to reverse the forced-assimilation policies in place since the Dawes Act of 1887 (see p. 400). The Indian Reorganization Act of 1934 (the "Indian New Deal") encouraged tribes to establish local self-government, helped stop the loss of Indian lands, and revived tribes' interest in their identity and culture. Nearly 200 tribes established new governments under its provisions, although 77 others refused to reorganize.

Battling Bankers and Big Business

Reformist New Dealers were determined from the outset to curb the "money changers" who had played fast and loose with gullible investors before the Wall Street crash of 1929. The Hundred Days Congress passed the Truth in Securities Act (Federal Securities Act), which required promoters to transmit to the investor sworn information regarding the soundness of their stocks and bonds, even though the buyer might never read the fine print.

In 1934 Congress took further steps to protect the public against fraud, deception, and inside manipulation. It authorized the Securities and Exchange Commission (SEC), which was designed as a watchdog administrative agency. Stock markets henceforth were to operate more as trading marts and less as gambling casinos.

New Dealers likewise directed their fire at public utility holding companies, those super-corporations. When Chicagoan Samuel Insull's multibillion-dollar financial empire crashed in 1932, citizens rebelled against pyramidal business structures controlled with a minimum of capital. The Public Utility Holding Company Act of 1935 delivered a "death sentence" against this type of fatty growth.

The TVA Harnesses the Tennessee River

Inevitably, the sprawling electric-power industry attracted the fire of New Deal reformers. Within a few decades it had risen from nothingness to a behemoth with an investment of $13 billion. As a public utility, it reached directly and regularly into the pocketbooks of millions of consumers for vitally needed services. Ardent New Dealers accused it of gouging the public with excessive rates, especially since it owed its success to having secured, often for a song, priceless waterpower sites from the public domain.

The tempestuous Tennessee River provided New Dealers with a rare opportunity. With its tributaries, the river drained a badly eroded area about the size of England, and one containing some 2.5 million of the most poverty-stricken people in America. The federal government already owned valuable properties at Muscle Shoals, where it had erected plants for needed nitrates in World War I. By developing the hydroelectric potential of the entire area, Washington could combine the immediate advantage of putting thousands of people to work with a long-term project for reforming the power monopoly.

An act creating the Tennessee Valley Authority (TVA) was passed in 1933 by the Hundred Days Congress. This far-ranging enterprise was largely a result of the steadfast vision and unflagging zeal of Senator George W. Norris of Nebraska, after whom one of the mighty dams was named. From the standpoint of "planned economy," the TVA was by far the most revolutionary of all New Deal schemes.

New Dealers pointed with pride at the amazing achievements of the TVA. To an impoverished area it brought not only cheap power but full employment, low-cost housing, abundant cheap nitrates, restoration of eroded soil, reforestation, improved navigation, and flood control. The TVA also attempted to establish a "yardstick" for measuring the fair cost of producing and distributing electricity.

Exulting New Dealers agitated for parallel enterprises in the valleys of the Columbia, Colorado, and Missouri rivers. Hydroelectric power from federally built dams would drive the growth of the urban West, and the waters they diverted would nurture agriculture in the previously bone-dry western deserts. But conservative reaction against the "socialistic" New Deal would confine the TVA's brand of federally guided resource management and comprehensive regional development to the Tennessee Valley.

Housing Reform and Social Security

Gratifying beginnings had meanwhile been made by the New Deal in housing construction. To speed recovery and better homes, Roosevelt set up the Federal Housing Administration (FHA) as early as 1934. The building industry was to be stimulated by small loans to householders. So popular did the FHA prove to be that it was one of the few "alphabetical agencies" to outlast the age of Roosevelt.

Congress bolstered the program in 1937 by authorizing the United States Housing Authority (USHA)—an agency designed to lend money to states or communities for low-cost construction. Although units for about 650,000 low-income people were started, new building fell tragically short of needs. New Deal efforts to expand the project ran head-on into vigorous opposition from real estate promoters, builders, and landlords ("slumlords"), to say nothing of anti–New Dealers who attacked what they considered down-the-rathole spending. Nonetheless, for the first time in a century the slum areas in America ceased growing and even shrank.

Incomparably more important was the success of New Dealers in the field of unemployment insurance and old-age pensions. Their greatest victory was the epochal Social Security Act of 1935—one of the most complicated and far-reaching laws ever to pass Congress. To cushion future depressions, the measure provided for federal-state unemployment insurance. To provide security for old age, specified categories of retired workers were to receive regular

payments from Washington, ranging from $10 to $85 a month (later raised) and financed by a payroll tax on both employers and employees. Provision was also made for the blind, the physically handicapped, delinquent children, and other dependents.

Social Security was largely inspired by the example of some of the more highly industrialized nations of Europe. In the agricultural America of an earlier day, there had always been farm chores for all ages, and the large family had cared for its own dependents. But in an urbanized economy, at the mercy of boom-and-bust cycles, the government was now recognizing its responsibility for the welfare of its citizens. By 1939 over 45 million persons were eligible for Social Security benefits, and in subsequent years further categories of workers were added and the payments to them periodically increased.

A New Deal for Unskilled Labor

The NRA blue eagles, with their call for collective bargaining, had been a godsend to organized labor. As New Deal expenditures brought some slackening of unemployment, labor began to feel more secure and hence more self-assertive. A rash of walkouts occurred in the summer of 1934, including a paralyzing general strike in San Francisco that was broken only when outraged citizens resorted to vigilante tactics.

When the Supreme Court axed the blue eagle, a Congress sympathetic to labor unions undertook to fill the vacuum. The fruit of its deliberations was the Wagner, or National Labor Relations, Act of 1935. This trailblazing law created a powerful new National Labor Relations Board for administrative purposes and reasserted the right of labor to engage in self-organization and to bargain collectively through representatives of its own choice. The Wagner Act proved to be one of the real milestones on the rocky road of the U.S. labor movement.

Under the encouragement of a highly sympathetic National Labor Relations Board, a host of unskilled workers began to organize themselves into effective unions. The leader of this drive was beetle-browed, domineering, and melodramatic John L. Lewis, boss of the United Mine Workers. In 1935 he succeeded in forming the Committee for Industrial

Later Major New Deal Measures, 1933–1939
(Items in parentheses indicate secondary purposes.)

Recovery	Relief	Reform
(CWA)	FDR establishes Civil Works Administration (CWA), Nov. 9, 1933	
Gold Reserve Act, Jan. 30, 1934, authorizes FDR's devaluation, Jan. 31, 1934		
		Securities and Exchange Commission (SEC) authorized by Congress, June 6, 1934
(Reciprocal Trade Agreements)	(Reciprocal Trade Agreements)	Reciprocal Trade Agreements Act, June 12, 1934
(FHA)	National Housing Act, June 28, 1934, authorizes Federal Housing Administration (FHA)	(FHA)
(Frazier-Lemke Act)	Frazier-Lemke Farm Bankruptcy Act, June 28, 1934	
(Resettlement Administration)	FDR creates Resettlement Administration, April 30, 1935	
(WPA)	FDR creates Works Progress Administration (WPA), May 6, 1935, under act of April 8, 1935	
(Wagner Act)	(Wagner Act)	(Wagner) National Labor Relations Act, July 5, 1935
		Social Security Act, August 14, 1935
		Public Utility Holding Co. Act, Aug. 26, 1935
(Soil Conservation Act)	Soil Conservation and Domestic Allotment Act, Feb. 29, 1936	
(USHA)	(USHA)	U.S. Housing Authority (USHA) established by Congress, Sept. 1, 1937
(Second AAA)	Second Agricultural Adjustment Act, Feb. 16, 1936	
(Fair Labor Standards)	(Fair Labor Standards)	Fair Labor Standards Act, June 25, 1938
		Reorganization Act, April 3, 1939
		Hatch Act, Aug. 2, 1939

Organization (CIO) within the ranks of the skilled-craft American Federation of Labor. But skilled workers, ever since the days of the ill-fated Knights of Labor in the 1880s, had shown only lukewarm sympathy for the cause of unskilled labor, especially blacks. In 1936, following inevitable friction with the CIO, the older federation suspended the upstart unions associated with the newer organization.

Nothing daunted, the rebellious CIO moved on a concerted scale into the huge automobile industry. Late in 1936 the workers resorted to a revolutionary technique known as the sit-down strike: they refused to leave the factory buildings of General Motors at Flint, Michigan, and thus prevented the importation of strikebreakers. Conservative respecters of private property were scandalized. The CIO finally won a resounding victory when its union, after heated negotiations, was recognized by General Motors as the sole bargaining agency for its employees.

Roosevelt's "Coddling" of Labor

Unskilled workers now pressed their advantage. The United States Steel Company, hitherto an impossible nut for labor to crack, averted a costly strike when it voluntarily granted rights of unionization to its CIO-organized employees. But the "little steel" companies fought back savagely. Citizens were shocked in 1937 by the Memorial Day massacre at the plant of the Republic Steel Company in South Chicago. In a bloody fracas, police fired upon pickets and workers, leaving the area strewn with several dead and wounded.

A better deal for labor continued when Congress, in 1938, passed the memorable Fair Labor Standards Act (Wages and Hours Bill). Industries involved in interstate commerce were to set up minimum-wage and maximum-hour levels. Specific goals were forty cents an hour (later raised) and a forty-hour week. Labor by children under sixteen was forbidden; under eighteen, if the occupation was dangerous. These reforms were bitterly though futilely opposed by many industrialists, especially by those southern textile manufacturers who had profited from low-wage labor.

In later New Deal days, labor unionization flourished; "Roosevelt wants you to join a union" was the rallying cry of professional organizers. The president received valuable support at ballot-box time from labor leaders and many appreciative working men and women. One mill worker remarked that Roosevelt was "the only man we ever had in the White House who would know that my boss is an s.o.b."

The CIO surged forward, breaking completely with the A.F. of L. in 1938. On that occasion the *Committee* for Industrial Organization was formally

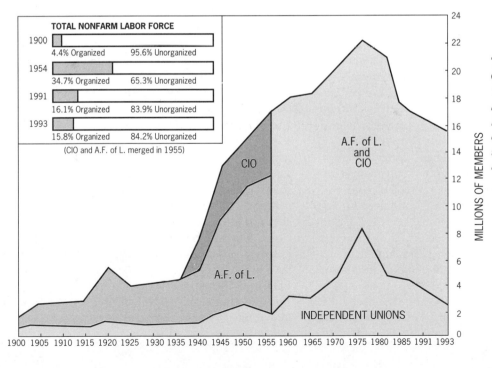

The Rise of Organized Labor, 1900–1993 *The percentage of the total labor force that was organized increased until 1954, and it has declined ever since.*

TOTAL NONFARM LABOR FORCE

1900		
4.4% Organized	95.6% Unorganized	
1954		
34.7% Organized	65.3% Unorganized	
1991		
16.1% Organized	83.9% Unorganized	
1993		
15.8% Organized	84.2% Unorganized	

(CIO and A.F. of L. merged in 1955)

MILLIONS OF MEMBERS

A.F. of L. and CIO

CIO

A.F. of L.

INDEPENDENT UNIONS

1900 1905 1910 1915 1920 1925 1930 1935 1940 1945 1950 1955 1960 1965 1970 1975 1980 1985 1991 1993

reconstituted as the *Congress* of Industrial Organizations (the new CIO), under the high-handed presidency of John L. Lewis. By 1940 the CIO could claim about 4 million members in its constituent unions, including some 200,000 blacks.

Landon Challenges "the Champ" in 1936

As the presidential campaign of 1936 neared, the New Dealers were on top of the world. They had achieved considerable progress, and millions of "relievers" were grateful to their bountiful government. The exultant Democrats renominated Roosevelt on a platform squarely endorsing the New Deal.

To run against "the Champ" Roosevelt, the Republicans settled on Alfred M. Landon, the sincere, homespun governor of Kansas. Landon himself was a moderate inclined to accept some New Deal reforms, although not Social Security. But the Republican platform vigorously condemned the New Deal for its radicalism, experimentation, confusion, and "frightful waste." The Republican campaign became fatally linked to embittered former President Hoover, who called for a "holy crusade for liberty," and the American Liberty League, a group of wealthy conservatives formed to fight "socialistic" New Deal schemes and "that man" Roosevelt.

Such reactionary rhetoric provided a made-to-order target for FDR. Angry enough to stretch sheet iron, Roosevelt took to the stump to denounce "economic royalists" who "hide behind the flag and the Constitution." "I welcome their hatred," he proclaimed.

A landslide overwhelmed Landon, as the demoralized Republicans carried only two states, Maine and Vermont. The popular vote was 27,752,869 to 16,674,665; the electoral count was 523 to 8—the most lopsided in 116 years. Democratic majorities were again returned to Congress. Jubilant Democrats could now claim more than two-thirds of the seats in the House, and a like proportion in the Senate.

The battle of 1936, perhaps the most bitter since Bryan's in 1896, partially bore out Republican charges of class warfare. Even more than in 1932, the needy economic groups were lined up against the so-called greedy economic groups. CIO units contributed generously to FDR's campaign chest. Many left-wingers turned to Roosevelt, as the customary third-party protest vote sharply declined. Blacks, several million of whom had also enjoyed welcome relief checks, had by now largely shaken off their traditional allegiance to the Republican party. To them, Lincoln was "finally dead."

FDR won primarily because he appealed to the forgotten man, whom he never forgot. Roosevelt in fact had forged a powerful and enduring coalition of the South, the blacks, the urbanites, and the poor. He proved especially effective in marshaling the support of the multitudes of New Immigrants—mostly the Catholics and Jews who had been clogging the great cities since the turn of the century. These once-scorned newcomers, with their now-numerous sons and daughters, had at last come politically of age. In the 1920s, only 4 percent of federal judgeships went to Catholics; Roosevelt appointed Catholics to 25 percent of the judiciary positions.

Conflict over the Court

Bowing his head to the sleety blasts, Roosevelt took the presidential oath on January 20, 1937, instead of the traditional March 4. The Twentieth Amendment to the Constitution had been ratified in 1933 (see Appendix). It swept away the postelection lame duck session of Congress and shortened by six weeks the awkward period before inauguration.

Flushed with victory, Roosevelt interpreted his reelection as a mandate to continue New Deal reforms. But in his eyes the cloistered old men on the supreme bench, like fossilized stumbling blocks, stood stubbornly in the pathway of progress. In nine major cases involving the New Deal, the Roosevelt administration had been defeated seven times. The Court was ultraconservative, and six of the nine judges in black were over seventy. As luck would have it, not a single member had been appointed by FDR in his first term.

Roosevelt—his "Dutch up"—viewed with mounting impatience what he regarded as the obstructive conservatism of the Court. Some of these

Old Guard appointees were hanging on with a senile grip, partly because they felt it their patriotic duty to curb the "socialistic" tendencies of that "radical" in the White House.

To overcome such obstructionism, Roosevelt suddenly announced, early in 1937, a scheme to expand the Supreme Court. He bluntly asked Congress for legislation to add a new justice to the Supreme Court for every member over seventy who would not retire. The maximum membership could then be fifteen. In presenting his plan, Roosevelt inaccurately alleged that the Court was far behind in its work.

Congress and the nation were promptly convulsed over the scheme to "pack" the Supreme Court with a "dictator bill," which one critic called "too damned slick." Franklin "Double-crossing" Roosevelt was savagely condemned for attempting to break down the delicate checks and balances among the three branches of the government.

The Court had meanwhile seen the ax hanging over its head. Whatever his motives, Justice Roberts, formerly regarded as conservative, began to vote on the side of his liberal colleagues. "A switch in time saves nine" was the classic witticism inspired by this change. By a five to four decision, the Court, in March 1937, upheld the principle of a state minimum wage for women, thereby reversing its stand on a different case a year earlier. In succeeding decisions, the Court, more sympathetic to the New Deal, upheld the National Labor Relations Act (Wagner Act) and the Social Security Act.

Such rulings made the Court-packing scheme seem unnecessary as well as dangerous, and Roosevelt suffered his first major legislative defeat at the hands of his own party in Congress. Yet in losing this battle, Roosevelt incidentally won his campaign. The Court, as he had hoped, became markedly more friendly to New Deal reforms. Furthermore, a succession of deaths and resignations enabled him to make nine appointments to the tribunal.

Yet in a sense FDR lost both the Court battle and the war. He so aroused conservatives of both parties in Congress that few New Deal reforms were passed after 1937, the year of the fight to pack the Supreme Court. With this catastrophic miscalcula-tion, he squandered much of the political goodwill that had carried him to such a resounding victory in the 1936 election.

The Twilight of the New Deal

Roosevelt's first term, from 1933 to 1937, did not banish the depression from the country. Unemployment stubbornly persisted in 1936 at about 15 percent, down from the grim 25 percent of 1933 but still miserably high. Despite the inventiveness of New Deal programs and the billions of dollars in "pump-priming," recovery had been dishearteningly modest, though the country seemed to be inching its way back to economic health.

Then, in 1937, the economy took another sharp downturn, a surprisingly severe depression-within-a-depression that the president's critics quickly dubbed the "Roosevelt recession." In fact, government policies had caused the nosedive, as Social Security taxes began to bite into payrolls and as the administration cut back on spending to try to achieve a balanced budget, in accordance with orthodox economic doctrine.

Only at this late date did Roosevelt at last frankly and deliberately embrace the recommendations of the British economist John Maynard Keynes. In April 1937, FDR announced a bold program to stimulate the economy by planned deficit spending. Although the deficits were still relatively small, this abrupt policy reversal toward "Keynesianism" marked a turning point in the government's relation to the economy.

Facing an increasingly conservative Congress, Roosevelt pushed only a few reform measures after 1937. His proposal to reorganize the national administration became caught up in the fight over the Supreme Court, and was passed only in diluted form in 1939. That same year Congress also passed the much-heralded Hatch Act, which barred most federal employees from active political campaigning and prohibited the use of government funds for political purposes.

By 1938 the New Deal had clearly lost most of its early momentum. Magician Roosevelt could find few spectacular new reform rabbits to pull out of his tall silk hat. In the congressional elections of 1938 the Republicans, for the first time, cut heavily into the unwieldy New Deal majorities in Congress, though failing to gain control of either house.

The international crisis that came to a boil in 1938–1939 shifted public attention away from domestic reform, and no doubt helped save the political hide of the Roosevelt "spendocracy." The New Deal, for all practical purposes, had shot its bolt.

New Deal or Raw Deal?

Foes of the New Deal condemned its alleged radicalism, bureaucratic confusion and waste, creation of an oppressive big government, and economic failures. New Dealers conceded some weaknesses, but defended their record as a necessary and effective response to the depression.

To some conservatives, the New Deal was a radical attempt to make America over in a Bolshevik-Marxist image. They condemned "Rooseveltski" for bringing to Washington "crackpot" college professors, leftist "pinkos," and outright communists. The Hearst newspapers assailed

> The Red New Deal with a Soviet seal
> Endorsed by a Moscow hand,
> The strange result of an alien cult
> In a liberty-loving land.

Other critics accused Roosevelt of bringing too many bright young Jewish leftists to Washington ("The Jew Deal"), or even asserted that Roosevelt himself was Jewish ("Rosenfeld").

More widespread was the charge that the New Deal brought bureaucracy, waste, and a welfare-state mentality that undermined the old American virtues of individualism, thrift, self-reliance, and limited government. As the federal government expanded into a giant bureaucracy, with hundreds of thousands of employees and a federal pill for every ill, the states faded farther into the background. Promises of balancing the federal budget were forgotten as the national debt proceeded to skyrocket from $19,487,000,000 in 1932 to $40,440,000,000 by 1939. Critics charged that the lavish benefactions of the "handout state" were turning once-self-reliant Americans into relief-seeking loafers, with wishbones larger than their backbones.

Hardheaded businesspeople, most of whom were Republicans, bitterly attacked what they saw as the New Deal's governmental oppression and regimentation, its class warfare, and Roosevelt's one-man rule. Private enterprise, they charged, was being stifled by an interventionist big government, a "planned economy," and "creeping socialism." The worker and the farmer were being favored, while government fomented hatred against those who

Unemployment, 1929–1942 *The cold figures can only begin to suggest the widespread human misery caused by mass unemployment. One man wrote to a newspaper in 1932: "I am forty-eight; married twenty-one years; four children, three in school. For the last eight years I was employed as a Pullman conductor. Since September, 1930, they have given me seven months of part-time work. Today I am an object of charity. . . . My small, weak, and frail wife and two small children are suffering and I have come to that terrible place where I could easily resort to violence in my desperation."*

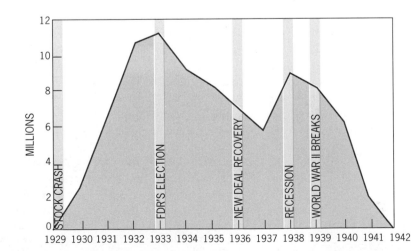

"met a payroll." Roosevelt's aggressive leadership, especially the Court-packing plan, smacked of dictatorship.

The most damning indictment of the New Deal was that it had failed to cure the depression. Despite some $20 billion poured out in six years of deficit spending and lending, many economists believed that better results would have been achieved by even greater deficit spending. The New Deal, some believed, had merely administered aspirin, sedatives, and Band-Aids, with the result that in 1939 millions of dispirited men and women were still unemployed. Not until World War II—the greatest pump-primer of all—increased the national debt from $40 billion in 1939 to $258 billion in 1945 was the unemployment headache solved.

New Dealers staunchly defended their record. Admitting that there had been bureaucratic inefficiency and waste, they argued that it had been trivial in view of the immense sums spent and the obvious need for haste. The New Deal, they insisted, had relieved a crisis by demonstrating that the Washington regime was to be used, not feared. By federal action America's economic system was kept from collapse, citizens were kept from mass hunger and enabled to retain their self-respect, and a fairer distribution of national income was achieved.

Though hated by business tycoons, FDR should have been their patron saint, so his admirers claimed. He deflected popular resentments against business and may have saved the American system of free enterprise. Roosevelt's quarrel was not with capitalism but with capitalists; he purged American capitalism of some of its worst abuses so that it might be saved from itself. He may even have headed off a more radical swing to the left by a mild dose of what was mistakenly condemned as "socialism." The head of the American Socialist party, when once asked if the New Deal had carried out the Socialist program, reportedly replied that it had indeed—on a stretcher.

Roosevelt, like Jefferson, provided reform without a bloody revolution—at a time when some foreign nations were suffering armed uprisings and when many Europeans were predicting either communism or fascism for America. He was upbraided by the left-wing radicals for not going far enough, and by the right-wing radicals for going too far.

Choosing the middle road, he has been called the greatest American conservative since Hamilton. He was in fact Hamiltonian in his espousal of big government, but Jeffersonian in his concern for the forgotten man. Demonstrating anew the value of powerful presidential leadership, he exercised that power to relieve the erosion of the nation's greatest physical resource—its people. He helped preserve democracy in America at a time when democracies abroad were disappearing down the sinkhole of dictatorship. And in playing this role he unwittingly girded the nation for its part in the gruesome war that loomed on the horizon—a war in which democracy the world over would be at stake.

Varying Viewpoints

The New Deal has stirred hot debate since its beginnings in 1933. Some contemporaries like Herbert Hoover, and some historians like Edgar E. Robinson, condemned Roosevelt's program as a "socialistic" break from American traditions. But until the 1960s, the great majority of historians approved of the political values of the New Deal and praised its accomplishments.

Arthur M. Schlesinger, Jr., portrayed the New Deal as a dramatic climax to a reform tradition reaching back through progressivism and populism to the age of Jackson. In an equally sympathetic but different vein, Richard Hofstadter viewed the New Deal as a bold response to a severe crisis and hence a triumphant departure from the old reform tradition. Another pro-Roosevelt scholar dubbed the New Deal the "Third American Revolution."

In the past few decades, several New Left historians have challenged this orthodox interpretation. They see the New Deal as neither bold nor innovative but simply as a conservative holding action to shore up sagging capitalism. The Roosevelt program, these scholars charge, did not promote recovery, redistribute wealth, improve race relations, or reform American business.

The consensus seems to be somewhere in the middle. As William Leuchtenburg has put it, the New Deal engineered a "half-way revolution." It was neither outright radical nor simply conservative, but it did initiate changes in the party system, labor relations, and the economic and social role of the federal government that significantly transformed American life.

SELECT READINGS

Primary Source Documents

James Agee and Walker Evans, *Let Us Now Praise Famous Men* (1940), brilliantly evokes the misery of the depression in words and photographs. Franklin D. Roosevelt's dramatic "First Inaugural Address" (1933), in Henry Steele Commager, ed., *Documents of American History,* captured the imagination of the distressed nation. Less successful was Roosevelt's "Radio Address on Supreme Court Reform" (1937), in Richard Hofstadter, *Great Issues in American History.* See also Dorothy Thompson's attack on the Court plan in the Washington *Star,* February 10, 1937.* Clifford Odets's play *Waiting for Lefty* (1935) and John

Steinbeck's novel *The Grapes of Wrath* (1939) exemplify the literature stimulated by the Great Depression.

Secondary Sources

A masterly summation is William E. Leuchtenburg, *Franklin D. Roosevelt and the New Deal, 1932–1940* (1963). Briefer and more critical of the limitations of reform is Paul Conkin, *The New Deal* (rev. ed., 1975). A detailed biography is Frank Freidel, *Franklin D. Roosevelt* (4 vols., 1952–1973). A sympathetic and perspective family portrait is Joseph Lash, *Eleanor and Franklin* (1971). Brilliantly pro-FDR are the three volumes of Arthur M. Schlesinger, Jr., *The Age of Roosevelt: The Crisis of the Old Order* (1957), *The Coming of the New Deal* (1959), and *The Politics of Upheaval* (1960). The social impact of the depression is vividly etched in Studs Terkel, *Hard Times* (1970), Ann Banks, *First Person America* (1980), and James Gregory, *American Exodus: The Dust Bowl Migration and Okie Culture in California* (1989). Of special interest are Lois Scharf, *To Work and to Wed: Female Employment, Feminism, and the Great Depression* (1980), and Susan Ware, *Beyond Suffrage: Women in the New Deal* (1981). On Eleanor Roosevelt, see Scharf's *Eleanor Roosevelt: First Lady of American Liberalism* (1987) and Blanche Wiesen Cook's *Eleanor Roosevelt: A Life* (1992). Alan Brinkley

brilliantly chronicles *Voices of Protest: Huey Long, Father Coughlin, and the Great Depression* (1982). Ellis Hawley, *The New Deal and the Problem of Monopoly* (1966), is a superb analysis of the conflicting currents of economic policy in the Roosevelt administration. A comprehensive assessment by several noted scholars is Harvard Sitkoff, ed., *Fifty Years Later: The New Deal Evaluated* (1985). Especially good on intellectual history are Richard H. Pells, *Radical Visions and American Dreams: Culture and Social Thought in the Depression Years* (1973), and Daniel Aaron, *Writers on the Left* (1961). A trenchant appraisal of the New Deal legacy is Steven Fraser and Gary Gerstle, eds., *The Rise and Fall of the New Deal Order* (1989).

CHAPTER 36

Franklin D. Roosevelt and the Shadow of War, 1933–1941

The epidemic of world lawlessness is spreading. When an epidemic of physical disease starts to spread, the community approves and joins in a quarantine of the patients in order to protect the health of the community against the spread of the disease. . . . There must be positive endeavors to preserve peace.

Franklin D. Roosevelt, Chicago quarantine speech, 1937

FDR's First Foreign Policy Steps

Roosevelt's early foreign policy was intended to serve his schemes for domestic recovery. This was demonstrated by his actions at the London Economic Conference in the summer of 1933. Sixty-six nations had gathered to attack the depression by stabilizing national currencies. But Roosevelt, unwilling to subordinate his gold-juggling policies to an international agreement that might tie his hands, torpedoed the conference with an explosive message that scolded the delegates for even trying to stabilize currencies. The conference probably would have failed to produce a wonder-drug cure for the world's economic maladies, but the devil-take-the-hindmost attitude of Roosevelt plunged the world even deeper into narrow isolationism and extreme nationalism—a trend that played directly into the hands of power-mad dictators.

Roosevelt's formal recognition of the Soviet regime in 1933 also stemmed partly from domestic considerations. As a liberal, Roosevelt did not share the conservative belief that the Bolshevik regime would collapse. He was also willing to gamble that an enriching trade with the Soviet Union might aid the depression-ridden United States.

Ironically, the Great Depression helped make possible better relations with Latin America. Yankee economic imperialism south of the border had cooled off as thousands of investors in Latin "securities" became sackholders rather than stockholders. Roosevelt's "Good Neighbor" policy, announced in his inaugural address, was partly based on the fact that there were now fewer dollars to be protected by the rifles of the hated marines. With thirsty dictators seizing power in Europe and Asia, Roosevelt was also eager to line up Latin Americans to help defend the Western hemisphere. Embittered neighbors would be potential tools of transatlantic aggressors.

Roosevelt made clear at the outset that he renounced armed intervention, particularly the vexatious corollary to the Monroe Doctrine devised by

U.S. Marines in Haiti
Franklin Roosevelt withdrew U.S. marines from Haiti in 1934 as part of his Good Neighbor policy toward Latin America. The marines had been sent to the Caribbean island nation by Woodrow Wilson in 1914 (see page 456).

his cousin Theodore Roosevelt. At the Seventh Pan-American Conference at Montevideo, Uruguay, in 1933, the U.S. delegation formally accepted nonintervention.

Deeds followed words. The last marines departed from Haiti in 1934, and the same year Cuba was freed from the hobbling Platt Amendment. The hope-inspiring Good Neighbor policy received its acid test in Mexico, where the seizure of Yankee oil properties in 1938 brought vehement demands for armed intervention from American investors. But Roosevelt successfully resisted the clamor, and a settlement was finally threshed out in 1941.

Spectacular success crowned Roosevelt's Good Neighbor policy. His earnest attempts to inaugurate a new era of friendliness, though hurting some U.S. bondholders, paid rich dividends in goodwill among the peoples to the south. The Colossus of the North now seemed less a vulture and more an eagle.

Philippine Freedom and Free Trade

The Great Depression, otherwise a blight, actually brightened hopes for Philippine independence. In the crisis, American taxpayers, organized labor, and U.S. sugar interests saw the islands as an economic

liability or threat. Congress therefore in 1934 passed the Tydings-McDuffie Act, which promised independence after a twelve-year preparation period. United States military installations, except naval bases, were to be relinquished. The intent of this action was not so much to free the Philippines, but to free America *from* the Philippines, which now seemed only a vulnerable Achilles' heel in East Asia.

Intimately associated with good neighborism, and also popular in Latin America, was the reciprocal trade policy of the New Dealers. Its chief architect was idealistic Secretary of State Cordell Hull, a high-minded Tennessean of the low-tariff school. Like Roosevelt, he believed that trade was a two-way street; that a nation can sell abroad only as it buys abroad; that tariff barriers choke off foreign trade; and that trade wars beget shooting wars.

Responding to the Hull-Roosevelt leadership, Congress passed the Reciprocal Trade Agreements Act in 1934. Designed in part to lift American export trade from the depression doldrums, this enlightened measure was aimed at both relief and recovery. Roosevelt was empowered to lower existing tariff rates by as much as 50 percent, provided that the other country involved was willing to respond with similar reductions.

Secretary Hull, whose zeal for reciprocity was unflagging, succeeded in negotiating pacts with twenty-one countries by the end of 1939. During these same years, U.S. foreign trade increased appreciably.

Impulses Toward Isolationism

Post-1918 chaos in Europe, followed by the Great Depression, fostered the ominous concept of totalitarianism. The individual was nothing; the state was everything. The Communist USSR led the way, with the crafty and ruthless Joseph Stalin finally emerging as dictator. Blustery Benito Mussolini, a swaggering Fascist, seized the reins of power in Italy during 1922. And Adolf Hitler, a fanatic with a toothbrush mustache, plotted and harangued his way into control of Germany in 1933 with liberal use of the "big lie."

Jut-jawed Mussolini, seeking both glory and empire in Africa, brutally attacked Ethiopia in 1935 with bombers and tanks. But Hitler was the most dangerous dictator because he combined tremendous power with impulsiveness. A frustrated Austrian house painter, with hypnotic talents as an orator and leader, he had led the Nazi party to power in Germany by making political capital of the Treaty of Versailles and the depression-spawned unemployment. In 1936 the Nazi Hitler and the Fascist Mussolini allied themselves in the Rome-Berlin axis.

International gangsterism was likewise spreading in East Asia, where imperial Japan was on the make. Like Germany and Italy, Japan was a so-called have-not power. Like them, it resented the ungenerous Treaty of Versailles. Like them, it demanded additional space for its teeming millions, cooped up in their crowded island nation. Determined to find a place in the Asian sun, Tokyo terminated the Washington Naval Treaty in 1934, and the following year in London torpedoed all hope of naval disarmament by walking out on the multipower arms limitation conference.

Isolationism, long festering in America, received a strong boost from these alarms abroad. Though disapproving of the dictators, Americans still believed that their encircling seas conferred a kind of mystic immunity. They were continuing to suffer the disillusionment born of their participation in World War I, which they now regarded as a colossal blunder. They likewise cherished bitter memories of the ungrateful and defaulting debtors. As early as 1934 a spiteful Congress had passed the Johnson Debt Default Act, which prevented debt-dodging nations from borrowing further from the United States.

As the gloomy 1930s lengthened, an avalanche of lurid articles and books condemning the munitions manufacturers as war-fomenting "merchants of death" poured forth from American presses. A Senate committee, headed by Senator Gerald Nye of North Dakota, was appointed in 1934 to investigate the "blood business." By sensationalizing evidence regarding America's entry into World War I, the senatorial probers tended to shift the blame away from the German submarine onto the American bankers and arms manufacturers. Because the munitions makers had obviously made money out of the war, many a naive citizen leaped to the illogical conclusion that these scavengers had caused the war in order to make money. This kind of reasoning suggested that if the profits could only be removed from the arms traffic—"one hell of a business"—the country could keep out of any future world conflict.

Responding to overwhelming popular pressure, Congress made haste to legislate the nation out of war. Action was spurred by the danger that Mussolini's Ethiopian assault would plunge the world into a new bloodbath. The Neutrality Acts of 1935, 1936, and 1937, taken together, stipulated that *when the president proclaimed* the existence of a foreign war, certain restrictions would automatically go into effect. No American could legally sail on a belligerent ship, sell or transport munitions to a belligerent, or make loans to a belligerent.

Storm-cellar neutrality proved to be tragically shortsighted. Through statutory neutrality, America served notice that it would make no distinction between brutal aggressors and innocent victims. By striving to hold the scales even, it actually overbalanced them in favor of the dictators, who had armed themselves to the teeth. By declining to use its vast industrial strength to aid its democratic friends and

What Next? *The western European democracies looked on helplessly as Nazi Germany swallowed up Austria and part of Czechoslovakia in 1938. Hitler's juggernaut seemed unstoppable.*

defeat its totalitarian foes, America helped to spur the aggressors along their blood-spattered path of conquest.

The Spanish Civil War of 1936–1939—a proving ground and dress rehearsal in miniature for World War II—was a painful object lesson in the folly of neutrality-by-legislation. Spanish rebels, who rose against the left-leaning republican government in Madrid, were headed by fascistic General Francisco Franco. Generously aided by his fellow conspirators, Hitler and Mussolini, he undertook to overthrow the established Loyalist regime, which in turn was assisted on a smaller scale by the Soviet Union. This pipeline from communist Moscow offended many Americans, especially Roman Catholics.

In accordance with previous American practice, the Loyalist government should have been free to purchase desperately needed munitions in the United States. But Congress, with the encouragement of Roosevelt and with only one dissenting vote, amended the existing neutrality legislation so as to apply an arms embargo to both Loyalists and rebels.

Uncle Sam thus sat on the sidelines while Franco, abundantly supplied with arms and men by his fellow dictators, strangled the republican government of Spain. The democracies, including the United States, were so determined to stay out of war that they helped to condemn a fellow democracy to death. In so doing they further encouraged the dictators to take the dangerous road that led over the precipice to World War II.

Appeasing Japan and Germany

Sulfurous war clouds had meanwhile been gathering in tension-taut East Asia. In 1937 the Japanese militarists, at the Marco Polo Bridge near Peking, touched off the explosion that led to a full-dress invasion of China. In a sense this attack was the curtain raiser of World War II.

Roosevelt declined to invoke the recently passed neutrality legislation, noting that the so-called China incident was not an officially declared war. If he had put the existing restrictions into effect, he would have cut off the tiny trickle of munitions on which the Chinese were desperately dependent. The Japanese, of course, could continue to buy mountains of war supplies in the United States.

In Chicago—unofficial isolationist "capital" of America—Roosevelt delivered his sensational "Quarantine Speech" in the autumn of 1937. Alarmed by the recent aggressions of Italy and Japan, he called for some "positive endeavors" to "quarantine" the aggressors—presumably by economic embargoes. One immediate result was a cyclone of protest from isolationists and other foes of involvement; they feared that a moral quarantine would lead to a shooting quarantine. Startled by this angry response, Roosevelt retreated and sought by less direct means to curb the dictators.

America's deepening isolationism was further demonstrated in December 1937, when Japanese aviators bombed and sank an American gunboat, the

Panay, in Chinese waters. In the days of 1898, when the *Maine* went down, this outrage might have provoked war. But instead of striking back, Americans accepted with relief the Japanese apology and indemnity, and turned their backs on the plight of American civilians in China.

More immediately menacing was Adolf Hitler. In 1935 he had openly flouted the Treaty of Versailles by introducing compulsory military service in Germany. The next year he boldly marched into the demilitarized German Rhineland, likewise contrary to the detested treaty, while France and Britain looked on in an agony of indecision. Lashing his following to a frenzy, Hitler undertook to persecute and then exterminate the Jewish population in the areas under his control. In the end, he wiped out about 6 million innocent victims, mostly in gas chambers (see "Makers of America: Refugees from the Holocaust," pp. 534–535). Calling upon his people to sacrifice butter for guns, he whipped the new German air force and mechanized ground divisions into the most devastating military machine the world had yet seen.

Suddenly, in March 1938, Hitler bloodlessly occupied German-speaking Austria, his birthplace. The democratic powers, wringing their hands in despair, prayed that this last grab would satisfy his passion for conquest.

But like a drunken reveler calling for madder music and stronger wine, Hitler could not stop. Intoxicated by his recent gains, he began to make bullying demands for the German-inhabited Sudetenland in neighboring Czechoslovakia. British and French leaders, eager to avoid war, frantically arranged a conference with Hitler and Mussolini at Munich, Germany, in September 1938, where they consented to Hitler's demand. Europeans and Americans alike hoped that these concessions would bring "peace in our time." Indeed, Hitler publicly promised that the Sudetenland "is the last territorial claim I have to make in Europe."

"Appeasement" of the dictators, symbolized by the ugly word *Munich,* turned out to be merely surrender on the installment plan. It was like giving a cannibal a finger in the hope of saving an arm. In March 1939, scarcely six months later, Hitler suddenly erased the rest of Czechoslovakia from the map, contrary to his solemn promises. The democratic world was again stunned.

Hitlerian Belligerence and U.S. Neutrality

Joseph Stalin, the sphinx of the Kremlin, was a key to the peace puzzle. When efforts to secure a mutual defense treaty with Britain and France fell through in the summer of 1939, Stalin astounded the world by signing, on August 23, 1939, a nonaggression treaty with the German dictator. The notorious Hitler-Stalin pact meant that, contrary to hopes of wishful thinkers in western Europe, the two dictators would join hands to share the spoils rather than destroy each other.

World War II was only hours away. Hitler, intensifying the pressure, demanded from neighboring Poland a return of the areas wrested from Germany after World War I. Failing to secure satisfaction, he sent his mechanized divisions crashing into Poland at dawn on September 1, 1939. Honoring their commitments, Britain and France promptly declared war, but they were powerless to aid Poland, which was quickly divided between Hitler and his partner in crime, Stalin. Long-dreaded World War II was now fully launched, and the long truce of 1919–1939 had come to an end.

Americans were overwhelmingly anti-Nazi and anti-Hitler, but they were desperately determined to stay out of war; they were not going to be "suckers" again. Neutrality promptly became a heated issue in the United States. Britain and France urgently sought American airplanes and weapons, but the Neutrality Act of 1937 raised a sternly forbidding hand. Roosevelt summoned Congress into special session, and after hectic debate it came up with the makeshift Neutrality Act of 1939. This law provided that henceforth the European democracies might buy American war materials, but only on a "cash-and-carry" basis—that is, they would have to pay for munitions in cash and transport them in their own ships.

Despite its defects, this unneutral neutrality law clearly favored the democracies against the dic-

Refugees from the Holocaust

Fed by Adolf Hitler's genocidal delusions, anti-Semitism bared its fangs in the 1930s, spreading out across Europe as Nazi Germany seized Austria, Czechoslovakia, Poland, and France. Eluding the jackboots of Hitler's bloodthirsty S.S. (*Schutzstaffel,* an elite military and police force), some 150,000 European Jews fled the Third Reich for America between 1935 and 1941. Among those seeking refuge were many of Europe's greatest scientists, artists, and intellectuals. They included some of the world's premier nuclear physicists: Albert Einstein, the Nobel laureate whose plea to President Roosevelt helped initiate the top-secret American atomic bomb project; Leo Szilard, who helped construct the first atomic weapon at Los Alamos; and Edward Teller, creater of the first hydrogen bomb. Also escaping at the eleventh hour were Hannah Arendt, a leading authority on totalitarianism, psychoanalyst Erich Fromm, painter Marc Chagall, and composer Kurt Weill.

These exiled luminaries found a settled Jewish community in America, the descendant of the successive waves of immigrants from Germany and eastern Europe who had arrived between the mid-nineteenth century and 1920. By 1935 most Jews had entered the middle class. Children of immigrant tailors and peddlers, they had risen to white-collar jobs, meanwhile founding numerous institutions to ease their adjustment to American life. Despite such success, the American Jewish community was not pre-

A Survivor of the Holocaust *A Polish Jew is reunited with his sister in the United States in 1946. He was lucky to have lived; most Polish Jews perished at Hitler's hands.*

pared for the catastrophe of Hitler's Holocaust in Europe.

Jews had long fought to convince their fellow Americans of their loyalty, and many now feared that a bold advocacy of intervention in Europe during the isolationist 1930s would undo their years of effort. Some American Jews, frightened by the scurrilous radio broadcasts of Father Charles Coughlin, worried about a new burst of anti-Semitism. Internal bickering between the cautious American Jewish Conference and the more aggressive American Jewish Congress also compromised the political effectiveness of the American Jewish community, hampering efforts to persuade the Roosevelt administration to rescue the European Jews.

Even so, many American Jews lobbied the federal government—but to no avail. In 1941 Congress rejected a bill that would have granted 20,000 German-Jewish children entry to the United States. At the same time, the State Department suppressed early reports of Hitler's plan to exterminate the Jews, and after the führer's sordid final solution became known in America, the War Department rejected pleas to bomb the gas chambers. Military officials maintained that a raid on Auschwitz or Dachau would divert essential military resources and needlessly extend the war. Thus only a lucky few escaped the Nazis, whereas 6 million died in one of history's most ghastly testimonials to the human capacity for evil.

---

tators—and was so intended. Because the British and French navies controlled the Atlantic, the European aggressors could not send their ships to buy America's munitions. The United States not only improved its moral position but simultaneously helped its economic position. An overseas demand for war goods brought a sharp upswing from the recession of 1937–1938, and ultimately solved the decade-long unemployment crisis. (See the chart on p. 524.)

The Fall of France and the Destroyer Deal (1940)

The months following the collapse of Poland, while France and Britain marked time, were known as the "phony war." An ominous silence fell on Europe, as Hitler shifted his victorious divisions from Poland for a knockout blow at France. Inaction during this anxious period was relieved by the Soviets, who wantonly attacked neighboring Finland in an effort to secure strategic buffer territory.

An abrupt end to the phony war came in April 1940, when Hitler, again without warning, overran his weaker neighbors, Denmark and Norway. Hardly pausing for breath, the next month he launched an unannounced assault on Holland and Belgium, followed by a paralyzing blow at France. By late June, France was forced to surrender, but not until Mussolini had pounced on its rear for a jackal's share of the loot. Only by the so-called miracle of Dunkirk did the British manage to evacuate the bulk of their shattered army. The crisis providentially brought forth an inspired leader in Prime Minister Winston Churchill, the bulldog-jawed orator who nerved his people to fight off the fearful air bombings of their cities.

France's sudden collapse shocked Americans out of their daydreams. Stout-hearted Britons, singing "There'll Always Be an England," were all that stood between Hitler and the end of constitutional government in Europe. If Britain went under, Hitler would have at his disposal the workshops, shipyards, and slave labor of western Europe. He might even have the powerful British fleet as well. This frightening possibility, which seemed to pose a dire threat to American security, steeled the American people to a tremendous effort.

Roosevelt now moved with electrifying energy and dispatch. He called upon an already debt-burdened nation to build huge air fleets and a two-ocean navy, which could also check Japan. Congress, jarred out of its apathy, within a year appropriated the astounding sum of $37 billion, more than the total cost of fighting World War I. Congress also passed a conscription law on September 6, 1940, the first peacetime draft in American history.

Before the fall of France in June 1940, Washington had generally observed a technical neutrality.

Destroyer-Bases Deal

But now the wisdom of neutrality seemed increasingly questionable.

As the Battle of Britain raged in the air over the British Isles, debate intensified in the United States over what foreign policy to embrace. Supporters of aid to Britain formed propaganda groups, the most potent of which was the Committee to Defend America by Aiding the Allies. The isolationists, both numerous and sincere, were by no means silent. Determined to avoid bloodshed at all costs, they organized the America First Committee. Their basic philosophy was "the Yanks are not coming," and their most effective speechmaker was the famed aviator Colonel Charles A. Lindbergh who, ironically, had narrowed the Atlantic in 1927.

Britain was in critical need of destroyers, for German submarines were again threatening to starve it out with attacks on shipping. Roosevelt moved boldly; on September 2, 1940, he agreed to transfer to Great Britain fifty old destroyers left over from World War I. In return, the British promised to hand over to the United States eight valuable defensive base sites, stretching from Newfoundland to South America. These strategically located outposts were

to remain under the Stars and Stripes for ninety-nine years.

Shifting warships from a "neutral" United States to a belligerent Britain was, beyond question, a flagrant violation of neutral obligations. Public opinion polls demonstrated that a majority of Americans were determined to provide the battered British with "all aid short of war."

FDR Shatters the Two-Term Tradition (1940)

In the midst of this crisis came the distracting presidential election of 1940. The Republican convention in Philadelphia was miraculously swept off its feet by Wendell L. Willkie, a German-descended Indiana public utilities corporation lawyer who was a complete novice in politics. With the galleries in Philadelphia wildly chanting, "We want Willkie," the delegates finally accepted this political upstart as the only candidate who could possibly beat Roosevelt. The magnetic Willkie was opposed not so much to the New Deal as to its extravagances and inefficiencies. Democratic critics branded him "the rich man's Roosevelt" and "the simple, barefoot Wall Street lawyer."

Democrats fretted while Roosevelt delayed until the last minute the announcement of his decision to challenge the sacred two-term tradition. Despite what he described as his personal yearning for retirement, he avowed that in so grave a crisis he owed his experienced hand to the service of his country and humanity.

With the country already badly split between interventionists and isolationists, Willkie could have widened the breach with a violent attack on Roosevelt's aid-to-Britain policies. But the Republican candidate refrained from assailing the president's interventionism and accepted the essential premises of an internationalist foreign policy: help the victims of aggression, stay out of war, strengthen the nation's defenses. For his part, Roosevelt stayed close to the White House and generally ignored Willkie. But in a speech in Boston he did emphatically declare that "your boys are not going to be sent into any foreign wars"—a pledge that later came back to plague him.

A Campaign Poster from the Election of 1940 *Roosevelt emerged as the only president ever to break the two-term tradition.*

Roosevelt triumphed, although Willkie ran a strong race. The electoral count was 449 to 82. The popular vote was much closer—27,307,819 to 22,321,018.

Congress Passes the Landmark Lend-Lease Law

By late 1940 embattled Britain was nearing the end of its financial tether; its credits in America were being rapidly consumed by insatiable war orders. But Roosevelt, who had bitter memories of the wrangling over the Allied debts of World War I, was determined, as he put it, to eliminate "the silly, foolish, old dollar sign." He finally hit on the scheme of lending or leasing American arms to the reeling democracies. When the shooting was over, to use his comparison, the guns and tanks could be returned, just as one's next-door neighbor would return a garden hose when a threatening fire was put out. But isolationist Senator Robert Taft retorted that lending arms was like lending chewing gum: "You don't want it back." Who wants a chewed-up tank?

The lend-lease bill, patriotically numbered 1776, was entitled "An Act Further to Promote the Defense of the United States." The underlying concept was "Send guns, not sons" or "Billions, not bodies." America, so President Roosevelt promised, would be the "arsenal of democracy." It would send a limitless supply of arms to the victims of aggres-

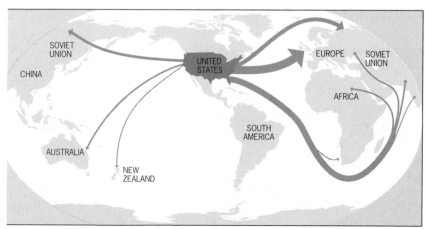

Main Flow of Lend-Lease Aid (width of arrows indicates relative amount) *The proud but desperate British prime minister, Winston Churchill, declared in early 1941: "Give us the tools and we will finish the job." Lend-lease eventually provided the British and other Allies with $50 billion worth of "tools."*

sion, who in turn would finish the job and keep the war on their side of the Atlantic. Isolationists assailed the lend-lease bill as "the blank-check bill." Senator Burton Wheeler called it "the new triple-A [Agricultural Adjustment Act] bill"—a measure designed to "plow under every fourth American boy." Nevertheless, lend-lease was finally approved in March 1941 by sweeping majorities in both houses of Congress.

Lend-lease was one of the most momentous laws ever to pass Congress; it was a challenge hurled squarely into the teeth of the Axis dictators. America eventually sent about $50 billion worth of arms and equipment—much more than the cost to it of World War I—to those nations fighting aggressors. By its very nature, lend-lease marked the abandonment of any pretense of neutrality. It was no destroyer deal arranged privately by Roosevelt. The bill was universally debated, over drugstore counters and cracker barrels, from California to Maine; and the sovereign citizens at last spoke through convincing majorities in Congress. Lend-lease had the somewhat incidental result of gearing the nation's own factories for all-out war production. The enormously increased capacity thus achieved helped to save America's own skin when, at long last, the shooting war burst around its head.

Hitler himself evidently recognized lend-lease as an unofficial declaration of war. Until then, Germany had avoided attacking U.S. ships; memories of America's decisive intervention in 1917–1918 were still fresh in German minds. But after the passing of lend-lease there was less point in trying to curry favor with the United States. On May 21, 1941, the *Robin Moor,* an unarmed American merchant ship, was torpedoed and destroyed by a German submarine in the South Atlantic, outside a war zone. The sinkings had started, but on a limited scale.

Hitler's Assault on Russia Spawns the Atlantic Charter

Two globe-shaking events marked the course of World War II before the assault on Pearl Harbor in December 1941. One was the fall of France in June 1940; the other was Hitler's invasion of the Soviet Union a year later, in June 1941.

The scheming dictators Hitler and Stalin had been uneasy yoke-fellows under the ill-begotten Nazi-Soviet pact of 1939. As masters of the double-cross, neither trusted the other.

Out of a clear sky, on June 22, 1941, Hitler launched a devastating attack on his Soviet neighbor. Sound American strategy dictated speedy aid to Moscow while it was still afloat. Roosevelt immediately promised assistance and backed up his words by making some military supplies available. Several months later, interpreting the lend-lease law to mean that the defense of the USSR was essential for the defense of the United States, he extended $1 billion in lend-lease—the first installment on an ultimate total of $11 billion. Meanwhile, the valor of the Red Army, combined with the white paralysis of an early Russian winter, had halted Hitler's invaders at the gates of Moscow.

With the surrender of the Soviet Union still a dreaded possibility, the drama-charged Atlantic Conference was held in August 1941. British Prime Minister Winston Churchill, with cigar embedded in his cherubic face, secretly met with Roosevelt on a warship off the foggy coast of Newfoundland.

The most memorable offspring of this get-together was the eight-point Atlantic Charter. Suggestive of Wilson's Fourteen Points, the new covenant outlined the aspirations of the democracies for a better world at war's end. It promised that there would be no territorial changes contrary to the wishes of the inhabitants (self-determination). It further affirmed the right of a people to choose their own form of government and, in particular, to regain the governments abolished by the dictators. Among various other goals, the charter declared for disarmament and a peace of security, pending "a permanent system of general security" (a new League of Nations).

U.S. Destroyers and Hitler's U-Boats Clash

Lend-lease shipments of arms to Britain on British ships were bound to be sunk by German wolf-pack submarines. If the intent was to get the munitions to Britain, not to dump them into the ocean, the freighters would have to be escorted by U.S. warships. Britain simply did not have enough destroyers.

The fateful decision to convoy was taken in July 1941. Roosevelt issued orders to the navy to escort lend-lease shipments to Iceland. The British would then shepherd them the rest of the way.

Inevitable clashes with submarines ensued on the Iceland run, even though Hitler's orders were to strike American warships only in self-defense. In September 1941, the U.S. destroyer *Greer,* provocatively trailing a German U-boat, was attacked by the undersea craft, without damage to either vessel. Roosevelt then proclaimed a shoot-on-sight policy. On October 17 the escorting destroyer *Kearny,* while engaged in a battle with U-boats, lost eleven men when it was crippled but not sent to the bottom. Two weeks later the destroyer *Reuben James* was torpedoed and sunk off southwestern Iceland, with the loss of more than 100 officers and men.

Neutrality was still inscribed on the statute books, but not in American hearts. Congress, responding to public pressures and confronted with a shooting war, voted in mid-November 1941 to pull the teeth from the now useless Neutrality Act of 1939. Merchant ships could henceforth be legally armed, and they could enter the combat zones with munitions for Britain. Americans braced themselves for wholesale attacks by Hitler's submarines.

The Surprise Assault at Pearl Harbor

The blowup came, not in the Atlantic, but in the faraway Pacific. This explosion should have surprised no close observer, for Japan, since September 1940, had been a formal military ally of Nazi Germany—America's shooting foe in the North Atlantic.

Japan's position in East Asia had grown more perilous by the hour. It was still mired down in the costly and exhausting China incident, from which it could extract neither honor nor victory. Its war machine was fatally dependent on immense shipments from the United States of steel, scrap iron, oil, and aviation gasoline. Such assistance to the Japanese aggressor was highly unpopular in America. But Roosevelt had resolutely held off an embargo, lest he goad the Tokyo warlords into a descent upon the oil-rich and weakly defended Dutch East Indies (present-day Indonesia).

Washington, late in 1940, finally imposed the first of its embargoes on Japan-bound supplies. This blow was followed in mid-1941 by a "freezing" of Japanese assets in the United States and a cessation of all shipments of gasoline and other sinews of war. As the oil gauge dropped, the squeeze on Japan grew steadily more nerve-wracking.

Japanese leaders were faced with two painful alternatives. They could either knuckle under to the Americans or break out of the embargo ring by a desperate attack on the oil supplies and other riches of Southeast Asia.

Final tense negotiations with Japan took place in Washington during November and early December of 1941. The State Department insisted that the Japanese clear out of China but, to sweeten the pill, offered to renew trade relations on a limited basis. Japanese imperialists, after waging a bitter war against the Chinese for more than four years, were unwilling to lose face by withdrawing at the behest of the United States. Faced with capitulation or continued conquest, they chose the sword.

Officials in Washington, having "cracked" the top-secret code of the Japanese, knew that Tokyo's decision was for war. But the United States, as a democracy committed to public debate and action by Congress, could not shoot first. Roosevelt, misled by Japanese ship movements in the western Pacific, evidently expected the blow to fall on British Malaya or on the Philippines. No one in high authority in Washington seems to have believed that the Japanese were either strong enough or foolhardy enough to strike Hawaii.

But the paralyzing blow struck Pearl Harbor, while Tokyo was deliberately prolonging negotiations in Washington. Japanese bombers, winging in from distant aircraft carriers, attacked without warning on the "Black Sunday" morning of December 7, 1941. It was a date, as Roosevelt told Congress, "which will live in infamy." About 3,000 casualties were inflicted on American personnel; many aircraft were destroyed; the battleship fleet was virtually wiped out when all eight of the craft were sunk or otherwise immobilized; and numerous small vessels were damaged or destroyed. Fortunately for America, the three priceless aircraft carriers happened to be outside the harbor.

CHRONOLOGY

1933	FDR torpedoes the London Economic Conference.
	United States recognizes the Soviet Union.
	FDR declares Good Neighbor policy toward Latin America.
1934	Reciprocal Trade Agreements Act.
1935	Mussolini invades Ethiopia.
	First U.S. Neutrality Act.
1936	Second U.S. Neutrality Act.
1936–1939	Spanish Civil War.
1937	U.S. Neutrality Act of 1937.
	Panay incident.
	Japan invades China.
1938	Hitler seizes Austria.
	Munich Conference.
1939	Nazi-Soviet pact.
	Hitler seizes Czechoslovakia.
	World War II begins in Europe with Hitler's invasion of Poland.
	U.S. Neutrality Act of 1939.
1940	Fall of France.
	Hitler invades Denmark, Norway, the Netherlands, and Belgium.
	Unites States invokes first peacetime draft.
	Battle of Britain.
	Bases-for-destroyers deal with Britain.
	FDR defeats Willkie for presidency.
1941	Lend-Lease Act.
	Hitler attacks the Soviet Union.
	Atlantic Charter.
	Japan attacks Pearl Harbor.

An angered Congress, the next day, officially recognized the war that had been "thrust" upon the United States. The roll call in the Senate and House fell only one vote short of unanimity. Germany and Italy, allies of Japan, spared Congress the indecision of debate by declaring war on December 11, 1941. This challenge was formally accepted on the same day by a unanimous vote of both the Senate and the House. The unofficial war was now official.

America's Transformation from Bystander to Belligerent

Japan's *hara-kiri* gamble in Hawaii paid off only in the short run. True, the Pacific fleet was largely destroyed or immobilized, but the sneak attack aroused and united America as almost nothing else could have done. To the very day of the blowup, a strong majority of American still wanted to keep out of war. But the bombs that pulverized Pearl Harbor blasted the isolationists into silence. The only thing left to do, growled isolationist Senator Wheeler, was "to lick hell out of them."

But Pearl Harbor was not the full answer to the question as to why the United States went to war. This treacherous attack was but the last explosion in a long chain reaction. Following the fall of France, Americans were confronted with a devil's dilemma. They desired above all to stay out of the conflict; yet they did not want Britain to be knocked out. They wished to halt Japan's conquests in East Asia—conquests that menaced not only American trade and security but international peace as well. To keep Britain from collapsing, the Roosevelt administration felt compelled to extend the unneutral aid that invited attacks from German submarines. To keep Japan from expanding, Washington undertook to cut off vital Japanese supplies and invite possible retaliation. Rather than let democracy die and dictatorship rule supreme, a strong majority of citizens were evidently determined to support a policy that might lead to war. It did.

Clearheaded Americans had come to the conclusion that no nation was safe in an era of international anarchy. Appeasement—the tactic of throwing the weaker persons out of the sleigh to the pursuing wolves—had been tried, but it had merely whetted dictatorial appetites. Power-drunk dictators had flouted international law and decency. Asserting the philosophy that might makes right, they had cynically negotiated nonaggression treaties with their intended victims, merely to lull them into a false sense of security. Most Americans were determined to stand firm—and let war come if it must—because they were convinced that with ruthless dictators on the loose the world could not long remain half-enchained and half-free.

Varying Viewpoints

After World War II ended in 1945, many historians were convinced that tragedy could have been averted if only the United States had awakened earlier from its isolationist illusions. These scholars condemned the policies and attitudes of the 1930s as a "retreat from responsibility." Much of the historical writing in the postwar period contained the strong flavor of medicine to ward off another infection by the isolationist virus.

This approach fell into disfavor in the 1960s during the Vietnam War, when many American policy makers defended their actions in Southeast Asia by making dubious comparisons to the decade before World War II. Some scholars responded by arguing that the lessons of the 1930s—especially about the need to avoid appeasement and to take quick and decisive action against aggressors—could not properly be applied to any and all subsequent situations. One controversial product of this line of thinking was Bruce Russett's *No Clear and Present Danger*, which argued that the United States had no clearly defined national interests at stake in 1941, and that both the nation and the world might have been better off without U.S. intervention.

Although few scholars fully accept Russett's conclusions, more recent writing on American entry into World War II has tended to avoid finding in that episode lessons for posterity. Attention has focused, rather, on the wisdom or folly of specific policies, such as Washington's hard line toward Tokyo throughout 1941, when the possibility of a negotiated settlement with Japan perhaps existed. P. W. Schroeder's *The Axis Alliance and Japanese-American Relations, 1941* makes that point with particular force. Other historians debate whether Franklin Roosevelt was really a bold interventionist struggling against Congress and public opinion or a reluctant figure who shared much of the traditional isolationist credo. Robert Dallek's encyclopedic study of Roosevelt's foreign policy portrays Roosevelt as a shrewd and calculating internationalist, whereas Donald Cameron Watt's *How the War Came* depicts him as a myopic and ill-informed leader who overestimated his own peacemaking abilities and, like most other Americans, only belatedly awakened to the menace of totalitarianism.

SELECT READINGS

Primary Source Documents

Franklin D. Roosevelt's "Quarantine the Aggressors" speech (1937), in Richard Hofstadter, *Great Issues in American History,* revealed what would become the goal of the president's foreign policy in succeeding years. See also Roosevelt's "Press Conference on Lend-Lease" (1940), in *The Public Papers and Addresses of Franklin D. Roosevelt, 1940 Volume* (1941), pp. 606–608.* For opposition to lend-lease, see the speech of January 12, 1941, by Montana Senator Burton K. Wheeler, *Congressional Record,* 77 Cong., 1 sess., Appendix, pp. 178–179.* Charles A. Lindbergh elaborated the isolationist position in the *New York Times,* April 24, 1941, p. 12.*

Secondary Sources

Indispensable and comprehensive is Robert Dallek, *Franklin D. Roosevelt and American Foreign Policy, 1932–1945* (1979). A useful brief survey is John E. Wiltz, *From Isolation to War, 1931–1941* (1968). Isolation is ably handled in Manfred Jonas, *Isolationism in America, 1935–1941* (1966), Thomas Guinsburg, *The Pursuit of Isolationism in the United States Senate from Versailles to Pearl Harbor* (1982), and Robert A. Divine, *The Reluctant Belligerent* (1965). Sympathetic to the isolationists is Wayne S. Cole, *Roosevelt and the Isolationists, 1932–1945* (1983). On Good Neighborism consult Bryce Wood, *The Making of the Good Neighbor Policy* (1961), and Irwin F. Gellman, *Good Neighbor Diplomacy* (1979). For East Asia, see Dorothy Borg, *The United States and the Far Eastern Crisis of 1933–1938* (1964), P. W. Schroeder, *The Axis Alliance and Japanese-American Relations, 1941* (1958), and Akira Iriye and Warren Cohen, eds., *American, Chinese, and Japanese Perspectives on Wartime Asia, 1931–1949* (1990). The Japanese attack on Pearl Harbor is considered in Gordon W. Prange, *At Dawn We Slept* (1981), and Michael Slackman, *Target: Pearl Harbor* (1990). A provocative analysis of the reasons (or lack of them) for United States entry into the conflict is Bruce Russett, *No Clear and Present Danger* (1972). See also Donald Cameron Watt, *How War Came: The Immediate Origins of the Second World War, 1938–1939* (1989).

CHAPTER 37

America in World War II, 1941–1945

Never before have we had so little time in which to do so much.

Franklin D. Roosevelt, 1942

The Allies Trade Space for Time

The United States was plunged into the inferno of World War II with the most stupefying and humiliating military defeat in its history. In the dismal months that ensued, the democratic world teetered on the edge of disaster.

Japan's fanatics forgot that whoever stabs a king must stab to kill. A wounded but still potent American giant pulled itself out of the mud of Pearl Harbor, grimly determined to avenge the bloody treachery. "Get Hirohito first" was the cry that rose from millions of infuriated Americans, especially on the Pacific Coast. These outraged souls regarded America's share in the global conflict as a private war of vengeance in the Pacific, with the European theater a kind of holding operation.

But Washington, in the so-called ABC-1 agreement with the British, had earlier and wisely adopted the grand strategy of "getting Hitler first." If America diverted its main strength to the Pacific, Hitler might crush both the Soviet Union and Britain and then emerge unconquerable in Fortress Europe. But

if Germany was knocked out first, the combined Allied forces could be concentrated on Japan, and its daring game of conquest would be up. Meanwhile, enough American strength would be sent to the Pacific to prevent Japan from digging in too deeply.

The get-Hitler-first strategy was the solid foundation on which all American military strategy was built. But it encountered much unwarranted criticism from Americans who thirsted for revenge against Japan. Aggrieved protests were also registered by shorthanded American commanders in the Pacific and by Chinese and Australian allies. But President Roosevelt, a competent strategist in his own right, wisely resisted these pressures.

Given time, the Allies seemed bound to triumph. But would they be given time? True, they had on their side the great mass of the world's population, but the wolf is never frightened by the number of the sheep.

Time, in a sense, was the most needed munition. Expense was no limitation. The overpowering

The Japanese

In 1853 the American commodore Matthew Perry sailed four gunboats into Japan's Uraga Bay and demanded that the nation open itself to diplomatic and commercial exchange with the United States. Within two decades of Perry's arrival, Japan's government had launched the nation on an ambitious program of industrialization and militarization designed to make it the economic and political equal of the Western powers.

As Japan rapidly modernized, its citizens increasingly took ship for America. A steep land tax drove more than 300,000 Japanese farmers off their land. In 1884 the Meiji government permitted Hawaiian planters to recruit contract laborers from among this displaced population. By the 1890s, many Japanese were sailing beyond Hawaii to the ports of Long Beach, San Francisco, and Seattle.

Between 1885 and 1924, roughly 200,000 Japanese migrated to Hawaii, and around 180,000 more ventured to the U.S. mainland. They were a select group: because Japan's government saw overseas Japanese as representatives of their homeland, it strictly regulated emigration. Thus Japanese immigrants to America arrived with more money and better education than their European counterparts.

Nor was this exclusively a male migration. The Japanese government, wanting to avoid the problems of an itinerant bachelor society that it observed among the Chinese in the United States, actively promoted women's migration. Although most Japanese immigrants were young men in their twenties and thirties, thousands of women also ventured to Hawaii and the mainland as contract laborers or "picture brides," so called because their courtship had consisted exclusively of an exchange of photographs with their prospective husbands.

Japanese-American Evacuees, 1942 *This farm family in Los Angeles County was "relocated" shortly after this photograph was taken.*

In Hawaii most Japanese labored on the vast sugarcane plantations. On the mainland they initially found migratory work on the railroads or in fish, fruit, or vegetable canneries. A separate Japanese economy of restaurants, stores, and boardinghouses soon sprang up in cities to serve the immigrants' needs.

From such humble beginnings, many Japanese—particularly those on the Pacific Coast—quickly moved into farming. In the late nineteenth century, the spread of irrigation shifted California agriculture from grain to fruits and vegetables, and the invention of the refrigerated railcar opened hungry new markets in the East. The Japanese, with centuries of experience in intensive farming, arrived just in time to take advantage of these developments.

Their many small vegetable- and fruit-growing operations prospered.

But the very success of the Japanese proved a lightning rod for trouble. On the West Coast, Japanese immigrants had long endured racist barbs and social segregation. Increasingly, white workers and farmers, jealous of Japanese success, pushed for immigration restrictions. Bowing to this pressure, President Theodore Roosevelt in 1908 negotiated the "Gentlemen's Agreement," under which the Japanese government voluntarily agreed to limit emigration. In 1913 the California legislature denied Japanese immigrants already living in the United States the right to own land.

Discriminated against in their adopted homeland, Japanese immigrants (the "Issei," from the Japanese word for *first*) became more determined than ever that their American-born children (the "Nissei," from the Japanese word for *second*) would succeed. Japanese parents encouraged their children to learn English, to excel in school, and to get a college education. Many Nissei grew up in two worlds, a fact they often recognized by Americanizing their Japanese names. Although education and acculturation did not protect the Nissei from the hysteria of World War II, those assets did give them a springboard to success in the postwar era.

---

problem confronting the nation was to retool itself for all-out war production, while praying that the dictators would not meanwhile crush the democracies. Haste was all the more imperative because the highly skilled German scientists might turn up with unbeatable weapons, including rocket bombs and perhaps even atomic arms.

America's task was far more complex and backbreaking than during World War I. It had to feed, clothe, and arm itself, as well as transport its forces to regions as far separated as Britain and Burma. More than that, it had to send a vast amount of food and munitions to its hard-pressed allies, who stretched all the way from the USSR to Australia. Could the American people, reputedly "gone soft," measure up to this colossal responsibility? Was democracy "rotten" and "decadent," as the dictators sneeringly proclaimed?

The Shock of War

National unity was no worry, thanks to the electrifying blow by the Japanese at Pearl Harbor. Prewar controversies melted away, while millions of Italian-Americans and German-Americans loyally supported the nation's war program. In contrast to World War I, when the patriotism of millions of New Immigrants was hotly questioned, World War II actually speeded the assimilation of many ethnic groups into American society. Immigration had been choked off for almost two decades before 1941, and America's ethnic communities were now composed of well-settled members, whose votes were crucial to Franklin Roosevelt's Democratic party. Consequently, there was virtually no governmental witch-hunting of minority groups, as had happened in World War I.

A painful exception was the plight of some 110,000 Japanese-Americans, concentrated on the Pacific Coast (see "Makers of America: The Japanese," pp. 544–545). The Washington top command, fearing that they might act as saboteurs for Japan in case of invasion, forcibly herded them together in concentration camps, though about two-thirds of them were American-born U.S. citizens. This brutal precaution was both unnecessary and unfair, as the loyalty and combat record of Japanese-Americans proved to be admirable. But a wave of post–Pearl Harbor hysteria, backed by the long historical swell of anti-Japanese prejudice on the West Coast, temporarily robbed many Americans of their good sense—and their sense of justice. The internment camps deprived these uprooted Americans of dignity and basic rights; the internees also lost hundreds of millions of dollars in property and foregone earnings. The wartime Supreme Court in 1944 upheld the constitutionality of the Japanese relocation in *Korematsu* v. *U.S.* But more than four decades later, in 1988, the U.S. government officially apologized for its actions and approved the payment of reparations of $20,000 to each camp survivor.

The war prompted other changes in the American mood. Many programs of the once-popular New Deal were wiped out by the conservative Congress elected in 1942, and even President Roosevelt declared in 1943 that "Dr. New Deal" was going into retirement to be replaced by "Dr. Win-the-War." The era of New Deal reform was over.

World War II was no idealistic crusade, as World War I had been. The Washington government emphasized action rather than propaganda. According to opinion polls during the war, a majority or near-majority of citizens confessed to having "no clear idea what the war is about." All Americans knew was that they had a dirty job on their hands

and that the only way out was forward. They went about their bloody task with astonishing efficiency.

Building the War Machine

The war crisis made the drooping American economy snap to attention. Massive military orders—over $100 billion in 1942 alone—almost instantly soaked up the idle industrial capacity of the still-lingering Great Depression. Orchestrated by the War Production Board, American factories poured forth an avalanche of weaponry: 40 billion bullets, 300,000 aircraft, 76,000 ships, 86,000 tanks, and 2.6 million machine guns.

Farmers, too, rolled up their sleeves and increased their output. The armed forces drained the farms of workers, but heavy new investment in agricultural machinery and improved fertilizers more than made up the difference. In 1944 and 1945, blue-jeaned farmers hauled in record-breaking billion-bushel wheat harvests.

These wonders of production also brought economic strains. Full employment and scarce con-

Mexican *Braceros* Headed for New Mexico Cotton Fields, 1940s *During World War II, tens of thousands of migrant workers were brought into the United States to perform agricultural labor. Many received low pay and lived in poor and crowded conditions.*

sumer goods fueled a sharp inflationary surge in 1942. The Office of Price Administration eventually brought ascending prices under control with extensive regulations. Rationing held down the consumption of critical goods such as meat and butter, though some "black marketeers" and "meatleggers" cheated the system. The War Labor Board (WLB) imposed ceilings on wage increases.

Labor unions, whose memberships grew from about 10 million to more than 13 million workers during the war, fiercely resented the government-dictated wage ceilings. Despite the no-strike pledges of most major unions, a rash of labor walkouts plagued the war effort. Threats of lost production through strikes became so worrisome that Congress, in June 1943, passed the Smith-Connally Anti-Strike Act, which authorized the federal government to seize and operate tied-up industries. Under the Smith-Connally Act, Washington took over the coal mines and, for a brief period, the railroads. Yet work stoppages accounted for less than one percent of the total working hours of the United States' wartime laboring force.

Manpower and Womanpower

The armed services enrolled nearly 15 million men in World War II—and some 216,000 women, who were employed for noncombat duties. Best known of these "women in arms" were the WACS (army), WAVES (navy), and SPARS (Coast Guard).

Despite draft exemptions for key categories of industrial and agricultural workers, military needs left the nation's farms and factories so drained of personnel that new workers had to be found. An agreement with Mexico in 1942 brought thousands of Mexican agricultural workers, called *braceros,* across the border to harvest the fruit and grain crops of the West. The *bracero* program outlived the war by some twenty years, becoming a fixed feature of the agricultural economy in many western states.

Even more dramatic was the march of women onto the factory floor. More than 6 million women took up jobs outside the home; over half of them had never before worked for wages. Many of them were mothers, and the government was obliged to set up some 3,000 day-care centers to care for "Rosie the

Riveter's" children while she drilled the fuselage of a heavy bomber or joined the links of a tank track. When the war ended, Rosie and many of her sisters wanted to keep working and often did. The war thus measurably contributed to an eventual revolution in the roles of women in American society.

Yet the war's impact on women's lives frequently has been exaggerated. The great majority of women—especially those with husbands at home or with small children to care for—did not work for wages in the wartime economy but continued in their traditional roles. In both Britain and the Soviet Union, a far greater percentage of women were pressed into industrial service, as the gods of war laid a much heavier hand on those societies than they did on the United States. The main result of wartime experience for women appeared to be not economic liberation but the postwar rush into suburban domesticity and the mothering of the "baby boomers" who were born by the tens of millions in the decade and a half after 1945. America was destined to experience a revolution in women's status later in the postwar period, but the roots of that upheaval are only faintly traceable to the war years.

The war also proved to be a demographic cauldron, churning and shifting the American population. Many of the 15 million men and women in uniform, having seen new sights and glimpsed new horizons, chose not to go home again at war's end. War industries sucked people into boomtowns such as Los Angeles, Detroit, Seattle, and Baton Rouge. California's population grew by nearly 2 million. The South experienced especially dramatic changes. The states of the old Confederacy received a disproportionate share of defense contracts, including nearly $6 billion of federally financed industrial facilities. Here were the origins of the postwar boom in the "Sunbelt."

Despite this economic stimulus in the South, some 1.6 million blacks left the land of their ancient enslavement to seek jobs in the war plants of the West and North (see "Makers of America: The Great African-American Migration," pp. 566–567). Forever after, race relations constituted a national, not a regional, issue. Explosive tensions developed over employment, housing, and segregated facilities. Black leader A. Philip Randolph, head of the Brotherhood of Sleeping Car Porters, threatened a massive "Negro march on Washington" in 1941 to demand equal opportunities for blacks in war jobs and in the armed forces. Roosevelt's response was to issue an executive order forbidding discrimination in defense industries. In addition, the president established the Fair Employment Practices Commission (FEPC) to monitor compliance with his edict. Blacks were also drafted into the armed forces, though primarily in service rather than combat units. But in general the war helped to embolden blacks in their long struggle for equality. Membership in the National Association for the Advancement of Colored People (NAACP) shot up almost to the half-million mark, and a new militant organization, the Congress of Racial Equality (CORE), was founded in 1942.

The northward migration of African-Americans accelerated after the war, thanks to the advent of the mechanical cotton picker—an invention whose impact rivaled that of Eli Whitney's cotton gin. Overnight, the Cotton South's historic need for cheap labor disappeared. Their labor no longer required in Dixie, some 5 million black tenant farmers and sharecroppers headed north in the three decades after the war. Within a single generation, a near-majority of African-Americans gave up their historic homeland and their rural way of life. By 1970 half of all blacks lived outside the South, and *urban* had become almost a synonym for *black*.

The war also prompted an exodus of Native Americans from the reservations. Thousands of Indian men and women found war work in the cities

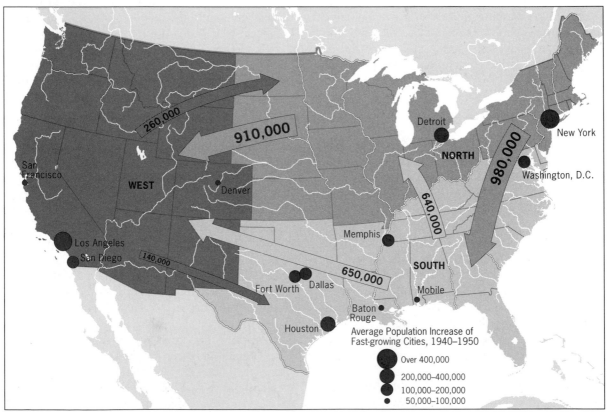

Internal Migration in the United States During World War II *Few events in American history have moved the American people about so massively as World War II. The West and the South boomed, and several war-industry cities grew explosively. Some 1.3 million migrants from the South were blacks.*

or answered Uncle Sam's call to arms. More than 90 percent of Indians resided on reservations in 1940; four decades later more than half lived in cities.

The sudden rubbing against one another of unfamiliar peoples produced some distressingly violent friction. In 1943 young "zoot-suit"–clad Mexicans and Mexican-Americans in Los Angeles were viciously attacked by Anglo sailors who cruised the streets in taxicabs, searching for victims. At almost the same time, an even more brutal race riot that killed twenty-five blacks and nine whites erupted in Detroit.

Holding the Home Front

Despite these ugly episodes, Americans on the home front suffered little from the war, compared with the peoples of the other fighting nations. By war's end much of the planet was a smoking ruin. But in America the war invigorated the economy and lifted the country out of a decade-long depression. The gross national product vaulted from less than $100 billion in 1940 to more than $200 billion in 1945. Corporate profits and disposable personal income approximately doubled during the war. Despite wage ceilings, overtime pay fattened pay envelopes. On December 7, 1944, the third anniversary of Pearl Harbor, Macy's department store rang up the biggest sales day in its history. Americans had never had it so good—and they wanted it a lot better.

The hand of government touched more American lives more intimately during the war than ever before. The war, perhaps even more than the New Deal, pointed the way to the post-1945 era of big-government interventionism. Millions of men and women worked for Uncle Sam in the armed forces or defense industries, and their personal needs were cared for by government-sponsored housing projects, day-care facilities, and health plans. The Office of Scientific Research and Development channeled hundreds of millions of dollars into university-based scientific research, establishing the partnership between the government and universities that underwrote America's technological and economic leadership in the postwar era.

The flood of war dollars—not the relatively modest rivulet of New Deal spending—at last swept the plague of unemployment from the land. War, not enlightened social policy, cured the depression. As the postwar economy continued to depend dangerously on military spending for its health, many observers saw in the years 1941–1945 the origins of a "warfare-welfare state."

The conflict was phenomenally expensive. The wartime bill amounted to more than $330 billion—ten times the direct cost of World War I and twice as much as *all* previous federal spending since 1776. Despite an expanded income tax and higher tax rates, only about two-fifths of the war costs were paid from current revenues. The remainder was borrowed. The national debt skyrocketed from $49 billion in 1941 to $259 billion in 1945.

The Rising Sun in the Pacific

Early successes of the Japanese militarists were breathtaking: the Tokyo warlords realized that they would have to win quickly or lose slowly. Simultaneously with the assault on Pearl Harbor, the Japanese launched widespread and uniformly successful attacks on various bastions in the Pacific and East Asia. These included the American outposts of Guam, Wake Island, and the Philippines, as well as the British-Chinese port of Hong Kong, and British Malaya, with its critically important supplies of rubber and tin.

Nor did the Japanese stop there. The soldiers of the emperor, plunging into the snake-infested jungles of Burma, cut the famed Burma road. This was the route over which the United States had been trucking a trickle of munitions to the armies of the Chinese generalissimo Jiang Jieshi (Chiang Kai-shek) who was still resisting the Japanese invader in China. Thereafter, intrepid American aviators were forced to fly a handful of war supplies to Jiang "over the hump" of the towering Himalaya Mountains from the India-Burma theater. Meanwhile, the Japanese had lunged southward against the oil-rich Dutch East Indies, which speedily fell to the assailant.

In the Philippines, General Douglas MacArthur's resistance effectively slowed the Japanese advance for five months. Twenty thousand American troops and a larger force of Filipinos withdrew to a

United States Thrusts in the Pacific, 1942–1945 *American strategists had to choose among four proposed plans for waging the war against Japan:*

1. Defeating the Japanese in China by funneling supplies over the Himalayan "hump" from India.

2. Carrying the war into Southeast Asia (a proposal much favored by the British, who could thus regain Singapore).

3. Heavy bombing of Japan from Chinese air bases.

4. "Island-hopping" from the South Pacific to within striking distance of the Japanese home islands. This strategy, favored by General Douglas MacArthur, was the one finally emphasized.

strong defensive position at Bataan, where they held off violent Japanese attacks until the inevitable surrender on April 9, 1942. MacArthur himself was ordered to depart secretly for Australia, but proclaimed as he departed, "I shall return." The battered prisoners of war were treated with vicious cruelty in the eighty-five-mile Bataan death march. The island fortress of Corregidor, in Manila Harbor, held out until May 6, 1942, when it surrendered and left Japanese forces in complete control of the Philippine archipelago.

Japan's High Tide at Midway

The aggressive warriors from Japan, making hay while the Rising Sun shone, pushed relentlessly southward. They invaded the turtle-shaped island of

New Guinea, north of Australia, and landed on the Solomon Islands, from which they threatened Australia itself. Their onrush was finally checked by a crucial naval battle in the Coral Sea, in May 1942. An American carrier task force, with Australian support, inflicted heavy losses on the victory-flushed Japanese. For the first time in history, the fighting was all done by carrier-based aircraft; and neither fleet saw or fired a shot directly at the other.

Japan next undertook to seize Midway Island, more than 1,000 miles northwest of Honolulu. From this strategic base, it could launch devastating assaults on Pearl Harbor, and perhaps force the weakened American Pacific fleet into destructive combat. An epochal naval battle was fought near Midway, June 3–6, 1942. Admiral Chester W. Nimitz, a high-grade naval strategist, directed a smaller but skillfully maneuvered carrier force, under Admiral Raymond A. Spruance, against the powerful invading fleet. The fighting was all done by aircraft, and the Japanese broke off action after losing four vitally important carriers.

The smashing success at Midway, combined with the Battle of the Coral Sea, turned the tide of Japan's conquest. But the thrust of the Japanese into the eastern Pacific did net them America's fog-girt islands of Kiska and Attu, in the Aleutian archipelago, off Alaska. This easy conquest aroused fear of an invasion of the United States from the northwest. Much American strength was consequently diverted to the defense of Alaska, including the construction of the "Alcan" highway through Canada.

Yet the Japanese imperialists, overextended in 1942, suffered from "victory disease." Their appetites were bigger than their stomachs. If they had only dug in and consolidated their gains, they would have been much more difficult to dislodge.

American Leapfrogging toward Tokyo

Following the heartening victory at Midway, the United States for the first time was able to seize the initiative in the Pacific. In August 1942 American ground forces gained a toehold on Guadalcanal Island, in the Solomons, in an effort to protect the lifeline from America to Australia through the Southwest Pacific. After several desperate sea battles for naval control of the area, the Japanese troops evacuated Guadalcanal in February 1943.

American and Australian forces, under General MacArthur, meanwhile had been hanging on grimly to the southeastern tip of New Guinea, the last buffer protecting Australia. Aided by American naval forces, MacArthur eventually fought his way through the green jungle hell and completed the conquest of New Guinea by August 1944.

The United States Navy, with marines and army divisions doing the meat-grinder fighting, had meanwhile been "leapfrogging" the Japanese islands in the Pacific. Rather than proceed on a broad front and carefully protect their flanks, the new American strategy of island hopping called for bypassing the most heavily fortified Japanese posts, capturing nearby islands, setting up airfields on them, and then neutralizing the enemy bases through heavy bomb-

ing. Deprived of supplies from the homeland, Japan's outposts would slowly wither on the vine—as they did.

With Admiral Nimitz skillfully coordinating the efforts of naval, air, and ground units, the American attacks achieved brilliant success. In May and August 1943, Attu and Kiska in the Aleutians were easily retaken. In November 1943 "Bloody Tarawa" and Makin in the Gilberts fell after suicidal resistance, and key outposts in the Marshall group succumbed after savage fighting in January and February 1944. The retaking of Guam and other spacious islands in the Marianas in July and August 1944 provided airfields for America's new B-29 superbombers to conduct round-trip bombing raids on Japan's home islands. With these unsinkable aircraft carriers now available, virtual round-the-clock bombing of Japan began in November 1944.

The Allied Halting of Hitler

Early setbacks for America in the Pacific were paralleled in the Atlantic. Hitler had entered the war with a formidable fleet of ultramodern submarines, which ultimately operated in "wolf packs" with frightful effect. During ten months of 1942 more than 500 merchant ships were reported lost—111 in June alone—as ship destruction far outran construction. Not until the spring of 1943 did the Allies clearly gain the upper hand against the U-boat.

Meanwhile, the turning point of the land-air war against Hitler had come late in 1942. The British, who had launched a 1,000-plane raid on Cologne in May, were joined by the American air force in cascading bombs on German cities. The Germans under Marshal Erwin Rommel—"the Desert Fox"—had driven across the hot sands of North Africa into Egypt, perilously close to the Suez Canal. A breakthrough would have spelled disaster for the Allies. But late in October 1942, the British general Bernard Montgomery delivered a withering attack at El Alamein, west of Cairo. With the aid of several hundred hastily shipped American Sherman tanks, he speedily drove the enemy back to Tunisia, more than 1,000 miles away.

On the Soviet front, the unexpected successes of the Red Army gave a new lift to the Allied cause. In September 1942, the Soviets halted the German

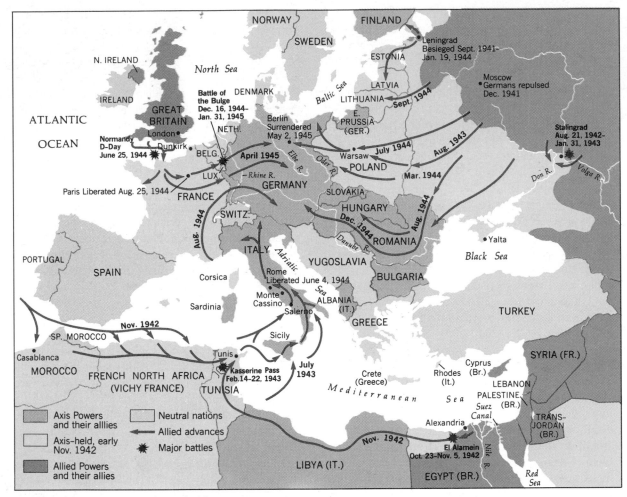

World War II in Europe and North Africa, 1939–1945

steamroller at rubble-bestrewn Stalingrad, graveyard of Hitler's hopes. In November 1942, the resilient Soviets unleashed a crushing counteroffensive, which was never seriously reversed. A year later, Stalin had regained about two-thirds of the blood-soaked Soviet Motherland wrested from him by the German invader.

North Africa and Italy

Soviet losses were already staggering in 1942. By war's end, the grave had closed over some 20 million Soviet soldiers, and the country had been laid waste. It is small wonder that Soviet leaders never ceased to

clamor for a second front. Many Americans, including FDR, were eager to begin a diversionary invasion of France in 1942 or 1943, because they feared that the Soviets might make a separate peace with Hitler and leave the western Allies to face Hitler's fury alone. But British military planners, remembering their fearful losses in 1914–1918, were not enthusiastic about a frontal assault on German-held France. It might end in complete disaster. They preferred to attack Hitler's Fortress Europe through the "soft underbelly" of the Mediterranean. Faced with British reluctance, the Americans reluctantly agreed to postpone a massive invasion of Europe.

An invasion of French-held North Africa was a

compromise second front. The highly secret attack, launched in November 1942, was headed by a gifted and easy-smiling American general, Dwight D. ("Ike") Eisenhower. The surprise landing was highly successful. After savage desert fighting, the remnants of the German-Italian army were trapped in Tunisia and surrendered in May 1943.

Skeptical Soviets scoffed at this second-rate second front. At Casablanca, in newly occupied French Morocco, President Roosevelt met with Winston Churchill in January 1943 to plan strategy. The Big Two agreed to step up the Pacific war, invade Sicily, increase pressure on Italy, and insist on an "unconditional surrender" of the enemy. Designed to reassure the ultrasuspicious Soviets, who feared separate Allied peace negotiations, "unconditional surrender" proved to be one of the most controversial policies of the war. The main criticism was that it steeled the enemy to fight to a last-bunker resistance. Although there was some truth in these charges, no one can prove that "unconditional surrender" shortened or lengthened the war. But by helping to destroy the German government utterly, the harsh policy immensely complicated the problems of postwar reconstruction.

Following the Casablanca strategy, American, British, and Canadian forces captured Sicily in August 1943. In September 1943, while Allied troops were pouring onto the toe of the Italian boot, Mussolini was deposed and a new Rome government surrendered unconditionally.

But if Italy dropped out of the war, the Germans did not drop out of Italy. Hitler's well-trained troops resisted the Allied invaders in some of the filthiest, bloodiest, and most frustrating fighting of the war. After a touch-and-go assault on the Anzio beachhead, Rome was taken on June 4, 1944. But it was not until May 2, 1945, only five days before Germany's official surrender, that the several hundred thousand Axis troops in Italy laid down their arms and became prisoners of war.

Eisenhower's D-Day Invasion of France

The Soviets had never ceased to clamor for an all-out second front. Plans for a major Allied invasion were finally settled at a conference of Stalin, Churchill,

and Roosevelt in Teheran, Iran, held from November 28 to December 1, 1943. The Soviets agreed to coordinate attacks on Germany from the east with the prospective Allied assault from the west.

Preparations for the cross-channel invasion of France were gigantic. Britain's fast-anchored isle virtually groaned with munitions, supplies, and troops, as nearly 3 million fighting men were readied. As the United States was to provide most of the Allied warriors, the overall command was entrusted to an American, General Eisenhower.

French Normandy, less heavily defended than other parts of the European coast, was pinpointed for the invasion assault. On D-Day, June 6, 1944, the enormous operation, which involved some 4,600 vessels, unwound. Stiff resistance was encountered from the Germans, who had been misled by a feint into expecting the blow to fall farther north. The Allies had already achieved mastery of the air over France. They were thus able to block reinforcements by crippling the railroads, while worsening German fuel shortages by bombing gasoline producing plants.

The Allied beachhead, at first clung to with fingertips, was gradually enlarged, consolidated, and reinforced. After desperate fighting, the invaders finally broke out of the German iron ring at the base of the Normandy peninsula. Most spectacular were the lunges across France by American armored divisions, brilliantly commanded by blustery and profane General George S. ("Blood 'n' Guts") Patton. The retreat of the German defenders was hastened when an American-French force landed in August 1944 on the southern coast of France and swept northward. With the assistance of the French "underground," Paris was liberated in August 1944.

Allied forces rolled irresistibly toward Germany. The first important German city (Aachen) fell to the Americans in October 1944, and the days of Hitler's "thousand-year *Reich*" were numbered.

FDR: The Fourth-Term-ite of 1944

The presidential campaign of 1944 came awkwardly as the awful conflict roared to its climax. Victory-starved Republicans nominated short, mustachioed Thomas Dewey, the popular governor of New York. A former prosecutor, Dewey was only forty-two years old, causing one veteran New Dealer to sneer that the candidate had cast his diaper into the ring. Dewey was a mild internationalist, and the Republican platform called for an unstinted prosecution of the war and for the creation of a new international organization to maintain peace.

FDR, aging under the strain but still the "indispensable man," was nominated by acclamation for a fourth term. Most of the Democratic convention's attention focused on the vice presidency. Roosevelt's third-term vice president, former agriculture secretary Henry A. Wallace, had a strong liberal following. Conservative Democrats developed a "ditch Wallace" movement that gained tremendous momentum and finally won Roosevelt's blessing. The vice-presidential nomination then went to smiling and self-assured Senator Harry S Truman of Missouri, who had recently attained national visibility by conducting an investigation of wasteful war expenditures.

A dynamic Dewey took the offensive in the campaign, proclaiming in his beautiful baritone voice that it was "time for a change" after "twelve long years" of New Dealism. Roosevelt was too involved in directing the war to spare much time for speechmaking. But in the closing weeks of the campaign, he left his desk for the stump. He was eager to show himself, even in chilling rains, to spike well-founded rumors of failing health.

Democrats relied heavily on the new Political Action Committee of the CIO, which provided union funds and workers for the ticket. Roosevelt, as customary, won a sweeping victory: 432 to 99 in the Electoral College, 25,606,585 to 22,014,745 in the popular totals. Elated, he quipped that "the first twelve years are the hardest."

The Last Days of Hitler

By mid-December 1944, the month after Roosevelt's fourth-term victory, Germany seemed to be wobbling on its last legs. The Soviet surge had penetrated eastern Germany. Allied aerial "blockbuster" bombs,

A Nazi Concentration Camp *These gaunt survivors of the Nazi concentration camp at Evensee, Austria, greeted their liberators from the U.S. Third Army on May 7, 1945. Scanty food and wretched sanitation claimed almost as many lives in the death camps as the dreaded gas chambers. Though the world had some knowledge of these conditions before the war's end, the full revelation of Hitler's horrors as the Allies overran Germany in the spring of 1945 stunned and sickened the invading troops.*

making the "rubble bounce" on an around-the-clock schedule, were falling like giant hailstones on cities, factories, and transportation arteries. The German western front seemed about to buckle under the sledgehammer blows of the United States and its allies.

Hitler then staked everything on one last throw of his reserves. Secretly concentrating a powerful force, he hurled it, on December 16, 1944, against the thinly held American lines in the heavily befogged and snow-shrouded Ardennes forest. Caught off guard, the outmanned Americans were driven back, creating a deep "bulge" in the Allied line. The ten-day penetration was finally halted after the 101st Airborne Division had stood firm at the vital bastion of Bastogne. The commander, Brigadier General A. C. McAuliffe, defiantly answered the German demand for surrender with one word: "Nuts." Reinforcements were rushed up, and the last-gasp Hitlerian offensive was at length bloodily stemmed in the Battle of the Bulge.

In March 1945, forward-driving American troops reached Germany's Rhine River, where, by incredibly good luck, they found one strategic bridge undemolished. Pressing their advantage, General Eisenhower's troops reached the Elbe River in April 1945. There, a short distance south of Berlin, American and Soviet advance guards dramatically clasped hands.

The conquering Americans were horrified to find blood-bespattered concentration camps, where the German Nazis had engaged in scientific mass murder of "undesirables," including an estimated 6 million Jews. The federal government had long been informed about Hitler's campaign of genocide against the Jews and had been reprehensibly slow to take steps against it—such as bombing the rail lines that carried the victims to the camps. But until the war's end, the full dimensions of the Holocaust had not been known. When the details were revealed, the whole world was aghast.

The vengeful Soviets, clawing their way forward from the east, reached Berlin in April 1945. After desperate house-to-house fighting, followed by an orgy of pillage and rape, they captured the bomb-shattered city. Adolf Hitler, after a hasty marriage to his mistress, committed suicide in an underground bunker on April 30, 1945.

Tragedy had meanwhile struck the United States. President Roosevelt, while relaxing at Warm Springs, Georgia, suddenly died from a massive cerebral hemorrhage on April 12, 1945. Leaderless citizens discussed the future anxiously, as bewildered, unbriefed Vice President Truman took the helm.

On May 7, 1945, what was left of the German government surrendered unconditionally. May 8 was officially proclaimed V-E Day—Victory in Europe Day—and it was greeted with frenzied rejoicing in the Allied countries.

Japan Dies Hard

Japan's rickety bamboo empire meanwhile was tottering. American submarines—"the silent service"—were sending the Japanese merchant marine to the bottom so fast that they were running out of prey. All told, these underseas craft destroyed 1,042 ships, or about 50 percent of Japan's entire life-giving merchant fleet.

Giant bomber attacks were more spectacular. Launched from Saipan and other captured Marianas, they were reducing the enemy's fragile cities to cinders. The massive fire-bomb raid on Tokyo, March 9–10, 1945, was annihilating. It destroyed over 250,000 buildings, gutted a quarter of the city, and killed an estimated 83,000 persons—a loss comparable to that later inflicted by atomic bombs.

General MacArthur was also on the move. Completing the conquest of jungle-draped New Guinea, he headed northwest for the Philippines, en route to Japan, with 600 ships and 250,000 men. In a scene well staged for the photographers, he splashed ashore at Leyte Island, on October 20, 1944. Manila was taken in March 1945, but the Philippines were not finally conquered until July, after bitter fighting against holed-in Japanese that took a toll of over 60,000 American casualties.

Tokyo's still-menacing navy was at last subdued in the gigantic clash at Leyte Gulf (October 23–26, 1944). Japan was through as a sea power. With American fleets now commanding the western Pacific, a steel vise was tightening mercilessly around

Japan. In March 1945 the tiny but strategic island of Iwo Jima was captured in a bitter assault that cost 4,000 American lives. The island of Okinawa, defended by Japanese soldiers fighting with incredible courage from their caves, was finally taken in June 1945 after 80,000 American casualties and far heavier Japanese losses. The U.S. Navy, which covered the invasion, sustained severe damage when Japanese suicide pilots began crashing their bomb-laden planes onto the decks of the invading fleet, sinking over thirty ships and damaging scores more.

Atomic Awfulness

Strategists in Washington were meanwhile planning an all-out invasion of the main islands of Japan—an invasion that presumably would cost hundreds of thousands of American (and even more Japanese) casualties. Tokyo, recognizing imminent defeat, had secretly sent peace feelers to Moscow, which had not yet entered the East Asian war. But bomb-scorched Japan still showed no outward willingness to surrender *unconditionally* to the Allies.

The Potsdam conference, held near Berlin in July 1945, sounded the death knell of the Japanese. There President Truman, still new on his job, met in a seventeen-day parley with Joseph Stalin and the British leaders. The conferees issued a stern ultimatum to Japan: surrender or be destroyed. American bombers showered the grim warning on Japan in tens of thousands of leaflets, but no encouraging response was forthcoming.

America had a fantastic ace up her sleeve. Early in 1940, after Hitler's wanton assault on Poland, Roosevelt was persuaded by American and exiled scientists, notably German-born Albert Einstein, to push ahead with gigantic preparations for unlocking the secret of an atomic bomb. Congress, at Roosevelt's blank-check request, blindly made available nearly $2 billion.

The huge atomic project was pushed feverishly forward, as American know-how and industrial power were combined with the most advanced scientific knowledge. Much technical skill was provided by British and refugee scientists, who had fled to America from the torture chambers of the dictators. Finally, in the desert near Alamogordo, New Mexico,

on July 16, 1945, the experts detonated the first awesome and devastating atomic device.

With Japan still refusing to surrender, the Potsdam threat was fulfilled. On August 6, 1945, a lone American bomber dropped one atomic bomb on the military-base city of Hiroshima, Japan. In a blinding flash of death, followed by a mushroom-shaped cloud, about 180,000 persons were left killed, wounded, or missing. Some 70,000 of them died instantaneously. Sixty-thousand more soon perished from burns and radiation disease.

Two days later, on August 8, Stalin entered the war against Japan, exactly on the deadline date previously agreed upon with his allies. Soviet armies speedily overran the depleted Japanese defenses in Manchuria and Korea in a six-day "victory parade" that involved several thousand Soviet casualties. Stalin was evidently determined to be in on the kill, lest he lose a voice in the final division of Japan's holdings.

Frantically resisting Japanese, though facing atomization, still did not surrender. On August 9, American aviators, dropped a second atomic bomb on the naval-base city of Nagasaki. The explosion took a horrible toll of about 80,000 people killed or missing.

At last Japan could endure no more. On August 10, 1945, Tokyo sued for peace on one condition: that Hirohito, the bespectacled Son of Heaven, be allowed to remain on his throne as nominal emperor. Despite their "unconditional surrender" policy, the Allies accepted this condition on August 14, 1945. The formal surrender took place on the battleship *Missouri* on September 2, 1945.

The Allies Triumphant

World War II proved to be terribly costly. American forces suffered some 1 million casualties, about one-third of which were deaths. Compared with other wars, the proportion killed by wounds and disease was sharply reduced, owing in part to the use of blood plasma and "miracle" drugs, notably penicillin.

America was fortunate in emerging with its mainland virtually unscathed. Much of the rest of the world was bomb-pocked, rubble-strewn, and

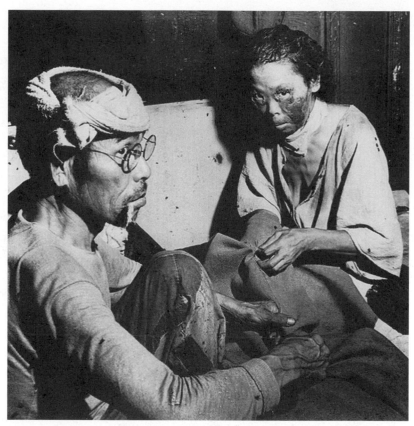

Hiroshima Atomic Bomb Survivors, 1945 *This Japanese man and woman suffered severe burns from the atomic bomb dropped on their city on August 6, 1945.*

impoverished. America alone was untouched and healthy—oiled and muscled like a prize bull, standing astride the world's ruined landscape.

This complex conflict was the best-fought war in America's history. Though unprepared for it at the outset, the nation was better prepared than for the others, partly because it had begun to buckle on its armor about a year and a half before the war officially began. In the end the United States showed itself to be resourceful, tough, adaptable—able to accommodate itself to the tactics of an enemy who was relentless and ruthless.

American military leadership proved to be of the highest order. A new crop of war heroes emerged in brilliant generals like Eisenhower, MacArthur, and Marshall (chief of staff) and in imaginative admirals like Nimitz and Spruance. President Roosevelt and Prime Minister Churchill, as kindred spirits, collaborated closely in planning strategy. "It is fun to be in the same decade with you," FDR once cabled Churchill.

Industrial leaders were no less skilled, for marvels of production were performed almost daily. Assembly lines proved as important as battle lines; and victory went again to the side with the most smokestacks. Enemy forces were devastated by the volume of American-made bayonets, bullets, bazookas, and bombs. Hitler and his Axis coconspirators had chosen to make war with machines, and the ingenious Yankees could ask for nothing better. They demonstrated again, as they had in World War I, that the American way of war was simply more—more men, more weapons, more machines, more technology, and more money than any enemy could hope to match. From 1940 to 1945, the output of American factories was simply phenomenal.

Hermann Goering, a Nazi leader, had sneered, "The Americans can't build planes—only electric

CHRONOLOGY

1941	The United States declares war on Japan.		"Zoot-suit" riots in Los Angeles.
	Germany declares war on the United States.		Race riot in Detroit.
			Japanese driven from Guadalcanal.
	Randolph plans black march on Washington.		Teheran conference
		1944	*Korematsu* v. *U.S.*
	Fair Employment Practices Commission (FEPC) established.		D-Day invasion of France.
			Battle of the Marianas.
1942	Japanese-Americans sent to concentration camps.		Roosevelt defeats Dewey for presidency.
	Japan conquers the Philippines.	1944–1945	Battle of the Bulge
	Battle of the Coral Sea.	1945	Roosevelt dies; Truman assumes presidency.
	Battle of Midway.		
	United States invades North Africa.		Germany surrenders.
	Congress of Racial Equality (CORE) founded.		Battles of Iwo Jima and Okinawa.
			Potsdam conference.
1943	Allies hold Casablanca conference.		Atomic bombs dropped on Hiroshima and Nagasaki.
	Allies invade Italy.		Japan surrenders.
	Smith-Connally Anti-Strike Act.		

iceboxes and razor blades." Democracy had given its answer, as the dictators, despite long preparation, were overthrown and discredited. It is true that an unusual amount of direct control was exercised over the individual by the Washington authorities during the war emergency. But the American people preserved their precious liberties without serious impairment.

Varying Viewpoints

The United States emerged militarily triumphant in 1945. But one event threatened to tarnish the crown of moral victory: the atomic bombing of Japan. America is the only nation ever to have used an atomic weapon in war, and some critics noted cynically that the bomb was dropped not on European enemies but on people of a non-white race. A few scholars, notably Gar Alperovitz, have further charged that the holocaust at Hiroshima and Nagasaki was not the final shot of World War II but the first salvo in the Cold War. Alperovitz notes that the Japanese were already defeated in the summer of 1945 and were attempting to arrange a *conditional* surrender. President Truman ignored those attempts and unleashed his horrible new weapon, so the argument goes, not only to defeat Japan but also to frighten the Soviets into less aggressive behavior.

Could the use of the atomic bomb have been avoided? Few policy makers even asked this at the time, as Martin J. Sherwin's studies have shown. United States leaders wanted to end the war as quickly as possible, for many reasons, and the bomb undoubtedly hastened the devastating conclusion. It also strengthened the American hand against the Soviet Union, but that was not the *primary* reason for the fateful decision to proceed with the nuclear incineration of two Japanese cities. Nevertheless, remorse and misgivings about those horrible bombbursts continue to plague the nation's conscience.

SELECT READINGS

Primary Source Documents

For background on the date that will live in infamy, see *Pearl Harbor Attack: Hearings Before the Joint Committee on the Investigation of the Pearl Harbor Attack,* 79th Congress, 1st Session (1946).* Vivid portraits of the fighting are found in Ernie Pyle's *Here Is Your War* (1943) and *Brave Men* (1944). On the atomic bomb, consult the reactions of the *Nippon Times* (August 10, 1945),* the *Christian Century* (August 29, 1945),* and President Truman's justification of the bombing in *Memoirs of Harry S Truman* (1955).*

Secondary Sources

A scholarly discussion of the home front is John M. Blum, *V Was for Victory: Politics and American Culture During World War II* (1976). Studs Terkel has compiled an interesting oral history of the war experience in *The Good War* (1984). On women, see William H. Chafe, *The American Woman: Her Changing Social, Economic, and Political Roles, 1920–1970* (1972). On blacks, see Neil A. Wynn, *The Afro-Americans and the Second World War* (1976). The military history of the war is capably handled in Albert Russell Buchanan, *The United States and World War II* (2 vols., 1964). High strategy is developed in Kent R. Greenfield, *American Strategy in World War II* (1963). A good introduction to wartime diplomacy is Gaddis Smith, *American Diplomacy During the Second World War* (1965). Also valuable are Robert Dallek's work, cited in the preceding chapter; John L. Gaddis, *The United States and the Origins of the Cold War, 1941–1947* (1972); and two "revisionist" studies that are highly critical of American policy: Gabriel Kolko, *The Politics of War: The World and United States Foreign Policy, 1943–1945* (1968), and Lloyd Gardner, *Architects of Illusion: Men and Ideas in American Foreign Policy, 1941–1949* (1970). The war in Asia is covered in Jonathan Utley, *Going to War with Japan, 1937–1941* (1985); Akira Iriye, *Power and Culture: The Japanese-American War, 1941–1945* (1981); Ronald H. Spector's gracefully written *Eagle Against the Sun: The American War with Japan* (1985); and John W. Dower, *War Without Mercy: Race and Power in the Pacific War* (1986). Paul Fussell contrasts actual combat and wartime rhetoric in *Wartime: Understanding and Behavior in the Second World War* (1989). On the atomic bomb, see Richard G. Hewlett and Oscar E. Anderson, Jr., *The New World* (1962), Martin J. Sherwin, *A World Destroyed: The Atomic Bomb and the Grand Alliance* (1975), and Richard Rhodes, *The Making of the Atomic Bomb* (1986). Paul Boyer's *By the Bomb's Early Light* (1985) analyzes the bomb's impact on the American mind.

CHAPTER 38

The Cold War Begins, 1945–1952

America stands at this moment at the summit of the world.

Winston Churchill, 1945

Postwar Economic Anxieties

The American people, 140 million strong, cheered the blinding atomic climax of World War II in 1945. But when the shouting faded away, countless men and women began to worry about their future. Four fiery years of war had not entirely driven from their minds the painful memories of twelve desperate years of the Great Depression.

The decade of the 1930s had left deep scars. Joblessness and insecurity had dampened the marriage rate. Babies went unborn as pinched budgets and sagging self-esteem wrought a sexual depression in American bedrooms. The war had banished the blight of depression, but grim-faced observers warned that peace would bring the return of hard times.

The faltering economy in the initial postwar years threatened to confirm the worst predictions of the doomsayers who foresaw another Great Depression. Real gross national product (GNP) slumped sickeningly in 1946 and 1947 from its wartime peak.

With the removal of price controls, prices giddily levitated by 33 percent in 1946–1947. An epidemic of strikes swept the country, as 4.6 million laborers conducted work stoppages during 1946 alone.

The growing muscle of organized labor deeply annoyed many conservatives. They had their revenge against labor's New Deal gains in 1947, when a Republican-controlled Congress (the first in fourteen years) passed the Taft-Hartley Act over President Truman's vigorous veto. Labor leaders condemned the act as a "slave-labor law." It outlawed the closed (all-union) shop, made unions liable for damages resulting from jurisdictional disputes, and required union leaders to take a noncommunist oath.

The Democratic administration meanwhile took steps of its own to forestall an economic downturn. It sold war factories and other government installations to private businesses at fire sale prices. It secured passage in 1946 of the Employment Act, which created a three-member Council of Economic

561

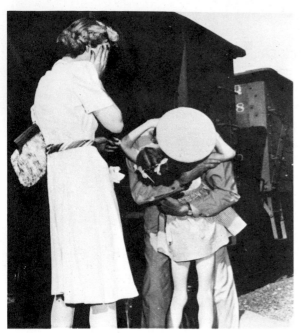

Daddy Comes Home

Advisers to provide the president with data and recommendations on how to "promote maximum employment, production, and purchasing power."

Most dramatic was the passage of the Serviceman's Readjustment Act of 1944, better known as the GI Bill of Rights or the GI Bill. Enacted partly out of fear that the employment markets would never be able to absorb 15 million returning veterans at war's end, the GI Bill made generous provisions for sending the former soldiers to school. In the postwar decade, some 8 million veterans advanced their education at Uncle Sam's expense. The majority attended technical and vocational schools, but colleges and universities were crowded to the blackboards as more than 2 million ex-GIs stormed the halls of higher learning. The total eventually spent for education was some $14.5 billion in taxpayer dollars. The act also enabled the Veterans Administration (VA) to guarantee about $16 billion in loans for veterans to buy homes, farms, and small businesses. By raising educational levels and stimulating the construction industry, the GI Bill powerfully nurtured the robust and long-lived economic expansion that

eventually took hold in the late 1940s—and that deeply shaped the entire history of the postwar era.

The Long Economic Boom, 1950–1970

The GNP began to climb haltingly in 1948. Then, beginning about 1950, the American economy surged onto a dazzling plateau of sustained growth that was to last virtually uninterrupted for nearly two decades. America's economic performance became the envy of the world. National income nearly doubled in the 1950s and almost doubled again in the 1960s, shooting through the trillion-dollar mark in 1973. Americans, some 6 percent of the world's people, were enjoying about 40 percent of the planet's wealth.

As the gusher of prosperity poured forth its riches, Americans drank deeply from the gilded goblet. Millions of depression-pinched souls sought to make up for the sufferings of the 1930s. They determined to "get theirs" while the getting was good. A people who had once considered a chicken in every pot the standard of comfort and security now hungered for two cars in every garage, swimming pools in their backyards, vacation homes, and gas-guzzling recreational vehicles. The size of the "middle class," defined as households earning between $3,000 and $10,000 a year, doubled from pre–Great Depression days and included 60 percent of the American people by the mid-1950s. By the end of that decade, the vast majority of American families owned their own car and washing machine, and nearly 90 percent owned a television set—a gadget invented in the 1920s but virtually unknown until the late 1940s. In another revolution of sweeping consequences, almost 60 percent of American families owned their own homes by 1960, compared with less than 40 percent in the 1920s. A nation of renters had become a nation of homeowners.

Of all the beneficiaries of postwar prosperity, none reaped greater rewards than women. More than ever, urban offices and shops provided them with a bonanza of employment, as the service sector of the economy dramatically outgrew the old industrial and manufacturing sectors. Women accounted for one-fourth of the American workforce at the end of World War II, and for nearly half the labor pool five decades later. Yet even as they continued their march into the workplace in the 1940s and 1950s, popular culture glorified the traditional feminine roles of homemaker and mother. The clash between the demands of suburban housewifery and the realities of employment eventually sparked a feminist revolt in the 1960s.

Nothing loomed larger in the history of the post–World War II era than this fantastic eruption of affluence. It did not enrich all Americans, and it did not touch all people evenly, but it transformed the lives of a majority of citizens and molded the agenda of politics and society for at least two generations. What propelled this unprecedented economic explosion?

The Second World War itself provided a powerful stimulus. While other countries had been ravaged by years of fighting, the United States had used the war crisis to fire up its smokeless factories and rebuild its depression-plagued economy. America had almost effortlessly come to dominate the ruined global landscape of the postwar period. Yet perhaps the very ease of this ascent to the summit of the world economy rendered the country unfit to stay there for long—as the economic crises of the 1970s would eventually suggest.

Ominously, much of the glittering prosperity of the 1950s and 1960s rested on the underpinnings of colossal military budgets, leading some critics to speak of a "permanent war economy." The economic upturn of 1950 was fueled by massive appropriations for the Korean War, and defense spending accounted for some 10 percent of the GNP throughout the ensuing decade. Pentagon dollars primed the pumps of high-technology industries such as aerospace, plastic, and electronics, and also financed much of the scientific research and development that spurred the economy.

Cheap energy also fed the economic boom. American and European companies that controlled the flow of abundant petroleum from the Middle East kept their prices low, and Americans consequently doubled their consumption of the seemingly

Agribusiness *Expensive machinery of the type shown here made most of American agriculture a capital-intensive, phenomenally productive big business by the 1990s—and sounded the death knell for many small-scale family farms.*

inexhaustible oil in the quarter-century after the war. Anticipating a limitless future of low-cost fuels, they flung out endless ribbons of highways, installed air-conditioning in their homes, and spread electrical cables everywhere to activate the tools of workers on factory floors.

With the forces of nature thus increasingly harnessed in their hands, workers chalked up spectacular gains in productivity—the amount of output per hour of work. In the two decades after the outbreak of the Korean War in 1950, productivity increased at an average rate of more than 3 percent per year. Gains in productivity were also enhanced by the rising educational level of the workforce. By 1970 nearly 90 percent of the school-age population was enrolled in educational institutions—a dramatic contrast with the opening years of the century, when only half of this age group had attended school. Better educated and better equipped, workers in 1970 could produce nearly twice as much in an hour's labor as they had done in 1950. Productivity was the key to prosperity. Rising productivity in the 1950s and 1960s virtually doubled the average American's standard of living in the postwar quarter-century.

Also contributing to the vigor of the economy were some momentous changes in the nation's basic economic structure. Conspicuous was the accelerating shift of the workforce out of agriculture, which achieved productivity gains virtually unmatched by any other economic sector. Farmers whose forebears had busted sod with oxen or horses now plowed their fields in air-conditioned tractor cabs, listening on their stereophonic radios to weather forecasts or the latest Chicago commodities market quotations. Once the mighty backbone of the agricultural republic, and still some 15 percent of the labor force at the end of World War II, farmers made up about 2 percent of the American population by the 1990s—yet they fed much of the world.

The Smiling Sunbelt

The convulsive economic changes of the post-1945 period shook and shifted the American people, amplifying the population redistribution set in motion by World War II. As immigrants and westward-trekking pioneers, Americans had always been a people on the move, but they were astonishingly footloose in the postwar years. For some three decades after 1945, an average of 30 million persons changed residences every year. Families especially felt the strain, as distance divided parents from children, and brothers and sisters from one another. One sign of this kind of stress was the phenomenal popu-

Population Increase in the Sunbelt States, 1950–1990 *States with figures higher than 50 percent were growing faster than the national average. Note that "sunbelt" is a loose geographical concept, as some Deep South states had very little population growth, while the mountain and Pacific states were booming.*

America on the Move, 1953 *Millions of Americans migrated to the suburbs and the Sunbelt in the years after World War II. Here a new housing development has just opened near Los Angeles.*

larity of advice books on child rearing, especially Dr. Benjamin Spock's *The Common Sense Book of Baby and Child Care.* First published in 1945, it instructed millions of parents during the ensuing decades in the kind of homely wisdom that was once transmitted naturally from grandparent to parent, and from parent to child.

Especially striking was the growth of the "Sunbelt"—a fifteen-state area stretching in a smiling crescent from Virginia through Florida and Texas to Arizona and California. This region increased its population at a rate nearly double that of the old industrial zones of the Northeast (the "frost belt").

A Niagara of federal dollars accounted for much of the Sunbelt region's new prosperity, even though, ironically, southern and western politicians led the cry against government spending. By the 1990s the South and West were annually receiving some $125 billion more in federal funds than the Northeast and Midwest. Northeasterners and their allies from the hard-hit region of the Ohio Valley tried to rally political support with the sarcastic slogan "The North shall rise again."

These dramatic shifts of population and wealth further broke the historic grip of the North on the nation's political life. Every elected occupant of the White House since 1960 has hailed from the Sunbelt, and the region's congressional representation rose as its population grew. With their devotion to unregulated economic growth, the Sunbelters were redrawing the republic's political map.

The Rush to the Suburbs

In all regions, America's modern migrants—if they were white—fled from the cities to the burgeoning

The Great African-American Migration

So many black southerners took to the roads during World War II that local officials could not keep track of the migrants passing through the towns. Black workers on the move—a vast population with no addresses and no telephone numbers—crowded into boardinghouses, camped out in cars, and clustered in the juke joints of roadside America en route to a new, uncertain future in the cities of the North and West.

Southern cotton fields and tobacco plantations had yielded but slender sustenance to African-American farmers, most of whom labored as tenants and sharecroppers. The Great Depression was yet another setback, for many tenants were evicted from their land. With few other opportunities in the depression-ravaged country, dispossessed former sharecroppers toiled as seasonal farm laborers or found themselves without work, without shelter, and without hope for the future.

The shiny new war plants and busy shipyards of the South offered little to African-Americans. In 1940 and 1941 the labor-hungry war machine soaked up white unemployment but commonly denied jobs to southerners with the "wrong" skin color. Fed up with such discrimination, many African-Americans headed for shipyards, factories, foundries, and fields north of the Mason-Dixon line, where their willing hands found work in abundance.

Angered by the racism that drove their people from the South, black leaders pressured President Roosevelt into declaring that "there shall be no discrimination in the employment of workers in defense industries or government because of race, creed, color, or national origin." This executive order was but a tenuous, rudimentary step; still, many African-

Headed North *Dispossessed African-Americans leaving Florida.*

Americans were heartened to see a presidential response to their protests. The war experience emboldened the civil rights movement, adding momentum and tactical knowledge to the cause. NAACP leader Walter White concluded that the war "immeasurably magnified the Negro's awareness of the disparity between the American profession and practice of democracy. . . ."

By war's end, many African-Americans made new homes in the North and Far West, shifting the heart of America's black community from southern plantations to northern cities. There they competed for scarce housing in overcrowded slums and paid outrageous rents to secure a foothold in the few neighborhoods of northern cities that would admit them.

The entire nation was now grappling with the evil of racism, as bloody World War II–era riots in Detroit, New York, and other cities tragically revealed. Although the trek to northern cities was an economic boon for most African-Americans, it did not end the intractable national problem of black poverty. Black teenage unemployment, a scourge to this day, dates from World War II. Southern farms, though providing the barest subsistence, had been all too generous in dispensing work to all members of the family—work not so readily found by African-American youth in today's decaying northern cities.

---

new suburbs. Government policies encouraged this momentous move. Federal Housing Authority (FHA) and VA home-loan guarantees made it more economically attractive to own a home in the suburbs than to rent an apartment in the city. Tax deductions for interest payments on home mortgages provided additional financial incentive. And government-built highways that sped commuters from suburban homes to city jobs further facilitated this mass migration. By 1960 one of every four Americans dwelt in suburbia, and the same leafy neighborhoods held more than half the nation's population as the century neared its end.

The construction industry boomed in the 1950s and 1960s to satisfy this demand. Pioneered by innovators such as the Levitt brothers, whose first "Levittown" sprouted on New York's Long Island in the 1940s, builders developed efficient new techniques for constructing mass-produced housing. Critics wailed about the aesthetic monotony of the suburban "tract" developments, but eager homebuyers nevertheless moved into them by the millions.

"White flight" to the green suburbs left the inner cities—especially in the Northeast and Midwest—black, brown, and broke. Migrating blacks from the South filled up the city neighborhoods abandoned by the departing white middle class (see "Makers of America: The Great African-American Migration," pp. 566–567). Taxpaying businesses fled with their affluent customers from downtown shops to suburban shopping malls, another post–World War II invention.

The Postwar Baby Boom

Of all the changes in postwar America, none was more dramatic than the "baby boom"—the huge leap in the birthrate in the decade and a half after 1945. Confident young men and women tied the nuptial knot in record numbers at war's end and began immediately to fill the nation's empty cradles. They thus touched off a demographic explosion that added more than 50 million bawling babies to the nation's population by the end of the 1950s. The soaring birthrate finally crested in 1957 and was followed by a deepening birth dearth. By 1973 fertility rates had dropped below the point necessary to maintain existing population figures. If the trend persisted, only further immigration would lift the American population above its 1990 level of some 250 million.

This boom-or-bust cycle of births begot a bulging wave along the American population curve. As the oversize postwar generation grew to maturity, it was destined—like the fabled pig passing through the python—to strain and distort many aspects of American life. Elementary-school enrollments, for example, swelled to nearly 34 million pupils in 1970. Then began a steady decline, as the onward-marching age group left in its wake closed schools and unemployed teachers.

Truman: The "Gutsy" Man from Missouri

Presiding over the opening of the postwar period was the "accidental president"—Harry S Truman.

What Next? 1946 *This cartoon expresses the feeling of many Americans that their new president was overwhelmed, even bamboozled, by his job.*

"The moon, the stars, and all the planets" had fallen on him, he remarked when he was called upon to shoulder Roosevelt's awesome burdens of leadership. Trim and owlishly bespectacled, with his graying hair and friendly, toothy grin, Truman was called "the average man's average man." Even his height—5 feet 9 inches—was average. The first president in many years without a college education, he had farmed, served as an artillery officer in France during World War I, and failed as a haberdasher. He then tried his hand at precinct-level Missouri politics, through which he rose from a judgeship to the U.S. Senate. Though a protégé of a notorious political machine in Kansas City, he had managed to keep his own hands clean.

The problems of the postwar period were staggering, and the firm-mouthed new president initially approached his tasks with becoming humility. Gradually gaining confidence to the point of cockiness, he

displayed courage, decisiveness, and willingness to fight. Though amateurish as a public speaker at first, he finally developed into one of the most effective "give 'em hell" orators of his generation.

Yet by degrees the defects of Truman's common clay became painfully apparent. He permitted designing old associates of the "Missouri gang" to gather around him and, like Grant, was stubbornly loyal to them when they were caught with cream on their whiskers. On occasion, he would send critics hot-tempered and profane "s.o.b." letters. Most troubling, in trying to demonstrate to a skeptical public his decisiveness and power of command, he was inclined to go off half-cocked or stick mulishly to a wrongheaded notion.

But if Truman was sometimes small in the small things, he was often big in the big things. He had down-home authenticity, few pretensions, rock-solid probity, and a lot of that old-fashioned character trait called moxie. Not one to dodge responsibility, he placed a sign on his White House desk that read, "The buck stops here." Among his favorite sayings was, "If you can't stand the heat, get out of the kitchen."

Yalta: Bargain or Betrayal?

Vast and silent, the Soviet Union continued to be the great enigma. The conference in Teheran in 1943, where Roosevelt had first met Stalin on a man-to-man basis, had done something to clear the air, but much had remained unresolved—especially questions about the postwar fates of Germany, Eastern Europe, and Asia.

A final fateful conference of the Big Three had taken place in February 1945 at Yalta. At this former tsarist resort on the relatively warm shores of the Black Sea, Stalin, Churchill, and the fast-failing Roosevelt reached momentous agreements. Stalin agreed that Poland, with revised boundaries, should have a representative government based on free elections—a pledge he soon broke. Bulgaria and Romania were likewise to have free elections—a promise also flouted. The Big Three further announced plans for fashioning a new international peacekeeping organization—the United Nations.

The most painful decisions at Yalta concerned Moscow's entry into the war against Japan. Uncertain of the untested atomic bomb, and expecting frightful American casualties in the projected assault on Japan, the Americans were willing to offer inducements to the Soviets to come into the war and pin down Japanese troops in Manchuria and Korea.

Horse-trader Stalin was in a position at Yalta to exact a high price. He agreed to attack Japan within three months after the collapse of Germany; and he later fulfilled this pledge in full. In return, the Soviets were promised the southern half of Sakhalin Island, Japan's Kurile Islands, and railroad and industrial concessions in Manchuria.

As it turned out, Moscow's entry into the war was unnecessary to defeat Japan. Critics quickly concluded that Stalin's aid had not been needed, and charged that the dead Roosevelt's concessions had undermined Jiang Jieshi and contributed to his overthrow by the Chinese communists four years later.

Roosevelt's defenders countered that Stalin's mighty red army could have secured much more of China, and that the Yalta conference really set limits to his ambitions. Apologists for Roosevelt also noted that Soviet troops had already occupied much of Eastern Europe, and a war to throw them out was unthinkable.

The fact is that the Big Three at Yalta were not drafting a comprehensive peace settlement; at most they were sketching general intentions and testing one another's reactions. In the case of Poland, Roosevelt admitted that the Yalta agreement was "so elastic that the Russians can stretch it all the way from Yalta to Washington without ever technically breaking it." More specific understandings among the wartime allies—especially the two emerging superpowers, the United States and the Soviet Union—awaited the arrival of peace.

The United States and the Soviet Union

History provided little hope that America and the Soviets would reach cordial understandings about the shape of the postwar world. Mutual suspicions were ancient, abundant, and deep. Communism and capitalism were historically hostile social philoso-

phies. The United States had refused officially to recognize the Bolshevik revolutionary government in Moscow until 1933. America had also aroused Soviet suspicions by its delays in opening a second front against Germany, by freezing its ally out of the project to develop atomic weapons, and by abruptly terminating vital lend-lease aid in 1945 and spurning Moscow's plea for a $6 billion reconstruction loan.

Different visions of the postwar world also separated the two superpowers. Stalin aimed above all to guarantee the security of the Soviet Union by establishing friendly governments along its western border, especially in Poland. By maintaining an extensive Soviet sphere of influence in Eastern and Central Europe, the USSR could protect itself and consolidate its revolutionary base as the world's leading communist country.

To many Americans, that "sphere of influence" looked like an ill-gained "empire." They remembered the earlier Bolshevik call for world revolution, and doubted whether Stalin's emphasis on "spheres" could be reconciled with Franklin Roosevelt's Wilsonian dream of a decolonized, demilitarized, and democratized world.

Even the ways in which the United States and the Soviet Union resembled each other were troublesome. Both countries had been largely isolated from world affairs before World War II. Both nations had a history of conducting a kind of "missionary" diplomacy—of trying to export to all the world the political doctrines precipitated out of their respective revolutionary origins.

Unaccustomed to their great-power roles, America and the USSR suddenly found themselves staring eyeball-to-eyeball over the prostrate body of battered Europe—a Europe that had been the traditional center of international affairs. In these circumstances, some kind of confrontation was virtually unavoidable. In a fateful progression of events, marked often by misperceptions as well as by genuine conflicts of interest, the two powers provoked each other into a tense standoff known as the Cold War. Enduring four and a half decades, the Cold War not only shaped Soviet-American relations; it overshadowed the entire postwar international order in every corner of the globe.

Shaping the Postwar World

Despite these obstacles, the United States did manage at war's end to erect some of the structures that would support Roosevelt's vision of an open world. Meeting at Bretton Woods, New Hampshire, in 1944, the Western Allies established the International Monetary Fund (IMF) to encourage world trade and the International Bank for Reconstruction and Development (World Bank) to promote economic growth in war-ravaged and underdeveloped areas. In contrast to its behavior after World War I, the United States took the lead in creating these important international bodies.

Meeting in San Francisco in April 1945, representatives from fifty nations at the United Nations Conference fashioned a charter that strongly resembled the old League of Nations Covenant. It featured a Security Council dominated by the Big Five powers (the United States, Britain, the USSR, France, and China), each of whom had the right of veto, and an assembly that could be controlled by smaller countries. The U.S. Senate overwhelmingly approved the document on July 28, 1945.

"Witnesses for the Prosecution," 1945

The United Nations had some gratifying initial successes. It helped preserve peace in Iran, Kashmir, and other trouble spots. It played a large role in creating the new Jewish state of Israel. The U.N. Trusteeship Council guided former colonies to independence. Through such arms as UNESCO (United Nations Educational, Scientific, and Cultural Organization), FAO (Food and Agricultural Organization), and WHO (World Health Organization), the U.N. brought benefits to peoples the world over. But it proved far less successful in controlling the fearsome new technology of the atom. The Soviets rejected an American proposal in 1946 for a U.N. agency to prevent the manufacture of nuclear weapons, and the atomic clock therefore ticked ominously on.

The Problem of Germany

Hitler's ruined *Reich* posed especially thorny problems for all the wartime Allies. They agreed only that the cancer of Nazism had to be cut out of the German body politic, which involved punishing Nazi leaders for war crimes. The Allies tried twenty-two top culprits at Nuremberg, Germany, during 1945–1946 for crimes against the laws of war and humanity. Justice, Nuremberg-style, was harsh. Twelve of the accused Nazis swung from the gallows, and seven were sentenced to long jail terms.

Beyond punishing the top Nazis, the Allies could agree on little about postwar Germany. Some American Hitler-haters wanted to deindustrialize Germany, while the Soviets sought to extract enormous reparations from the Germans. Both these desires clashed headlong with the reality that an industrial, healthy German economy was indispensable to the recovery of Europe. The Americans soon came to appreciate that fact, but the fearful Soviets resisted all efforts to revitalize Germany.

Along with Austria, Germany had been divided at war's end into four military occupation zones, each assigned to one of the Big Four powers (France, Britain, America, and the USSR). Before long, it was apparent that Germany would remain indefinitely divided. West Germany eventually became an independent country, wedded to the West. East Germany, along with other Soviet-domi-

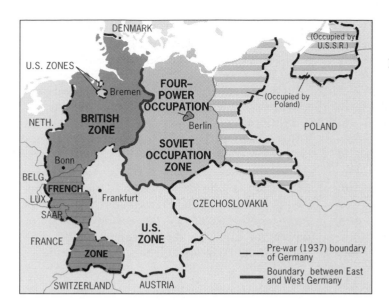

Postwar Partition of Germany

nated Eastern European countries, became nominally independent "satellite" states bound to the Soviet Union. Eastern Europe virtually disappeared from Western sight behind the "iron curtain" of secrecy and isolation for more than four decades.

With Germany now split in two, there remained the problem of the rubble heap known as Berlin. Lying deep within the Soviet zone (see map above), this beleaguered isle in a red sea had been broken, like Germany as a whole, into sectors occupied by troops of each of the four victorious powers. In 1948, the Soviets abruptly choked off all rail and highway access to Berlin, evidently hoping that the Allies would be starved out.

Berlin became a hugely symbolic issue for both sides. The Americans organized a gigantic airlift in the midst of hair-trigger tension. For nearly a year they ferried thousands of tons of supplies to the grateful Berliners. The Soviets, their bluff dramatically called, finally lifted their blockade in May 1949. In the same year the governments of the two Germanies, East and West, were formally established. The Cold War had icily congealed.

Crystallizing the Cold War

A crafty Stalin also probed the West's resolve at other sensitive points, including oil-rich Iran. In 1946 he broke an agreement to remove his troops from Iran's northernmost province. Truman sent off a stinging protest, and the Soviet dictator backed down.

Moscow's hard-line policies in Germany, Eastern Europe, and the Middle East wrought a psychological Pearl Harbor. Any remaining goodwill from the period of comradeship-in-arms evaporated in a cloud of dark mistrust. "I'm tired of babying the Soviets," Truman remarked privately in 1946, as attitudes on both sides began to harden frostily.

Truman's piecemeal responses to various Soviet challenges took on intellectual coherence in 1947, with the formulation of the "containment doctrine." Crafted by a brilliant young diplomat and Soviet specialist, George F. Kennan, this concept held that the Soviet Union, whether tsarist or communist, was relentlessly expansionary. But the Kremlin was also cautious, Kennan argued, and the flow of Soviet power into "every nook and cranny available to it" could be stemmed by "firm and vigilant commitment."

Kennan's advice seemed to require a globe-girdling strategy of military and political preparedness. Truman embraced this advice when he formally and publicly adopted a "get-tough-with-Russia" policy in 1947. His first dramatic move was triggered by word that heavily burdened Britain could no longer bear the financial and military load of defending

Greece against communist pressures. If Greece fell, Turkey would presumably collapse and the strategic eastern Mediterranean would pass into the Soviet orbit.

The president went before Congress on March 12, 1947, and requested support for what came to be known as the Truman Doctrine. Specifically, he asked for $400 million to bolster Greece and Turkey, which Congress quickly granted. More generally, he declared that "it must be the policy of the United States to support free peoples who are resisting attempted subjugation by armed minorities or outside pressures"—a sweeping and open-ended commitment of vast and worrisome proportions. Critics then and later charged that the Truman Doctrine committed the United States to back "anticommunist" despots, needlessly polarized the world into pro-Soviet and pro-American camps, and unwisely construed the Soviet threat as primarily military in nature. Apologists for Truman have explained that it was Truman's fear of a revised isolationism that led him to exaggerate the Soviet threat and to cast his message in the charged language of a holy global war against godless communism—a description of the Cold War that straightjacketed future policy makers who would seek to tone down Soviet-American competition and animosity.

A threat of a different kind loomed in Western Europe—especially France, Italy, and Germany. Still suffering from the hunger and economic chaos spawned by the war, these key nations were in grave danger of being taken over from the inside by Communist parties that could exploit these hardships. The bold American response came on June 5, 1947, when Secretary of State George C. Marshall offered American financial assistance for European economic recovery. The democratic nations of Europe enthusiastically accepted the so-called Marshall Plan at a Paris conference in July 1947.

The U.S. Congress at first balked at the Marshall Plan's proposal for spending $12.5 billion over four years in sixteen cooperating countries. But a Soviet-sponsored communist coup in Czechoslovakia finally spurred the legislators to action, and they voted the initial appropriations in April 1948. Truman's Marshall Plan was a spectacular success. American dollars pumped reviving blood into the economic veins of the anemic West European

nations. Within a few years, an "economic miracle" drenched Europe in prosperity. The Communist parties in Italy and France lost ground, and these two keystone countries were saved from communism.

A resolute Truman made another fateful decision in 1948. Access to Middle Eastern oil was crucial to European recovery and, increasingly, to the U.S. economy. Yet the Arab oil countries adamantly opposed the creation of the Jewish State of Israel in the British mandate territory of Palestine. Defying Arab wrath and his own State and Defense departments, Truman officially recognized the state of Israel on May 14, 1948. Truman's policy of strong support for Israel would vastly complicate U.S. relations with the Arab world in the decades ahead.

America Begins to Rearm

The Cold War, the struggle to contain Soviet communism, was not war, but it was not peace. The standoff with the Kremlin banished the dreams of tax-fatigued Americans that tanks could be beaten into automobiles.

The Soviet menace spurred the unification of the armed services as well as the creation of a huge new national security apparatus. Congress in 1947 passed the National Security Act, creating the Department of Defense. The uniformed heads of each service were brought together as the Joint Chiefs of Staff.

The National Security Act also established a National Security Council (NSC) to advise the president on security matters, and a Central Intelligence Agency (CIA) to coordinate the government's foreign fact gathering. The "Voice of America," authorized by Congress in 1948, began beaming American radio broadcasts behind the iron curtain. In the same year, Congress resurrected the military draft, providing for the conscription of selected young men from nineteen to twenty-five years of age. The overshadowing presence of the Selective Service System played a major role in shaping young people's educational, marital, and career plans in the following quarter-century. One shoe at a time, a war-weary America was reluctantly returning to a war footing.

The Soviet threat was also forcing the United States to join with the democracies of Western Europe in a defensive military alliance. On April 4,

1949, representatives of twelve nations signed the historic North Atlantic Pact, which stipulated that an attack on one member by an aggressor would be an attack on all. Over last-ditch isolationist opposition, the U.S. Senate ratified the treaty on July 21, 1949, by a vote of eighty-two to thirteen.

The epochal pact served notice on Moscow that an attack on any of the signatories would be resisted. The North Atlantic Treaty Organization (NATO), which expanded to fifteen members by 1955, gradually built up an army for defensive purposes. For America, the willingness to join a peacetime military alliance, despite ancient tradition, revealed a tormenting concern over Soviet aggressions.

Reconstruction and Revolution in Asia

Reconstruction in Japan was simpler than in Germany, primarily because it was largely a one-man show. The occupying American army, with General Douglas MacArthur as a kind of Yankee mikado, implemented his program for the democratization of Japan with stunning success. The Japanese saw that good behavior and the adoption of democracy would speed the end of occupation—as it did. A MacArthur-dictated constitution, adopted in 1946, paved the way for a phenomenal economic recovery that within a few decades made Japan one of the world's mightiest industrial powers.

If Japan was a success story for American policy makers, the opposite was true in China, where a bitter civil war had raged for years between Nationalists and communists. Washington had halfheartedly supported the Nationalist government of Generalissimo Jiang Jieshi in his struggle with the Communists under Mao Zedong (Mao Tse-tung). But ineptitude and corruption within the generalissimo's regime cost him his people's confidence and enabled the communist armies to sweep to victory late in 1949. Jiang was forced to flee with the remnants of his force to the last-hope island of Taiwan.

The collapse of Nationalist China was a depressing defeat for America and its allies in the Cold War. At one fell swoop nearly one-fourth of the world's population—some 500 million people—was swept into the communist camp. The Republicans charged that President Truman and his British-

appearing secretary of state, Dean Acheson, had "lost China." Democrats heatedly replied that when a regime has forfeited the support of its people, no amount of outside help will save it. Truman, the argument ran, did not "lose" China because he never had China to lose.

More bad news came in September 1949, when President Truman shocked the nation by announcing that the Soviets had exploded an atomic bomb—approximately three years earlier than many experts had thought possible. To outpace the Soviets in nuclear weaponry, Truman ordered the development of the "H-bomb" (hydrogen bomb)—a city-smashing device many times more lethal than the atomic bomb. The United States exploded its first hydrogen device on a South Pacific atoll in 1952, despite warnings from some scientists that the H-bomb was so powerful that "it becomes a weapon which in practical effect is almost one of genocide." Not to be outdone, the Soviets exploded their first H-bomb in 1953, and the nuclear arms race entered a perilously competitive cycle. Nuclear "superiority" became a dangerous and elusive dream, as each side tried to outdo the other in the scramble to build more destructive weapons. If the Cold War had ever blazed into a hot war, there might be no world left for the communists to communize or the democracies to democratize—a chilling thought that restrained both camps. Peace through mutual terror brought a shaky stability to the superpower standoff.

Ferreting Out Alleged Communists

One of the most active Cold War fronts was at home, where a new anti-red chase was in full cry. In 1947 Truman launched a massive "loyalty" program. A Loyalty Review Board investigated more than 3 million federal employees, some 3,000 of whom either resigned or were dismissed, none under formal indictment.

Individual states likewise became intensely security conscious. Loyalty oaths in increasing numbers were demanded of employees, especially teachers. The gnawing question for many earnest Americans was, Could the nation continue to enjoy traditional freedoms in a Cold War climate?

In 1949 eleven communists were convicted of advocating the overthrow of the American govern-

Ethel and Julius Rosenberg Outside Court, 1951 *The Alger Hiss case and the Rosenberg case became highly emotional symbols of alleged communist subversion in America. Even some people who believed the Rosenbergs guilty of spying for the Soviet Union protested their death sentences to no avail.*

ment under the Smith Act of 1940. In 1948, Congressman Richard M. Nixon, a member of the House Committee on Un-American Activities, led the chase after Alger Hiss, a prominent ex–New Dealer and a distinguished member of the "eastern establishment." Accused of being a communist agent in the 1930s, Hiss met his chief accuser before the committee and denied everything. But Hiss was caught in embarrassing falsehoods, convicted of perjury in 1950, and sentenced to five years in prison.

In February 1950 Senator Joseph R. McCarthy, a Wisconsin Republican, spectacularly charged that there were scores of known communists in the State Department. He proved utterly unable to substantiate his accusation, and many Americans, including President Truman, began to fear that the red hunt was turning into a witch-hunt. Nevertheless, in 1950 Congress passed, over Truman's veto, the McCarran Internal Security Bill, which, among other provi-

sions, authorized the president to arrest and detail suspicious persons during an "internal security emergency."

The stunning success of Soviet scientists in developing an atomic bomb was presumably due, at least in part, to the cleverness of communist spies in stealing American secrets. In 1951, two American citizens, Julius and Ethel Rosenberg, were convicted of espionage. Their sensational trial and eventual electrocution in 1953, combined with sympathy for their two orphaned children, began to sour some sober citizens on the excesses of the red-hunters.

Democratic Divisions in 1948

Attacking high prices and "High-Tax Harry" Truman, the Republicans had won control of Congress in the congressional elections of 1946. Their prospects had seldom looked rosier as they gathered in Philadelphia to choose their 1948 presidential candidate. They noisily renominated warmed-over New York Governor Thomas E. Dewey, still as debonair as if he had stepped out of a bandbox.

Also gathering in Philadelphia, Democratic politicos looked without enthusiasm on their hand-me-down president and sang, "I'm Just Mild About Harry." But their "dump Truman" movement collapsed when war hero Dwight D. Eisenhower refused to be drafted. The peppery president, unwanted but undaunted, was then chosen in the face of violent opposition by southern delegates. They were alienated by his strong stand in favor of civil rights for blacks, who now mustered many votes in the big-city ghettoes of the North.

Truman's nomination split the party wide open. Embittered southern Democrats from thirteen states, like their fire-eating forebears of 1860, met in their own convention, in Birmingham, Alabama, with Confederate flags brashly in evidence. Amid scenes of heated defiance, these "Dixiecrats" nominated Governor J. Strom Thurmond of South Carolina on a States' Rights party ticket.

To add to the confusion within Democratic ranks, former vice president Henry A. Wallace threw his hat into the ring. Having parted company with the administration over its get-tough-with-Russia policy, he was nominated at Philadelphia by the new Progressive party—a bizarre collection of disgruntled former New Dealers, starry-eyed pacifists, well-meaning liberals, and communist-fronters.

Wallace, a vigorous if misguided liberal, assailed Uncle Sam's "dollar imperialism" from the stump. This so-called Pied Piper of the Politburo took an apparently pro-Soviet line that earned him drenchings with rotten eggs in hostile cities. But to many Americans, Wallace raised the only hopeful voice in the deepening gloom of the Cold War.

With the Democrats deeply split three ways and the Republican congressional victory of 1946 just past, Dewey's victory seemed assured. Succumbing to overconfidence engendered by his massive lead in public opinion polls, the cold, smug Dewey confined himself to dispensing soothing-syrup generalities like, "Our future lies before us."

The seemingly doomed Truman, with little money and few active supporters, had to rely on his "gut-fighter" instincts and folksy personality. Whistle-stopping the country to deliver some 300 "give 'em hell" speeches, he lashed out at the Taft-Hartley "slave labor" law and the "do-nothing" Republican Congress while whipping up support for his program of civil rights, improved labor benefits, and health insurance. "Pour it on 'em, Harry!" cried increasingly large and enthusiastic crowds, as the pugnacious president rained a barrage of verbal uppercuts on his opponent.

On election night the *Chicago Tribune* ran off an early edition with the headline, "DEWEY DEFEATS TRUMAN." But in the morning it turned out that "President" Dewey had embarrassingly snatched defeat from the jaws of victory. Truman had swept to a stunning triumph, to the complete bewilderment of politicians, pollsters, prophets, and pundits. Even though Thurmond took away 39 electoral votes in the South, Truman won 303 electoral votes, primarily from the South, Midwest, and West. Dewey's 189 electoral votes came principally from the East. The popular vote was 24,179,345 for Truman, 21,991,291 for Dewey, 1,176,125 for Thurmond, and 1,157,326 for Wallace. To make the victory sweeter, the Democrats regained control of Congress as well.

Truman's victory rested on farmers, workers, and blacks, all of whom saw threats from the Republicans. Republican overconfidence and Truman's lone-wolf, never-say-die campaign also won him the support of many Americans who admired his "guts." No one wanted him, someone remarked, except the people.

Smilingly confident, Truman sounded a clarion note, in the fourth point of his inaugural address, when he called for a "bold new program" ("Point Four"). The plan was to lend U.S. money and technical aid to underdeveloped lands to help them help themselves. Truman wanted to spend millions to keep underprivileged peoples from becoming communists rather than to spend billions to shoot them after they had become communists. This far-seeing program was officially launched in 1950, and it brought badly needed assistance to impoverished countries, notably in Latin America, Africa, the Middle East, and East Asia.

At home, Truman outlined a sweeping "Fair Deal" program in his 1949 message to Congress. It called for badly needed housing, full employment, a higher minimum wage, better farm price supports, new TVAs, and an extension of Social Security. But most of the Fair Deal fell victim to congressional opposition from Republicans and southern Democrats. The only major successes came in raising the minimum wage, providing for public housing in the Housing Act of 1949, and extending old-age insurance to many more beneficiaries in the Social Security Act of 1950.

The Korean Volcano Erupts (1950)

Korea, the Land of the Morning Calm, heralded a new and more ominous phase of the Cold War—a shooting phase—in June 1950. When Japan collapsed in 1945, Soviet troops had accepted the Japanese surrender north of the thirty-eighth parallel on the Korean peninsula, and American troops did likewise south of that line. Both superpowers professed to want reunification of Korea, but, as in Germany, each helped to set up rival regimes above and below the parallel. When the Soviets and Americans withdrew in 1949, the entire peninsula was a bristling armed camp.

Secretary of State Acheson seemed to wash his hands of the dispute early in 1950, when he declared that Korea was outside the essential United States defense perimeter in the Pacific. But when North Korean army columns rumbled across the thirty-eighth parallel on June 25, 1950, and quickly pushed the South Koreans into a tiny defensive area around Pusan, President Truman sprang into the breach. The invasion seemed to provide devastating proof of a fundamental premise in the "containment doctrine" that shaped Washington's foreign policy: that even a slight relaxation of America's guard was an invitation to communist aggression somewhere.

The Korean invasion also provided the occasion for a vast expansion of the American military. Truman's National Security Council had recommended in a document of 1950 (known as National Security Council Memorandum Number 68, or NSC-68) that the United States should quadruple defense spending. Buried at the time, NSC-68 was resurrected by the Korean crisis. Truman now ordered a massive military buildup, well beyond what was necessary for the immediate purposes of the war. Soon the United States had 3.5 million men under arms and was spending $50 billion per year on the defense budget—some 13 percent of the GNP.

The Military Seesaw in Korea

Rather than fight his way out of the southern Pusan perimeter, MacArthur launched a daring amphibious landing behind the enemy's lines at Inchon. This bold gamble, on September 15, 1950, succeeded brilliantly; within two weeks the North Koreans had

retreated pell-mell behind the "sanctuary" of the thirty-eighth parallel. Truman's avowed intention was to restore South Korea to its former borders, but the pursuing South Koreans had already crossed the thirty-eighth parallel, and there seemed little point in permitting the North Koreans to regroup and come again. The U.N. Assembly tacitly authorized a crossing by MacArthur, whom President Truman ordered northward, provided that there was no intervention in force by the Chinese or Soviets.

The Americans thus raised the stakes in Korea, and in so doing, they quickened the fears of another potential player in this dangerous game. The Chinese communists had publicly warned that they would not sit idly by and watch hostile troops approach the strategic Yalu River boundary between Korea and China. But MacArthur pooh-poohed all predictions of an effective intervention by the Chinese and reportedly boasted that he would "have the boys home by Christmas."

MacArthur guessed wrong. In November 1950 hordes of Chinese "volunteers" fell upon his rashly overextended lines and hurled the U.N. forces reeling back down the peninsula. The fighting now sank into a frostbitten stalemate on the icy terrain near the thirty-eighth parallel.

An imperious MacArthur, humiliated by this rout, pressed for drastic retaliation. He favored a blockade of the China coast and bombardment of

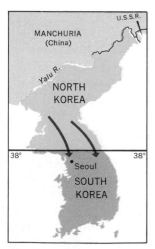 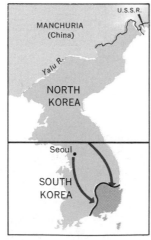 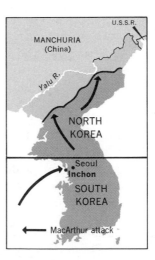 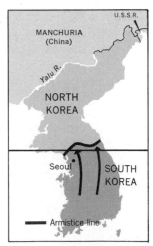

The Shifting Front in Korea

CHRONOLOGY

1944	Servicemen's Readjustment Act (GI Bill).
	Bretton Woods economic conference.
1945	Spock publishes *The Common Sense Book of Baby and Child Care.*
	Yalta conference.
	United Nations established.
1945–1946	Nuremberg war crimes trials in Germany.
1946	Employment Act creates Council of Economic Advisers.
	Iran crisis.
1946–1948	Tokyo war crimes trials.
1947	Truman Doctrine.
	Marshall Plan.
	Taft-Hartley Act.
	National Security Act creates Department of Defense, National Security Council (NSC), and Central Intelligence Agency (CIA).
1948	United States officially recognizes the state of Israel.
	Hiss case begins.
	Truman defeats Dewey for presidency.
1948–1949	Berlin crisis.
1949	NATO established.
	Communists defeat Nationalists in China.
1950	American economy begins postwar growth.
	McCarthy red hunt begins.
	McCarran Internal Security Act passed over Truman's veto.
1950–1953	Korean War.
1951	Truman fires MacArthur.
	Rosenbergs convicted of treason.
1952	United States explodes first hydrogen bomb.
1957	Postwar peak of U.S. birthrate.
1973	U.S. birthrate falls below replacement level.

Chinese bases in Manchuria. But Washington policy makers, with anxious eyes on Moscow, refused to enlarge the already costly conflict. The chairman of the Joint Chiefs of Staff declared that a wider clash in Asia would be "the wrong war, at the wrong place, at the wrong time, and with the wrong enemy." Europe, not Asia, was the administration's first concern; and the USSR, not China, loomed as the more threatening foe.

Two-fisted General MacArthur felt that he was being asked to fight with one hand tied behind his back. He sneered at the concept of a "limited war" and insisted that "there is no substitute for victory."

When the general began to take issue publicly with presidential policies, Truman had no choice but to remove the insubordinate MacArthur from command (April 11, 1951). The imperious war hero, a legend in his own mind, returned to an uproarious welcome, while Truman was condemned as a "pig," an "imbecile," a "Judas," and an appeaser of "Communist Russia and Communist China." In July 1951 truce discussions began in a rude field tent near the firing line but were almost immediately snagged on the issue of prisoner exchange. They dragged on unproductively for nearly two years—while men continued to die.

Varying Viewpoints

Who was to blame for starting the Cold War? For nearly a generation after World War II, American historians generally agreed that the suspicious and grasping Soviets were almost solely responsible. This "orthodox" appraisal fitted comfortably with the traditional view of the United States as a God-blessed land with an idealistic foreign policy. But in the 1960s a revisionist interpretation began to flower, powerfully reinforced by revulsion against American atrocities in Vietnam. "New Left" revisionists attempted to reverse the orthodox view. They argued that the Soviets had understandably defensive intentions at the end of World War II and that the United States had behaved aggressively and irresponsibly. Moderate revisionists blamed Truman for abandoning Roosevelt's conciliatory approach to Moscow, while radical revisionists like the Kolkos found the roots of American aggression before Truman's time in long-standing policies of economic expansion.

In the 1970s a "postrevisionist" interpretation emerged. Historians of this school, among them

John L. Gaddis and Melvyn P. Leffler, concede that American foreign policies and domestic politics also helped precipitate the conflict. They note how the constraints of domestic politics and the miscalculations of U.S. leaders led a nation in search of security to seek a "preponderance" of power, thus exacerbating U.S.-Soviet relations and precipitating the arms race. Insisting, however, that national self-interest is not necessarily immoral and that the mistakes of U.S. leaders were understandable, writers of this persuasion still place most of the blame for the Cold War on the Soviet Union.

The great unknown, of course, is Soviet intentions. Were Soviet aims purely defensive in the immediate postwar years, or did the Kremlin have a design for global conquest? Was there an opportunity for reconciliation following Stalin's death in 1953? With the end of the Cold War and the promised opening of Soviet archives, scholars are eagerly pursuing answers to such questions.

SELECT READINGS

Primary Source Documents

George F. Kennan's "long telegram," *Foreign Relations of the United States, 1946* (Vol. 6, 1969, pp. 696–709),* outlined the containment doctrine that would form the foundation of American foreign policy in the Cold War era. Harry S Truman first applied the containment doctrine when he enunciated the Truman Doctrine, *Congressional Record*, 80th Congress, 1st Session, p. 1981 (1947).* Joe McCarthy's vitriol can be found in his *McCarthyism: The Fight for America* (1952).*

Secondary Sources

Lucid overviews of the postwar years can be found in Eric Goldman, *The Crucial Decade and After: America, 1945–1960* (1961), William H. Chafe, *The Unfinished Journey: America Since World War II* (1986), John Patrick Diggins, *The Proud Decades: America in War and Peace,*

1941–1960 (1988), William O'Neill, *American High: The Years of Confidence, 1945–1960* (1986), and William Leuchtenburg, *A Troubled Feast: American Society Since 1945* (updated ed., 1983). Harold G. Vatter gives a valuable account of *The United States Economy in the 1950s* (1963). The rise of the Sunbelt is dramatically portrayed by Kirkpatrick Sale, *Power Shift* (1975), and Kevin Phillips, *The Emerging Republican Majority* (1970). Suburbia is the subject of Herbert J. Gans, *The Levittowners* (1967), Zane Miller, *Suburb* (1981), Carol O'Connor, *A Sort of Utopia: Scarsdale, 1891–1981* (1983), and Kenneth T. Jackson's sweeping synthesis, *Crabgrass Frontier* (1986). On the baby boom and its implications, consult Richard A. Easterlin, *Birth and Fortune: The Impact of Numbers on Personal Welfare* (1980), Landon Y. Jones, *Great Expectations: America and the Baby Boom Generation* (1980), and Michael X.

Delli Carpini, *Stability and Change in American Politics: The Coming of Age of the Generation of the 1960s* (1986). On the origins of the Cold War, see the titles cited in Chapter 37 by John L. Gaddis, Lloyd Gardner, Gar Alperovitz, Martin J. Sherwin, Herbert Feis, and Gabriel Kolko. Consult also Gaddis's *Strategies of Containment* (1982) and Joyce and Gabriel Kolko's *The Limits of Power: The World and United States Foreign Policy, 1945–1954* (1972), which roundly condemns Washington's actions. For an ambitious revisionist synthesis, see Thomas McCormick, *America's Half-Century: U.S. Foreign Policy in the Cold War* (1989). Useful surveys of the diplomatic history of the period, all of them in varying degrees critical of American policy, are Stephen Ambrose, *Rise to Globalism: American Foreign Policy Since 1938* (rev. ed., 1983), Walter LaFeber, *America, Russia and the Cold War, 1945–1984* (5th ed., 1985), and Daniel Yergin, *Shattered Peace* (1977). Among the most comprehensive postrevisionist studies is Melvyn P. Leffler, *A Preponderance of Power: National Security, the Truman Administration, and the Cold War* (1992). Broader accounts that include discussion of domestic events are Donald R. McCoy, *The Presidency of Harry S Truman* (1984), Alonzo L. Hamby, *Beyond the New Deal: Harry S Truman and American Liberalism* (1973), Barton J. Bernstein, ed., *Politics and Policies of the Truman Administration* (1970), and Robert J. Donovan, *Conflict and Crisis: The Presidency of Harry S Truman* (1977). Korea is discussed in David Rees, *Korea: The Limited War* (1964), Callum A. MacDonald, *Korea: The War Before Vietnam* (1986), Bruce Cummings, ed., *Child of Conflict: The Korean-American Relationship, 1943–1953* (1983), and Bruce Cummings and Jon Halliday, *Korea: The Unknown War* (1988). On the "red scare" at home, see Richard M. Freeland, *The Truman Doctrine and the Origins of McCarthyism* (1971), and Thomas Reeves, *The Life and Times of Joe McCarthy* (1982), as well as David M. Oshinsky, *A Conspiracy so Immense: The World of Joe McCarthy* (1983). Daniel Bell, ed., *The Radical Right* (1963), places McCarthyism in a larger context. See also David W. Reinhard, *The Republican Right Since 1945* (1983). Examinations of the impact of the Cold War on American culture include Victor Navasky, *Naming Names* (1980), Nora Sayre, *Running Time: The Films of the Cold War* (1982), Nancy Schwartz, *The Hollywood Writers' Wars* (1982), Ellen Schrecker, *No Ivory Tower: McCarthyism and the Universities* (1986), Michael P. Rogin, *McCarthy and the Intellectuals* (1967), and Richard H. Pells, *The Liberal Mind in a Conservative Age* (1985).

CHAPTER 39

The Eisenhower Era,
1952–1960

*Every warship launched, every rocket fired signified . . . a theft from those who hunger and
are not fed, those who are cold and are not clothed.*

Dwight D. Eisenhower, April 16, 1953

The Advent of Eisenhower

Democratic prospects in the presidential election of 1952 were blighted by the military deadlock in Korea, Truman's clash with MacArthur, war-bred inflation, and whiffs of scandal from the White House. Dispirited Democrats, convening in Chicago, nominated a reluctant Adlai E. Stevenson, the witty, eloquent, and idealistic governor of Illinois.

Republicans enthusiastically chose General Dwight D. Eisenhower on the first ballot. As "Ike's" running mate the convention selected California Senator Richard M. Nixon, who had distinguished himself as a relentless red-hunter.

Eisenhower was already the most popular American of his time, as "I Like Ike" buttons everywhere testified. Striking a grandfatherly, nonpartisan pose, Eisenhower left the rough campaigning to Nixon, who relished pulling no punches. The vice-presidential candidate lambasted his opponents with charges that they had cultivated corruption, caved in on Korea, and coddled communists. He particularly blasted the intellectual ("egghead") Stevenson as "Adlai the appeaser," with a "Ph.D. from [Secretary

of State] Dean Acheson's College of Cowardly Communist Containment."

The outcome of the presidential election of 1952 was never really in doubt. Given an extra prod by Eisenhower's last-minute pledge to go personally to Korea to end the war, the voters massively declared for "Ike." He garnered 33,963,234 votes to Stevenson's 27,314,992. He cracked the solid South wide open, ringing up 442 electoral votes to 89 for his opponent. "Ike" not only ran far ahead of his ticket but pulled enough Republicans into office on his military coattails to ensure GOP control of the new Congress by a paper-thin margin.

True to his campaign pledge, President-elect Eisenhower undertook a flying three-day visit to Korea in December 1952. But even a glamorous "Ike" could not immediately budge the peace negotiations off dead center. Seven long months later, after Eisenhower had threatened to use atomic weapons, an armistice was finally signed but was repeatedly violated in succeeding decades.

The brutal and futile fighting had lasted three

years. About 54,000 Americans lay dead, joined by more than a million Chinese, North Koreans, and South Koreans. Tens of billions of American dollars had been poured down the Asian sinkhole. Yet this terrible toll in blood and treasure bought only a return to the conditions of 1950; Korea remained divided at the thirty-eighth parallel. Americans took what little comfort they could from the fact that communism had been "contained" and that the bloodletting had been "limited" to something less than full-scale global war. The shooting had ended, but the Cold War remained rigidly unthawed.

"Ike" Takes Command

In Dwight Eisenhower, the man and the hour apparently met. The nation sorely needed a respite from twenty years of depression and war. Yet the American people in the 1950s unexpectedly found themselves dug into the front lines of the Cold War abroad and dangerously divided at home over the issues of communist subversion and civil rights. They longed for reassuring leadership. "Ike" seemed ready to give it to them.

As a military commander, Eisenhower had cultivated a leadership style that self-consciously projected an image of sincerity, fairness, and optimism. He enjoyed remarkable success in harmonizing the efforts of potentially quarrelsome allies. He had been widely perceived during the war as an "unmilitary" general, and in the White House he similarly struck the pose of an "unpolitical" president, serenely above the petty partisan fray. He also shrewdly knew that his greatest "asset" was his enjoyment of the "affection and respect of our citizenry," as he confided to his diary in 1949.

"Ike" thus seemed ideally suited to soothe the anxieties of troubled Americans, much as a distinguished and well-loved grandfather brings stability to his family. He played this role well as he presided over a decade of shaky peace and shining prosperity. Yet critics charged that he unwisely hoarded the "asset" of his immense popularity, rather than spend it for a good cause (especially civil rights), and that he cared much more for social harmony than for social justice.

One of the first problems with which Eisenhower had to contend was the swelling popularity and fearful power of Senator Joseph R. McCarthy, the anticommunist "crusader." McCarthy had crashed into the limelight in February 1950, when he charged in a public speech that Secretary of State Dean Acheson was knowingly employing 205 Communist party members in the State Department. Pressed to reveal the names, McCarthy at first conceded that there were only fifty-seven genuine communists, and in the end failed to find even one. His Republican colleagues nevertheless realized the political usefulness of this kind of attack on the Democratic administration. Ohio Senator John Bricker reportedly said, "Joe, you're a dirty s.o.b., but there are times when you've got to have an s.o.b. around, and this is one of them."

McCarthy flourished in the seething Cold War atmosphere of suspicion and fear. He was not the first nor even the most effective anti-red, but he was surely the most ruthless, and he did the most damage to American traditions of fair play and free speech.

For the next four years, "low-blow Joe" proved a master at manipulating the media and playing upon the anxieties of politicians and the public. The careers of countless government officials, writers, actors, and others were ruined after McCarthy had named them, often unfairly, as communists or communist sympathizers. Democrats, he charged, "bent to the whispered pleas from the lips of traitors." General George Marshall, former army chief of staff and ex-secretary of state, was denounced as "part of a conspiracy so immense and an infamy so black as to dwarf any previous venture in the history of man."

Politicians trembled in the face of such onslaughts, especially when opinion polls showed that a majority of the American people approved of McCarthy. Eisenhower privately loathed McCarthy but publicly tried to stay out of his way. Trying to appease the brash demagogue from Wisconsin, Eisenhower allowed him, in effect, to control personnel policy at the State Department. One baleful result was severe damage to the morale and effectiveness of the professional foreign service. In particular, McCarthyite purges deprived the government of a number of Asian specialists who might have

Exposing "Reds" *Senator McCarthy makes a point at the army-McCarthy hearings in 1954 while army counsel Joseph Welch ponders a reply. McCarthy declared in a speech in 1951: "Let me assure you that regardless of how high-pitched becomes the squealing and screaming of those left-wing, bleeding-heart, phony liberals, this battle is going to go on."*

counseled a wiser course in Vietnam in the fateful decade that followed.

McCarthy finally bent the bow too far when he attacked the U.S. Army. The embattled military men fought back in thirty-five days of televised hearings in the spring of 1954. The political power of the new medium of television was again demonstrated as up to 20 million Americans watched in fascination as the boorish, surly McCarthy cut his own throat by parading his essential meanness and irresponsibility. A few months later the Senate condemned him for "conduct unbecoming a member," and three years later McCarthy died unwept and unsung. But *McCarthyism* passed into the English language as a label for the dangerous forces of unfairness and fear that a democratic society can unleash only at its peril.

Desegregating the South

America counted some 15 million black citizens in 1950, two-thirds of whom still made their homes in the South. There they lived bound by the iron folkways of a segregated society. A rigid set of antiquated rules known as Jim Crow laws governed all aspects of their existence, from the schoolroom to the restroom.

Blacks everywhere in the South not only attended segregated schools but were compelled to use separate public toilets, drinking fountains, restaurants, and waiting rooms. Trains and buses had "whites only" and "colored only" seating. Only about 20 percent of eligible southern blacks were registered to vote, and fewer than 5 percent in some Deep South states such as Mississippi and Alabama.

Where the law proved insufficient to enforce this regime, vigilante violence did the job. Six black war veterans, claiming the rights for which they had fought overseas, were murdered in the summer of 1946. A Mississippi mob lynched black fourteen-year-old Emmett Till in 1955 for allegedly leering at a white woman. It is small wonder that a black clergyman declared that "everywhere I go in the South the Negro is forced to choose between his hide and his soul."

In his notable book of 1944, *An American Dilemma,* Swedish scholar Gunnar Myrdal had exposed the contradiction between America's professed belief that all men are created equal and its sordid treatment of black citizens. There had been token progress in race relations since the war—Jack Roosevelt ("Jackie") Robinson, for example, had cracked the racial barrier in big-league baseball when the Brooklyn Dodgers signed him in 1947. But for the most part, the national conscience still slumbered, and blacks still suffered.

Increasingly, however, African-Americans refused to suffer in silence. The war had generated a new militancy and restlessness among many members of the black community. The National Association for the Advancement of Colored People (NAACP) had for years pushed doggedly to dismantle the legal underpinnings of segregation and now enjoyed some success. In 1944 the Supreme Court ruled the "white primary" unconstitutional, thereby undermining the status of the Democratic party in the South as a white persons' club. And in 1950, NAACP chief legal counsel Thurgood Marshall (himself later a Supreme Court justice) wrung from the High Court a ruling that separate professional schools for blacks failed to meet the test of equality.

On a chilly day in December 1955, Rosa Parks, a college-educated black seamstress, made history in Montgomery, Alabama. She boarded a bus, took a seat in the "whites only" section, and refused to give it up. Her arrest for violating the city's Jim Crow statutes sparked a yearlong black boycott of the city buses and served notice throughout the South that blacks would no longer submit meekly to the absurdities and indignities of segregation.

The Montgomery bus boycott also catapulted to prominence a young pastor at Montgomery's Dexter Avenue Baptist Church, the Reverend Martin Luther King, Jr. Barely twenty-seven years old, King seemed an unlikely champion of the downtrodden and disfranchised. Raised in a prosperous black family in Atlanta and educated partly in the North, he had for most of his life been sheltered from the grossest cruelties of segregation. But his oratorical skill, his passionate devotion to biblical and constitutional conceptions of justice, and his devotion to the nonviolent principles of India's Mohandas Gandhi were destined to thrust him to the forefront of the black revolution that would soon pulse across the South—and the rest of the nation.

Rosa Parks at Last Sits in the Front of the Bus, 1956 *Ms. Parks had been arrested on December 1, 1955, for sitting in front of white passengers, a violation of Montgomery, Alabama's segregation laws. To secure the humble right to sit where they pleased, Montgomery's blacks staged a lengthy and eventually successful boycott of the city's bus lines—and in the process launched the modern civil rights movement.*

Martin Luther King, Jr., and His Wife Coretta Arrested
King and his wife were arrested for the first time in Montgomery, Alabama, in 1955 while organizing a bus boycott.

Seeds of the Civil Rights Revolution

In 1946, President Harry Truman commissioned a report on blacks entitled "To Secure These Rights." Following the report's recommendations, Truman in 1948 ended segregation in federal civil service and ordered "equality of treatment and opportunity" in the armed forces. The military brass at first protested that "the army is not a sociological laboratory," but military manpower shortages in Korea forced the integration of combat units, without the predicted loss of effectiveness. Yet Congress stubbornly resisted passing civil rights legislation, and Truman's successor, Dwight Eisenhower, showed no real signs of interest in the racial issue. Within the government, that left only the judicial branch as an avenue of advancement for civil rights.

Breaking the path for civil rights progress was broad-jawed Chief Justice Earl Warren, former governor of California. Elevated to the supreme bench by Eisenhower, Warren shocked the president and other traditionalists with his active judicial intervention in previously taboo social issues. Publicly snubbed and privately criticized by President Eisenhower, Warren persisted in encouraging the Court to apply his straightforward populist principles to its interpretation of the Constitution: in short, legislation by the judiciary, in default of legislation by Congress.

The unanimous decision of the Warren Court in *Brown* v. *Board of Education of Topeka, Kansas,* in May 1954 was epochal. In a forceful opinion, the learned justices ruled that segregation in the public schools was "inherently unequal" and thus unconstitutional. The uncompromising sweep of the decision startled conservatives like an exploding time bomb, for it reversed the Court's earlier declaration of 1896 in *Plessy* v. *Ferguson* (see p. 343) that "separate but equal" facilities were allowable under the Constitution. That doctrine was now dead. Desegregation, the justices insisted, must go ahead with "all deliberate speed."

The border states generally made reasonable efforts to comply with this ruling, but in the Deep South diehards organized massive resistance against the Court's attack on the sacred principle of separate but equal. Several states diverted public funds to hastily created private schools, for there the integration order was more difficult to apply. Throughout the South, white citizens' councils, sometimes with fire and hemp, thwarted attempts to make integration a reality. Ten years after the Court's momentous ruling, fewer than 2 percent of the eligible blacks in the Deep South states were sitting in classrooms with whites.

Crisis at Little Rock

President Eisenhower was little inclined toward promoting integration. He shied away from employing his vast popularity and the prestige of his office to educate white Americans about the need for racial justice. He had advised against integration of the armed forces in 1948 and criticized Truman's call for a permanent Fair Employment Practices Commission. He complained that the Supreme Court's decision in *Brown* v. *Board of Education* had upset "the customs and convictions of at least two generations of Americans," and he steadfastly refused to issue a public statement endorsing the Court's conclusions. "I do not believe," he explained, "that prejudices, even palpably unjustifiable prejudices, will succumb to compulsion."

But in September 1957 "Ike" was forced to act. Orval Faubus, the governor of Arkansas, mobilized the National Guard to prevent nine black students from enrolling in Little Rock's Central High School. Confronted with a direct challenge to federal authority, Eisenhower sent troops to escort the children to their classes.

In the same year, Congress passed the first Civil Rights Act since Reconstruction days. Eisenhower characteristically reassured a southern senator that the legislation represented "the mildest civil rights bill possible." It set up a permanent Civil Rights Commission to investigate violations of civil rights and authorized federal injunctions to protect voting rights.

Blacks meanwhile continued to take the civil rights movement into their own hands. Martin Luther King, Jr., formed the Southern Christian Leadership Conference (SCLC) in 1957. It aimed to mobilize the vast power of the black churches on behalf of black rights. This was an exceptionally shrewd strategy, because the churches were the largest and best-organized black institutions that had been allowed to flourish in a segregated society.

More spontaneous was the "sit-in" movement launched on February 1, 1960, by four black college freshmen in Greensboro, North Carolina. Without a detailed plan or institutional support, they demanded service at a whites-only Woolworth's lunch counter. Observing that "fellows like you make our race look bad," the black waitress refused to serve them. But they kept their seats and returned the next day with nineteen classmates. The following day, eighty-five students joined in; by the end of the week, a thousand. Like a prairie fire, the sit-in movement burned swiftly across the South, swelling into a wave of wade-ins, lie-ins, and pray-ins to compel equal treatment in restaurants, transportation, employment, housing, and voter registration. In April 1960, southern black students formed the Student Non-Violent Coordinating Committee (SNCC, pronounced "snick") to give more focus and force to these efforts. Young and impassioned, SNCC members would eventually lose patience with the more stately tactics of the SCLC and the even more deliberate legalisms of the NAACP.

Eisenhower Republicanism at Home

The balding, sixty-two-year-old General Eisenhower had entered the White House in 1953 pledging his administration to a philosophy of "dynamic conservatism." Above all, he strove to balance the federal budget and guard the republic from what he called "creeping socialism." Eisenhower supported the transfer of control over offshore oil fields from the federal government to the states. "Ike" also tried to curb the TVA by encouraging a private power company to build a generating plant to compete with the massive public utility spawned by the New Deal. His secretary of health, education, and welfare condemned free distribution of Salk antipolio vaccine as "socialized medicine."

Eisenhower responded to the Mexican government's worry that illegal Mexican immigration to the United States would undercut the *bracero* program of legally imported farm workers inaugurated during World War II (see p. 547). In a massive roundup of illegal aliens, as many as 1 million Mexicans were apprehended and returned to Mexico in 1954.

In yet another of the rude and arbitrary reversals that have long afflicted the government's relations with Native Americans, Eisenhower sought to cancel the tribal preservation policies of the "Indian New Deal," in place since 1934 (see p. 400). He proposed to "terminate" the tribes as legal entities and to return to the assimilationist goals of the

Dawes Severalty Act (see p. 400). But most tribes resisted termination, and the policy was abandoned in 1961.

Eisenhower Republicans obviously could not unscramble all the eggs that had been cooked by New Dealers and Fair Dealers for twenty long years. In many ways, Eisenhower accepted and even advanced New Dealish programs. During his presidency, Social Security benefits were extended and the minimum wage raised to one dollar an hour. In a public works project that dwarfed anything the New Deal had ever dreamed of, Eisenhower also backed a $27 billion plan to build 42,000 miles of sleek, fast, interstate highways. The construction of these modern, multilane roads created countless construction jobs and speeded the suburbanization of America.

Despite his good intentions, Eisenhower managed to balance the budget only three times in his eight years in office, and in 1959 he incurred the biggest peacetime deficit thus far in American history. Yet critics blamed his fiscal timidity for aggravating several business recessions during the decade, especially the sharp downturn of 1957–1958, which left more than 5 million workers jobless. Economic troubles helped to revive the Democrats, who regained control of both houses of Congress in 1954. Unemployment jitters also helped to spark the merger of the A. F. of L. and the CIO in 1955.

A "New Look" in Foreign Policy

Mere "containment" of communism was condemned in the 1952 Republican platform as "negative, futile and immoral." Incoming Secretary of State John Foster Dulles promised not merely to stem the red tide but to "roll back" its gains and "liberate captive peoples." At the same time, the new administration promised to balance the budget by cutting military spending.

How were these two contradictory goals to be reached? Dulles answered with a "policy of boldness" in early 1954. The genial President Eisenhower would relegate the army and the navy to the back seat and build up an air fleet of super-bombers with city-flattening nuclear bombs. These fearsome weapons would be equipped to inflict "massive retaliation" on the Soviets if they got out of hand. The advantages of this new policy were thought to be its paralyzing nuclear impact and its cheaper price tag when compared with conventional forces—"more bang for the buck."

Both aspects of the touted "new look" in foreign policy were delusions. In 1956 the Hungarians rose up against their Soviet masters and appealed in vain to the United States for aid. To his dismay, Eisenhower also discovered that the aerial and atomic hardware necessary for "massive retaliation" was also staggeringly expensive. Military costs shot skyward. In 1960, as Eisenhower was about to leave office, he sagely but ironically warned against the dangerous growth of a "military-industrial complex" that his own policies had nurtured.

The Vietnam Nightmare

Europe, thanks to the Marshall Plan and NATO, seemed reasonably secure by the early 1950s, but East Asia was a different can of worms. Nationalist movements had sought for years to throw off the French colonial yoke in Indochina, inspired in part by Woodrow Wilson's doctrine of self-determination and by Franklin Roosevelt's anticolonialism.

Cold War events dampened the dreams of anticolonial Asian peoples. Their leaders—including the Vietnamese nationalist leader Ho Chi Minh—became increasingly communist while the United States became increasingly anticommunist. By 1954, American taxpayers were financing nearly 80 percent of the costs of a bottomless French colonial war in Indochina. The United States' share amounted to about $1 billion a year.

Despite this massive aid, French forces continued to crumble under guerrilla onslaughts. In March 1954 a key French garrison was trapped hopelessly in the fortress of Dienbienphu. The new "policy of boldness" was now put to the test. Secretary Dulles, Vice President Nixon, and the chairman of the Joint Chiefs of Staff favored intervention with American bombers to help bail out the beleaguered French. But Eisenhower, wary about another war in Asia soon after Korea, and correctly fearing British non-support, held back.

Dienbienphu fell, and a multination conference at Geneva roughly halved Vietnam at the seventeenth parallel, supposedly temporarily. The victorious Ho Chi Minh in the north consented to this arrangement on the assurance that Vietnam-wide elections would be held within two years. In the south a pro-Western government under Ngo Dinh Diem was soon entrenched at Saigon. The Vietnamese never held the promised elections, primarily because the communists seemed certain to win, and Vietnam remained a dangerously divided country.

Eisenhower promised economic and military aid to the conservative Diem regime, provided that it undertook certain social reforms. Change came at a snail's pace, but American aid continued, as communist guerrillas heated up their campaign against Diem. The Americans had evidently backed a losing horse, but saw no easy way to call off their bet.

East Asia, 1955–1956

Cold War Crises

The United States had initially backed the French in Indochina, in part to win French approval of a plan to rearm Western Germany. Despite French fears, the Germans were finally welcomed into the NATO fold in 1955. In the same year, the East European countries and the Soviets signed the Warsaw Pact, creating a red military counterweight to the newly bolstered NATO forces in the West.

Despite these hardening military lines, the Cold War seemed to be thawing a bit in 1955. In May the Soviets rather surprisingly agreed to end their occupation of Austria. A summit conference in July produced little progress on the burning issues, but it bred a conciliatory "spirit of Geneva" that caused a modest blush of optimism to pass over the face of the Western world. Hopes rose further the following year when Soviet Communist party boss Nikita Khrushchev, a burly ex–coal miner, publicly denounced the bloody excesses of Joseph Stalin, the dictator dead since 1953.

Violent events late in 1956 ended the post-Geneva lull. When the liberty-loving Hungarians struck for their freedom, they were ruthlessly overpowered by Soviet tanks while the Western world looked on in horror.

Fears of Soviet penetration in the Middle East also heightened Cold War tensions. The government of Iran, supposedly influenced by the Kremlin, began to resist the power of the gigantic Western companies that controlled Iranian petroleum. In response, the American Central Intelligence Agency (CIA) engineered a coup in 1953 that installed the youthful shah of Iran as a kind of dictator. Though successful in the short run in securing Iranian oil for the West, the American intervention left a bitter legacy of resentment among many Iranians. More than two decades later, they took their revenge on the shah and his American allies (see pp. 628–629).

The Suez crisis proved far messier than the swift strike in Iran. President Nasser of Egypt, an ardent Arab nationalist, had obtained tentative offers of American and British aid to build a dam on the Nile, but when Nasser began to flirt openly with the communist camp, Secretary of State Dulles dramatically withdrew the dam offer. Nasser promptly regained face by nationalizing the Suez Canal, owned chiefly by British and French stockholders.

Nasser's action placed a razor's edge at the jugular vein of Western Europe's oil supply. America's apprehensive British and French allies, coordinating their blow with one from Israel, staged a joint assault on Egypt late in October 1956.

For a breathless week, the world teetered on the edge of an abyss. The French and British, who had kept the United States in the dark before their invasion, had made a fatal miscalculation—that America would supply them with oil while their Middle Eastern supplies were disrupted. But to their unpleasant surprise, a furious President Eisenhower resolved to let them "boil in their own oil" and refused to release emergency supplies. The oilless allies resentfully withdrew their troops.

The Suez crisis marked the last time in history that the United States could brandish its oil weapon. As recently as 1940, the United States had produced two-thirds of the world's oil, but by 1948 America had become a net oil importer. Its days as an oil power clearly were numbered as the economic and strategic importance of the Middle East oil region grew dramatically.

The U.S. president and Congress proclaimed the Eisenhower Doctrine in 1957, pledging U.S. military and economic aid to Middle Eastern nations threatened by communist aggression. The real threat to U.S. interests in the Middle East, however, was not communism but nationalism. The Arab countries increasingly resolved to reap for themselves the lion's share of the enormous oil wealth that Western companies pumped out of the scorching Middle Eastern deserts. In a portentous move, Saudi Arabia, Kuwait, Iraq, and Iran joined with Venezuela to form the Organization of Petroleum Exporting Countries (OPEC). In the next two decades, OPEC's stranglehold on the Western economies would tighten.

Round Two for "Ike"

The election of 1956 was a replay of the 1952 contest, with President Eisenhower pitted against Adlai Stevenson. Democrats were hard pressed to find issues with which to attack the popular Eisenhower in a time of peace and prosperity. The voters gave a

resounding endorsement to Eisenhower. He piled up an enormous majority of 35,590,472 to Stevenson's 26,022,752; in the Electoral College the count was 457 to 73. But Eisenhower's victory was a distinctly personal one: he failed to win either house of Congress for his party.

In fragile health, Eisenhower began his second term as a part-time president. Critics charged that he had his hands on his golf clubs, fly rod, and shotgun more often than on the levers of power.

A key area in which the president bestirred himself was labor legislation. Congressional investigations revealed scandalous revelations of gangsterism in high unionist echelons, especially the Teamsters Union. The AFL-CIO had already expelled the Teamsters for choosing leaders like tough-fisted James R. Hoffa, who was later convicted for jury tampering, served part of his sentence, and disappeared—evidently the victim of the gangsters with whom he had consorted. Legislation was clearly needed to keep collective bargaining from becoming collective bludgeoning. Eisenhower persuaded Congress in 1959 to pass the Landrum-Griffin Act, which forced financial reforms in union operations and outlawed "secondary boycotts."

Soviet scientists astounded the world on October 4, 1957, by lofting into orbit around the globe a beep-beeping "baby moon" (*Sputnik I*), weighing 184 pounds. A month later they topped their own ace by sending aloft a larger satellite (*Sputnik II*), weighing 1,120 pounds and carrying a dog.

This amazing scientific breakthrough shattered American self-confidence. America had seemingly taken a back seat in scientific achievement. Envious "backward" nations laughed at America's discomfiture, all the more so because the Soviets were occupying outer space while American troops were occupying the high school in Little Rock.

Military implications of these man-made satellites proved sobering. If the Soviets could fire heavy objects into outer space, they could reach America with intercontinental ballistic missiles. Experts testified that America's manned bombers were still a powerful deterrent, but heroic efforts were needed if the "missile gap" was not to widen.

"Rocket fever" swept the nation. After humiliating and well-advertised failures (the Soviets concealed theirs), the Americans regained some prestige four months after the initial Soviet space triumph. They managed to put into orbit a grapefruit-sized satellite weighing 2.5 pounds.

The *Sputnik* spur led to a critical comparison of the American educational system, already under fire as too easygoing, with that of the Soviet Union. A strong move developed in the United States to replace "frills" with solid subjects—to substitute square root for square dancing. Congress rejected demands for federal scholarships, but late in 1958 the National Defense and Education Act (NDEA) authorized $887 million in loans to needy college students and in grants for the improvement of teaching the sciences and languages. Exploring the space between the ears seemed necessary if America was going to catch up with the Soviet Union in exploring outer space.

The Continuing Cold War

The fantastic race toward nuclear annihilation continued unabated. Humanity-minded scientists urged that nuclear tests be stopped before the atmosphere became so polluted as to produce generations of deformed mutants. The Soviets, after completing an intensive series of exceptionally "dirty" tests, proclaimed a suspension in March 1958, and urged the Western world to follow. Beginning in October 1958, Washington did halt both underground and atmospheric testing. But attempts to regularize such suspensions by proper inspection sank on the reef of mutual suspicion.

Thermonuclear suicide seemed nearer in July 1958, when both Egyptian and communist plottings threatened to engulf Western-oriented Lebanon. After its president had called for aid under the Eisenhower Doctrine, the United States boldly landed several thousand troops and helped restore order without taking a single life.

Khrushchev, no doubt feeling his missile-muscles, deliberately provoked an even more ominous crisis over Berlin—"a bone in the throat," he said—in November 1958. Annoyed by this pro-Western oasis in a communist desert, he gave the three West-

"What's So Funny?" *Premier Khrushchev gloats over "Ike's" spying discomfiture.*

ern powers (Britain, France, the United States) six months to pull their troops out of West Berlin. The Soviet East German satellite would then take over, and if the West resisted, Moscow would rush to the aid of its puppet. This could only mean World War III. But Eisenhower and Dulles, remembering the perils of appeasement, staunchly refused to yield.

The burly Khrushchev, seeking new propaganda laurels, was eager to meet with Eisenhower and pave the way for a "summit conference" with Western leaders. Despite grave misgivings as to any tangible results, the president invited him to America in 1959. Arriving in New York, Khrushchev appeared before the U.N. General Assembly and dramatically resurrected the ancient Soviet proposal of complete disarmament. But he offered no practical means of achieving this end.

A result of this tour was a meeting at Camp David, the presidential retreat in Maryland. Khrushchev emerged saying that his ultimatum for the evacuation of Berlin would be extended indefinitely. The relieved world gave prayerful but premature thanks for the "spirit of Camp David."

The Paris summit conference, scheduled for May 1960, turned out to be an incredible fiasco. Both Moscow and Washington had publicly taken a firm stand on the burning Berlin issue, and neither could risk a public backdown. Then, on the eve of the conference, an American U-2 spy plane was shot down deep in the heart of Russia. After bungling bureaucratic denials in Washington, "honest Ike" took the unprecedented step of assuming personal responsibility. Khrushchev stormed into Paris filling the air with invective, and the conference collapsed before it could get off the ground.

Cuba's Castroism Spells Communism

An ill-timed "goodwill" tour by Vice President Nixon through South America in 1958 reaped a harvest of spit and spite. After being stoned, spat upon, and shouted down at Lima, Peru, Nixon narrowly escaped serious injury from a mob in Caracas, Venezuela. Latin Americans bitterly resented Uncle Sam's lavishing billions of dollars on Europe, while doling out only millions to the poor relations to the south. They also chafed at Washington's continuing habit of intervening in Latin American affairs—as in a CIA-directed coup that ousted a leftist government in Guatemala in 1954. On the other hand, Washington continued to support—even decorate—bloody dictators who claimed to be combating communists.

Most ominous of all was the communist beachhead in Cuba. The ironfisted dictator Batista had encouraged huge investments of American capital, and Washington in turn had given him some support. When black-bearded Dr. Fidel Castro engineered a revolution early in 1959, he denounced the Yankee imperialists and began to expropriate valuable American properties in pursuing a land-distribution program. Washington, finally losing patience, released Cuba from "imperialistic slavery" by cutting off the heavy imports of Cuban sugar. Castro retaliated with further wholesale confiscations of Yankee property and in effect made his left-wing dictatorship an economic and military satellite of Moscow. Washington broke diplomatic relations with Cuba early in 1961.

Americans talked seriously of invoking the Monroe Doctrine before the Soviets set up a communist base only 90 miles from their shores. Khrushchev angrily proclaimed that the Monroe Doctrine was dead and indicated that he would shower missiles upon the United States if it attacked his good friend Castro.

Kennedy versus Nixon in 1960

Republicans faced up to the presidential campaign of 1960 without great optimism, for they had taken a bad beating in the midterm congressional elections of 1958. Vice President Nixon was the Republican heir apparent. The "old" Nixon had been a no-holds-barred campaigner, especially in assailing Democrats and left-wingers. The "new" Nixon who appeared in 1960 was represented as a mature, seasoned statesman. Nixon gained stature with his global travels. A photograph of him pointing his index finger at Khrushchev during their "kitchen debate" in Moscow in 1959 was cited as proof that he knew how to stand up to the Russians. Nixon was nominated on the first ballot at the Republican convention in Chicago; his running mate was handsome Henry Cabot Lodge, Jr., of Massachusetts.

Emerging the winner from the Democratic primaries and the Los Angeles convention was John F. Kennedy, a tall, youthful, tooth-flashing millionaire senator from Massachusetts. In a marriage of convenience designed to appease the South, Kennedy chose as his running mate Senator Lyndon B. Johnson of Texas, who had been his closest rival for the nomination.

Because Kennedy was a Roman Catholic, bigotry inevitably showed its snarling face. Smear artists revived the ancient charges that the Pope would control the White House, arousing misgivings in the Protestant Bible Belt South. Kennedy denied that he

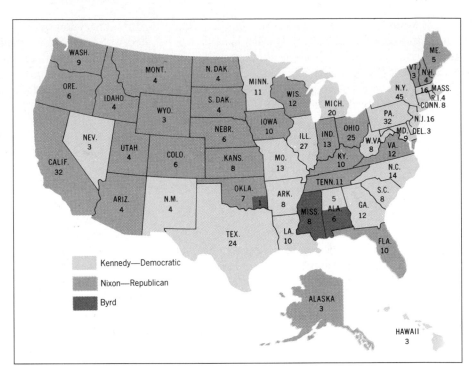

Presidential Election of 1960 (with electoral vote by state) *Kennedy owed his hairbreadth triumph to his victories in twenty-six of the forty largest cities— and to Lyndon Johnson's strenuous campaigning in the South, where Kennedy's Catholic religion may have been a hotter issue than his stand on civil rights.*

would be swayed by Rome, and asked if some 40 million Catholic Americans were to be condemned to second-class citizenship from birth. In the end, the religious issue largely canceled itself out. If many southern Democrats stayed away from the polls because of Kennedy's Catholicism, northern Democrats in unusually large numbers supported Kennedy because of the bitter attacks on their Catholic faith.

Kennedy insisted that the Soviets, with their nuclear bombs and *Sputniks,* had gained on America in prestige and power. Nixon replied that the nation's prestige had not slipped, although Kennedy was causing it to do so by his unpatriotic talk. A series of television debates between the contestants may well have tipped the scales. Many viewers found Kennedy's glamour and vitality far more appealing than Nixon's tired and pallid appearance.

Kennedy won the election with a rather comfortable electoral vote margin of 303 to 219, but with a breathtakingly close popular margin of only 118,574 votes out of over 68 million cast. Like Franklin Roosevelt, Kennedy ran well in the large

industrial centers, where he had strong support from workers, Catholics, and African-Americans. (He had solicitously telephoned the pregnant Coretta King, whose husband, Martin Luther King, Jr., was then imprisoned in Georgia for participating in a sit-in.) Despite losing a few seats, the Democrats swept both houses of Congress by wide margins.

An Old General Fades Away

President Eisenhower, the aging "dynamic conservative," continued to enjoy extraordinary popularity up until the final curtain. Despite Democratic gibes about "eight years of golfing and goofing," of "putting and puttering," Eisenhower was universally admired and respected for his dignity, decency, sincerity, goodwill, and moderation.

Pessimists had predicted that Eisenhower would be a seriously crippled lame duck during his second term, owing to the barrier against reelection erected by the Twenty-second Amendment, ratified in 1951 (see the Appendix). In truth, he displayed more vigor, more political know-how, and more aggressive leadership during his last two years as president than ever before. For an unprecedented six years, from 1955 to 1961, Congress remained in Democratic hands, yet Eisenhower established unusual control over it. He wielded the veto 169 times, and only twice was he overridden by the required two-thirds vote.

America was fabulously prosperous in the Eisenhower years, despite pockets of poverty and unemployment, recurrent recessions, and perennial farm problems. To the north the vast St. Lawrence waterway project, constructed jointly with Canada and completed in 1959, had turned the cities of the Great Lakes into bustling ocean seaports.

"Old Glory" could now proudly display fifty stars. Alaska attained statehood in 1959, as did Hawaii. Alaska, though gigantic, was thinly populated and noncontiguous, but these objections were overcome in a Democratic Congress that expected Alaska to vote Democratic. Hawaii had ample population (largely of Asian descent), advanced democratic institutions, and more acreage than Rhode Island, Delaware, or Connecticut.

Though a crusading general, Eisenhower as president mounted no moral crusade for civil rights.

This was perhaps his greatest failing. Yet he had done far more than grin away problems and tread water. As a Republican president, he had further woven the reforms of the Democratic New Deal and Fair Deal into the fabric of national life. As a former general, he had exercised wise restraint in his use of military power and had soberly guided foreign policy away from countless threats to peace. He had ended one war and avoided all others. As the decades lengthened, appreciation of him grew.

Consumer Culture in the Fifties

The 1950s witnessed a huge expansion of the middle class and the blossoming of a consumer culture. Diner's Club introduced the plastic credit card in 1950, and four years later the first McDonald's hamburger stand opened in San Bernardino, California. Also in 1955, Disneyland opened its doors in Anaheim, California. These innovations—easy credit, high-volume "fast-food" production, and new forms of recreation—were harbingers of an emerging new lifestyle of affluence that was in full flower by the decade's end.

Crucial to the development of that lifestyle was the rapid rise of the new technology of television.

The Original McDonald's, San Bernardino, California, 1955 *The birth of McDonald's heralded the arrival of the "fast-food" industry, a characteristic feature of the consumer-oriented economy that flourished in post–World War II America.*

Only six TV stations were broadcasting in 1946; a decade later 442 stations were operating. TV sets were rich people's novelties in the 1940s; but 7 million sets were sold in 1951. By 1960 virtually every American home had one, in a stunning display of the speed with which new technologies can pervade and transform modern societies. By the mid-1950s advertisers annually spent $10 billion to hawk their wares on television, while critics fumed that the wildly popular new mass medium was degrading the public's aesthetic, moral, political, and educational standards.

Popular music was also dramatically transformed in the fifties. The chief revolutionary was Elvis Presley, a white singer born in 1935 in Tupelo, Mississippi. Fusing black rhythm and blues with white bluegrass and country styles, he created a new musical idiom known forever after as rock and roll. Rock was "crossover" music, carrying its heavy beat and driving rhythms across the cultural divide that separated black and white musical traditions. Listening and dancing to it quickly became a kind of religious rite for the millions of baby boomers coming of age in the 1950s.

Traditionalists were repelled by Presley, and they found much more to upset them in the affluent decade. Movie star Marilyn Monroe, with her ingenuous smile and mandolin-curved figure, helped to popularize—and commercialize—new standards of sensuous sexuality. So did *Playboy* magazine, first published in 1955. As the decade closed, Americans were well on their way to becoming free-spending consumers of mass-produced, standardized products, advertised on the electronic medium of television and often sold for their alleged sexual allure.

Many critics lamented the implications of this new consumerist lifestyle. Harvard sociologist David Riesman criticized the postwar generation as conformists in *The Lonely Crowd* (1950), as did William H. Whyte, Jr., in *The Organization Man*. Novelist Sloan Wilson explored a similar theme in *The Man in the Gray Flannel Suit* (1955). Harvard economist John Kenneth Galbraith questioned the relation between private wealth and the public good in a series of books beginning with *The Affluent Society* (1958) and extending to *Economics and the Public Purpose* (1973). The postwar explosion of prosperity,

CHRONOLOGY

1952	Eisenhower defeats Stevenson for presidency.
1953	CIA-engineered coup installs shah of Iran.
1954	French defeated in Vietnam.
	SEATO formed.
	Army-McCarthy hearings.
	Brown v. *Board of Education.*
	CIA-sponsored coup in Guatemala.
1955	Montgomery bus boycott begins; emergence of Martin Luther King, Jr.
	Geneva summit meeting.
	Warsaw Pact signed.
	A. F. of L. merges with CIO.
1956	Soviets crush Hungarian revolt.
	Suez crisis.
	Eisenhower defeats Stevenson for presidency.
1957	Little Rock school desegregation crisis.
	Civil Rights Act passed.
	Southern Christian Leadership Conference (SCLC) formed.
	Eisenhower Doctrine.
	Soviet Union launches *Sputnik* satellite.
1958	U.S. troops sent to Lebanon.
	NDEA authorizes loans and grants for science and language education.
1958–1959	Berlin crisis.
1959	Castro leads Cuban revolution.
	Landrum-Griffin Act.
	Alaska and Hawaii attain statehood.
1960	U-2 incident sabotages Paris summit.
	Sit-in movement for civil rights begins.
	Kennedy defeats Nixon for presidency.

Galbraith claimed, had produced a troublesome combination of private opulence amid public squalor. Americans had televisions in their homes but garbage in their streets. They ate rich food but breathed foul air. Galbraith's call for social spending to match private purchasing proved highly influential in the 1960s.

Sociologist Daniel Bell, in *The Coming of Post-Industrial Society* (1973) and *The Cultural Contradictions of Capitalism* (1976), found even deeper paradoxes of prosperity. The hedonistic "consumer ethic" of modern capitalism, he argued, might undermine the older "work ethic" and thus destroy capitalism's very productive capacity. Collusion at the highest level of the military-industrial complex was the subject of *The Power Elite* (1956), an influential piece of modern muckraking by radical sociologist C. Wright Mills, who became a hero to New Left student activists in the 1960s.

Varying Viewpoints

Liberal historians, reflecting a Democratic bias that is widespread in academic circles, have portrayed the 1950s as the time of the "great postponement." These critics condemn Eisenhower as visionless and passive, and lament the failure of the decade to carry forward vigorously the programs of the New Deal. But to other scholars the Eisenhower era has begun to appear in a more favorable light. Antidotes to the liberal conventional wisdom have come both from conservatives, who view "Ike's" presidency as an island of calm between the noisy clashes of the Truman years and the convulsive upheavals of the 1960s, and from radicals, who stress his restraint at the time of Dienbienphu and his desire to control the military-industrial complex. In recent years some scholars, notably Fred I. Greenstein, have argued that Eisenhower's public nonchalance masked decisive and adept behind-the-scenes leadership.

SELECT READINGS

Primary Source Documents

Earl Warren's decision in *Brown* v. *Board of Education of Topeka,* 347 U.S. 492–495 (1954),* altered the course of race relations in the United States. It also sparked the opposition of 100 southern congressmen, *Congressional Record,* 84th Congress, 2d Session, pp. 4515–4516 (1956).* Eisenhower's farewell address (1961)* warned of the dangers of the military-industrial complex. John Kenneth Galbraith criticized the consumer culture in *The Affluent Society* (1958).*

Secondary Sources

The era is surveyed readably in several works, including Eric F. Goldman, *The Crucial Decade—and After: America, 1945–1960* (1961), Richard Polenberg, *One Nation Divisible: Class, Race, and Ethnicity in the United States Since 1938* (1980), William Leuchtenberg. *A Troubled Feast: American Society Since 1945* (updated ed., 1983), William H. Chafe, *The Unfinished Journey: America Since World War II* (1985), and more succinctly in Charles C. Alexander, *Holding the Line: The Eisenhower Era, 1952–1961* (1975). Eisenhower the man is the subject of Stephen Ambrose's two-volume biography, *Eisenhower: Soldier, General of the Army, President-Elect, 1890–1952* (1983) and *Eisenhower: The President* (1984). Fred I. Greenstein portrays Ike as the master of *The Hidden Hand Presidency* (1982). Robert A. Divine, *Eisenhower and the Cold War* (1981), praises his diplomatic restraint. The background and consequences of the Supreme Court's 1954 desegregation decision are ably presented in Richard Kluger, *Simple Justice: The History of* Brown v. Board of Education (1976), and Raymond Wolters, *The Burden of Brown: Thirty Years of School Desegregation* (1984). Especially rich are Taylor Branch, *Parting the Waters: America in the King Years, 1954–1963* (1988), and David J. Garrow, *Bearing the Cross: Martin Luther King, Jr., and the Southern Christian Leadership Conference* (1986). For one man's experience of integration, see Jules Tygiel, *Baseball's Great Experiment: Jackie Robinson and His Legacy* (1983). Relevant memoirs and biographies include William O. Douglas, *The Court Years, 1939–1975* (1980); G. Edward White, *Earl Warren* (1982); Jerome E. Edwards, *Pat McCarran* (1982); John Bartlow Martin, *Adlai Stevenson* (2 vols., 1976–1977); and Townsend Hoopes, *The Devil and John Foster Dulles* (1973). On the election of 1960, see Theodore H. White's colorful *The Making of the President, 1960* (1961). For more on cultural developments during the 1950s, see Lary May, ed., *Recasting America: Culture and Politics in the Age of the Cold War* (1989); Elaine May, *Homeward Bound: American Families in the Cold War Era* (1988); and Tino Balio, ed., *Hollywood in the Age of Television* (1990).

CHAPTER 40

The Stormy Sixties, 1960–1968

In the final analysis it is their war. They are the ones who have to win it or lose it . . . the people of Vietnam.

John F. Kennedy, September 1963

Kennedy's New Frontier

Complacent and comfortable as the 1950s closed, Americans elected in 1960 a young, vigorous president who pledged "to get the country moving again." As the new decade opened, neither the nation nor the new president had any inkling of just how action-packed it would be, both at home and abroad. The 1960s would bring a sexual revolution, a civil rights revolution, the emergence of a youth culture, a devastating war in Vietnam, and the beginnings, at least, of a feminist revolution. By the end of the stormy sixties, many Americans would yearn nostalgically for the comparative calm of the fifties.

Hatless and topcoatless in the 22°F chill, John F. Kennedy delivered a stirring inaugural address on January 20, 1961. Tall, elegantly handsome, speaking crisply and with staccato finger jabs at the air, Kennedy personified the youth, glamor, and vigor of the new administration.

From the outset Kennedy inspired high expectations, especially among the young. His challenge of a "New Frontier" quickened patriotic pulses. He brought a warm heart to the Cold War when he proposed the Peace Corps, an army of idealistic and mostly youthful volunteers to bring American skills to underdeveloped countries.

Kennedy came into office with narrow Democratic majorities in Congress. Southern Democrats threatened to team up with Republicans and ax New Frontier proposals such as medical assistance for the aged and increased federal aid to education.

Another vexing problem was the economy. Kennedy had campaigned on the theme of revitalizing the economy after the recessions of the Eisenhower years. His administration helped negotiate a noninflationary wage agreement in the steel industry in early 1962. The assumption was that the companies, for their part, would keep the lid on prices.

Almost immediately, steel management announced significant price increases, thereby seemingly demonstrating bad faith. The president erupted in wrath, remarking that his father had once said that "all businessmen were sons of bitches." He called the "big steel" men onto the White House carpet and unleashed his Irish temper. Overawed, the steel operators backed down.

The steel episode provoked fiery attacks by big business on the New Frontier, but Kennedy soon appealed to believers in free enterprise when he announced his support of a general tax-cut bill. He chose to stimulate the economy by slashing taxes and putting more money directly into private hands. When he announced his policy before a big business group, one observer called it "the most Republican speech since McKinley."

Kennedy also promoted a multibillion-dollar project to land a man on the moon. When skeptics objected that the money could best be spent elsewhere, Kennedy answered them in a speech at Rice University in Texas: "But why, some say, the moon? . . . And they may well ask, why climb the highest mountain? Why, thirty-five years ago, fly the Atlantic? Why does Rice play Texas?" Twenty-four billion dollars later in 1969, two American astronauts triumphantly planted human footprints on the moon's dusty surface.

Rumblings in Europe

A few months after settling into the White House, the new president met Soviet Premier Khrushchev at Vienna, in June 1961. The tough-talking dictator adopted a belligerent attitude, threatening to cut off Western access to Berlin. Though visibly shaken, the president refused to be bullied, and on his return requested an increase in the military budget and called up reserve troops for the possible defense of Berlin. The Soviets backed off from their most bellicose threats but suddenly began to construct the Berlin Wall in August 1961. A barbed-wire-and-concrete barrier, the "Wall of Shame" looked to the free world like a gigantic enclosure around a concentration camp. The wall stood for almost three decades, an ugly scar symbolizing the post–World War II division of Europe into two hostile camps.

Kennedy meanwhile turned his attention to Western Europe, now miraculously prospering after the Marshall Plan and the growth of the Common Market. He finally secured passage of the Trade Expansion Act in 1962, authorizing tariff cuts of up to 50 percent to promote trade with Common Market countries. This legislation led to the so-called Kennedy Round of tariff negotiations, concluded in 1967, and to a significant expansion of European-American trade.

But not all of Kennedy's ambitious designs for Europe were realized. American policy makers were dedicated to an economically and militarily united "Atlantic Community," with the United States the dominant partner. But they found their way blocked by towering, stiff-backed Charles de Gaulle, president of France. De Gaulle deemed the Americans unreliable in a crisis, so he tried to preserve French freedom of action by developing his own small atomic force. Despite the perils of nuclear proliferation or Soviet domination, de Gaulle demanded an independent Europe, free of Yankee influence.

Foreign Flare-ups and "Flexible Response"

Special problems for U.S. foreign policy emerged from the worldwide decolonization of European overseas possessions after World War II. Many of the newcomer nations from once-colonial Asia and Africa were critical of U.S. foreign policy, while some became battlegrounds between the noncommunist and the communist worlds.

Sparsely populated Laos, freed of its French colonial overlords in 1954, was festering dangerously by the time Kennedy came into office. The Eisenhower administration had drenched this jungle kingdom with dollars, but failed to cleanse the country of an aggressive communist element. A red Laos, many observers feared, would be a river on which the influence of communist China would flood into all of Southeast Asia.

As the Laotian civil war raged, Kennedy's military advisers seriously considered sending in American troops. But the president found that he had insufficient forces to put out the fire in Asia and still honor his commitments in Europe. Kennedy thus sought a diplomatic escape hatch in the fourteen-power Geneva conference, which imposed a shaky peace in Laos in 1962.

These "brushfire wars" intensified the pressure for a shift away from Secretary Dulles's dubious doctrine of "massive retaliation." Kennedy felt hamstrung by the knowledge that in a crisis he had the devil's choice between humiliation and nuclear incineration. With Defense Secretary McNamara, he pushed the strategy of "flexible response"—that is, developing an array of military options that could be precisely matched to the scope and importance of the crisis at hand. To this end, Kennedy increased spending on conventional military forces and bolstered the Special Forces (Green Berets). They were an elite anti-guerrilla outfit trained to survive on snake meat and to kill with scientific finesse.

Stepping into the Vietnam Quagmire

The doctrine of flexible response seemed sane enough, but it contained lethal logic. It potentially lowered the level at which diplomacy would give way to shooting. It also provided a mechanism for a progressive, and possibly endless, stepping-up of the use of force. Vietnam soon presented a grisly demonstration of these dangers.

The corrupt and right-wing Diem government in Saigon, despite a deluge of American dollars, had ruled shakily since the partition of Vietnam in 1954. Anti-Diem agitation, spearheaded by the local communist Viet Cong and encouraged by the red regime in the north, noisily threatened to topple the pro-American government from power. In a fateful decision late in 1961, Kennedy ordered a sharp increase in the number of "military advisers" (U.S. troops) in South Vietnam.

American forces had allegedly entered Vietnam to foster political stability—to help protect Diem from the communists long enough to allow

Vietnam and Southeast Asia

"Backbone" *United States supports South Vietnam.*

him to enact basic social reforms favored by the Americans. But the Kennedy administration eventually despaired of the reactionary Diem and encouraged a successful coup against him in November 1963. Ironically, the United States thus contributed to a long process of political disintegration that its original policy had meant to prevent. Kennedy still told the South Vietnamese that it was "their war," but he had made dangerously deep political commitments. By the time of his death, he had ordered more than 15,000 American men into the far-off Asian slaughter pen. A graceful pullout was becoming increasingly difficult.

Cuban Confrontations

Although the United States regarded Latin America as its backyard, its southern neighbors feared and resented the powerful Colossus of the North. In 1961 Kennedy extended the hand of friendship with the Alliance for Progress (*Alianza para el Progreso*), hailed as a Marshall Plan for Latin America. But results were disappointing; there was little alliance and even less progress. American handouts had little positive impact on Latin America's immense social problems.

President Kennedy also struck below the border with the mailed fist. He had inherited from the Eisenhower administration a CIA-backed scheme to topple Fidel Castro from power by invading Cuba with anticommunist exiles. On a fateful April 17, 1961, some 1,200 exiles landed at Cuba's Bay of Pigs. When the invasion bogged down, the bullet-riddled band of anti-Castroites surrendered. President Kennedy assumed full responsibility for the failure, remarking that "victory has a hundred fathers, and defeat is an orphan."

The Bay of Pigs blunder, along with continuing American covert efforts to assassinate Castro and overthrow his government, naturally pushed the Cuban leader even further into the Soviet embrace. Wily Chairman Khrushchev lost little time taking full advantage of his Cuban comrade's position just 90 miles off Florida's coast. In October 1962, aerial photographs taken by American spy planes revealed that the Soviets were secretly and speedily installing nuclear-tipped missiles in Cuba.

Kennedy and Khrushchev now began a nerve-wracking game of "nuclear chicken." The president, on October 22, 1962, ordered a naval "quarantine" of Cuba and demanded immediate removal of the threatening missiles. He also served notice on Khrushchev that any attack on the United States from Cuba would be regarded as coming from the Soviet Union, and would trigger nuclear retaliation against the Russian heartland. For an anxious week, Americans waited while Soviet ships approached the patrol line established by the U.S. Navy off Cuba. The world teetered breathlessly on the brink of global atomization.

In this tense eyeball-to-eyeball confrontation, Khrushchev finally flinched. On October 28 he agreed to a partially face-saving compromise, by which he would pull the missiles out of Cuba. The United States in return agreed to end the quarantine and not invade the island.

Fallout from the Cuban missile crisis was considerable. A humiliated Khrushchev was ultimately hounded out of the Kremlin and became an "unperson." Kennedy, apparently sobered by the appalling risks he had just run, pushed harder for a nuclear test-ban treaty with the Soviet Union. After prolonged negotiations in Moscow, a pact prohibiting trial nuclear explosions in the atmosphere was signed in late 1963. Another barometer indicating a thaw in the Cold War was the installation (August 1963) of a Moscow-Washington "hot line," permitting immediate teletype communication in case of crisis.

Most significant was Kennedy's speech at the American University, Washington, D.C., in June 1963. The president urged Americans to abandon a view of the Soviet Union as a devil-ridden land filled with fanatics, and instead to deal with the world "as it is, not as it might have been had the history of the last eighteen years been different." Kennedy thus tried to lay the foundations for a realistic policy of peaceful coexistence with the Soviet Union. Here were the modest origins of the policy that later came to be known as *détente*.

The Struggle for Civil Rights

Kennedy had campaigned with a strong appeal to black voters, but he proceeded gingerly to redeem his promises. Although he had pledged to eliminate racial discrimination in housing "with a stroke of the pen," it took him nearly two years to find the right pen. Civil rights groups meanwhile sent thousands of pens to the White House in an "Ink for Jack" protest against the president's slowness.

Political concerns stayed the president's hand on civil rights. Elected by a wafer-thin margin and with shaky control over Congress, Kennedy needed the support of southern legislators to pass his economic and social legislation, especially his medical and educational bills. He believed, perhaps justifiably, that those measures would eventually benefit black Americans at least as much as specific legislation on civil rights. Bold moves for racial justice would have to wait.

But events soon scrambled these careful calculations. Following the wave of sit-ins that surged across the South in 1960, groups of Freedom Riders fanned out to end segregation in facilities serving interstate bus passengers. A white mob torched a Freedom Ride bus near Anniston, Alabama, in May 1961, and Attorney General Robert Kennedy's personal representative was beaten unconscious in another anti–Freedom Ride riot in Montgomery. When southern officials proved unwilling or unable to stem the violence, Washington dispatched federal marshals to protect the Freedom Riders.

Reluctantly but fatefully, the Kennedy administration had now joined hands with the civil rights

Freedom Ride, 1961   *Rampaging whites near Anniston, Alabama, burned this bus carrying an interracial group of Freedom Riders on May 14, 1961.*

movement. For the most part, the relationship between Martin Luther King, Jr., and the Kennedys was a fruitful one. Encouraged by Robert Kennedy, and with financial backing from Kennedy-prodded private foundations, SNCC and other civil rights groups inaugurated a Voter Education Project to register the South's historically disfranchised blacks.

Integrating southern universities threatened to provoke wholesale slaughter. Some desegregated painlessly, but the University of Mississippi ("Ole Miss") became a volcano. A twenty-nine-year-old air force veteran, James Meredith, encountered violent opposition when he attempted to register in October 1962. In the end President Kennedy was forced to send in 400 federal marshals and 3,000 troops to enroll Meredith in his first class—in colonial American history.

In the spring of 1963, Martin Luther King, Jr., launched a campaign against discrimination in Birmingham, Alabama, the most segregated big city in America. Although they constituted nearly half the city's population, blacks made up fewer than 15 percent of the city's voters. Previous attempts to crack rigid racial barriers had produced more than fifty cross burnings and eighteen bomb attacks since 1957. "Some of the people sitting here will not come back alive from this campaign," King advised his organizers. Events soon confirmed this grim prediction. Watching developments on television screens, a horrified world saw peaceful civil rights marchers repeatedly repelled by police with attack dogs and electric cattle prods. Most fearsome were the high-pressure water hoses directed at the civil rights demonstrators. Special monitor guns delivered water with enough force to knock bricks loose from buildings or strip bark from trees at a distance of 100 feet. The hoses bowled little children down the street like tumbleweed.

Jolted by these vicious confrontations, President Kennedy delivered a memorable televised speech to the nation on June 11, 1963. He called the situation a "moral crisis" and pleaded for new civil rights legislation to protect black citizens. On the very night of that stirring appeal a white gunman shot down Medgar Evers, a Mississippi civil rights worker. In August, Martin Luther King, Jr., led 200,000 black and white demonstrators on a peaceful "March on Washington" in support of the proposed civil rights legislation. Still the violence continued. In September 1963 an explosion blasted a Baptist church in Birmingham, killing four black girls who had just finished a lesson called "The Love That Forgives."

The Killing of Kennedy

Violence haunted America in the mid-1960s, and it stalked onto center stage on November 22, 1963. While riding in an open limousine in downtown Dallas, Texas, President Kennedy was shot in the head by a concealed rifleman and died within seconds. As a stunned nation nursed its grief, the tragedy grew still more unbelievable. The alleged assassin, a furtive figure named Lee Harvey Oswald, was himself shot to death in front of the television cameras by a self-appointed avenger, Jack Ruby. So bizarre were the events surrounding the two murders that even an elaborate official investigation conducted by Chief Justice Warren could not quiet all doubts and theories about what had really happened. Vice President Johnson, sworn in as president on a waiting airplane in Dallas, managed a dignified and efficient transition, pledging continuity with his slain predecessor's policies.

For several days, the nation was steeped in sorrow. Not until then did many Americans realize how fully their young, vibrant president and his captivating wife had cast a spell over them. Chopped down in his prime after only slightly more than 1,000 days in the White House, Kennedy was acclaimed more for the ideals he had enunciated and the spirit he had kindled than for the concrete goals he had achieved. He had laid one myth to rest forever—that a Catholic could not be trusted with the presidency of the United States. Mass was celebrated only once in the White House—the day of his funeral.

In later years revelations about Kennedy's womanizing and allegations about his involvement with organized crime figures blighted his reputation. But despite those accusations, his vigor, charisma, and idealism made him an inspirational figure for the generation of Americans who came of age in the

1960s—including Bill Clinton, who as a boy briefly met President Kennedy and was himself elected president in 1992.

The LBJ Brand on the Presidency

The torch had now passed to craggy-faced Lyndon Baines Johnson, a Texan who towered 6 feet 3 inches. He could move political mountains or checkmate opponents as the occasion demanded, using what came to be known as the "Johnson treatment"—a flashing display of backslapping, flesh-pressing, and arm-twisting that overbore friend and foe alike.

As president, Johnson quickly shed the conservative coloration of his Senate years to reveal a still-living liberal underneath. Seeking to carry on his predecessor's legacy, Johnson rammed Kennedy's stalled tax cut and civil rights bills through Congress, and added proposals of his own for a billion-dollar "War on Poverty."

Johnson's nomination by the Democrats in 1964 was a foregone conclusion. He had dubbed his domestic program the "Great Society"—a sweeping set of New Dealish economic and welfare measures aimed at transforming the American way of life. Public support for LBJ's antipoverty war was aroused by Michael Harrington's *The Other America* (1962), which revealed that in affluent America 20 percent of the population—and over 40 percent of the black population—suffered in poverty.

The Republicans, convening in San Francisco, nominated box-jawed Senator Barry Goldwater of Arizona, a bronzed and bespectacled champion of rock-ribbed conservatism. The American stage was thus set for a historic clash of political principles.

Goldwater's forces had galloped out of the Southwest to ride roughshod over the moderate Republican "eastern establishment." Goldwater attacked the federal income tax, the Social Security system, the Tennessee Valley Authority, civil rights legislation, the nuclear test-ban treaty, and, of course, the Great Society. His fiercely dedicated followers proclaimed: "In Your Heart You Know He's Right," which prompted the Democratic response, "In Your Guts You Know He's Nuts."

Johnson cultivated the image of a resolute statesman by seizing upon the Tonkin Gulf episode early in August 1964. Unbeknownst to the American public or Congress, U.S. Navy ships had been cooperating with South Vietnamese gunboats in provocative raids along the coast of North Vietnam. Two of these American destroyers were allegedly fired upon by the North Vietnamese on August 2 and 4, although exactly what happened remains unclear. Later investigations strongly suggested that the North Vietnamese fired in self-defense on August 2, and that the "attack" of August 4 never happened. Johnson later quipped, "For all I know, the Navy was shooting at whales out there."

Johnson nevertheless promptly called the attacks "unprovoked" and moved swiftly to make political hay out of this episode. He ordered a "limited" retaliatory air raid against the North Vietnamese bases, proudly proclaiming that he sought "no wider war"—thus implying that the trigger-happy Goldwater did. Johnson also used the incident to spur congressional passage of the all-purpose Tonkin Gulf Resolution. With only two dissenting votes in both houses, the lawmakers virtually abdicated their war-declaring powers and handed the president a blank check to use further force in Southeast Asia.

The towering Texan rode to a spectacular victory in November 1964. The voters were herded into Johnson's column by fondness for the Kennedy legacy, faith in Great Society promises, and fear of Goldwater. A stampede of 43,129,566 Johnson votes trampled the Republican ticket, with its 27,178,188 supporters. The tally in the Electoral College was 486 to 52. Goldwater carried only his native Arizona and five other states—all of them, significantly, in the racially restless South. Johnson's record-breaking 61 percent of the popular vote swept lopsided Democratic majorities into both houses of Congress.

The Great Society Congress

Johnson's victory temporarily smashed the conservative coalition of southern Democrats and northern Republicans. A wide-open legislative road stretched before the Great Society programs, as the president skillfully ringmastered his two-to-one Democratic majorities. Congress poured out a flood of legislation, comparable only to the output of the New Dealers in the Hundred Days Congress of 1933, as Johnson at last delivered on long-delayed Democratic promises of social reform. The Office of Economic Opportunity, the front line of the Great Society's War on Poverty, had its appropriation doubled to nearly $2 billion. Congress granted more than $1 billion to redevelop the gutted hills of Appalachia and voted a slightly greater amount for aid to elementary and secondary schools.

Other landmark laws flowed from Johnson's "hip-pocket Congress." Medicare for the elderly became a reality in 1965. Although it was a bitter pill for the American Medical Association to swallow, the system was welcomed by millions of older Americans who were being pushed into poverty by skyrocketing medical costs.

A tireless Johnson also prodded the Congress into creating two new cabinet offices: the Department of Transportation and the Department of Housing and Urban Development (HUD). He named the first black cabinet member in the nation's history, noted economist Robert C. Weaver, to be secretary of HUD. Other noteworthy laws established a National Endowment for the Arts and Humanities, designed to lift the level of American cultural life, and still others sweepingly reformed the long-criticized quota system for immigrants.

Great Society programs came in for harsh political attack in later years. Conservatives charged that poverty could not be papered over with greenbacks; yet the poverty rate did decline measurably in the ensuing decade. Medicare dramatically reduced poverty among America's elderly, and Project Head Start notably improved the educational performance of underprivileged youth. Lyndon Johnson was not fully victorious in the war against poverty, but he did win several noteworthy battles.

The Black Revolution Explodes

In Johnson's native South, the walls of segregation were crumbling, but not fast enough for long-suffering blacks. The Civil Rights Act of 1964 gave the federal government more muscle to enforce school desegregation orders and to prohibit racial discrimination in all kinds of public accommodations and employment. But the problem of voting rights remained. In Mississippi, which had the largest black minority of any state, only about 5 percent of eligible blacks were registered to vote. The lopsided pattern was similar throughout the South. Ballot-denying devices like the poll tax, literacy tests, and bare-faced intimidation still barred black people from the political process.

Beginning in 1964, opening up the polling booths became the chief goal of the black movement in the South. The Twenty-fourth Amendment, ratified in January 1964, abolished the poll tax in federal elections (see the Appendix). Blacks joined hands with white civil rights workers—many of them student volunteers from the North—in a massive voter-registration drive in Mississippi during the "Freedom Summer" of 1964. Singing "We Shall Overcome," they zealously set out to soothe generations of white anxieties and black fears.

But events soon blighted bright hopes. In late June 1964, one black and two white civil rights workers disappeared in Mississippi. Their badly beaten bodies were later found buried beneath an earthen dam. In August an integrated "Mississippi Freedom Democratic Party" delegation was denied its seat at the national Democratic convention.

Early in 1965 Martin Luther King, Jr., resumed the voter-registration campaign in Selma, Alabama. State troopers with tear gas and whips assaulted King's peaceful demonstrators. A Boston Unitarian minister was killed, and a few days later a white Detroit woman was shotgunned to death by Klansmen on the highway near Selma.

As the nation recoiled in horror before these violent scenes, President Johnson, speaking in soft southern accents, delivered a memorable address on television. What happened in Selma, he insisted, concerned all Americans, "who must overcome the crippling legacy of bigotry and injustice." Then, in a stirring adaptation of the anthem of the civil rights movement, the president concluded: "And we shall overcome." Following words with deeds, Johnson speedily shepherded through Congress the landmark

Voting Rights Act of 1965, signed into law on August 6. It outlawed literacy tests and sent federal voter registrars into several southern states.

The passage of the Voting Rights Act, exactly 100 years after the conclusion of the Civil War, climaxed a century of awful abuse and robust resurgence for African-Americans in the South. The act did not end discrimination and oppression overnight, but it placed an awesome lever for change in blacks' hands. Black southerners now had power and began to wield it without fear of reprisals. In the following decade, for the first time since emancipation, African-Americans began to migrate *into* the South.

Black Rage

The Voting Rights Act of 1965 marked the end of an era in the troubled history of the black movement—the era of civil rights campaigns, focused on the South and led by peaceable moderates such as Martin Luther King, Jr. Just five days after President Johnson signed the new voting law, a bloody riot exploded in Watts, a black ghetto in Los Angeles. The week-long violence left 31 blacks and 3 whites dead, more than 1,000 people injured, and hundreds of buildings charred and gutted.

Increasingly, violent voices began to be heard in the black movement. Rising bitterness was highlighted by the career of Malcolm X, a brilliant Black Muslim preacher who favored black separatism and condemned the "blue-eyed white devils." In early 1965, he was cut down by black gunmen while speaking to a large crowd in New York City.

The moderation of Martin Luther King, Jr., came under heavy fire from younger black radicals, such as Trinidad-born Stokely Carmichael of the Student Non-Violent Coordinating Committee (SNCC). Carmichael urged giving up peaceful demonstrations and pursuing "Black Power."

The phrase "Black Power" frightened many whites. Levelheaded advocates of Black Power intended the slogan to describe a broad-front effort to *exercise* the political rights gained by the civil rights movement. But for a time, Black Power seemed to be simply a justification for pillage and

arson. City-shaking riots erupted in Newark, New Jersey, in the summer of 1967, taking twenty-five lives, and in Detroit, Michigan, where federal troops restored order after forty-three people had died in the streets. Black rioters burned down their own neighborhoods, attacking not so much white people as the symbols of white domination. These included the landlord's property, police officers, and even fire fighters, who had to battle blacks chanting, "Burn, baby, burn."

Riotous tactics angered white Americans, who now threatened to retaliate with their own "backlash" against ghetto arsonists and killers. Inner-city anarchy baffled many northerners, who had considered racial problems a purely "southern" question. But black concerns had moved north—as had nearly half the nation's black people. In the North the Black Power movement now focused less on civil rights and more on economic demands. Black unemployment, for example, was nearly double that for whites. These problems seemed even less likely to be solved peaceably than the struggle for voting rights in the South.

Despair deepened when the magnetic and moderate voice of Martin Luther King, Jr., was forever silenced by a sniper's bullet in Memphis, Tennessee, on April 4, 1968. A martyr for justice, he had bled and died against the peculiarly American thorn of race. The killing of King cruelly robbed the American people of one of the most inspirational leaders in their history at a time when they could least afford to lose him. This outrage triggered a nationwide orgy of ghetto-gutting and violence that cost over forty lives.

Rioters noisily made news, but thousands of other blacks quietly made history. Their voter registration had shot upward, and by the late 1960s there were several hundred black elected officials in the Old South. Cleveland, Ohio, and Gary, Indiana, had elected black mayors. By 1972 nearly half of southern black children sat in integrated classrooms. Actually, more schools in the South were integrated than in the North. About a third of black families had risen economically into the ranks of the middle class—though an equal proportion remained below the "poverty line." King left a shining legacy of racial progress, but he was cut down when the job was far from completed.

Combating Communism in Two Hemispheres

Violence at home eclipsed Johnson's legislative triumphs, whereas foreign flare-ups threatened his political life. Discontented Dominicans rose in revolt against their military government in April 1965. Johnson speedily announced that the Dominican Republic was the target of a Castrolike coup by "Communist conspirators," and he dispatched some 25,000 American troops to restore order. But the evidence of a communist takeover was fragmentary at best. Johnson was widely condemned, at home and in Latin America, for his temporary reversion to the officially abandoned "gunboat diplomacy." Critics charged that the two-fisted Texan was far too eager to back right-wing regimes with bayonets.

About the same time, Johnson was floundering deeper into the monsoon mud of Vietnam. Viet Cong guerrillas attacked an American air base at Pleiku, South Vietnam, in February 1965. The president immediately ordered retaliatory bombing raids against military installations in North Vietnam and for the first time ordered attacking U.S. troops to land. By the middle of March 1965, the Americans had "Operation Rolling Thunder" in full swing— regular full-scale bombing attacks against North Vietnam. Before 1965 ended, some 184,000 American troops were slogging through the jungles and rice paddies of South Vietnam searching for black-clad guerrillas.

Johnson had now taken the first fateful steps down a slippery path. He and his advisers believed that a fine-tuned, step-by-step escalation in American force would drive the enemy to defeat with a minimum loss of life. But the enemy matched every increase in American firepower with more men and more wiliness in the art of guerrilla warfare.

The South Vietnamese themselves were meanwhile becoming spectators in their own war, as the fighting became increasingly Americanized. Corrupt and collapsible governments succeeded each other in Saigon with bewildering rapidity. Yet American officials continued to talk of defending a faithful demo-

The Agony of War, 1965 *A U.S. marine carries a South Vietnamese baby to safety. The child was wounded by American jets during the opening stages of a military operation at Cape Batangan, Vietnam.*

cratic ally. Washington spokespeople also defended the action as a test of Uncle Sam's "commitment" and of the reliability of his numerous treaty pledges to resist communist encroachment. Persuaded by such thinking, Johnson steadily raised the military stakes in Vietnam. By 1968 he had poured more than half a million troops into Southeast Asia, and the annual bill for the war was exceeding $30 billion. Yet the end was nowhere in sight.

Vietnam Vexations

America could not defeat the enemy in Vietnam, but it seemed to be defeating itself. World opinion grew increasingly hostile; the blasting of an underdeveloped country by a mighty superpower struck many critics as obscene. Several nations expelled American Peace Corps volunteers. Disgusted European allies complained that they were being neglected militarily and punished economically, as America exported war-bred inflation to its European trading partners. Haughty Charles de Gaulle, ever suspicious of American reliability, ordered NATO off French soil in 1966.

Overcommitment in Southeast Asia also tied America's hands elsewhere. Capitalizing on American distraction in Vietnam, the Soviet Union expanded its influence in the Mediterranean area, especially in Egypt. Tiny Israel humiliated the Soviet-backed Egyptians in a devastating Six-Day War in June 1967. The Middle East was becoming an ever more dangerously packed powder keg that the war-plagued United States was powerless to defuse.

Domestic discontent also festered as the Vietnamese entanglement dragged on. Antiwar demonstrations had begun on a small scale with campus "teach-ins" in 1965, and gradually these protests mounted to tidal-wave proportions. As the long arm of the military draft dragged more and more young men off to the Asian slaughter pen, resistance stiffened. Thousands of draft registrants fled to Canada; others publicly burned their draft cards. Hundreds of thousands of chanting marchers filled the streets of New York, San Francisco, and other cities. Many Americans felt pangs of conscience at the ghastly spectacle of their countrymen burning peasant huts and blistering civilians with napalm.

Opposition in Congress to the Vietnam involvement centered in the influential Senate Committee on Foreign Relations, headed by Senator J. William Fulbright of Arkansas. A constant thorn in the side of the president, he staged a series of widely viewed televised hearings in 1966 and 1967, during which prominent personages aired their views, mostly antiwar. Gradually the public came to feel that it had been lied to about both the causes and the "winnability" of the war. A yawning "credibility gap" opened between the government and the people. New flocks of antiwar "doves" were hatching daily.

By early 1968 the brutal and futile struggle had become the longest and most unpopular foreign war in the nation's history. Casualties, including both killed and wounded, already exceeded 100,000. More bombs had been dropped on Vietnam than on all enemy territory in World War II. Evidence mounted that America had been entrapped in an Asian civil war, fighting against highly motivated rebels who were striving to overthrow an oppressive regime. Yet Johnson clung to his basic strategy of stepping up the pressure bit by bit. He stubbornly assured doubting Americans that he could see "the light at the end of the tunnel." But to growing numbers of Americans, it seemed that Johnson was bent on "saving" Vietnam by destroying it.

Vietnam Topples Johnson

Hawkish illusions that the struggle was about to be won were shattered by a blistering communist offensive launched in late January 1968, during Tet, the Vietnamese New Year. At a time when the Viet Cong were supposedly licking their wounds, they suddenly and simultaneously mounted savage attacks on twenty-seven key South Vietnamese cities, including the capital, Saigon. Although eventually beaten off with heavy losses, they demonstrated anew that victory could not be gained by Johnson's strategy of gradual escalation. With an increasingly insistent voice, American public opinion demanded a speedy end to the war. Opposition grew so vehement that President Johnson could feel the very foundations of government shaking under his feet.

American military leaders responded to the Tet attacks with a request for 200,000 more troops. The size of the request staggered many policy makers. Johnson himself now began to doubt the wisdom of continuing on his raise-the-stakes course.

Meanwhile, Senator Eugene J. McCarthy of Minnesota was sharply challenging the president from within his own party for the 1968 Democrat presidential nomination. McCarthy, a sometime poet and devout Catholic, gathered a small army of antiwar college students who helped him gain 42 percent of the Democratic vote in the New Hampshire presidential primary on March 12. Four days later, Senator Robert F. Kennedy of New York, the murdered president's younger brother and by now himself a "dove" on Vietnam, threw his hat into the ring. The charismatic Kennedy, heir to his fallen brother's mantle of leadership, stirred a passionate response among workers, African-Americans, Hispanics, and young people.

These startling events abroad and at home were not lost on LBJ. In a bombshell television address on March 31, 1968, he announced that he would freeze American troop levels and scale down the bombing. He also startled his vast audience by firmly declaring that he would not be a candidate for the presidency in 1968.

Johnson's "abdication" had the effect of preserving the military status quo. The United States could maintain the maximum *acceptable* level of military activity in Vietnam with one hand, while trying to negotiate a settlement with the other. North Vietnam shortly agreed to negotiations in Paris, but progress was glacially slow, as prolonged bickering developed over the very shape of the conference table.

The Presidential Sweepstakes of 1968

Summer in 1968 was one of the hottest political seasons in the nation's history. Johnson's heir apparent for the Democratic nomination was Vice President Hubert Humphrey, who loyally supported LBJ's Vietnam policies through thick and thin, and therefore received support from the White House–dominated party apparatus. Senators McCarthy and Kennedy meanwhile dueled through several state primaries, with Kennedy's bandwagon gathering ever-increasing speed. But on June 5, 1968, on the night of an exciting victory in the California primary, Kennedy was shot to death by a young Arab immigrant.

Antiwar forces, deprived by an assassin of their leading candidate, streamed into Chicago for the Democratic convention in August 1968. Mayor Richard Daley responded by arranging for barbed-wire barricades around the convention hall, as well as calling in thousands of police and National Guard troops. Some militant demonstrators baited the officers in blue as "pigs" and hurled bags of filth at police lines. As people the world over watched on television, the exasperated "peace officers" broke into a "police riot," clubbing and manhandling innocent and guilty alike. Acrid tear gas fumes hung over

the city even as Humphrey steamrollered to a first-ballot nomination. The Humphrey forces blocked the dovish McCarthyites' attempt to secure an antiwar platform plank and rammed through their own declaration that armed force would be relentlessly applied until the enemy showed more willingness to negotiate.

Scenting victory over the divided Democrats, the Republicans convened in plush Miami Beach and nominated former vice president Richard Nixon, who arose from his political grave to win the nomination. As a "hawk" on Vietnam and a right-leaning middle-of-the-roader on domestic policy, Nixon could please Goldwater conservatives and was acceptable to party moderates. He appealed to southern whites and the "law and order" element when he tapped as his running mate Maryland Governor Spiro T. Agnew, noted for his tough stands against dissidents and black militants. The Republican platform called for victory in Vietnam and a strong anticrime policy.

Adding color and confusion to the campaign was the third-party candidacy of former Alabama Governor George C. Wallace. Wallace attacked the "pointy-headed bureaucrats," and taunted hecklers as "bums" who needed a bath. He called for prodding blacks back into their place. He and his running mate, former air force general Curtis LeMay, also proposed smashing the North Vietnamese to smithereens by "bombing them back to the Stone Age."

There was little to choose between Humphrey and Nixon on Vietnam. Both candidates were committed to keeping on with the war until the enemy would settle for an "honorable peace," which seemed to mean an American victory. The millions of doves had no place to roost, and many refused to vote at all. Humphrey, scorched by the LBJ brand, went down to defeat as a prisoner of his chief's policies.

Nixon, who had lost a cliff-hanger to Kennedy in 1960, won one in 1968. He garnered 301 electoral votes with 43.4 percent of the popular tally (31,785,480), as compared with 191 electoral votes and 42.7 percent of the popular votes (31,275,166) for Humphrey. Wallace won an impressive 9,906,473 popular votes and 46 electoral votes, all from five

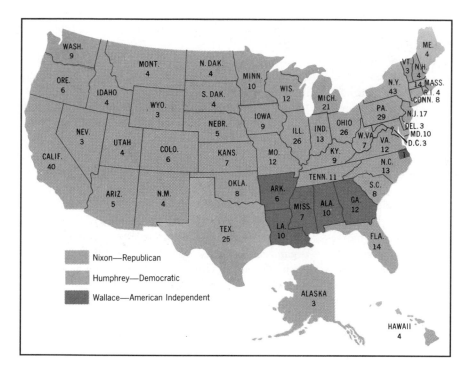

states of the Deep South, four of which the Republican Goldwater had carried in 1964.

The Obituary of Lyndon Johnson

Talented but tragedy-struck Lyndon Johnson returned to his Texas ranch in January 1969, and died there four years later. His party was defeated and his "me-too" Hubert Humphrey was repudiated.

Yet Johnson's legislative leadership for a time had been remarkable. No president since Lincoln had worked harder or done more for civil rights. None had shown more compassion for the poor, blacks, and the ill-educated. But by 1966 Johnson was already sinking into the Vietnam quicksands. Great Society programs began to wither on the vine, as soaring war costs sucked tax dollars into the military machine. Johnson had promised both guns and butter but could not keep that promise. Ever-creeping inflation blighted the prospects of prosperity, and the War on Poverty met resistance as stubborn as the Viet Cong and eventually went down to defeat. Great want persisted alongside great wealth.

The Southeast Asian quagmire engulfed Johnson's noblest intentions. Committed to some degree by his two predecessors, he had chosen to defend the American foothold and enlarge the conflict rather than be run out. He was evidently persuaded by his brightest advisers, both civilian and military, that a "cheap" victory was possible. It would be achieved by massive aerial bombing and large, though limited, troop commitments. His decision not to escalate the fighting still more offended the hawks, and his refusal to back off altogether antagonized the doves. Like the Calvinists of colonial days, luckless Lyndon Johnson was damned if he did and damned if he did not.

The Cultural Upheaval of the 1960s

The struggles of the 1960s against racism, poverty, and the war in Vietnam had momentous cultural consequences. The decade came to be seen as a watershed dividing two distinct eras in terms of values, morals, and behavior. Launched in youthful idealism, many of the decade's reform movements sputtered out in violence and cynicism. Students for a

Democratic Society (SDS), once at the forefront of the antipoverty and antiwar campaigns, had by decade's end spawned an underground terrorist group called the Weathermen. Peaceful civil rights demonstrations had given way to blockbusting urban riots. What started as apparently innocent experiments with drugs such as marijuana and LSD had fried many youthful brains and spawned a loathsome underworld of drug lords and addicts.

Everywhere in 1960s America a negative attitude toward all kinds of authority began to take hold. Disillusioned by the discovery that their society was not free of racism, sexism, imperialism, and oppression, many young people lost their traditional moral rudders. Neither families nor churches nor schools seemed to be able to define values and shape behavior with the certainty of shared purpose that many people believed had once existed. This upheaval even churned the tradition-bound Roman Catholic church, among the world's oldest and most conservative institutions. Clerics abandoned their Roman collars and the Latin Mass, folk songs replaced Gregorian chants, and meatless Fridays became ancient history. No matter what the topic, conventional wisdom and inherited ideas came under fire. "Trust no

one over thirty" was a popular sneer of rebellious youth.

Skepticism about authority had deep historical roots in American culture, and it had even bloomed in the supposedly complacent and conformist 1950s. "Beat" poets such as Allen Ginsberg and iconoclastic novelists like Jack Kerouac had voiced dark disillusion with the materialistic beliefs of "establishment" culture in the Eisenhower era. In the movie *Rebel Without a Cause* (1955), the attractive young actor James Dean seemed to personify the restless frustration of many young people.

The disaffection of the young reached crisis proportions in the tumultuous 1960s. One of the first organized protests against established authority broke out at the University of California at Berkeley in 1964, in the so-called Free Speech Movement. Prompted by seething resentment against the war in Vietnam, many sons and daughters of the middle class turned to mind-bending drugs, tuned in to "acid rock," and dropped out of "straight" society. Others "did their own thing" in communes or "alternative" institutions. *Patriotism* became a dirty word. Beflowered women in trousers and long-haired men with earrings heralded the rise of a self-conscious

Los Angeles "Love-In," 1967
One feature of the late 1960s was the "love-in," a large gathering of young people to express their desire for "love, not hate" in the world. At this "love-in" in a Los Angeles park in March, 1967, several thousand young people sang, danced, read poetry, and made speeches. Police reported that the youthful throng was "peaceful but noisy."

counterculture vehemently opposed to traditional American ways.

Sexual attitudes also seemed drastically altered as women's roles rapidly changed and as increasing numbers of women and men engaged in premarital intimacies. The introduction of the birth control pill in 1960 made unwanted pregnancies much easier to avoid and further fed the "sexual revolution." Legal sanctions against obscenity and pornography withered away, and profanity and nudity became almost obligatory on stage and screen. Old taboos against homosexuality crumbled as gay people proudly demanded sexual tolerance. Only widening worries in the 1980s about sexually communicated diseases such as genital herpes and AIDS (acquired immunodeficiency syndrome) would slow the sexual revolution.

Straitlaced guardians of respectability denounced the self-indulgent romanticism of the "flower children" as the beginning of the end of modern civilization. Sympathetic observers hailed the "greening" of America—the replacement of materialism and imperialism by a new consciousness of human values. But the upheavals of the 1960s could be largely attributed to three Ps: the youthful population bulge, protest against racism and the Vietnam War, and the apparent permanence of prosperity. As the decade flowed into the 1970s, the flower children grew older and had children of their own, the civil rights movement fell silent, the war ended, and economic stagnation blighted the bloom of prosperity. Young people in the 1970s seemed more concerned with finding jobs in the system than with tearing the system down. The counterculture appeared in retrospect to be not the road to the future but a historical blind alley. But if it had not managed fully to replace older values, it had weakened their grip, perhaps permanently.

CHRONOLOGY

1961	Berlin crisis and construction of the Berlin Wall.
	Bay of Pigs.
	Alliance for Progress.
	Kennedy sends "military advisers" to South Vietnam.
1962	Pressure from Kennedy results in a rollback of steel prices.
	Laos neutralized.
	Cuban missile crisis.
1963	Anti-Diem coup in South Vietnam.
	Civil rights march in Washington, D.C.
	Kennedy assassinated; Johnson assumes presidency.
1964	Johnson defeats Goldwater for presidency.
	War on Poverty begins.
	Twenty-fourth Amendment (abolishing poll tax in federal elections) ratified.
	Civil Rights Act.
	Tonkin Gulf Resolution.
1965	Great Society legislation.
	Voting Rights Act.
	U.S. troops occupy Dominican Republic.
1965–1968	Race riots in U.S. cities.
	Escalation of the Vietnam War.
1967	Six-Day War between Israel and Egypt.
1968	Tet offensive in Vietnam.
	Martin Luther King, Jr., and Robert Kennedy assassinated.
	Nixon defeats Humphrey and Wallace for presidency.
1969	Astronauts land on moon.

Varying Viewpoints

Why did the United States become so deeply immersed in the Vietnam quagmire? Three different explanations have been proposed. The first, appraising Vietnam in the context of the Cold War "containment" policy, portrays the Southeast Asian war as simply another instance of American response to the menace of the communist "monolith." Had the United States refused to resist the enemy in Vietnam, other nations of the free world would have lost faith in America's will and would eventually have tumbled like "dominoes" into the Soviet bloc. The official defense of American policy at the time essentially rested on this explanation.

The second explanation does not question the anticommunist thrust of U.S. foreign policy but holds that Vietnam was a mistaken application of that policy. We should have known better, this argument goes, than to have taken over from the French their unwinnable war against a colonial people seeking to overthrow Western control.

Underrating of enemy strength, misguided military strategy, and the fear of appearing "soft on communism" have all been advanced as reasons why American policy makers pursued such an ill-advised course of action. This view can be found in the work of George Herring and John Lewis Gaddis.

The third interpretation is the New Left revisionist perspective, best represented by Gabriel Kolko. It maintains that the Vietnam War was but the logical (and near-fatal) consequence of U.S. "imperialism." In this view, America feels that it must resist all left-leaning challenges to the existing world order so as to protect its access to overseas markets and raw materials. Significantly, this explanation bears some resemblance to the official defense of U.S. policy. But New Left proponents reverse the official value judgment by holding that American economic domination, and even capitalism itself, is not worth preserving.

SELECT READINGS

Primary Source Documents

Norman Mailer paints vivid portraits of the 1968 conventions in *Miami and the Siege of Chicago* (1968) and of the March on Washington in his *Armies of the Night* (1968). Martin Luther King, Jr.'s *Letter from Birmingham Jail* (1963)* eloquently defends the civil rights movement. The progress of the war in Vietnam is chronicled in *The Pentagon Papers* (1971).*

Secondary Sources

The tumultuous decade of the sixties is treated in William L. O'Neill, *Coming Apart: An Informal History of America in the 1960s* (1971), and in Allen Matusow, *The Unraveling of America* (1984), as well as in the surveys cited in Chapter 39. On Kennedy, see Theodore C. Sorenson, *Kennedy* (1965), and Arthur M. Schlesinger, Jr., *A Thousand Days* (1965), both appreciative accounts by insiders. More criti-

cal is Henry Fairlie, *The Kennedy Promise* (1973). A two-volume biography by Herbert Parmet is *Jack: The Struggles of John F. Kennedy* (1980) and *JFK: The Presidency of John F. Kennedy* (1983). See also James N. Giglio, *The Presidency of John F. Kennedy* (1990), and Michael Beschloss, *The Crisis Years: Kennedy and Khrushchev, 1960–1963* (1991). Eric Goldman, *The Tragedy of Lyndon Johnson* (1969), is a sympathetic yet critical account of the Johnson presidency. In the same vein, with a psychoanalytic touch, is Doris Kearns, *Lyndon B. Johnson and the American Dream* (1976). A concise study is Paul Conkin's *Big Daddy from the Pedernales* (1986). Robert Dallek's *Lone Star Rising* (1991) is masterful on LBJ's prepresidential career. The conditions that called forth the Great Society are movingly described in Michael Harrington, *The Other America: Poverty in the United States* (1962). James Patterson summarizes *America's Struggle Against Poverty* (1981). Two superb chronicles of the civil rights movement focusing on King are Taylor Branch, *Parting the Waters: America in the King Years, 1954–1963* (1988), and David J. Garrow, *Bearing the Cross: Martin Luther King, Jr., and the Southern Christian Leadership Conference* (1986). The racial upheavals of the decade are discussed in Harvard Sitkoff, *The Struggle for Black Equality, 1954–1980* (1981), and Clayborne Carson, *In Struggle: SNCC* [Student Non-Violent Coordinating Committee] *and the Black Awakening of the 1960s* (1981). On the New Left, consult two volumes by Todd Gitlin, *The Sixties: Years of Hope, Days of Rage* (1987) and *The Whole World Is Watching: Mass Media in the Making and Unmaking of the New Left* (1980), James Miller, *"Democracy Is in the Streets": From Port Huron to the Sea of Chicago* (1987), Sara Evans, *Personal Politics* (1979), David Harris, *Dreams Die Hard* (1982), and Tom Hayden, *Reunion* (1988). On Vietnam, consult Ronald Spector, *The United States Army in Vietnam* (1984), and Stanley Karnow's encyclopedic *Vietnam: A History* (1983).

Concise accounts are George Herring, *America's Longest War* (1986), and Marilyn B. Young, *The Vietnam Wars, 1945–1990* (1991). Neil Sheehan, *A Bright Shining Lie: John Paul Vann and America in Vietnam* (1988), is a gripping account of one unorthodox commander. The emergence of a youth culture in the 1960s is illuminated in three studies by Kenneth Keniston, *The Uncommitted* (1965), *Young Radicals* (1968), and *Youth and Dissent* (1971). Popular books indicating the mood of the 1960s include Theodore Roszak, *The Making of a Counter-Culture* (1969), and Charles Reich, *The Greening of America* (1970). Also intriguing on the 1960s is Morris Dickstein, *The Gates of Eden: American Culture in the Sixties* (1977). A lucid survey of the intellectual history of the postwar era is Richard Pells, *The Liberal Mind in a Conservative Age* (1984). Sexual changes are scrutinized in Daniel Yankelovich, *The New Morality* (1974), Morton Hunt, *Sexual Behavior in the 1970s* (1974), and Paul Robinson, *The Modernization of Sex* (1976).

CHAPTER 41

The Stalemated Seventies, 1968–1980

*In all my years of public life, I have never obstructed justice. People have got to know
whether or not their president is a crook. Well, I'm not a crook; I earned everything I've got.*

Richard Nixon, 1973

The Economy Stagnates in the 1970s

As the 1960s lurched to a close, the fantastic quarter-century economic boom of the post–World War II era also showed signs of petering out. By increasing their productivity, American workers had doubled their average standard of living in the twenty-five years since the end of World War II. Now, fatefully, productivity gains slowed to the vanishing point. The entire decade of the 1970s did not see a productivity advance equivalent to even one year's progress in the preceding two decades. At the new rate, it would take 500 more years to bring about another doubling of the average worker's standard of living. The rising baby-boom generation faced the depressing prospect of a living standard that would be lower than that of their parents.

What caused the sudden slump in productivity? Some observers cited the increasing presence in the workforce of women and teenagers, who typically had fewer skills than male adult workers and were less likely to take the full-time, long-term jobs in which skills might be developed. Other commentators blamed declining investment in new machinery, the heavy costs of compliance with government-imposed safety and health regulations, and the general shift of the economy from manufacturing to services, in which productivity gains were allegedly more difficult to achieve.

The Vietnam War also precipitated painful economic distortions. The disastrous conflict in Southeast Asia drained tax dollars from needed improvements in education, deflected scientific skill and manufacturing capacity from the civilian sector, and touched off a sickening spiral of inflation. Sharply rising oil prices in the 1970s also fed inflation, but its deepest roots lay in government policies of the 1960s—especially Lyndon Johnson's insistence on simultaneously fighting the war in Vietnam and funding the Great Society programs at home, all without a tax increase to finance the added expenditures. The cost of living more than tripled in the dozen years following Richard Nixon's inauguration, in the longest and steepest inflationary cycle in American history.

Other weaknesses in the nation's economy were also laid bare by the abrupt reversal of America's financial fortunes in the 1970s. The competitive advantage of many American businesses had been so enormous after World War II that they had small incentive to modernize plants and seek more efficient methods of production. The defeated German and Japanese people had meanwhile scratched their way out of the ruins of war and built wholly new factories with the most up-to-date technology and management techniques. By the 1970s their efforts paid handsome rewards, as they came to dominate industries such as steel, automobile, and consumer electronics—fields in which the United States had once been unchallengeable.

For all these reasons, the postwar wave of robust economic growth had clearly crested by the early 1970s. At home and abroad, the "can do" American spirit gave way to a new sense of limits. The stifling realization hung over the country like a pall. It frustrated both policy makers and citizens who keenly remembered the growth and optimism of the quarter-century since World War II. But now a stalemated, unpopular war and a stagnant, unresponsive economy heralded the end of the self-confident postwar era. With it ended the liberal dream, vivid since New Deal days, that an affluent society could spend its way to social justice.

Nixon "Vietnamizes" the War

Inaugurated on January 20, 1969, Richard Nixon urged the American people, torn with dissension over Vietnam and race relations, to "stop shouting at one another." Yet the new president seemed an unlikely conciliator of the clashing forces that appeared to be ripping American society apart. Solitary and suspicious by nature, he could be brittle and testy in the face of opposition. He also harbored bitter resentments against the "liberal establishment" that had cast him into the political darkness for much of the preceding decade. Yet Nixon brought one hugely valuable asset with him to the White House—his broad knowledge and thoughtful expertise in foreign affairs.

The first burning need of American foreign policy was to quiet the public uproar over Vietnam. President Nixon's announced policy—called "Vietnamization"—was to withdraw the 540,000 U.S. troops in South Vietnam over an extended period.

THE NIXON WAVE

The Nixon Wave *During Richard Nixon's presidency, Americans experienced the first serious inflation since the immediate post–World War II years. The inflationary surge grew to tidal-wave proportions by the late 1970s, when the consumer price index rose at annual rates of more than 10 percent.*

The South Vietnamese—with American money, weapons, training, and advice—could then gradually take over the burden of fighting their own war.

The so-called Nixon Doctrine thus evolved. It proclaimed that in the future, Asians and others would have to fight their own wars without the support of large bodies of American ground troops.

Nixon sought not to end the war but to win it by other means, without the further spilling of American blood. But even this much involvement was distasteful to the American doves, many of whom demanded a withdrawal that was prompt, complete, unconditional, and irreversible. Antiwar protestors staged a massive national Vietnam moratorium in

October 1969, as nearly 100,000 people jammed the Boston Common and some 50,000 filed by the White House carrying lighted candles.

Undaunted, Nixon launched a counteroffensive by appealing to the "silent majority" who presumably supported the war. Though ostensibly conciliatory, Nixon's appeal was in fact deeply divisive. His intentions soon became clear when he unleashed tough-talking Vice President Agnew to attack the "nattering nabobs of negativism" who demanded quick withdrawal from Vietnam. Nixon himself in 1970 sneered at the antiwar demonstrators as "bums."

By January 1970 the Vietnam conflict had become the longest in American history and, with some 40,000 killed and over 250,000 wounded, the third most costly foreign war in the nation's experience. Black and white soldiers floundered through booby-trapped swamps and steaming jungles, often unable to distinguish friend from foe among the black-clad peasants. Drug abuse, mutiny, and sabotage reduced the army's fighting effectiveness. Domestic disgust with the war was further deepened in 1970 by revelations that in 1968 American troops had massacred innocent women and children in the village of My Lai. Even soldiers in the field shared the general disillusion. Increasingly desperate for a quick end to the demoralizing conflict, Nixon widened the war in 1970 by attacking Vietnam's neighbor, Cambodia.

"Cambodianizing" the Vietnam War

Without consulting Congress, Nixon suddenly ordered American forces on April 29, 1970, to invade Cambodia, which was officially neutral but had long been used as a staging area by the North Vietnamese and Viet Cong. Restless students nationwide responded to the Cambodian invasion with rock throwing, window smashing, and arson. At Kent State University in Ohio, National Guard troops killed four students; at Jackson State College in Mississippi, the highway patrol killed two students.

Nixon withdrew the American troops from Cambodia after two months. In America the invasion deepened the bitterness between hawks and doves,

as right-wing groups physically assaulted leftists. Disillusionment with "whitey's war" increased ominously among African-Americans in the armed forces. The Senate (though not the House) overwhelmingly repealed the Gulf of Tonkin blank check that Congress had given Johnson in 1964 and sought ways to restrain Nixon.

In the spring of 1971, mass rallies and marches once more erupted from coast to coast. New combustibles fueled the fires of antiwar discontent in June 1971, when the *New York Times* published a top-secret Pentagon study of America's involvement in the Vietnam War, "leaked" to the *Times* by former Pentagon official Daniel Ellsberg, that laid bare the blunders and deceptions of the Kennedy and Johnson administrations, especially the provoking of the 1964 North Vietnamese attack in the Gulf of Tonkin. As the antiwar firestorm flared ever higher, Nixon grew more daring in his search for an exit from Vietnam.

Nixon in Beijing (Peking) and Moscow

With bold insight, Nixon concluded that the road out of Vietnam ran through Beijing and Moscow. Nixon astutely perceived that tensions between the Chinese and the Soviets afforded the United States an opportunity to play off one antagonist against the other—and to enlist the aid of both in pressuring North Vietnam into peace. Nixon's thinking was reinforced by his national security adviser, Dr. Henry Kissinger, who negotiated secretly with North Vietnamese officials in Paris while preparing the president's path to Beijing and Moscow.

Nixon, heretofore an uncompromising anticommunist, startled the nation with his historic journey to China in February 1972, which paved the way for improved relations between Washington and Beijing. Nixon next traveled to Moscow in May 1972 to play his "China card" in a game of high-stakes diplomacy in the Kremlin. The Soviets, hungry for American foodstuffs and haunted by the fear of intensified rivalry with an American-backed China, were ready to deal.

Nixon's visits ushered in an era of détente, or relaxed tensions, and produced several significant agreements. First was the great grain deal of 1972, by

Balancing Act   *Nixon treads delicately between the two communist superpowers in 1973, holding some of the wheat with which he enticed both into détente.*

which the food-rich United States agreed to sell the Soviets at least $750 million worth of wheat, corn, and other cereals. In the far more important military sphere, the two superpowers agreed to an antiballistic missile (ABM) treaty, which limited each nation to two clusters of defensive missiles. Another significant pact was a SALT (for Strategic Arms Limitations Talks) agreement to freeze the numbers of long-range nuclear missiles for five years.

These accords, both ratified in 1972, constituted a long-overdue first step toward slowing the arms race. Yet even though the ABM treaty forbade elaborate defensive systems, the United States forged ahead with the development of "MIRVs" (Multiple Independently Targeted Reentry Vehicles), designed to overcome any defense by "saturating" it with large numbers of warheads, several to a rocket. Predictably, the Soviets proceeded to "MIRV" their own missiles, and the arms race ratcheted up to a still

more perilous plateau, with over 16,000 nuclear warheads deployed by both sides in the 1980s.

Nixon's détente diplomacy was, on the whole, successful. By checkmating and co-opting the two great communist powers, the president had cleverly set the stage for America's exit from Vietnam. But the concluding act in that wrenching tragedy still remained to be played.

Nixon on the Home Front

Nixon had lashed out during the campaign at the "permissiveness" and "judicial activism" of the Supreme Court presided over by Chief Justice Earl Warren. Following his appointment in 1953, the jovial Warren had led the Court into a series of decisions that drastically affected civil rights, criminal law, the practice of religion, and the structure of political representation. Among the most controversial decisions were the case of *Miranda* (1966), which gave accused criminals the right to remain silent, and a set of decisions in 1962 and 1963 prohibiting required prayers and Bible readings in public schools on the basis of the First Amendment separation of church and state. Because these divisive decisions affected stubborn social problems, the Court came under endless criticism, the bitterest since New Deal days.

Fulfilling campaign promises, President Nixon undertook to change the Court's philosophical complexion. Taking advantage of several vacancies, he sought appointees who would strictly interpret the Constitution, cease "meddling" in social and political questions, and not coddle radicals or criminals. The Senate in 1969 speedily confirmed his nomination of white-maned Warren E. Burger of Minnesota to succeed the retiring Earl Warren as chief justice. Before the end of 1971 the Court counted four conservative Nixon appointments out of nine members.

Yet Nixon was to learn the ironic lesson that many presidents have learned about their Supreme Court appointees: once seated on the high bench, the justices are fully free to think and decide according to their own beliefs, not the president's expectations. The Burger Court that Nixon shaped proved reluctant to dismantle the liberal rulings of the Warren

Court; it even produced the most controversial judicial opinion of modern times, the *Roe* v. *Wade* decision in 1973, which legalized abortion (see p. 639).

Veto hatchet in hand, Nixon was frequently at odds with the Democratic Congress. When the legislators passed what he regarded as "budget-busting" appropriations over his veto, he simply impounded (that is, refused to spend) the funds. Impoundment was but one glaring example of Nixon's presidential expansion of constitutional powers at the expense of the legislative branch.

With Congress often in a balky mood, Nixon enjoyed scant success in his efforts to reform the welfare system. He fared better in his campaign for a "revenue-sharing" bill that provided for a return of $30 billion in federal revenues to the states over a period of five years. Among the commendable legacies of the Nixon years was the creation of the Environmental Protection Agency (EPA) in 1970. Inspired in part by author Rachel Carson's enormously effective *Silent Spring* (1962), the environmental movement eventually pushed through the Clean Air Act of 1970, the Clean Water Act of 1972, and Superfund, a 1980 law aimed at cleaning toxic dumps.

Worried about creeping inflation (then running about 5 percent), Nixon overcame his distaste for economic controls and imposed a ninety-day wage and price freeze in 1971. Seeking to stimulate the nation's sagging exports, he stunned the world by taking the United States off the gold standard and devaluing the dollar. These moves effectively ended the "Bretton Woods" (see p. 570) system of international currency stabilization that had functioned since World War II.

Congress worried about inflation, too, and in a fateful decision voted in 1972 to raise Social Security benefits and provide for automatic increases when the cost of living rose more than 3 percent in any year. Designed to protect the elderly and disabled against the ravages of inflation, this legislation actually helped to fuel the inflationary fire that raged out of control later in the decade.

Elected as a minority president, with only 43 percent of the vote in 1968, Nixon devised a clever but cynical plan—called the "southern strategy"—to achieve a majority in 1972. His Supreme Court nominations constituted an important part of this plan. The southern strategy emphasized an appeal to white voters by soft-pedaling civil rights and openly opposing school busing to achieve racial balance. But as fate would have it, foreign policy dominated the presidential campaign of 1972.

The Nixon Landslide of 1972

Vietnam continued to be the burning issue. Nearly four years had passed since Nixon had promised, as a presidential candidate, to end the war and "win" the peace. Yet in the spring of 1972 the fighting escalated anew to alarming levels when the North Vietnamese, heavily equipped with foreign tanks, burst through the demilitarized zone separating the two Vietnams. Nixon reacted promptly by launching massive bombing attacks on strategic centers in North Vietnam, including Hanoi, the capital. Gambling heavily on Soviet and Chinese forbearance, he also ordered the dropping of contact mines to blockade the principal harbors of North Vietnam.

The continuing Vietnam conflict spurred the rise of South Dakota Senator George McGovern to the 1972 Democratic nomination. McGovern's promise to pull the remaining American troops out of Vietnam in ninety days earned him the backing of the large antiwar element in the party. But his appeal to racial minorities, feminists, leftists, and youth alienated the traditional working-class backbone of his party. Moreover, the discovery, shortly after the convention, that McGovern's running mate, Missouri Senator Thomas Eagleton, had undergone psychiatric care forced Eagleton's removal from the ticket and further doomed McGovern's candidacy.

Nixon's campaign emphasized that he had wound down the "Democratic war" in Vietnam from some 540,000 troops to about 30,000. His candidacy received an added boost just twelve days before the election when the high-flying Dr. Kissinger announced that "peace is at hand" in Vietnam and that an agreement would be settled in a few days.

Nixon won the election in a landslide. His lopsided victory encompassed every state except Massachusetts and the nonstate District of Columbia. He piled up 520 electoral votes to 17 and a popular majority of 47,169,911 votes to 29,170,383. Nixon's claim that the election gave him an unprecedented mandate for his policies was weakened by Republican election losses in both the House and Senate.

The dove of peace, "at hand" in Vietnam just before the balloting, took flight after the election, when Nixon refused to be stampeded into accepting terms that had obvious loopholes. After the fighting on both sides had again escalated, he launched a furious two-week bombing of North Vietnam. This merciless pounding resulted in substantial losses of America's big B-52 bombers, but it drove North Vietnamese negotiators to agree to cease-fire arrangements on January 23, 1973, nearly three months after peace was prematurely proclaimed.

Nixon hailed the face-saving agreement as "peace with honor," but the boast rang hollow. The United States was to withdraw its remaining 27,000 or so troops and could reclaim some 560 American prisoners of war. The North Vietnamese were allowed to keep some 145,000 troops in South Vietnam, where they still occupied about 30 percent of the country. To many observers, the shaky "peace" seemed little more than a thinly disguised American retreat.

Watergate Woes

Nixon's election triumph was soon sullied by the so-called Watergate scandals. On June 17, 1972, some two months before his renomination, a bungled burglary had occurred in the Democratic headquarters, located in the Watergate apartment-office complex in Washington. Five men were arrested inside the building with electronic "bugging" equipment in their possession. They were working for the Republican Committee for the Re-election of the President—popularly known as CREEP—which had managed to raise tens of millions of dollars, often by secretive, unethical, or unlawful means. CREEP had also engaged in a "dirty tricks" campaign of unethical espionage and sabotage, including faked documents, directed against Democratic candidates in the campaign of 1972.

The Watergate break-in was only the tip of an iceberg in a slimy sea of corruption that made the Grant and Harding scandals look almost respectable. The scandal in Washington also provoked the improper or illegal use of the Federal Bureau of Investigation and the Central Intelligence Agency. Even the Internal Revenue Service was called upon by Nixon's aides to audit or otherwise harass political opponents and others who had fallen into disfavor. A White House "enemies list" turned up that included innocent citizens who were to be hounded or prosecuted in various ways. In the name of national security, Nixon's aides had authorized a burglary of the files of Dr. Daniel Ellsberg's psychiatrist, so great was the determination to convict the man who had "leaked" the Pentagon Papers. This was the most notorious exploit of the White House "plumbers unit," created to plug up leaks of confidential information.

A select Senate committee, headed by the aging Senator Sam Ervin of North Carolina, conducted a prolonged and widely televised series of hearings in 1973–1974. John Dean III, a former White House lawyer with a remarkable memory, testified glibly and at great length as to the involvement of the top echelons in the White House, including the president, in the cover-up of the Watergate break-in. Dean in effect accused Nixon of the crime of obstructing justice. But the committee then had only the unsupported word of Dean against White House protestations of innocence.

The Great Tape Controversy

A bombshell exploded before Senator Ervin's committee in July 1973 when a former presidential aide reported the presence in the White House of bugging equipment, installed under the president's authority. President Nixon's conversations, in person or on the telephone, had been recorded on tape without notifying the other parties that electronic eavesdropping was taking place.

Nixon had emphatically denied prior knowledge of the Watergate burglary or involvement in the cover-up. Now Dean's sensational testimony could be checked against the White House tapes, and the Senate committee could better determine who was telling the truth. But for months Nixon flatly refused to produce the taped evidence. He took refuge behind various principles, including separation of powers and executive privilege.

The anxieties of the White House deepened when Vice President Spiro Agnew was forced to resign in October 1973, having been accused of taking bribes or "kickbacks" from Maryland contractors while governor and also as vice president. President Nixon himself was now in danger of being removed by the impeachment route, so Congress invoked the Twenty-fifth Amendment (see Appendix) to replace Agnew with a twelve-term congressman from Michigan, Gerald ("Jerry") Ford.

Ten days after Agnew's resignation came the famous "Saturday night massacre" (October 20, 1973). Archibald Cox, a Harvard law professor appointed as a special prosecutor by Nixon in May, issued a subpoena for relevant tapes and other documents from the White House. Nixon thereupon ordered the firing of Cox and then accepted the resignations of the attorney general and the deputy attorney general because they had refused to fire Cox.

The Secret Bombing of Cambodia and the War Powers Act

As if Watergate were not enough, the constitutionality of Nixon's continued aerial battering of Cambodia came under increasing fire. In July 1973 America was shocked to learn that the U.S. Air Force had already secretly conducted some 3,500 bombing raids against North Vietnamese positions in Cambodia. They had begun in March 1969 and had continued for some fourteen months prior to the open American incursion in May 1970. The most disturbing feature of these sky forays was that, while they were going on, American officials, including the president, were avowing that Cambodian neutrality was being respected. Countless Americans began to wonder what kind of representative government they had if they were fighting a war they knew nothing about.

Defiance followed secretiveness. After the Vietnam cease-fire in January 1973, Nixon openly carried on his large-scale bombing of communist forces in order to help the rightist Cambodian government. This stretching of presidential war-making powers met furious opposition from the public and from a clear majority of both houses of Congress, which repeatedly tried to stop the bombing by cutting off appropriations. But Nixon's vetoes of such legislation were always sustained by at least one-third plus one vote in the House. Finally, with appropriations running short, Nixon agreed to a compromise in June 1973 whereby he would end the Cambodian bombing six weeks later and seek congressional approval of any future action in that bomb-blasted country.

Congressional opposition to the expansion of presidential war-making powers by Johnson and Nixon led to the War Powers Act in November 1973. Passed over Nixon's veto, it required the president to report to Congress within forty-eight hours after committing troops to a foreign conflict or "substantially" enlarging American combat units in a foreign country. Such a limited authorization would have to end within sixty days unless Congress extended it for thirty more days.

Compelling Nixon to end the bombing of Cambodia in August 1973 was but one manifestation of what came to be called the "New Isolationism." The draft had ended in January 1973, although it was retained on a standby basis. Future members of the armed forces were to be well-paid volunteers—a change that greatly eased tensions among youth. Insistent demands arose in Congress for reducing American armed forces abroad, especially because some 300,000 troops remained in Europe more than a quarter of a century after Hitler's downfall. But President Nixon, fearful of a weakened hand in the high-stakes game of power politics, headed off all serious attempts at troop reduction.

The Arab Oil Embargo and the Energy Crisis

Adding to Nixon's problems, the long-rumbling Middle East erupted anew in October 1973, when the rearmed Syrians and Egyptians unleashed surprise attacks on Israel. Kissinger, who had become secretary of state in September, hastily flew to Moscow in an effort to restrain the Soviets, who were supplying the attackers. Believing that the Kremlin was poised to fly combat troops to the Suez area,

Nixon placed America's nuclear forces on alert and ordered a gigantic airlift of nearly $2 billion in war materials to the Israelis. This assistance helped save the day, as the Israelis brilliantly turned the tide and threatened Cairo until American diplomacy brought about an uneasy cease-fire.

America's policy of backing Israel against its oil-rich neighbors exacted a heavy penalty. Late in October 1973, the Arab nations suddenly clamped an embargo on oil for the United States and other countries supporting Israel. Americans had to suffer through a long winter of lowered thermostats and speedometers. Lines of automobiles at service stations lengthened as tempers shortened and a business recession deepened.

The "energy crisis" suddenly energized a number of long-deferred projects. Congress approved a costly Alaska oil pipeline and a fifty-five-miles-per-hour speed limit in order to save fuel. Agitation mounted for heavier use of coal and nuclear power, despite the environmental threat posed by these energy sources.

The five months of the Arab "blackmail" embargo in 1974 clearly signaled the end of an era—a period of cheap and abundant energy. American oil production peaked in 1970 and then began an irreversible decline. Blissfully unaware of their dependence on foreign suppliers, Americans, like revelers on a binge, had more than tripled their oil consumption since the end of World War II. The number of automobiles increased two and a half times between 1949 and 1972.

So by 1974 America was addicted to oil and extremely vulnerable to any interruption in supplies. That stark fact colored the diplomatic and economic history of the 1980s and 1990s. The Middle East loomed ever larger on the map of America's strategic interests, until the United States in 1990 at last found itself pulled into a shooting war with Iraq to protect its oil supplies.

The Middle Eastern sheiks had approximately quadrupled their price for crude oil after lifting the embargo in 1974. Huge new oil bills jeopardized the American balance of trade and payments. Various sectors of the economy, including Detroit's carmak-

ers, began their slow, grudging adjustment to the rudely dawning age of energy dependency. But full reconciliation to that uncomfortable reality was a long time coming.

The Unmaking of a President

Political tribulations added to the nation's cup of woe in 1974. The continuing impeachment inquiry cast damning doubts on Nixon's integrity. Responding at last to the House Judiciary Committee's demand for the Watergate tapes, Nixon agreed in the spring of 1974 to the publication of "relevant" portions of the tapes, declaring that these would vindicate him. But substantial sections of the wanted tapes were missing, while Nixon's frequent obscenities were excised with the phrase "expletive deleted."

Nixon, the Law-and-Order Man

Confronted with demands for the rest of the material, Nixon flatly refused. On July 24, 1974, the president suffered a disastrous setback when the Supreme Court unanimously ruled that "executive privilege" gave him no right to withhold from the special prosecutor portions of tapes relevant to criminal activity. Skating on thin ice over hot water, Nixon reluctantly complied.

The House Judiciary Committee pressed ahead with its articles of impeachment. The key vote came late in July 1974, when the committee adopted the first article, which charged obstruction of "the administration of justice," including Watergate-related crimes. Two other articles were later approved by the committee accusing Nixon of having abused the powers of his office and of having shown contempt of Congress by ignoring lawful subpoenas for relevant tapes and other evidence.

Seeking to soften the impact of inevitable disclosure, Nixon voluntarily took a step, on August 5, 1974, that had a devastating effect on what remained of his credibility. He now made public three subpoenaed tapes of conversations with his chief aide on June 23, 1972. One of them had him giving orders, six days after the Watergate break-in, to use the CIA to hold back an inquiry by the FBI. Now Nixon's own tape-recorded words convicted him of having been an active party to the attempted cover-up, in itself the crime of obstructing justice. More than that, he had solemnly told the American people on television that he had known nothing of the Watergate cover-up until about nine months later.

The public backlash proved to be overwhelming. Republican leaders in Congress concluded that the guilty and unpredictable Nixon was a loose cannon on the deck of the ship of state. They frankly informed the president that his impeachment by the full House and removal by the Senate were foregone conclusions, and that he would do best to resign.

Left with no better choice, Nixon choked back his tears and announced his resignation in a dramatic television appearance on August 8, 1974. In his Farewell Address, Nixon admitted having made some "judgments" that "were wrong" but insisted that he had always acted "in what I believed at the time to be the best interests of the nation." Unconvinced, Americans would change the song "Hail to the Chief" to "Jail to the Chief."

The nation had survived a wrenching constitutional crisis, which proved that the impeachment machinery forged by the founding fathers could work when public opinion overwhelmingly demanded that it be made to work. The principles that no person is above the law and that presidents must be held to strict accountability for their acts were strengthened. The United States of America, on the eve of its two-hundredth birthday as a republic, had given an impressive demonstration of self-discipline and self-government to the rest of the world.

The First Unelected President

Gerald Rudolph Ford, the first man to be made president solely by a vote of Congress, entered the blackened White House, in August 1974, with serious handicaps. He was widely—and unfairly—suspected of being little more than a dim-witted former college football player. President Johnson had sneered that "Jerry" was so lacking in brainpower that he "could not walk and chew gum at the same time." Worse, Ford had been selected, not elected, vice president, following Spiro Agnew's resignation in disgrace. The sour odor of illegitimacy hung about this president without precedent.

Then, out of a clear sky, Ford granted a complete pardon to Nixon for any crimes he may have committed as president, discovered or undiscovered. Democrats were outraged, and lingering suspicions about the pardon cast a dark shadow over Ford's prospects of being elected president in his own right in 1976.

Ford at first sought to deepen the so-called détente with the Soviet Union that Nixon had crafted. In July 1975 President Ford joined leaders from thirty-four other nations in Helsinki, Finland, to sign several sets of historic accords. One group of agreements officially wrote an end to World War II by finally legitimizing the Soviet-dictated boundaries of Poland and other East European countries. In return, the Soviets signed a "third basket" of agree-

The Vietnamese

At first glance, the towns of Westminster and Fountain Valley, California, seem to resemble other California communities nearby. Tract homes line residential streets; shopping centers flank the busy thoroughfares. But these are no ordinary American suburbs. Instead, they make up "Little Saigons," vibrant outposts of Vietnamese culture in the contemporary United States.

Before South Vietnam fell in 1975, few Vietnamese ventured across the Pacific. Only in 1966 did United States immigration authorities even designate "Vietnamese" as a separate category of newcomers, and most early immigrants were the wives and children of U.S. servicemen. But as the communists closed in on Saigon, many Vietnamese, particularly those who had worked closely with American or South Vietnamese authorities, feared for their future. Gathering together as many of their extended-family members as they could assemble, thousands of Vietnamese fled for their lives. In a few hectic days in 1975, some 140,000 escaped before the approaching gunfire, a few dramatically clinging to the bottoms of departing helicopters. Another 60,000 less fortunate escaped at the same time over land and sea to Hong Kong and Thailand, where they waited nervously for permission to move on.

To accommodate the refugees, the U.S. government set up camps across the nation. Arrivals were crowded into army barracks affording little room and less privacy. These were boot camps not for military service but for assimilation into American society. A rigorous program trained the Vietnamese in English, forbade children from speaking their native language in the classroom, and even immersed them

From Vietnam to California *Vietnamese immigrants sometimes had a difficult time adjusting to American life. But like immigrants before them, many Vietnamese achieved success in small businesses and shops serving their own ethnic community.*

in American slang. Many resented this attempt to mold them and strip them of their culture.

Their discontent boiled over when authorities prepared to release the refugees from camps and board them with families around the nation. The resettlement officials had decided to find a sponsor for each Vietnamese family—an American family that would provide food, shelter, and assistance for the refugees until they could fend for themselves. But the Vietnamese people cherish their traditional extended families—grandparents, uncles, aunts, and cousins living communally with parents and children. The refugees were dispersed to Iowa, Illinois, Pennsylvania, New York, Washington, and California. As soon as they could, they relocated, hastening to established Vietnamese enclaves around San Francisco, Los Angeles, and Dallas.

Soon a second throng of Vietnamese immigrants pushed into these Little Saigons. Fleeing from the ravages of poverty and from the oppressive communist government, these stragglers had poured themselves and their few possessions into little boats, hoping to reach Hong Kong or get picked up by ships. Eventually, many of these "boat people" reached the United States. Usually less educated than the first arrivals and receiving far less resettlement aid from the U.S. government, they were, however, more willing to start at the bottom. Today these two groups total more than half a million people. Differing in experience and expectations, the Vietnamese share a new home in a strange land. Their uprooting is an immense, unreckoned consequence of America's longest war.

ments, guaranteeing more liberal exchanges of people and information between East and West and protecting certain basic "human rights." The Helsinki accords kindled small dissident movements in Eastern Europe and even in the USSR itself, but the Soviets soon poured ice water on these sputtering flames of freedom. Moscow's restrictions on Jewish emigration had already, in December 1974, prompted Congress to add punitive restrictions to a U.S.–Soviet trade bill.

West Europeans, especially the West Germans, cheered the Helsinki conference as a milestone of détente. But in the United States critics increasingly charged that détente was proving to be a one-way street, with American grain and technology flowing across the Atlantic to the USSR and little of comparable importance flowing back.

Despite these difficulties, Ford at first clung stubbornly to détente. But the American public's fury over Moscow's double-dealing so steadily mounted that by the end of his term the president was refusing even to pronounce the word *détente* in public. The thaw in the Cold War was threatening to prove chillingly brief.

Victory for North Vietnam

Early in 1975 the North Vietnamese gave full throttle to their long-expected drive southward. President Ford urged Congress to vote still more weapons for Vietnam, but his plea was in vain, and without the crutch of massive American aid, the South Vietnamese quickly and ingloriously collapsed.

The dam burst so rapidly that the remaining Americans had to be frantically evacuated by helicopter, the last of them on April 29, 1975. Also rescued were about 140,000 South Vietnamese, most of them so dangerously identified with the Americans that they feared a bloodbath by the victorious communists. Ford compassionately admitted these people to the United States, adding further seasoning to the melting pot. Eventually some 500,000 arrived (see "Makers of America: The Vietnamese," pp. 624–625).

Passing the Buck *A cruel, satirical view of where responsibility for the Vietnam debacle should be laid.*

America's longest, most frustrating war thus ended, not with a bang, but with a whimper. In a technical sense the Americans had not lost the war; their client nation had. The United States had fought the North Vietnamese to a standstill and had then withdrawn its troops in 1973, leaving the Vietnamese to fight their own war, with generous shipments of costly American aircraft, tanks, and other munitions. The estimated cost to America was $118 billion in current outlays, along with some 56,000 dead and 300,000 wounded. The people of the United States had in fact provided just about everything, except the will to win—and that could not be injected by outsiders.

Technicalities aside, the United States had lost more than a war. It had lost face in the eyes of foreigners, lost its own self-esteem, lost confidence in its military prowess—and lost much of the economic muscle that had made possible its global leadership since World War II. Americans reluctantly came to realize that their power, as well as their pride, had been deeply wounded in Vietnam and that recovery would be slow and painful.

The Bicentennial Campaign and the Carter Victory

America's two-hundredth birthday, in 1976, fell during a presidential election year—a fitting coincidence for a proud democracy. Gerald Ford energetically sought nomination for the presidency in his own right and won the Republican nod at the Kansas City convention.

The Democratic standard-bearer was fifty-one-year-old James Earl Carter, Jr., a dark-horse candidate who galloped out of obscurity during the long primary elections season. A former Georgia governor who insisted on humble "Jimmy" as his first name, this born-again Baptist touched many people with his down-home sincerity. Untainted by ties with a corrupt and cynical Washington, Carter ran against the memory of Nixon and Watergate as much as he ran against Ford. His most effective campaign pitch was his promise that "I'll never lie to you."

Carter squeezed out a narrow victory on election day, with 51 percent of the popular vote. The electoral count stood at 297 to 240. The winner swept every state except Virginia in his native South. Especially important were the votes of African-Americans, 97 percent of whom cast their ballots for Carter.

After the colorful inaugural ceremonies of January 20, 1977, Jimmy Carter waved off the official black limousine and walked, hand in hand with his wife, Rosalyn, down Pennsylvania Avenue to his new home at the White House. This act symbolized his common touch, and the new president's popularity remained exceptionally high during his first few months in office.

With hefty Democratic majorities in both houses of Congress, hopes ran high that the stalemate of the Nixon-Ford years between a Republican White House and a Democratic Capitol Hill would now be ended. At first, Carter enjoyed notable political success, as Congress granted his requests to create a new Cabinet-level Department of Energy and to cut taxes by some $18 billion in 1978.

But Carter's honeymoon did not last long. An inexperienced outsider, he had campaigned against the Washington "establishment," and he never quite made the transition to being an insider himself. He repeatedly rubbed congressional fur the wrong way, and critics charged that he isolated himself in a shallow pool of fellow Georgians.

Carter's Humanitarian Diplomacy

As a committed Christian, President Carter displayed from the outset an overriding concern for human rights as the guiding principle of his foreign policy. He verbally lashed the dictatorial regimes of Cuba and Uganda, among others, and cut foreign aid to the repressive governments in Uruguay, Argentina, and Ethiopia. But he stopped short of punitive actions against other offending nations, such as South Korea and the Philippines, presumably because they were too vital to American security to risk insulting. In the African nations of Rhodesia (later Zimbabwe) and South Africa, Carter and his eloquent United Nations ambassador, Andrew Young, championed the oppressed black majority.

Carter's diplomacy successfully concluded two treaties designed to turn over to Panama complete ownership and control of the Panama Canal by the year 2000. The president's most spectacular foreign policy achievement came in September 1978 when he invited President Anwar Sadat of Egypt and Prime Minister Menachem Begin of Israel to the presidential retreat at Camp David, Maryland, in an attempt to prevent another blowup in the misery-drenched Middle East. After thirteen days, Carter, skillfully serving as go-between, persuaded the two visitors to sign an accord (September 17, 1978) that held considerable promise of peace. Israel agreed in principle to withdraw from territory conquered in the 1967 war, and Egypt in return promised to respect Israel's borders. Both parties pledged themselves to sign a formal peace treaty within three months.

Despite these dramatic accomplishments, trouble stalked Carter's foreign policy. Overshadowing all international issues was the ominous reheating of the Cold War with the USSR. Détente fell into disrepute as thousands of Cuban troops, assisted by Soviet advisers, appeared in Angola, Ethiopia, and elsewhere in Africa to support revolutionary factions. Arms-control negotiations with Moscow stalled in the face of this Soviet military meddling.

Carter's Economic and Energy Woes

Adding to Carter's mushrooming troubles was the failing health of the economy. A stinging recession during Gerald Ford's presidency had temporarily slowed inflation, but virtually from the moment of Carter's inauguration, prices resumed their dizzying ascent, driving the inflation rate well above 13 percent by 1979. The Organization of Petroleum Exporting Countries (OPEC) nearly doubled its petroleum charges, and the soaring bill for imported oil pushed America's balance of payments deeply into the red (an unprecedented $40 billion in 1978).

Yawning deficits in the federal budget, reaching nearly $60 billion in 1980, further aggravated the U.S. economy's inflationary ailments. The elderly and other Americans living on fixed incomes suffered from the shrinking dollar. People with money to lend pushed interest rates ever higher, hoping to protect themselves from being repaid in badly depreciated dollars. The prime rate (the rate of interest that banks charged their very best customers) vaulted to an unheard-of 20 percent in early 1980. The high cost of borrowing money shoved small businesses to the wall and strangled the construction industry.

Carter diagnosed America's economic disease as stemming primarily from the nation's costly dependence on foreign oil. Unfortunately, his legislative proposals in April 1977 for energy conservation met with congressional hostility and a blaze of indifference among the American people, who had already forgotten the long gasoline lines of 1973.

Events in Iran jolted Americans out of their complacency about energy supplies in 1979. The imperious Mohammed Reza Pahlevi, installed as shah of Iran with help from America's CIA in 1953, had long ruled his oil-rich land with a will of steel. His repressive regime was finally overthrown in January 1979 in a violent revolution spearheaded by Muslim fundamentalists. The crippling upheavals of the revolution soon spread to Iran's oil fields. As Iranian oil supplies stopped flowing, shortages appeared, petroleum prices rose steeply, and Americans once more found themselves waiting impatiently in long lines at gas stations or allowed to buy gasoline only on specified days.

Seeking to take political advantage of the calamity, Carter began in April 1979 to lift price controls from domestically produced oil, a move designed both to curtail consumption and to increase production. As the oil crisis deepened, the president sought ways to advance still further his energy goals. In July 1979 Carter retreated to Camp David, where he remained largely out of public view for ten days. Like a royal potentate of old summoning the wise men of the realm for their counsel in a time of crisis, Carter called in over 100 leaders from all walks of life to give him their views. Meanwhile, the nation waited anxiously for the results of these extraordinary deliberations.

When he finally came down from the mountaintop on July 15, 1979, Carter stunned and perplexed the nation by chiding his fellow citizens for falling into "moral and spiritual crisis" and for being too concerned with "material goods." When he finally arrived at his energy proposals, Carter called for a ten-year, $140 billion federal program to develop synthetic fuels, limit foreign oil imports, and encourage the substitution of coal for oil. A few days later, the president let drop another shoe when he fired four cabinet secretaries and circled the wagons of his Georgian advisers more tightly about the White House. Critics began to wonder aloud whether Carter, the professed man of the people, was losing touch with the popular mood of the country.

Foreign Affairs and the Iranian Imbroglio

Hopes for a less dangerous world rose slightly in June 1979, when President Carter met with Soviet leader Leonid Brezhnev in Vienna to sign the long-stalled SALT II agreements, limiting the levels of lethal strategic weapons in the Soviet and American arsenals. But conservative critics of the president's defense policies, deeply suspicious of the Soviet Union, unsheathed their long knives to carve up the SALT Treaty when it came to the Senate for debate in the summer of 1979.

Political earthquakes in the petroleum-rich Persian Gulf region finally buried all hopes of ratifying the treaty. On November 4, 1979, a howling mob of rabidly anti-American Muslim militants stormed the United States embassy in Teheran, Iran, and took all of its occupants hostage. World opinion hotly condemned the diplomatic felony in Iran, while Americans agonized over both the fate of the hostages and the stability of the entire Persian Gulf region. The Soviet army then aroused the West's worst fears on December 27, 1979, when it blitzed into the mountainous nation of Afghanistan, next door to Iran, and appeared to be poised for a thrust at the oil-jugular of the gulf.

President Carter reacted vigorously to these alarming events. He slapped an embargo on the export of grain and high-technology machinery to the USSR, called for a boycott of the upcoming Olympic Games in Moscow, and requested that young people (including women) be made to register for a possible military draft. Proclaiming that the United States would "use any means necessary, including force," to protect the Persian Gulf against Soviet incursions, Carter grimly conceded that he had misjudged the Soviets. The SALT Treaty became a dead letter in the Senate. Meanwhile, the Soviet army met unexpectedly stiff resistance in Afghanistan and became bogged down in a nasty guerrilla war that came to be called "Russia's Vietnam."

The Iranian hostage crisis was Carter's—and America's—bed of nails. The captured Americans languished in cruel captivity, while the nightly news broadcasts showed humiliating scenes of Iranian mobs burning the American flag and spitting upon effigies of Uncle Sam.

Carter at first tried to apply economic sanctions and the pressure of world opinion against the Iranians. But the president's frustration grew as the

political upheaval in Iran ground on relentlessly. Carter at last ordered a daring rescue mission. A highly trained commando team penetrated deep into Iran's sandy interior, but when equipment failures prevented some members of the team from reaching their destination, the mission had to be scrapped. As the commandos withdrew, two of their aircraft collided, killing eight of the would-be rescuers.

The disastrous failure of the rescue raid proved anguishing for Americans. The episode seemed to underscore the nation's helplessness and even incompetence in the face of a mortifying insult to the national honor. The stalemate with Iran dragged on throughout the rest of Carter's term in office, providing an embarrassing backdrop to the embattled president's struggle for reelection.

Varying Viewpoints

Richard Nixon may well be the most controversial political personality in recent American history. He built his career on the most inflammatory issues of the day, from red-chasing in the 1940s and 1950s to the Vietnam War in the 1960s; and the Watergate episode ended his public life with the most explosive constitutional crisis in over a century. Ever combative and resourceful, he antagonized his enemies and cultivated his followers with unremitting energy and skill. Hence, there are few "objective" accounts of the Nixon years; passion still guides the pens of most writers, producing assessments that are either bitterly critical or aggressively apologetic. Thus it may be some time before historians can make a balanced appraisal of Nixon's role (though an impressive beginning has been made by Stephen E. Ambrose in *Nixon,* 2 vols., 1987 and 1989). The stain of Watergate, for example, has almost blotted from the record Nixon's initiatives in foreign policy, especially toward China. Whatever the final judgment, it seems that historians will be unforgiving of the wounds that Watergate inflicted on the American body politic. Trust in elected leaders is an essential but fragile ingredient in a democracy, and that trust was badly undermined by the Watergate revelations.

SELECT READINGS

Primary Source Documents

Richard Nixon's vision of the international order is delineated in his *RN: The Memoirs of Richard Nixon* (1978).* The articles of impeachment reported against Nixon can be found in *House of Representatives Report No. 93–1305,* 93d Congress, 2d Session, pp. 1–2 (1974).* Opposing opinions on the Panama Canal treaty were voiced by Cyrus Vance and Ronald Reagan, *Hearings Before the Committee on Foreign Relations,* United States Senate, 95th Congress, 1st Session, pp. 10–15, 96–103 (1977).

Secondary Sources

The most comprehensive account of Nixon's early career is Stephen E. Ambrose, *Nixon: The Education of a Politician (1913–1962)* (1987). See also his *Nixon: The Triumph of a Politician, 1962–1972* (1989). Nixon's intriguing personality is examined in Garry Wills, *Nixon Agonistes: The Crisis of the Self-Made Man* (1970). Rowland Evans, Jr., and Robert D. Novak discuss *Nixon in the White House: The Frustrations of Power* (1971). Valuable background on American foreign policy in the Nixon years can be found in David P. Calleo and Benjamin Rowland, *America and the World Political Economy* (1973). Retrospectives on Vietnam include George C. Herring, *America's Longest War* (1979), and William Shawcross's chilling account of Cambodia, *Sideshow* (2d ed., 1981). Shawcross is vigorously rebutted in Henry Kissinger's rich memoir, *White House Years* (1979). Arthur M. Schlesinger, Jr., traces the growth of *The Imperial Presidency* (1973). The Watergate crisis is vividly described in two books by Carl Bernstein and Robert Woodward, *All the President's Men* (1974) and *The Final Days* (1976). "Jerry" Ford is analyzed by his former press secretary in J. F. ter Horst, *Gerald Ford and the Future of the Presidency* (1974). For a sharply critical view, see Clark Mollenhoff, *The Man Who Pardoned Nixon* (1976). On Jimmy Carter, see David Kucharsky, *The Man from Plains* (1984), and Clark Mollenhoff's more negative *The President Who Failed: Carter Out of Control* (1980). On Central American policy, see Richard Fagen, *The Nicaraguan Revolution* (1981), Walter LaFeber, *Inevitable Revolutions: The United States in Central America* (1983), and LaFeber's *Panama Canal: The Crisis in Historical Perspective* (1990). The catastrophe in Iran is described in Michael Ledeen and William Lewis, *Debacle: The American Failure in Iran* (1981), and in Gary Sick, *All Fall Down* (1986).

CHAPTER 42

The Resurgence of Conservatism, 1981–1995

It will be my intention to curb the size and influence of the federal establishment and to demand recognition of the distinction between the powers granted to the federal government and those reserved to the states or to the people.

Ronald Reagan, Inaugural Address, 1981

The Triumph of Conservation

Bedeviled abroad and becalmed at home, Carter's administration struck many Americans as bungling and befuddled. Carter's inability to control "double-digit" inflation was especially damaging.

Disaffection with Carter's apparent ineptitude ran deep even in his own Democratic party, where an "ABC" (Anybody But Carter) movement gathered steam, especially among liberal inheritors of the New Deal tradition. They found their champion in Senator Edward Kennedy of Massachusetts, who in late 1979 declared his intention to contest Carter's renomination. Carter finally emerged the winner after a series of bruising primary elections, but the Democratic party was left divided and in disarray.

Meanwhile, delighted Republicans decorously proceeded to select their presidential nominee. Ronald Reagan, the perennial darling of the right wing, easily outdistanced his rivals and secured the nomination he had sought for a decade.

The hour of the conservative right seemed at last to have arrived. Census figures confirmed that the average American was older than in the stormy

1960s and much more likely to live in the South or West, the traditional bastions of the "old right." The conservative cause drew added strength from the emergence of a "new right" movement. Spearheading the new right were evangelical Christian groups such as the Moral Majority, who enjoyed startling success as political fundraisers and organizers. Many new-right activists were especially agitated about so-called social issues such as abortion, the Equal Rights Amendment, pornography, homosexual rights, and especially affirmative action. They championed prayer in the schools and tougher penalties for criminals. Together, the old and new right added up to a powerful political combination.

Of all the social issues, affirmative action was among the most politically explosive. President Johnson had signed an executive order in 1965 requiring employers on federal contracts to take "affirmative action" to ensure that underprivileged minorities, as well as women, were hired. Affirmative-action programs quickly became obligatory in countless American corporations that did business with the government and in colleges and universities that received federal scholarship aid and research funding.

But in the 1970s, as the economy slowed and opportunities narrowed, white anxiety about advancing minorities intensified. White workers and white students increasingly raised the cry of "reverse discrimination," charging that employers and admissions officers put more weight on racial or ethnic background than on ability or achievement. One white Californian, Allan Bakke, made headlines in 1978 when the Supreme Court upheld his claim that his application to medical school had been turned down because of an admissions program that partially favored minority people. Many conservatives cheered the decision as affirming the principle that justice is color-blind.

The Election of Ronald Reagan, 1980

Ronald Reagan was well suited to lead the gathering conservative crusade. Reared in a generation whose values were formed well before the upheavals of the 1960s, he naturally sided with the new right on social issues. In economic and social matters alike, he denounced the activist government and failed "social engineering" of the 1960s. As his early political hero Franklin Roosevelt had championed the "forgotten man" against big business, the Republican Reagan championed the "common man" against big government. He aimed especially to win over working-class and lower-middle-class white voters from the Democratic column by implying that the Democratic party had become the exclusive tool of its minority constituents.

An actor turned politician, Reagan enjoyed enormous popularity with his crooked grin and "aw-shucks" manner. Facing a badly battered Jimmy Carter, the Republican candidate proved to be a formidable campaigner. Reagan attacked the incumbent's fumbling performance in foreign policy and blasted the "big-government" philosophy of the Democratic party (a philosophy that Carter did not fully share).

Carter's spotty record in office was no defense against Reagan's popular appeal. On election day the Republican rang up a spectacular victory, bagging

The New Right Wing   *Republican conservatives scored a double victory in 1980, winning control of both the White House and the Senate. Aided by conservative Democratic "boll weevils," they also dominated the House of Representatives, and a new era of conservatism dawned in the nation's capital.*

over 51 percent of the popular vote, while 41 percent went to Carter and 7 percent to independent candidate John Anderson. The electoral count stood at 489 for Reagan and 49 for Carter. Equally startling, the Republicans gained control of the Senate for the first time in twenty-five years. Democratic liberals who had been "targeted" for defeat by well-heeled new-right groups went down like dead timber in the conservative windstorm that swept the country.

Carter showed dignity in defeat. An unusually intelligent, articulate, and well-meaning president, he had been hampered by his lack of managerial talent and had been badly buffeted by events beyond his control, such as the soaring price of oil, runaway inflation, and the galling insult of the continuing hostage crisis in Iran. If Carter was correct in believing that the country was suffering from a terrible "malaise," he never found the right medicine to cure the disease.

The Reagan Revolution

Reagan's arrival in Washington was triumphal. The Iranians contributed to the festive mood by releasing the hostages on Reagan's inauguration day, January 20, 1981, after 444 days of captivity. The new president, a hale and hearty sixty-nine-year-old, was devoted to fiscal fitness. A major goal of Reagan's political career was to reduce the size of the government by shrinking the federal budget and slashing taxes. Years of New Deal–style tax-and-spend programs, Reagan quipped, had created a federal government that reminded him of the definition of a baby as a creature who was all appetite at one end, with no sense of responsiblity at the other.

By the early 1980s, this antigovernment message found a receptive audience. From 1960 to 1980, federal spending had risen from about 18 percent of the gross national product to nearly 23 percent. After four decades of advancing New Deal and Great Society programs, a strong countercurrent took hold. Californians staged a "tax revolt" in 1978 (known by its official title, Proposition 13) that slashed property taxes and forced painful cuts in government services. The California "tax quake" jolted other state capitals and rocked even Washington, D.C. Ronald Reagan had ridden this political shock wave to presidential victory in 1980 and now proceeded to rattle the "welfare state" to its very foundation.

With near-religious zeal, Reagan set out to persuade Congress to legislate his smaller-government policies into law. He proposed a new federal budget that necessitated cuts of some $35 billion, mostly in social programs such as food stamps and federally funded job-training centers. Reagan worked naturally in harness with the Republican majority in the Senate, while in the Democratic House he effectively wooed a group of mostly southern conservative Democrats (dubbed "boll weevils"), who abandoned their own party's leadership to follow the president.

Then on March 20, 1981, a deranged gunman shot the president as he was leaving a Washington hotel. A .22-caliber bullet penetrated beneath Reagan's left arm and collapsed his left lung. Also severely wounded in the attack was Reagan's press secretary James Brady, who later became a strong advocate of gun control. With admirable courage and with impressive physical resilience for a man his age, Reagan recovered rapidly from his violent ordeal. Twelve days after the attack, he walked out of the hospital and returned to work. When he appeared a few days later on national television to address the Congress and the public on his budget, the outpouring of sympathy and support was enormous.

The Battle of the Budget

Swept along on a tide of presidential popularity, Congress swallowed Reagan's budget proposals, approving expenditures of some $695 billion. To hit those financial targets, drastic surgery was required, and Congress plunged its scalpel deeply into Great Society–spawned social programs. Reagan's triumph amazed political observers, especially defeated Democrats. The new president had descended upon Washington like an avenging angel of conservatism. He sought nothing less than the dismantling of the welfare state and the reversal of the political evolution of the preceding half-century. Reagan's impressive performance demonstrated the power of the presidency with a skill not seen since Lyndon Johnson's day. Out the window went the textbooks that had concluded, largely on the basis of the stalemate of the 1970s, that this office had been eclipsed by a powerful, uncontrollable Congress.

Reagan hardly rested to savor the sweetness of his victory. The second part of his economic program called for deep tax cuts, amounting to 25 percent across-the-board reductions over a period of three years. Thanks largely to Reagan's skill as a television performer and the continued defection of the "boll weevils" from the Democratic camp, the president again had his way. In August 1981 Congress approved a set of sweeping tax reforms that lowered individual tax rates, virtually eliminated federal estate taxes, and created new tax-free savings plans for small investors. Reagan's "supply-side" economic advisers assured him that the combination of budgetary discipline and tax reduction would stimulate new investment, boost productivity, and foster dramatic economic growth.

But at first supply-side economics seemed to be a beautiful theory mugged by a gang of brutal facts, as the economy slid into its deepest recession since the 1930s. Unemployment reached nearly 11 percent in 1982, businesses folded, and several bank failures jolted the nation's entire financial system. The automobile industry, once the brightest jewel in America's industrial crown, reported losses in the hundreds of millions of dollars.

Ignoring the Democratic critics who charged that the president's budget cuts favored only the well-to-do, Reagan and his economic advisers serenely waited for their supply-side economic policies ("Reaganomics") to produce the promised results. The supply-siders seemed to be vindicated when a healthy economic recovery finally got under way in 1983. Yet the economy of the 1980s was not uniformly sound. For the first time in the twentieth century, income gaps widened between the richest and the poorest Americans. The poor got poorer and the very rich grew fabulously richer, while middle-class incomes largely stagnated. Symbolic of the new income stratification was the emergence of "yuppies," or young urban professionals. Though numbering only about 1.5 million people, yuppies showcased the values of materialism and the pursuit of wealth that flourished in the high-rolling 1980s.

Some economists located the sources of the economic upturn neither in the president's budget cuts and tax reforms nor in the go-get-'em avarice of the yuppies, but in his massive expenditures for the military. Reagan cascaded nearly 2 trillion budget dollars onto the Pentagon in the 1980s, asserting the need to close the "window of vulnerability" in the armaments race with the Soviet Union. Ironically, this conservative president thereby plunged the government into a red-ink bath of deficit spending that made the New Deal look downright stingy. Federal budget deficits topped $100 billion in 1982, and the government's books were nearly $200 billion out of balance in every year from 1983 to 1985. Massive government borrowing to cover these deficits kept interest rates high, and high interest rates in turn pushed the value of the dollar to record altitudes in international money markets. The soaring dollar dealt crippling blows to American exporters, as the American international trade deficit reached a record $152 billion in 1987. The masters of international commerce and finance for a generation after World War II, Americans suddenly became the world's heaviest borrowers in the global economy of the 1980s.

Reagan Renews the Cold War

Hard as nails toward the Soviet Union in his campaign speeches, Reagan saw no reason to soften up after he checked in at the White House. He immediately warned that the Soviets stood "prepared to commit any crime, to lie, to cheat" in pursuit of their goals of world conquest, and he later characterized the Soviet empire as "the focus of evil in the modern world."

Reagan believed in negotiating with the Soviets—but only from a position of overwhelming strength. Accordingly, his strategy for dealing with Moscow was simple: by enormously expanding U.S. military capabilities, he could force the Kremlin leaders either to embark upon a fantastically costly new round in the arms race or to come to the bargaining table and dance to Reagan's tune.

This strategy resembled a riverboat gambler's ploy. It wagered the enormous sum of Reagan's defense budgets on the hope that the other side would not call Washington's bluff and initiate a new cycle of arms competition. Reagan played his trump card in this deadly game in March 1983 when he announced his intention to pursue a high-technology missile defense system called the Strategic Defense Initiative (SDI), popularly known as Star Wars. The plan called for orbiting battle stations in space that could fire laser beams or other forms of concentrated energy to vaporize intercontinental missiles on lift-off. Although most scientists considered this an impossible goal, the deeper logic of SDI lay in its fit with Reagan's overall Soviet strategy. By pitching the arms contest onto a stratospherically high plane of technology and expense, it would further force the Kremlin's hand.

By emphasizing defense rather than offense, SDI upset four decades of strategic thinking about nuclear weaponry. But many experts feared that Star Wars research might be astronomically costly, ultimately unworkable, and fatally destabilizing to the distasteful but effective "balance of terror" that had kept the nuclear peace since World War II. Scientific and strategic doubts combined to constrain congressional funding for SDI through the remainder of Reagan's term.

Soviet-American relations further nosedived in late 1981 when the government of Poland, needled by a popular union movement called Solidarity, clamped martial law on the troubled country. Seeing

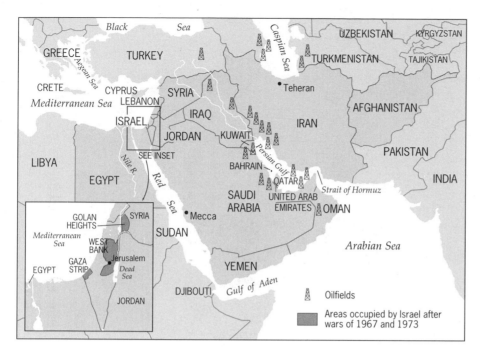

The Middle East *A combination of political instability and precious petroleum resources has made the region from Egypt to Afghanistan an "arc of crisis."*

the heavy fist of the Kremlin inside this Polish iron glove, Reagan imposed economic sanctions on Poland and the USSR alike.

Dealing with the Soviet Union was additionally complicated by the inertia and ill health of the aging oligarchs in the Kremlin, three of whom died between late 1982 and early 1985. Relations grew even more tense when the Soviets, in September 1983, blasted a Korean airliner from the skies, plunging hundreds of civilians, including many Americans, to their deaths in the frigid Sea of Okhotsk. By the end of 1983, all arms-control negotiations with the Soviets were broken off. The deepening chill in the Cold War was further felt in 1984, when USSR and Soviet-bloc athletes boycotted the Olympic Games in Los Angeles.

Troubles Abroad

The volatile Middle Eastern pot continued to boil ominously. Israel badly strained its bonds of friendship with the United States by continuing to allow new settlements to be established in the occupied territory of the Jordan River's West Bank.

Israel further raised the stakes in the Middle East in June 1982 when it invaded neighboring Lebanon, seeking to suppress once and for all the guerrilla bases from which Palestinian fighters harassed beleaguered Israel. The Palestinians were bloodily subdued, but Lebanon, already pulverized by years of episodic civil war, was plunged into armed chaos. President Reagan was obliged to send American troops to Lebanon in 1983 as part of an international peace-keeping force, but their presence did not bring peace. A suicidal bomber crashed an explosives-laden truck into a U.S. marine barracks on October 23, 1983, killing 239 marines. President Reagan soon thereafter withdrew the remaining American troops, while miraculously suffering no political damage from this horrifying and humiliating attack. His mystified Democratic opponents began to call him a "Teflon president," to whom nothing hurtful could stick.

Central America, in the United States' own backyard, also rumbled menacingly. A leftist revolution had deposed the longtime dictator of Nicaragua in 1979. President Carter had tried to ignore the anti-American rhetoric of the revolutionaries, known as

Central America and the Caribbean *This region of historical importance to the United States experienced dramatic political upheavals in the 1970s, 1980s, and 1990s.*

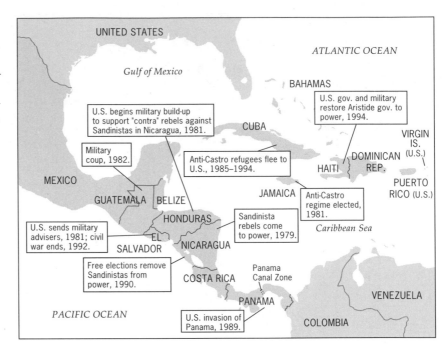

UNITED STATES

ATLANTIC OCEAN

Gulf of Mexico

BAHAMAS

U.S. gov. and military restore Aristide gov. to power, 1994.

CUBA

U.S. begins military build-up to support "contra" rebels against Sandinistas in Nicaragua, 1981.

Military coup, 1982.

Anti-Castro refugees flee to U.S., 1985–1994.

VIRGIN IS. (U.S.)

DOMINICAN REP.

HAITI

PUERTO RICO (U.S.)

MEXICO

GUATEMALA   BELIZE

JAMAICA

Anti-Castro regime elected, 1981.

HONDURAS

Caribbean Sea

U.S. sends military advisers, 1981; civil war ends, 1992.

EL SALVADOR

Sandinista rebels come to power, 1979.

NICARAGUA

Free elections remove Sandinistas from power, 1990.

COSTA RICA

Panama Canal Zone

VENEZUELA

PACIFIC OCEAN

PANAMA

U.S. invasion of Panama, 1989.

COLOMBIA

"Sandinistas," and to establish good diplomatic relations with them. But Reagan took their words at face value and hurled back at them some hot language of his own. He accused the Sandinistas of turning their country into a forward base for Soviet and Cuban military penetration of all of Central America. Brandishing photographs taken from high-flying spy planes, administration spokespeople claimed that Nicaraguan leftists were shipping weapons to revolutionary forces in tiny El Salvador, torn by violence since a coup in 1979.

Reagan sent military "advisers" to prop up the pro-American government of El Salvador. He also provided covert aid, including the CIA-engineered mining of harbors, to the "contra" rebels opposing the anti-American Sandinista government of Nicaragua. Reagan also flexed his military muscles elsewhere in the turbulent Caribbean. In a dramatic display of American might, in 1983 he dispatched a heavy-firepower invasion force to the island of Grenada, where a military coup had killed the prime minister and brought Marxists to power. Swiftly overrunning the tiny island, American troops vividly demonstrated Reagan's determination to assert the

dominance of the United States in the Caribbean, just as Theodore Roosevelt had done.

Round Two for Reagan

A confident Ronald Reagan, bolstered by a buoyant economy at home and by the popularity of his muscular posture abroad, handily won the Republican nomination in 1984 for a second White House term. His opponent was Democrat Walter Mondale, who made history by naming as his vice-presidential running mate Congresswoman Geraldine Ferraro of New York. She was the first woman ever to appear on a major party presidential ticket. But even this dramatic gesture could not salvage Mondale's candidacy. On election day Reagan walked away with 525 electoral votes to Mondale's 13, winning everywhere except in Mondale's home state of Minnesota and the District of Columbia. Reagan also overwhelmed Mondale in the popular vote—52,609,797 to 36,450,613.

Shrinking the federal government and reducing taxes had been the main objectives of Reagan's first term; foreign policy issues dominated the news

The Americans Invade Grenada, 1983 *United States forces easily overran the tiny Caribbean island-nation, thwarting a Marxist takeover.*

in his second term. The president soon found himself contending for the world's attention with a charismatic new Soviet leader, Mikhail Gorbachev, installed as chairman of the Soviet Communist party in March 1985. Gorbachev was personable, energetic, imaginative, and committed to radical reforms in the Soviet Union. He announced two policies with sweeping, even revolutionary, implications. *Glasnost,* or "openness," aimed to ventilate the secretive, repressive stuffiness of Soviet society by introducing free speech and a measure of political liberty. *Perestroika,* or "restructuring," was intended to revive the moribund Soviet economy by adopting many of the free-market practices—such as the profit motive and an end to subsidized prices—of the capitalist West.

Both *glasnost* and *perestroika* required that the Soviet Union shrink the size of its enormous military machine and redirect its energies to the civilian economy. That requirement, in turn, necessitated an end to the Cold War. Gorbachev accordingly made warm overtures to the West, including an announcement in

April 1985 that the Soviet Union would cease to deploy intermediate-range nuclear forces (INF) targeted on Western Europe, pending an agreement on their complete elimination. He pushed this goal when he met with Reagan at their first of four summit meetings, in Geneva in November 1985. A second summit meeting in Reykjavik, Iceland, in October 1986 broke down in stalemate, but at a third summit in Washington, D.C., in December 1987, the two leaders at last signed the INF Treaty, banning all intermediate-range nuclear missles from Europe.

Reagan and Gorbachev capped their new friendship in May 1988 at a final summit in Moscow. There President Reagan, who had entered office condemning the lying, cheating "evil empire" of Soviet communism, warmly praised Gorbachev. Reagan, the consummate cold warrior, had been flexible and savvy enough to seize a historic opportunity to join with the Soviet chief to bring the Cold War to a kind of conclusion. For this history would give both leaders high marks.

The Iran-Contra Imbroglio

Two foreign policy problems seemed insolvable to Reagan: the continuing captivity of a number of American hostages, seized by Muslim extremist groups in bleeding, battered Lebanon; and the continuing grip on power of the left-wing Sandinista government in Nicaragua. The president repeatedly requested that Congress provide military aid to the "contra" rebels fighting against the Sandinista regime. Congress repeatedly refused, and the administration grew increasingly frustrated, even obsessed, in its search for a means to help the contras.

Unbeknown to the American public, some Washington officials saw a possible linkage between the two thorny problems of the Middle Eastern hostages and the Sandinistas. In 1985 American diplomats secretly arranged arms sales to the embattled Iranians in return for Iranian aid in obtaining the release of American hostages held by Middle Eastern terrorists. At least one hostage was eventually set free. Meanwhile, money from the payment for the arms was diverted to the contras. These actions brazenly violated a congressional ban on military aid to the Nicaraguan rebels—not to mention Reagan's repeated vow that he would never negotiate with terrorists.

News of these secret dealings broke in November 1986 and ignited a firestorm of controversy. President Reagan claimed he was innocent of wrongdoing and ignorant about the activities of his subordinates, but a congressional committee condemned the "secrecy, deception, and disdain for the law" displayed by administration officials and concluded that "if the president did not know what his national security advisers were doing, he should have."

The Iran-contra affair cast a dark shadow over Reagan's record on foreign policy and tends to obscure the president's achievement in establishing a new relationship with the Soviets. Although the several Iran-contra investigations presented damaging revelations of Reagan's weaknesses and laziness as a chief executive, he remains among the most popular and beloved presidents in modern American history.

Reagan's Economic Legacy

Ronald Reagan had taken office vowing to invigorate the American economy by rolling back government regulations, reducing taxes, and balancing the budget. He did ease many regulatory rules, and he pushed major tax-reform bills through Congress in 1981 and 1986. But a balanced budget remained grotesquely out of reach. The combination of tax reduction and huge increases in military spending opened a vast "revenue hole" of $200 billion in annual deficits. In his eight years in office Reagan added nearly 2 trillion dollars to the national debt— more than all his predecessors combined.

The staggering deficits of the Reagan years assuredly constituted a dismal economic failure. And because foreign lenders, especially the Japanese, financed so much of the Reagan-era debt, the deficits virtually guaranteed that future generations of Americans would have to either work harder than their parents or lower their standard of living, or both, to pay their foreign creditors.

But if the deficits represented an economic failure, they also constituted, strangely enough, a kind of political triumph. By making new social spending both practically and politically impossible, they achieved one of Reagan's paramount goals: slowing the growth of government and blocking or even repealing the social programs begun in the era of Lyndon Johnson's Great Society. They achieved, in short, Reagan's highest political objective: the containment of the welfare state. Ronald Reagan thus ensured the long-term perpetuation of his values to a degree that few presidents have managed to achieve. For better or worse, the consequences of Reaganomics would be large and durable.

Culture Wars

Reagan's legacy also was likely to be lasting with respect to the social issues that first helped get him elected president in 1980. The courts became his principal instrument in his battles against affirmative action and abortion, the two great icons of the liberal political culture that Reaganism repudiated. By the time he left office, Reagan had appointed a near-majority of all sitting judges. Equally important, he had named three conservative-minded justices to the Supreme Court. They included Sandra Day O'Connor, a brilliant Stanford Law School graduate who was sworn in on September 25, 1981, as the first woman justice in the Court's nearly 200-year history.

The Court showed its newly conservative coloration in 1984, when it decreed, in a case involving Memphis fire fighters, that union rules about job seniority could outweigh affirmative-action concerns in guiding promotion policies in the city's fire department. In two cases in 1989 *(Ward's Cove Packing* v. *Antonia* and *Martin* v. *Wilks),* the Court made it more difficult to prove that an employer practiced racial discrimination in hiring, and made it easier for white males to argue that they were the victims of reverse discrimination. Congress passed legislation in 1991 that partially reversed the effects of these decisions.

The vexed issue of abortion also reached the Court in 1989. In the case of *Roe* v. *Wade* in 1973, the Supreme Court had prohibited states from making laws that interfered with a woman's right to an abortion during the early months of pregnancy. For nearly two decades, that decision had been the bedrock principle on which "pro-choice" advocates built their case for abortion rights. It had also provoked bitter criticism from Roman Catholics and various "right-to-life" groups who wanted a virtually absolute ban on all abortions. In *Webster* v. *Reproductive Health Services,* the Court in July 1989 did not entirely overturn *Roe,* but it seriously compromised *Roe*'s protection of abortion rights. By approving a Missouri law that imposed certain restrictions on abortion, the court signaled that it was inviting the states to legislate in an area from which *Roe* had previously forbidden them to legislate.

Right-to-life advocates were at first delighted by the *Webster* decision. But the Court's ruling also jolted pro-choice organizations into a new militancy. Bruising, divisive battles loomed in state legislatures across the country over the abortion issue. This painful cultural conflict was also part of the Reagan-era legacy.

The Agony of Abortion   *Pro-life and pro-choice demonstrators hold signs on the steps of the Supreme Court building. Abortion emerged in the 1980s and 1990s as perhaps the most morally charged and divisive issue in American society since the struggle over slavery in the nineteenth century.*

Referendum on Reaganism in 1988

Republicans lost control of the Senate in the off-year elections of November 1986. Hopes rose among Democrats that the "Reagan revolution" might be showing signs of political vulnerability at last. The newly Democratic majority in the Senate flexed its political muscle in 1987 when it rejected Robert Bork, the president's ultraconservative nominee for a Supreme Court vacancy. Democrats also relished the prospect of making political hay out of both the Iran-contra scandal and the allegedly unethical behavior that tainted an unusually large number of key members of Reagan's administration.

Disquieting signs of economic trouble also seemed to open political opportunities for Democrats. The "twin towers" of deficits—the federal budget deficit and international trade deficit—continued to mount ominously. Falling oil prices blighted the economy of the Southwest, slashing real estate values and undermining hundreds of savings and loan (S&L) institutions. The damage to the S&Ls was so massive that a federal rescue operation was eventually estimated to carry a price tag of well over $500 billion. A wave of mergers, acquisitions, and leveraged buyouts washed over Wall Street, leaving many brokers and traders mega-rich and many companies saddled with mega-debt. A cold spasm of fear struck the money markets on "Black Monday," October 19, 1987, when the leading stock market index plunged 508 points—the largest one-day decline in history. This crash, said *Newsweek* magazine, heralded "the final collapse of the money culture . . . , the death knell of the 1980s." But as Mark Twain famously commented about his own obituary, this announcement proved premature.

Hoping to cash in on these ethical and economic anxieties, a batch of Democrats—dubbed the "seven dwarfs" by derisive Republicans—chased after their party's 1988 presidential nomination. Black candidate Jesse Jackson, a rousing speech maker who hoped to forge a "rainbow coalition" of minorities and the disadvantaged, campaigned energetically. But the Democratic nomination in the end went to the coolly cerebral governor of Massachusetts, Michael Dukakis. Republicans nominated Reagan's vice president, George Bush, who ran largely on the Reagan record of tax cuts, strong defense policies, toughness on crime, opposition to abortion, and a long-running if hardly robust economic expansion. Dukakis made little headway with the ethical and economic issues, and came across to television viewers as almost supernaturally devoid of passion. On election day the voters gave him just 40,797,905 votes to 47,645,225 for Bush. The Electoral College count was 112 to 426.

George Bush and the End of the Cold War

George Herbert Walker Bush was born with a silver spoon in his mouth. His father had served as a U.S. senator from Connecticut, and young George enjoyed a first-rate education at Yale. After service in World War II, he amassed a modest fortune in the oil business in Texas. His deepest commitment, however, was to public service; he left the business world to serve briefly as a congressman and then held various posts in several Republican administrations, including emissary to China, ambassador to the United Nations, director of the Central Intelligence

George Bush on the Campaign Trail *After eight years as Ronald Reagan's vice president, Bush won the White House in 1988 by defeating Democrat Michael Dukakis.*

Agency, and vice president. He capped this long political career when he was inaugurated as president of the United States in January 1989, promising to work for "a kinder, gentler America."

In the first months of the Bush administration, the communist world commanded the planet's fascinated attention. Astoundingly, it seemed that everywhere in the communist bloc the season of democracy had arrived.

In China hundreds of thousands of prodemocracy demonstrators thronged Beijing's Tienanmen Square in the spring of 1989. They were dispersed, however, in June of that year, when China's aging and autocratic rulers brutally crushed the movement. Tanks rolled over the crowds, and machine-gunners killed hundreds of protesters. World opinion roundly condemned the bloody suppression of the Chinese democratic movement, and President Bush joined in the criticism. Yet despite angry demands in Congress for punitive restrictions on trade with China, the president insisted on maintaining normal relations with Beijing.

Stunning changes also shook Eastern Europe in 1989. Long oppressed by puppet regimes propped up by Soviet guns, the region was revolutionized in just a few startling months. The Solidarity movement in Poland led the way when it toppled Poland's communist government in August. With dizzying speed, communist regimes collapsed in Hungary, Czechoslovakia, East Germany, and even hyperrepressive Romania. In December 1989, jubilant Germans danced atop the hated Berlin wall, symbol of the division of Germany, and all of Europe, into two armed and hostile camps. The wall itself soon came down, heralding the imminent end of the forty-five-year-long Cold War. With the approval of the victorious Allied powers of World War II, the two Germanies, divided since 1945, were at last reunited in October 1990.

Most startling of all were the changes that swept the heartland of world communism, the Soviet Union. Mikhail Gorbachev's policies of *glasnost* and *perestroika* had set in motion forces that raged out of control. Old-guard hardliners, in a last-gasp effort to preserve the tottering communist system, attempted to overthrow Gorbachev in August 1991. With the support of Boris Yeltsin, president of the Russian

Republic (one of several republics that composed the Union of Soviet Socialist Republics), Gorbachev foiled the plotters. But in December 1991 Gorbachev resigned as president, and the Soviet Union dissolved into fifteen sovereign republics, with Russia the most powerful. To varying degrees, all the new governments repudiated communism and embraced democratic reforms and free-market economies.

The demise of the Soviet Union wrote a spectacular and surprising finish to the Cold War. More than four decades of nail-biting tension between the two nuclear superpowers, the Soviet Union and the United States, evaporated when the USSR dismantled itself. With the Soviet Union swept into the dustbin of history, and communism all but extinct, President Bush spoke hopefully of a "new world order" in which democracy would reign and diplomacy would take the place of weaponry.

But the disintegration of the Soviet Union turned out to pose thorny new questions. Control of the formidable Soviet nuclear arsenal by the successor states and enforcement of arms-control agreements with the United States were by no means guaranteed. Waves of nationalistic fervor and long-suppressed ethnic and racial hatred rolled across the vast lands of the former Soviet empire. In 1995 the Russian army waged a brutal war of suppression against rebels in the territory of Chechnya. Ethnic warfare flared in other former communist countries as well, notably in the misery-drenched territory of former Yugoslavia, which was wracked by vicious civil wars and "ethnic cleansing" against minorities.

The cruel and paradoxical truth was revealed: the ironfisted communist regimes of Eastern Europe, whatever their sins, had at least bottled up the ancient ethnic antagonisms that were the region's peculiar curse and that now erupted in all their historic fury. As civil wars and economic collapse sent refugees fleeing westward, the nations of Western Europe, notably Germany, were themselves threatened by economic and ethnic tensions directed especially against various newcomers. For more than four decades the Western democracies had feared the *strength* of the Eastern bloc; now, ironically, they saw their well-being threatened by the *weakness* of the former communist lands.

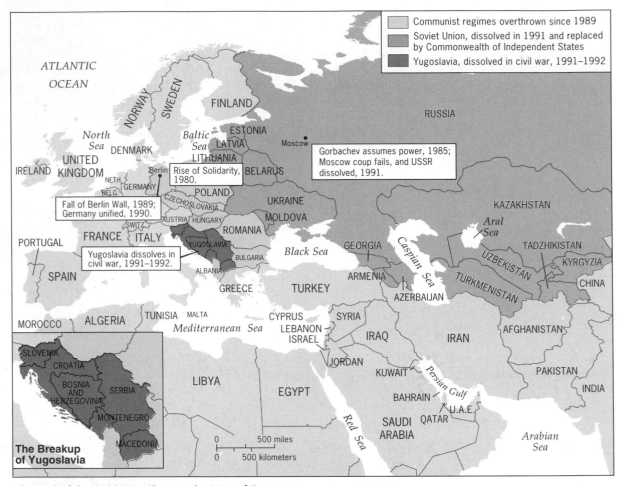

Communist regimes overthrown since 1989

Soviet Union, dissolved in 1991 and replaced by Commonwealth of Independent States

Yugoslavia, dissolved in civil war, 1991–1992

Rise of Solidarity, 1980.

Gorbachev assumes power, 1985; Moscow coup fails, and USSR dissolved, 1991.

Fall of Berlin Wall, 1989; Germany unified, 1990.

Yugoslavia dissolves in civil war, 1991–1992.

The Breakup of Yugoslavia

The End of the Cold War Changes the Map of Europe

Lithuanians Demand Independence, 1991 *Lithuanian demonstrators are shown here in the capital city of Vilnius before a visit by Soviet President Mikhail Gorbachev in January 1991. The sign says, "Freedom and Independence for Lithuania" in Russian. Within a year, Lithuania and all the former Soviet republics achieved that goal.*

The end of the Cold War also proved a mixed blessing for the United States. With the Soviet threat now canceled, the major justification for American internationalism ended, and the nation's traditional isolationist feeling began to reassert itself. The Soviet-American rivalry had also deeply shaped the U.S. economy through military contracts in industries such as aerospace. The economic cost of beating swords into plowshares became painfully apparent in 1991, when the Pentagon announced the closing of thirty-four military bases and canceled a $52 billion order for a navy attack plane. The problems of weaning the U.S. economy from its decades of reliance on military spending, especially in defense-dependent areas like southern California, tempered the euphoria of Americans as they welcomed the Cold War's finale.

The Persian Gulf War

Sadly, the end of the Cold War did not mean the end of all wars. President Bush flexed the United States' still-intimidating military muscle in tiny Panama in December 1989, when he sent airborne troops to capture dictator and drug lord Manuel Noriega.

Still more ominous events in the summer of 1990 severely tested Bush's dream of a democratic and peaceful new world order. On August 2, Saddam Hussein, the brutal and ambitious ruler of Iraq, sent his armies to overrun Kuwait, a tiny, oil-rich desert sheikdom on Iraq's southern frontier.

Oil fueled Saddam's aggression. Financially exhausted by its eight-year war with Iran that had ended in stalemate in 1988, Iraq needed Kuwait's oil

U.S. Soldiers in Iraq, 1991   *American GIs celebrate their swift victory in the Persian Gulf War.*

Operation Desert Storm: The Ground War

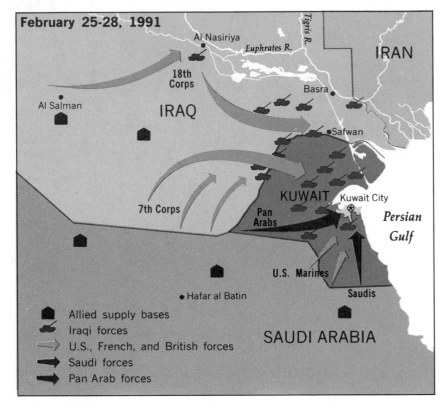

to pay its huge war bills. Saddam's larger design was iron-fisted control over the entire oil-rich Persian Gulf region. With his hand thus firmly clutching the world's economic jugular vein, he dreamed of dictating the terms of oil supplies to the industrial nations, and perhaps of totally extinguishing the Arabs' enemy, Israel.

On August 2, 1990, Iraq's formidable invading army of some 100,000 men roared into Kuwait. The swiftness and audacity of the Iraqi invasion was stunning, but the world responded just as swiftly. The U.N. Security Council unanimously condemned the invasion on August 3, 1990, and demanded the immediate and unconditional withdrawal of Iraq's troops. In November, the Security Council delivered an ultimatum to Iraq: leave Kuwait by January 15, 1991, or U.N. forces would "use all necessary means" to expel the Iraqi army.

In a logistical operation of astonishing com-plexity, meanwhile, the United States spearheaded a massive international military deployment on the sandy Arabian peninsula. As the January 15 deadline approached, some 539,000 U.S. soldiers, sailors, and pilots—many of them women and all of them members of the new, post-Vietnam, all-volunteer American military—had swarmed into the Persian Gulf region. They were joined by nearly 270,000 troops, pilots, and sailors from twenty-eight other countries in the coalition opposed to Iraq.

A war of nerves set in as diplomats explored every avenue to resolve the crisis peacefully. Historians will debate whether continued economic sanctions might eventually have brought Saddam to his knees; but all hopes seemed dashed by a dramatic eleventh-hour meeting in Geneva, Switzerland, on January 9, 1991, between U.S. Secretary of State James Baker and the Iraqi foreign minister. The U.S. Congress thereupon voted regretfully on January 12 to approve the use of force. The time bomb of war now ticked off its final few beats.

On January 16, 1991, the United States and its U.N. allies unleashed a hellish air war against Iraq. For thirty-seven days, warplanes pummeled targets in occupied Kuwait and in Iraq itself. Iraq responded to this pounding by launching several dozen "Scud" short-range ballistic missiles against military and civilian targets in Saudi Arabia and Israel. These missile attacks claimed several lives but did no significant military damage.

Yet if Iraq made but a feeble military response to the air campaign, the allied commander, the beefy and blunt American general Norman ("Stormin' Norman") Schwarzkopf, took nothing for granted. Saddam, who had threatened to wage "the mother of all battles," had the capacity to inflict awful damage. Iraq had stockpiled tons of chemical and biological weapons, including poison gas and the means to spread epidemics of anthrax, and Saddam might use them at any minute.

Saddam's tactics also included ecological warfare; he released a gigantic oil slick into the Persian Gulf to forestall amphibious assault and ignited hundreds of oil-well fires whose smoky plumes shrouded the ground from aerial view. Faced with these horrifying tactics, Schwarzkopf's strategy was starkly simple: soften the Iraqis with relentless bombing, then suffocate them on the ground with a tidal-wave rush of troops and armor.

On February 23 the dreaded and long-awaited land war began. Dubbed "Operation Desert Storm," it lasted only four days—the "hundred-hour war." With the Iraqi forces grounded or destroyed, Schwarzkopf had secretly moved a huge force far across the desert to the extreme western end of the Iraqi fortifications. With lightning speed it penetrated deep into Iraq, outflanking the occupying forces in Kuwait and blocking the enemy's ability either to retreat or to reinforce. Allied casualties were amazingly light whereas much of Iraq's remaining fighting force was quickly destroyed or captured. On February 27 Saddam accepted a cease-fire, and Kuwait was liberated.

For a brief moment in the war's victorious afterglow, President Bush enjoyed enormous popular approval. Yet he came perilously close to snatching moral defeat from the jaws of military victory. When Iraq's minority Kurds and Shiite Arabs heeded Bush's call to rise up against Saddam Hussein, the diabolical dictator ruthlessly crushed them while the United States looked on helplessly. Worse, the war had failed to dislodge Saddam from power. When the smoke cleared, he had survived to menace to world another day. The perpetually troubled Middle East knew scarcely less trouble after Desert Storm had ceased to thunder, and the United States, for better or worse, found itself more deeply entangled in the region's web of mortal hatreds and intractable conflicts.

Bush on the Home Front

In his inaugural address, George Bush pledged that he would work for a "kinder, gentler America." He redeemed that promise in part when he signed the Americans with Disabilities Act (ADA) in 1990, a landmark law prohibiting discrimination against the 43 million U.S. citizens with physical or mental disabilities. The president also signed a major water projects bill in 1992 that put the interests of the environment ahead of agriculture, especially in California's heavily irrigated Central Valley. As for Bush's promise to become the "education president," it went largely unredeemed. Critics charged, with increasing heat, that Bush, for all his triumphs in foreign policy, seemed to lack interest in domestic affairs.

The president did continue to aggravate the explosive "social issues" that had so divided Americans throughout the 1980s, especially the nettlesome questions of affirmative action and abortion. Bush challenged the legality of college scholarships targeted for racial minorities, and only reluctantly approved a watered-down civil rights bill in 1991 that was designed to make it easier for employees to prove they were victims of discrimination.

Most provocatively, in 1991 Bush nominated for the Supreme Court the conservative African-American jurist Clarence Thomas, a notorious critic of affirmative-action policies. Although Thomas refused to reveal his views on abortion and other controversial issues, his nomination was loudly opposed by labor, civil rights, and women's organizations. Reflecting these bitter divisions, the Senate Judiciary Committee concluded its hearings with a divided seven to seven vote and forwarded the matter to the Senate without a recommendation.

Then, in early October 1991, just days before the Senate was scheduled to vote, it was suddenly revealed that a University of Oklahoma law professor, Anita Hill, had accused Thomas of sexual harassment. The Senate Judiciary Committee was forced to reopen its hearings. For days, a prurient American public sat glued to their television sets as Hill graphically detailed her charges of sexual improprieties and Thomas angrily responded. In the end, by a 52–48 vote, the Senate narrowly confirmed Thomas as the second African-American ever to sit on the supreme bench. While many Americans hailed Hill as a heroine for her role in raising the issue of sexual harassment, Thomas maintained that her unproved allegations amounted to "a high-tech lynching for uppity blacks who in any way deign to think for themselves, to do for themselves." Enraged by the Thomas nomination and by Bush's opposition to abortion, many women turned sharply against the president.

Still more damaging to President Bush's political health, the economy sputtered and stalled almost at the outset of his administration. By 1992 the unemployment rate exceeded 7 percent, while the federal budget deficit continued to mushroom, topping $250 billion in each year of Bush's presidency. In a desperate attempt to stop the hemorrhage of red ink, Bush and Congress agreed in 1990 to a budget that included $133 billion in new taxes.

Bush's 1990 tax and budget package added up to a political catastrophe. In his 1988 presidential campaign, Bush had belligerently declared, "Read my lips—no new taxes." Now he had flagrantly broken that campaign promise. Worse, his repudiation of his no-tax pledge failed to produce the desired economic result. As deficits continued to mount, the recession deepened. Disgusted with the intractable budgetary crisis, the stagnant economy, and the apparent paralysis of the federal government, many citizens became increasingly disillusioned with all political incumbents.

Bill Clinton: The First Baby-Boomer President

The slumbering economy and the rising anti-incumbent spirit spelled opportunity for Democrats, frozen out of the White House for all but four years since 1968. In a bruising round of primary elections, Governor William Jefferson Clinton of Arkansas weathered blistering accusations of womanizing and draft evasion to emerge as his party's standard-bearer, with Senator Albert Gore of Tennessee as his vice-presidential running mate.

Clinton claimed to be a "new" Democrat, chastened by his party's long exile in the political wilderness. Clinton and other centrist Democrats attempted to point Democrats away from their traditional antibusiness, dovish, champion-of-the-underdog orientation. Clinton campaigned vigorously, especially on promises to stimulate the economy, reform the welfare system, and overhaul the nation's scandalously expensive and inefficient health-care system.

Trying to wring one more win out of the social issues that had underwritten the presidential victories of Reagan and Bush, the Republican convention in Houston dwelled stridently on "family values" as it renominated George Bush and Vice President J. Danforth Quayle for a second term. A dispirited Bush tried to attack Clinton's character and take credit for the end of the Cold War. He proudly cited his leadership role in the Persian Gulf War and touted his achievement in negotiating the North American Free Trade Agreement (NAFTA), which created a free-trade zone encompassing Canada, the United States, and Mexico.

But fear for the economic problems of the future swayed more voters than pride in the foreign policies of the past. The purchasing power of the average worker's paycheck had actually declined

Presidential Election of 1992
(with electoral vote by state)

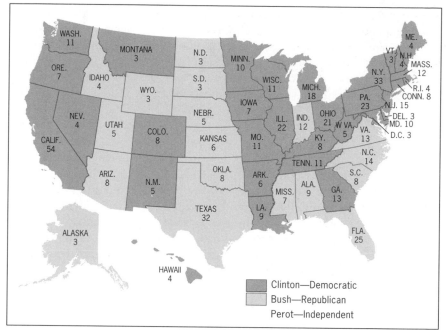

Clinton—Democratic
Bush—Republican
Perot—Independent

during Bush's presidency. Reflecting pervasive economic unease and the virulence of the throw-the-bums-out national mood, nearly 20 percent of voters cast their ballots for independent presidential candidate H. Ross Perot, a "billionaire populist" from Texas who proudly boasted that he had never held any public office.

With a record turnout of voters on election day, the final tally gave Clinton 43,728,275 popular votes and 370 in the Electoral College. Bush polled 38,167,416 popular and 168 electoral votes. Perot won no electoral votes but did gather 19,237,247 in the popular count—the strongest showing for an independent or third-party candidate since Theodore Roosevelt ran on the Bull Moose ticket in 1912. Democrats also racked up clear majorities in both houses of Congress.

Bill Clinton and Albert Gore represented the first successful all-southern ticket since Andrew Jackson and John C. Calhoun in 1828. Clinton was also the first president since Franklin D. Roosevelt not to have served in the armed forces. And he was the first baby boomer to ascend to the White House,

President Bill Clinton and Hillary Rodham Clinton, 1993
The public partnership of the president and the first lady reminded many Americans of the similar roles played by Franklin Delano Roosevelt and his wife, Eleanor. As with Eleanor Roosevelt, Hillary Rodham Clinton's involvement in political affairs stirred both praise and criticism.

a distinction reflecting the electoral profile of the U.S. population, 70 percent of which was composed of Americans who had been born after World War II. The nation and the world looked to Clinton to see whether his generation's record would match the history that their parents had made in the post–World War II epoch that had come to a close.

Clinton Takes the Reins

Youthful and vigorous, the new president consciously tried to model his administration after that of his political hero, John Kennedy. But Clinton's term got off to a rocky start when his first two nominees for attorney general were forced to withdraw because they had employed illegal immigrants. Clinton finally found an attorney general, Janet Reno, and the rest of his cabinet displayed more diversity of gender, race, and ethnicity than any previous administration.

Clinton also stirred controversy by proposing to lift the ban on homosexuals in the military. The president's plan was fiercely opposed by many in Congress and the Pentagon. A brittle compromise on the issue—"Don't ask, don't tell"—was arranged in July 1993, leaving almost no one satisfied.

Clinton partially recovered from these early stumbles with his handling of the economy. To control the exploding deficit, he proposed a set of spending cuts and tax increases designed to reduce the deficit by $500 billion over five years. Republicans in Congress fiercely attacked the tax increases, but Clinton's Democratic allies held firm and passed the bill by narrow margins, with Vice President Albert Gore breaking a 50-50 tie in the Senate.

The U.S. economy, which had lingered in the doldrums since 1989, gradually began to regain strength. The gross domestic product (GDP) picked up steam in late 1993 and hummed along through 1994. The annual deficits declined, and unemployment dropped from nearly eight percent to under five percent by early 1995. Many of the new jobs were relatively low-paying positions in the service sector, and pockets of severe unemployment and underemployment remained, especially in California and New England, where continuing defense budget cuts hit hard. But the manufacturing sector, by introducing modernized technology and new management techniques, reversed its decades-long decline and added muscle to the economic recovery, especially in the industrial Midwest. Remarkably, inflation stayed under control even as the economy heated up, though the cautious Federal Reserve Board steadily raised interest rates to guarantee that the inflation beast would stay chained down.

Clinton also sought to develop freer international trade. The keystone of his effort was the North American Free Trade Agreement (NAFTA), which would reduce trade barriers among the United States, Mexico, and Canada. Prodded by Clinton, as well as by NAFTA's original proponent, George Bush, Congress overrode anxious opposition from organized labor and Ross Perot to pass NAFTA in November 1993.

Political Trouble

With public opinion initially on his side, Clinton boldly proclaimed his determion to fix the nation's inefficient and fabulously expensive health-care system. In a daring and unprecedented step, he put his wife and political partner, Hillary Rodham Clinton, in charge of designing health-care reform. But the Clintons mistakenly relied on a task force of "experts" who took nearly a year to come up with a jerry-built
proposal involving bureaucratically cumbersome government-sponsored "health-care alliances." An easy target for attack by zealous Republicans and legions of lobbyists, the Clintons' plan died in Congress in October 1994 without even coming to a vote.

An aroma of scandal compounded Clinton's political woes. Several administration officials came under investigation for financial malfeasance, including agriculture secretary Mike Espy and housing secretary Henry Cisneros. Clinton's outspoken surgeon general, Joycelyn Elders, was forced to resign over controversial remarks about sex education. Worst of all, President Clinton was himself embroiled in charges of financial and sexual misbehavior, all dating from his days as governor of Arkansas.

Clinton's inexperience in foreign affairs and his lack of a military record also made him vulnerable to

CHRONOLOGY

1980	Reagan defeats Carter for presidency.
1981	Iran releases American hostages.
	"Reaganomics" spending and tax cuts passed.
	Sandra Day O'Connor appointed to Supreme Court.
1981–1988	United States aids antileftist forces in Central America.
1982	Recession hits U.S. economy.
1983	Russians shoot down Korean airliner.
	U.S.-Soviet arms-control talks break off.
	U.S. marines killed in Lebanon.
	U.S. invasion of Grenada.
1984	Reagan defeats Mondale for presidency.
1985	U.S.-Soviet arms-control talks resume.
	Mikhail Gorbachev comes to power in Soviet Union.
	First Reagan-Gorbachev summit meeting, in Geneva.
1986	Gramm-Rudman-Hollings Act.
	Iran-contra scandal revealed.
1987	508-point stock market crash.
	INF Treaty signed.
1988	Fourth Reagan-Gorbachev summit meeting, in Moscow.

	Bush defeats Dukakis for presidency.
1989	Supreme Court tightens affirmative-action rules and relaxes protection of abortion rights.
	Chinese government suppresses prodemocracy demonstrators.
	Eastern Europe throws off communist regimes.
	United States invades Panama to capture dictator–drug lord Manuel Noriega.
1990	Sandinistas voted out of power in Nicaragua.
	Iraq invades Kuwait.
	Five-year budget agreement passed.
	Americans with Disabilities Act (ADA).
1991	Persian Gulf War.
	U.S. economy enters recession.
	Soviet Union dissolves.
1992	Clinton defeats Bush for presidency.
1993	Congress pases NAFTA agreement.
1994	Republicans win control of Congress for first time in forty years.

critics. After U.S. troops on a relief mission to Somalia suffered casualties in October 1993, Clinton had them quickly withdrawn. As the grotesquely barbaric war in Bosnia dragged on, the Clinton administration found itself paralyzed, alternating between stern threats of U.S. action and a reluctance to become involved in the beleaguered United Nations effort in that country. Relations with the new Russia remained shakey, especially when Boris Yeltsin's government launched a brutal attack on the breakaway province of Chechnya in 1994. Political turmoil and economic collapse in Mexico in late 1994 forced emergency U.S. aid and raised questions about the promised benefits of NAFTA. Even Clinton's most successful foreign policy effort, the U.S.-sponsored restoration to power of Haiti's elected leader, Jean-Bertrand Aristide, earned the president little credit as an international leader.

Republicans Win Congress

Throughout Clinton's term, energetic Republican critics kept up a drumbeat of criticism that gradually began to take hold with the public. Aided by Clinton's own errors and their powerful new allies on the right-wing "talk radio" air waves, militant conservatives mounted an aggressive assault on the president and the "corrupt liberal Congress" as the 1994 midterm congressional elections approached.

In their boldest move, all Republican House candidates pledged if elected to enact swiftly the "Contract with America," a ten-point platform that promised congressional reforms, a balanced-budget amendment, and drastic reductions in the size and power of the federal government. The Republican gamble paid off spectacularly, as the GOP won a majority in the Senate and gained control of the House of Representatives for the first time in forty years.

Radiating confidence, the new Republican congressional majority marched into Washington in January 1995 determined to cut the federal government down to size and restore long-lost power to the states. Led by their loquacious speaker, Newt Gingrich of Georgia, the House Republicans rammed almost all of their "Contract with America" through the lower chamber in the first hundred days. The more deliberative and cautious Senate seemed inclined to slow Gingrich's legislative juggernaut. In March 1995 it defeated the balanced-budget amendment by one vote and began to take a harder look at the House's welfare and tax-cut proposals.

Meanwhile, President Clinton and the demoralized Democrats were reduced largely to the role of spectators in the national political arena. Some commentators saw in the 1994 election's outcome a final death knell for the era of political liberalism and "big government." A few even predicted the decline of the modern American presidency, powerfully sustained since the days of Franklin Roosevelt through Republican and Democratic administrations alike. Historians would exercise their customary role by waiting for further evidence to come in before drawing conclusions. But few doubted that the drama of American public life had taken another surprising turn.

Varying Viewpoints

The Reagan era is only beginning to receive scholarly scrutiny by historians, but debate has already crystallized around a central question: did Reagan's presidency mark a revolutionary departure from the half-century-long course of American political, economic, and social development that began with the New Deal? Pro-Reagan authors such as Martin Anderson claim that it did. They cite Reagan's achievements in slowing the growth of the federal government, reducing taxes, deregulating business, blunting affirmative action, and attacking abortion. Some writers of this persuasion also credit Reagan's assertive foreign policy with bringing about the end of the Cold War.

Critics of Reagan, among them Richard Reeves, counter that the Reagan era constituted a mere detour in the long-term advancement of liberal programs such as government economic regulation and the enlargement of welfare services. Only the passage of time will definitively settle this argument.

Many observers claim that in the long run history will award to Mikhail Gorbachev, not Ronald Reagan, top honors for ending the Cold War. It was the internal development of communist society itself, not the threat of American competition, they argue, that led to *glasnost* and *perestroika.* American policies may have accelerated the course of events in the communist bloc, they concede, but did not fundamentally cause them.

SELECT READINGS

Primary Source Documents

The debate over "Reaganomics" can be followed in Reagan's nationally televised address of July 27, 1981, *Weekly Compilation of Presidential Documents,* Vol. 17, no. 31,* and in the critical response of the *New York Times,* August 2, 1981.* See also the comments of Budget Director David Stockman, in William Greider, *The Education of David Stockman and Other Americans* (1982). On arms control, see the pastoral letter of the National Council of Catholic Bishops and the reply of Albert Wohlstetter in Charles Kegley and Eugene Wittkopf, eds., *The Nuclear Reader* (1985). On Central American policy, see Reagan's remarkable speech of March 16, 1986.* The inside workings of the Iran-contra scandal can be studied in *The Tower Commission Report* (1987).

Secondary Sources

Ronald Reagan is portrayed in Bill Boyarsky, *Reagan: His Life and Rise to the Presidency* (1981), Lou Cannon, *Reagan* (1982), Laurence Barrett, *Gambling with History* (1984), Fred Greenstein, *The Reagan Presidency* (1983), and Robert Dallek, *Ronald Reagan: The Politics of Symbolism* (1984). Reagan's economic policies are discussed in Paul C. Roberts, *The Supply-Side Revolution* (1984), and are sharply criticized in David A. Stockman, *The Triumph of Politics: Why the Reagan Revolution Failed* (1986). The debate over nuclear policy is covered in R. James Woolsey, *Nuclear Arms* (1984), Strobe Talbott, *The Russians and Reagan* (1984), and Charles Kegley and Eugene Wittkopf, eds., *The Nuclear Reader* (1985). The neoconservative movement is best elucidated by the writings of its leaders. See Norman Podhoretz, *Breaking Ranks* (1979), and Irving Kristol, *Reflections of a Neoconservative* (1983). For a critical view, consult Peter Steinfels, *The Neoconservatives*

(1979). Two studies of affirmative action are Allan P. Sindler, *Bakke, DeFinis and Minority Admissions* (1978), and J. Harvie Wilkinson, *From Brown to Bakke* (1979). A group of young Democrats offered a "neo-liberal" response to the neoconservative challenge. See Gary Hart, *A New Democracy* (1983), and Paul Tsongas, *The Road from Here* (1981). Kevin P. Phillips is insightful about the implications of the conservative revival in *Post-Conservative America* (1982). Useful books on the role of religion in modern politics include Robert Booth Fowler, *A New Engagement: Evangelical Political Thoughts, 1966–1976* (1982), Robert Wuthnow, *The New Christian Right* (1983) and *The Restructuring of American Religion* (1989), and Richard John Neuhaus, *The Naked Public Square: Religion and Democracy in America* (1984). Critical of Reagan are William Leuchtenburg, *In the Shadow of FDR: From Harry Truman to Ronald Reagan* (1983), Paul D. Erickson, *Reagan Speaks: The Making of an American Myth* (1985), Garry Wills, *Reagan's America: Innocents at Home* (1987), Ronnie Duggar, *On Reagan* (1983), June Mayer and Doyle McManus, *Landslide: The Unmaking of the President, 1984–88* (1988), and Richard Reeves, *The Reagan Detour* (1985). More balanced are two books by John L. Palmer, *The Reagan Record* (co-edited with Isabel V. Sawhill, 1984) and *Perspectives on the Reagan Years* (1986). Important topics in foreign policy are covered in Walter LaFeber, *Inevitable Revolutions* (2d ed., 1984), which discusses Central America; Robert Pastor's more probing study, *Condemned to Repetition: The United States and Nicaragua* (1987); and Bob Woodward, *Veil: The Secret Wars of the CIA* (1987). For Bill Clinton, see David Maraniss, *First in His Class: A Biography of Bill Clinton* (1995).

CHAPTER 43

The American People
Face a New Century

As our case is new, so we must think anew and act anew. We must disenthrall ourselves, and then we shall save our country.

Abraham Lincoln, 1862

The Weight of History

Two hundred years old in 1976, the United States was both an old and a new nation. It boasted one of the longest uninterrupted traditions of democratic government of any country on earth. Indeed, it had pioneered the techniques of mass democracy and was, in that sense, the oldest modern polity. As one of the earliest countries to industrialize, America had also dwelled in the modern economic era longer than most nations.

But the republic was in many ways still youthful as well. American society continued to be rejuvenated by fresh waves of immigrants, full of energy and ambition. The economy, despite problems, generated new jobs in the 1980s and 1990s at a rate of nearly 2 million per year. Innovation, entrepreneurship, and risk taking—all characteristics of youth—were honored national values. The whole world seemed to worship the icons of American youth culture—downing soft drinks and donning blue jeans, listening to rock or country-and-western music, even adapting indigenous sports such as baseball and bas-

ketball. In the realm of consumerism, American products seemed to have Coca-Colonized the globe.

The history of American society also seemed to have special global significance as the third millennium of the Christian era approached. Americans were a pluralistic people who had struggled for centuries to achieve tolerance and justice for many different religious, ethnic, and racial groups. Their historical experience could offer valuable lessons to the rapidly internationalizing planetary society that was emerging in the late twentieth century.

In politics, economics, and culture, the great social experiment of democracy was far from completed as the United States faced its future. Much history remained to be made as the country entered its third century of nationhood. But men and women make history only within the framework bequeathed to them by earlier generations. For better or worse, they march forward along time's path bearing the burdens of the past. Knowing when they have come to a truly new turn in the road, when they can lay part of their burden down, and when they cannot, or should not—all this constitutes the kind of wisdom that only historical study can provide.

New Economic Patterns

The changing character of the economy at the century's end exemplified the sometimes dazzling rapidity of movement in modern American society. As early as 1956, white-collar workers had outnumbered blue-collar workers, marking the passage from an industrial to a postindustrial era. In the following decades, employment in the older manufacturing industries increased only modestly and by the 1970s was even decreasing in depressed "smokestack" industries such as steel. The fastest-growing employment opportunities were in the service sector—notably information processing, medical care, communications, teaching, merchandising, and finance. Growing especially lustily was government, which, despite Reagan-era cutbacks, employed about one in seven working Americans in the 1990s.

White-collar workers constituted some 80 percent of the workforce in the 1990s. They proved far less inclined to join labor unions than their blue-collar cousins, and by 1990 only about 16 percent of workers were unionized, down from a high point of nearly 35 percent in the 1950s. Organized labor withered along with the smokestack industries in which it had flourished.

America's economic well-being in the new century would depend as never before on harnessing scientific knowledge. High-technology industries such as aerospace, biological engineering, and especially electronics defined the business frontier. From its crude beginnings with Germany's "V-2" rockets at the end of World War II, rocketry had advanced to place astronauts on the moon in the 1960s and produce a reusable space shuttle in the 1980s, and inspire talk of a man landing on Mars in the next century. But the breakthroughs had also equipped the United States and the Soviet Union with bristling arsenals of intercontinental nuclear weapons.

When scientists unlocked the secrets of molecular genetic structure in the 1950s, the road lay open to breeding new strains of high-yield, bug- and weather-resistant crops and to curing hereditary diseases. As technical mastery of biological and medical

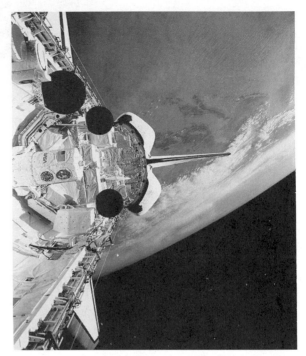

Earth Viewed from Space, 1992   *Although not as active as it was during the 1960s, the U.S. space program continues to perform valuable scientific experiments and to obtain distant observations of Earth. Orbiting equipment of the Atmospheric Laboratory for Applications and Science is shown here above the Sahara Desert and the Atlas Mountains of northern Africa.*

techniques advanced, unprecedented ethical questions emerged. Should the human gene pool itself be "engineered"? What principles should govern the allocation of human organs for lifesaving transplants, or of scarce dialysis machines, or of artificial hearts? Was it wise in the first place to spend money on such costly devices rather than devoting society's resources to improved sanitation, maternal and infant care, and nutritional and health education? Who was the rightful parent of a child born to a "surrogate mother" or conceived by artificial insemination?

The invention of the transistor in 1948 touched off a revolution in electronics, especially in computers. This revolution was less ethically vexing than the upheaval in biology, but it had profound social and economic consequences. Transistors and, later, printed circuits on silicon wafers made possible dramatic miniaturization and phenomenal computational speed. By the 1990s an inexpensive calculator contained more computer power than the room-size early models. Computers utterly transformed age-old business practices such as billing and inventory control, and opened new frontiers in areas such as airline scheduling, high-speed printing, telecommunications, and space navigation—not to mention complex military weapons systems such as Ronald Reagan's Strategic Defense Initiative (SDI).

United States Steel Corporation, formed in 1901, had been the flagship company of America's early-twentieth-century industrial revolution, which emphasized heavy industry and the building of the nation's economic infrastructure. Companies that could efficiently produce the basic building blocks of an industrial civilization reaped the greatest rewards. In turn, General Motors was the leading firm in the shift to the economy of mass consumerism that first appeared in the 1920s and flourished in the 1950s. In this phase of economic development, success depended on the high-volume production of inexpensive, standardized consumer products. In the postindustrial economic order emerging by the 1970s, the awesome rise of International Business Machines (IBM) symbolized yet another shift. The computer's capacity to store, manipulate, and communicate vast quantities of data heralded the birth of the "information age."

In the century's last decade, even IBM showed signs of obsolescence. The electronics revolution accelerated fantastically in the information age, spawning hundreds of relatively small firms such as Apple, Intel, Microsoft, and Sun Microsystems. These nimble newcomers outmaneuvered and outcompeted the lumbering, bureaucracy-bound IBM in the information and telecommunications marketplace. Some observers suggested that lean, entrepreneurial companies would eventually dominate the economic landscape by better adapting to the dizzying pace of technological change.

The United States in the New International Economy

The information age is also the international age. Computerized telecommunication technology threatened the old dominance of New York and London in international finance and created a global network

of capital flows with powerful centers in Tokyo, Hong Kong, and other new concentrations of monetary muscle. In the blink of an eye, businesspeople could girdle the planet with transactions of prodigious complexity. Japanese bankers might sell wheat contracts in Chicago and instantly direct the profits to buying oil shipments from the Persian Gulf offered by a broker in Holland.

With some reluctance, the United States dove headlong into this newly internationalized economy. When OPEC quadrupled the price of oil in 1974 and tripled it again in 1979, an era ended. Americans could no longer count on an ever-expanding stream of cheap, plentiful energy to fuel their economic growth. Neither could the United States ever again seriously consider a policy of economic isolation, as it had tried to do in the decades between the two world wars. For most of its history, America's foreign trade had accounted for less than 10 percent of the gross national product (GNP). But driven by the necessity to pay for huge foreign oil bills, that figure rose rapidly in the 1970s, until by 1990 some 27 percent of the GNP depended on foreign trade. In turn, the nation's new economic interdependence meant that the United States could not dominate international trade and financial arrangements as easily as it could in the immediate post–World War II decades. In the new century, international leadership will have

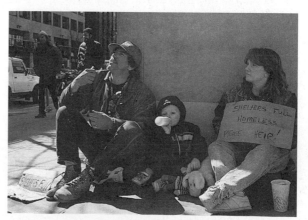

A Homeless Family in Washington, D.C. *Despite many efforts by public and private agencies to provide housing and shelter for the poor, the problems of homelessness remained severe in America's major cities in the 1990s.*

to give way to international partnership. And Americans, once happily insulated behind their ocean moats, will now have to master foreign languages and learn more about foreign cultures if they want to prosper in the twenty-first century.

The United States remained the largest national economy in the world in the early 1990s. Still, Japan showed few signs of slowing its own fantastic economic growth, and the integration of the European Community in 1992 created a powerful rival.

Americans were still prosperous in the century's last decade. Median family income stood near $33,000. Even those Americans with incomes below the government's official poverty level enjoyed a standard of living higher than that of two-thirds of the rest of humankind. But Americans were no longer the world's wealthiest people, as they had been in the years right after World War II. Citizens of several other countries enjoyed higher average per capita incomes, and many nations boasted more equitable distributions of wealth. The richest 20 percent of Americans in the 1990s still raked in nearly half the nation's income, whereas the poorest 20 percent received about 5 percent. Somewhat surprisingly, that disparity had changed little over the course of the century, despite New Deal and Great Society reforms and the supposedly leveling influence of the income tax. The gap between rich and poor even widened somewhat in the 1980s. In 1989 the median family income for Hispanics was 35 percent below that for whites. African-Americans fared more poorly still, earning some 44 percent less than their white counterparts. Thirty-two million Americans remained mired in poverty—a depressing indictment of the inequalities still afflicting an affluent and allegedly egalitarian republic.

The Feminist Revolution

All Americans were caught up in the great economic changes of the late twentieth century, but no group was more profoundly affected than women. When the century had opened, women made up about 20 percent of all workers. Over the next five decades they increased their presence in the labor force at a fairly steady rate, except for a temporary spurt during World War II. Then, beginning in the 1950s, women's entry into the workplace accelerated dramatically. By 1990 nearly half of all workers were women, and the majority of working-age women held jobs outside the home. Most astonishing was the upsurge in employment of mothers. In 1950, 90 percent of mothers with children under the age of six did not work for pay. But by the 1990s, a majority of women with children as young as one year old were wage earners.

What underlay this epochal change? Much of the explanation was to be found in the shifting composition of the American economy. Of some 40 million new jobs created in the three decades after 1950, more than 30 million were in the service sector. Women filled most of those positions and in the process became the principal employment beneficia-

"WELL, IT'S ABOUT TIME"

The Justice Is a Lady *This cartoon hails Sandra Day O'Connor's appointment to the Supreme Court in 1981.*

ries of the emerging postindustrial era. Higher wages relative to the value of time spent at home also increased the attractiveness of work.

Exploding employment opportunities for women unleashed a ground swell of social and psychological transformations that mounted to tidal-wave proportions as the century lengthened. Feminist Betty Friedan gave focus and fire to women's feelings and launched the modern women's movement in 1963 when she published *The Feminine Mystique,* a runaway best-seller and a classic of feminist protest literature. She spoke in rousing accents to millions of able, educated women who applauded her indictment of the stifling boredom of suburban housewifery. Many of those women were already working for wages, but they struggled against the guilt and frustration of leading an "unfeminine" life as defined by the postwar "cult of domesticity."

Feminists now complained that they had to bring home the bacon and then cook it too. They protested against gender segregation, overturning many barriers that guarded historic citadels of masculinity. Numerous all-male strongholds, including Yale, Princeton, West Point, Annapolis, and the Air Force Academy, yielded to the forces of feminism. Soon women were flying airplanes and orbiting in

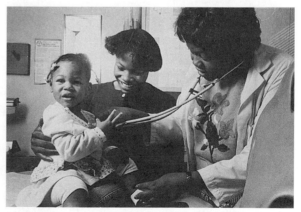

Women's World: Something Old, Something New   *By the 1990s, revolutionary changes in the economy and in social values had opened new career possibilities to women—from military officer to medical doctor—while not fully emancipating them from their traditional duties as mothers and homemakers.*

outer space. They governed states and cities, wrote Supreme Court decisions, and sat in both houses of Congress.

Despite ridicule from "male chauvinists," the women's cause made notable headway. Forward-looking feminists founded the National Organization for Women (NOW) in 1966 as a kind of civil rights advocacy group for women. In its Title VII, the Civil Rights Act of 1964 prohibited sexual discrimination by employers. Lyndon Johnson's executive order on affirmative action in 1965 proved as useful to women as it did to blacks and other minorities. Soon several corporations, including giant American Telephone and Telegraph (AT&T), were forced to provide back wages to female employees who had not been receiving equal pay for equal work, and to abolish hiring and promotion practices that discriminated against women.

Despite such legal victories, many feminists remained frustrated. Women continued to receive lower wages than men in corresponding jobs, and they tended to concentrate in a few low-skill, low-prestige, low-paying occupations (the "pink-collar ghetto"). Although they made up more than half the population, women in 1992 accounted for only 22 percent of lawyers and judges (up from 5 percent in 1970) and 18 percent of physicians (up from 10 percent in 1970). Overt sexual discrimination explained some of this occupational segregation, but most of it seemed attributable to the greater burdens of parenthood on women than on men. Women were far more likely than men to interrupt their careers to bear and raise children, and even to choose less demanding career paths to allow for fulfilling those traditional roles. Employers increasingly had to provide day-care and other child-support services for women workers, and Congress considered legislation to aid working mothers.

As the feminist revolution surged in the 1990s, it touched men's lives as well as women's. Some employers provided paternity leave in addition to maternity leave, recognition of the shared burdens of the two-worker household. Traditional female responsibilities such as cooking, laundry, and child care were increasingly regarded as men's tasks. Recognizing the new realities of the modern American household, Congress passed a Family Leave Bill in

Percentage of Working Married Women with Children (Husband Present), 1948–1989

Year	Total Percentage	No Children Under 18	Children 6–17 Only	Children Under 6
1948	22.0	28.4	26.0	10.8
1950	23.8	30.3	28.3	11.9
1955	27.7	32.7	34.7	16.2
1960	30.5	34.7	39.0	18.6
1965	34.7	38.3	42.7	23.3
1970	40.8	42.2	49.2	30.3
1980	50.1	46.0	61.7	45.1
1984	52.8	47.1	65.4	51.8
1989	57.8	50.5	72.5	58.4

1993, mandating support for working mothers as well as fathers.

The Fading Family

The nuclear family, once prized as the foundation of society and nursery of the republic, suffered heavy blows in postwar America. Divorce rates doubled in the decade after 1965, and by the 1990s one out of every two marriages ended in divorce. Seven times more children were affected by divorce than at the turn of the century, and kids who commuted between separated parents were becoming commonplace.

Traditional families were not only falling apart at an alarming rate but also increasingly slow to form in the first place. The proportion of adults living alone tripled in the three decades after 1950, and by 1990 nearly one-third of women age twenty-five to twenty-nine had never been married. In 1960, 5 percent of all births were to unmarried women, but by 1990 one out of six white babies, one out of three Hispanic babies, and an astounding two out of three African-American babies were born to single mothers. Every fourth child in America was growing up in a household that lacked two parents. Some critics claimed that this collapse of the traditional family was a deeper cause of poverty than any shortcomings in the economic or the political system.

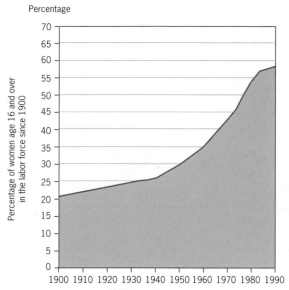

Percentage

Percentage of women age 16 and over in the labor force since 1900

Women in the Labor Force, 1900–1990

Born and raised without the family support enjoyed by their forebears, Americans were also increasingly likely to be lonely in their later years. Most elderly people in the 1990s depended on government Social Security payments, not on their loved ones, for their daily bread. The great majority of them drew their last breaths not in their own homes but in hospitals and nursing facilities. From youth to old age, the role of the family was dwindling.

Americans were living longer than ever before. A person born at the dawn of the century could expect to survive fewer than fifty years, but a white male born in the 1990s could anticipate a life span of more than seventy-two years. His white female counterpart would probably outlive him by seven years. (The figures were slightly lower for non-whites, reflecting differences in living standards, especially diet and health care.) The census of 1950 recorded that women for the first time made up a majority of Americans, thanks largely to greater female longevity. Miraculous medical advances lengthened and strengthened lives. Noteworthy were the development of antibiotics after 1940 and Dr. Jonas Salk's discovery in 1953 of a vaccine against a dreaded crippler, polio.

Longer lives spelled more older people. One American in nine was over sixty-five years of age in the 1990s, and projections were that one of every six

Child rearing, the family's foremost function, was being increasingly assigned to "parent-substitutes" at day-care centers or schools—or to television, the modern age's "electronic babysitter." Estimates were that the average child by age sixteen had watched up to 15,000 hours of TV—more time than was spent in the classroom.

Senior Power *"Senior citizens" coalesced into one of America's most politically powerful interest groups in the last decades of the twentieth century. In 1989 they successfully induced Congress to repeal a program that required the elderly to pay a share of the insurance costs for treatment of catastrophic illnesses.*

Government Expenditures for Social Welfare, 1930–1990 *"Social welfare" includes unemployment and old-age insurance, medical insurance, and veterans' benefits. The skyrocketing costs from the mid-1960s onward reflect the increasing size (and political clout) of the elderly population, who were the main beneficiaries of Great Society programs such as Medicare.*

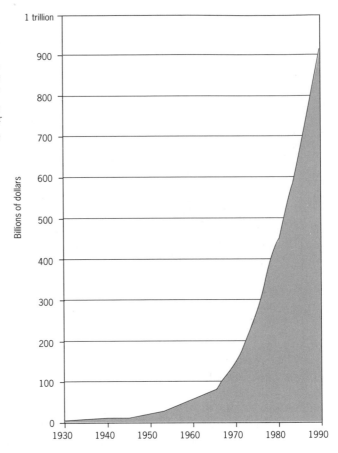

would be in the "sunset years" by 2030, as the median age rose toward forty. This aging of the population raised a host of political, social, and economic questions. Elderly people formed a potent electoral bloc that successfully lobbied for government favors. In 1977 the "wrinkled radicals" scored a major victory when the California legislature abolished mandatory retirement at age sixty-five, and the following year the federal Congress passed similar legislation.

These triumphs for senior citizens symbolized the fading of the youth culture that had colored the American scene in the first three post–World War II decades. Medical gains also brought fiscal strains, especially in the Social Security system, established in 1935 to provide income for retired workers. When Social Security began, most of the labor force continued to work after age sixty-five. By century's end,

only 20 percent did, and a majority of the elderly population relied exclusively on Social Security checks for their living expenses. Benefits had risen so high, and the ratio of active workers to retirees had dropped so low, that drastic adjustments were necessary. The problem was intensified in the 1970s, when a compassionate Congress dramatically increased retirement benefits at a time when productivity growth was stalled.

Without greater productivity, larger payments to retirees could only mean smaller paychecks for workers. Three-quarters of all employees in the 1990s paid higher Social Security taxes than income taxes (an individual paid a maximum of $5,238 in Social Security taxes in 1992).

Thanks to the political clout of the elderly, the share of the GNP spent on health care for people over sixty-five almost doubled in the twenty years after the enactment of Medicare legislation in 1965. This growth in medical payments for the old far outstripped the growth of educational expenditures for the young. A war between the generations loomed, as the ratio of workers to retirees fell to about 2 to 1 by the end of the century. Extending the working lifetime of the still-active elderly was one way of averting the crisis.

The New Immigration

Newcomers flooded into modern America. They washed ashore in waves that swelled in size after the Immigration and Nationality Act of 1965 had abolished the old quota system based on national origins (see p. 479). The new law made it easier for entire families to migrate and established special categories for political refugees. The result was a massive surge in immigration, which averaged over half a million legal entrants a year in the 1970s and 1980s. Probably an even larger number of "undocumented" migrants annually slipped across the U.S. border, and they may have added up to an astonishing 8 million people by 1985, prompting calls for restrictive legislation. In 1994 California voters passed a highly controversial measure, Proposition 187, designed to deny medical, welfare, and educational benefits to illegal immigrants. Legal and undocumented entrants together accounted for the heaviest inflow of immigrants in America's experience. In striking contrast to the historic pattern of immigration, Europe contributed far fewer people than did the teeming countries of Asia and Latin America, especially Mexico.

What prompted this new flocking to America? The truth is that the newest immigrants came for

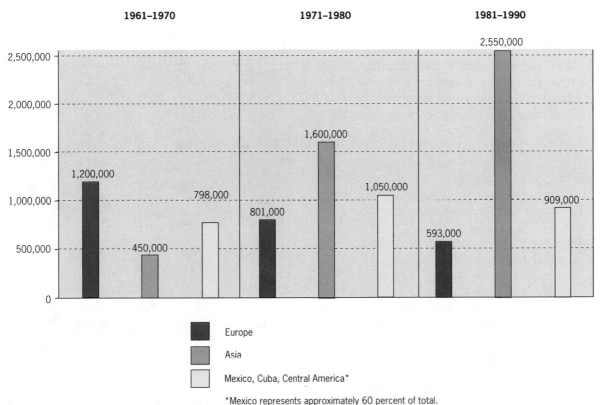

1961–1970   **1971–1980**   **1981–1990**

Legend:
- Europe
- Asia
- Mexico, Cuba, Central America*

*Mexico represents approximately 60 percent of total.

Recent Immigration by Area of Origin, 1961–1990

many of the same reasons as the old. They typically left countries where populations were growing rapidly and where agricultural and industrial revolutions were shaking people loose from old habits of life—conditions almost identical to those in nineteenth-century Europe. They came to America, as previous immigrants had done, in search of jobs and economic opportunity.

The Southwest, from Texas to California, felt the immigrant impact especially sharply, as Mexican migrants concentrated heavily in that region. In 1990 Hispanics made up 25 percent of the population in Texas, Arizona, and California and almost 40 percent in New Mexico—amounting to a demographic *reconquista* of the lands lost by Mexico in the war of 1846.

The size and geographic concentration of the Hispanic population in the Southwest had few precedents in the history of American immigration. Most previous groups had been so thinly scattered across the land that they had little choice but to learn English and make their way in the larger U.S. society, however much they might have longed to preserve their native language and customs. But Hispanic-Americans might succeed in creating a truly bicultural zone in the booming southwestern states. Many of them have championed bilingual education and stayed in close cultural contact with their native country south of the border.

Old-stock Americans worried about the capacity of the modern United States to absorb this new immigrant mass. Yet foreign-born persons accounted for less than 10 percent of the nation's population in the 1990s—a far smaller proportion than the historical high point of 15 percent recorded in the census of 1910. Somewhat inconsistently, critics charged both that illegal immigrants robbed citizens of jobs and that they dumped themselves on the welfare rolls at the taxpayers' expense. In fact, studies showed that immigrants took jobs scorned by Americans and that they paid many times more dollars in taxes (withholding and Social Security taxes, as well as sales taxes) than they claimed for welfare payments. The real worry was that unscrupulous employers could take cruel advantage of undocumented workers, who were without recourse to legal protection. The Immigration Reform and Control Act of 1986 attempted to choke off illegal entry by penalizing employers of undocumented aliens and by granting amnesty to many of those already here.

Ethnic Pride

Thanks both to continued immigration and to their own high birthrate, Hispanic-Americans were becoming an increasingly important minority (see "Makers of America: The Latinos," pp. 664–665). The census of 1990 counted about 22 million Hispanics. They included some 12 million Chicanos, or Mexican-Americans, mostly in the Southwest, as well as more than 2 million Puerto Ricans, chiefly in the Northeast, and about 1 million Cubans in Florida.

Chicana Pride *A Mexican-American girl celebrates her cultural heritage at the Texas Folklife Festival in San Antonio.*

Flexing their political muscles, Hispanics elected mayors of Miami, Denver, and San Antonio. After years of struggle, the United Farmworkers Organizing Committee (UFWOC), headed by soft-spoken and charismatic César Chávez, succeeded in improving working conditions for the mostly Chicano "stoop laborers" who followed the cycle of planting and harvesting across the American West. Hispanic influence seemed likely to grow, as suggested by the increasing presence of Spanish-language ballots and television broadcasts. Hispanic-Americans, newly confident and organized, might well become the nation's largest ethnic minority, outnumbering even African-Americans, by the turn of the century.

Other ethnic groups also grew more conscious of their unique identity in postwar America. The fire under the melting pot seemed to flicker out in the 1960s. Descendants of European immigrants, long thought to have been fused into the national amalgam, began to assert their unalloyed separateness. Ethnic stereotyping became a hazardous occupation, and dialect jokes fell into malodorous disrepute.

Asian-Americans made giant strides in the post–World War II era. By the 1980s, they were America's fastest-growing minority. Their numbers nearly doubled in that decade alone, thanks to heavy immigration. Once feared and hated as the "yellow peril" and consigned to the most menial and degrading jobs, citizens of Japanese and Chinese ancestry were now counted among the most prosperous of Americans. Even by 1970 Japanese family income stood at 32 percent, and Chinese family income at 12 percent, *above* the national average.

Indians, the original Americans, shared in the general awakening of "cultural nationalism." The 1990 census counted some 1.5 million Native Americans, half of whom had left their reservations to live in cities. Meanwhile, unemployment and alcoholism had blighted reservation life.

Militant members of the American Indian Movement (AIM) seized the Indian Bureau in Washington in 1972. The next year heavily armed Indians occupied the ghost-haunted village of Wounded Knee, South Dakota (see p. 400), and held it for two months amid national publicity. Lawyers replaced warriors as various tribes sought, with some success, to regain long-lost fishing rights or to secure multi-million-dollar payments for land "stolen" by whites.

The Urban Jungle

The "alabaster cities" of song and story grew more sooty and less safe in the closing decades of the century. Polluted air and crime in the streets were among the curses of urban life. The rate of violent crimes committed in cities increased threefold in the 1960s and reached an all-time high in the drug-infested 1980s. Statistically, murder victims in 1991 fell at the rate of one every 21 minutes; burglaries occurred every 10 seconds; 4 cars were stolen every minute; every 5 minutes a woman was raped. By 1990, America imprisoned a larger fraction of its citizens than any country in the world. Frightened urbanites cowered like nightly prisoners in their locked and bolted apartments. When New Yorker Bernhard Goetz, on December 22, 1984, gunned down four black youths who allegedly tried to mug him in a subway, he became a folk hero, and a court later exonerated him of assault charges.

Racial and ethnic tensions exacerbated the problems of American cities. These stresses were especially evident in Los Angeles, which, like New York a century earlier, was a magnet for immigrants, mostly from Asia and Latin America. When in 1992 a mostly white jury exonerated white Los Angeles police officers of beating a black suspect, the ethnic neighborhoods of South Central Los Angeles erupted in rage. Arson and looting laid waste to entire city blocks, scores of people were killed, and many local Asian shopkeepers were attacked.

Feeding the urban violence was a seemingly endless epidemic of drug addiction. The 1960s witnessed the addition of marijuana, LSD, and other hallucinogens to the traditional substances, such as alcohol and heroin, that many Americans had long abused. Cocaine became the intoxicant of choice among affluent users in the 1970s. By the 1980s "crack," derived from cocaine, raced like a plague through the nation's inner cities.

American cities had always held an astonishing variety of ethnic and racial groups, but in the late twentieth century, minorities made up a majority of the population of many American cities, as whites

The Latinos

Today Mexican food is handed through fast-food drive-up windows in all fifty states, Spanish-language broadcasts fill the airwaves, and the Latino community has its own telephone book, the *Spanish Yellow Pages.* Latinos send representatives to Congress and mayors to city hall, record hit songs, paint murals, and teach history. Hispanic-Americans, among the fastest-growing segments of the United States population, include Puerto Ricans, frequent voyagers between their native island and northeastern cities; Cubans, many of them refugees from the communist dictatorship of Fidel Castro, concentrated in Miami and southern Florida; and Central Americans, fleeing the ravages of civil war in Nicaragua and El Salvador.

But the most populous group of Latinos derives from Mexico. The first significant numbers of Mexicans began heading for *el Norte* (the North) around 1910, when the upheavals of the Mexican Revolution stirred and shuffled the population into more or less constant flux. Their northward passage was briefly interrupted during the Great Depression, when thousands of Mexican nationals were deported. But immigration resumed during World War II, and since then a steady flow of legal immigrants has passed through border checkpoints, joined by countless millions of their undocumented countrymen and countrywomen stealing across the frontier on moonless nights.

For the most part, these Mexicans came to work in the fields, following the ripening crops northward through the summer and autumn. Others gathered in the cities of the Southwest—El Paso, Los Angeles, Houston, and San Bernardino. There they found regular work, even if racial discrimination often confined them to manual labor. Houses may have been shabby in the *barrios,* but these Mexican neighbor-

Cuban Refugees Arriving in the United States, 1980
These Cuban exiles arrived in Key West in crowded shrimp boats that carried hundreds of other refugees at the same time.

hoods provided a sense of togetherness, a place to raise a family, and the chance to join a mutual aid society. Such societies, or *Mutualistas,* sponsored baseball leagues, helped the sick and disabled, and defended their members against discrimination.

Mexican immigrants lived so close to the border that their native country acted like a powerful magnet, drawing them back time and time again. Mexicans frequently returned to see relatives, and relatively few became U.S. citizens. In addition, the Mexican government sometimes intervened to discourage Mexicans from becoming citizens of their adopted country by promoting Mexicanization programs among the immigrants, including parades to celebrate *Cinco de Mayo* (Fifth of May), Mexican independence day. Since World War II, this American-born second generation has carried on the fight

for political representation, economic opportunity, and cultural autonomy.

Fresh arrivals from Mexico and from other Latin American nations daily swell the Hispanic communities across America. As the United States heads toward the twenty-first century, it is taking on a pronounced Spanish accent.

---

fled to the suburbs. More than three-fourths of African-Americans lived in cities by the 1990s, whereas only about one-fourth of whites did. The most desperate black ghettos, housing a seething "underclass" in the inner core of the old industrial cities, were especially problematic. Successful blacks who had benefited from the civil rights revolution of the 1950s and 1960s followed whites to the suburbs, leaving a residue in the old ghetto of the poorest poor. Without a middle class to sustain community institutions such as schools, the inner cities seemed bereft of leadership, cohesion, resources, and hope.

In Black America

The desperate poor in America's inner cities represented a sorry—and dangerous—social failure that eluded any known remedy. But other segments of the African-American community had clearly prospered in the wake of the civil rights gains of the 1950s and 1960s, though they still had a long hill to climb before reaching full equality. Perhaps a third of blacks were now counted in the middle class. The number of black elected officials had risen almost to the 7,500 mark by 1995, including more than 1,200 in the Old South, some three dozen members of Congress, and the mayors of Detroit, Philadelphia, Washington, Cleveland, Birmingham, Oakland, Kansas City, and Seattle. Voting tallies in many of these cities demonstrated that successful black politicians were moving beyond isolated racial constituencies

and into the political mainstream by appealing to a wide variety of voters. In 1989 Virginians, only 15 percent of whom were black, chose L. Douglas Wilder as the first African-American elected to serve as a state governor.

By 1970 the black-white income gap had noticeably narrowed, as black families earned on the average about 64 percent of the income of their white counterparts. But black economic gains had flowed in large part from general prosperity rather than from any basic redistribution of the nation's wealth or the permanent eradication of racism. When the economy faltered in the 1970s, the gap began to widen again. Blacks once more suffered from the age-old stigma of being "the last hired and the first fired." African-American unemployment in the 1990s was nearly triple that of whites, and among black teenagers more than one in three found it almost impossible to land any kind of job.

Single women headed over half of black families, or almost three times the rate for whites. Understandably, a majority of these husbandless and jobless women depended on welfare to feed their children. As social scientists increasingly emphasized the importance of the home environment for success in school, it became clear that many fatherless, impoverished African-American children continued to suffer from educational handicaps that were difficult to overcome. Black youths in the 1990s still had about one year less schooling than whites of the same age and were less than half as likely to earn college degrees.

White Backlash   *"Soiling of Old Glory."* Anti-busing *demonstration in Boston, April 1976.*

Education remained the principal fighting front for African-Americans still struggling for their share of the American dream, and the North was soon transformed into the main educational battleground. There segregated schools often resulted not from overt discrimination but from segregated neighborhoods. Many white parents had moved to the suburbs to ensure better schools for their children. Now they felt deeply threatened by court-ordered busing that seemed to deprive them unfairly of their hard-bought advantages. Violent confrontations shook cities such as Boston in the 1970s, when school officials tried to achieve racial balance by busing. A new wave of "white flight" swept many metropolitan areas, as families fled not just to more distant suburbs but to private schools. In some northern cities, the public school system was being virtually abandoned to black pupils.

The Life of the Mind

Despite the mind-sapping chatter of the "boob tube," Americans in the late twentieth century were better educated than ever before. The GI Bill of Rights paid the college fees of millions of veterans in the 1940s and 1950s, thus stimulating a vast expansion of higher education. By the 1990s colleges were awarding nearly a million degrees a year, and one person in four in the twenty-five to thirty-four-year-old age group was a college graduate.

This expanding mass of educated people lifted the economy to more advanced levels while creating consumers for "high culture." Americans annually made some 300 million visits to museums in the 1990s and boasted about 1,000 opera companies and 1,500 symphony orchestras. Despite television, people bought books in record numbers, especially after the "paperback explosion" of the 1960s, when more than a million volumes a day were being sold.

In a reaction against 1960s liberalism, there emerged in the 1970s a small but influential group of intellectuals known as "neoconservatives." Their ranks included Norman Podhoretz, editor of *Commentary* magazine, and Irving Kristol, editor of the *Public Interest.* Neoconservatives championed free-market capitalism liberated from government restraints, and they tended to take a tough stance on foreign policy. They also questioned liberal welfare programs and affirmative-action policies and called for a reaffirmation of traditional values of individualism and the centrality of the family. The neoconservatives' hour seemed to have arrived with the election of Ronald Reagan in 1980.

In fiction writing, some of the pre–World War II realists continued to ply their trade, notably Ernest Hemingway in *The Old Man and the Sea* (1952). A Nobel laureate in 1954, Hemingway was dead by his own duck gun in 1961. John Steinbeck, another prewar writer who produced graphic portrayals of American society, received the Nobel Prize for literature in 1962, the seventh American to be so honored.

Brutal realism also characterized the earliest novels that portrayed soldierly life in World War II, such as Norman Mailer's *The Naked and the Dead* (1948) and James Jones's *From Here to Eternity* (1951). But as time passed, realistic writing fell from favor. Authors tended increasingly to write of the war and other topics in fantastic and even psychedelic prose. Joseph Heller's *Catch-22* (1961) dealt with the improbable antics and anguish of American airmen in the wartime Mediterranean. A savage satire, it made readers hurt when they laughed. The supercharged imagination of Kurt Vonnegut, Jr., poured forth works of puzzling complexity in sometimes impenetrably inventive prose.

Pennsylvania-born John Updike described the white middle class at bay in books such as *Rabbit Run* (1960) and *Couples* (1968), as did Massachusetts-bred John Cheever in *The Wapshot Chronicle* (1957) and *The Wapshot Scandal* (1964). Louis Auchincloss wrote elegantly of upper-class New Yorkers. Gore Vidal contributed a series of intriguing historical novels as well as several impish and always iconoclastic works, including *Myra Breckenridge* (1968), about a reincarnated transsexual. Together, these writers constituted the rear guard of an older, WASP* elite that had long dominated American writing.

Writers on the Margin

The most striking development in postwar American letters was the rise of younger authors, many of whom represented the "marginal" regions and ethnic groups now coming into their own. William Kennedy nostalgically evoked the urban past in a series of novels about his native Albany, New York. Larry McMurtry wrote about the small-town West, and lovingly recollected the end of the cattle-drive era in *Lonesome Dove* (1985). Tom Wolfe turned from journalism to fiction with a wicked satire on modern New York, *The Bonfire of the Vanities* (1987). Raymond Carver wrote understated and powerful stories about working-class life in the Northwest. Annie Dillard, Ivan Doig, and Jim Harrison re-created the gritty frontier history of that same verdant region. Wallace Stegner, the acknowledged dean of western writers, continued to produce works that far transcended their regional themes. Norman MacLean, a former English professor, left two unforgettable accounts of his boyhood in Montana: *A River Runs Through It* (1976) and *Young Men and Fire* (1992). The South boasted a literary renaissance led by veteran Mississippi author William Faulkner, who was a Nobel Prize recipient in 1950. Fellow Mississippians Walker Percy and Eudora Welty grasped the falling torch from the falling Faulkner, who died in 1962. Tennessean Robert Penn Warren immortalized Louisiana politico Huey Long in *All the King's Men* (1946). Flannery O'Connor wrote

perceptively of her native Georgia, and Virginian William Styron confronted the harsh history of his home state in a controversial fictional representation of an 1831 slave rebellion, *The Confessions of Nat Turner* (1967).

Books by black authors also made the best-seller lists, beginning with Richard Wright's chilling portrait of a black Chicago killer in *Native Son* (1940). Ralph Ellison depicted the black person's quest for personal identity in *Invisible Man* (1952), one of the most moving novels of the postwar era. James Baldwin won plaudits as a novelist and essayist, particularly for his sensitive reflections on the racial question in *The Fire Next Time* (1963). Black nationalist LeRoi Jones, who changed his name to Imamu Armiri Baraka, crafted powerful plays such as *Dutchman* (1964). Playwright August Wilson retold the history of African-Americans in the twentieth century, with special emphasis on the psychic costs of the northward migration (*Fences,* 1986; *Joe Turner's Come and Gone,* 1988). Toni Morrison, in novels such as *Beloved* (1987), gave fictional voice to the experience of black women. Native Americans, too, achieved literacy recognition. Kiowa author N. Scott Momaday won a Pulitzer Prize for his portrayal of Indian life in *House Made of Dawn* (1968). James Welch wrote movingly about his Blackfoot ancestors in *Fools Crow* (1986).

Asian-American authors also flourished, among them playwright David Hwang and essayist Maxine Hong Kingston, whose *China Men* (1980) imaginatively reconstructed the obscure lives of the earliest Chinese immigrants. Amy Tan's *The Joy Luck Club* (1989) explored the sometimes painful relationship between immigrant Chinese parents and their Asian-American children.

Women writers and women's themes forged to the fictional forefront as the feminist movement advanced. Californian Joan Didion explored the empty despair of contemporary life in works like *Play It as It Lays* (1970); and Joyce Carol Oates, in a series of novels, grotesquely portrayed the pervasive violence that afflicts modern America. The rising interest in feminist and African-American themes revived the popularity of a 1930s writer, Zora Neale Hurston, who is known especially for her naturalistic novel *Their Eyes Were Watching God,* first published in 1937.

---

*White Anglo-Saxon Protestant.

Especially bountiful was the outpouring of books by Jewish novelists. Some critics quipped that a knowledge of Yiddish was becoming necessary to understand much of the dialogue in American novels. J. D. Salinger painted an unforgettable portrait of a sensitive, upper-class, Anglo-Saxon adolescent in *Catcher in the Rye* (1951), but other Jewish writers found their favorite subject matter in the experience of lower- and middle-class Jewish immigrants. Philip Roth wrote comically about young New Jersey suburbanites in *Goodbye, Columbus* (1959) and penned an uproarious account of a sexually obsessed middle-aged New Yorker in *Portnoy's Complaint* (1969). Roth poignantly described his father's terminal illness in *Patrimony* (1991). Chicagoan Saul Bellow contributed masterful sketches of Jewish urban and literary life in landmark books such as *The Adventures of Augie March* (1953), *Herzog* (1962), *Humboldt's Gift* (1975), and *More Die of Heartbreak* (1987). Bellow became the eighth American Nobel laureate for literature in 1977. Isaac Bashevis Singer emigrated to America from Poland in the 1930s and continued to write in Yiddish. He won the Nobel Prize for literature in 1978. E. L. Doctorow employed Old Testament themes in his fictional account of atomic spies Julius and Ethel Rosenberg, *The Book of Daniel* (1971), and imaginatively drew on other modern historical materials in *Ragtime* (1975), *World's Fair* (1985), and *Billy Bathgate* (1989).

Cultural Landmarks

Poetry also flourished in the postwar era, though poets, too, were often highly critical, even deeply despairing, about the shape of American life. Older poets were still active, including cantankerous Ezra Pound, jailed after the war in a U.S. army detention center near Pisa, Italy, for alleged collaboration with the Fascists. Connecticut insurance executive Wallace Stevens and New Jersey pediatrician William Carlos Williams continued after 1945 to pursue "second careers" as prolific poets. But younger poets were coming to the fore during the postwar period. Pacific northwesterner Theodore Roethke wrote lyrically about the land until his death by drowning in Puget Sound in 1963. Robert Lowell, descended from a long line of patrician New Englanders, sought

to apply the wisdom of the Puritan past to the perplexing present in allegorical poems like *For the Union Dead* (1964). Troubled Sylvia Plath wrote the moving verses of *Ariel* (1966) and a disturbing novel, *The Bell Jar* (1963), but her career was cut short when she took her own life in 1963. Another brilliant poet of the period, John Berryman, ended it all in 1972 by leaping from a Minnesota bridge onto the frozen bank of the Mississippi River. Writing poetry seemed to be a dangerous occupation in modern America. The life of the poet, it was said, began in sadness and ended in madness.

Playwrights were also active, especially Tennessee Williams, with his series of sordid dramas about psychological misfits struggling to hold themselves together amid the disintegrating forces of modern life. Noteworthy were *A Streetcar Named Desire* (1947) and *Cat on a Hot Tin Roof* (1955). Arthur Miller brought to the stage searching probes of American values, notably in *Death of a Salesman* (1949). In the 1960s Edward Albee exposed the snarling underside of middle-class life in *Who's Afraid of Virginia Woolf?* (1962). In the 1980s, David Mamet analyzed the barbarity of American capitalism in plays such as *American Buffalo* and *Glengarry Glen Ross,* in which he crafted a kind of poetry from the sludge of American slang.

New York became the art capital of the world after World War II, as well-heeled Americans supported a large number of painters and sculptors. The Ford Foundation also became a major patron of the arts, as did the federal government after the creation of the tax-supported National Endowment for the Arts in 1965. The open and tradition-free American environment seemed especially congenial to the experimental mood of much modern art. Jackson Pollock pioneered abstract expressionism in the 1940s and 1950s, flinging paint onto huge canvases stretched on his studio floor. Realistic representation went out the window, as artists like Pollock and Willem de Kooning strove to create "action paintings" that expressed the painter's individuality and made the viewer a creative participant in defining the painting's "meaning." Pop artists in the 1960s, notably Andy Warhol, depicted everyday items of consumer culture, such as soup cans. Robert Rauschenberg made elaborate collages out of objects such as cardboard boxes and newspaper clippings.

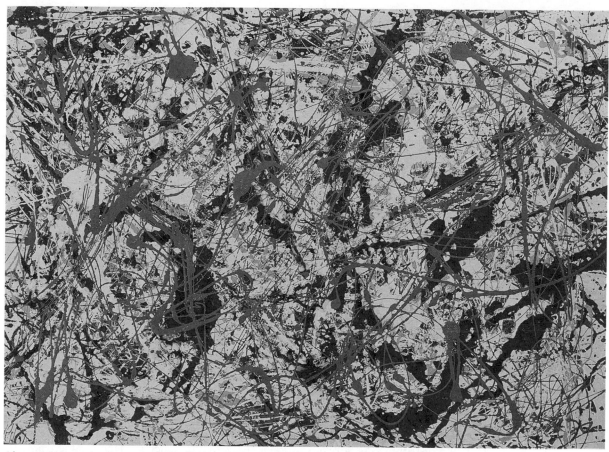

Abstract Expressionism *Post–World War II American painters like Jackson Pollock abandoned traditional subject matter altogether and emphasized pure form, color, and line. Their movement, called abstract expressionism, made New York City the art capital of the world.*

Claes Oldenburg tried to stun viewers into a new visual awareness with unfamiliar versions of familiar objects, such as giant plastic sculptures of pillow-soft telephones.

Architecture also benefited from the building boom of the postwar era. Old master Frank Lloyd Wright produced strikingly original designs, as in the round-walled Guggenheim Museum in New York. Louis Kahn employed stark geometric forms and basic building materials like brick and concrete to make beautiful, simple buildings. Eero Saarinen, the son of a Finnish immigrant, contributed a number of imaginative structures, including two Yale University residential colleges that evoked the atmosphere of an Italian hill town. Chinese-born I. M. Pei designed numerous graceful buildings on several college campuses, as well as the John F. Kennedy Library in

Boston. Philip Johnson artfully created an intimate feeling within huge edifices like New York City's Seagram Building and the New York State Theater at Lincoln Center, New York.

The American Prospect

The American spirit surged with vitality as the nation headed toward the close of the twentieth century, but grave problems continued to plague the republic. Women still fell short of first-class economic citizenship, and society groped for ways to adapt the traditional family to the new realities of women's work outside the home. A whole generation after the civil rights triumphs of the 1960s, full equality remained an elusive dream for countless Americans of color. The scourge of drug abuse afflicted all sectors of U.S.

society but wreaked its cruelest damage in hopeless underclass neighborhoods of the inner city.

Powerful foreign competitors began to challenge America's premier economic status. Successive presidential administrations, Democratic and Republican alike, searched somewhat in vain for the instrument with which to revive productivity growth and stimulate the economy.

Environmental concerns clouded the country's energy future. Coal-fired electrical generating plants helped form acid rain and probably contributed to the "greenhouse effect," an ominous warming of the planet's atmosphere. The unsolved problem of radioactive waste disposal hampered the development of nuclear power plants. The planet was being drained of oil, and disastrous accidents, such as the grounding and subsequent oil spill of the giant tanker *Exxon Valdez* in 1989 in Alaska's pristine Prince William Sound, demonstrated the ecological risks of oil exploration and transportation at sea.

Some Americans, soured on the false satisfactions of wealth and anxious to set the globe on the path to ecological stability, welcomed the prospect of a "no-growth" economy. But enlarging the economic pie had historically been Americans' way of appeasing the appetites of various groups for a richer life. Because of fabulous growth, they had happily been spared bitter battles over the distribution of a relatively fixed supply of this world's goods. No-growth would change the rules of the political game, with consequences that no one could foresee. And for the great majority of the world's aspiring peoples who still plowed with oxen and nightly went to bed hungry, no-growth seemed a cruel joke perpetrated by the privileged few who had already grown fat and happy.

America was born as a revolutionary force in a world of conservatism; for much of this century it had stood as a conservative force in a world of revolutionism. It has held aloft the banner of liberal democracy in a world buffeted by revolutions of left and right, including communism, nazism, and fascism. But much that is revolutionary remains in the liberal democratic legacy, and Americans have pioneered in the revolutions against colonialism, racism, sexism, ignorance, and poverty that have swept the planet in the past half-century. And as the human family grows at an alarming rate on a shrinking globe, America's revolutionary heritage does not lack for new challenges.

The task of cleansing Spaceship Earth of its abundant pollutants—including nuclear weapons—is the urgent mission confronting the American people in the closing years of the present century—in many ways "the American century." At the same time, new opportunities beckon both in outer space and on inner-city streets, at the artist's easel and in the concert hall, at the inventor's bench and in the scientist's laboratory, and in the unending quest for social justice, individual fulfillment, and international peace. The challenges facing Americans are formidable, at home and abroad, but so is the republic. As the twentieth century approaches its sunset, the people of the United States can still proudly claim, in the words of Lincoln, that they and their heritage represent "the last best hope of earth."

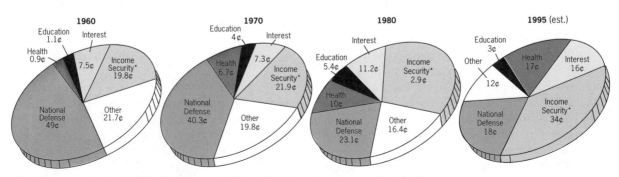

* Includes Social Security payments to the elderly and disabled, unemployment compensation, and welfare.
Note the shifting emphasis in the budget from defense spending to health and income security.
This shift was sharply checked by the Reagan administration.

The Federal Budget Dollar and How It Is Spent, by Major Category

CHRONOLOGY

1980	Reagan defeats Carter for presidency.
	Iran releases American hostages.
	"Reaganomics" spending and tax cuts passed.
	Sandra Day O'Connor appointed to Supreme Court.
1981–1991	United States aids antileftist forces in Central America.
1982	Recession hits U.S. economy.
1983	Reagan announces Star Wars plan.
	Russians shoot down Korean airliner.
	U.S. marines killed in Lebanon.
	U.S. invasion of Grenada.
	U.S.-Soviet arms-control talks break off.
1984	Reagan defeats Mondale for presidency.
1985	Mikhail Gorbachev comes to power in Soviet Union.
	First Reagan-Gorbachev summit meeting, in Geneva.
1986	Iran-contra scandal revealed.
	Second Reagan-Gorbachev summit meeting, in Reykjavik, Iceland.
1987	508-point stock-market plunge.
	Third Reagan-Gorbachev summit meeting, in Washington, D.C.; INF Treaty signed.
1988	Fourth Reagan-Gorbachev summit meeting, in Moscow.
	Bush defeats Dukakis for the presidency.
1989	Supreme Court tightens affirmative-action rules and relaxes protection of abortion rights.
	Chinese government suppresses prodemocracy demonstrators.
	Webster v. *Reproductive Health Services.*
	Eastern Europe throws off communist regimes.
	United States invades Panama.
	Berlin Wall torn down.
1990	Sandinistas voted out of power in Nicaragua.
	Nelson Mandela freed from South African prison after twenty-seven years.
	Iraq invades Kuwait.
	East and West Germany reunite.
1991	Persian Gulf War.
	Attempted coup to oust Gorbachev fails.
	Clarence Thomas appointed to Supreme Court.
	Gorbachev resigns as Soviet president.
	Soviet Union dissolves.

1992   Peace comes to El Salvador.

Twenty-seventh Amendment (prohibiting congressional pay raises from taking effect until an election seats a new session of Congress) ratified.

Planned Parenthood v. *Casey.*

Clinton defeats Bush and Perot for presidency.

U.S. joins U.N. military effort in Somalia.

1993   Congress passes Clinton's budget and tax plan.

North American Free Trade Agreement (NAFTA) approved.

U.S. forces suffer casualties in Somalia.

Israel and the Palestine Liberation Organization (PLO) sign peace agreement.

Federal agents raid cult headquarters in Waco, Texas.

1994   Congress fails to pass Clinton health care plan.

U.S. forces withdraw from Somalia.

U.S. diplomatic and military effort restores Aristide to power in Haiti.

Republicans win control of House and Senate for first time in forty years.

1995   House Republicans pass provisions of the "Contract with America."

Economic crisis in Mexico brings U.S. aid package.

U.S. economy continues growth.

Varying Viewpoints

The self-confident post–World War II era of affluence at home and unparalleled power abroad ended in the 1970s. The Vietnam War, the civil rights movement, and feminist revolt shattered the postwar social order in the 1960s, and by the opening of the 1970s the American social landscape clearly had changed permanently. During that same decade, the United States lost its undisputed international economic and strategic preeminence, and even the drastic Reagan policies of the 1980s could not fully restore the country to its immediate postwar position.

But if the postwar era has passed, it is not clear how to characterize the historical events of the closing quarter of the century. The shape of the quarter-century after World War II seems so sharply etched that it overshadows all efforts to define the contemporary age. Most observers, in fact, habitually invoke the postwar epoch in their efforts to understand the present. They call it the postindustrial era, the post–New Deal era, or the post–Cold War era. Only the future can judge whether the end of the twentieth century was the long twilight of what historian William O'Neill called the "American high" of the post-1945 decades or whether it has a distinctive identity in its own right.

SELECT READINGS

Primary Source Documents

On the changing family, consult Dr. Benjamin Spock, *Baby and Child Care* (1957),* and Betty Friedan, *The Feminine Mystique* (1963).*

Secondary Sources

A useful overview can be found in William H. Chafe, *The Unfinished Journey: America Since World War II* (1986). The 1960s get special attention in William O'Neill, *Coming Apart: An Informal History of America in the 1960s* (1971). The problems of cities are examined in Jon C. Teaford, *The Rough Road to Renaissance: Urban Revitalization in America, 1940–1985* (1990), and Larry Bennett, *Fragments of Cities: The New American Downtowns and Neighborhoods* (1990). America's international economic role is analyzed in David P. Calleo, *The Imperious Economy* (1982). See also Richard J. Barnet, *The Alliance: America-Europe-Japan, Makers of the Postwar World* (1983). George Masnick and Mary Jo Bane, The *Nation's Families: 1960–1990* (1980), is rich in statistical information. For a brilliant discussion of the same subject from an economic perspective, see Victor R. Fuchs, *How We Live* (1983), and his *Women's Quest for Economic Equality* (1988). The evolving social participation of women is clearly spelled out by William H. Chafe in *The American Woman: Her Changing Social, Economic, and Political Roles, 1920–1970* (1972). Consult also Gayle Graham Yates, *What Women Want: The Ideas of the Movement* (1975), Susan M. Bianchi, *American Women in Transition* (1987), Marian Faux, *Roe vs. Wade* (1988), and Susan Faludi's provocative best-seller, *Backlash: The Undeclared War Against American Women* (1991). Several ethnic minority groups are examined in Daniel P. Moynihan and Nathan Glazer, *Beyond the Melting Pot* (1963), and Thomas Sowell, *Ethnic America* (1981). Consult also Andrew Levison, *The Working-Class Majority* (1974). On blacks, see Harvard Sitkoff, *The Struggle for Black Equality, 1954–1880* (1981). Regarding Native Americans, consult Alvin M. Josephy, *Now That the Buffalo Have Gone: A Study of Today's American Indians* (1982), and Vine DeLoria's *Custer Died for Your Sins* (1969). On Mexican-Americans, see Matt S. Meier and Feliciano Rivera, *The Chicanos* (1972), and Richard Rodriguez's poignant memoir, *Hunger of Memory* (1982). The newest immigrants are the subjects of David M. Reimers, *Still the Golden Door: The Third World Comes to America* (1986). John W. Aldridge, *After the Lost Generation* (1951), looks at the earliest post–World War II writers. On postwar literature see Tony Tanner, *City of Words* (1971), and Alfred Kazin, *Bright Book of Life* (1973). On the arts, consult Edward Lucie-Smith, *Late Modern: The Visual Arts Since 1945* (1969). On television, see David Marc, *Demographic Vistas: Television in American Culture* (1984). Long-term economic trends are interpreted in David F. Noble, *Forces of Production* (1984), Daniel Bell, *The Coming of Post-Industrial Society* (1973), and Charles F. Sabel and Michael J. Piore, *The Second Industrial Divide* (1984). For an acerbic comment on the 1970s, see Christopher Lasch, *The Culture of Narcissism* (1979). Lasch extends his sharp social criticism in *The Revolt of the Elites and the Betrayal of Democracy* (1994). A sensitive and intriguing study of the values of modern Americans is Robert N. Bellah, *Habits of the Heart: Individualism and Commitment in American Life* (1985). See also Allan Bloom, *The Closing of the American Mind* (1987).

APPENDIX

DECLARATION OF INDEPENDENCE
In Congress, July 4, 1776

The Unanimous Declaration of the Thirteen United States of America

[Bracketed material in color has been inserted by the authors. For adoption background, see p. 96.]

When, in the course of human events, it becomes necessary for one people to dissolve the political bands which have connected them with another, and to assume, among the powers of the earth, the separate and equal station to which the laws of nature and of nature's God entitle them, a decent respect to the opinions of mankind requires that they should declare the causes which impel them to the separation.

We hold these truths to be self-evident: That all men are created equal; that they are endowed by their Creator with certain unalienable rights; that among these are life, liberty, and the pursuit of happiness; that, to secure these rights, governments are instituted among men, deriving their just powers from the consent of the governed; that whenever any form of government becomes destructive of these ends, it is the right of the people to alter or to abolish it, and to institute new government, laying its foundation on such principles, and organizing its powers in such form, as to them shall seem most likely to effect their safety and happiness. Prudence, indeed, will dictate that governments long established should not be changed for light and transient causes; and accordingly all experience hath shown that mankind are more disposed to suffer, while evils are sufferable, than to right themselves by abolishing the forms to which they are accustomed. But when a long train of abuses and usurpations, pursuing invariably the same object, envinces a design to reduce them under absolute despotism, it is their right, it is their duty, to throw off such government, and to provide new guards for their future security. Such has been the patient sufference of these colonies; and such is now the necessity which constrains them to alter their former systems of government. The history of the present King of Great Britain is a history of repeated injuries and usurpations, all having in direct object the establishment of an absolute tyranny over these states. To prove this, let facts be submitted to a candid world.

He has refused his assent to laws, the most wholesome and necessary for the public good. [See royal veto, p. 81.]

He has forbidden his governors to pass laws of immediate and pressing importance, unless suspended in their operation till his assent should be obtained; and, when so suspended, he has utterly neglected to attend to them.

He has refused to pass other laws for the accommodation of large districts of people [by establishing new counties], unless those people would relinquish the right of representation in the legislature, a right inestimable to them, and formidable to tyrants only.

He has called together legislative bodies at places unusual, uncomfortable, and distant from the depository of their public records, for the sole purpose of fatiguing them into compliance with his measures. [e.g., removal of Massachusetts Assembly to Salem, 1774]

He has dissolved representative houses repeatedly, for opposing, with manly firmness, his invasions on the rights of the people. [e.g., Virginia Assembly, 1765]

He has refused for a long time, after such dissolutions, to cause others to be elected; whereby the legislative powers, incapable of annihilation, have returned to the people at large for their exercise; the state remaining, in the mean time, exposed to all the dangers of invasions from without and convulsions within.

He has endeavored to prevent the population [populating] of these states; for that purpose obstructing the laws for naturalization of foreigners; refusing to pass others to encourage their migration hither, and raising the conditions of new appropriations of lands. [e.g., Proclamation of 1763, p. 77]

He has obstructed the administration of justice, by refusing his assent to laws for establishing judiciary powers.

He has made judges dependent on his will alone, for the tenure of their offices, and the amount and payment of their salaries. [See Townshend Acts, p. 84]

He has erected a multitude of new offices, and sent hither swarms of officers to harass our people and eat out their substance. [See enforcement of Navigation Laws, pp. 80–81.]

He has kept among us, in times of peace, standing armies, without the consent of our legislatures. [See p. 83.]

He has affected to render the military independent of, and superior to, the civil power.

He has combined with others to subject us to a jurisdiction foreign to our constitution, and unacknowledged by our laws, giving his assent to their acts of pretended legislation:

> For quartering large bodies of armed troops among us [see Boston Massacre, p. 84];
>
> For protecting them, by a mock trial, from punishment for any murders which they should commit on the inhabitants of these states [see 1774 Act, p. 86];
>
> For cutting off our trade with all parts of the world [see Boston Port Act, p. 86];
>
> For imposing taxes on us without our consent [see Stamp Act, p. 83];
>
> For depriving us, in many cases, of the benefits of trial by jury;
>
> For transporting us beyond seas, to be tried for pretended offenses;
>
> For abolishing the free system of English laws in a neighboring province [Quebec], establishing therein an arbitrary government, and enlarging its boundaries, so as to render it at once an example and fit instrument for introducing the same absolute rule into these colonies [Quebec Act, p. 86];
>
> For taking away our charters, abolishing our most valuable laws, and altering fundamentally the forms of our governments [e.g., in Massachusetts, p. 86];
>
> For suspending our own legislatures, and declaring themselves invested with power to legislate for us in all cases whatsoever [see Stamp Act repeal, p. 83].

He has abdicated government here, by declaring us out of his protection and waging war against us [Proclamation, p. 94].

He has plundered our seas, ravaged our coasts, burned our towns, and destroyed the lives of our people [e.g., the burning of Falmouth (Portland), p. 94].

He is at this time transporting large armies of foreign mercenaries [Hessians, p. 94] to complete the works of death, desolation, and tyranny already begun with circumstances of cruelty and perfidy scarcely paralleled in the most barbarous ages, and totally unworthy of the head of a civilized nation.

He has constrained our fellow-citizens, taken captive on the high seas [by impressment], to bear arms against their country, to become the executioners of their friends and brethren, or to fall themselves by their hands.

He has excited domestic insurrection among us [i.e., among slaves], and has endeavored to bring on the inhabitants of our frontiers the merciless Indian savages, whose known rule of warfare is an undistinguished destruction of all ages, sexes, and conditions.

In every stage of these oppressions we have petitioned for redress in the most humble terms; our repeated petitions have been answered only by repeated injury [e.g., pp. 93–94]. A prince, whose character is thus marked by every act which may define a tyrant, is unfit to be the ruler of a free people.

Nor have we been wanting in our attentions to our British brethren. We have warned them, from time to time, of attempts by their legislature to extend an unwarrantable jurisdiction over us. We have reminded them of the circumstances of our emigration and settlement here. We have appealed to their native justice and magnanimity; and we have conjured them, by the ties of our common kindred, to disavow these usurpations, which would inevitably interrupt our connections and correspondence. They, too, have been deaf to the voice of justice and of consanguinity [blood relationship]. We must, therefore, acquiesce in the necessity which denounces [announces] our separation, and hold them, as we hold the rest of mankind, enemies in war, in peace friends.

We, therefore, the representatives of the United States of America, in General Congress assembled, appealing to the Supreme Judge of the world for the rectitude of our intentions, do, in the name and by the authority of the good people of these colonies, solemnly publish and declare, That these United Colonies are, and of right ought to be, FREE AND INDEPENDENT STATES; that they are absolved from all allegiance to the British crown, and that all political connection between them and the state of Great Britain is, and ought to be, totally dissolved; and that, as free and independent states, they have full power to levy war, conclude peace, contract alliances, establish commerce, and do all other acts and things which independent states may of right do. And for the support of this declaration, with a firm reliance on the protection of Divine Providence, we mutually pledge to each other our lives, our fortunes, and our sacred honor.

[Signed by]   JOHN HANCOCK [President]
                                               [and fifty-five others]

CONSTITUTION OF
THE UNITED STATES OF AMERICA

[Boldface headings and bracketed explanatory matter and marginal comments (both in color) have been inserted for the reader's convenience. Passages that are no longer operative are printed in italic type.]

PREAMBLE

On "We the people,"
see p. 187n.
We the people of the United States, in order to form a more perfect union, establish justice, insure domestic tranquillity, provide for the common defense, promote the general welfare, and secure the blessings of liberty to ourselves and our posterity, do ordain and establish this CONSTITUTION for the United States of America.

Article I.   Legislative Department

Section I.   Congress

Legislative power vested in a two-House Congress. All legislative powers herein granted shall be vested in a Congress of the United States, which shall consist of a Senate and a House of Representatives.

Section II.   House of Representatives

1. The people elect representatives biennially. The House of Representatives shall be composed of members chosen every second year by the people of the several States, and the electors [voters] in each State shall have the qualifications requisite for electors of the most numerous branch of the State Legislature.

2. Who may be representatives. No person shall be a Representative who shall not have attained to the age of twenty-five years, and been seven years a citizen of the United States, and who shall not, when elected, be an inhabitant of that State in which he shall be chosen.

3. Representation in the House based on population; census. Representatives and direct taxes[1] shall be apportioned among the several States which may be included within this Union, according to their respective numbers, *which shall be determined by adding to the whole number of free persons, including those bound to service for a term of years* [apprentices and indentured servants], *and excluding Indians not taxed, three-fifths of all other persons* [slaves].[2] The actual enumeration [census] shall be made within three

See 1787
compromise,
pp. 113–115.

See 1787 compromise
p. 115.

---

[1] Modified in 1913 by the 16th Amendment re income taxes.

[2] The word *slave* appears nowhere in the Constitution; *slavery* appears in the 13th Amendment. The three-fifths rule ceased to be in force when the 13th Amendment was adopted in 1865 (see p. 295 and text of Amendments following).

years after the first meeting of the Congress of the United States, and within every subsequent term of ten years, in such manner as they shall by law direct. The number of Representatives shall not exceed one for every thirty thousand, but each State shall have at least one Representative; *and until such enumeration shall be made, the State of New Hampshire shall be entitled to choose three, Massachusetts eight, Rhode Island and Providence Plantations one, Connecticut five, New York six, New Jersey four, Pennsylvania eight, Delaware one, Maryland six, Virginia ten, North Carolina five, South Carolina five, and Georgia three.*

4. Vacancies in the House are filled by election. When vacancies happen in the representation from any State, the Executive authority [governor] thereof shall issue writs of election [call a special election] to fill such vacancies.

See Johnson trial, p. 333; Nixon trial preliminaries, pp. 622–623.

5. The House selects its Speaker; has sole power to vote impeachment charges (i.e., indictments). The House of Representatives shall choose their Speaker and other officers; and shall have the sole power of impeachment.

Section III.   Senate

1. Senators represent the states. The Senate of the United States shall be composed of two Senators from each State, *chosen by the legislature thereof,*[1] for six years; and each Senator shall have one vote.

2. One-third of Senators chosen every two years; vacancies. *Immediately after they shall be assembled in consequence of the first election, they shall be divided as equally as may be into three classes. The seats of the Senators of the first class shall be vacated at the expiration of the second year, of the second class at the expiration of the fourth year, and of the third class at the expiration of the sixth year,* so that one-third may be chosen every second year; *and if vacancies happen by resignation or otherwise, during the recess of the legislature of any State, the Executive* [governor] *thereof may make temporary appointments until the next meeting of the legislature, which shall fill such vacancies.*[2]

3. Who may be Senators. No person shall be a Senator who shall not have attained to the age of thirty years, and been nine years a citizen of the United States, and who shall not, when elected, be an inhabitant of that State for which he shall be chosen.

4. The Vice-President presides over the Senate. The Vice-President of the United States shall be President of the Senate, but shall have no vote, unless they be equally divided [tied].

5. The Senate chooses its other officers. The Senate shall choose their other officers, and also a President *pro tempore,* in the absence of the Vice-President, or when he shall exercise the office of President of the United States.

See Johnson trial, p. 333.

6. The Senate has sole power to try impeachments. The Senate shall have the sole power to try all impeachments. When sitting for that purpose, they shall be on oath or affirmation. When the President of the United States is tried, the Chief Justice shall preside:[3] and no person shall be convicted without the concurrence of two-thirds of the members present.

7. Penalties for impeachment conviction. Judgment in cases of impeachment shall not extend further than to removal from office, and disqualification to hold and enjoy any

---

[1] Repealed in favor of popular election in 1913 by the 17th Amendment.

[2] Changed in 1913 by the 17th Amendment.

[3] The Vice-President, as next in line, would be an interested party.

office of honor, trust or profit under the United States: but the party convicted shall nevertheless be liable and subject to indictment, trial, judgment and punishment, according to law.

Section IV.   Election and Meetings of Congress

1. Regulation of elections. The times, places and manner of holding elections for Senators and Representatives shall be prescribed in each State by the legislature thereof; but the Congress may at any time by law make or alter such regulations, except as to the places of choosing Senators.

2. Congress must meet once a year. The Congress shall assemble at least once in every year, and such meeting *shall be on the first Monday in December, unless they shall by law appoint a different day.*[1]

Section V.   Organization and Rules of the Houses

1. Each house may reject members; quorums. Each house shall be the judge of the elections, returns and qualifications of its own members, and a majority of each shall constitute a quorum to do business; but a smaller number may adjourn from day to day, and may be authorized to compel the attendance of absent members, in such manner, and under such penalties, as each house may provide.

See "Bully" Brooks case, pp. 285–286.
2. Each House makes its own rules. Each house may determine the rules of its proceedings, punish its members for disorderly behavior, and with the concurrence of two-thirds, expel a member.

3. Each House must keep and publish a record of its proceedings. Each house shall keep a journal of its proceedings, and from time to time publish the same, excepting such parts as may in their judgment require secrecy; and the yeas and nays of the members of either house on any question shall, at the desire of one-fifth of those present, be entered on the journal.

4. Both Houses must agree on adjournment. Neither house, during the session of congress, shall, without the consent of the other, adjourn for more than three days, nor to any other place than that in which the two houses shall be sitting.

Section VI.   Privileges of and Prohibitions upon Congressmen

1. Congressional salaries; immunities. The Senators and Representatives shall receive a compensation for their services, to be ascertained by law and paid out of the treasury of the United States. They shall in all cases except treason, felony and breach of the peace, be privileged from arrest during their attendance at the session of their respective houses, and in going to and returning from the same; and for any speech or debate in either house, they shall not be questioned in any other place [i.e., they shall be immune from libel suits].

2. A Congressman may not hold any other federal civil office. No Senator or Representative shall, during the time for which he was elected, be appointed to any civil office under the authority of the United States, which shall have been created, or the emoluments whereof shall have been increased, during such time; and no person holding any

---

[1] Changed in 1933 to January 3 by the 20th Amendment (see p. 496 and text of Amendments).

office under the United States shall be a member of either house during his continuance in office.

Section VII.   Method of Making Laws

See 1787 compromise, p. 115.

1. Money bills must originate in the House. All bills for raising revenue shall originate in the House of Representatives; but the Senate may propose or concur with amendments as on other bills.

President Nixon, more than any predecessors, "impounded" billions of dollars voted by Congress for specific purposes, because he disapproved of them. The courts generally failed to sustain him, and his impeachment foes regarded wholesale impoundment as a violation of his oath to "faithfully execute" the laws.

2. The President's veto power; Congress may override. Every bill which shall have passed the House of Representatives and the Senate, shall, before it become a law, be presented to the President of the United States; if he approve he shall sign it, but if not he shall return it with his objections to that house in which it shall have originated, who shall enter the objections at large on their journal, and proceed to reconsider it. If after such reconsideration two-thirds of that house shall agree to pass the bill, it shall be sent, together with the objections, to the other house, by which it shall likewise be reconsidered, and if, approved by two-thirds of that house, it shall become a law. But in all such cases the votes of both houses shall be determined by yeas and nays, and the names of the persons voting for and against the bill shall be entered on the journal of each house respectively. If any bill shall not be returned by the President within ten days (Sundays excepted) after it shall have been presented to him, the same shall be a law, in like manner as if he had signed it, unless the Congress by their adjournment prevent its return, in which case it shall not be a law [this is the so-called pocket veto].

3. All measures requiring the agreement of both Houses go to President for approval. Every order, resolution, or vote to which the concurrence of the Senate and House of Representatives may be necessary (except on a question of adjournment) shall be presented to the President of the United States; and before the same shall take effect, shall be approved by him, or being disapproved by him, shall be repassed by two-thirds of the Senate and House of Representatives, according to the rules and limitations prescribed in the case of a bill.

Section VIII.   Powers Granted to Congress

Congress has certain enumerated powers:

1. It may lay and collect taxes. The Congress shall have power to lay and collect taxes, duties, imposts, and excises, to pay the debts and provide for the common defense and general welfare of the United States; but all duties, imposts and excises shall be uniform throughout the United States;

2. It may borrow money. To borrow money on the credit of the United States;

3. It may regulate foreign and interstate trade. To regulate commerce with foreign nations, and among the several States, and with the Indian tribes;

For 1798 naturalization, see pp. 133–134.

4. It may pass naturalization and bankruptcy laws. To establish an uniform rule of naturalization, and uniform laws on the subject of bankruptcies throughout the United States;

5. It may coin money. To coin money, regulate the value thereof, and of foreign coin, and fix the standard of weights and measures;

6. It may punish counterfeiters. To provide for the punishment of counterfeiting the securities and current coin of the United States;

7. It may establish a postal service. To establish post offices and post roads;

8. It may issue patents and copyrights. To promote the progress of science and useful arts by securing for limited times to authors and inventors the exclusive right to their respective writings and discoveries;

See Judiciary Act of 1789, p. 125.

9. It may establish inferior courts. To constitute tribunals inferior to the Supreme Court;

10. It may punish crimes committed on the high seas. To define and punish piracies and felonies committed on the high seas [i.e., outside the three-mile limit] and offenses against the law of nations [international law];

11. It may declare war; authorize privateers. To declare war,[1] grant letters of marque and reprisal,[2] and make rules concerning captures on land and water;

12. It may maintain an army. To raise and support armies, but no appropriation of money to that use shall be for a longer term than two years;[3]

13. It may maintain a navy. To provide and maintain a navy;

14. It may regulate the army and navy. To make rules for the government and regulation of the land and naval forces;

See Whiskey Rebellion, pp. 127–128.

15. It may call out the state militia. To provide for calling forth the militia to execute the laws of the union, suppress insurrections, and repel invasions.

16. It shares with the states control of militia. To provide for organizing, arming, and disciplining the militia, and for governing such part of them as may be employed in the service of the United States, reserving to the States respectively the appointment of the officers, and the authority of training the militia according to the discipline prescribed by Congress;

17. It makes laws for the District of Columbia and other federal areas. To exercise exclusive legislation in all cases whatsoever, over such district (not exceeding ten miles square) as may, by cession of particular States, and the acceptance of Congress, become the seat of government of the United States,[4] and to exercise like authority over all places purchased by the consent of the legislature of the State, in which the same shall be, for the erection of forts, magazines, arsenals, dock-yards, and other needful buildings;—and

Congress has certain implied powers:

This is the famous "Elastic Clause"; see p. 127.

18. It may make laws necessary for carrying out the enumerated powers. To make all laws which shall be necessary and proper for carrying into execution the foregoing powers, and all others powers vested by this Constitution in the government of the United States, or in any department or officer thereof.

Section IX.   Powers Denied to the Federal Government

See 1787 slave compromise, p. 115.

1. Congressional control of slave trade postponed until 1808. *The migration or importation of such persons as any of the States now existing shall think proper to admit shall not be prohibited by the Congress prior to the year 1808; but a tax or duty may be imposed on such importation, not exceeding $10 for each person.*

---

[1] Note that the President, though he can provoke war (see the case of Polk, pp. 247–249) or wage it after it is declared, cannot declare it.

[2] Papers issued private citizens in wartime authorizing them to capture enemy ships.

[3] A reflection of fear of standing armies earlier expressed in the Declaration of Independence.

[4] The District of Columbia, 10 miles square, was established in 1791 with a cession from Virginia (see p. 110).

See Lincoln's unlawful suspension, pp. 301–302.

2. The writ of habeas corpus[1] may be suspended only in case of rebellion or invasion. The privilege of the writ of habeas corpus shall not be suspended, unless when in cases of rebellion or invasion the public safety may require it.

3. Attainders[2] and ex post facto laws[3] forbidden. No bill of attainder or ex post facto law shall be passed.

4. Direct taxes must be apportioned according to population. No capitation [head or poll tax], or other direct, tax shall be laid, unless in proportion to the census or enumeration herein before directed to be taken.[4]

5. Export taxes forbidden. No tax or duty shall be laid on articles exported from any State.

6. Congress must not discriminate among states in regulating commerce. No preference shall be given by any regulation of commerce or revenue to the ports of one State over those of another; nor shall vessels bound to, or from, one State, be obliged to enter, clear, or pay duties in another.

7. Public money may not be spent without congressional appropriation; accounting. No money shall be drawn from the treasury, but in consequence of appropriations made by law; and a regular statement and account of the receipts and expenditures of all public money shall be published from time to time.

8. Titles of nobility prohibited; foreign gifts. No title of nobility shall be granted by the United States: and no person holding any office of profit or trust under them, shall, without the consent of the Congress, accept of any present, emolument, office, or title, of any kind whatever, from any king, prince, or foreign state.

Section X.   Powers Denied to the States

Absolute prohibitions on the states:

1. The states are forbidden to do certain things. No State shall enter into any treaty, alliance, or confederation; grant letters of marque and reprisal [i.e., authorize privateers]; coin money; emit bills of credit [issue paper money]; make anything but gold and silver coin a [legal] tender in payment of debts; pass any bill of attainder, ex post facto,[5] or law impairing the obligation of contracts, or grant any title of nobility.

On contracts, see Fletcher v. Peck, p. 170.

Conditional prohibitions on the states:

2. The states may not levy duties without the consent of Congress. No State shall, without the consent of the Congress, lay any imposts or duties on imports or exports, except what may be absolutely necessary for executing its inspection laws: and the net produce of all duties and imposts, laid by any State on imports or exports, shall be for the use of the treasury of the United States; and all such laws shall be subject to the revision and control of the Congress.

Cf. Confederation chaos, p. 111.

3. Certain other federal powers are forbidden the states except with the consent of Congress. No State shall, without the consent of Congress, lay any duty of tonnage [i.e.,

---

[1] A writ of habeas corpus is a document that enables a person under arrest to obtain an immediate examination in court to ascertain whether he is being legally held.

[2] A bill of attainder is a special legislative act condemning and punishing an individual without a judicial trial.

[3] An ex post facto law is one that fixes punishments for acts committed before the law was passed.

[4] Modified in 1913 by the 16th Amendment (see text of following Amendments).

[5] For definitions, see footnotes 3 and 4.

duty on ship tonnage], keep [non-militia] troops or ships of war in time of peace, enter into any agreement or compact with another State, or with a foreign power, or engage in war, unless actually invaded, or in such imminent danger as will not admit of delay.

Article II.   Executive Department

Section I.   President and Vice-President

1. The President the chief executive; his term. The executive power shall be vested in a President of the United States of America. He shall hold his office during the term of four years,[1] and, together with the Vice-President, chosen for the same term, be elected as follows:

See 1787 compromise, pp. 113–115.

2. The President is chosen by electors. Each State shall appoint, in such manner as the legislature thereof may direct, a number of electors, equal to the whole number of Senators and Representatives to which the State may be entitled in the Congress; but no Senator or Representative, or person holding an office of trust or profit under the United States, shall be appointed an elector.

A majority of the electoral votes needed to elect a President. *The electors shall meet in their respective States, and vote by ballot for two persons, of whom one at least shall not be an inhabitant of the same State with themselves. And they shall make a list of all the persons voted for, and of the number of votes for each; which list they shall sign and certify, and transmit sealed to the seat of government of the United States, directed to the President of the Senate. The President of the Senate shall, in the presence of the Senate and House of Representatives, open all certificates, and the voted shall then be counted. The*

See Burr-Jefferson disputed election of 1800, pp. 139–141.

person having the greatest number of votes shall be the President, if such number be a majority of the whole number of electors appointed; and if there be more than one who have such majority, and have an equal number of votes, then the House of Representatives shall immediately choose by ballot one of them for President; and if no person have a majority, then from the five highest on the list the said house shall in like manner choose the President. But in choosing the President the votes shall be taken by States, the representation from each State having one vote; a quorum for this purpose shall consist of a member or members from two-thirds of the States, and a majority of all the States shall be necessary to a choice. In every case, after the choice of the President, the person having the

See Jefferson as Vice-President in 1796, p. 131.

greatest number of votes of the electors shall be the Vice-President. But if there should remain two or more who have equal votes, the Senate shall choose from them by ballot the Vice-President.[2]

3. Congress decides time of meeting of Electoral College. The Congress may determine the time of choosing the electors and the day on which they shall give their votes; which day shall be the same throughout the United States.

To provide for foreign-born like Alexander Hamilton, born in the British West Indies.

4. Who may be President. No person except a natural-born citizen, *or a citizen of the United States at the time of the adoption of this Constitution,* shall be eligible to the office of President; neither shall any person be eligible to that office who shall not have attained to the age of thirty-five years, and been fourteen years a resident within the United States [i.e., a legal resident].

---

[1] No reference to re-election; for anti-third term 22d Amendment, see text of Amendments following.

[2] Repealed in 1804 by the 12th Amendment (see text of Amendments following).

Modified by Amendments XX and XXV.

5. Replacements for President. In case of the removal of the President from office or of his death, resignation, or inability to discharge the powers and duties of the said office, the same shall devolve on the Vice-President, and the Congress may by law provide for the case of removal, death, resignation, or inability, both of the President and Vice-President, declaring what officer shall then act as President, and such officer shall act accordingly, until the disability be removed, or a President shall be elected.

6. The President's salary. The President shall, at stated times, receive for his services a compensation, which shall neither be increased nor diminished during the period for which he shall have been elected, and he shall not receive within that period any other emolument from the United States, or any of them.

7. The President's oath of office. Before he enter on the execution of his office, he shall take the following oath or affirmation;—"I do solemnly swear (or affirm) that I will faithfully execute the office of the President of the United States, and will to the best of my ability preserve, protect and defend the Constitution of the United States."

Section II. Powers of the President

See Cabinet evolution, p. 124.

1. The President has important military and civil powers. The President shall be commander in chief of the army and navy of the United States, and of the militia of the several States, when called into the actual service of the United States; he may require the opinion, in writing, of the principal officer in each of the executive departments, upon any subject relating to the duties of their respective offices, and he shall have power to grant reprieves and pardon for offenses against the United States, except in cases of impeachment.[1]

For President's removal power, see p. 333.

2. The President may negotiate treaties and nominate federal officials. He shall have power, by and with the advice and consent of the Senate, to make treaties, provided two-thirds of the Senators present concur; and he shall nominate, and by and with the advice and consent of the Senate, shall appoint ambassadors, other public ministers and consuls, judges of the Supreme Court, and all other officers of the United States, whose appointments are not herein otherwise provided for, and which shall be established by law: but the Congress may by law vest the appointment of such inferior officers, as they think proper, in the President alone, in the courts of law, or in the heads of departments.

3. The President may fill vacancies during Senate recess. The president shall have power to fill up all vacancies that may happen during the recess of the Senate, by granting commissions which shall expire at the end of their next session.

Section III. Other Powers and Duties of the President

For President's personal appearances, see pp. 454–455.

Messages; extra sessions; receiving ambassadors: execution of the laws. He shall from time to time give to the Congress information of the state of the Union, and recommend to their consideration such measures as he shall judge necessary and expedient; he may, on extraordinary occasions, convene both houses, or either of them, and in case of disagreement between them, with respect to the time of adjournment, he may adjourn them to such time as he shall think proper; he shall receive ambassadors and other public min-

---

[1] To prevent the President's pardoning himself or his close associates, as was feared in the case of Richard Nixon. See pp. 586–587.

isters; he shall take care that the laws be faithfully executed, and shall commission all the officers of the United States.

See Johnson's acquittal, p. 333; also Nixon's near impeachment, pp. 622–623.

Section IV.   Impeachment

Civil officers may be removed by impeachment. The President, Vice-President and all civil officers[1] of the United States shall be removed from office on impeachment for, and on conviction of, treason, bribery, or other high crimes and misdemeanors.

Article III.   Judicial Department

Section I.   The Federal Courts

See Judiciary Act of 1789, p. 125.

The judicial power belongs to the federal courts. The judicial power of the United States shall be vested in one Supreme Court, and in such inferior courts as the Congress may from time to time ordain and establish. The judges, both of the Supreme and inferior courts, shall hold their offices during good behavior, and shall, at stated times, receive for their services a compensation which shall not be diminished[2] during their continuance in office.

Section II.   Jurisdiction of Federal Courts

1. Kinds of cases that may be heard. The judicial power shall extend to all cases, in law and equity, arising under this Constitution, the laws of the United States, and treaties made, or which shall be made, under their authority;—to all cases affecting ambassadors, other public ministers and consuls;—to all cases of admiralty and maritime jurisdiction;—to controversies to which the United States shall be a party;—to controversies between two or more States;—*between a State and citizens of another State,*[3]—between citizens of different States;—between citizens of the same State claiming lands under grants of different States, and between a State, or the citizens thereof, and foreign states, citizens or subjects.

2. Jurisdiction of the Supreme Court. In all cases affecting ambassadors, other public ministers and consuls, and those in which a State shall be party, the Supreme Court shall have original jurisdiction.[4] In all the other cases before mentioned, the Supreme Court shall have appellate jurisdiction,[5] both as to law and fact, with such exceptions, and under such regulations, as the Congress shall make.

3. Trial for federal crime is by jury. The trial of all crimes, except in cases of impeachment, shall be by jury; and such trial shall be held in the State where the said crimes shall have been committed; but when not committed within any State, the trial shall be at such place or places as the Congress may by law have directed.

---

[1] I.e., all federal executive and judicial officers, but not members of Congress or military personnel.

[2] In 1978, in a case involving federal judges, the Supreme Court ruled that diminution of salaries by inflation was irrelevant.

[3] The 11th Amendment (see text of Amendments following) restricts this to suits by a state against citizens of another state.

[4] I.e., such cases must originate in the Supreme Court.

[5] I.e., it hears other cases only when they are appealed to it from a lower federal court or a state court.

Section III.   Treason

See Burr trial, pp. 146–147.

1. Treason defined. Treason against the United States shall consist only in levying war against them, or in adhering to their enemies, giving them aid and comfort. No person shall be convicted of treason unless on the testimony of two witnesses to the same overt act, or on confession in open court.

2. Congress fixes punishment for treason. The Congress shall have power to declare the punishment of treason, but no attainder of treason shall work corruption of blood, or forfeiture except during the life of the person attainted.[1]

Article IV.   Relations of the States to One Another

Section I.   Credit to Acts, Records and Court Proceedings

Each state must respect the public acts of the others. Full faith and credit shall be given in each State to the public acts, records, and judicial proceedings of every other State.[2] And the Congress may by general laws prescribe the manner in which such acts, records, and proceedings shall be proved [attested], and the effect thereof.

Section II.   Duties of States to States

1. Citizenship in one state is valid in all. The citizens of each State shall be entitled to all privileges and immunities of citizens in the several States.

This stipulation is sometimes openly flouted. In 1978 Governor Jerry Brown of California, acting on humanitarian grounds, refused to surrender to South Dakota an American Indian, Dennis Banks, who was charged with murder in an armed uprising.

2. Fugitives from justice must be surrendered by the state to which they have fled. A person charged in any State with treason, felony, or other crime, who shall flee from justice, and be found in another State, shall on demand of the executive authority [governor] of the State from which he fled, be delivered up, to be removed to the State having jurisdiction of the crime.

Basis of fugitive slave laws; see p. 272.

3. Slaves and apprentices must be returned. *No person held to service or labor in one State, under the laws thereof, escaping into another, shall, in consequence of any law or regulation therein, be discharged from such service or labor, but shall be delivered up on claim of the party to whom such service or labor may be due.*[3]

Section III.   New States and Territories.

E.g., Maine (1820); see p. 169.

1. Congress may admit new states. New States may be admitted by the Congress into this Union; but no new State shall be formed or erected within the jurisdiction of any other State; nor any State be formed by the junction of two or more States, or parts of

---

[1] I.e., punishment only for the offender; none for his heirs.

[2] E.g., a marriage valid in one is valid in all.

[3] Invalidated in 1865 by the 13th Amendment (see text of Amendments following).

States, without the consent of the legislatures of the States concerned as well as of the Congress.[1]

2. Congress regulates federal territory and property. The Congress shall have power to dispose of and make all needful rules and regulations respecting the territory or other property belonging to the United States; and nothing in this Constitution shall be so construed as to prejudice any claims of the United States, or of any particular State.

Section IV.	Protection to the States

United States guarantees to states representative government and protection against invasion and rebellion. The United States shall guarantee to every State in this Union a republican form of government, and shall protect each of them against invasion; and on

See Cleveland and the Pullman strike, pp. 408–409.

application of the legislature, or of the executive [governor] (when the legislature cannot be convened), against domestic violence.

Article V.   The Process of Amendment

The Constitution may be amended in four ways. The Congress, whenever two-thirds of both houses shall deem it necessary, shall propose amendments to this Constitution, or, on the application of the legislatures of two-thirds of the several States, shall call a convention for proposing amendments, which, in either case, shall be valid to all intents and purposes, as part of this Constitution, when ratified by the legislatures of three-fourths of the several States, or by conventions in three-fourths thereof, as the one or the other mode of ratification may be proposed by the Congress; provided *that no amendments which may be made prior to the year one thousand eight hundred and eight shall in any manner affect the first and fourth clauses in the ninth section of the first article,*[2] and that no State, without its consent, shall be deprived of its equal suffrage in the Senate.

Article VI.   General Provisions

This pledge honored by Hamilton, pp. 125–126.

1. The debts of the Confederation are taken over. All debts contracted and engagements entered into, before the adoption of this Constitution, shall be as valid against the United States under this Constitution, as under the Confederation.

2. The Constitution, federal laws, and treaties are the supreme law of the land. This Constitution, and the laws of the United States which shall be made in pursuance thereof; and all treaties made, or which shall be made, under the authority of the United States, shall be the supreme law of the land; and the judges in every State shall be bound thereby, anything in the Constitution or laws of any State to the contrary notwithstanding.

3. Federal and state officers bound by oath to support the Constitution. The Senators and Representatives before mentioned, and the members of the several State legislatures, and all executive and judicial officers, both of the United States and of the several States, shall be bound by oath or affirmation to support this Constitution; but no religious test

---

[1] Loyal West Virginia was formed by Lincoln in 1862 from seceded Virginia. This act was of dubious constitutionality and was justified in part by the wartime powers of the President. See p. 281.

[2] This clause, re slave trade and direct taxes, became inoperative in 1808.

shall ever be required as a qualification to any office or public trust under the United States.

Article VII.   Ratification of the Constitution

See 1787 irregularity, pp. 115–116.   **The Constitution effective when ratified by conventions in nine states.** The ratification of the conventions of nine States shall be sufficient for the establishment of this Constitution between the States so ratifying the same.

Done in Convention by the unanimous consent of the States present, the seventeenth day of September in the year of our Lord one thousand seven hundred and eighty-seven and of the Independence of the United States of America the twelfth. In witness whereof we have hereunto subscribed our names.
[Signed by]

G° WASHINGTON
Presidt and Deputy from Virginia
[and thirty-eight others]

AMENDMENTS TO THE CONSTITUTION

Amendment I.   Religious and Political Freedom

For background of Bill of Rights, see pp. 124–125.   **Congress must not interfere with freedom of religion, speech or press, assembly, and petition.** Congress shall make no law respecting an establishment of religion,[1] or prohibiting the free exercise thereof; or abridging the freedom of speech, or of the press; or the right of the people peaceably to assemble, and to petition the government for a redress of grievances.

Amendment II.   Right to Bear Arms

The people may bear arms. A well-regulated militia being necessary to the security of a free State, the right of the people to keep and bear arms [i.e., for military purposes] shall not be infringed.[2]

Amendment III.   Quartering of Troops

See Declaration of Independence and British quartering above.   **Soldiers may not be arbitrarily quartered on the people.** No soldier shall, in time of peace, be quartered in any house without the consent of the owner, nor in time of war, but in a manner to be prescribed by law.

Amendment IV.   Searches and Seizures

A reflection of colonial grievances against Crown.   **Unreasonable searches are forbidden.** The right of the people to be secure in their persons, houses, papers, and effects, against unreasonable searches and seizures, shall not be violated, and no [search] warrants shall issue but upon probable cause, supported by oath or affirmation, and particularly describing the place to be searched, and the persons or things to be seized.

---

[1] In 1787 "an establishment of religion" referred to an "established church," or one supported by all taxpayers, whether members or not. But the courts have often acted under this article to keep religion, including prayers, out of the public schools.

[2] The courts, with "militia" in mind, have consistently held that the "right" to bear arms is a limited one.

Amendment V.

When witnesses refuse to answer questions in court, they routinely "take the Fifth Amendment."

Right to Life, Liberty, and Property

The individual is guaranteed certain rights when on trial and the right to life, liberty, and property. No person shall be held to answer for a capital, or otherwise infamous crime, unless on a presentment [formal charge] or indictment of a grand jury, except in cases arising in the land or naval forces, or in the militia, when in actual service in time of war or public danger; nor shall any person be subject for the same offense to be twice put in jeopardy of life or limb; nor shall be compelled in any criminal case to be a witness against himself, nor be deprived of life, liberty, or property, without due process of law; nor shall private property be taken for public use [i.e., by eminent domain] without just compensation.

Amendment VI.

See Declaration of Independence above.

Protection in Criminal Trials

An accused person has important rights. In all criminal prosecutions, the accused shall enjoy the right to a speedy and public trial, by an impartial jury of the State and district wherein the crime shall have been committed, which district shall have been previously ascertained by law, and to be informed of the nature and cause of the accusation; to be confronted with the witnesses against him; to have compulsory process [subpoena] for obtaining witnesses in his favor, and to have the assistance of counsel for his defense.

Amendment VII.

Suits at Common Law

The rules of common law are recognized. In suits at common law, where the value in controversy shall exceed twenty dollars, the right of trial by jury shall be preserved, and no fact tried by a jury shall be otherwise re-examined in any court of the United States, than according to the rules of the common law.

Amendment VIII.

Bail and Punishments

Excessive fines and unusual punishments are forbidden. Excessive bail shall not be required, nor excessive fines imposed, nor cruel and unusual punishments inflicted.

Amendment IX.

Amendments IX and X were bulwarks of Southern states' rights before the Civil War.

Concerning Rights Not Enumerated

The people retain rights not here enumerated. The enumeration in the Constitution, of certain rights, shall not be construed to deny or disparage others retained by the people.

Amendment X.

A concession to states' rights, p. 127.

Powers Reserved to the States and to the People

Powers not delegated to the federal government are reserved to the states and the people. The powers not delegated to the United States by the Constitution, nor prohibited by it to the States, are reserved to the States respectively, or to the people.

Amendment XI.

Suits Against a State

The federal courts have no authority in suits by citizens against a state. The judicial power of the United States shall not be construed to extend to any suit in law or equity, commenced or prosecuted against one of the United States by citizens of another state, or by citizens or subjects of any foreign state. [Adopted 1798.]

Amendment XII.   Election of President and Vice-President

1. Changes in manner of electing President and Vice-President; procedure when no presidential candidate receives electoral majority. The electors shall meet in their respective States, and vote by ballot for President and Vice-President, one of whom, at least, shall not be an inhabitant of the same State with themselves; they shall name in their ballots the person voted for as President, and in distinct ballots the person voted for as Vice-President, and they shall make distinct lists of all persons voted for as President, and of all persons voted for as Vice-President, and of the number of votes for each, which lists they shall sign and certify, and transmit sealed to the seat of government of the United States, directed to the President of the Senate;—the President of the Senate shall, in the presence of the Senate and House of Representatives, open all the certificates and the votes shall then be counted;—the person having the greatest number of votes for President shall be the President, if such number be a majority of the whole number of electors appointed; and if no person have such majority, then from the persons having the highest numbers not exceeding three on the list of those voted for as President, the House of Representatives shall choose immediately, by ballot, the President. But in choosing the President, the votes shall be taken by States, the representation from each State having one vote; a quorum for this purpose shall consist of a member or members from two-thirds of the States, and a majority of all the States shall be necessary to a choice. And if the House of Representatives shall not choose a President whenever the right of choice shall devolve upon them, before *the fourth day of March*[1] next following, then the Vice-President shall act as President, as in the case of death or other constitutional disability of the President.

2. Procedure when no vice-presidential candidate receives electoral majority. The person having the greatest number of votes as Vice-President shall be the Vice-President, if such number be a majority of the whole number of electors appointed; and if no person have a majority, then from the two highest numbers on the list the Senate shall choose the Vice-President; a quorum for the purpose shall consist of two-thirds of the whole number of Senators, and a majority of the whole number shall be necessary to a choice. But no person constitutionally ineligible to the office of President shall be eligible to that of Vice-President of the United States. [Adopted 1804.]

Forestalls repetition of 1800 electoral dispute, pp. 139–140.

See 1876 disputed election, pp. 342–343.

See 1824 election, pp. 179–180.

Amendment XIII.   Slavery Prohibited

Slavery forbidden. 1. Neither slavery[2] nor involuntary servitude, except as a punishment for crime whereof the party shall have been duly convicted, shall exist within the United States, or any place subject to their jurisdiction.

2. Congress shall have power to enforce this article by appropriate legislation. [Adopted 1865.]

For background, see pp. 310–311.

Amendment XIV.   Civil Rights for Ex-slaves,[3] etc.

1. Ex-slaves made citizens; U.S. citizenship primary. All persons born or naturalized in the United States, and subject to the jurisdiction thereof, are citizens of the United States

For background, see pp. 324–328.

---

[1] Changed to January 20 by the 20th Amendment (see text of Amendment following).

[2] The only explicit mention of slavery in the Constitution.

[3] Occasionally an offender is prosecuted under the 13th Amendment for keeping an employee or other person under conditions approximating slavery.

For corporations as "persons," see pp. 365–366.

Abolishes three-fifths rule for slaves, Art. I, Sec. II, para. 3.

and of the State wherein they reside. No State shall make or enforce any law which shall abridge the privileges or immunities of citizens of the United States; nor shall any State deprive any person of life, liberty, or property, without due process of law; nor deny to any person within its jurisdiction the equal protection of the laws.

2. When a state denies citizens the vote, its representation shall be reduced. Representatives shall be apportioned among the several States according to their respective numbers, counting the whole number of persons in each State, excluding Indians not taxed. But when the right to vote at any election for the choice of Electors for President and Vice-President of the United States, Representatives in Congress, the executive and judicial officers of a State, or the members of the legislature thereof, is denied to any of the male inhabitants of such State, being twenty-one years of age and citizens of the United States, or in any way abridged, except for participation in rebellion, or other crime, the basis of representation therein shall be reduced in the proportion which the number of such male citizens shall bear to the whole number of male citizens twenty-one years of age in such State.

Leading ex-Confederates denied office. See p. 329.

3. Certain persons who have been in rebellion are ineligible for federal and state office. No person shall be a Senator or Representative in Congress, or Elector of President and Vice-President, or hold any office, civil or military, under the United States, or under any State, who, having previously taken an oath, as a member of Congress, or as an officer of the United States, or as a member of any State legislature, or as an executive or judicial officer of any State, to support the Constitution of the United States, shall have engaged in insurrection or rebellion against the same, or given aid or comfort to the enemies thereof. But Congress may, by a vote of two-thirds of each house, remove such disability.

The ex-Confederates were thus forced to repudiate their debts and pay pensions to their own veterans, plus taxes for the pensions of Union veterans, their conquerors.

4. Debts incurred in aid of rebellion are void. The validity of the public debt of the United States, authorized by law, including debts incurred for payment of pensions and bounties for services in suppressing insurrection or rebellion, shall not be questioned. But neither the United States nor any State shall assume or pay any debt or obligation incurred in aid of insurrection or rebellion against the United States, or any claim for the loss or emancipation of any slave; but all such debts, obligations, and claims shall be held illegal and void.

5. Enforcement. The Congress shall have power to enforce, by appropriate legislation, the provisions of this article. [Adopted 1868.]

Amendment XV.

Suffrage for Blacks

For background, see pp. 324–328.

Black males are made voters. 1. The right of citizens of the United States to vote shall not be denied or abridged by the United States or by any State on account of race, color, or previous condition of servitude.

2. The Congress shall have power to enforce this article by appropriate legislation. [Adopted 1870.]

Amendment XVI.

Income Taxes

Congress has power to lay and collect income taxes. The Congress shall have power to lay and collect taxes on incomes, from whatever source derived, without apportionment among the several States, and without regard to any census or enumeration. [Adopted 1913.]

Amendment XVII. Direct Election of Senators

Senators shall be elected by popular vote. 1. The Senate of the United States shall be composed of two Senators from each State, elected by the people thereof, for six years; and each Senator shall have one vote. The electors in each State shall have the qualifications requisite for electors of [voters for] the most numerous branch of the State legislatures.

2. When vacancies happen in the representation of any State in the Senate, the executive authority of such State shall issue writs of election to fill such vacancies: Provided, that the Legislature of any State may empower the executive thereof to make temporary appointments until the people fill the vacancies by election as the Legislature may direct.

3. This amendment shall not be so construed as to affect the election or term of any Senator chosen before it becomes valid as part of the Constitution. [Adopted 1913.]

Amendment XVIII. National Prohibition

For background, see p. 480.

The sale or manufacture of intoxicating liquors is forbidden. 1. *After one year from the ratification of this article the manufacture, sale, or transportation of intoxicating liquors within, the importation thereof into, or the exportation thereof from the United States and all territory subject to the jurisdiction thereof, for beverage purposes, is hereby prohibited.*

2. *The Congress and the several States shall have concurrent power to enforce this article by appropriate legislation.*

3. *This article shall be inoperative unless it shall have been ratified as an amendment to the Constitution by the legislatures of the several States, as provided by the Constitution, within seven years from the date of the submission thereof to the States by the Congress.*

[Adopted 1919; repealed 1933 by 21st Amendment.]

Amendment XIX. Woman Suffrage

For background, see pp. 237, 390, 439, 466.

Women guaranteed the right to vote. 1. The right of citizens of the United States to vote shall not be denied or abridged by the United States or by any State on account of sex.

2. The Congress shall have power to enforce this article by appropriate legislation. [Adopted 1920.]

Amendment XX. Presidential and Congressional Terms

Shortens lame-duck periods by modifying Art. I, Sec. IV, para. 2.

1. Presidential, vice-presidential, and congressional terms of office begin in January. The terms of the President and Vice-President shall end at noon on the 20th day of January, and the terms of Senators and Representatives at noon on the 3d day of January, of the years in which such terms would have ended if this article had not been ratified; and the terms of their successors shall then begin.

2. New meeting date for Congress. The Congress shall assemble at least once in every year, and such meeting shall begin at noon on the 3d day of January, unless they shall by law appoint a different day.

3. Emergency presidential and vice-presidential succession. If, at the time fixed for the beginning of the term of the President, the President-elect shall have died, the Vice-President-elect shall become President. If a President shall not have been chosen before the time fixed for the beginning of his term, or if the President-elect shall have failed to qualify, then the Vice-President-elect shall act as President until a President shall have qualified; and the Congress may by law provide for the case wherein neither a President-elect nor a Vice-President-elect shall have qualified, declaring who shall then act as President, or the manner in which one who is to act shall be selected, and such persons shall act accordingly until a President or Vice-President shall have qualified.

4. The Congress may by law provide for the case of the death of any of the persons from whom the House of Representatives may choose a President whenever the right of choice shall have devolved upon them, and for the case of the death of any of the persons from whom the Senate may choose a Vice-President whenever the right of choice shall have devolved upon them.

5. Sections 1 and 2 shall take effect on the 15th day of October following the ratification of this article.

6. This article shall be inoperative unless it shall have been ratified as an amendment to the Constitution by the Legislatures of three-fourths of the several States within seven years from the date of its submission. [Adopted 1933.]

Amendment XXI.   Prohibition Repealed

For background, see p. 515.

1. 18th Amendment repealed. The eighteenth article of amendment to the Constitution of the United States is hereby repealed.

2. Local laws honored. The transportation or importation into any State, Territory, or Possession of the United States for delivery or use therein of intoxicating liquors, in violation of the laws thereof, is hereby prohibited.

3. This article shall be inoperative unless it shall have been ratified as an amendment to the Constitution by conventions in the several States, as provided in the Constitution, within seven years from the date of the submission thereof to the States by the Congress. [Adopted 1933.]

Amendment XXII.   Anti-Third Term Amendment

Sometimes referred to as the anti-Franklin Roosevelt amendment.

Presidential term is limited. 1. No person shall be elected to the office of President more than twice, and no person who has held the office of President, or acted as president, for more than two years of a term to which some other person was elected President shall be elected to the office of President more than once. But this article shall not apply to any person holding the office of President when this article was proposed by the Congress [i.e., Truman], and shall not prevent any person who may be holding the office of President, or acting as President, during the term within which this article becomes operative [i.e., Truman] from holding the office of President or acting as President during the remainder of such term.

2. This article shall be inoperative unless it shall have been ratified as an amendment to the Constitution by the legislatures of three-fourths of the several States within seven years from the date of its submission to the States by the congress. [Adopted 1951.]

Amendment XXIII.   District of Columbia Vote

Designed to give the District of Columbia three electoral votes and to quiet the century-old cry of

1. Presidential Electors for the District of Columbia. The District constituting the seat of Government of the United States shall appoint in such manner as the Congress may direct:

A number of electors of President and Vice-President equal to the whole number of Senators and Representatives in Congress to which the District would be entitled if it

"No taxation without representation." Yet the District of Columbia still has only one non-voting member of Congress.

were a State, but in no event more than the least populous State; they shall be in addition to those appointed by the States, but they shall be considered for the purposes of the election of President and Vice-President, to be electors appointed by a State; and they shall meet in the District and perform such duties as provided by the twelfth article of amendment.

2. Enforcement. The Congress shall have the power to enforce this article by appropriate legislation. [Adopted 1961.]

Amendment XXIV.   Poll Tax

Designed to end discrimination against blacks and other poor folk. An aspect of the civil rights crusade under President Lyndon Johnson. See p. 604.

1. Payment of poll tax or other taxes not to be prerequisite for voting in federal elections. The right of citizens of the United States to vote in any primary or other election for President or Vice-President, for electors for President or Vice-President, or for Senator or Representative in Congress, shall not be denied or abridged by the United States or any State by reason of failure to pay any poll tax or other tax.

2. Enforcement. The Congress shall have the power to enforce this article by appropriate legislation. [Adopted 1964.]

Amendment XXV.   Presidential Succession and Disability [1] (1967)

1. Vice-President to become President. In case of the removal of the President from office or of his death or resignation, the Vice-President shall become President.[2]

2. Successor to Vice-President provided. Whenever there is a vacancy in the office of the Vice-President, the President shall nominate a Vice-President who shall take office upon confirmation by a majority vote of both Houses of Congress.

3. Vice-president to serve for disabled President. Whenever the President transmits to the President pro tempore of the Senate and the Speaker of the House of Representatives his written declaration that he is unable to discharge the powers and duties of his office, and until he transmits to them a written declaration to the contrary, such powers and duties shall be discharged by the Vice-President as Acting President.

Gerald Ford was the first "appointed President," See pp. 621, 623.

4. Procedure for disqualifying or requalifying President. Whenever the Vice-President and a majority of either the principal officers of the executive departments or of such other body as Congress may by law provide, transmit to the President pro tempore of the Senate and the Speaker of the House of Representatives their written declaration that the President is unable to discharge the powers and duties of his office, the Vice-President shall immediately assume the powers and duties of the office as Acting President.

Thereafter, when the President transmits to the President pro tempore of the Senate and the Speaker of the House of Representatives his written declaration that no inability exists, he shall resume the powers and duties of his office unless the Vice-President and a majority of either the principal officers of the executive department[s] or of such other body as Congress may by law provide, transmit within four days to the President

---

[1] Passed by a two-thirds vote of both Houses of Congress in July 1965; ratified by the requisite three-fourths of the state legislatures, February 1967, or well within the seven-year limit.

[2] The original Constitution (Art. II, Sec, I, para. 5) was vague on this point, stipulating that "the powers and duties" of the President, but not necessarily the title, should "devolve" on the Vice-President. President Tyler, the first "accidental President," assumed not only the powers and duties but the title as well.

pro tempore of the Senate and the Speaker of the House of Representatives their written declaration that the President is unable to discharge the powers and duties of his office. Thereupon Congress shall decide the issue, assembling within forty-eight hours for that purpose if not in session. If the Congress, within twenty-one days after receipt of the latter written declaration, or, if Congress is not in session, within twenty-one days after Congress is required to assemble, determines by two-thirds vote of both Houses that the President is unable to discharge the powers and duties of his office, the Vice-President shall continue to discharge the same as Acting President; otherwise, the President shall resume the powers and duties of his office.

Amendment XXVI.   Lowering Voting Age (1971)

A response to the current revolt of youth; see p. 617.

1. Ballot for eighteen-year olds. The right of citizens of the United States, who are eighteen years of age or older, to vote shall not be denied or abridged by the United States or by any State on account of age.

2. Enforcement. The Congress shall have power to enforce this article by appropriate legislation.

An American Profile:
The United States and Its People

Growth of U.S. Population and Area

| Census | Population of United States | Increase over the Preceding Census | | Land Area (Sq. Mi.) | Pop. per Sq. Mi. | Percent of Pop. in Urban and Rural Territory | |
		Number	Percent			Urban	Rural
1790	3,929,214			867,980	4.5	5.1	94.9
1800	5,308,483	1,379,269	35.1	867,980	6.1	6.1	93.9
1810	7,239,881	1,931,398	36.4	1,685,865	4.3	7.2	92.8
1820	9,638,453	2,398,472	33.1	1,753,588	5.5	7.2	92.8
1830	12,866,020	3,227,567	33.5	1,753,588	7.3	8.8	91.2
1840	17,069,453	4,203,433	32.7	1,753,588	9.7	10.8	89.2
1850	23,191,876	6,122,423	35.9	2,944,337	7.9	15.3	84.7
1860	31,433,321	8,251,445	35.6	2,973,965	10.6	19.8	80.2
1870	39,818,449	8,375,128	26.6	2,973,965	13.4	24.9	75.1
1880	50,155,783	10,337,334	26.0	2,973,965	16.9	28.2	71.8
1890	62,947,714	12,791,931	25.5	2,973,965	21.2	35.1	64.9
1900	75,994,575	13,046,861	20.7	2,974,159	25.6	39.7	60.3
1910	91,972,266	15,997,691	21.0	2,973,890	30.9	45.7	54.3
1920	105,710,620	13,738,354	14.9	2,973,776	35.5	51.2	48.8
1930	122,775,046	17,064,426	16.1	2,977,128	41.2	56.2	43.8
1940	131,669,275	8,894,229	7.2	2,977,128	44.2	56.5	43.5
1950	150,697,361	19,028,086	14.5	2,974,726*	50.7	64.0	36.0
1960[†]	179,323,175	28,625,814	19.0	3,540,911	50.6	69.9	30.1
1970	203,235,298	23,912,123	13.3	3,536,855	57.5	73.5	26.5
1980	226,504,825	23,269,527	11.4	3,536,855	64.0	73.7	26.3
1990	248,709,873	22,164,068	9.8	3,536,855	70.3	74.1	25.9

* As remeasured in 1940; shrinkage offset by increase in water area.
† First year for which figures include Alaska and Hawaii.
Source: Census Bureau, *Historical Statistics of the United States,* updated by relevant *Statistical Abstract of the United States.*

Characteristics of the U.S. Population

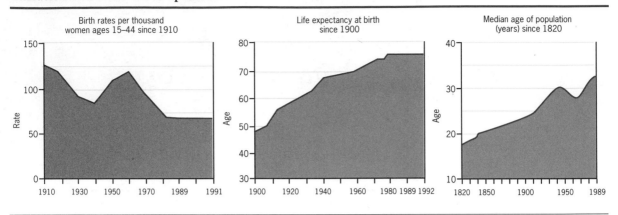

Birth rates per thousand women ages 15–44 since 1910

Life expectancy at birth since 1900

Median age of population (years) since 1820

Sources: *Historical Statistics of the United States* and *Statistical Abstract of the United States,* relevant years.

Changing Lifestyles in the Twentieth Century

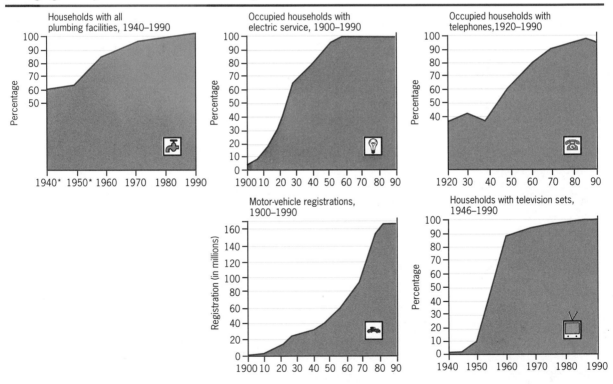

Households with all plumbing facilities, 1940–1990

Occupied households with electric service, 1900–1990

Occupied households with telephones, 1920–1990

Motor-vehicle registrations, 1900–1990

Households with television sets, 1946–1990

* Except for 1940 and 1950, figures are for "all plumbing facilities" (not defined in source). For 1940, figure is for flush toilet, inside structure, private use (64.7 percent had flush toilet, and private and/or shared inside structure, and 60.9 percent had installed bath or shower). For 1950, figure designates units with private toilet and bath, and hot running water (flush toilet, private or shared inside structure is 74.3 percent; installed bathtub or shower, 72.9 percent)

Sources: *Historical Statistics of the United States* and *Statistical Abstract of the United States,* relevant years.

Characteristics of the U.S. Labor Force

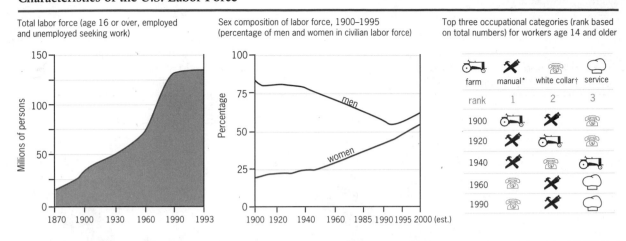

Total labor force (age 16 or over, employed and unemployed seeking work)

Sex composition of labor force, 1900–1995 (percentage of men and women in civilian labor force)

Top three occupational categories (rank based on total numbers) for workers age 14 and older

* Manual workers = operators, fabricators, and laborers plus precision production, craft, and repair.

† White collar workers = managerial and professional plus technical, sales, and administrative support.

Sources: *Historical Statistics of the United States* and *Statistical Abstract of the United States,* relevant years, and Department of Labor Statistics, *Handbook of Labor Statistics,* relevant years.

Leading Economic Sectors (Various Years)

Percentage of value added contributed

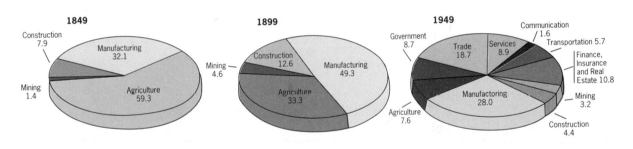

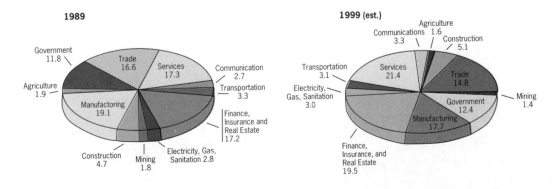

Sources: *Historical Statistics of the United States* and *Statistical Abstract of the United States,* relevant years.

Per-Capita Disposable Personal Income in Constant (1982) Dollars, 1929–1990

Comparative Tax Burdens (Percentage of Gross Domestic Product paid as taxes in major industrial countries, 1991)

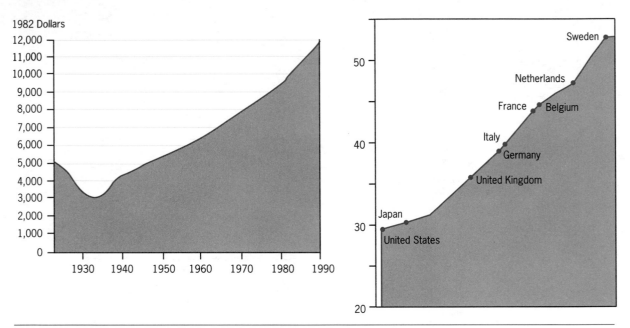

Sources: *Historical Statistics of the United States* and *Statistical Abstract of the United States.*

Value of Imports by Place of Origin (Millions of Dollars)

| Year | Western Hemisphere | | Europe | | Asia | | Australia and Oceania | Africa |
	Total	Canada	Total	U.K.	Total	Japan		
1900	224	39	441	160	146	33	29	11
1910	503	95	806	271	210	66	20	17
1920	2,424	612	1,228	514	1,397	415	80	150
1930	1,195	402	911	210	854	279	33	68
1940	1,089	424	390	155	981	158	35	131
1950	5,063	1,960	1,449	335	1,638	182	208	494
1960	6,864	2,901	4,268	993	2,721	1,149	266	534
1970	16,928	11,092	11,395	2,194	9,621	5,875	871	1,113
1980	78,687	41,459	48,039	9,842	80,299	30,714	3,392	34,410
1990	158,280	91,372	108,896	20,288	207,144	89,655	5,765	15,869

Value of U.S. Exports by Destination

Year	Western Hemisphere		Europe		Asia		Australia and Oceania	Africa
	Total	Canada	Total	U.K.	Total	Japan		
1900	227	95	1,040	534	68	29	41	19
1910	479	216	1,136	506	78	22	34	19
1920	2,553	972	4,466	1,825	872	378	172	166
1930	1,357	659	1,838	678	448	165	108	92
1940	1,501	713	1,645	1,011	619	227	94	161
1950	4,902	2,039	3,306	548	1,539	418	151	376
1960	7,684	3,810	7,398	1,487	4,186	1,447	514	793
1970	15,612	9,079	14,817	2,536	10,027	4,652	1,189	1,580
1980	74,114	35,395	71,372	12,695	60,168	20,792	4,876	9,060
1990	136,757	82,967	113,034	23,484	120,257	48,585	9,964	7,951

Principal Exports 1900–1990 (Leading Three Exports by Value in Dollars)

Year	First	Second	Third
1900	cotton	wheat and wheat flour	meat products
1910	cotton	machinery	petroleum and products
1920	cotton	wheat and wheat flour	petroleum and products
1930	machinery	cotton	petroleum and products
1940	machinery	iron and steel mill products	petroleum and products
1950	machinery	cotton	automobiles*
1960	machinery	automobiles*	wheat and wheat flour
1970	machinery	automobiles*	wheat and wheat flour
1980	machinery	road motor vehicles*	metals and manufactures
1990	automobiles, motor vehicles*	office machinery, computers	aircraft*

* includes parts

U.S. Foreign Trade, Ratio of Raw Materials to Manufactured Goods

| | U.S. Domestic Exports | | U.S. General Imports | |
Year	Percentage of Raw Materials	Percentage of Manufactured Goods	Percentage of Raw Materials	Percentage of Manufactured Goods
1900	41.3	58.7	44.7	55.3
1910	40.0	60.0	46.4	53.6
1920	34.7	65.3	44.8	55.2
1930	26.7	73.3	45.8	54.2
1940	13.7	86.3	51.0	49.0
1950	26.8	73.2	47.7	52.3
1960	21.8	78.2	31.4	68.6
1970	27.0	73.0	31.0	69.0
1980	29.6	70.4	45.0	55.0
1990*	20.8	79.2	19.6	80.4

* Petroleum accounts for 55 percent of raw material imports.

Value of Exports and Imports and Status of the Balance of Trade

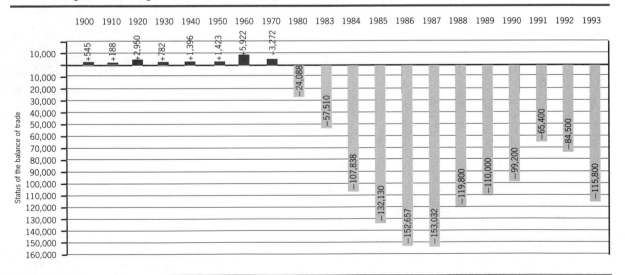

Sources for tables and graph: *Historical Statistics of the United States* and *Statistical Abstract of the United States,* relevant years.

Tariff Levies on Dutiable Imports, 1821–1990 (Ratio of Duties to Value of Dutiable Imports)

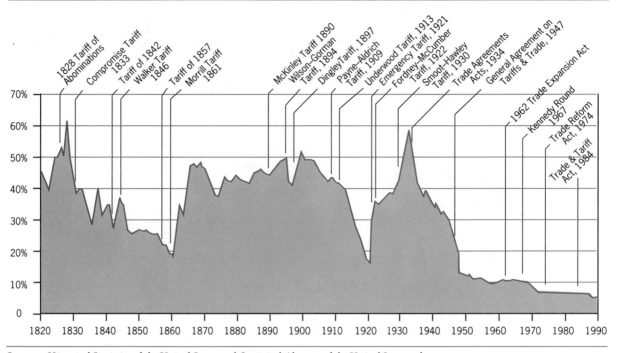

Sources: *Historical Statistics of the United States* and *Statistical Abstract of the United States,* relevant years.

Gross National Product in Current and Constant (1982) Dollars, 1900–1990

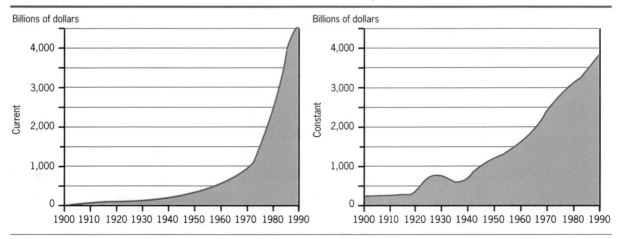

Source: *1991 Economic Report of the President.*

Presidential Elections*

Election	Candidates	Parties	Popular Vote	Electoral Vote
1789	GEORGE WASHINGTON	No party designations		69
	John Adams			34
	Minor Candidates			35
1792	GEORGE WASHINGTON	No party designations		132
	John Adams			77
	George Clinton			50
	Minor Candidates			5
1796	JOHN ADAMS	Federalist		71
	Thomas Jefferson	Democratic-Republican		68
	Thomas Pinckney	Federalist		59
	Aaron Burr	Democratic-Republican		30
	Minor Candidates			48
1800	THOMAS JEFFERSON	Democratic-Republican		73
	Aaron Burr	Democratic-Republican		73
	John Adams	Federalist		65
	Charles C. Pinckney	Federalist		64
	John Jay	Federalist		1
1804	THOMAS JEFFERSON	Democratic-Republican		162
	Charles C. Pinckney	Federalist		14
1808	JAMES MADISON	Democratic-Republican		122
	Charles C. Pinckney	Federalist		47
	George Clinton	Democratic-Republican		6
1812	JAMES MADISON	Democratic-Republican		128
	DeWitt Clinton	Federalist		89
1816	JAMES MONROE	Democratic-Republican		183
	Rufus King	Federalist		34
1820	JAMES MONROE	Democratic-Republican		231
	John Q. Adams	Independent Republican		1
1824	JOHN Q. ADAMS (Min.)[†]	Democratic-Republican	108,740	84
	Andrew Jackson	Democratic-Republican	153,544	99
	William H. Crawford	Democratic-Republican	46,618	41
	Henry Clay	Democratic-Republican	47,136	37
1828	ANDREW JACKSON	Democratic	647,286	178
	John Q. Adams	National Republican	508,064	83
1832	ANDREW JACKSON	Democratic	687,502	219
	Henry Clay	National Republican	530,189	49
	William Wirt	Anti-Masonic	33,108	7
	John Floyd	National Republican		11
1836	MARTIN VAN BUREN	Democrat	762,678	170
	William H. Harrison	Whig		73
	Hugh L. White	Whig	736,656	26
	Daniel Webster	Whig		14
	W. P. Mangum	Whig		11

* Candidates receiving less than 1 percent of the popular vote are omitted. Before the 12th Amendment (1804), the Electoral College voted for two presidential candidates, and the runner-up became vice president. Basic figures are taken primarily from *Historical Statistics of the United States, 1789–1945* (1949), pp. 288–290; *Historical Statistics of the United States, Colonial Times to 1957* (1960), pp. 682–683; and *Statistical Abstract of the United States, 1969* (1969), pp. 355–357.

[†] "Min." indicates minority president—one receiving less than 50 percent of all popular votes.

Presidential Elections (Continued)

Election	Candidates	Parties	Popular Vote	Electoral Vote
1840	WILLIAM H. HARRISON	Whig	1,275,016	234
	Martin Van Buren	Democratic	1,129,102	60
1844	JAMES K. POLK (Min.)*	Democratic	1,337,243	170
	Henry Clay	Whig	1,299,062	105
	James G. Birney	Liberty	62,300	
1848	ZACHARY TAYLOR	Whig	1,360,099	163
	Lewis Cass	Democratic	1,220,544	127
	Martin Van Buren	Free Soil	291,263	
1852	FRANKLIN PIERCE	Democratic	1,601,274	254
	Winfield Scott	Whig	1,386,580	42
	John P. Hale	Free Soil	155,825	
1856	JAMES BUCHANAN (Min.)*	Democratic	1,838,169	174
	John C. Fremont	Republican	1,341,264	114
	Millard Fillmore	American	874,534	8
1860	ABRAHAM LINCOLN (Min.)*	Republican	1,867,198	180
	Stephen A. Douglas	Democratic	1,379,434	12
	John C. Breckinridge	Democratic	854,248	72
	John Bell	Constitutional Union	591,658	39
1864	ABRAHAM LINCOLN	Union	2,213,665	212
	George B. McClellan	Democratic	1,802,237	21
1868	ULYSSES S. GRANT	Republican	3,012,833	214
	Horatio Seymour	Democratic	2,703,249	80
1872	ULYSSES S. GRANT	Republican	3,597,132	286
	Horace Greeley	Democratic and Liberal Republican	2,834,125	66
1876	RUTHERFORD B. HAYES (Min.)*	Republican	4,036,298	185
	Samuel J. Tilden	Democratic	4,300,590	184
1880	JAMES A. GARFIELD (Min.)*	Republican	4,454,416	214
	Winfield S. Hancock	Democratic	4,444,952	155
	James B. Weaver	Greenback-Labor	308,578	
1884	GROVER CLEVELAND (Min.)*	Democratic	4,874,986	219
	James G. Blaine	Republican	4,851,981	182
	Benjamin F. Butler	Greenback-Labor	175,370	
	John P. St. John	Prohibition	150,369	
1888	BENJAMIN HARRISON (Min.)*	Republican	5,439,853	233
	Grover Cleveland	Democratic	5,540,309	168
	Clinton B. Fisk	Prohibition	249,506	
	Anson J. Streeter	Union Labor	146,935	
1892	GROVER CLEVELAND (Min.)*	Democratic	5,556,918	277
	Benjamin Harrison	Republican	5,176,108	145
	James B. Weaver	People's	1,041,028	22
	John Bidwell	Prohibition	264,133	
1896	WILLIAM MCKINLEY	Republican	7,104,779	271
	William J. Bryan	Democratic	6,502,925	176
1900	WILLIAM MCKINLEY	Republican	7,207,923	292
	William J. Bryan	Democratic;Populist	6,358,133	155
	John C. Woolley	Prohibition	208,914	

[†] "Min." indicates minority president—one receiving less than 50 percent of all popular votes.

Presidential Elections (Continued)

Election	Candidates	Parties	Popular Vote	Electoral Vote
1904	THEODORE ROOSEVELT	Republican	7,623,486	336
	Alton B. Parker	Democratic	5,077,911	140
	Eugene V. Debs	Socialist	402,283	
	Silas C. Swallow	Prohibition	258,536	
1908	WILLIAM H. TAFT	Republican	7,678,908	321
	William J. Bryan	Democratic	6,409,104	162
	Eugene V. Debs	Socialist	420,793	
	Eugene W. Chafin	Prohibition	253,840	
1912	WOODROW WILSON (Min.)*	Democratic	6,293,454	435
	Theodore Roosevelt	Progressive	4,119,538	88
	William H. Taft	Republican	3,484,980	8
	Eugene V. Debs	Socialist	900,672	
	Eugene W. Chafin	Prohibition	206,275	
1916	WOODROW WILSON (Min.)*	Democratic	9,129,606	277
	Charles E. Hughes	Republican	8,538,221	254
	A. L. Benson	Socialist	585,113	
	J. F. Hanley	Prohibition	220,506	
1920	WARREN G. HARDING	Republican	16,152,200	404
	James M. Cox	Democratic	9,147,353	127
	Eugene V. Debs	Socialist	919,799	
	P. P. Christensen	Farmer-Labor	265,411	
1924	CALVIN COOLIDGE	Republican	15,725,016	382
	John W. Davis	Democratic	8,386,503	136
	Robert M. La Follette	Progressive	4,822,856	13
1928	HERBERT C. HOOVER	Republican	21,391,381	444
	Alfred E. Smith	Democratic	15,016,443	87
1932	FRANKLIN D. ROOSEVELT	Democratic	22,821,857	472
	Herbert C. Hoover	Republican	15,761,841	59
	Norman Thomas	Socialist	881,951	
1936	FRANKLIN D. ROOSEVELT	Democratic	27,751,597	523
	Alfred M. Landon	Republican	16,679,583	8
	William Lemke	Union, etc.	882,479	
1940	FRANKLIN D. ROOSEVELT	Democratic	27,244,160	449
	Wendell L. Willkie	Republican	22,305,198	82
1944	FRANKLIN D. ROOSEVELT	Democratic	25,602,504	432
	Thomas E. Dewey	Republican	22,006,285	99
1948	HARRY S TRUMAN (Min.)*	Democratic	24,105,812	303
	Thomas E. Dewey	Republican	21,970,065	189
	J. Strom Thurmond	States' Rights Democratic	1,169,063	39
	Henry A. Wallace	Progressive	1,157,172	
1952	DWIGHT D. EISENHOWER	Republican	33,936,234	442
	Adlai E. Stevenson	Democratic	27,314,992	89
1956	DWIGHT D. EISENHOWER	Republican	35,590,472	457
	Adlai E. Stevenson	Democratic	26,022,752	73
1960	JOHN F. KENNEDY (Min.)*	Democratic	34,226,731	303
	Richard M. Nixon	Republican	34,108,157	219

† "Min." indicates minority president—one receiving less than 50 percent of all popular votes.

Presidential Elections (Continued)

Election	Candidates	Parties	Popular Vote	Electoral Vote
1964	LYNDON B. JOHNSON	Democratic	43,129,484	486
	Barry M. Goldwater	Republican	27,178,188	52
1968	RICHARD M. NIXON (Min.)*	Republican	31,785,480	301
	Hubert H. Humphrey, Jr.	Democratic	31,275,166	191
	George C. Wallace	American Independent	9,906,473	46
1972	RICHARD M. NIXON	Republican	45,767,218	520
	George S. McGovern	Democratic	28,357,688	17
1976	JIMMY CARTER	Democratic	40,828,657	297
	Gerald R. Ford	Republican	39,145,520	240
1980	RONALD W. REAGAN	Republican	43,201,220	489
	Jimmy Carter	Democratic	34,913,332	49
	John B. Anderson	Independent	5,581,379	0
1984	RONALD W. REAGAN	Republican	52,609,797	525
	Walter Mondale	Democratic	36,450,613	13
1988	GEORGE BUSH	Republican	47,917,341	426
	Michael Dukakis	Democratic	41,013,030	112
1992	WILLIAM CLINTON	Democratic	43,728,275	370
	George Bush	Republican	38,167,416	168
	H. Ross Perot	Independent	19,237,247	

[†] "Min." indicates minority president—one receiving less than 50 percent of all popular votes.

Presidents and Elected Vice Presidents

Term	President	Vice President
1789–1793	George Washington	John Adams
1793–1797	George Washington	John Adams
1797–1801	John Adams	Thomas Jefferson
1801–1805	Thomas Jefferson	Aaron Burr
1805–1809	Thomas Jefferson	George Clinton
1809–1813	James Madison	George Clinton (d. 1812)
1813–1817	James Madison	Elbridge Gerry (d. 1814)
1817–1821	James Monroe	Daniel D. Tompkins
1821–1825	James Monroe	Daniel D. Tompkins
1825–1829	John Quincy Adams	John C. Calhoun
1829–1833	Andrew Jackson	John C. Calhoun (resigned 1832)
1833–1837	Andrew Jackson	Martin Van Buren
1837–1841	Martin Van Buren	Richard M. Johnson
1841–1845	William H. Harrison (d. 1841) John Tyler	John Tyler
1845–1849	James K. Polk	George M. Dallas
1849–1853	Zachary Taylor (d. 1850) Millard Fillmore	Millard Fillmore
1853–1857	Franklin Pierce	William R. D. King (d. 1853)

Presidents and Elected Vice Presidents (Continued)

Term	President	Vice President
1857–1861	James Buchanan	John C. Breckinridge
1861–1865	Abraham Lincoln	Hannibal Hamlin
1865–1869	Abraham Lincoln (d. 1865) Andrew Johnson	Andrew Johnson
1869–1873	Ulysses S. Grant	Schuyler Colfax
1873–1877	Ulysses S. Grant	Henry Wilson (d. 1875)
1877–1881	Rutherford B. Hayes	William A. Wheeler
1881–1885	James A. Garfield (d. 1881) Chester A. Arthur	Chester A. Arthur
1885–1889	Grover Cleveland	Thomas A. Hendricks (d. 1885)
1889–1893	Benjamin Harrison	Levi P. Morton
1893–1897	Grover Cleveland	Adlai E. Stevenson
1897–1901	William McKinley	Garret A. Hobart (d. 1899)
1901–1905	William McKinley (d. 1901) Theodore Roosevelt	Theodore Roosevelt
1905–1909	Theodore Roosevelt	Charles W. Fairbanks
1909–1913	William H. Taft	James S. Sherman (d. 1912)
1913–1917	Woodrow Wilson	Thomas R. Marshall
1917–1921	Woodrow Wilson	Thomas R. Marshall
1921–1925	Warren G. Harding (d. 1923) Calvin Coolidge	Calvin Coolidge
1925–1929	Calvin Coolidge	Charles G. Dawes
1929–1933	Herbert C. Hoover	Charles Curtis
1933–1937	Franklin D. Roosevelt	John N. Garner
1937–1941	Franklin D. Roosevelt	John N. Garner
1941–1945	Franklin D. Roosevelt	Henry A. Wallace
1945–1949	Franklin D. Roosevelt (d. 1945) Harry S Truman	Harry S Truman
1949–1953	Harry S Truman	Alben W. Barkley
1953–1957	Dwight D. Eisenhower	Richard M. Nixon
1957–1961	Dwight D. Eisenhower	Richard M. Nixon
1961–1965	John F. Kennedy (d. 1963) Lyndon B. Johnson	Lyndon B. Johnson
1965–1969	Lyndon B. Johnson	Hubert H. Humphrey, Jr.
1969–1973	Richard M. Nixon	Spiro T. Agnew
1973–1977	Richard M. Nixon (resigned 1974) Gerald R. Ford	Spiro T. Agnew; Gerald R. Ford Nelson Rockefeller
1977–1981	Jimmy Carter	Walter F. Mondale
1981–1985	Ronald Reagan	George Bush
1985–1989	Ronald Reagan	George Bush
1989–1993	George Bush	J. Danforth Quayle III
1993–	William Clinton	Albert Gore, Jr.

Ratification of the Constitution

Admission of States to the Union

State	Date	Order of Admission	State	Date of Admission	Order of Admission	State	Date of Admission
1 Delaware	Dec. 7, 1787	14	Vermont	March 4, 1791	33	Oregon	Feb. 14, 1859
2 Pennsylvania	Dec. 12, 1787	15	Kentucky	June 1, 1792	34	Kansas	Jan. 29, 1861
3 New Jersey	Dec. 18, 1787	16	Tennessee	June 1, 1796	35	West Virginia	June 20, 1863
4 Georgia	Jan. 2, 1788	17	Ohio	March 1, 1803	36	Nevada	Oct. 31, 1864
5 Connecticut	Jan. 9, 1788	18	Louisiana	April 30, 1812	37	Nebraska	March 1, 1867
6 Massachusetts	Feb. 7, 1788	19	Indiana	Dec. 11, 1816	38	Colorado	Aug. 1, 1876
(inc. Maine)		20	Mississippi	Dec. 10, 1817	39	North Dakota	Nov. 2, 1889
7 Maryland	Apr. 28, 1788	21	Illinois	Dec. 3, 1818	40	South Dakota	Nov. 2, 1889
8 South Carolina	May 23, 1788	22	Alabama	Dec. 14, 1819	41	Montana	Nov. 8, 1889
9 New Hampshire	June 21, 1788	23	Maine	March 15, 1820	42	Washington	Nov. 11, 1889
10 Virginia	June 26, 1788	24	Missouri	Aug. 10, 1821	43	Idaho	July 3, 1890
11 New York	July 26, 1788	25	Arkansas	June 15, 1836	44	Wyoming	July 10, 1890
12 North Carolina	Nov. 21, 1789	26	Michigan	Jan 26, 1837	45	Utah	Jan. 4, 1896
13 Rhode Island	May 29, 1790	27	Florida	March 3, 1845	46	Oklahoma	Nov. 16, 1907
		28	Texas	Dec. 29, 1845	47	New Mexico	Jan. 6, 1912
		29	Iowa	Dec. 28, 1846	48	Arizona	Feb. 14, 1912
		30	Wisconsin	May 29, 1848	49	Alaska	Jan. 3, 1959
		31	California	Sept. 9, 1850	50	Hawaii	Aug. 21, 1959
		32	Minnesota	May 11, 1858			

Estimates of Total Costs and Number of Battle Deaths of Major U.S. Wars*

	Total Costs** (Millions of Dollars)	Original Costs	Number of Battle Deaths
Vietnam Conflict	352,000	140,600	47,318[†]
Korean Conflict	164,000	54,000	33,629
World War II	664,000	288,000	291,557
World War I	112,000	26,000	53,402
Spanish-American War	6,460	400	385
Civil War { Union only	12,952	3,200	140,414
Civil War { Confederacy (est.)	N.A.	1,000	94,000
Mexican War	147	73	1,733
War of 1812	158	93	2,260
American Revolution	190	100	6,824

* Deaths from disease and other causes are not shown. In earlier wars especially, owing to poor medical and sanitary practices, non-battle deaths substantially exceeded combat casualties.

** The difference between total costs and original costs is attributable to continuing postwar payments for such items as veterans' benefits, interest on war debts, etc.

[†] 1959–1983

Sources: *Historical Statistics of the United States, Statistical Abstract of the United States,* relevant years, and *The World Almanac and Book of Facts, 1986.*

Photo Credits

politan Museum of Art. Gift of I. N. Phelps Stokes, Edward S. Hawes, Alice Mary Hawes, Marion Augusta Hawes, 1937; p. 167, Maryland Historical Society

Chapter 14
p. 178, The Nelson-Atkins Museum of Art, Kansas City, Missouri (Purchase: Nelson Trust); p. 181, United States Weekly Telegram; p. 184, New York Historical Society; p. 187, Tennessee State Library and Archives

Chapter 15
p. 194, Boston Public Library; p. 198, Texas State Library; p. 203, Boatman's National Bank of St. Louis

Chapter 16
p. 210, Culver Pictures; p. 212, Cincinnati Historical Society; p. 214, The New York Public Library; p. 215, Yale University Art Gallery, Gift of George Hoadley, B.A. 1801; p. 220, *Harper's Weekly,* 1868; p. 223, The Bettmann Archive

Chapter 17
p. 230, Library of Congress; p. 233, Smithsonian Institution, Division of Cultural History; p. 236, Brown Brothers; p. 241, Harvard University, Cambridge

Chapter 18
p. 249, Missouri Historical Society; p. 251 (right and left) Collection Photothèque Musée de'Homme; p. 253, National Portrait Gallery/Smithsonian Institution

Chapter 19
p. 259, Institute of Texas Culture; p. 262, *Yankee Doodle;* p. 266, Bancroft Library, University of California, Berkeley

Chapter 20
p. 273, Library of Congress; p. 274, The Granger Collection; p. 276, The Brooklyn Museum, gift of Miss Gwendolyn O. L. Conkling; p. 280, Republican cartoon

Chapter 21
p. 284, New-York Historical Society; p. 285, Courtesy, The New York Public Library, Astor, Lenox, and Tilden Foundations; p. 288, Illinois State Historical Library

Chapter 22
p. 299, New-York Historical Society; p. 300, John Johnson Collection/ Philadelphia Museum of Art; p. 303, Museum of the City of New York

Chapter 23
p. 310, Library of Congress; p. 312, Library of Congress; p. 314 (left and right) National Archives; p. 317, *Harper's Weekly,* 1863; p. 319, Lincoln Museum, Ft. Wayne, Indiana

Chapter 24
p. 324, Library of Congress; p. 325, Library of Congress; p. 327 The Granger Collection, p. 329, Thomas Nast, *Harper's Weekly,* 1866

Chapter 25
p. 338, Thomas Nast, *Harper's Weekly,* 1871; p. 344, Amon Carter Museum; p. 348, *Puck*

Chapter 26
p. 358, Historical Pictures/Stock Montage; p. 360, Library of Congress; p. 366, *The Verdict,* January 22, 1900, New York Public Library; p. 368, Culver Pictures, Inc.; p. 370, Culver Pictures, Inc.

Chapter 27
p. 376, Library of Congress; p. 378, Culver Pictures, Inc.; p. 381, Sophia Smith Collection, Smith College; p. 387, Amherst College Library

Chapter 28
p. 397, National Archives; p. 398, Archives & Manuscripts Division of the Oklahoma Historical Society; p. 404, Grant Heilman; p. 407, Library of Congress; p. 410 (left) Culver Pictures, Inc., (right) Nebraska State Historical Society

Chapter 29
p. 420, Chicago Historical Society; p. 423, Library of Congress; p. 424, By permission of the Houghton

Index

Italic page numbers indicate illustrations.